P9-EJJ-289

HANDBOOK OF RESEARCH IN EDUCATION FINANCE AND POLICY

Sponsored by the American Education Finance Association (AEFA), this groundbreaking new handbook assembles in one place the existing research-based knowledge in education finance and policy, thereby helping to define this evolving field of research and practice. It provides a readily available resource for anyone seriously involved in education finance and policy in the United States and around the world.

The *Handbook* traces the evolution of the field from its initial focus on school *inputs* (per pupil expenditures) and the revenue sources (property taxes, state aid programs) used to finance these inputs to a focus on educational *outcomes* (student achievement) and the larger policies used to achieve them. It shows how the current decision-making context in school finance inevitably interacts with those of governance, accountability, equity, privatization, and other areas of education policy. Because a full understanding of the important contemporary issues requires insights from a variety of perspectives, the *Handbook* draws on contributors from a variety of disciplines. While many of the chapters cover complex state-of-the-art empirical research, the authors explain key concepts in language that non-specialists can understand.

HANDBOOK OF RESEARCH IN EDUCATION FINANCE AND POLICY

Edited by

Helen F. Ladd and Edward B. Fiske

Routledge
Taylor & Francis Group
NEW YORK AND LONDON

First published 2008
by Routledge
270 Madison Ave, New York, NY 10016

Simultaneously published in the UK
by Routledge
2 Park Square, Milton Park, Abingdon, Oxon OX14 4RN

Routledge is an imprint of the Taylor & Francis Group, an informa business

Transferred to Digital Printing 2010

© 2008 American Education Finance Association

Typeset in Times and Helvetica by EvS Communication Networx, Inc.

All rights reserved. No part of this book may be reprinted or reproduced or utilised in any form or by any electronic, mechanical, or other means, now known or hereafter invented, including photocopying and recording, or in any information storage or retrieval system, without permission in writing from the publishers.

Trademark Notice: Product or corporate names may be trademarks or registered trademarks, and are used only for identification and explanation without intent to infringe.

Library of Congress Cataloging in Publication Data
Handbook of research on education finance and policy / [edited by] Helen F. Ladd and Edward B. Fiske.
p. cm.
Includes bibliographical references and index.
1. Education--Finance--Handbooks, manuals, etc. I. Ladd, Helen F.
II. Fiske, Edward B.
LB2824.H36 2007
379.1'210973--dc22
2007028453

ISBN 10: 0-805-86144-0 (hbk)
ISBN 10: 0-805-86145-9 (pbk)
ISBN 10: 0-203-96106-4 (ebk)

ISBN 13: 978-0-805-86144-0 (hbk)
ISBN 13: 978-0-805-86145-7 (pbk)
ISBN 13: 768-0-203-96106-3 (ebk)

CONTENTS

II. MAKING MONEY MATTER

Section Editors: Jennifer King Rice and Amy Ellen Schwartz

III. PROMOTING EQUITY AND ADEQUACY

Section Editor: Leanna Stiefel

IV. CHANGING PATTERNS OF GOVERNANCE AND FINANCE

Section Editor: Andrew Reschovsky

VII. SPECIAL CIRCUMSTANCES

SECTION EDITOR: DAVID H. MONK

VIII. HIGHER EDUCATION

SECTION EDITORS: DAVID W. BRENEMAN AND MICHAEL S. MCPHERSON

Contributors

GENERAL EDITORS

Helen F. Ladd is the Edgar Thompson Professor of Public Policy Studies and professor of economics at Duke University. As the co-chair of the National Academy of Sciences Committee on Education Finance from 1996–1999, she co-edited a set of background papers, *Equity and Adequacy in Education Finance* and the final report, *Making Money Matter: Financing America's Schools*. She is also the editor of *Holding Schools Accountable: Performance-Based Reform in Education* (Brookings Institution, 1996) and the author of several books and many articles on education policy. She is on the editorial board of *Education Finance and Policy* and a co-editor of the *Journal of Policy Analysis and Management*.

Edward B. Fiske is a former Education Editor of the *New York Times* who has written extensively on school reform both in the United States and in developing countries for UNESCO, the World Bank, USAID, the Academy for Educational Development, the Asia Society and other organizations. The editor of *Smart Schools, Smart Kids* (Simon & Schuster), he is also the editor of the *Fiske Guide to Colleges* and the author of numerous other books on college admissions. Fiske and Ladd are co-authors of *When Schools Compete: A Cautionary Tale*, a study of market-based school reforms in New Zealand, and *Elusive Equity: Education Reform in Post-Apartheid South Africa,* both published by Brookings Institution Press.

SECTION EDITORS

David W. Breneman is University Professor, Newton and Rita Meyers Professor in Economics of Education, and Dean of the Curry School of Education at the University of Virginia. A former president of Kalamazoo College, he has written extensively on the economics of higher education as well as public policy toward education.

James W. Guthrie is Professor of Public Policy and Education and Chair of the Department of Leadership and Policy at Peabody College of Vanderbilt University. He is also Director of the National Center on Performance Incentives at Vanderbilt and served in 2006 as the President of the American Education Finance Association.

Michael Kirst is Emeritus Professor of Education and Business Administration at Stanford University. A policy generalist, Kirst has published articles on school finance politics, curriculum politics, intergovernmental relations, and education reform policies. He was a member of the California State Board of Education from 1975 to 1982 and its president from 1977 to 1981.

Henry M. Levin is the William Heard Kilpatrick Professor of Economics and Education and Director of the National Center for the Study of Privatization (NCSPE), Teachers College, Columbia University and the David Jacks Professor of Education and Economics, *Emeritus*, Stanford University, where he served on the faculty from 1968-1999. A specialist in the economics of education, he is a recipient of the Outstanding Service Award from the AEFA.

Susanna Loeb is an associate professor of education at Stanford University and the Director of the Institute for Research on Education Policy and Practice. She specializes in the economics of education and the relationship between schools and federal, state, and local policies. She is also an associate professor of business (by courtesy) at Stanford, co-Director of Policy Analysis for California Education, and a faculty research fellow at the National Bureau of Economic Research.

Michael S. McPherson is President of the Spencer Foundation. A nationally known economist whose expertise focuses on the interplay between education and economics, he is a former president of Macalester College in St. Paul, Minnesota. He previously served as chair of the economics department and dean of the faculty at Williams College.

David H. Monk is Professor of Educational Administration and Dean of the College of Education at the Pennsylvania State University. He consults widely on matters related to educational productivity and the organizational structuring of schools and school districts. A Past President of the AEFA, he is co-editor of *Education Finance and Policy.*

Andrew Reschovsky is Professor of Public Affairs and Applied Economics, University of Wisconsin-Madison. He has conducted research and published articles on tax policy, educational finance, and intergovernmental relations. He has also served as an advisor to the government of South Africa on local government fiscal reform and educational finance. He is a member of the Board of Directors of the AEFA and on the editorial board of *Education Finance and Policy.*

Jennifer King Rice is Associate Professor in the Department of Education Policy and Leadership at the University of Maryland. Her research draws on the discipline of economics to explore education policy questions concerning the efficiency, equity, and adequacy of U.S. public education. Her current work focuses on teachers as a critical resource in the education process. She is currently President of the AEFA.

Amy Ellen Schwartz is Professor of Public Policy, Education and Economics, and Director of the Institute for Education and Social Policy, Wagner Graduate School of Public Service and Steinhardt School, New York University. An applied microeconomist, her current work in education focuses on urban high schools, the education of immigrants and issues in school finance, including the cost of small schools and weighted student funding. She is President-Elect of the AEFA.

Leanna Stiefel is Professor of Economics at the Robert F. Wagner Graduate School of Public Service, New York University. Her research on education finance and policy has been published as books such as *The Measurement of Equity in School Finance* (with Robert Berne) and *Measuring School Performance and Equity* (co-edited). A past president of the AEFA, she received its outstanding service award in 2005.

AUTHORS

Bruce D. Baker is Associate Professor, Department of Educational Leadership and Policy Studies, University of Kansas.

Thomas R. Bailey is the George and Abby O'Neill Professor of Economics and Education and Director of the National Center for Postsecondary Research, Teachers College, Columbia University.

Daphna Bassok is a Doctoral Candidate, School of Education, Stanford University.

Sandy Baum is Professor of Economics, Skidmore College, and Senior Policy Analyst, the College Board.

Clive Belfield is Assistant Professor of Economics, Queens College, City University of New York and Co-Director of the Center for Benefit-Cost Studies in Education, Teachers College, Columbia University.

Eric P. Bettinger is Associate Professor of Economics, Case Western Reserve University.

Robert Bifulco is Associate Professor of Public Policy, University of Connecticut.

Kevin Booker is Researcher, Mathematica Policy Research.

Donald Boyd is Deputy Director of the Center for Policy Research, and Senior Fellow at the Rockefeller Institute of Government, University at Albany.

Brian O. Brent is Associate Dean of Graduate Studies, Warner Graduate School of Education and Human Development, University of Rochester.

Dominic J. Brewer is Professor, Rossier School of Education, University of Southern California.

Katrina Bulkley is Associate Professor of Educational Leadership, Montclair State University.

Jay G. Chambers is Senior Research Fellow and Managing Director, American Institutes for Research.

Sean P. Corcoran is Assistant Professor of Educational Economics, New York University.

Thomas A. Downes is Associate Professor of Economics, Department of Economics, Tufts University.

William D. Duncombe is Professor of Public Administration, Department of Public Administration, Maxwell School of Citizenship and Public Affairs, Syracuse University.

Eric R. Eide is Associate Professor. Department of Economics. Brigham Young University.

William N. Evans is Keough-Hesburgh Professor of Economics, University of Notre Dame.

Edward B. Fiske, former Education Editor of the *New York Times,* is an education writer and editor.

David N. Figlio is the Knight-Ridder Professor of Economics, University of Florida.

Patricia Gándara is Professor of Education and Co-Director, Civil Rights Project/Provecto Derechos Civiles, University of California at Los Angeles.

Margaret Goertz is Professor of Education Policy and Co-Director, Consortium for Policy Research in Education, University of Pennsylvania.

Brian Gill is Senior Social Scientist, Mathematica Policy Research.

Jessica Goldberg is Doctoral Candidate, Department of Economics, University of Michigan.

Dan Goldhaber is Principal Investigator, Center on Reinventing Public Education and Research Professor, Evans School of Public Affairs, University of Washington.

Nora E. Gordon is Assistant Professor of Economics, University of California at San Diego.

Preston C. Green is Associate Professor of Educational Law, Department of Education Policy Studies and Penn State-Dickinson School of Law, Penn State University.

James W. Guthrie is Professor of Public Policy and Education, Chair of the Department of Leadership and Policy, Peabody College, Vanderbilt University, and Director of the National Center on Performance Incentives, Vanderbilt University.

Jesse Hahnel is a J.D. Candidate, Stanford Law School.

Janet S. Hansen is Senior Policy Researcher, RAND Corporation.

Jenifer J. Harr is Senior Research Analyst, the American Institutes for Research.

Douglas N. Harris is Assistant Professor of Educational Policy Studies, University of Wisconsin-Madison.

Guilbert C. Hentschke is Richard T. Cooper and Mary Catherine Cooper Chair in Public School Administration, Rossier School of Education, University of Southern California.

Stephen P. Heyneman is Professor of Public Policy and International Education, Peabody College, Vanderbilt University.

Eric A. Houck is Assistant Professor of Educational Administration, University of Georgia.

Rebecca Jacobsen is a Doctoral Candidate in Politics and Education, Teachers College, Columbia University.

Kieran M. Killeen is Associate Professor, Department of Education, University of Vermont.

William S. Koski is Eric and Nancy Wright Professor of Clinical Education and Professor of Law, Stanford Law School.

Ally Kuzin is Dean's Fellow, Rossier School of Education, University of Southern California.

Helen F. Ladd is Edgar Thompson Professor of Public Policy Studies and Professor of Economics, Sanford Institute of Public Policy, Duke University.

Hamilton Lankford is Professor of Educational Administration and Policy, University at Albany.

Henry M. Levin is the William Heard Kilpatrick Professor of Economics and Education, and Director of the National Center for the Study of Privatization (NCSPE), Teachers College, Columbia University

Paul E. Lingenfelter is President, State Higher Education Executive Officers, Boulder, CO.

Susanna Loeb is Associate Professor of Education, Stanford University.

Chad R. Lykins is Research Associate, Peabody College, Vanderbilt University.

William F. Massy is President, the Jackson Hole Higher Education Group, Inc., and Professor Emeritus, Stanford University.

Patrick J. McEwan is Associate Professor of Economics, Wellesley College.

Therese J. McGuire is the Beatrice Foods Professor in Strategic Management, Northwestern University.

Gary Miron is Chief of Staff, the Evaluation Center, and Professor of Education, Western Michigan University.

Michelle B. Nayfack is Dean's Fellow, Rossier School of Education, University of Southern California.

Allan Odden is Professor of Educational Leadership and Policy Analysis, School of Education, University of Wisconsin-Madison, and Co-Director of the Consortium for Policy Research in Education.

Leslie E. Papke is Professor of Economics, Michigan State University.

Tom Parrish is Managing Director, American Institutes for Research.

Lawrence O. Picus is Professor of Education Finance and Policy, Rossier School of Education, University of Southern California.

David N. Plank is Executive Director, Policy Analysis for California Education, University of California.

Sean F. Reardon is Associate Professor of Education, Stanford University.

Jennifer King Rice is Associate Professor of Education, Department of Education Policy and Leadership, University of Maryland.

Joseph P. Robinson is a Doctoral Candidate, School of Education, Stanford University.

Richard Rothstein is a Research Associate, Economic Policy Institute.

Russell W. Rumberger is Professor of Education, Gervitz Graduate School of Education, University of California, Santa Barbara.

Kai A. Schafft is Assistant Professor of Education and Director, Center on Rural Education and Communities, Penn State University.

Amy Ellen Schwartz is Professor of Public Policy, Education and Economics, and Director of the Institute for Education and Social Policy, Wagner Graduate School of Public Service and Steinhardt School, New York University.

John W. Sipple is Associate Professor, Department of Education, Cornell University.

BetsAnn Smith is Associate Professor of Educational Administration, Michigan State University.

Jeffrey Smith is Professor of Economics, University of Michigan and Research Associate, National Bureau of Economic Research (NBER).

Matthew G. Springer is Assistant Professor, Peabody College Vanderbilt University.

Leanna Stiefel is Professor of Economics, Wagner Graduate School of Public Service, New York University.

James Wyckoff is Professor of Public Administration, Public Policy and Economics, Rockefeller College of Public Affairs and Policy, the University at Albany.

Kenneth K. Wong is Professor of Political Science, Brown University.

John Yinger is Trustee Professor of Public Administration and Economics, Maxwell School, Syracuse University.

Ron Zimmer is Economist, Rand Corporation.

Preface

The purpose of this *Handbook of Research in Education Finance and Policy* is to assemble in one place the existing research-based knowledge in education finance and policy, and thus to help define the current state of this evolving field of research and practice. The *Handbook* is being published on behalf of the American Education Finance Association (AEFA) and is the official handbook of the Association.

The *Handbook* is intended to serve as an accessible resource for current and future members of the AEFA as well as anyone else seriously involved in education finance and policy, including academic researchers, practitioners at all levels of government in the United States and elsewhere, lawyers involved in education finance, and representatives of teacher unions. We hope that the volume will serve as a valuable resource for graduate students in professional degree programs in education and policy schools, as well as Ph.D. candidates in a variety of related fields.

The American Education Finance Association was established in 1975 with a clear-cut focus on a discrete set of issues relating to school finance policy and practice. These were issues that could be examined and understood more or less in their own terms and without reference to broader issues of educational policy. As described in the Introduction, this original vision has now undergone considerable evolution, and it is generally recognized that educational finance as a field must engage a much broader and more complex set of policy issues than in the past. In recognition of that change, the Association has recently established a new journal called *Education Finance and Policy*, published by MIT press. The first issue appeared in early 2006.

The AEFA Board of Directors approved the concept of the association's first *Handbook* in April 2005 and recruited Helen F. Ladd and Edward B. Fiske to serve as general editors. The handbook is truly a collective effort. Ladd and Fiske provided the conceptual framework for the volume and drafted the initial prospectus with input from the Board. The general editors recruited 11 Section Editors and worked closely with them to refine the list of topics to be included within each section. The section editors then identified one or more authors for each of the chapters, and they worked closely with the general editors to assure that each chapter met high quality standards with respect not only to substance but to the clarity and accessibility of the writing. All in all, 71 persons, including the general editors and many of the section editors, contributed as authors to the 40 chapters in the volume.

Assembling a manuscript of this breadth and depth is a monumental task. The Association is deeply indebted to Helen (Sunny) Ladd and Edward (Ted) Fiske, who devoted countless hours to ensuring a clear, accessible, and comprehensive treatment of education finance and policy issues. A *Handbook* of this caliber would not have been possible without their powerful intellectual leadership, tireless attention to detail, and unwavering commitment to quality.

The Association also is grateful for the hard work and enthusiasm of the section editors as well as to the many contributors to this volume. Finally, thanks go to Lane Akers at Routledge; Stewart Pether, project editor at Taylor & Francis; and the staff of EvS for their assistance in the production of this volume.

Introduction

Helen F. Ladd and Edward B. Fiske

Publication in 1983 of *A Nation at Risk*, the controversial report of the National Commission on Excellence in Education, was a milestone in American education. The report, which deplored the pervasive "mediocrity" of schooling in the United States, resonated with the concerns that many Americans had regarding the quality of education that their children were receiving. It placed education policy firmly on the national political agenda—where it has remained ever since. The search for ways to foster quality in education became a preoccupation of political and educational leaders and policy makers at the local, state, and national levels. This concern about educational quality in turn had major consequences for the field of education research, whose practitioners were increasingly called upon to provide intellectual backup for policy decisions.

Education research can take many forms and range across many different topics. One fundamental distinction is between research that examines what goes on at the student level within a classroom and research that focuses on the structures that shape the conditions within which teachers and students interact. This *Handbook of Research in Education Finance and Policy* focuses on research of the latter type. In particular, it concentrates on the financing and governance systems that are used to create and sustain the conditions necessary for promoting desirable educational outcomes.

Education finance emerged as a formal field of study at the beginning of the 20th century. What we now think of as *traditional* school finance focused primarily on the inputs of education—teachers and other human resources, textbooks, school busses, and the like—and the revenue sources used to finance these inputs. In its early years, the field of education finance attracted a limited number of academic specialists; its practitioners tended to be accountants who were employed by state governments and whose engagement with policy makers was usually limited to annual or biennial deliberations over state budgets and appropriation bills.

A principal role of early education finance experts was to construct formulas for distributing monies raised through state and local taxes across districts and among schools. They grappled with issues such as the large variation in per pupil spending across school districts, the viability of the local property tax as a major revenue source for schools, and the design of state aid programs to equalize revenue and spending across districts.

The 1954 *Brown v. Board of Education* decision ending school segregation put an end to separate school systems for black and white students, and, starting with the 1971 *Serrano vs. Priest* case in California, a series of school finance court cases challenged reliance on the property tax to finance public education. Suddenly school finance was no longer the preserve of a few scholars and a bevy of government technicians. The lines between school finance and education policy blurred, and the technicalities of distributing education funds were complicated by broader policy concerns about equity. School finance as a field expanded rapidly to include specialized attorneys, political activists, sociologists, union representatives, economists, and statistical and measurement experts. No longer solely the province of accountants and economists, school finance evolved into a field of multidisciplinary scholarship.

In the 1980s the work of school finance—like the entire field of education policy of which it had now become a part—took off in additional new directions. First came *A Nation At Risk*. Then, in 1989, President George H. W. Bush convened the country's governors for an Education Summit on the campus of the University of Virginia—the only such occasion since President Theodore Roosevelt had assembled state governors to talk about the environment—to adopt a set of national goals for U.S. education. Policy makers and practitioners at the state and national levels began looking for ways to realize these goals. By necessity, discussions of school finance became increasingly intertwined with questions of broad educational policy.

This evolution continued into the 1990s and the early years of the 20th century. A turning point was enactment by Congress of the No Child Left Behind Act of 2001 (NCLB), which substantially altered the role of the federal government in the day-to-day functioning of local schools. Among other things, NCLB required school districts to administer tests in core academic subjects and imposed sanctions on schools in which substantial proportions of students in various categories failed to pass these tests. Students in "failing" schools were given the option of taking their public funding to another school.

TRENDS IN NATIONAL EDUCATION POLICY

NCLB represented the political culmination of three major trends in national education policy over the previous two decades—each of which had major financial implications and produced new grist for the field of education finance.

The first was *standards-based reform*, a movement that stressed the need for ambitious educational outcomes and coherent policy structures to attain them. A major component of this trend is the shift away from a focus on inputs and processes to educational outcomes. Consistent with the shift from inputs to outputs was a change in the agenda of school finance research and policy from concerns about whether per pupil revenues were equitably distributed across school districts to concerns about whether resources were adequate to achieve the desired outcome standards.

The second was the push for *new forms of educational governance*. These include school-based management, charter schools, and more parental choice within the public school system as well as the possibility of greater use of public funding in the form of school vouchers for private schooling. These new forms contrast with the former "factory model" of education predicated on the view that one size school can serve the needs of all students. New governance structures inevitably require new approaches to financing schools.

The third was increased emphasis on raising the *productivity* of the education system. Such an emphasis is a byproduct of the increasing concern with educational outcomes and draws attention to the concepts of accountability, incentives, and competition. This focus on productivity forces policy makers to ask not only how revenues are generated and distributed but how they can be used most effectively in the pursuit of the desired educational outcomes.

In short, a field that for the better part of a century could be defined as *education finance* has evolved into the field of *education finance and policy*—a phrase that by no coincidence found its way into the title of the American Education Finance Association's new journal, *Education Finance and Policy*.

Contemporary education finance and policy have evolved in other ways as well. No longer is there a sharp break between the K–12 education process and what happens to students before the primary and after the secondary school experiences. Scholars are now examining issues related to what students bring to the classroom as a result of their family backgrounds and pre-school education as well to what happens to students after they graduate from high school.

Consistent with the growing connectedness of individuals and institutions around the world, researchers in the field of education finance and policy have increasingly recognized that there is now an international marketplace of ideas related to education policy and education reform. Scholars now routinely search for insights from the experience of other countries on topics such as school choice. Policy makers and researchers look to data from international organizations to compare educational achievement levels across countries. Both developed and developing countries are working together to promote greater access to quality education for all children around the world.

Finally, academics and others working in the field of education finance and policy now have an abundance of data that was not available to their predecessors. These data include national survey data on students, data from randomized field research such as the Tennessee class size experiment, and state and local administrative data sets that include repeated observations on whole populations of students. The availability of administrative data has significantly increased the quality of empirical work in this field.

STRUCTURE OF THE *HANDBOOK*

We have organized this *Handbook of Research in Education Finance and Policy* to reflect not only the evolution of the field but how each of the trends highlighted above have shaped content and methods. The seven chapters in Section I, *Perspectives on Education Finance and Policy*, edited by James W. Guthrie and Michael Kirst, establish the central theme that the field of education finance and policy is no longer the province of accountants and economists alone. Given the reality that decisions regarding school finance inevitably interact with those of governance, accountability, and other areas of education policy, a full understanding of the important contemporary issues requires insights from a variety of perspectives.

Thus the *Handbook* opens with a series of chapters that provide different perspectives on the field. The chapters in Section I show, among other things, how growing federal involvement in the delivery of education has altered relationships between the various levels of government, and how the public has frequently held broader expectations for schools than legislators and other policy makers. Other chapters describe the growing importance of market-based and other economic concepts in education policy, the impact of litigation on issues such as equity and adequacy, and the emergence of sophisticated quantitative research methods. A final chapter highlights the growing importance of global trends in education finance.

Section II, *Making Money Matter*, edited by Jennifer King Rice and Amy Ellen Schwartz, explores the growing concern with productivity in education, a concept that has various meanings but is fundamentally concerned with using available resources most effectively to realize desired student outcomes. While researchers from a variety of disciplines have used various methods to examine the relationship between education inputs and outcomes, much of the recent research on productivity draws heavily on the concept of the education production function as developed by economists.

In general, policy makers and researchers have recognized three types of strategies to improve educational outcomes: (1) changing the quality or quantity of key inputs such as teachers, (2) improving the productivity of existing resources though better education technologies, and (3) introducing incentives embedded in high stakes accountability policies or market-based reforms. Although researchers and policy makers alike have identified quality teachers as the single most important educational resource provided to students, the empirical relationship between specific measurable teacher qualifications and student performance is often elusive. Likewise, research shows that the effectiveness of incentives is largely a function of the design elements built into them, such as the outcomes that are included in an accountability system or who is eligible for a school voucher program. While theory suggests that all three strategies hold promise for improving student outcomes, continued research is needed to promote a better understanding of how resources matter in different contexts and for different types of students.

Section III, *Promoting Equity and Adequacy,* edited by Leanna Stiefel, explores the all-important sea change that occurred around 1990 when the focus shifted from an *implied* to an *explicit* focus on achieving fairness and effectiveness in educational outputs. Previously, for example, states used foundation formulas to set a level of funding that would provide for the basic education of all children. Fairness was measured in terms of inputs, mostly expenditures or revenues, and output goals were only implied. With the advent of school finance court cases based on *adequacy,* the focus has shifted to outputs and, specifically, to the levels of financial and other resources needed to achieve specific learning outcomes.

Despite the passage of more than 15 years, the design of systems to achieve and measure outputs is still in its infancy. We can see this infancy and lack of knowledge in both measures of adequacy (four very different measures are commonly employed) and in the multiplicity of methods for calculating the cost of educating students with different needs. We still know relatively little about the production function in education, including what role schools themselves can have in affecting outputs. Likewise, we have limited knowledge of the impact on learning of factors outside of the school walls, such as family resources and health issues, and the sorts of resources needed to compensate for outside-of-school deficiencies. Thus our ability to define the level of funding needed to achieve "adequate" education remains constrained.

The five chapters in Section IV, *Changing Patterns of Governance and Finance,* edited by Andrew Reschovsky, focus on the evolution of funding and governance in elementary and secondary public education. Up through the first half of the last century, nearly all of the financial resources needed to fund schools came from local governments. During the past 30 years, however, state governments have emerged as the largest single source of education funding and, more recently, financial contributions from the federal government and from private sources, foundations, and individual donations, have come to play an increasingly important role.

Research provides strong evidence that, starting with the *Serrano v. Priest* decision in 1971 in California, legal challenges to state funding systems have led to an increased state share of support for schools and an increase in funding equity, usually through increased funding to low-spending districts. On the negative side, widespread enactment of tax and spending limitations (TELS) has placed limits on local government revenues and, evidence shows, lowered student academic performance. Money and governance are clearly related. In a number of states, the increased role of state funding of education came with increased control by the state over the governance of the schools. This control took the form of requirements to take specific steps to improve the academic performance of students and in some states, of restrictions on how local school districts spent money and on their ability to raise local taxes. This section also explores how demographic changes, especially the aging of the baby boom generation, may result in increased opposition to the property tax as a source of education funding. Whether decreased political support for the local funding of education will occur and whether the state or federal government, or private-sector donors, will compensate for a diminished local role are all questions for future research.

The chapters in Section V, *Educational Markets and Decentralization,* edited by Henry M. Levin, describe a concept that appears to be clear from its language but is elusive in that it takes many different forms in practice. Virtually all schools produce both private benefits for families and public ones that benefit larger social entities such as a communities, regions, or nations through higher productivity, democratic functioning, and social cohesion. The key starting point for researchers is to recognize that different forms of schooling, such as traditional public schools, charter schools, private schools, and home schooling, emphasize different combinations of public and private components and benefits.

These chapters explore the various approaches to privatization, including charter schools, voucher programs, and—the most privatized form of education—home schooling. They take note of the recent trend both in the U.S. and internationally to devolve the management of schools from centralized to decentralized levels, often to individual schools. A private industry of Education Management Organizations, or EMOs, has arisen to manage schools. Above all, this section of the *Handbook* shows that there are many forms of privatization, and that predictions of their consequences are not straightforward. Research shows, for example, that the capacity of EMO's either to improve student performance or to generate profits has yet to be demonstrated. The details of each approach weigh heavily on the probable outcomes, and evaluations of results are challenging and often indeterminate.

Section VI, *Race, SES and Achievement Gaps*, edited by Susanna Loeb, explores what is known about the relationships between family background and educational outcomes, focusing particularly on the reasons for these relationships and on policies designed to break the often deleterious link between the two. The various authors examine the research on patterns of achievement differences across racial and ethnic groups and among students of high and low socioeconomic status. Research has shown, for example, that systematic differences in development and ability emerge long before children enter school, and those children who start school at a disadvantage are likely to remain behind their peers throughout school and beyond. Further, the research evidence in the section shows that policies both contribute to and have the potential to reduce achievement gaps between groups. Advances in research have highlighted the importance of the early childhood environment as a contributing factor to school readiness gaps. Nonetheless, implementing programs that meaningfully narrow the differences in school readiness has been a major challenge.

Once children enter school, they are faced with resource differences that often contribute to the gaps. Research shows, for example, that the least-qualified teachers typically teach in the schools with the highest concentration of disadvantaged students for a variety of reasons related primarily to teachers' preferences with regard to compensation and working conditions. Research presented in this section suggests a number of promissing approaches to reducing achievement gaps. These include early childhood interventions, reducing segregation, providing financial incentives to attract teachers willing to work in challenging settings, and improving the working conditions in such schools.

Section VII, *Special Circumstances*, edited by David H. Monk, addresses the education of children who are in special circumstances that arise from certain combinations of geography, history, and the incidence of particular populations of students. It begins with a review of funding for students with disabilities and describes the lively debates that have surrounded both the diagnosis of their needs and the determination of the appropriate school response. Research in special education has shown the critical importance of establishing coherent links between special and general education funding.

Successive chapters highlight new insights into the educational situation of students with limited or non-existent English language skills and examine the particular needs and characteristics of students in rural schools. The section concludes with a review of student transience, an important but largely unappreciated source of costs for schools. Population transience is a significant sociological concept that has been the focus of numerous sociological studies, including some that focus on schools.

Finally, Section VIII, *Higher Education,* edited by David W. Breneman and Michael S. McPherson, looks at recent trends in the financing of higher education, most notably the key policy issues relating to access and retention, affordability, accountability, educational quality assessment and linkages to K–12 education. The various chapters discuss the decline that began in the early 1990s in the share of state revenues devoted to higher education as well as concerns about affordability and the pricing of potential students out of the market. They explore the various economic theories and potential explanations for the rising economic price to the consumer of higher education and show why it is so difficult for legislators to put the brakes on these increases.

Still other chapters describe what research has shown about the financial rates of return to graduates of various types of colleges, programs, and majors as well as the impact of federal and state tuition assistance programs, and their private counterparts run by private foundations and institutions. Finally, the section looks at growing efforts to link higher education more explicitly to K–12 preparation in the form of remediation at the collegiate level, the growing use of dual-enrollment programs and efforts to align high school graduation requirements with college entrance requirements.

LOOKING AHEAD

Our goal as general editors was to produce a *Handbook* that would review the research on education finance and policy in a comprehensive, balanced, and accessible manner. With the help of a dedicated set of section editors, who have devoted countless hours to their tasks, we believe we have collectively achieved this goal.

This volume is comprehensive in that it covers topics of traditional, current, and emerging interest. Traditional concerns include the evaluation of revenue sources, the distribution of inputs across school districts, and the design of state aid distribution formulas. Among the current issues are the use of the school as the basic unit for accountability and management, and the overarching concern with educational outcomes. Emerging issues include the challenges of dealing with students who have special needs, such as transient students or language minority students, and the growing relevance of international comparisons and experiences. Running through all of these trends is a recognition that education is a continuous, even seamless, process that begins well before kindergarten and extends to higher education and beyond.

The *Handbook* is balanced in that, in the selection of authors and the writing of chapters, we have sought to reflect the wide range of methodological approaches and conclusions that characterize the field of education finance and policy. While not shying away from controversy, we have tried to avoid pushing any particular point of view. We thank the contributors, many of whom have strong opinions on the topics about which they are writing, for taking this objective seriously.

Finally, we have paid special attention to the need to make the *Handbook* accessible to the growing audience of scholars, policy makers, and practitioners with an interest in education finance and policy. While many of the chapters cover complex state-of-the-art empirical research, we have worked with authors to explain key concepts in language that non-specialists can understand, in many cases providing technical details in appendices. This volume deals with issues that are important to all Americans—students, parents, employers, and citizens as well as to education specialists and researchers—in the early years of the 21st century. Our hope is that the wealth of factual information, data, and wisdom to be found in these chapters will make a significant contribution to improving the quality of education in the United States.

I

PERSPECTIVES ON EDUCATION FINANCE AND POLICY

Section Editors

James W. Guthrie and Michael Kirst

1

History and Scholarship Regarding United States Education Finance and Policy

Matthew G. Springer, Eric A. Houck, and James W. Guthrie

INTRODUCTION

America's first generation of education funding systems provided land to stimulate popular provision of schooling. Today, state funding mechanisms have evolved into a complex array of policy levers ranging from pupil weighting schemes and interlocking systems of property, income and sales taxation to provisions for vouchers, tax credits and home school certificates. Scholars and policy makers routinely deal with issues ranging from how to promote more equitable distribution of education resources within states to the relationships (or lack thereof) between various "purchased inputs" and academic performance.

Ironically, even though contemporary education finance issues are more complex than their 19th century predecessors, there is much about them that has a familiar ring. Much of modern education finance policy is rooted in questions that have persisted for over 100 years. For example, in 1906, Elwood P. Cubberley in *School Funds and Their Apportionment,* the work that launched the scholarly study of education finance, noted "However desirable and even necessary it may be to provide more money with which to maintain the schools of a state, a still more important question is how to distribute this money so as to secure the best results."

Like generations of education finance researchers to follow, Cubberley was concerned with the manner in which governments generate and distribute revenues for schools, and with the results that flow therefrom. Although he likely did not anticipate the full spectrum of issues now confronting education finance scholars and policy makers—economic concepts such as efficiency or productivity come to mind—Cubberley's distillation of fundamental issues is as relevant today as it was over a century ago.

This chapter has a twofold purpose: (1) to describe the historic evolution of American education finance policy; and (2) building upon this historic platform, to explain the modern day integration of education finance with larger issues of education policy. In the process, the chapter reviews basic education governance structures and revenue generation and resource distribution mechanisms upon which American public education now depends. This discussion sets the stage for an examination of the three public values shaping the direction of contemporary educational finance and policy: equity, efficiency, and liberty.

HISTORIC AND CONTEMPORARY CONTEXT OF EDUCATION FINANCE AND POLICY

Financial support for K–12 education is one of the nation's major objects of public expenditure. School spending, as a percent of Gross Domestic Product (GDP), has increased steadily since 1936, with more than a four-fold increase in per-pupil terms in constant dollars since 1966 (see Figure 1.1).[1] A 2005 international comparison ranked the United States first among 27 OECD (Organization for Economic Co-operation and Development) nations in terms of annual total education expenditures as a percentage of GDP and country wealth (see Figure 1.2). This steady stream of rationally justified and politically accepted expansions in school services and attendant increases in school spending has led some to conclude that the system is operating inefficiently, thus advocating for reform efforts to focus on productivity.

However, a reader should not view the above-depicted resource trajectory as evidence that school spending has simply spiraled out of control. One reason for the fulsome increase of school costs has been the expansion of expectations within the larger policy system. These include increased high school graduation rates and consequent reduced incidence of school drop outs; the addition of costly auxiliary services such as meals, transportation, and guidance; the far greater inclusion of previously neglected populations such as disabled, limited English-speaking, and immigrant students; and a recent interest in the provision of preschool education for students.

Public education continues to be increasingly labor intensive and, not coincidentally, resistant of efforts to substitute capital for labor. Whereas economic sectors such as agriculture, transportation, manufacturing, communication, and finance have become increasingly capital intensive, schooling has moved in the opposite direction by adding labor and increasing the quality of that labor. Since 1970 the national average pupil-teacher ratio (see Figure 1.3) has decreased from 22.3 to an estimated 15.4 in 2007 (National Center for Education Statistics, 2004), the pro-

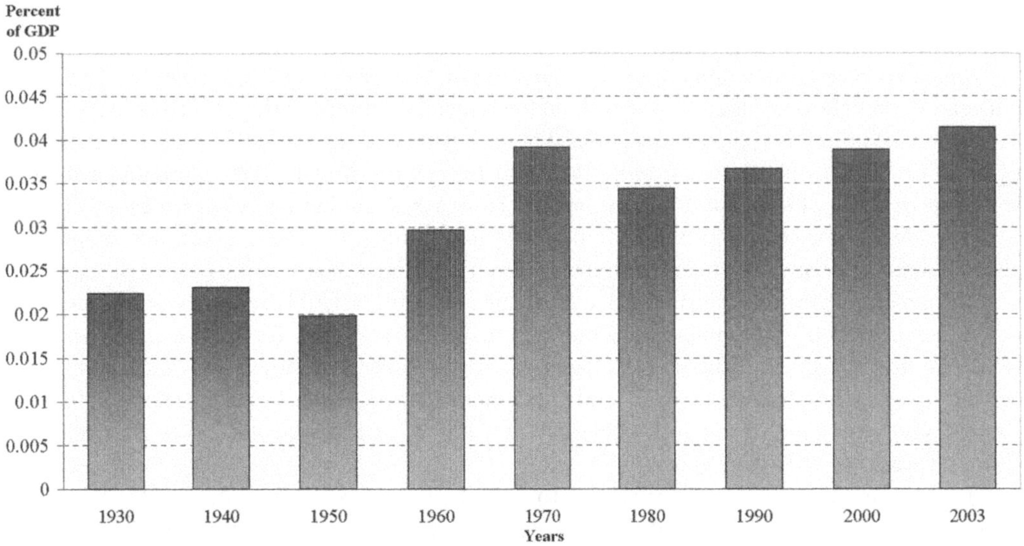

FIGURE 1.1. Federal, State, and Local K–12 Education Expenditures as a percentage of GDP in Current Dollars (1930–2003).

Source: U.S. Department of Education, National Center for Education Statistics, Biennial Survey of Education in the United States, 1919–20 through 1949–50; Statistics of State School Systems, 1959–60 and 1969–70; Revenues and Expenditures for Public Elementary and Secondary Education, 1979–80; and The NCES Common Core of Data (CCD), "National Public Education Financial Survey," 1989–90 through 2002–03.

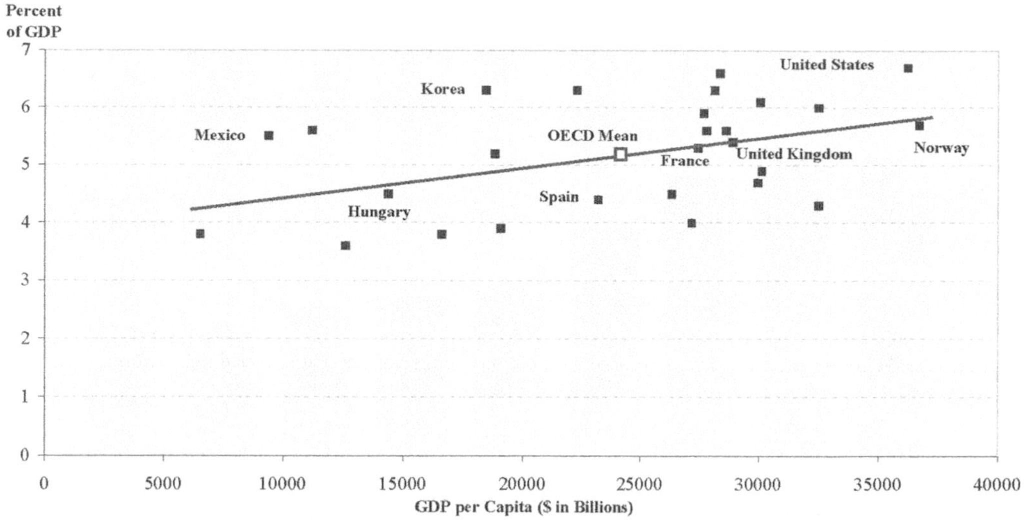

FIGURE 1.2. Linear Relationship between Total Expenditures as a percentage of GDP and Country Wealth for 27 OECD Countries (2002).

Source: Organization for Economic Cooperation and Development (OCED), Center for Educational Research and Innovation (2005). Education at a Glance: OECD Indicators, 2005, tables B1.1, B2.1c, and X2.1. Data from OECD Education Database, previously unpublished tabulation (August 2005).

portion of teachers with masters degrees and beyond (see Figure 1.4) has risen from 23.1 percent to 56 percent, and median years of teaching experience has increased from 11 to 14 (National Center for Education Statistics, 2005).

These conditions, the provision and expansion of school services, a preference that schooling be more efficient, and an omnipresent desire that students learn more and go to school for a

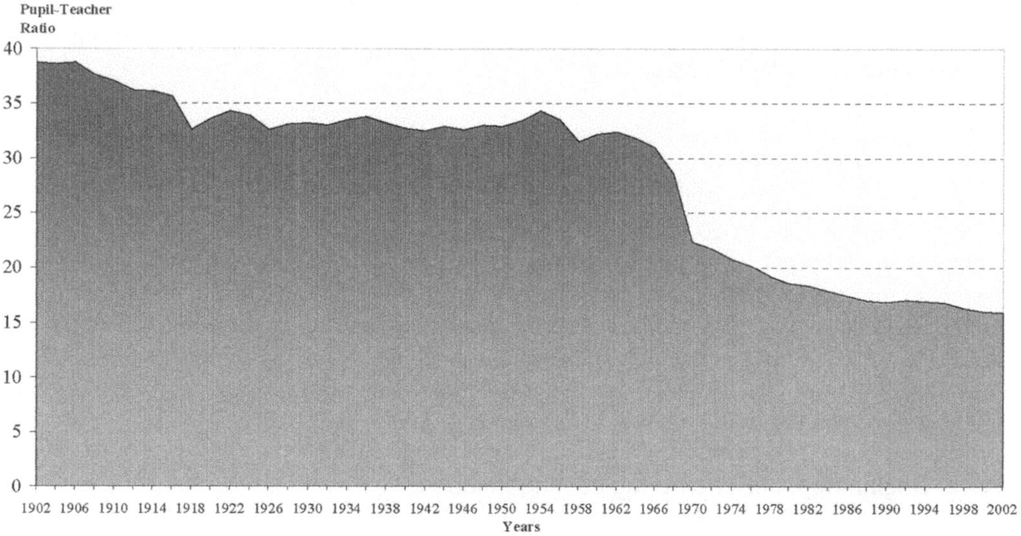

FIGURE 1.3. Pupil–Teacher Ratio in United States K–12 Public Education (1902–2002).

Source: U.S. Census, Statistical Abstract: Bicentenial Edition—Social Studies—Education; U.S. Census Statistical Abstract: 1971—Education Section Table 173; and NCES Digest of Education Statistics 2005 Table 63.

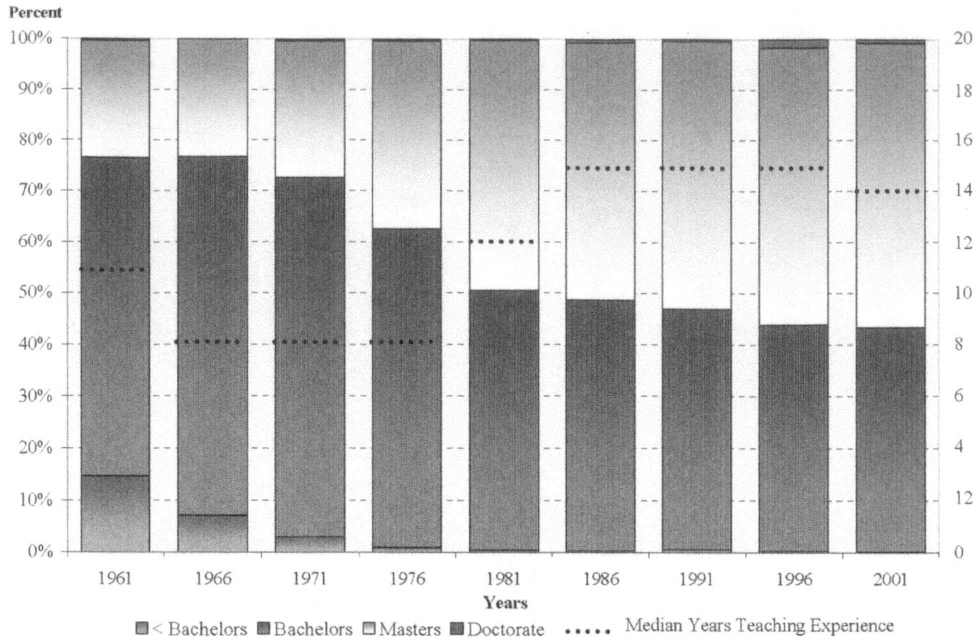

FIGURE 1.4. Degrees Held and Median Years Teaching Experience for K–12 Public School Teachers (1961–2001).

Source: National Education Association, Status of the American Public School Teacher, 2000.

longer period of time, are illustrative of the policy struggles that have characterized American public schooling since its inception. What distinguishes the early part of the 21st century, however, is that the amplitude or valence of these sometimes conflicting expectations has vastly intensified. The growing significance of formal education, both for societal and individual well-being, has thrust education finance policy, and the research that accompanies it, into the forefront of the education policy and scholarly arenas.

EDUCATION GOVERNANCE, REVENUE GENERATION, AND RESOURCE DISTRIBUTION

For more than 150 years, schooling has been a public good provided, at taxpayer expense, free of charge to the immediate user. Education governance in K–12 public education is a function of the inter-jurisdictional dynamics put in place by the United States Constitution at the end of the 18th century. The taxation and resource distribution mechanisms upon which American K–12 public education now depends was a product of this governance system and was itself shaped in the industrial period from the mid-19th to the mid-20th centuries.

Federal Beginnings and Their Long Lasting Influence

The United States is one of only a handful of nations that rely upon a decentralized administrative and financing model rather than a national or central governmental system, to operate and govern education. Because the framers of the Constitution did not explicitly specify education as a federal government responsibility, the logic of the 10th Amendment places plenary authority for schools with state governments. States, however, have delegated significant responsibility for financing and operating the nation's approximate 14,000 public school districts and 96,000 traditional public schools.

Political and economic support for schooling long has involved a mixture of federal, state, and local governmental actors and actions. Figure 1.5 shows that the role of federal, state, and local governmental entities in generating revenue and distributing resources has varied across time. Broadly speaking, local districts now provide approximately 42.8 percent of total funding, the federal government 8.5 percent, and state governments the remaining 48.7 percent (National Center for Education Statistics, 2005).

Early federal policy provided land for use in establishing schools, as land was one of the few resources easily at hand. As early as 1783, when England's King George III's Proclamation of Cessation of Hostilities culminated in the Paris Peace Treaty (1783), there was official reference to use of public lands to support schools (Barr, et al. 1970). Since the Ordinance of 1785 (later known as the Northwest Ordinance of 1787), when the Continental Congress appropriated public lands to establish schools, federal land grants have served as a cornerstone for federal involvement in education. Such grants also provided a working model for state initiatives that induced local districts to establish an educational system.

It was not until the 1900s, and particularly the latter part of the 20th century, however, that the federal government began to appropriate money in a manner that forcefully influenced education policy. Each of these federal initiatives—from 1917 to the present—reflected federal educational priorities, and each has influenced schools in the United States to the extent that vestiges of early efforts are still visible in today's educational operations. Federal funding priorities for public schools have sought to ensure flows of scarce workforce talent (the 1917 Smith Hughes Act, the 1958 National Defense Education Act), to expand access and equity (Title I of the 1965 Elementary and Secondary Education Act), and to promote school reform (1998 Comprehensive School Reform Act, provisions of the 2001 No Child Left Behind). Federal involvement is most notable by the growth in the federal share of revenue provided to schools following the mid-

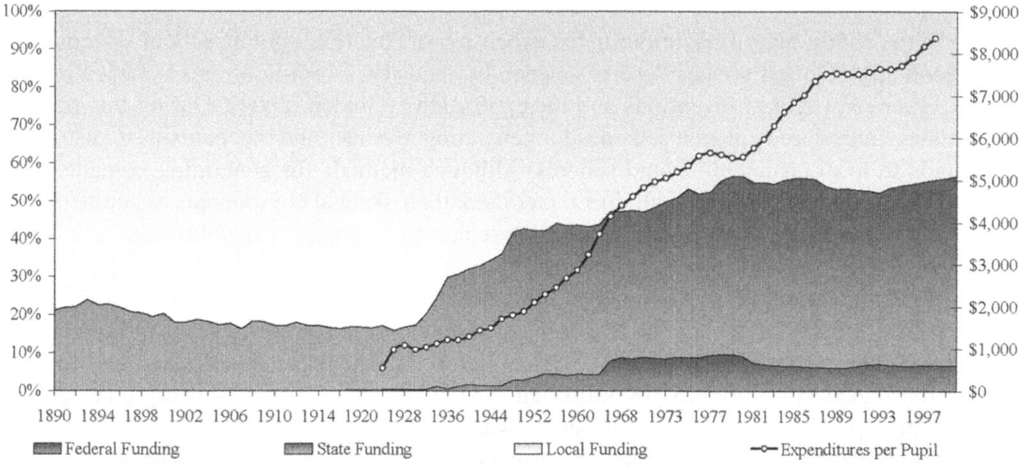

FIGURE 1.5. Education Revenue by Source and Per-Pupil Expenditure in Constant Dollars (1890–2000).

Source: U.S. Department of Education, National Center for Education Statistics, Biennial Survey of Education in the United States, 1919–20 through 1955–56; Statistics of State School Systems, 1957–58 through 1969–70; Revenues and Expenditures for Public Elementary and Secondary Education, 1970–71 through 1986–87; The NCES Common Core of Data (CCD), "National Public Education Financial Survey," 1987–88 through 2002–03.

1960s implementation of the Elementary and Secondary Education Act, as can be seen in Figure 1.5.

Because United States Constitutional authority for education was allocated, at least by default, to state government, and because state constitutions specify varying levels of commitment to education, revenue generation and distribution schemes vary widely across states. There are, in effect, 50 school finance systems operating nationwide, and even more if one considers the District of Columbia and the various federally-overseen trust Territories and Department of Defense Schools. Add to this list the many private religious and independent schools, and one begins to understand the remarkable complexity of United States school governance.

Constitutional authority for education is lodged principally with state legislative bodies. However, as education has ascended as a public policy priority over the last quarter of the 20th century, increasing numbers of governors have adopted education reform as a major element of their policy portfolio. For example, prior to becoming presidents of the United States, James Earl "Jimmy" Carter, Jr., William Jefferson Clinton, and George W. Bush were aggressive education reformists in their respective states. Beginning with education finance equity in the early 1970s and extending to education finance adequacy today, state courts too have become increasingly active in overseeing education matters.

While federal and state involvement undoubtedly shaped early education policy, it was local townships and communities that bore principal responsibility for developing means to generate education revenue. This arrangement reflected Americans' generally high regard for local government and a belief that individual freedom is best protected if government remains in the hands of small, presumably self-concerned communities. Indeed, every state except Hawaii has delegated major responsibility for operating and financing public schools to local school districts.

Many districts have local taxing authority, set salary levels for employees, allocate teachers and students across schools, and advocate for funding of capital construction. Local funding comes from property taxation and some local option sales taxation. Funds for capital construction are also raised by issuing bonds.

Industrialization's Contributions

Starting in the 1850s, industrialization fueled expansion of America's public school system. The "new" economy involved greater "use of science by industry, a proliferation of academic disciplines, a series of critical inventions and their diffusion" (Golden, 2004). During this period, policy makers introduced taxation schemes for generating revenues and mechanisms to distribute these funds to local communities and schools. Although methods for generating revenues and distributing resources have continually been modified, their skeletal components assembled during a century long time starting in the 1850s have remained comparatively unbroken.

Generating Revenues. Taxation is the main method of revenue generation for public education. For the 2002–2003 school year, general revenues of public elementary and secondary school in the United States amounted to $449 billion. Of this amount local, state, and federal sources contributed $192 billion, $218 billion, and $38 billion, respectively. Seventy-nine percent of the revenue provided by local governments was raised through property taxes. Sixty-eight percent of the revenue provided by state governments resulted from general formula assistance that includes revenue from state income and sales taxes.

Distributing Resources. In an effort to promote the provision and expansion of public schooling, the first generation of finance scholars began studying and developing intergovernmental fiscal arrangements and criteria for distributing revenue to compensate communities for differences in local property wealth. Scholars such as Elwood P. Cubberley of Stanford University, Arthur B. Moehlman of the University of Michigan, Henry C. Morrison of the University of Chicago, Harlan Updegraff of the University of Pennsylvania, and George D. Strayer, Robert Murray Haig, and Paul R. Mort of Teachers College not only contributed to an expansion of scholarship, but also had substantial practical influence upon policies that states adopted to generate and distribute revenues to local school districts (Johns, 1938; Moehlman, 1925, 1932; Morrison, 1924, 1930, 1932; Mort, 1924, 1926, 1932; Updegraff, 1922; Updegraff & King, 1922).

Three of the most common early methods for public school resource distribution were: (1) flat grants, (2) foundation programs, and (3) equalization plans. The modern versions of these school funding strategies are discussed in Picus, Odden, and Goertz in this volume.

Flat Grants. When states began appropriating money to local communities to assist with the cost of schooling, they typically allocated equal amounts of money to each community, regardless of the number of school age children or its ability to raise money locally. The flat grant approach to resource distribution was intended to guarantee that each locality have at least one public elementary school. While flat grant distribution systems are rare today, by the 1930s, 38 states were distributing flat grants to districts based on a count of all school-age children (Guthrie, Springer, Rolle, and Houck, 2007).

Policy makers assumed that schooling in excess of this minimum would benefit only the individual recipient or the community in which he or she resided. They further assumed that added spending, above the flat grant amount, was a local luxury to be indulged in as each community saw fit, and not to be subsidized by the state. Under these assumptions, the flat grant is a satisfactory wealth equalizer. It does not equalize for differences in need or cost, which is a different matter, to be discussed later. Since the amount of the flat grant is presumed to be sufficient to cover the education level the state believes to be minimally necessary; and, since the same grant is provided to all students equally and raised by taxes levied at a uniform rate on all residents of the state, there is nothing inherently unequal about it. Improvements in educational services, then, were seen simply as matters of increasing minimum expectations. This policy improvement, Cubberley asserted, should be made "without reference to whether or not a portion of its communities will be unable, unaided, to meet the demands" (1906, p. 17).

A practical problem with flat grants, however, is that states had no scientific means for determining the appropriate dollar amount per student. Instead, the size of the flat grant was determined by the political process, and, because there are many other demands on the state treasury, is inevitably lower than the resource level at which school advocates believe a proper education can be purchased. Moreover, flat grants have historically lacked any consideration of the diversity of students in enrolled in districts, and they have also funded districts within a state the same regardless of size and made no distinction between urban and rural contexts (Waterman, 1932; Mort, 1933). Early efforts to adjust for student populations divided district valuation by the number of elementary school classrooms (Mort, 1933). However, wide discrepancies were found between rural and urban districts (Mort and Lawler, 1938). No state now depends solely on flat grants as a means of financing the state share of educational costs. The last state to rely upon such a method, Connecticut, adopted an equalizing plan in 1975.

Foundation Plan. George D. Strayer and Robert M. Haig (1923) were the first to publish descriptions of the practical problems with the administration of flat grants and to propose a solution. In a report to the Educational Finance Inquiry Commission based on a study of New York State, they proposed a system that captured a portion of the local property tax for state purposes. Their proposal has since become known as the foundation program, or the Strayer-Haig plan.

In a foundation program, just as with a flat grant, a state specified the dollar amount per student to which each school district was entitled. Presumptively, this was the amount of money per pupil necessary to guarantee a minimally adequate education. At the time of the foundation plan's conception, there were few systematic efforts to ensure that the dollar amount prescribed was sufficient to provide a foundational level of schooling. More often than not, the foundation dollar amount was an outcome of the political process. In this scenario, state legislatures, predisposed to a certain level of taxation or constrained by the level of revenue available, initially established a revenue pool and then, through division, determined the per pupil amount of the foundation.

As with the flat grant, and indeed all resource distribution schemes, there are practical problems with the foundation plan. First, despite a certain "elegance," foundation plans assume that the foundation spending is the dollar amount necessary for a minimally adequate education, although there is no way of determining such a benchmark with precision (Benson, 1961, p. 205). Second, if the tax rate mandated for the required local effort is set low, the aggregate amount of the funding appropriation required from state sources may be more than the state can afford.

On the other hand, if the required local tax rate is high so that less money is required from the state, a substantial number of districts will raise more than the foundation guarantee at the local tax required rate, and hence lose eligibility for state aid. Theoretically, a state could use a foundation plan and "recapture" excess district level funds. Recent evidence from Texas, however, suggests that attempts to enact recapture in an education finance system have caused negative capitalization because districts are loathe to contribute their tax dollars for funding in other districts (Hoxby and Kuziemko, 2004). Nechyba (1996) noted that, when housing markets are sufficiently settled, the effect might be small in magnitude. Finally, the Strayer-Haig plan was criticized for its equal treatment of pupil as units of funding, for the lack of leeway, which would ensure than even wealthy districts received a modicum of state aid (Mort and Reusser, 1951), and for the lack of incentives for local effort (Benson, 1961).

Percentage Equalizing Plan. A percentage equalizing plan employs a different philosophy than flat grants and foundation programs. Essentially, percentage equalizing plans define equity as equal access to finances for education. The state's responsibility under this plan is to ensure that district level effort to support schools is equally rewarded regardless of any individual district's property wealth. The state backs up this promise by subsidizing the tax effort of poorer districts.

Adoption of percentage equalizing was first urged by Updegraff and King (1922) around the same time Strayer and Haig advocated the foundation plan. However, it was not until Benson (1961) popularized the percentage equalizing concept that states began to adopt the approach. It is interesting to note that the Strayer-Haig plan became the dominant state funding mechanism plan, whereas percentage equalizing was never widely adopted. Only Iowa, Massachusetts, Maine, New York, Pennsylvania, Rhode Island, Utah, and Wisconsin adopted a form of percentage equalizing.

Like the other plans, percentage equalizing has suffered from practical problems. First, if the local district is responsible for deciding the size of its education budget and the state thereafter guarantees equal access to funds, there are no budgetary size restrictions. For example, a district with a very high aid ratio will spend a large amount of money simply because it knows that an additional dollar of local taxes will bring in an additional $10 or $20 of state money at very little financial cost to its citizenry. Second, the percentage equalizing formula, like that of the foundation plan, carries the possibility that some districts will receive no equalization money at all, or worse, be forced to contribute to the state instead.

In 2005, 34 states relied on a foundation program and 9 states relied upon some form of a percentage equalization plan. Five states used weighted funding based on census percentages, and North Carolina retained a heavily modified grant program. Hawaii, which functions as a single district, relies upon a full state assumption plan.

MODERN EDUCATION FINANCE: THE PURSUIT OF EQUALITY, EFFICIENCY, AND LIBERTY

Four scholarly publications, two highly visible national reports, and two court decisions signal the onset of the modern era in education finance and policy. These eight scholarly documents and public pronouncements have shaped education finance and propelled the field of education finance onto its current center stage of American education policy setting. Key questions confronting researchers and policymakers have included themes of equity, efficiency and liberty. In short, researchers have asked: Are some students systematically disadvantaged by school finance structures? Is the public getting the most they can expect from the expenditures they invest in public education? Are school systems maximizing parental choice in school attendance decisions? The rest of the chapters in this section address these issues in turn, providing a backdrop for some of the chapters to follow.

The Quest for Equality

Despite the continual formulaic tweaking of funding programs throughout the early 1900s, the fact remained that localities raised differential amounts of funds for education because state funding systems allowed local contributions. In latter part of the mid-1900s, school finance researchers began to understand that such funding arrangements provided a systematic disadvantage to specific classes of citizens and sought to develop legal arguments to address this disparity. *Private Wealth and Public Education,* by John E. Coons, William H. Clune, and Stephen D. Sugarman (1970), and *Rich Schools: Poor Schools*, by Arthur Wise (1970), became path-breaking volumes. Though written independently, both books targeted property related resource disparities within states as an injustice and constructed a constitutional argument, based on the Fourteenth Amendment's equal protection clause, by which resource disparities could become a productive province for adjudication. This scholarship, undertaken within the context of the 1960s Civil Rights movement, facilitated the equity quest of the 1960s and the judicial mindset of modern education finance that continues to this day.

In the 1971 case of *Serrano v. Priest*, plaintiffs argued that poor citizens received unequal treatment as a class of citizens from the state of California's school finance system. The *Serrano* court ruled in their favor, finding the state funding system of California unconstitutional because of unequal treatment of poor citizens. In legal parlance, the *Serrano* court treated poor citizens as a "suspect class", which gave the state a high hurdle to pass in proving the state funding system constitutional. However, in 1973, the United States Supreme Court's decision in *San Antonio Independent School District v. Rodriguez* ruled against the *Serrano*-style argument and thereby, at least for now, neutralized finance equity as a federal constitutional matter.

Nevertheless, the legal reasoning based on state equal protection constructs by Wise and Coons, Clune, and Sugarman continued to prevail at the state level. The artful arguments constructed by these scholars came to be termed Proposition One: *The quality of a child's schooling should not be a function of wealth, other than the wealth of the state as a whole*. It is this formulation that provided the judicial system with a purchase on remedy, a criterion by which equity reforms can be judged and served as a foundation for much school finance research around issues of equality of access to educational resources (Guthrie, Springer, Rolle, and Houck, 2007). Proposition One does not specify any appropriate spending level per pupil. Rather, it takes the opposite approach and specifies what the pattern of finance distribution should *not* be. Whatever an appropriate level, it should not be a function of local or personal wealth.

Prior to the formulation of Proposition One, courts avoided education finance litigation for fear that there were no manageable solutions to finance inequality. This judicial reluctance was reinforced by seemingly daunting issues of definition and measurement. Just how was one to measure the wealth of the state as a whole? How could one tell if a state was complying with a judicial decree to render its education finance system equitable?

The next signal contribution was made by another set of education finance scholars, Robert Berne and Leanna Stiefel. In their 1984 scholarly volume, *The Measurement of Equity in School Finance*, Berne and Stiefel specify multiple definitions of equity, methodological procedures for measuring equity, and explored empirical issues in resource allocation that facilitated plaintiffs' pursuit of greater equalization in the distribution of school funding. Ultimately, their work changed the debate about school finance from theoretical (or *ex ante*) analysis to more concrete (or *ex post*) terms. Berne and Stiefel's measurements and conceptual framework allowed researchers to measure the equity of funds as they had been generated and distributed, thereby giving lawyers and judges both a means to measure the effect of a system as well as a manner of defining how a system had to change in order to meet constitutional muster.

The legal logic constructed by the Coons team and Wise, buttressed by the measurement contributions of Berne and Stiefel, had an enormous effect on education finance and policy. Court cases alleging equal protection violations were filed in literally dozens of states, and by the 1990s 36 states had faced equity-based challenges (Springer, Liu, and Guthrie, 2006). Legislatures in many states—sometimes in response to or in anticipation of, a judicial decision, or in hopes of forestalling an unfavorable judicial decision—began devising new distribution arrangements to reduce inter-district per pupil spending disparities.

This combination of state level judicial and legislative efforts aimed at reducing resource disparities had significant impact on the distribution of school resources. In 1998, for example, Murray, Evans, and Schwab published a comprehensive analysis of the impact of court-mandated reform on resource distribution. They generated a nationwide panel dataset with more than 16,000 district observations and estimated a series of econometric models to assess whether funding disparities had decreased within and between states between 1972 and 1992. Murray and colleagues found that as a result of court-mandated reform intrastate inequality was dampened to the point that disparities between states were grater than disparities within states. They also found that spending rose in the lowest and median spending school districts and remained constant in the highest spending districts; and they showed how increased spending was a result of higher taxes and not a reallocation of resource from other government expenditure categories such as hospitals, health care, and highways. See Section III of this volume for a more comprehensive review of education finance equity.

The Quest for Adequacy (Equity II)[2]

While the intrastate equity movement dominated education finance and policy during the 1960s, 1970s, and 1980s, it failed to address the amounts of money deemed necessary or adequate for students to achieve state constitutional guarantees; nor did it suggest means by which districts could spend resources more wisely in order to generate desired outcomes. It was a more general education policy movement in latter part of the 20th century that allowed school finance as a field to begin to tackle these difficult issues.

The standards-based reform movement, based on a theory of systemic alignment (Smith and O'Day, 1991), allowed policy makers to move from questions of resource distribution to resource use. Smith and O'Day articulated a vision for education policy by which state level policy defined the knowledge and skills that students would acquire, as well as assessments to measure the attainment of that knowledge and those skills. Local districts would align curriculum and instruction with state standards, and prove their acquisition through performance on state level assessments. In this system, policies, curriculum and assessments would be aligned in the service of teaching and learning. The adoption of a systemic framework allowed education policy to refine its focus on broader issues of aligning the work of local, state and federal education officials—often around notions of educational accountability. Two questions arise when researchers inquire regarding the use of revenues. First, do funding levels provide sufficient support to schools in attaining achievement goals? That is, are the funds adequate to the expectations of the system? And, second, are educational funds expended in a manner that makes efficient use of taxpayer dollars?

A Kentucky Supreme Court decision in *Rose v. Council for Better Education* (1989) shifted school finance discussion from the conventional notion of equity—which focused on the measuring the distribution of resources—towards a new concept called resource adequacy or Equity II—which focuses on the relationships between funding and the actual education delivered to students. Adequacy seeks to "backward map" policy expectation to arrive at more precise levels of student funding (Clune, 1995).

While the definition of an "adequate" education varies from state-to-state, based on the language in a state's education clause, education finance adequacy generically infers that a sufficient level of resources be available to all students, thus providing them opportunity at least to reach a level of proficiency defined by state standards (Guthrie, Springer, Rolle, Houck, 2007; Ladd and Hansen, 1999; Odden and Clune, 1998).

State courts have had substantial influence in placing the issue of funding adequacy on the policy agenda (West and Peterson, 2007). As of 2006, 36 states had the constitutionality of their funding mechanism challenged on adequacy grounds; of these challenges, 24 were ruled unconstitutional (Springer and Guthrie, 2007). In 2005 alone, high-court decisions were handed down in Kansas and Texas, and a decision with national implication was awaiting appeal in South Carolina. Trial court decisions were pending in Alaska and Missouri, and new cases were coming to trial in Connecticut, Georgia, Nebraska, and Washington.

Scholars have proposed four methods of approximating the cost of education programs and services in order to specify an adequate educational opportunity. These are the econometric or cost function approach, the successful schools or "empirical" approach, the state-of-the-art or research-based approach, and professional judgment models. Approximately 58 cost studies have been conducted in 39 states as of January 2006, and at least 20 cost studies in 14 states have been undertaken between January 2004 and December 2005 (Springer and Guthrie, 2007).

Each of these methods for determining the cost of an adequate educational opportunity has strengths and weaknesses. Some authors argue that, given the current state of the art, it is not possible to construct credible estimates. (Hanushek, 2007, 2006, 2005; Springer and Guthrie, 2007; Guthrie and Springer, 2007). A more detailed discussion of measuring adequacy is discussed in Downes and Stiefel of this volume.

The Quest for Efficiency

Efficiency as a concept focuses on the relationship between spending and educational processes and outcomes. Prior to the 1960s, researchers conceived educational efficiency in terms of standardization and consolidation. It was deemed less efficient, for example, to have a 30-member school board made up of representatives from each neighborhood in a city than to have a nine-member school board comprised of more broad-minded professionals (see, for example, Tyack, 1971). Similarly, the single salary schedule for teachers was deemed by school leaders such as William T. Harris as a more equitable and efficient manner of compensation than of negotiating individual teacher contracts. Harris also saw age grading—the process of placing students in a school grade based on their chronological age—as an efficient policy for creating city-wide school systems. These and other efforts are well chronicled by Raymond Callahan in his 1962 classic, *Education and the Cult of Efficiency* (Callahan, 1962).

Under the guise of accountability, another movement coalesced around ideas of efficiency in the late 1960s. The principal impetus for this efficiency movement was the federally sponsored report, *Equality of Educational Opportunity*, the prime author of which was the renowned sociologist James S. Coleman.

Congress commissioned the oft-referenced "Coleman Report" to document the depth of resource inequality that separated black and white schools. Although Coleman found abundant inequality, his study also found that more variation in performance could be attributed to home and social environments than to school. The net effect of the Coleman report was to trigger a conflagration of controversy regarding the possibility that student achievement was less a function of the amount of school resources, than it was a function of external environmental factors. Researchers sought to determine if schooling (and school funding) mattered for students, and to more precisely determine what the relationship was between educational spending and attainment.

Despite Coleman's efforts to dampen the firestorm, the popular press, took these research findings to mean that dollars for schooling did not make a difference. The Nixon administration capitalized on the Coleman report and attendant publicity to call for greater efficiency in the operation of America's schools and to extol the virtues of school accountability, getting greater output within the confines of existing funds (Grant, 1973; Welsh, 1972). While followers of the 1960s accountability and efficiency movement attempted to establish specific educational goals, clearly affix responsibility for reaching those goals, precisely measure whether goals had been met, and, often calculate the cost incurred (Murphy and Cohen, 1974; House, 1974), their efforts were largely over shadowed by the momentum of the previously described equity movement.

Another development during the efficiency movement followed the 1983 release of *A Nation at Risk* report, which decried the American public education system as unresponsive and inefficient. As a consequence, education research and policy concentrated seriously on the efficient production of educational outcomes pioneered by scholars subsequent to the Coleman report. Contrary to academic interest in efficiency spawned by the Coleman report, interest in the issue of efficiency has remained an influential concept in guiding education finance policy. Most notably, one can observe a commitment to ideas of efficiency in the federal government's No Child Left Behind Act and its insistence on added levels of student achievement, generally within existing spending boundaries; in essence, greater efficiency from the system.

For researchers seeking the impact of the marginal dollar on educational productivity, two arguments, perhaps predictably, emerged from this research: that money matters in producing educational outcomes (Hedges, Laine, and Greenwald, 1994; Laine, Greenwald, and Hedges, 1996) and, conversely, that money does not matter in producing educational outcomes (Finn, 1983; Hanushek, 1991; Mann and Inman, 1984; Walberg and Walberg, 1994). Hanushek, by counting the number of statistically significant findings over a number of school finance studies, argued that prior education finance studies revealed few situations in which additional spending was related to improved outcomes. Hedges, Laine and Greenwald criticized Hanushek's "vote-counting" methods as overly simple and, using a statistical technique known as meta-analysis, found cases in which additional funding did improve student's outcomes.[3] The debate was summarized and extended in the 1996 volume, *Does Money Matter?* (Burtless, 1996), and most concede today that money may be necessary in many situations; however, one cannot be sure what the precise dollar amount is required for sufficiency. Newer research, instead of seeking relationships between dollars and outcomes, seeks to identify the effect of "purchased inputs"—such as teacher characteristics—and outcomes. These initiatives are discussed more fully below.

Policy proposals to increase educational productivity, that is, to gain additional output for constant levels of inputs, have centered on governance and market incentive. One such incentive, accountability, once popular, has reemerged in the early 21st century, most notably with reauthorization of the nation's omnibus Elementary and Secondary Education Act of 1965 in the No Child Left Behind Act (NCLB). The central objective of NCLB is that all traditional public school students, and defined subgroups thereof (e.g., race/ethnicity, free reduced price lunch status, and special education), reach academic "proficiency" by the 2013–2014 school year. NCLB monitors progress toward meeting academic "proficiency" through Adequate Yearly Progress (AYP) calculations, a series of minimum competency performance targets that must be met by schools and school districts to avoid sanctions of increasing severity. In theory, NCLB's threat of sanctions increases the motivation for schools and school districts to elevate learning opportunities for traditionally low-performing students and student subgroups.

Although considerable interest and controversy surrounds NCLB, surprisingly little empirical research has examined its impact. This deficiency is due in large part to data limitations and to the fact that minimum competency accountability programs were not as potent a feature of state public education systems until federal enactment of NCLB in 2002. To date, most scholarly research has examined pre-NCLB accountability programs at the state level, concentrating on the association between accountability programs and mean achievement growth (Carnoy and Loeb, 2002; Hanushek and Raymond, 2005). A growing body of research is interested in system-gaming and/or opportunistic behavior under minimum competency accountability programs (Figlio and Getzler, 2002; Figlio, 2006; Jacob and Levitt, 2003; Porter, Linn, and Trimble, 2005). A more detailed discussion of education accountability is discussed in Figlio and Ladd in this volume.

Perhaps the largest unaltered area of education finance is that of teacher salaries. The single salary schedule, that pays teachers based on years of experience and education level, has been a nearly universal feature of American K–12 school districts since the 1930s (Kershaw and McKean, 1962; Protsik, 1995). Policy makers have recognized that research suggests a marginal correlation, at best, between these two variables and student outcomes (Hanushek, 2003), and have coupled this recognition with the fact that the single salary schedule applies to roughly 95 percent of the nation's approximate 3.1 million public school teachers (Podgursky, 2007). As a result, there is growing interest in merit- or performance-based compensation schemes in K–12 public education. Although merit-based pay programs date back to Great Britain in the early-1700s, and similar educator compensation reform efforts have been experimented with in the United States periodically since the 1920s (Hall and Stucker, 1971; Murnane and Cohen, 1985), most programs were short lived. Research highlighted the difficulty inherent in creating reliable processes for identifying effective teachers (particularly with respect to the measurement of teachers' value-added contributions), elimination of preferential treatment during evaluation processes, and standardization of assessment systems across schools (Murnane and Cohen, 1985; Hatry, Greiner, and Ashford, 1994).

One pay reform strategy that has gained some traction is knowledge- and skill-based pay. Knowledge-and skill-based pay programs, such as those designed by the Consortium for Policy Research in Education (CPRE), reward teachers for acquisition of new skills and knowledge presumably related to better instruction. Administrators link salary increases to external evaluators and assessments (e.g., the Praxis III and National Board for Professional Teaching Standards) that gauge the degree to which an individual teacher has reached a specific level of competency (Odden and Kelley, 1996). Although proponents argue that these strategically-focused rewards can broaden and deepen teachers' content knowledge of core teaching areas and facilitate attainment of classroom management and curriculum development skills (Odden and Kelly, 1996), evidence that the training and credentials being rewarded in these systems actually improve student outcomes is inconclusive (Ballou and Podgursky, 2000; Hanushek and Rivkin, 2004). Another option is to link teacher pay directly to student performance.

The direct evaluation literature on such "pay-for-performance" plans is slender; nevertheless, as noted in a recent survey of teacher pay policy and research by Podgursky and Springer (2007), it is sufficiently promising to support more extensive field trials and policy experiments. The National Center on Performance Incentives at Vanderbilt University, for example, has implemented the nation's first randomized field trial specifically designed to examine the impact of financial incentives for teachers on student achievement and institutional and organizational dynamics. Moreover, the federal government's Teacher Incentive Fund (TIF) supports efforts to develop and implement performance-based teacher and principal compensation systems in high-need schools. Evidence generated from this experiment and other initiatives nationwide will answer persistent questions about the efficacy of dramatically altering the national paradigm for teacher compensation.

The Quest for Liberty

The notion of liberty, or the opportunity to choose among schooling options, gained currency in American education policy upon publication of Milton Friedman's (1964) voucher proposal in *Capitalism and Freedom*. Subsequent scholars engaged Friedman's ideas to develop and articulate policy options for family educational choice in the modern era. Although private schools have been available since the inception of the republic, available to those who could afford them, and their existence legally legitimated by the 1926 Supreme Court case *Pierce v. Society of Sisters*, choice has never been systematically included as a policy value for all citizens.

Coons and Sugarman (1971) identified the "family versus professional dispute" as the distinguishing question of liberty argument. The family versus professional dispute recognizes that the family's right to make decisions in the best interest of their child can come into conflict with educators' professional obligation to make similar decisions. One example might be student assignment, where a parental desire for schooling closer to home can conflict with an educators' desire for racially or socio-economically balanced student populations. Although this impulse towards family choice was motivated by a deep concern for impoverished children and families often trapped in low-performing urban public school systems, resultant choice-oriented policy proposals were envisioned for all parents (Coons and Sugarman, 1971, 1978). By overcoming enforced uniformity, it is hypothesized that the infusion of choice, or liberty, into the public education system creates a competitive market where pressures to compete among institutions leads to increased instructional innovation and student achievement (Chubb and Moe, 1990; Hess, 2002). The empirical justification of this argument that was first established by Hoxby (2002) has been challenged by Rothstein (2004) and others.

The market as an arbiter of educational quality is a powerful notion in current policy debate.

Within this context, Guthrie and colleagues (2007) defined a continuum along which school choice options are best viewed, moving from the incremental (e.g. magnet school programs, intradistrict transfers) to moderate (e.g. charter schools) and then more bold initiatives (e.g. vouchers). Each of these forms of school choice is described briefly below.

Magnet Schools. Magnet schools have sought to entice parents to voluntarily send their children to schools which offered innovative academic programs. The trade off was that the parents would be contributing to efforts to desegregate the school without mandatory student assignment policies. As incremental choice measures that seek to draw students from across a school district into specialized and/or rigorous programs, magnet schools have been used to desegregate districts and provide parental choice. Magnet school popularity received a boost in 1975 when the United States Supreme Court ruled in *Morgan v. Kerrigan* that magnet schools were an acceptable method of racially desegregating school districts. Indeed, between 1982 and 1992, the number of schools offering magnet programs nearly doubled (Goldring and Smrekar, 2000).

Charter Schools. The charter school movement began legislatively in 1991 in Minneapolis, Minnesota. Since this time the charter school movement has gained significant momentum. A 2002 report identified 2,348 charter schools operating in the United States, enrolling 1.2 percent of all school students (National Center for Education Statistics, 2003).

State charter school laws vary widely (Wong and Shen, 2007). Some states restrict the number of charters that can be in operation at any one time. Such restrictions are usually part of a legislative compromise in which charter advocates accept a limited number in order to obtain the right to open charter schools at all. Often, professional educators are intimidated by notions of choice, perhaps fearful that parents will not choose public schools. Consequently, their advocacy groups lobby intensely to restrict formation of charter schools. Other states stipulate charters may operate only on behalf of at-risk students who already attend failing schools.

Despite these variations in state enabling laws, several common elements emerge. Charter schools have an independent governance structure under which decisions are made at the school level without an intervening layer of the school district, and, in keeping with their specific missions, they enjoy reduced state regulation. Charter schools have a mandate to succeed and face sanctions for failure, including revocation of the school charter.[4]

A second measure of charter school success is the extent to which charters create educational marketplaces and spur levels of competition sufficient to improve public schools. Despite wide variation in charter school characteristics, common elements include: an independent governance structure; reduced or eliminated state regulation of mission; direct parental control over policies and procedures through planning teams or other means; and a mandate to succeed with sanctions for failure, including revocation of the school charter (Finn, Manno, and Vanourek, 2000). Research by Booker et al. (forthcoming) suggests that greater penetration of the market by charter schools is associated with improved public school performance in Texas, while Bifulco and Ladd (2004) do not find similar effects in North Carolina. Research also suggests that charters inspire innovation in surrounding schools, but that a degree of political ill will inhibits the transfer of innovative practices to surrounding schools (Teske et al., 2001).

Vouchers. Voucher proposals have sought to make the portability of K–12 educational funding comparable to that of federal funding for higher education—where educational loans for college tuition are made directly to the student rather than to any other institution or governmental entity—by placing the control of educational funds with parents and families. Vouchers flow directly from Friedman's arguments. Funds are provided directly to families for use in purchasing educational services in the private market. The theory behind voucher programs is similar to that of charters—private schools may increase student achievement, and market penetration and resultant competition may spur public school improvement. In the United States, findings from experimental and quasi-experimental studies have been mixed. An early study of the nation's first education voucher experiment, the Milwaukee's (WI) Parental Choice Program, found no significant differences between voucher students and public school students (Witte, et al., 1997). Other studies of the Milwaukee data have found a positive voucher effect in math scores, but not in reading (Rouse, 1997). A second randomized study in multi-sites by Howell and Peterson (2002, 2004) found achievement effects for voucher students that were limited by subject area and students racial background, although this research has been reanalyzed resulting in a contrary conclusion (Krueger and Zhu, 2002).

The liberty argument, however, does not require that choice options perform better than traditional public schools. Rather, as long as the performance of these alternative options is commensurate with that of traditional public schools, enhanced parental choice serves as the policy value. The current accountability context and contemporary educational policy debate reflects the salience of this notion. NCLB sanctions, for example, in enfranchising students to "opt out" of their present school and to select another, reflects the adoption of market principles in the education policy mainstream.

CONCLUSION

Over the course of 150 years, the financing of schools has moved from the provision of land and through a period of actuarial and political skill, to a point where issues of school finance intersect with and overlay many major policy initiatives in the United States. The range and depth of the issues examined constitute a long journey from the issues conceived by Cubberley in 1906. Better data, better methods, and better understanding of policy development have brought the field of education finance into a new era in which expectation for finance policy are aligned with education policy more broadly defined. Nonetheless, it is prudent to reflect again upon Cubberley's initial concerns, and fitting that he should have the last word:

> With the strong educational demand everywhere manifest for an improvement in educational conditions, ... the time is opportune, in many states, for a reopening of the question of providing adequate school revenue and for the revision of the general apportionment plan. The author would be glad if the principles laid down in the following pages should provide of service in formulating future legislation on the subject (p. 4).

NOTES

1. There was a .14 dollar drop in 1976.
2. Ladd and Hansen's 1999 National Council of Research volume, *Making Money Matter: Financing America's Schools* was the first to refer to the second round of equity concerns, dealing with the adequacy of available resources, as "Equity II."
3. Meta-analysis is a technique that conceptually recreates and combined databases from previously published studies and re-conducts analysis on this large database. Meta-analysis as a method is more fully described in this volume by McEwan.
4. Adapted from Finn, Manno, and Vanourek (2000).

REFERENCES

Ballou, D. and Podgursky, M. (2000). Reforming teacher preparation and licensing: What does the evidence show? *Teachers College Record*, 101(1), 5–26.

Barr, W. et al. (1970). Financing public elementary and secondary school facilities in the United States. *National Educational Finance Project Special Study No. 7.*

Benson, C.S. (1961). *The economics of public education*. New York: Houghton Mifflin.

Berne, R. and Stiefel, L. (1984). *The measurement of equity in school finance: Conceptual, methodological, and empirical dimensions*. Baltimore, MD: Johns Hopkins University Press.

Bifulco, R. and Ladd, H.F. (2004). The impact of charter schools on student achievement: Evidence from North Carolina . *Journal of Education Finance and Policy, 1*(1), pp. 50–91.

Booker, K., Gilpatrick, S., Gronberg, T., and Jansen, D. (forthcoming). The effect of charter schools on traditional public school students in Texas: Are children who stay behind left behind.

Burtless, G. (1996) *Does money matter? The effect of school resources on student achievement and adult success*. Washington, DC: The Brookings Institution.

Callahan, R.E. (1962). *Education and the cult of efficiency: A study of the social forces that have shaped the administration of the public schools.* Chicago: The University of Chicago Press.

Chubb, J. and Moe, T. (1990). *Politics, markets and America's Schools.* Washington, WA: Brookings Institution.

Carnoy, M. and Loeb, S. (2002). Does external accountability affect student outcome? *Education Evaluation and Policy Analysis, 24*(4), 305–331.

Clune, W. H. (1995). Educational adequacy: A theory and its remedies, 28 *University of Mich. J. L. Reform* 481.

Coleman, J.S., Campbell, E.Q., Hobson, C.J., McPartland, F., Mood, A M., Weinfeld, F.D., et al, (1966). *Equality of educational opportunity.* Washington, DC: U.S. Government Printing Office.

Coons, J. and Sugarman, S. (1971). *Family choice in education: A model state system for vouchers*. Berkeley, CA: Institute of Governmental Studies.

Coons, J. and Sugarman, S. (1978). *Education by choice: The case for family control.* Los Angeles, University of California Press.

Coons, J.E., Clune, W.H., and Sugarman, S.D. (1970). *Private wealth and public education.* Cambridge, MA: Harvard University Press.

Cubberley, E. P. (1906). *School funds and their apportionment*. New York: Teachers College Press.

Darling-Hammond, L., and Youngs, P. (2002). Defining "highly qualified teachers": What does "scientifically-based research" actually tell us? *Educational Researcher,* December, 13–25.

Elementary and Secondary Education Act (1965).

Erekson, O.H. et al. (2002). Fungibility of lottery revenues and support of public education. *Journal of Education Finance*, *28*, 301–312.

Figlio, D. (2006). Testing crime and punishment. *Journal of Public Economics, 90*(4–5), 837–851.

Figlio, D. and Levitt, S. (2003). *Accountability, ability, and disability: Gaming the system* (working paper 9307). Cambridge, MA: National Bureau of Economic Research.

Finn, C. (1983). "Why NIE cannot be." *Kappan*, 64(6, February), 407–410.

Finn, C., Manno, B.V., and Vanourek, G. (2000). *Charter schools in action: Renewing public education.* Princeton, NJ: Princeton University Press.

Friedman, M. (1964) Capitalism and freedom. Chicago: University of Chicago Press.

Golden, M. (2004). Technology's potential promise for enhancing student learning. *T.H.E. Journal, 31*(12), 42.

Goldring, E. and Smrekar, C. (2000). Magnet schools and the pursuit of racial balance. *Education and Urban Society, 33*(1), 17–35.

Grant, G. (1973). Shaping social policy: The politics of the Coleman Report. *Teachers College Record, 75*(1) 17–54.

Guthrie, J.W. Springer, M .G., Rolle, R. A., and Houck, E. A. (2007). *Modern Educational Finance and Policy*. Chicago: Allyn and Bacon.

Guthrie, J.W. and Springer, M.G. (2007). Courtroom Alchemy: Adequacy Advocates Turn Guesstimates into Gold. *Education Next, 7*(1), 20–27.

Hall, G. R. and Stucker, J. P. (1971). *Performance contracting in education: An introductory overview.* Santa Monica, CA: RAND.

Hanushek, E. (1991). When school finance "reform" may not be a good policy. *Harvard Journal on Legislation, 28*, 423–456.

Hanushek, E. (2005). Pseudo-science and a sound basic education: Voodoo statistics in New York. *Education Next, 5*(4), 67–73.

Hanushek, E. (2006). *Courting failure: How school finance lawsuits exploit and harm our children.* Stanford, CA: Hoover Institution Press.

Hanushek, E. (2007). The confidence men: Selling adequacy: Making millions. *Education Next, 7*(3), 73–78.

Hanushek, E. A. (2003). The failure of input-based schooling policies, *Economic Journal, 113*(485), F64–98.

Hanushek, E. and Raymond, M. (2005). Does school accountability lead to improved student performance? *Journal of Policy Analysis and Management, 24*(2), 297–327.

Hanushek, E. A. and Rivkin, S. G. (2004). How to improve the supply of high quality teachers. In D. Ravitch (ed.), *Brookings papers on educationalpPolicy 2004* (pp. 7–25), Washington, DC: Brookings Institution Press.

Hatry, H. P., Greiner, J. M., and Ashford, B. G. (1994). *Issues and case studies in teacher incentive plans* (2nd ed.). Washington, DC: Urban Institute Press.

Hedges, L.V., Laine, R.D., and Greenwald, R. (1994). Does money matter? A meta-analysis of studies of the effects of differential school inputs on student outcomes. *Educational Researcher, 23*(3), 5–14.

Hess, F.M. (2002) *Revolution at the margins: The impact of competition on urban school systems.* Washington, DC: Brookings Institution Press.

House, J.S. (1974). Understanding social factors and inequalities in health: 20th century progress and 21st century prospects. *Journal of Health and Social Behavior, 43*, 2.

Howell, W.G. and Peterson, P.E. (2002). *The Education Gap: Vouchers and Urban Schools.* Washington, DC: Brookings Institution Press.

Hoxby, C.M. (2002). How school choice affects the achievement of public school students. In Paul Hill (ed.), *Choice with equity.* Stanford, CA: Hoover Institution Press.

Hoxby, C. and Kuziemko, I. (2004). *Robin Hood and his not-so-merry plan: Capitalization and the self-destruction of Texas' school finance equilization plan* (working paper 10722). Cambridge, MA: National Bureau of Economic Research.

Johns, R. L. (1938). *An index of the financial ability of local school divisions to support public education.* Montgomery: Alabama State Department of Education.

Kershaw, J.A. and McKean, R.N. (1962). Teacher shortages and salary schedules. New York: McGraw-Hill.

Kreuger, A.B. and Zhu, P. (2002). *Another look at the New York City voucher experiment.* (Working paper 9418). Cambridge, MA: National Bureau of Economic Research.

Ladd, H. F. and Hansen, J. S. (1999). Making money matter: Financing America's schools. Washington, DC: National Academy Press.

Laine, R.D., Greenwald, R., and Hedges, L.V. (1996). Money does matter: A research synthesis of a new universe of education production function studies. In L. Picus and J. Wattenbarger (eds.), *Where does the money go*? (pp. 44–70). Thousand Oaks, CA: Corwin Press.

Mann, D. and Inman, D. (1984). Improving education with existing resources: The instructionally effective schools' approach. *Journal of Education Finance 10*(2), 259–269.

Moehlman, A.B. (1925). *Public education in Detroit.* Bloomington, IL: Public School Publishing.

Moehlman, A.B. (1932). Public school accounting. *Review of Educational Research,* 2(2), 99–104.

Morrison, H.C. (1924*). The financing of public schools in the State of Illinois. Report of the educational finance inquiry commission IX.* New York: MacMillan Company.

Morrison, H.C. (1930). *School revenue.* Chicago: University of Chicago Press.

Morrison, H.C. (1932). *The management of the school money.* Chicago: The University of Chicago Press.

Mort, P.R. (1924). *The measurement of educational need.* New York: Columbia University Press.
Mort, P.R. (1926). *State support for education.* New York: Teachers College.
Mort, P.R. (1932). *State support for education.* Washington, DC: The American Council on Education.
Mort, P.R. (1933). State support for Public Education, A report by the National Survey of School Finance. Washington, DC: American Council on Education.
Mort, P.R. and Lawler, E.S. (1938). Comparison of the ability of rural and urban areas to support education. *The Elementary and School Journal, 28*(5), 337–343.
Mort, P.R. and Reusser, W.C. (1951). *Public school finance: Its background, structure, and operation.* New York: McGraw-Hill.
Murnane, R.and Cohen, D.K. (1985) The merits of merit pay. *The Public Interest 80* (Summer).
Murphy, J.T., and Cohen, D.K. (1974). Accountability in education: The Michigan experience. *The Public Interest, 36*, 53–82.
Murray, S.E., Evans, W.N., Schwab, R.M. (1998) Education Finance Reform and the Distribution of Education Resources. *American Economic Review, 88*(4), 789–812.
National Center for Education Statistics. (2005). Washington, DC: U.S. Department of Education.
National Commission on Excellence in Education (NCEE) (1983). *A Nation at Risk: The imperative for educational reform.* Washington, DC: U.S. Department of Education.
National Defense Education Act (1958).
Nechyba, T. (1996). A computable general equilibrium model of intergovernmental aid. *Journal of Public Economics, 62*(3), 363–397.
No Child Left Behind Act (2001).
Northwest Ordinance (1787).
Odden, A. and Clune, W. (1998). School finance systems: Aging structures in need of renovation. *Educational Evaluation and Policy Analysis, 20*(3), 157–177.
Odden, A. and Kelley, C. (1996). *Paying teachers for what they know and do: New and smarter compensation strategies to improve.* Corwin Press
Pierce v. Society of Sisters (1925). 268 U.S. 510.
Podgursky, M. (2007). Teams versus bureaucracies: Personal policy, wage-setting, and teacher quality in traditional public, charter, and private schools. In M. Berends, M. G. Springer, and H. Halberg (Eds.) *Charter schools outcomes.* Mahwah, NJ: Earlbaum (in press).
Podgursky, M. and Springer, M. G. (2007). Teacher pay policies: A review. *Journal of Policy Analysis and Management.*
Porter, A., Linn, R. L., & Trimble, C. S. (2005). The effects of state decisions about NCLB adequate yearly progress targets. *Educational Measurement: Issues and Practice.* Winter, 32–39.
Protsik, J. (1995). History of teacher pay and incentive reforms. *Consortium for Policy Research in Education.* Madison, WI: Finance Center.
Rose v. Council for Better Education, 790 S.W. 2d 186 (Ky. 1989).
Rouse, C. E. (1998). Private school vouchers and student achievement: An evaluation of the Milwaukee parental choice program. *Quarterly Journal of Economics, 113,* 553–602.
Rothstein, R. (2004). *Class and schools. Using social, economic, and educational reform to close the black-white achievement gap.* Washington, DC: The Economic Policy Institute, and New York: Teachers College, Columbia University.
San Antonio v. Rodriguez, 411 U.S. 1, 93 1278 (S. Ct. 1973).
Serrano v. Priest, 5 Cal. 3d 584 (1971).
Smith, M. and O'Day, J. (1991). Systemic school reform. In S. H. Fuhrman and B. Malen (Eds.), *The politics of curriculum and testing* (pp. 233–268). Bristol, PA: Falmer Press.
Smith-Hughes Act. (1917).
Solmon, L., Park, K., and Garcia, D. (2001). *Does charter school attendance improve test scores? The Arizona results.* Goldwater Institute, March.
Springer, M.G. and Guthrie, J.W. (2007). The politicization of the school finance legal process. In M.R. West and P.E. Peterson (eds.), *School money trials: The legal pursuit of educational adequacy* (pp. 102–131). Washington, DC: Brookings Institute.

Springer, M. G., Lin, K., and Guthrie, J. W. (2005). *The impact of court-mandated reform on resource distribution: Is there anything special about adequacy?* (working paper no. 12). Nashville, TN: Peabody Center for Education Policy.

Strayer, G. and Haig, R. (1923). *Financing of education in the State of New York.* New York: Macmillan.

Stiefel, L. (2006). Insight from hindsight: The new education finance of the xext decade, *Education Finance and Policy*, *1*(4): 383–395.

Teske, P. et al. (2001). Can charter schools change traditional public schools?, in P. Peterson and D. Campbell (eds.), *Charters, vouchers and public education.* Washington, DC: Brookings Institution.

Updegraff, H. and King, L.A. (1922). *Survey of the fiscal policies of the State of Pennsylvania in the field of education.* Philadelphia: University of Pennsylvania.

Updegraff, H. (1922). Report of the Committee on Participation of teachers in management. *The Elementary School Journal*, *22*(10), 783–788.

Walberg, H.J. and Walberg, H. (1994). *Losing local control. Educational Researcher*, *23*(5), 19–26.

Waterman, I.R. (1932). Equalization of the burden of support for education. *University of California Publications in Education*, *6*(5), 285–358.

Welsh, J. (1972). Funds for research: A complex issue. *Educational Researcher 1*(4), 17–18.

West, M. R., and Peterson, P. E. (Eds.) (2007). *School money trials: The legal pursuit of educational adequacy.* Washington, DC: Brookings Institute.

Wise, A. (1970). *Rich schools, poor schools.* Chicago: University of Chicago Press.

Witte, J.F. (1998). The Milwaukee voucher experiment. *Educational Evaluation and Policy Analysis, 20,* 229–251.

Wong, K.K. and Shen, F.X. (2007). Charter law and charter operation: Re-examining the charter school marketplace, in M. Berends, M.G. Springer, and H.J. Walberg (eds.), *Charter school outcomes.* Mahwah, NJ: Erlbaum.

2

The Role of Economics in Education Policy Research

Dominic J. Brewer, Guilbert C. Hentschke, Eric R. Eide, with Ally Kuzin and Michelle B. Nayfack

INTRODUCTION

Over the last quarter century, the discipline of economics has taken on growing importance in education research and policy. More and more frequently economists are seen in positions of influence within the education, academic and policy community. For example, economists Eric Hanushek and Carolyn Hoxby serve on the National Board for Education Sciences, the flagship advisory group for the U.S. Department of Education's (ED) research agenda, and economists dominate the ED's peer review panels for education policy research. Economists are faculty members in the Schools of Education at leading research institutions such as Harvard, Stanford, Columbia, University of Southern California, and Vanderbilt. Topics on the economics of education make up a sizeable part of conference agendas for the American Education Finance Association (AEFA) and the Association for Public Policy Analysis and Management (APPAM).[1] There is also evidence that the economics of education has grown rapidly as a field within economics during recent years. Numerous scholarly journal articles are published in leading economics journals such as the *American Economic Review*, the *Quarterly Journal of Economics*, and the *Journal of Human Resources*, among others. *Economics of Education Review*, an academic journal devoted entirely to research on education economics has seen increasing numbers of articles from senior "star" economists in recent years. Although hard to quantify precisely, it certainly appears that economists have more to say about educational issues than in the past.

The reasons for the growing importance of economics in the education policy arena are numerous. In the past, scholars and policy makers have tended to view education and economics as separate realms, with education being a public good and economics focusing more on private goods. Economics has been characterized as cold and impersonal due to its focus on rational self-interested individuals and cost-benefit decision making, which on the surface appear to be unrelated to the social and moral values critical to educating children. Since the 1983 publication of *A Nation at Risk,* which highlighted the deficiencies of the U.S. education system, the distance between the two realms has narrowed. It is well documented that better educated workers have more favorable labor market outcomes than those with less schooling. Moreover, a well-educated labor force is critical for a nation to compete in an increasingly global economy that rewards knowledge and skills. The economic realities, both for individuals and the country, associated with the level and quality of education are therefore apparent, and they provide the incentives to providers for improvement of education services and to households to pursue higher quality schooling. Given that the study of incentives, choice, and competition lie at the heart of economics, economists have become more relevant to the education reform debate.

In particular, economists have contributed substantially to the study of market-based reforms in education. Economists have studied the effects of competition in the educational marketplace generally (Goldhaber and Eide, 2002, 2003; Hoxby, 1999, 2003, 2004; Rouse, 1998, 2006; Brewer, 1996) as well as specific school choice programs such as charter schools, which provide public funds to independent entities operating under a contract with a designated authorizing agency (Bettinger, 2005; Bifulco and Ladd, 2006; Zimmer et al., 2003) and voucher schemes in which parents may use public funds at almost any school (Angrist et al., 2002, 2006; Gill et al., 2001). Much of the school choice debate is fueled by political and philosophical rhetoric without regard to evidence, and so the empirical contributions from economic studies are potentially useful in informing the debate. Many of these issues are reviewed in the section of this volume on educational markets and decentralization, edited by Henry Levin.

Another reason for the rising prominence of economics in education research and policy is the focus on standard- and outcomes-based accountability that has dominated the policy environment in K–12 education for the past fifteen years. This movement towards accountability in education plays to economists' strengths in a number of ways. First, there has been increasing attention to resource allocation decision making at the school level, taking a view of educational organizations as enterprises, and those running them as entrepreneurs (see, for example, Ouchi and Segal, 2003). Second, in order to understand educational policy in an era of accountability, it is necessary to consider more explicitly the way in which actors in a large complex system respond to the incentives they face, e.g., teachers reacting to merit pay incentives, or schools facing competition from one another. Third, as part of building accountability systems, states, districts and schools have become much more interested in the collection of data on outcomes, and making them available in a way that permits their use in decision making. The federal government, through the National Center for Education Statistics, has also developed a systematic and extensive data program. The collection, in particular, of large-scale individual-level longitudinal data (most notably, *High School and Beyond* (HSB) and the *National Educational Longitudinal Study of 1988* (NELS, p. 88)), provided an unparalleled opportunity for economists to join their quantitative sociologist, psychologist and political science colleagues in 'mining' the rich data to investigate all sorts of educational phenomena.[2] The data, combined with econometric know-how, permitted the use of more sophisticated statistical analyses in studying education topics.

While economists' utilization of improved data and econometric modeling contributed to raising the level of quantitative education research, the difficulty of teasing out solid cause-and-effect findings using multivariate non-experimental methods helped push education research towards randomized experimental trials. With the Institute of Education Sciences (IES) strongly promoting this trend, it has had a marked influence on the field of education research. Further, given the expense and difficulty of actually carrying out true randomized experiments, economists have creatively used quasi-experimental methods, leading to a host of interesting and well done studies of educational policies and programs.[3] The influx of economists into education research has undoubtedly focused attention on the importance of rigorous research design, as well as spurred interest in quantitative as opposed to qualitative methods.

Although the contribution of economics to education policy research is significant, it is perhaps too early to judge its long-run impact. In this chapter we provide an overview of basic economic concepts relevant to education research and highlight some recent work that illustrates how the application of economic principles has been useful in understanding educational phenomena. We do not intend to provide textbook-like coverage of the main building blocks of economics, nor do we offer a comprehensive survey of the hundreds of books, articles, and papers using economics that might fall under the scope of "education finance and policy research." Rather, we seek to characterize what we believe to be the major foci of this work. We begin with an overview of foundational principles of economics relevant to education. We then discuss three major areas in which economics can usefully be applied to understanding educational issues: the relationship between education and the economic success of individuals; the way in which society should allocate education; and the behavior of educational organizations as economic enterprises.

THE GROWING USE OF FUNDAMENTAL ECONOMICS PRINCIPLES IN EDUCATION

Economics is often defined as "the study of the allocation of scarce means to satisfy competing ends" (Becker as quoted by Walberg and Bast, 2003, p. 182). Economists study how individuals, organizations, and societies employ time, money, and effort. In the case of education, economists are interested in how society organizes and uses resources to produce various types of knowledge and skills through formal schooling and distributes them to various groups in society. This broad definition means that many social and political challenges can fall under the purview of economics. John Maynard Keynes once wrote that economics was a "way of thinking" and it is this lens that has been brought to bear on a wide array of topics related to education. Perhaps the best modern illustration of this view is the bestselling book *Freakonomics* (2005), authored by University of Chicago economist Steven D. Levitt and Stephen J. Dubner. *Freakonomics* addresses topics such as what schoolteachers and sumo wrestlers have in common, why drug dealers still live with their moms and thc impact of *Roe v. Wade* on violent crime, none of which are conventional economics topics. Along the same lines, economics blogs such as those of George Mason University economists Tyler Cowen and Alex Tabarrok (http://www.marginalrevolution.com) and Harvard economist Greg Mankiw (http://www.gregmankiw.blogspot.com) are gaining mainstream popularity by non-economists who are interested in economic issues.

Economists typically begin an explanation of observed phenomena by building a theory or a model in order to simplify reality and highlight key characteristics. A model contains a set of assumptions, and yields predictions, *ceteris paribus* (all other things being equal). Often this abstraction causes concern among non-economists, but such simplifications are essential to understanding real world settings. Economists would argue that what matters is whether the predictions of a model are correct on average rather than whether the assumptions underlying it are realistic. Economics, then, sits firmly within the tradition of theory-testing scientific method-based disciplines: a question is framed; a model/theory developed to explain behavior; and the hypotheses or predictions of that model/theory are then tested empirically using real world data. Economics is often described as concerned with "positive" rather than "normative" issues, where the former are empirically testable and the latter are dependent on value judgments.[4] Because of the emphasis on hypothesis testing, economists almost always use research designs that are quantitative in nature, attempting to discern whether predictions of cause and effect are true, and whether they are generalizable.

Economic theories are typically built on three basic foundations: scarcity, rationality, and optimization. *Scarcity* refers to the assumption that individuals and society will never have enough resources to completely satisfy their unlimited wants. *Rationality* refers to people's ability to make decisions in a systematic and purposeful way. It implies a "consistency of response to general economic incentives and an adaptability of behavior when those incentives change" (Ehrenberg and Smith, 2006, p. 4). The last assumption is the idea of *optimization*—either profit or goal maximization in reference to organizations or utility maximization in reference to individuals. Individuals and groups have a particular goal—be it happiness, profit, or something else—and will make choices that will maximize benefits, subject to the constraints that they face. Again, these underlying assumptions often cause angst for non-economists who incorrectly conclude that economists only care about "selfish" or "self-interested" individuals. Economists view personal "values" much more broadly, and use them to help explain individual behavior. In this vein, the "altruistic" values of Mother Theresa and the "wealth accumulating" values of Donald Trump help explain the utility maximizing behavior of both.

Economics at its most general asserts that in order to make sense of the world's complexity it is useful to believe that behavior is motivated by the desire to achieve some sort of goal and that people behave consistently in trying to achieve that goal. Economists don't say that explaining *why* people (or institutions) have certain goals is or isn't important, but they do usually leave that task to other disciplines like psychology. Similarly, although economists are interested in *how* people and institutions behave subject to the constraints they face and the context they find themselves in, they don't tend to delve too deeply into how those constraints were formed or whether the context is "just." Again, other disciplines—history, philosophy, sociology, and political science—tend to have more to say on those topics.

Economics, then, is a framework for helping understand the behavior of individuals and organizations in allocating resources. Using this perspective, economists have examined a wide range of education-related topics, and in the remainder of this chapter we discuss three of the major questions of interest. First, how much education should an individual acquire? Second, how should education be produced and allocated by a society? Third, can we be more efficient in organizing the production of education? We discuss each of these in turn.

HOW MUCH EDUCATION SHOULD AN INDIVIDUAL ACQUIRE? THE RELATIONSHIP BETWEEN LEARNING AND EARNING

One of the most common areas of research for economists dealing with education has been the link between schooling and various individual outcomes, especially those associated with the labor market. Economists typically view education (and training) as an individual investment decision designed to achieve a monetary return in the labor market. This notion of "human capital" has a rich history, with early economists like Adam Smith, John Stuart Mill, and Alfred Marshall suggesting that individuals' skills could contribute to their economic status. In 1776, Smith laid the foundation for human capital theory when he wrote that human effort lies at the root of all wealth. In 1848, Mill built upon Smith's notion; he considered human abilities as "means to wealth." Modern-day human capital theory has further extended the central insight through the pioneering work of Schultz (1963), Becker (1964), and Mincer (1958, 1962).

Underlying the concept is the idea that the knowledge and skills acquired through educational investments increase human productivity enough to justify the costs incurred in acquiring them. Investments in human capital take place primarily during three life stages: early childhood when learning is predominately controlled by parents and early schooling experiences; late adolescence, when students attend high school, college or vocational training programs; and during the working years, when adults receive on-the-job training or attend night school or complete on-line courses. (These stages are, of course, more characteristic of "developed" than "developing" countries.) At each stage of investment, one may incur costs in the form of out-of-pocket expenses, foregone earnings, and psychic costs associated with the pressure of studying and examinations. Benefits accrue later in life through enhanced earnings in the labor market, access to better jobs, a higher likelihood of being employed, and better health. There are also psychic benefits from enhanced social status and the prestige associated with higher levels of education. Although individuals' motivation for pursuing schooling may differ, and the psychic costs and benefits may be quite varied depending on personality and other traits, economists hypothesize that, other things equal, the more education acquired, the higher the earnings achieved after the schooling is completed.

Prima facie evidence for human capital theory is to be found in the strong positive relationship between education levels and earnings that exist in almost every developed country. For example, the most recent data available from the U.S. Census Bureau shows those investing in more education earn higher salaries over their lifetime. Generally, earnings rise with education level and they increase at an increasing rate in the immediate post-education years, continue to increase at a slower pace, and then flatten as individuals approach retirement (Ehrenberg and Smith, 2006). This general pattern of earnings by education level holds for almost all sub-groups, including men and women, and different racial and ethnic groups, but it is the differences among these groups that often fuels education policy debates about the distribution of education subsidies and services. As Table 2.1 shows, whites earn considerably more than other races regardless of level of education.

Such raw statistics do not, of course, prove that education *causes* higher earnings because we cannot rule out the possibility that other factors are responsible for the positive relationship that is observed.[5] For this reason, economists have devoted considerable attention to the challenge of estimating the returns to schooling taking account of these other factors. Returns to investments in education have been estimated since at least the late 1950s. Analysis of such returns generally reveals a consistent positive relationship between investment in education and increased earnings

TABLE 2.1
Earnings in 2003 by Educational Attainment of Workers 18 Years and Over, by Age, Sex, Race, and Hispanic Origin: 2004

Both Sexes 18 years and over	*Total*	*High School*			*College*		
Year round Full time workers		*Not High School Graduate*	*Graduate, including GED*	*Some College, No degree*	*Bachelors degree*	*Master's degree*	*Professional degree*
All Races Mean Earnings	$46,444	$25,328	$34,057	$39,817	$60,664	$73,024	$129,297
White Alone Mean Earnings	$47,786	$25,733	$35,084	$40,991	$62,436	$73,752	$134,402
Non-Hispanic White Alone Mean Earnings	$50,597	$29,893	$36,333	$41,763	$63,395	$74,126	$136,849
Black Alone Mean Earnings	$35,761	$22,364	$28,981	$33,061	$48,167	$64,595	$94,007
Asian Alone Mean Earnings	$51,333	$25,817	$30,089	$36,745	$55,559	$73,342	$115,524
Hispanic (of any race) Mean Earnings	$31,323	$22,364	$27,708	$35,504	$49,280	$65,013	$89,053

Source: U.S. Census Bureau, Current Population Survey. Internet Release Date: March 2005.

for individuals, with an estimate of the average rate of return to an additional year of schooling of about 10%. Estimating such rates of return proves to be very complicated statistically, given that individuals are free to choose their education levels. Significant advances have been made over the past three decades both in available data and in statistical techniques that have permitted more reliable estimates of the causal effect of schooling on earnings. These approaches range from use of innovative statistical models that rely on instrumental variables (see McEwan this volume) and to studies of twins (Ashenfelter and Krueger, 1994; Ashenfelter and Rouse, 1998; Behrman et al., 1994; Card, 1995, 1999).

Continued interest in estimating returns to education has been spurred in part in recent years by interest in what appears to be an increasing return to higher levels of education. Several studies have examined the changes in education-related wage differentials over time (e.g., changes in average earnings of high school graduates relative to average earnings of college graduates), and have begun to explore the underlying reasons for the shift (e.g., Murnane et al., 1995; Brewer et al., 1999; Grogger and Eide, 1995). Such research has implications, potentially, for education policy. For example, it suggests policies designed to encourage students to stay in school as long as possible, and to gain access to postsecondary institutions, have considerable economic benefit for some students. It also suggests that policy adjustments enhancing the content and quality of schooling (e.g., in terms of curriculum, resource allocation, teacher quality and so on) might be worthwhile in order to take advantage of rising economic returns (e.g., Brewer et al., 1999; Grogger and Eide, 1995).

In addition, recent studies have focused on more contextualized estimates of the return to schooling. They have, for example, examined the return to different type of education diplomas and degrees (e.g., Kane and Rouse, 1993), to different college majors (e.g., Eide, 1994, 1997; Grogger and Eide, 1995), and to different types of institutions (e.g., Brewer et al., 1999; Dale and Krueger, 2002). These finer grained studies are of more interest to the policy community because they begin to "unpack" the simplifying notion that all years of schooling are equivalent. This work reflects increasing attention of economists to institutional and policy-relevant factors in rate of return studies.

Economists have also highlighted the strong correlations between educational levels and a number of other private and public social benefits. Individuals who have invested in education and job-training often have more job stability, have improved health (e.g., exercise regularly, smoke less, and eat better), are more likely to receive employer-provided health insurance and pension benefits, and are more inclined to vote and have generally increased social and cultural capital that often enables upward mobility (Cohn and Geske, 1990; Wolfe and Zuvekas, 1997). Additionally, poverty rates are strongly correlated to educational attainment. This linkage between education and an array of positive outcomes that benefit society as a whole, means that there is a great deal of interest in encouraging investments in education—in other words, not leaving the decision to acquire additional schooling entirely to individuals (Karoly, 2001). The extent and type of government involvement in the provision of education is the subject of the next section.

Producing and Allocating Education Services: The Emerging Role of Markets

The discussion thus far has focused on returns to education at the individual level. However, there is also general consensus that national investments in education lead to economic growth (for a review of the literature, see Sturm, 1993). Although the measures of economic growth vary they all support national investments in education and job-training (Hanushek and Kimko, 2000). Countries spend a sizable percentage of their gross domestic product (GDP) on education each year (see Figure 2.1). In 2003, the United States invested 7.5% of its GDP in education.

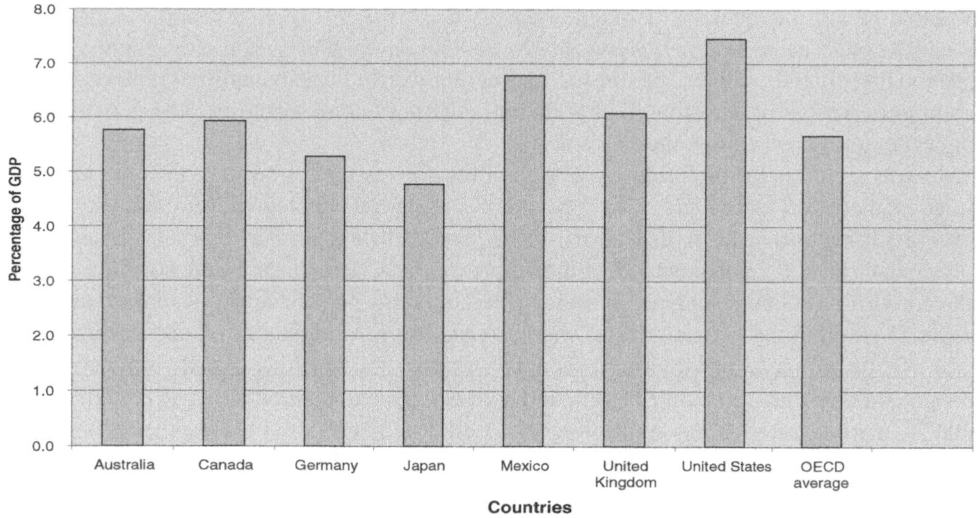

FIGURE 2.1 Education as a Percentage of GDP, 2003, by OECD Country.
Source: http://www.oecd.org.

Having a high level of national income devoted to education is generally regarded as beneficial to a country and society. Educational spending can be undertaken by *private* individuals and by governments through *public* expenditures, and the decision as to how education at different age levels should be allocated is a central issue in public policy, and at its core, is an economic decision about how best to produce and allocate scarce resources. In studying this broad question, economists have focused a good deal of attention on two different approaches—those associated with "production functions" (essentially technical relationships akin to engineering) and those associated with organizational forms (essentially tradeoffs between markets and hierarchies, or organizational design).

Economists generally assume that goods and services are produced in accordance with some technical relationship that combines different inputs (sometimes called "factors of production") to produce the desired output(s). Goods and services may get allocated in many different ways—by tradition, force, or lottery, for example. In modern societies, resources are allocated either by markets, by governments, or frequently through the interplay of both. Most goods and services in the U.S. economy are allocated by markets, but K–12 schooling has traditionally been allocated by government at the federal, state, and local levels, with postsecondary education allocated by some combination of markets and government. As concerns about the effectiveness of existing schools have risen, policy makers have questioned the central role and functions of government in the allocation of educational resources, and have recently turned more toward market-related mechanisms such as contracting out, charter schools, and vouchers.

A market is a collection of buyers who purchase and sellers who produce and sell goods and services; the interaction of buyers and sellers results in the possibility of exchange and, hence, in the allocation of goods and services. The transaction is facilitated through agreement on price. A simple depiction of a market, typically unveiled in any basic economics class, shows a downward "demand curve" and an upward sloping "supply curve." Sellers want to maximize profits, while buyers want to maximize satisfaction based on their preferences and budget constraints. The higher the market price, the more of a good or service a seller is willing to supply, but the lower quantity of that same good or service a buyer will demand, other things being equal. The function of a market is to adjust price to accommodate changes in supply and demand as efficiently as possible. When the quantity demanded equals the quantity supplied market equilibrium is achieved. Markets act to keep prices low. Producers that fail to offer consumers what they want or charge too high a price, will lose business and eventually close. The dynamics of markets requires a continuous process of adjustments that includes shortages and surpluses, and consumers and producers entering and exiting the market.[6]

Markets are often the preferred method for allocating resources because they are able to co-ordinate many buyers and sellers, give consumers considerable influence over price and quantity, and avoid relying on a handful of arbitrary decision makers. Under many circumstances, markets are the most *efficient* mechanism for allocating resources. This means that no more could be produced with the same resources, and the same could not be produced with less resources. It is important to note that efficiency is a specific criterion for judging an allocation mechanism. It does *not*, for example, make judgments about whether the resulting distribution of resources meets goals other than satisfying buyers and sellers—for example, whether it is "fair" or "equitable." Clearly, education has multiple goals (Gill et al., 2001) and these other goals need to be considered in deciding what is the "best" mechanism for allocating education from society's standpoint.

Market failure occurs when markets do not efficiently organize production or allocate goods/services to consumers. Markets fail for several reasons. First, *market power* may arise when a supplier of a good/service has the ability to control price. A monopoly is an example of such market power. Perfectly competitive markets have many buyers and sellers, so no single buyer or seller has a big impact on price. While certain inputs to schooling may be more characteristic of "perfect markets" than others (e.g., school supplies), markets in K–12 schooling are quite "imperfect" and for a variety of reasons above and beyond the number of buyers and sellers in the marketplace.

Second, when consumers have *incomplete information* about price and product quality, the market cannot respond efficiently and correctly. This is important because parents may or may not choose schools based on outputs important for broader society. There is some evidence for example, that many parents care not only about student achievement but the social and racial profile of a schools' students, preferring settings where there are most students like their own child. Hence, although their preferences may be satiated in a market setting, some may judge that these preferences are not desirable from society's standpoint.

Third, *externalities* exist when consumption or production has an indirect effect on others that is not reflected in market prices. In the case of education, the decision maker (e.g., an individual potential student) does not bear all the costs or reap all the rewards from his or her action. Even though society may benefit more from an educated person, the person making the educational decisions may not see those benefits as his or her own. Thus, the good (education) will be underprovided from the perspective of the market. This presence of social benefits arising from basic education is perhaps the chief reason why governments have typically viewed education to be so important to the life chances of individuals that they have made it compulsory at elementary and secondary levels.

Fourth, markets may fail for *public goods*—those that can be made available to additional people without additional cost (a situation economists label non-rival consumption) and, once provided, are difficult to prevent others from consuming (a characteristic economists label as non-excludability). Schooling is to some degree a public good. As with externalities, markets will tend to undersupply public goods.

The likelihood of market failure, and in particular concern about the likely under consumption of education by private individuals from society's standpoint, as well as the importance of educational goals other than efficiency, has historically led to significant government intervention in the education sector. Indeed, in most countries, schooling at the K–12 level at least (and in many nations, postsecondary education too) has been allocated almost exclusively by the government. We can usefully break down the role of government into three functions—regulation, financing, and operation. Distinguishing between these roles is critical because arguments for and against government involvement (e.g., based on equity goals or externalities) need not require the government to take on responsibility for all three roles.

Regulation can take different forms including setting safety standards, mandating curriculum or student assessments, and requiring minimum teacher credentials. *Financing* can be in the form of direct funding to schools or various forms of financial aid to individuals, such as tax credits or school vouchers. Direct funding to schools more directly supports the "supply side" of schooling, while aid to individuals more directly supports the "demand side." Revenues for schooling are likely to be generated from general taxation, rather than user fees, such that there is no clear relationship between receipt of the service and the payment for it. This simple fact is critical because it puts the responsibility for paying for education on a much broader constituency than simply those who directly consume it. The government may also directly oversee the *operation* of educational enterprises, meaning that the delivery units are embedded within a larger governmental infrastructure controlled by political mechanisms, "owned" by the state, and in which the employees are civil servants.

Historically, school operation has encompassed regulation, finance and operation in a vertically integrated public sector "system." Further, because government-operated schools have been designed to serve all students in a geographic area, within that locality they constitute a virtual monopoly. From a market perspective, this fact means that schools do not face competitive pressure to keep quality high and costs down. In addition, many families (particularly low income and minority families) do not have much choice over the schooling options for their children. The system is also biased toward public production; private production is possible, but families using private schools still have to pay taxes.

Recent educational reforms are to some extent characterized by an attempt to "unbundle" regulation, finance, and operation. From its early origins in local communities, publicly-provided schooling at the elementary level spread to the high school level and beyond. The central role of government was not seriously challenged during this expansion. This situation was challenged nearly a half century ago when Nobel Laureate Milton Friedman (1962) questioned the fundamental premise that government was the best agent for allocating schooling, and called for a system of private vouchers by which individual parents would be free to select any school for their children using government financial support. Such a system would enhance individual liberty. Further, Friedman argued that if schools had to compete for students, over time they would become more efficient and more effective.[7]

Over the course of the subsequent half century, changing household and schooling conditions fostered an array of arguments by others about the merits of specific elements of Friedman's proposition (Hentschke, 2007). Chief among them was whether, and the degree to which, vouchers should be provided in higher amounts for children from lower income households and, therefore, "means-tested." In the early 1970s, for example, as concerns about household income inequality and social justice rose to the fore, John Coons and Steve Sugarman (1971) suggested that poor parents needed to be given greater choices than their wealthier counterparts in order to help ensure equal access to quality schooling and that means tested vouchers were an appropriate method of achieving that goal.

With these salvos from the right and the left of the political spectrum, coupled with a growing recognition that governments were themselves self-interested economic actors in the education business, interest in alternatives to a government monopoly as the underpinning of the K–12 system began to be discussed more frequently and openly. Finally, with the growing concern about the nation's economic health in the late 1970s and early 1980s, policy makers began to question the effectiveness of the nation's K–12 system, and entertain much more radical reforms than in the past.

Consequently, over the past two decades there have been various attempts to introduce elements of market-based resource allocation into K–12 education in the United States. Needless to say, these have attracted a great deal of attention from economists. The variants of market-based reform are complex—ranging from tax credit schemes, to magnet schools, to controlled choice programs, to charter schools and voucher programs. Although we cannot provide an overview of all reforms, each contains some market-based elements, and a few require our attention due to their current scope and scale. Several chapters in this volume contain a detailed review of the evidence on each.

Beginning with the contracting out of non-core services to private vendors, state governments have gradually eroded the coupling of public school finance and public operation. The most significant reform in this regard has been the emergence of charter schools. Charter schools can be started by educators, parents, community groups or others, who enter into a performance contract with an authorizing agency, usually a local school district (Brewer and Wohlstetter, 2006). Forty states and the District of Columbia permit charter schools and they serve more than a million students across the country. Many states allow existing public schools to convert to charter status; laws also allow charter schools to start from scratch. The school's performance contract spells out how the school will be organized and governed, how students will be taught, and the performance goals that will be achieved at the end of the contract period.

Charter schools are public schools of choice; educators, parents, and students choose to be there rather than being assigned by a district office and these stakeholders have considerable autonomy to decide the school mission, how students will be taught and how resources will be used. The theory of action underlying the charter school concept proposes that if schools are empowered to make their own decisions and they are schools of choice that must attract educators to work and families to attend them, then the schools will work to innovate to improve teaching and learning.

There have also been a handful of attempts at a more explicit ("demand side") market-oriented reform, in the form of "vouchers" along the lines originally envisaged by Friedman and Coons and Sugarman. These have included privately funded voucher schemes (e.g., in New York City) and small state-sponsored public schemes (e.g., in Milwaukee, Cleveland, and Florida). At the time of this writing, a school voucher program in Utah, which would provide every child in the state with a school voucher worth between $500 and $3,000, was recently passed by the legislature and is awaiting voter approval. If this bill is approved by the Senate, it will become America's first universal statewide voucher program.

The evidence on the effects of these attempts to move away from government regulation, financing and operation of K–12 schooling, is growing. Needless to say, many of the findings are specific to the particular state (e.g., charter school legislation) or program context (e.g., whether a voucher is targeted to particular kinds of students), so making generalizations is difficult. One of the most comprehensive examinations to date of the effectiveness of voucher and charter programs (Gill et al, 2001) examined the available empirical evidence on voucher and charter programs in terms of their effects on five policy areas: academic achievement, choice, equitable access, integration, and preparation for civic responsibilities. The implications of these findings are that "In some contexts—such as high poverty cities with substantial African-American populations, or communities that have dysfunctional public schools—targeted voucher programs may produce discrete benefits" (p. xviii).

Moreover, "such programs will not be a silver bullet that will rescue urban education, but they are unlikely to produce the negative consequences that voucher opponents fear." The evidence on charter schools is more problematic to summarize because charter programs are relatively new, and they vary markedly across states. Nevertheless, the study finds that charters do satisfy certain parental demands, and while achievement results are mixed, there are signs of promise.[8] Betts and Hill (2006) review the methodology underlying many charter achievement studies and suggest that while progress has been made, there is a still a long way to go before stronger evidence on charter effects will be forthcoming.

In an attempt to understand the empirical evidence of the impact of private sector competition on the educational marketplace, Goldhaber and Eide (2003) provide an overview of the research that focuses on the potential achievement effects of greater private sector competition on K–12 schools. In particular, they explore the various methodologies and data that have been used to assess the relative effectiveness of public and private schools. They discuss the strengths and shortcomings of different approaches, and based on this, speculate as to what is known and not known about the impact of increased choice and competition. They find that although many of the methodologies used to assess the effects of particular interventions, such as educational vouchers, are sound, they likely fail to capture the general equilibrium consequences of enhanced choice due to their limited and partial implementation. As a result, many of the questions we would want answered to inform policy making remain unknown. Taken together, these studies suggest that while voucher and charter school programs do hold some promise, it is too early for a definitive answer regarding their long term benefits or costs to students. Since there are no large scale voucher programs in operation in the United States, and charter schools continue to be a small fraction of the total number of schools in most states, claims as to improvements in the overall effectiveness of schools remain unsubstantiated.

OPENING THE "BLACK BOX": UNDERSTANDING THE INNER WORKINGS OF ORGANIZATIONS

In addition to studies of links between learning and earning and to the overall production and distribution of educational services, economists have sought to better understand organized work, including education. This investigation has taken two different forms. One is to treat education as a "production function" wherein schooling inputs are processes and outputs produced. In this formulation schooling processes occur within a "black box." The second approach explicitly looks inside the "black box" and examines the organization as a web of interpersonal "contracts" wherein individuals seek to coordinate others (and are in turn coordinated by others) in the performance of work. This latter arena is most often referred to either as "transaction cost economics" (accounting for the newly recognized costs of coordination or transactions) or as applications of "principal-agent theory" (seeking to capture the complex issues of delegation of decision rights between bosses or principals, and their subordinates or agents). The first perspective has been applied more rigorously to research in education, while the second has been applied more implicitly to issues of education governance. The impact of both perspectives on education policy is notable if mixed.

Economists often use an input-output framework to help think about schooling. The main inputs may include teachers, administrators, supplies, and facilities while the main "outputs" are student achievement (i.e., knowledge, skills). Schools transform a set of inputs into a set of outputs using a "production function." This simple abstraction is very complex in practice in education (Goldhaber and Brewer, 1997b; Rice and Schwartz, this volume). For example, it is hard to identify and measure all inputs and outputs of schooling. Multiple outputs (e.g., basic skills, vocational skills, creativity, attitude) are valued, may accrue in a cumulative manner, and may only be discernable many years into the future. Inputs can be hard to measure, and the dimensions most easily measurable may not capture the important features of that input adequately (e.g., teacher "quality" is not well captured by proxies such as years of experience or qualifications; Goldhaber, this volume). Non-school inputs, such as peer influence and family background clearly affect how much students learn. And outputs are themselves joint products, i.e., students experience multiple teachers and carry with them knowledge from other classes and from home. The value of the production function approach, however, is as a framework for thinking about what manipulable resources really make a difference for student outcomes, and as such it focuses attention on how schooling should be organized so as to get the most "bang for the buck."

Many studies have attempted to determine the relationship between inputs and outputs as currently exists in the United States. Researchers estimate statistical models using data on inputs and outputs across many students either at one point in time or over time, often focusing on a particular input such as teachers (e.g., Boyd et al., 2005; Dee, 2004; Loeb and Page, 2000; Ehrenberg and Brewer, 1994; Goldhaber and Brewer, 1997b, 2000b), class size (Ehrenberg et al., 2001), or others. There have been numerous often-cited reviews of this large literature, notably by Hanushek. His (in)famous conclusion is that, based on this literature there is "no consistent relationship" between most measured school inputs and student achievement (Hanushek, 1997). Although this conclusion has been disputed in terms of meta-analytic techniques (e.g., Greenwald et al., 1996), this view has become widely accepted among economists, and utilized by defendants in school finance litigation against increases in school spending. It does not imply that schools or teachers "don't matter." Indeed, the evidence is that they do raise the overall level of student achievement, and that unmeasured characteristics of schools and teachers can account for significant variation in achievement from school to school and teacher to teacher. But it does suggest that under the existing organizational structure of public schools in the United States, additional resources are unlikely to generate significant improvements in student achievement.

Information on productivity gains attributable to any change in school inputs is interesting for policymakers, but in principle is not sufficient for taking action because the *costs* of changing inputs has to be considered. Because any program or policy uses both tangible resources like facilities, equipment and materials and non-tangible ones, like time and energy of the staff, there are opportunity costs involved. (Opportunity costs refer to the resources used for any given activity that entail sacrificing what we might have gained from using the resources for another purpose.) Identifying all the ingredients that comprise an intervention, policy or program (including personnel, facilities, equipment and materials), placing a value on each, and summing all the costs, is time consuming and rarely done (McEwan and McEwan, 2003).

One particularly salient area in which education economists (typically trained in public finance) have played a role is in the study of school finance reforms that have dramatically affected the level and allocation of educational resources (e.g., Corcoran and Evans, this volume). Beginning with *Serrano v. Priest* in California, many states have experienced challenges and changes to their system of school finance. According to Murray et al. (1998), 43 states have challenged the constitutionality of the public school finance system. Many of these states shifted local funding to the state level in response to court mandates. Murray and colleagues found that such education-finance reform efforts had three main results: decreased within-state inequality; reduced inequality by increasing spending at the bottom of the distribution while leaving spending at the top unchanged; and increased spending for education possibility through higher taxes. Loeb (2001), in her review of school finance reform points out that not only did the shifting of local funding to state funding affect the allocation of educational resources, the structure of the school finance system is also important. She compared those with pure state funding, state funding with unlimited local supplementation, and state funding with limited local supplementation and concluded that indeed the type of state funding system strongly affects education spending. These recent studies serve simply to illustrate the involvement of economics researchers in the school finance arena.

The second economics-oriented perspective on organizations, achieved largely through applied principal-agent theory, was originally conceived by economist Nobel Laureate Ronald Coase in the early 1930s, who argued that markets and hierarchies, heretofore examined as separate topics, were in effect, substitutes for each other. The factors in a specific firm or division of a firm that made one alternative superior to another were often associated with the differing costs of coordination (the costs associated with transactions among individuals). This perspective has been applied most widely in recent years by Oliver Williamson and, even more recently, by Walter Powell and others who extended the argument to include a third substitutable form of organization, alliances or networks. Although the nature of the research carried out by these economists was often not quantitatively grounded, it nonetheless has had a profound effect on managerial thinking in all organizations, including thinking about education. These authors provide many of the arguments about current educational policies involving outsourcing, public-private partnerships, charter schools, vouchers, and accountability systems.

Regulation through standards- and outcomes-based accountability has become, in rhetoric at least, the prevailing mechanism favored by policymakers, although it takes different forms in different states (see Figlio and Ladd, this volume). For example, most accountability systems explicitly measure student outcomes, and they make information on outcomes available to parents and the public in order to permit judgments about school performance. In some cases, states allow parents some ability to respond to this information (e.g., through the receipt of supplemental services, or through switching schools). Some schemes incorporate explicit monetary rewards for school leaders and/or teachers, based on student performance.

The passage of the federal No Child Left Behind Act of 2001 (NCLB) brought national attention to the issue of accountability in schools, and in the process drew much greater attention to the incentives influencing the behaviors of educators, especially teachers, principals, and school district superintendents and boards. As such, NCLB accountability embodies much of the framework that economists refer to as agency theory (Moe, 1984; Ferris and Winkler, 1991). Per agency theory "principals" ("superiors" in organizations, e.g., school superintendents) seek to ensure that "agents" ("subordinates" in organizations, e.g., school principals) carry out the "principal's" goals, in recognition of four primary factors that make this difficult. These four problematic factors between principals and agents are fundamental and apply in varying degrees to the vast majority of relationships between "superiors" and "subordinates" in organized society. An *adverse selection problem* occurs when "principals" (e.g., school superintendents) are not fully informed about the abilities and values of the "agents" (e.g., school principals) and select agents that are not the best choice. A *diverse objectives problem* occurs when agents pursue their own objectives at the expense of pursuing the principals' objectives. This problem is compounded when compliance is achieved only by costly monitoring and controlling of the agents. An *information asymmetry problem* occurs when information within the accountability relationship is not evenly distributed. The agent typically has the information advantage. Finally, a *weak incentives problem* occurs when principals lack sufficient decision rights to cause the agents to either share principals' values or to behave as if they did. Many critiques of NCLB and state accountability implementation address, often implicitly, these classic principal-agent problems and argue for changes that address them (Hentschke and Wohlstetter, 2004).

Accountability systems vary along many dimensions, but their overriding purpose (effective delegation of authority and responsibility) is generally accepted. While much of the debate over NCLB centers on whether standardized testing is the right measure of student performance, it is still unclear whether current forms of accountability actually improves student achievement. Carnoy and Loeb (2003) recently reviewed accountability systems in 50 states and analyzed whether the "strength"—degree to which principal-agent issues are addressed—of these accountability systems is related to student gains in achievement (measured by the NAEP mathematics test in 1996–2000). They found that students in high-accountability states (where attempts to remedy potential principal-agent problems were incorporated into legislation) showed greater gains on the NAEP 8th grade math test than students in states with low-accountability. These gains did not apply to any other grade levels and the effects of high-accountability also did not apply to higher retention or lower high school completion rates. Figlio and Rouse (2005) also found a complex picture in their study of the effects of accountability on school performance. Focusing on low-performing schools facing the threat of voucher assignment, they found that some of the claims for large-scale improvement in these schools can be explained by other factors such as changing student characteristics. (For further discussion of the empirical evidence, see Figlio and Ladd in this volume.)

The question of whether current forms of accountability improve student achievement is not easily answered by available data, but is likely to be a question that continues to fascinate economists seeking both to understand and to improve the performance of educators (in their roles as principals and agents) within and among the organizations and systems of education.

CONCLUDING THOUGHTS

In this chapter, we argue that economics, as a framework for understanding the allocation of resources, and human and organizational behavior more generally, has made important contributions to the study of educational policy. The core importance of economics in education, especially vis á vis other social sciences, lies in its conceptual structure and the scientific approaches applied by economists to their research, fueled by the increasing availability of quantitative data on all aspects of the educational enterprise. As policy makers continue to focus on reform strategies that rely at least to some extent on economic foundations, as information technology and the global economy continues to evolve in a way that appears to dramatically change the kinds of skills students need and the jobs available to them, the linkage between education and economics is likely to continue to grow.

As our review of some of the major education economics topics has suggested, the contributions and the impact of economics on education (past and projected) is uneven. The concept of human capital, for example, is well established, and has expanded beyond simple rate of return calculations to considerations useful for policymakers—for example, in determining the relative contributions of different types of institution or programs of study. The interplay between markets, regulation and individual and organizational performance in education has attracted considerable academic interest, and that is expected to continue, albeit frustrated by the absence of large-scale demonstrations of different structures of the sort that would permit more definitive statements about what works. Applying economics to policies affecting the design of education organizations has been a mixed bag. With some exceptions, production function and cost effectiveness studies have had limited policy impact. Agency theory and transaction cost economics, intuitively appealing concepts, have not yet been rigorously applied to education organizations. However, as the education world begins to "flatten" (more privatized outsourcing, joint venturing, unbundling of education service provision along with increased entrepreneurial behavior in education responding to greater consumer choice), this field should be expected to grow.

Needless to say, our view is that the increasing use of economics concepts in analyses of education policy is a positive development, in terms of helping improve the overall rigor of education research, in providing educators and policy makers evidence on different strategies for improving schooling, and indeed, with providing some of the conceptual frameworks for those strategies. As we look to the future, considering simultaneously the discipline of economics and the field of education policy, there seem to us to be a number of particularly promising areas where progress could be made.

First, the increasing issue of property rights and the economics of intellectual property will expand as for-profit providers enter K–12 education in greater proportions. Second, as income inequality continues to expand, the relationship of educational programs to other human and social services and poverty reduction strategies will likely resurface as a research and policy area. Third, economic globalization will undoubtedly spread further into the education sector, as schooling at all levels increasingly is framed as a tradable, commodified service, suggesting that aspects of macroeconomics might become more useful. This, in turn, suggests something more than the fact that education policy makers and economists will be increasingly "approaching each other." Rather it suggests that both may well focus more attention simultaneously on education's connections to the larger economic context within which it operates and on the incentives influencing the behavior of individuals deep within the education enterprise, a perspective suggested by the work of 2006 Nobel laureate economist Edmund Phelps (2006). It should be a stimulating period of intellectual activity.

NOTES

1. See http://www.aefa.cc and http://www.appam.org for sample agendas. AEFA provides for perhaps the biggest gathering of education economists. The AEFA journal *Education Finance and Policy* is edited by two economists. The largest educational research organization, American Education Research Association (AERA; http://www.aera.net), remains relatively immune to the influence of economists, although its leading applied journal *Educational Evaluation and Policy Analysis* occasionally features research authored by economists.
2. There are dozens of studies by economists using these data. For example, the data were used to examine issues of teacher quality and certification (Ehrenberg and Brewer, 1994; Goldhaber and Brewer, 1997, 2000), tracking (Rees et al, 1996), returns to education (Brewer et al, 1999; Grogger and Eide 1995; Eide 1994, 1997), the role of community colleges (Hilmer, 1998), the determinants of student achievement (Eide and Showalter, 1998), teacher race, gender and ethnicity (Ehrenberg et al, 1994), and numerous other topics.
3. The search for methods to approximate experimental designs has been advanced greatly in recent years. For example, regression discontinuity design (RDD) borrowed from psychology has been used in a number of recent educational policy studies by economists (Jacob and Lefgren, 2004a, 2004b; Chay et al, 2005).
4. This is not to suggest that economists have not formulated extensive arguments favoring or opposing specific initiatives. Consider as one illustration the vociferous debates about school vouchers, despite a dearth of empirical studies. It is to suggest, however, that descriptive work is valued more highly, perhaps due to its relative scarcity.
5. The screening hypothesis, for example, posits that schooling is just a mechanism through which individuals with traits that are valued by employers are sorted into jobs that pay higher wages. In this model, more schooling may just be a way to demonstrate to employers that workers are disciplined and motivated, as opposed to representing increased human capital attainment.
6. It should be apparent that in *any* market, this means firms will be opening and closing, causing dis-

ruption. In a school setting, this raises concerns because the dislocations caused by the opening and closing of schools, affects children and their families. For a competitive environment to work well in a K–12 school setting, attention must be paid to the incentives for good producers to grow enrollments, and protections for students who may be forced out of a failing school.

7. Friedman's impact on education policy debates was fueled at least as much by the manner in which the ideas were communicated as well by the idea itself. Despite the Friedman's contributions as an author, arguably most people became acquainted with his ideas through television, especially his 1980 10-part series, *Free to Choose*, which aired three times on public television and continues to air today via free Internet video-stream (http://www.ideachannel.tv). (John Fund, "TV's Evangelist for Capitalism," *Wall Street Journal*, 1/31/07, p. D10). The ongoing policy debate over education vouchers illustrates the complexity of linkages between research and policy.
8. A comprehensive up-to-date summary of charter achievement studies may be found at http://www.ncsrp.org/cs/csr/print/csr_docs/achstud.htm.

REFERENCES

Angrist, J., Bettinger, E., & Kremer, M. (2006). Long-term educational consequences of secondary school vouchers: Evidence from administrative records in Colombia. *American Economic Review, 96*(3), 847–862.

Angrist, J., Bettinger, E., Bloom, E., King, E., & Kremer, M. (2002). Vouchers for private schooling in Columbia: Evidence from randomized natural experiment. *American Economic Review 92*(5), 1535–1558.

Ashenfelter, O., & Krueger, A. (1994). Estimates of the economic return to schooling from a new sample of twins. *American Economic Review*, *84*, 1157–1174.

Ashenfelter, O., & Rouse, C. (1998). Income, schooling and ability: Evidence from a new sample of identical twins. *Quarterly Journal of Economics*, *113*, 253–284.

Becker, G.S. (1964). *Human Capital—A theoretical and empirical analysis, with special reference to education*. New York: National Bureau of Economic Research.

Behrman, J., Rosenzweig, M., & Taubman, P. (1994). Endowments and the allocation of schooling in the family and in the marriage market: The twins experiment. *Journal of Political Economy,102*, 1131–1174.

Bettinger, E.P. (2005). The effect of charter schools on charter students and public schools. *Economics of Education Review*, 24(2), 133–147.

Betts, J., & Hill, P. (2006), *Key issues in studying charter schools and achievement: A review and suggestions for national guidelines.* Seattle, WA: National Charter School Research Project Charter School Achievement Consensus Panel.

Bifulco, R. & Ladd, H. (2006, Winter). The impact of charter schools on student achievement: Evidence from North Carolina. *Journal of Education Finance and Policy, 1*(1), 778– 820.

Boyd, D., Lankford, H., Loeb, S., & Wyckoff, J. (2005). The draw of home: How teachers' preferences for proximity disadvantage urban schools. *Journal of Policy Analysis and Management*, *24*(1), 113–132.

Brewer, D.J. (1996). Career paths and quit decisions: Evidence from teaching. *Journal of Labor Economics,* 14(2), 313–339.

Brewer, D.J., & Wohlstetter, P. (2005, Winter). Charter schools come of age. *Urban Ed, 15–19.*.

Brewer, D.J., Eide, E.R., & Ehrenberg, R.G. (1999). Does it pay to attend an elite private college? Cross-cohort evidence on the effects of college type on earnings. *Journal of Human Resources*, *34*(1), 104–123.

Card, D. (1995). Using geographic variation in college proximity to estimate the return to schooling. In L.N. Christofides, E.K. Grant, & R. Swidinsky (Eds.), *Aspects of Labor Market Behaviour: Essays in Honour of John Vanderkamp*. Toronto: University of Toronto Press.

Card, D. (1999). The causal effect of education on wages. In O. Ashenfelter & D. Card (Eds.), *Handbook of Labor Economics, Vol. 3*. Amsterdam: Elsevier.

Carnoy, M., & Loeb, S. (2003). Does external accountability affect student outcomes? A cross-state analysis. *Education Evaluation and Policy Analysis, 24*(4), 305–331.

Chay, K., McEwan, P.J., & Urquiola, M. (2005). The central role of noise in evaluating intervention that use test scores to rank schools. *American Education Review, 95*(4), 1237–1258.

Cohn, E., & Geske, T. (1990). *The Economics of Education.* New York: Pergamon Press.

Coons, J., & Sugarman, S. (1971). Family choice in education: A model state system for vouchers. *California Law Review, 59,* 321–438.

Dale, S.B., & Krueger, A.B. (2002, November). Estimating the payoff to attending a more selective college: An application of selection on observables and unobservables. *Quarterly Journal of Economics, 117*(4), 1491–1528.

Dee, T.S. (2004). Teachers, Race and Student Achievement in a Randomized Experiment, The *Review of Economics and Statistics, 86*(1), 195–210.

Ehrenberg, R.G., & Brewer, D.J. (1994). Do school and teacher characteristics matter? Evidence from high school and beyond. *Economics of Education Review, 13*(1), 1–17.

Ehrenberg, R.G., & Smith, R. (2006). *Modern labor economics: Theory and public policy* (9th ed.). Reading, MA: Addison-Wesley.

Ehrenberg, R.G., Brewer, D.J., Gamoran, A., & Willms, D. (2001, November). Does class size matter? *Scientific American, 285*(5), 66–73.

Eide, E.R. (1994). College major choice and changes in the gender wage gap. *Contemporary Economic Policy, 12*(2), 55–63.

Eide, E.R. (1997). Accounting for race and gender differences in college wage premium Changes. *Southern Economic Journal, 63*(4), 1039–1050.

Eide, E.R., & Showalter, M.S. (1998). The effect of school quality on student performance: A quantile regression approach. *Economics Letters*, 58(3), 345–350.

Ferris, J., & Winkler, D. (1991). Agency theory and decentralization. In R. Prud'homme (Ed.) *Public finance with several layers of government.* The Hague: Foundation Journal.

Figlio, D.N., & Rouse, C.E. (2005). Do accountability and voucher threats improve low-performing schools? NBER Working Papers 11597, National Bureau of Economic Research.

Friedman, M. (1962). *Capitalism and freedom.* Chicago: University of Chicago Press.

Gill, B.P., Timpane, P.M., Ross, K.E., & Brewer, D.J. (2001). *Rhetoric versus reality: What we know and what we need to know about vouchers and charter schools.* Santa Monica, CA: RAND.

Goldhaber, D.D., & Brewer, D.J. (2000a). Does teacher certification matter? High school teacher certification status and student achievement. *Educational Evaluation and Policy Analysis*, *22*(2), 129–145.

Goldhaber, D.D., & Brewer, D.J. (2000b). Teacher certification and student achievement. *Educational Evaluation and Policy Analysis, 22*(2), 129–145.

Goldhaber, D.D., & Brewer, D.J. (1997a). Evaluating the effect of teacher degree level on educational performance. In W. Fowler (Ed.), *Developments in school finance, 1996.* Washington, DC: U.S. Department of Education, National Center for Education Statistics.

Goldhaber, D.D., & Brewer, D.J. (1997b). Why don't schools and teachers seem to matter? Assessing the impact of unobservables on educational productivity. *Journal of Human Resources, 32*(2), 505–523.

Goldhaber, D.D., & Eide, E.R. (2002). What do we know (and need to know) about the impact of school choice reforms on disadvantaged students? *Harvard Educational Review*, *72*(2), 157–176.

Goldhaber, D.D., & Eide, E.R. (2003). Methodological thoughts on measuring the impact of private sector competition on the educational marketplace. *Educational Evaluation and Policy Analysis, 25*(2), 217–232.

Greenwald, R., Hedges, L.V., & Laine, R.D. (1996). The effect of school resources on student achievement. *Review of Educational Research, 66*(3), 361–396.

Grogger, J., & Eide, E.R. (1995). Changes in college skills and the rise in the college wage premium. *Journal of Human Resources, 30*(2), 280–310.

Hanushek, E., & Kimko (2000). Schooling, labor force quality, and the growth of nations. *American Economic Review, 90*(5), 1184–1208.

Hanushek, E. (1997). Assessing the effects of school resources on student performance: An update. *Educational Evaluation and Policy Analysis, 19*(2), 141–164.

Hentschke, G. (2007). The role of government in education – enduring principles, new circumstances and the question of 'shelf-life.' In L. Ealy & R. Endlow (Eds.), *Liberty and Learning: Friedman's Voucher Idea at Fifty.* Washington, DC: Cato Institute.

Hilmer, M.J. (1998). Post-secondary fees and the decision to attend a university or a community college. *Journal of Public Economics, 67*(3), 348–372.

Hornbeck, D.W., & Salamon, L.M. (Eds.). (1991). *Human capital and America's future.* Baltimore: The Johns Hopkins University Press.

Hoxby, C. (1999). The productivity of schools and other local public goods producers. *Journal of Public Economics, 74*(1), 1–30.

Hoxby, C. (2003). Does competition among public schools benefit students and taxpayers? *The American Economic Review, 90*(5), 1209–1238.

Hoxby, C. (2004). School choice and school competition: Evidence from the United States. *Swedish Economic Policy Review, 10*, 11–66.

Jacob, B., & Lefgren, L. (2004a). Remedial education and student achievement: A regression-discontinuity analysis. *Review of Economics and Statistics, 86*(1), 226–244.

Jacob, B., & Lefgren, L. (2004b). The impact of teacher training on student achievement: Quasi-experimental evidence from school reform efforts in Chicago. *Journal of Human Resources, 39*(1), 50–79.

Kane, T.J., & Rouse, C. (1993). Labour market returns to two- and four-year college: Is a credit a credit and do degrees matter? *American Economic Review, 83*(3), 600–613.

Karoly, L. (2001). Investing in the future: Reducing poverty through human capital investments. In S.H. Danziger & R.H. Haveman (Eds.), *Understanding Poverty* (pp. 314–356). Cambridge, MA: Harvard University Press.

Levitt, S.D., & Dubner, S.J. (2005). *Freakonomics: A rogue economist explores the hidden side of everything.* New York: HarperCollins Publisher, Inc.

Loeb, S., & Page, M. (2000). Examining the link between teacher wages and student outcomes: The importance of alternative labor market opportunities and non-pecuniary variation. *Review of Economics and Statistics, 82*(3).

Loeb, S. (2001, May). Estimating the effects of school finance reform: A framework for a federalist system. *Journal of Public Economics,* 80(2).

McEwan, E.K., & McEwan, P. J. (2003). *Making sense of research: What's good, what's not, and how to tell the difference.* Thousand Oaks, CA: Corwin Press, Inc.

Mincer, J. (1958). Investment in human capital and personal income distribution. *Journal of Political Economy, 66*, 281–302.

Mincer, J. (1962). On-the-job training: Costs, returns and some implications. *Journal of Political Economy* (Supplement), *70*, 50–79.

Moe, T. (1984). The new econmics of organization. *American Journal of Political Science, 28*, 739–777.

Murnane, R.J., Willett, J.B. & Levy, F. (1995, May). The growing importance of cognitive skills in wage determination. *Review of Economics and Statistics*, MIT Press, *77*(2), 251–266.

Murray, S.E., Evans, W.N., & Schwab, R.M. (1998). Education finance reform and the distribution of education resources. *American Economic Review, 88*(4), 789–812.

Ouchi, W., & Segal, L. (2003) *Making schools work : A revolutionary plan to get your children the education they need.* New York: Simon and Schuster.

Phelps, E.S. (2006, October 10). Dynamic capitalism. *Wall Street Journal,* p. A14. Retrieved from http://online.wsj.com/article/SB116043974857287568.htm.

Rees, D., Argys, L., & Brewer, D.J. (1996). Detracking America's schools: Equity at zero cost?" *Journal of Policy Analysis and Management,* 15(4), 623–645.

Rouse, C.E. (1998). Schools and student achievement: More on the Milwaukee parental choice program. *Economics Policy Review, 4*(1), 61–78.

Rouse, C.E. (2006). Do accountability and voucher threats improve low-performing schools? *Journal of Public Economics, 90*, 239–255.

Schultz, T.W. (1963). *The economic value of education.* New York: Columbia University Press.

Sturm, R. (1993) *How do education and training effect a country's economic performance? A literature survey.* Santa Monica, CA: RAND.

Walberg, H.J., & Bast, J.L. (2003) *Education and capitalism: How overcoming our fear of markets and economics can improve America's schools*. Hoover Institution Press, Stanford.

Wolfe B., & Zuvekas, S. (1997). Nonmarket outcomes of schooling. *International Journal of Educational Research, 27*(6), 491–501.

Zimmer, R., Buddin, R., Chau, D., Daley, G.A., Gill, B., Guarino, C.M., et al, (2003). *Charter school operations and performance: Evidence from California.* Santa Monica, CA: RAND.

3

The Past, Present, and Possible Futures of Educational Finance Reform Litigation

William S. Koski and Jesse Hahnel

For more than thirty years, the judiciary has been shaping the educational finance terrain and debate. Seizing upon arcane and often indeterminate state constitutional language, state supreme courts have invalidated the educational finance schemes of state legislatures and ordered those systems reformed in accordance with constitutional strictures. Through 2005, school finance lawsuits have been filed in 45 of the 50 states, with challengers prevailing in 24 of 43 cases that resulted in a judicial decision (National Access Network, 2005a, 2005b). Although early litigation focused on the development of the right to equal per pupil funding, or at least a school finance scheme not dependent upon local property wealth, more recent litigation has sought to define qualitatively the substantive education to which children are constitutionally entitled.

This chapter explores the intellectual and legal foundations of the school finance reform litigation of recent decades, the legal and reform theories that have evolved in those litigations, and the potential directions that this litigation might move in the future. Though the future of school finance reform through the courts remains uncertain, there can be no doubt that this experiment in judicial federalism has generated heated debate and affected education finance policy making in those states in which courts have intervened.

THE PAST (PART I): THE INTELLECTUAL AND LEGAL ROOTS OF SCHOOL FINANCE LITIGATION

Rooted in the hallowed principle of local control, public schools have traditionally relied on local property taxes as their primary funding source. Naturally, as property tax bases vary among districts, so do the property tax revenues available to schools. Although the extent of the inter-district inequality in educational funding resulting from this property-tax-based system had long been recognized by educational finance experts, it received little outside attention until the late 1960s, when social activists and scholars began to notice the differences in educational resources available to students in different districts. Buoyed by recent victories in the Warren Supreme Court, these reform-minded scholars and activists began to look to federal law and litigation as a potential tool to remedy the unfair distribution of school funding.

The Legal Environment

Prior to the landmark *Brown v. Board of Education* decision in 1954,[1] courts rarely intervened in educational policy making and practice. With that decision, the U.S. Supreme Court ushered in the Equal Protection Revolution that quickly spread from the unlawful segregation of children based on race to the differential treatment of other "suspect classes," such as women and religious minorities, and the state's denial of other "fundamental rights," such as the right to vote, to an attorney in criminal cases, and, perhaps, to equal educational opportunity.

By the time scholars and advocates began turning their attention to the issue of unequal school funding, the U. S. Supreme Court had begun employing two distinct approaches to claims asserted under the Equal Protection Clause.[2] The first and more relaxed standard of review under the Equal Protection Clause, known as the "rational review" test, upholds legislation so long as it reflects some rational relation between the state's policy objective and the means the regulation uses to achieve that objective. Most legislation falls under this category. The second approach, requiring closer scrutiny of the law by the Court, is triggered when either a "fundamental right" is at stake or the state employs a "suspect classification." Legislation subject to strict scrutiny is unconstitutional unless the state provides a compelling interest to which the challenged legislation is narrowly tailored as well as showing that the interest cannot be satisfied by any other means.[3]

Whether education was a "fundamental right" was a question that had not been considered by the Court, but *Brown* had deemed it "perhaps the most important function of state and local government."[4] And while race was clearly recognized as a suspect class, by the late 1960's the Court had also begun to show a marked antipathy toward legislative classifications that discriminated on the basis of wealth.[5] The legal groundwork had been laid. To scholars and advocates alike, school finance systems that provided fewer educational opportunities to children solely because they lived in property-poor communities appeared easy targets for this new jurisprudence. However, unlike a poll tax, the courts could not simply strike down the school finance scheme without providing guidance towards a constitutional replacement. At least, this was the conventional wisdom on the subject.

Strategies and Proposed Standards

In the late 1960s, several legal scholars and advocates began preparing the assault on school finance systems that provided vastly different educational opportunities to children. Although differing slightly on the details, all agreed that the legal basis for the attack was the Equal Protection Clause of the Fourteenth Amendment, while the proper forum would be the federal courts, as those courts seemed more willing to protect rights and liberties than their relatively complacent state counterparts. Where these scholars and advocates disagreed was in their interpretation of the specific constitutional wrong in the system and the judicial standards for constitutional compliance; i.e., the meaning of "equality of educational opportunity." From this early thinking, four contenders emerged: per-pupil spending equality or "horizontal equity;" needs-based funding equality or "vertical equity;" equal opportunity for an equal outcome or "effective equality;" and the "fiscal neutrality" principle. This intellectual history is reviewed here because the questions raised by these early thinkers are still debated today.

One Scholar, One Dollar—Horizontal Equity. As a doctoral student, Arthur Wise became one of the early architects of the assault on the inequality produced by educational finance systems (Wise, 1967). To Wise, the central evil of educational finance schemes was their classification of students based upon the accident of geography and socio-economic status. He reasoned that because education finance schemes classify students on the basis of the school district in which they reside, and because such classification largely determines the quality of the educational opportunity students receive, educational finance schemes that rely on local property tax bases unlawfully discriminate against children in low property wealth districts.

Mindful that courts would have to fashion a definition of equal educational opportunity to guide legislative remedies, he reasoned that they would most likely select a "negative definition" of equality of educational opportunity. Such a negative definition would require that a child's educational opportunity should depend upon neither her parents' economic circumstances nor her location within the state. The difficulty with this definition, Wise noted, is that it provides legislatures little guidance as to what constitutes a constitutional educational finance system. To be safe, Wise concluded, courts would likely adopt the "basic standard of equal dollars per pupil" (p. 159).[6] Simplicity of application aside, however, the "one scholar, one dollar" standard appeared to many, including Wise, unsatisfying. It failed to account for the differential costs of doing business among districts, the differing needs of students, and the differing pressures on municipal budgets for social services. To rectify this deficiency, Wise suggested that courts might stray from this absolute equality standard to allow deviations in spending for different classifications of students.

Student Needs—Vertical Equity. Writing at about the same time as Wise, Harold Horowitz of the University of California, Los Angeles Law School was crafting a slightly different legal theory to attack educational finance schemes and preparing an arguably more ambitious standard for equality of educational opportunity under the Fourteenth Amendment (Horowitz, 1966; Horowitz & Neitring, 1968). Horowitz argued that equal protection jurisprudence could support a claim to strike down the state's educational finance scheme where "a school board, though providing substantially the same educational programs and services in all schools, fails to provide programs and services which adequately compensate for the inadequate educational preparation of culturally deprived children" (Horowitz, 1966, p. 1148). Relying on empirical evidence that children in schools in "disadvantaged" neighborhoods perform poorly on academic achievement tests and receive fewer educational resources, Horowitz maintained that such children could only enjoy "equality" if they received "special programs, adapted to the specific needs of these children" (pp. 1166–1167).[7] As a judicial standard, however, vertical equity was thought to be unmanageable, as it seems to require a student-by-student analysis and remedy.

Equal Opportunity for an Equal Outcome—Effective Equity. Perhaps the most aggressive standard for equality of educational opportunity to arise from the early Equal Protection scholarship is David Kirp's (1968) call for effective equality. Kirp argued that "[a] reconsideration of effective equality in the light of recent and extensive educational research studies ... suggests that the state's obligation to provide an equal educational opportunity is satisfied only if each child, no matter what his social background, has an equal chance for an equal educational outcome, regardless of disparities of cost or effort that the state is obliged to make in order to overcome such differences" (p. 636). To achieve this goal, two remedial schemes appeared to Kirp most promising: integration and resource reallocation aimed at effective equalization. Kirp argued that redistricting local school districts such that poor and minority youth would be integrated among their wealthier and whiter peers would "do most to better the chances of the poor, presently locked into predominantly lower class schools" (p. 661). But what about those districts for which such redistricting would be politically or geographically infeasible due to the sheer density of concentrated poverty among minority children and the resistance of wealthy suburbs? Kirp's response was reallocation of resources pursuant to the principle of effective equalization—resources should be allocated to ensure children of different social backgrounds have the same academic success.

Theoretically, a meaningful distinction exists between the needs-based standard proposed by Horowitz and the outcomes-oriented standard proposed by Kirp. Horowitz would have the state compensate for educational deprivation and needs without regard to outcome, whereas Kirp's model—much like modern adequacy "costing-out" models discussed below—would focus on outcomes and the resources necessary for each student to reach the same high outcome. In practice, however, the connection between specific educational inputs and outcomes was unknown, creating a great deal of ambiguity in judicial standards. This ambiguity of standards was *and is* inevitable where theory outpaces empirical knowledge of what it takes to provide equal chances for equal outcomes or an adequate education.

Fiscal Neutrality. Jack Coons, William Clune, and Stephen Sugarman saw fiscal neutrality as the remedy for ambiguity. Less than two pages into their seminal work, *Private Wealth and Public Education* (1970), Coons, Clune, and Sugarman set forth their modest and clear standard for what would constitute a constitutional provision of educational opportunities within a state: "The quality of public education may not be a function of wealth other than the wealth of the state as a whole" (p. 2). What they then called Proposition One, and what would later be dubbed the "fiscal neutrality" principle, is a simple negative statement of what the state could not do—discriminate against students on the basis of the wealth of the community in which they live. Mindful of the complexity and contradictions inherent in defining equality of educational opportunity, Coons, Clune, and Sugarman designed this principle in a way that boils down to one simple measure: dollars. The availability of those dollars could not depend upon the wealth of one's neighbors. Because the fiscal neutrality principle prohibited, rather than demanded, certain forms of state action, it allowed the courts to spark a major reform in educational finance policy while permitting the legislature to tackle the intricate difficulties of designing a fair and efficient system. A court could at once be activist *and* restrained. Finally, the negative statement of fiscal neutrality largely sidestepped the complex and ever-controversial issue of whether and how money matters in education, then known as the cost-quality debate. Under the Coons, Clune, and Sugarman formula, there was no need to demonstrate the link between educational resources and educational outcomes.

The fiscal neutrality principle did not mandate compensation for prior inadequate schooling, "cultural disadvantage," or natural (in)abilities. Nor did it prevent some localities from choosing to spend more on their children's education than others, so long as that choice was not dependent upon the wealth of a municipality. Indeed, Coons, Clune, and Sugarman saw the fact that some communities could tax themselves at higher rates to provide more educational resources to their children as a strength of their proposal. It would encourage educational experimentation, enhance local control, and recognize the independence and liberty interests that communities and parents should enjoy.

Unfortunately, the fiscal neutrality principle could do very little for those districts that needed the most help. By the late 1960s, educational failure had become synonymous with large, urban, minority districts. Children in such districts often faced multiple handicapping conditions, ranging from deep and persistent poverty to racial and cultural isolation to greater rates of physical, emotional, and mental disabilities. Paradoxically, those districts often enjoyed greater than average commercial or industrial property wealth; the problem was not the tax base, but the tax rate. Urban residents already taxed themselves to the limit to pay for municipal services that included amplified law enforcement, social services programs, and waste disposal. Suffering from such "municipal overburden," urban communities simply could not afford to increase their taxes.

Yet fiscal neutrality as a principle was unconcerned with this problem. Judicial modesty and manageability were the touchstones for judicial intervention and the guiding principles behind Proposition One. The courts should only apply a negative test for constitutionality of an educational finance system, and they should refuse to prescribe specific components of equality of educational opportunity. This decision was best left to the legislature, Coons, Clune, and Sugarman argued.

This modesty put Coons, Clune, and Sugarman directly at odds with the more ambitious proposals to equalize opportunities of rich and poor children. From the work of Wise, Horowitz, Kirp, and Coons, Clune, and Sugarman, four theoretically distinct principles for judicial intervention in educational financing emerged. This chapter now considers how the courts grappled, and continue to grapple, with these standards.

THE PAST (PART II): THE EVOLUTION OF EDUCATIONAL FINANCE REFORM LITIGATION

Presented with an issue ripe for reform and armed with coherent and potentially winning legal strategies, educational finance reform advocates took their cases to court. Since 1968, according to the standard narrative, school finance litigation has developed in three waves (Heise, 1995b; Thro, 1989). Though the three waves are hardly monolithic and may be criticized for their descriptive accuracy (Koski, 2003; Ryan & Saunders, 2004), this standard narrative provides a common language to consider the shifting legal underpinnings of school finance litigation. In addition to the shift in legal doctrine, the wave narrative traces a shift from equity to adequacy in the distributional paradigm underlying school finance reform. This section describes the evolution of educational finance reform litigation in three waves.

The First Wave: Federal Equal Protection Litigation (1970–73)

Launched in the late 1960s, successful school finance litigation initially adopted the strategies developed by Wise and Coons, Clune, and Sugarman by focusing on the federal constitution's Equal Protection Clause and the theory that per-student funding should be substantially equal, or at least not dependent upon the wealth of the school district in which the student resided. After enjoying initial success in at least two federal district courts[8] and the California Supreme Court in *Serrano v. Priest (Serrano I)*,[9] the federal equal protection theory was quashed by the U.S. Supreme Court in *San Antonio Independent School District v. Rodriguez*.

At issue in *Rodriguez* was Texas's system of educational finance, which relied almost exclusively on local property tax wealth and resulted in local school districts receiving radically unequal levels of educational funding. The questions before the Court were whether such a system violated the federal Equal Protection Clause and, more specifically, whether poor children in poor school districts formed a suspect classification, or whether education was a fundamental interest under the federal Constitution. Finding neither a suspect classification in poverty nor a fundamental interest in education, a 5–4 majority of the Court applied the "rational relationship" test to Texas's school finance plan and held that the state's interest in local control over education easily supported the school funding scheme, unequal as it was. Though the Court left open the door to a federal constitutional claim against a state policy that deprived children of some basic floor of educational opportunity, *Rodriguez* effectively shut the door on federal school finance litigation under the U.S. Constitution to date.

The Second Wave: State "Equity" Litigation (1973–89)

Undaunted and capitalizing on the federalist structure of the judicial system, school finance reformers turned to state constitutions as sources of educational rights and school finance reform. Only thirteen days after the Supreme Court handed down *Rodriguez,* the New Jersey Supreme Court ushered in the second wave of school finance cases with its discovery of educational rights in state constitutions.[10] Although the *Robinson v. Cahill* court based its decision solely on the state's education article, which imposed on the state legislature a duty to provide a "thorough and efficient" education to the state's children, the critical aspect of the case was the newfound reliance on state constitutional arguments. Thereafter, most state high courts relied heavily on their state education article, at times employing it in conjunction with the state's constitutional equality provision, when finding the state's school spending scheme unconstitutional.[11]

The essence of the claim in second-wave cases was the equity of school funding schemes. Specifically, the courts primarily sought to achieve either horizontal equity among school districts, such that per-pupil revenues were roughly equalized by the state, or at least fiscal neutrality, such that the revenues available to a school district would not depend solely on the property wealth of the school district.[12] Unfortunately for plaintiffs in second-wave cases, the courts were mostly unreceptive to their claims: plaintiffs prevailed in only 7 of the 22 final decisions in second-wave cases.

Beyond the win–loss record, several modest conclusions can be made as to the impact of second-wave, equity-minded educational finance litigations. First, in those states in which the state's high court overturned the educational finance system, per-student spending across districts has become more equal (Evans, et al., 1997, 1999; Murray, et al., 1998). Second, this greater equity has in part been realized by greater funds being targeted to less wealthy school districts (Evans, et al., 1997, 1999; Murray, et al., 1998). Third, while some have argued that this increased equity has come at the expense of limiting overall growth in educational spending or reducing the state's educational spending compared to other states,[13] others have concluded that educational spending in the wake of a successful challenge to the school finance scheme increased school funding.[14] Finally, a declaration that the educational finance system is unconstitutional typically leads to greater centralization in educational spending.[15]

The Third Wave: State "Adequacy" Litigation (1989–Present)

The third wave was launched by the Kentucky Supreme Court in 1989 when it found in the education article of its state constitution not an entitlement to educational equity, but rather an entitlement to a substantive level of educational quality.[16] Interpreting its thorough and efficient clause, the court held that the state legislature must provide its students with an adequate education, defined as one that instills in its beneficiaries seven capabilities, including, for example, sufficient oral and written communication skills to enable them to function in a complex and rapidly changing society.[17] Though equity litigation has not been abandoned, *Rose* is considered the bellwether for the legal and rhetorical shift from equity to adequacy (Thro, 1989).

"Adequacy" as a distributional principle differs from any of those proffered by the early school finance scholars seeking to define "equality of educational opportunity." An adequate education is understood to mean a specific qualitative level of educational resources or, focusing on the outcomes object, a specific level of resources required to achieve certain educational outcomes based on external and fixed standards. It is a measure that does not compare the educational resources or outcomes of students with each other; rather, it looks only to some minimally required level of resources for all students. Notably, in the context of adequacy lawsuits, the very same education articles that supported equity claims in the second wave would now be deployed for adequacy claims in the third wave.

One might argue that the move from equity to adequacy was a strategic necessity. Rather, the adequacy principle based on state education articles possesses many advantages over the equity principle based either on state equality provisions or education articles. First, by relying upon the education provision of the state constitution, judges would be less likely to create spillover effects in other areas of public policy. Changing the black-letter law of equal protection might invalidate not only locally financed education, but all other locally funded government services—a decision the scope of which courts were unprepared to order.

Second, adequacy arguments seem to flow naturally from the language of education articles, which generally require that the legislature provide a "thorough and efficient,"[18] "uniform,"[19] or even "high quality"[20] education to its children. The court need not bend the language of these provisions beyond recognition to reach the adequacy standard or search for elusive "fundamental rights" and "suspect classes."

Third, a standard that relies on absolute rather than relative levels of educational opportunity would, at least in theory, avoid the ire of the state's political and economic elite. A constitutional floor of adequacy permits local districts to provide their children more than what the court deems an "adequate" education. Similarly, an adequacy standard seems to intrude less upon the value of local control. The decision-making authority of well-to-do districts need not be curtailed simply because of a court order to the state that a poor school district be provided resources. Indeed, giving that school district the financial wherewithal to improve itself enhances local control.

Fourth, an adequacy standard may, at first blush, simply be more appealing to certain norms of fairness and opportunity. Modern American society views education as a key to economic success and social mobility. It is not much of a stretch to say that social and economic inequality are better tolerated in this country *because* Americans believe that the necessary tools for success are provided through public education. When one learns that some children are not receiving even the minimally adequate education that will help them better their lot, one feels that an injustice has been perpetrated. But Americans do not seem to feel this way if one child—most often their own—receives a *better* education than another child, so long as that "other child" is getting an "adequate" education.

Finally, at least upon initial examination, the adequacy standard appears to enjoy a clarity that equality of educational opportunity lacks. Nettlesome concerns about input versus outcome equity and vertical versus horizontal equity are avoided. All the legislature needs to do is define what constitutes an adequate education and provide districts with the resources and conditions necessary to deliver that level of education.

Normatively, however, the shift from adequacy to equity might be seen as troubling. Education as a private good possesses strong positional aspects, with one's employment opportunities and socio-economic status depending (in large part) not on one's absolute level of academic achievement but on one's place in the educational distribution. Policies and constitutional holdings that mandate higher achievement but tolerate or even exacerbate already existing educational disparities only serve to further disadvantage the educationally underserved (Koski & Reich, 2006).

More pragmatically, the adequacy standard may provide no more clarity than ineffable equity standards. State constitutions provide legislatures, and ultimately courts, virtually no guidance as to what constitutes an adequate education. There is no agreed-upon list of public education goals (is it producing civic-minded democratic citizens, or productive contributors to the economy?).

There is no standard for the skills, competencies, and knowledge necessary to serve those goals of an adequate education.[21] Finally, even if the legislature and courts were to craft those standards from whole cloth, how do we determine what resources will produce the desired outcomes? And what background characteristics of students ought to be considered in distributing those resources (e.g., linguistic, economic, and/or genetic disadvantages)? This chapter next considers how courts have addressed these issues in modern adequacy litigation.

THE PRESENT: ISSUES IN MODERN EDUCATIONAL FINANCE REFORM LITIGATION

This section explores modern "adequacy" school finance litigation with a focus on how that litigation has developed in conjunction with the standards-based reform movement. Concurrently, it examines the difficult question of how courts have approached the challenge of crafting a remedy for the constitutional deprivation of an adequate or equal education.

Adequacy Litigations, Standards-Based Reform, and the "New Accountability"

Parallel to recent adequacy litigation, state legislatures have embraced the now-inseparable policies of standards-based reform and accountability for student outcomes. Put simply, the standards-based reform movement has sought, among other things, to combat low educational expectations for poor and minority children. By establishing challenging educational content standards that define what all children should know and be able to do, standards-based reform aims to raise the level of all children's achievement to what the state determines is "proficient" (read: "adequate").

Beginning a decade or so ago, standards-based reform or the push for accountability has been supplemented by an additional policy lever—accountability of schools and students for performance on standards-referenced achievement tests. This "new accountability" in public education provides for rewards or sanctions to schools, administrators, teachers, and students according to their success in meeting achievement goals. At one end of the spectrum, successful schools are provided with commendations and, sometimes, monetary rewards. At the other end, failing schools may be offered technical assistance and temporary improvement grants, while persistently failing schools may be subject to state takeover or reconstitution. At a minimum, school and district performances on standards-based assessments are published and subjected to public scrutiny.

Standards-based accountability programs, like the federal No Child Left Behind Act, though promising to raise the performance of poor and minority children and close the achievement gap, are frequently criticized for failing to provide the necessary educational resources and conditions for all children to achieve at world-class levels (Elmore, 2003). This is where the new adequacy litigation and new accountability movements are beginning to embrace each other in courtrooms. Scholars and advocates have argued that it is institutionally appropriate for courts to hold states accountable under state constitutional education articles for providing the resources necessary for children to learn at the levels authorized by legislatures and often established by executive branches.

Although no state court has gone so far as to constitutionalize state educational standards, many judges are citing as evidence of educational inadequacy the failure of students to reach proficiency on state-mandated tests.[22] Whether at the point of identifying the substantive entitlement to an education (the skills and capacities all children should receive) or designing the appropriate remedy (costing-out an adequate education based on student need or providing specific interventions and programs geared toward achieving the standards-based outcomes), courts are beginning to compel policy makers to flesh-out the substantive entitlement to an education, sometimes based on states' own expected educational outcomes.

System-Wide Reform: What Is the Remedy for an Unconstitutional Funding Scheme?

Although some courts have held the issue of educational adequacy to be non-justiciable, a matter best left to the legislative branch, these decisions are in the minority.[23] As explored above, courts are increasingly finding it within their power, indeed their duty, to rule on the constitutionality of their state's method of financing education. But often that is all they do. Having found the funding system in violation of their state's constitution, separation of powers concerns have led most courts to simply instruct the legislature to fix the problem.[24]

In some states, this inter-branch dialogue has led to meaningful education reform. But where legislatures appear politically unmotivated or unable to enact a constitutional funding scheme, some courts have taken a more active role. Unwilling to be complicit in their state's failure to provide a constitutionally adequate education, they have ordered a range of remedies, from simply imposing deadlines upon the legislature to ordering specific, comprehensive, system-wide reform. Some of these more expansive, and often controversial, remedies and their legal underpinnings are explored below.

Costing-Out. State funding for education has historically been a product of political deal making, economic pressures, and the struggle among competing interests for limited state resources. Costing-out is an attempt to tie educational funding to the actual amount needed to provide every child a constitutionally adequate education. Many legislatures have conducted costing-out studies independent of judicial intervention, but others have done so only in response to threats of litigation, settlements, judicial orders to enact a new and constitutional system of educational funding, or occasionally, specific orders to conduct such studies.

Costing-out remedies are a logical extension of adequacy claims. If the court finds the state to be violating its constitutional obligation to fund an adequate educational system, it must know how much more before it can order more funding. A costing-out study can inform that question. The pathbreaking case in this respect is *Campbell v. State*, in which the Wyoming Supreme Court directed the legislature to define the "basket" of education every Wyoming child should receive, to undertake a "cost of education" study to determine the actual cost of providing such a basket, and to fund such an educational system.[25] Other state courts have followed, with New York, Arkansas, and Ohio all ordering the legislature to conduct costing-out studies as a prerequisite to funding an adequate educational system.[26]

Although *adequacy* claims naturally lead to costing-out remedies, costing out sometimes results from *equity* claims.[27] In Arizona, a federal court twice ordered costing-out studies performed in response to Equal Education Opportunities Act (EEOA) claims, though these costing-out studies were done only for English Language Learners.[28] Costing-out studies have also resulted from state equal protection claims, as legislatures act to provide a "rational basis" for their funding decisions.[29]

As prevalent as costing-out studies have become, they are not without their critics, who focus not on the need for such studies but rather on the feasibility of obtaining accurate and reliable results.[30] Nonetheless, recognizing the imperfections in the studies but also the need for a rational method of determining necessary educational resources, courts and legislatures continue ordering and implementing costing-out studies.

Programmatic Mandates. While many courts have hesitated to intrude on the legislative domain by directing them to fund education on the basis of a costing-out study, a few courts have gone further and directed their legislature to fund and implement specific educational programs found necessary under the state constitution. The leading cases in this vein are New Jersey's *Abbott* decisions where, after a period of "inter-branch dialogue" spanning over twelve years, the court finally made clear (i.e. ordered) what was required.[31] Among the most expansive of the programmatic mandates ordered by the court was implementation of Success for All, a whole-school reform program for elementary schools.[32] Other mandated programs include interventions aimed at reducing dropout rates; school-to-work and college-transition programs; summer-school, after-school, and school nutrition programs for which there is demonstrated need; and art, music, and special education programs beyond those required as part of the reform plan.[33] More recently, courts are going beyond K–12 education and mandating early enrollment kindergarten and preschool.[34] This is hardly surprising: evidence suggests that remedial programs are more effective and less costly when intervention occurs at a young age (Barnett, & Jung, & Lamy, 2005).

Remedies Focusing on Subclasses of Children. Just as some courts have ordered remedies focused on subsets of the educational offerings (programmatic remedies), others have ordered remedies focused on subsets of students. This most often takes the form of courts focusing adequacy opinions on the plight of at-risk children, with remedies tailored to "ensuring that 'at-risk' students are afforded a chance to take advantage of their constitutionally-guaranteed opportunity to obtain a sound basic [adequate] education."[35] In some instances, a case has been brought by students protected by specific legislative mandates. For instance, English Language Learners have prevailed under the EEOA[36] and children with disabilities have prevailed under the Individuals with Disabilities Education Act (IDEA).[37] The underlying claim—inadequate or unequal educational opportunities—remains the same, but the remedy—extra programs or funding—is directed toward a subclass of students.

Race is a subclass to which courts pay especially close attention, and when issues of educational equity and racial segregation mix the resulting remedy might be neither programmatic nor financial in nature. In a particularly innovative suit, plaintiff schoolchildren in Hartford, Connecticut claimed that the racial isolation of the Hartford public schools prevented them from receiving substantially equal educational opportunity as guaranteed by the state's education and equal protection clauses.[38] Reading these two clauses together, the Connecticut Supreme Court agreed. It held the state's creation of school boundaries to be the most important factor contributing to the racial disparity between Hartford and the surrounding suburbs and ruled that "the existence of extreme racial and ethnic isolation in the public school system deprives schoolchildren of a substantially equal educational opportunity and requires the state to take further remedial measures."[39] Underlying this ruling was an understanding that a child's educational experience is defined by more than just the programs provided by the state, it includes, perhaps most importantly, the child's interaction with his peers.

But the Connecticut case is an outlier, and even it did not force the state to redraw or redefine district boundaries. The parties agreed to a settlement requiring the state to create eight new inter-district magnet schools in Hartford, provide additional seats in suburban schools for minority public school students from Hartford, and provide increased funding for inter-district cooperative programs,[40] a far cry from a truly inter-district, regional solution. Moreover, in a similar suit, the New York Court of Appeals recently held the state not "responsible for the demographic makeup of every school district... [as this] would... subvert the important role of local control and participation in education." It concluded that "if the State truly puts adequate resources into the classroom, it satisfies its constitutional promise under the Education Article, even though student performance remains substandard."[41] This opinion envisions a very different future for judicial involvement in educational finance litigation, one in which the state is found to be supplying a constitutional educational system despite perpetual substandard performance—low performance being a product of socio-economic factors for which children, not the state, are responsible.

Whether it be costing out, specific programmatic remedies, or a focus on subclasses of children, courts and advocates appear to appreciate that increased funding for schools is insufficient. Inequities persist, and disadvantaged children remain without their constitutionally guaranteed adequate education. The following section explores the possible futures of educational finance litigation by considering suits brought on behalf of educational units other than the district; i.e., suits brought by individual schools, students, and states. The section concludes with thoughts on the continuing role, if any, of courts in educational finance reform.

THE POSSIBLE FUTURES OF EDUCATIONAL FINANCE REFORM LITIGATION

To this point in the chapter, all plaintiffs (with the exception of those filing under federal statutes) have claimed that their state's method of distributing funds to local school districts violates the state or federal constitution. But state financing of education is only part of the problem. As education litigation matures, its scope is expanding. Gone are the days when the only legal relationship in question is that between the state and its districts. This section examines current and possible educational finance litigation involving the legal relationships between students, schools, districts, states, and finally, the nation.

The School as the Focal Point for Litigation and Remedial Efforts

If a state has a constitutional obligation to provide every child an adequate education, why should an individual school not bring a suit claiming inadequate resources and funding? Manageability concerns have led some courts to reject this legal approach on the basis that, given absent evidence that the state is under-funding the district as a whole, the school has no claim against the state.[42] But what if the state is not underfunding the district? What if the district is misallocating its resources and underfunding the school? Is it possible for a school to bring suit against its district? Is such district misallocation even a problem?

Recent research suggests that "variations of per pupil funding within districts are often greater than the within-state variations that have been found unconstitutional" (Roza & Hill, 2004). A primary reason for such intra-district inequality is the use of Teacher Salary Cost Averaging (TSCA), a practice by which teachers are paid "directly" by the district, with each school given the authority to hire a number of teachers proportionate to the school's enrollment, independent of salary constraints. Because teacher's salaries are usually independent of the difficulty of their teaching assignment, there is an incentive among teachers to teach in easier, more affluent schools. Moreover, the more "affluent" schools are often staffed with more experienced, more expensive teachers. Thus, schools serving low-income, minority students frequently receive substantially less funds than schools serving more affluent, Anglo students, even after Title I and other categorical funds are taken into account.[43] While suits challenging the constitutionality of TSCA are rare,[44] more might be forthcoming.

Charter Schools. In the last decade, charter schools have grown from an oddity to an established feature of the educational landscape; as of September 2006 there were over 4,000 charter schools serving over a million students (The Center for Education Reform, 2006). A number of common finance issues impact both charter and non-charter schools: because charter schools are usually funded by the state according to the state's education finance formula—which itself may produce inequitable or inadequate funding—intra-state inequalities affect charter schools, as does inadequate funding. On the other hand, some finance problems are unique to charter schools. While charter schools are not subject to TSCA, they are usually responsible for their facility costs. Because they often receive little or no extra money to pay for their building, many spend close to 20% of their core funding securing a facility (Sugerman, 2002; Premack, 2001). This leaves them with less to spend on individual students, perhaps leading to future claims of inadequate funding or funding incapable of financing educational opportunities equal to those in the district's non-charter schools. Such adequacy or equity claims by charter schools could usher in the next wave of educational finance litigation.

The Student as the Focal Point for Litigation and Remedial Efforts

While schools seek funding appropriate to their student population, another class of plaintiffs—individual students in failing and/or underfunded schools—has emerged as potential claimants, with the result being a remedy individualized to the aggrieved student. Voucher advocates argue that since the constitutional right to an adequate education is that of the child rather than the district or the school, the funding (based on a weighted student formula) should flow to the child, not the district or the school. Possessing the funding necessary to secure a constitutionally adequate education, the student would be free to seek it at the school of her choice.

This is not a hypothetical case; it is already in the courts. In New Jersey, a class action was recently filed on behalf of children in high-poverty, low-performing school districts seeking vouchers for each family worth the weighted student formula value of their children, "so they may attend a functioning public or private school" (Alliance for School Choice, 2006). A similar lawsuit has been filed in Georgia, where three parents have sought to join Georgia's adequacy suit, but seek a voucher remedy similar to the one above (Donsky, 2005). Interestingly, in both cases, the plaintiffs seek another remedy in the alternative: the elimination of compulsory attendance zones forcing students to attend a school in the district of their residence (Alliance for School Choice, 2006; Donsky, 2005).

The liability arguments in these two voucher cases are identical to the adequacy arguments discussed throughout this chapter. All are brought under state constitutional provisions; the difference is the remedy sought. But school choice claims are increasingly being brought under federal statutory law as well. The No Child Left Behind Act (NCLBA) requires "program improvement schools" to offer their students the option of transferring to a non-improvement school.[45] NCLB's implementing regulations require the district to provide a choice of more than one such school.[46] An administrative complaint was recently brought against the Los Angeles Unified School District alleging failure to inform parents of their right to transfer their child under NCLB's school choice provision and illegally discouraging and denying transfers.[47] As more schools fall into "improvement" status, this provision of NCLB will undoubtedly be used more often to leverage school choice.

Inter-State Inequality as the Focal Point for Litigation and Remediation

Even when adjusted for cost-of-living differences, per-pupil spending varies dramatically between states, with states containing more economically disadvantaged, minority, and English language learner students likely to spend less (Liu, 2006). In fact, "disparities between states accounts for more of the variation in district per-pupil spending nationally than disparities within states" (Liu, 2006). While this could reflect a preference for less educational spending, data indicate that it is more a function of ability than willingness to pay (Liu, 2006). Absent substantial federal aid aimed at equalizing educational opportunities, children in wealthier states will continue receiving educational opportunities superior to those in poorer states.

The difficulty is that the likeliest source of legal rights to remedy inter-state inequality, the U.S. Constitution, appears to most advocates to have been foreclosed by the *Rodriguez* decision. Recently, however, Goodwin Liu has suggested a legal argument for establishing a Congressional "duty"—though not an actionable "right"—to ameliorate such inter-state inequalities. Arguing the Citizenship Clause of the 14th Amendment constitutes a "font of substantive rights," with the affirmative nature of the Clause acting to expand Congress's enforcement power beyond protecting national citizenship from state invasion, he concludes that "the constitutional grant of congressional power to enforce the national citizenship guarantee implies a constitutional duty of enforcement" (Liu, 2006). While Liu uses legislative history from the period directly subsequent to enactment of the 14th Amendment to buttress the validity of this interpretation (Liu, 2006), recent increased involvement of the federal government (through legislation such as the NCLB, IDEA, and EEOA) in the traditionally local matter of public schooling makes claims of adequate educational opportunities being a component of citizenship all the more reasonable. While not providing a source of action to aggrieved individuals, the paper serves to remind national legislators of their moral and constitutional responsibility to abet inter-state educational equity.

From refocusing litigation and remedial reform from school districts to schools and individual students, to seeking to combat the large inequalities in educational spending among states, the future of educational finance litigation may look very different from its past. It is not clear whether the recent upsurge in judicial activity will continue, or whether courts are showing signs of fatigue.

The Continuing Role of the Judiciary in Educational Finance Policy Making

Though advocating a litigation strategy to attack the manifest unfairness of property-tax-based educational finance schemes, Coons, Clune, and Sugarman (1970) were equally wary of the courts intervening in the complex social policy arena of educational finance without clear standards. As the previous section demonstrates, courts have frequently failed to heed that advice and have become entangled in frequently lengthy and often contentious policy-making "dialogues" with state legislatures. The inevitable question is whether, and if so how, courts will help shape the future of educational finance and policy.

There is no doubt that the role of the judiciary in what Abram Chayes (1976) famously called "public law litigation" differs dramatically from traditional litigation among private parties. Ever since at least *Brown v. Board*, courts, under the authority of state and federal constitutional and sometimes statutory mandates, have been called upon to reform and superintend complex institutions such as schools and prisons in equally complex social policy arenas such as child welfare and police practices. In educational finance reform cases, state supreme courts have become deeply enmeshed in the policy-making process. Whether it is exercising the judicial "veto" over a school finance scheme, directing that a legislature "cost-out" an adequate education, or even prescribing specific educational reforms such as preschool for all, courts are making forays into policy making that was traditionally left to legislatures.

For some, this dialogue between the judiciary and the political branches is a logical, if not healthy, role for the branch charged with protecting constitutional values (Jaffe, 1991). James Liebman and Charles Sabel (2003) have recently argued that in these school reform cases the judiciary is beginning to create public forums in which the political branches, educational insiders, and "new publics" (coalitions of civic-minded outside reformers) can "discuss comprehensive reforms of American education that draw on linked innovations in school governance, performance measurement, and the reconceptualization of the teaching profession and pedagogy" (p. 280). In this model, courts assume a coordinating and oversight role, enabling the new publics to reform educational finance policy once powerful interests have been "disentrenched" by judicial decisions. Whether this will become the norm in educational finance litigation is, however, unknown, as some are much less sanguine about this new role for the judiciary.

Indeed, the courts have come under increasing scrutiny and even attack for intervening in and invalidating educational finance policy (Starr, 2005). Courts have been criticized for crafting unmanageable constitutional standards, straying beyond their expertise, ignoring the separation of powers, and calling into question the very legitimacy of the judicial institution. Faced with such challenges, courts may choose a very different future from that lauded by Liebman and Sabel. Since the inception of educational finance reform litigation, many courts have avoided the complex waters of school finance policy by invoking the "political question doctrine" or citing to concerns about the separation of powers.[48] Perhaps a more chilling example for would-be judicial reformers, however, is the risk of being ineffectual in the reform process. Some argue that the Ohio educational finance reform litigation provides a cautionary tale, a tale in which, after repeatedly striking down the state's educational finance reform system and being rebuffed by the legislature (and potentially facing a constitutional crisis), the Ohio Supreme Court relinquished jurisdiction over the matter.[49]

Whether the judiciary will ambitiously pursue the role of participant in a school reform dialogue with policy makers and other "new publics" or whether courts, feeling fatigued from 30 years of litigation and not infrequent legislative recalcitrance, will withdraw from the school finance debate remains to be seen. What is known, however, is that the last few decades of educational finance reform litigation have permanently injected the "constitutional" values of equality and adequacy into that debate.

NOTES

1. 347 U.S. 483, 493 (1954).
2. See, e.g., *Shapiro v. Thompson*, 394 U.S. 618 (1969); *McGowan v. Maryland*, 366 U.S. 420 (1961).
3. *Shapiro*, 394 U.S. 618; see also *Griffin v. Illinois*, 351 U.S. 12 (1956); *Douglas v. California*, 372 U.S. 353 (1963); *Harper v. Virginia State Board of Elections*, 383 U.S. 663 (1966); *Kramer v. Union Free School District No. 15*, 395 U.S. 621 (1969).
4. *Brown,* 347 U.S. at 493.
5. *Harper*, 383 U.S. at 668 ("Lines drawn on the basis of wealth or property, like those of race . . . , are traditionally disfavored.").
6. In their seminal work on the measurement of equality in educational finance, Robert Berne and Leanna Stiefel later called this standard "horizontal equity" (Berne & Stiefel, 1984).
7. In Berne and Stiefel's (1984) terminology, this is deemed "vertical equity."
8. *Rodriguez v. San Antonio Indep. Sch. Dist.*, 337 F. Supp. 280 (W.D. Tex. 1971), rev'd, 411 U.S. 1 (1973); *Van Dusartz v. Hatfield*, 334 F. Supp. 870 (D. Minn. 1971).
9. 487 P.2d 1241 (Cal. 1971), aff'd after remand, 557 P.2d 929 (Cal. 1976). *Serrano I* is widely recognized as the case all equity litigations sought to emulate. There, the California Supreme Court considered the now-infamous discrepancy in funding between the Baldwin Park and Beverly Hills school districts. In 1968–69, Beverly Hills enjoyed a per-pupil assessed valuation of $50,885, while the largely minority Baldwin Park suffered a $3,706 valuation. These disparities were naturally reflected in per-pupil expenditures: where Beverly Hills lavished $1,231.72 on each of its students, whereas Baldwin Park could afford to spend only $577.49 per student. This difference prevailed in spite of the fact that

Baldwin Park taxed itself more aggressively than Beverly Hills. Based on the federal Equal Protection Clause, the California Supreme Court found that education was a "fundamental right" and poverty a "suspect classification." Therefore, judicial "strict scrutiny" should apply. California could provide no compelling state interest for the local property-tax-based finance system nor demonstrate that the system was narrowly tailored to achieve the state's interests. Although the court found the funding system unconstitutional under the federal Constitution, the court would later reconsider the matter and again find the state's funding scheme unconstitutional under the state constitution. *Serrano v. Priest*, 557 P.2d 929 (Cal. 1976) (*Serrano II*).

10. *Robinson v. Cahill*, 303 A.2d 273, 282 (N.J. 1973).
11. See, e.g., *Seattle Sch. Dist. No. 1 v. State*, 585 P.2d 71 (1978) (finding the state's school finance system unconstitutional under the state's education article); *Washakie County Sch. Dist. No. One v. Herschler*, 606 P.2d 310 (Wyo. 1980) (bolstering the state's equality provision with the state's education article to find the funding system unconstitutional); *Dupree v. Alma Sch. Dist. No. 30*, 651 S.W.2d 90, 93 (Ark. 1983) (finding that an analysis of the education article reinforces the holding that the funding system was unconstitutional under the equality provision).
12. This usually meant greater state-level involvement in educational funding through state-guaranteed tax base plans or, on rare occasion, state-backed equal yield plans, a.k.a. district power equalization, that sought to recapture "excess" revenues from wealthy districts.
13. See Evans, et al. 1999, pp. 74–75 (noting that California has achieved finance equity through leveling down high revenue districts); Joondeph, 1995 (concluding that California's *Serrano* decision depressed educational spending in the state); Heise, 1995a (finding a negative relationship between judicial intervention in Connecticut's school finance policy and overall state educational spending); Sonstelie, et al. 2000 ("[S]pending per pupil in California between 1969 and 1998 fell about 15% relative to the average for the other states."). It should be noted, however, that some of the evidence for this proposition comes from California; a state in which school funding has been further stymied by the property-tax-capping effects of Proposition 13. See Silva & Sonstelie, 1995.
14. See Hickrod et al. 1992, Evans et al. 1999.
15. See Evans, et al. 1999.
16. *Rose v. Council for Better Educ.*, 790 S.W.2d 186, 205–13 (Ky. 1989).
17. *Rose*, 790 S.W.2d at 212.
18. See, e.g., N.J. CONST. art. VIII, § 4, cl. 1 ("The Legislature shall provide for maintenance and support of a thorough and efficient system of free public schools . . . .").
19. See, e.g., WIS. CONST. art. X, § 3 ("The legislature shall provide by law for the establishment of district schools, which shall be as nearly uniform as practicable.").
20. See e.g., ILL. CONST. art. X, § 1 ("The State shall provide for an efficient system of high quality public educational institutions and services.").
21. For a discussion of the difficulties in establishing an "adequacy" standard, see Koski & Levin, 2000.
22. See, e.g., *Campaign for Fiscal Equity v. State*, 801 N.E.2d 326, 332 (N.Y. 2003) (*CFE II*) (relying on the New York Regents' "Learning Standards" in finding that the state had not provided the constitutionally required "sound, basic education"); *Montoy v. Kansas*, 102 P.3d 1160, 1164 (2005) (relying on the Kansas school accreditation standards, which incorporate student performance measures, in determining that the state's school funding scheme did not provide a constitutionally "suitable" education).
23. Florida and Rhode Island are typical of states holding any judicial ruling on educational adequacy to constitute an impermissible foray into the legislative realm. See, e.g., Coalition for Adequacy and Fairness in *School Funding, Inc. v. Chiles*, 680 So.2d 400 (Fla. 1996); *City of Pawtucket v. Sundlun*, 662 A.2d 40 (R.I. 1995).
24. See, e.g., *Horton v. Meskill*, 376 A.2d 359 (Conn. 1977); *Brigham v. State*, 692 A.2d 384 (Vt. 1997).
25. *Campbell I*, 907 P.2d at 1279 (indicating that the opportunity for a quality education should include small class sizes, ample, appropriate provisions for at-risk students, and meaningful standards and assessments).
26. See *CFE II*, 100 N.Y.2d at 930; *Lake View School District v. Huckabee*, 91 S.W.3d 472, 508–509 (Ark. 2002) (*Lake View IV*); *DeRolph I*, 677 N.E.2d at 747.

27. Indeed, both *Campbell I* and *Lake View IV* can be viewed as hybrid adequacy-equity cases, with both courts using strong equity language. See *Campbell I*, 907 P.2d at 1278 (holding that under Wyoming's equal protection clause "an equal opportunity for a proper education necessarily contemplates the playing field will be leveled so each child has an equal chance for educational success."); *Lake View IV*, 91 S.W.3d at 499 (holding it to be the General Assembly's constitutional duty to "provide equal educational opportunity to every child in this state.").
28. See *Flores v. Arizona*, 160 F.Supp.2d 1043, 1047 (Ariz. 2000) (*Flores III*); *Flores v. Arizona*, 2002 U.S. Dist. LEXIS 23178, 8 (Ariz. 2002) (*Flores V*). Plaintiffs in these cases claimed the state was denying English Language Learners (ELL) equal educational opportunities and was failing to take appropriate action to overcome language barriers that impeded equal participation by ELL students in the state's educational programs. The federal court agreed and ordered the state implement a costing-out study to determine the cost of an appropriate ELL program, and then to supply the funding.
29. See *Tennessee Small School Systems v. McWhorter*, 851 S.W.2d 139 (Tenn. 1993) (*Small Schools I*) (enacting the Educational Improvement Act based on a court-ordered costing-out study in an equity litigation).
30. While most scholars view costing out as an inexact and evolving methodology, some argue that it's so susceptible, and subject to, manipulation, that it ought not be used by judicial decision makers (Hanushek, 2006). For example, the Professional Judgment Model produces different results depending on the professionals chosen, the Similar Schools approach is susceptible to data based manipulation, and the Cost Function Model is highly sensitive to technical assumptions. Competing studies using similar methodologies produce radically different results (Guthrie & Springer, 2007).
31. See *Abbot v. Burke*, 710 A.2d 450, 473– 474 (N.J. 1998) (*Abbot V*).
32. See *Abbot V*, 710 A.2d at 457 (explaining that this was an effort to change the way educational decisions are made, rather than add reform piecemeal).
33. Id. at 473– 474.
34. See Id. (ordering the state to provide full-day kindergarten for five year olds and a half day preschool program for three and four year olds); *Abbot v. Burke*, 748 A.2d 82 (N.J. 2000) (*Abbot VI*) (further detailing the type of preschool to be provided); see also Circuit Court Decision 93–CP–31–0169, 162 (S.C. 2005) (holding that "students in the Plaintiff Districts are denied the opportunity to receive a minimally adequate education because of the lack of effective and adequately funded early childhood intervention programs designed to address the impact of poverty on their educational abilities and achievements."); but see *Lake View IV*, 91 S.W.3d at 501 (holding "implementation of pre-school programs… [to be] a public-policy issue for the General Assembly to explore and resolve."); *Hoke County v. State*, 599 S.E.2d 365, 391– 95 (N.C. 2004) (holding "specific court-imposed remedies… [to be]… inappropriate at this juncture…").
35. *Hoke County*, 599 S.E.2d at 390.
36. See, e.g., *Flores v. Arizona*, 48 F.Supp.2d 937 (Ariz. 1999) (*Flores I*).
37. See, e.g., *Vaughn G. v. Mayor and City Council of Baltimore*, Civ. Action No. MJG–84–1911 (M.D. 1996); *Emma C. v. Eastin*, 985 F. Supp 940 (N.D.Cal. 1997).
38. *Sheff v. O'Neill*, 678 A.2d 1267 (Conn. 1996).
39. Id. at 1281.
40. See OLR Research Report at http://www.cga.ct.gov/2003/olrdata/ed/rpt/2003-R-0112.htm (Conn. 2003).
41. *Paynter v. State*, 797 N.E.2d 1225, 1229 (N.Y. 2003). It should be noted that Connecticut, unlike New York, had previous rulings establishing a strong right to substantially equal educational opportunities. See *Horton v. Meskill*, 376 A.2d 359 (Conn. 1977) (*Horton I*).
42. *NYCLU v. State*, 791 N.Y.S.2d 507, 511 (2005) (rejecting the claims of a group of 27 schools outside New York City by holding that "in identifying specific schools that do not meet minimum standards, plaintiffs do not allege any district wide failure . . . in seeking to require the State to assess and rectify the failings of individual schools, plaintiffs' theory would subvert the important role of local control and participation in education").
43. In a study of Baltimore, Cincinnati, and Seattle, high-poverty, low-performing schools employed

teachers whose salaries were lower than average (Roza & Hill, 2004). In Houston, high-poverty, low-performing schools were found to be receiving significantly less funding than low-poverty, high-performing schools (Roza & Miles, 2002).

44. To the authors' knowledge only one such claim has been litigated: *Rodriguez v. Los Angeles Unified School District*, No. C 611–358, Superior Court of the State of California for the County of Los Angeles, with a consent decree entered August 25th, 1992.
45. P.L. 107–100, Sec. 1111, (b)(2)(D)(ii).
46. *Federal Register*, Vol. 67, no. 231, Sec. 200.44 (a)(4)(i), 2002.
47. *Coalition On Urban Renewal and Education and Alliance for School Choice v. Los Angeles Unified School District*, Complaint for Failure to Provide "Understandable and Uniform" Notice and Explanation to Parents of their School Choice Rights and for Denying and Discouraging Public School Transfers Under the No Child Left Behind Act.
48. See, e.g., *Hornbeck v. Somerset County Bd. Of Educ.*, 458 A.2d 758, 790 (M.D. 1983) ("[I]t is not within the power or province of members of the Judiciary to advance their own personal wishes or to implement their own personal notions of fairness under the guise of constitutional interpretation. The quantity and quality of educational opportunities to be made available to the State's public school children is a determination committed to the legislature . . . ."); *Britt v. North Carolina Bd. of Educ.*, 357 S.E.2d 432, 437 (Ct. App.), appeal dismissed 361 S.E.2d 71 (N.C. 1987) (holding that good law or bad law, wise or unwise, the question of what type of education to provide to North Carolinians is for the legislature, not the courts); *Committee for Educ. Rights v. Edgar*, 174 Ill. 2d 1, 28 (1996) ("What constitutes a "high quality" education, and how it may best be provided, cannot be ascertained by any judicially discoverable or manageable standards"); *City of Pawtucket v. Sundlun*, 662 A.2d 40, 59 (R.I. 1995) ("The volume of litigation and the extent of judicial oversight provide a chilling example of the thickets that can entrap a court that takes on the duties of a Legislature.").
49. See *DeRolph v. State*, 677 N.E. 2d 733 (Ohio 1997) (*DeRolph I*); *DeRolph v. State*, 728 N.E.2d 993 (Ohio 2000) (*DeRolph II*); *DeRolph v. State*, 754 N.E.2d 1184 (Ohio 2001) (*DeRolph III*); *DeRolph v. State*, 780 N.E.2d 529 (Ohio 2002) (*DeRolph IV*); *State v. Lewis*, 789 N.E.2d 195 (Ohio 2003) (*DeRolph V*).

REFERENCES

Augenblick, J., & Myers, J. (1997, July). *Recommendations for a Base Figure and Pupil-Weighted Adjustments to the Base Figure for Use in a New School Finance System in Ohio*. Columbus, Ohio: Ohio Department of Education.

Barnett, W. S., Jung, K., & Lamy, C. (2005). *The Effects of State Prekindergarten Programs on Young Children's School Readiness in Five States*. New Brunswick, NJ: The National Institute for Early Education Research.

Berne, R., & Stiefel, L. (1984). *The Measurement of Equity in School Finance*. Baltimore, MD: Johns Hopkins University Press.

Chalk, R., Hansen, J. S., & Ladd, H. F. (Eds.). (1999). *Equity and Adequacy in Education Finance: Issues and Perspectives*. Washington, DC: National Academy Press.

Chayes, A. (1976). The Role of the Judge in Public Law Litigation. *Harvard Law Review*, 89, 1289–1316.

Coons, J. E., Clune, W. H., & Sugarman, S. (1970). *Private Wealth and Public Education*. Cambridge, MA: Belknap Press.

Donsky, P. (2005, January 28). Fed-Up Father Jarvis Suit for Better Schools. *Atlanta Journal Constitution*, D1.

Elmore, R. (2003). Accountability and Capacity. In M. Carnoy, R. Elmore, & L. S. Siskin (Eds.), *High Schools and the New Accountability* (pp. 195–209). New York: Routledge.

Evans, W. N., Murray, S. E., & Schwab, R. M. (1997). Schoolhouses, Courthouses, and Statehouses After *Serrano*. *Journal of Policy Analysis and Management*, 16, 10–31.

Evans, W. N., Murray, S. E., & Schwab, R. M. (1999). The Impact of Court-Mandated School Finance Reform. In R. Chalk, J. S. Hansen, & H. F. Ladd (Eds.), *Equity and Adequacy in Education Finance: Issues and Perspectives* (pp. 72–98). Washington, DC: National Academy Press.

Guthrie, J. W., & Springer, M. G. (2007). *Adequacy's Politicalization of the School Finance Legal Process.* In Peterson, P. E. & West, M. R. (Eds.), *School Money Trials: The Legal Pursuit of Educational Adequacy.* Washington, DC: Brookings Institution Press.

Hanushek, E. A. (2006). Science Violated: Spending Projections and the "Costing Out" of an Adequate Education. In E. A. Hanushek (Ed.), *Courting Failure: How School Finance Lawsuits Exploit Judges' Good Intentions and Harm our Children* (pp. 257–311). Stanford, CA: Hoover Press.

Heise, M. (1995a). State Constitutional Litigation, Educational Finance, and Legal Impact: An Empirical Analysis. *University of Cincinnati Law Review*, 63, 1735–1765.

Heise, M. (1995b). State Constitutions, School Finance Litigation, and the "Third Wave": From Equity to Adequacy. *Temple Law Review,* 68, 1151–1172.

Hickrod, A. et al. (1992). The Effect of Constitutional Litigation on Education Finance: A Preliminary Analysis. *Journal of Education Finance*, 18, 180.

Hill, P. T., & Roza, M. (2004). *How Within-District Spending Inequities Help Some Schools Fail.* Washington, DC: Brookings Paper on Education Policy.

Horowitz, H. (1966). Unseparate But Unequal: The Emerging Fourteenth Amendment Issue in Public School Education. *UCLA Law Review,* 13, 1147–1172.

Horowitz, H., & Neitring, D. (1968). Equal Protection Aspects of Inequalities in Public Education and Public Assistance Programs from Place to Place Within a State. *UCLA Law Review*, 15, 787–816.

Jaffe, M. (1991). Guaranteeing a State Right to a Quality Education: The Judicial-Political Dialogue in New Jersey. *Journal of Law and Education*, 20, 271–313.

Joondeph, B. W. (1995). The Good, the Bad, and the Ugly: An Empirical Analysis of Litigation Prompted School Finance Reform. *Santa Clara Law Review*, 35, 793–797.

Kim, J., & Sunderman, G. L. (2004). *Does NCLB Provide Good Choices for Students in Low Performing Schools*, Cambridge, MA: The Civil Rights Project, Harvard University.

Kirp, D. L. (1968). The Poor, the Schools, and Equal Protection. *Harvard Educational Review*, 38, 635–668.

Koski, W. S. (2003). Of Fuzzy Standards and Institutional Constraints: A Re-examination of the Jurisprudential History of Educational Finance Reform Litigation. *Santa Clara Law Review*, 43, 1185–1298.

Koski, W. S. (2004). The Politics of Judicial Decision-Making in Educational Policy Reform Litigation. *Hastings Law Journal*, 55, 1077–1233.

Koski, W. S., & Levin, H. M. (2000). Twenty-Five Years After Rodriguez: What Have We Learned? *Teachers College Record*, 102, 480.

Koski, W. S., & Reich, R. (2006). When Adequate Isn't: The Shift from Equity to Adequacy in Educational Law and Policy and Why It Matters. *Emory Law Journal,* 56, 545–618.

Liebman, J. S., & Sabel, C. (2003). A Public Laboratory Dewey Barely Imagined: The Emerging Model of School Governance and Legal Reform. *New York University Review of Law & Social Change*, 28, 183–304.

Liu, G. (2006). Education, Equality, and National Citizenship. *Yale Law Journal,* 116, 330–411.

Murray, S. E., et al. (1998). Education Finance Reform and the Distribution of Education Resources. *American Economic Review,* 88 789–811.

Miles, K. H., & Roza, M. (2002). *Moving Toward Equity in School Funding within Districts.* Providence, RI: Annenberg Institute for School Reform at Brown University.

National Access Network. (2006, June). *A Costing Out Primer.* Retrieved October 18, 2006, from http://www.schoolfunding.info/resource_center/costingoutprimer.php3

National Access Network. (2005a, November). *"Equity" and "Adequacy" School Funding Court Decisions.* Retrieved November 29, 2005, from http://www.schoolfunding.info/litigation/equityandadequacytable10-04-05.pdf

National Access Network. (2005b, November). *Litigations Challenging the Constitutionality of K-12 Funding in the 50 States.* Retrieved November 29, 2005, from http://www.schoolfunding.info/litigation/In-Process%20Litigations-09-2004.pdf

National School Boards Association. (2005, February). *Atlanta parents join lawsuit seeking to have Georgia's education system declared unconstitutional.* Retrieved October 18, 2006, from http://www.nsba.org/site/doc_cosa.asp?TRACKID=&VID=50&CID=451&DID=35349
Premack, E. (2001). *California Charter School Finance: A Guide for Charter Schools and Charter Granting Agencies* (2000–2001 ed.). Sacramento, CA: Premack.
Roza, M., & Hill, P. T. (2004). How Within-District Spending Inequities Help Some Schools Fail. In *Brookings Papers on Education Policy, 2004.* Washington, D.C.: Brookings Institution Press.
Ryan, J. E., & Saunders, T. (2004). Foreword to Symposium on School Finance Litigation: Emerging Trends or New Dead Ends. *Yale Law & Policy Review*, 22, 463–480.
Silva, F., & Sonstelie, J. (1995). Did Serrano Cause a Decline in School Spending? *National Tax Journal*, 48, 199–221.
Sonstelie, J., Brunner, E., & Ardon, K. (2000). *For Better or For Worse? School Finance Reform in California.* Retrieved September 1, 2006, from http://www.ppic.org/content/pubs/report/R_200JSR.pdf
Starr, K.W. (2005, October). *The Judiciary and the Uncertain Future of Adequacy Remedies: A Look to the Past.* Paper presented at Adequacy Lawsuits: Their Growing Impact on American Education, Kennedy School of Government, Harvard University, Cambridge, MA.
Sugerman, S. D. (2002). *Charter School Funding Issues.* Retrieved October 18, 2006, from http://epaa.asu.edu/epaa/v10n34.html
Symposium. (1991). Investing in Our Children's Future: School Finance Reform in the '90s. *Harvard Journal on Legislation*, 28, 293–568.
Symposium. (1994). Issues in Educational Law and Policy. *Boston College Law Review,* 35, 543–680.
Symposium. (1995). Adequacy Litigation in School Finance. *University of Michigan Journal of Law Reform*, 28, 481–680.
Symposium. (2004). School Finance Litigation. *Yale Law & Policy Review*, 22, 463–657.
The Center for Education Reform. (2006, September). *National Charter School Data.* Retrieved October 18, 2006, from http://www.edreform.com/_upload/CER_charter_numbers.pdf
Thro, W. E. (1989). To Render Them Safe: The Analysis of State Constitutional Provisions in Public School Finance Litigation. *Virginia Law Review*, 75, 1639–1679.
Thro, W. E. (1994). Judicial Analysis During the Third Wave of School Finance Litigation: The Massachusetts Decision as a Model. *Boston College Law Review*, 35, 597–617.
Wise, A. (1967). *Rich Schools, Poor Schools: The Promise of Equal Educational Opportunity.* Chicago, IL: University of Chicago Press.

4

Education Finance from the Perspective of Politics, Political Cultures and Government Structures

James W. Guthrie and Kenneth K. Wong

INTRODUCTION

A popular perception of politics is that it is a process that determines who gets what and when or who pays and who benefits. Viewed more abstractly, politics is a process by which a collective (a tribe, an organization, a people) allocates what it considers to be of value. The kinds of items or conditions that are valued include resources such as material objects, personal or public privilege, public symbols, access, power and participation. All human societies have procedures for deciding how to allocate these values. What distinguishes open and closed societies is the extent to which the political rules governing these decisions, and the breadth of political participation, are explicit and popularly agreed upon.

Modern media and cynical pundits promote a perverted view of American politics by periodically suggesting that contemporary political activities are somehow unseemly and political officials inevitably self-serving. This is a regrettable perspective. The alternatives to an open political system are dictatorships and oligarchies in which the same distributive dimensions exist but where the decision processes are dominated by far fewer and almost assuredly less civic-minded powerbrokers.

POLITICS AND POLITICAL SYSTEMS

Education in both K–12 and postsecondary sectors in the United States is an enormously expensive undertaking that accounts annually for 6 to 8 percent of the dollar value of the nation's total annual production of goods and services, or Gross Domestic Product.[1] Huge numbers of individuals are directly and indirectly affected by the education system; they range from parents, school and college enrollees, employees and vendors to those more remotely engaged, such as citizens who pay taxes and vote on education issues. Given the magnitude of the resources at stake, the extensive spectrum of participants and benefactors, and the widely perceived long run significance of education to the overall society, it is no wonder that executive and legislative branch officials—as well as a seemingly infinite number of interest groups and advocates, at the federal, state and local levels—spend vast amounts of time lobbying for, or deliberating upon, education issues.

The political process takes place within a context of overarching cultural perspectives and societal values, specialized spheres of interests and expertise, and governmental arrangements. This context can shape the nature of the political process and its outcomes and is, of course, reciprocal. The outcomes of the political process also shape the larger society and governmental arrangements.

Today's political actions frame the societal context for tomorrow's issues. David C. Easton (1953) was the first to portray the political process and its reciprocal relationship with the larger society as a system comprised of varying parts, each of which was capable of exerting influence upon the other. Most notably, Easton captured the important interactions between the larger society, the political processes, the centrality of government, and the feedback loop that results when a set of political outputs influences a subsequent set of political demands. In other words, the political issues of today, and the formal political system's responses to them, set the stage for a subsequent wave, possibly a reactive one, of political dynamics.

Moreover, to add yet another layer of complexity, political dynamics can also be shaped by the particular issue at hand. For example, proposals to expand the number of charter schools or to increase local school district property taxes are likely to motivate different sets of political actors and to lead to different forms of political engagement. A variety of policy spheres and specialized interests can catalyze political processes and structural arrangements and fuse them in unique combinations.

Politics involves various processes, values, interest groups, spheres of policy perception and governmental arrangements. Even though these components are continually evolving and reciprocally shaping and reshaping each other—this chapter consciously separates them in order to describe the fundamental elements of politics more clearly. The reader should understand, though, that this separation is artificial and that political reality involves a booming, buzzing cacophony of complexity. Below is a practical illustration of a condition of long historical standing and continued contemporary significance that illustrates the interactions between the components of political systems.

Illustrating the Interaction of Structure and Process

In 1647, The Commonwealth of Massachusetts enacted Ye Olde Deluder Satan Act. This colonial-era legislation specified that each community would have a specialized governmental body overseeing schools, that local school boards would be comprised of laypersons, and that they would have property taxing authority. The fact that property wealth was ill distributed geographically was of little consequence in colonial times.

Today, vast differences exist in the amounts of assessed value per pupil across different local school districts, and these contribute to substantial differences in local school district spending. Many years later, the fact that Massachusetts, the rest of New England, and much of the remainder of the nation adopted this structural feature triggered heated legislative debate and litigation over matters of education finance equalization. Uneven wealth distribution in turn contributes to otherwise unusual coalitions of low wealth school districts, such as those in rural and urban areas, that, while having little else in common, cooperate in order to influence legislative and judicial financial distribution outcomes.

PUBLIC VALUES AND POLITICAL PROCESSES

Figure 4.1 depicts a triangle within a rectangle. Each side of the inner triangle represents a core value historically crucial to American democracy: equality, efficiency, and liberty. These three values are deeply embedded in the public ideology and political ecology of the United States, and each is continually and collectively reinforced in the nation's public symbols and political rhetoric. The outer sides of the rectangle represent forces at work in the larger society. Changes in these external forces may trigger disequilibrium in the political system and provide an opportunity for a macro political shift in policy direction.

The three public values—equality, efficiency, and liberty—are often represented as symbols, and public officials frequently refer to them as ideals to be maximized. Whereas the three values are held dear in the abstract, however, they are often in direct conflict in practice. To pursue equality to its absolute metaphysical limit is to substantially restrict liberty. To eschew equality and to pursue only choice or liberty runs the risk of creating wealth and social class extremes sufficient to jeopardize social and political stability. Finally, while efficiency may well be furthered by choice and liberty, unfettered pursuit of efficiency may jeopardize equality.

Liberty, which is the ability of individuals and groups to choose and to maximize personal preferences, is often seen as the higher goal. Equality, the restriction of differences, for its own sake can be empty. To be sure, a democracy must strive to achieve and maintain equality of opportunity. Few contend, however, that absolute material equality, with all of its likely trappings of drab sameness, is an end in itself. If everyone had the same clothes, cars, houses, and food, there might be equality, but tedium might well be the order of the day. Absolute equality, or at least the pretense of such, was the hallmark of the former Soviet Union. Its ultimate downfall was a function of an inept system of individual and collective performance incentives, distance

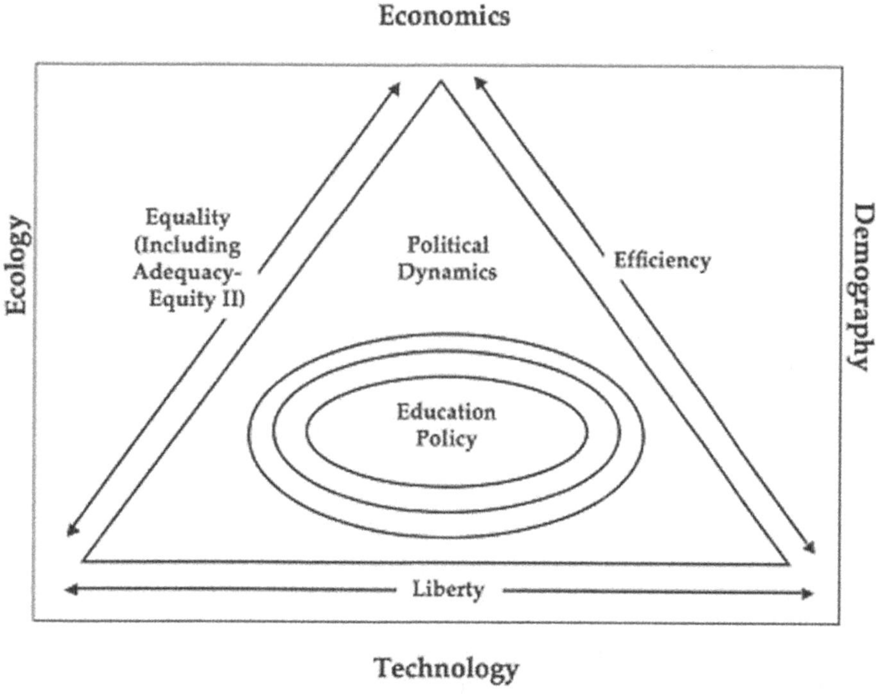

FIGURE 4.1

between ideological aspirations for citizen equality and the material corruption of its leaders, and its inability to provide consumers with choice.

Similarly, efficiency, the pursuit of maximal output while striving to minimize inputs, usually is taken to be an instrumental or mediating goal. Efficiency for its own sake has little intrinsic value. However, the conservation of resources so as to have more of something, be it material or psychic, would seem to contribute to enhanced choice or liberty.

Thus each of the three values, or the practical expressions sought by their proponents, competes with the other two in a political system. For much of the post-World War II period the American political system concentrated upon the pursuit of equality. This was particularly true in education, starting with school racial desegregation following the U.S. Supreme Court's landmark 1954 decision in *Brown v. Board of Education*. Subsequent federal enactments such as the 1965 Elementary and Secondary Education Act, the 1976 Education for all Handicapped Children Act, gender equity requirements contained in Title VI of the 1966 Higher Education Act, state court school finance equalization decisions, such as *Serrano v. Priest* in California and *Robinson v. Cahill* in New Jersey, and immigrant education decisions such as *Plyler v. Doe*, illustrate the half century of policy concern for educational equality.

While equality was ascendant as a policy consideration between World War II and the turn of the 21st century, concerns for liberty and efficiency were by no means eclipsed. For example, tax limitation movements, charter school and voucher proposals and demands for greater market play in education have been on the policy agenda at all levels of government since the 1980s. Contemporary concern for efficiency and productivity in the education system is also evident in enactment of the No Child Left Behind Act in 2001, federal Teacher Incentive Fund legislation, and state pay-for-performance teacher pay plans.

Equilibrium Theory

Systems, whether they be biological, ecological, or political, seek balance or stability and strive continually to adjust to their external environments. This tendency is known as homeostasis. A major function of the political system is to maintain a balance between the preferences of proponents of the three core values and their practical expression in day-to-day activities and conditions. For example, an emphasis upon equality that results in a restriction of choice or an erosion of liberty may provoke a reaction. Similarly, too great a concern for equality of school spending may motivate some parents to seek private schooling for their children, while too great a concern for liberty may alienate those who perceive themselves disadvantaged by choice and may lead to pressure for a restoration of concern for equality.

Within the value triangle depicted in Figure 4.2 are multiple interests, each of which may be associated with a different perception of what constitutes a just balance between the three values. This figure displays the interest spheres of parents, students, and the polity, any one of whom may have a different view of what is equitable, efficient, or liberating when it comes to education policy.

Micro Politics

The "iron triangle of politics" influences strongly what has come to be labeled incremental or micro politics—the ceaseless day-to-day actions and adjustments of local, state and federal officials and interest groups, to maintain the stability of the political system. The iron triangle involves three categories of political actors: (1) self-interested advocates for change or direct recipients of prospective benefits, (2) policy makers who concentrate in this specialized policy sphere, and (3)

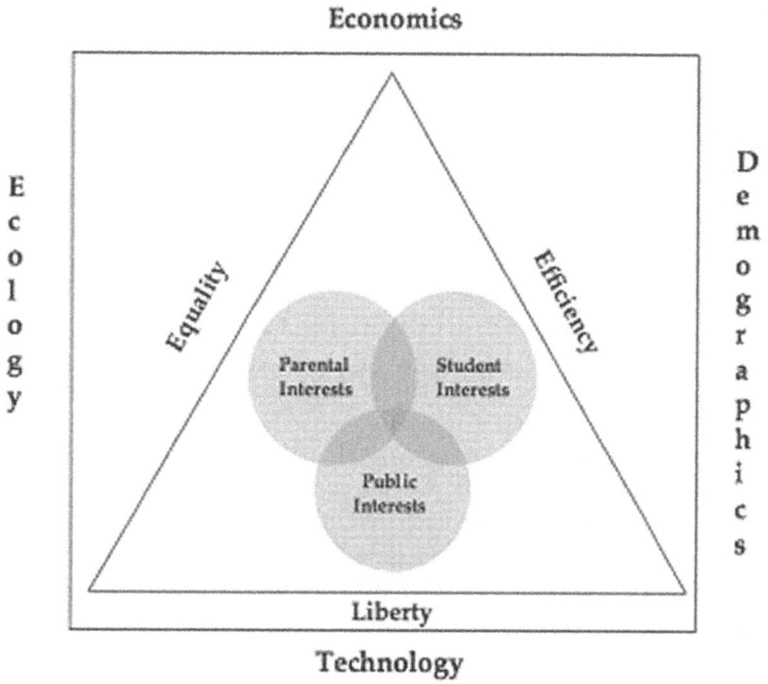

FIGURE 4.2

executive branch officials and bureau workers who administer the programs connected with these interests. When it comes to incremental politics, these three parties are the dominant actors.

To illustrate the iron triangle in operation, consider a set of local school districts that desire a change in the state's school finance formula. However altruistic the banners under which they mobilize, proponents are also likely to be organizational, and possibly personal, beneficiaries of the changes they seek. These distribution formula issues are unlikely to attract the attention of the larger political system involving political parties, the governor, the speaker, or the full legislature. Rather, these micro issues are more likely to be settled within the smaller domain of the iron triangle. However, if the desired formula alternations have substantial cost consequences and could lead to major redistributions of existing resources among districts, then the issue may exceed the boundary of the iron triangle and come to the attention of the larger political system.

More generally, much of the political system's routine activity is engaged with maintaining a homeostatic condition. Micro adjustments are continually being made to finance formulas, to higher education student financial aid or to institutional appropriation levels so as to maintain stability in the system. On selected occasions, however, a more dramatic change takes place. The issue may become partisan and provoke political parties to take positions regarding the issue. A governor, a mayor, the full state legislature or the full city council may get engaged. Kingdon (1995) labels this latter condition "High Politics."

High Politics

Certain dynamics can upset the value balance and shift the emphasis of a political system in such a way that it produces new or significantly altered policies. Returning to Figure 4.2, one can see a peripheral rectangle, each side of which represents one of four change vectors: technology, economics, demographics and ecology. A significant change on any one of these forces can distort the public value balance, trigger altered policies and, eventually, provoke a search for a recalibrated policy equilibrium. Following are illustrations of this process at work.

Technological innovation is a major source of system imbalance and, hence, a principal trigger of new policies. Here is a dramatic example that had major consequences for the nation's education system through the latter half of the 20th century. In the 1950s Stanford University researcher Carl Dejerassi invented a reliable birth control pill for women. Few could have predicted the eventual consequences of this pharmaceutical invention. These included a sustained decline in the birthrate, vastly expanded workforce participation by women, increased demand for out-of-home child care services, reliance upon television for entertaining children and youth, possible erosion of the two-parent nuclear family, or at least a diminution in the proportion of such units in the overall population, widespread relaxation of prior prohibitions regarding premarital and extramarital sex, and a reduction of the ratio of children to adults in society.

These changes, in turn, contributed to policy demands for publicly subsidized child care, extension of public school kindergarten and pre-school programs, new child welfare laws, added reliance on equal protection laws to ensure women equitable treatment in the workplace. Other effects included proposals for increased regulation of television offerings, a greater openness to overseas immigration to enable the workforce to keep pace with the job demands of a vastly expanding economy, and the expanded consumption capacity associated with two income earners in many households.

Examples abound of the reciprocal effects of technological innovation and economic change, and of the combined effect of these two forces upon policy demands. The acceleration of a global economy in the 1990s resulted from the convergence of a number of electronic innovations leading to formation of the World Wide Web and the Internet. These new communication and information transfer technologies liberated capital, creative ideas and talent from national boundaries. Companies and other organizations, including even international terrorist groups, could now draw upon ideas and recruits from overseas in a never ceasing quest for means to lower manufacturing and production costs. The outsourcing of jobs itself reverberated through the United States policy system as electoral candidates and government officials debated and sought means for regulating or limiting the flow of offshore jobs.

Ecological conditions can have a profound impact on policy, including education policy. While the intense ecological attention that is presently paid to global warming and carbon emissions has elevated ecological issues into the realm of high politics, there are on-the-ground examples of ecological consequences for schooling. For example, proponents of charter schools saw the policy confusion that followed the 2006 Gulf Coast disasters triggered by Hurricane Katrina as a political opportunity to push their cause. The result has been major restructuring of the city's public school system, with regular public schools diminished in authority and enrollment, and the ascendance of charter schools (Waldman, 2007). How long this solution will remain in place is unclear.

Preconditions for Macro Policy Change

Scholars continually probe the primordial ooze from which political actions stem in search of precursors that facilitate or portend significant policy change. Two engaging theories have emerged, both centered on a notion of disequilibrium. When the political system is somehow out of balance, significant policy change is more likely.

Kingdon (1995) stresses the alignment of problems, proposals, and politics, three conditions that conventionally occur independent of the other. A problem occurs when a sufficient proportion of the body politics becomes concerned about an unfilled preference or a political demand. In education, for example, presently there are many proposals for market incentives and arrangements for generating greater competition among schools. Such proposals are often formulated in the absence of a particular problem. They are proposals, some say, in search of a problem to which their proponents can attach them. Politics is the set of circumstances and processes by which, on occasion, problems and proposals find one another.

Kingdon contends that change occurs when there is an alignment of political opportunity, the presence of a policy champion and a set of predetermined solutions that match the problem. The overwhelming 1964 electoral victory of Lyndon Baines Johnson over Republican opponent Barry Goldwater for president of the United States supplied Johnson with a huge congressional majority, one so large as to ensure passage of his legislative agenda with hardly a debate. This window of political opportunity facilitated Johnson's long-standing predisposition to take leadership on issues of poverty and education. He had previously established a blue ribbon task force that created a slate of education ideas. The overwhelming Democratic Party majority rapidly approved these ideas, the principal feature of which was the 1965 Elementary and Secondary Education Act. Johnson had a set of proposals. Having a window of political opportunity enabled him to attach his proposals to a newly defined problem, the eradication or diminution of poverty.

Baumgartner and Jones (1993, 2002) offer a different set of hypotheses regarding dramatic policy redirection. Their concern is with the fact that most policymaking is incremental, controlled by circumstances and by actors connected with the previously mentioned iron triangle of interest groups, bureaucrats and decision makers. However, from time to time dramatic and deep changes in policy do occur. Baumgartner and Jones label this condition *punctuated equilibrium*—long periods of policy stability interrupted by major alterations to the system. Stability is maintained through the creation of interest group coalitions that can dominate an issue or an already implemented solution to an issue. These dominating positions rely heavily for their sustenance upon the manipulation of policy images, which are generally connected to core political values; i.e., equality, liberty, or efficiency. The manipulation of images combines empirical information and popular appeals. These images can be easily communicated and are transmitted directly and simply through campaign commercials and electoral rhetoric.

McDonnell (2007) provides the following explanation of the change dynamic espoused by Baumgartner and Jones:

> A primary reason changes occur is that those opposed to the policy monopoly or excluded from it constitute slack resources (opposition) policy entrepreneurs can mobilize. They do so through a redefinition of the dominant policy image using ideas that challenge it and capture the imagination of the media, policymakers, and the public. They provide new understandings of policy problems and new ways of conceptualizing solutions. These ideas can fuel powerful changes as they are communicated through a variety of rhetorical mechanisms, including stories about decline or negative consequences resulting from the current policy monopoly and stories of hope about what can be accomplished with a new framing of the policy problem and solution.

POLITICAL CULTURES

The political system has five identifiable cultural components, or self-adopted lenses through which political actors often view reality and attempt to shape it. These political cultures influence the manner in which advocates for a particular change will define a problem or seek predetermined solutions. The unique components of each culture also shape the instruments and processes by which participants attempt to implement and oversee policy. The five political cultures are: legislative, regulative, legal, professional, and markets.

Legislative

This is the culture conventionally associated with policy making. Deliberative bodies, such as legislatures, city councils, and school boards, confer about issues and render recorded decisions. These politically-made rules may be the product of intense controversy characterized by complicated and protracted lobbying by various parties at interests. The activity may have been partisan and linked to identifiable political parties. The newly enacted policy may alter some existing circumstance, add new service, elevate taxes or acknowledge some important symbolic issue. Whatever the policy, its construction is characterized by the principal components of the political process: coalition building and bargaining.

Regulative

Regulation, too, is a widely perceived component of politics. Many individuals believe that regulations derive singularly from enactments by deliberative bodies. In short, they think of "regulations" as detailed rules authorized by, and flowing from, relatively abstract policy enactments, something of a bureaucratic follow-on to conventional politics. There is some accuracy to this perception, but by itself it is insufficient.

Operating agencies of the executive branch also have a political momentum, and sometimes an interest predisposition, of their own. Some of the rules they develop and promulgate stem solely from the momentum of bureaucratic practices and only remotely from explicit political enactments. There is a large organization imperative which specifies that if there is to be a hierarchy of authority, with some individuals enjoying greater decision-making power than others, then there must be rules to enforce the division of labor, specialization of tasks, and an expectation that all similarly situated clients will be treated similarly.

The distinguishing characteristics of the regulatory political culture are codification, rationality, rigidity, specialization, hierarchy, standardization and efforts to appear objective and independent. Anyone who has had military experience will have encountered a regulatory political culture. Military procedures may eventually be linked to statutory authority, but often one must follow the policy "food chain" to very high levels to identify the overarching authority. In fact, the military is quite capable of generating rules all by itself, as are educational institutions. Public universities and school districts have many sets of rules that, however well intentioned and effective, are a product of bureaucratic, and thus not necessarily openly political, processes.

Legal

Courts and legal procedures comprise a third major cultural component of the political system. Their identifying features are an ability to frame an issue in keeping with longstanding, judicially sanctioned doctrines, a resort to adversarial techniques, adherence to precedent, appeals to higher authority, and proscribed sets of procedural activities known only to a restricted cadre of certified technicians, lawyers.

Professional

The professional culture is the political culture that may be least visible to the general public. From this culture stem procedures and decisions derived from self-reinforcing sets of beliefs of professional participants, not necessarily from court decisions, bureaucratic rules or political enactments. Distinguishing characteristics are actions taken to restrict entry into the field, protect clients, enhance standards, advance knowledge in a field, and insulate the profession from overtly partisan or selfish interests. Examples include peer evaluation procedures for assessing performance of university professors, peer review among research organizations to determine a manuscript's publishability or fundability of a proposed project, or grading policies for student performance in an institution of higher education or a secondary school.

Markets

This political culture is distinguished by a fundamental assumption that clients are sufficiently informed and motivated to operate in their own self interests and that, in the process of doing so, will promote the public long run interests as well. Market oriented political cultures certainly have room for rules generated in other spheres. For example, few who believe in deregulating the airline industry would also completely eliminate Federal Aviation Administration rules regarding pilot training or aircraft maintenance. However, the weight of a restrictive argument, from a marketeer's point of view, must be heavily in favor of regulation. Further, open choice among services or products, open competition for consumers' resources, access to capital, and a free flow of information are seen as the sine qua non that should shape policy.

GOVERNMENT STRUCTURES

The United States Constitution became fully operational in 1790. It provides the nation with its fundamental governing charter, the collectively affirmed set of rules and structures within which the political process operates. The framers of the Constitution did not envision a national system of education. Indeed, Article I, Section 8 of the U.S. Constitution does not list education among the "enumerated powers" that Congress enjoys, and the Tenth Amendment grants states autonomy in virtually all domestic affairs, including education. Moreover, the sovereignty ceded to the states was not dependent on the federal government but instead stems from a state's citizenry. Consistent with this view, in *The Federalist Papers*, first published during 1787 and 1788 (Hamilton, Madison, & Jay, 1961), James Madison wrote, "The federal and state governments are in fact but different agents and trustees for the people, constituted with different powers, and designed for different purposes" (No. 46. p. 296).

Such a multilevel governance structure was further maintained by local customs, practice and belief. In his description of the American democracy in the mid-nineteenth century, Alexis de Tocqueville (2000) opened his seminal treatise by referring to the local government's "rights of individuality." Observing the state-local relations in the New England townships, the visiting French observer wrote, "Thus it is true that the tax is voted by the legislature, but it is the township that apportions and collects it; the existence of a school is imposed, but the township builds it, pays for it, and directs it" (p.63). Thus public education was primarily an obligation internal to the state. The division of power within the federal system was so strong that it continued to preserve state control over its internal affairs, including the de jure segregation of schools, for many decades following the Civil War.

Federal constitutional silence regarding education, coupled with the social contract philosophy expressed most directly in the Tenth Amendment,[2] means that plenary authority for the formation and operation of education system rests in the hands of states. At the time states were establishing elementary schools, primitive transportation and communication arrangements rendered centralized governance difficult. Hence, a great deal of authority for schools was initially ceded to local governments. This tradition of local control of schools persists, though in vastly attenuated form, today. In fact, whatever the actual degree of local control, the ideology remains powerful symbolically and rhetorically in the conduct of education politics. Thus, even though states are most intensely empowered on matters of education governance and operation, the federal government and local authorities are also involved. This layering renders American education far more complicated structurally and politically than virtually any other nation in the world. The overwhelming proportion of other nations, democracies included, relies upon national systems of education.

Vertically Distributed Power in the U.S. Education System

Historically, the federal government has taken a permissive role in education that is consistent with what political scientist Morton Grodzins characterized as "layer cake" federalism. Grodzins was referring to the United States' three governmental strata—local, state, and federal—as the cake layers. One practical expression of the layering is the varying amount of resources contributed by each level of government. The variation is wide across states, but the national average involves state governments paying for about 50 percent of the expense of public education, local governments about 40 percent, and the federal government, as the junior partner, contributing approximately 10 percent.

Starting in the mid-20th century, however, a number of events converged to reorient the federal role to a more activist posture. The Servicemen's Readjustment Act of 1944 (otherwise known as the G.I. Bill) assisted returning veterans in financing their higher education. Also, in 1958, a year after the Soviet Union launched its Sputnik satellite into orbit, Congress enacted the National Defense Education Act, which authorized federal funds for math, science and language instruction at the pre-college level. The 1954 landmark Supreme Court ruling in *Brown v. Board of Education* and the Congressional enactment of the 1964 Civil Rights Act sharpened the federal attention to the needs of disadvantaged students. In addition, the federal government adopted a major antipoverty education program in 1965, Title I of the 1965 Elementary and Secondary Education Act (ESEA).

The expanding modern federal role notwithstanding, the 50 states continue to assume constitutional and policy authority over much of the domain of public education through constitutionally established state-level school boards. Though far from uniform, selection of state board members is largely by appointment. Governors in 31 states appoint the boards, while elsewhere the process also involves the legislature. Board members in 20 percent of states are elected on either a partisan or non-partisan basis. Even where state school boards are elected the board selects most chief state school officers. No state any longer maintains both an elected board and an elected chief state school officer.

Despite interstate variation in governing tradition and culture (Elazar 1972; Wirt 1977), local districts are seen as agencies of the state educational system and exercise only those powers granted to them by the state. States enjoy substantial control over compulsory attendance, accreditation, curriculum, graduation standards, and housekeeping matters such as the school calendar, records and accounting procedures.

In practice, local governments exercise control over critical resources. Localities can select their own political representatives, decide on fiscal policies, and define the scope of their services. Today, there are approximately 14,000 local school districts governing over 90,000 schools across the nation. Although an overwhelming majority of school boards are popularly elected, those in Baltimore, Boston, Chicago, Cleveland, New York, Oakland, Philadelphia, Trenton, and several other cities are appointed either by the mayor or jointly by the mayor and the state's governor (Wong et al, 2007). There are also county systems, principally in the south, that have appointed school boards. Local districts generally maintain control over district organization, instructional personnel, pupil-teacher ratios, staff recruitment and extracurricular activities. Nonetheless, on school funding and accountability issues, the balance of power has shifted toward greater state control in recent years. At the middle of the 20th century, the balance of revenue provision highly favored local sources. By the end of the 20th century, states were the principal providers of school revenues.

HORIZONTALLY DISTRIBUTED POWER IN THE U.S. EDUCATION SYSTEM

State level legislative politics play an important role in shaping educational policy because states are central to taxation, expenditure and constituent concerns, and school legislation often constitutes part of a larger revenue package. Over 80 percent of state education monies are distributed through formulas written by lawmakers; arriving at these formulas involves considerable political give and take and the building of political coalitions.

Coalitions are particularly difficult to create in some circumstances, especially when legislative authority in the education sector is fragmented. In their comparative state study, Rosenthal and Fuhrman (1981) found that education committee chairs quite often do not overlap with the membership on the ways and means and appropriations committees. In each budgetary cycle, education has to compete with other major policy domains, such as welfare assistance, criminal justice and transportation. Both K–12 and postsecondary education are usually in competition for limited government resources. Given this fragmentation, newly adopted education programs may not be fully funded. Likewise, partisan disagreements between the legislature and the governor's office, as well as between the two houses within a legislature, can present political obstacles when enacting spending and taxing bills. State boards of education seldom play an important role in this political part of the political process.

Conflict is often embedded in urban-suburban-rural divisions within legislatures. An example is Illinois, where the longstanding legislative feud between Chicago and the remainder of the state has been a crucial factor in shaping state revenue and spending policy that affects Chicago schools. Suburban and rural legislators rarely voted for tax increases to provide additional aid to the Chicago schools. Racial factors may further contribute to these cleavages.

Influence of Non-Governmental Actors

Policy makers at the state and district level must also deal with competing demands from multiple organized groups with an interest in educational policy, including, most notably, the two major national teachers unions (McDonnell and Pascal, 1979; Moe, 2002; Loveless, 2001). The American Federation of Teachers (AFT), which has its roots in the labor movement and belongs to the AFL-CIO, is active primarily in urban districts in the northeast and the Midwest. The much larger National Education Association (NEA), whose roots as a professional education association date back to the 19th century, organizes teachers in most other districts.

In his study of the Chicago's teachers' union, an AFT affiliate, Grimshaw (1979) suggested that the AFT typically goes through two phases in its relationship with a local school administration. During the initial organizing phase, when formal bargaining recognition is the objective, the local union largely cooperates with the district and state administration in return for a legitimate role in the policy-making process. Cole (1969) found, for example, that the desire for formal union recognition, where such had never before existed, was a key objective in the 1960 teachers' strike in New York City. In the second phase, which Grimshaw (1979) characterizes as "union rule," the union typically looks to the national union leadership for technical support and political guidance. This support makes it possible for the union to become independent of local and state political leadership and to engage in tough bargaining with the school management over better compensation and working conditions. Consequently, Grimshaw (1979) argued that policy makers "no longer are able to set policy unless the policy is consistent with the union's objectives" (p.150).

Policy makers must also contend with an increasingly well-organized taxpaying public, a substantial portion of which no longer has children in the public schools (Kirst and Garms, 1980). The aging population has exacerbated the competition for funds between public education and other sectors such as transportation, public safety, community development and health care. Discontent with property taxes became widespread during the time of the much-publicized 1978 campaign for Proposition 13 in California. Thirty-nine of the 67 tax or spending limitation measures on state ballots across the nation between 1978 and 1983 were approved (Citrin, 1984). In communities with a substantial representation of retirees, such as those in Florida, referenda for school taxes have met with greater resistance than in settings with larger proportions of households with children.

More recently, business-organized lobbying groups have been successful in pushing goals such as higher academic standards, strong accountability measures and, in some case, alternative ways of delivering schooling services, including privatization or creating charter schools.

NO CHILD LEFT BEHIND: AN EXAMPLE OF POLITICAL DYNAMICS

The No Child Left Behind Act (NCLB), enacted in 2001, is a massively influential piece of legislation. Its various provisions insinuate the federal government into the warp and woof of American education—all the way into the classroom and, the interactions between teachers and students. In addition to its massive practical impact, however, NCLB also illustrates the manner in which abstractions such as systems theory, iron triangles, policy spheres, policy cultures, policy champions, high politics, and punctuated equilibrium come together in the reality of education finance and governance.

Consistent with the previously cited writings of Baumgartner and Jones and Kingdon, President George W. Bush took advantage of alterations in global economic and technological conditions to shape a new popular image of American education. He succeeded in using this new image to diminish public sympathy toward the prevailing Clinton administration interpretation of equality and to promote, in its place, a new concept of equality that furthered the value of efficiency.[3] Bush and his advisers took advantage of a new policy system equilibrium, repurposed efficiency ideas they had long held, and insinuated their enaction into federal policy through NCLB.

Content

No Child Left Behind is, technically speaking, an amendment of the Elementary and Secondary Education Act (ESEA). It authorizes federal funding for public school districts and utilizes a modification of the ESEA funding formula to distribute approximately $20 billion in federal funds to states based on multipliers of current school spending levels and numbers of low-income students. However, NCLB is far more than a vehicle for funneling federal dollars to schools. In exchange for added financing, NCLB mandates performance targets, exhorting states and school districts to propel 95 percent of their students to levels of reading and mathematics proficiency by the 2013–2014 school year. Exhortations such as this have been promoted previously, including previous re-authorization of ESEA. What is different with NCLB is that it also mandates state measurement systems by which schools can be held accountable for making "Adequate Yearly Progress" (AYP) toward the 2014 goal. When they fail to meet academic performance targets, schools are subjected to sanctions, including a provision that their student may opt to receive federally funded vouchers to attend other public or even private schools.

NCLB has additional accountability provisions that render it unique in the history of federal aid to education. The Adequate Yearly Progress performance measurement system does not deal simply with mean or average performance. It mandates test measures of various categories of historically neglected students, low income and predominantly non-white. Therefore, a school cannot easily hide behind high or accelerating achievement scores of middle-class students and overlook otherwise frequently neglected low-income students. Also, NCLB requires all districts to provide parents with annual report cards on district and school performance in meeting or failing AYP.

Beginnings

NCLB was one of the most prominent proposals of the first Administration of President George W. Bush and was submitted to Congress shortly after his initial inauguration in 2001. The act's principal ideas had been previously honed during Bush's two terms as Governor of Texas, an eight-year administration that had mounted a sustained effort to reform education and had shaped a slate of accountability ideas as their major change instrument.

The Bush team trumpeted the need for higher academic standards and more accountability in the education system. In his presidential campaign and early in his administration, Bush discussed the outsourcing of jobs, the trade deficit, the alarming economic gains of nations such as China. The same kinds of threats had previously been discussed in the 1983 report, *A Nation at Risk*. That report, drafted by the National Commission on Excellence in Education and released by the U.S. Department of Education during the Reagan administration, marked the beginning of a nationwide focus on academic performance. Its recommendations comprised the basis for federal and state efforts to improve the quality and performance of public schools that continues to this day.

The Bush team did not openly disparage equality as a value or policy objective. Rather, they diminished or diluted the previously dominating rhetoric regarding the need for expensive added services for disadvantaged students, a legacy of the predecessor Clinton Administration, and replaced it with the notion that inequality of opportunity came about not because of a lack of educational services. President Bush was fond of saying that poor and otherwise disadvantaged students were unintended victims of the soft prejudice of low expectations.

By returning to themes of higher standards and accountability previously proposed in *A Nation At Risk,* Bush and colleagues altered the prevailing policy paradigm. They employed new rhetoric in a manner that was persuasive to the body politic, and constructed a new policy attractive to a majority of Congress. In so doing, the Bush Administration punctured the previously prevailing policy paradigm; equality, and replaced it with their agenda regarding efficiency.

EVOLVING POLITICS OF PERFORMANCE-BASED ACCOUNTABILITY

The 2001 enactment and subsequent implementation of the No Child Left Behind Act represents one of the great political ironies in American history. NCLB is a direct policy descendent of *A Nation at Risk*, which had been promoted by President Ronald Reagan as part of his attempt to reduce the federal government's role in education. Now, NCLB is unquestionably the most powerful federal influence on American education ever imagined. The twist and turns of political fate are not easily predicted.

At the time of the release of *A Nation at Risk,* President Reagan was striving to reduce the status and authority of the U.S. Department of Education, and thereby shrink the federal role in education. Reagan's education agenda included enacting tuition tax credits for parents of children attending parochial schools and passage of a Constitutional amendment that would permit prayer in public schools.[4] In an interview with the *New York Times* during his first month as Reagan's U.S. Secretary of Education, Terence Bell pledged his commitment to the president's proposal to abolish the department, saying that he was "not sure that we need department-level cabinet status" (*New York Times*, Feb. 3, 1981, p.13.) Bell did little in practice to push this agenda, however, and by 1987, the Reagan administration had begun to abandon its six-year effort to reduce federal spending in education—a shift that coincided with the appointment of a pragmatic former Tennessee Republican Senator Howard Baker, as the White House chief of staff (Fiske, 1987, p. A14).

Reagan's drive toward government-wide efficiency and budgetary restraint posed a political challenge to Lyndon Baines Johnson's Great Society legacy, the formerly powerful prevailing policy paradigm that had focused mainly on equity and access. In mediating the tension between efficiency and equity, *A Nation at Risk* proposed an alternative paradigmatic view that focused on quality and standards. In that report, members of the National Commission asserted America's academic flabbiness rendered the United States vulnerable to economic dominance by foreign nations and that it would be in the nation's long run best interest to raise academic standards in public schools and institutions of higher education. The report made no mention of any of the major educational initiatives proposed by the Reagan White House, nor was it sympathetic with the Congressional recommendation for an increase in educational spending. Instead, *A Nation at Risk* left unsettled the question of the amount and types of resources the nation may need in order to reverse the declining trend of its public school system's educational performance. Instead of terminating the federal role in education, the Commission called upon the federal government to lead the movement toward "creating a learning society."

While it was one among many reports that addressed school quality during the early 1980s, *A Nation at Risk* offered a necessary, even provocative, comprehensive framework with which to reassess the role of the federal government. Its recommendations on school quality and standards played an important role in reshaping the way the federal government designed its largest program in elementary and secondary education, No Child Left Behind.

For example, *A Nation at Risk's* recommendations on academic expectations, curriculum, use of time and teacher quality were featured in all the modern era legislative changes to the ESEA, including the 1994 Improving America's Schools Act_and the 2001 NCLB (Wong and Nicotera, 2004).

Post-NCLB Enactment Political Dynamics

Passage of the No Child Left Behind Act in 2001 changed the terms of political engagement among key institutional actors involved in education. The enactment of NCLB reflected growing public support for holding schools and districts accountable for academic performance, and its accountability-oriented, centrist approach to education drew bipartisan support. Clearly, Republican lawmakers were ready to abandon the 1994 Newt Gingrich-inspired policy platform of dismantling federal involvement. Instead, with NCLB, they chose substantially to broaden federal expectations on outcome-based accountability in public education. In supporting the NCLB, Congressional Republicans gave their strong endorsement to a core concern of the Bush Presidency, namely raising student achievement.

To be sure, Bush was able to bank on that fact that Republicans controlled not only the presidency but also both branches of the Legislature. He also benefited from the political rapport associated with the first months of a new administration and the widespread public confidence with the federal government in the context of the tragic events of September 11, 2001.

NCLB formally identifies school choice as an option for school restructuring, an indication of relying on the demand side to drive school improvement. Consistent with the Republican Party's platform, Bush advocated for greater "consumer" choice during his 2000 presidential campaign, which included school vouchers for private schools. His administration was willing to compromise, however, to make sure that annual testing was adopted. Instead, a more limited set of choice arrangements were enacted as part of the provisions for corrective action. When schools fail in consecutive years to meet the Adequate Yearly Progress requirement, students in those schools are granted access to supplementary tutorial service and charter schools.

Challenges to NCLB

Politics has elements in common with physics. For every political action there is something of a reaction, though it may not be equal or precisely opposite. NCLB illustrates this condition. From the moment NCLB was submitted as a bill in Congress, powerful opponents have attempted to prevent its enactment, eviscerate its implementation, or prevent its reauthorization. The opponents, principally, are comprised of professional education groups for which the concepts of accountability are threatening. Secondarily, opponents are school administrators who have found implementing the massive act daunting and seek either to mitigate testing and accountability provisions or to delay implementation of the adequate yearly progress schedule. Other criticisms involve the allegation that NCLB, with its insistence upon elevating reading and mathematics test scores, has unduly restricted the school curriculum, and specifically has driven out creative subjects such as the arts and literature. In addition, critics contend the Act has such a large number of under defined components (e.g., that every child deserves a highly qualified teacher) that federal regulations outstrip practical or research knowledge. It is not known, for example, what in reality comprises a highly qualified teacher.

The first legal challenge to NCLB came from local school districts in Michigan, Texas, and Vermont and from the National Education Association. These plaintiffs argued that NCLB imposed federal mandates without adequate financial support. In November 2004, a federal judge in the U.S. District Court for the Eastern District of Michigan rejected the challenge and ruled that Congress had the authority to specify policy conditions on states (Janofsky 2005, p. A14). In another suit against the United States Department of Education, Connecticut sought full financial support from the federal government to implement the NCLB. It claimed that the Department had acted in an "arbitrary and capricious manner" in deciding on state requests for waivers and exemption (Janofsky, 2005, A14). For example, Connecticut cited rejection of the state's request for testing the students every other year instead of annually. Such intergovernmental conflicts over specific NCLB provisions are likely to continue.

In the face of such local and state resistance, the United States Department of Education has relaxed some requirements on a case-by-case basis. For example, Chicago succeeded in gaining federal approval to provide its own after school tutoring programs for students in schools that failed the average yearly progress standards rather than rely on outside vendors as prescribed by the legislation. In a series of private meetings between the Chicago Mayor Richard Daley and U.S. Secretary of Education Margaret Spellings, a compromise was reached. In return for permission to continue its supplemental services, the city agreed to reduce barriers for private vendors to provide tutorial services. When Secretary Spellings formally announced the compromise in early

September of 2005 in Chicago, Mayor Daley hailed the efforts as the "beginning of a new era of cooperation" across levels of government in education (see *New York Times*, Sept. 2, 2005, p. A11). Similar waivers were subsequently granted in New York City, Boston, Memphis and elsewhere. In effect, it appears that the United States Department of Education, in order to constrain criticisms and gain re-authorization of NCLB, has adopted a posture of greater flexibility and has been tailoring regulations more to the particular circumstances of local school districts.

CONCLUSION

It is desirable to have a theory of action that facilitates prediction. Who will be the next U.S. President? What will be the eventual political system response to the threat of global warming? What will be the next big domestic policy initiative? Will there ever be peace in the Middle East? And so on. Politics, or at least political theory, presently lacks a precise set of predictive postulates. The best one can do is to rely upon a rear view mirror approach and try retrospectively to understand and explain the flow of political events.

This chapter has sought to contribute to the development of a predictive capacity by laying out a multilevel and multistage theory of politics, explaining the dynamics by which this theory operates within the multilayered governmental structure fostered by the United States Constitution, and illustrating the interaction of politics and government by reference to the No Child Left Behind Act. Deeper understanding of these various interactions may enable policy makers, eventually, both to tailor policies more to public preferences and, possibly, more forcefully contribute to the public's well being.

NOTES

1. Only health care provision and government debt annually involve larger government appropriations.
2. The powers not delegated to the United States by the Constitution, nor prohibited by it to the States, are reserved to the States respectively, or to the people.
3. The Bush campaign's attention to education came at a time when public confidence in schools had been declining for more than a 30-year period. In 1977, for example, 53 percent of the public revealed a high level of confidence with public education. By May 2005, the confidence level fell to only 37 percent (Public Agenda, 2006). However, the public seemed not ready to give up reforming the existing system of public schools. According to the Gallup Poll conducted in the summer of 2003, 73 percent of survey respondents wanted to reform the existing public school system, while only 25 percent preferred alternative approaches such as school vouchers.
4. A reduced federal government role in education reappeared as a policy objective in 1994 under the leadership of Republican House Speaker, Newt Gingrich, of Georgia. However, Gingrich's agenda was never fulfilled, prior to his ouster as Speaker. Indeed, by 2001, the No Child Left Behind Act had virtually gone one-hundred-and-eighty degrees in the opposite direction, propelling massive federal government intervention in state governance of education and local school district operation.

REFERENCES

Baumgartner, F. & Jones, B. (1993). *Agendas and instability in American politics*. Chicago: The University of Chicago Press.
Baumgartner, F. R. & Jones, B. D. (Eds.) (2002). *Policy dyanmics.* Chicago: University of Chicago Press.

Citrin, J. (1984). Introduction: The legacy of Proposition 13. In T. Schwadron (Ed.), *California and the American tax revolt.* Berkeley and Los Angeles: University of California Press.

Cole, S. (1969). The *unionization of teachers: A case study of the United Federation of Teachers.* New York: Praeger.

de Tocqueville, A. (2000). *Democracy in America.* (H. Mansfield & D. Winthrop, Trans., Ed.). Chicago: University of Chicago Press. (Original work published 1835/1840)

Easton, D. (1953). *The political system.* New York: Knopf.

Easton, D. (1981). *The political system: An inquiry into the state of political science* (2nd ed.). New York: Alfred Knopf.

Eberling, E. (1999). Massachusetts Education Laws of 1642, 1647, and 1648. In R. J. Altenbaugh (Ed.), *Historical Dictionary of American Education.* Greenwood Press.

Education Secretary Bell's view of a department in transition. (1981, February 3). *New York Times*, pp. 11, 13.

Elazar, D. (1972). *American federalism: A view from the states* (2nd ed.). New York: Crowell.

Elementary and Secondary Education Act of 1865, Pub L., No. 89–10, Sec 201, 79 Stat. 27. (1965). Codified as amended at 20 U.S.C. Sec 6301. (2002).

Fiske, E. (1987, June 11). Bennett, in shift, urging an end to drive for big education cuts. *New York Times*, p. A14.

Grimshaw, W. (1979). *Union rule in the schools.* Lexington, MA: D.C. Heath.

Hamilton, A., Madison, J., & Jay, J. (1961). *The Federalist papers.* New York: Mentor. (Original work published 1787/1788).

Improving America's Schools Act of 1994, P.L. No. 103–382. (1994).

Janofsky, M. (2007). Educational accountability as a presidential priority: No Child Left Behind and the Bush presidency. In Wong & Sunderman (Eds.), *Journal of Federalism*, A14.

Jennings, J. (1998). *Why national standards and tests? Politics and the quest for better schools.* Thousand Oaks, CA: Sage.

Kingdon, J. W. (1995). Agendas, alternatives, and public policies (2nd ed.). New York: Harper Collins.

Kirst, M. & Garms, W. (1980). *The political environment of school finance policy in the 1980's: A decade of conflict.* Cambridge, MA: Ballinger.

Loveless, T. (2001). How well are American students learning? *Report on Education*, I(2), 6–16. Washington, DC: Brookings Institution, Brown Center.

McDonnell, L. (2007). *Creating the political conditions for major changes in school finance policy.* Danial C. Evans School of Public Affairs.

McDonnell, L. and Pascal, A. (1979*). Organized teachers in American schools.* Santa Monica, CA: Rand Corporation.

Moe, T. M. (2002). The structure of school choice. In P. T. Hill (Eds.), *Choice with equity* (pp. 179–212). Stanford, CA: Hoover Institution Press.

No Child Left Behind Act of 2001, P.L. No. 107–110. (2002).

Public Agenda. (2006) Accessed on November 1, 2006, from http://www.publicagenda.org/issues

Rosenthal, A. & Fuhrman, S. (1981). *Legislative education leadership in the States.* Washington, DC.: Institute for Educational Leadership.

Wirt, F. (1977). School policy culture and state decentralization. In J. Scribner (Ed.), *The politics of education.* Chicago: University of Chicago Press.

Wong, K.K. et al, (2007). *The education mayor.* Washington DC: Georgetown University Press.

Wong & Nicotera (2004). Educational quality and policy redesign: Reconsidering the NAR and Federal Title I Policy. *Peabody Journal of Education, 39*(1), 87–104.

5

Educational Goals: A Public Perspective

Richard Rothstein and Rebecca Jacobsen[1]

Contemporary education policy stresses "accountability" but defines the goals of public education narrowly, usually holding schools accountable only for adequate standardized test scores in mathematics and reading. Yet because public schools provide collective benefits, such as a common set of democratic values, Americans have historically defined schools' goals more expansively.

As this chapter shows, a careful review of the history of American educational thought demonstrates that policymakers have always believed that schools should be held accountable for students having sufficient background in history and world and civic affairs to exercise the rights and responsibilities of citizenship, and for students having the organizational skills and proficiency in decision-making and cooperative behavior that will allow them to participate thoughtfully in the democratic processes of their communities and nation. Americans want students to have sufficient appreciation of literature and of the visual, musical and performing arts to be able to engage in fulfilling adult leisure activities. Policy makers have regularly held that schools should also graduate students with habits of intellectual curiosity, creative imagination, and personal discipline—patience, persistence, and self-confidence—which enhance both workplace productivity and personal fulfillment. Graduates should know how to resolve personal and social conflicts peaceably and in a manner that reconciles competing interests with justice and fairness.

Our historical review finds that Americans expect schools to make students familiar with the many ethnic traditions that their peers bring to diverse communities. Youths should graduate with a broad knowledge of science—not only to choose technical careers if they wish, but also because public problems on which citizens in a democracy must deliberate require scientific insight for intelligent resolution. Further, schools are expected to inspire young people to develop habits of exercise, hygiene and nutrition that lead to lifelong physical fitness; schools should teach enough about physiology and sexuality for youths to lead healthy and responsible teen and adult lives.

The contemporary near-exclusive emphasis on basic academic skills is an historic aberration. Widely publicized contemporary surveys show that Americans do expect students to graduate with the literary and mathematical skills that enable them to enroll in college or technical school or to succeed in vocations of their choice. Yet these surveys also find support for the idea that assessment and accountability systems should include more than these skills alone.[2]

PRE-TWENTIETH CENTURY GOALS OF EDUCATION

When the Founding Fathers called for public education, their motives were mostly political. Instruction in reading was the way to teach citizens to make wise political decisions. History instruction was thought to teach students good judgment, to help them learn from prior generations' mistakes and successes, and to inspire character traits like honesty, integrity and compassion. The Founders had no doubt that education could produce good character, and it would never have occurred to them that reading and arithmetic alone would itself guarantee good citizenship.

In 1749 Benjamin Franklin proposed that Pennsylvania establish a public school that should, he said, "place as much emphasis on physical as on intellectual fitness because 'exercise invigorates the soul as well as the body.'" As for academics, Franklin thought history particularly important, because "questions of right and wrong, justice and injustice, will naturally arise" as students debate historical issues "in conversation and in writing." They should also discuss current controversies, developing logic and reasoning.[3]

George Washington's goals for public schools were also political and moral. In his first message to Congress, he advocated public schools that would teach students "to value their own rights," and "to distinguish between oppression and the necessary exercise of lawful authority." His farewell address warned that because public opinion influences policy in a democracy, "it is essential that public opinion should be enlightened" by schools teaching virtue and morality. He wanted to go further, but his speechwriter (Alexander Hamilton) cut from the address a proposal for a national public university that would encourage tolerance of diversity: integrating students of different backgrounds to show them there is no basis for "jealousies and prejudices."[4]

Thomas Jefferson thought universal public education was needed primarily to prepare voters to exercise wise judgment. He wanted not what we now call civics education—learning how bills are passed, how long a president's term is, and so on. Rather, he thought schools could prepare voters to think critically about candidates and choose wisely. And he insisted that a graduate should have learned "to observe with intelligence and faithfulness all the social relations under which he shall be placed."[5]

In 1787, the Northwest Ordinance provided funds for new states to establish public schools. To enter the union, states were required to adopt a commitment to public education. Indiana's 1816 constitution, for example, asserted that education is "essential to the preservation of a free government," and instructed the legislature to establish schools and to enact other policies to promote "arts, sciences, commerce, manufacture and natural history; and.... countenance and encourage the principles of humanity, honesty, industry and morality."[6]

Early 19th century labor unions insisted that public schools for the poor should include not only basic reading and arithmetic, but the more important intellectual development whose achievement characterized schools for the wealthy. An 1830 workingmen's committee, for example, examined Pennsylvania's urban public schools, mostly serving the poor. The committee denounced urban schools for instruction that "extends [no] further than a tolerable proficiency in reading, writing, and arithmetic..." Equality, the committee concluded, is but "an empty shadow" if poor children do not get an "equal education.... in the habits, in the manners, and in the feelings of the community."[7]

In 1837, Horace Mann was elected Secretary of the newly created Massachusetts Board of Education and thereafter wrote 12 annual reports to encourage support for public schools. One report stressed the importance of vocal music, not only because musical notes have mathematical relationships, but because it was a social equalizer (in contrast to other arts, it required no expensive materials or equipment) and encouraged pacific and unifying sentiments—patriotism, for example.[8] Another of Mann's reports, following a visit to Europe, concluded that education in reading and arithmetic did not alone ensure democratic values. Prussian students were literate, after all, but supported autocracy. Mann concluded that Massachusetts schools should not be held accountable for academics alone but must inculcate democratic moral and political values so that literacy will not be misused.[9]

TWENTIETH CENTURY VIEWS

As schooling expanded in the twentieth century, the federal Bureau of Education commissioned a 1918 report, *The Cardinal Principles of Secondary Education*. Although some contemporary historians have promoted the notion that the *Cardinal Principals* turned American education away from academic skills,[10] this is an exaggeration. In fact, the document asserted that "much of the energy of the elementary school is properly devoted to teaching certain fundamental processes, such as reading, writing, arithmetical computations, and the elements of oral and written expression" and that secondary schools should be devoted to applying these skills. But the document argued that academics were not enough; continuing in the tradition of the Founding Fathers and Horace Mann, it urged a balanced approach to education goals.

As its first goal, the committee listed physical activity, instruction in personal hygiene and in public health. Its second goal was academic skills. Third was preparation for traditional household roles of husbands and wives. Fourth was vocational education, including selection of jobs appropriate to each student's abilities and interests, and maintenance of good relationships with fellow workers.

Like the Founders, the committee emphasized in its fifth goal the need for civic education: preparation for participation in neighborhoods, towns or cities, states, and nation. *The Cardinal Principals* devoted more space to civic education than to any other goal, stressing that schools should teach "good judgment" in political matters and that students can only learn democratic habits if classrooms and schools are run with democratic methods. Even the study of literature should "kindle social ideals."

The sixth goal was "worthy use of leisure," or student appreciation of literature, art, and music. And lastly, the seventh goal, ethical character, was described as paramount in a democratic society. It included developing a sense of personal responsibility, initiative, and the "spirit of service."[11]

Two decades later, the National Education Association (NEA), then a quasi-governmental group that included not only teachers but all professionals and policy makers in education, considered how schools should respond to the Great Depression.[12] The NEA warned in 1938: "[T]he safety of democracy will not be assured merely by making education universal;" in other words, simply by making all Americans literate. "The task is not so easy as that. The dictatorships [Germany, Italy, Japan and the Soviet Union] have universal schooling and use this very means to prevent the spread of democratic doctrines and institutions" (p. 16). Democratic values and habits would not flow automatically from proficiency in reading and math. Schools, it went on, should also teach morality: justice and fair dealing, honesty, truthfulness, maintenance of group understandings, proper respect for authority, tolerance and respect for others, habits of cooperation, and work habits such as industry and self-control, along with endurance and physical strength.

Prefiguring our contemporary dilemmas, the 1938 report went on to warn that tests measuring only "basic skills may recognize objectives of education which are relatively unimportant." Rather, we should evaluate schools by measures such as whether graduates are "sympathetic in the presence of suffering and indignant in the presence of injustice," show "greater concern about questions of civic, social, and economic importance," are "living in accordance with the rules of health," and appreciate "their rich inheritance in art, literature, and music."

Another two decades had passed when the Rockefeller Brothers Fund convened leaders to make public policy recommendations. Nelson Rockefeller (subsequently New York's governor and Gerald Ford's vice-president) chaired the project; Henry Kissinger (later secretary of state) was staff director. The 1958 Rockefeller Report asserted: "Our conception of excellence must embrace many kinds of achievement.... There is excellence in abstract intellectual activity, in art, in music, in managerial activities, in craftsmanship, in human relations, in technical work." Testing was important for sorting future scientists and leaders. But, the panel warned that "[d]ecisions based on test scores must be made with the awareness of the.... qualities of character that are a necessary ingredient of great performance [:].... aspiration or purpose.... courage, vitality or determination."[13]

For the last 30 years, litigants have argued that states are obliged to finance an "adequate" education and state courts have had to define what this means. True to American traditions, courts have proposed definitions that went beyond adequacy measured by math and reading test scores alone.

The earliest such decision was issued by the New Jersey Supreme Court, finding, in 1976, a constitutional requirement for a "thorough and efficient education" where graduates become "citizens and competitors in the labor market." The Court later elaborated, stating,

> Thorough and efficient means more than teaching.... skills... It means being able to fulfill one's role as a citizen, a role that encompasses far more than merely registering to vote. It means the ability to participate fully in society, in the life of one's community, the ability to appreciate music, art, and literature, and the ability to share all of that with friends....

These are goals sought by wealthy districts, the court said, and must be pursued in low-income areas as well.[14]

EFFORTS TO SYNTHESIZE GOALS: 1950s TO 1990s

This chapter is not the first to review goals of American education and conclude that an excessive stress on basic academic skills violates a national consensus. In the late 1950s, a University of Chicago team synthesized all education goals it could identify that had previously been embraced by Americans. Led by Lawrence Downey, the researchers polled 15 representative communities in the nation and in Canada, surveying educators and members of service, social, labor, management, church, ethnic and racial-justice organizations. Nearly 1,300 educators and 2,500 non-educators were asked to sort cards on which 16 alternative education goals were described, and place these cards in order of relative importance.

For elementary schools, educators ranked "intellectual skills" (defined as the skill to acquire and transmit information, as opposed to the possession of knowledge) as the highest priority. Next was development of a desire for knowledge, or "love of learning." Third was students' ability to cooperate with others in day-to-day life. Fourth was creativity, fifth was moral integrity, sixth was good citizenship (including knowledge of both rights and duties), and seventh was emotional health and stability. Nine other goals followed, with lesser importance. Top priorities were similar for high schools, except that creativity was ranked higher than cooperation, and emotional health and stability higher than citizenship. The non-educator community leaders established similar, though not identical priorities.[15]

In 1975, John Goodland commenced a review of American public education that culminated in his 1983 book, *A Place Called School*. Analyzing goals that had been embraced by state and local boards of education and commissions that had studied education, Goodlad defined a consensus on the goals of education that included, among other outcomes, basic academic skills; vocational preparation (including positive attitudes towards work and habits of good workmanship); problem solving skills and intellectual curiosity; interpersonal skills such as respect, trust, and cooperation; citizenship, including a willingness to participate in national and community political life; emotional and physical well-being; and moral and ethical character, including a commitment to "strengthen the moral fabric of society."[16]

As demands have recently grown for school accountability based on test scores, some scholars and officials have sounded alarms about the potential for high stakes basic skill tests to distort curricula. In 1987, a committee of the National Academy of Education issued this warning:

> At root here is a fundamental dilemma. Those personal qualities that we hold dear—resilience and courage in the face of stress, a sense of craft in our work, a commitment to justice and caring in our social relationships, a dedication to advancing the public good in our communal life—are exceedingly difficult to assess. And so, unfortunately, we are apt to measure what we can, and eventually come to value what is measured over what is left unmeasured. The shift is subtle, and occurs gradually. It first invades our language and then slowly begins to dominate our thinking. It is all around us, and we too are a part of it. In neither academic nor popular discourse about schools does one find nowadays much reference to the important human qualities noted above. The language of academic achievement tests has become the primary rhetoric of schooling. (p. 64)

Citing this warning, the Department of Education's National Center for Education Statistics (NCES) proposed, in 1991, a national indicator system that reflected this balance of education goals. NCES urged that, in addition to academic competence in core subjects, measured "learner outcomes" should include tolerance, comprehending pluralism, self-direction, responsibility, commitment to craft, and other measures.[17] Subsequently, NCES commissioned the design of a variety of "input, output, outcome, and efficiency" indicators. The American Institutes for Research produced an inventory of such indicators,[18] but did not define their relative importances, and NCES never proceeded to develop such a system. As the testing frenzy grew in the 1990s, the intent was forgotten.

CURRENT CONSENSUS ON THE GOALS OF EDUCATION

This chapter's authors attempted, in 2005, a new synthesis of education goals that had been established through 250 years of American history. We defined eight broad goal areas that seemed to be prominent in each era, although certainly emphases changed from generation to generation. We then presented these goals to representative samples of American adults, of school board members, state legislators, and school superintendents and asked respondents to assign a relative importance to each of the goal areas.[19] Because giving weights to eight categories is too cognitively complex a task for a telephone interview, respondents worked either over a secure website or, if they were without computor access, over a device provided to them and attached to their television sets. Average responses of all adults, board members, legislators, and superintendents were very similar. If an accountability system were to hold public schools responsible for bringing students to the end of their school careers with a balanced set of outcomes, this is

TABLE 5.1

Goal Area	*Relative Importance (Weights, in %)*[20]
Basic Academic Skills in Core Subjects Reading, writing, math, knowledge of science and history.	22
Critical Thinking and Problem Solving Able to analyze and interpret information, use computers to develop knowledge, apply ideas to new situations.	18
Social Skills and Work Ethic Good communication skills, personal responsibility, the ability to get along well with others, and work with others from different backgrounds.	12
Citizenship and Community Responsibility Know how government works, how to participate in civic activities like voting, volunteering, and becoming active in communities.	11
Physical Health A foundation for lifelong physical health, including good habits of exercise and nutrition.	9
Emotional Health Tools to develop self-confidence, respect for others, and the ability to resist peer pressure to engage in irresponsible personal behavior.	9
The Arts and Literature Participate in and appreciate the musical, visual, and performing arts and developing a love of literature.	9
Preparation for Skilled Work Vocational, career, and technical education that will qualify youth for skilled employment that does not require a college degree.	10

how the system would have to be structured, at least according to the surveyed groups presented in Table 5.1.

It is curious that these survey findings articulate goals embraced by state representatives and school board members, public officials who have been aggressive in recent years about demanding accountability only for basic skills. The gap between goal preferences expressed in our surveys and educational standards established through political processes reflects a widespread policy incoherence.

CONTEMPORARY GOAL DISPLACEMENT

As this chapter is written (Spring, 2007), federal law (No Child Left Behind, or NCLB) holds all elementary schools, regardless of student characteristics, accountable for achieving proficiency in reading and math. By demanding that schools report achievement for racial, ethnic and economic subgroups, the accountability system aims to shine a light on schools that "leave children behind."

By basing sanctions solely on math and reading, however, the law creates incentives to narrow education goals by limiting time spent on other important curricular objectives. Research has shown that this re-orientation of instruction disproportionately affects low-income and minority children, so achievement gaps may actually widen in domains for which schools are not now held accountable.

The Council for Basic Education (CBE) surveyed school principals in the fall of 2003 and found that schools with more minority students were more likely than schools with fewer such students to find extra time for math and reading, by reducing instruction in history, civics, geography, the arts, and foreign languages.[21] And a 2005 survey by the Center on Education Policy found that 97 percent of high-poverty districts had new minimum time requirements for reading, while only 55 percent of more affluent districts had them.[22] Where districts had adopted such minimum time policies, about half had reduced attention to social studies, 43 percent had reduced art and music, and 27 percent reduced physical education.[23] Thus, although NCLB aims to narrow achievement gaps in math and reading, its unintended consequence is to widen gaps in other curricular areas.

This is how one former teacher describes her changed classroom activities:

> From my experience of being an elementary school teacher at a low-performing urban school in Los Angeles, I can say that the pressure became so intense that we had to show how every single lesson we taught connected to a standard that was going to be tested. This meant that art, music and even science and social studies were not a priority and were hardly ever taught. We were forced to spend ninety percent of the instructional time on reading and math. This made teaching boring for me and was a huge part of why I decided to leave the profession.[24]

In testimony before a U.S. Senate committee, the historian David McCullough observed: "Because of No Child Left Behind, sadly, history is being put on the back burner or taken off the stove altogether in many or most schools, in favor of math or reading."[25] Retired Supreme Court Justice Sandra Day O'Connor co-chairs a "Campaign for the Civic Mission of Schools" which laments that, under NCLB, "as civic learning has been pushed aside, society has neglected a fundamental purpose of American education, putting the health of our democracy at risk."[26]

GETTING ACCOUNTABILITY BACK ON TRACK

What would an accountability system look like if it created incentives for schools to pursue a balanced set of goals?

It would certainly include standardized tests of academic skills. Other standardized tests should be added. For example, tests of physical fitness (like upper body strength) and simple measures of body weight can be standardized to shed light on the efficacy of schools' physical education programs. Schools that sacrifice essential physical education for excessive drill in math and reading would lose incentives for such practices with accountability so structured.

Balanced accountability should also utilize measures that are more difficult to standardize but equally valid. Student writing and analysis of contemporary issues, student performances in the arts, in scientific experimentation, in debates, should also be included. School accountability does not require such assessments of each student every year, but only of a random sample drawn periodically.

Accountability also requires less immediate measures that nonetheless reflect on school adequacy. As most states have adopted (or are in the process of adopting) unique student identifier systems, it has become possible to link data from surveys of representative groups of young adults to the efficacy of schools they attended. By such means school civics programs can be judged by whether graduates register and vote, participate as community volunteers, or contribute to charity. Survey data can indicate the adequacy of students' literacy instruction by the standard of whether, as young adults, they read for pleasure. Surveys can also indicate the adequacy of students' physical education in part by whether, as young adults, they exercise regularly.

Balanced accountability also requires school inspections, differing from today's accreditation procedures. Inspection teams should include, in addition to professional educators, representatives of elected officials, businesses, labor, and community groups. Inspectors should judge whether students are engaged in group activities likely to develop the teamwork so valued by employers, or whether classroom discussions aim to develop critical thinking that leads to intelligent voting.

We are a long way from developing an accountability system that is true to American traditions and to our contemporary goals for public schools. We could move towards such a system, but test-based accountability is taking us in the opposite direction.

NOTES

1. Research for this chapter was supported by the Teachers College Campaign for Educational Equity. Views expressed in this chapter are those of the authors alone, and do not necessarily represent positions of Teachers College, Columbia University.
2. See, for example, the Gallup-Phi Delta Kappa annual public opinion surveys about public education; e.g., Lowell C. Rose and Alec M. Gallup, 2006. "The 38th Annual Phi Delta Kappa/Gallup Poll of the Public's Attitudes Toward the Public Schools." *Phi Delta Kappan* 88 (1), September: 41–56, Tables 37 and 38.
3. Benjamin Franklin. 1749. *Proposals Relating to the Education of Youth in Pensilvania.* Facsimile Reprint. Philadelphia: University of Pennsylvania Press (1931). Also, Lorraine Smith Pangle and Thomas L. Pangle, 2000. "What the American Founders Have to Teach Us About Schooling for Democratic Citizenship." In Lorraine M. McDonnell, P. Michael Timpane, and Roger Benjamin, eds. *Rediscovering the Democratic Purposes of Education.* University Press of Kansas.
4. George Washington. 1790. "First Annual Address," January 8. In Fred L. Israel, ed. 1966. *The State of the Union Messages of the Presidents, Volume I, 1790–1860.* New York: Chelsea House-Robert Hector Publishers; George Washington. 1796. "The Farewell Address," September 17. In Burton Ira Kaufman, ed. 1969. *Washington's Farewell Address. The View from the 20th Century.* Chicago: Quadrangle Books; Joseph J. Ellis. 2001. *Founding Brothers. The Revolutionary Generation.* New York: Alfred A. Knopf, 2001, p. 154.
5. Thomas Jefferson et al, 1818. "Report of the Commissioners Appointed to Fix the Site of the University of Virginia, etc." In Roy J. Honeywell, 1964. *The Educational Work of Thomas Jefferson.* New York: Russell and Russell; Appendix J. Also, Jennings L. Wagoner, Jr., 2004. *Jefferson and Education.* Chapel Hill: The University of North Carolina Press.
6. Thorpe, op. cit., Vol. 2, p.1068 (Constitution of Indiana, 1816, Article IX).
7. Cited in Lawrence A. Cremin. 1951. *The American Common School. An Historic Conception.* New York: Bureau of Publications, Teachers College, Columbia University.
8. Mann, Horace. 1845. *Eighth Annual Report of the Board of Education together with the Eighth Annual Report of the Secretary of the Board.* Boston: Dutton and Wentworth, State Printers.
9. Mann, Horace. 1844. *Seventh Annual Report of the Board of Education together with the Seventh Annual Report of the Secretary of the Board.* Boston: Dutton and Wentworth, State Printers.
10. See for example Diane Ravich. 2000. *Left Back: A Century of Battles Over School Reform.* New York: Simon and Schuster.
11. Commission on the Reorganization of Secondary Education. *Cardinal Principals of Secondary Education.* Department of the Interior, Bureau of Education, Bulletin No. 35. (Washington, D.C.: Government Printing Office, 1918).
12. Educational Policies Commission. 1938. *The Purposes of Education in American Democracy.* Washington, DC: National Education Association of the United States and the American Association of School Administrators.
13. Rockefeller Brothers Fund. 1958. *The Pursuit of Excellence: Education and the Future of America.*

The "Rockefeller Report" on Education. Special Studies Project Report V. New York: Rockefeller Brothers Fund.

14. *Abbott v. Burke II.* 119 N.J. 287; 575 A.2d 359 (1990).
15. Downey, Lawrence William. 1960. *The Task of Public Education. The Perceptions of People.* Chicago: Midwest Administration Center, The University of Chicago.
16. John I. Goodlad. 1979, 1994. *What Schools Are For.* 2nd Ed. Phi Delta Kappa Educational Foundation; John I. Goodlad. 1984. *A Place Called School: Prospects for the Future.* New York: McGraw Hill.
17. Alan D. Morgan, et al. 1991. *Education Counts. An Indicator System to Monitor the Nation's Educational Health.* U.S. Department of Education, National Center for Education Statistics, NCES 91–634, September.
18. Lauri Peternick, Andrew Cullen, John Guarnera, Erin Massie, and Adrienne Siegendorf. 1999. "Developing a Dynamic Indicator System: Measuring the Input, Output, Outcome, and Efficiency of School Systems." Draft, January. Washington, D.C.: Pelavin Research Center, The American Institutes for Research.
19. A full description of the survey methodology and detailed results will appear in a forthcoming publication by the authors.
20. The weights shown are a simple average of the average responses for each of the four surveyed groups.
21. Claus von Zastrow, with Helen Janc. 2004. *Academic Atrophy. The Condition of the Liberal Arts in America's Public Schools.* (Washington, D.C.: Council for Basic Education). Mr. Von Zastrow (personal correspondence) provided additional data.
22. Center on Education Policy. 2006. *From the Capital to the Classroom. Year 4 of the No Child Left Behind Act.* (Washington, D.C.: author).
23. Center on Education Policy. 2005. *From the Capital to the Classroom. Year 3 of the No Child Left Behind Act.* (Washington, D.C.: author).
24. Jacquelyn Duran. 2005. "An Adequate Teacher: What Would the System Look Like?" Term Paper, Teachers College, Columbia University, Course ITSF 4151, December.
25. Sam Dillon. 2005. "From Yale to Cosmetology School, Americans Brush Up on History and Government." *New York Times*, September 16.
25. Campaign for the Civic Mission of Schools. 2006. *Call to Action.* April 17. http://www.civicmissionofschools.org/.

6

Quantitative Research Methods in Education Finance and Policy

Patrick J. McEwan

INTRODUCTION

Researchers in education finance and policy rely on a myriad of quantitative methods. The most common include regression analysis, a mainstay of social science research, but they increasingly include experimental or quasi-experimental methods (McEwan & McEwan, 2003; Shadish, Cook, & Campbell, 2002). These methods are particularly suited to addressing research questions about the causal relationship between a policy or program and education outcomes.[1] Do school finance reforms increase the equity of school expenditures? Does attending a private instead of a public school improve students' achievement? Does financial aid increase the probability that students attend college? This chapter describes a range of quantitative methods that can be used to address causal questions, placing special emphasis on the methods' rationale, intuition, and pitfalls.

METHODS FOR WHAT?

Defining Research

In 2002, following a request of the U.S. Department of Education, the National Research Council (NRC) defined principles of scientific inquiry in education research (Shavelson and Towne, 2002, pp. 54–73). To paraphrase the NRC report, education research should: (1) pose important questions; (2) investigate them empirically, with appropriate research methods; (3) provide an explicit answer, after assessing and discarding plausible alternatives; (4) replicate and generalize the answers across contexts; and (5) do so in a transparent and professionally accountable way. The greatest controversy lies in the definition of "important" research questions, which shapes views on "appropriate" methods. Shavelson and Towne (2002) define three categories of questions: (1) descriptive (what is happening?), (2) causal (does it work?), and (3) process (how does it work?).

Descriptive research establishes or refutes patterns in the data, inspires theoretical explanations of the observed facts, guides the design of causal research, and provides better context for interpreting and generalizing causal results. Causal research tests for cause-and-effect relationships, rather than mere correlations, between policy interventions and policy outcomes. It helps test, refine, and possibly discard theoretical explanations of empirical regularities in education. Most practically, it helps policy makers assess the relative merits of interventions and allocate resources to better ones, however defined. Process research inquires why a policy intervention does or does not affect policy outcomes. Did a single component of the intervention not work? Was it implemented well or poorly? Did teachers, students, or other participants respond by altering their behavior? To the extent that it unpacks the mechanisms explaining a "black box" causal effect, process research helps establish whether the same result can be replicated elsewhere.

Choosing Research Methods

The choice of a research method hinges on the question posed. Descriptive research employs standard quantitative techniques (Tukey, 1977) to describe the central tendency and dispersion of single variables (e.g. school expenditures or teacher characteristics) and their statistical association with other variables (e.g. student characteristics or test scores). Descriptive research also employs qualitative techniques—including case studies, ethnographies, or pragmatic reportage—to describe classrooms, schools, legislation, and political contexts.

Causal research uses mostly quantitative techniques, especially variants of regression analysis, to isolate the unique contribution of a policy to an education outcome. Regression methods are increasingly combined with, or supplanted by, experimental or quasi-experimental research methods, described below. Causal research employs qualitative methods less commonly, despite the potential applications (King, Keohane, & Verba, 1994).

Finally, process research is conducted with mixed, but frequently qualitative methods. In the best of cases, process research is built into an existing causal research designs. For example, researchers have employed qualitative methods, especially teacher interviews and classroom observations, to explain the large or small effects of reduced class sizes (Zahorik et al., 2000), Catholic school attendance (Bryk, Lee, & Holland, 1993), and whole-school reform (Cook et al., 1999; Cook et al., 2000).

The Emerging Importance of Causal Research

This chapter emphasizes quantitative methods for causal inference. In particular, it discusses regression analysis and related statistical techniques, as well as increasingly popular experimental and quasi-experimental research designs for analyzing the causal impact of policy interventions. It does so because these methods are foundational in modern research on education finance and policy, as evidenced by other chapters in the *Handbook*. Even so, some important methodological innovations have been slow to filter down to the day-to-day practice of education policy researchers, in part because the methods are confined to specialized or highly technical journal articles.

At least two factors have spurred the growing interest in valid causal research. First, policy makers are increasingly interested in policies or programs that have been rigorously shown to cause improvements in student outcomes. The interests of policy makers, in turn, have been shaped by an increasing federal emphasis on "scientific" research in education (Shavelson & Towne, 2002; U.S. Department of Education, 2003). For example, the U.S. Department of Education allocates grants to state and local education agencies for the implementation of reading programs, but only if they have been shown to "work."[2]

Second, education researchers have access to increasingly rich data sources that facilitate the application of additional methods (for examples, see Dee, Evans, & Murray, 1999; Loeb & Strunk, 2003). The data fall into three broad categories: (1) national samples of students;[3] (2) state and local administrative data that include repeated observations on a population of students;[4] and

(3) site-specific, fieldwork-based data such as the Tennessee STAR class size experiment. The second and third categories have been a particular catalyst to recent education policy research, because they facilitate better methods described below (Loeb & Strunk, 2003).

What This Chapter Does Not Address

Given the chapter's limited scope, it does not address three issues. First, the chapter does not discuss the application of quantitative methods to descriptive- or process-oriented research questions. Second, the chapter does not describe qualitative methods, despite their evident or potential merits in addressing descriptive, causal, or process questions. Third, it does not discuss a few quantitative methods that, while used by policy researchers, are the subject of their own specialized literatures. These include cost-benefit and cost-effectiveness analysis (Levin and McEwan, 2001; 2002), meta-analytic techniques for summarizing the results of many studies (Cooper & Hedges, 1994), and methods of measuring and comparing student achievement (Crocker & Algina, 1986; Kolen & Brennan, 2004).

DEFINITIONS OF RESEARCH TERMS

The results of cause-testing research, regardless of the method, are commonly judged by two criteria: *internal validity* and *external validity* (Cook & Campbell, 1979; Meyer, 1995; Shadish et al., 2002). A result is internally valid when it identifies a believable causal link between a policy or program and an education outcome. (The policy or program is often generically called a *treatment.*) A causal result is externally valid when it can be generalized to modified versions of the policy treatment, to alternate measures of student outcomes, to diverse populations of students or schools, or to different policy contexts. Much of the following discussion—and recent policy debates—emphasize the importance of improving internal validity (Barrow & Rouse, 2005; U.S. Department of Education, 2003). However, an internally valid result may be of little use to policy makers if it cannot be usefully generalized.

To take one example, California's large-scale and costly class size reduction was inspired by small-scale research in Tennessee that demonstrated positive—and internally valid—effects on student achievement (Mosteller, 1995; Krueger, 1999). Unlike the Tennessee research, California's large-scale implementation substantially increased demand for teachers. Statewide, deteriorating teacher quality appears to have offset the positive effects of class size reduction, resulting in a substantially modified version of the policy (Jepsen & Rivkin, 2002). The California experience highlights the trade-offs that often exist between internal and external validity.

The causal effect of a policy treatment is the difference between students' outcomes when treated, and the same students' outcomes when not treated. The latter is simply called the *counterfactual.* Short of procuring a time machine, it cannot be observed because treatments cannot be undone. Instead, research methods are employed to "create reasonable approximations to the physically impossible counterfactual" (Shadish et al., 2002, p. 5).[5] Researchers typically estimate counterfactual outcomes by identifying a separate group of untreated students, called a *control group* or *comparison group* (the former term is sometimes reserved for randomized experiments, but is used loosely). Members of the control or comparison group should be similar to their treated counterparts, in every respect but for exposure to the treatment.

In practice, the groups are often dissimilar, in ways that affect the outcomes of interest but have nothing to do with the treatment (i.e., students' families have different incomes, because higher-income families were more or less likely to choose the treatment). If this occurs, then the mean outcomes of comparison students incorrectly estimate the policy counterfactual. Thus, a simple difference in the average outcomes of treatment and comparison students can yield a misleading estimate of the treatment's causal effect, and is said to suffer from *selection bias*. Selection bias is a pervasive challenge to internal validity, and the research methods discussed below are aimed at lessening it (on related challenges, see Shadish et al., 2002; Meyer, 1995).

Researchers use two broad methods, sometimes in combination, to ensure that members of treatment and control/comparison groups are similar, on average. First, they make statistical controls for observed differences between students, often using regression analysis. Second, they influence how students are assigned to treatment and control groups. Cause-testing research is often lumped into three broad categories: *experimental, quasi-experimental,* and *non-experimental*. The essential difference among categories is the degree of control exerted by the researcher over who is assigned to the policy treatment (whether students, teachers, schools, districts, or states), and who is assigned to the control/comparison group.

In experimental research—often referred to as a randomized, controlled trial (RCT)—the assignment is entirely determined by luck of the draw, as in a researcher's flip of a coin. In quasi-experimental research, the broadest category of research, assignment may contain elements of randomness or purposeful assignment by the researcher, but some might be due to the individual choices of students, parents, or administrators (called *selection*). In non-experimental research, the researcher exerts absolutely no influence, and assignment is entirely due to selection. When greater control is exerted, then causal results often possess greater internal validity. The following sections develop this point.

METHODS FOR ANSWERING CAUSAL QUESTIONS

Statistical Controls for Observed Variables

Suppose that researchers collect non-experimental data from students who attend either private or public schools, but were not encouraged or coerced to do so by researchers. Their causal question is whether attending private school improves test scores.[6] A naïve researcher would simply estimate the difference between the average test scores of private students and public students, and ascribe it to the causal effect of school type. But the difference could be explained by pre-existing differences in students that are the result of selection. For one, private students in tuition-paying schools have higher incomes, on average, which might be associated with higher test scores.

Regression Analysis. Regression analysis is the first line of defense against this kind of selection bias.[7] A basic regression model can be written as:

$$A_i = \beta_0 + \beta_1 P_i + \beta_2 X_i + \varepsilon_i,$$

where A represents the test score of each student in the entire sample (the subscript i might range from 1 to 1000); P indicates whether a student attends a private school ($P = 1$) or public school ($P = 0$);[8] X indicates the value of a control variable, like family income, that one wishes to hold constant; and ϵ is an error term unique to each student. The error term captures the notion that test scores vary, for unobserved reasons, even among students attending the same school type and with the same incomes.

Using the method of ordinary least squares, researchers estimate the regression coefficients β_0, β_1, and β_2. In the absence of controls for X, the estimate of β_1 would be interpreted as the average difference between private and public students' achievement (the naïve estimate from before). Upon controlling for X, it is the average difference *holding constant family income*. The immediate question is whether the difference can now be interpreted as the causal effect of private school attendance.

The causal interpretation rests on an assumption of regression analysis: that private school attendance (P), controlling for X, is uncorrelated with positive or negative shocks in test scores captured in the error term, ϵ.[9] What could produce such correlations? Suppose the existence of an unmeasured variable, M, that gauges parent motivation. Further suppose that children of motivated parents disproportionately attend private schools (M and P are positively correlated, even controlling for X) and that the children of motivated parents obtain higher test scores (M and A are positively correlated, even controlling for X).

In regressions that do not control for M, the net result is that attending private schools tends to be accompanied by positive shocks in students' test scores, the (non-causal) influence of greater unobserved motivation among their parents. In this example, estimates of the coefficient β_1 would be "too big" because of selection bias, leading to overly optimistic causal conclusions about private school effects. Yet, selection bias could also work in the opposite direction, depending on the sign of partial correlations between the excluded variable(s), the dependent variables (A), and the key treatment variable (P).[10] Omitting variables like M creates no bias in estimates of β_1 if (1) the omitted variables are uncorrelated with A, or (2) the omitted variables are uncorrelated with P.[11]

In non-experimental research settings like this, researchers have few remaining options. One is to collect and control for additional variables in the regression, but that is cold comfort to users of existing data sets. Even controlling for hundreds of variables proves unconvincing in many contexts. For example, the archetypal non-experimental study in education policy regresses student test scores on student, family, and school variables.[12] The third category often includes a key policy variable such as class size or student/teacher ratio. Yet, test scores (say, at the end of grade 6) are the cumulative product of family and school "inputs" received by students from birth onwards (Todd & Wolpin, 2003). Data sets, even detailed longitudinal ones, can never fully and accurately measure all inputs. Variables like class size are probably correlated with unobserved variables that determine achievement, and estimates of their causal effects are unpredictably biased upward or downward.[13]

In test score regressions, researchers often resort to controlling for test score measurements taken at earlier moments in students' careers (say, at the beginning of grade 6). By controlling for pre-tests in so-called value-added regressions, researchers hope to implicitly control for all inputs that affected test scores until that moment, thereby reducing the scope of bias. Nonetheless, there is no guarantee that omitted variables during the sixth grade, or earlier ones not captured by error-ridden pre-tests, do not continue to bias estimates.[14]

Propensity Score Matching. An alternative and increasingly popular method of controlling for observed variables is propensity score matching (for recent examples in education policy, see Behrman, Cheng, & Todd, 2004; Black & Smith, 2004; Hong & Raudenbush, 2006; Shapiro & Trevino, 2004). Researchers first estimate a propensity score for each student (or other unit) in the sample (Rosenbaum & Rubin, 1983). The score is a predicted probability that students receive a treatment, given their observed characteristics. So, in the prior example, researchers would estimate probabilities, using a probit or logit regression, that students attend a private school, given their family income (X) and other observed variables thought to influence propensities.

Then, each private student is matched to a "similar" public student, based exclusively on values of their propensity scores.[15] If students cannot be matched to a counterpart, then they are discarded from the sample (this might happen, for example, if children of millionaires, or with other observed characteristics, *always* attend private schools). Estimates of private school effects are based on comparisons of average outcomes across students in propensity-score matched treatment and control groups.

The method's virtues are at least twofold (Ravallion, 2005). First, it imposes no arbitrary assumption of linearity on the relationships between outcomes, policy variables, and other controls, as in the previous section's regression model. Second, it removes treated (or untreated) students from the sample that have no obvious "match" in the other group. Intuitively, the observed uniqueness of such students implies that they are also unique in unobserved ways that could introduce selection bias.

Yet, like regression analysis, the causal interpretation of propensity score matching results rests on the unverifiable assumption that no unobserved variables are correlated with outcomes and with the probability of receiving a treatment. In this regard, it is no panacea for causal research. Some empirical comparisons suggest that linear regression analysis and propensity score matching yield similar results (Godtland et al., 2004; Vandenberghe & Robin, 2004).[16]

Randomized Assignment

In the 1990s, researchers in education policy grew disenchanted with the ability of statistical controls for observed variables to eliminate selection bias in non-experimental data.[17] A turning point was the widespread analysis and debate of results from a randomized experiment in Tennessee that identified the causal effect of smaller class sizes on student test scores.[18] At the time, Krueger (1999) opined that "one well-designed experiment should trump a phalanx of poorly controlled, imprecise observational studies based on uncertain statistical specification" (p. 528). His opinion reflected a broader movement in empirical economics to focus less on the rote application of statistical tools, and more on the quality of counterfactual reasoning deployed by researchers (Angrist & Krueger, 1999; Glewwe & Kremer, 2006).[19]

In the classic instance of randomized assignment, researchers flip a coin to determine which students are treated, and which are not (note that teachers, schools, districts, or even entire towns could also be randomly assigned). Thus, each student's probability of receiving the treatment is an identical 0.5.[20] The virtue of this approach is that it balances, by design, the distribution of students' observed and unobserved characteristics across treatment and control groups. The two groups are not identical, of course, but they should be similar, on average.[21] Because control group members are similar, except for their exposure to a treatment, they provide an ideal counterfactual estimate of outcomes. For this reason, randomized experiments are commonly asserted to be the "gold standard" method of answering causal research questions.

To obtain an internally valid estimate of causal effects, one estimates the mean difference between the outcomes of treated and untreated units (a pleasant irony of experiments is that credible causal conclusions are obtained with unsophisticated statistical methods). One could further apply regression analysis to control for observed differences between groups. If randomization proceeded without a hitch, then doing so is not strictly necessary to eliminate selection bias,[22] although it reduces the standard errors of estimates of causal effects.

Besides class size, randomized experiments have been used to explore the effects of multiple policy treatments on student test scores. These include teacher performance incentives (Glewwe, Ilias, & Kremer, 2003), whole-school reform (Borman et al., 2005; Cook, et al., 2000), and private school vouchers in New York City (Howell & Peterson, 2002; Krueger & Zhu, 2004), among many other topics.[23]

In the New York voucher experiment, it was not feasible to randomly assign students to attend a private school. Rather, researchers randomly awarded private school tuition vouchers to some students, and the treatment consisted of a "voucher offer." In practice, not all students offered a voucher actually used it to attend a private school; by the same token, some students denied a voucher still attended a private school. This highlights a common feature of almost all social experiments: a subset of randomly assigned participants do not comply with the initial assignment.

This is not a fatal flaw of the research design. One option is simply to compare the outcomes (test scores, in this case) of the full treatment and control groups as initially assigned, regardless of whether or not they take up the voucher offer. This yields an unbiased estimate of the aptly-named "intent-to-treat." Though not an estimate of the effect of actually using a voucher to attend a private school, it provides valuable information to policy-makers. To further recover the effect of using a voucher—the effect of the "treatment-on-the-treated"—researchers can use additional methods, including instrumental variables methods discussed in a later section.

Randomized experiments are not without pitfalls (for varied opinions, see Burtless, 1995; Heckman, 1995). One common critique is that attrition from treatment or control groups could re-introduce selection bias into experimental estimates. In a voucher experiment, for example, one might be concerned that students leave the experimental sample, perhaps because they did not receive a voucher offer and chose to move to a district outside the research site. Attrition creates bias in experimental mean comparisons, to the extent that differential attrition across treatment and control groups changes the balance of observed and unobserved characteristics (i.e., all higher income students in the control group leave the sample to attend private schools in another city). To be fair, attrition is a widespread problem in social science research, and is not confined to randomized experiments.

A second critique is that experiments, especially small-scale ones, yield causal conclusions of limited external validity (Shadish et al., 2002). As one example, it is unlikely that treatments affect all students similarly. A typical randomized experiment identifies the average causal effect among heterogeneous students (some of whom are strongly affected, and others not at all). Researchers with large enough samples can estimate causal effects within subsamples of students, perhaps dividing them by location, income, or race. Yet, even average effects in experimental samples may not be generalizable to the average student in the entire population, since initial samples are not always a random draw. In fact, many experiments pragmatically begin with volunteers, whether students (Howell & Peterson, 2002) or schools (Cook et al., 2000). Results from volunteer students or schools may be harder to generalize to the broader population.

Though increasingly common, one might ask why "gold-standard" experiments are not used more often in education research (Cook, 2002). In education finance, some policy treatments are not amenable to randomized assignment. These include, for example, revised formulas for collecting and distributing education revenues that are imposed by courts or state legislatures. The close links of researchers to state-specific policy environments, and a desire to maximize the external validity of results, have focused attention on quasi-experimental methods for causal inference.

Other policies, such as test-based accountability, reward teachers and schools for their causal effect, or lack thereof, on student achievement. In such instances, randomized assignment can *never* be practically used to obtain such effects among the entire population of public schools, teachers, and students. As a consequence, recent state accountability laws rely on a mélange of quasi- and non-experimental approaches to assess teachers' and schools' "value-added."

Discontinuity Assignment

One of the most credible quasi-experimental methods is the regression-discontinuity design (RDD).[24] In the RDD, researchers assign students to treatment or control groups on the basis of a single assignment variable—often a test score, but potentially any continuous variable—and a specified cutoff value. To provide an illustration, suppose that a thousand students vie for college financial aid by taking a pre-test (the assignment variable). Students with scores of 50 or above (the cutoff) receive aid, and those with scores below 50 do not. Note that assignment is not randomized, as in the flip of coin, but neither is it due to selection. This provides sufficient leverage to identify the causal effect of financial aid on some students' subsequent outcomes.

The causal effect is estimated by comparing the outcomes of treatment and control students whose values of the assignment variables are close to 50.[25] The intuition is that such students should be very similar, not just in their values of the pre-test, but in other observed and unobserved ways. At the very least, observed and unobserved characteristics of the students should not vary *sharply* in the vicinity of the cutoff. In short, control students (just to the left of the cutoff) provide a good counterfactual estimate of outcomes for treated students (just to the right). Thus, any sharp—or discontinuous—changes in outcomes near the cutoff can be attributed to the financial aid treatment.

The intuition of this approach is best understood with a visual analogy. In the absence of any treatment, suppose that one graphed a scatterplot of a college post-test on the y-axis against the pre-test on the x-axis. The scatterplot and a best-fitting line would likely indicate a positive relationship. They key point is that one would not anticipate a sharp break or discontinuity in the absence of the treatment. When the treatment is applied, perhaps accompanied by a break in outcomes near the cutoff, one's confidence is bolstered that it has a causal interpretation.

Among a growing litany of topics in education policy, the RDD has been applied to estimate the effects of class size reduction (Angrist & Lavy, 1999; Urquiola, 2006), college financial aid (Kane, 2003; van der Klaauw, 2002), early childhood education (Gormley & Gayer, 2005; Ludwig & Miller, 2007), teacher training (Jacob & Lefgren, 2004), and compensatory education for disadvantaged children (Chay et al., 2005).

A hallmark of recent papers is that researchers do not specify cutoffs or implement the assignment process. Instead, researchers take advantage of cutoff-based assignment that administrators used to allocate resources in a transparent, fair, or efficient way (i.e., needy or meritorious students receive financial aid, low-scoring schools receive assistance or sanctions and high-scoring ones receive rewards, less-effective teachers receive training, and so on). The unintended usefulness of such rules to researchers has only recently been noted in many cases, even when discontinuity assignment has a long history, as in the Head Start program (Ludwig & Miller, in press).

What are the potential pitfalls of using discontinuity-based assignment? The most serious, related to internal validity, is that students, or others subject to discontinuity assignment, are familiar with the potential intervention, the assignment variable, and the value of the cutoff. If they have incentives to receive the treatment, or not, then they may well attempt to manipulate their values of the assignment variable (Lee, in press; McCrary, in press). As in the non-experimental context, the concern is that manipulation may introduce selection bias into estimates of causal effects. For example, suppose that students with rich parents are aware of financial aid assignment rules and obtain extra pre-test tutoring for their children. The result is that treated children, just to the right of the cutoff, also happen to be somewhat wealthier, and perhaps more likely to attend college even without the treatment.

Precise manipulation of many continuous assignment variables is actually harder than it might seem (Lee, in press). While most families can probably influence their child's pre-test score, random errors in testing make it unlikely that they can affect it within a very narrow band of scores around the assignment cutoff. Students within this narrow band contribute the most to estimates of causal effects, implying that assignment variable manipulation must be very precise to bias regression-discontinuity effects.[26] To test for manipulation, researchers typically search for suspicious clustering of students on either side the cutoff (McCrary, in press). They also compare students' observed characteristics near the cutoff, which should vary smoothly across the break, in the absence of manipulation.

Instrumental Variables

In the majority of cases, the assignment of students, schools, or other units to policy treatments is neither random nor based on values of an observed assignment variable. Besides controlling for observed characteristics, what remaining methods are available to identify the causal effect of policies on outcomes? One of most popular in the last decade has been instrumental variables (see Wooldridge, 2002, 2006; Angrist & Krueger, 1999).

In non-experimental data, the receipt of policy treatments is usually correlated with unobserved characteristics of individuals that affect outcomes. Therein lies the empirical dilemma. Yet, some individuals in the sample might receive a treatment because of luck or because they were encouraged to do so for reasons unrelated to outcomes. The challenge is to base estimates of causal effects entirely on "clean" variation in treatment status—that is, variation uncorrelated with unobserved characteristics that affect outcomes. It is easier said than done.

One must identify an instrumental variable, or instrument, that fulfills two conditions (Bound, Jaeger, & Baker, 1995; Wooldridge, 2002, 2006). First, it must be strongly correlated with the probability of receiving an intervention. This condition, straightforward to test in the data, is needed to ensure that the instrument actually induces students to alter their treatment status. Second, the instrument cannot be correlated with unexplained variation in the outcome variable (that is, the variation in outcomes that remains after controlling for other independent variables). The validity of the second assumption, more complicated to empirically test, usually rests upon the compelling reasoning of the researcher.

In applications to education policy, instruments are often related to features of geography or students' location, which are assumed to be "random" in some regard, and thus viable candidates to fulfill the second condition. Towards estimating private school effects, Figlio and Ludwig (2000) show that the availability of subway transportation in metropolitan areas affects the probability that families, especially poorer ones, choose private schools. Using this as an instrumental variable, their analysis suggests that private school attendance has strong effects on reducing some risky teenage behaviors. Their analysis must assume that transportation availability, of the instrument, is uncorrelated with student outcomes, controlling for other variables like family income.

Hoxby (2000) estimates the effects of competition among public school districts on students' outcomes like test scores.[27] She measures competition as the concentration of public school districts within metropolitan areas, where areas dominated by a few districts are assumed to be less competitive. The measure of competition is likely correlated with unobserved features of local students, schools, and communities that affect test scores. Hoxby argues that the number of streams in metropolitan areas (the instrumental variable) increases competition, because higher transportation costs led many areas to fragment into smaller school districts. The IV results suggest that metropolitan competition (induced by streams) has strong effects on test scores, based on the assumption that local geography is not correlated with unexplained test scores. Rothstein (2005) critiques the assumption that the instrumental variable is uncorrelated with unexplained student outcomes, as well as the measurement of the streams variable.

In each example, the validity of the second condition is hard to prove, and counter-examples easy to invent. (Do metropolitan areas with extensive subways have progressive mayors that invest in public schools? Do metropolitan areas with many streams and districts also have greater segregation by race or socioeconomic status that lowers achievement?) In the most convincing IV analyses, there are a priori reasons to believe that instruments are uncorrelated with unexplained outcomes.

Difference-in-Differences

Difference-in-differences (DD) methods attempt to control for unobserved variables that bias estimates of causal effects, aided by longitudinal data collected from students, school, districts, or states. Researchers employ two varieties of longitudinal data. Panel data track the progress of the same students or teachers in successive months or years. Repeated cross-section data follow *different* groups of individuals (e.g., second-graders in successive years) that are clustered within the same schools, districts, or states.

The logic of DD causal inference is best communicated with an example based on repeated-cross section data (for its empirical implementation, see Dee & Levine, 2004). Of two states, Massachusetts and Maine, suppose that the former implements a finance reform—increasing state financing of local public school districts—and the latter does not. To estimate the reform's impact on district outcomes in Massachusetts, a naïve approach would compare outcomes across states, within a single year of post-reform data. The comparison is likely biased by selection, since unobserved differences across states could also affect outcomes.

Now consider the same comparison of outcomes, but within an earlier, pre-reform year of data. Evidently any differences in outcomes cannot be attributed to a Massachusetts reform that has yet to occur. Pre-reform differences in outcomes are perhaps due to unobserved differences across states that contaminated the previous, naïve estimate. To control for these unobserved variables, the DD estimate of the reform's effect subtracts the second difference from the first. The remaining "difference-in-differences" could be plausibly attributed to the reform. For this to be credible, the *change* in Maine's outcomes must be a good counterfactual for Massachusetts'. Yet, suppose that Massachusetts' outcomes rose more quickly than other states, even before the reform, because of economic growth due to a strong biotech industry. The DD will nonetheless attribute faster outcome growth in the treated state to the causal effect of reform.

In light of this pitfall, one of the best ways to assess the internal validity of DD results is to compare the trends of outcome variables across treatment and control groups *before* application of the treatment (Angrist & Krueger, 1999; Meyer, 1995). Evidence of similar trends bolsters confidence in the DD assumption. Dee and Levine (2004) estimated the effect of Massachusetts' state finance reform on districts' per-pupil state revenues. As controls, they used districts in Maine and Connecticut, which did not apply reforms, over the same pre- and post-reform period. DD estimates showed significant effects of the reform on local revenues. To support the use of these comparison groups, they showed that the outcome variables had similar trends in the three states in years prior to the reform.

There are many variants of DD analyses, depending on the context, research question, and data.[28] Dynarski (2003) estimates the effect of government-provided college subsidies on college attendance. She takes advantage of the fact that Social Security Administration used to provide large college subsidies to children with deceased parents, but abruptly stopped doing so, beginning with the high school class of 1982. Dynarski identifies students with deceased parents—the treatment group—who graduated from high school before and after the change, and students without deceased parents—a comparison group never eligible for the benefits—over the same period. The DD estimates suggest large effects of subsidies on college attendance.

Researchers increasingly apply DD methods to student-level panel data on test scores, applying a similar logic of causal inference. Some students' outcomes are observed before and after exposure to a treatment. Their outcomes are compared to students never exposed to the treatment. Rouse (1998) provides a lucid example of this approach in her re-analysis of data from the Milwaukee voucher program. The treatment group consists of students, observed before and after their selection to receive a private school voucher. The comparison groups consist of (1) students who were denied a private school voucher or (2) students in public schools who never applied for one. The DD estimates suggest that treated students have faster gains in math scores, but not in reading, than students in both comparison groups. The necessary assumption, as in previous analyses, is that treated students would have had trends in achievement similar to untreated students in the absence of the treatment.[29]

Combining Methods to Improve Causal Inference

Researchers often apply multiple methods in the same study to bolster confidence in causal results. Almost every study employs statistical controls for family and student characteristics that affect outcomes. In experiments, the RDD, and a few DD applications, controls are not essential since careful control group selection alone should be enough to remove selection bias.[30] However, the further inclusion of controls in such studies provides a handy check of internal validity, since it should not substantially alter estimates of causal effects.[31]

Researchers often combine DD methods with experiments (Krueger & Zhu, 2004; Skoufias, 2005), the RDD (Chay et al., 2005; Jacob & Lefgren, 2004), and IV (Kuziemko, 2006; Loeb & Page, 2000). In experiments and the RDD, there should be no initial difference in pre-treatment outcomes across treatment and control groups, so using longitudinal data is not strictly necessary to control for selection bias.[32] But again, it provides a useful check of internal validity, and might improve the internal validity of research with a great deal of sample attrition.

Finally, researchers combine IV methods with randomized experiments and the RDD, especially to address imperfect compliance of students with random or cutoff-based assignment to policy treatments.[33] Returning to the previous example of New York's voucher experiment, students were randomly assigned to receive a voucher offer, but not all students accepted the offer and actually attended a private school. To recover an estimate of the treatment-on-the-treated (i.e., the effect of actually attending a private school), researchers used the voucher offer as an instrument for private school attendance (Howell & Peterson, 2002; Krueger & Zhu, 2004). The instrument plausibly fulfills both conditions: (1) it is correlated with private school attendance, and (2) the initial random assignment of the offer ensures that it is not correlated with unexplained outcomes. The resulting IV estimate provides a credible estimate of the effect of private school attendance on those induced to accept it by the voucher offer.[34]

CONCLUSIONS

This chapter has described quantitative research methods used to estimate the causal effect of policies on education outcomes. Some, like regression analysis with non-experimental data, are ubiquitous but not always capable of delivering strong causal conclusions. Others, like experimental and discontinuity research designs, are increasingly common in education finance and policy, but are still relatively under-utilized.

Good causal research is a necessary but not sufficient condition for designing and implementing good policy, a point not always clear in recent debates (U.S. Department of Education, 2003). Notwithstanding this chapter's emphasis on rigorous causal research methods, it does not address methods for answering descriptive or process questions nor does it review qualitative research methods (King, Keohane, & Verba,1994). Both can be eminently "scientific" (Shavelson & Towne, 2002) and deserve serious attention from newer generations of researchers in education finance and policy.

NOTES

1. For methodological reviews in education policy, see Angrist (2004), Barrow and Rouse (2005), Glewwe and Kremer (in press), Hanushek (2002), Ludwig (2001), and McEwan and McEwan (2003). Angrist and Krueger (1999), Meyer (1995), and Ravallion (2001; 2005) provide reviews in the context of social policy. Shadish, Cook, and Campbell (2002) and its predecessors (Campbell & Stanley, 1963; Cook & Campbell, 1979) are canonical references in evaluation research.
2. The federally funded "What Works Clearinghouse" sifts through education research and harshly judges its ability to derive valid causal inferences about the impact of education programs. Within the Department of Education, the grant-making Institute for Education Sciences favors research proposals that use research methods able to credibly demonstrate causal impacts, notably randomized experiments and regression-discontinuity designs.
3. National samples, notably NELS:88, have been collected by the National Center for Education Statistics (NCES) and are available from their Web site (http://www.nces.ed.gov).
4. These include data from Chicago Public Schools (Jacob & Lefgren, 2004), Texas (Hanushek et al., 2007), North Carolina (Bifulco & Ladd, 2006), Florida (Sass, 2006), and teachers in New York state (Lankford, Loeb, & Wyckoff, 2002).
5. Shadish et al. (2002) describe the history of the counterfactual reasoning. It has been formalized by statisticians, especially Donald Rubin (Holland, 1986), in a framework that has been adopted by econometricians (Wooldridge, 2002, pp. 603–607; Angrist, 2004; Ravallion, 2005), and applied in recent research on education finance and policy.
6. For reviews of similar research, see McEwan (2000), Ladd (2002), and Neal (2002).
7. In this chapter, regression analysis implies ordinary least-squares regression (OLS). For basic discussions, see Wooldridge (2006) or Stock and Watson (2003). In education policy, it is common to apply multilevel or hierarchical models (Raudenbush & Bryk, 2002; Somers, McEwan, & Willms, 2004) that model error components and account for the potential correlation of errors within classrooms, schools, communities, or states. In so doing, they avoid understating standard errors of coefficients and over-stating their statistical significance. (The models do not necessarily, as is sometimes assumed, remove selection bias.) Economists are more likely to report OLS coefficient estimates accompanied by adjusted Huber-White standard errors that allow for arbitrary correlations among units within clusters (Wooldridge, 2002). In comparisons, OLS with adjusted standard errors and other multilevel models yield similar results, though OLS with standard errors *not* adjusted for clustering can dramatically underestimate standard errors (Angeles & Mroz, 2001). This issue is not discussed further, but the research cited in this chapter generally reports cluster-adjusted standard errors.
8. This assumes a binary policy intervention (treated or not), though the discussion can be generalized to continuously-measured policy interventions (e.g. class sizes of 1 to 50).
9. Formally, the assumption is that $\text{cov}(P_i, \varepsilon_i) = 0$.
10. It is common for researchers to conjecture about the direction of bias, in concert with the oft-reasonable presumption that selection on unobserved characteristics, like motivation, might work in the same direction as selection on observed characteristics, like family income (e.g. Somers et al., 2004). For a rigorous application of this reasoning to the effects of private school attendance on test scores, see Altonji, Elder, and Taber (2005).
11. The goal of randomized experiments is to ensure that the second condition holds by design.
12. For reviews of such studies in the United States, see Greenwald, Hedges, and Laine (1996), Hanushek (1997; 2002), and Krueger (2003). Reviews of international studies include Fuller and Clarke (1994), Hanushek (1995), and Glewwe and Kremer (2006).
13. Urquiola (2006) documents that disadvantaged, rural students in Bolivia, by virtue of their location, are

more likely to attend smaller classes. Presuming that some features of "disadvantage" are unobserved, and lead to lower test scores, regression-based estimates of the causal effect of small-class treatments are biased towards finding no effect. For related arguments focusing on the United States, see Boozer and Rouse (2001).

14. See Hanushek (1986) and Barrow and Rouse (2005). Boardman and Murnane (1979) and Todd and Wolpin (2003) formally analyze conditions under which pre-test controls may eliminate bias in test score regressions.
15. One could literally match units "by hand," based on a small number of observed characteristics. Doing so becomes increasingly difficult as the number of observed characteristics and matching categories increases. Propensity score matching provides a solution to this "curse of dimensionality." Matching algorithms and related analyses are still a topic of debate; for reviews, see Ravallion (2005) and the citations therein.
16. As a counter-example Black and Smith (2004) find that regression and propensity estimates of the effects of college quality on wages are similar in a sample of men, but not women.
17. A growing literature finds that non-experimental statistical approaches, including regression and propensity score matching, do a poor job of replicating experimental results (Agodini & Dynarski, 2004; Glewwe et al., 2004; Glazerman, Levy, & Myers, 2003).
18. See Mosteller (1995) and Krueger (1999). In developing-country research, a similar role was played by the large-scale experimental evaluation of PROGRESA, a Mexican program that awarded cash payments to families in exchange for participating in health and education programs (Skoufias, 2005).
19. The opinion is not limited to researchers in education policy or economics. The statistician David Freedman (1991) remarked that "regression models make it all too easy to substitute technique for work" (p. 300), and called on researchers to expend more "shoe leather" in the pursuit of the convincing counterfactual reasoning and data.
20. A coin flip or similar mechanism is only the simplest approach to designing randomized assignment. The essential point is that students or other units have well-defined probabilities of being assigned to the treatment. On the design, implementation, and analysis of randomized experiments, see Orr (1999) and Duflo, Glennerster, and Kremer (2006).
21. Indeed, one of the key tests for determining whether randomization "worked" is to test, and hopefully not reject, the null hypothesis of no average differences in observed characteristics across treatment and control group units. If there are differences, it could indicate random, but unlikely noise (like the person who flips a coin and gets heads 10 times in row). More perniciously, it could indicate attempts to manipulate random assignment, which is most likely in settings where researchers do not administer random assignment, and where individuals or other units have incentives to be treated or untreated (McEwan & Olsen, 2007).
22. In terms of the previous regression framework, randomized assignment ensures that the treatment (e.g., P) is uncorrelated with the error term, ϵ.
23. For overviews of experimentation in the United States, see Borman (2002) and, in developing countries, Glewwe and Kremer (2006).
24. See Hahn, Todd, and van der Klauuw (2001), Lee (in press), and Shadish et al. (2002). On the design's use and independent discovery in several disciplines, see Cook (in press). Cook and Wong (in press) and Buddelmeyer and Skoufias (2003) compare experimental and RDD estimates of the same programs. They find close correspondence, suggesting that the internal validity of RDD results is high.
25. See Chay, McEwan, and Urquiola (2005) and van der Klaauw (2002). The sample of students (or other assigned units) is often small near cutoffs, limiting the statistical precision of comparisons. Thus, researchers frequently apply parametric or non-parametric regression analysis to larger samples of data, further away from the cutoff (on techniques, see van der Klaauw, 2002; McCrary & Royer, 2006). Regressions control for an indicator of eligibility (i.e., pre-test above the cutoff) and additional controls for smooth functions of the assignment variable, often a quadratic or cubic function (Chay et al., 2005).
26. Such manipulation is perhaps more likely when using discrete assignment variables that individuals or organizations—with incentives to obtain or avoid treatment—can precisely set. For example, many

researchers note that day of birth is an assignment variable, and that children born after a specified assignment cutoff date are subject to treatments, like delaying school enrollment by one year (McCrary & Royer, 2006; McEwan & Shapiro, in press). Of course, motivated parents can manipulate day of birth by cesarean section or induced labor. While such manipulation might seem unlikely, Dickert-Conlin and Chandra (1999) show that U. S. parents precisely time year-end births to obtain tax benefits.

27. Belfield and Levin (2002) summarizes the empirical literature on competition.
28. One of the most common uses in economics, and increasingly so in education finance and policy, is to use repeated cross-section data on all 50 states, during periods in which some states were exposed to reform (perhaps at different times), and other states were not. The strategy has been applied, for example, to the effects of state accountability reforms (Hanushek & Raymond, 2005) and state finance reforms (Murray, Evans, & Schwab, 1998).
29. The assumption is not always tenable in student panel data on test scores. Suppose that students are more likely to apply to charter schools after experiencing slower test score growth in public schools than other students. If they switch to charter schools, a DD estimate of charter school effects could mistake this pre-existing trend for part of a charter school "effect." With more than two years of data, researchers can implement more complicated models that compare changes in test score *gains* rather than levels (Bifulco & Ladd, 2006; Hanushek et al., 2007; Sass, 2006). Repeated cross-section studies have employed a similar strategy, controlling for unit-specific linear time trends (see, e.g., the state-level studies of Loeb & Page, 2000 and Hanushek & Raymond, 2005).
30. This is not the case in common applications of IV, since fulfilling the second condition (instruments uncorrelated with *unexplained* outcomes) is more likely to be fulfilled when researchers have used controls to already explain much of the variance in outcomes.
31. For applications to experiments, regression-discontinuity, and DD, see Krueger (1999), Chay et al., (2005), and Dynarski (2003), respectively.
32. In experiments, this includes the full treatment and control groups in experiments; in the RDD, it includes smaller groups close to the cutoff.
33. For examples of experiments, see Krueger and Zhu (2004) and Rouse (1998). On the RDD, see van der Klaauw (2002).
34. In the analogous RDD case, units do not always comply with their initial cutoff-based assignment to treatment or control groups. RDDs with perfect compliance are called "sharp" designs, and those with imperfect compliance are "fuzzy" (Shadish et al., 2002). In the earlier example, families whose child is ineligible for financial aid (by virtue of obtain a pre-test score below 50) may nonetheless lobby to have the decision overturned. Other families may turn down the assigned treatment. Researchers can apply IV (as described in van der Klaauw, 2002 or Chay et al., 2005) to estimate a local version of the effect of the treatment-on-the-treated.

REFERENCES

Agodini, R., & Dynarski, M. (2004). Are experiments the only option? A look at dropout prevention program. *Review of Economics and Statistics, 86*(1), 180–194.

Altonji, J. G., Elder, T. E., & Taber, C. R. (2005). Selection on observed and unobserved variables: Assessing the effectiveness of Catholic schools. *Journal of Political Economy, 113,* 151–184.

Angeles, G., & Mroz, T. A. (2001). *A guide to using multilevel models for the evaluation of program impacts.* Measure Evaluation Working Paper 01–33. Chapel Hill, NC: Carolina Population Center, University of North Carolina.

Angrist, J. D. (2004). American education research changes tack. *Oxford Review of Economic Policy, 20*(2), 198–212.

Angrist, J. D., & Krueger, A. B. (1999). Empirical strategies in labor economics. In O. Ashenfelter & D. Card (Eds.), *Handbook of Labor Economics* (Vol. 3A). Amsterdam: Elsevier.

Angrist, J. D., & Lavy, V. (1999). Using Maimonides' rule to estimate the effect of class size on scholastic achievement. *Quarterly Journal of Economics, 114*(2), 533–575.

Barrow, L., & Rouse, C. E. (2005). *Causality, causality, causality: The view of education inputs and outputs from economics.* Working Paper 2005–2015. Chicago: Federal Reserve Bank of Chicago.

Behrman, J. R., Cheng, Y., & Todd, P. E. (2004). Evaluating preschool programs when length of exposure to the program varies: A nonparametric approach. *Review of Economics and Statistics, 86*(1), 108–132.

Belfield, C., & Levin, H. M. (2002). The effects of competition between schools on educational outcomes: A review for the United States. *Review of Educational Research, 72*(2), 279–341.

Bifulco, R., & Ladd, H. F. (2006). The impacts of charter schools on student achievement: Evidence from North Carolina. *Education Finance and Policy, 1*(1), 50–90.

Black, D. A., & Smith, J. A. (2004). How robust is the evidence on the effects of college quality? Evidence from matching. *Journal of Econometrics, 121*(1-2), 99–124.

Boardman, A. E., & Murnane, R. J. (1979). Using panel data to improve estimates of the determinants of educational achievement. *Sociology of Education, 52*(2), 113–121.

Boozer, M., & Rouse, C. (2001). Intraschool variation in class size: Patterns and implications. *Journal of Urban Economics, 50*(1), 163–189.

Borman, G. D. (2002). Experiments for educational evaluation and improvement. *Peabody Journal of Education, 77*(4), 7–27.

Borman, G. D., Slavin, R. E., Cheung, A., Chamberlain, A., Madden, N., & Chambers, B. (2005). The national randomized field trial of Success for All: Second-year outcomes. *American Educational Research Journal, 42,* 673–696.

Bound, J., Jaeger, D. A., & Baker, R. (1995). Problems with instrumental variable estimation when the correlation between the instruments and endogenous explanatory variable is weak. *Journal of the American Statistical Association, 90*(430), 443–450.

Bryk, A. S., Lee, V. E., & Holland, P. B. (1993). *Catholic schools and the common good.* Cambridge, MA: Harvard University Press.

Buddelmeyer, H., & Skoufias, E. (2003). *An evaluation of the performance of regression discontinuity design on PROGRESA.* Discussion Paper No. 827. IZA.

Burtless, G. (1995). The case for randomized field trials in economic and policy research. *Journal of Economic Perspectives, 9*(2), 63–84.

Campbell, D. T., & Stanley, J. C. (1963). *Experimental and quasi-experimental designs for research.* Chicago: Rand McNally.

Chay, K. Y., McEwan, P. J., & Urquiola, M. (2005). The central role of noise in evaluating interventions that use test scores to rank schools. *American Economic Review, 95*(4), 1237–1258.

Cook, T. D. (2002). Randomized experiments in educational policy research: A critical examination of the reasons the educational evaluation community has offered for not doing them. *Educational Evaluation and Policy Analysis, 24*(3), 175–199.

Cook, T. D. (in press). Waiting for life to arrive: A history of the regression-discontinuity design in psychology, statistics, and economics. *Journal of Econometrics.*

Cook, T. D., & Campbell, D. T. (1979). *Quasi-experimentation: design and analysis issues for field settings.* Boston: Houghton Mifflin.

Cook, T. D., Habib, F. N., Phillips, M., Settersten, R. A., Shagle, S. C., & Degirmencioglu, S. M. (1999). Comer's School Development Program in Prince George's County, Maryland: A theory-based evaluation. *American Educational Research Journal, 36*(3), 543–597.

Cook, T. D., Murphy, R. F., & Hunt, H. D. (2000). Comer's School Development Program in Chicago: A theory-based evaluation. *American Educational Research Journal, 37*(2), 535–597.

Cook, T. D., & Wong, V. C. (in press). Empirical tests of the validity of the regression discontinuity design. *Annales d'Economie et de Statistique.*

Cooper, H., & Hedges, L. V. (Eds.). (1994). *The handbook of research synthesis.* New York: Russell Sage Foundation.

Crocker, L., & Algina, J. (1986). *Introduction to classical and modern test theory.* Fort Worth: Harcourt Brace Jovanovich.

Dee, T. S., Evans, W. N., & Murray, S. E. (1999). Data watch: Research data in the economics of education. *Journal of Economic Perspectives, 13*(3), 205–216.

Dee, T. S., & Levine, J. (2004). The fate of new funding: Evidence from Massachusetts' education finance reforms. *Educational Evaluation and Policy Analysis, 26*(3), 199–215.

Dickert-Conlin, S., & Chandra, A. (1999). Taxes and the timing of births. *Journal of Political Economy, 107*(1), 161–177.

Dynarski, S. M. (2003). Does aid matter? Measuring the effect of student aid on college attendance and completion. *American Economic Review, 93*(1), 279–288.

Duflo, E., Glennerster, R., & Kremer, M. (2006). *Using randomization in development economics research: A toolkit.* Unpublished manuscript, MIT.

Figlio, D. N., & Ludwig, J. (2000). *Sex, drugs, and Catholic schools: Private schooling and non-market adolescent behaviors.* Working Paper No. 7990. Cambridge, MA: National Bureau of Economic Research.

Freedman, D. A. (1991). Statistical models and shoe leather. *Sociological Methodology, 21,* 291–313.

Fuller, B., & Clarke, P. (1994). Raising school effects while ignoring culture? Local conditions and the influence of classroom tools, rules, and pedagogy. *Review of Educational Research, 64*(1), 119–157.

Glazerman, S., Levy, D. M., & Myers, D. (2003). Nonexperimental versus experimental estimates of earnings impacts. *Annals of the American Academy of Political and Social Science, 589*(1), 63–93.

Glewwe, P., & Kremer, M. (2006). Schools, teachers, and education outcomes in developing countries. In E. A. Hanushek & F. Welch (Eds.), *Handbook of the Economics of Education* (Vol. 2, pp. 945–1017). Amsterdam: Elsevier.

Glewwe, P., Ilias, N., & Kremer, M. (2003). *Teacher incentives.* Working Paper No. 9671. Cambridge, MA: National Bureau of Economic Research.

Glewwe, P., Kremer, M., Moulin, S., & Zitzewitz, E. (2004). Retrospective vs. prospective analyses of school inputs: The case of flip charts in Kenya. *Journal of Development Economics, 74,* 251–268.

Godtland, E. M., Sadoulet, E., de Janvry, A., Murgai, R., & Ortiz, O. (2004). The impact of farmer field schools on knowledge and productivity: A study of potato farmers in the Peruvian Andes. *Economic Development and Cultural Change, 53,* 63–92.

Gormley, W. T., & Gayer, T. (2005). Promoting school readiness in Oklahoma: An evaluation of Tulsa's Pre-K program. *Journal of Human Resources, 40*(3), 533–558.

Greenwald, R., Hedges, L. V., & Laine, R. D. (1996). The effect of school resources on student achievement. *Review of Educational Research, 66*(3), 361–396.

Hahn, J., Todd, P., & van der Klaauw, W. (2001). Identification and estimation of treatment effects with a regression-discontinuity design. *Econometrica, 69*(1), 201–209.

Hanushek, E. A. (1986). The economics of schooling: Production and efficiency in public schools. *Journal of Economic Literature, 24*(3), 1141–1177.

Hanushek, E. A. (1995). Interpreting recent research on schooling in developing countries. *World Bank Research Observer 10*(2), 227–246.

Hanushek, E. A. (1997). Assessing the effects of school resources of student performance: An update. *Educational Evaluation and Policy Analysis, 19*(2), 141–164.

Hanushek, E. A. (2002). Publicly provided education. In A. J. Auerbach & M. Feldstein (Eds.), *Handbook of Public Economics* (Vol. 4, pp. 2045–2141). Amsterdam: Elsevier.

Hanushek, E. A., Kain, J. F., Rivkin, S. G., & Branch, G. F. (2007). Charter school quality and parental decision making with school choice. *Journal of Public Economics, 91*(5–6), 823–848.

Hanushek, E. A., & Raymond, M. E. (2005). Does school accountability lead to improved student performance? *Journal of Policy Analysis and Management, 24*(2), 297–327.

Heckman, J. J. (1995). Assessing the case for social experiments. *Journal of Economic Perspectives, 9*(2), 85–110.

Holland, P. W. (1986). Statistics and causal inference. *Journal of the American Statistical Association, 81*(396), 945–960.

Hong, G., & Raudenbush, S. W. (2006). Evaluating Kindergarten retention policy: A case study of causal inference for multilevel observation data. *Journal of the American Statistical Association, 101*(475), 901–910.

Howell, W. G., & Peterson, P. E. (2002). *The education gap: Vouchers and urban schools.* Washington, DC: The Brookings Institution Press.

Hoxby, C. M. (2000). Does competition among public schools benefit students and taxpayers? *American Economic Review, 90*(5), 1209–1238.

Jacob, B. A., & Lefgren, L. (2004). The impact of teacher training on student achievement: Quasi-experimental evidence from school reform efforts in Chicago. *Journal of Human Resources, 39*(1), 50–79.

Jepsen, C., & Rivkin, S. (2002). *What is the tradeoff between smaller classes and teacher quality?* Working Paper No. 9205. Cambridge, MA: National Bureau of Economic Research.

Kane, T. J. (2003). *A quasi-experimental estimate of the impact of financial aid on college-going.* Working Paper No. 9703. Cambridge, MA: National Bureau of Economic Research.

King, G., Keohane, R. O., & Verba, S. (1994). *Designing social inquiry: Scientific inference in qualitative research.* Princeton, NJ: Princeton University Press.

Kolen, M. J., & Brennan, R. L. (2004). *Test equating, scaling, and linking: Methods and practices* (2nd ed.). New York: Springer.

Krueger, A. B. (1999). Experimental estimates of education production functions. *Quarterly Journal of Economics, 114*(2), 497–532.

Krueger, A. B. (2003). Economic considerations and class size. *Economic Journal, 113*(485), F34–F63.

Krueger, A. B., & Zhu, P. (2004). Another look at the New York City voucher experiment. *American Behavioral Scientist, 47*(5), 658–698.

Kuziemko, I. (2006). Using shocks to school enrollment to estimate the effect of school size on student achievement. *Economics of Education Review, 25*(1), 63–75.

Ladd, H. F. (2002). School vouchers: A critical view. *Journal of Economic Perspectives, 16*(4), 3–24.

Lankford, H., Loeb, S., & Wyckoff, J. (2002). Teacher sorting and the plight of urban schools: A descriptive analysis. *Educational Evaluation and Policy Analysis, 24*(1), 37–62.

Lee, D. S. (in press). Randomized experiments from non-random selection in U.S. House elections. *Journal of Econometrics.*

Levin, H. M., & McEwan, P. J. (2001). *Cost-effectiveness analysis: Methods and applications* (2nd ed.). Thousand Oaks, CA: Sage.

Levin, H. M., & McEwan, P. J. (Eds.). (2002). *Cost-effectiveness and educational policy.* Larchmont, NY: Eye on Education.

Loeb, S., & Page, M. E. (2000). Examining the link between teacher wages and student outcomes: The importance of alternative labor market opportunities and non-pecuniary variation. *Review of Economics and Statistics, 82*(3), 393–408.

Loeb, S., & Strunk, K. (2003). The contribution of administrative and experimental data to education policy research. *National Tax Journal, 56*(2), 415–438.

Ludwig, J. (2001). Problems in the estimation of school effects: Insights from improved models. In D. H. Monk, H. J. Walberg, & M. C. Wang (Eds.), *Improving educational productivity* (Vol. 1, pp. 209–236). Greenwich, CT: Information Age Publishing.

Ludwig, J., & Miller, D. L. (2007). Does Head Start improve children's life chances? Evidence from a regression discontinuity design. *Quarterly Journal of Economics, 122*(1), 159–208.

McCrary, J. (in press). Manipulation of the running variable in the regression-discontinuity design: A density test. *Journal of Econometrics.*

McCrary, J., & Royer, H. (2006). *The effect of maternal education on fertility and infant health: Evidence from school entry laws using exact date of birth.* Unpublished manuscript, University of Michigan.

McEwan, E. K., & McEwan, P. J. (2003). *Making sense of research.* Thousand Oaks, CA: Corwin.

McEwan, P. J. (2000). The potential impact of large-scale voucher programs. *Review of Educational Research, 70*(2), 103–149.

McEwan, P. J., & Olsen, R. (2007). *Admission lotteries in charter schools.* Unpublished manuscript, Wellesley College and Urban Institute.

McEwan, P. J., & Shapiro, J. (in press). The benefits of delayed primary school enrollment: Discontinuity estimates using exact birth dates. *Journal of Human Resources.*

Meyer, B. D. (1995). Natural and quasi-experiments in economics. *Journal of Business and Economic Statistics, 13*(2), 151–161.

Mosteller, F. (1995). The Tennessee study of class size in the early school grades. *The Future of Children, 5*(2), 113–127.

Murray, S. E., Evans, W. N., & Schwab, R. M. (1998). Education-finance reform and the distribution of education resources. *American Economic Review, 88*(4), 789–812.

Neal, D. (2002). How vouchers could change the market for education. *Journal of Economic Perspectives, 16*(4), 25–44.

Orr, L. L. (1999). *Social experiments.* Thousand Oaks, CA: Sage.

Ravallion, M. (2001). The mystery of the vanishing benefits: An introduction to impact evaluation. *World Bank Economic Review, 15*(1), 115–140.

Ravallion, M. (2005). *Evaluating anti-poverty programs.* Policy Research Working Paper No. 3625. Washington, DC: World Bank.

Raudenbush, S. W., & Bryk, A. S. (2002). *Hierarchical linear models: Applications and data analysis methods* (2nd ed.). Thousand Oaks, CA: Sage.

Rosenbaum, P. R., & Rubin, D. B. (1983). The central role of the propensity score in observational studies for causal effects. *Biometrika, 70*(1), 41–55.

Rothstein, J. (2005). *Does competition among public schools benefit students and taxpayers? A comment on Hoxby (2000).* Working Paper No. 11215. Cambridge, MA: National Bureau of Economic Research.

Rouse, C. E. (1998). Private school vouchers and student achievement: An evaluation of the Milwaukee Parental Choice Program. *Quarterly Journal of Economics, 113*(2), 553–602.

Sass, T. R. (2006). Charter schools and student achievement in Florida. *Education Finance and Policy, 1*(1), 91–122.

Shadish, W. R., Cook, T. D., & Campbell, D. T. (2002). *Experimental and quasi-experimental designs for generalized causal inference.* Boston: Houghton Mifflin.

Shapiro, J., & Trevino, J. M. (2004). *Compensatory education for disadvantaged Mexican students: An impact evaluation using propensity score matching.* Policy Research Working Paper 3334. Washington, DC: World Bank.

Shavelson, R. J., & Towne, L. (Eds.). (2002). *Scientific research in education.* Washington, DC: National Academy Press.

Skoufias, E. (2005). *PROGRESA and its impacts on the welfare of rural households in Mexico.* Research Report No. 139. Washington, DC: International Food Policy Research Institute.

Somers, M.-A., McEwan, P. J., & Willms, J. D. (2004). How effective are private schools in Latin America? *Comparative Education Review, 48,* 48–69.

Stock, J. H., & Watson, M. W. (2003). *Introduction to econometrics.* Boston: Addison-Wesley.

Todd, P. E., & Wolpin, K. I. (2003). On the specification and estimation of the production function for cognitive achievement. *Economic Journal, 113*(485), F3–F33.

Tukey, J. W. (1977). *Exploratory data analysis.* Reading, MA: Addison-Wesley.

Urquiola, M. (2006). Identifying class size effects in developing countries: Evidence from rural Bolivia. *Review of Economics and Statistics, 88*(1), 171–177.

U.S. Department of Education. (2003). *Identifying and implementing educational practices supported by rigorous evidence: A user friendly guide.* Washington, DC: U.S. Department of Education, Institute of Education Sciences.

van der Klaauw, W. (2002). Estimating the effect of financial aid offers on college enrollment: A regression-discontinuity approach. *International Economic Review, 43*(4), 1249–1286.

Vandenberghe, V., & Robin, S. (2004). Evaluating the effectiveness of private education across countries: A comparison of methods. *Labour Economics, 11,* 487–506.

Wooldridge, J. M. (2002). *Econometric analysis of cross section and panel data.* Cambridge, MA: MIT Press.

Wooldridge, J. M. (2006). *Introductory econometrics: A modern approach* (3rd ed.). Thomson South-Western.

Zahorik, J., Molnar, A., Ehrle, K., & Halbach, A. (2000). Smaller classes, better teaching? Effective teaching in reduced-size classes. In S. W. M. Laine & J. G. Ward (Eds.), *Using what we know: A review of the research on implementing class-size reduction initiatives for state and local policymakers* (pp. 53–73). Oak Brook, IL: North Central Regional Educational Laboratory.

7

The Evolution of Comparative and International Education Statistics

Stephen P. Heyneman and Chad R. Lykins

INTRODUCTION

An argument ensued between M. Dottrens and Jean Piaget at a board meeting of the Institute of Statistics in Geneva in 1933.[1] Dottrens proposed an international survey to record what countries were doing in education. Piaget was against it. He said: "L'expérience nous a montre qu'il est extrêmement difficile d'établir des tableaux statistiques comparables" (Smyth, 1996, p. 4). Piaget had a point. At that time there was no common definition on what education meant, how schooling might differ from ad hoc learning, or how to distinguish educational levels. The meanings of vocational and general education varied between and within nations. There were 115 different ways to define literacy and 133 different ways to classify educational attainment by age group (Smyth, 2005, p. 13). Dottrens, however, apparently won the argument on grounds that, in spite of the procedural complexities and the danger of receiving misleading results, the demand to know what countries are doing in education was simply irresistible.

These same arguments have re-occurred with regularity in the last 74 years. Though those who agree with Dottrens' claim have lost many battles in the interim, they have all but won the war. The record of advancement in geographical coverage and qualitative depth in comparative education statistics has been unidirectional. From counting schools in 1933 to videotaping teaching styles and capturing unit expenditures, the story of educational measurement and the resulting debates over its unprecedented findings is one true sign that there has been progress in education research. This extraordinary growth, both in the quantity and the quality of educational data, has brought fresh—and sometimes contentious—insights into perennial questions concerning the financing of education. The goal of this chapter is to explore the history of this growth and what it means for the study of some key questions in education finance.

EDUCATION COMPARISONS IN OECD COUNTIES

The Origin of Descriptive Education Statistics

The first attempt to compare educational expenditures internationally was made in 1937 by the International Bureau of Education (IBE). Their report presented seven tables illustrating national budgets, number of primary and secondary schools, and teachers and students in 58 countries. In

May of 1946, the United States submitted to the UNESCO Preparatory Commission a proposal to establish an international statistical service which should "assist in the co-ordination, standardization and improvement of national education statistics, the technology of its standardization, and should provide advice to member countries and international organizations on general questions relating to collection, interpretation and dissemination of education statistics" (Smyth, 1996, p. 7). The proposal was adopted. Consequently, a meeting of experts was called in November of 1951, to work on details of the world's first education statistical service.

The barriers to its operations were substantial. Prior education statistics consisted of only country-by-country "illustrations." There was insufficient agreement on terms and procedures to make comparisons. Recognizing this lack of agreement, the committee developed the first International Standard Classification of Education (ISCED) document which defined a school and established standards for classifying primary, secondary, higher and vocational education in 1953. It also provided the first definitions of education finance. These included definitions for *receipts* (cash received or made available for schools, including appropriations, subventions, fees, cash value of property received as gifts), *expenditures, recurring expenditures*, *capital expenditures* and *debt service* (Smyth, 1996, p. 18). Under each category, moreover, there were lengthy descriptions of each concept and details concerning proper tabulation. These initial iterations resulted in the compendious *World Surveys of Education* published in 1955, 1958, 1961, 1966, and 1971.

Despite significant improvements in education statistics between 1933 and 1971, there were still no indicators of education achievement or outcomes. Nor were there reliable indicators of teaching technologies, student attitudes, labor market activities, or unit expenditures. This lack became the focus of international attention and debate beginning in the 1970s and continuing to the present.

The Origin of Cross National Tests of Academic Achievement

The effort to compare academic achievement across countries was among the most controversial aspects of international education statistics. At first, the use of surveys for cross national education research was just an experiment, born from a chance visit by Torsten Husen (from the University of Stockholm) to the University of Chicago in the mid-1950s. There Husen met Professors Benjamin Bloom (Curriculum), C. Arnold Anderson (Sociology) and Mary Jean Bowman (Economics). They agreed that the world should be seen as a single educational laboratory. From this meeting emerged the idea—novel at the time—to sponsor an informal academic association promoting surveys of education *achievement*. The group was called the International Association for the Evaluation of Educational Achievement (IEA). For reasons of diplomacy, it was headquartered in Sweden. In 1959, the IEA published the first results from a pilot survey of a test consisting of 120 items covering reading comprehension, geography, science, mathematics, and non-verbal ability administered to non-representative samples of 9,918 13-year-old students in 12 countries (Postlewaite, 1975, p. 1). Since then there have been 33 cross-national studies of academic achievement, 29 of which have been sponsored by the IEA (Figure 7.1.).

Problems emerged from the beginning. It was a significant challenge for academics to manage an enterprise of such political and institutional complexity. There were difficulties in agreeing on common definitions, methodologies, sampling, and techniques for managing data. There were hurdles in obtaining sufficient resources from participating countries and donors with widely divergent economic circumstances. And there were severe pressures to meet strict schedules of implementation. These spawned numerous assessments of the benefits and drawbacks of the cross-national enterprise (Heyneman, 2004a, 2004b; Chromy, 2002; Floden, 2002; Linn, 2002;

Sponsor	Description	Countries	Year(s) Conducted
IEA	First International Mathematics Study (FIMS)	12 countries	1964
IEA	Six Subjects Study:		1970–1971
	Science	19 systems	
	Reading	15 countries	
	Literature	10 countries	
	French as a foreign language	8 countries	
	English as a foreign language	10 countries	
	Civic Education	10 countries	
IEA	First International Science Study (FISS) (part of Six Subjects Study)	19 countries	1970–1971
IEA	Second International Mathematics Study (SIMS)	10 countries	1982
IEA	Second International Science Study (SISS)	19 systems	1983–1984
ETS	First International Assessment of Educational Progress (IAEP-I, Mathematics and Science)	6 countries (12 systems)	1988
ETS	Second International Assessment of Educational Progress (IAEP-II, Mathematics and Science)	20 countries	1991
IEA	Reading Literacy (RL)	32 countries	1990–1991
IEA	Computers in Education	22 countries	1988–1989
		12 countries	1991-1992
Statistics Canada	International Adult Literacy Survey (IALS)	7 countries	1994
IEA	Preprimary Project:		
	Phase I	11 countries	1989–1991
	Phase II	15 countries	1991–1993
	Phase III (longitudinal follow up of Phase II sample)	15 countries	1994–1996
IEA	Language Education Study	25 interested countries	1997
IEA	Third International Mathematics and Science Study (TIMSS):	45 countries	1994–1995
	Phase I	About 40	1997–1998
	Phase II (TIMSS-R)		
IEA	Civic Education Study	28 countries	1999
OECD	Program for International Student Assessment	32 countries	2000 (reading) 2003 (math) 2006 (science)

FIGURE 7.1 Selected International Comparative Studies in Education: Scope and Timing.
Source: Chromy (2002).

Rowen, 2002; Smith, 2002; Postlewaite, 1999; Goldstein, 1995; Horvitz, 1992; Medrich and Griffith, 1992; Olkin and Searls, 1985).

The surveys did, however, help stimulate debate over new questions and theories from a wide variety of disciplines including sociology, philosophy, child and cognitive psychology, economics, pedagogy, and education policy (Medrich and Griffith, 1992; Purves and Levine, 1975; Tomlinson and Tuijnman, 1994; Phillips, 1991; IEA, 1990). For instance, Robert Thorndike observed that the variables which differentiate students are not the same as those which differentiate countries. On the basis of international comparisons, he once argued that parental help may be a sign of student ineptitude (Thorndike, 1975, p. 102). Benjamin Bloom noted that students who do poorly are those who are not interested in studying (Bloom, 1975, p. 80). Contrary to the theory that elite education systems would have higher achievement, William Platt found that achievement does not decline as universal schooling and rates of retention go up. He also found that achievement stems from certain cognitive domains rather than others (Platt, 1975, p. 40). Each new study seemed to offer a new range of dependent variables, for instance the use of computers in classrooms and achievement scores for those studying French and English as a foreign language, mathematics, science, civics, reading, and writing (IEA, 2001, 1993, 1992a, 1992b, 1976, 1975, 1973).

The informality of IEA as an organization proved to be a significant obstacle to the carrying out of each survey. From the first meeting in Chicago in the mid–1950s up to the publication of the Second International Study of Science (SIMS) in 1982, IEA had remained an association of academic institutes unaffiliated with governmental agencies. In centralized systems, such as in France and Japan, the member institutes happened to be sponsored by governments. But in the United States, as well as in many low- and middle-income countries, the representative to the IEA was an independent professor with no official capacity.[2] After the 1982 results suggested that the United States was behind other industrial democracies, the U.S. Department of Education was called to account by Congress, only to discover that the U.S. samples for SIMS were not nationally representative. The National Center for Education Statistics (NCES) and the National Science Foundation concluded that for political as well as professional reasons, this lack of representativeness should not re-occur. Any international study in which the United States participates (particularly with such visibility) henceforth must insure that the data meet normal standards of representativeness, reliability, and validity. Thus, the timely delivery of the IEA Third International Mathematics and Science Study (TIMSS) became a high federal priority. Coordinated with the stated U.S. goals of being first in math and science (Vinovskis, 1999), the TIMSS study was the most ambitious and expensive enterprise undertaken by the IEA, and its results have generated debate that should extend well into the future (Beatty, 1997; Peak, 1997, 1996; Ravitch, 2003; Baker and LeTendre, 2005). But how could the federal government enforce its standards upon a private voluntary organization of which it was not even an official member?

THE ORIGIN AND PURPOSES OF BICSE

In 1988 two agencies (the National Science Foundation and the U.S. Department of Education) decided to sponsor the Board on International Comparative Studies Education (BICSE) through the National Academy of Sciences. The board was given four main objectives: (1) to suggest technical principles which could be internationally enforced; (2) to guide U.S. agencies on the types of studies of highest priority;[3] (3) to ensure the efficient management of any studies in which U.S. students might be studied; and (4) to sensibly coordinate the necessary financing and management of the infrastructure necessary to make international studies viable over the long run. The BICSE committee was influential globally over the next dozen years. While many nations did not feel comfortable working with the U.S. government in education,[4] they listened more attentively to the views of a committee of the National Academy of Sciences because it was perceived to be professionally competent and politically neutral.

BICSE's first report, distributed in 1990, consists of a series of reasons why a country might wish to engage in international comparative work in education and the kinds of studies that might be useful. The report includes rationales for studies of academic achievement as well as a wide range of educational questions using descriptive, qualitative, observational techniques (Bradburn and Gilford, 1990). The eclectic nature of the list helped overcome some of the misgivings of the academic community. The report laid out a series of principles for international standards in areas such as technical validity, research neutrality, sampling, access to schools, instrument construction and administration, analysis, reporting, and dissemination. Unlike textbook and other academic sources for these standards, the BICSE report had a scientific imprimatur which influenced public agencies financing U.S. participation in international studies, agencies in the participating countries cooperating with the United States, and inter-governmental agencies (such as OECD, UNESCO, and the World Bank).

The next BICSE report, three years later, went well beyond the first and outlined the international structures required to put a larger and more professional agenda of studies into effect (Gilford, 1993). It included sections dealing with problems of comparability across nations, financing requirements, and suggestions for improving the international infrastructure for cross national research. As a result of these first two reports and the multiple informal discussions surrounding them, IEA was transformed from an informal 'academic club' to a professional multi-national agency. It initiated and enforced a dues structure, technical procedures for implementing studies, and formal sanctions for participating countries which did not adhere to them.[5] BICSE published additional reports on the range of international studies available (National Research Council, 1995), how to get the most out of re-analyses (National Research Council, 1999) and how to use cross national studies in the making of educational policy (National Research Council, 2002).

However successful BICSE was in establishing a consensus among nations, cross-national studies continued to be challenged for many reasons. Some believed that the United States was at a systematic disadvantage because it had higher enrollment rates and comprehensive schooling, while other participating countries with lower enrollment rates and elitist systems (and thus unrepresentative samples) enjoyed artificially high scores (Rotberg, 1990). This stimulated a powerful, personal reply from some BICSE committee members (Bradburn, Haertel, et al., 1991).

THE ORIGIN OF OECD AS A LEADER IN EDUCATION STATISTICS

The U.S. federal government became a strong supporter of cross national education research following the publication of *A Nation at Risk* (National Commission on Excellence in Education, 1983). Among other things, the report claimed that international comparisons indicated that the United States had surrendered in the battle to create the most knowledgeable citizenry in the world. The U.S. government decided to utilize the Organization for Economic Cooperation and Development (OECD) to spearhead an initiative to improve international education statistics.[6]

An acrimonious meeting took place one year after the publication of a *Nation at Risk.* The U.S. delegate from the Center for Educational Research and Innovation (CERI) board challenged OECD to undertake a project to quantify educational quality with measures for curriculum standards, costs, sources of financing, learning achievement, and employment trends.[7] The reaction among the OECD staff at that time was one of shock and suspicion that quantification of educational quality and especially cross national testing constituted a right-wing political tactic, and an abrogation of professional standards.[8] Like Piaget in 1933, they believed that education was specific to each culture, and therefore could not be measured between cultures. They argued that the process of quantification would oversimplify and misrepresent a nation's education system. Many assumed that the demand for such information would shift as soon as the political party of the U.S. presidency changed.[9] It is now clear that this was not the case. In the 20-year interim, the OECD helped pioneer the International Education Indicators project which led to an annual report titled *Education at a Glance*—the most highly demanded of all OECD publications (OECD, 2002).[10]

The Origin of IAEP, PISA, and IALS

Another important topic of discussion at the BICSE meetings concerned whether the U.S. should participate (and help generate) curriculum-based international tests, or whether they should pioneer a new international initiative concentrating largely on a criterion-based achievement test variable roughly analogous to the National Assessment of Educational Progress (NAEP). The original IEA studies which had generated a myriad of explanatory variables were thought to be superior in the sense that they could offer a wide variety of hypotheses.[11] But the IEA style of studies required a decade to generate, were extraordinarily complex to implement, and were expensive. Policy makers said they wanted a faster turn-around with data, including trend data, delivered on time, and collected more frequently.[12]

The U.S. Department of Education agreed to a trial of a NAEP-like international project utilizing the same center that had been administering the NAEP at the Education Testing Service. A new project, called the International Assessment of Educational Progress (IAEP), saw to it that instruments were developed and data collected, analyzed, and reported for more than a dozen countries, within a record time of three years. The measure of academic achievement was developed centrally and based largely on what a student was supposed to perform at a given age level instead of being developed from an analysis of each country's curriculum (IAEP, 1992, 1991).

Many in the international education community felt that the IAEP project was misguided in its decision to determine, without sufficient analysis of local curricula, what a student should be able to do. Although BICSE recommended that the United States participate in both styles of analysis, it was not clear whether the cost of double participation could be justified. However, the timeliness, credibility, and immediate demand for information from the international indicator project helped insure that it would have a future. Since the IEA seemed reluctant to engage in an enterprise that monitored achievement without studying its antecedents in depth, the task for developing the new project was assigned to OECD. It would later develop into the Program of International Student Assessment (PISA) (OECD, 2004a).

PISA has proven to be a wide-ranging and valuable assessment. Among its chief innovations is the introduction of a cross-curricular problem-solving component. It examines students' capacity "to understand problems situated in novel and cross-curricular settings, to identify relevant information or constraints, to represent possible alternatives or solution paths, to develop solution strategies, and to solve problems and communicate the solutions" (OECD, 2004b, p. 3). This component helps balance the heavy weight previous assessments placed on memorized knowledge. Yet interestingly, the rankings in PISA were largely similar to those in previous surveys. Reading ability was divided into five levels of proficiency. Of the 39 countries participating in the PISA project, only 5 percent of the 13-year-old school children in Peru could read above the international mean whereas 75 percent of the 13 year old students in Korea could read above the international mean. The United States, with 60 percent of its 13-year-old students above the mean, was ranked 15th (Figure 7.2.).

OECD was also encouraged to develop a new survey to gauge adult literacy, newly defined as a performance indicator.[13] The results of the International Adult Literacy Study (IALS) were startling. Several nations, such as Poland, which had heretofore been known for having very effective educational systems, had pockets of genuine illiteracy among its adult population and a generally low level of literate performance relative to what had been expected. Only 2.9 percent of the adults surveyed in Poland performed at Level 4 literacy.[14] The United States, which lags behind many counties in elementary and high school surveys, had 17.3 percent of its adult population performing at Level 4, compared to only 12.3 percent in Germany, 14.6 percent in Netherlands, roughly 9 percent in Switzerland (OECD, 2005). Furthermore, no country except

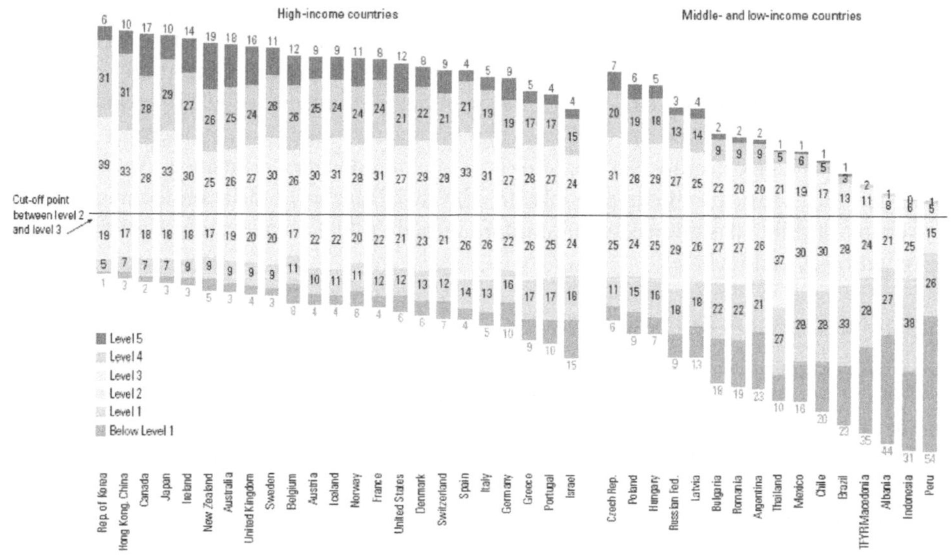

FIGURE 7.2 Percentage of 15-Year-Old Students in Five Proficiency Levels of Reading, 2000–2002.
Source: UNESCO (2005b), *EFA Global Monitoring Report 2005: The Quality Imperative*. Montreal: UNESCO.

Sweden had more than 5 percent of its adults surveyed perform at Level 5. These findings added new urgency to debates concerning adult education across the globe.

Origin of Date on Education Expenditures

Descriptive data on education expenditures was also an important product of the effort to improve education statistics (Sherman, 1982, 1981). The first education finance comparability study was completed for ten countries in 1995 and twenty countries in 1999. After a series of improvements in design and clarity of definitions, the survey was updated using trend data in 2002 and 2004. Today, an expert group governs the collection and reporting of education finance data at OECD.[15] They focus on data whose quality is relatively consistent across geographical regions and which can be collected in a timely manner (Charbonnier, 2005a).

Six financial indicators meet these criteria: (1) expenditures/student; (2) expenditures on primary, secondary, and tertiary educational institutions relative to GDP; (3) relative proportions of the public and private investment in educational institutions; (4) total public expenditures on education; (5) support for students and households through public subsidies; and (6) expenditures on institutions by service category (technical, general, secondary, etc.) and by resource category (public and private). Three new indicators are under development—a metric combining expenditure and performance, an empirical listing of who pays and who benefits from university education, and an indicator of cost/university graduate (Charbonnier, 2005a).

Explanation for the Success of the OECD Project

One key to the success of the OECD effort has been the way in which quality was controlled. Instead of being engineered by a single central authority, quality, and efficiency of implementation was established on the principle of informed peer pressure. Because each nation's reputations depended on the findings, each nation worked hard to make sure that the results meet commonly accepted standards of rigor. All partners have equally enforced adherence to time schedules and quality control. This distributed control allowed the OECD to remain comfortably in its traditional role of neutral coordinator of the interests of member countries while still ensuring technical precision. It also has allowed the OECD to explore terrain opened up by member states. The United States, for instance, in the sponsorship of work on educational finance (Sherman, 1982, 1981; Barro, 1998, 1996) has made possible, for the first time, consensus on technical matters. This consensus-building has allowed regular international collection and analysis of data on education expenditures and finance.

The Use of International Education Statistics

Since the beginning, public officials have often used international studies of academic achievement not as an opportunity to better understand the nature of learning, but as a means of motivating internal reforms in the name of global competition. The results of the Second International Science Study (SIMS) in the 1980s showed that the United States was at best a mediocre performer. Japanese students were reported to learn over 60 percent of what they were taught while the American students learned only 40 percent (Baker, 1993, p. 19). Findings that the U.S. scores were low by comparison to other countries were pervasive and consistent, causing some to suspect that the data might have been mishandled by the federal government so as to generate greater support for educational reform (Bracey, 1996),[16] a hypothesis that was rejected by others (Baker, 1997). Some wondered if it was fair to compare a large and complex nation such as the United States with smaller more homogeneous nations. If states are treated as nations,[17] five of the ten highest scoring nations in 13-year-old math proficiency were U.S. states. These included Iowa (ranked 2nd in the world), North Dakota (3rd), Minnesota (5th), Maine (8th), and New Hampshire (9th) (National Center for Education Statistics, 1996, p. 155).

BICSE helped organize and ensure the timely delivery of the IEA Third International Mathematics and Science Study (TIMSS). But when results appeared in 1995, the United States was again found to be a low achiever. In terms of increases in math between the 4th and the 8th grades, the U.S. gain (93) was significantly lower than Thailand (168); in this the United States ranked last among the 24 nations in the sample (Martin, Gregory, and Stemler, 1999). Much of the problem of U.S. scores was attributed to the breadth of the curriculum, which allegedly precluded the necessary depth (Schmidt, McKnight, and Raizen, 1997). However more recent analyses suggest that national achievement scores in math and science are only vaguely related to characteristics of the curriculum (Baker and LeTendre, 2005, p. 162).

With the follow up administrations of TIMSS in 1999 and 2003 (and one expected in 2007), the U.S. placement may be becoming more difficult to interpret (Martin, Gregory and Stemler, 1999). Eighth grade scores in math and science were higher in 2003 than in 1995 relative to the other 21 countries. However, fourth-grade scores were lower in 2003 than in 1995 compared to other countries (Gonzales, Guzman et. al., 2004). New, more comprehensive data have allowed the posing of new questions and concerns. Instead of using average achievement scores across nations, now it is common to ask which nation is more successful at closing gaps in educational disadvantage among students.[18] In this the United States ranks 18th among the 24 wealthy industrial democracies (UNICEF, 2002).

Does an increase in education spending increase children's math and science performance? Since the work of James S. Coleman and others (1966) and Christopher Jencks (1972) in the United States, it has been common to conclude that schools, especially public schools, are relatively ineffective and inefficient at raising their levels of performance. Drawing on new interna-

Country	Change in Math and Science Score 1970–1994	Increase in Real Spending Per Pupil 1970–1994	Increase in Real GDP/Capita 1970–1994
Austria	–2.3	269.8	46.4
New Zealand	–9.7	222.5	24.3
France	–6.0	211.6	60.7
Italy	1.3	125.7	74.6
Germany	–4.8	108.1	66.8
Japan	–1.9	103.3	100.7
United Kingdom	–8.2	76.7	58.3
Belgium	–4.7	64.7	68.0
Netherlands	1.7	36.3	52.9
United States	0	33.1	70.5
Sweden	4.3	28.5	35.1

FIGURE 7.3 Percentage Changes in Test Scores and Real Expenditures Per Pupil 1970-1994.
Source: UNESCO (2004), *2005 EFA Monitoring Report: The Quality Imperative*. Paris: UNESCO, p. 65.

tional data available in the 1970s, one study across 29 countries found that the explanatory power of children's social background varied by country, and in poorer countries was exceeded by the explanatory power of school quality (Heyneman and Loxley, 1983). These results suggested that when highly motivated, children from impoverished backgrounds can use the school system to overcome the exigencies of their social status.

The availability of additional cross national data in the late 1990s allowed several new analyses (Harris, 2007; Baker, Goesling, and LeTendre, 2003; Gameron and Long, 2006; Hayneman, 2005). These new analyses suggest that the "Heyneman-Loxley Effect" (low impact of social background and high impact of school quality in low-income countries and the reverse in high-income countries) continues. With respect to the modest impact of new resources on achievement (e.g., between 1970–1994), Austria increased real spending per pupil by 269 percent, but its math and science scores declined by 2.3 percent over the same time period. New Zealand increased its spending per pupil by 222 percent, yet its math and science scores declined by 9.7 percent (Figure 7.3.).

Estimates of the impact of school resources on achievement tend to be greater in developing countries than in the United States. For instance, teacher education is a positive and statistically significant predictor of student performance in 56 percent of the estimates for developing countries but in only 9 percent of those in the United States (see Figure 7.4). School resources is a positive and statistically significant predictor of math and science achievement in 65 percent of the studies conducted in developing countries but in only 9 percent of those conducted in the United States.[19]

The existence of new, high quality, international data sets continues to generate innovative hypotheses about the nature of American schooling. Some have combined the different data sets from school achievement (TIMSS and PISA) with adult literacy (IALS) and have begun to ask questions of new kinds. Might differing forms of social segregation in education (between and within schools and classrooms) be related to social gaps in adult literacy? Using social segregation within school systems, for instance, countries seem to fall into groups. The Nordic and East Asian nations have the lowest levels of social inequality in schools; English-speaking nations

	% Positive and Significant	
	United States[a]	Developing Countries[b]
Real Classroom Resources		
Pupil/Teacher Ratio (PTR)	14	27
Teacher Education	9	56
Teacher Experience	29	35
Financial Resources		
Teacher Salaries	20	31
Expenditures Per Pupil	27	50
Other		
Facilities	9	65

a. Based on 376 production function estimates.
b. Based on 96 production function estimates.

FIGURE 7.4 Effect of Key Resources on Student Performance.
Source: UNESCO (2004), *2005 EFA Monitoring Report: The Quality Imperative*. Paris: UNESCO, p. 65.

have a much greater level and German-speaking countries (Germany and Austria) have the highest level. Social segregation within school systems is associated with differences in adult literacy. Perhaps Germany's practice of segregating students into secondary schools with terminal functions (rare in Europe) helps explain the high levels of inequality in German adult literary (Green, Preston, and Janmaat, 2006, p. 125).

Some researchers have combined new international data sets on achievement with other sources of information on school curriculum and textbooks (Heyneman, 2006a). Mathematics textbooks and curricula today cover more topics and in more depth (Cummings, Knipe et. al., 2007). For many years, schools have emphasized higher order cognitive skills. Now it is being suggested that an emphasis on higher order cognitive skills has begun to boost average IQ scores. This suggests that the power of schools and of school systems to affect human behavior may have been underestimated (Cummings et. al., 2007).

Perhaps the biggest puzzle is not whether these new theories of school performance in an international context are necessarily correct, but rather how they have come to exist at all. How did the world go from a debate in 1933 over whether one could even count schools to a debate over the influences of schools into adulthood and across generations? The existence of new and improved statistics has facilitated new questions and new theories, and has justified the effort of the agencies and the individuals who have been involved.

EDUCATION OUTSIDE OF THE OECD COUNTRIES

Of the pupils enrolled in schools around the world, only 12 percent are enrolled in OECD countries. If high quality educational statistics were to be confined to OECD countries, 88 percent of the pupils and schools in the world would be left out.

The Role of UNESCO

Country-specific descriptive educational statistics are the responsibility of each Ministry of Education. The office of statistics in UNESCO circulates a template with instructions on their collection. It includes common definitions and suggests standards for quality control. These statistics are then published annually. The International Institute of Education Planning, a sub-unit of UNESCO, is responsible for training public officials in education planning including the application of UNESCO statistical templates. UNESCO receives data from each member state, and then has the responsibility to determine its accuracy. If the data appear to be below an acceptable standard, or if there are important questions about the data, UNESCO will inquire about its origins. In instances where corrections cannot be made or when the data appear to be particularly implausible, UNESCO reserves the right to not publish a country's statistics in its annual statistical yearbook.[20]

During the debt crises in the 1980s, the quality of schooling in low and in many middle income countries declined (Heyneman and Fuller, 1989).[21] The quality of education statistics also declined. Figures on rates of enrollment and on numbers of teachers became increasingly untrustworthy. The statistics division within UNESCO faced declining budgetary support and increasing difficulties monitoring the quality of statistics from low-income countries. When statistics of questionable quality were received, fewer professionals were available to intervene. The declining quality of education statistics began to hamper the ability of nations to accurately review their own priorities and the ability of international organizations to provide assistance (Heyneman, 1998, 1997a, 1997b). The mounting inadequacies in educational statistics stymied international cooperation by making it difficult to accurately identify the sources of problems and the means of amelioration (Heyneman, 1999, 1993a).

BICSE was constituted primarily to improve the comparability of the United States with other industrial democracies. But BICSE members became increasingly aware that American trade and social interests included Brazil, Russia, China, Indonesia, India, and many other countries which were not OECD members. Hence, it became necessary to extend the interests of BICSE to improving the quality of statistics in non-OECD countries. In an effort to become informed as to the current status of education statistics in UNESCO, a BICSE consultant (supported by the World Bank) argued that the decline in the quality of education statistics was a serious problem even to the United States (Puryear, 1995; Heyneman, 2003a).

The U.S. government was not a member of UNESCO, but it made informal contact,[22] and through BICSE, helped sponsor a specialized assessment of UNESCO's statistics capacity. The study was highly critical of UNESCO's handling of statistics, but was also careful to set out feasible organizational options to improve the situation (Guthrie and Hansen, 1995). These options were adopted by a special UNESCO commission chaired by Jo Ritzen, the Minister of Education from the Netherlands. The division of education statistics was reconfigured to become an independent institute, chaired by the ex-president of the British Statistical Association, staffed with newly acquired professionals, and relocated from Paris to Montreal. The improvement in UNESCO's statistics capacity in the interim has been significant (Brown and Micklewright, 2004; UNESCO, 2005a).

Despite this marked improvement in the professionalism of its publications (see for instance UNESCO, 2005a), the reconfiguration has not gone to the root of the problem, which is the poor state of education statistics generated by many of the countries themselves. Of the 196 countries reporting, 30 percent (59) did not have acceptable data on enrollment as recently as 1999. This includes 40 percent (18) of countries in Sub-Saharan Africa. When independent household surveys were employed to counter-check the accuracy of government enrollment statistics in Sub Saharan Africa 68 percent (17) were found to have significantly lower enrollment rates than were submitted, causing UNESCO to questions "the reality of enrollment statistics in a good number of countries" (UNESCO, 2002, p. 49).

Improving education statistics in low-income countries cannot be achieved through UNESCO alone. Precedent had been set by the speedy and effective collaboration within OECD countries. This experience might be useful more broadly.[23]

In 1996, the World Bank helped finance a program of collaboration between OECD and UNESCO. The result, called the World Education Indicators (WEI) Project, allowed non-OECD countries to develop indicators comparable to those of OECD countries. Many of the countries most eager to collaborate (Russia, China, Pakistan, India, Brazil, and Indonesia) were of such size that in 2002, the OECD publication *Education at a Glance* could claim to cover roughly two thirds of the world's population (OECD, 2002).

In the 1970s and 1980s, IEA surveys of academic achievement were greeted with skepticism by those in the international education community who worried that middle and low-income countries would not benefit from an academic Olympics. With the broadening of objectives and insights, and the creation of regional surveys of achievement, their hesitancy has been modified. Publications such as *Sub-Saharan Africa Regional Report* (UNESCO, 2001b) and *Latin America and the Caribbean Regional Report* (UNESCO, 2001a), and similar reports from the Southern and Eastern African Consortium for Monitoring Educational Quality (SACMEQ) have proved useful in assessing countries with financial and cultural similarities (Heyneman, 1993b). On reflection today, educational leaders from developing countries can see the advantages of having participated in international surveys of academic achievement (Brunner, 2005). In the future, an increasing variety of countries will likely participate in these surveys. International agencies are likely to continue to sponsor their regular participation.

Education-For-All

Among the more important international objectives has been the achievement of universal enrollment at least in primary school. Since the end of WWII, universal primary enrollment has been achieved in 85 countries, including most of Latin America, Europe and Central Asia, much of East Asia, and Iraq, Tunisia, Jordan, Algeria, Botswana, Gabon, Lesotho, South Africa, Swaziland, Togo, and Uganda (UNESCO, 2002, p. 46). Nine nations remain with gross enrollment rates below 70 percent, although there are many additional countries where recent data are not sufficient to determine enrollment rates. Despite significant progress, most countries fall short of the standard of universal completion of grade nine. In West and Central Africa and in South Asia about one third of the deficit in completion rates can be attributed to dropouts; in Central America and in Eastern and Southern Africa, dropouts constitute 70 percent of the missing completers; in Europe and Central Asia and in Latin American dropouts constitute 80 percent and 92 percent, respectively (Pritchett, 2004, p. 181). The remainder is accounted for by those who repeat.

The main problem is not lack of access to primary education but progress through the grades once access has been obtained. While some national school systems have been found to operate efficiently despite low levels of resources (Heyneman, 2004a), it is also the case that low resources often constitute the largest explanation for low achievement (Heyneman and Loxley, 1983). Low achievement is one cause of dropping out of school, and the differences from one school to another in available resources may be one of the principal causes of low achievement (Heyneman, 2004a).

Using newly available financial data from UNESCO, we have taken the level of expenditures on education as a percentage of gross domestic product (GDP) and the allocation to education (in $US). We divided the population of school age children by educational expenditures to find the expenditures for each school age person, and have ranged the countries by their place on a world spectrum (Figure 7.5).

Low-income countries are able to allocate to education only a small fraction of what a high-

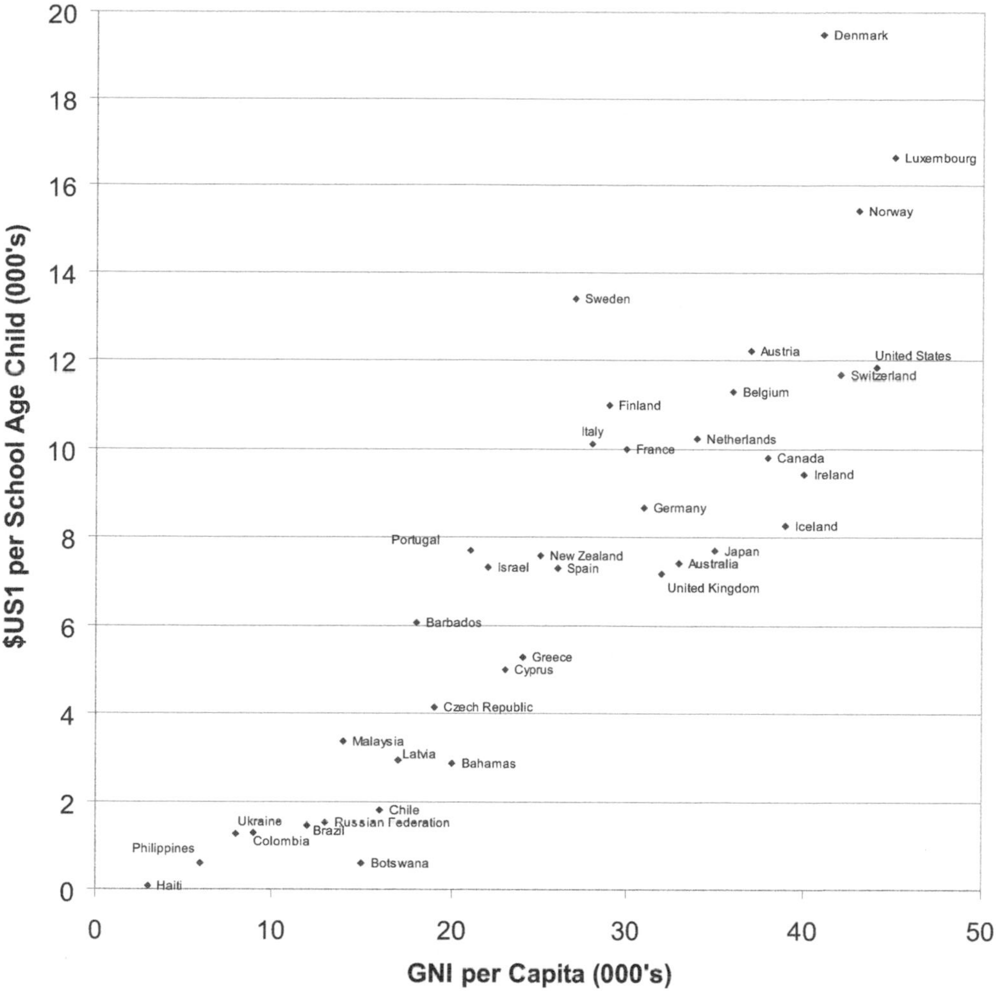

FIGURE 7.5 Equity of International Educational Resources.

income country might allocate. Bangladesh spends about $157/school age person/year. This compares unfavorably with Azerbaijan ($486), Brazil ($1450), and the Netherlands ($19,468). To mitigate this widespread inequality, the international community has declared that completion of basic education at a reasonable standard of quality is a fundamental right for all children. At a summit in Thailand in 1990, Education-For-All was adopted as a global priority.[24] Development assistance agencies and countries themselves were expected to allocate more resources to education and a higher percentage of education resources to basic education. Early in the 1990s, however, many scholars realized that the statistical capacity was too weak to monitor changes in basic education and that many of the Education-For-All objectives, such as achieving basic levels of literacy and numeracy, were simply impossible to prove (Bloom, 2005). This lack of direct proof stimulated UNESCO to create proxy measures of education progress (UNESCO, 2004, Appendix 1, p. 236).

Yet despite a weak statistical capacity, it was not a secret that the targets established in 1990 would not be reached (UNESCO, 2004, 2002; World Bank, 2005), and that new aims would have to be given. Debate ensued over how much Universal Basic Education would cost. UNESCO estimated that it would cost $US 4.3 billion (UNESCO, 2004, p. 136). UNICEF estimated that it would cost $US 4.9 billion (Heyneman, 2004c). The World Bank has estimated that it would cost $US 8.4 billion (World Bank, 2005). The difference among the estimates reflects differing positions regarding minimum per student expenditures, whether enrollment or completion is taken as the objective, whether only the 47 poorest or all developing countries are included, and whether special funds are set aside for AIDS orphans (Glewwe and Zhao, 2006).

The barrier to achieving Education-for-All objectives may have little to do with its cost and more to do with the political will of the participants. The portion of foreign aid allocated to education has not changed in two decades. It accounts for 6 percent of new commitments in USAID and 8 percent in the World Bank (Heyneman, 2006a). Some scholars suggest that the recipient countries have not reallocated public expenditures toward education in part because the opportunities for rent-seeking are fewer in education than in other sectors with more capital expenditures (Corrales, 2006).[25]

Role of the World Bank

Two factors have limited the World Bank since it began education lending. One was the use of manpower forecasting, which held an analytic monopoly between 1962 and 1980. Because justifications for public expenditures could only be made for vocational and technical education, the Bank confined lending to those areas. Primary education was largely excluded,[26] as was lending to improve the arts and sciences in tertiary education. Secondary education could be justified if the schools could be equipped with metal shops, wood shops and domestic science laboratories for girls. Although adding these facilities more than doubled the unit expenditures, these practical skills, it was argued, were necessary to offset the overemphasis on academic subjects which, according to Bank staff, led to educated unemployment (Heyneman, 2003b). The second handicap was the relative absence of experienced education staff. To alleviate this latter problem in 1977, the World Bank established the Education Finance Division in UNESCO with staff assigned to work on World Bank operations.[27]

Disagreements quickly emerged over issues of sector policy. As the designated education agency within the UN system, UNESCO argued that it alone should be responsible for education policy. Representatives to UNESCO were ministers of education. The Bank worried that UNESCO would advocate for education without sufficient emphasis on cost containment or efficiency. Representatives to the World Bank were ministers of finance. The Bank believed that its direct link to the financial ministries placed it in a better position to make economically feasible education policy. In the 1970s, the Bank began to acquire its own education policy staff and establish its own education sector policy.

Bank staff also came to recognize that the monopoly of manpower forecasting was creating distortions in the lending program. As a remedy, the Bank hired staff who understood the economic technique of rate-of-return analysis so that it could begin to integrate economic rates of return into its education sector work. Because this new technique utilized changes in monetary productivity, the benefits of education could be calculated for any level including primary education and not be confined to vocational or technical education. The changes in the Bank's methodologies, announced in the Education Policy Paper of 1980, allowed the Bank for the first time to include assistance to all levels of education and, theoretically, to any educational purpose whether vocational or academic. As a result, the Bank's analytic work led it to become a leader in the Rates of Return to Education studies.

The Bank's analyses have consistently found that the *public* Rates of Return to Education tend to be greatest for investments made in primary rather than higher education and for low-income countries (Psacharopoulos, Tan, and Jimenez, 1986; Psacharopoulos, 1994). This was the case in part because of the very low levels of investment in the quality of primary education. Based on these findings, the Bank began recommending that countries shift public expenditures from higher education to elementary education; that the private share of the costs for higher education should be increased; and that loans should be made available for those who cannot afford the newly increased fees (World Bank, 1995, 1994).

Many borrowing countries, particularly in Sub Saharan Africa, objected to the suggestion that they reduce public expenditures on higher education on the grounds that they would not be able to develop expertise in vital areas such as health, agricultural engineering, and general science, and would end up being continuously dependent upon the advice of those who share neither their culture nor the national priorities. As the use of RORE grew in importance, some researchers objected to the Bank's interpretations.[28] They argued that while there were numerous problems in the RORE calculations, the real issues lay in how the results were interpreted and how recommendations were made to countries. Low public returns to higher education might imply that the efficiency or quality of higher education should be improved. Instead of suggesting that the solution lay in a reduction of public expenditures, the solution may well lie in an increase in the effectiveness of public expenditures (Heyneman, 1995).[29] Some argued that economic returns are an ancillary result of education, and that the true returns come in other forms, such as social cohesion (Merrett, 1971; Heyneman, 2000).

These criticisms began to call into question the credibility of the Bank's analytic staff. In response, the Bank contracted an external panel of higher education experts to write a new report on higher education. This report concluded that the earlier interpretations had seriously underestimated the non-monetary benefits of higher education (Task Force on Higher Education and Society, 2000, 2004). Following the recommendations of the Task Force, the Bank began to incorporate non-monetary rationales into the deliberations over lending strategies, and now offers RORE as one among many sources of information as to how best to invest in education. The role or RORE in the Bank's lending policy is now to highlight potential problems, rather than to rigidly define priorities (Heyneman, 2003b).

The World Bank's owners insist on policy conditionality; hence conditioning lending on an efficient allocation of public expenditures is a normal Bank responsibility.[30] Policy conditionality may include environmental safeguards for a transport project or merit pay in an education project. Technical staff of the Bank believe the conditions are necessary for a successful investment. The problem is that investments have failed because the conditions, on hindsight, were based on false premises (Bennell, 1996; Colclough, 1996; Heyneman, 2003b, 2006b).

SUMMARY

Education finance would be remiss to forget either Piaget's caution or Dottrens' confidence toward international comparisons in education. Piaget was correct when he outlined the several obstacles to obtaining useful, comparable knowledge about education systems. But looking back, it is easy to see that his list of "obstacles" has functioned as a catalogue of challenges rather than a series of insurmountable impasses. The first of these accomplishments was the development of the International Standard Classification of Education (ISCED) in 1951, which ensured that all members of the international community had a commensurable set of definitions. With this conceptual groundwork laid, the next challenge was to create indicators which gave the clearest picture of, to paraphrase Dottrens, "what other countries were doing." In the 1970s, significant advancements were made in this area—for the first time, reliable measurements of education achievement and outcomes (and not just inputs) were included in international comparisons.

Since the 1970s, the refinement of measurements of outcomes has become the dominant interest in international comparative education. While the United States and other OECD countries have the longest history of measuring and comparing themselves, there has been a surge in participation by non-OECD countries as well. Much of this positive trend has been made possible by the influx of foreign aid. Yet, as Dollar and Pritchett show (1998), a disturbing portion of foreign aid has failed to yield significant improvements in recipient nations' ability to monitor their own education systems. The aspirations motivating Education-For-All offer hope that future findings will serve the international community just as well as Piaget's caution—as a list of goals to accomplish, rather than a series of excuses to abandon the comparative project.

Debates about the validity and purposes of cross-national statistics are a sign of a healthy research community. Governments, traders, and humanitarians will continue to pressure scholars to expand the breadth and depth of statistical projects throughout the world. If the past is any indicator of the future, the new theories and insights produced by this research will justify these efforts.

Important progress in the quality of education statistics has been made outside of OECD countries. The former Soviet Union, the countries of eastern and central Europe, and the emerging democracies in Latin American and Asia have demanded, and often achieved, equal partnership in cross-national educational exercises. Nevertheless, many important areas of the world have made little progress in their ability to gather and analyze important information about their own educational systems. The future dilemma is stark: will educational progress be left unmeasured or will these nations be supplied with the resources and the regulatory environment to join others in their cross-national efforts to monitor educational progress?

NOTES

1. Dottrens and Piaget were Swiss educational psychologists. Dotterns served on the Board of Directors of the International Bureau of Education (IBE); Piaget served as IBE's director for 40 years. The International Bureau of Education was founded in Geneva in 1925 as a non-governmental educational organization. In 1929 it allowed countries to join as members. Today, the IBE is a specialized agency within UNESCO.
2. The United States was represented on the IEA General Assembly by Richard Wolff of Teachers College, Columbia University.
3. There were three main concerns: the use of (1) academic achievement versus other dependent variables; (2) curriculum-based (IEA) studies of achievement versus census-based (ETS and OECD) studies of achievement; and (3) empirical as opposed to qualitative (video-taping) models of schooling.
4. Reasons for reluctance varied. They included a feeling of imposition from a well-funded dominant authority and a tendency to associate some educational policies which encourage competition with neo-liberal political views.
5. The most serious sanction was for a country to be left off of the official report, and allocated space "below the line" indicating that there were sufficient technical reasons to declare their results non-comparable. This sanction was enforced, for instance, in cases where sampling was not representative of the country.
6. The United States had withdrawn from UNESCO, the second international agency with an education statistics mandate.
7. The CERI is an advisory body for the education and labor branch of the OECD.
8. Personal communication with OECD officials in 1984.
9. When assessing U.S. policy trends, one common mistake of Europeans is to underestimate the importance of local officials in setting the national education agenda. The extent to which the U.S. president

can, without the support of local officials, set a national educational agenda, is less than in many European countries.

10. The publication *Education at a Glance* reports annually on trends in enrollment, finance, and changes in management structures across OECD countries.
11. From the beginning the IEA-sponsored studies were controlled by academics, not policy makers, hence IEA project managers felt that they could afford the time to gather information on a wide variety of influences on academic achievement. These included separate instruments for school principals, students and teachers; a separate analysis of school curriculum and (occasionally) cases studies of classroom pedagogy in each participating country.
12. Clare Burstall, Director of the National Foundation for Education Research in England and Wales (1983–1993), made this case to a meeting of the BICSE Board in Washington, D.C.
13. The UNESCO definition of literacy was vague and applied with unpredictable variation. As a result, for purposes of literacy statistics, the world had been divided into two groups: OECD and non-OECD (Heyneman, 1998).
14. Literacy was divided into five levels of proficiency, and countries were assessed by what percentage of the population had achieved levels five, four or three (the three top proficiency levels).
15. Current work includes the clarification of systems of pensions, student loans, interest payments, research and development and ancillary services (Charbonnier, 2005b).
16. Both scholars and politicians, however, had to acknowledge that the performance of American students relative to students in other industrialized democracies was considerably better in reading than it was in math and science (Elley, 1992).
17. This is not an irrational comparison. Minnesota for instance, has a population equivalent to Norway.
18. Educational disadvantage is a compendium of the percentage of children scoring below a fixed international benchmark in surveys of reading literacy of 15-year-olds, math and science literacy of 15-year-olds, and math and science eighth-grade achievement.
19. These comparisons do not account for the possibility that there may be variations in the quality of the studies.
20. This "right of refusal" is used by all UN statistical agencies with mixed success. When the Soviet Union dissolved, each of the 15 republics argued that their own definitions and calculations for current accounts and currency reserves were superior to those of the IMF. The IMF simply left blank the figures which were not calculated in accordance with their standards. Within a few years, all 15 republics had accepted the IMF guidelines. Leaving figures for a nation's education enrollment blank may not create the same problem as leaving blank the nation's statistics on current accounts or currency reserves.
21. In Latin America the 1980s are referred to as the "lost decade."
22. With expenses covered by the World Bank, Jeanne Griffith from the National Center for Education Statistics met with senior officials of UNESCO in Paris in the winter of 1994.
23. It is more complex and more difficult to achieve collaboration between international agencies than it is to achieve collaboration between different agencies, for instance, of the U.S. federal government.
24. The Education-For-All initiative was sponsored by UNESCO, UNDP, UNICEF, and the World Bank. The latter was a reluctant participant. Similar global conferences had been used to force countries and multilateral lending institutions into making financial commitments to special interests without consultation with fiscal authorities. In the case of Education-For-All, agreements were signed by Ministers of Education who have no fiscal authority. Hence, commitments involving a reallocation of public resources were null and void from the beginning. Also, see chapter by Fiske and Ladd in this volume.
25. "Rent seeking" in this case refers to the opportunity to use a government office to collect illegal fees or bribes ("rents"). It is argued that the opportunity to collect rents is higher in capital intensive sectors such as infrastructure rather than in the labor-intensive sectors such as education.
26. Exceptions were made for community primary schools equipped with facilities for community meetings and other facilities for adult education.
27. A similar cooperative program was established by the World Bank in the Food and Agricultural Organization (FAO).

28. See for instance: Barnett and Finnemore (1999), Bennell (1996), Colclough (1996), International Labor Office (1996), Carnoy (1995), Hinchliffe (1993), Biersteker (1992), Helleiner (1992), Colclough and Manor (1991), and Merrett (1971).
29. While public returns to investments in higher education were commonly lower than public returns to primary education, it was also common to find that private returns to higher education were lower than public returns because of the high public subsidies in higher education. In fact, higher education was often free of tuition whereas in primary education tuition was common.
30. The international development banks are owned by its member states. Countries own differing shares, much like a private equity company.

REFERENCES

Baker, D. P., Goesling, B., & LeTendre, G. (2003). Socioeconomic Status, School Quality and National Economic Development: A Cross-National Analysis of the 'Heyneman-Loxley' Effect. *Comparative Education Review, 46*(3), 291–313.

Baker, D. P., & LeTendre, G. (2005). *National Differences, Global Similarities: World Culture and the Future of Schooling*. Stanford, CA: Stanford University Press.

Baker, D. P. (1993). Compared to Japan, the U.S. is a low achiever, really. *Educational Researcher, 22*(3), 18–20.

Baker, D. P. (1997). Good News, Bad News, and International Comparisons: Comment on Bracey. *Educational Researcher, 26*(3), 16–17.

Barnett, M., & Finnemore, M. (1999). The Politics Power and Pathologies of International Organizations. *International Organization, 53,* 699–732.

Barro, S. M. (1996). *The International Education Expenditures Comparability Study* Washington D.C.: SMB Economic Research Incorporated (January).

Barro, S. M. (1998). *The Prospects for Developing Internationally Comparable Education Finance Statistics for Latin American Countries.* Washington, D.C.: SMB Economic Research Incorporated (March).

Beatty, A. (ed.) (1997). *Learning from TIMSS: Results of the Third International Mathematics and Science Study*. Washington, D.C.: National Academy Press.

Bennell, P. (1996). Using and Abusing rates of return: A critique of the World Bank's 1995 education sector review. *International Journal of Education Development, 16*, 235–248.

Biersteker, T. (1992). The Triumph of neoclassical economics in the developing world: policy convergence and the basis of governance in the international economic order. In J. Rosenau & E.O. Czempiel (Eds.), *Governance Without Government*. Cambridge: Cambridge University Press, 102–131.

Bloom, B. S. (1975). Implications of the IEA Studies for Curriculum and Instruction. In A. C. Purves & D. U. Levine (Eds.), *Educational Policy and International Assessment: Implications of the IEA Surveys of Achievement.* Berkeley: McCrutchan Publishing Corporation, 65–84.

Bloom, D. E. (2005). Global education: facts and data for measuring progress toward universal basic and secondary education. Paper prepared for the Project on Universal Basic and Secondary Education, Academy of Arts and Sciences, Cambridge, MA.

Bracey, G. W. (1996). International Comparisons and the Condition of American Education. *Educational Researcher*, *25*(1), 5–11.

Bradburn, N., & Gilford, D. M. (Eds.) (1990). *A Framework and Principles for International Comparative Studies in Education*. Washington, D.C.: National Academy Press.

Bradburn, N., Haertel, E., Schwille, J., & Torney-Purta, J. (1991). A Rejoinder to 'I never promised you first place'. *Phi Delta Kappan* (June), 774–777.

Brown, G., & Micklewright, J. (2004). *Using International Surveys of Achievement and Literacy: A View from the Outside*, Montreal: UNESCO Institute of Statistics.

Brunner, J. J. (2005). Comparative Research and Public Policy: From Authoritarianism to Democracy. *Peabody Journal of Education, 80*(1), 100–107.

Carnoy, M. (1995). Structural Adjustment and the Changing Face of Education. *International Labour Review, 134,* 653–673.

Charbonnier, E. (2005a). Trends in the Financing of Education. Presentation to the Annual Meeting of the American Education Finance Association. Louisville, Kentucky, (March).

Charbonnier, E. (2005b). OECD Initiatives to Improve International Comparison of Education Statistics. Presentation to the Annual Meeting of the American Education Finance Association. Louisville, Kentucky (March).

Chromy, R.R. (2002). Sampling issues in design, conduct and interpretation of international comparative studies of school achievement. In National Research Council (Ed.), *Methodological advances in cross-national surveys of educational achievement.* Washington, D.C.: National Academy Press, 80–117.

Colclough, C. (1996). Education and the Market: Which parts of the neo-liberal solution are correct. *World Development, 24,* 589–610.

Colclough, C., & Mannor, J. (1991). *States of Markets: Neo Liberalism and the Development Policy Debate.* Oxford: Clarendon Press.

Coleman, J. S., Campbell, E. Q., Hobart, C. J., McPartland, J., Mood, A. M., Weinfall, F., & York, R. F. (1966). *Equality of Educational Opportunity.* Washington D.C.: U.S. Government Printing Office, Department of Health, Education and Welfare.

Corrales, J. (2006). Political Obstacles to Expanding and Improving Schooling in Developing Countries. In J. E. Cohen, D. E. Bloom, & M. B. Malin (Eds.), *Educating All Children: A Global Agenda.* Boston: MIT Press, 231–303.

Cummings, E., Knipe, H., Collins, J., Baker, D., & Gamson, D. (2007). The Increasing Rigor of Elementary Mathematics Textbook Content During the Twentieth Century. Paper presented to the Annual Meeting of the American Education Research Association, Chicago (April).

Dollar, D., & Pritchett, L. (1998). *Assessing Foreign Aid: What Works and What Doesn't and Why.* New York: Oxford University Press.

Elley, W. (1992). *How in the World Do Students Read?* Hamburg (Germany): Grindeldruck GMBH.

Floden, R.E. (2002). The Measurement of the opportunity to learn. In National Research Council (Ed.), *Methodological advances in cross-national surveys of educational achievement.* Washington, D.C.: National Academy Press, 231–267.

Gamoran, A., & Long, D. (2006). Equality of Educational Opportunity: A 40 Year Perspective. Wisconsin Center for Education Research Working Paper no. 2006–9, Madison, Wisconsin.

Gilford, D. M. (Ed.) (1993). *A Collaborative Agenda for Improving International Comparative Studies in Education.* Washington, D.C.: National Academy Press.

Glewwe, P., & Zhao, M. (2006). The Cost of Providing Universal Basic Education by 2015: An Evaluation of Cost Estimates. In J. E. Cohen, D. E. Bloom, & M. B. Malin, (Eds.), *Educating all Children: A Global Agenda.* Boston: MIT Press, 415–495.

Goldstein, H. (1995). *Interpreting international comparisons of student achievement.* Paris: UNESCO.

Gonzales, P., Guzman, J., Partelow, L., Pahlke, E., Jocelyn, L., Kastberg, D., & Williams, T. (2004). *Highlights From the Trends in International Mathematics and Science Study: TIMSS 2003* Boston.: TIMSS & PIRLS International Study Center, Lynch School of Education, Boston College.

Green, A., Preston, J., & Janmaat, J. (2006). *Education, Equality and Social Cohesion: A Comparative Analysis.* Hampshire: Palgrave Macmillan.

Guthrie, J. W., & Hansen, J. S. (eds.) (1995). *World Wide Education Statistics: Enhancing UNESCO's Role.* Washington, D.C.: National Academy Press.

Harris, D. (2007). Diminishing Marginal Returns and the Production of Education: An International Analysis. *Education Economics* (Forthcoming).

Helleiner, G. (1992). The IMF, The World Bank, and Africa's Adjustment and external debt problems: An unofficial view. *World Development, 20,* 779–792.

Heyneman, S. P. (1993a). Educational Quality and the Crisis of Education Research. *International Review of Education, 39*(6), 511–517.

Heyneman, S. P. (1993b). Comparative Education: Issues of Quantity, Quality and Source. *Comparative Education Review, 37* (November), 372–388.

Heyneman, S. P. (1995). The Economics of Education: Disappointments and Potential. *UNESCO Prospects XXV* (4) (December), 559–583.
Heyneman, S. P. (1997a). The Quality of Education in the Middle East and North Africa. *International Journal of Education Development, 17*(4), 449–466.
Heyneman, S. P. (1997b). Economic Development and the International Trade in Education Reform. *UNESCO Prospects, XXVII* (4) (December), 501–531.
Heyneman, S. P. (1998). Educational Cooperation Between Nations for the 21st Century, in J. Delors (Ed.) *Education for the Twenty-First Century: Issues and Prospects*. Paris: UNESCO.
Heyneman, S. P. (1999). The Sad Story of UNESCO's Education Statistics. *International Journal of Education Development, 19*(January), 65–74.
Heyneman, S. P. (2000). From the Party/State to Multi-Ethnic Democracy: Education and Social Cohesion in the Europe and Central Asia Region. *Educational Evaluation and Policy Analysis, 21*(4) (Summer), 173–191.
Heyneman, S. P. (2003a). What the United States Needs to Learn from UNESCO. *UNESCO Prospects, XXXIII* (1) (March),7–11.
Heyneman, S. P. (2003b). The History and Problems of making Education Policy at the World Bank 1960–2000. *International Journal of Education Development, 23*, 315–337.
Heyneman, S. P. (2004a). International Education Quality. *Economics of Education Review, 23,* 441–452.
Heyneman, S. P. (2004b). The Use of Cross-National Comparisons for Local Education Policy. *Curriculum Inquiry, 34*(3), 345–352.
Heyneman, S. P. (2004c). On the International Dimension of Education and Social Justice. *Journal of Education* (Boston University), *185*(3), 83–103.
Heyneman, S. P. (2005). Student Background and Student Achievement: What is the Right Question? *American Journal of Education, 112* (November), 1–9.
Heyneman, S. P. (2006a). The Effectiveness of Development Assistance in Education: An Organizational Analysis. *Journal of International Cooperation in Education* (Hiroshima), *9*(1), 7–25.
Heyneman, S. P. (2006b). The Use of Textbooks in a Modern Education System. In C. B. Bralavsky (Ed.), *Textbooks and Quality Learning for All: Some Lessons Learned from International Experiences*. Geneva: UNESCO?International Bureau of Education.
Heyneman, S. P. & Loxley, W. (1983). The Effect of Primary School Quality on Academic Achievement in Twenty-Nine High- and Low-Income Countries. *American Journal of Sociology, 88*(6) (May), 1162–1194.
Heyneman, S. P. & Fuller, B. (1989). Third World School Quality: Current Collapse, Future Potential. *Educational Researcher 18*(2) (March), 12–19.
Hinchcliffe, K. (1993). Neo-liberal prescriptions for education finance: unfortunately necessary or inherently desirable? *International Journal of Education Development, 13,* 183–187.
Horvitz, D. (1992). Improving the quality of international education surveys. Draft prepared for the Board on International Comparative Studies in Education. Washington, D.C.: National Research Council.
Ilon, L. (2002). Agent of Global Markets or Agent of the Poor? The World Bank's Education Sector Strategy Paper. *International Journal of Education Development, 22*(5), 475–483.
International Association for the Evaluation of Education Achievement (IEA). (1973). *Science Education in 19 Countries: An empirical Study*. Stockholm: IEA.
IEA. (1975). *Civic Education in Ten Countries, an Empirical Study*. Stockholm: IEA.
IEA. (1976). *The IEA Six Subject Survey: An Empirical Study of Education in 21 Countries*. Stockholm: IEA.
IEA. (1990). *Thirty Years of International Research: An Annotated Bibliography of IEA Publications (1960–1990).* Netherlands: IEA.
IEA. (1992a). *Computers in American Schools, 1992 An Overview*. Minneapolis: University of Minnesota, Department of Sociology.
IEA. (1992b). *How in the World Do Students Read? IEA Study of Reading Literacy*. Netherlands: IEA.
IEA. (1993). *Schools, Teachers, Students and Computers: A Cross National Perspective*. Netherlands: IEA.

IEA. (2001). *Citizenship and Education in 28 Countries: Civic Knowledge and Engagement at Age Fourteen*. Netherlands: IEA.

International Assessment of Educational Progress (1991). *The 1991 IAEP Assessment: Objectives for Mathematics, Science and Geography*. Princeton: Center for the Assessment of Educational Progress, Educational Testing Service.

International Labor Office (1996). *Impact of Structural Adjustment on the Employment and Training of Teachers*. Geneva: International Labor Office.

Jencks, C., Smith, M., Ackland, H., Bane, M. J., Cohen, D., Gintis, H., Heyns, B., & Michelson, S. (1972). *Inequality: A Reassessment of the Effect of Family and Schooling in America*. New York: Basic Books.

Linn, R. L. (2002). The Measurement of student achievement in international studies. In National Research Council (Ed.), *Methodological advances in cross-national surveys of educational achievement*. Washington D.C.: National Academy Press.

Martin, M., Gregory, K., & Stemler, S. (1999). TIMSS Technical Report. Boston International Study Center.

Medrich, E. A. & J. E. Griffith (1992). *International mathematics and science assessments: What have we learned*? Washington D.C.: U.S. Department of Education, Office of Educational Research and Improvement.

Merrett, S. (1971). Rate of Return to Education: A Critique. In R. Wykstra (Ed.), *Education and the Economics of Human Capital*. New York: Free Press, 196–213.

National Center for Education Statistics. (1996). *Education in States and Nations: Indicators Comparing U. S. States with Other Industrialized Countries in 1991*. Washington, D.C.: U.S. Department of Education.

National Commission on Excellence in Education. (1983). *A Nation at Risk: The imperative on education reform*. Washington, D.C.: U.S. Government Printing Office

National Research Council. (1995). International *Comparative Studies in Education: Descriptions of Selected Large-Scale Assessments and Case Studies*. Washington D.C.: National Academy Press.

National Research Council. (1999). Next Steps for TIMSS: Directions for secondary analysis. Washington, D.C.: National Academy Press.

National Research Council. (2002). *Understanding Others, Educating Ourselves: Getting More from International Comparative Studies in Education*. Washington, D.C.: National Academy Press.

Organization for Economic Cooperation and Development (OECD). (2002). *Education at a Glance 2002*. Paris: OECD.

OECD. (2004a). *Learning for Tomorrow's World: First Results from PISA 2003*. Paris: OECD.

OECD. (2004b). *Problem Solving for Tomorrow's World: First Measures of Cross-Curricular Competencies from PISA 2003*. Paris: OECD.

OECD. (2005). *Literacy, Economy and Society: Results of the First International Adult Literacy Survey*. Ottawa: OECD.

Olkin, I., & Searls, D.T. (1985). Statistical aspects of international assessments of science and education. Paper presented at the conference on Statistical Standards for International Assessments in Pre-College Science and Mathematics,Washington, D.C.

Peak, L. (1996). *Pursuing Excellence: A Study of Eighth-Grade Mathematics and Science Teaching, Learning, Curriculum and Achievement in International Context: Initial Findings for the Third International Mathematics and Science Study*. Washington, D.C.: National Center for Educational Statistics.

Peak, L. (1997). *Pursuing Excellence: A Study of U.S. Fourth-Grade Mathematics and Science Achievement in International Context: Initial Findings for the Third International Mathematics and Science Study*. Washington, D.C.: National Center for Education Statistics.

Phillips, D. (Ed.) (1991). *Lessons of Cross-National Comparisons of Education*. Oxford Studies in Comparative Education. Wallingford: Triangle Books Ltd.

Platt, W. J. (1975). Policy Making and International Studies in Educational Evaluation. In A. C. Purves & D. U. Levine (Eds.), *Educational Policy and International Assessment: Implications of the IEA Surveys of Achievement*. Berkeley, CA: McCrutchan Publishing Corporation, 33–59.

Postlewaite, N. (1975). The Surveys of the International Association for the Evaluation of Educational Achievement (IES). In A. C. Purves & D. U. Levine (Eds.), *Educational Policy and International*

Assessment: Implications of the IEA Surveys of Achievement. Berkeley, CA: McCrutchan Publishing Corporation, 1–33.
Postlewaite, N. (1999). *International Studies of academic achievement: Methodological Issues* Hong Kong: University of Hong Kong.
Pritchett, L. (2004). Access to Education. In A. M. Levine & M. J. Bane (Eds.), *Global Crisis, Global Solutions*. Cambridge: Cambridge University Press, 252–276.
Psacharopoulos, G. (1994). Returns to investment in education: a global update. *World Development, 22*(9), 1325–1343.
Psacharopoulos, G., Tan, J.P., & Jiminez, E. (1986). Financing Education in Developing Countries: An Exploration of Policy Options. Washington, D.C.: The World Bank.
Puryear, J.M. (1995). International Education Statistics and Research: Status and Problems. *International Journal of Education Development, 15*(1), 79–91.
Purves, A. C. & Levine, D. U. (Eds.) (1975). *Educational Policy and International Assessment: Implications of the IEA Surveys of Achievement.* Berkeley, CA: McCutchan Publishing Corporation.
Ravitch, D. (Ed.) (2003). *Brookings Papers on Education Policy.* Washington, D.C.: The Brookings Institution.
Rotberg, I. (1990). I Never Promised you First Place. *Phi Delta Kappan* (December), 296–303.
Rowen, B. (2002). Large-scale, cross-national surveys of educational achievement: Promises Pitfalls and possibilities. In A. C. Purves & D. U. Levine (Eds.), *Educational Policy and International Assessment: Implications of the IEA Surveys of Achievement.* Berkeley: McCrutchan Publishing Corporation, 321–353.
Schmidt, W., McKnight, C., & Raizen, S. (1997). *A Splintered Vision: An Investigation of U.S. Science and Mathematics Education.* Lansing, MI: National Research Center for the Third International Mathematics and Science Study, Michigan State University.
Sherman, J. D. (1981). Federal Education Policy in Australia: Implications for the U.S. School Finance project working paper. Washington, D.C.: National Institute of Education, (March).
Sherman, J. D. (1982). Public Finance of Private Schools: Observations from Abroad. Stanford Institute for Research on Educational Finance and Governance. Stanford, CA: Stanford University.
Smith, M.S. (2002). Drawing inferences for national policy from large-scale cross national education surveys. In National Research Council (Ed.), *Methodological advances in cross-national surveys of educational achievement*. Washington, D.C.: National Academy Press, 251–321.
Smyth, J. (1996). The Origins, Purposes and Scope of the International Standard Classification of Education. Paper submitted to the ISCED-revision task force. Paris: UNESCO (February) (Mimeographed).
Smyth, J. (2005). UNESCO's International Literacy Statistics 1950–2000. Paris: Mimeographed, 15.
Task Force on Higher Education and Society. (2000). *Higher Education In Developing Countries: Perils and Promise.* Washington, D.C.: The World Bank.
Task Force on Higher Education and Society. (2004). Moderated Discussion: The Task Force on Higher Education and Society. *Comparative Education Review, 48*(1), 70–88.
Thorndike, R. L. (1975). The Relation of School Achievement to Differences in the Backgrounds of Children. In A. C. Purves & D. U. Levine (Eds.), *Educational Policy and International Assessment: Implications of the IEA Surveys of Achievement.* Berkeley, CA: McCrutchan Publishing Corporation, 93–104.
Tomlinson, T., & Tuijnman, A. (eds.) (1994). *Education Research and Reform: An International Perspective.* Washington, D.C.: U. S. Department of Education.
UNICEF. (2002). *A League Table of Educational Disadvantage in Rich Nations.* Innocenti Report Card Issue 4 (November). Florence, Italy.
United Nations Education, Scientific and Cultural Organization (UNESCO). (1955). *World Survey of Education, Volume I: Educational Organization and Statistics.* Paris: UNESCO.
UNESCO. (1958). *World Survey of Education, Volume II: Primary Education.* Paris: UNESCO.
UNESCO. (1961). *World Survey of Education, Volume III: Secondary Education.* Paris: UNESCO.
UNESCO. (1966). *World Survey of Education, Volume IV: Higher Education.* Paris: UNESCO.
UNESCO. (1971). *World Survey of Education, Volume V: Educational Policy, Legislation and Administration Education.* Paris: UNESCO.

UNESCO. (2001a). *Latin American and the Caribbean Regional Report.* Paris: UNESCO.
UNESCO. (2001b). *Sub-Saharan Africa Regional Report.* Paris: UNESCO.
UNESCO. (2002). *Education for All: Global Monitoring Report 2002.* Paris: UNESCO.
UNESCO. (2004). *Education for All: Is the World on Track?* Paris: UNESCO.
UNESCO. (2005a). *Global Education Digest 2005. Comparing Education Statistics across the World.* Montreal: UNESCO Institute of Statistics.
UNESCO. (2005b). *EFA Global Monitoring Report 2005: The Quality Imperative.* Montreal: UNESCO.
Vinovskis, M. A. (1999). *The Road to Charlottesville: The 1989 Education Summit.* Washington, D.C. National Goals Panel.
World Bank. (1994). *Higher Education: The Lessons of Experience.* Washington, D.C.: The World Bank
World Bank. (1995). *Priorities and Strategies for Education.* Washington D.C.: The World Bank.
World Bank. (2005). *Achieving Education for All by 2015. Simulation Results for 47 Low-Income Countries.* Washington, D.C.: World Bank.

II

MAKING MONEY MATTER

Section Editors

Jennifer King Rice and Amy Ellen Schwartz

8

Toward an Understanding of Productivity in Education

Jennifer King Rice and Amy Ellen Schwartz

The growing national interest in the academic performance of public school students has heightened interest in understanding how schools, teachers, and other educational resources can be marshaled to improve student performance. Because the public demand for improved public school outcomes is not matched by a similar willingness to increase spending, there is considerable interest in increasing the bang we get for the public education buck or, put differently, in increasing the productivity of public schools and educational institutions in the United States.

Determining the level of funding needed to accomplish our educational goals has become a central focus of the policy debate in education. Some contend that schools can "do better" by using resources more effectively say, by moving school personnel out of administrative positions and into classrooms, or by focusing curricula on academic fundamentals like reading and mathematics rather than arts or physical education. Others argue that better performance requires additional resources to decrease class size, attract more qualified teachers, or provide teacher professional development. Public pressures have spawned a plethora of research examining the relationship between educational resources and student performance, shedding light on the production of education and, at the same time, highlighting substantial gaps in our knowledge. Can we increase test scores by reducing class size? Would it be better (or cheaper) to increase the number of teacher aides instead? Should we invest in professional development for teachers or lengthen the school day (or year)? These are, essentially, questions about the productivity of school resources.

Borrowing from the economics of manufacturing, research on productivity in education often focuses on estimating an "education production function" that links school inputs to educational outcomes and identifies the impact of changes in inputs (e.g., teachers) on student outcomes (e.g., achievement as measured by test scores). While the application of economic tools has been fruitful, understanding the productivity of schools is considerably more complicated than the relatively simple analogy to manufacturing suggests. In manufacturing, "productivity" is typically defined and measured as the amount of output produced per unit of input used. This seemingly straightforward concept is riddled with complexities when applied to education. For instance, questions surround the appropriate outputs of education. What should schools produce and how should we measure the quality and quantity of the "product"? Should we focus on basic functional competencies or critical thinking skills? Will standardized tests suffice to measure progress and if so, what sort of tests? What about civic responsibility, economic self-sufficiency, cultural awareness, and social and economic mobility? How do we account for those outcomes? Answering these questions extends well beyond the domain of research and requires a broader social consensus on the fundamental goals of public education. The absence of such a consensus complicates the measurement of productivity in education.

Identifying and measuring inputs is equally challenging. What are the inputs to the production of education? The spectrum of educational resources or inputs is wide and varied across communities. While purchased inputs, such as teachers, school buildings, or books are easily identified, non-purchased inputs, including donated goods and services, are less obvious but no less critical to student success.

Of course, measuring inputs and outputs is only the first step in understanding the factors that drive differences in productivity across schools and school districts and, ultimately, identifying ways to make improvements. Put differently, researchers aim to peek inside the "black box" of education and examine the technology of production to understand what schools *do* with their resources, how these choices influence the relationships between inputs and outputs and, ultimately, what changes can be made to improve that relationship. Thus, research on productivity in education might consider the implications of different choices related to curriculum (e.g. whole language vs. phonics), the organization of schools (e.g., K–8 or K–5 and 6–8), the size of schools and classes, policies toward teachers (e.g., hiring, tenure, and compensation policies), and so on. As might be expected, operationalizing these constructs and developing appropriate measures to study them present theoretical and empirical challenges.

Finally, researchers have struggled with understanding the role that students themselves play in the production process. Clearly, student differences in ability, level of motivation, and aspirations are important determinants of educational outcomes. These student characteristics may be shaped by school policies or programs at the same time that they influence the kinds of policies or programs that the schools adopt. Thus, disentangling the causal pathways that link resources to outcomes is complicated by the responses of students (and parents, teachers, and others) in ways that may complement or hinder the intentions of school policies.

The goal of this chapter is to describe and discuss the theoretical foundations and empirical contributions of research on productivity in education. We aim to provide a sense of the depth and breadth, the complexity and challenges of this field of research. At the outset, we recognize that "productivity" means different things to different people, and we describe some of the research traditions that have examined the relationship between educational resources and student outcomes. In the section that follows, we narrow our discussion to the economist's notion of the education production function, and discuss the key empirical debates and conceptual issues. We conclude with a discussion of the role of research on productivity in education in supporting multiple, competing social goals of public education in the United States.

CHARACTERIZING THE RESEARCH ON PRODUCTIVITY IN EDUCATION

The concept of productivity in education has various meanings but is fundamentally concerned with the quantity and quality of educational outcomes that result from a given investment of resources. While research on productivity is often considered to be part of the discipline of economics, scholars from multiple research traditions have used a range of methods to study various questions concerning the relationship between inputs and outcomes in education. These methods often involve trade-offs between the generalizability offered by large-scale quantitative studies and the in-depth context-specific findings of smaller scale qualitative research. From a methodological perspective, the most promising approach may involve mixed-methods where complementary approaches compensate for the weaknesses inherent in each (Rice, 2001). Ladd and Hansen (1999, p. 139–140) offer three "lenses" to characterize this "large and unwieldy body of research" (Monk, 1990, p. 315).

First, the institutional perspective on schools and educational productivity includes studies that examine how broad education policies can influence the will and capacity of schools to use their resources more productively. Much policy interest has been paid to the possibility of improving outcomes by intensifying the "pressure" placed on schools and school districts through incentives embedded in standards-based accountability and market-based reforms. High stakes accountability policies that rely heavily on student testing to promote better performance within traditional public education systems have become pervasive across education systems throughout the nation. These systems often link the results of standardized tests to sanctions or rewards for schools and school personnel. The underlying logic is that such systems improve outcomes by inducing schools to eliminate waste which may arise because of malfeasance, lethargy, or ineptitude (of myriad kinds); because the absence of clear standards have led to a misalignment between the goals of the schools and the state; or because innovative educators have not been motivated to find new and better ways to accomplish those goals.[1] In 2002, the No Child Left Behind Act made such a system national, but many states had enacted some sort of accountability system prior to that year, providing researchers the opportunity to gain insight into the effectiveness of these reforms. While theory suggests that strengthened incentives in high stakes accountability systems leads to improved performance (Hanushek, 1994; Koretz, 1996), the effectiveness of these policies depends on a number of design elements including the measurement of school performance, the treatment of highly mobile and disabled students, the assessment of student subgroups within schools, the accountability time period, and the breadth and focus of the accountability system (Figlio & Ladd, this volume).

Another institutional approach aimed at improving productivity is to introduce market-based reforms that expand the choices of students and families beyond traditional public education systems. Market-based reforms increase competition for students between schools and create incentives for schools to increase performance to attract more and/or better students and the funds they bring to the school. Theoretically, market-based reforms also free schools from the bureaucratic demands of a public system, allowing them to be more innovative and productive. These options—including charter schools, public funding for private schools, and private management of public schools—are sometimes components of high stakes accountability policies, so the two approaches are not mutually exclusive. Theories about the power of markets to improve school performance date to the 1950's arguments advanced by Milton Friedman. Despite the promising theoretical basis for market-based reforms as a mechanism for improving productivity (Friedman, 2002), research indicates that the effectiveness of these strategies is contingent on a range of design factors. Perhaps most important are the effects of these policies on conventional public schools and on the broad set of purposes for public education. Existing research suggests cautious optimism (Gill & Booker, this volume).

A second lens for viewing the relationship between education resources and outcomes are studies of educational practices. Studies of educational practices look inside the "black box" (Ladd & Hansen, 1999; Rice, 2001) to examine the inner workings of schools and school systems with the goal of identifying the organizational conditions, educational resources, and instructional strategies associated with high performance. Anthropologists, sociologists, psychologists, and others have used a range of research traditions to empirically identify factors associated with effective schools that might be replicated in other environments to improve performance. These studies—often characterized as school effects studies, process-product studies, and outlier studies—employ qualitative and quantitative methods to identify key factors associated with higher-than-expected performance, given the demographic characteristics of the school. Often focusing on urban contexts, researchers select schools serving similar student populations, but differing significantly in student achievement, with the goal of identifying characteristics that distinguish effective from ineffective schools (e.g., Brookover et al., 1979; Edmonds, 1981). Taken together, this body of research has generated a five-factor model of effective schools: strong building leadership, shared instructional focus, safe and orderly school climate, high expectations for student learning, and data-based decision making (Edmonds, 1979, 1981). While this model was influential in education policy and reform efforts in the 1980s (Teddlie & Stringfield, 1991; General Accounting Office, 1989), scholars have identified a number of limitations associated with this body of work including limited independent variables, concerns about the validity of outcome measures, instability of effects over time, lack of attention to contextual factors, and a heavy reliance on student and teacher perceptions (Good & Brophy, 1986; Purkey & Smith, 1983).

More recent studies of educational practices focus on approaches to school reform that are consistent with key principles emerging from this body of research, such as the importance of high standards for all students, the need for good curriculum and teaching, and the role of school staff in school improvement efforts (Smith, et al., 1996). Following years of top-down reform efforts, education policies based on effective schools research emphasized schools as the unit of change (Tyack & Cuban, 1995). For instance, school-based management (Malen, Ogawa, & Kranz, 1990; Tyack, 1993; Wohlstetter & Odden, 1992) that prioritizes school-level decision making, and whole school reform models (Wong & Wang, 2002) that emphasize the school as the unit for comprehensive reform became popular strategies. However, studies examining the effectiveness of these approaches were undermined by uneven implementation, insufficient data and methods of analysis, and the lack of attention to contextual factors (Summers & Johnson, 1996; Bodilly, 1998; Wong & Wang, 2002). Further, the effects of these reforms need to be considered in light of their costs to make determinations about productivity (Rice, 2002).

The third lens, input-output research, aims to isolate a causal relationship between school resources and student outcomes, usually measured by test scores. This line of research dates back to the 1966 Equality of Educational Opportunity Study, which concluded that schools have little influence on student achievement, independent of family background (Coleman, et al., 1966). With the availability of better data systems and the development of more sophisticated analytic methods, the past four decades have seen these studies evolve into increasingly sophisticated statistical analyses known as education production function research. While this research has examined the impact of multiple resources (e.g., school facilities, computers, and technology), much of the research in this area has focused on teachers, both their quality and their quantity, which fundamentally determines class size. In the next section we discuss the research on the education production function, highlighting the critical conceptual issues, the key empirical findings, and the contentious debates that have surrounded this field of research.

THE EDUCATION PRODUCTION FUNCTION

Education production functions have been used to address a set of fairly straightforward policy questions:

- How much will outcomes increase if we increase resources by some amount? (e.g., how much will test scores increase if we decrease class size by ten percent?)

- Can schools deliver better outcomes with existing resources or will better outcomes require more resources? (e.g., can we increase performance by eliminating waste or improving efficiency?)
- How much more will it cost to increase outcomes by a desired amount or to a desired level? (e.g., what will it cost to meet standards on state proficiency tests?)

Answering these questions requires an understanding of the production "process"—the inputs and outputs and the relationship between them—and also an understanding of the prices that schools must pay for these inputs (e.g., teacher salaries) and the extent to which schools (or school personnel) are "wasteful" or "inefficient." We begin with a discussion of outputs in education and turn quickly to our central concerns—defining and measuring school inputs; inefficiency and waste; and a more formal mathematical presentation of the production function. We conclude with discussion of productivity and social values.

School Outputs

The starting point for any study of productivity in education is the definition and measurement of outcomes. In general, purposes of education are to produce individuals who can contribute to the economic, political, civic, social, and cultural institutions in our society. As such, we expect high school graduates to have acquired a wide range of competencies, skills, and personal qualities. These ideas are consistent with those of early proponents of public education including Horace Mann and Thomas Jefferson (Rothstein, this volume). Further, they reflect international efforts to identify the array of "key competencies that contribute to a successful life and a well-functioning society" (Rychen & Salganik, 2003). Research on the productivity of education resources, however, typically focuses on a narrow set of measures driven, in large part, by the quantity, accessibility, and quality of available data.

Some studies estimate the effect of education investments on long-term *outcomes* like employment and earnings (e.g., Betts, 1996; Bishop, 1991; Card & Krueger, 1996) and civic participation (Dee, 2004). Using earnings as the outcome has a particular appeal because it delivers an estimate of the impact of education resources that is denominated in dollars, making it easy to estimate the rate of the return on the investment, which then can be compared with the rates of return associated with other sorts of public investments (e.g., health care, social services). The difficulty with using earnings, or any distal outcome measure, however, lies in the challenges of isolating the specific effect of the public school from other factors, like labor market conditions or the availability of college opportunities that may shape these outcomes in the time between graduation from public school and the measurement of the outcome.

The more typical alternative is to focus on shorter-term *outputs* like student achievement measures (generally in math and reading for elementary schools or math and science for high school) and high school graduation rates. While this set of commonly used output measures reflects a narrow view of the broad range of purposes for public education, these measures are consistent with the current emphasis of accountability systems on student test scores (also see Rothstein, this volume). And, although there continues to be some policy interest in understanding test score *levels*, measuring educational output requires controlling, in some way, for the student's prior educational performance or attainment. One way to estimate the value added by a particular resource to student performance is to measure output as the gain in student performance (that is, the increase in test scores between years). An alternative is to include prior performance as a control variable in regression analysis, which is particularly attractive for studies that focus on non-test score outcomes such as graduation rates.

School Inputs

As described earlier, education output reflects not only the impacts of school inputs but also the influences of families, communities, and individuals. Consequently, isolating the specific contributions of school inputs such as class size, teachers, or computers—the focus of much research on productivity in education—requires accounting for the contributions of peers, family and communities. These outside-of-school influences are interesting and important in their own right and a significant body of research examines the impact of home or community based inputs including health care, parenting practices, and home environment on outcomes. (See Rothstein 2006 for a discussion of the role of these factors as determinants of student performance.) That said, most of the policy research—and the policy debate—focuses on school inputs since the public sector bears much of the responsibility for ensuring equity and efficiency in provision, and it wields considerable power in determining those inputs. Thus, while family practices undoubtedly shape student performance, school districts have little ability to influence out-of-school practices and have much wider latitude in changing school inputs.

Notice that school inputs into the education process include a wide range of resources, both purchased and donated—teachers, guidance counselors, school buildings, buses, books, computers, paper, and so on—and there is wide variation in the quality and character of these inputs. Thus, measuring the quantity and quality of inputs can be difficult and, as a result, data of this kind are relatively scarce. Consequently, many researchers have relied upon spending data, which can be viewed as providing a summary measure of the amount of inputs used, and which easily yields estimates of the improvements associated with each dollar spent.[2]

For a variety of reasons, however, measures of spending fall short of representing the quantity and quality of resources that students actually receive. As a result, studies examining the effect of per pupil expenditures on student performance and eventual labor market outcomes, taken together, have been frustratingly inconsistent in their findings. While Hanushek (1986) finds little consistent evidence that school expenditures have a statistically (much less substantively) significant impact on test scores, Hedges, Laine, and Greenwald (1994) are more sanguine in their reading of the evidence, finding that spending may, in contrast, be important. By calling into questions Hanushek's "vote-counting" methodology of tabulating research findings, Krueger (2002) demonstrates that other approaches to weighting studies lead to a more consistent and positive story about the effect of resources on student achievement.[3] Despite the intense policy debates and considerable heat generated about whether or how much "money matters," few people would argue that money *never* matters. For instance, it is hard to imagine that anyone would argue seriously that cutting spending back by fifty or seventy five percent would have no impact on educational outcomes. On the other hand, it is equally hard to imagine a serious argument that money *is always* the answer or that doubling spending would be expected to double outputs.

Ultimately, the failure to reach consensus may reflect inadequacy in the framing of the question. As described above, the relationship between dollars expended and output realized is not direct. Instead, money "matters" because (or to the extent that) it changes the quantity and/or quality of inputs used in the production of education. Thus, recent research has moved away from examining the level of spending to focus on understanding the impact of *what* the money buys (e.g. school buildings, school leadership, instructional resources, computers, teachers) and on understanding why (or how) *prices or costs vary.* Much of this work focuses on three key determinants of school spending and outcomes: class size, teacher qualifications, and teacher salaries.

While debate continues, new evidence on the impact of class size and teacher quality on student performance is mounting and consensus may be emerging. New methods yield increasingly convincing evidence that class size matters, improving upon existing studies which had largely relied upon the variations in class sizes across schools in U.S. districts to estimate the impacts. Angrist and Lavy (1999) investigated this issue using data on Israeli public schools where significant differences in class sizes emerge because of small, essentially random, differences in the number of students in a grade; maximum class size is 40 students. These researchers found significant and substantial increases in test scores of reducing class size. Equally important has been the evidence from the Tennessee STAR class size experiment. Researchers randomly assigned students and teachers in grades K–3 to small classes (13–17 students), regular classes (22–26 students), or regular classes with a full-time teacher's aide in addition to the classroom teacher to study the effect of the assignment on student test scores. This sort of randomized experiment has been heralded by some as the "gold standard" of social science methods.

Despite the hope that the STAR experiment would settle the class size debate, controversy has surrounded the interpretation of the STAR results. Many interpret the results as indicating a positive effect of reducing class size (see Finn & Achilles,1999; Nye, Hedges, & Konstantopolous, 1999). Hanushek (1999) is unpersuaded, arguing that the implementation of the experiment was flawed—leading to unmeasured differences between the students in small and large classes, for example—and that no significant impact of reduced class size is demonstrated. That said, Hanushek (2002) acknowledges that "class size reductions are beneficial in specific circumstances—for specific groups of students, subject matters, and teachers" (p. 38). At the same time, there is a growing recognition that class size reduction is not a 'magic bullet' for improving academic performance. As demonstrated by California's large scale class size reduction initiative, reducing class size requires an increase in the need for teachers (and classroom space), which may carry unintended consequences for schools, even while test scores may rise overall (Jepsen & Rivkin, 2002). Thus, while the class size debate continues, it seems to have become more nuanced, focusing on when, where, and for whom class size reduction makes most sense. (See chapters by Krueger, Hanushek, and Rice in Mishel & Rothstein, 2002, for more information.)

While teachers are clearly the most important educational resource provided to students and research increasingly finds that the quality of teachers matters significantly to student performance (Rivkin, Hanushek, & Kain, 1998; Sanders, 1998), evidence on the relationship between specific teacher qualifications and student performance is mixed and inconclusive, undermining policies that rely on teacher qualifications as indicators of teacher quality (Rice, 2003; Goldhaber, this volume). Alternatives to improve teacher quality include policies focused on relaxing requirements for entry into the profession ("teacher gateway policies") and policies aimed at improving the effectiveness of existing teachers ("teacher workforce policies") (Goldhaber, this volume; Boyd, et al., this volume).

Much of the existing research on teacher effectiveness and qualifications focuses quite narrowly on the contributions of an individual teacher to the gains made by the students in his or her own current classroom. In contrast, other school personnel may also play a role in determining the performance of single student. In their study examining the effect of teacher education and preparation on student performance in high school math and science, Monk and King (1994) distinguished between different levels of teaching resources in a school: (1) the "proximate" teacher who is the currently-assigned instructor in a particular subject; (2) the immediate past teacher in the subject; (3) the set of previous teachers a student had had in a particular subject over some period of time; and (4) the set of all teachers in a school who teach courses in a given subject. One argument for pursuing the school-level effects of teacher qualifications is that teachers learn from one another, so any negative effect associated with having a low quality teacher might be reduced if there are other teachers who are supportive, more knowledgeable and more skilled. A second theory is that students interact with and learn from teachers other than those to whom they are directly assigned. Using national data, the researchers found that it is the cumulative effect of the set of teachers that a student has had over time that affects student achievement, particularly in math. This study demonstrates the importance of moving beyond the narrow linking of each student to one teacher in productivity analyses to consider the role of other personnel—say subject area teachers, teaching support personnel, guidance counselors, or principals—in determining student performance.

In addition, recent research examines differences in the costs of purchased inputs, particularly teachers, and focuses on *what a dollar buys.* This research has been motivated, in part, by an interest in explaining how and why a dollar spent in one location has a different impact on outcomes than a dollar spent elsewhere, or how and why a dollar spent in one year may have a different impact than a dollar spent some years later. Ultimately, the key question is whether these differences can be explained by differences in the price of acquiring inputs—due to differences in labor markets, for example—or by differences in the productivity of these inputs.

There is broad consensus that the cost of educational inputs varies geographically due to differences in local labor markets, house prices, transportation costs, energy prices, and the like. For example, it is widely accepted that the cost of building a new school will be higher in San Francisco, where property values and construction costs are relatively high, than in Cleveland, where these costs are more modest. Further, the high cost of housing and competitive labor markets make it likely that a higher salary will be needed to hire a well-trained teacher in New York City than in a more affordable place like Tallahassee. Despite the intuitive appeal, measuring cost differentials is difficult due, essentially, to the scarcity of geographically detailed data on the prices and quality of inputs purchased. Nonetheless, some headway has been made and various estimates of geographic cost differentials in education, mostly focused on teachers, now exist. A prime example is the Geographic Cost of Education Index (GCEI) developed by Chambers (1998) which adjusts salary differentials for differences in worker and workplace characteristics. States have also implemented their own cost-of-education indices to compensate school districts for geographic variations in cost—mostly associated with teacher salaries—that result from factors beyond the control of school districts (e.g., Taylor, et al., 2002). (For a relatively recent example, see Allegretto, Corcoran, & Mishel, 2004.)

As noted above, related research has addressed changes in costs over time. There may be some consensus among economists, if not more widely, that the education sector may suffer from what is called *Baumol's cost disease.* According to this theory, labor-intensive sectors, such as education, will experience lower productivity growth relative to other sectors like manufacturing, which rely more on capital and machines than on human interactions for production. The implication is that technological change in making cars and computers will make them cheaper over time (controlling for quality), while technological change in personnel-intensive industries like education, nursing, and hospital care, will be slower, making the products of these sectors relatively more expensive over time.

Finally, it is important to consider the role of students in their own education, and the way in their motivation and behavioral responses shape the output of schools. Put simply, students (and parents) are not passive translators of education inputs into outputs. Instead, the process by which the inputs are translated into outputs depends critically upon behavior and ignoring this response may confound our understanding of productivity in education. If, for example, schools provide more books for students to read at home and parents or students respond by decreasing the number of books acquired from the library, then the impact of the school book program may be small or insignificant even if having more books at home increases student reading *ceteris paribus.* (See Todd & Wolpin, 2003, for more on this point.) Unfortunately, much of the research on productivity yields average effects that typically do not account for the differences across students in motivation and behavioral responses to resources.

A Note on Inefficiency and Waste

We should note that in our discussion thus far we have devoted little attention to the possibility that resources are wasted or that there is inefficiency in public education. Considerable research recognizes this possibility (e.g., Hoxby, 1995; Duncombe & Yinger, 1999). One reason that schools may be wasteful or inefficient is the possibility of a mismatch between the goals of the school personnel and the goals implicit in the formulation of the production function. For instance, the school may be aiming to maximize graduation rates while policymakers and analysts are gauging efficiency in terms of producing SAT scores as an output. If these two outputs are highly correlated, then the differences may matter little. If not, this mismatch between goals and measured outputs can matter a good deal. A second reason that our assumption may not hold is that schools may be constrained by policies or institutions, such as work rules for faculty and staff or building construction and maintenance, that prevent them from making the best use of their resources in ways that are unobserved by the researcher. A third possibility is that inefficiency arises because of poor motivation, malfeasance, or inadequate information about the levels of outputs. Or, special interest groups might be able to influence school policies in ways that benefit themselves at the expense of others. As an example, Rose and Sonstelie (2007) argue that the premium paid to experienced teachers is inefficiently high because of the influence of the teachers union. Clearly, the prospect of improving performance by eliminating waste or reducing inefficiency is an attractive policy option, suggesting that we can get more without additional resources. Unfortunately, the evidence on this remains controversial, although new research on measuring efficiency and on policies that reduce waste and enhance efficiency is promising (see, for example, Stiefel et al., 2005; Figlio & Ladd, this volume).

The Education Production Function: A Mathematical Treatment

An education production function typically takes the following general form:[4]

(1) $A_{it} = g(F_{it}, S_{it}, P_{it}, O_{it}, I_{it})$, where

- A_{it} = a vector of educational outcomes for the ith student at time t;
- F_{it} = a vector of family background characteristics relevant to the ith student at time t;
- S_{it} = a vector of school inputs relevant to the ith student at time t;
- P_{it} = a vector of peer or fellow-student characteristics relevant to the ith student at time t;
- O_{it} = a vector of other external influences (e.g., community) relevant to the ith student at time t;
- I_{it} = a vector of characteristics of the ith student relevant at time t.

and g(.) is the transformation that captures the technology linking them. This formulation is conceptually comprehensive in that it includes a wide array of possible inputs (school, community, family, peer, and individual across time) and outcomes (achievement as well as other more difficult to measure outcomes such as civic competencies and cultural tolerance). To be clear, these vectors may include variables that measure characteristics from prior periods, including, but not limited to, the student's prior education experiences, or home environment in early childhood. Such variables are designed to account the cumulative nature of the education process. A common way for researchers to control for these prior experiences is to include only the student's previous academic performance on the ground that this measure sufficiently captures all their effects. This assumption is not fully satisfying and a growing body of research treats prior year experiences with greater nuance (e.g., Todd & Wolpin, 2003).

When prior year achievement is included, equation 1 can be interpreted as a value-added model. In this case, the estimated coefficients indicate how each of the explanatory variables in the current period influence achievement, controlling for the achievement that the student brings to the classroom. An alternative way of specifying a value added model is to substitute the gains in output (e.g., the change in test scores from one year to the next) for the level of output in equation 1. While these models are flexible in principle, limitations in methods and the availability of data on both inputs and outputs can be significant in practice.

In many applications, the production function is estimated using regression analysis and assumes a linear relationship between the inputs and the outputs[5]:

$$(2)\ A_{it} = b_0 + b_1F_{it} + b_2S_{it} + b_3P_{it} + b_4O_{it} + b_5I_{it}$$

Thus, the regression yields estimates of b_0, an intercept, and b_1, b_2 b_3, b_4, b_5 which measure the increase in the outcome Ait that results from a one unit change in the corresponding input Fit, S_{it}, P_{it}, O_{it}, I_{it}, respectively.[6] Notice that the estimates of b_1, b_2 b_3, b_4, b_5 are key productivity measures, capturing what economists call the marginal product of the inputs.[7] The parameter, b_2, is of particular interest for education policymakers because it measures the change in output that is due to a change in school inputs. As an example, if we specify S_{it} as spending per pupil, then b_2 will provide an estimate of the impact on outcomes of increasing spending per pupil by a dollar.

Estimating a production function requires identifying a set of schools that are sufficiently similar that we can summarize their production process using a single production function. The schools can differ in the level or mix of the inputs they use, their output level, community factors, and so on, but in estimation we assume that the parameters of the production function that summarize the average relationship between variables is the same for all. Often production functions are estimated using data on all of the schools in a particular district or state, or using data on a sample of schools from across the nation. The sample is typically limited further, distinguishing between elementary, middle, and high schools, and separating schools serving primarily special education students, or schools in their first year of operation. Further analyses often focus on particular populations of students (e.g., low income, special education) or subjects (e.g., mathematics, reading) within those schools.

Using several years of data for the same set of schools is particularly attractive because it allows the specification to include a school fixed effect (a school specific intercept) which means the impact is estimated using the differences in inputs and outputs experienced by the same school over time and controls for any unobserved, time-invariant features of schools that might not be fully captured by the other variables. Although this method controls for persistent differences among schools, it does not control for changes over time in factors such as school leadership or school curricula. That said, longitudinal analyses can be very powerful and can provide insight that would be difficult to disentangle using only cross-sectional data.

This framework clarifies that increasing output can be accomplished in two very distinct ways: (1) by changing the quantities of the inputs—increasing the quantity of at least one input, potentially substituting for another input, and (2) by increasing the marginal products of the inputs.[8] This distinction is important and often obscured in policy discussions. As an example, the first method might involve increasing the number of teachers while decreasing the number of paraprofessionals. An example of the second approach would be to introduce new instructional practices that help students do better given existing inputs. Research on productivity in education explores both kinds of interventions.

Productivity researchers have begun to recognize that numerous levels of decision making simultaneously occur at any point in the educational process, and all have potential impacts on the productivity of the entire enterprise. In other words, the complexity of schooling is manifest in the interlocking and nested nature of its production function. The educational process is a function of student and family characteristics as well as policies and practices at multiple organizational levels: students are nested in classrooms, classrooms are nested in schools, and schools are nested in districts. Further, the education system is nested in a broader social and economic policy context. These influences are all operating simultaneously to create the whole educational experience for each pupil. The current challenge for productivity research is to incorporate the various actors in and levels of the process, and to disentangle their effects on pupil outcomes.

While the education production function can serve as a powerful conceptual and analytic tool for understanding the relationship between inputs and outcomes, this approach has not been fully embraced by the education community. Critics have raised concerns about its emphasis on average effects across schools, its lack of attention to the process of educating students (i.e., what happens inside the black box), and its apparent neglect of the role of students in their own education. New research methodologies and data collection that allow education production function studies to address these concerns and/or pair production function studies with qualitative analyses that provide depth and context are attractive and likely to be given greater attention in the future.

PRODUCTIVITY IN THE BROADER CONTEXT OF SOCIAL VALUES

Underlying this chapter is the assumption that productivity research can help guide policymakers in their efforts to improve the allocation and use of educational resources. Specifically, productivity research provides information about the relationships between educational inputs and outcomes, and when this type of information is coupled with data on costs, it can guide policymakers seeking to identify the most efficient policy alternative. Clearly, this approach has much to offer in the current policy environment that gives high priority to accountability and efficiency, particularly if the outcomes measured are consistent with the goals sought. However, efficiency is not the only goal underlying the financing of public education. The pursuit of equity has also been an enduring concern of education finance policy and research.

While the link between productivity research and the goal of efficiency has always been apparent, the connection between productivity research and the goal of equity has grown more direct as the concept of equity has evolved from a focus on educational inputs (e.g., equal dollars per pupil) to an emphasis on outcomes. This shift is most apparent in the adequacy movement, which promotes funding systems that provide "sufficient resources to ensure students an effective opportunity to acquire appropriately specified levels of knowledge and skills" (Guthrie & Rothstein, 2001, p. 103). As such, adequacy-based reform requires clearly specified and measurable academic proficiencies expected of all students, and information on the educational inputs required to provide all students the opportunity to meet those standards. So, specifying and evaluating adequacy requires knowledge of the education production function, i.e., the process by which inputs are systematically transformed into desired outcomes.

In addition, funding an adequate system of education requires information on how much it costs to provide educational opportunities for all students to meet standards. This focus on the costs of an adequate education introduces questions about the resources required to educate students with a variety of learning styles and needs across different kinds of communities. The work on this topic reveals the importance of efficiency as a prerequisite for adequacy determinations (Duncombe & Yinger, 1999). An adequate funding system should offer additional aid to districts that face higher-than-average education costs due to factors outside of their control, but not to districts whose costs are high due to inefficiency. Again, knowledge of the production process is needed to make these determinations.

While progress is being made in the study of productivity in education and, specifically, using education production functions, much remains to be learned about what resources, in what quantities, and under what circumstances lead to learning. Perhaps the greatest promise of adequacy-based school reform is that it will promote a greater accumulation of knowledge about the relationship between school inputs and student outcomes. This task may involve efforts that both improve the quality of production function research and expand the range of research brought to bear on these matters. The research on class size reduction, for example, suggests that we need to draw on a range of research designs, including but not limited to production function studies, to gain a clear understanding of these relationships and whether and how context shapes them. The key to improving student achievement through specific investments lies in reaching a more refined understanding of the resources themselves, for whom they matter most, under what circumstances, and at what cost. Such work is critical to the promotion of efficiency, equity, and adequacy in public education.

NOTES

1. In some sense, these kinds of reforms aim at getting schools back on the production frontier, rather than at moving along the frontier.
2. Public expenditures on education are substantial. In 2003, more than $511 billion, or 4.7% of the U.S. Gross Domestic Product, was dedicated to elementary and secondary education. The average total expenditure per pupil ranged from $5,969 in Utah to $14,419 in Washington, D.C., with a national average of $9,299 (U.S. Department of Education, 2005).
3. Krueger's (2002) critique of Hanushek's methodology centered on the way in which the various studies were weighted in Hanushek's analysis. Essentially, Hanushek labeled each estimate of an effect as a "study," so that one article could have several estimates, or studies, that are factored into Hanushek's count of positive, negative, or statistically insignificant (positive and negative) effects. Krueger argues that Hanushek's approach weights the various studies by the number of different estimates of the effect of a particular variable they include. Further, he contends that studies that report negative or statistically insignificant findings are more likely to include more estimates than those that find statistically significant positive effects.
4. This specification follows Levin (1976). A similar specification can be found in Hanushek (1986).
5. Technically, an econometric specification of (2) would include an error term recognizing the potential for random events to influence the educational outcome.
6. In principle, this interpretation is correct only if the model is fully and correctly specified such that the estimates are unbiased.
7. In principle, all inputs should have a positive marginal product. That is, increasing the level of any one input will increase the amount of output produced. So, increasing the number of teachers or books, say, always leads to an increase in output, even if it's small. This is less restrictive than it may seem and essentially reflects an underlying assumption that there is, in the language of economics, "free disposal," meaning that any input that does not make a positive contribution can be disposed of at no cost.
8. The first implies movement along the production function; the second implies changing the production function.

REFERENCES

Allegretto, S. A., Corcoran, S. P., & Mishel, L. (2004). *How does teacher pay compare? Methodological challenges and answers.* Economic Policy Institute, Washington, D.C.

Angrist, J., 7 Lavy, V. (1999). Using Maimonides' rule to estimate the effect of class size on scholastic achievement. *Quarterly Journal of Economics*

Betts, J. (1996). Is there a link between school inputs and earnings? Fresh scrutiny of an old literature. In Burtless, Gary. (Ed.). *Does money matter: The effect of school resources on student achievement and adult success.* Washington, D.C.: Brookings.

Bishop, J. H. (1991). Achievement, test scores, and relative wages. In M. Kosters (Ed.), *Workers and their wages: Changing patterns in the United States.* Washington, D.C.: American Enterprise Institute Press.

Bodilly, S. J. (1998). Lessons from new American schools scale-up phase: Prospects for bringing designs to multiple schools. Santa Monica, CA: Rand.

Brookover, W.B ., Beady, C., Flood, P., Schweitzer, J., & Wisenbaker, J. (1979). *Schools, social systems and student achievement: Schools can make a difference.* New York: Praeger.

Card, D., & Krueger, A.B. (1996). Labor market effects of school quality: Theory and evidence. In G. Burtless (ed.), *Does money matter: The effect of school resources on student achievement and adult success*, 97–140. Washington, D.C.: Brookings.

Chambers, J. G. (1998). *Geographic variations in the prices of public school inputs.* Washington, DC: U.S. Department of Education, National Center for Education Statistics, Working Paper No. 98–104.

Coleman, J. S., Campbell, E. Q., Hobson, C. J., McPartland, A.M., Weinfeld, F. D., & York, R. L. (1966). *Equality of Educational Opportunity.* Washington, D.C.: U.S. Department of Health, Education, and Welfare.

Dee, T. (2004). Are there civic returns to education? *Journal of Public Economics, 88*(9), 1697–1720.

Duncombe, W. D., & Yinger J. (1999). Performance standards and educational cost indices: You can't have one without the other. In J. Ladd, R. Chalk, J. & Hansen (eds.), *Equity and adequacy in education finance: Issues and perspectives.* National Research Council: Washington, DC.

Edmonds, R. R. (1979). Effective schools for the urban poor. *Educational Leadership, 37*(10), 15–24.

Edmonds, R. R. (1981). Making public schools effective. *Social policy,* 12, 56–60.

Finn, J. D., & Achilles, C. M. (1999). Tennessee's class size study: Findings, implications, and misconceptions. *Educational Evaluation and Policy Analysis, 21*(2), 97–110.

Friedman, M. (2002). *Capitalism and freedom, fortieth anniversary edition.* Chicago, IL: University of Chicago Press

General Accounting Office. (1989). *Effective schools programs: Their extent and characteristics.* (GAO Publication No. HRD 89–132BR). Washington, D.C.: U.S. Government Printing Office.

Good, T., & Brophy, J. E. (1986). School effects. In Merlin L. Wittrock (ed.). *Handbook of research on teaching*, 3rd edition (pp. 570–602). New York: McMillan.

Guthrie, J. W. & Rothstein, R. (2001). A new millennium and a likely new era of education finance. In S. Chaikind & W. J. Fowler (eds.), *Education finance in the new millennium,* 99–120. Larchmont, NY: Eye on Education.

Hanushek, E. A. (1986). The economics of schooling: Production and efficiency in the public schools. *Journal of Economic Literature. 24*(3), 1141–1178.

Hanushek, E. A. (1994). *Making schools work: Improving performance and controlling costs.* Washington, D.C.: Brookings.

Hanushek, E. A. (1999). Some findings from an independent investigation of the Tennessee STAR experiment and from other investigations of class size effects. *Educational Evaluation and Policy Analysis, 21*(2), 143–164.

Hanushek, E. A. (2002). Evidence, politics and the class size debate. In Mishel, L. & Richard R., (eds.), *The class size debate* (p. 37–65). Washington, D.C.: The Economic Policy Institute.

Hedges, L. V., Laine, R. D., & Greenwald, R. (1994). Does money matter? A meta-analysis of studies of the effects of differential school inputs on student outcomes. *Educational Researcher, 23*(3), 5–14.

Hoxby, C. M., (1995, September). Is there an equity-efficiency trade-off in school finance? Tiebout and a theory of the local public goods producer. NBER Working Paper No. W5265.

Jepsen, C. & Rivkin, S. (2002). *Class size reduction, teacher quality, and academic achievement in California public elementary schools*. San Francisco: Public Policy Institute of California.

Koretz, D. (1996). Using student assessments for educational accountability. In E. A. Hanushek . & D. W. Jorgenson (eds.). *Improving America's schools: The role of incentives*. Washington, D.C.: National Academy Press.

Krueger A. B. (2002). Understanding the magnitude and effect of class size on student achievement. In L. Mishel R. Richard (eds.), *The class size debate* (pp. 7–36). Washington, D.C.: The Economic Policy Institute.

Ladd, H. F., & Hansen, J. (Eds.). (1999). *Making money matter: Financing America's schools*. Washington, D.C.: National Academy Press.

Levin, H. M. (1976). Concepts of economic efficiency and educational production. In J.T. Froomkin, D.T. Jamison, & R. Radner (eds.), *Education as an industry*. Cambridge, MA: Ballinger.

Malen, B., Ogawa, R., &. Kranz, J. (1990). What do we know about school-based management? A case study of the literature-a call for research. In W. H. Clune & J. F. Witte (eds.), *Choice and control in American education, Volume 2: The practice of decentralization and school restructuring* (pp. 289–342). Briston, PA: Falmer Press.

Mishel, L., & Rothstein, R. (Eds.). (2002) *The class size debate*. Washington, D.C.: The Econmic Policy Institute.

Monk, D. H. (1990). *Educational finance: An economic approach*. New York: McGraw Hill.

Monk, D. H., & King, J. K. (1994). Multilevel teacher resource effects on pupil performance in secondary mathematics and science: The case of teacher subject-matter preparation. In R. Ehrenberg (ed.), *Choices and consequences: Contemporary policy issues in education* (pp. 29–58). Ithaca, NY: ILR Press.

Nye, B., Hedges, L. V., & Konstantopoulos, S. (1999). The long-term effects of small classes: A five-year follow-up of the Tennessee class size experiment. *Educational Evaluation and Policy Analysis, 21*(2), 127–142.

Purkey, S. C., & Smith, M .S. (1983). Effective schools: A review. *Elementary School Journal, 83*, 427–452.

Rice, J. K. (2001). Illuminating the black box: The evolving role of education productivity research. In S. Chaikind & W. Fowler (eds.), *Education finance in the new millennium, 2001 Yearbook of the American Education Finance Association* (pp. 121–138). Larchmont, NY: Eye on Education.

Rice, J. K. (2002). Making economically-grounded decisions about comprehensive school reform models: Considerations of costs, effects, and contexts. In M. C. Wang & K. K. Wong (eds.), *Efficiency and equity issues in Title I schoolwide program implementation* (pp. 29–55). Greenwich, CT: Information Age Publishing, Inc.

Rice, J. K. (2003). *Teacher quality: Understanding the effectiveness of teacher attributes*. Washington, D.C.: Economic Policy Institute

Rivkin, S. G., Hanushek, E. A., & Kain, J. F. (1998). *Teachers, schools, and academic achievement*. National Bureau of Economic Research, Working Paper 6691.

Rose, H., & Sonstelie, J. (2007). School board politics, school district size and the bargaining power of teachers' unions. Unpublished manuscript.

Rothstein, R. (2006). *Class and schools: Using social, economic, and educational reform to close the black-white achievement gap*. Washington, D.C.: Teacher College Press and Economic Policy Institute.

Rychen, D. S., & Slaganik, L. (2003). *Key competencies for a successful life and a well-functioning society*. Toronto: Hogrefe & Huber.

Sanders, W. L. (1998). Value-added assessment. *The School Administrator, 55*(11), 24–32.

Smith, M. S., Scoll, B. W., & Link, J. (1996). Research-based school reform: The Clinton administration's agenda. In E. A. Hanushek & D. W. Jorgenson (eds.). *Improving America's schools: The role of incentives*. Washington, D.C.: National Academy Press.

Stiefel, L., Schwartz, A. E., Rubenstein, & Zabel, J. (2005). *Measuring school performance and efficiency*. Larchmont, NY: Eye on Education Press.

Summers, A., & Johnson, A. W.. (1996). The effects of school-based management plans. In Board on Science, Technology, and Economic Policy. E.A. Hanushek & D.W. Jorgenson, (eds.), *Improving America's schools: The role of incentives* (pp. 75–96). Commission on Behavioral and Social Sciences and Education, National Research Council. Washington, D.C.: National Academy Press.

Taylor, L. L., Alexander, C. D., Gronberg, T. J., Jansen, D. W., & Keller, H. (2002). Updating the Texas cost of education index. *Journal of Education Finance., 28*(2), 261–284.

Teddlie, C., & Stringfield, S. (1993). *Schools make a difference: lessons learned from a 10-year study of school effects.* New York: Teachers College Press.

Todd, P., & Wolpin, K. (2003). On the specification and estimation of the production function for cognitive achievement. *Economic Journal,* F3–F33.

Tyack, D. (1993). School governance in the United States: Historical puzzles and anomalies. In J. Hannaway & M. Carnoy (eds.), *Decentralization and School improvement: Can we fulfill the promise?* (pp. 1–32). San Francisco: Jossey-Bass.

Tyack, D., & Cuban, L.. (1995). *Tinkering toward Utopia: A century of public school of reform.* Cambridge, MA: Harvard University Press.

U.S. Department of Education. (2005). *Digest of education statistics.* Washington, D.C.: Institute for Education Sciences, U.S. Department of Education.

Wohlstetter, P., & Odden, A.. (1992). Rethinking school-based management policy and research. *Educational Administration Quarterly, 28*(4):529–549.

Wong, M. C., & Wang. K. K. (Eds.). (2002). *Efficiency and equity issues in Title I schoolwide program implementation* (pp. 29–55). Greenwich, CT: Information Age Publishing.

9

Teachers Matter, But Effective Teacher Quality Policies Are Elusive

Dan Goldhaber

THE VALUE OF TEACHER QUALITY

For most, it comes as no surprise that research has consistently shown that teachers can have profound effects on their students. Hanushek (1992), for instance, finds that the quality of a teacher can make the difference of a *full year's* learning growth. Research dating all the way back to the "Coleman Report" (Coleman, 1966) has shown teacher quality to be the most important *schooling* factor influencing student achievement.[1] Recent findings, based on better data and more rigorous statistical methods, have confirmed that the quality of the teacher in the classroom remains the most important schooling factor predicting student outcomes, and have furthermore shown that there is considerable variation in quality between teachers (Goldhaber, 2007; Rivkin, Hanushek, & Kain, 2005; Rockoff, 2004; Sanders & Horn, 1998; Sanders & Rivers, 1996; Wright, Horn, & Sanders, 1997).[2]

Teacher quality is a common term that may be clear in concept, but has been used to mean many different things. Some measure quality based on the credential or set of credentials that a teacher holds. For instance, the No Child Left Behind (NCLB) Act specifically denotes that "highly qualified teachers" are those who hold a bachelor's degree, obtain full certification from their state, and demonstrate competency in each subject they teach (as defined by the state).[3] Others focus on teacher practices in the classroom to gauge teacher quality or use the behavior or learning (measured in a variety of ways) of students as a metric for teacher quality. Likewise, teacher quality has been studied and measured using a variety of both qualitative and quantitative approaches from case study observations of teachers, to teacher reports of practices, to "value-added production function" studies that attempt to use statistical methods to isolate the contributions that teachers make toward student achievement and/or relate particular teacher attributes to student achievement.[4] Teachers no doubt contribute in many different ways to students' intellectual and emotional growth, implying that their quality could be measured along any number of dimensions. While admittedly a narrow conception of what teachers do, in this chapter I primarily focus on research that employs a production function approach to assess the relationship between teacher characteristics and student achievement. Throughout the chapter, I use the term "teacher quality" to refer to a teacher's value-added contribution in producing measurable gains for students on standardized exams (or other easily quantifiable student outcomes, such as high school graduation). I focus on this measure of teacher quality with the belief that effective teachers may have a range of attributes, strategies, and skills, some quite different from one another, that contribute to student achievement on tests, which does in fact represent an important measure of genuine learning.

Unfortunately for policy makers, a large body of research suggests that teacher quality (as defined above), while an important predictor of student success, is not strongly associated with readily observable teacher characteristics like degree and experience levels (Hanushek, 1986, 1997). This point is well-illustrated by some research I conducted with colleagues (Goldhaber, Brewer, & Anderson, 1999) that first estimated the overall impact of teachers on students, then parsed out which part could be explained by specific teacher characteristics and which part was attributable to less-easily quantifiable teacher attributes (e.g., whether they are enthusiastic and hard working).[5] We found that teachers account for approximately 8.5 percent of the variation in students' tenth grade achievement.[6] But, the impact of unobservable teacher attributes (i.e., those that are not included in the dataset) dwarf that of objective, observable, easily measured attributes such as degree and experience levels: less than 5 percent of the variation in teacher quality is explained by such quantifiable characteristics.

Different studies reach varying conclusions as to the extent to which teacher quality can be predicted by readily observable teacher characteristics.[7] A nuanced reading of the research literature suggests that some readily identifiable characteristics do predict success in the classroom. In particular, measures of academic proficiency or cognitive ability, such as a teacher's performance on standardized tests (e.g., licensure tests or the SAT or the selectivity of the colleges she graduated from), and subject specific training (e.g., a degree in mathematics) in a teacher's specialty area appear to be predictors of teacher quality.[8] However, an important theme emerging from the newest, most sophisticated educational production function studies is that, when it comes to teachers, there is far more variation in the effectiveness of teachers who hold a particular credential than there is between teachers with different credentials. In other words, even when a particular characteristic does predict teacher quality in a statistical sense, there are greater differences between teachers who share a common characteristic or credential than there are differences between teachers with different characteristics or credentials.

In this chapter, I briefly explore the research linking teachers and students and the policy implications of this research. I focus on several pre-service and in-service teacher policy interventions: (1) the growing use of alternative certification, (2) efforts to "professionalize" the teacher workforce through the voluntary certification of teachers by the National Board for Professional Teaching Standards (NBPTS), and (3) experimentation with alternative compensation plans (e.g., merit pay).

The chapter is organized as follows. In the next section, I provide a brief overview of research findings that link teacher quality to readily observable teacher credentials and characteristics. In the third section, I discuss the "more variation within than between" theme in greater detail, explore what this might mean for state and local policy makers who play a role in shaping the teacher workforce, and set it in the context of the major trends in educational policies designed to enhance teacher quality through manipulation of pre-service requirements ("teacher gateway policies"). I conclude by specifically examining the implications of the research for policies designed to affect teachers who are in the workforce ("teacher workforce policies").

TEACHER QUALITY AND READILY OBSERVABLE TEACHER CHARACTERISTICS

Teacher quality does not appear to be *strongly* correlated across educational contexts (e.g., subjects, grade-levels, etc.) with any readily observable and easily quantifiable attributes, such as licensure status or degree level. This is not an uncontroversial assertion: education researchers have come to different conclusions based on different studies (and sometimes based on reviews of the same studies), and one can generally find educational research "evidence" in support of a particular position on the relationship between teachers and students. Furthermore, it is clear that there are some significant contextual gaps in terms of what we know about the relationships between various teacher characteristics and student achievement. For example, most of the studies on teacher content knowledge tend to focus on student math and reading achievement at the secondary level (Goldhaber, 2004). With these caveats as a backdrop, I offer a brief summary of the educational production function literature linking teacher characteristics and student achievement.

Years of Teaching Experience

Teacher experience, and its value as a predictor of teacher effectiveness in the classroom, has been studied extensively. For example, a 1986 review article by Eric Hanushek reports findings from 109 studies that include teacher experience as an explanatory variable. Of the 109 studies, 40 find experience to be a statistically significant predictor of teacher effectiveness and of these, 33 find a significant positive effect. While it is plausible that a positive finding on experience results not from a causal relationship between experience and student outcomes, but from the tendency of more-experienced teachers to be matched with classes composed of higher-achieving students (e.g., due to seniority transfer policies) (Hanushek, 1986). In fact, recent empirical work utilizing more-sophisticated econometric approaches to account for this potential problem tends to confirm that teachers do become more effective as they gain experience early on in their careers.[9]

A problem with the great majority of studies of teacher experience is that they implicitly, through their modeling techniques, treat every year of teaching experience as though it is the same. They do this despite the fact that there may be substantial differences between, for instance, the impact of experience gained between the first and second year of teaching and experience gained between the twenty-fifth to the twenty-sixth year of teaching. Indeed, some more nuanced educational productivity studies have found that not every year of teacher experience has the same impact on teacher effectiveness as every other year. Early studies, such as Murnane (1975) and Murnane and Phillips (1981) show non-linear experience impacts on teacher productivity with teachers showing significant productivity benefits from early career experience gains that tend to taper off after five or so years. This finding has grown more convincing as increasingly detailed longitudinal data has become available, allowing researchers to examine the impacts of experience gains at different points in a teacher's career while accounting for the fact that teachers of varying experience levels are likely not randomly assigned to students of varying abilities (Clotfelter, Ladd, & Vigdor, 2006; Goldhaber, 2007; Kane, Rockoff, & Staiger, 2006; Rivkin et al., 2005; Rockoff, 2004).[10]

The magnitude of the teacher-experience effect differs from one study to the next, but most studies that account for non-random match of teachers and students, and that allow for non-linearities in the relationship between teacher experience and student achievement, suggest that a teacher tends to become significantly more effective in each of the first 3 to 5 years of his or her career, with the gains from experience being larger in math.[11] The positive findings on teacher experience span different grade-levels and subjects and thus appear to be robust to different teaching contexts.

Degree Level and Subject-Matter Knowledge

There is relatively little evidence that teacher degree level per se is a good proxy for teacher quality. Hanushek's 1986 review found the expected statistically significant, positive relationship between teacher degree level and student achievement in only about 5 percent of reviewed studies and about the same number showed a statistically significant, negative effect—roughly what one might expect simply by chance.[12]

Were it the case that teacher degree-level has a large effect on teacher quality it likely would not be so difficult to detect it. Furthermore, since more-credentialed teachers tend to be assigned to higher-achieving students (Clotfelter et al., 2006; Lankford Loeb, & Wyckoff, 2002), one would expect that if a bias exists in the estimates of the effect of teacher degree it would be an upward bias, implying that many studies likely overstate the findings on experience.

There *is* evidence that a teacher's degree level may matter in some specific contexts. In particular, Goldhaber and Brewer's analyses present a more nuanced portrait of the impact of teacher degrees in those grades (1997a, 1997b). They find that a teacher's advanced degree is not generally associated with increased student learning from the eighth to the tenth grade, but that having an advanced degree in math and science for math and science teachers does appear to influence students' achievement (1997b).[13] This was not, however, true for English and history degrees when focusing on student achievement in English/reading and history.

Goldhaber and Brewer's findings in math and science are broadly consistent with research by Monk (1994) and Monk and King (1994). They find that subject-matter training in math and science predicts teacher quality. Specifically, they find that each additional course a teacher has taken in math improves student mathematics achievement by about three quarters of one percent of a standard deviation, and similar science preparation increases student achievement in science by up to two thirds of one percent of a standard deviation. Assuming a math or science major requires ten to eleven courses in subject, this would roughly be the equivalent to seven to eight percent of the standard deviation in math achievement and around six to seven percent in science, very similar in size to Goldhaber and Brewer's findings.

Importantly, Monk and King find the impact of subject-specific training depends on the context of the classes taught. Specifically, their results suggest that the number of math and science courses taken by teachers while in college had an impact on sophomores' and juniors' achievement in math and science, but the effect is non-linear and teacher coursework had a larger impact if a teacher is teaching a more-advanced course.

There is relatively little empirical evidence suggesting a strong relationship between subject-matter training of teachers and student achievement at the elementary level, and the existing evidence is less conclusive. Eberts and Stone (1984) address this relationship and find no statistically significant relationship between the number of math courses taken by teachers and their 4th grade students' achievement in math. Similarly, Hill, Rowan, and Ball (2005) do not find a relationship between the number of math methods and content courses (they group these together) a teacher has completed and student gains in mathematics (in the 1st and 3rd grades). They do, however, find that teachers who have more demonstrated mathematical knowledge (based on their performance on a subject-matter test) produce larger gains. They estimate that a 1 standard deviation increase in teacher math knowledge increases student achievement by 2 to 4 points on the Terra Nova test, which, expressed as a function of average monthly student growth, is equivalent to about a half month's worth of learning gains.[14] In contrast, they do not find any significant effect for a teacher's reading knowledge on student performance in reading.

Licensure/Certification Status and Pedagogical Preparation

States regulate who may become a teacher through their licensure policies. The primary purpose of these policies is to assure the public that individuals in the teaching profession have at least the minimal standard of teaching competence to be qualified to begin practicing in the profession.[15] Most licensure system require that prospective teachers complete a standard set of college-level courses in pedagogy and/or in the subject they wish to teach, and for them to demonstrate competence by passing one or more standardized tests. However, there is also great variation among states in the specific requirements to enter teaching, either through both traditional and alternative routes. Furthermore, there is likely to be considerable within state variation in the quality and content of teacher training programs as these programs can differ substantially from one another in terms of educational philosophies and approaches (Wilson, Floden, & Ferrini-Mundy, 2001).

Recent reviews of licensure studies have reached very different conclusions and have helped to spur a public debate over the role of the state in regulating the teacher labor market. Walsh (2001) investigates over 200 studies on licensure and finds the process to be deeply flawed. Walsh concludes the research on the teacher attributes correlated with teacher quality "does not show that certified teachers are more effective teachers than uncertified teachers" (p. iv). Darling-Hammond (2002) refutes Walsh's conclusions writing that: "Given the crudeness of the measure [certification], it is perhaps remarkable that so many studies have found significant effects of teacher certification."[16]

Notwithstanding the more than 200 studies cited in these reviews, there is relatively little high-quality empirical research on the effectiveness of teacher preparation programs and licensure due primarily to a lack of good data for such studies. The overwhelming majority of these cited studies do not directly link teacher licensure status or pedagogical preparation to student achievement at the teacher-student level (instead they all rely on aggregated data or link licensure to outcomes such as teacher beliefs, teaching style, or behavior in the classroom). In fact, in a recent comprehensive review of empirical papers relating teacher characteristics to student achievement, Wayne and Youngs (2003) found only two papers on the impacts of teacher licensure that were rigorous enough (i.e., they were peer-reviewed, used longitudinal student-level achievement data, and controlled for prior student achievement and student SES) to meet the requirements for inclusion in their review: Goldhaber and Brewer (1997a) and Goldhaber and Brewer (2000).[17]

Both Goldhaber and Brewer studies find evidence at the high school level of positive student achievement effects of in math of having a teacher who is certified in math, as opposed to being certified in another area. They do not, however, find statistically significant effect of science teacher certification on science achievement (they did not examine certification in other areas).[18] But, Goldhaber and Brewer do not find significant differences in achievement between students with teachers who hold standard state certification in math, and thus have received pedagogical preparation, and those with emergency certification in math (or other subjects), who likely do not receive pedagogical training.[19] A more recent study (Dee & Cohodes, 2005) focusing on 8th grade students finds results that are almost identical to those of Goldhaber and Brewer's at the 10th and 12th grades: assignment to a math teacher who is certified in her subject is predicted to increase student achievement by about 10 percent of a standard deviation, but there are no similarly statistically significant findings for science, social studies, or English. Croninger et al.'s study (2007) of elementary school teachers suggests that certification status is not predictive of teacher quality in math or reading.

More recently, several studies have focused on differences between traditionally certified teachers and a prominent alternative certification program: Teach For America (TFA). One of the goals of TFA is to recruit candidates who may not otherwise consider teaching. TFA recruitment focuses on academic aptitude and leadership experience and does not require that applicants complete education training in college. In fact, TFA explicitly states, "A degree in or coursework in education has no bearing on a candidate's chances of admission [to TFA]" (http://www.teachforamerica.org/tfa/FAQ).[20]

Several studies have examined TFA and non-TFA teachers in the Houston Independent School

District (Darling-Hammond et al., 2005; Raymond and Fletcher, 2002) and reached somewhat different conclusions from one another. Raymond and Fletcher use results on the TAAS exam (the former Texas student achievement test) to compare the performance of students with TFA teachers to students with traditional teachers. They consistently find that TFA teachers perform comparably in reading with other new teachers (both certified and uncertified), and outperform other new teachers in math by roughly 10 percent of a standard deviation. They also find that the distribution of student scores with TFA teachers is more narrowly centered around the mean than for non-TFA teachers, and conclude from this that TFA teachers have more predictable classroom ability.

Darling-Hammond et al. find more mixed evidence on TFA teachers versus other teachers in general (including both certified and uncertified teachers), but strongly conclude that certification makes a difference for teacher quality. In particular, they note that uncertified TFA teachers (as most are initially) are less effective than fully certified teachers (and about as effective as other uncertified teachers), but TFA teachers who become certified do about as well as, and in some cases outperform, other certified teachers.[21]

Neither study accounts for the potential for non-random sorting of teachers across classrooms, nor do they allow for non-linear experience effects—both important considerations.[22] Less-than-fully credentialed teachers are likely to be teaching in more difficult work settings, so failure to account for this could bias the estimates of the effects of these teachers downward. Furthermore, the effects of the certification variables in the model (e.g., uncertified, TFA status, etc.) may well be confused with the impact of teacher experience: the way the models are specified opens the possibility that the positive effects of early career experience could inappropriately be attributed to the effects of a teacher becoming certified.[23]

One of the most methodologically sound studies of TFA is conducted by Glazerman, Mayer, and Decker (2006). What makes this study unique and the findings convincing is its experimental design: students are randomly assigned to TFA and non-TFA teachers.[24] Glazerman et al. find that students with TFA teachers do no worse in reading and do better in math than the students of non-TFA teachers. Specifically, in the TFA—non-TFA comparison (where non-TFA includes both certified and uncertified teachers), the authors find statistically significant positive effects in the growth of math scores of 15 percent of a standard deviation, but no significant effects in the growth of reading scores. More striking is the finding that these results held whether the comparison teachers were novice or experienced, and certified or uncertified, with statistically significant effect sizes ranging from 9 to 26 percent of a standard deviation in mathematics, depending on the comparison. None of these effects were statistically significant for reading in any of the comparisons.

Another study that accounts for the potential nonrandom match of teachers to schools is that of Boyd et al. (2005a), which examines the performance of teachers in New York City (in grades 3–8, in math and English language arts) who enter the teacher workforce though various alternative pathways relative to that of teachers who obtained a traditional teacher license. The alternative pathways Boyd et al. consider include Teach For America, the NYC Teaching Fellows program, and the Teaching Opportunity Program (two alternative programs that are specific to NYC). Overall, students of TFA teachers were found to have gains similar to those of traditionally certified teachers, but students of teachers who entered through one of the other alternate pathway had slightly lower gains. The authors also provide evidence that the effects of having a TFA teacher are different across grades, with TFA teachers being relatively more effective in higher grade levels (the differences in the effect sizes are small and not consistently statistically significant, so not worth reporting).[25]

One of the major fault lines in the research on the effectiveness of TFA teachers (and other alternative licensure programs) has been over defining an appropriate comparison group to TFA teachers. While some argue that the only appropriate comparison to make is TFA teachers to traditionally (fully) licensed teachers, others believe that this does not paint an accurate picture because it is unrealistic to assume that TFA teachers are the relevant alternative to traditionally licensed teachers and vice versa. The TFA program, by design, tends to place teachers in schools that have great difficulty hiring traditionally licensed teachers and, in the absence of other policy changes (e.g., increases in teacher salaries), hiring officials for these types of schools often have to make choices between various types of alternatively licensed teachers—and sometimes between alternatively licensed teachers and other options, such as long-term substitutes. Thus, my own view is that, while an interesting comparison, the TFA or alternatively licensed teacher versus the traditionally licensed teacher comparison is not really the relevant one for making policy decisions. Rather, the other teachers, certified or not, who are also employed in the schools employing TFA teachers are the appropriate comparison group.

More importantly, new research suggests that there is far greater variation between teachers who enter the workforce with the same credential than between teachers who hold different credentials, which implies there may be a benefit to focusing on in-service teacher policies as opposed to pre-service policies, like certification. This issue is discussed in greater detail below.

Teacher Test Performance and Demonstrated Academic Proficiency

Academic proficiency covers a diverse set of teacher attributes—teacher performance on tests of verbal ability, teacher licensure, or college entrance exams to the selectivity of the undergraduate institutions attended by teachers—all of which likely provide some underlying measure of academic competence or ability. While there are fewer studies predicting student achievement that include measures of teacher academic proficiency than those that include degree and experience levels, the existing research is relatively consistent in showing a positive relationship between the two (Goldhaber, 2004). For example, in a 1996 review by Greenwald, Hedges, and Laine, 12 of the 24 studies that include a measure of teacher ability (their term) show a positive, statistically significant relationship between teacher ability and student achievement, and in only 4 percent did they find a statistically significant, negative relationship, and Hanushek suggests that "[t]he only reasonably consistent finding seems to be that "smarter" teachers do better in terms of student achievement … [h]owever, … elements of teaching skill are not easily identified or measured. Indeed, given our current knowledge of the achievement process, it appears that teacher performance is quite idiosyncratic" (Hanushek, 1981, p. 29).

Most of the research on academic proficiency is based on teacher performance on some type of standardized test. Several aggregate-level studies (e.g., Ferguson, 1991, 1998; Ferguson & Ladd, 1996) find a positive relationship between teacher scores on some type of exam (e.g., a licensure or SAT test) and student achievement. The magnitude of the effects from these aggregated-level studies tend to be quite large: a one standard deviation increase in the distribution of teacher test scores is found to lead to a 10–25 percent of a standard deviation increase in student achievement.

While the above studies seem to suggest a strong and quite large relationship between teacher performance on exams and student achievement, this is in part due to the fact that the effect is judged relative to the variation in student achievement at the *district level* (it would be smaller judged against the variation in achievement of students). But, it is also true that all rely on aggregated data, and the aggregation of the data may lead to an overestimate of the relationships as it is unclear whether higher-scoring teachers lead to higher-scoring students or whether affluent districts, which tend to have higher-achieving students, tend to hire teachers with higher scores or assign them to more advanced classes.[26] Educational production function studies tend to find far stronger relationships between resources and student achievement the more aggregated the data and, as Hanushek Rivkin, and Taylor (1996) show, these studies are more likely to suffer from "aggregation bias" due to problems such as the correlation between the effect in question and omitted factors (e.g., state education policies).

Several more recent papers that explore the relationship between teacher performance on licensure exams and student achievement using disaggregated data find a significant but smaller relationship between teacher performance on licensure exams (the Praxis tests used in North Carolina) and student achievement and, importantly, show that the distribution of teachers across schools and students can greatly influence the magnitude of estimated effects.[27] Clotfelter et al. (2006) analyze this relationship for fifth-grade students and find that a 1 standard deviation increase in a teacher's average test score is predicted to increase students' reading achievement by 1.1 percent of a standard deviation, and to increase math achievement by 1.8 percent of a standard deviation.[28] Furthermore, they convincingly show that the distribution of teachers across schools greatly influences the estimates of the effects of teacher characteristics like their licensure scores. Goldhaber (2007) focuses on elementary grades (4th–6th) and estimates the value of licensure tests as a signal of teacher effectiveness. He finds consistent evidence that teachers who pass the licensure tests are, on average, more effective, but the difference between those who pass and those who fail is relatively small: increasing student achievement by 4 to 6 percent of a standard deviation. However, licensure tests appear to provide information about teacher quality beyond the simple pass/fail signal, as there is a positive relationship between a teacher's performance on licensure tests and student achievement even among teachers who have all met the state standards for passing the exam. Like Clotfelter et al., Goldhaber's study confirms the importance of accounting for teacher sorting by showing that the estimates of the relationship between teacher licensure and student achievement are far higher when one does not account for the nonrandom distribution of teachers across schools and classrooms.

Advanced Credentials: NBPTS Certification

Several new research studies (Cavalluzzo, 2004; Goldhaber and Anthony, 2007; Vandevoort et al. (2004) suggest that the National Board for Professional Teaching Standards (NBPTS) certification provides an indicator of teacher quality. All three find positive effects of having an NBPTS-certified teacher in both math and reading tests, though the magnitude of the estimated effects differs. Cavalluzzo, who focuses on the mathematics achievement of high school students in the 9th and 10th grades, finds that, all else equal, students with an NBPTS-certified teacher gain 12 percent of a standard deviation more than other students on a year-end exam. Goldhaber and Anthony study students in grades 3–5, and find that having an NBPTS-certified teacher is predicted to improve student achievement (outside of the year that a teacher becomes certified) by about 5 percent of a standard deviation (in both subjects). Since research suggests that NBPTS certified teachers, on average, perform substantially better on licensure tests than non-NBPTS teachers and tend to be teaching in more advantaged educational settings (Goldhaber, Anthony, & Perry, 2004), one might hypothesize that the NBPTS effect is simply a reflection of nonrandom student-teacher matching or that all the information provided by NBPTS certification status could be garnered by knowing a teacher's licensure test performance. This turns out not to be the case. Goldhaber and Anthony's study suggests that the estimated effect is influenced by student-teacher matching, but not solely attributed to it, and that the NBPTS credential provides information beyond that conveyed by other objective teacher attributes, including licensure test performance. Finally, the Vandervoort, Amrein-Beardsley, and Berliner study (2004), which focuses on students in grades 2 through 6, suggests that, when averaged across grade and subject area (math, reading, and language), students with an NBPTS certified teacher gain 12 percent of a standard deviation more than other students.[29]

Not all the research on NBPTS teachers shows such positive effects. A more recent large-scale quantitative study (Sanders, Alston, & Wright 2005) generally finds little evidence of statistically significant, positive, NBPTS effects.[30] The differences in findings between this and the aforementioned NBPTS studies may be explained by differences in datasets, methodology employed, or the fact that NBPTS itself has gone through some changes (e.g., in 2001 there was a change in the weighting of different assessments used to judge NBPTS candidates). But, what is interesting about the Sanders et al. study is the emphasis on the fact that there is greater variation in teachers who receive the NBPTS credential than between NBPTS and non-NBPTS teachers. As Sanders et al. (2005) state, "the variation among teachers within the same certification status was significantly large such that whatever small average differences there were between teachers in different certification status categories were rather meaningless in comparison." (p. 2). I explore the implication of this emerging theme in research findings in the next two sections of the chapter.

MORE VARIATION WITHIN THAN BETWEEN AND TEACHER GATEWAY POLICIES

The findings discussed above suggest that a teacher's readily observable characteristics (e.g., licensure status) are a relatively weak screen for teacher quality. This makes crafting policies designed to ensure a basic level of teacher quality based on pre-service credentials difficult: simply put, there do not appear to be readily quantifiable paper credentials that strongly predict teacher quality. Several recent papers aptly illustrate this conclusion. The aforementioned Goldhaber (2007) paper on teacher licensure tests shows that there is far more variation between teachers who either pass or fail the North Carolina licensure test than there is between all those who pass and all those who fail. Kane et al. (2006) investigate the relationship between a teacher's route into the classroom (e.g., traditional certification, TFA, Teaching Fellows Program) and student achievement, and find that there is much more variation in teacher quality within a route to the classroom than there is between routes.

The finding that paper credentials, such as certification, do not sharply delineate good teachers from bad is quite prevalent in research. In fact, it is perfectly consistent with the research previously cited (Goldhaber et al., 1999; Nye et al., 2004) showing that the portion of teacher quality that is explained by commonly measured attributes such as degree and experience levels is dwarfed by that explained by any number of more subtle, and less-easily quantified teacher attributes. Even when a particular teacher attribute meets the standard of being "statistically significant," it is far from a guarantee that a teacher holding that attribute would be considered an effective teacher.

Teachers, of course, come in "package form," implying that they may tend to have groups of attributes or credentials. And, as Clotfelter et al. (forthcoming) show, even if individual teacher credentials don't appear to accurately predict teacher quality, it is conceivable that groups of credentials do. Still, one logical implication flowing out of the finding that paper credentials do not accurately predict teacher quality is that policies ought to deemphasize the certification filter of individuals into the teacher workforce and place far greater emphasis on teacher performance in the classroom, based on actual classroom performance (I discuss this in greater detail in the next section). This suggestion, which has been made by a number of researchers (Ballou & Podgursky, 1998; Gordon, Kane, & Staiger, 2006; Hanushek & Rivkin, 2003), is consistent with states' growing reliance on alternative certification programs that permit individuals with divergent pre-service experiences to move into the teaching profession, at least briefly (many programs require teachers to obtain "full" state certification within a few years of teaching).[31] The idea is that by relaxing the gateway (state-level) requirements for entering teachers, local school districts will be provided the opportunity to evaluate a greater number of teachers based on their actual performance, thus allowing districts to make more informed decisions about whether to retain them and how much compensation to provide them.

While a relaxation of the certification gateway may seem a sensible shift in policy emphasis in light of the research findings described in this chapter, it is important to note that changes in pre-service requirements have ambiguous impacts on the quality of teachers in the workforce, and there are likely important distributional impacts (Boyd et al., 2007; Goldhaber, 2004). For example, a relaxation of the certification gateway might ultimately improve the average quality of the teacher workforce, but allow more very low-quality teachers into the workforce, at least for a time, in the process.[32] Is this a worthy tradeoff? Clearly this is a judgment call that will depend on how one values the potential harm done by having more low-quality teachers in the workforce as compared to the potential benefit of having high-quality teachers in the workforce.

Furthermore, a relaxation of the certification gateway raises questions about an important mediating factor in determining the quality of the teacher workforce: the link between teacher certification policies and the quality of the teacher workforce in the local school system at the point of hire. After certification, local school systems act as a second gateway in determining the composition of the teacher workforce; therefore, how apt they are in selecting teachers is an important mediating factor in determining the quality of the teacher workforce (Goldhaber, 2004). In theory at least, local hiring officials have the capacity to garner extensive information about teacher candidates—information that may go a long way toward explaining the significant variation researchers observe for teachers who are in the labor force. Unfortunately, school system hiring processes are largely a black box operation to researchers, at least in terms of the available systemic information about the efficacy of the specific processes schools (or districts) use in selecting among teacher applicants (DeArmond & Goldhaber, 2005).

The little evidence that does exist suggests that the hiring processes could be better. Ballou (1996), for instance, conducts research on the likelihood that teachers with various attributes are hired, and finds that districts do not appear to value measures of academic proficiency: teacher applicants who attended "above average" colleges are found to be significantly less likely to be hired than were applicants who had attended "below average colleges." Furthermore, Ballou finds that teacher attributes such as undergraduate GPA and subject specialties have only a small effect on an applicant's probability of being hired. The available empirical evidence suggests that public schools tend to rely on local labor pools to find teachers (Boyd et al., 2005b) and, though they do have preferences when it comes to hiring teacher candidates (Boyd et al., 2003), they rely on the presence of teacher licensure as a primary means of screening among applicants. They then look to graduation from a state-approved teacher education program as a secondary means of winnowing out the applicant field (U.S. Department of Education, 1996).

Research suggests that new teachers have relatively few interactions with school-based personnel during the hiring process (Liu & Johnson, 2006; Strauss et al., 2000). Few school systems—less than 10 percent in a recent study (Liu, 2003)—require prospective teachers to demonstrate their craft through the teaching of a sample lesson. Instead, districts rely on transcripts, letters of reference, and resumes (Balter & Duncombe, forthcoming) and many—perhaps as many as 2,000 school districts, though the actual number is unknown (Metzger & Wu, in press)—rely on relatively short structured interviews to help make hiring decisions. There does not appear to be any independent analysis suggesting that these teacher interview instruments (e.g., the Urban Teacher Selection "Star" Teacher Interview and Gallup's Teacher Perceiver Interview protocol) can be used to detect teacher quality.[33]

The lack of knowledge about the effectiveness of local school systems' teacher selection processes is troubling. Better knowledge about these processes would provide insights about the merits of tightening or loosening the teacher certification gateway.

TEACHER WORKFORCE POLICIES

Shaping a high-quality teacher workforce through legislative and regulatory policies has proven thus far to be an elusive goal. It is difficult if not impossible to address the teacher quality issue through federal or state mandates given the apparent weak link between paper credentials and student outcomes, which makes choosing the "right" teachers an imprecise endeavor. Illustrate this point with an example from my own work on NBPTS certification. As I described above, work with a colleague (Goldhaber & Anthony, 2007) finds that a teacher being NBPTS-certified has a statistically significant impact on student achievement and the effect, about 5 percent of a standard deviation, is non-trivial. But, what does this mean for NBPTS status as a predictor of teacher quality? To answer this question, in follow-up work (Goldhaber, 2006), I estimate the total impact that teachers in the study have on their students and divide the sample of teachers into those who are NBPTS-certified and those who are not.[34] This simulation shows that teachers who become NBPTS-certified are likely to have larger teacher impacts than the average teacher in the sample, but not terribly consistently: 59 percent of NBPTS-certified teachers have above-average effects in math, and 56 percent have above-average effects in reading—certainly more than what one would expect from a teacher taken from the workforce at random (50 percent), but far from an overwhelming percentage of the NBPTS-certified population as a whole.

One conclusion that could be drawn from the considerable heterogeneity in teacher effectiveness is that schools ought to craft and emphasize policies that evaluate teachers based on their actual in-service practices and performance. There are various types of reforms along these lines. For example, it is not too controversial to suggest that the type of professional development offered to teachers be tailored to individual teacher needs. More controversial are calls for changes in teacher-tenure policies that diminish the up-front (often after three years) teacher job security that exists in many districts (Johnson & Donaldson, 2006). Also contentious is the notion that pay systems ought to be restructured, either so they are more closely aligned to teacher productivity, so-called "merit pay" (Ballou & Podgursky, 1993; Hanushek & Rivkin, 2003; Teaching Commission, 2006), or so that they encourage teachers to acquire key teaching skills, "knowledge and skills pay" (Odden & Wallace, 2007).[35]

The NBPTS model probably represents the most prominent and significant of these teacher workforce policies. Supporters of NBPTS believe it plays an important role in professionalizing teaching and ultimately will increase students' learning by helping to change the culture in schools and spread productive teaching practices. As of 2005 there were over 47,500 NBPTS-certified teachers. The cost to society of these teachers depends on the extent of support and services they receive from states or school districts. Rice (forthcoming), in a case study of four NBPTS support programs, estimates that the participant cost—including, for instance, the payment of the application fee, administrative infrastructure and mentoring costs—of these programs ranges from about $18,000 to $31,000 per participant. And, Goldhaber and Anthony (2007) estimate that the investment to-date in the NBPTS model, either through application fees or direct government or foundation grant funding, has exceeded $400 million.

The financial support for NBPTS shows that it has been broadly accepted as a workable and productive educational policy. But, as I described above, it is clear that, at least as measured by the standardized test achievement of students in a teacher's classroom, NBPTS certification represents a somewhat imprecise targeting of effective teachers.[36] For this reason there are many who argue for policies that more narrowly focus on benchmarking teacher performance based on student achievement on tests and then, based on this, crafting policies that encourage effective teachers to remain in the profession and weak performers to either improve or leave the profession. One of the most popular and controversial of these is merit pay, a reform that has been in the news quite a bit as of late, with several big-city school systems (Denver and Houston among them) opting to experiment with this particular alternative teacher compensation policy.

Research on merit pay provides a mixed picture of its efficacy: efforts by school districts to offer merit pay to their teachers have been largely deemed unsuccessful in practice (Ballou, 2001; Goldhaber, 2002; Hatry, Greiner, & Ashford ,1994; Murnane & Cohen, 1986). The "failure" of merit pay programs is due to one or more issues. Unions (and often teachers) typically oppose this pay structure so it can lead to both political strife and problems with teacher morale. It is difficult and controversial to identify those teachers deserving of a merit bonus, and as a result, in many systems so many teachers receive bonuses that the pay system becomes unaffordable. On the other hand, some research has actually suggested that merit pay, either targeted toward individual teachers (Dee & Keys, 2004; Figlio & Kenny, 2005; Lavy, 2002) or designed as a school-based incentive (Clotfelter & Ladd, 1996), can lead to better student achievement.

While policies designed to reward teachers for their contribution toward students' performance, such as merit pay, sound sensible and straightforward, they presume an ability to accurately measure classroom performance. There are in fact ample technical challenges when it comes to measuring individual teacher performance. For example, there are legitimate questions as to whether value-added teacher models ought to include adjustments for differences in the backgrounds of a teacher's students (Ballou, Sanders, & Wright, 2004; McCaffrey et al., 2004). Furthermore, there is little research to date on the extent to which teacher effectiveness, measured by student achievement gains, is a stable characteristic and one would not want to inappropriately reward or sanction a teacher, or expend professional development resources, based on what may only be a 'statistical blip.' Is a teacher who is very effective in one year likely to be effective in the next? Is a teacher who is very effective in teaching math likely also to be effective in teaching reading? Is a teacher who is effective with advantaged students likely also to be effective in teaching disadvantaged students? The answers to these types of key questions are knowable, but we are only at the leading edge of answering them.[37]

In the case of teacher-tenure reforms, there is substantial political opposition from the teachers' unions that wield considerable power in many states and localities (Moe, 2005), especially in the context of collective bargaining rights (Hess, Maranto, & Milliman, 2000). These same political forces appear to limit the use of merit pay (Goldhaber et al., 2006), or any alternative to the single salary schedule (Johnson & Donaldson, 2006; Johnson & Kardos, 2000). The use of merit pay is clearly also hampered by the technical issues described above and the fact that a significant proportion of the teacher workforce is not teaching in an area that is covered by state-mandated student assessment tests, the gains from which are often proposed as a benchmark for evaluating teacher performance.[38] Research on professional development shows that it can, at times and in some contexts, have an impact on teacher performance, but, by and large, the typical one-shot workshops that are often offered to teachers have failed to lead to performance changes (Cohen & Hill, 2000; Garet et al., 2001; Kennedy, 1998).[39]

So, does all this suggest that teacher workforce reforms face insurmountable hurdles? I would argue that it's too early to tell—we do not yet know enough to determine the feasibility of using student achievement data to drive workforce policies. But, policy makers from a number of states and localities have clearly taken the position that the devil they don't know is better than the devil they do, at least in the context of teacher compensation. Denver and Houston are examples of localities that have embarked on high-profile experiments with pay-for-performance, Minnesota and Florida are moving in that direction at the state level, and the new Teacher Incentive Fund from the U. S. Department of Education encourages these types of experiments. Ideally, policy makers, regardless of their position on these particular reforms, will encourage research on their effects so we can learn from these experiments. This would move the debate about workforce reforms from one that is largely based on inferences about the lack of efficacy of pre-service policies to one based on demonstrated effects of specific teacher-workforce policies and programs.

NOTES

1. Here and henceforth the terms "student achievement" and "student outcomes" should be treated as synonymous with "value-added gains on achievement tests". The term "teacher quality" refers to the ability of teachers to produce such gains on achievement tests.
2. Both Rivkin et al. (2005) and Rockoff (2004) find that a one-standard deviation increase in teacher quality is estimated to raise student achievement in reading and math by about 10 percent of a standard deviation. Furthermore, this effect swamps other educational resource interventions— being equivalent to a reduction in class size of 10 to 13 students (Rivkin et al., 2005).
3. For specific legal definition of "highly qualified teachers" see No Child Left Behind Act, Title IX, Sec. 901, Part A, Sec. 9101.23.
4. For more background on educational production function methods and studies, see Goldhaber and Brewer (1997a, 1997b), Hanushek (1979), or Todd and Wolpin (2003).
5. Specifically, we estimated the contribution of unobservable teacher effects by calculating the incremental contribution to explained variation of adding teacher fixed effects to an educational production function model that includes school fixed effects and observable student and class covariates.
6. This estimate falls squarely within the range of estimates reported by Nye, Konstantopoulos, and Hedges (2004) from 18 different studies.
7. Rivkin et al. (2005), for instance, finds about 10 percent is explained by such characteristics. For a summary of this literature see, for example, Darling-Hammond (2000), Rice (2003), Wayne and Youngs (2003) or Wilson, Floden, and Ferrini-Mundy (2001).
8. Non-random attrition from the teacher labor force could also lead to biased estimates of the coefficient on teacher experience.
9. The fact that teachers of varying experience levels are likely not randomly assigned to students of varying abilities can lead researchers to misattribute the impact of student-teacher matching to teacher experience (or any other observable teacher characteristic), but this issue can be dealt with using appropriate statistical techniques given a particular data structure.
10. Specifically, Rivkin et al. (2005) estimate that elementary and middle school students (in 4th–7th grades) of teachers with no prior experience are about 3–5 percent of a standard deviation worse off in both math and reading than those with teachers who have one year of experience. In contrast, the gain from the increased experience achieved by going from the 1st to the 2nd year of teaching is smaller (and borderline statistically significant) at around 2 to 3 percent of a standard deviation. Rivkin et al. find little gain in experience beyond year two of teaching. Clotfelter et al. (2006; forthcoming) find similar results. In math they find a gain between the first and second year of teaching of between 5 to 7 percent of a standard deviation, and in reading the gain ranges from 2 to 4 percent of a standard deviation. The Rivkin et al. study includes student and school fixed effects, while the Clotfelter et al. includes student lagged test scores.
11. Follow-up studies by Hanushek reach similar conclusions about the effects of teacher degree and experience levels. As an example, in Hanushek's 1989 review, teachers' advanced degrees predicted higher levels of student achievement in only 13 of the 183 studies reviewed, and there was a *negative*

relationship in 6 of the 13 studies. Even the Greenwald et al. (1996) review, which reaches far more positive conclusions about the ability to predict teacher quality based on teacher attributes, only finds a statistically significant, positive association between teacher degree and student achievement in 15 percent of the cases (and a statistically significant, negative effect in 13 percent of the cases).

12. Specifically, they find that a teacher having an undergraduate major in math increases students' math achievement by about 5 percent of a standard deviation and having a Masters degree in math increases students' math achievement by an additional 4 percent of a standard deviation. A teacher having an undergraduate science major increases students' achievement in science by 9 percent of a standard deviation (they did not find a statistically significant effect for advanced degrees in science). The same results were not found to be true for teachers of English or history, where the authors do not find college major (or subject area of a Masters degree) to influence student achievement.
13. Hill et al. did not report the student post-test standard deviation so it is not possible to present conventional effect sizes that are comparable to those specified elsewhere in this report.
14. I use the terms "licensure" and "certification" interchangeably (except when discussing NBPTS certification) as is the practice in education research.
15. Darling-Hammond (2002) wrote that Walsh's 2001 report "dismissed or misreported much of the existing evidence in order to argue that teacher education makes no difference to teacher performance or student learning, and that students would be better off without state efforts to regulate entry into teaching or to provide supports for teachers' learning" (p. 60). A rejoinder by Walsh to Darling-Hammond refutes this assertion.
16. For examples of other reviews, see Wilson et al. (2001) and Clift and Brady (2005).
17. They find that there is roughly a 10 percent of a standard deviation increase in math scores for high school students whose math teacher is fully licensed in math.
18. Emergency certification can be issued to teachers who have not satisfied all of the requirements necessary to obtain a standard certificate.
19. Upon selection to the TFA program, TFA corps members must complete a five-week summer training institute at one of the regional centers. Following the summer institute, teachers must comply with any other state and/or local requirements for certification such as passing required certification exams or continuing coursework during their teaching assignment. The exact requirements vary depending on the local agreements that districts have made with TFA. See http://www.teachforamerica.org/tfa/certification.html for more information.
20. The effect sizes (relative to traditionally certified teachers) for uncertified TFA teachers range from –0.03 to –0.30 of a standard deviation in reading and math, while the effect sizes for certified TFA teachers range from 0 to 0.11 of a standard deviation.
21. Nor do they account for clustering of students within classes, which is likely to influence the level of statistical significance of their findings (i.e., the precision of their estimates are likely overstated).
22. Aside from concerns about their effectiveness, a second concern about TFA teachers is their high rate of attrition out of the teacher labor market. A number of studies highlight issues associated with the attrition rate out of teaching. Teacher turnover has received substantial attention in research because of the costs associated with finding and hiring teachers as well as potential impacts on student performance. Besides the relatively short (formal two–year) time commitment that TFA teachers make to teach, there are other reasons to expect that TFA teachers would have high turnover rates. For instance, research has found that teachers have higher rates of attrition if they are teaching in urban schools (Levinson, 1988; Hanushek et al., 2004), if they are from strong academic undergraduate institutions (Murnane & Olsen, 1989, 1990), if they are secondary science teachers (Murnane & Olsen, 1989, 1990), and if their level of specific human capital (i.e., they have training specifically applicable for teaching, such as an education major) is low relative to their general human capital (Grissmer & Kirby, 1992).
23. Because these students are randomly assigned, one would not expect the match between teachers and students to result in any systematic differences in the estimates of student achievement growth.
24. Kane et al. (2006) is another recent study (using New York City data) that compares TFA teachers to teachers who enter the workforce through alternate routes. The findings from this study are similar to

those in Boyd et al.: differences in teacher performance by route (TFA or other) are generally quite small. In fact, this research shows that the differences between routes are small relative to the differences between teachers within each of these routes.

25. Aggregation also limits the ability to detect differential teacher effects on different types of students.
26. A few individual student-level studies focus on other measures of academic proficiency. Ehrenberg and Brewer (1994), for instance, include a measure of the selectivity of a teacher's undergraduate institution (based on the Barron's college ratings) in their model and find that students learn more from teachers who attended more-selective undergraduate institutions. They found that an increase of one selectivity category would increase white students' gain scores by about 0.4 points and black students' scores by about 1.5 points. This is to be compared with a mean white student gain score in the sample of 0.56 points. Rowan, Chiang, and Miller (1997), using individual-level student data from the National Educational Longitudinal Study of 1988 (NELS), find that whether a teacher correctly answers *the single mathematics question* on the NELS survey predicts their students' performance on a mathematics test. Answering correctly is estimated to increase student achievement by 2 percent of a standard deviation.
27. Goldhaber (forthcoming) focuses on elementary grades (3rd–5th) and finds roughly similar results: a 1 standard deviation change in teacher test-score performance is predicted to increase student test scores by slightly less than 1 percent of a standard deviation in reading and slightly less than 4 percent of a standard deviation in math.
28. A number of studies on NBPTS-certified teachers and their impacts on student learning are ongoing at the time of this writing. The results of these writings should be available as they are published at http://www.nbpts.org/research/index.cfm.
29. NBPTS-certified teachers tend to have positive effects, but they are small and generally do not reach conventional levels of statistical significance.
30. For more information on the growing use of alternative certification and changes in eligibility requirements to teach, see, for instance, NASDTEC Manual (2002), *The Teaching Commission* (2006), or National Center for Alternative Certification website (http;//www.teach-now.org).
31. The implication of this is that the variation in teacher quality is increased as a consequence of the relaxation of certification requirements.
32. Based on a review of the evidence, Metzger and Wu (in press) conclude that there is little empirical evidence that these instruments are related to (any measure of) teacher effectiveness.
33. To measure the total teacher impact, I estimate a model that includes teacher fixed effects and then predict the size of each teacher's fixed effect. The findings from this simulation should be interpreted with caution, since the "teacher effect" is based only on a three-year panel of matched teachers and students, and the simulation discussed below does not account for either the size of individual teacher effects nor the statistical precision to which they are measured.
34. Calls to reform teacher compensation are not new; in fact, most of the *Nation at Risk* recommendations called for the link between teacher pay and performance (Odden & Wallace, 2007).
35. NBPTS and its supporters likely would suggest that NBPTS certified teachers do far more than just increase student learning on standardized tests.
36. As Kane and Staiger (2002) illustrate in the case of measuring school-level performance, there is a substantial amount of "noise" resulting from test measurement error or the luck of the draw in students.
37. See, for instance, Aaronson, Barrow, and Sander (2003), Ballou et al. (2004), and Koedel and Betts (2005), as recent studies that focus on some of these issues.
38. New research suggests there may be alternatives to using student tests as the primary benchmark for teacher performance. Research by Jacob and Lefgren (2006), for instance, suggests that principals generally do a good job of distinguishing the most- and least-effective teachers. Regardless of the accuracy of measuring teacher performance, simply knowing that there exists some type of teacher performance-based accountability may itself change behavior.
39. Research on professional development has focused both on the form or delivery that in-service training takes (e.g., who leads in-service training, whether the training is a one-shot workshop or more time intensive with follow-up) and on the content of the training (e.g., subject-matter, working with special

education students, or classroom management techniques). There are a tremendous number of studies on these issues, but most of them are either small-sample case studies or they focus on the impact of training on teacher attitudes or instructional practices. Those studies that do focus on measures of student achievement tend to be methodologically weak. For example, few studies include the types of school, teacher, and student background controls that are common in the educational production function studies.

REFERENCES

Aaronson, D., Barrow, L., & Sander, W. (2003). *Teachers and student achievement in the chicago public high schools.* Federal Reserve Bank of Chicago, Working Paper Series: WP-02–28.

Ballou, D. (1996). Do public schools hire the best applicants? *Quarterly Journal of Economics, 111*(1), 97–133.

Ballou, D. (2001).Pay for performance in public and private schools. *Economics of Education Review, 20,* 51–61.

Ballou, D., & Podgursky, M. (1993). Teachers' attitudes toward merit pay: Examining conventional wisdom. *Industrial and Labor Relations Review, 47*(1), 50–61.

Ballou, D., & Podgursky, M. (1998). The case against teacher certification. *Public Interest, 132,* 17–29.

Ballou, D., Sanders, W., & Wright, P. (2004). Controlling for student background in value-added assessment of teachers. *Journal of Educational and Behavioral Studies, 29*(1), 37–65.

Balter, D., & Duncombe, W. (forthcoming). Recruiting highly qualified teachers: Do district recruitment practices matter? *Public Finance Review.*

Boyd, D., Lankford, H., Loeb, S., & J. Wyckoff. (2003). *Analyzing the determinants of the matching public school teachers to jobs: Estimating compensating differentials in imperfect labor markets.* NBER Working Paper No. 9878.

Boyd, D., Grossman, P., Lankford, H., Loeb, S., & Wyckoff, J. (2005a). How changes in entry requirements alter the teacher workforce and affect student achievement. Retrieved September 11. 2007, from the New York State School Finance Reform online archive: http://finance.tc-library.org/Content.asp?abstract=true&uid=1771.

Boyd, D., Lankford, H., Loeb, S., & Wyckoff, J. (2005b). The draw of home: How teachers' preferences for proximity disadvantage urban schools. *Journal Analysis of Policy Analysis and Management, 24*(1), 113–132.

Boyd, D., Goldhaber, D., Lankford, H., & Wyckoff, J. (2007). The effect of certification and preparation on teacher quality. *Future of Children, 17*(1), 45–68.

Cavalluzzo, L. C. (2004). Is national board certification an effective signal of teacher quality? The CNA Corporation. Retrieved September 11, 2007 from http://www.cna.org/documents/CavaluzzoStudy.pdf.

Clift, R. T., & Brady, P. (2005). Research on methods courses and field experiences. In M. Cochran-Smith & K. Zeichner (Eds.), *Studying teacher education: The report of the AERA panel on research and teacher education* (pp. 309–424). Mahwah, NJ: Erlbaum.

Clotfelter, C. T., & Ladd. H. F.. (1996). Recognizing and rewarding success in public schools. In H. F. Ladd (Ed.), *Holding schools accountable: Performance-based reform in education* (pp. 23–63). Washington, D.C.: The Brookings Institution

Clotfelter, C. T., Ladd, H. F., & Vigdor, J. (2006). Teacher-student matching and the assessment of teacher effectiveness. *Journal of Human Resources, 41*(4), 778–820.

Clotfelter, C. T., Ladd, H. F., & Vigdor, J. (forthcoming). Teacher credentials and student achievement: Longitudinal analysis with student fixed effects." *Economics of Education Review.* (A longer version of this paper is also available as NBER Working Paper 12828, How and why do teacher credentials matter for student achievement?")

Cohen, D. K., & Hill, C. (2000). Instructional policy and classroom performance: The mathematics reform in California. *Teachers College Record, 102*(2), 294–343.

Coleman, J. S. (1966). *Equality of educational opportunity*. Washington, D.C.: U.S. Dept. of Health, Education, and Welfare, Office of Education.

Croninger, R. G., Rice, J. K., Rathbun, A., & Nishio, M.. (2007).Teacher qualifications and early learning: Effects of certification, degree, and experience on first-grade student achievement. *Economics of Education Review, 26*(3), 312–324.

Darling-Hammond, L. (2000). Teacher Quality and Student Achievement: A Review of State Policy Evidence. *Education Policy Analysis Archives, 8*(1). Retrieved September 5, 2006, from http://epaa.asu.edu/epaa/v8n1.html.

Darling-Hammond, L. (2002). Research and rhetoric on teacher certification: A response to "Teacher Certification Reconsidered," *Education Policy Analysis Archives, 10*(36). Retrieved September 5, 2006, from http://epaa.asu.edu/epaa/v10n36.html.

Darling-Hammond, L., Holtzman, D. J., Gatlin, S. J., & Heilig, J. V. (2005). Does teacher preparation matter? Evidence about teacher certification, Teach for America, and teacher effectiveness. *Education Policy Analysis Archives, 13*(42). Retrieved September 5, 2006, from http://epaa.asu.edu/epaa/v13n42.html.

DeArmond, M., & Goldhaber, D. (2005). The Back Office: The Neglected Side of Teacher Quality. *Education Week, 24*(22), 31–32.

Dee, T., &. Cohodes, S. (2005). Out-of-Field Teachers and Students Achievement: Evidence from "Matched-Pairs" Comparisons. Unpublished manuscript.

Dee, T. S., & Keys, B. J. (2004). Does merit pay reward good teachers? Evidence from a randomized experiment. *Journal of Policy Analysis and Management, 23*(3), 471–488.

Eberts, R. W., & Stone, J. A. (1984). *Unions and public schools: the effect of collective bargaining on American education*. Lexington, MA, Lexington Books.

Ehrenberg, R. G., & Brewer, D. J. (1994). Do school and teacher characteristics matter? Evidence from high school and beyond. *Economics of Education Review, 13*(1), 1–17.

Ferguson, R. F. (1991). Paying for public-education — New evidence on how and why money matters. *Harvard Journal on Legislation, 28*(2), 465–498.

Ferguson, R. F. (1998). Can schools narrow the Black-White test score gap?. In C. Jencks & M. Phillips (Eds.), *The Black-White test score gap* (pp. 318–374). Washington, D.C.: The Brookings Institution.

Ferguson, R. F., & Ladd, H. F. (1996). How and why money matters: An analysis of Alabama schools. In H. F. Ladd (Ed.), *Holding schools accountable: performance-based reform in education* (pp. 265–298). Washington, D.C.: The Brookings Institution.

Figlio, D. N., & Kenny, L. W. (2005). Do individual teacher incentives boost student performance? Working Paper.

Garet, M. S., Porter, A. C., Desimone, L., Birman, B. F., & Yoon, K. S.. (2001). What makes professional development effective? Results from a national sample of teachers. *American Educational Research Journal, 38*(4), 915–945.

Glazerman, S., Mayer, D. P., & Decker, P. T. (2006). Alternative routes to teaching: The impacts of Teach for America on student achievement and other outcomes. *Journal of Policy Analysis and Management, 25*(1), 75–96.

Goldhaber, D. (2002). Teacher quality and teacher pay structure: What do we know, and what are the options? *Georgetown Public Policy Review, 7*(2), 81–94.

Goldhaber, D. (2004). Why do we license teachers? In F. Hess, A. Rotherham, & K. Walsh (Eds.), *A qualified teacher in every classroom: Appraising old answers and new ideas* (pp. 81–100). Cambridge, MA: Harvard Education Press.

Goldhaber, D. (2006). National Board teachers are more effective, but are they in the classrooms where they're needed the most? *Education Finance and Policy, 1*(3), 372–282.

Goldhaber, D. (2007). Everyone's doing it, but what does teacher testing tell us about teacher effectiveness? *Journal of Human Resources, 42*(4), 765–794.

Goldhaber, D. (forthcoming). Teacher licensure tests and student achievement: Is teacher testing an effective policy? In D. Chaplin & J. Hannaway (Eds.), *Learning from longitudinal data in education*. Washington, D.C.: UI Press.

Goldhaber, D., & Anthony, E. (2007). Can teacher quality be effectively assessed? National Board Certification as a signal of effective teaching. *Review of Economics and Statistics, 89*(1), 134–150.

Goldhaber, D., Anthony, E., & Perry, D. (2004). NBPTS certification: Who applies and what factors are associated with success? *Educational Evaluation and Policy Analysis, 26*(4), 259–280.

Goldhaber, D., & Brewer, D. J. (1997a). Why don't schools and teachers seem to matter? Assessing the impact of unobservables on educational productivity. *Journal of Human Resources, 32*(3), 505–523.

Goldhaber, D., & Brewer, D. J. (1997b). Evaluating the effect of teacher degree level on educational performance. In J. W. Flower (ed.), *Developments in school finance 1996* (pp. 197–210). Washington, D.C., National Center for Education Statistics..

Goldhaber, D., & Brewer, D. J. (2000). Does teacher certification matter? High school teacher certification status and student achievement. *Educational Evaluation and Policy Analysis, 22*(2), 129–145.

Goldhaber, D., Brewer, D. J., Anderson, D. (1999). A three-way error components analysis of educational productivity. *Education Economics, 7*(3), 199–208.

Goldhaber, D., Player, D., DeArmond, M., & Choi, H. J. (2006). Why do so few public school districts use merit pay? Working paper.

Gordon, R., Kane, T. J., & Staiger, D. O. (2006). Identifying effective teachers using performance on the job. The Hamilton Project: Discussion Paper 2006–01. Washington, D.C.: Brookings Institution. Retrieved September 11, 2007, from http://www.brook.edu/views/papers/200604hamilton_1.pdf.

Greenwald, R., Hedges, L. V., & Laine, R. D. (1996). The effect of school resources on student achievement. *Review of Educational Research, 66*(3), 361–396.

Grissmer, D. W. & Kirby, S. N. (1992). Patterns of attrition among Indiana teachers, 1965–1987 (Report No. R-4076-LE). Santa Monica, CA, The RAND Corporation.

Hanushek, E. A. (1979). Conceptual and empirical issues in the estimation of education production functions. *Journal of Human Resources, 14*(3), 351–388.

Hanushek, E.A. (1981). Throwing money at schools. *Journal of Policy Analysis and Management, 1*, 19–41.

Hanushek, E. A. (1986). The economics of schooling: Production and efficiency in public schools. *Journal of Economic Literature, 24*(3), 1141–1177.

Hanushek, E. A. (1989). The impact of differential expenditures on school performance. *Educational Researcher, 18*(4), 45–51,62.

Hanushek, E. A. (1992). The trade-off between child quantity and quality. *Journal of Political Economy,* 100(1), 84–117.

Hanushek, E. A. (1997). Assessing the effects of school resources on student performance: An update. *Educational Evaluation and Policy Analysis, 19*(2), 141–164.

Hanushek, E.A., & Rivkin, S. G. (2003). How to improve the supply of high quality teachers. Brookings Papers on Education Policy.

Hanushek, E. A., Rivkin, S. G., & Taylor, L. L. (1996). Aggregation and the estimated effects of school resources. *Review of Economics and Statistics, 78*(4), 611–627.

Hanushek, E. A., Kain, J. F., & Rivkin, S. G. (2004). Why public schools lose teachers. *Journal of Human Resources, 39*(2), 326–354.

Hatry, H. P., Greiner, J. M., & Ashford, B. G. (1994). *Issues and case studies in teacher incentive plans* (2nd ed.). Washington, D.C.: The Urban Institute Press.

Hess, F. M., Maranto, R., & Milliman, S. (2000). Resistance in the trenches: What shapes teachers' attitudes toward school choice? *Educational Policy, 14*(2), 195–213.

Hill, H. C., Rowan, B., & Ball, D. L. (2005). Effects of teachers' mathematical knowledge for teaching on student achievement. *American Educational Research Journal,* 42(2), 371–406.

Jacob, B., & Lefgren, L. (2006). When principals rate teachers. *Education Next, 6*(2): 59–64.

Johnson, S. M., & Donaldson, M. L. (2006). The effects of collective bargaining on teacher quality. In J. Hannaway & A. J. Rotherham (Eds.), *Collective bargaining in education* (pp. 111–140). Cambridge, MA: Harvard Education Press.

Johnson, S. M., & Kardos, S. M. (2000). Reform bargaining and its promise for school improvement. In T. Loveless (Ed.), *Conflicting missions? Teachers unions and educational reform* (pp. 7–46). Washington, D.C.: Brookings Institution Press.

Kane, T. J., & Staiger, D. O. (2002) The promise and pitfalls of using imprecise school accountability measures. *Journal of Economic Perspectives, 16*(4), 91–114.
Kane, T. J., Rockoff, J. E., & Staiger, D. O. (2006). What does certification tell us about teacher effectiveness? Evidence from New York City. Working Paper.
Kennedy, M. (1998). Form and substance in in-service teacher education. Research Monograph, Vol. 13. Madison: University of Wisconsin.
Koedel, C., & Betts, J. (2005). Re-examining the role of teacher quality in the educational production function. Working Paper: University of California, San Diego.
Lankford, H., Loeb, S., & Wyckoff, J. (2000). The labor market for public school teachers: A descriptive analysis of New York State's teacher workforce. New York State Educational Finance Research Consortium.
Lankford, H., Loeb, S., & Wyckoff, J. (2002). "Teacher Sorting and the Plight of Urban Schools: A Descriptive Analysis." *Educational Evaluation and Policy Analysis*, 24(1), 38–62.
Lavy, V. (2002). Evaluating the effect of teachers' group performance incentives on pupil achievement. *Journal of Political Economy,* 110, 1286–1317.
Levinson, A. (1988). Reexamining teacher preferences and compensating wages. *Economics of Education Review,* 7(3), 357–364.
Liu, E. (2003). *New teachers' experiences of hiring: Preliminary findings from a four-state study*. American Educational Research Association, Chicago, Harvard Graduate School of Education.
Liu, E., & Johnson, S. M. (2006). New teachers' experiences of hiring: Late, rushed, and information-poor. *Educational Administration Quarterly, 42(*3), 324–360.
McCaffrey, D. F., Lockwood, J. R., Kortez, D. M., & Hamilton, L. S. (2003). *Evaluating Value-Added Models for Teacher Accountability*. Santa Monica, CA: RAND Corporation.
McCaffrey, D. F., Lockwood, J. R., Kortez, D. M., Louis, T. A., & Hamilton, L. S. (2004). Models for value-added modeling of teacher effects. *Journal of Educational and Behavioral Statistics, 29*(1), 67–102.
Metzger, S. A., & Wu, M.-J. (in press). Commercial teacher selection instruments: The validity of selecting teachers through beliefs, attitudes, and values. *Review of Educational Research.*
Moe, T. (2005). Political control and the power of the agent. Unpublished manuscript, Stanford University.
Monk, D. H. (1994). Subject area preparation of secondary mathematics and science teachers and student achievement. *Economics of Education Review,* 13(2), 125–145.
Monk, D., & Rice, J. K. (1994). Multi-level teacher resource effects on pupil performance in secondary mathematics and science: The role of teacher subject matter preparation. In R. G. Ehrenberg (Ed.), *Contemporary policy issues: Choices and consequences in education* (pp. 29–58). Ithaca, NY: ILR Press.
Murnane, R. J. (1975). *The impact of school resources on the learning of inner city children.* Cambridge, MA: Balinger Publishing Company.
Murnane, R. J., & Cohen, D. K. (1986). Merit pay and the evaluation problem: Why most merit pay plans fail and a few survive. *Harvard Education Review, 56*(1), 1–17.
Murnane, R. J., & Olsen, R. J. (1989). The effects of salaries and opportunity costs on duration in teaching: Evidence from Michigan. *Review of Economics and Statistics, 71*(2), 347–352.
Murnane, R. J., & Olsen, R. J. (1990). The effects of salaries and opportunity costs on length of stay in teaching: Evidence from North Carolina. *Journal of Human Resources, 25*(1), 106–124.
Murnane, R. J., & Phillips, B. R. (1981). Learning by doing, vintage, and selection: Three pieces of the puzzle relating teaching experience and teaching performance. *Economics of Education Review, 1*(4), 453–465.
NASDTEC Manual (2002). *The NASDTEC manual on the preparation and certification of educational personnel* (6th ed.). Sacramento, CA: National Association of State Directors of Teachers Education and Certification.
Nye, B., Konstantopoulos, S., & Hedges, L. V. (2004). How large are teacher effects? *Educational Evaluation and Policy Analysis 26***,** 237–258.
Odden, A., & Wallace, M. (2007). *Rewarding Teacher Excellence: A teacher compensation handbook for state and local policy makers.* Madison: University of Wisconsin, Consortium for Policy Research in Education.

Raymond, M. E., & Fletcher, S. (2002). Teach for America: An evaluation of teacher differences and student outcomes in Houston, Texas. *Education Next, 2*(1), 62–69.

Rice, J. K. (forthcoming). National board certification as professional development: What does it cost and how does it compare?" Manuscript under review at *EEPA*.

Rice, J. K. (2003). Investing in teacher quality: A framework of estimating the cost of teacher professional development. In W. Hoy & C. Miskel (Eds.), *Theory and research in educational administration*, volume 2 (pp. 209–233). Greenwich, CT: Information Age Publishing.

Rivkin, S., Hanushek, E. A., & Kain, J. F. (2005). Teachers, schools and academic achievement. *Econometrica,* 73(2), 417–458.

Rockoff, J.E. (2004). The Impact of Individual Teachers on Student Achievement: Evidence from Panel Data. *American Economic Review,* 94(2), 247–252.

Rowan, B., Chiang, F. S., & Miller, R. J. (1997). Using research on employees' performance to study the effects of teachers on students' achievement. *Sociology of Education, 70*(4), 256–284.

Sanders, W., & Horn, S. (1998). Research findings from the Tennessee value-added assessment system (TVAAS) database: Implications for educational evaluation and research. *Journal of Personnel Evaluation in Education, 12*(3), 247–256.

Sanders, W. L., & Rivers, J. C. (1996). Cumulative and residual effects of teachers on future student academic achievement. Knoxville: University of Tennessee Value-Added Research and Assessment Center. Research Progress Report:

Sanders, W. L., Alston, J. J., & Wright, S. P. (2005). Comparison of the effects of nbpts certified teachers with other teachers on the rate of student academic progress. Retrieved September 11. 2007 from http://www.nbpts.org/UserFiles/File/SAS_final_NBPTS_report_D_-_Sander s.pdf.

Strauss, R. P., Bowes, L. R., Marks, M. S., & Plesko, M. R. (2000). Improving teacher preparation and selection: lessons from the Pennsylvania experience. Economics of Education Review, 19(4), 387–415.

Teaching Commission (2006). *Teaching at tisk: Progress & potholes*. Final Report, Spring 2006.

Todd, P. E., & Wolpin, K. I. (2003). On the specification and estimation of the production function for cognitive achievement. *Economic Journal, 113*(485), F3–33.

U.S. Department of Education (1996). *Out of the lecture hall and into the classroom: 1992–93 college graduates and elementary/secondary school teaching,* NCES Report 96–899. Washington, D.C.: National Center for Education Statistics.

Vandevoort, L. G., Amrein-Beardsley, A., & Berliner, D. C. (2004). National board certified teachers and their students' achievement. *Education Policy Analysis Archives, 12*(46).

Walsh, K. (2001). *Teacher certification reconsidered: Stumbling for quality*. Baltimore, Abell Foundation.

Wayne, A. J., & Youngs, P. (2003). Teacher characteristics and student achievement gains: A review. *Review of Educational Research 73*(1), 89–122.

Wilson, S., R. Floden, R., & Ferrini-Mundy, J. (2001). *Teacher preparation research: Current knowledge, gaps, and recommendations.* Seattle: Center for the Study of Teaching and Policy, University of Washington.

Wright, P. S., Horn, S. P., & Sanders, W. L. (1997). Teacher and classroom context effects on student achievement: Implications for teacher evaluation. *Journal of Personnel Evaluation in Education, 11*(1), 57–67.

10

School Accountability and Student Achievement

David N. Figlio and Helen F. Ladd

Demands for more accountability and results-based incentive systems in K–12 education come from many directions and currently dominate much of the education policy discussion at both the state and federal levels (Ladd, 1996; Ladd & Hansen, 1999; Peterson & West, 2003). Accountability in education is a broad concept that could be addressed in many different ways: using political processes to assure democratic accountability, introducing market-based reforms to increase accountability to parents and children, developing peer-based accountability systems to increase the professional accountability of teachers, or using administrative accountability systems designed to drive the system toward higher student achievement. This chapter focuses on this last approach and pays particular attention to programs that focus on the individual school as the primary unit of accountability.

The accountability systems of interest here operate within the traditional public school system and rely heavily on student testing (Elmore, Abelmann, & Fuhrman, 1996; Clotfelter & Ladd, 1996; Hanushek & Raymond, 2003). Most emblematic is the federal No Child Left Behind Act (NCLB), which became law in 2002. NCLB requires states to test students in reading and mathematics in grades three to eight, as well as in one high school grade. In addition, it requires states to assess schools on the basis of whether their students (both in the aggregate and by subgroup) are making adequately yearly progress (AYP) toward the ultimate goal of 100 percent proficiency by 2014, and it imposes consequences on schools and districts that fail to make AYP. This law is the most recent incarnation of a bipartisan standards-based reform movement that emerged from a historic 1989 summit in Charlottesville, Virginia, between President George H.W. Bush and the state governors. That meeting generated a set of national education goals that were subsequently embedded in the Clinton administration's 1994 Goals 2000: Educate America Act. NCLB differs from that act by its far heavier emphasis on accountability and its significantly greater federal intrusion into the operations of individual schools and districts.

School-based accountability programs preceded NCLB in many states. As of 2001, 45 states published report cards on schools, and 27 of them rated schools or identified low-performing ones (*Education Week, Quality Counts,* 2001). Several states (e.g., North and South Carolina, Texas, Kentucky and Florida) as well as districts such as Chicago, Dallas and Charlotte-Mecklenburg, also had full school-based accountability programs in which they rated schools based on their students' performance, provided rewards either to schools or to teachers for improved performance, and provided some combination of sanctions and assistance to low-performing schools.[1]

THE RATIONALE FOR SCHOOL-BASED ACCOUNTABILITY

The current school-based accountability efforts emerged from the broader standards-based reform movement that began in the 1980s (O'Day & Smith, 1993). Standards-based reform involves the setting of clear, measurable and ambitious performance standards in a set of core academic subjects for students at various ages, aligning curriculum to these standards, and establishing high expectations for students to meet them. Assessment of students is a key component of standards-based reform. These assessments are used to measure student progress toward mastery of the standards and also the effectiveness of the schools they attend. The goal is to provide incentives for schools to raise student achievement.

In the context of standards-based reform, accountability is only one part of a larger policy package. Accountability—whether for schools, students, teachers or districts—can also be viewed as a stand-alone policy. One rationale for such a policy comes from comparisons to the private sector where business firms focus attention on results and rely on benchmarking procedures to measure progress. Another rationale is provided by the economists' model of the principal-agent problem. In such a model, school administrators and teachers may underperform because the state policy makers do not have a good means of monitoring them. It follows that student achievement would improve if state policy makers could monitor the teachers and school administrators more effectively.

School accountability systems serve as a mechanism for counteracting this principal-agent problem. By assessing schools against a common metric, policy makers generate independent information about the performance of schools and school districts. This common yardstick then allows policy makers to compare each school's performance to that of another school or to an external standard. By measuring, reporting and, in many cases, attaching positive consequences to strong school performance and negative consequences to weak performance, policy makers provide incentives for schools and school districts to focus attention on what is being measured and possibly to change the way in which they deliver education.[2]

The measurement and reporting of a school's progress allows policy makers to assess how successful a school has been in meeting the state's achievement goals. Although some researchers (e.g., Lavy, 2007) and policymakers favor accountability for individual teachers—through, for example, merit- or performance-based pay—rather than for schools, others view accountability at the school level as preferable both because it promotes collaboration among teachers and because schools have more opportunities than do individual teachers to enact the types of changes in resource allocation and practices that may be needed to raise student achievement (Ladd, 2001). Though accountability at the district level clearly has a place, exclusive accountability at that level could mask considerable differences in performance across schools within a district.

Most administrative accountability systems measure only a very small fraction of the educational outcomes that stakeholders value. The outcomes in such systems typically include student achievement as measured by test scores in only the core subjects of math and reading, supplemented in some cases (as under NCLB) with some non-test-based measures such as student attendance or graduation rates. As documented by Rothstein (this volume), educational stakeholders value a much broader range of academic outcomes as well as other outcomes such as citizenship. Thus, the narrow focus of administrative accountability systems on test results in math and reading clearly privileges one narrow set of outcomes over others.

DESIGN MATTERS

How a school accountability system is designed can have a significant impact on the nature of and the strength of the incentives that schools face to raise student achievement in the tested subjects. Moreover the design can affect which students are likely to receive the most additional attention.

Measuring School Performance

Broadly speaking, two main approaches have been used to measure school performance. The first is "status" measures in which schools are judged based on their levels of performance, typically measured by average test scores or by the fraction of students attaining certain proficiency levels. The second is "growth" or "value-added" measures in which schools are rated on how much they improve individual students' performance from one year to the next (Hanushek & Raymond, 2003). The simplest way to measure achievement growth, or value added, is to use gains in student test scores from one year to the next. In some cases, those gains, averaged across all students in the school, are then compared to the gains in test scores that are predicted for that school given the achievement level of its students in the prior year. More refined measures of value added can be based on regression models, with or without additional statistical controls for student characteristics (Clotfelter & Ladd, 1996; Ladd & Walsh, 2002). States and local school districts have used variations of both the status and the growth approach (Hanushek & Raymond, 2003). Although NCLB requires that schools be evaluated in terms of their "Adequate Yearly Progress" toward the ultimate goal of 100 percent proficiency, such "progress" is measured based on comparisons of aggregate levels of student performance from one year to the next. Thus, NCLB is essentially a status model not a growth model. The U.S Department of Education has recently given a few states the authority to introduce some growth elements into the basic approach.[3]

The two types of measures have somewhat different goals and generate somewhat different incentives. Status-based systems that focus on the percent of students who achieve at proficient levels seek to encourage schools to raise performance at least to that level. This approach is appealing to many policy makers because it sets the same target for all groups of students and because it encourages schools to focus attention on the set of low-performing students who in the past may have received little attention. Status-based systems also have the advantage of being transparent.

The goal of the growth model approach is to encourage schools to improve the performance of their students independently of the absolute level of that achievement. Such an approach is appealing to many people because of its perceived fairness. It explicitly takes into account the fact that where students end up is heavily dependent on where they start and the fact that the starting points tend to be highly correlated on average with family background. At the same time, the use of the growth model approach may raise political concerns, both because the public may find the approach less transparent than the status approach and because some see it as a way of letting schools with low average performance off the hook.

Systems using status and growth models generate different incentives in part because they lead to different rankings of schools. Many schools deemed ineffective based on their aggregate performance levels may actually have quite high "value added" and vice versa (Clotfelter & Ladd, 1996; Ladd & Walsh, 2002; Kane & Staiger, 2002; and Stiefel et al., 2005). Some accountability systems (e.g., North Carolina's) encourage both high levels of performance and high test score growth, by focusing on both levels and gains (Ladd & Zelli, 2002).

In addition, the two approaches send different signals about which students deserve more attention. Under a status-based system designed to encourage schools to raise student performance to some threshold level, the position of the threshold matters. A challenging performance threshold—one that would be consistent with the high aspirations of the standards-based reform movement, for example—would provide incentives for schools to focus attention on a larger group of students than would be the case with a lower threshold. Evaluating schools on the basis of value added, by contrast, provides a stronger incentive for schools to expend effort on the entire student body. In such a system, however, schools may have an incentive to focus attention on the more advantaged students because the test score gains of those students are likely to exceed those of the less advantaged students (Ladd & Walsh, 2002; Richards & Sheu, 1992).

Under either approach, random errors in the measurement of student performance can generate inconsistent rankings of schools over time—a factor that weakens incentives for improvement. That is especially true for small schools because the smaller is the number of students in the school, the larger is the school-wide average measurement error, and hence the less consistent the school's ranking is likely to be from one year to the next. Schools deemed to be improving at one point in time are often found to be declining the next year due to measurement error (Kane & Staiger, 2002). The problem of measurement error is exacerbated when schools are rated based on the growth model because it requires test scores for more then one year. The danger is that personnel in such schools may receive such inconsistent signals from one year to the next that they have little incentive to respond in a constructive way.

Neither approach to measuring school performance captures what economists call school efficiency—the effectiveness with which schools use their resources to maximize student outcomes, given the students they serve. According to the "education production function" model, student achievement is determined by the characteristics of the student and his or her classmates, the school's resources (including the quantity and qualifications of the teachers), and the efficiency with which those resources are used. Because efficiency cannot be observed directly, it must be inferred from statistical analysis that controls both for the resources available to the school and the characteristics of the students being served (Stiefel et al., 2005).

If the goal of an accountability system is to induce schools to use the resources they have more effectively, then, in principle, schools should be rated on their efficiency, not simply on the level or growth of their students' achievement. The problem is that the data requirements for such efficiency measures are often daunting and the statistical techniques can be complex (Ladd & Walsh, 2002; Stiefel et al., 2005).

In contrast to a measure of school efficiency, the status and growth measures provide information on whether or not schools are meeting expectations for either the level of or the growth in achievement with no attention to what accounts for that performance. Although inefficient use of available resources may be one reason for poor performance, another could well be that the resources available to the school are insufficient for the school to meet the accountability standard given the profile of the students in the school. In the latter case, it is neither fair nor likely to be productive for state or federal policy makers to blame the teachers or other school personnel for the poor performance of the school's students (Ladd & Walsh, 2002). Thus, accountability and the financing of schools are closely intertwined.

Treatment of Mobile Students and Students with Disabilities

A second design issue relates to decisions about which students to include within the accountability system. The state of Florida, for example, has taken two different tacks with regard to students who move in and out of schools. In its 1999 accountability system, Florida based school evaluations both on stable students and also on students who recently arrived in the school. The following year, however, school ratings were based only on students present in the school for the entire school year up to the testing date. These rule changes influenced the sets of schools identified as low- or high-quality (Figlio & Lucas, 2004). Although NCLB limits the students counted for a school's proficiency goals to those in the evaluated school for the full academic year, transient students are included in aggregate totals for the purposes of public reporting, and still count for district proficiency goals.

NCLB mandates that students with disabilities and those with limited proficiency in English be included in calculations of a school's Adequate Yearly Progress (and also as a separate subgroup). Once again policies differ across states. Virginia, for example, which adopted its inclusion rules before NCLB, applies the same inclusion criteria as required by the federal law. Florida, in contrast, excludes all students with disabilities, even those who take tests, from the school-level aggregates used to measure performance.

As a result, the student populations used to evaluate schools under NCLB differ from those used in its own accountability system. Excluding students with disabilities from school accountability measures is likely to lead schools to pay less attention to their performance than they would to other students. The incentives to do so, however, are less strong in states that use a growth model.

State policy makers face clear tradeoffs with respect to the treatment of these special populations. On the one hand, schools with large fractions of mobile and disabled students in many cases have a legitimate argument that holding them accountable for the academic achievement of such challenging-to-educate students puts them at an unfair disadvantage relative to other schools with fewer disabled students. On the other hand, excluding students on the basis of *classification* provides schools with an incentive to selectively reclassify or move students in order to look better against performance metrics. The evidence is quite clear that schools have responded to accountability pressures in this way (see, e.g., Cullen & Reback, forthcoming; Deere & Strayer 2001; Figlio & Getzler, forthcoming; Jacob, 2005). Thus, while the incentives to reclassify low-performing students as students with disabilities are small under NCLB, such incentives may still exist under state policy.[4]

We note, however, that these accountability-driven incentives for reclassifying students interact with school finance systems in complicated ways. For instance, in states that compensate school districts for disabled students on the basis of predicted—rather than actual—disability caseloads, a district that reclassifies a student as disabled to avoid having that student counted for the purposes of accountability will generate higher costs for the district because it is responsible for the full costs of providing special services for the student. In states that compensate school districts for the extra costs of educating students who are specifically classified as disabled, in contrast, the finance system will exacerbate any incentives to overclassify students provided by the accountability system.

Subgroups Within a School

Another design issue specifically related to NCLB involves the treatment of multiple subgroups within a school. Under NCLB, a school is held accountable not only for the performance of the full student body, but also for the performance of subgroups of students defined by their race, income and disability status. Because of the small size of many subgroups, this subgroup requirement exacerbates the problems of measurement error highlighted by Kane & Staiger (2002). Nonetheless, NCLB requires such disaggregation on the ground that it provides incentives for schools to pay attention to members of each subgroup and thereby prevents schools from leaving particular groups of children behind.

States have the authority under NCLB to determine the minimum size of subgroups that are separately measured and reported, and states have set very different thresholds. Thresholds vary from five students in Maryland to as many as 50 to 200 students depending on the size of the school in Texas.

The identification of subgroups, and the attendant issue of the size requirements for subgroup identification, influences the likelihood that a school will meet all of the AYP criteria. When the subgroup size thresholds are low, the more racially heterogeneous schools will have more measured subgroups and will face greater risks of low accountability ratings compared to more homogeneous schools because any negative random error in any single subgroup is sufficient to lead to a negative rating for a school. Using national data, Stullich et al. (2006) show that among schools that missed AYP in 2004, 23 percent missed because of the failure of a single subgroup and 18 percent missed because of insufficient achievement of two or more subgroups. Given the correlation between subgroups (e.g., those based on race and free lunch eligibility), one can reasonably assume that subgroup size requirements were responsible for anywhere from one-fifth to one-third of the failure to make AYP among the schools that missed it.

Setting the size of the subgroup thresholds involves a clear policy trade-off. On the one hand, a higher threshold increases the accuracy with which school performance is measured. On the other hand, a higher threshold means that large segments of a school's population could fall under the radar screen, an outcome that would be inconsistent with the goals of NCLB. A recent and highly-publicized Associated Press analysis, for example, reported that 1.9 million students are not counted under their racial and ethnic subgroups, including more than one-third of Asian students and nearly half of Native American students (Bass, Dizon, & Feller, 2006). A potential alternative to the subgroup requirement would be to focus special attention on the segment of the school's students that performed at a low level in the previous year and to track that group's growth. This segment would likely include a large fraction of the economically disadvantaged and racial minority students, and so might capture the spirit of the NCLB law without exacerbating the problem of measurement error.

Accountability Time Period

A fourth design issue is the relevant time period for accountability. Kane and Staiger (2002) demonstrate, both conceptually and with data, that substituting multi-year moving averages for year-by-year analysis considerably reduces the instability of the measures of school performance over time, and thereby provides schools with more consistent incentives to raise student performance. Hence, accountability systems based on a single year of data (or growth from one year to the next)—as is largely the case in both NCLB and state accountability systems—are likely to misjudge the performance of schools. Increasing the flexibility through which schools are evaluated reduces the likelihood that measurement error will artificially punish deserving schools, though it increases the likelihood that schools may get credit for performance that is unwarranted.

Figlio (2005) simulates how permitting accountability to apply to periods longer than a year affects the set of schools likely to be sanctioned under the NCLB Act. His simulations show that the fraction of schools sanctioned under the year-by-year system is approximately 20 percent higher than it would be under a system based on a three-year time period. In addition, he demonstrates that shifting to the longer time period reduces the rate at which schools are likely to be sanctioned more for racially heterogeneous schools with multiple subgroups than for other schools. Thus, extending the time period to three years reduces the random variation within subgroups and allows for a more accurate picture of trends in student performance within a student category.

Breadth and Focus of the Accountability System

State accountability systems differ in the number and types of tests, or other performance indicators, they include. The use of tests in multiple subjects complicates the incentives provided by the accountability system. While mathematics and reading test scores, for instance, tend to move together over time within a school, Figlio (2004) shows that the correlation between changes from one cohort to the next in one test relative to another test is quite weak. Therefore, accountability systems that require schools to meet particular criteria on multiple outputs may be difficult to attain, especially if the standards are set appropriately high.

This issue arises whenever schools must meet performance targets in more than one subject and is particularly a problem when the targets are defined in terms of growth. Potential fixes to the measurement error problem include aggregating multiple outcomes into a single indicator or evaluating schools on multiple criteria separately without requiring standards to be met (or improvements to be realized) in every year. As revised in 2002, for example, Florida's accountability system evaluates schools on the basis of a hybrid of reading, writing and mathematics test scores.

The available evidence strongly supports the conclusion that schools tend to concentrate their attention on the subjects tested and on the grades that have high-stakes tests (Deere & Strayer, 2001; Ladd & Zelli, 2001; Stecher et al., 1998; Figlio, 2006a). Other studies (e.g., Hamilton, Berends, & Stecher, 2005; Jones et al., 1999; Koretz et al., 1996; Koretz & Hamilton, 2006; Linn, 2000; Stecher et al., 1998; Stecher et al., 2000) show that teachers and schools tend to narrow the curriculum and shift their instructional emphasis from non-tested to tested subjects, while earlier work by Shepard and Dougherty (1991) and Romberg, Zarinnia, and Williams (1989) suggest that teachers focus more on tested content areas within specific subjects. In related work, Chakrabarti (2005) presents evidence that schools may concentrate their energies on the most easily-improved areas of instruction, rather than on subjects across the board.

In principle, accountability systems could be expanded to incorporate other measures of school performance besides student performance on state tests. Hanushek and Raymond (2003) construct a hierarchy of non-test indicators of school performance, ranked on the basis of their relevance and likely alignment to objective measures of school progress. For instance, they argue that certain measures such as the drop-out rate, graduation rate,[5] number of students in advanced courses, percent of students passing end-of-course exams, retention rate, student mobility and suspension rate, are relatively closely related to student achievement. Other variables, however, such as college entrance exam scores, course offerings, number of computers, number of non-credentialed teachers, parental satisfaction, school crime rate, principal mobility or teacher mobility, are only weakly related to student achievement. To the extent that the goal of the accountability system is to increase student achievement, therefore, some of these measures would be more appropriate than others as elements of an accountability program.

WHY ACCOUNTABILITY MIGHT NOT INCREASE STUDENT ACHIEVEMENT

The preceding discussion predicts that school accountability programs will increase student achievement, although the magnitude of the predicted effects for particular groups of students or types of schools may well differ depending on how the system is designed. For several reasons, however, school accountability systems might not generate higher achievement.

Improving Measured, but Not Generalizable, Achievement

In any monitoring situation, those being monitored face incentives to appear as effective as possible against the metric being assessed. Thus, the concern arises that teachers might teach so narrowly to the high-stakes test that little or no generalizable learning would take place (Koretz & Barron, 1998). Typically, though, as long at the high-stakes tests reflect material that policy-makers and society consider important, teaching to the test would still be expected to improve student learning in the tested areas, at least to some extent. In a few cases, however, reported gains may be completely bogus. Jacob and Levitt (2004), convincingly demonstrate, for example, that a small fraction of Chicago teachers responded to accountability pressures in that city by engaging in outright cheating in order to boost measured student test performance.

A common way to examine whether student learning has increased is to measure achievement using a low-stakes test, that is, one with no specific consequences for schools. A natural test for that purpose is the National Assessment of Educational Progress (NAEP), which has been administered to a nationally representative random sample of students since the early 1970s and to representative samples of students in grades four and eight in most states since the 1990s. That test serves as the basis for much of the empirical work discussed later in this chapter. The downside to measuring achievement using scores from a test with no consequences for students or teachers is that students may not take the test sufficiently seriously to do their best work. Unless student effort differs from one administration of the low-stakes test to the next, however, changes in performance on the low-stakes test should provide a reasonable estimate of gains in student learning.

The accountability experience in Texas illustrates the importance of this distinction between performance on high and low-stakes tests. After a series of education reforms starting in the early 1980s, Texas introduced in 1990 a criterion-referenced testing program called the Texas Assessment of Academic Skills (TAAS) that was designed to shift the focus from minimum skills to higher-order thinking skills (Haney, 2000). By 1994, tests were being administered annually to all students in three to eight and students had to pass a tenth grade test to graduate. The state then used passing rates on the TAAS, along with dropout rates and student attendance rates, to hold individual schools accountable for their students' performance. Schools were held accountable not only for the overall pass rate in the school but also for the pass rates of four student subgroups: African-Americans, Hispanics, whites, and economically disadvantaged students.

Between 1994 and 1998, TAAS scores in both math and reading increased quite dramatically, suggesting that the accountability program had a large and positive impact on student achievement. Klein et al. (2000), however, showed that the large gains on TAAS did not translate into comparably large gains in the lower-stakes Texas NAEP scores. In general, the gains in NAEP scores were about a third the size of the gains in TAAS scores.

Further, the TAAS and NAEP results generate conflicting stories about how accountability affected racial achievement gaps in Texas. In particular, the gaps between blacks and whites based on the TAAS scores in fourth grade reading and math and eighth grade math decreased significantly between 1994 and 1998, while the comparable gaps based on the NAEP increased slightly (Klein et al., 2000, pp. 10–11). Similar patterns also emerge for Hispanics. Klein et al. speculate that the reasons for the differing patterns for TAAS and NAEP results is that Texas teachers may be teaching very narrowly to the TAAS and that the schools serving minority students may be doing so even more than other schools.

Additional evidence on whether the transferability of knowledge from high-stakes to low-stakes tests emerges from Jacob's 2005 study of accountability in Chicago. Jacob compared achievement gains for fourth and eighth graders in math as measured by scores on the district's high-stakes test to those on a comparable, but low-stakes, test administered by the state of Illinois. Those comparisons show that gains for eighth graders generalized to the state test but that those for fourth graders did not.[6]

Manipulating the Test Pool and Other Strategic Behavior

Schools may engage in strategies that artificially improve test scores by changing the group of students subject to the test. The most widely studied behavior of this type is the selective assignment of students to special education programs. As mentioned above, many studies show that schools tend to classify low-achievers as learning disabled in the context of accountability systems. Though there may be some debate about whether the greater rates of classification are undesirable in all cases, nonetheless, they highlight the possibility that schools are manipulating the testing pool specifically to inflate measured school performance. Figlio's (2006b) finding that some Florida schools changed their discipline and suspension patterns around the time of the testing in ways consistent with the goal of improving test-takers' average scores reinforces this concern.

Schools may engage in other types of strategic behavior that affect student performance. For example, Figlio and Winicki (2005) demonstrate that schools change their meals programs at the time of the tests in an apparent attempt to raise performance on high-stakes examinations, while Anderson and Butcher (2006) find that schools subject to accountability pressure are more apt than other schools to sell soft drinks and snacks through vending machines. Finally, Boyd et al. (2002) illustrate how high-stakes testing in certain grades in New York altered which teacher taught in particular grades and schools. It is not clear, however, whether the altered distribution of teachers should be interpreted as strategic behavior on the part of school officials designed to affect test scores.

Many of these behaviors are less likely to occur in growth model accountability systems than in status-based systems. The reason is that in the growth approach, the manipulative behavior that increases student achievement in one year would make it more difficult for the school to attain accountability goals the following year. No such tradeoff arises in status-based accountability systems.

Failure to Respond to Incentives

Implicit in accountability systems is the assumption that administrators and teachers will respond to external incentives—whether those incentives are in the form of bonuses, positive recognition or negative sanctions—by changing their behavior in ways consistent with the goals of the accountability system. If the external rewards or sanctions are not strong enough to override any internal professional incentives for principals and teachers to do what they think best, it is possible that they would not respond and student achievement would not change. Moreover if the incentives of the accountability incentives "crowd out" the natural intrinsic incentives (Frey, 2000), student achievement could decline.

As indicated by the preceding discussion of strategic behavior by both teachers and principals, however, it is clear that accountability systems can be powerful tools for changing behavior. Ladd and Zelli's (2002) survey-based analysis of elementary school principals in North Carolina provides further confirmation of the power of that state's system to change the behavior of school principals. Many, though not all, of their responses were in line with state goals. The more crucial question is whether schools have the capacity and knowledge to respond in ways that increase student achievement.

Lack of Capacity to Respond Productively

For many reasons, schools may not have the capacity to respond in ways desired by state or federal policy makers. Some schools may have insufficient resources to effect serious change in student outcomes, others may lack the leadership required for significant change, and teachers may lack the necessary skills and knowledge to meet the expectations of an accountability system that require rates of increase far larger than historical experience has shown to be feasible, as is the case with NCLB. Thus, it could be that one of the major assumptions underlying stand-alone accountability programs—namely that teachers are underperforming because of insufficient monitoring of their behavior—is incorrect. If, instead, school level resources are inadequate or if teachers simply do not have the knowledge or the support needed to raise student achievement to the more ambitious levels required by the accountability system, even strong incentives for them to do so will do little to increase student learning.

Moreover, even if schools had the know-how to generate improved student outcomes, the fact that accountability systems tend to focus so heavily on short-term achievement gains may interfere with the ability of schools to make the investments in capacity that could potentially lead to higher student achievement in the future.

Strategic Behavior by States and Fiscal Interactions under NCLB

States, themselves, may also respond strategically to federally imposed accountability pressures in ways antithetical to higher achievement. At the same time that NCLB delegates to them the task of defining proficiency standards, it imposes penalties on schools and districts that fail to make adequate progress toward those standards. Consequently, states have incentives to set low proficiency levels. Peterson and Hess (2005) document the low level of concordance between their students progress toward state-defined proficiency and their performance on the NAEP. States such as South Carolina that set very high standards for their students find themselves with large fractions of schools deemed in need of improvement, while states such as Texas that set low standards have few such schools. This interaction between state-set standards and the likelihood that their schools will face sanctions has the potential to lead, in Peterson and Hess's words, to a "race to the bottom" in terms of setting proficiency standards.

A final potentially adverse effect on achievement works through funding provisions. Under NCLB, districts that are sanctioned for low performance are required to use their Title I grants to pay for privately-provided supplemental services and for transportation for students who choose to opt out of failing schools. Figlio (2003) shows that the districts with the highest fractions of minority and low-income students are likely to lose the most Title I funding under this provision. Unless the district or the state replaces that funding with other revenue, NCLB could reduce the instructional resources available to students in those districts, which could potentially have adverse effects on student achievement.

Summary

Thus, despite the theoretical prediction that school accountability systems will improve student achievement—at least for certain segments of the school population—such gains are not a foregone conclusion. In some cases schools may focus on test scores to the exclusion of transferable knowledge or may end up with less funding for instruction. Potentially most important, schools may lack the knowledge and capacity to produce significant gains in student achievement.

THE EFFECTS OF ACCOUNTABILITY ON STUDENT ACHIEVEMENT

Measuring the effects of test-based accountability systems on student achievement is not a simple task. When such systems are part of a larger standards-based reform effort, it is difficult to separate the effects of the accountability system from those of other components of the reform package. In addition, researchers face the challenge of finding appropriate control groups to determine what would have happened to student achievement in the absence of the accountability system. In practice, researchers have used a variety of empirical strategies to address these challenges.

A few recent studies (Cronin et al., 2005, using longitudinal student-level data; and Lee, 2006, using aggregated NAEP data) have tried to determine the achievement effects of NCLB. The short time period since that federal law was implemented limits the conclusions that can be drawn from such studies. More compelling studies of how accountability affects student achievement are based on the state and local accountability systems that preceded NCLB. This research includes district or state specific-studies as well as cross-state studies that measure achievement using the NAEP.results. Researchers conducting district and state-specific studies (Richards & Sheu, 1992; Ladd, 1999; Smith & Mickelson, 2000; Jacob, 2005; Haney, 2000; Klein et al., 2000; Figlio & Rouse, 2006) have used a combination of state or district-wide trends in achievement, along with trends or patterns in school and student level achievement in other comparable districts or states, to sort out how the specific accountability system in that district or state affected student achievement. The main advantages of district and state studies is that the analysis is firmly focused on a specific, well-defined accountability system. Some of the studies, particularly those for particular states, are hampered by the difficulty of predicting what would have happened to student achievement in the absence of the state's accountability system,[7]

Cross-state studies (e.g., the methodologically sophisticated work by Carnoy & Loeb, 2002, 2005; Hanushek & Raymond, 2005; and earlier work by Amrein & Berliner, 2002; Amrein-Beardley & Berliner, 2003; Rosenhine, 2003; Braun, 2004) make use of the variation across states in the nature or timing of accountability systems. Although the conclusions of cross-state studies are sensitive to how accountability policies are defined as well as to methodological considerations such as the determination of control groups, the findings of cross-state studies are likely to be less idiosyncratic and more generalizable than those that emerge from the analysis of a specific program.

Though no one approach or study is flawless and many inconsistencies remain, taken as a whole, the body of research suggests the following conclusions.

Results by Subject

Estimated positive achievement effects of accountability systems emerge far more clearly and frequently for math than for reading. This pattern is particularly clear when the outcome measure is based on a national test, such as NAEP, but it also emerges in some of the district or state level studies such as Figlio and Rouse (2006). In part this pattern reflects the fact that some authors report results only for math, although that is presumably because of the smaller effects for reading. The larger effects for math are intuitively plausible and are consistent with findings from other policy interventions such as voucher programs (Bettinger & Zimmer, this volume) and tax and expenditure limitations (Downes & Figlio, this volume). Compared to reading skills, math skills are more likely to be learned in the classroom, the curriculum is well defined and sequenced, and there is less opportunity for parents to substitute for what goes on the classroom (Cronin, 2005, p. 58).

One exception to this finding of larger effects for math emerges from Jacob's 2005 study of accountability in Chicago, where the positive effects for low-performing students were somewhat stronger in reading than in math. This finding, however, is based on results from the district's high-stakes test rather than from a low-stakes state or national test, and may well reflect the particular characteristics of Chicago's accountability system.

Size and Policy Significance of the Estimated Effects

The most compelling cross-state study (Hanushek & Raymond, 2005) finds that the introduction of an accountability system with consequences for schools during the 1990s raised eighth grade student test scores on the NAEP by about 3.2 scale points.[8] The study does not distinguish between effects on reading and on math. The effect is about a fifth of the 16.2 point standard deviation of average eighth grade average scores across states, but would be a far smaller fraction of the deviation across individual students, which is the way effect sizes are more commonly measured in the education literature. Thus the effect is modest at best. This conclusion is similar to that reported by Lee (2006) based on his meta-analysis of 12 cross-state studies completed between 1994 and 2004.

Other studies suggest that accountability systems are associated with at most small or non-existent gains in reading achievement when achievement is measured by national tests, but positive gains when reading achievement is measured by local high-stakes tests. In math, the estimated gains are consistently somewhat larger, as measured both by national tests or local high-stakes tests.

In addition, one careful cross-state study (Carnoy & Loeb, 2002) shows that the relationship between the strength of a state accountability system and student performance on NAEP math is stronger at the basic level than at the proficient level. Given that NCLB calls for performance at the proficient rather than the basic level, this finding suggests that even the strongest current state-level accountability systems may have little success in raising students to levels required under NCLB—except to the extent that states maintain proficiency levels far below the NAEP standards. Consistent with that conclusion, but inconsistent with findings by Hanushek and Raymond (2005), other studies indicate that even though high-stakes tests may be associated with gains in math scores at the fourth grade level, they may not be associated with gains as students progress from fourth grade to eighth grade and, hence, as the students confront more challenging material.

Estimated Effects by Racial Group

The studies generate mixed results by racial group, with at least one study (Carnoy & Loeb, 2002) for the late 1990s finding larger effect sizes on passing rates at the basic level on NAEP for black and Hispanic students than for white students. Other studies with different outcome measures find different patterns. In particular, Hanushek & Raymond (2005) find essentially no effects of accountability on the eighth grade achievement of black students, but positive effects for Hispanic students, patterns that are consistent with early findings by racial group for seventh graders in Dallas (Ladd, 1999). Effects of accountability on racial achievement gaps are similarly mixed. The Hanushek and Raymond study finds that state accountability systems may have reduced the gap for Hispanics but raised it for blacks. The two recent national studies find little effect of NCLB on racially defined achievement gaps.

Other Differential Effects

Some evidence from the district or state-specific studies suggests that the schools at the bottom of the performance distributions exhibit the greatest gains under an accountability system. This conclusion emerges from both Chicago (Jacob 2005) and Florida (Figlio & Rouse, 2006). Working in the other direction is the finding from the Cronin et al. (2005) national study that the effects of high stakes are greater for the higher scoring students.

Estimated Effects over Time

The evidence suggests that accountability systems generated larger effects on achievement in the late 1990s than in the early 1990s, although Carnoy and Loeb (2005) suggest that their effectiveness may now be declining. The larger estimated effects in the late 1990s relative to the early 1990s are consistent with the observation that the programs introduced in the late 1990s were typically more ambitious than those introduced earlier in the decade. The possibility that the size of the effects is now declining suggests either that accountability generates decreasing marginal returns over time within a state, or that the early state adopters were the most likely to benefit from accountability given their low initial test scores. A related potential explanation is that the early adopters were also more likely than later adopters—primarily those who introduced accountability in response to federal legislation—to embed their accountability systems in comprehensive standards-based reform packages that included other elements such as additional funding or professional development for teachers. Although some of the studies control for certain elements of comprehensive reforms such as changes in funding, no study controls fully for all the components such as the development of organizational capacity, and investments in the capacity of teachers. In any case, both the recent decline and these possible explanations should be viewed as speculative at this time. More research would be useful.

FUTURE RESEARCH

Much of the empirical evidence of the achievement effects reviewed in this paper comes from cross-state studies that are "black-box" analyses designed to determine whether test-based accountability systems have raised student achievement. With the exception of Hanushek and Raymond (2005), such studies shed little light on the mechanisms through which accountability exerts its effects. In that study the authors are able to distinguish the effects of accountability systems that have consequences from those that do not. Other studies generate conclusions about stronger versus weak accountability systems but with little attention to the details of the system design or of the rewards and sanctions associated with it. In addition, few studies explore the policy contexts in which accountability is likely to be more or less successful. An important exception is Loeb and Strunk's (2007) paper that explores the degree to which schools respond to accountability incentives in situations in which they have or do not have local control.

A logical next step would be for researchers to explore in more detail the relationship between particular elements of accountability systems and student performance, and to examine the nature of the state-level conditions most favorable to the success of accountability systems. We believe that the most productive research on this topic will be based on student-level analyses within individual states—which will permit the careful analysis of specific provisions of accountability systems—combined with replications of the analyses in other states to determine the generalizability of the findings.

NOTES

1. The concentration of early accountability efforts in the South was motivated by southern governors' desire to foster economic development; the fact that for historical reasons state governments in the South typically had more authority over education finance and governance than in other parts of the country and hence were in a position to impose accountability; and that teachers unions, which might have opposed accountability programs, were not a major factor in most southern states.
2. Such information may also facilitate improved monitoring by another important set of stakeholders in the education system, namely parents. Whether by complaining about poor performance or by threatening to withdraw their child from the school, parents could potentially use the publicly provided information on school performance to induce their children's schools to improve.
3. Under a new pilot program currently in use in Delaware, North Carolina and Tennessee, with future plans for Arkansas and Florida, states have the flexibility to give credit to schools for students who move from below basic to basic levels of proficiency, so long as the primary NCLB attributes of annual testing and subgroup reporting, coupled with continuously increasing student achievement are met.
4. Consistent with this conclusion, during the 1990s, Texas and North Carolina, both of which had highly touted state accountability systems, excluded increasingly large number of students from the NAEP tests, thereby biasing upward the observed gains in NAEP scores in those states (Amrein & Berliner, 2002; Braun, 2004).
5. Graduation rates are used to calculate high school AYP under NCLB.
6. Data were not available for a comparable analysis of reading scores.
7. However, some studies (e.g., Figlio & Rouse, 2006; Figlio, 2006b) focus not on overall achievement but rather on how specific provisions of Florida's accountability system affect student achievement.
8. Even this study is not free from criticism. The study identifies the effects of accountability systems by making use of the variation in their time of introduction. The choice of specific starting dates for some of the states, including key states such Florida and North Carolina, creates some cause for concern. Hence, replications of this study would be useful.

REFERENCES

Amrein, A. and D. Berliner. 2002, March 28. "High states testing, uncertainty and student learning." *Education Policy Analysis Archives* 10(18). Retrieved from: http://epaa.asu.edu/epaa/v10n18/ accessed September 14, 2006.

Anderson. P., and K. Butcher. 2006. "Reading, writing, and refreshments: Are school finances contributing to children's obesity?" *Journal of Human Resources* 41(3), 467–494.

Amrein-Beardley, A. and D. Berliner. 2003. "Re-analysis of NAEP math and reading scores in states with and without high-stakes tests: Responses to Rosenshine." *Education Policy Analysis Archives* 11(25).

Bass, F., N. Dizon, and B. Feller. 2006. "Schools skirt 'No Child Left Behind' rule." Associated Press, April 17.

Boyd, D., H. Lankford, S. Loeb, and J. Wyckoff. 2002. "Do high-stakes tests affect teachers' exit and transfer decisions? The case of the 4th grade test in New York State." Working paper, Stanford University.

Braun, H. 2004. "Reconsidering the impact of high-stakes testing." *Education Policy Analysis Archives* 12(1). Retrieved from: http://epaa.asu.edu/epaa/v12n1/ (43 pages) accessed September 14, 2006.

Carnoy M., S. Loeb, and T. Smith. 2001. "Do higher scores in Texas make for better high school outcomes?" CPRE Research Report no. RR-047. Philadelphia: Consortium for Policy Research in Education.

Carnoy, M. and S. Loeb. 2002. "Does external accountability affect student outcomes?: A cross-state analysis." *Educational Evaluation and Policy Analysis* 24(4), 305–331.

Carnoy, M. and S. Loeb. 2005. "Revisiting external accountability effects on student outcomes: A cross-state analysis of NAEP reading and math results in the 1990s and early 2000s." Paper prepared for the Learning from Longitudinal Data in Education Conference, May. Washington, D.C.: The Urban Institute.

Chakrabarti, R. 2005. "Do public schools facing vouchers behave strategically?" Working paper, Harvard University.

Clotfelter, C. and H. Ladd. 1996. "Recognizing and rewarding success in public schools." In H. Ladd, (ed.). *Holding Schools Accountable: Performance-Based Reform in Education* (pp. 23–64). Washington, D.C.: Brookings Institution Press.

Cronin, J., G. G. Kingsbury, M. S. MCall, and B. Rocoe. 2005, April. "The impact of the NCLB act on student achievement and growth: 2005 edition. Technical Report. Northwest Evaluation Association.

Cullen, J. and R. Reback. Forthcoming. "Tinkering towards accolades." In T. Gronberg and D. Jansen (eds.). *Advances in Microeconomics*.

Deere, D. and W. Strayer. 2001. "Putting schools to the test: School accountability, incentives and behavior." Working paper, Texas A&M University.

Elmore, R., C. H. Abelmann, and S. H. Fuhrman. 1996. "The new accountability in state education reform: From Process to Performance." In H. F. Ladd, (ed.). *Holding schools accountable: Peformance-based reform in education.* Washington, D.C.: Brookings Institution Press.

Donovan, C., D. Figlio, and M. Rush. 2006. "Cramming: The effects of school accountability on college-bound students." NBER working paper 12628.

Figlio, D. 2003. "Fiscal implications of school accountability initiatives." *Tax Policy and the Economy* 17.

Figlio, D. 2005. "Measuring school performance: Promise and pitfalls." In L Stiefel et al. (Eds.), *Measuring School Performance and Efficiency: Implications for Practice and Research, 2005*. Yearbook of the American Education Finance Association. Larchmont, NY: Eye on Education.

Figlio, D. 2006a. "School responses to accountability pressure: Cross-state evidence from the Schools and Staffing Surveys." Working paper, University of Florida.

Figlio, D. 2006b. "Testing, crime and punishment." *Journal of Public Economics* 90(4), 837–851.

Figlio, D. and L. Getzler. Forthcoming. "Accountability, ability and disability: Gaming the system?" In T. Gronberg and D. Jansen (eds.), *Advances in microeconomics*.

Figlio, D. and C. Rouse. 2006. "Do accountability and voucher threats improve low-performing schools?" *Journal of Public Economics* 90(1), 239–255.

Figlio, D. and J. Winicki. 2005. "Food for thought? The effects of school accountability plans on school nutrition." *Journal of Public Economics* 89(2), 381–394.

Fredericksen, N. 1994. *The influence of minimum competency tests on teaching and learning*. Princeton, NJ: Educational Testing Services.

Frey, B. 2000. "Motivation and human behaviour." In P. Taylor-Gooby (ed.), *Risk, trust and welfare* (pp. 31–50). Basingstoke, UK: Macmillan.

Fuller, B., K. Gesicki, E. Kang, and J. Wright. 2006. "Is the NCLB Act Working?: The reliability of how states track achievement." Policy Analysis for California Education (PACE). Working Paper 06–01.

Grissmer, D. and A. Flanagan. *Exploring rapid achievement gains in North Carolina and Texas*. Washington, D.C.: National Education Goals Panel.

Hamilton, L., M. Berends, and B. Stecher. 2005. "Teachers' responses to standards-based accountability." Santa Monica, CA: RAND Corporation.

Haney, W. 2000. "The myth of the Texas miracle in education." *Educational Policy Analysis Archives* 8(41).

Hanushek, E. and M. Raymond. 2003. "Lessons about the Design of State Accountability Systems." In P. E. Peterson and M. R. West, (eds.). *NCLB?: The politics and practice of school accountability.* Washington, D.C.: Brookings Institution Press.

Hanushek, E. and M. Raymond. 2005. "Does school accountability lead to improved school performance?" *Journal of Policy Analysis and Management* 24(2), 297–329.

Jacob, B. 2001. "Getting tough? The impact of high school graduation exams." *Educational Evaluation and Policy Analysis* 23(2), 99–121.

Jacob, B. 2005. "Accountability, incentives and behavior." *Journal of Public Economics.*

Jacob, B. and S. Levitt. 2004. "Rotten apples." *Quarterly Journal of Economics.*

Jones, M. G., B. Jones, B. Hardin, L. Chapman, T. Yarbrough, and M. Davis. 1999. "The impact of high-stakes testing on teachers and students in North Carolina." *Phi Delta Kappan* 81(3), 199–203.

Kane, T. and D. Staiger. 2002. "Improving school accountability systems." NBER working paper.

Klein, S., L. Hamilton, D. McCaffrey, and B. Stecher. 2000. "What do test scores in Texas tell us?" *Education Policy Analysis Archives* 9(49). Retrieved from: http://epaa.asu.edu/epaa/v8n49/ accessed August 16, 2006.

Koretz, D., S. Barron, K. Mitchell, and B. Stecher. 1996. *Perceived effects of the Kentucky Instructional Results Information System (KIRIS).* Santa Monica, CA: RAND Coporation, MR-792-PCT/FF.

Koretz, D. and S. Barron. 1998. "The validity of gains on the Kentucky Instructional Results Information System (KIRIS)." Working paper, RAND Corporation.

Ladd, H.F. and J. Hansen. 1999. *Making money matter: Financing America's schools.* Washington, D.C: National Academy Press.

Ladd, H. 1999. "The Dallas school accountability and incentive program: An evaluation of its impacts on student outcomes." *Economics of Education Review.*

Ladd, H. 2001. "School-based educational accountability systems: The promise and the Pitfalls." *National Tax Journal* 54(2), 385–400.

Ladd, H. and E. Glennie. 2001. "A replication of Jay Greene's voucher effect study using North Carolina data." In Carnoy, M. (ed.). *Do school vouchers improve student performance?* (pp. 49–52). Washington, D.C.: Economic Policy Institute.

Ladd, H. and Walsh, R. 2002. "Implementing value-added measures of school effectiveness: Getting the incentives right." *Economics of Education Review* 21(1), 1–17.

Ladd, H. and F. Zelli. 2002. "School-based accountability in North Carolina: The responses of school principals" *Education Administration Quarterly.*

Ladd, H. 1996. *Holding schools Aacountable: Performance based reform in education.* Washington, D.C.: Brookings Institution Press.

Lavy, Victor. 2007. "Using performance-based pay to improve the quality of teachers". In "Excellence in the Classroom," *The Future of* Children 17(1), Spring.

Linn, R. L. 2000. "Assessments and Accountability." Educational Researcher, 29(2), 4–16.

Loeb, S. and K. Strunk. 2007. "Accountability and local control: Response to incentives with and without authority over resource allocation and generation." *Education Finance and Policy* 2(1), 10–39.

O'Day , J. A. and M. S. Smith. 1993. "Systemic reform and educational opportuity." In S. Fuhrman (ed.), *Designing coherent education policy: Improving the system* (pp. 250–312). San Francisco: Jossey Bass.

Pedulla, J., L. Abrams, G. Madaus, M. Russell, M. Ramos, and J. Miao. 2003. "Perceived effects of state-mandated testing programs on teaching and learning: Findings from a national survey of teachers." Boston: National Board on Educational Testing and Public Policy.

Peterson, P. and F. Hess. 2005. "Keeping an eye on state standards." *Education Next.*

Peterson . P. E. and M. R. West. 2003. *NCLB? The politics and practice of school accountability.* Washington, D.C.: Brookings Institution Press.

Richards, C. and T. Sheu. 1992. "The South Carolina School Incentive Reward Program: A policy analysis." *Economics of Education Review* 11(1), 71–86.

Romberg, T., E. Zarinnia, and S. Williams. 1989. "The influence of mandated testing on mathematics instruction: Grade 8 teachers' perceptions." Madison: National Center for Research in Mathematical Science Education, University of Wisconsin-Madison.

Shepard, L. and K. Dougherty. 1991. "Effects of high-stakes testing on instruction." Working paper, ERIC.

Stecher, G., S. Barron, T. Kaganoff, and J. Goodwin. 1998. "The effects of standards-based assessment on classroom practices: Results of the 1996–97 RAND survey of Kentucky teachers of mathematics and writing." Los Angeles: Center for Research on Evaluation, Standards and Student Testing.

Stecher, B., S. Barron, T. Chun, and K. Ross. 2000. "The effects of the Washington state education reform on schools and classrooms." Los Angeles: Center for Research on Evaluation, Standards and Student Testing.

Stiefel, L. A. E. Schwartz, R Rubinstein, and J. Zabel, eds. 2005. *Measuring school performance and efficiency: Implications for practice and research.* American Education Finance Association 2005 Yearbook. Larchmont, NY: Eye on Education.

Stullich, S., L. Eisner, J. McCrary, and C. Roney. 2006. "National assessment of Title I: Interim report." Washington, D.C.: U.S. Department of Education.

11

School Competition and Student Outcomes

Brian Gill and Kevin Booker

INTRODUCTION

An entire section of this volume is devoted to issues related to school choice and educational privatization, including charter schools, the public funding of private schools, and educational management organizations that operate public schools under contract. Nonetheless, the use of market forces in education is an appropriate topic for this section as well, because market-based educational policies may affect the productive use of resources across the educational system. In particular, many supporters of market-based approaches believe that the competitive pressures they create will promote an increase in school productivity (see, e.g., Friedman, 1955; Chubb and Moe, 1990; Hoxby, 2000). If so, benefits might be seen not only by students enrolled in schools of choice (whether private, charter, or privately managed), but also by students who remain in conventional public schools and by taxpayers. At the same time, the adoption of market mechanisms in schooling raises questions about the extent to which schools operating under a competitive model will productively serve public as well as private purposes (see, e.g., Wells, 1993; Wolf and Macedo, 2004; Fiske and Ladd, 2000; Gill et al., 2001; Gutmann, 1987; Fuller, Elmore, and Orfield, 1996; Levin, 2000). How will competition affect the stratification of students across schools, by race, social class, and ability? Will privately operated schools effectively promote education in the knowledge, skills, and values needed for effective citizenship in a democracy?

This chapter does not address the productivity of market-based schools (e.g., voucher schools, charter schools, or privately managed schools) as measured by the math and reading achievement of their own students; we leave that issue to the chapters in Section V of this volume. Instead, we address issues related to the effects of competition on conventional public schools and on the traditional public purposes of education, including student integration and the education of citizens.

A variety of different kinds of policies can promote market forces in education, potentially producing competitive effects. Scholarships that subsidize tuition at private schools, usually known as vouchers, have been proposed in a variety of forms for at least fifty years. Publicly-funded voucher programs are currently operating in Ohio, Florida, and Milwaukee, Wisconsin. Some states use state income tax policy to subsidize private-school tuition payments indirectly. This subsidy can involve permitting deductions or credits for families paying private-school tuition or, as Arizona, Pennsylvania, and Florida have done in recent years, giving tax credits to individuals or businesses that contribute to privately-operated scholarship/voucher programs. Over the last fifteen years, the most popular market-based policy intervention in state legislatures around the country has been the creation of charter schools—publicly funded and publicly regulated schools that are privately operated (i.e., operated autonomously, outside the direct control of local public officials) and enrolled by student/parent choice. Charter schools are now permitted in at least 40 states. Meanwhile, competition might also result from choices among conventional public schools, whether created by intra- or inter-district open enrollment policies or simply arising from families' options to set up residence in different school districts. Economists typically refer to this latter form of choice as Tiebout choice after the economist who first described the process of voting with one's feet for public services.

Whether competition in the K–12 education market will produce positive results has been a matter of great theoretical debate for half a century, since Milton Friedman (1955) proposed a voucher system. Supporters of competition argue that it will give families a wider range of choices and make schools more responsive to their customers. This kind of responsiveness should lead to an increase in school productivity, under the assumption that parents and students will choose the most-effective schools.

But K–12 education has characteristics that have led skeptics of market solutions to doubt that competition will produce desirable outcomes. Markets are effective tools for generating efficient distributions of private goods. But markets that efficiently allocate private goods often under-supply public goods. For two centuries, a primary justification for the public support of education has been the understanding that an educated citizenry, socialized in common civic values and equipped with the skills to be economically productive, is a public good. Although no one in mainstream politics seriously questions public funding for education, proposals for competition and privatization raise a question about whether public purposes will be served through the pursuit of private ends.

Educational consumers—parents—are presumably generally interested in sending their children to schools that are academically effective. Nonetheless, market failure might occur in the educational marketplace because both schools and parents are often interested not only in the quality of schools, but also in the characteristics of the student body. If schools have the implicit or explicit ability to select their students, or if parents select schools based partly on peer characteristics, then competition could increase stratification by ability, race, and socioeconomic status (see Wells, 1993; Fiske and Ladd, 2000; Epple and Romano, 2000; Schneider et al., 1997). Moreover, the fact that education is compulsory distinguishes it from most market goods: Some parents and students are likely to be passive choosers who will be disadvantaged in a marketplace where others are active choosers. In addition, schools might pursue strategies to make themselves effective selectors of students rather than productive educators. And some parents and schools might care very much about promoting particularistic private values (such as, for example, football or religion) rather than academic effectiveness and civic socialization.

In addition, conventional public schools are not institutionally designed to respond effectively to market pressures (see, e.g., Hess, 2002). Governed by democratically elected officials, they were set up to respond to political signals rather than market signals. School choice, however, may actually undermine schools' political responsiveness by promoting "exit" over "voice" for the most-active families. Because schooling is compulsory (unlike most market goods and services), there will always be a population of "non-choosers" whose fate is left to the conventional public schools (or to other schools of last resort, whatever they might be). Those students and their schools might be left substantially worse off if all of the most-motivated and best-informed families have exited to schools of choice.

Questions about the potential benefits of market forces and its potential harms cannot be resolved theoretically. Empirical evidence is needed to determine the extent to which competition can increase school productivity, on the one hand, and the extent to which it may produce stratification, sectarianism, and inequity, on the other hand. Choice and competition in education challenge the "common school" ideal that has been the model for American public education since the time of Horace Mann (Gill et al., 2001). This ideal model assumes that the public purposes of education demand that students in a community be educated under a common roof with a curriculum that promotes a common set of values. Departure from the common school ideal does not mean that the values associated with it are being abandoned, but it raises a critical empirical question about whether market competition can serve those values as well as (or better than) publicly-operated schools can.

COMPETITION AND STUDENT ACHIEVEMENT

We begin by examining the evidence of the effects of educational competition on public schools' productivity as measured by students' test scores.

Competitive Effects of Charter Schools

Charter schools have been in operation in the United States for only a decade and a half, and the empirical evidence on their competitive effects on student achievement in conventional public schools has grown substantially in the last five years. Table 11.1 summarizes several recent studies of the competitive effects of charter schools.

Hoxby (2002) examined the effect of charter schools on standardized test scores for surrounding public schools in Michigan and Arizona between 1992–93 and 1999–2000 in 4th and 7th grades. She identified districts as facing significant charter competition where at least 6 percent of the public school students in the district were attending charter schools. Using school-level data and school fixed effects, Hoxby compared the trend in average achievement growth in districts that face charter competition with the trend at the same districts prior to facing charter competition. In both states, average achievement growth was slightly higher for 4th grade math and reading at schools that face charter competition (by a statistically significant margin). In 7th grade, there was no significant charter competition effect except in math in Arizona.

Bettinger (2005) also examined the effect of charter school competition on changes in average test scores for conventional public schools in Michigan. He examined 4th grade math and reading scores from 1992–93 through 1998–99, aggregated to the school level. Bettinger measured the degree of charter competition that a school faces by the number of charter schools within a five-mile radius of the school. He found a small positive charter competition effect on reading scores after two or more years of having charter schools nearby, but all of the other estimated charter effects were statistically insignificant. Bettinger suggested that this small positive effect on school-level results is as likely to be the result of a favorable population change as an actual effect on the achievement of students: Average test scores in conventional public schools would increase automatically if charter schools drew away a disproportionate number of low-achieving students.

Booker et al. (2006) examined the effect of charter competition on math and reading test score gains in Texas between 1995–96 and 2003–04, with longitudinal student-level data for grades 4–8, using school-student fixed effects to control for time-invariant school and student characteristics. They measured the degree of charter competition that a public school faces by

TABLE 11.1
Studies of Competitive Effect of Charter Schools

Author	*Sites Included*	*Time Period Covered*	*Subjects and Grades Included*	*Measure of Charter Competition*	*Estimation Method*	*Results*
Hoxby (2002)	Michigan, Arizona	1992–93 through 1999–00	Math and Reading, Grades 4 and 7	Indicator for at least 6% of district students attending charters	School-level differences-in-differences, with the change in school average test score as the dependent variable	Positive effect of charter competition on math and reading
Bettinger (2005)	Michigan	1992–93 through 1998–99	Math and Reading, Grade 4	Number of charters within a 5-mile radius	School-level panel, with the school average test score as the dependent variable, controlling for the school's lagged average test score	Mostly finds no effect of charter competition on math or reading
Booker et al. (2006)	Texas	1995–96 through 2003–04	Math and Reading, Grades 4–8	Number of charters within a 5-mile radius	Student-level panel with school-student fixed effects, with the student's change in test score as the dependent variable	Positive effect of charter competition on math and reading
Buddin and Zimmer (2004)	Six large California districts	1997–98 through 2001–02	Math and Reading, Grades 2–11	Number of charters within a 2.5-mile radius	Student-level panel with school-student fixed effects, with the student's change in test score as the dependent variable	No effect of charter competition on math or reading
Bifulco and Ladd (2005)	North Carolina	1995–96 through 2001–02	Math and Reading, Grades 3–8	Number of charters within a 2.5-mile radius	Student-level panel with student fixed effects, with the student's change in test score as the dependent variable	No effect of charter competition on math or reading
Sass (2005)	Florida	1999–00 through 2002–03	Math and Reading, Grades 3–10	Number of charters within a 2.5-mile radius	Student-level panel with school-student fixed effects, with the student's change in test score as the dependent variable	Positive effect of charter competition on math, no effect on reading

the number of charter schools within a five- or ten-mile radius of the school. They found a positive and statistically significant effect of charter competition on student math and reading test score gains, larger at the five-mile radius than the ten-mile radius—limited to schools that had below-average achievement at baseline. The charter competition effect was largest for black and Hispanic students.

Buddin and Zimmer (2004) performed a similar (school-student fixed effects) analysis of the systemic effects of charter schools in California, using longitudinal student-level data from grades 2–11 from six large school districts for 1997–98 through 2001–02. They used a variety of different measures of charter competition, including whether the school has a charter within a 2.5-mile radius, and the number of charter schools within a 2.5 mile radius. They found no significant effect of charter schools on student achievement growth at surrounding public schools.

Bifulco and Ladd (2005) likewise used longitudinal, student-level data and a fixed-effects strategy to analyze charter competition effects. They examined math and reading scores for students in North Carolina from 1995–96 through 2001–02, in grades 3–8. They measured the degree of charter competition a school faced by the number of charter schools within a 2.5 mile radius, as well as the distance to the nearest charter. They found no significant effects of charter competition on student math and reading performance in surrounding conventional public schools, but were careful to note that the finding might simply reflect the limited amount of competition posed by the state's 100 charter schools.

Sass (2005) used a similar data set and method to examine charter competition effects in Florida. He looked at students in grades 3–10, for the period of 1999–2000 through 2002–03, and he also used the number of charter schools within a 2.5-mile radius as a measure of charter competition. He found a positive and statistically significant effect of charter competition on the math gains in nearby schools, but no significant effects on performance in reading.

Several different explanations could potentially account for the positive competitive effect observed in some of these studies. The first possibility is that competitive pressure induces conventional public schools to increase their educational productivity. Alternately, competitive pressure may simply encourage a narrower focus on raising test scores. A third possibility relates to peer effects. If, as Bettinger suggests, charter schools attract students with lower-than-average achievement levels, the outflow of students to charter schools would not only produce an automatic increase in average achievement results in the conventional public schools, but could also produce gains for individual students who benefit from an increase in the average achievement levels of their peers. Still another possibility is that conventional public schools may experience an increase in per-pupil resources, if the resources lost with the departure of the charter students are less than the district's average expenditures.

Taken as a whole, these studies provide evidence that in some states, the availability of charter schools leads to higher achievement in nearby conventional public schools. Although some studies have found no such effect, none of the studies have found a negative effect. Future studies are needed to investigate further the cause of this effect, and whether it varies depending on the design of the charter law and the flow of funding.

COMPETITIVE EFFECTS OF VOUCHER PROGRAMS

Table 11.2 summarizes the results of studies of the competitive effects of voucher programs in Milwaukee, Cleveland, and Washington DC and a large-scale, quarter-century-old voucher program in Chile.

TABLE 11.2
Studies of Competitive Effect of Vouchers

Author	*Sites Included*	*Time Period Covered*	*Subjects and Grades Included*	*Estimation Method*	*Results*
Hoxby (2002)	Milwaukee	1996–97 through 1999–00	Math and Reading, Grade 4	School-level differences-in-differences, with the change in school average test score as the dependent variable	Positive effect of voucher threat on math and reading
Chakrabarti (2005)	Milwaukee, Florida	1989–90 through 1996–97 (Milwaukee), 1998–99 through 2001–02 (Florida)	Grade 3 Reading and Grade 5 Math (Milwaukee), Grade 4 Math and Grade 5 Reading (Florida)	School-level panel, with school average test score as the dependent variable, including school fixed effects	Milwaukee: Small positive effect of voucher threat on math and reading Florida: Positive effect of school receiving an F grade on math and reading
Greene (2003)	Florida	2001–02 through 2002–03	Math, Reading and Writing, Grades 3–10	School-level analysis of changes in average test scores by cohort	Positive effect of school receiving an F grade on math and writing, no effect on reading
West and Peterson (2005)	Florida	2002–03 through 2004–05	Math and Reading, Grades 3–5	Student-level analysis, with student's test score as the dependent variable	Positive effect of school receiving an F grade on math and reading scores on high-stakes tests but not low-stakes tests
Figlio and Rouse (2004)	Florida	1998–99 through 1999–00	Grade 4 Math and Grade 5 Reading	Student-level analysis, with the student's change in test score as the dependent variable, including school fixed effects	Small positive effect of being classified as a low-performing school on high-stakes math and reading test results, but no effect on low-stakes test results
Greene and Winters (2006)	Washington, DC	2003–04 through 2004–05	Math and Reading, Grades 3, 5, 8 and 10	School-level analysis, with the school average test score as the dependent variable, controlling for the school's lagged average test score	No effect of voucher threat on math or reading
Hsieh and Urquiola (2001)	Chile	1981–82 and 1989-–90	Math and Reading, Grade 4	School-level analysis of changes in average test scores	No effect of vouchers on math and reading
McEwan and Carnoy (2000)	Chile	1989-90 through 1995-96	Math and Reading, Grade 4	Student-level analysis, with the student's test score as the dependent variable	Positive effect of vouchers on math and reading in Santiago, but for country as a whole no aggregate effects

The Milwaukee voucher program, enacted in 1990, provides students from low-income families with vouchers that can be used to attend private schools. For each student using a voucher, the school district loses approximately 30 percent of the state aid associated with that pupil. In 1998 the size of the program expanded dramatically, when an enrollment cap was raised from 1.5 percent of the total student population to 15 percent, and religious schools were allowed to participate, substantially increasing the available supply of spaces. It now enrolls over 15,000 voucher students in over 100 private schools.

Hoxby (2002) and Chakrabarti (2005) examined the competitive impact of the Milwaukee voucher program. Using school-level data, Hoxby compared the average fourth grade math and reading performance of schools prior to wide-spread voucher use (1996–97) and after (1999–2000). She found that average achievement in both subjects improved the most at Milwaukee public schools with a high percentage of voucher-eligible students, as compared with schools with fewer voucher-eligible students and with schools outside of Milwaukee. Chakrabarti used a similar method and likewise found larger gains in public schools with the largest number of voucher-eligible students. As in Bettinger's study of the competitive effects of charter schools, however, the results of these studies could be driven by population changes in the schools rather than actual improvements in student achievement, if the voucher schools are attracting low-achieving students (see Ladd, 2002).

The federal government created a program providing a $7,500 voucher to low-income students in Washington DC, beginning in the 2004–05 school year. Greene and Winters (2006) found no impacts on public-school achievement in the first year of the program's operation. They suggest the absence of competitive impact is due to the small size of the program (enrolling 2,000 students in the first year), the fact that this is the first year it has been in place, and the fact that it was designed to have little funding impact on the public schools.

Florida's Opportunity Scholarship Program, launched in 1999–2000, was created as an integral part of the state's high-stakes testing regime: It made students in the lowest-rated Florida public schools (those that received "F" grades two years in a row) eligible for vouchers. During the first couple of years of the Florida voucher program, most of the schools that received an F grade improved in the next year, and thus avoided the voucher threat. In 1999–2000, 76 schools received their first F grade, but all of them improved the following year and received at least a D grade in 2000–01. In later years some schools received consecutive F grades and their students became eligible for vouchers.

Using a variety of different methods, Greene (2003), West and Peterson (2005), Chakrabarti (2005), and Figlio and Rouse (2004) all found evidence that scores on Florida's state accountability test increased in public schools subject to the voucher threat. But two of the studies (West and Peterson, 2005; Figlio and Rouse, 2004) found no evidence of a similar effect on low-stakes test results in the same schools, leaving some doubt about whether the effects are related to narrow, test-taking skills. Moreover, even if the gains on the high-stakes test represent genuine learning, it is unclear whether the effects can be attributed to the voucher threat per se. Given that the voucher threat is an integral part of the high-stakes testing program, there is ultimately no way to distinguish the effect of the voucher component from the effect of the complete accountability system. The safe conclusion is that the high-stakes testing system as a whole has induced rising high-stakes test scores in targeted schools, and that the voucher threat may contribute to the incentives created by the high-stakes regime. Indeed, the fact that the strongest evidence of a positive competitive effect of vouchers comes from Florida is probably related to the design of the program, which gives public schools a clear incentive to respond by raising test scores (unlike in Milwaukee and Washington DC) (Chakrabarti, 2005).

Voucher programs have been implemented outside the United States. With respect to the competitive effects of vouchers, Chile has received more scholarly attention than other countries. Beginning in 1981, Chile gave every student the option to use a voucher to attend a private school, and made public school funding directly related to the school's enrollment. In response, more than a thousand new private schools opened in Chile, and private school enrollment increased from 20 percent to 40 percent.

Hsieh and Urquiola (2001) compared aggregate math and reading scores in 1982, before widespread voucher usage, to those in 1990 after the voucher use was widespread. They found no evidence of overall achievement gains across the educational sector. McEwan and Carnoy (2000) used a national student-level panel dataset to estimate the impact on public school achievement of having competition from private schools serving voucher students. They found some evidence of a positive effect of voucher competition on math and reading scores in the Santiago metropolitan area, but slightly negative effects in the rest of the country. They speculated that the positive effects in Santiago could be due to higher population density there, making private school competition more effective. Their results are consistent with finding no aggregate effect for the country as a whole.

During the 1990s, the government of Sweden instituted a variety of education reforms nationwide, aiming to decentralize educational authority, permit parental choice in schooling, and promote competition among schools. Among other changes, the reforms created new subsidies for students to attend private schools; in metropolitan areas, the proportion of Swedes enrolled in private schools increased substantially (Bjorklünd, 2005). In a 2005 volume, Anders Bjorklünd and colleagues report that decentralization, choice, and competition produced small positive achievement effects for most students in Sweden. They also sound a note of caution, however: Disparities in academic achievement in Sweden also increased—modestly—at the same time.

In sum, evidence on the competitive effects of vouchers remains limited, but the existing evidence provides reason for cautious optimism. No studies have found substantial negative effects, and a few have provided preliminary evidence of positive effects. Evidence from Chile and Sweden suggests the importance of examining differential impacts for different groups of schools and students, as well as average impacts. Finally, the specific design of voucher programs is likely to be important in determining whether they have competitive effects.

TIEBOUT COMPETITION AND STUDENT ACHIEVEMENT

One of the most widespread potential sources of school competition is competition among public schools themselves. One source of this public school competition would be "Tiebout choice," describing residential choices made by parents, which may be based partly on the quality of the public schools in that neighborhood. This could induce indirect competition among school districts, as they compete for additional local property tax revenues and per-student funding.

Hoxby (2000) assessed the impact of public school competition on student achievement by examining nationwide variation in the amount of public school choice available in different metropolitan areas. Because local school district structure is related to other factors that influence student achievement, Hoxby used the number of rivers and streams in the metropolitan area as an instrument, in order to determine the portion of variation in public school choice that is independent of other factors affecting student performance. She found that having more public school choice is related to higher levels of student performance, controlling for other local characteristics. Rothstein (2005), however, found that Hoxby's results were not robust across different specifications.

Using data for elementary schools in the San Francisco Bay area, Bayer and McMillan (2005) estimated the change in demand each school faces in response to a change in that school's quality. They related this measure of local competitiveness to student achievement, controlling for observable school characteristics, and found that a one standard deviation increase in the competitiveness of a school's local market was associated with a 0.15 standard deviation increase in school performance.

In sum, the competitive effect of Tiebout choice on student achievement is not yet clear; different studies have produced conflicting results. Examining the effect of this kind of naturally occurring choice is very difficult, because it is impossible to conduct a randomized experiment or even to observe changes in student achievement before and after an intervention occurs. In consequence, causal inferences are problematic. The competitive effect of Tiebout choice is therefore likely to remain a matter of debate—and further empirical inquiry—for some time to come.

COMPETITION, INTEGRATION, AND CIVIC SOCIALIZATION

Although a growing number of studies has attempted to measure the effects of competition on achievement in math and reading, relatively little attention has been devoted to the effects of competition on two of the traditional public purposes of schooling: social integration and civic socialization. Because choice and competition represent fundamental departures from the common-school model for the provision of public education—a model intended (at least in its ideal) to promote integration and civic socialization—empirical evidence on these issues is especially important.

Competition and Student Sorting

A few scholars have used theoretical models to predict the effects of school-choice policies on the distribution of students. Epple and Romano (1998) predicted that flat-rate educational vouchers would increase the stratification of students by wealth and ability, in the absence of constraints on tuition and admissions policies in private schools. High-income, well-informed, motivated parents would find their way to private schools that would be seeking high-achieving, motivated students whose families could afford to "top off" the voucher with additional tuition payments. In a later paper, however, the same authors concluded that school-choice policies could be designed in ways to "reap the benefits of increased competition without increased stratification" (Epple and Romano, 2002, abstract) In particular, they predict that voucher policies could avoid increasing stratification of students by requiring participating private schools to accept the voucher as full payment of tuition (i.e., to prohibit "topping off" the voucher with additional tuition payment—a prohibition that is in fact incorporated in some existing voucher policies) and by varying the voucher amount to provide larger scholarships to students with greater educational needs (much as the state of Florida does in its McKay scholarship program for students with disabilities).

School-choice policies may have different effects on integration in neighborhoods than on integration in schools. Nechyba (1999, 2000, 2003) used theoretical models to predict that vouchers should reduce residential stratification, because they cut the link between school quality and residential location for families using them. Access to vouchers to attend private schools will make some families more willing to live in communities with low-performing public schools—communities that otherwise would be populated largely with low-income families. Ferreyra (2007) found similar results when simulating the effects of a high-value, universally available voucher for residents of Chicago.

Few studies have systematically examined the effects of charter schools on the stratification of students. Some reports (e.g., Frankenberg and Lee, 2003) have descriptively compared the racial/ethnic composition of charter schools and conventional public schools in their states. Such studies, however, cannot estimate the effect of charter schools on integration, because they provide no evidence on how students would be distributed in the absence of charter schools. Moreover, they sometimes compare enrollments in charter schools with district-wide or state-wide averages, without recognizing that charter schools often open in neighborhoods that are highly segregated.

Three studies in four states have carefully examined stratification issues related to charter schools, and all have found some evidence that charter schools may increase stratification by race. Bifulco and Ladd (2006) found that charter schools in North Carolina have contributed to an increase in racial stratification, with both white students and black students becoming more racially isolated. Among students observed transferring from conventional public schools to charter schools, black students tended to move to charter schools where blacks constituted a larger majority of the enrollment (72%, versus 53% in the schools they left), while white students tended to move to charter schools where blacks constituted a smaller minority of the enrollment (18%, versus 28% in the schools they left).

Booker et al. (2006) found that in California and Texas, black students transferring from conventional public schools to charter schools tended to move to schools with higher proportions of their own racial group and lower levels of racial/ethnic integration. Movements of white and Hispanic students, by contrast, had mixed effects on schools' integration. In Texas, white students moved to charter schools with higher proportions of their own group and lower levels of integration, while Hispanics moved to schools with lower proportions of their own group students and slightly higher levels of integration. In California, white and Hispanic students alike moved to charter schools with smaller proportions of their own group and higher levels of integration.

Ross (2005) examined statewide data in Michigan, and found that the exposure of black and Hispanic students to white students in conventional public schools declined in districts that had large proportions of students (7% or more) enrolling in charter schools. She concluded that charter schools were leading to increases in racial stratification in Michigan.

Scholars have not used student-level data to examine the effects on racial and ethnic distributions of movements of students from public to private schools under the voucher programs that have been operating in Milwaukee, Cleveland, Florida, and Washington DC. In three of these cities, however, studies have compared existing levels of racial stratification in voucher and charter schools. Fuller and colleagues (Fuller and Mitchell, 1999, 2000; Fuller and Greiveldinger, 2002) found that students participating in the Milwaukee voucher program (after its expansion to include religious schools) were slightly less likely to be in schools that are highly stratified racially than were students in public schools. Students in religiously affiliated voucher schools were substantially less likely to be racially isolated than were those in secular voucher schools. This difference among the voucher schools may not be attributable to religious status per se, but might have occurred because religious schools were more likely to be pre-existing private schools that included tuition-paying students as well as low-income voucher students.[1]

In Cleveland, Greene (1999) found a mixed picture: Voucher students in Cleveland were slightly less likely to attend schools enrolling over 90 percent minority students, but they were more likely to attend schools enrolling over 90 percent white students. As compared with public-school students in the city of Cleveland and in the surrounding suburbs, Cleveland voucher students were more likely to attend schools with racial distributions near the region-wide average. Similarly, Greene and Winters (2006) found that students participating in the federally funded voucher program in Washington DC were more likely to attend schools reflective of the racial distribution of the population of the metropolitan area than were students who remained in DC public schools. In addition, voucher students were less likely to be enrolled in schools with more than 90 percent of their students from a single racial group.

Other evidence of the effects of school-choice policies on the stratification of students is available from policies in place outside the United States. New Zealand created a comprehensive system of universal choice among publicly supported schools in 1991, while giving the schools substantial autonomy in operations—thereby creating a competitive market in education. The system allows oversubscribed schools to choose students. Ladd and Fiske (2001) found that the resulting distribution of students across schools in New Zealand was highly stratified by ethnicity, with Maori and Pacific Islander students disproportionately concentrated in schools that are not in high demand.

Willms (1996) examined sorting effects over a decade after the introduction of school choice in Scotland in 1991. Unlike the system in New Zealand, Scotland's system is not a universal choice system, but one that permits choices by families seeking them out. Willms found that choosing parents tended to move their children to schools with higher achievement levels and higher socioeconomic status than the assigned schools they left. In consequence, communities with high proportions of students making active choices saw the largest increases in stratification by socioeconomic status in schools.

In sum, studies of the effects of school choice on the sorting of students suggest that stratification across schools may increase under some circumstances. It also appears likely, however, that the stratification effects of school choice programs differ depending on the local context and the policy design. In particular, universally available school choice programs may reduce integration across racial/ethnic or socioeconomic lines, but programs targeted to low-income families could conceivably increase integration, particularly if implemented in communities where public schools are presently highly stratified.

Nearly all of the empirical studies of the effect of school competition on student stratification take as their starting point the assumption that the school is the appropriate unit of analysis. But student sorting can occur within schools as well as between schools. If integration is to benefit students, presumably it requires that they interact in the classroom, the cafeteria, and the gym, rather than having separate educational experiences that happen to occur under the same roof. In many large public high schools, social factors and the sorting of students into discrete academic "tracks" combine to make students' daily interactions less integrated than schoolwide counts of students might suggest.[2] Unfortunately, no studies have compared the internal integration of charter schools, voucher schools, and conventional public schools. One study (Greene and Mellow, 1998) compared integration in cafeterias in samples of public and private schools in two unnamed cities, and found that private-school students were somewhat more likely than public-school students to have students of differing racial/ethnic groups sitting in close proximity. Whether this finding would generalize to other cities, and whether it predicts what would occur under policies promoting school choice, are unclear. More research on integration inside schools is much needed.

Competition and Civic Socialization

Integration has typically been regarded as a public good under the assumption that students who are exposed to others of different backgrounds will develop a sense of tolerance and a wider community allegiance. This assumption is implicit in the common-school model: The education of students in common is presumed to foster healthy civic attitudes. Moreover, the common-school model also expects that healthy civic attitudes will be promoted because public schools are ultimately accountable to democratically elected officials, who will ensure that the schools have a curriculum that explicitly promotes civic values (see McDonnell, Timpane, and Benjamin, 2000).

Despite these longstanding assumptions about the benefits of the common-school model, there is little empirical evidence on the point. Meanwhile, few scholars studying vouchers and charter schools have examined civic outcomes (Gill et al., 2001). The debate about school choice and civic values has been conducted almost entirely in the legal arena, where advocates on both sides have argued whether permitting public funding to go to religiously-affiliated private schools violates provisions of state and federal constitutions. The constitutional debate makes no reference to empirical evidence on the civic outcomes produced by publicly and privately operated schools, and it obscures the possibility that the issue may extend beyond religion, affecting charter schools as well as private schools.

Only one study has compared charter schools and conventional public schools in terms of effects on students' attainment of civic skills and knowledge. Buckley and Schneider (2004) used results from telephone surveys of students in grades seven through twelve to compare the values, civic participation, and knowledge of charter students and students in conventional public schools in the District of Columbia. They found that charter students were significantly more likely than students in conventional public schools to perform community service, while they had no greater probability of participating in clubs or sports. Charter students were marginally significantly more likely to take part in a debate or discussion and to speak at a community meeting. They found no differences between charter students and students in conventional public schools in terms of political tolerance. Buckley and Schneider's findings regarding the potential advantages of charter schools for civic skills and community service are provocative, but given the high rate of attrition from the sample and the difficulty of controlling for selection bias, they should be viewed as tentative.

No studies have yet examined the effects of voucher programs on civic outcomes, but three studies have assessed the effects of private schools. Campbell (2001) and Belfield (2003) used data from two different waves of the National Household Education Survey (NHES) to examine the effects of public and private schools on students' civic skills, civic confidence, political knowledge, political tolerance, and participation in community service. Using a cross-sectional regression analysis that controlled for a wide range of student, family, and school characteristics with 1996 NHES data, Campbell found that Catholic schools (but not other private schools) had a positive effect on community service. Catholic schools were also associated with greater civic skills and civic knowledge. Catholic schools, other religious schools, and secular private schools were all found to have advantages over public schools for civic confidence (i.e., confidence in one's ability to write a letter to a government official or to make a statement at a public meeting). Catholic schools and secular private schools had students with greater political tolerance than did public schools, while students in non-Catholic religious private schools had less political tolerance. Belfield (2003) found similar results using similar methods and data from a subsequent administration of the NHES in 1999.

Godwin, Godwin, and Martinez-Ebers (2004) surveyed high school students in public schools and fundamentalist Christian schools in one metropolitan area, and compared the political values and attitudes of students in both types of schools in 10th grade and 12th grade. Controlling for various family characteristics, 10th grade students in fundamentalist Christian schools had lower scores than did public-school students in terms of some measures of tolerance. Because the 12th grade cohort of students in fundamentalist schools exhibited substantially higher levels of tolerance, however, the difference in tolerance between grades 10 and 12 in fundamentalist schools exceeded that in the public schools. The authors interpret this quasi-longitudinal result to suggest that "Fundamentalist schools appear to be as successful as public schools in teaching the values necessary to assume the burdens of citizenship in a democratic society" (p. 1109).

In the absence of randomized designs and true longitudinal data, all three of the studies on civic socialization in private schools should be viewed as providing only suggestive rather than conclusive evidence. Nonetheless, the studies so far provide little evidence to confirm fears that privately operated schools might promote attitudes unsuitable to socialization in a democracy. In some instances, they suggest reason for optimism that some kinds of privately operated schools could actually improve public outcomes.[3]

Such optimism also gains support from the experience of European countries that have long experience with public funding of privately operated religious schools. In some countries—notably the Netherlands—providing public support for the religious education preferences of parents has been regarded not as a threat to civic unity but as an essential support for it. A recent collection of essays edited by Wolf and Macedo (2004) describes the history, politics, and policy behind the varied systems of public support for private schools that exist in the Netherlands, Belgium, Germany, France, the United Kingdom, and Alberta, Canada—as well as some empirical evidence on the effects of the private schools on civic values. The chapter by Dronkers (2004) reviews empirical evidence from studies of private schools across continental Europe, finding no evidence that the religious schools promote different civic values than do the government-operated schools. As all of the case study essays in the volume make clear, however, the "private" religious schools that receive public funding in European countries are subject to far more regulation than are private schools in the United States. In Europe, public funding has come with extensive public regulation. Whether this kind of regulation is necessary to ensure the promotion of civic outcomes in private schools is unclear. And whether it would be constitutionally permissible and politically acceptable in the United States is also unclear. Nonetheless, at minimum the other countries provide useful examples for considering how U.S. policy makers might promote civic purposes in privately managed and religious schools.

POLICY IMPLICATIONS AND FUTURE RESEARCH

Competitive effects—positive or negative—are among the most important outcomes that may be produced by educational privatization and school choice. Effects on students remaining in conventional public schools could easily dwarf direct effects on students who make use of school-choice policies. Moreover, privatization of the governance of schools may have implications for the public purposes of schooling that are not often considered in research on school-choice programs. A few studies, however, have provided some guidance on these issues.

Existing research on charter schools and voucher programs suggests reason for cautious optimism about their competitive effects on the achievement of students in conventional public schools: Several studies have found positive competitive effects, and none have found negative effects. The literature provides more reason for concern about the effect of school choice on the stratification of students across schools. Some varieties of choice programs appear to increase stratification by race or socioeconomic status.

Surprisingly little empirical evidence is available on the effect of competition and privatization on one of the long-recognized public purposes of education: the socialization of citizens. There is as yet no empirical evidence that supports the hypothesis that serving this public purpose requires schools that are publicly governed. The very limited research base suggests the intriguing possibility that some kinds of privately operated schools may promote tolerant attitudes, civic knowledge, and community service more effectively, on average, than do conventional public schools. But the evidence on this point is thin indeed, and researchers have not had the opportunity to apply the kinds of longitudinal methods that have been used to assess impacts on math and reading achievement.

Indeed, more research on all of these points would help to clarify the effects of competition on a variety of outcomes and under a variety of circumstances. Effects on outcomes other than math and reading achievement are especially in need of more study. Competitive, decentralized models of K–12 education delivery such as those represented by charter schools and vouchers involve a fundamental departure from the standard, "common school" model that has dominated American schooling for the past two centuries, so the relative absence of attention to the public purposes that the common-school model aims to achieve is especially notable.

Additional research should also more deeply explore the measurement of competition and competitive effects. Future work could include closer attention to patterns of integration inside schools as well as between them. In addition, the measure of competition itself merits examination. Levacic (2004) points out that structural measures of competition, such as the percentage of students in an area attending alternative schools or the number of alternative schools within a specified geographic area, are not necessarily related to the degree of competitive pressure actually felt by the decision-makers at the public school or district. Examining schools in England, she finds that the degree of competition perceived by school officials has a strong positive effect on student performance but that structural measures of competition do not.

Despite the limitations of the existing evidence on the effects of competition, enough exists to provide some guidance to policymakers. The specific design of a program of educational competition is likely to matter. The effect of school choice on integration will depend substantially on what students and schools are eligible to participate in the program. Some choice programs that are open to all students have had the effect of increasing the stratification of students across schools. Voucher programs that are targeted to low-income students, by contrast, have the potential to reduce stratification. That outcome will occur if they succeed in bringing low-income and minority students into private schools that presently enroll higher-income, tuition-paying students.

Other predictions about the effects of policy design may not follow directly from the existing empirical literature, but can be logically inferred with plausible assumptions. For example, universally-available voucher programs that provide small scholarships (i.e., less than is necessary to pay full tuition at many private schools) could easily exacerbate stratification by subsidizing upper-income families who can afford to pay tuition above the scholarship amount. And choice programs that allow participating schools to select their students might have more-negative effects on stratification than would programs that require participating schools to accept all applicants (or to choose randomly among them if they are oversubscribed). Finally, choice programs may have more success in inducing improved achievement in conventional public schools if they are explicitly designed with that aim in mind, by incorporating accountability systems (as does Florida's A+ Schools program), by removing some constraints on public schools that might reduce their ability to compete, or by increasing financial incentives for improvement by ensuring that educational funds follow each student to whatever school he or she attends.

Less can be said with confidence about the specific policy levers that might promote favorable effects on civic socialization. Too little is known about the effects of different kinds of schools on this outcome. At minimum, it would make sense for choice programs to attempt to measure civic socialization in participating schools and to make public any information about the civic components of schools' missions and curricula.

Indeed, provision of good information about schools—going beyond achievement results in reading and mathematics—should be viewed as an essential component of any educational program based on choice and competition. High-quality information for consumers (i.e., parents and students) is a critical ingredient for the effective operation of markets. Better information therefore merits serious attention from policymakers interested in educational competition—not only because additional research is needed on the effectiveness of choice programs and schools, but also because information is itself a fundamental component of a competition-based system.

NOTES

1. Chakrabarti (2005) also examined student sorting in Milwaukee, but her data came from the early 1990s, when the Milwaukee voucher program enrolled very small numbers of students and before it included religiously-affiliated schools.
2. On the disproportionate representation of racial/ethnic minority students in lower academic tracks, see Oakes (1985); Gamoran (1987); Oakes (1990); Braddock (1990); Braddock and Dawkins (1993).
3. If privately operated schools had the effect of increasing educational attainment, they might have an indirect and positive effect on civic outcomes as well. Dee (2004) has found that greater educational attainment may increase voter participation, civic knowledge, and support for free speech. Whether charter schools or voucher schools increase the educational attainment of their students has not yet been empirically examined.

REFERENCES

Bayer, Patrick and Robert McMillan. 2005. *Choice and Competition in Local Education Markets*. Cambridge, MA: National Bureau of Economic Research.

Belfield, Clive R. 2003. "Democratic Education Across School Types: Evidence from the NHES99." Occasional Paper #73, Teachers College, Columbia University.

Bettinger, Eric P. 2005. "The Effect of Charter Schools on Charter Students and Public Schools." *Economics of Education Review* 24: 133–147.

Bifulco, Robert and Helen F. Ladd. 2006. "The Impact of Charter Schools on Student Achievement: Evidence from North Carolina." *Journal of Education Finance and Policy* 1, Winter: 50–90.

Bjorklünd, Anders, Per-Anders Edin, Peter Fredriksson, and Alan Krueger. 2005. *The Market Comes to Education in Sweden: An Evaluation of Sweden's Surprising School Reforms*. New York: Russell Sage Foundation.

Booker, Kevin, Scott Gilpatric, Timothy Gronberg, and Dennis Jansen. 2006. "The Effect of Charter Schools on Traditional Public School Students in Texas: Are Children Who Stay Behind Left Behind?" Working paper, Texas A&M University.

Braddock, Jomills H. 1990. *Tracking: Implications for Race-Ethnic Subgroups*. Baltimore, MD: Center for Research on Effective Education for Disadvantaged Students, Johns Hopkins University.

Braddock, Jomills H. and Marvin Dawkins. 1993. "Ability Grouping, Aspirations, and Achievement: Evidence from the National Educational Longitudinal Study of 1988." *Journal of Negro Education* 62: 324–336.

Buckley, Jack, Simona Kucsova, and Mark Schneider. 2003. "Building Social Capital in the Nation's Capital: Can Charter Schools Build a Foundation for Cooperative Behavior?" Unpublished.

Buckley, Jack and M. Schneider. 2004. "Do Charter Schools Promote Student Citizenship?" Occasional Paper #91, National Center for the Study of Privatization in Education, Columbia University.

Buddin, Richard, and Ron Zimmer.2004. "Is Charter School Competition in California Improving the Performance of Traditional Public Schools?" Santa Monica, CA: RAND Corporation, WR–297–EDU, 2005. Online only: http://www.rand.org/publications/WR/WR297/.

Campbell, David E. 2001. "Bowling Together: Private Schools, Serving Public Ends." *Education Next* 1: 55–61.

Chakrabarti, Rashid. 2005. "Impact of Voucher Design on Public School Performance: Evidence from Florida and Milwaukee Voucher Programs." Working paper, Harvard University.

Chubb, John E., and Terry M. Moe. 1990. *Politics, Markets, and America's Schools.* Washington DC: Brookings Institution.

Dee, Thomas S. 2004. "Are There Civic Returns to Education?" *Journal of Public Economics* 88: 1697–1720.

Dronkers, Jaap. 2004. "Do Public and Religious Schools Really Differ: Assessing the European Evidence." In Patrick Wolf and Stephen Macedo, eds., *Educating Citizens: International Perspectives on Civic Values and School Choice*. Washington DC: Brookings Institution Press.

Epple, Dennis and Richard Romano. 1998. "Competition between Private and Public Schools, Vouchers, and Peer-Group Effects." *The American Economic Review* 88: 33–62.

Epple, Dennis and Richard Romano. 2000. "Neighborhood Schools, Choice, and the Distribution of Educational Benefits." NBER Working Paper #W7596.

Epple, Dennis and Richard Romano. 2002. "Educational Vouchers and Cream Skimming." NBER Working Paper #9354.

Ferreyra, Maria Marta. 2007. "Estimating the Effects of Private School Vouchers on Multidistrict Economies." *American Economic Review* 97: 789–817.

Figlio, David N. and Cecilia Ellen Rouse. 2004. "Do Accountability and Voucher Threats Improve Low-Performing Schools?" NBER working paper revised August, 2004.

Fiske, Edward B. and Helen F. Ladd. 2000. *When Schools Compete: A Cautionary Tale*. Washington DC: Brookings Institution Press.

Frankenberg, Erica and Chungmei Lee. 2003. "Charter Schools and Race: A Lost Opportunity for Integrated Education." *Educational Policy Analysis Archives* 11(32). Available at: http://epaa.asu.edu/epaa/v11n32.

Friedman, Milton. 1955. "The Role of Government in Education." In *Economics and the Public Interest*, edited by Robert A. Solo. Piscataway, NJ: Rutgers University Press.

Fuller, Bruce, R. F. Elmore, and G. Orfield. 1996. *Who chooses? Who looses? Culture, institutions, and the unequal effects of school choice*. New York: Teachers College Press.

Fuller, Howard L., and Deborah Greiveldinger. 2002. "The Impact of School Choice on Racial Integration in Milwaukee Private Schools." Milwaukee, WI: American Education Reform Council. Available at: http://www. schoolchoiceinfo.org.

Fuller, Howard L., and George A. Mitchell. 1999. "The Impact of School Choice on Racial and Ethnic Enrollment in Milwaukee Private Schools." Milwaukee, WI: Institute for the Transformation of Learning, Marquette University. Available at: http://www. schoolchoiceinfo.org.

Fuller, Howard L., and George A. Mitchell. 2000. "The Impact of School Choice on Integration in Milwaukee Private Schools." Milwaukee, WI: Institute for the Transformation of Learning, Marquette University. Available at http://www.schoolchoiceinfo. org/servlets/SendArticle/4/integ1299.pdf.

Gamoran, Adam. 1987. "The Stratification of High School Learning Opportunities." *Sociology of Education* 60:135–155.

Gill, Brian P., Michael Timpane, Karen E. Ross, and Dominic J. Brewer. 2001. *Rhetoric Versus Reality: What we Know and What we Need to Know about Vouchers and Charter Schools.* Santa Monica, CA: RAND.

Godwin, R. Kenneth, Jennifer R. Godwin, and Valerie Martinez-Ebers. 2004. "Civic Socialization in Public and Fundamentalist Schools." *Social Science Quarterly* 85: 1097–1111.

Greene, Jay P. and N. Mellow. 1998. "Integration where it counts: A Study of Racial Integration in Private School Lunchrooms." Presented at the Meeting of the American Political Science Association, Boston, MA., September. Available online at: http://www.schoolchoices.org/roo/jay1.htm.

Greene, Jay P. 1999. "The Racial, Economic, and Religious Context of Parental Choice in Cleveland." Paper presented at the Association for Public Policy Analysis and Management. Washington DC, November.

Greene, Jay P. and Marcus A. Winters. 2003. "When Schools Compete: The Effects of Vouchers on Florida Public School Achievement." Education Working Paper, Center for Civic Innovation at the Manhattan Institute, August.

Greene, Jay P. and Marcus A. Winters. 2006. "An Evaluation of the Effect of D.C.'s Voucher Program on Public School Achievement and Racial Integration after One Year." Education Working Paper, Center for Civic Innovation at the Manhattan Institute, January.

Gutmann, Amy. 1987. *Democratic Education*. Princeton, NJ: Princeton University Press.

Hess, F. M. 2002. *Revolution at the Margins: The Impact of Competition on Urban School Systems*. Washington DC: Brookings Institution Press.

Hsieh, Chang-Tai and Miguel Urquiola. 2001. "When Schools Compete, how do they Compete? An Assessment of Chile's Nationwide School Voucher Program." Presented at UCLA/RAND Joint Labor and Population Workshop, Santa Monica, CA. November 20.

Hoxby, Caroline M. 2000. "The Battle Over School Choice." PBS. Available at http://www.pbs.org/wgbh/pages/frontline/shows/ vouchers/interviews/hoxby.html.

Hoxby, Caroline. 2002. "School Choice and School Productivity (Or Could School Choice be a Tide that Lifts all Boats?)." NBER Working Paper #8873, April 2002.

Ladd, Helen F. 2002. "School Vouchers: A Critical View." *Journal of Economic Perspectives* 16: 3–24.

Ladd, Helen F. and Edward B. Fiske. 2001. "The Uneven Playing Field of School Choice: Evidence from New Zealand." *Journal of Policy Analysis and Management* 20: 43–64.

Levacic, Rosalind. 2004. "Competition and the Performance of English Secondary Schools: Further Evidence." *Education Economics* 12: 177–193.

Levin, Henry M. 2000. *A Comprehensive Framework for Evaluating Educational Vouchers*. New York: National Center for the Study of Privatization of Education, Teachers College, Columbia University.

Macedo, S. and P. Wolf. 2004. Introduction to Educating Citizens: International Perspectives on Civic Values and School Choice, co-edited by Patrick J. Wolf and Stephen Macedo, with David Ferrero and Charles Venegoni. Washington DC: Brookings Institution Press.

McDonnell, Lorraine, P., Michael Timpane, and Roger Benjamin (eds.). 2000. *Rediscovering the Democratic Purposes of Education*. Lawrence, KS: University of Kansas Press.

McEwan, Patrick J., and Martin Carnoy. 2000. "The Effectiveness and Efficiency of Private Schools in Chile's Voucher System." *Educational Evaluation and Policy Analysis* 22: 213–239.

Nechyba, Thomas J. 1999. "School Finance Induced Migration and Stratification Patterns: the Impact of Private School Vouchers." *Journal of Public Economic Theory* 1: 5–50.

Nechyba, Thomas J. 2000. "Mobility, Targeting, and Private-School Vouchers." *The American Economic Review* 90: 130–146.

Nechyba, Thomas. 2003. "School Finance, Spatial Income Segregation, and the Nature of Communities." *Journal of Urban Economics* 54: 61–88.

Oakes, Jeannie. 1985. *Keeping Track: How Schools Structure Inequality*. New Haven, CT: Yale University Press.

Oakes, Jeannie. 1990. *Multiplying Inequalities: The Effects of Race, Social Class, and Tracking on Opportunities to Learn*. Santa Monica, CA: RAND.

Ross, Karen E. 2005. "Charter Schools and Integration: The Experience in Michigan." J. Betts & T. Loveless (eds.) in *Getting Choice Right: Ensuring Equity and Efficiency in Education Policy* (pp. 146–175). Washington DC: The Brookings Institution.

Rothstein, Jesse. 2005. "Does Competition Among Public Schools Benefit Students and Taxpayers? A Comment on Hoxby (2000)." NBER Working Paper #11215 (March 2005).

Sass, Tim R. 2005. "Charter Schools and Student Achievement in Florida." Working paper, Florida State University.

Schneider, Mark, Paul Teske, Christine Roch, and Melissa Marschall. 1997. "Networks to Nowhere: Segregation and Stratification in Networks of Information About Schools." *American Journal of Political Science* 41:1201–1223.

Wells, A.S. 1993. *Time to choose: America at the crossroads of school choice policy*. New York: Hill and Wang.

West, Martin R. and Paul E. Peterson. 2005. "The Efficacy of Choice Threats within School Accountability Systems: Results from Legislatively Induced Experiments." Paper presented before the Annual Conference of the Royal Economic Society, University of Nottingham, March 23.

Willms, J. Douglas. 1996. "School Choice and Community Segregation: Findings from Scotland." In *Generating School Stratification: Toward a New Research Agenda*, edited by Alan C. Kerckhoff. Boulder, CO: Westview Press.

Wolf, Patrick J., and Stephen Macedo, with David Ferrero and Charles Venegoni, eds. 2004. *Educating Citizens: International Perspectives on Civic Values and School Choice.* Washington DC: Brookings Institution Press.

III

PROMOTING EQUITY AND ADEQUACY

Section Editor

Leanna Stiefel

12

Conceptions of Equity and Adequacy in School Finance

Bruce D. Baker and Preston C. Green

INTRODUCTION

This chapter provides an overview of recent literature on conceptions of educational equity and adequacy applied to state school finance policy in the United States. Equity conceptions deal primarily with variations or relative differences in educational resources, processes and outcomes across children, whereas adequacy conceptions attempt to address in more absolute terms, how much funding, how many resources or what quality of educational outcomes are sufficient to meet state constitutional mandates. State constitutions address explicitly state legislatures' responsibility toward public schooling. The fact that the U.S. Constitution does not do so, however, leads to significant limitations for resolving inequities or inadequacies in public schooling nationwide. Equity and adequacy remain issues governed primarily by state courts and legislatures.

The chapter draws on work by scholars in the areas of public finance, law and school finance policy. We begin the second section with a discussion of Robert Berne and Leanna Stiefel's framework for evaluating school finance policy introduced in 1984 following initial waves of legal challenges to state school finance policies. We then trace the roots of the conceptions laid out by Berne and Stiefel, including the public finance policy roots of horizontal and vertical equity and early legal theories of equal educational opportunity. We conclude the second section by exploring in greater depth the intersection between conceptions of school finance equity and federal and state constitutional and statutory protections for the rights of individuals and groups.

The third section of this chapter addresses vertical equity and the intersection between conceptions of vertical equity and educational adequacy. We point out that vertical equity and adequacy conceptions are separable but have largely been folded into one as a matter of legal convenience in the context of state education clause challenges to school finance formulas. The fourth section provides a synthesis of equity and adequacy concepts in relation to law. The final section addresses issues for future consideration.

ORIGINS OF EQUITY CONCEPTIONS IN SCHOOL FINANCE

School finance policy lies at the intersection of the fields of public finance, law and other social sciences. As first comprehensively framed by Robert Berne and Leanna Stiefel in 1984, school finance equity may be viewed from either or both the perspectives of the *taxpayer* or the *child*. Because equity measurement evaluates the distribution of objects, there exists the critical underlying question—across which units of organization should the distribution of objects be evaluated? Ideally, equity would be measured across each individual child or taxpayer using precise measures of the educational inputs available to each child or tax burden shouldered by each individual taxpayer. Most U.S. states organize public schooling into local education agencies, or school districts with school buildings within districts. Hawaii, which operates as a single statewide district, is the notable exception.[1] In most U.S. states, the primary role for the intermediate governance unit—the school district—is financial management, including authority over local taxation for annual operations of schools and infrastructure.[2] State government interventions to resolve inequities have been designed primarily to compensate inequities in revenue raising capacity across school districts (see Picus, Geortz and Odden, this volume, for more detail).[3] State aid is allocated primarily to districts rather than to schools or children. As such, most school finance distributional analyses focus on distribution across school districts, masking potentially large disparities across school buildings and children within buildings.[4]

Berne and Stiefel offer the following four guiding questions for evaluating equity in school finance: Who? What? How? How Much? Under the question of *who*, various constituents might be addressed, including children, teachers or taxpayers. Most often, children, clustered within school districts, have been the emphasis in school finance equity analyses.

Under the question of *what*, one may focus on (a) financial inputs to schooling; (b) resources purchased with fiscal inputs that include teachers, equipment, materials, supplies as well as facilities and transportation; (c) educational processes, including time spent on specific activities, student participation rates in specific courses of study; or (d) student outcomes, ranging from measures of academic achievement to measures of economic productivity. In practice, analyses have focused on the first of these: financial inputs to schooling, usually per pupil expenditure, measured at the school district (local education agency) level.[5] Further, most analysts have evaluated state-level systems of financing public education, excluding children in private and home schooling. Cross-state analyses have been relatively rare, as have analyses that include private schooling or more recently charter schooling.[6]

In response to the question of *how*, Berne and Stiefel adapted public finance concepts of horizontal equity defined as the *equal treatment of equals*, and vertical equity defined as the *unequal treatment of unequals,* and added to these concepts *equal educational opportunity.* Berne and Stiefel defined equal opportunity to include what is now typically called fiscal neutrality. Fiscal neutrality means that variations in resources across children should not be a function of the wealth of the community in which a child happens to live. Horizontal equity states that resources should be equally available to all students attending school within a state, provided all students have equal needs. Vertical equity applies to those cases where specific students or groups of students have identifiably different educational needs and where meeting those needs requires additional resources.

The *how* much question requires statistical measures, which can be distinguished by their emphasis on different ranges of the resource distribution.[7] These measures address questions such as how much variation in resources across similarly situated students is acceptable? How much variation across differently situated students is necessary and on what basis?

Historical Origins of the Berne and Stiefel Framework

Theories underlying Berne and Stiefel's framework came from two discrete sources that were adapted for evaluating the raising of public education revenue and distribution of expenditures across public schools. The first of these sources was public finance principles applied to tax policy. The second was legal theory. Given this context, the frameworks addressed herein are unique to the public education system in the United States, a nation where defining educational rights has been left largely to the states and where no broader guarantee of education as a basic human right is explicitly acknowledged (see Fiske and Ladd, this volume, for contrast with developing countries).

Public Finance Origins

Though applied by Berne and Stiefel to the expenditure side of the school finance equation, the basic concepts of *horizontal* and *vertical* equity were drawn from a lengthy literature in public finance that focuses on tax policy. Within the context of this literature, horizontal equity refers to the equal treatment of equals and is a concept around which there is little dispute. Simons (1950, p. 8) notes that "[i]t is generally agreed that taxes should bear similarly upon all people in similar circumstances."

Like its counterpart in school finance, the concept of vertical equity in tax policy is more controversial. In general, vertical equity (VE) in tax policy refers to the progressiveness of a tax, or how much more certain individuals should be asked to pay in taxes, and on what basis. The well-known public finance economist, Richard Musgrave (1990), notes:

> VE (Vertical Equity) on the contrary is inherently controversial. An appropriate pattern of differentiation must be chosen but people will disagree on its shape. Whereas HE (Horizontal Equity) is a minimal rule of fairness, VE (Vertical Equity) is a matter of social taste and political debate. (p. 113)

Further, some argue that there is little or no need for a separate conception of vertical equity, if horizontal equity applies specifically to *equal treatment* only of *equals.* As such, horizontal equity accepts that unequals should be treated unequally. Musgrave (1959) suggests that "the requirements of horizontal and vertical equity are but different sides of the same coin" (p. 161).

Scholars of tax policy suggest two possible standards for determining the fair treatment of taxpayers that are unequal: (a) the benefit standard, and (b) the ability standard. Under the benefit standard, individuals or groups who stand to reap the greatest benefit from a tax should pay higher taxes. Under the ability standard, individuals with greater ability to pay a tax should pay higher taxes relative to their income, as would be the case with a progressively structured income tax.[8] In the tax policy context, one is still left with the value laden concern over just how progressive is progressive enough? We suggest at a later point that this vertical equity question is more easily answered in the context of modern public education finance.

Legal Origins

Providing additional backdrop to Berne and Stiefel's framework was the emergence of early legal theories on how best to challenge and resolve significant disparities across school districts, schools or groups of students in the quality of public schooling. Specifically, in the late 1960s legal theorists explored how one might challenge disparities in the quality of schooling across children, disparities that persisted through the period of racial integration of public schooling in the first few decades following *Brown v. Board of Education.* A flurry of activity emerged in the late 1960s following implementation of the Civil Rights Act of 1964, the Elementary and Secondary Education Act (1965) and release of the Coleman Report, *Equality of Educational Opportunity* (1966).

Even in their early stages, challenges to school finance formulas required evaluating the nature as well as the existence of disparities. Were differences in resource distribution related to legitimate vertical equity concerns? Were they simply arbitrary? Or were these disparities associated with some factor courts could identify as offensive, such as race or ethnicity? The political wounds of *Brown v. Board* still being fresh and the remedy response slow if not entirely stalled in some states, scholars sought ways to define disparities across groups without reference to race (Ryan, 1999).

Thus, legal theorists of the late 1960s suggested frameworks for evaluating variation in educational resources, with the particular goal of showing that resource variation deprived classes of students (including groups classified by race) of access to their fundamental right to education. Unfortunately, because such a fundamental right was not explicitly spelled out in the U.S. Constitution, the possibility of federal court challenges to the overall adequacy of educational funding and the scope of subsequent equal protection challenges was severely limited.[9]

Early frameworks sought to build on the Supreme Court's treatment of the Equal Protection Clause in the 1950s and 1960s (Enrich, 1995). Especially important were the Court's emphasis on the importance of education in American life (*Brown v. Board*), especially the Court's suggestion that governments had an affirmative duty to ensure that governmental services were equally available to all.

Horowitz (1966) suggested that variations in resources that were geographically arbitrary should be considered by courts to violate equal protection—the principle of *Geographic Uniformity.* Coons, Clune and Sugarman (1969), building on this argument, proposed the principle of *fiscal neutrality* (discussed by Berne and Stiefel). They argued that children in property-poor school districts were discriminated against by state policies that allowed heavy reliance on local property taxation for public schooling.

Coons, Clune and Sugarman's framework provided the basis for arguments in two seminal early school finance cases: *Serrano v. Priest* in California state court and *San Antonio Independent School District v. Rodriguez* in federal court. Both were equal protection challenges, and both challenged disparities in funding across school districts that resulted from differences in local taxable property wealth and local taxing decisions under state policy. The California State Supreme Court agreed that education was a fundamental right and, further, that property-wealth related disparities in school district funding were unacceptable, in part on the assumption that wealth was a suspect class and that differential treatment by wealth should be reviewed under strict scrutiny. The U.S. Supreme court viewed wealth-related school funding disparities in Texas differently. It ruled that under the U.S. Constitution, education was not a fundamental right and further that individuals residing in property poor school districts were not a suspect class; therefore only rational basis scrutiny was required. Ultimately, the U.S. Supreme Court accepted that the State of Texas had a legitimate interest in maintaining locally controlled taxation for public schooling and chose not to overturn the state's school finance policy.

Arguably, *Rodriguez* was not the best case for early federal court application of Coons, Clune and Sugarman's framework because it could be too easily shown, in Texas in particular, that taxable property wealth per pupil at the school district level was not highly associated with financial well-being of individual families and children residing in those districts. Testimony in *Rodriguez* revealed the complexities of evaluating the relationship between school funding and community attributes. Unfortunately, while these complexities were somewhat context specific, the court's ruling in the case was broad, shutting off all future Federal court challenges to property-wealth related disparities in educational funding. While the arguments failed in federal court, there were some additional early successes in state courts beyond *Serrano*.[10]

TABLE 12.1
Aligning Equity Conceptions and Laws

School Finance Inequality	*Governing Laws (Federal)*	*Governing Laws (State)*
Horizontal	Constitution—Equal Protection Clause	Constitution—Equal Protection Clause, Education Clause
Vertical	Statutes—IDEA (Individuals with Disabilities Education Act), EEOA (Equal Educational Opportunity Act)	Constitution—Education Clause

Conceptions of Inequality under the Law

Table 12.1 summarizes the intersection of equity concepts and the law. In short, horizontal inequities may be challenged in either state or federal courts as violating an individual's constitutional rights to equal protection under laws. Further, education articles in some state constitutions specify to a higher level, the *uniformity* of educational opportunities to which all children in a state should have access. We also discuss in this section the difficulties in articulating arguments for *appropriately different* treatment under equal protection frameworks. In general, such arguments fail because equal protection clauses are assumed to guarantee only equal treatment (in terms of inputs and processes), but not equal outcomes. Under federal law, a handful of statutes provide for appropriately different treatment. In state law, constitutional education articles have been interpreted as requiring appropriately different treatment.

The Equal Protection Clause of the Fourteenth Amendment, §1 of the U.S. Constitution provides the primary basis for evaluating *equal treatment* under laws.

> No state shall make or enforce any law which shall abridge the privileges or immunities of citizens of the United States; nor shall any state deprive any person of life, liberty, or property, without due process of law; nor deny to any person within its jurisdiction the equal protection of the laws.

In short, the equal protection clause provides primarily for the equal treatment of individuals by federal, state and local governments. In school finance, the equal protection clause provides primarily for protection against violation of the principle of horizontal equity—equal treatment of equals. However, that protection generally applies only to the most extreme cases of obvious, inappropriate differential treatment (Green and Baker, 2002). For example, when a state government adopts a policy that creates differential treatment across individuals, that policy is only in violation of equal protection if the state cannot provide a *rational basis* for the policy.[11]

A variety of types of differential treatment exist across local school districts in state school finance policies ranging from allowance of local control over property taxation to complex aid allocation schemes that provide vastly different funding levels across districts. In *Rodriguez*, plaintiffs challenged the allowance of local control over taxation for public schooling as yielding inappropriate and discriminatory disparities in educational quality. In *Rodriguez*, the U.S. Supreme Court accepted that the preservation of local authority to levy property taxes was sufficient rational basis for financial disparities across Texas school districts.[12] Not all fiscal disparities across local public school districts share this immunity. A sparse string of U.S. Supreme Court and Federal Circuit Court cases[13] since *Rodgriguez* indicates that funding differences across students may not always meet the rational basis standard, as did the local control argument in *Rodriguez* (Green and Baker, 2002).

Because the rational basis standard is a low standard for a government to meet in justifying its policies, early legal theorists sought ways to heighten the standard of judicial review by arguing that school funding disparities both discriminated against specific groups of students (referred to in the law as a suspect class) and deprived those students of some minimally adequate level of education that should be considered a fundamental right. Equal protection concerns, especially in federal court, are most easily articulated when a specific identifiable group of students, and exclusively that group, are deprived outright of access to a specific educational opportunity. Where expenditure variation falls along a continuum, the point of deprivation is harder to identify. Further, discrimination becomes harder to prove where deprivation falls irregularly though still systematically (the legal term for which is disparate effect), rather than explicitly, exclusively and intentionally across certain students.

In *Rodriguez,* the U.S. Supreme Court accepted this categorical view of equal protection—deprivation or not—but reasoned that no such deprivation of *minimally adequate education* existed in Texas at the time. Wise (1976) critiqued the *Rodriguez* court's evaluation that the Texas school finance system assured a "basic education for every child in the state." The court's evaluation on this point was based solely on minimum compliance with the Texas Educational Code. Wise noted that the *Rodriguez* court used this logic of categorical evaluation of equal protection to gloss over the "substantial financial and educational inequalities in the Texas system," thereby allowing the court to "escape ruling on the quality of education received by poor children in the state" (p. 470).

While the courts have permitted states to make accommodations to promote vertical equity, it has been more difficult to argue that the equal protection clause guarantees individuals a right to appropriately different treatment. Appropriately different treatment requires one to address the questions of (a) who should receive that treatment, (b) on what basis and (c) how much differential treatment is sufficient?

Early federal district court challenges regarding the rights of children with disabilities to participate in public schooling focused solely on obtaining equal access to the general education classroom rather than on obtaining appropriately different treatment such that students with disabilities might receive some *benefit* from participation.[14] In the 1970s, Congress codified rights to appropriately differentiated treatment for children with disabilities in the Education for All Handicapped Children Act P.L. 94–142[15] and children with limited English proficiency in the Equal Educational Opportunities Act of 1974 (EEOA). Section 1703(f) of the EEOA provides: "[N]o state shall deny equal educational opportunity to an individual on account of his or her race, color, sex, or national origin, by the failure by an educational agency to take appropriate action to overcome language barriers that impede equal participation by its students in its instructional programs" (EEOA, 2006).[16]

Legal scholars in recent years have rediscovered the argument that the Due Process Clause of the Fourteenth Amendment also provides a basis for promoting vertical equity, but only in conjunction with state policies. Due process analysis shifts the focus from inputs to outcomes, but it does so in categorical terms: deprivation or not. Where state constitutions identify education as a property interest (because the U.S. Constitution does not), and where states adopt outcome standards that measure attainment of that property interest, such as high stakes testing for graduation, appropriately different treatment may be required to ensure that children have equal opportunity to access their property interest.[17]

Most often, concerns about vertical equity for groups other than children with disabilities have been dealt with in the context of state constitutional education clauses and, more specifically, in the context of challenges to the adequacy of state financing under those clauses. Increasingly, state courts are infusing outcome standards into their evaluations of sufficiency of schooling inputs, thereby compelling the provision of vertical equity. We reserve the third section of this chapter for addressing the intersection of vertical equity and educational adequacy. We argue that the two, while increasingly coupled in the context of state school finance litigation and in some scholarly literature, remain importantly separable concerns.

THE SHIFT FROM INPUT EQUITY TO OUTCOME EQUITY IN SCHOOL FINANCE

The shift toward greater emphasis on vertical equity is in large part associated with a shift away from a focus on the *equality of educational inputs* toward the *equality of educational outcomes*. The publication of James Coleman's report, *Equality of Educational Opportunity,* in 1966 is often cited as a major turning point. Among other things, Coleman and colleagues highlighted the strength of the influence of family background characteristics on student outcomes and the relative insensitivity of student outcomes to school and district resources.

In the immediate aftermath of the Coleman Report (1966), Garms and Smith (1970), in pioneering work, used school-level data from New York State to estimate a crude, regression-based education cost function model. Their goal was to estimate the costs of achieving specific student outcome levels on standardized reading and math assessments, given a rich set of student background characteristics. Garms and Smith note that "equality of educational opportunity is usually thought of as allowing all school districts to offer, with a reasonable tax effort, at least a minimum standard school program" (p. 304). They then note that "the realization is coming gradually that even if state aid programs were to distribute money to school districts in such a way that all districts would have an equal expenditure per pupil with equal local tax effort, we would still not be guaranteeing equality of educational opportunity" (p. 304). The authors posit that "[e]quality of educational opportunity exists when the average achievement of groups is roughly equal. This definition recognizes a duty of the public schools, as servants of society, to attempt to overcome environmental deficiencies that are not the fault of the individual students" (p. 305). That is, in 1970, Garms and Smith further proposed an outcome-based definition as the value system for measuring vertical equity, and proposed and applied an empirical model for identifying "who" requires differential treatment and "how much."

While shifting focus toward educational outcomes, the Coleman report raised questions that would linger through current school finance litigation about the tenuous nature of the relationship between schooling quality—as measured by student outcomes—and financial inputs to schooling. Does money matter? Will equal inputs lead to equity defined in terms of educational outcomes? Or are differential inputs needed to account for different needs, and is the approach recommended by Garms and Smith a reasonable way to close achievement gaps across student groups? Early state court cases overturning funding disparities accepted that expenditures on schooling were related to educational quality: "[we] accept the proposition that the quality of educational opportunity does depend in substantial measure upon the number of dollars invested."[18] Later state court cases addressed more directly the assumptions that (a) money in general does matter for improving student outcomes and (b) money may matter more for some children than for others, which represents an endorsement of the concept of vertical equity.[19]

Vertical Equity as Outcome Equity: Setting the "How Much" Standard

Recall that in the tax policy literature no standard provides a decisive answer to the question of "how much" progressiveness is enough. Arguably, in school finance policy, the "how much" question is easier to address. At least at the conceptual level, how much, in terms of the differential inputs required for groups with different educational needs, can be defined in terms of the relative sufficiency of those resources toward improving equity of educational outcomes. Those outcomes may be measured either in normative terms or against specific criteria. Such criteria might include acceptable minimum performance on state assessments, graduation rates or successful matriculation to and participation in postsecondary education. In that sense, vertical equity as a school finance conception might simply be redefined as horizontal equity of outcomes or horizontal equity of opportunity to achieve a defined outcome. Stated differently, equality of outcomes requires differentiation of inputs.

Shifting the focus toward outcomes, however, raises the question of which outcomes are of greatest interest. The most common outcome in school finance litigation is student achievement as measured by state standardized test scores. Test scores have become the centerpiece of school finance litigation in part because of their role in state performance-based accountability systems. Further, most statistical analyses of the costs of achieving state mandated educational outcome levels have focused on the costs either of achieving specific test score levels on state assessments or on the costs of achieving specific percentages of children scoring proficient or higher on state assessments. Less attention has been paid to longer term outcomes such as college attendance and completion, future earnings or harder-to-measure *quality of life outcomes* addressed in disability literature (Turnbull, Turnbull, Wehmeyer and Park, 2003). In contrast to the narrow focus on test scores in cost studies, judicial decrees based on state education clauses have expressed a far broader conception of the desired outcomes of schooling, focusing most often on economic and civic participation.

Despite the failure of equal outcome claims in federal courts under the equal protection clause, this outcome perspective remains the most conceptually, empirically and legally viable approach for addressing the "how much" question of vertical equity. To accept an alternative view, such as requiring state and local governments to provide only *reasonable accommodations* in terms of educational inputs, where those inputs may knowingly be insufficient to promote equal or adequate outcomes, is to suggest that state governments should be granted wide latitude to establish different outcome standards for some children than for others.

The federal No Child Left Behind Act of 2001 (NCLB) provides further clarity on this point by requiring that states adopt outcome measurement systems which apply to all eligible students. Further, NCLB requires that states not only monitor achievement gaps across children by race, ethnicity, language proficiency and poverty, but that states close achievement gaps between these groups over time. Most states have now promulgated systems of outcome measurement and accountability compliant with NCLB, and some have gone beyond NCLB requirements to tie measures of individual students' achievement to the granting of a high school diploma.

The allowance of numerous accommodations and exceptions under NCLB for children with disabilities along with the independent statutory framework (IDEA) for classified children means there are two separate systems for determining vertical equity for children with disabilities: one outcome-based (NCLB) and one due process and predominantly input-based (IDEA). In part this difference reflects the practical concern over the extreme cases in which a child's disabilities are so severe that no level of resources would be sufficient to generate a high academic outcome. The conflict can only be resolved with significant resources targeted to those extreme cases, coupled with standards so low as to be meaningless for most children.

Educational Adequacy and Vertical Equity

Due to failures of "equal protection" doctrine under the U.S. Constitution to guarantee vertical equity, arguments for vertical equity have found their recent legal home in state education clause challenges, which increasingly focus on the *adequacy* of funding provided by states to local public school districts. Typically, adequacy is measured in terms of whether funding is sufficient for children in schools to achieve state-mandated minimum outcome levels (based on systems promulgated under NCLB). These accountability systems vary across states. Where outcome equity is emphasized, differentiation of inputs across districts with different proportions of hard-to-educate children is required.

On the heels of William Clune's influential work on *The Shift from Equity to Adequacy in School Finance* (1994), Julie Underwood (1995) framed vertical equity as synonymous with educational adequacy. Underwood asserts that each individual child requires a specific set of educational programs and services to achieve the desired educational outcomes for that child. As such, those inputs are necessarily differentiated. In fact, under this conception, while horizontal equity theoretically exists, it may not exist in practice, since no two children's educational needs are exactly the same.

Underwood's framework, while useful, applies under very limited conditions. It applies only to vertical equity pertaining to individual student educational needs, and it requires that a level of desired educational outcome be specified for each child or all children. Underwood's framework is primarily an adequacy framework, pegged to a specific level of outcome, with emphasis on state mandated outcome levels.

Beyond individual students' needs, conditions that influence vertical equity apply to concentrations of children from economically disadvantaged backgrounds, children with limited English language proficiency, minority student concentrations or average peer group prior achievement level. While Underwood's conception addresses the student's individual needs, her approach fails to acknowledge the potential effects of peers on students' individual outcomes and of different costs of improving those outcomes as peer composition varies. Underwood's conception also fails to address the fact that costs of outcomes vary due to labor market costs (especially the cost of attaining sufficient quantity of teachers of specific quality) and economies of scale (whereby some districts have high costs due to small enrollments), among other things. Individual student background attributes are but one small piece of a complex integrated puzzle in which the specific educational needs of individual students interact with the composition of students' peer groups and with the context in which children are schooled. These factors affect comprehensively the costs of achieving specific educational outcomes.

For any specific level of outcome, inputs must be distributed in a vertically equitable way to achieve that outcome. However, vertical equity remains separable from adequacy in that vertical equity is a purely relative concept. Vertical equity of inputs is necessary for providing either equal opportunity to achieve a specific outcome, or equal outcomes.[20]

Koski and Reich (2006) offer an alternative rationale for a more pure conception of vertical equity. Koski and Reich argue that the quality of educational outcomes is largely relative because education is primarily a competitive *positional good.* Hirsch (1976) describes positional competition as follows:

> By positional competition is meant competition that is fundamentally for a higher place within some explicit or implicit hierarchy and that thereby yields gains for some only by dint of loss for others. Positional competition, in the language of game theory, is a zero-sum game: what winners win, losers lose. (p. 52)

If education is considered to be a competitive positional good, the extent of disparity in educational outcomes above a minimum outcome standard codified in state policies matters a great deal. Baker (2005) describes variation in educational opportunity above the minimum standard as *opportunity surplus*. Under a *vertical equity as adequacy* conception, it matters only whether individuals have sufficient resources to achieve a state mandated minimum outcome level. That is, only opportunity deficits must be erased. Opportunity surpluses are considered non-offensive.

Koski and Reich argue, however, that the value of achieving that minimum standard is largely contingent on the variation of education opportunities above it. In a system where children are guaranteed only minimally adequate K–12 education, but where many receive far superior opportunities, those with only minimally adequate education will have limited opportunities in higher education or the workplace. Based on the concerns expressed by Wise (1976), it is likely that the least fair state school finance systems in the nation might surpass the minimum adequacy standard by allowing no one school or child to fall below a meaningless minimum outcome threshold, while allowing dramatic degrees of opportunity surplus beyond that minimum threshold.

As with a *reasonable accommodations* view of vertical equity, the minimum adequacy compromise constitutes a state endorsement of different outcome standards leading to different life opportunities for different children. While some compromise may be an unavoidable reality of school finance policy, the compromise need not be embedded into the framework for evaluating fairness in state school finance policies. Evaluation frameworks are better built on pure equity conceptions, with compromises left for political deliberation over school finance and judicial evaluation of constitutional compliance.

SYNTHESIS AND SUMMARY

We conclude this chapter with a framework in which we synthesize legal and theoretical developments in evaluating the fairness and equity in state school finance formulas. We suggest that the evaluation of the equity and adequacy of modern state school finance formulas might be best addressed through the following four questions, approached sequentially:

1. Is there variation in educational inputs such as per pupil expenditures across districts and children?
2. What is the nature of that variation? From a legal standpoint, it remains relevant to discern whether variation in resources across school districts is (a) related to fiscal capacity and local control issues, (b) related to vertical equity or marginal cost issues or (c) otherwise unjustifiable variation created by legislative actions. While disparities resulting from local control remain largely immune to Federal Court challenge under *Rodriguez*, other disparities are not and may still be challenged.
3. Is the school finance system generally progressive or regressive with respect to assumed need factors? That is, all else equal, do school districts and schools with greater shares of children in poverty, limited English proficient children and children with disabilities have more resources per pupil than districts with fewer of these children? More broadly, are resource levels higher in those schools and districts that by virtue of their student populations, labor market conditions and other factors outside control of school officials have higher costs of achieving educational outcomes. Do those who need more receive more?[21]
4. Does the school finance system provide enough resources such that children in those schools where costs of educational outcomes are higher have equal and/or sufficient opportunity to achieve desired outcome levels.

Table 12.2 reframes these questions in relation to existing law. The first question above and part of the second are addressed by Standard One, drawing primarily the work of early legal theorists including Wise (1968) and Coons, Clune and Sugarman (1969). This baseline standard asks whether there is variation in resources that might be considered an equal protection violation and second whether that variation is specifically related to issues such as state granted local authority to raise supplemental per pupil revenues. Notably, most concerns addressed under this standard cannot be addressed in Federal court as a violation of equal protection, but may be addressed under state equal protection clauses.

The second standard in Table 12.2 is the pure vertical equity or equal outcomes standard. Under the second standard, outcome equality is purely relative. For example, if the "average" student in a state receives a quality of education sufficient to provide a 25 percent chance of achieving an adequate educational outcome, so too should the child from economically disadvantaged background, the child with limited English proficiency or the child with disabilities.[22] Whether a 25 percent chance is constitutionally adequate is addressed under the third and fourth standards.

Pure vertical equity can be accomplished in a system that is adequate for none (according to judicial or legislative interpretation of state constitutional mandate). Taking this argument to the extreme, pure vertical equity can be achieved when all children are deprived entirely of schooling. However, pure vertical equity can also be violated in a system that is adequate for all. As such, it makes practical sense to couple vertical equity and adequacy conceptions.

Conceptually, the Equal Educational Opportunities Act (EEOA) and the Individuals with Disabilities Education Act (IDEA) provide statutory frameworks for advocating pure vertical equity. That is, one should be able to apply IDEA to advocate for educational opportunities for children with disabilities to be similar to educational opportunities for other children in the state, no more, no less. However, practical application of IDEA tends to be linked to external standards of "adequate" services for children with disabilities, but only for children with disabilities. This creates a legal protection imbalance across student groups that potentially compromises pure vertical equity. Pure vertical equity standards may also be useful for state level judicial review under equal protection clauses in states where state constitutional adequacy concerns are non-justiciable. These claims still face the uphill battle of convincing courts that an equal outcomes standard is practicable.

Standard three provides an integrated conception of vertical equity and adequacy, which might also be framed as an *adequacy compromise* view of vertical equity. Wise (1976) identified this compromise very early on, noting:

> From the beginning, some said that school finance lawsuits should not be argued on the basis of equal protection but on the basis of substantive due process. Such an approach implies that the cases would be concerned with minimum levels of protection to be afforded to children in the schools. The equal protection clause is much more encompassing, creating a demand for the equal treatment of equals. A substantive due process interpretation would mean only that protection needs to be provided up to a certain level. (p. 477)

The third standard of the framework is necessarily tied to a state constitutionally guaranteed minimum outcome adequacy standard.

The *vertical equity as adequacy* standard is perhaps the most common approach in modern school finance "adequacy" litigation under state education clauses. This standard, however, applies best to substantive due process claims where a specific property interest—minimally adequate educational outcome—is identified and where some students are deprived of access to that interest. The primary emphasis under the *vertical equity as adequacy* standard is that children

TABLE 12.2
Finance Equity Synthesis Framework

Level/ Standard	*School Finance Conception*	*Central Question*	*Federal Law*	*State Law*
One	Horizontal Equity & Fiscal Neutrality	Are there differences in resources unrelated to educational need?	C[1] – Equal protection	C – Equal Protection & Education Clause
Two	Pure Vertical Equity (equal outcomes)	Are there sufficient differences in resources to accommodate educational need, measured against equity of outcomes standard?	S[2] – EEOA, IDEA	C – Education Clause
Three	Vertical Equity as Adequacy (equitable and/or sufficient opportunity to achieve minimum outcomes)	Do all groups of children have sufficient resources to support equal opportunity to achieve minimum outcome standards?	C – Due process (contingent on property interest) S – EEOA, IDEA	C – Due process & Education Clause
Four	Adequacy	Is aggregate funding sufficient for children to achieve minimum outcome standards?		C – Education Clause

Note: [1] C = Constitutional; [2] S= Statutory

who would otherwise have less likelihood of achieving their property interest of adequate educational outcomes, must be provided sufficient additional resources to increase their opportunities. Deprivation must be eliminated. From a practical perspective, *opportunity surpluses* are viewed as non-offensive under this standard.

This third standard is likely the most immediately practical standard in modern school finance litigation for making marginal improvements to pure vertical equity. However, this standard can only legitimately improve vertical equity where the outcome standard is sufficiently high. Where the outcome standard is very low, the state's most vulnerable children will be guaranteed only sufficient opportunity to achieve a meaningless quality of education, while others obtain far more and are better positioned for access to higher education and the work force. While opportunity deficits are erased by lowering the outcome standard, the magnitude of opportunity surpluses increases.

Under the third standard, vertical equity is achieved only where all children have access to adequate opportunities. Pure vertical equity can be maintained with this standard but only if no children have surpluses beyond this level. Typically, however, pure vertical equity is compromised under the third standard by the existence of opportunity surpluses.

The fourth and final standard is the pure adequacy standard, decoupled from vertical and horizontal equity. This standard asks broadly whether a state legislature has allocated sufficient funding statewide for a constitutionally sufficient share of the state's children to achieve a constitutionally adequate educational outcome. Under a pure adequacy standard, the distribution—across districts, schools or children—of either educational inputs or educational outcomes is largely irrelevant; such a standard may violate either or both principles of horizontal and vertical equity so long as a sufficient amount of funding is allocated for a sufficient share of the state's children to succeed. This standard applies only under state constitutional education clauses and only where state courts have determined pure adequacy arguments to be justiciable.

In most cases, adequacy conceptions are linked to either or both horizontal and vertical equity. Early school finance litigation and early foundation aid formulas strove to achieve horizontally equitable and minimally adequate fiscal inputs across school districts and the children they serve. More recently, school finance adequacy litigation using state education clauses has striven to better target fiscal resources to high need settings such that students have adequate opportunity to achieve state mandated outcomes. This is a *vertical equity as adequacy* standard.

However, recent state school finance litigation has also revealed a judicial preference to identify the aggregate amount of money that would constitute an adequate education. In some cases, state courts have laid out remedy frameworks that address only the aggregate amount of additional statewide funding—regardless of distribution across districts, schools or children—required to achieve a constitutionally adequate system. In other cases, courts have shifted their unit of analysis from statewide school finance reform to the allocation of sufficient funding for a single school district, regardless of the distribution of funding statewide relative to that district. (See Appendix A.1 for a delineation between *pure adequacy, horizontal equity as adequacy* and *vertical equity as adequacy*).

Pure educational adequacy is the least well-defined standard and least justiciable for at least two reasons. First, applying this standard requires judges and legislators to establish a precise operational definition of legislative obligation toward the state's children—or any subset of them—from generally ambiguous state constitutional language. So too does the vertical equity as adequacy standard. Second, educational adequacy as an independent standard is also not linked to any particular guiding legal principle regarding treatment of individuals in American society, most of which address concerns over equal treatment rather than adequate treatment. Even where adequacy concerns make their way into American law, as in defining *property interests* in due process litigation, the central concern of the courts has been whether individuals or groups have been unfairly and inequitably deprived of access to that interest, and not whether the average person's *property* is sufficient or adequate. Further, one cannot overlook entirely that education is substantially a competitive positional good, such that one child's *adequate* education is necessarily made less adequate by the ability of other children to gain access to more. Educational adequacy as an independent standard provides little guarantee that our nation's most vulnerable children will be provided equal opportunities, through publicly financed schooling, to become involved civic participants and economically productive citizens.

DIRECTIONS FOR FUTURE RESEARCH AND DEVELOPMENT

We have presented in this chapter the perspective that the shift in interest from educational inputs toward educational outcomes adds clarity to conceptions and measurement of vertical equity. We have suggested that the "who" and "how much" questions of vertical equity analysis may be addressed by measuring precisely the marginal costs of achieving specific educational outcomes across students and settings. Further, we have suggested that such measures might provide the basis for future legal challenges centered primarily on vertical equity conceptions. Yet the shift in emphasis from financial inputs toward educational outcomes requires that we now pay much greater attention to the desired outcomes of schooling in America and how we measure those outcomes. Alternatively, the current policy focus on educational outcomes necessitates a rethinking of school finance.

Numerous researchers since Garms and Smith (1970) have attempted to estimate statistically how the cost of achieving specific educational outcomes varies across individual students, groups of students and educational settings. Invariably, in the current context of state standards and accountability systems, those studies have based their models on state tests of academic achievement, typically including only reading and mathematics achievement. The literature on the extent to which state reading and math tests have predictive validity toward labor market outcomes or even postsecondary outcomes remains sparse. Further, while courts have repeatedly emphasized *civic participation* as a critical goal of public schooling, few states include assessments of civic knowledge in their testing and little is known about the relationship between current testing and civic outcomes. The void between broad judicial interpretations of state constitutional mandates with respect to educational outcomes and how we measure those outcomes in practical context and empirical models is vast.

It stands to reason that the "who" and "how much" questions of vertical equity analysis might be answered differently in any given state under different outcome objectives. Where college matriculation and completion are the outcome of interest, marginal costs of achieving those outcomes across children and settings may differ from marginal costs of closing test score achievement gaps. The new emphasis on vertical equity, either in pure form or with respect to minimally adequate outcomes, requires far greater attention to the desired outcomes of schooling and how we measure them.

Others have presented a compelling argument that the overemphasis on measurable student achievement outcomes in math and reading has led to an excessive narrowing of educational programming for children requiring the greatest effort to improve those specific outcomes (Rothstein, 2006). Where minimally adequate educational outcomes are defined only in terms of test scores in reading and math, broader, richer educational opportunities are reserved for a privileged few for whom the minimally adequate reading and math test scores are but a incidental right of passage. As discussed above, we should seek to broaden outcome measurement to reduce the extent to which such problems occur. However, inequities in the breadth or depth of curriculum are unlikely to be remedied by simply adding outcome assessments for each and every possible course of study from Advanced Calculus to Advanced Jazz Improvisation. More than likely, effectively evaluating inequities in the breadth of curricular opportunities will require continued focus on educational inputs, as well as outcomes.

NOTES

1. Hawaii's school system is often described as a single school district. Baker and Thomas (2006) describe the system as direct state control over schools, where only the state legislature has taxing and revenue raising authority for those schools.
2. Often only that level of authority granted directly by state legislative action. Increasingly, school districts are being encouraged to decentralize control over the expenditure side of financial management, allocating lump sums to individual schools through *weighted student formulas* and granting increased budget authority to those schools. Even in the most aggressively decentralized forms of this model, as implemented in Seattle, personnel contracts remain managed at the district level and the total budget constraint is dictated by district level available revenue. For more extensive discussion and analysis see Baker and Thomas (2006).
3. See also, John Yinger (2004)
4. In New York State, for example, a cross-district distributional analysis would fail to capture disparities that may exist across more than on third of the state's children because they all attend schools within a single district. Hawaii has generally been exempted from distributional analysis despite significant inequities in financial resources and teacher quality across Hawaii schools (Baker and Thomas, 2006).
5. Exceptions include Stiefel, Rubenstein and Berne (1998).
6. See Murray, Evans and Schwab (1998)

APPENDIX 12A.1

Category	*Concept*	*Distribution/ Level*	*Explanation*
Equity			
	Horizontal Equity	Inputs are equal, outcomes unequal (unless all children are equals or distributed equally). The absolute level of inputs provided or outcomes achieved is unimportant.	Local education agencies and the children they serve have comparable access to education resources.
	Vertical Equity	Inputs are unequal, outcomes are equal. The absolute level of inputs provided or outcomes achieved is unimportant.	Resources are distributed such that children with greater needs receive sufficiently more than children with lesser needs, where sufficiently more specifically means enough more to achieve equal educational outcomes.
Adequacy/Sufficiency			
	Educational Adequacy	Distribution of inputs or outcomes is irrelevant. The absolute level of available resources is sufficient (statewide).	There is enough total funding allocated by any specific level of government (usually state) to produce sufficient educational outcomes, on average. An adequate share of children statewide score proficient or higher. Does not guarantee nor prohibit horizontal equity, vertical equity or vertical equity as adequacy. Outcome failure may be disproportionate and district level performance inadequate in higher need districts.
	Horizontal Equity as Adequacy	Inputs are equal, outcomes unequal (unless all children are equals or distributed equally). The absolute level of available resources is sufficient (statewide).	A purely adequate aggregate sum of resources is divided evenly across districts and/or pupils. Does not provide vertical equity or vertical equity as adequacy. Outcome failure will remain disproportionate unless all children have equal needs (or groups of children distributed across districts) and district level performance will remain inadequate in higher need districts.
	Vertical Equity as Adequacy	Inputs are unequal, outcomes unequal (unless pure vertical equity is achieved). The absolute level of available resources is sufficient in each district or school.	Each district is allocated a sufficient floor of funding such that a sufficient share of children in that district can achieve adequate educational outcomes (preferably down to school level). District level outcomes should be increased to minimally adequate levels in high need districts, but outcome failure may remain disproportionate cross higher versus lower need districts.
Neutrality			
	Local Demand		Variations in educational resources across local public schools under the same state constitutional umbrella should not be related to differences in local tastes, income or the price of raising an additional $1 of revenue for local public schools.
	Political		Variations in educational resources across local public schools under the same state constitutional umbrella should not be related to purely political preferences that cannot be validated as legitimately associated with vertical equity goals.

7. For example, measures which evaluate spending at the top and bottom of the distribution only (ranges and range ratios), the pattern of distribution across all districts (coefficients of variation, Gini coefficients, or distribution just among those districts in the lower half of the distribution (McLoone indices)).
8. The two are not entirely irreconcilable. Adam Smith argued that individuals "ought to contribute to the support of the government, as nearly as possible, according to their respective abilities [ability-to-pay taxation]; that is, in proportion to the revenue which they respectively enjoy under the protection of the state [benefit taxation]" (Smith, 1904, p. 310 in Steuerle, 1999).
9. While on the one hand, equal protection challenges address in a purely relative sense the different treatment of otherwise similarly situated individuals, courts commonly evaluate differential treatment in terms of deprivation with respect to some minimum standard, as in deprivation of the right to vote. Unlike the right to vote, it is much more difficult to discern at what point along the education quality continuum deprivation has occurred. More discussion on this topic occurs at a later point.
10. See *DuPree v. Alma Sch. Dist. No. 30*, 651 S.W.2d 90 (Ark. 1983); *Horton v. Meskill*, 376 A.2d 359 (Conn. 1977); *Pauley v. Kelley*, 255 S.E.2d 859 (W.Va. 1979); *Robinson v. Cahill*, 303 A.2d 273 (N.J. 1973); *Seattle Sch. Dist. No. 1 v. State*, 585 P.2d 71 (Wash. 1978); *Washakie County Sch. Dist. No. 1 v. Herschler*, 606 P.2d 310 (Wyo. 1980).
11. See *Northwestern Sch. Dist. v. Pittenger*, 397 F. Supp. 975, 978–79 (W.D.Pa. 1975) (finding that two provisions of Pennsylvania school code, which granted sparsity payment subsidies to some school districts, but not to others, based on their low population densities did not violate the Equal Protection Clause).
12. This momentous judicial decision is one example among many that provides states wide latitude in allowing if not promoting disparities in educational quality across children. Such disparities are legally permissible under the U.S. Constitution and persist in many states where state courts have chosen also not to intervene. But, such disparities are not morally, ethically or even economically *good public policy.*
13. Including *Plyler v. Doe* (1982) and *Papasan v. Allain* (1986) and at the 10th Circuit court level, *Robinson v. Kansas.*
14. *Mills v. Board of Educ. of Dist. of Columbia,* 348 F. Supp. 866 (D.D.C. 1972); *Pennsylvania Ass'n for Retarded Children v. Commonwealth,* 34 F. Supp. 1257 (E.D. Pa. 1971).
15. P.L. 94–142, now IDEA, provides for vertical equity by granting detailed due process rights to parents of students with disabilities to consult with school officials, qualified experts and other mediators toward the establishment of an individualized educational program (IEP), which complies with the spirit of providing a *Free and Appropriate Education* in the *Least Restrictive Environment,* for the child with one or more specific disabilities. Decades of case law affirm the emphasis on the process guarantees rather than specific, uniform guarantees on the extent of differentiation or required outcomes.
16. EEOA (Equal Educational Opportunities Act) compels states and local school districts to assist students toward the specific outcome of overcoming language barriers. While no Supreme Court precedent exists, in *Castaneda v. Pickard* (1981), the Fifth Circuit Court of Appeals articulate a three-pronged test for evaluating compliance with EEOA, specifically including whether the differential treatment is sufficient to actually overcome children's language barriers (Baker, Markham and Green, 2004). Applying the *Castaneda* test, a federal district court in *Flores v. Arizona* (2000) ruled that Arizona's provision of $150 per LEP student violated the EEOA by failing to provide these students with an adequate education. That is, conceivably, under EEOA states or local school districts might be compelled to provide not only some level of vertical equity accommodation for children with limited English proficiency, but accommodation sufficient to produce a given level of outcome—overcoming the language barrier.
17. Substantive due process arguments are subtly but importantly different from the equity of outcomes framework rejected by the Supreme Court in *Missouri v. Jenkins* (1995), a long running and well known school desegregation case. In *Missouri v. Jenkins* plaintiffs argued that additional resources and interventions should be kept in place in Kansas City Missouri School District until equity of outcomes was achieved. First, the argument was framed in terms of equal protection, not substantive due process. Second, emphasis was on achieving "equal outcomes," which, as we discuss at a later point, requires

pure vertical equity whereas substantive due process claims require equal opportunity to achieve some minimum outcome, or *vertical equity as adequacy.*

18. *Robinson v. Cahill,* 62, N.J., 473, 303 A2d 273, 277.
19. One particularly bold proclamation to this effect was provided by district court judge Terry Bullock in *Montoy v. Kansas.* In defense, Defendants simply argue "money doesn't matter." Without regard to the constitutional mandate that there be adequate funds for a suitable education and that those funds be equitably divided, the defense seems to say: there is no correlation between spending and student learning, so what's all the fuss. "Money doesn't matter?" That dog won't hunt in Dodge City! *Montoy II,* 2003 WL 22902963.
20. Except in the special case where that outcome is "nothing" or "0." The unique feature of this case is that first, the theoretical cost of achieving nothing, is nothing. And, that cost does not vary by students or context.
21. For a comprehensive view on how one might measure, with relative precision whether resources are sufficient to achieve desired outcomes, see the chapter in this volume by William Duncombe and John Yinger.
22. If the student's IEP states that the student is capable of achieving a state standard.
23. Horizontal equity violations resulting from local control over property taxation governed by *Rodriguez.*
24. In the summer of 2005, the Kansas Supreme Court in *Montoy v. Kansas* issued a specific remedial order that an additional $142 million be added to the finance formula, providing no direction as to where that funding should be added, despite evidence in the trial record and language in their own previous decisions that would suggest that most if not all of the funding should be targeted toward vertical equity objectives. The $142 million aggregate figure was drawn from the aggregate spending increase recommended by the legislature's 2002 cost study on the trial record. The court explained further that "we will consider, among other remedies, ordering that, at a minimum, the remaining two-thirds ($568 million) in increased funding based upon the A&M study be implemented for the 2006–07 school year" (p. 941). Ultimately, the court accepted legislation that added $148 million statewide, much of which was allocated toward factors that compromised rather than advanced vertical equity. Similar logic was adopted by the Kansas Supreme Court in their final dismissal of *Montoy v. State* in the summer of 2006.
25. In *Campaign for Fiscal Equity v. New York,* the state's Appellate Division has taken a similar but narrower view that the state must allocate a range of aggregate funding to New York City schools in particular, without regard for whether the statewide system achieves vertical or horizontal equity. "The record establishes a range of between $4.7 billion and $5.63 billion, a difference of $930 million, in additional annual operating funds, that would satisfy the State's constitutional education funding obligations" (p. 2).
26. That is, if we falsely assume that children across districts are "equals" requiring only equal treatment. Notably, even pure horizontal equity is more nuanced concept than this, requiring that "equals" be treated equally.

REFERENCES

Baker, B.D. (2005). Nebraska's State School Finance Policy Fails to Provide Equal Opportunity for Nebraska School Children. Expert Testimony provided on behalf of plaintiff districts in the case of *Douglas County School District v. Heinemann.* Omaha, NE: Baird-Hold Law Firm.

Baker, B.D., & Duncombe, W.D. (2004). Balancing District Needs and Student Needs: The Role of Economies of Scale Adjustments and Pupil Need Weights in School Finance Formulas. *Journal of Education Finance 29*(2): 97–124.

Baker, B.D., & Green, P.C. (2005) Tricks of the Trade: Legislative Actions in School Finance that Disadvantage Minorities in the Post-Brown Era. *American Journal of Education 111* (May): 372–413.

Baker, B.D., Markham, P., & Green, P.C. (2004–Winter). A Comprehensive Legal and Empirical Framework for Evaluating State Financial Aid for the Provision of Services to English Language Learners.

Annual Meeting of the National Association for Bilingual Education (NABE), Albuquerque, NM.
Baker, B.D., & Thomas, S. L. (2006). *Evaluation of Hawaii's Weighted Student Funding*. Honolulu: Hawaii State Board of Education.
Berne, R., & Stiefel, L. (1984). *The Measurement of Equity in School Finance*. Baltimore, MD: Johns Hopkins Press.
Bradbury, K.L., Ladd, H., Perrault, M., Reschovsky, A., & Yinger, J. (1984). State Aid to Offset Fiscal Disparities Across Communities. *National Tax Journal* 37(2): 151–170.
Campaign for Fiscal Equity v. State, 801 N.E.2d 326 (N.Y. 2003).
Coleman, J. et al. (1966). *Equality of Educational Opportunity*. Washington, DC: U.S. Government Printing Office.
Coons, J.E., Clune, W.H., & Sugarman, S.D. (1969). Educational Opportunity: A workable constitutional test for state financial structures. *California Law Review* 57 (2) 305–421.
Duncombe, W., & Johnston, J. (2004) The Impacts of School Finance Reform in Kansas: Equity is in the Eye of the Beholder. In John Yinger (ed.) *Helping Children Left Behind: State Aid and the Pursuit of Educational Equity*, pp. 147–194. Cambridge, MA. MIT Press.
Enrich, P. (1995). Leaving Equality Behind: New Directions in School Finance Reform. *Vanderbilt Law Review 48*:101–94.
Equal Educational Opportunities Act, 20 U.S.C. §§ 1701–21 (2006).
Flores v. Arizona, 172 F. Supp. 2d 1225 (D.Ariz. 2000).
Green, P.C., & Baker, B.D. (2002). Circumventing *Rodriguez*: Can plaintiffs use the Equal Protection Clause to challenge school finance disparities caused by inequitable state distribution policies? *Texas Forum on Civil Liberties and Civil Rights 7*(2): 141–165.
Garms, W.I., & Smith, M.C. (1970). Educational Need and its Application to State School Finance. *Journal of Human Resources 5*(3): 304–317.
Hirsch, F. (1976). *Social Limits to Growth*. Cambridge, MA: Harvard University Press.
Horowitz, H. (1966) .Unseparate but Unequal: The Emerging Fourteenth Amendment Issue in Public School Education. *UCLA Law Review 13*: 1147–1172.
Koski, W.S., & Reich, R. (2006). Why "Adequate" isn't: The retreat from equity in educational law and policy and why it matters. *Emory Law Review 56*(3): 545–618.
Mort, P.R., & Reusser, W.C. (1951). *Public School Finance*. New York, McGraw-Hill.
Murray, S.E., Evans, W.N, & Schwab, R.M. (1998) Education Finance Reform and the Distribution of Education Resources. *American Economic Review 88*(4) 789–812.
Musgrave, R.A. (1959). *The Theory of Public Finance*. New York, McGraw-Hill.
Musgrave, R.A. (1990). Horizontal Equity Once More. *National Tax Journal 43*(2): 113–122.
Rothstein, R. (2003). The Price of High Standards. Equality in Education 50 Years after *Brown v. Board of Ed*. New York: Teachers College of Columbia University. http://www.tc.columbia.edu/news/article.htm?id=6199.
Ryan, J. (1999). Schools, Race, and Money. *Yale Law Journal 109*: 249–316.
Simons, H. (1950). *Federal Tax Reform*. Chicago: University of Chicago Press.
Smith, A. (1904). *An Inquiry into the Nature and Causes of the Wealth of Nations*, edited by Edwin Cannan. Vol. II. London: Cambridge University Press.
Stiefel, L., Rubenstein, R., & Berne, R. (1998). Intra-District Equity in Four Large Cities: Data, Methods and Results. *Journal of Education Finance 23*(4): 447–467.
Steuerle, C. E. (1999). *An Equal (Tax) Justice for All*. Washington, DC: Tax Policy Center of the Urban Institute and Brookings Institution. Available at http://www.taxpolicycenter.org/publications/template.cfm?PubID=7947; accessed August 1, 2006.
Strayer, G.D., & Haig, R.M (1924). *The Financing of Education in the State of New York*, pp. 173–175. New York, Report of the Educational Finance Inquiry Commission.
Turnbull, H.R., Turnbull, A., Wehmeyer, M., & Park, J. (2003). A Quality of Life Framework for Special Education Outcomes. *Remedial and Special Education 24*(2): 67–74.
Underwood, J.K. (1995). School Finance Adequacy as Vertical Equity. *University of Michigan Journal of Law Reform 28*(3): 493–519.

U.S.Constitution, Ammendment XIV, §1.

Wise, A. (1968). *Rich Schools, Poor Schools: The Promises and Pitfalls of Equal Education Opportunity.* Chicago: University of Chicago Press.

Wise, A.E. (1976). Minimum Educational Adequacy: Beyond School Finance Reform. *Journal of Education Finance 1*(4): 468–483.

Yinger, J. (ed.) (2004). *Helping Children Left Behind: State Aid and the Pursuit of Educational Equality.* Cambridge, MA: MIT Press.

13

Measuring Equity and Adequacy in School Finance

Thomas A. Downes and Leanna Stiefel

INTRODUCTION

Over the past 35 years, researchers have devoted significant effort to developing ways to measure two important goals of state school finance systems: the promotion of equity and, more recently, the provision of adequacy. Equity, as the term is traditionally used in the school finance literature, is a relative concept that is based on comparisons of spending across school districts. An equitable finance system is one that reduces to a "reasonable level" the disparity in spending across a state's districts. Adequacy, in contrast, is an absolute concept that requires that spending reach some minimum threshold level in each district. An adequate school finance system is one that provides sufficient spending to give students in each district an opportunity to meet state standards of performance. Thus, adequacy focuses only on the bottom part of the distribution of spending, with no attention to variations above the threshold needed for adequacy. Although general definitions are straightforward, quantifying the measures needed to judge either the equity or the adequacy of a school finance system is a challenge.

We refer the reader to other chapters in this section for discussion of some considerations that arise in the design of school finance systems to address adequacy or equity concerns. For example, Baker and Green (chapter 12, this volume) develop the legal, economic, and school finance *concepts* of equity and adequacy, while we focus on how researchers and policy analysts have translated those concepts into *quantitative measures*. In addition, we do not discuss in any detail the specific ways to adjust the quantitative measures for differences in prices of inputs across school districts, the differential costs of educating students who have educational disadvantages, or the higher costs experienced by districts with exceptionally small enrollments. The various ways of measuring these *cost differentials* are developed by Duncombe and Yinger (chapter 14, this volume). All of the measures of equity and adequacy that we describe can be, and usually are, adjusted for such cost differentials. Nor do we discuss the specifics of how school finance formulas have evolved to address issues of equity and adequacy; instead we refer the reader to Picus, Goertz, and Odden (chapter 15, this volume). Our emphasis is on how conceptions of equity and adequacy are translated into specific numerical measures.

The chapter is organized as follows. In the first section, we discuss statistical measures of school finance equity. In the second section, we identify issues that cut across the four main methods for measuring adequacy, and we then present and analyze those four methods. The third section deals with the incentives that accompany the introduction of adequacy into state intergovernmental aid formulas. In the next section, we highlight particular areas in need of further research.

MEASURING SCHOOL FINANCE EQUITY

As described by Baker and Green (chapter 12, this volume), equity concepts are often separated into horizontal and vertical equity. Horizontal equity refers to how well students who are similar in their characteristics are treated relative to one another. Vertical equity refers to the degree to which students who differ from others, due to educational disadvantages such as poverty or due to differing fiscal capacities of their school districts, are treated appropriately differently.

While the equity concepts are defined in terms of the treatment of individuals, school finance systems are designed for districts not individuals. Thus the concepts are translated from the individual to the district level. The concept of fiscal neutrality offers one example of how the individual-based concept of vertical equity is translated into a district-based equity concept. In particular, an aid system is said to be fiscally neutral if differences in the fiscal capacity of districts do not result in differences in per pupil spending (Louis, Jabine, and Gerstein, 2003).

Horizontal Equity Measures

In their early work, Berne and Stiefel (1984) identified eleven possible statistical measures to quantify the degree of horizontal equity in spending per pupil across school districts within a state.[1] The Berne-Stiefel equity measures summarize the variation in per pupil spending across school districts.

Berne and Stiefel discuss the differences in measures in terms of the values inherent in them.[2] One value reflects whether all districts, as opposed to only a subset of districts, are included in the measure. Another value is whether the measure places a heavy emphasis on the lowest spending districts. Yet a third value gauges whether equal proportional changes in spending (for example, a 5 percent increase in every district's per pupil spending) leaves the equity of the system unchanged. Although such a change in spending would leave all districts (sorted from low to high) in the same *relative* position, spending in the higher spending districts would rise by a larger *absolute* amount. Some equity measures remain unchanged after such proportional changes while others indicate that equity has declined.[3] Measures that remain unchanged after proportional changes are appropriate for making comparisons across states whose levels of spending differ approximately by proportional amounts.

Examples of how common equity statistics reflect some of these values follow. The range measures the difference in spending per pupil between the highest and lowest spending districts. The range is easy to understand but it ignores all districts in the middle of the distribution, is sensitive to extreme outliers, and indicates greater inequity with equal percentage increases in spending. A second related statistic, the federal range ratio, corrects some of the problems of the range. It measures the ratio of resources per pupil in the district at the top 95th percent to the district at the bottom 5th percent of the distribution. In contrast to the range, the federal range ratio is not sensitive to extreme outliers and does not indicate greater inequity when there are equal proportional changes in spending in all districts. If state policy makers' goal is to constrain districts to small differences in spending per pupil, the federal range ratio serves as a good indicator of how well that goal is being achieved.

Another measure, the McLoone index, focuses attention on the bottom of the distribution.

It compares the sum of actual spending in all districts that spend less per pupil than the median district to what total spending would be in those districts if their spending were brought up to the median. The higher is the resulting ratio, the less is the inequity. Thus, the McLoone index ignores any districts whose spending is above the median. Implicit in its construction is the idea that spending by the upper half of the districts is irrelevant to achieving school finance equity.

Other measures, such as the coefficient of variation, the Gini coefficient, the Theil measure, and the standard deviation of the logarithm of spending per pupil are based on per pupil spending in all districts. These measures do not change when there are equal proportional increases in all districts' spending per pupil.

Berne and Stiefel tracked the behavior of the eleven equity measures over eight years in Michigan and eleven years in New York State and found that four groups of measures could be formed based on similarity in the patterns among them. The range, restricted range and variance were in one group; the coefficient of variation, Gini coefficient, Theil measure, standard deviation of logarithms[4] and relative mean deviation were in a second; the federal range ratio and the McLoone index each formed their own third and fourth groups.[5] Thus analysts who wish to provide a comprehensive picture of the equity of a school finance system need choose only one measure from each group.

Vertical Equity Measures

To quantify vertical equity and fiscal neutrality, Berne and Stiefel developed two approaches. One approach uses regression analysis to relate spending per pupil at the district level to factors that cause cost differentials (such as the percent of students in poverty) or, in the case of fiscal neutrality, to property wealth per pupil. Higher coefficients on the cost factors imply that spending is higher in districts with above-average proportions of costly-to-educate students and, hence, that the interdistrict pattern is more vertically equitable than if the estimated coefficients were lower. In the equation to test for fiscal neutrality, small coefficients on the wealth variable imply that per pupil spending in wealthy districts is not much higher than in poor districts and, hence, that the finance system is relatively equitable along that dimension.

The second approach converts per pupil spending into spending per weighted student, where the weights are based on the differential costs associated with each type of student compared to students with average costs. The horizontal equity measures based on weighted students can then be used to assess the degree of vertical equity.[6]

The importance of the choices that researchers make when choosing a particular statistic and a particular equity concept are highlighted by some of the sharp differences in two much publicized equity rankings, one produced by *Education Week* as part of its *Quality Counts* report, and the other generated by the Education Trust. For example, in *Education Week*'s 2005 ranking of the 50 states, New Jersey was 33rd, while the Education Trust ranking for that year placed New Jersey 2nd. The differences for Massachusetts and New York were more stark. Massachusetts was 50th according to *Education Week* and 1st according to the Education Trust; New York was 3rd according to *Education Week* and 50th according to the Education Trust. The differences emerge because the two organizations chose different equity statistics for their rankings (Costrell, 2005) and also used different concepts of equity. The ranking produced by *Education Week* is determined by the state's McLoone index, generated using spending, *with no adjustment for cost differentials,* which is a horizontal equity measure. The primary measure used by the Education Trust is the spending gap between districts with the highest and the lowest poverty rates, which not only differs from the McLoone index as a statistic, but is also a version of a vertical equity measure. It relates spending per pupil to the percent of poor students in two groups of districts.

For states like New Jersey and Massachusetts, the Education Trust measure can provide a very different picture than does the McLoone index, because high-poverty districts spend above the median. The rankings diverge for a state like New York because the state has one very large district with a high poverty rate and spending at the state median. These examples emphasize two fundamental points: the statistical measure of equity can make a difference, and measures of horizontal and vertical equity cannot be compared to one another.

MEASURING SCHOOL FINANCE ADEQUACY

The spending that is deemed adequate in a particular school district in a particular state depends upon the context in that state. The state's constitution, and the interpretation of that constitution by the state's courts and elected leaders, ultimately determine what is adequate (Briffault, 2006). In some states, such as New Jersey and Kentucky, the courts have been relatively prescriptive in translating the language of the state constitution into specific adequacy standards and in specifying the steps policy makers need to take to meet those standards. In other states, like Alabama and Ohio, the courts have given policy makers more discretion both to establish the standards and to choose the policies designed to insure that all students have access to an adequate education (Briffault, 2006). In yet other states, the courts have not been involved at all; instead legislators and governors have designed school finance systems that aim to achieve adequacy.

The goal of any method of calculating adequate spending is to determine the "cost" of achieving a specified level of student performance, that is, the least amount of per pupil spending needed to achieve that level of student performance. The main approaches for "costing-out" a specified level of student performance are the professional judgment or resource cost model approach, the successful district approach, the whole school design approach, and the district cost function approach. Given the common goal of these approaches, all explicitly or implicitly build on the idea of a "production function for education" or an efficient relationship between student outcomes and spending. When the goal is calculation of adequate spending, researchers reverse this production function relationship; that is, they relate spending to outcomes instead of relating outcomes to spending. A multiplicity of approaches have been developed to calculate adequate spending because the technology that links school inputs to student achievement is not well understood.

Most state policy makers set standards establishing levels of academic performance (or outcomes) that the students in each district are expected to attain.[7] Differences across districts in input prices, student needs, and district characteristics (i.e., cost differentials) mean some districts will need to spend more than others to achieve the standards (Duncombe and Lukemeyer, 2002). Thus, the process of calculating adequate levels of spending usually is undertaken in two steps regardless of the methodology that underlies the actual calculations (Duncombe, 2002). In the first step, researchers determine the spending level needed to attain the state-established student performance requirements in at least one district, often labelled a benchmark district. In the second step, researchers adjust the spending in the benchmark district to reflect the cost differentials present in other districts.

Professional Judgment/Resource Cost Model Approach

In the standard application of the professional judgment approach, researchers consult with professional educators ("experts") to decide the level of spending per pupil that is required to achieve an adequacy standard in a prototypical school with pre-defined characteristics. Examples of characteristics generally include the total enrollment in the school, the percentage of students who are poor, and the percentage who are English language learners. The experts provide detailed information on the inputs needed to achieve the adequacy standard, based on their best judgments from their own experiences, and researchers combine estimates from panels of such experts to arrive at "best practice" or benchmark schools and districts. Spending for the benchmark district (or districts) is then adjusted for cost differentials, typically though the use of input price and cost indexes

The quality of the estimates generated by this method is based heavily on the process involved. Panels of experts generally meet for several days allowing time for detailed discussion and debate about what is needed to achieve pre-defined standards. Their calculations are often passed to other panels that look at several estimates all together and choose which ones to recommend. Sometimes the original panels are asked to reconvene after all have done their work to reconcile their estimates with those of others.

Some practitioners of the professional judgment approach, including Guthrie and Rothstein (1999) and the American Institutes for Research and Management Analysis and Planning (AIR/MAP) team of Chambers, Guthrie, and Smith (AIR/MAP, 2004), argue that research should be used to guide the deliberations of the panels. In New York in 2004, for example, panels were provided with "an objective description of mainstream educational research as background for [their] deliberations." In principle, providing panel members with a summary of the consensus in the literature could constrain the panel deliberations in reasonable ways. Panel members might feel a need to justify any deviations between the resource mixes they propose and those that the educational research literature suggests are effective.[8] In reality, however, because of the lack of consensus in the literature on the strength of the links between school inputs, such as class size and teacher characteristics, and student performance, any "description of mainstream educational research" is likely to be either uninformative or colored by the biases of the researcher preparing that description.

A major problem with the professional judgment approach is that participants in the panels are not asked to contemplate trade-offs, which means that they tend to adopt a pie-in-the-sky view of the world. Sonstelie (2001), Rose, Sonstelie, Reinhard, and Heng (2003), and Rose, Sonstelie, and Richardson (2004) suggest that this problem can be avoided if a two-step approach is used, with professionals first being asked to make resource allocation choices given a series of different budgets and then being asked to indicate which of the budgets would enable them to satisfy certain standards. To support this approach, Rose, Sonstelie, and Richardson (2004) document cases in which, given explicit outcome standards, the same set of professionals made different resource recommendations when they did and did not face explicit budget constraints.

Finally, the professional judgment approach suffers from two forms of human bias: self-serving behavior and habit. Some of the experts may have their own reasons for wanting funding to be high or low and thus may make recommendations that serve their own purposes but not necessarily the purpose of the project. While the remaining experts on the panel could counter this bias, the absence of a budget constraint substantially reduces the incentive for any participants to argue strenuously for compromises.

In addition, the experts are using their experience of current classrooms, schools, and districts, which may or may not be a good base for understanding what is required to meet state standards. If the professionals are given a standard that few, if any, districts are attaining, then their estimates of the resources needed are not likely to be accurate.

Several of the existing professional judgment studies highlight the extent to which the results are dependent on personal experience. For example, in a report that uses the professional judgment methodology to cost out an adequate education in Nebraska, Augenblick and Myers (2003)

include a table that summarizes, for elementary schools in a relatively large school district, the personnel recommendations generated by professional judgment panels in Nebraska, Kansas, Maryland, and Montana. The extent of variation in the recommendations is striking, even though contexts were intended to be very similar. Because the professional judgment method typically imposes constraints on class size, the recommended number of teachers did not vary dramatically across the states. But the number of teacher aides per 1,000 students ranged from 0 in Maryland to 25.7 in Nebraska. The number of librarians and media specialists ranged from 2 in Maryland to 5 in Kansas, and the guidance counselors ranged from 1.4 in Nebraska to 5 in Kansas. Total personnel recommended ranged from 80 in Maryland to 102.9 in Nebraska.

While in theory these differences could reflect differences in state standards, in this case, the standards used by Augenblick and Myers (2003) for Montana and Nebraska were very similar, as were the characteristics of the prototype schools and the students they served. Further, in Montana, the output standards presented to the professional judgment panels were based on statewide performance results, not on district-specific performance information. As a result, professionals with experience in high-performing or low-performing schools or districts would have little, if any, experience on which to draw to determine the resources needed for a prototypical school to achieve the performance gains specified in the standard.

Successful District Approach

The successful district approach builds on the plausible idea that districts already meeting a state's performance standard will be spending an amount that is at least sufficient to provide an adequate education. To implement this method, researchers identify districts (not schools) presently meeting the standard and then measure how much these districts are spending.[9] To mitigate the influence of extraordinary cases and to reduce the possibility that districts with inefficiently high spending affect adequacy estimates, most practitioners eliminate an arbitrary percentage of outlier districts (those that spend the least and the most). For the remaining benchmark districts, average (either mean or median) per pupil spending is calculated. Finally, to determine what spending is needed to meet the standard in districts outside the benchmark group, per pupil spending is adjusted for differences in such determinants of costs as the size of the districts, the types of students served, and the salaries of teachers.

Basing adequacy calculations on the spending of districts that have already attained the standard has considerable intuitive appeal. The successful districts approach, however, may fail to produce an accurate estimate because districts that have attained the standard may not be representative of "typical" districts, particularly if the standard is high. In other words, the districts that are meeting standards are not a random sample of all districts. They may differ in terms of measurable characteristics, such as their wealth or the types of students they serve, and in unobservable ways that are related to the cost of achieving the standard. Duncombe and Lukemeyer (2002) document that in New York State the extent to which successful districts are atypical in measurable ways, both in terms of property wealth and the share of high needs students, increases as the standard increases. While researchers have implemented various ad hoc approaches to account for the fact that successful districts represent a select group, they have not agreed on a standard method for addressing this limitation.

Whole School Design Approach

Proponents of the whole school design approach (Odden, 1997; Odden and Busch, 1998) argue that experience from successful school reform efforts can be used to determine the expenditures needed to provide an adequate education. For example, Odden (1997) uses the expenditures for schools participating in the Modern Red Schoolhouse program to generate an estimate of the amount that would be needed to provide an adequate education.[10] He chooses the Modern Red Schoolhouse program because of its claimed success in improving student performance. Other examples of whole school reforms could be used as well, such as Success for All or Accelerated Schools.

This approach has the virtue of providing both an estimate of what must be spent to provide an adequate education and a model of reform that can be adopted by districts that have yet to attain the standard. For any particular school district, however, the estimate of what must be spent to provide an adequate education may be flawed for two reasons. First, few studies using experimental or other causal designs have been performed to test the effectiveness of the various reforms. (For a summary of research on the quality and effectiveness of 22 comprehensive reform models, see CSQR, 2005.) Without such evaluations, there is little rigorous proof that whole school reforms will improve student performance. Second, and related in terms of validity, the estimate of the cost of adequacy is often based on evidence from a highly select sample. For example, if the only schools that had implemented the Modern Red Schoolhouse program were in an urban setting, the calculated implementation costs might be a poor indicator of the spending needed to implement the program in a rural setting. Some evidence on whole school reform methods indicates that reforms may be very successful in some settings but may fail in others, in part because of unique features of those successful settings.

School District Cost Function Approach

Researchers who use the cost function approach apply economic theory to understand the behavior of local governments and to explain variation in expenditures across school districts. Specifically, these researchers use as their starting point the concept of a production function for education, in which educational outcomes (Q) are a function of inputs (X). Implicit in this production relationship is a cost function:

$$C = pX = c(Q,p,A)$$

where C is cost per pupil, p consists of input prices, X consists of inputs to the production process, Q consists of outputs of the production process, A consists of variables that measure attributes of the school district and its students that influence its costs, and c(.) is the functional form relating costs to its determinants.[11] The cost function gives the cost of obtaining each set of outputs, conditional on input prices and district and student characteristics.

When asked to calculate adequate spending, economists typically turn to this method (see, for example, Imazeki and Reschovsky, 2006). When advising policy makers, however, researchers have been reluctant to recommend the use of this method because it is both difficult to explain and not transparent.[12]

With this method, estimates of the extent to which certain factors contribute to cost variation is determined by relating variation in per pupil expenditures to variation in output levels, input prices, student characteristics, and district characteristics. Information for step one (establishing a benchmark district) and step two (adjusting the benchmark to reflect cost differentials) are estimated together. As examples, outputs may include student performance standards such as test scores or graduation rates; input prices may include teacher and other personnel salaries; student characteristics may include percentages of students who are poor, English language learners, and disabled; and district characteristics may include size, density and perhaps rural or urban location. In addition, in order for these models to represent cost functions, a measure of district efficiency should be included since *costs* represent minimum per pupil spending for given output levels while *per pupil expenditure*, which is the dependent variable used in the empirical analysis, represents actual per pupil spending for given output levels (see Duncombe and Yinger, chapter 14 of this volume, for further explication). Researchers use econometric methods and historical data on school district expenditures, outcomes, and student and district characteristics to estimate a cost function (for examples, see Downes and Pogue, 1994; Duncombe, Ruggiero, and Yinger, 1996; Reschovsky and Imazeki, 2003).

Duncombe (2002) uses this approach in a study of New York State. In estimating the cost function, he measures student performance in each district by scores on 4th and 8th grade math and English tests as well as state high school exams in math and English (Regents' exams). After generating estimates of the cost function, he calculates how much a district with the mean value of each determinant of costs (a benchmark district) would have to spend to reach a particular performance standard. Adequate spending in other districts is calculated by multiplying spending in the benchmark district by a cost index, which has been calculated for each district using the cost function estimates.

This approach has the virtue of estimating one equation that can incorporate different output standards and different student characteristics, should these factors change in the future. In addition, because the estimates are generated using statistical procedures, analysts can calculate confidence intervals for adequacy numbers. There are, however, at least four problems with this approach. First, the method requires high quality data. If the data are imprecisely measured or incomplete, generating accurate results will be difficult.[13] For example, in theory outputs should be measures of value-added or gains in performance from one year in a grade to the next year in the next grade. However, often performance measures in a previous year for a previous grade are unavailable; instead, measures from several years in the past must be substituted. As another example, poverty of students is generally represented by the percentage of students receiving free or reduced price lunch, but this may not be an accurate measure of student deprivation, especially at the high school level, where students are reluctant to sign up for the federal lunch program even when they are eligible.

Second, measuring the efficiency with which districts deliver education is not straightforward and while researchers have tried several methods, such as indexes based on data envelopment analysis or indexes representing the degree of competition facing each district, still no widely accepted method exists. For example, Duncombe (2002) includes in his cost function an explicit measure of inefficiency in resource use, based on a data envelopment analysis (DEA).[14] Each district's cost index is calculated with that district's efficiency measure replaced with the average level of efficiency. Downes and Pogue (1994) also outline methods that could be used to generate cost indexes. They argue that the fixed-effects estimation methodology they use could, indirectly, account for some unobserved determinants of costs, unobserved outputs, and inefficiency. (See Duncombe, Ruggiero, and Yinger, 1996; Imazeki and Reschovsky, 2005, for more detail and other approaches.)

Third, theory does not indicate a specific "functional form" for the regression model and researchers obtain different results depending on the particular functional form they use. For example, in Texas two groups of researchers obtained different results in part because they used different functional forms. One group used a modified Cobb-Douglas specification, which generated a spending equation that was linear in logarithms, while the other used a trans-log specification, resulting in an equation that involved many interactions of the logarithms of inputs and prices on the right hand side. Although these differences are quite technical, each specification has its origins in economic theory about organizational behavior, and, theoretically, one is not more correct than the other (Reschovsky and Imazeki, 2005; Gronberg et al., 2005).

Finally, the method has a "black box," quality to it. This means that although the cost function methodology allows researchers to determine an overall level of spending needed for adequacy, the methodology does not specify how resources should be allocated to produce the standard desired.

USING EQUITY/ADEQUACY MEASURES TO DESIGN SCHOOL FINANCE SYSTEMS

The amount each district would need to spend to provide an adequate education is a critical component of most state or federal intergovernmental aid formulas (Sonstelie, 2004). As a result, methods used to determine the adequate level of spending should explicitly address certain design features that have been discussed in the intergovernmental aid literature. This section contains a brief discussion of these design considerations; more expansive discussion of design considerations can be found in Louis, Jabine, and Gerstein (2003).

Before turning to these specific design features, we mention again one pervasive reality common to all methods of estimating adequate spending amounts: because in most states numerous districts are far from meeting existing standards, all costing-out methodologies must project "outside" the information currently available for at least some districts. Since this problem is unavoidable, researchers would do well to make explicit the inherent unreliability of the adequacy calculations for some districts. Checks on reliability that we discuss below could help reduce, but not eliminate, some of the lack of reliability.

The Incentive Problem

In the intergovernmental aid literature, broad consensus exists that state aid should not compensate local jurisdictions for factors that can be influenced by the behavior of the governments receiving aid (Louis, Jabine, and Gerstein, 2003). For example, in the literature on aid to provide compensation for the costs associated with special education, much attention has been paid to the fact that school districts have an incentive to identify too many students as requiring services. This incentive occurs when an aid formula compensates districts for the number of students that the district itself identified as needing special education services (Cullen, 2003). Many states have responded to the existence of these problematic incentives by modifying their aid formulas. Under the modified formulas the aid a district receives does not depend directly on the number of students that the district has identified as needing special education services. As a result, some districts may not be compensated fully for the cost of serving students needing special education services.

In theory, then, the calculation of the amount each district would need to spend in order to provide adequate services should be independent of the choices that a district makes. In practice, breaking the link between aid and district choices may be very difficult to do, since many of the factors that account for cross-district variation in district costs are also affected by district choices. A commonly cited example is district size, which depends on decisions to pursue consolidation. District size is not the only cost factor that could create problems; some observers argue that even such cost factors as the fraction of students eligible for school lunch subsidies can be influenced by how aggressively districts seek to identify eligible students.

Downes and Pogue (1994) and Duncombe (2002) argue that one strategy state policy makers can pursue to avoid the effects of adverse incentives of this type when designing aid formulas is to make cost adjustments dependent on regional or statewide averages rather than the actual measures of a district's discretionary factors. While this approach would mitigate the incentive problem, since district behavior can have little or no influence on regional or statewide averages, the approach also leads to incomplete adjustment for cost variation.

A second alternative is to turn to the research literature for evidence on the extent to which district behavior is sensitive to these incentives. The research by Lankford and Wyckoff (1996) on the extent to which special education assignments by districts in New York were sensitive to the incentives in the aid formula offers a nice example of the kind of research that can guide policy makers.[15] If research indicates that district behavior is not particularly responsive to these incentives, then full compensation is warranted. Further research on responsiveness of school districts to incentives will help improve the ability of policy makers to design aid formulas that compensate for cost variation without providing perverse incentives.

Updating the Adequacy Calculations

Almost any method that could be used to determine adequate spending levels will be time-consuming and potentially costly. The natural inclination will be to use the results of the initial study as the basis of aid calculations for several years, with the only substantive year-to-year changes being inflation adjustments that are uniform across the state. Following this natural inclination could, however, lead to lack of adequate funding for many districts.

Over time, new data will become available, characteristics of districts will take on different values, and simple inflation adjustments will not account for these changes. Since most methods use a process that can incorporate new data on characteristics, recalculating adequate spending amounts can be done easily no matter which method is used. For example, new counts of students in poverty can be inserted into indexes that adjust for student cost differences without re-estimating the entire cost function. As a result, the initial adequacy study will not need to be fully replicated on a yearly basis, only updated.

State standards are also likely to evolve. Depending on the method used to determine the spending levels needed to satisfy the standards, adjusting for changes in these standards may be difficult. If, as is the case with the cost function methodology, the method incorporates information on student performance without being dependent on a specific performance standard, a change in standards can be handled as easily as can new data. If, as is the case with the professional judgment methodology, spending in the benchmark district is determined in reference to specific standards, then a change in the standards necessitates a new adequacy study.

NEEDED FURTHER RESEARCH

Eric Hanushek, in a pair of papers (2005a, 2005b), questions the scientific underpinnings of the methods used to calculate the cost of an adequate education. Most of the criticisms made by Hanushek echo concerns noted above. But Hanushek goes further, contending that these concerns are of sufficient magnitude to render meaningless any adequacy calculation based on existing methodologies. He concludes that:

> Decisions on how much to spend on education are not scientific questions, and they cannot be answered with methods that effectively rule out all discussions of reforms that might make the school system more efficient. (Hanushek, 2005b, 73)

Duncombe (2006) has responded to Hanushek's criticism by arguing that, while the political process should determine the achievement and equity standards in each state, technical analysis using one of the methodologies described above should be the basis for determining the dollars that should flow to each school district. If the methodologies are flawed, researchers should work to eliminate those flaws. To do this, and to check the scientific merit of the methodologies, researchers utilizing any of the methodologies should evaluate the reliability and accuracy of their results, Duncombe (2006) argues. He suggests steps that could be used to evaluate the reliability, statistical conclusion validity, construct validity, predictive validity, and internal validity of the results. One critical task for researchers is to execute these steps and then to use the results of the reliability and validity checks to improve the methodologies.

Duncombe (2006) focuses on strategies that could be applied within the confines of a single methodology. Since in several states multiple methodologies have been applied, this situation provides researchers with an opportunity to determine the consistency of the results from different methodologies. Downes (2004) provides an example of relatively crude consistency checks; Baker (2006) offers a model for more sophisticated consistency checks. Such consistency checks may help to highlight correctable flaws in a methodology and also to illustrate the degree of imprecision involved in determining adequate funding.

Another fruitful avenue for research is to explore the benefit of combining one or more of the methodologies. For example, such a hybrid method could combine elements of the successful schools, cost function, and professional judgment methodologies (Downes, 2004; Bradbury, 2004). The successful schools methodology could be used to identify districts that appear to be meeting the standard with little waste (inefficiency). Using data from these districts, the cost function methodology could be used to generate estimates of the amount of spending each district would need in order to provide an adequate education.[16] Then, following the logic of Rose, Sonstelie, and Richardson (2004), these estimates could be used to generate budget constraints under which the professionals would need to operate. The professionals would be asked if, given the resources implied by the cost function methodology, achieving the state standards is feasible.

Using the professional judgment approach in a checking-the-estimates capacity can solve one of the flaws of the cost function approach by making the process by which adequate spending levels are determined more transparent. Combining the methodologies also can mitigate the effect of the inherent flaw in the professional judgment approach, which is that it relies exclusively on people's experience. Using the successful districts methodology to select the sample may provide one mechanism for avoiding the possibility that the cost function estimates are flawed as a result of the inclusion of data from school districts that are operating inefficiently. Only experimentation with such hybrid methods will make it possible to determine if these methods work and if they provide us with any useful information about the validity of the individual methodologies.

Yet a further area for future research is the application of adequacy models to intra-district (cross-school) distributions of resources. School finance aid flows from states to districts and districts then make decisions about resources that students in each school receive. If districts aim to promote the achievement of state standards, logically the distribution of resources to schools would reflect the resources needed to allow students to reach adequacy. Could methods for determining adequate resource levels for districts be applied to schools as well? Such applications are not obviously appropriate. While it may be possible to estimate school-level equations that relate expenditures per pupil to student and school characteristics (such as the percent of pupils in poverty or school enrollment), one would need to make an argument for interpreting the estimated results as a cost function. Schools, like districts, are not necessarily cost minimizing organizations. As a result, they may not operate efficiently. Thus, as with the district cost functions, problems arise because of the absence of agreed-upon ways of correcting for inefficiency. (See Schwartz, Stiefel, and Bel Hadj Amor, 2005, for some seminal work in this area.) In addition, while price differentials may exist across schools, it is not clear how to interpret these differences in those districts where teachers are all paid on one scale and the central district purchases most inputs for all schools.

Finally, although adequacy is currently a more prominent public goal than equity, many policy makers continue to believe that equity in school finance is important as well. (See Koski and Reich, 2006, for a philosophical/legal argument in favor of an equity emphasis.) Under certain circumstances, however, the two goals for school finance systems may be in conflict. For example, a low state standard for performance could lead a state to provide low levels of funding to meet an adequacy goal. At the same time, if the state does not restrict spending by wealthy districts from their own funds, then some standards of equity would be violated.

Alternatively, if a state restricts high spending districts in an effort to reduce dispersion in resources (aiming to achieve equity across a system that includes high as well as low spending districts), would local districts subvert the effort? For example, would richer citizens or those more interested in consuming education services opt out of publicly provided education—or opt to spend less on public education—than they would have before the equity goal was pursued? While the link between changes in the school finance system and the decision to opt out of publicly-provided education has been discussed (see, for example, Fischel, 1989, 1996; Downes and Schoeman, 1998; Sonstelie, Brunner, and Ardon, 2000; Evans, Murray, and Schwab, 1999), further research is needed into the links between changes in the structure of the school finance system and the broad range of private responses to those changes.

School finance analysts have been engaged in measuring equity of systems for well over thirty years, while the measurement of adequacy is more recent. There is much room for continued research on how to measure adequacy, especially on how to combine existing measures to capture the best features of each.

NOTES

1. The eleven measures are the range, restricted range, federal range ratio, relative mean deviation, McLoone index, variance, coefficient of variation, standard deviation of logarithms, Gini coefficient, Theil's measure, and Atkinson's index (p. 19).
2. Berne and Stiefel (1984, p. 23) present these value judgments as a series of eight questions with yes or no answers for each of the eleven equity measures they identify.
3. This value is often labeled relative inequality aversion in the broader literature on measures of inequality.
4. More fully stated, the standard deviation of the logarithm of per pupil spending and the relative mean deviation of per pupil spending.
5. The Atkinson index changes groups depending on the value of one of its parameters, which can be set by the analyst in order to focus on the lower, the upper, or the middle of the distribution of spending per pupil.
6. Student counts are higher in districts with many weighted students, making their spending per (weighted) student lower.
7. Grubb (2006) argues that what is adequate depends on whether the courts and policy makers determine if the concept of adequacy is applied to access, to funding, to resources, or to outcomes. For example, if the concept is applied to access, then the standards that are relevant are minimum school standards, such as accreditation standards. If the adequacy concept is applied to outcomes, then the standards that are relevant are student performance standards established by state law. Many courts, such as the courts in Nevada and Montana, have applied the concept of adequacy to access and to outcomes. In such contexts, both minimum school standards and performance standards are relevant.
8. The Evidence-Based Approach is a variant of the Professional Judgment Methodology in which a panel

of researchers is first convened to produce a report that summarizes the relevant educational research. This report is then used to guide the work of the professional judgment panels, with the panels being required to justify any deviations between their recommendations and the consensus summarized in the report (Odden, Picus, Goertz, and Fermanich, 2006).

9. Often spending is limited to that devoted to "regular" education programs, with spending for special education or English language learners or compensatory help removed.
10. See http://www.mrsh.org (accessed February 11, 2007) for more information on the components of this reform model, which focuses on six areas of school organization.
11. The functional form of a regression equation is the precise mathematical equation used by the researcher when that researcher estimates the regression equation (Schmidt, 2005).
12. Bradbury, et al. (1984) represents an exception to this practice. The estimated cost adjustments provided in that paper were used in the construction of a formula to allocate a portion of the aid to cities and towns in Massachusetts.
13. Data imprecision is not a problem that is unique to the cost function methodology; even the data that is generated by experts participating in professional judgment panels is likely to be imprecise. So any estimate of adequate spending is likely to be subject to error. In fact, as already pointed out, one of the virtues of the cost function approach is that the methodology can provide a statistical estimate of the magnitude of the error.
14. DEA is an operations research technique used to determine whether an organization is producing the most of at least one of its outputs from its inputs. It is similar to input/output analysis and is explained more fully in Duncombe and Yinger (chapter 14, this volume).
15. Lankford and Wyckoff (1996) find what they describe as "at best weak support for the notion that New York school districts alter special education classifications in response to the financial incentives of the state aid formula" (pp. 238–239). In particular, for two of the three special education placement settings they consider, they find a no link between the dollar increase in excess-cost aid that results from an additional weighted special education student (holding total enrollment constant) and total special education enrollment. For the third placement setting, the elasticity of special education enrollment with respect to the dollar increase in special education aid is only 0.02.
16. This method will work only if there are a large number of districts meeting the standard and there is substantial variation among them.

REFERENCES

American Institutes for Research and Management Analysis and Planning, Inc. [AIR/MAP]. (2004). The New York Adequacy Study: 'Adequate' Education Cost in New York State. Unpublished report.

Augenblick and Myers, Inc. (2002). Calculation of the Cost of an Adequate Education in Montana in 2001–2002 Using the Professional Judgment Approach. Denver: Unpublished report.

Augenblick and Myers, Inc. (2003). Calculation of the Cost of an Adequate Education in Nebraska in 2002–2003 Using the Professional Judgment Approach. Denver: Unpublished Report.

Baker, B.D. (Fall 2006). Evaluating the Reliability, Validity and Usefulness of Education Cost Studies. *Journal of Education Finance, 32,* 170–201.

Berne, R., & Stiefel, L. (1984). *The Measurement of Equity in School Finance: Conceptual, Methodological and Empirical Dimensions.* Baltimore: Johns Hopkins University Press.

Bradbury, K.L. (2004). Discussion. In D. Monk & J. Wyckoff (Eds.), *Symposium Proceedings 2004, Education Finance and Organizational Structure in New York State Schools* (pp. 89–97). Albany, NY: Rockefeller College of Public Affairs and Policy, University at Albany.

Bradbury, K.L., Ladd, H.F., Perrault, M., Reschovsky, A., & Yinger, J. (June 1984). State Aid to Offset Fiscal Disparities Across Communities. *National Tax Journal, 37,* 151–170.

Briffault, R. (Fall Semester 2006). Adding Adequacy to Equity: The Evolving Legal Theory of School Finance Reform. Columbia University Law School Public Law and Legal Theory Research Paper Series

Research Paper No. 06-111and Princeton University Program in Law and Public Affairs Research Paper Series Research Paper No. 06–013.

Chambers, J.G. (February 1998). Geographic Variations in the Public Schools' Costs. National Center for Education Statistics Working Paper No. 98–100.Washington, DC: U.S. Department of Education, National Center for Education Statistics.

Costrell, R.M. (Summer 2005). Equity v. Equity: Why Education Week and the Education Trust Don't Agree. *Education Next, 5*(3), 77–81.

Cullen, J.B. (August 2003). The Impact of Fiscal Incentives on Student Disability Rates. *Journal of Public Economics, 87,* 1557–1589.

CSQR Center Report on Elementary School Comprehensive Reform Models. (November, 2005). Washington, DC: American Institutes for Research.

Downes, T.A. (2004). What Is Adequate? Operationalizing the Concept of Adequacy for New York. In D. Monk & J. Wyckoff (Eds.), *Symposium Proceedings 2004, Education Finance and Organizational Structure in New York State Schools* (pp. 23–39). Albany, NY: Rockefeller College of Public Affairs and Policy, University at Albany.

Downes, T.A., & Pogue, T.F. (March 1994). Adjusting School Aid Formulas for the Higher Costs of Educating Disadvantaged Students. *National Tax Journal, 47,* 83–102.

Downes, T. A., & Pogue, T. F. (December 2002). How Best to Hand Out Money: Issues in the Design and Structure of Intergovernmental Aid Formulas. *Journal of Official Statistics, 18,* 329–352.

Downes, T.A., & Schoeman, D. (1998). School Financing Reform and Private School Enrollment: Evidence from California. *Journal of Urban Economics, 43,* 418–443.

Downes, T.A., & Zabel, J. (July 2002). The Impact of School Quality on House Prices: Chicago 1987–1991. *Journal of Urban Economics, 52,* 1–25.

Duncombe, W. (February 2002). Estimating the Cost of an Adequate Education in New York. Center for Policy Research Working Paper Number 44, Maxwell School of Citizenship and Public Affairs, Syracuse University.

Duncombe, W. (Fall 2006). Responding to the Charge of Alchemy: Strategies for Evaluating the Reliability and Validity of Costing-Out Research. *Journal of Education Finance, 32,* 137–169.

Duncombe, W.D., & Lukemeyer, A. (March 2002). Estimating the Cost of Educational Adequacy: A Comparison of Approaches. Mimeograph, Syracuse University.

Duncombe, W., Ruggiero, J., & Yinger, J. (1996). Alternative Approaches to Measuring the Cost of Education. In H.F. Ladd (Ed.), *Holding Schools Accountable* (pp. 327–356). Washington, DC: Brookings Institution.

Duncombe, W.D., & Yinger, J. (January 2001). Does School District Consolidation Cut Costs? Center for Policy Research Working Paper Number 33, Maxwell School of Citizenship and Public Affairs, Syracuse University.

Duncombe, W.D., & Yinger, J. (1999). Performance Standards and Educational Cost Indexes: You Can't Have One without the Other. In H.F. Ladd, R. Chalk, & J.S. Hansen (Eds.), *Equity and Adequacy in Education Finance: Issues and Perspectives* (pp. 260–297). Washington, DC: National Academy Press.

Eom, T.H., Duncombe, W., & Yinger, J. (October 2005). *Unintended Consequences of Property Tax Relief: New York's STAR Program.* Center for Policy Research, Maxwell School, Syracuse University.

Evans, W.N., Murray, S.E., & Schwab, R.M. (February 1999). Public School Spending and Private School Enrollment. Mimeograph, University of Maryland, College Park.

Fischel, W.A. (1989). Did Serrano Cause Proposition 13? *National Tax Journal, 42,* 465–473.

Fischel, W.A. (1996). How Serrano Caused Proposition 13. *Journal of Law and Politics, 12,* 607–645.

Gronberg, T.J., Jensen, D.W., Taylor, L.L., & Booker, K. (2005). State Outcomes and School Costs: The Cost Function Approach plus Technical Appendix. Texas A and M University, Draft.

Grubb, W.N. (February 2006). What Should Be Equalized? Litigation, Equity, and the 'Improved' School Finance. Mimeograph. University of California, Berkeley.

Guthrie, J.W. (2001). Twenty-First Century Education Finance: Equity, Adequacy, and the Emerging Challenge of Linking Resources to Performance. Mimeograph, Vanderbilt University.

Guthrie, J.W., & Rothstein, R. (1999). Enabling 'Adequacy' to Achieve Reality: Translating Adequacy into State School Finance Arrangements. In H.F. Ladd, R. Chalk, & J.S. Hansen (Eds.), *Equity and Adequacy in Education Finance: Issues and Perspectives* (pp. 209–259). Washington, DC: National Academy Press.

Hanushek, E. A. (October 2005a). The Alchemy of 'Costing Out' an Adequate Education. Program for Education Policy and Governance Working Paper 05–28, Taubman Center for State and Local Government and Center for American Political Studies, Harvard University.

Hanushek, E. A. (Fall 2005b). Pseudo-Science and a Sound Basic Education: Voodoo Statistics in New York. *Education Next, 4,* 67–73.

Iatarola, P., & Stiefel, L. (2003). Intradistrict Equity of Public Education Resources and Performance. *Economics of Education Review, 22* (1) 60–78.

Imazeki, J., & Reschovsky, A. (2006). Does No Child Left Behind Place a Fiscal Burden on States? Evidence from Texas. *Education Finance and Policy, 1* (2), 217–246.

Imazeki, J., & Reschovsky, A. (2005). Assessing the Use of Econometric Analysis in Estimating the Costs of Meeting State Education Accountability Standards: Lessons from Texas. Lafollette School Working Paper No. 2005–005, http://www.lafollette.wisc.edu/publications/workingpapers.

Koski, W.S., & Reich, R. (2006). When "Adequate" isn't: The retreat from equity in educational law and policy and why it matters. *Emory Law Review, 56* (3), 545–617.

Lankford, H., & Wyckoff, J.H. (1996). The Allocation of Resources to Special Education and Regular Instruction. In H.F. Ladd (Ed.), *Making Schools Accountable: Performance-Based Approaches to School Reform* (pp. 221–257).Washington, DC: Brookings Institution.

Loeb, S., & Socias, M. (forthcoming). Federal Contributions to High-Income School Districts: The Use of Tax Deductions for Funding K–12 Education. *Economics of Education Review.*

Louis, T.A., Jabine, T.B., & Gerstein, M. (Eds.). (2003). *Statistical Issues in Allocating Funds by Formula.* Washington, DC: National Academies Press.

Odden, A.R. (1997). *The Finance Side of Implementing New American Schools.* Alexandria, VA: Report for the New American Schools.

Odden, A.R., & Busch, C. (1998). *Financing Schools for High Performance.* San Francisco: Jossey-Bass.

Odden, A.R., & Picus, L.O. (2007). *School Finance: A Policy Perspective.* New York: McGraw Hill.

Odden, A., Picus, L.O., Goertz, M., & Fermanich, M. (2006). *An Evidence Based Approach to School Finance Adequacy in Washington.* North Hollywood, CA: Lawrence O. Picus and Associates (April 1 version).

Reschovsky, A., & Imazeki, J. (2003). Let No Child Be Left Behind: Determining the Cost of Improving Student Performance. *Public Finance Review, 31,* 263–290.

Rose, H., Sonstelie, J., Reinhard, R., & Heng, S. (2003). *High Expectations, Modest Means: The Challenge Facing California's Public Schools.* San Francisco: Public Policy Institute of California.

Rose, H., Sonstelie, J., & Richardson, P. (2004). *School Budgets and Student Achievement: The Principal's Perspective.* San Francisco, CA: Public Policy Institute of California.

Rubenstein, R. (2003). National Evidence on Racial Disparities in School Finance Adequacy. In W.J. Fowler Jr. (Ed.), *Developments in School Finance: 2001–02* (pp. 91–109). Washington, DC: National Center for Education Statistics.

Schmidt, S. (2005). *Econometrics.* New York: McGraw-Hill.

Schwartz, A.E., Stiefel, L., & Bel Hadj Amor, H. (2005). Measuring School Performance Using Cost Functions. In L. Stiefel et al., *Measuring School Performance and Efficiency: Implications for Practice and Research* (pp. 67–91). Larchmont, NY: Eye on Education.

Sonstelie, J. (2001) Toward Cost and Quality Models for California's Public Schools. In J. Sonstelie & P. Richardson (Eds.), *School Finance and California's Master Plan for Education* (pp. 103–123). San Francisco: Public Policy Institute of California.

Sonstelie, J. (2004). Financing Adequate Resources for New York Schools. In D. Monk & J. Wyckoff (Eds.), *Symposium Proceedings 2004, Education Finance and Organizational Structure in New York State Schools* (pp. 41–60). Albany, NY: Rockefeller College of Public Affairs and Policy, University at Albany.

Sonstelie, J., Brunner, E., & Ardon, K. (2000). *For Better or Worse? School Finance Reform in California.* San Francisco: Public Policy Institute of California.

State Aid Work Group, New York State Education Department. (January 2004). Regents Proposal on State Aid for School Districts for 2004–2005. Albany, NY: Unpublished report.

Taylor, L.L., & Keller, H. (2003). Competing Perspectives on the Cost of Education. In W.J. Fowler Jr. (Ed.), *Developments in School Finance: 2001–02* (pp. 111–126). Washington, DC: National Center for Education Statistics.

Underwood, J. (1995). School Finance Adequacy as Vertical Equity. 28 U. Mich. J. L. Ref 493.

14

Measurement of Cost Differentials

William D. Duncombe and John Yinger

INTRODUCTION

The evaluation of education cost differentials across school districts has been an important topic in education finance research for decades (Fowler and Monk, 2001). Interest in this topic has grown in recent years with the emergence of adequacy as the primary standard in school finance litigation and the growth of state accountability systems that focus on student performance. Each of these developments calls attention to the fact that some districts must spend more than others to obtain the same performance; that is, to education cost differentials. The link between research and policy on this topic is not well developed, however; existing state aid formulas usually contain ad hoc cost adjustments that fall far short of the across-district cost differences estimated by scholars. The objective of this chapter is to synthesize the research literature on education cost differences across school districts and to discuss the implications of this literature for state education aid formulas. The material in this chapter complements the discussions of equity and adequacy in chapters 12 and 13.

The term "cost" in economics refers to the minimum spending required to produce a given level of output. Applied to education, cost represents the minimum spending required to bring students in a district up to a given average performance level. Education costs can be affected by three categories of factors, each of which is outside of school district control: (1) geographic differences in resource prices, (2) district size, and (3) the special needs of some students. In this chapter, we address the principal methods for estimating the cost impacts of each of these factors. These impacts need not be the same, of course, for every measure of student performance.

While states commonly adjust their basic operating aid programs for differences in the capacity of school districts to raise revenue, typically measured by property wealth or income, few states systematically adjust these programs for cost differences across districts. Instead, cost adjustments tend to be confined to ancillary aid programs or to be ad hoc. This is a critical limitation because the success of a basic operating aid formula in providing the funds needed for an adequate education in each district, however defined, is linked to the accuracy of the cost adjustment. If the adequacy standard is defined as access to a minimum set of resources, then the basic aid formula needs to account for geographic variation in resource prices. If the adequacy standard is defined as a minimum level of student performance, then the basic aid formula also requires cost adjustments for district size and student needs.

Because cost adjustments may vary with the measure(s) of student performance or with conditions in a state, standard cost adjustments are not available. Instead, each state needs to estimate its own cost adjustments or else settle for approximate adjustments based on studies in similar states. Estimating cost adjustments is a challenging enterprise that requires clear judgments about state educational objectives, good data, and technical expertise. These challenges are the subject of this chapter.

The focus here is on cost differentials across school districts, not across individual schools. School districts are the primary budget decision making units, and taxing power and budget authority lie with district officials. Accordingly, state school finance systems are focused on distributing education aid to school districts, not schools, in most cases. Recent research has highlighted inequity in the distribution of resources across schools within large urban school districts (Roza and Hill, 2004; Stiefel, Rubenstein, and Berne, 1998) and some districts have introduced formula-based distribution formulas (weighted student formulas) to improve the equity of intra-district resource allocation (Odden, 1999). The measures of cost differentials due to student needs discussed in this chapter would also be appropriate for intra-district funding formulas.

The chapter is organized roughly in line with the major cost factors. We begin by discussing briefly the one method that can produce estimates for all three types of cost factors—education cost functions. We then turn to looking at other methods for estimating geographic resource price differences, the cost effects of enrollment size, and the cost impacts of various student characteristics. Each section describes the most frequently used methods, discusses their strengths and weaknesses, and provides key references for more detailed information.

EDUCATION COST FUNCTIONS

To estimate the relationship between spending, student performance, and other important characteristics of school districts, many education researchers employ one of the key tools of production theory in microeconomics, namely, a cost function. Cost is defined as the spending required to reach a given level of student performance using current best practices. Cost cannot be directly observed, however, so cost functions are estimated using district spending (usually operating spending per pupil) as the dependent variable. Spending may deviate from cost because some school districts are inefficient, that is, they deviate from current best practices. As a result, cost functions need to be estimated with controls for school district efficiency, if possible.

More formally, education costs, C, depend on (1) student performance (S), (2) resource prices (W), such as teacher salaries, (3) enrollment size (N), and (4) student need measures (P), which are discussed in detail below; that is, $C = f(S, W, N, P)$. Now let e stand for school district efficiency in delivering S. Without loss of generality, we can set the value of e at 1.0 in an efficient district, so that it has a value between zero and one in a district that does not use current best practices. With this scaling, we can write the cost/efficiency equation that scholars estimate as:

$$E = \frac{C}{e} = \frac{f(S,W,N,P)}{e} \quad (1)$$

This formulation makes it clear that a district that does not use best practices ($e < 1$) must spend more than an efficient district ($e = 1$) to achieve the same level of performance (S), all else equal.

Equation (1) has been widely used in various forms because it addresses many fundamental questions of interest to scholar and policy makers. For example, a cost function measures how much a given change in teacher salaries, district enrollment, or student needs affect the cost of achieving a particular level of student performance at a given level of efficiency. The cost function methodology has been refined over the last few decades, and cost function studies have been undertaken for several states.[1]

In order to estimate equation (1) using multiple regression analysis, researchers must address several methodological challenges. The first challenge is to identify a performance objective and find data to measure it (*S*). One common approach, for example, is to select the performance measure or measures that are most central to a state's school accountability system, which typically include student performance on state-administered tests and perhaps graduation rates. Other studies select available test-score information, usually on math and English scores in a variety of grades. In addition, these measures of student performance are determined simultaneously with district spending, so they need to be treated as endogenous when equation (1) is estimated.[2]

Many production function studies (and a few state accountability systems) focus not on levels of student performance, as measured, say, by the share of students passing a state test, but instead on the change in student performance over time, often referred to as a value-added measure. This approach is difficult to implement in a cost study, however, because a value-added approach requires test score information on the same cohort in different grades—information that is not generally available. "Value-added" measures that compare different cohorts in the same grade provide noisy signals, particularly in small school districts (Kane and Staiger, 2002).[3]

A second methodological challenge is to control for school district efficiency (*e*). The problem is that efficiency cannot be directly observed, so a researcher must select a method to control for efficiency indirectly. Several approaches, each with limitations, have appeared in the literature. One approach is to estimate the cost function with district fixed effects, which control for all district characteristics, including any part of efficiency, which do not vary over time (Downes and Pogue, 1994). The limitations of this approach are that it cannot control for district efficiency if it varies over time and that, by removing all cross-section variation it undermines a researcher's ability to estimate the impact of *S*, *W*, *N*, and *P* on costs.

Another efficiency approach is to estimate a cost frontier based on the lowest observed spending for obtaining any given student performance, to calculate each district's deviation from this spending as an index of inefficiency, and then to control for this measure in an estimated cost function (Duncombe, Ruggiero, and Yinger, 1996; Duncombe and Yinger, 2000; Reschovsky and Imazeki, 2001).[4] A limitation of this approach is that this index of "inefficiency" reflects both cost and efficiency differences across districts. As a result, this approach may lead to underestimated coefficients of cost variables, such as student poverty, because a portion of the impact of these variables on costs may be captured by the estimated coefficient of the "inefficiency" index.

The final efficiency approach in the literature is to identify factors that have a conceptual link to efficiency and then to control for them in a cost function regression. A limitation of this approach is that these conceptual links cannot be directly tested. Nevertheless, a strong case can be made for the inclusion of two types of efficiency controls. First, some district characteristics might influence the incentives for voters to monitor school officials or for school officials to adopt best practices. For example, Imazeki and Reschovsky (2004b) control for efficiency using a measure of competition from other public schools, which might influence the behavior of school officials. Second, some district characteristics, such as median household income or tax price, might influence voters' demand for measures of school-district performance other than *S*. Because efficiency can only be defined relative to specific measures of school-district performance, in this case *S*, any spending to obtain other measures of performance is, by definition, inefficient.[5] Income and tax price are examples of variables that help control for this type of inefficiency (Duncombe and Yinger, 2000, 2005a, 2005b).

A third challenge is to select a functional form for the cost model. This form reflects underlying assumptions about the technology of production, such as the degree of substitution between inputs, economies of scale, and the interaction between school and non-school factors. Most education cost studies have used a simple multiplicative cost function, which works well in practice but which imposes limits on both factor substitution and economies of scale.[6] By contrast, Gronberg et al. (2004) use a flexible cost function that does not impose significant restrictions on production technology. This approach adds many variables to the cost model, however, which makes it more difficult to identify cost effects with precision.[7]

Despite the empirical challenges involved in estimating cost functions, they have some clear advantages over other methods of estimating cost differentials. First, they use actual historical data and statistical methodology to separate the impact of factors outside and within district control on the cost of reaching student performance levels. Second, they can provide measures of overall cost differentials across districts as well measures of individual cost factors (resource prices, enrollment, and student needs) that can be used in state aid formulas. Some scholars have criticized cost functions on the grounds that their technical complexity makes them difficult for state policy makers to understand.[8] One of the objectives of this chapter is to explain the intuition behind cost functions to help make them more accessible to policy makers. After all, complex statistical procedures are accepted in some policy arenas, such as revenue forecasting and program evaluation, and we see no reason why they could not become accepted in the design of state education aid formulas.

In the following sections we describe the use of cost functions and other methods to estimate cost differentials for resource prices, economies of size, and student needs.

GEOGRAPHIC VARIATION IN RESOURCE PRICES

The impact of geographic variation in the prices of goods and services on the purchasing power of school districts has been recognized for decades (Brazer and Anderson, 1974; Chambers, 1978). Eleven states incorporate geographic cost of education indices (GCEI) into their school funding formulas (Huang, 2004) and the National Center for Education Statistics (NCES) has sponsored the development of GCEI for all school districts in the country using two different methods (Chambers, 1997; Taylor and Fowler, 2006).

Controlling for the compensation a district must offer to attract personnel of a given quality is particularly important for accurate cost estimation, because personnel compensation makes up a large share, well over half, of a district's budget.[9] In this section, we discuss the reasons for variation in resource prices and review the four most common approaches for estimating GCEI. Each of these approaches attempts to measure the extent to which the cost of personnel varies across districts based on factors outside of districts' control—not on variation in districts' generosity.

Variation in the price of inputs other than personnel has been largely ignored in the literature. This remains an important topic for future research.

Reasons for Geographic Variation in Resource Prices

The prices school districts must pay for resources can differ across school districts for several reasons: (1) cost-of-living, (2) labor market conditions, (3) local amenities, and (4) working conditions for employees. The higher the cost-of-living in an area, defined as the resources required to purchase a standard bundle of goods and services, the more school districts in the area must pay to attract employees of a given quality. Local labor market conditions can also affect the salaries districts are required to pay. If an area's unemployment rate for professionals is relatively high, for example, then teachers and school administrators may have relatively limited choices of alternative jobs. Under these circumstances new teachers and administrators will be more apt to accept school district offers with lower salaries and benefits.

School employees, like other employees, may also be willing to sacrifice some compensation to have ready access to amenities, such as access to cultural events and business services; proximity to coastline, lakes, mountains, and parks; access to good highways, airports, and rail transportation; and access to good state or local public services.

Finally, the salary required to attract instructional and administrative personnel may depend on the working conditions in the school district, which depend both on school policies and on student characteristics. Working conditions that teachers care about may include factors under district control, such as school size, class size, professional development spending, availability of instructional materials, school leadership and culture. Districts may be able to trade off spending on factors related to working conditions against increased teacher compensation. Working conditions for teachers may also be influenced by factors outside district control, such as the socio-economic backgrounds of their students. Research on teacher mobility indicates that teacher employment decisions can be influenced by characteristics of the students they are teaching (Hanushek, Kain, and Rivkin, 2001, 2004; Scafidi, Sjoquist, and Stinebrickner, forthcoming; Falch and Strom, 2005; Ondrich, Pas, and Yinger, forthcoming).

Cost-of-Living (COL) Index

The cost-of-living (COL) approach estimates price differences for a "market-basket" of goods and services across geographic areas (Duncombe and Goldhaber, 2003). For each factor in the market basket, price data is collected by geographic area and a market basket is identified using data on consumer expenditure patterns. The final COL index is the spending required to purchase the market basket in each location relative to the state or national average. The use of a COL index as an education cost adjustment is based on the assumption that teachers compare real wages across districts, not nominal wages. This assumption implies that a high COL district cannot attract the same quality teachers as a low COL district without paying higher nominal wages.

The principal strengths of the COL approach are its conceptual simplicity and the fact that COL indices are based on private sector prices outside of district control (McMahon, 1996). This simplicity comes at a price, however. Even if a COL index accurately captures variation across locations in consumer prices and in the wages required to attract teachers, school personnel do not necessarily shop or live where they work.[10] In addition, COL indexes do not capture variation across districts in working conditions and local amenities, which can affect the compensation required to attract equal quality teachers. Moreover, COL data at the school district level are surprisingly difficult to obtain; existing national and state level COL indexes provide no insight into within-state COL variation (Nelson, 1991; McMahon, 1996). Colorado, Florida, and Wyoming have developed COL indices for their school aid calculations (Rothstein and Smith, 1997; Florida Department of Education, 2002; Wyoming Division of Economic Analysis, 1999; Colorado Legislative Council Staff, 2002).[11]

Competitive Wage Index (CWI)

Another approach to estimating a GCEI is to use information on variation in private sector salaries (or full compensation), particularly for occupations similar to teaching. The NCES recently published competitive wage index (CWI) estimates for all school districts in the United States (Taylor and Fowler, 2006). Some states, including Ohio, Massachusetts, New York, and Tennessee have used measures of average private wages as cost adjustments in their education aid formulas (Rothstein and Smith, 1997; Massachusetts Department of Education, 1999; New

York State Education Department, 2003; Eff and Eff, 2000; Ohio Department of Education, 2003).

One approach to developing a CWI is to use information on average salaries by occupation to construct a weighted average of salaries in occupations comparable to teaching, typically professional, managerial, or technical occupations (Rothstein and Smith, 1997). The major source for this data is the *Occupational Employment Survey* (OES) published by the U.S. Bureau of Labor Statistics, which is available for labor market areas. One disadvantage of this approach is that it assumes that private employees in these occupations are comparable on experience, education, and demographic factors across geographic areas.

A more appealing approach is to use detailed individual-level data on private employees to construct a private wage index that controls for employee characteristics. Taylor (2004) has applied this approach to Texas school districts and recently developed a CWI for all school districts in the country (Taylor and Fowler, 2006). Using data the 2000 Census of Population, Taylor and Fowler (2006) regress salaries of college graduates on demographic characteristics (age, gender, ethnicity, education, and hours worked), occupational categories, and indicator variables for labor market areas. The regression results are used to "predict the wages that a nationally representative person would earn in each labor market area" (Taylor and Fowler, 2006, p. 9). The CWI is obtained by dividing the predicted wage by the state or national average wage. This CWI can be updated for additional years by using the OES to estimate changes in wages across years by occupation and labor market area.

The comparable wage methodology is straightforward, and a carefully constructed CWI should capture the impact of cost-of-living, local amenities, and labor market conditions on the salary a district must pay to attract teachers of a given quality. The principle drawback to this methodology is that average private sector salaries are not likely to reflect differences in working conditions for teachers across districts. For example, private sector salaries in professional occupations are not likely to reflect the demographics of the student body in a district, the age and condition of school buildings, the extent of overcrowding in classrooms, and so on, which could be very important to the job choices of teachers.

Hedonic Teacher Cost Index (TCI)

A GCEI can also be estimated by separating the impact on teacher (or other employee) compensation of factors in and out of district control using statistical methods—and then to determine costs based only on external factors. What sets this approach apart from the others is that, to the extent possible with available data, it directly accounts for the effects of school working conditions on the salaries required to attract teachers to a district. Hedonic salary studies been conducted for several states, including Alaska, Maryland, and New York (Chambers et al., 2004b; Chambers, Taylor, and Robinson, 2003; Duncombe and Goldhaber, 2003; Duncombe, Lukemeyer and Yinger, 2003); however, only Texas, presently uses a hedonic-based cost adjustment in its aid formula (Alexander et al., 2000; Taylor, 2004). In addition, Chambers (1997) uses the hedonic approach to develop a teacher cost index for all school districts in the country; unfortunately, his data include only two variables related to a district's education environment, namely, district enrollment and the share of students from a minority group.

The hedonic salary approach involves estimating a multiple regression model in which employee salary (or salary plus fringe benefits) is regressed on teacher characteristics, working conditions under district control (such as school or class sizes), and factors outside district control that are related to cost-of-living, labor market conditions, local amenities, and school working conditions. Characteristics of teachers typically include education, experience, gender, race, type of assignment, and certification status. Some studies include other measures associated with teacher quality, such as certification test score performance and ranking of the college a teacher attended (Chambers, 1997; Duncombe, Lukemeyer and Yinger, 2003; and Duncombe and Goldhaber, 2003). Amenity variables typically include distance to a central city, climate and crime rates, and working-conditions. Other variables include district enrollment and student characteristics (e.g., race, language proficiency, and poverty).

Hedonic models are typically estimated with individual teacher-level data using standard multiple regression methods. To construct a personnel cost index, the coefficients for discretionary factors are multiplied by the state average value for that factor, while coefficients for external (i.e., non-discretionary) factors are multiplied by actual values for that district. The sum of these terms is the predicted salary required to attract an employee with average characteristics to a particular district, and the salary index compares this predicted salary to the state average.

Because they have the most complete controls, hedonic salary models could potentially to produce the most accurate TCI (teacher cost index), that is, the most accurate estimate of the salary required to attract teachers with given characteristics to work in a district. However, even hedonic estimates face several difficult challenges.

Perhaps the most difficult challenge is to fully control for teacher quality. Teacher characteristics included in existing studies capture several important dimensions of teacher quality, but these characteristics predict only a small share of variation in teacher quality as directly measured from teachers' impacts on the test scores of their students (Hanushek, Kain, and Rivkin, 2005). Moreover, teacher quality is likely to be negatively correlated with concentrated student disadvantage, so imperfect controls for teacher quality will bias the coefficients of the student disadvantage variables toward zero. As a result, hedonic studies may systematically understate the impact of concentrated student disadvantage on the compensation a district must pay to attract teachers of a given quality.

In addition, actual teacher salaries may not correspond in all districts to the minimum salaries required to attract teachers with certain characteristics into the district. Some districts could be overly generous or particularly inept in bargaining, for example. Differences between actual salaries and minimum required salaries are signs of district inefficiency, and they could lead to biased results in hedonic salary models if the (unobserved) factors that lead to inefficiency are correlated with the explanatory variables in the model.

Another challenge is that readily available COL measures may reflect discretionary district decisions. For example, housing prices often account for most of the variation in private prices across geographic areas but they may partially reflect differences in perceived education quality across districts. Using MSA level housing prices reduce this endogeneity (Duncombe and Goldhaber, 2003). Some hedonic studies have used the price of unimproved agricultural land as a COL measure to avoid the potential endogeneity of housing prices; however, agricultural land in central cities or inner ring suburbs often does not exist, and has to be imputed (Chambers et al., 2004b). Private sector salaries can serve as a proxy for COL, labor market conditions, and some amenities, but are likely to be influenced by housing prices (and education quality) as well.

Several studies have attempted to address potential biases in hedonic salary models. Teacher fixed effects models have been estimated to control for unobserved teacher quality differences (Taylor, 2004; Chambers, Taylor, and Robinson, 2003). To account for the possibility of omitted compensation or working condition variables, some studies have included an estimate of the turnover rate in the model (Chambers et al., 2004b; Duncombe and Goldhaber, 2003). Finally, a few hedonic studies have included variables to control for school district efficiency (Duncombe, Lukemeyer and Yinger, 2003; Duncombe and Goldhaber, 2003).

The TCI calculated from hedonic salary models tend to display relatively little variation, because most of the variation in teacher salaries is explained by key features of teacher salary schedules, usually education and experience, and because information on other determinants of teacher quality and on working conditions is incomplete.[12] The limited impact of working conditions on hedonic TCI runs counter to recent research on teacher labor markets, which finds that teacher mobility is influenced by the characteristics of the students they teach (Hanushek, Kain, and Rivkin, 2001; Scafidi, Sjoquist, and Stinebrickner, forthcoming; Falch and Strom, 2005; Ondrich, Pas, and Yinger, forthcoming). More research is needed to resolve this apparent contradiction.

Teacher Cost Indices from Cost Functions

Resource prices, particularly teacher salaries, are key variables in education cost functions. The coefficient on the teacher salary variable indicates the increase in costs required to maintain student performance levels when teacher salaries increase (holding other variables in the model constant). Using this coefficient and measure of teacher salaries by district it is possible to construct a teacher cost index (relative to the state average), which reflects variation in teacher salaries weighted by the impact of teacher salaries on spending.

Two different types of salary measures have been used in education cost functions: (1) private sector wage indices, such as a CWI (Reschovsky and Imazeki, 1998, 2001; Imazeki and Reschovsky, 2004a, 2004b), and (2) actual teacher salaries for teachers with similar education and experience levels. Recognizing that teacher salaries can be set simultaneously with spending levels in the annual budget process, studies using actual teacher salaries often treat them as endogenous variables in estimating the cost function (Duncombe and Yinger, 2000, 2005a, 2005b).[13] In these studies, the teacher salary index is based not on actual salary but instead on salary predicted on the basis of factors outside a district's control.

A teacher cost index derived from a cost function is similar in some respects to a CWI and should capture variation in employee compensation due to differences in cost-of-living, labor market conditions, and amenities across school districts. Because student characteristics are also included in the cost model, the teacher cost index is not likely to reflect the impact of working condition differences across school districts on the wages required to attract teachers.[14] This impact may appear, however, in the estimated coefficients of these student characteristics; if so, it will appear when teacher cost indexes and pupil weights (discussed below) are combined.

The strength of this approach is that it produces a teacher cost index that both reflects variation in key factors affecting teacher salaries and is weighted by the impact of teacher salaries on spending. The accuracy of this approach depends, however, on the quality of the cost-model controls for student disadvantage and school-district efficiency.

ENROLLMENT SIZE AND EDUCATION COSTS

The 90 percent drop in the number of school districts in the United States since 1938 represents one of the most dramatic changes in education governance and management in the twentieth century. While the pace of school district consolidation has slowed considerably since the early 1970s, some states still provide financial incentives to encourage school district consolidation (Gold, Smith, and Lawton, 1995; NCES, 2001). At the same time; however, operating aid formulas in a number of states compensate districts for small size or sparsity, thereby discouraging consolidation (Baker and Duncombe, 2004; Huang, 2004). In this section we briefly review the reasons for and the evidence on the relationship between costs and district size before discussing methods to estimate the cost effects of size.

Reasons Costs May Vary with Enrollment

Economies of scale are said to exist when the cost per unit declines as the number of units goes up. In the case of education, the focus has been on economies of size, which refer to a decline in per-pupil expenditure with an increase in district enrollment, controlling for other cost factors. Several explanations have been offered for economies of size in education (Haller and Monk, 1988). First, some district services, such as central administration, are relatively fixed in the sense that the same central administrative staff may be able to serve a significant range of enrollment without a degradation of service. Economies of size might exist if larger school districts are able to employ more specialized labor, such as science or math teachers, which could improve the quality of instruction at no additional cost. Furthermore, teachers may be more productive in a large school district because they can draw on the experience of many colleagues. In addition, large districts may be able to negotiate relatively low prices for bulk purchases of supplies and equipment or use their monosony power to negotiate lower wages for their employees.[15]

The existence of economies of size in education has been challenged for several reasons. First, some studies claim that the potential cost savings from consolidation are seldom realized because districts seldom lay off staff, salaries are often leveled-up across the merging districts, and transportation costs actually increase (Guthrie, 1979; Lee and Smith, 1997). Second, large school districts tend to have large schools, which, according to some studies, lead to lower student performance (Fowler and Walberg, 1991; Friedkin and Necochea, 1988; Haller, 1992; Lee and Smith, 1997) by damaging staff morale, student motivation and involvement in school, and parental involvement (Howley 1996; Cotton 1996).

Evidence on Economies of Size in Education

A large literature on economies of size in education has emerged over the last four decades. Since this literature has been covered in depth in existing literature reviews (Fox, 1981; Andrews, Duncombe, and Yinger, 2002), we only summarize the main findings. The vast majority of evidence on economies of size has come from the estimation of education cost functions. The early evidence on economies of size found sizeable economies with the cost-minimizing size for an urban district as high as 30,000 students (Fox, 1981). Recent cost function research, which have addressed a number of methodological limitations with early studies (Andrews, Duncombe, and Yinger, 2001), has also found that there may be sizeable economies of size in education, but that most of the cost savings from an increase in district enrollment are exhausted once enrollment levels of 2,000 to 4,000 pupils are reached. Surprisingly, few formal evaluations of the effects of school district consolidation on costs have been conducted (Howley, 1996). One exception is an evaluation of school district consolidations in New York from 1985 to 1997 (Duncombe and Yinger, forthcoming). They found sizeable savings in operating costs from the consolidation of two, very small districts (combined enrollment under 100 students), but that operating cost savings became relatively small (4% or less) when the consolidating districts had a combined enrollment of over 3,000.[16]

Methods for Estimating Cost Effects of Enrollment Size

A common method used by states to construct scale adjustments is to estimate the average district costs by enrollment class and then compare the average cost in a class to average costs in relatively large districts. Kansas used this strategy, for example, to develop "low enrollment weights," which are used in calculating operating aid (Duncombe and Johnston, 2004). The problem with this approach is that it does not consider factors other than enrollment size or sparsity; student performance, resource prices, topography, and student needs might affect spending differences across districts.

The cost function method provides the most direct way to determine the relationship between enrollment and costs. By controlling for student performance, resource prices, student needs, and efficiency; cost functions have the potential for isolating the effects of enrollment size on cost differences. The key decisions in estimating economies of size in a cost function is selecting measures of student counts, and the functional form of the relationship between cost and enrollment.

Student counts used in aid formulas generally are of three types: (1) enrollment, which is the count of all students at one point in time (usually the fall), (2) average daily membership (ADM), which is an estimate of the average enrollment over the course of the year, and (3) average daily attendance, which measures the average number of students actually attending school. In general, the difference between these student counts is quite small, except in the large cities where attendance rates are often lower.

The existence of economies of size implies a negative relationship between per pupil spending and enrollment at least over some range of enrollment. However, it is likely that the rate of decline in per pupil spending occurs more quickly at low enrollment levels than at higher enrollment levels because of relatively fixed costs, such as central administration. Several different functions have been used to account for the possible non-linear relationship between enrollment and per pupil cost. The most common approach is to use a quadratic function (the natural log of enrollment and its square) to model the relationship. Quadratic functions allow for the relationship between enrollment and per pupil costs to go from negative to positive, and cost function studies have found diseconomies of scale as well as economies of scale (Resckovsky and Imazeki, 1998, 2001; Imazeki and Reschovsky, 2004a, 2004b). In states with a few high enrollment school districts (e.g., New York), the quadratic function can lead to estimates of large diseconomies of scale; some studies have used cubic functions to reduce the effects of these large districts (Duncombe and Yinger, 2000; Duncombe, Ruggiero, and Yinger, 1996). To allow for a more flexible relationship between enrollment and per pupil costs, several cost function studies have used enrollment classes instead of a quadratic functions (Duncombe, Lukemeyer, and Yinger, 2003; Duncombe and Yinger, 2005a, 2005b). Flexible cost functions, such as translog functions, provide another alternative for specifying the enrollment-spending relationship by including both a quadratic term and a number of interaction terms between enrollment and other variables in the cost model (Gronberg et al., 2004).

Professional judgment studies can also be used to estimate the effects of size on costs. (See chapter 2, this volume, for a more detailed discussion of this approach.) In professional judgment studies, panels of education professionals are asked to estimate the resources required to produce a particular set of student performance results. Panels are typically asked to do estimates for prototypical schools or districts with different characteristics, such as enrollment size or poverty rates (Baker, 2005). The estimates for the prototypical districts can then be extrapolated to districts of different sizes to develop an economies-of-size estimate for all districts in a state. Using the results of professional judgment studies in several states, Baker (2005) found that the shape of the per-pupil cost curve relative to enrollment was similar to that found in cost function studies.

STUDENT DISADVANTAGE AND EDUCATION COSTS

Extensive research on the determinants of student success in school indicates that peer characteristics, family composition, parental education and employment status, as well as neighborhood characteristics can significantly affect student success (Coleman et al., 1966; Haveman and Wolf, 1994; Pollack and Ginther, 2003; Ferguson and Ladd, 1996; Jensen and Seltzer, 2000). In addition, student characteristics can affect the mobility decisions of teachers—and hence both the quality of teachers and the costs of teacher recruitment and training. Moreover, districts with a high concentration of students living in poverty or with limited English proficiency face much greater challenges than other districts with helping their students reach academic proficiency. In this section, we discuss the types of student characteristics considered in the literature, the methods available for estimating the additional costs required to bring disadvantaged students to a given performance level, and how states have accounted for student disadvantage in their aid formulas.

Measures of At-Risk Students

The term "at-risk" implies that a student is at a higher risk of failing to meet educational objectives than other students because of characteristics of the student or of his or her family or peers. The most widely used measure of "risk" or disadvantage is poverty. One key measure of poverty for education cost studies is the child poverty rate, defined as the share of school-age population (5- to 17-years-old) living in a poor household. The Census Bureau also provides intercensal estimates of child poverty.[17] An alternative poverty measure more commonly used in education research is the share of students that qualify for a free or reduced-price school lunch as part of National School Lunch Program administered by the U.S. Department of Agriculture.[18] This measure has the advantage over the census poverty measure in that it is updated annually, but it is based in part on decisions by families to apply for participation in the program and on decisions by school districts to offer and promote this service.[19] Particularly for elementary students, the percentage of students eligible for a free lunch is highly correlated with the child poverty rate.[20]

Other measures of student "risk" available in the decennial census include the share of children living with a single mother and the share of children living with a single mother who has an income below the poverty line and is not a high school graduate. States may also collect information on "Title 1" students (those eligible for Title 1 services) and student mobility rates.

Students with limited English proficiency (LEP) may also face significant challenges succeeding in school. Many states collect information on students who qualify for bilingual education programs or students that have been identified as needing language assistance. Unfortunately, however, there is no standard definition of LEP across states, and the LEP data in some states are of questionable accuracy. An alternative measure is available from the Census, which collects information on the number of children ages 5 to 17 who live in households where English is spoken "not well" or "not at all" or of children that are living in households that are "linguistically isolated."[21]

Students with disabilities or special needs generally require more resources than other students to reach the same student performance standards. To account for these extra costs, many states incorporate pupil weights or other adjustments for special needs students in their school aid formulas. Harr, Parrish, and Chambers (chapter 32, this volume), provide a detailed discussion of state policies, including aid formulas, to account for students with special needs.

Methods for Estimating Additional Costs to Educate Disadvantaged Students

In this section, we briefly explore some of the methods for estimating the extra costs required to educate disadvantaged students. These extra costs are often expressed as pupil weights.

Cost functions provide a direct way to estimate the impact of student disadvantage on the cost of education, holding student performance constant. To be specific, the coefficients on the variables measuring student disadvantages can be used to calculate pupil weights for each type of disadvantage (Duncombe and Yinger, 2005a). A weight of 1.0 indicates for a given type of student disadvantage that it costs 100 percent more to bring a student in that category up to given performance standards than the cost for a student without disadvantage. Poverty weights estimated from cost functions fall between 1.0 and 1.5 for states with large urban areas, such as Texas, New York, and Wisconsin, and between 0.6 and 1.0 for rural states (Duncombe and Yinger, 2005b; Duncombe, Lukemeyer, and Yinger, forthcoming).[22] One exception comes from the cost function study for Texas by Gronberg et al. (2004), which leads to weights for students in poverty between 0.23 and 0.31.[23]

Another approach for estimating the higher costs required to support at-risk students is to use professional judgment panels. These panels can be asked to estimate the required resources needed to reach student performance standards for schools with different levels of poverty (or LEP shares). The differential in costs across these prototype schools can be used to develop rough estimates of pupil weights by student type. Pupil weights from professional judgment panels are based on the judgments of professional educators, and may be sensitive to the instructions given to the panels and to the ability of panel participants to identify the extra programs that would be required to bring at-risk students up to the specified performance standard (Rose, Sonstelie, and Richardson, 2004).

Baker (2006) compared several professional judgment studies and cost function studies for the same state and found that pupil weights produced from professional judgment studies are generally lower than weights produced from cost function studies. In Kansas and New York, for example, poverty weights calculated using the results from professional judgment studies (Augenblick et al., 2001; Chambers et al., 2004a) are half those calculated in cost function studies (Duncombe and Yinger, 2005b; Duncombe and Yinger, 2005a).[24] One exception is the professional judgment study in Maryland done by Augenblick and Myers (2001), which estimated pupil weights of 1.0 or higher for poverty and LEP.

How States Adjust for Student Disadvantage

Almost all state governments have some type of aid program that provides additional funds to districts with a relatively high concentration of at-risk students. Some states include cost adjustments for poverty or LEP in their basic operating aid formula, some provide categorical aid programs for at-risk students, and a few use both of these strategies (Carey, 2002; Baker and Duncombe, 2004; Huang, 2004).

The costs of at-risk students are usually incorporated into operating aid programs through the use of pupil weights. The weighted-pupil approach is used to adjust the basic operating aid formula for poverty in 15 states, for students with limited English proficiency in 9 states, and for students with handicaps in 14 states (Duncombe and Yinger, 2005a). Most states use eligibility for the National School Lunch Program as their measure of poverty, but some states use Census poverty estimates or federal welfare eligibility. Carey (2002) found that the pupil weights used by states for students living in poverty range from 0.15 to 0.30.

With the exception of Maryland, which recently implemented an aid formula with a poverty weight from a study that used the professional-judgment method, no state we are aware of uses explicitly estimated pupil weights in its formula. Nevertheless, pupil weights have been estimated for many states and have been considered in many policy debates.

The cost adjustments discussed in this chapter are designed to apply to a school district's entire operating budget. Because categorical aid programs for at-risk students typically represent a small share of a district's budget, such programs are unlikely, by themselves, to provide needy districts with the funds they need to meet an adequacy standard. Most states have not yet recognized that incomplete cost adjustments in the operating aid formula combined with full cost adjustments applied to small categorical aid programs are not sufficient to meet an adequacy objective.

CONCLUSIONS AND DIRECTIONS FOR FUTURE RESEARCH

We find a broad consensus among scholars that the cost of achieving any given level of student performance is higher in some districts than in others because of (1) differences in the compensation needed to attract school personnel, (2) differences in enrollment size, and (3) differences in the concentration of disadvantaged students or those with special educational needs. We do not find a consensus, however, on the magnitude of these cost differences or on the best methods for estimating them. Instead, we observe an active literature with many different approaches to estimating costs and a lively debate about the strengths and weakness of each approach.

From our perspective, the core of this topic is the estimation of education cost models. Although scholars disagree about the details, these models are now widely used and have influenced the debate about state aid formulas in many states. The most difficult issue that arises in estimating these models is how to control for school-district efficiency. No consensus on the best approach has yet emerged and far more work on this topic is needed. Questions of variable selection and functional form also deserve more attention. Because they play such a critical role in state education aid formulas, pupil weights should continue to be a focus of this research.

A second focus of the literature has been on estimating teacher cost indexes. This topic also has important links to policy because a state aid formula cannot provide the resources needed to reach any student performance target without accounting for teacher costs. As we have shown, scholars have addressed this topic using a wide range of approaches with different strengths and weaknesses. The hedonic wage approach is the most appealing conceptually, but it also requires data that are often not available, and more research developing and comparing each of the approaches would be valuable.

Finally, we are struck by both the clear link between cost estimation and the objectives of most state education aid formulas and the need for more work to make cost studies accessible to policy makers. Complex statistical procedures are accepted in some policy arenas, such as the revenue forecasts used in budgeting, but are only beginning to be accepted in the design of state education aid formulas. Because careful estimates of cost differentials can help policy makers achieve their educational objectives, we believe that further efforts to make these estimates accessible would be valuable.

ACKNOWLEDGMENTS

We would like to thank Leanna Stiefel, Helen Ladd, and Ted Fiske for their excellent comments and suggestions on an earlier version of this chapter. We are fully responsible for any errors and omissions.

NOTES

1. Cost functions have been conducted for New York (Duncombe and Yinger, 2000, 2005a; Duncombe, Lukemeyer, and Yinger, 2003), Arizona (Downes and Pogue, 1994), Illinois (Imazeki, 2001), Texas

(Alexander et al., 2000; Imazeki and Reschovsky, 2004a, 2004b; Gronberg et al. 2004), Wisconsin (Reschovsky and Imazeki, 1998, 2001), Kansas (Duncombe and Yinger, 2005b), and Missouri (Duncombe, Lukemeyer, and Yinger, 2006).

2. More formally, equation (1) needs to be estimated with two-stage least squares regression, which requires additional "instruments." These instruments are variables that influence S but do not influence E directly. Recent studies use instruments that measure the determinants of the demand for S, such as socio-economic characteristics, in comparable school districts, which form a point of comparison for voters and school officials (Duncombe, Lukemeyer, and Yinger, 2006; Duncombe and Yinger, 2005a, 2005b). Many studies use a district's own income and tax-price as instruments. These instruments are not legitimate, however, because, as shown below, they are determinants of efficiency and therefore influence E directly. The choice of instruments is an important topic for future research.
3. In their studies of Texas, Imazeki and Reschovsky (2004a, 2004b) and Gronberg et al. (2004) use true measures of value-added across 1 or 2 years. Imazeki and Reschovsky (2004b) used value-added across two different testing instruments, the TAAS and TAKS. Gronberg et al. (2004) used a three-year average of value-added output measures to reduce noise in these measures.
4. The main method used with this approach is Data Envelopment Analysis (DEA). Ruggiero (1998) shows how to separate cost and efficiency factors in DEA, but his approach requires far more observations than are available for any state because each district must be compared with other districts that have the same performance *and* the same cost factors. A multi-stage DEA-based approach has been used by McCarty and Yaisawarng (1993), Ray (1991), and Ruggiero (2001). Another approach is a stochastic frontier regression (Alexander et al., 2000; Gronberg et al., 2004). Ondrich and Ruggiero (2001) show, however, that stochastic frontier regression produces the same results as an OLS regression except that the intercept has been shifted up to the frontier. As a result, this approach does not remove biases caused by omitting controls for efficiency.
5. In a cost-function context, it is not possible to separate inefficiency associated with "wasteful" spending from inefficiency associated with spending on performance measures other than those included in S. It follows that a given school district could be deemed inefficient in providing one measure of student performance, say math and English scores, and efficient in providing another, say art and music.
6. Most studies use a variant of the Cobb-Douglas function, which is multiplicative in form. The Cobb-Douglas function assumes that the elasticity of substitution between all inputs is equal to one, and that the elasticity for economies of scale is constant at all levels of output.
7. One of the most popular flexible cost functions used in empirical research is the translog cost function. A translog cost model includes squared terms for each input price and outcome, and adds interaction terms between all factor prices, and outcomes. Gronberg, et al. (2004) also include a number of interaction terms between outcomes, teacher salaries, and non-school factors. In all, they have over 100 variables in their cost function for Texas compared to 18 variables in the Texas cost model estimated by Imazeki and Reschovsky (2004b).
8. Downes (2004) argues that rejecting the cost function method because it is not easy to understand "means that other methodologies should be used in place of the cost function methodology, even if the cost function methodology is theoretically sound and is most likely to generate valid estimates of the spending levels needed to meet the standard. Taken to the extreme, this argument implies that, in choosing a method to determine adequate spending levels, one is better off choosing a method that is easy to understand but wrong rather than a method that is difficult to explain but produces the right answers" (p. 8).
9. Based on spending in the 2002-03 school year for all school districts in the United States, compensation (salaries and fringe benefits) represents 90 percent of current expenditures and 50 percent of total expenditures (NCES, 2003).
10. Colorado has recognized this possibility by calculating cost of living for "labor pool areas." Labor pool areas are designed to reflect where teachers in the district live, rather than where they work.
11. The geographic unit for construction of the index is counties for Florida and Wyoming, and counties and their neighboring counties for Colorado. For a detailed description of geographic cost adjustments used in other states see Appendix A in Duncombe and Goldhaber (2003).

12. Some hedonic salary studies have not included any measures of student characteristics (Chambers et al., 2004b), and a number of studies do not include measures of student poverty (Chambers, 1997; Chambers, Taylor, and Robinson, 2003; Taylor, 2004).
13. Specifically, the cost models are estimated with two-stage least squares regression, and "instruments" are identified for teacher salaries. Instruments have included private sector salaries, county population density, and teacher wages in surrounding or similar districts. The last of these instruments may not be appropriate if salaries in one district are influenced by salaries in nearby districts.
14. These conditions might be included if the index is based on predicted salaries and student characteristics are among the variables used to predict salaries. No study has investigated the magnitude of this effect, however.
15. Economies of scale can occur either because of increasing returns to scale, which arise when a one percent increase in inputs leads to a more than one percent increase in output, or because prices for certain resources used by the school district decline with the amount of resources used.
16. They did not find any evidence of economies of scale in capital spending. In addition, the economies of scale in operating spending were partially offset by large adjustment costs that faded out over time.
17. One comparison of intercensal estimates of child poverty and the decennial census in 1989 found that these measures at the county level varied by 17 percent on average. Information on estimation methodology, and predictive accuracy for the intercensal estimates of poverty are available from the Census Bureau at http://www.census.gov/hhes/www/saipe/schooltoc.html.
18. Children with incomes at or below 130 percent of the federal poverty line are eligible for a free lunch, and students between 130 and 185 percent of the poverty line are eligible for a reduced price lunch. In addition, households receiving Food Stamps, Aid to Dependent Children (ADC), Temporary Assistance to Needy Families (TANF), or the Food Distribution Program on Indian Reservations (FDPIR) are also eligible for a free lunch. A description of the program and eligibility requirements is available at http://www.fns.usda.gov/cnd/Lunch/AboutLunch/faqs.htm.
19. In a recent audit of free-lunch student counts, the Kansas Legislative Division of Post Audit (2006) found, based on a random sample of 500 free-lunch students, that 17 percent of free-lunch students were ineligible, and 3 percent of eligible students didn't apply.
20. Census child poverty in 2000 had a correlation equal to 0.8 with the K–6 free-lunch shares in New York (Duncombe, Lukemeyer, and Yinger, 2003), 0.7 with the K–12 free lunch shares in Kansas (Duncombe and Yinger, 2005b), and 0.93 with the K–12 subsidized lunch rates in Maryland (Duncombe and Goldhaber, 2003).
21. Language ability is estimated from the long form of the Census, in which individuals are asked if they speak a language other than English and are asked their ability to speak English. A household in which all members of the household 14 years or older do not speak English well and speak at least one other language than English are classified as linguistically isolated. See http://eddev01.pcci.com/sdds/ref00.asp.
22. The higher student poverty weights in urban states compared to rural states may reflect the possibility that student performance is significantly worse in high-poverty inner city schools than in high-poverty rural schools (Olson and Jerald, 1998). To account for the possible effects of concentrated urban poverty, Duncombe, Lukemeyer, and Yinger (forthcoming) included in their cost model for Kansas and Missouri an additional poverty variable, which is the percent free lunch students multiplied by pupil density (pupils per square mile). The found a statistically significant urban poverty effect in Missouri but not in Kansas.
23. These weights are our estimates based on the estimated range in marginal effects for free lunch students in Table 3 in Gronberg et al. (2004) divided by average spending per pupil. They should not be attributed directly to the authors of that study. These relatively low weights may be due in part to the fact that this study interacts the child poverty rate with several other variables. Several of these interaction terms are not statistically significant. An alternative way to separate cost and efficiency is developed by Ruggiero (1998, 2001) based on the two-step methods developed by McCarty and Yaisawarng (1993) and Ray (1991). In the first stage Ruggiero compares the spending per pupil of each district to a cost frontier (districts with equivalent outcomes and lower spending) using data envelopment analysis (DEA). The index produced from the first-stage DEA captures both inefficiency and cost differences

across districts. Ruggiero then regresses this index on a set of cost factors, and the predicted value from this regression is his estimate of cost of education index. The first-stage of this method uses a non-parametric method, data envelopment analysis, which can be sensitive to measurement error (Bifulco and Duncombe, 2002).

24. In New York, we developed poverty weights using information in the professional judgment study (Chambers et al., 2004a); these estimates should not be attributed to the authors of the study. Our estimates of poverty weights in this study range from 0.37 in middle school to 0.81 in elementary school (Duncombe and Yinger, 2004).

REFERENCES

Alexander, C. D., Gronberg, T. J., Jansen, D. W., Keller, H., Taylor, L. L., and Treisman, P. U. (2000). *A Study of uncontrollable variations in the costs of Texas public education.* A summary report prepared for The 77th Texas Legislature. Austin, TX: Charles A. Dana Center, The University of Texas at Austin.

Andrews, M., Duncombe W., and Yinger, J. (2002). Revisiting economies of size in education: Are we any closer to a consensus? *Economics of Education Review*, 21, 245–262.

Augenblick and Myers, Inc. (2001). *Calculation of the cost of an adequate education in Maryland in 1999–2000 using two different analytic approaches.* Prepared for the Maryland Commission on Education Finance, Equity, and Excellence (Thornton Commission).

Augenblick, J., Myers, J., Silverstein, J., and Barkis, A. (2001). *Calculation of the cost of an adequate education in Kansas in 2000–2001 using two different analytic approaches.* Submitted to the Legislative Coordinating Council, State of Kansas.

Baker, B. D. (2005). The emerging shape of educational adequacy: From theoretical assumptions to empirical evidence. *Journal of Education Finance*, 30, 259–287.

Baker, B. D. (2006). Evaluating the reliability, validity and usefulness of education cost studies. *Journal of Education Finance,* 32, 170–201.

Baker, B. and Duncombe, W. (2004). Balancing district needs and student needs: The role of economies of scale adjustments and pupil need weights in school finance formulas. *Journal of Education Finance*, 29, 195–221.

Bifulco, R. and Duncombe, W. (2002). Evaluating student performance: Are we ready for prime time? In J. W. Fowler (Ed.), *Developments in school finance: 2001–02* (pp. 127–153). Washington, DC: National Center for Education Statistics.

Brazer, H. E., and Anderson, A. (1974). A cost adjustment index for Michigan school districts. In E. Tron (Ed.), *Selected papers in school finance, 1975* (pp. 23–81). Washington, DC: U.S. Department of Education.

Carey, K. (2002). *State poverty based education funding: A survey of current programs and options for improvement.* Washington, DC, Center on Budget and Policy Priorities.

Chambers, J. G. (1978). Educational cost differentials and the allocation of state aid for elementary/secondary education. *Journal of Human Resources*, 13, 459–481.

Chambers, J. G. (1997). *A technical report on the measurement of geographic and inflationary differences in public school costs, Vol. III.* Washington, DC: National Center for Education Statistics.

Chambers, J., Taylor, L., and Robinson, J. (2003). *Alaska school district cost study: Volume I and II.* Report submitted to Legislative Budget and Audit Committee by American Institutes for Research [AIR].

Chamber, J. G., Parrish, T., Levin, J., Smith, J, Guthrie, J., and Seder, R. (2004a). *The New York adequacy study: Determining the cost of providing all children in New York an adequate education: Vol. 1—Final report.* Report submitted to the Campaign for Fiscal Equity by AIR/MAP.

Chamber, J. G., Parrish, T., Levin, J., Smith, J, Guthrie, J., Seder, R., and Taylor, L. (2004b). *The New York adequacy study: Determining the cost of providing all children in New York an adequate education: Technical appendices. Appendix J.* Report submitted to the Campaign for Fiscal Equity by AIR/MAP.

Coleman, J., et al. (1966). *Equality of educational opportunity.* Washington DC: U.S. Government Printing Office.

Colorado Legislative Council Staff (CLCS). (2002). *2001 school district cost-of-living study*. Memorandum from Deb Godshall, Assistant Director of CLCS to members of Colorado General Assembly, Feburary 25.

Cotton, K. (1996). Affective and social benefits of small-scale schooling. *Eric Digest*. EDO-RC-96-5.

Downes, T. (2004). What is adequate? Operationalizing the concept of adequacy in New York. Symposium paper for New York Education Finance Research Symposium. Albany, NY: Education Finance Research Consortium.

Downes, T. and Pogue, T. (1994). Adjusting school aid formulas for the higher cost of educating disadvantaged students. *National Tax Journal*, 67, 89–110.

Duncombe, W., and Goldhaber, D. (2003). *Adjusting for geographic differences in the cost of educational provision in Maryland*. Report submitted to the Maryland State Department of Education.

Duncombe, W. and Johnston, J. (2004). The impacts of school finance reform in Kansas: Equity is in the eye of the beholder. In J. Yinger (Ed.), *Helping children left behind: State aid and the pursuit of educational equity* (pp. 147–193). Cambridge, MA: MIT Press

Duncombe, W., Lukemeyer, A., and Yinger, J. (2003). Financing an adequate education: A case study of New York. In J. W. Fowler (Ed.), *Developments in school finance: 2001–02* (pp. 127–153). Washington, DC: National Center for Education Statistics.

Duncombe, W., Lukemeyer, A., and Yinger, J. (forthcoming). The No Child Left Behind Act: Have federal funds been left behind? *Public Finance Review*.

Duncombe, W., Ruggiero, J. and J. Yinger. (1996). Alternative approaches to measuring the cost of education. In H.F. Ladd (Ed.), *Holding schools accountable: Performance-based reform in education*. (pp. 327–356).Washington, DC: The Brookings Institution.

Duncombe, W. and Yinger, J.. (2000). Financing higher student performance standards: The case of New York State. *Economics of Education Review*, 19, 363–386.

Duncombe, W. and Yinger, J. (2004). Amicus Curiae Brief of William Duncombe and John Yinger, submitted to Supreme Court of the State of New York, County of New York, September 17.

Duncombe, W. and Yinger, J.. (2005a). How much does a disadvantaged student cost? *Economics of Education Review*, 24, 513–532.

Duncombe, W. and Yinger, J. (2005b). *Estimating the cost of meeting student performance outcomes adopted by the Kansas State Board of Education*. A study prepared for the Kansas Division of Legislative Post Audit.

Duncombe, W. and Yinger, J. (forthcoming). Does school consolidation cut costs? *Education Finance and Policy*.

Eff, E., and Eff, A. (2000). *How much should a teacher cost?: Comparing Tenessee school districts using hedonic housing price indices*. Unpublished paper.

Falch, T. and Strom, B. 2005. Teacher turnover and non-pecuniary factors. *Economics of Education Review*, 24, 611–631.

Ferguson, R. F., and Ladd, H. F. (1996). How and why money matters: An analysis of Alabama schools. In H. F. Ladd (Ed.), *Holding schools accountable: Performance-based reform in education*. (pp. 265–298). Washington, DC: The Brookings Institution.

Florida Department of Education. (2002). *2002 Florida level index*. Tallahassee, Fl: Author, http://www.firn.edu/doe/fefp/pdf/fpli2001.pdf.

Fowler, W. J. and Monk, D. H. (2001). *A primer for making cost adjustments in education*. NCES 2001-323. Washington, DC: U. S. Department of Education, Office of Educational Research and Improvement.

Fowler, W. and Walberg, H.J. (1991). School size, characteristics, and outcomes. *Educational Evaluation and Policy Analysis*, 13, 189–202.

Fox, W. F. (1981). Reviewing economies of size in education. *Journal of Educational Finance*, 6, 273–296.

Friedkin, N. E. and Necochea, J. (1988). School system size and performance: A contingency perspective. *Educational Evaluation and Policy Analysis*, 10, 237–249.

Gold, S. D., Smith, D.M., and Lawton, S. B. (1995). *Public school finance programs of the United States and Canada, 1993–94. Volume 1*. Albany, NY: Center for the Study of the States.

Gronberg, T., Jansen, W., Taylor, L., and Booker, K. (2004). *School outcomes and school costs: The cost function approach.* Available at: http://www.schoolfunding.info/states/tx/march4%20cost%20study.pdf.

Guthrie, J. W. (1979). Organization scale and school success. *Educational Evaluation and Policy Analysis,* 1, 17–27.

Haller, E. J. (1992). High school size and student indiscipline: Another aspect of the school consolidation issue? *Educational Evaluation and Policy Analysis*, 4, 145–156.

Haller, E. J. and Monk, D. H. (1988). New reforms, old reforms, and the consolidation of small rural schools. *Educational Administration Quarterly*, 24, 470–483.

Hanushek, E. A., Kain, J. F., and Rivkin, S. G. (2005). Teachers, schools, and academic achievement. *Econometrica*, 73, 417–458.

Hanushek, E. A., Kain, J. F., and Rivkin, S. G. (2004). The revolving door. *Education Next,* 4, 76–82.

Hanushek, E. A., Kain, J. F., and Rivkin, S. G. (2001). *Why public schools lose teachers.* National Bureau of Economic Research, Working Paper no. 8599, November.

Haveman, R. and Wolfe, B. (1994). *Succeeding generations: On the effects of investments in children.* New York: Russell Sage Foundation.

Howley, C. (1996). The academic effectiveness of small-scale schooling (An update). *Eric Digest,* Report No. EDO-RC-94-1.

Huang, Y. (2004). Appendix B: A guide to state operating aid programs for elementary and secondary education, In J. Yinger (Ed.) *Helping children left behind: State aid and the pursuit of educational equity*, (pp. 331–351). Cambridge, MA: MIT Press.

Imazeki, J. (2001). *Grade-dependent costs of education: Evidence from Illinois.* Draft paper. San Diego State University.

Imazeki, J. and Reschovsky, A. (2004a). School finance reform in Texas: A never ending story. In: J. Yinger (Ed.) *Helping children left behind: State aid and the pursuit of educational equity* (pp. 251–281). Cambridge, MA: MIT Press.

Imazeki, J. and Reschovsky, A. (2004b). *Estimating the costs of meeting the Texas educational accountability standards.* Available at: http://www.investintexasschools.org/schoolfinancelibrary/studies/files/2005/january/reschovsky_coststudy.doc

Jensen, B. and Seltzer, A. (2000). Neighborhood and family effects in education progress. *The Australian Economic Review*, 33, 17–31.

Kane, T.J. and Staiger, D.O. (2002). *The promise and pitfalls of using imprecise school accountability measures. Journal of Economic Perspectives*, 16, 91–114.

Kansas Legislative Division of Post Audit. (2006). *K–12 education: Reviewing free-lunch student counts as the basis for at-risk funding, part 1.* Topeka, KS: Author.

Lee, V. E. and Smith, J. B. (1997). High school size: Which works best and for whom? *Educational Evaluation and Policy Analysis,* 19, 205–227.

Massachusetts Department of Education. (1999). *An analysis of geographic differences in school operating and construction cost.* Boston, MA: Author, September 15.

McCarty, T. A. and Yaisawarng. (1993). Technical efficiency in New Jersey school districts. In H. O. Fried, C.A. Knox Lovell, and S. S. Schmidt (Eds.) *The measurement of productive efficiency: Techniques and applications* (pp. 271–287). New York: Oxford University Press.

McMahon, W. W. (1996). Interstate cost adjustments. In J. W. Fowler (Ed.), *Selected papers in school finance 1994* (pp. 89–114). Washington, DC: National Center for Education Statistics.

National Center for Education Statistics (NCES). (2001). *Public school finance programs of the United States and Canada: 1998–99.* NCES 2001-309. Washington DC: Author.

NCES. (2003). *Common core of data (CCD), National public education financial survey, 2002–03.* Washington DC: Author.

Nelson, F. H. (1991). An interstate cost-of-living index. *Educational Evaluation and Policy Analysis*, 13, 103–111.

New York State Education Department. (2003). *Recognizing high cost factors in the financing of public education: The calculation of a regional cost index.* Albany, NY: Author.

Odden, A. (1999). School-based financing in North America. In M.E. Goertz and A. Odden (Ed.), *School-Based Financing* (pp. 155–187). Thousand Oaks, CA: Corwin Press.

Ohio Department of Education. (2003). *Ohio's school foundation funding program*. Colombus, OH: Author.

Ondrich, J., Pas, E., and Yinger, J. (Forthcoming). The determinants of teacher attrition in upstate New York. *Public Finance Review.*

Ondrich, J. and Ruggiero, J. (2001). Efficiency measurement in the stochastic frontier model. *European Journal of Operational Research*, 129, 432–442.

Pollack, R. A. and Ginther, D. K. (2003). *Does family structure affect children's educational outcomes?* National Bureau of Economic Research, Working Paper no. 9628, April.

Ray, S. C. (1991). Resource use in public schools: A study of Connecticut. *Management Science,* 37, 1520–1628.

Reschovsky, A. and Imazeki, J. (1998). The development of school finance formulas to guarantee the provision of adequate education to low-income students. In J. W. Fowler (Ed.), *Developments in school finance: 1997* (pp. 123–147). Washington, DC: National Center for Education Statistics.

Reschovsky, A., and Imazeki, J. (2001). Achieving educational adequacy through school finance reform. *Journal of Education Finance*, 26, 373–396.

Roza, M. and Hill, P. (2004). How within-district spending inequalities help some schools to fail. In D. Ravitch (Ed.), *Brookings Papers on Education Policy* (pp. 201–227). Washington, DC: The Brookings Institution.

Rose, H., Sonstelie, J. and Richardson, P. (2004). *School budgetins and student achievement in California: The principal's perspective.* San Francisco: Public Policy Institute of California.

Rothstein, R. and Smith, J. (1997). *Adjusting Oregon education expenditures for regional cost differences: A feasibility study.* Submitted to Confederation of Oregon School Administrators. Management Analysis and Planning Associates, L.L.C.

Ruggiero, J. (1998). Non-discretionary inputs in data envelopment analysis. *European Journal of Operational Research*, 111, 461–468.

Ruggiero, J. (2001). Determining the base cost of education: An analysis of Ohio school districts. *Contemporary Economic Policy*, 19, 268–279.

Scafidi, B., Sjoquist, B., and Stinebrickner, T. (Forthcoming). Race, poverty, and teacher mobility. *Economics of Education Review.*

Stiefel, L., Rubenstein, R., and Berne, R. (1998). Intra-district equity in four large cities: Data, methods and results. *Journal of Education Finance*, 23, 447–467.

Taylor, L. (2004). *Adjusting for geographic variations in teacher compensation: Updating the Texas cost-of education index.* Austin, TX: Joint Select Committee on Public School Finance.

Taylor, L. L. and Fowler, W. J. (2006). *A comparative wage approach to geographic cost adjustment.* Washington, DC: U.S. Department of Education.

Wyoming Division of Economic Analysis. (1999). *The Wyoming cost of living index: Policies and procedures.* http://eadiv.state.wy.us/wcli/policies.pdf. Cheyenne, WY: Division of Economic Analysis, Department of Administration and Information, August.

15

Intergovernmental Aid Formulas and Case Studies

Lawrence O. Picus, Margaret Goertz, and Allan Odden

INTRODUCTION

Public education in the United States is big business. Revenue raised by all levels of government for K–12 education in 2003–04 amounted to nearly $450 billion (U.S. Department of Education, National Center for Education Statistics, 2006), and the National Education Association estimates total revenues exceeded $500 billion in 2005–06 (NEA, 2006). These revenues are raised as part of the larger federal fiscal system in the United States. Under this system governments at the local (such as cities and school districts), state, and federal levels all raise and spend public tax dollars.

Although responsibility for providing elementary and secondary education almost always rests with the nearly 15,000 local school districts across the nation, nearly half the financing for K–12 education is now provided by the governments of the 50 states. Only since the late 1970s has the state become an equal partner with local school districts in financing education. The federal role in education funding was negligible until passage of the Elementary and Secondary Education Act in the mid-1960s. Since that time between 7 and 9 percent of K–12 education funding has come from the Federal Government.

States are playing a more significant role in the finances of schools for a number of reasons. In response to lawsuits across the nation, states are agreeing to use their financial resources to equalize differences in the property tax—raising capacity of their school districts. As local taxpayers become more reluctant to increase property taxes to finance local services, including education, states step in and either provide additional funds for schools or use their resources to provide property tax relief. Often these two efforts work hand-in-hand, with increases in state revenues partially offsetting local property taxes and partially increasing educational spending. States have also initiated efforts to improve productivity and efficiency in school systems and to ensure adequate educational outcomes.

Local school districts traditionally finance almost all of their share of educational revenues through property taxes. Because property is fixed in location, and values tend to change slowly, such taxes offer relatively small units of government—such as school districts—a stable source of revenue (Monk & Brent, 1997). States that have a larger base upon which taxes can be levied have been able to use other taxes, especially sales and income taxes, to finance their operations. Moreover, these broad-based statewide taxes make it possible for the state to more efficiently ensure that educational spending in individual districts is a function of the wealth of the entire state and not of the individual school district.

Thus, there has been a shift from local sources to state sources, combined with a slight jump and then consistent percentage of federal funding beginning some 40 years ago. Simultaneously, the emphasis of school finance funding formulas has shifted from concern about equity to consideration of efficiency, and now, to adequacy.

Equity

School finance has long been concerned with the equitable distribution of funds to school districts. The traditional problem facing states in funding their schools is the diversity in size and financial capacity of the school districts within the state's boundaries. The most obvious challenge to the equitable distribution of funds to schools is the frequently large disparity in the ability of school districts to collect property taxes. Property taxes are typically assessed at a uniform rate within a taxing jurisdiction on all real property located within that jurisdiction's boundaries. The amount of money that can be raised for each pupil varies substantially among districts within any state.

In the late 1960s this variation in revenue per pupil was challenged under the equal protection clauses of the U.S. Constitution and state constitutions. Two legal challenges—*McInnis v. Shapiro* (293 F. Supp. 327 (N.O. Ill. 1968) aff'd.) in Illinois and *Burris v. Wilkerson* (310 F. Supp. 572 Virg. (1969), aff'd., 397 U.S. 44 (1970)) in Virginia—failed to establish a standard to assess and measure educational need. In 1970, Coons, Clune, and Sugarman proposed treating the use of property wealth per pupil as a suspect classification as a way to satisfy judicial scrutiny. This strategy was first used in the *Serrano* case in California (5 Cal. 3d 584, 487 P.2d 1241, 96 Cal. Rptr. 601 ([1971]).

The U.S. Supreme Court ruling in *Rodriguez v. San Antonio* in 1973 (411 U.S. 1) eliminated the use of the equal protection clause of the U.S. Constitution when the court declined to apply the strict scrutiny test. The court determined that education was not a fundamental right under the U.S. Constitution and that low property wealth was not a suspect class.

The focus of subsequent school finance litigation shifted to the states. Following the logic established in *Robinson v. Cahill* in New Jersey (62 N.J. 473, 303 A.2d 273) in 1976, state courts focused on the education clauses of their state constitutions. While the individual state clauses vary considerably (McUsic, 1991; Underwood, 1995), many state courts have used terms such as "thorough and efficient," "thorough and uniform," or "general and uniform" as the standard to which school finding systems must be held. Regardless of whether the courts ruled that systems were unconstitutional, most states moved to increase the equity of their school funding systems—generally through increases in overall education funding (Murray, Evans & Schwab, 1998; also see Corcoran & Evans, this volume).

Productivity

As spending for K–12 education increased in the 1980s and 1990s, policy makers and academics called for more effective use of the funds and better understanding of how dollars could lead to improvements in student learning. While most educators would say that additional money improves performance, the policy and research communities have been skeptical, and a substantial debate exists as to whether or not a statistical link between more spending and improved student outcomes can be established. Production function research constitutes the largest body of evidence on this question, and the results of this work are mixed.

Eric Hanushek (1981, 1986, 1989, 1994, 1997, 2002), who analyzed numerous studies and conducted several of his own, concludes that there is not a strong or consistent relationship between resources and student performance. Other researchers, however, (Hedges, Laine & Greenwald, 1994a, 1994b; Greenwald, Hedges & Laine, 1996a, 1996b; and Laine, Greenwald & Hedges, 1996) have reviewed the same studies and concluded that money can make a difference. Moreover, as research on specific instructional strategies that have higher per pupil costs, such as smaller class size, are conducted, evidence of their success suggests that a relationship between spending and student learning may exist. The lack of a clear statistical link between student performance and spending provided little motivation and evidence for changing school finance structures and led to alternative approaches in the courts by those unhappy with the way schools in their states were funded.

Adequacy

Beginning with court rulings in West Virginia (*Pauley v. Kelly*, 162 W. Va. 672, 259 S.E. 2d 859 [W. Va. 1979], on remand sub nom *Pauley v. Bailey*, C.A. No. 75-126; [Cir. Ct. Kanawha Cty., W. Va., May 11, 1982]), Washington (*Seattle Sch. Dist. No. 1 of King County v. State*, 90 Wn.2d 476, 585 P.2d 71 [1978]), and, most importantly, Kentucky (*Rose v. Council for Better Education*, 790 S.W. 2d 186 [Kent. 1989]), the adequacy movement took hold as the most common approach for challenging the school funding systems in the states. In recent years, adequacy challenges to school finance systems have been highly successful and there is a growing body of literature on how to determine what an adequate level of spending on education should be.

Adequacy is generally thought of as providing enough resources to allow each district and school to deploy a set of educational programs and strategies to ensure that each child has an equal opportunity to meet their state's educational performance standards. As described by Downes and Stiefel (this volume), four approaches to estimating adequacy have been developed to date—each with strengths and weaknesses. Significantly, the adequacy movement has begun to link school finance to measures of student performance. As school reformers focus on meeting educational standards, school finance analysts are seeking to understand the level of resources needed to give all students the opportunity to meet those standards, and what financing systems will ensure that those resources are available. Interest in adequacy has been encouraged by the growing number of successful law suits challenging state school funding systems and by state efforts to meet the requirements of the Federal No Child Left Behind Act, which requires all students meet state proficiency standards by 2014.

SCHOOL FINANCE FORMULAS

Since most school districts raise their own source revenue from property taxes, state aid formulas are designed to provide more state aid—for the same level of effort—to districts with low property wealth per pupil and less state aid to districts with higher property wealth per pupil. In this section we describe three general forms of school finance formulas: foundation programs, guaranteed tax bases (or power equalizing), and combination programs.

The fundamental goal of these formulas is to provide equal access to total revenues per pupil for school districts across a state. In some instances the goal is to insure a minimum level of per pupil revenue (achieved through a foundation program), while in other instances the goal is to provide equal resources for equal effort, leaving the choice of total per pupil spending to the local school district (achieved through a guaranteed tax base or GTB program). Combination programs join elements of foundation and GTB programs to equalize school district per pupil revenues by assuring a minimum revenue level in each district and providing equal access—at least up to some agreed upon level—to additional resources should local taxpayers want to make additional efforts on their own.

Foundation Programs[1]

In general, a foundation program establishes a minimum per pupil revenue level at a set property tax rate and then guarantees that districts levying that tax rate will receive the foundation level of revenue. State aid is then defined as the difference between the revenue guaranteed as a "foundation" and the amount raised locally by the established tax rate. The design of foundation programs raises several policy issues. The major issue is establishing the foundation level itself. In the past, this level has often been decided politically, based on the state revenue available for education in the budget year. The recent advances in school finance adequacy, however, provide methods for estimating what the foundation level should be.

In addition to the foundation level of funding, state policy makers need to agree on the required tax rate expected of local school districts, whether or not local school districts can exceed the revenue level established through the foundation program, what to do if a local school district's property tax revenues exceed the foundation guarantee at the minimum required tax rate, and whether or not to equalize revenues in excess of the foundation guarantee if districts elect to raise additional funds. This latter issue is discussed under combination programs below. In some states the "excess" revenues are subject to recapture—or redistribution to other school districts—while in other states, districts are allowed to keep all the additional funds they raise. In Texas, where recapture is not an option under the state's constitution (Picus & Hertert, 1993), the state devised a structure that requires wealthy districts either to transfer the value of part of their tax base to another school district for taxation purposes or to make payments to other districts or to the state when property tax revenues exceed the foundation guarantee.

Finally, adjustments should be made for differences in student needs and to compensate for differences in the costs of educational services and materials that are beyond the control of a school district. This later adjustment is the focus of chapter 14, this volume.

In simple terms, a foundation program provides aid to each school district in inverse relationship to its property wealth per pupil, as represented in the following equation:[2]

$$SAPP = FLPP - (RTR \times PVPP)$$

Where:

SAPP = state aid per pupil
FLPP = the foundation level of revenue per pupil
RTR = the tax rate each district is required to levy
PVPP = the property value per pupil of the school district

Thus, the amount of state aid given to a particular district is inversely proportional to the value of the district's per pupil property value. Under a foundation model, the foundation level (FLPP) and the required tax rate (RTR) are state policy decisions. Local districts can choose to spend more than the foundation level by taxing their own property value at a tax rate exceeding the required tax rate.

Arkansas provides an example of the use of such a formula. Based on a 2003 adequacy study, the Arkansas Legislature determined that the cost of funding an adequate education program amounted to $5,400 per pupil (Odden, Picus & Fermanich, 2003; and Odden, Picus & Goetz, 2006). This figure was then funded through a foundation program with a required property tax levy of 25 mills in each school district. To this foundation amount for the base program, Arkansas added two, major new categorical programs: $480 for each student eligible for free and reduced price lunch[3] and $195 for each English language learning student. Funds for students with mild and moderate disabilities were included in the calculation of the base foundation level of $5,400 per pupil.[4]

California has a variant of the foundation program known as the revenue limit. Each school district has a revenue limit determined on the basis of an historic formula. Although the revenue limits for the school districts enrolling over 95 percent of the students in the state are within a band of $300 by type of district,[5] some variation remains in the revenue limits across districts. In addition, this revenue limit does not include billions of dollars in additional categorical programs for special student or district circumstances that are part of the state funding system. Under Proposition 13, property taxes in California are limited to 1 percent of assessed value, which is further limited to a growth rate of 2 percent a year until a property is sold and reassessed at market value. The "local" property tax revenues are distributed to local taxing jurisdictions (including school districts) through a legislatively determined formula. Districts that do not generate sufficient property taxes to fund their revenue limit receive funding from the state to make up the difference.[6]

Foundation programs have several attractive features. They began as programs designed to provide a minimum quality education program, but, today they can be used to guarantee a higher quality program, perhaps one sufficient to meet the needs of an adequate education system, one in which students learn to high performance standards. For example, in states under an adequacy oriented court mandate, the foundation level could be set at the adequate base spending level as identified through an adequacy study. Foundation formulas are unique in having a base program guarantee as a critical variable. They are funded by a combination of state and local funds that link states and school districts in a fiscal partnership for funding public schools. They are also fiscal-capacity equalizing in that they provide state aid in an inverse relationship to local property value per pupil. They address the key structural problem of school finance—the disparity across districts in the local property tax base. Their key defect—at least from an equity perspetive—may be that they allow local spending above the foundation program, and if the base program is low, these local fiscal add-ons—financed entirely with local property tax revenues—restore some of the linkage between property wealth and education spending.

Guaranteed Tax Base Programs

Although foundation programs guarantee a fixed level of funding, Guaranteed Tax Base (GTB) programs assure a fixed level of revenue per pupil for a given tax rate. For example, if the guaranteed tax base is $600,000 of assessed value per pupil, a ten mill levy will raise $6,000 per pupil (a mill is a dollar of tax per $1,000 assessed value of property). A GTB program guarantees that any district whose wealth is less than $600,000 per pupil would receive state aid to make up the difference between $6,000 and what is raised through its property taxes. Mathematically this can be expressed as follows:[7]

$$SAPP = DTR \times (GTBPP - PVPP)$$

Where

SAPP = state aid per pupil (as above)

DTR = the district tax rate (note this is different from a required tax rate as used in the foundation program in that it is chosen by the district)
GTBPP = the property value per pupil level guaranteed to each district or the guaranteed tax base per pupil
PVPP = property value per pupil

Another way to look at this is to express total district revenue per pupil (TRPP) as follows:

TRPP = (DTR x PVPP) + (DTR x (GTBPP – PVPP))

Which can be simplified to be:

TRPP = DTR x GTBPP

Under the foundation program described above, the state sets the foundation spending level (FLPP) and the required tax rate (RTR) districts must levy to receive that funding, while under a GTB program, the state establishes the level of property value it will guarantee (GTBPP) and lets the district establish its own tax rate (DTR). The education spending preferences of each district dictate the tax rate and level of spending. All districts with property wealth per pupil below the GTBPP receive state aid.

Because a GTB program allows different local decisions on education per pupil spending levels, equality of spending is not its focus. Indeed, without a requirement for a minimum school tax rate, GTB programs do not even require a minimum education expenditure per pupil level. Still, in most situations where GTB programs have been enacted, they have increased expenditures in all but the school districts with the lowest tax rates. However, it should be emphasized that a GTB program is incompatible with the standard horizontal equity principal for students that requires equal spending per child. Instead it is a funding approach that offers a version of fiscal neutrality.

Initally implemented in a number of states in the 1970s to remedy the major source of school spending differences across states caused by unequal access to the local tax base, GTB programs were a highly visible policy alternative. They stimulated more education spending and produced what Odden and Picus (2008) term the "new" school finance equity issue. In the 1970s, property poor school districts usually had low spending per pupil even though they had high tax rates, while property rich districts usually had high spending per pupil with low tax rates. The GTB was expected to help poor districts by allowing them to lower their tax rates and simultanueously increase their spending. But in some states with GTB programs, (i.e., Illinois, Missouri, and Wisconsin), spending differences, though attenuated, continued to exist. But the patterns changed. Today in those states, property rich districts have high spending levels and high tax rates; average wealth districts tend to have average spending levels and average tax rates; and below average wealth districts tend to have below average spending and below average tax rates. Spending differences still exist, but they are driven by differences in local tax rates for schools. An issue for these states is whether such spending differences are a problem, even though not caused primarily by differences in the local property tax base for schools.

Combination Formulas

The discussion above suggests that efforts to ensure a minimum level of revenue to school districts are best served with foundation programs, while efforts to reduce the role of the local tax base in causing spending differences are best served though GTB formulas. As their name suggests, combination programs use the strengths of each approach to design a system that assures a minimum level of resources for all children, but provides an equitable way for any district that chooses to do so to increase its spending above the base foundation level. The foundation portion of the combined program first ensures a base spending level, usually above what had been a minimum level. This base spending level remedies a possible shortcoming of pure GTB programs that do not require a minimum spending level. The GTB portion of the combined program ensures equal education spending per pupil for equal tax rates above the foundation-required tax rate. This component remedies a defect of a minimum foundation program: unequalized spending above the foundation base.

Missouri has had a two-tiered, combination foundation and guaranteed tax base program since the late 1970s. When established, the Missouri formula set the foundation revenue level at just below the previous year's statewide average expenditure per pupil. For the second tier, the legislature used a GTB program, setting the wealth guarantee at that of the district at the 95th percentile of property wealth. Over time wealthy districts increased their tax rates to fund higher education expenditures, while low-wealth districts—despite the relatively lower local cost—did not. Consequently, funding the Guaranteed Tax Base Per Pupil (GTBPP) at the 95th precentile of property wealth did not over burden the state system. However, spending differences between the wealthy and poor districts increased because of different local preferences for education and willingness to pay.

The combination approach was used for other new school finance formulas established during the early 1990s. Both Texas and Kentucky, under court order to revise their school finance structures, enacted combination foundation and guaranteed tax base programs. In Texas, the 1989–90 foundation program provided a base spending or foundation level equal to about 42 percent of the statewide average expenditure per pupil. The guaranteed tax base program was set just below the statewide average per pupil property value. Texas placed a tax rate cap on the GTB component of the formula, providing GTB aid for just an extra 3.6 mills above the foundation required tax rate. Districts were also allowed to levy higher tax rates, for which revenues were derived solely from the local tax base up to a maximum of $1.50 per $100 of assessed value or 15 mills.

Kentucky enacted a similar, but three tiered combination program (see Picus, Odden, and Fermanich, 2004). The 1989–90 foundation base was set at about 77 percent of the statewide average per pupil spending. Kentucky also put a GTB on top of the foundation program, setting the wealth guarantee at about 150 percent of the statewide average. This GTB program, however, included two tiers, each with its own type of tax rate cap. The first tier limited the additional tax rate beyond which districts could not receive GTB aid by giving school boards the flexibility to increase spending (and thus the local tax rate) by 15 percent over the foundation base and still receive GTB aid. In addition, taxpayers could increase spending by a local vote (and thus the local tax rate) by another 30 percent of the total amounted generated by the foundation level and the first tier, but they would not be eligible for GTB aid for this second 30 percent spending boost. Thus, expenditures above the foundation base are limited to an additional 49.5 percent, 30 percent of which is fiscal-capacity equalized by a GTB.

As an example of how this works, suppose that the base foundation level were set at $1,000 per pupil. A district would receive this level of funding once it made the required tax effort. It would be allowed to increase its revenue to $1,150 per pupil (a 15% increase) and have that $150 equalized as well. If the district elected to spend beyond this level, it could increase total per pupil revenue by an additional 30 percent or an additonal $345 per pupil (30% of 1,150 is 345). This would bring the total available revenue to $1,495 per pupil.

A combination foundation and GTB program offers many advantages. Both components of the program require local matching funds and provide for fiscal capacity equalization. A base spending level is guaranteed, providing some element of expenditure equity. The ability to spend above the base is possible on an equal basis for rich and poor districts alike, thus providing the potential for a fiscally neutral system depending on the decisions made by local school districts (local choice). It will not break the relationship between wealth and expenditures, however, if wealthy districts continue to choose higher tax rates and thus higher spending. While a combination program is fiscally neutral in its design (*ex ante*), it may not be in its operation (*ex post*) due to local preferences and willingness to pay. If a state enacts a cap on the level of extra revenues, such as the 30 percent cap in Kentucky, the program might be more appealing to those who champion horizontal equity for children.

The second-tier GTB has in some instances functioned as an incentive to spend more, and primarily by above-average-wealth, suburban districts. As a result, the two-tier system, just like an unbridled GTB program, can create a system that generally results in combination with low-spending, low-tax-rate, low-wealth districts and, low-spending, high-tax-rate and high (or above-average) wealth districts. Some would not consider this to be a fair system.

The Cost Dimension

To this point the discussion has focused on equalizing access to dollars under the assumption that all students and school districts are alike in terms of needs. This, of course, is not the case and school funding systems generally adjust for differences in student characteristics and district characteristics—two issues over which the district has no control.

There is considerable evidence that students from different backgrounds require different levels of educational services. Today, state school finance formulas provide additonal resources for students from low-income households, for children who are English language learners, and for children with disabilities that impact their ability to learn and/or to participate in a regular school program.

There are two basic approaches for adjusting aid formulas for student characteristics. One method provides additonal aid in the form of categorical grants or aid intended to be used for the purpose of providing services for children with specific needs. Examples of such programs include funding for special education for children with disabilities and compensatory aid programs for children from low-income families. In both instances, districts receive additional dollars based on the number of children (and sometimes on the intensitiy of the needs of those children) to fund programs that meet the specific needs of those children.

A second approach is to "weight" children based on their identified needs. Thus in a state aid formula, children from low-income families might receive a weight of 1.25 and Limited English Proficient Children a weight of 1.10. When the enrollment of a district is determined, the total number of weighted students receive state funding. Details on incidence, needs, and costs of these programs are provided in sections VI and VII of this volume, and determination of the appropriate weights is a complex undertaking. Some states rely on relatively simple weighting schemes, offering one weight for low-income children, another for English-language learners, and a set of weights for special education based on the disabilities of children. Other states have established more complex weighting formulas, establishing varying weights for different grade levels, vocational education programs, or even variable rates for the concentration of low-income children in a school or district.

A number of district characteristics that affect the cost of education are beyond the control of local school authorities. Perhaps the most debated is price differences across a state (chapter

37, this volume). Adjustments in school finance formulas for price differences across geographic areas within a state are frought with political considerations. While it makes sense to compensate districts in high-cost areas for those additonal costs, it is often hard for policy makers to accept the reality that one dollar in one part of the state has less buying power than one dollar in another part of the state. State policy makers need to identify the best measure for determining cost differences in order to establish appropriate formula adjustments.

MEASURING EQUITY IN THE STATES

Longitudinal Analyses of Equity

How have school finance systems done over time in terms of equity objectives? A considerable body of literature addresses this question. Two examples presented here examine the impact of school funding formulas enacted in response to landmark court cases in Kentucky and New Jersey.

As described in the preceding section, Kentucky's school finance system (SEEK) combines foundation and GTB formulas. Picus, Odden and Fermanich (2004) found that the equity of Kentucky's funding system steadily improved between 1990–91 and 1999–2000 and that the state has achieved high levels of horizontal and vertical equity and fiscal neutrality. For example, the coefficient of variation (CV) for revenues per pupil decreased from 0.143 to 0.108. Similarly, the CV for revenues per weighted pupil (reflecting special student needs) dropped from 0.136 to 0.104. Analysis of the McLoone index, a measure of distribution at the low end of the revenue spectrum, shows there is a high degree of equity among those districts, rising from 0.94 to 0.96 for revenues per weighted pupil. Although the formula allows for up to a 50 percent difference in revenues per pupil for those districts that add both Tier I and Tier II revenues, the restricted range was less than $1,500 per pupil. Finally, the link between property wealth and revenue per pupil was nearly gone by 2000. The correlation between these two variables dropped more than 50 percent from 0.494 to 0.220. The elasticity, which measures the strength of this relationship, also decreased considerably from 0.15 to 0.07.

Thus, SEEK has achieved the equity goals set out by the legislature in 1990. The question remains, however, about whether Kentucky districts have adequate resources to allow students to meet state performance standards. Recent adequacy studies in that state suggested that the state would need to increase funding for education from between $740 million to as much as $2.1 billion (Picus, Odden & Fermanich, 2004; Odden, Fermanich & Picus, 2003; Verstegen, 2003).

New Jersey represents a particularly interesting case. In 17 decisions handed down over more than 30 years, the New Jersey Supreme Court has sought to ensure that all students in New Jersey, particularly in distressed urban areas, have equal access to a quality education. The decisions in *Robinson v. Cahill* and the initial decisions in *Abbott v. Burke* focused on equalizing educational spending, particularly between the state's poor urban and wealthy suburban school districts (Goertz & Edwards, 1999). In the absence of other measures, the Court used spending in the state's highest wealth districts as its benchmark for the level of resources needed to ensure equal educational opportunity in poor urban districts. In 1990 it ordered the legislature to design a funding system that would: (1) equalize spending for the *regular education program* between the state's poorer urban districts (*Abbott* districts) and property-rich districts; and (2) provide additional funds to meet the *special educational needs* of the urban districts in order to redress their disadvantages (*Abbott v. Burke*, 575 A.2d 359, 397 (1990); *Abbott v. Burke*, 643 A.2d 575 (1994); and *Abbott v. Burke*, 693 A.2d 417 (1997). The Court did not address spending disparities in poor rural or in middle class districts in the *Abbott* case.

To assess equity over time, Goertz and Weiss (2007) grouped New Jersey school districts into four categories: (1) the 30 *Abbott* districts; (2) low-wealth, non-*Abbott* (mostly rural) districts; (3) middle-income districts, and (4) high-wealth districts. In 1984–85, when the first *Abbott* decision was handed down, the *Abbott* districts spent a few hundred dollars per pupil more than the poor, non-*Abbott* districts (low wealth), but $800 dollars per pupil less than the middle wealth districts, and over $2,000 less than the high-wealth communities. The school tax rates in the *Abbott* districts were also nearly 50 percent higher than those in the high-wealth districts. At the same time, a $2,500 per pupil gap separated the low- and high-wealth districts.

By 2005–06, the *Abbott* districts were spending about $1,000 per pupil more than the high-wealth districts, and considerably more than both the poor non-*Abbott* ($3,600) and middle wealth ($2,850) districts, while levying much lower tax rates. While parity had been achieved between the *Abbott* and high-wealth districts, as intended by the Court, both spending and taxpayer disparities remained among the non-*Abbott* districts. The spending gap between the low- and high-wealth districts had widened slightly to $2,700 per pupil, while the gap between the middle- and high-wealth districts had grown to $2,000 per pupil. Taxpayers in low- and middle-wealth communities continue to raise fewer education dollars with higher tax rates. While changes in New Jersey's school finance system have done little to alleviate wealth-based disparities in education spending among the non-*Abbott* districts, they have made the distribution of education spending somewhat more equitable. Between 1984–85 and 2005–06, the coefficient of variation dropped from 0.183 to 0.165, the federal range ratio dropped from 0.816 to 0.655, and the McLoone index rose from 0.859 to 0.887, all of which represent movements toward greater equity. The coefficient of variation and federal range ratio remain high, however.

The legislature froze most categories of aid to non-*Abbott* districts between 2002 and 2007, driving up taxes in middle- and high-wealth communities. As a result, the governor and state legislature called for the development of a new funding formula. The formula must be equitable, based on the characteristics of a district's students and reflecting its ability to pay for education; adequate, as determined by a professional judgment panel study; and efficient, through the application of revenue caps, school district consolidation and stronger accountability measures (Joint Legislative Committee on Public School Funding Reform, New Jersey Legislature, November 15, 2006). The projected cost of the new formula is $1 billion.

Several studies have also analyzed the status of school finance equity across the 50 states (Stiefel & Berne, 1981; Brown et al., 1977; Evans, Murray, & Schwab, 1997; Murray, Evans, & Schwab, 1998; Odden & Augenblick, 1981; Odden, Berne, & Stiefel, 1979; Schwartz & Moskowitz, 1988; and Corcoaran & Evans, this volume). The early studies had conflicting results, depending on the time frame studied and on the equity object selected and statistic used.

The most comprehensive studies of school finance disparities analyzed 20 to 30 years of data and concluded that fiscal disparities had been reduced over this period but only by 16–25 percent and largely in those states with court cases (Evans, Murray, & Schwab, 1997; Murray, Evans, & Schwab, 1998; Corcoran & Evans, this volume). In addition, Murray, Evans, and Schwab (1998) show that, after adjusting for cost differences, the majority of fiscal differences, are caused by inter- rather than intrastate disparities. Thus even if all within-state disparities are eliminated, two-thirds of the disparities will remain, which supports Odden and Busch's (1998) conclusion that disparities across states exceed those within states. These studies, however, leave unanswered the question of whether additional money has improved student learning and performance. Understanding this link has been difficult. Below, we briefly discuss efforts to make the use of educational resources more efficient, and, following that, suggest how the growing adequacy movement may provide a path for improving student outcomes across all types of districts and among all students.

PRODUCTIVITY AND EFFICIENCY

In the 1990s, as the level of resources for K–12 education grew and the distribution of those resources became more equitable in many states, there was a growing interest in making sure schools made efficient use of educational resources. Research on the linkage between dollars spent and student outcomes led to few solid conclusions as to the best ways to spend money. Recent work on school finance adequacy has also sought ways to enhance the efficiency of how schools and school districts allocate and use their resources. It appears that seeking efficiencies within the instructional budget may offer more progress in this area. Developing school funding formulas that create incentives for these activities, while allowing local administrators and teachers ample flexibility in choosing the specific educational programs to use, is the challenge facing the design of school funding formulas in the future.

Pay for Performance

Over the years many have suggested that teacher pay be somehow tied to the performance of their students. While attractive on the surface, this suggestion has met with sound resistance from the teachers organizations, and thus far, has gained little traction in the policy environment. Moreover more recent research has suggested that rewarding teachers for their knowledge and skills may be an alternative way to encourage teachers to undertake strategies and actions that research suggests will lead to improved student performance (Odden & Wallace, 2007). To date successes in establishing teacher compensation systems that reward teachers for knowledge and skills have been implemented on a limited scale in a few school districts. While there have been efforts to institute state-wide knowledge and skill based pay systems at the state level—such as in Iowa—those efforts have yet to succeed. Results of current randomized experiments, such as that in Nashville, may provide more evidence for this on-going policy discussion. Designing state funding formulas that provide for enhanced salary flexibility on the part of local officials is a challenge facing the school finance and education policy communities.

ADEQUACY

School finance adequacy seeks to provide resources that are needed to insure that all students—or almost all students—can meet a state's learning goals and expectations. Four approaches have been developed to estimate school finance adequacy (see chapter 13, this volume). While adequacy studies have been conducted in many states, few states to date have used the findings from adequacy studies to design school funding systems. The small impact adequacy studies have had on funding systems is partly because the studies almost always call for substantial amounts of new money, much of it focused on parts of the state that are not politically strong. Two states that have implemented funding formulas on the basis of adequacy studies, Wyoming and Arkansas, are instructive of possible future trends in school finance.

Wyoming

Wyoming has perhaps more experience than any other state in designing and implementing school funding systems based on adequacy studies. Beginning in 1996 with a court ruling (*Campbell County v. Wyoming*) that required the state to define a proper education and fund the cost of that education, Wyoming has worked to estimate the costs of an adequate education and distribute funds to districts in a manner that will allow children to succeed.

Through two iterations five years apart, Wyoming policy makers used a professional judgment method to ascertain the level of resources needed to meet the standard established by the court (see Guthrie & Rothstein, 1999; and Guthrie et. al. 1997). In 2006, the state conducted an evidence-based assessment of school finance adequacy (Odden, Picus, et. al. 2005). Following the implementation of the latest study's recommendations, Wyoming school funding was among the highest of the 50 states. While significant gains in student performance appear to have been achieved when measured through the state's assessment system, results from the National Assessment of Educational Progress (NAEP), while improving, paint a less optimistic picture.

In response to growing school funding appropriations, the Wyoming Legislature has undertaken a two-year study of school district resource use. The state has asked its consultants to asses the instructional vision or goals of every school in the state and to compare how each school and school district use the resources allocated to them through the new funding model in relation to the way those funds were estimated. By visiting most of the schools in Wyoming, researchers hope to determine how schools are directing their resources to help students learn and to estimate how those decisions relate to the resource allocation components of the funding model. The results of this work will help policy makers better understand how dollars are actually used in schools to produce student learning. With this knowledge it may be possible to better fashion school finance formulas that offer local districts the flexibility to meet the needs of individual students, while at the same time holding school districts accountable for overall performance with resource use benchmarks to guide assessment of district success.

Arkansas

In response to court rulings in Arkansas, that state's legislature undertook an extensive evidence-based adequacy study in 2003 and updated that analysis in 2006 (Odden, Picus & Fermanich, 2003; Odden, Picus & Goetz, 2006). Following completion of the 2003 study, a special session of the Arkansas Legislature took the school-based funding estimates developed by Odden, Picus and Fermanich and converted that figure to a single per pupil figure, which was then appropriated and distributed to each school district in the state.

In 2006, Odden, Picus, and Goetz recalibrated the adequacy study and as part of that work visited a total of 107 schools across the state to ascertain how schools and school districts were using all of their revenues in relation to the adequacy model design. The researchers found that for the most part, schools were not implementing policies that would allocate resources as designed through the adequacy model, suggesting that a more focused set of expectations on the part of the legislature for the use of all school funds (new and existing resources) might be appropriate.

Other States

Research recently completed in Washington (Fermanich, Turner-Mangan, Odden, Picus, Gross & Rudo, 2006) supports this recommendation for a more focused set of expectations. Fermanich et al. conducted a successful schools analysis in the state of Washington as part of a comprehensive adequacy study done for Washington Learns, a legislatively established 18 month comprehensive study of pre-school through university education in Washington. Through that analysis, they identified nine successful school districts and 31 schools in those districts that showed dramatic improvement in student performance in recent years. Site visits to the districts and schools sought to understand the instructional goals and resource use decisions of each school. While local decisions varied to some extent, they were all highly correlated with the recommendations of the evidence base adequacy study that was also conducted for Washington Learns (Odden, Picus, et al., 2006).

Similarly, a set of four adequacy studies were conducted in New York in response to that state's court proceedings declaring funding for schools in New York City to be inadequate. While the recommendations from those studies ranged from $4.5 to 9.6 billion, New York's highest court recently ruled that the Legislature needs to appropriate an additional $1.93 billion to fully fund the New York City schools. The New York Court's ruling comes after 13 years of court action and many studies. It leaves the legislature with relatively little guidance beyond a minimum level of adequate funding for schools in New York City. The Legislature is still faced with finding the tax resources to meet this need, finding a way to distribute it to New York City and possibly other districts with similar needs, and continuing action on the part of stakeholders regarding what an adequate level of funding really might be. One problem may be that other than the expectation that the legislature must fund an adequate education for all children in New York City—and by extension one would assume all of the children in the state—members of the legislature have not been particularly involved in determining what constitutes adequacy. In both Wyoming and Arkansas, the final funding recommendations were developed in consultation with legislative committees, making acceptance of those funding levels by the full legislature a more straightforward task.

In summary, the experience of states faced with establishing school funding systems based on adequacy has been one of finding the additional funding called for by the adequacy studies that were conducted and then hoping that schools and school districts would use those funds in ways that improved student performance. Early models provided considerable local leeway to schools in how they used their educational resources, although recent findings in states with the most experience in school finance funding formulas based on adequacy studies suggests that a more categorical or directive approach to how money is used might receive more consideration from state policy-making bodies, particularly state legislatures, in the future.

CONCLUSIONS

This chapter has focused on the use of intergovernmental aid formulas in school finance. We traced the evolution of school funding formulas in the second half of the 20th century and the early years of the 21st century and showed how they have evolved from basic foundation programs to improve school funding equity through attempts to improve educational efficiency or productivity to today's adequacy movement and its attempt to define what resources are needed to ensure all students perform at high levels.

In many ways, the evolution of school funding formulas has been "circular." That is, if states can design funding formulas that provide each student with the resources they need to meet state performance expectations, the goals of horizontal and vertical equity will be met as well. Moreover, under an adequacy-based funding system, it seems possible to achieve the goals of fiscal neutrality as well. Adequacy raises the question of whether all the goals established for school finance formulas—equity, efficiency, productivity, and adequacy—can be met through a singular formula. And if formulas can be constructed to meet all of those goals, are they affordable by most states? If this turns out to be beyond the fiscal capacity of many states, what is the solution? Is there a federal role in assuring adequate educational resources are available for all children? And what are the implications of No Child Left Behind's achievement expectations for children?

As the courts, state policy makers, and education officials strive to improve student learning, developing a better understanding of how educational resources are translated into student learning is critical. We think that developing this understanding will require extensive and hard work in multiple schools across multiple districts and states to fully understand how resources matter over time. Operationalizing that understanding into school funding formulas will remain a challenge for the immediate future.

APPENDIX
Operation of State Aid Formulas

This appendix provides more detail on the operation of state aid formulas. It begins with the foundation program, continues with guaranteed tax base programs and finally offers a comparison of guaranteed tax base formulas with district power equalizing.

Foundation Program

A foundation program can be represented as follows:

$$SA_i = E^* - t_{min}(TB_i) \quad (1)$$

Where:

SA_i is the state aid per pupil in the *i*th district
E^* is the state-determined foundation level of education spending
t_{min} is the state-determined minimum tax rate that each district is required to levy
TB_i is the property tax base or wealth per pupil in the *i*th district

For example, if the state foundation guarantee (E*) were $2,000 per pupil and the minimum tax rate were 20 mills or two percent of property value, table 15A-1 summarizes state aid per pupil to each district (SA_i):

TABLE 15A.1
Foundation Program Computation Examples

District	*TB_i ($)*	*Local Revenue Per Pupil ($)*	*SA_i ($)*
A	50,000	1,000	1,000
B	100,000	2,000	0
C	500,000	10,000	(8,000)

In this example, District B is what is frequently called the zero aid district, that is it raises exactly the amount of revenue guaranteed by the foundation program and thus receives no state aid. This is an important concept as all districts with property wealth per pupil below the wealth of the zero aid district will receive some state aid, while all those with property wealth above the wealth of the zero aid district will not receive state aid through the foundation program.

A second issue identified in this table is how districts with wealth above the zero aid district should be handled. In the example above, District C raises $8,000 more than the foundation guarantee. The policy question facing the state is whether to recapture some or all of that revenue to distribute to other districts, or to let District C keep all of the additional revenue it collects at the state mandated tax rate.

Finally, state policy must determine whether or not school districts can exceed the minimum tax rate to increase spending, and if so whether or not those tax rate decisions will be equalized.

Guaranteed Tax Base

A guaranteed tax base is designed to assure that any district regardless of wealth will have as much revenue per pupil as the district with the guaranteed tax base, at any given tax rate. The formula for a GTB can be represented as:

$$SA_i = t_i(GTB\text{-}TB_i) \qquad (2)$$

Thus the total revenue for any school district is the sum of locally generated revenue plus its state aid as follows:

$$t_i(TBi) + t_i(GTB\text{-}TBi) = t_i(GTB) \qquad (3)$$

Unlike a foundation program where the amount of aid a district receives is fixed based on the state's policy decisions (foundation level and minimum tax rate), under a GTB a district can spend any level it chooses depending on the tax rate it establishes.

The GTB is the equivalent of the zero aid district identified in the foundation program above. That is the district with a wealth equal to the GTB receives no state aid, and for districts with property wealth above the GTB, the same questions about recapture that were identified in the foundation program description must be considered.

For those districts with wealth below the GTB, this program is effectively a matching program. If one represents total spending in the *i*th district as E_i, and assuming a district spends all its revenue, then:

$$E_i = t_i(GTB) \qquad (4)$$

and

$$t_i = E_i/GTB \qquad (5)$$

Substituting (5) into (4), we find:

$$SA_i = (1\text{-}TB_i/GTB)E_i \qquad (6)$$

On the surface, this would appear to give all districts the same tax base (at least those with wealth up to and including` the GTB). As Feldstein (1975) showed, that will not lead to the same level of spending in all districts due to a price effect (i.e. the variation in the "cost" to local taxpayers of providing one more dollar of spending to education will vary depending on property wealth of the district). However, as described above, the result of this price effect is not completely predictable. While we would expect low-wealth districts to increase their tax rates substantially because the state share of each dollar raised is high, in a number of states (Wisconsin and Missouri for example) we have found that it is the high-wealth districts that raise taxes to remain high spending while the low-wealth districts elect to reduce taxes and remain relatively low spending.

District Power Equalizing

Mathematically equivalent to the GTB is a formula generally known as District Power Equalizing or DPE. Under DPE, the state determines the level of subsidy or state aid to provide to the average wealth district rather than focusing on the tax capacity of school districts. A DPE formula can be expressed as:

$$SA_i = (1\text{- }P(TB_i/TB_{mean}))E_i \qquad (7)$$

Where

TB_{mean} is the average tax base or property wealth per pupil, and
P is a fraction between zero and one and represents the percentage of state funding for the average wealth district

If P = 1 and GTB = TB_{mean} then the DPE formula is equivalent to the GTB formula as expressed in equation (6).

NOTES

1. See Odden & Picus (2008) for more detailed descriptions of how all these formulas work.
2. The equations presented here are taken directly from Odden & Picus, 2008. Readers are referred to the appendix of this chapter for a more detailed discussion of the operation of state aid formulas.
3. The categorical program for free and reduced price lunch was actually more complex. The $480 per free and reduced price eligible pupil was for all schools with less than 70 percent of their enrollment qualifying for free and reduced price lunches. For schools with between 70 and 90 percent eligible students, the categorical grant was $960 per eligible student and for schools with over 90 percent free and reduced price lunch students, the categorical was $1,440 per eligible student.
4. Special education programs for children with mild and moderate disabilities were resourced trough local school sites, while services for children with severe disabilities were funded 100 percent by the state. In the actual funding model, all resources were converted into a per pupil foundation level and in the case of special education, three teacher positions were added to the number of teachers generated at a school of 500 students and funded at the state-wide average total compensation. These three teacher positions are included in the $5,400 per student foundation level.
5. In California school districts are divided into small and large districts in three categories: elementary, high school and unified for a total of six types of district. The $300 band referred to in the text is estimated for each of the six types of districts.
6. There are a small number of districts that raise more through property taxes than provided for through the revenue limit. For the most part they are allowed to keep these additional revenues. For some districts this represents a very small amount of money, but for a number of these so called "basic aid" districts, it is as much as 25 percent of their general fund budget.
7. See the Appendix A.1 for a more detailed description of these formulas.

REFERENCES

Adams, E. K. and Odden, A. (1981). "Alternative Wealth Measures." In K. Forbis Jordan & Nelda H. Cambron-McCabe (Eds.), *Perspectives in State School Support Programs* (pp. 143–165). Cambridge, MA: Ballinger.

Berne, R. and Stiefel., L. (1984). *The Measurement of Equity in School Finance*. Baltimore: Johns Hopkins University Press.

Berne, R. and Stiefel, L. (1999). Concepts of School Finance Equity: 1970 to Present. In Helen Ladd, Rosemary Chalk & Janet Hansen (Eds.), *Equity and Adequacy in Education Finance: Issues and Perspectives*. Washington, D.C.: National Academy Press.

Brown, L. L. et al. (1977). *School Finance Reform in the Seventies: Achievements and Failures*. Washington, D.C.: U.S. Department of Health, Education and Welfare, Office of the Assistant Secretary for Planning and Evaluation and Killalea Associates, Inc.

Campbell County School District v. State, 907 P2d 1238 (Wyo. 1995)

Chambers, J.G. (1995). Public School Teacher Cost Differences Across the United States: Introduction to a

Teacher Cost Index (TCI). In *Developments in School Finance*. Available at http://www.ed.gov/NCES/pubs/96344cha.html.

Coons, J. Clune, W. and Sugarman, S. (1970). *Private Wealth and Public Education*. Cambridge, MA: Belknap Press of Harvard University Press.

Evans, W. Murray, S. and Schwab, R. (1997). *State Education Finance Policy After Court Mandated Reform: The Legacy of Serrano.* 1996 Proceedings of the Eighty-Ninth Annual Conference on Taxation. Washington, D.C.: National Tax Association-Tax Institute of America.

Feldstein, M. (1975). Wealth Neutrality and Local Choice in Public Education. *American Economic Review, 64*, 75–89.

Fermanich, M., Turner-Mangan, M., Odden, A., Picus, L.O., Gross, B., and Rudo, Z. (2006). *Washington Learns: Successful District Study Final Report.* Prepared for the Washington Learns K-12 Advisory Committee, Olympia, WA. September. Available at http://www.washingtonlearns.wa.gov/materials/SuccessfulDistReport9-11-06Final_000.pdf

Fischel, W. (2006). "Why Voters Veto Vouchers: Public Schools and Community-Specific Social Capital," *Economics of Governance 7*, 109–132.

Fischel, W. (2002). "School Finance Litigation and Property Tax Revolts: How Undermining Local Control Turns Voters Away from Public Education." In William J. Fowler, Jr., editor, *Developments in School Finance, 1999–2000,* NCES 2002-316 (pp. 79–127). Washington, DC: U.S. Department of Education, National Center for Education Statistics.

Goertz, M. E. and Edwards, M. (1999). In search of excellence for all: The courts and New Jersey school finance reform. *Journal of Education Finance, 25*(1), 5–32.

Goertz, M. E. and Weiss, M. (2007). Money order in the Court: The promise and pitfalls of redistributing educational dollars through court mandates: The case of New Jersey. Paper presented at the annual meeting of the American Education Finance Association, Baltimore, MD.

Gold, S.D, Smith, D.M. and Lawton, S.B. (1995). *Public School Finance Programs of the United States and Canada: 1993–94.* New York: American Education Finance Association of Center for the Study of the States, The Nelson A. Rockefeller Institute of Government.

Greenwald, R., Hedges, L.V. and Laine, R.D. (1996b). Interpreting Research on School Resources and Student Achievement: A Rejoinder to Hanushek. *Review of Educational Research 66*(3), 411–416.

Greenwald, R., Hedges, L.V. and Laine, R.D. (1996a). The Effect of School Resources on Student Achievement. *Review of Educational Research 66*(3), 361–396.

Guthrie, J.W. and Rothstein, R. (1999). Enabling 'Adequacy' to Achieve Reality: Translating Adequacy into State School Finance Distribution Arrangements. In Helen Ladd, Rosemary Chalk & Janet Hansen (Eds.), *Equity and Adequacy in Education Finance: Issues and Perspectives* (pp. 209–259). Washington, D.C.: National Academy Press.

Guthrie, James, et al. (1997). *A Proposed Cost-Based Block Grant Model for Wyoming School Finance.* Davis, CA: Management Analysis and Planning Associates, LLC. Available at http://legisweb.state.wy.us/school/cost/apr7/apr7.htm, accessed June 30, 2007.

Hanushek, E.A. (1981). Throwing Money at Schools. *Journal of Policy Analysis and Management 1*(1), 19–41.

Hanushek, E.A. (1986). The Economics of Schooling: Production and Efficiency in Public Schools. *Journal of Economic Literature 24*(3), 1141–1177.

Hanushek, E.A. (1989). The Impact of Differential Expenditures on Student Performance. *Educational Researcher, 18*(4), 45–52.

Hanushek, E.A. (1994). Money Might Matter Somewhere: A Response to Hedges, Laine, and Greenwald. *Educational Researcher, 23*(3), 5–8.

Hanushek, E.A. (1997). Assessing the Effects of School Resources on Student Performance: An Update. *Educational Evaluation and Policy Analysis, 19*(2), 141–164.

Hanushek, E.A. (2002). Evidence, Politics and the Class Size Debate. In Lawrence Mishel & Richard Rothstein (Eds.), *The Class Size Debate* (pp. 37–65). Washington, DC: Economic Policy Institute.

Hedges, L.V., Laine, R.D. and Greenwald, R. (1994a). Does Money Matter? A Meta-Analysis of Studies of the Effects of Differential School Inputs on Student Outcomes. *Educational Researcher, 23*(3), 5–14.

Hedges, L.V., Laine, R.D. and Greenwald, R. (1994b). Money Does Matter Somewhere: A Reply to Hanushek. *Educational Researcher, 23*(3), 9–10.

Hoxby, C. M., (2002). "How School Choice Affects the Achievement of *Public* School Students." In Paul Hill (Ed.), *Choice with Equity*. Stanford, CA: Hoover Press.

Hoxby, C. M. (2001) "Rising Tide: New Evidence on Competition and the Public Schools," *Education Next, 1*(4).

Ladd, H. (1975). Local Education Expenditures, Fiscal Capacity and the Composition of the Property Tax Base. *National Tax Journal, 28*(2), 145–158.

Laine, R.D., Greenwald, R., and Hedges, L.V. (1996). Money Does Matter: A Research Synthesis of a New Universe of Education Production Function Studies. In Lawrence O. Picus & James L. Wattenbarger (Eds.), *Where Does the Money Go?: Resource Allocation in Elementary and Secondary Schools* (pp. 44–70), Thousand Oaks, CA: Corwin Press.

McMahon, W.W. (1994). Intrastate Cost Adjustment. In *Selected Papers in School Finance*. Available at http://www.ed.gov/NCES/pubs/96068ica.

McUsic, M. (1991). The Use of Education Clauses in School Finance Reform Litigation. Harvard *Journal on Legislation 28*(2), 307–340.

Monk, D.H. and Brent, B.O. (1997). *Raising Money for Schools: A Guide to the Property Tax.* Thousand Oaks, CA: Corwin Press.

Murray, S., Evans, W., and Schwab, R. (1998). Education Finance Reform and the Distribution of Education Resources. *American Economic Review, 88*(4), 789–812.

National Education Association. (2006). *Rankings and Estimates.* Washington, DC: The National Education Association, November.

Nelson, F. H., Rosenberg, B., and Van Meter, N. (2004). Charter School Achievement on the 2003 National Assessment of Educational Progress. Washington, DC: American Federation of Teachers. (August). Available at http://www.aft.org/pubs-reports/downloads/teachers/NAEPCharterSchoolReport.pdf, accessed June 30, 2007.

Odden, A. and Augenblick, J. (1981). *School Finance Reform in the States: 1981.* Denver: Education Commission of the States.

Odden, A. and Wallace, M. (2007). *How to Create World Class Teacher Compensation* St. Paul: Freeload Press. Available at: http://www.freeloadpress.com/bookDetail.aspx?bld=1077.

Odden, A. and Busch, C. (1998). *Financing Schools for High Performance: Strategies for Improving the Use of Educational Resources.* San Francisco: Jossey-Bass.

Odden, A., Berne, R., and Stiefel, L. (1979). *Equity in School Finance.* Denver: Education Commission of the States.

Odden, A., Goetz, M., and Picus, L.O. (2007). *How Close is the National Average Expenditure Per Pupil to Providing Adequate School Financing?* Seattle: University of Washington, Evans School of Public Affairs, School Finance Redesign Project.

Odden, A., Goetz, M., and Picus, L.O. (2007). *Paying for School Finance Adequacy with the National Average expenditure Per Pupil.* Working Paper 2. Seattle, WA: University of Washington, Evans School of Public Affairs, Center on Reinventing Public Education, School Finance Redesign Project.

Odden, A., Picus, L., Goetz, M., Turner Mangan, M., and Fermanich, M. (2006). *An Evidence Based Approach to School Finance Adequacy in Washington.* Prepared for the Washington Learns K-12 Advisory Committee, Olympia, WA. September. Available at: http://www.washingtonlearns.wa.gov/materials/EvidenceBasedReportFinal9-11-06_000.pdf, accessed July 12, 2007.

Odden, A., Picus, L.O., and Fermanich, M. (2003). *An Evidenced-Based Approach to School Finance Adequacy in Arkansas.* Submitted to the Joint Committee on Educational Adequacy of the Arkansas Legislature, Little Rock, AR.

Odden, A., Fermanich, M., and Picus, L.O. (2003). *A State-of-the-Art Approach to School Finance Adequacy in Kentucky.* Submitted to the Kentucky Department of Education, Frankfort, KY.

Odden, A.O., Picus, L.O., et. al. (2005). *An Evidence Based Approach to Recalibrating the Wyoming Block Grant School Funding Formula.* State of Wyoming, Legislative Service Office. Available at http://legisweb.state.wy.us/2005/interim/schoolfinance/Recalibration, accessed July 7, 2007.

Odden, A.O., Picus, L.O., and Goetz, M. (2006). *Recalibrating the Arkansas School Funding Structure: Final Report submitted to the Adequacy Study Oversight Sub-Committee of the House and Senate Interim Committees on Education of the Arkansas General Assembly.* North Hollywood, CA: Lawrence O. Picus and Associates.

Odden, Allan R., Picus, Lawrence O., Archibald, Sarah, Goetz, Michael, Mangan, Michelle Turner, and Aportela, Anabel. (2007). *Moving from Good to Great in Wisconsin: Funding Schools Adequately and Doubling Student Performance.* Madison, WI: University of Wisconsin, Wisconsin Center for Education Research, Consortium for Policy Research in Education.

Odden, A.R. and Picus, L.O. (2008). *School Finance: A Policy Perspective* (4th ed.). New York: McGraw Hill.

Picus, L.O. (2000). *Evaluation of Louisiana's School Finance System.* Prepared for the Louisiana School Finance Commission, Baton Rouge, LA.

Picus, L.O. (2001). Ten Year Equity Analysis of the Kansas School District Finance and Quality Performance Act. Prepared for the State of Kansas.

Picus, L.O. (2003). Trial testimony presented in *Hancock, v. Driscoll* (November 18, 2003).

Picus, L.O. (2004). Trial testimony presented in *Columbia Falls v. Montana* (January 22, 2004).

Picus, L.O. and Hertert, L. (1993). "Three Strikes and You're Out: Texas School Finance After Edgewood III." *Journal of Education Finance,* 18(4).

Picus, L.O., Odden, A., and Fermanich, M. (2004). Assessing the Equity of Kentucky's SEEK Formula: A 10-Year Analysis. *Journal of Education Finance, 29*(4), Spring 2004. 315–336.

Schwartz, M. and Moskowitz, J. (1988). *Fiscal Equity in the United States: 1984–85.* Washington, DC: Decision Resources Corporation.

Sherman, Joel. (1992). Review of School Finance Equalization Under Section 5(d) of P.L. 81-874, The Impact Aid Program. *Journal of Education Finance, 18*(1).

State v. Campbell County School District, 19 P.3d 518 (Wyo. 2001).

Stiefel, L. and Berne, R. (1981). "The Equity Effects of State School Finance Reforms: A Methodological Critique and New Evidence," *Policy Sciences, 13*(1), 75–98.

U.S. Department of Education, National Center for Education Statistics. (2006). *The Condition of Education 2006* (NCES 2006-071). Washington, DC: U.S. Government Printing Office.

Underwood, Julie. (1995). School Finance Litigation: Legal Theories, Judicial Activism, and Social Neglect. *Journal of Education Finance 20*(2), 143–162.

Verstegen, D. (1996). Concepts and Measures of Fiscal Inequality: A New Approach and Effects for Five States. *Journal of Education Finance, 22*(2), 145–160.

Verstegen, D. (2003) *Calculation of the Cost of an Adequate Education in Kentucky.* Prepared for the Council for Better Education, Inc., Frankfort Kentucky.

Yinger, J. (2002). *Helping Children Left Behind: State Aid and the Pursuit of Educational Equity.* Unpublished manuscript.

16

Education Equity in an International Context

Edward B. Fiske and Helen F. Ladd

INTRODUCTION

All countries face issues of educational equity. Depending on the country, the policy debate may focus on how to increase access to primary or secondary schools, how to reduce persistent achievement gaps between students of different genders, ethnic backgrounds or income levels, or how to reduce educational resource disparities between rural and urban areas of the country. Though all such issues are of interest to policy makers and researchers, we focus in this chapter on those areas of educational policy and research that are at the heart of the most widespread efforts at the international level to promote equity in education, particularly in developing countries.

Specifically, we begin with the international Education for All (EFA) movement. The main goal of EFA is to promote access to quality education for all students around the world. We then turn to two specific topics: efforts to promote gender equity by expanding educational opportunities for girls and efforts to promote fiscal equity by eliminating school fees. A leit-motif that runs through all three sections is the tradeoff that policy makers frequently confront between the competing values of greater access and enhanced quality.

EDUCATION FOR ALL

Although the international community has no formal constitution to serve as the basis for promoting educational equity across countries, a global consensus has emerged around a number of goals aimed at assuring that each country provides all of its children with a quality basic education. The most notable expression of this consensus has been the Education for All movement that grew out of the World Conference on Education for All in Jomtien, Thailand, in 1990.

Genesis of EFA

The idea of holding such a conference was first proposed in 1989 by James Grant, the administrator of the United Nations Children's Fund (UNICEF), who saw it as an opportunity to renew a worldwide commitment to meeting the learning needs of children, youth, and adults. He enlisted the support of the United Nations Educational Scientific and Cultural Organization (UNESCO) and the Educational and United Nations Development Program (UNDP). These three agencies then approached the World Bank, which agreed to establish an Inter-Agency Commission (IAC) with an Executive Committee and a small Executive Secretariat, located at UNICEF in New York, to prepare and organize the conference in Jomtien. The conference drew support from educators, policy makers, academics, and others from the United States and elsewhere who were concerned about inadequate provision of basic education in developing countries. Of particular concern was that more than 100 million children, at least 60 million of them girls, lacked access to primary schooling.

The IAC consulted with governments, major non-governmental organizations, and others, and prior to the conference it organized a series of nine regional consultations. Delegates from 155 member states of the U.N. and more than 150 organizations attended the conference and adopted a World Declaration on Education for All (henceforth the Jomtien Declaration) in which they pledged "to act cooperatively through our own spheres of responsibility, taking all necessary steps to achieve the goals of education for all." They also agreed on a Framework for Action that laid out strategies by which national governments, international organizations, bilateral aid agencies, non-governmental organizations and others could pursue these objectives (UNESCO, 1990).

The Jomtien Declaration was reaffirmed and updated a decade later, in 2000, by participants from 164 countries at the World Education Forum in Dakar, Senegal. They adopted a Dakar Framework for Action (henceforth the Dakar Framework) that laid out six specific goals for EFA, three of which set target dates (see box) (UNESCO, 2000a). The coordinating agency for the global effort to implement Education for All is the United Nations Economic, Social and Cultural Organization (UNESCO).

Much of the impetus behind the EFA movement grew out of a recognition that the prevailing model of piecemeal, donor-driven projects to improve education in developing countries had been unsuccessful (Schubert and Prouty-Harris, 2003). Such projects, typically, were too narrow in scope, did little to build local capacity to sustain educational improvements, and were designed

DAKAR GOALS (2000)

1. Expanding and improving comprehensive early childhood care and education, especially for the most vulnerable and disadvantaged children.
2. Ensuring that by 2015 all children, particularly girls, children in difficult circumstances, and those belonging to ethnic minorities, have access to and complete free and compulsory primary education of good quality.
3. Ensuring that the learning needs of all young people and adults are met through equitable access to appropriate learning and life-skills programs.
4. Achieving a 50 percent improvement in levels of adult literacy by 2015, especially for women, and equitable access to basic and continuing education for all adults.
5. Eliminating gender disparities in primary and secondary education by 2005, and achieving gender equality in education by 2015, with a focus on ensuring girls' full and equal access to and achievement in basic education of good quality.
6. Improving all aspects of the quality of education and ensuring excellence of all so that recognized and measurable learning outcomes are achieved by all, especially in literacy, numeracy and essential life skills.

with the priorities of donors rather than recipients in mind. A further spur to coordinated global action was the decline in both enrollments and the quality of education in Sub-Saharan Africa as documented in a 1988 World Bank assessment of the state of education in the region (World Bank, 1988).

The Conceptual Basis of Education Equity in EFA

The conceptual starting point for the cooperative international effort to promote educational equity in developing countries rests on three pillars: human rights, economic development, and poverty alleviation. The Universal Declaration of Human Rights, adopted by the United Nations in 1948, asserted that "everyone has a right to education." This principle has been reiterated in numerous subsequent international documents, including the 1979 Convention on the Elimination of All Forms of Discrimination Against Women and the 1989 Convention on the Rights of the Child.[1] The Jomtien Declaration begins by affirming that "every person—child, youth and adult—shall be able to benefit from educational opportunities designed to meet their basic learning needs."

The payoff in terms of the economic development that ensues from investing in basic education in developing countries has been widely documented (Psacharopoulos and Patrinos, 2002).[2] As we discuss in the next section, investments in the education of girls have been shown to be particularly effective in developing countries. Finally, investment in basic education is widely viewed as an essential tool in efforts to alleviate poverty. As part of its global anti-poverty strategy, the United Nations General Assembly in 2001 adopted a set of five Millennium Development Goals. Two of them—achieving universal primary education by 2015 and eliminating gender disparities in primary and secondary education by the same year—were education-specific and overlapped with the Dakar Goals (UNESCO, 2005, p. 28). UNESCO literature cites additional reasons for the international community's stake in educational equity, including global political and economic stability (UNESCO, 1997).

Defining EFA: Access Plus Quality

From the outset, proponents of EFA rejected a narrow conception of "basic education," such as the completion of a certain number of years of schooling, and opted instead for an inclusive definition. The Jomtien Declaration characterizes the content of basic education as the knowledge and skills "required by human beings to be able to survive, to develop their full capacities, to live and work in dignity, to participate fully in development, to improve the quality of their lives, to make informed decisions, and to continue learning." It adds that the scope of basic learning needs and how they should be met varies across countries and cultures and changes over time. (UNESCO, 1990). The expanded list of six goals adopted at Dakar was described as embracing "a holistic conception of educational development" (UNESCO, 2005, p. 28).

Jomtien inspired at least three major projects aimed at improving the quality of education in developing countries. In 1991, the United States Agency for International Development launched a decade-long Improving Educational Quality Project in 17 countries. The following year UNESCO and UNICEF initiated the Monitoring Learning Achievement project to track learning achievement around the world at the fourth grade level (UNESCO, 2000a). At the behest of the ministries of education of several Southern African countries, the Southern and Eastern Africa Consortium for Monitoring Educational Quality (SACMEQ) was created in 1995 both to monitor progress towards EFA quality goals and to develop local capacity to measure student achievement. (SACMEQ, 1993).

Despite such programs aimed at enhancing educational quality, most EFA efforts in the early 1990s focused on the narrower goal of expanding access to formal primary education, with progress measured in quantitative terms by trends in school attendance and rates of persistence. Little and Miller (2000) argue that the World Bank, UNICEF, and others saw this focus on access as a matter of technical and political convenience. Some critics viewed this initial emphasis on access as a retreat from the richness of the vision of Jomtien. They argued that getting students into schools was only part of the struggle for educational equity; equally important was the quality of instruction that they received once they were there (Delors et al., 1996). Concerns of this nature were expressed at the 1996 Amman Forum on EFA, called to offer a five-year review of progress since Jomtien, and by the mid-1990s the EFA movement was actively seeking a balance of access and quality (UNESCO, 1996). Some observers, however, believed the focus on access was appropriate. Carnoy (2004) argues, for example, that "some countries have such low levels of education … that simply increasing the average number of years of education attained may still be the most efficient strategy to follow."

The current renewed emphasis on quality is attributable in part to the relative success of efforts to expand primary enrollments. According to the 2005 Global Monitoring Report, for example, by 2001 net primary enrollment rates (see definition below) had increased in nearly every country whose enrollment rates at the beginning of the 1990s had been below 70 percent (UNESCO, 2004). Such successes, however, came with a price in the form of trade-offs between access and quality. In some countries and regions, particularly Sub-Saharan Africa, the rise in enrollments strained resources and resulted in substantially higher pupil-teacher ratios (UNESCO, 2004). Findings from the first stage of the MLA Project contributed to this growing concern with quality (Chinapah, 1997), and researchers found low levels of education and training among primary school teachers in Sub-Saharan Africa (Schleicher, Siniscalco and Postlethwaite, 1995). In 2000, the expanded commentary on the Dakar Framework cited "a lack of attention to the quality of learning" as one of several reasons for the failure to achieve the vision of EFA established at Jomtein (UNESCO, 2000a). Nonetheless, it is noteworthy that the two Millennium Development Goals relating to education—universal education and eliminating gender disparities—stress access rather than quality.

The 2006 EFA Global Monitoring Report also notes that since 2000 most attention has focused on the three of the six Dakar goals that are directly related to formal elementary education systems (universal primary education, gender parity and quality of education) while the other three (early childhood care and education, the learning needs of young people and adults, and adult literacy) have been "relatively neglected." The report points out that achieving the latter three goals typically requires the creation of new programs and that in most countries responsibility for such programs "does not fall neatly under the mandate of the Ministry of Education but rather is spread among several ministries" (p. 28). It also notes that governments tend to think of investments in young children as producing the greatest educational and political returns.

Measuring Progress toward EFA

One reason that access received particular emphasis in the early 1990s was that it was easier to measure than quality. Even today international organizations are struggling to develop quantitative measures of educational quality.

Measures of Access. The Framework for Action that emerged from Jomtien included a target of "universal access to, and completion of, primary education (or whatever higher level of education is considered 'basic') by the year 2000" (UNESCO, 1990). This goal of universal primary education (UPE) is typically measured by enrollment as captured by two ratios: gross enrollment ratio (GER) and net enrollment ratio (NER). Where they refer exclusively to primary education, the ratios are referred to as gross and net primary enrollment ratios—GPER and NPER. The GER is the ratio of the number of children enrolled at the primary or secondary school level, regardless of their age, to the number of children "officially corresponding to that level" (UNESCO, 2005). This ratio, expressed as a percent, can exceed 100 if there is early or delayed enrollment or grade repetition in an educational system. The NER reflects the percentage of age-appropriate children in the population who are enrolled in either primary or secondary school. A NER of 100 percent means that all eligible children are enrolled in school. UNESCO has also measured access through the survival rate to grade 5. A combination of a high NPER and high survival rate to grade 5 implies a high rate of primary school completion (Hewett and Lloyd, 2005).

Problems associated with these measures include the fact that NPERs are not entirely comparable across countries due to variation in length of their primary school cycles (5 to 7 years) as defined by UNESCO. Countries with longer cycles may have more difficulty reaching high NPERs. Questions have also been raised about the quality of the data from which the measures are calculated because of poor information systems in some countries and financial incentives for schools to inflate enrollment estimates (Hewett and Lloyd, 2005).

Measures of Quality. Compared to access, educational quality is far harder to define and measure. The prevailing understanding of quality education reflected in UNESCO documents derives from the Convention on the Rights of the Child (CRC) adopted by the General Assembly of the United Nations in 1989, Article 29 of which defines five proper aims of education. In brief, these are "the development of the child's personality, talents, and mental and physical abilities," "the development of respect for human rights and fundamental freedoms," "the development of respect for the child's parents" and her own and others' cultures, "the preparation of the child for responsible life in a free society," and "the development of respect for the natural environment" (United Nations, 1989). None of these is easy to quantify.

The Framework for Action that accompanied the Jomtien Declaration tried to address the quality issue by specifying a target of "improvement in learning achievement such that an agreed percentage of an appropriate age cohort (e.g., 80 percent of 14 year-olds) attains or surpasses a defined level of necessary learning achievement" (UNESCO, 1990). That approach, however, turned out to be unworkable. At the time of the EFA evaluation in preparation for the conference at Dakar, very few countries had set an achievement target, let alone met one, despite efforts to increase the capacity of developing countries to assess student achievement (UNESCO, 2000a). Thus, it was not until Dakar that UNESCO developed a working definition of quality by which countries' progress could be measured. The expanded commentary on Goal 6 of the Dakar Framework relating to quality education lists eight requirements of successful education programs, including well-trained teachers, active learning techniques, participatory governance and management and a "relevant curriculum that can be taught and learned in a local language." The Framework also laid out a specific target related to quality: "Improving every aspect of the quality of education and ensuring their excellence so that recognized and measurable learning outcomes are achieved by all, especially in literacy, numeracy, and essential life skills" (p. 17).

Despite the above reference to "recognized and measurable learning outcomes," it is significant that most of the measures used to define quality focus on inputs such as qualified teachers rather than on learning outcomes. One of the difficulties is that many developing countries do not participate in international tests such as TIMSS or PISA.[3] Efforts to refine the definitions and means of measuring quality education at the basic level are continuing. The 2005 Global

Monitoring Report, subtitled "The Quality Imperative," uses widely available input measures of educational quality and, to the extent possible, internationally comparable assessments of cognitive ability to assess of the state of school quality in developing countries (UNESCO, 2004).[4]

Progress in Access and Quality

In adopting the Dakar Framework for Action, the World Education Forum agreed to report progress toward the six goals. To facilitate such reporting, UNESCO in the 2003/4 Global Monitoring Report introduced the Education for All Development Index (EDI), a composite measure of a country's progress toward providing a basic, quality education to all its citizens. The EDI focused on four of the six goals: universal primary education, adult literacy, gender parity, and the quality of education. It excluded Goal 1 (early childhood care and education) on the grounds that reliable and comparable data are not available for most countries and Goal 3 (learning needs of youth and adults) because this objective "has not yet been sufficiently defined for quantitative measurement" (UNESCO, 2005, p. 252).

Proxies were chosen for each of the four goals that make up the EDI. Universal primary education (Goal 2) is measured by the primary net enrollment rate and adult literacy (Goal 4) by the literacy rate among individuals 15 and older. The proxy for gender parity (Goal 5) is a composite Gender Parity Index based on the arithmetical mean of primary and secondary gross enrollment ratios for boys and girls and the adult literacy rates for women and men. In the absence of data on learning outcomes that would be comparable across countries, the proxy for quality of education (Goal 6) is the proportion of students surviving to primary grade 5. For purposes of compiling an overall EDI score, each of the four goals was given equal weight. The index runs from 0 to 1, with countries having an index score of 0.95 judged to have achieved EFA or being close to doing so.

The 2006 Global Monitoring Report includes EDI scores in 2002 for the 122 countries for which data were available on all four of the component measures (Table A1.1, pp. 256–257). Of these, 45 countries were found to have reached the 0.95 threshold, 49 countries had EDI values between 0.80 and 0.94, and 28 countries had values below 0.80, which meant that "achieving EFA would require intervention throughout the school system." More than half of these low-performing countries are in Sub-Saharan Africa.

Between 1998 and 2002, the overall EDI index increased by 1.2 percent, a change that GMR 2006 characterized as "moderate" but that others might interpret as quite small. Based on trends between 1990 and 2002, UNESCO projected that, among the 163 countries for which 2002 data were available and for which projections could be run, 47 countries have already achieved universal primary education (UPE) and 20 others are likely to do so by 2015. In addition, 44 countries, mostly starting with low enrollment levels, may not achieve UPE but are making reasonable progress; while 20 others, mostly in Central and Eastern Europe and Central Asia, are facing declining NERs and are at risk of not achieving the goal (UNESCO, 2005).

GENDER EQUITY

Although multiple forms of internal inequities characterize the education systems of developing countries (Wils, Carrol and Barrow, 2005), only one particular form of inequity—that between genders—is singled out in both the Dakar Framework and the Millennium Development Goals. The Dakar Framework established two specific targets related to gender equity: (1) the elimination of all gender disparities in enrollment in primary and secondary education by 2005, and (2) gender equality in education by 2015. The 2005 Global Monitoring Report, which focuses on progress toward these goals, discusses these targets from two perspectives: fundamental human rights and economic development.

The educational rights perspective draws heavily on a background paper by Duncan Wilson, later published in the journal *Prospect* (Wilson, 2004). Wilson grounds his rights argument in the widespread ratification of the 1989 Convention on the Rights of the Child and the 1979 Convention on the Elimination of All Forms of Discrimination Against Women (CEDAW), both of which assert the right to gender equality in education, and he makes a distinction between parity and equality. Gender parity, in Wilson's view, refers to equal access to education and is easily captured in quantitative measures such as enrollment rates. By contrast, educational equality encompasses rights "in" and "through" education, such as equal treatment within schools and equal opportunities for developing one's talents, and is qualitative in nature. This distinction between parity and equity has clear parallels to the more general EFA discussion of the differences between access and quality.

The economic arguments for the importance of gender equality in education generally come in two varieties: those based on the private returns to education for girls and women and those based on positive externalities associated with expanding education for them. Studies of the private returns to education by King and Hill (1993), Psacharopoulos and Patrinos (2002), and Schultz (1995) have found that even though women on average earn less than men of the same age and education level, the return to a year's education for a woman is equal to, or slightly greater than, that for a man. Psacharopoulos and Patrinos find that women receive lower returns to primary education than men do (with returns of 13 percent and 20 percent, respectively), higher returns to secondary education (18 percent and 14 percent, respectively), and slightly higher returns to education without respect to level (10 percent and 9 percent, respectively). It should be noted that these rates of return are simply averages of the coefficients estimated in different studies and do not reflect any judgments as to the quality of the studies.

A more persuasive argument for the economic benefit of equal access for girls rests on evidence that the returns on investments in education at the primary level are higher than those for higher levels of education (Psacharopoulos and Patrinos, 2002; Schultz 2001). It follows that in countries where girls have little access to primary and basic secondary education, expanding their access to education would be a more efficient use of resources than expanding education without changing the gender gap. Compounding the situation is a "cross-effect" whereby increases in a husband's schooling lead to a reduction in his wife's labor supply. No reduction in a husband's labor supply is associated with an increase in the wife's education. All these returns to education are "private" in the sense that they are captured in wage rates and accrue directly to the participants. By educating girls, a country makes more productive use of its resources and thereby increases average income levels.

Schultz (2002) provides the most recent summary of evidence of significant positive externalities associated with investment in expanding education for women. He cites studies showing that increases in a mother's schooling are associated with greater improvements in outcomes for a family's children than are increases in the father's schooling. These outcomes include birth weight, child survival, nutrition, age at which schooling begins, and years of schooling by adulthood. Schultz also references the consistent finding that fertility is inversely related to women's schooling.

Whereas Schultz focuses on microeconomic evidence of the benefits of expanding schooling for women, others have tried to model the effect of gender equality in education on macroeconomic growth. All such empirical studies are subject to criticism because of the weaknesses of the quantitative measures used to test the theoretical models on which the empirical work is based, and the difficulties of controlling adequately for confounding factors. Early work by Barro and Lee (1994) and Barro and Sala-i-Martin (1995) found a negative effect of female primary and secondary education, measured in total years of schooling among the adult population, on GDP growth; but Dollar and Gatti (1999) showed that the inclusion of an indicator variable for Latin America, a relatively low growth region characterized by high female education, resulted in the disappearance of the negative effect. King and Hill (1993) and Knowles et al. (2002) found that greater gender inequality in education is associated with lower levels of Gross Domestic Product. Klasen (2002) found that 0.4 to 0.9 percentage points of the differences in annual per capita GDP growth rates between East Asia and Sub-Saharan Africa, South Asia and the Middle East over the period from 1960 to 1992 are attributable to differences in the gender gaps in education between the regions. This effect is estimated controlling for the level and growth of human capital.

Based on the literature, Abu-Ghaida and Klasen (2004) estimated the cost in foregone economic growth to 45 countries unlikely to meet the Millennium Development Goal of eliminating the gender disparity in primary and secondary education by 2015. They conclude that countries significantly off the track of meeting this goal could lose 0.1 to 0.3 percentage points in annual economic growth for the decade from 1995 to 2005 and an additional 0.4 percentage points annually from 2005 to 2015. Additionally, they estimate that these countries will record 0.1 to 0.6 more children per woman by 2015 than they would have had they met the MDG of gender equity and 32 more child deaths per 1000 children.

Obstacles to Gender Equity

Impediments to equality in education for women are numerous. They range from early marriage and pregnancy to adverse treatment when they do enroll in school, from biased textbooks and a dearth of female teachers to sexual harassment. In addition, due to their lower social status, girls in many countries are more vulnerable than boys to factors that reduce overall access to education. Faced with school fees and other cost pressures, for example, families are less likely to enroll a female child than they are a male child. Girls frequently bear the burden of caring for parents and others with HIV/AIDS. Chapter 3 of the 2003/4 *Global Monitoring Report* ("Why Are Girls Still Held Back?") provides a good summary of these obstacles to gender equity (UNESCO, 2003).

Most of the evidence of early marriage and pregnancy as barriers to educational access for women is qualitative and country- or region-specific (see cites in Wilson, 2004).[5] The nature of the relationship between marriage or early pregnancy and education may not be causal, of course; rates of early marriage are likely to be higher, and girls' participation in school is likely to be lower, in countries and regions with social norms that promote women's domesticity. But it is also the case that women in some countries are withdrawn from school specifically to marry (UNICEF, 2001).

Human rights reports have documented the prevalence of in-school abuse of girls in South African schools (Education Rights Project 2002 and Human Rights Watch 2001), and case studies of violence in schools in Jordan, Ethiopia, Malaysia, Israel, Slovakia, and several South American countries document that girls are disproportionately victimized by in-school violence in most of these countries (Ohsako 1997). More recently, Leach (2003) found not only that in-school violence against girls was high in secondary schools in Ghana, Malawi and Zimbabwe, but also that the boys and teachers who perpetrated the violence were usually not punished.

With respect to gender bias in educational curricula, much of the evidence is found in the national reports submitted to the United Nations Division for the Advancement of Woman by countries that have ratified CEDAW. In response to Article 10 of CEDAW, these reports must include information on gender equality in education, including assessments of girls' access to education, female drop-out rates, and gender stereotyping in curricula. Wilson (2004) cites the reports of Thailand and the Philippines from 1997 and 1996, respectively, as evidence of bias in curriculum.

Progress toward Gender Equity

The 2006 Global Monitoring Report provides the most recent data on progress toward the two-fold Dakar goal of gender equity. On the sub-goal of gender parity, only 49 of 149 countries for which data were available were judged to have achieved this goal by 2002 at both levels of schooling, with six others likely to do so by 2005 and eight more by 2015. It concluded, "Gender disparities in enrollment remain the rule rather than the exception, and present trends are insufficient for the Dakar goals to be met" (p. 71). Significantly, the report provides no data on progress toward the second sub-goal of achieving gender equality in education by 2015. To the contrary, the document states that "measuring and monitoring the broader aspects of equality in education is difficult" and concedes that the gender-specific index that it uses "does not fully reflect the second equality aspect of the EFA gender goal" (p. 254).[6]

FUNDING EQUITY: SCHOOL FEES

One of the thorniest issues related to funding equity in developing countries is the balancing of public and private funding in school finance. In contrast to practice in the United States and other developed countries where public schools are financed almost entirely with public revenue, families in developing countries are often asked to assume responsibility for a significant share of school funding through enrollment fees paid directly to schools or other schooling-related expenditures, such as text books and compulsory school uniforms. A survey by the World Bank of 79 of its client countries found that 77 of them required user fees in some form and that 69 had more than one type of fee (Kattan & Burnett, 2004), and a more extensive survey by the World Bank for the 2006 EFA Global Monitoring Report found that 89 of 103 countries had some form of school fees for primary school (UNESCO, 2005, p. 64).

Despite their prevalence, the international community is increasingly opposed to school fees, especially at the level of primary education. Critics argue that such fees keep some children from attending school, an unacceptable outcome for a service deemed by the international community to be a basic human right. Further, because a major purpose of primary education is to reduce poverty, a related concern is that, since school fees are likely to impose the greatest burdens on poor households, they are thus inherently unfair. Notably, the Dakar goals explicitly call for free and compulsory education of good quality.

Given the relatively large role that user fees currently play in the financing of education in many developing countries, their elimination raises a number of complex policy challenges that revolve around the access vs. quality dilemma. When fees are removed, alternative sources of revenue must be found not only to replace the revenue that would have been generated by school fees but also to cover the costs of sustaining quality for a larger group of enrolled students.

The Prevalence of User Fees for Primary Education

The World Bank survey of 79 countries indicates that, with the exception of Algeria and Uruguay, all of them impose some form of fee on parents of public school students.[7] In about a third of the countries, however, the fees are not sanctioned by the government and are, in fact, counter to national policy. Reported user fees include payments for tuition in the form of school registration and annual fees (30 countries), textbook charges (37), compulsory uniforms (39), PTA/community contributions (56) and activity fees (34) (Kattan & Burnett, 2004, p. 10). For the purposes of this survey, fees do not include payments for school meals or for private tutors.

The prevalence by type of fee varies across regions. Tuition fees are quite common in the former socialist countries and East Asia, including China, but are almost non-existent in Latin America. Fees for textbooks are the norm in all areas, but compulsory uniforms are much more prevalent in the former socialist countries than elsewhere. All types of fees are quite common in Africa, including contributions to community schools. In some countries in Central and West Africa, such as Chad, Togo and Mali, the absence of state schools in many rural areas has led to the private financing of community schools. Previously viewed as illegal, these schools are now increasingly recognized as necessary to compensate for the absence of state schools (Kattan & Burnett, 2004, p. 11).

Data from 12 developing countries derived from household surveys in the 1990s indicate that household spending on a broad array of school-related items accounted on average for over 20 percent of total public and private spending on primary education. For example, families often see a need to purchase private tutoring from teachers in order to assure that their children will receive the attention they need in situations where there are large classes. Countries in which the household contributions were particularly large include Tanzania (37 percent), India (43 percent), Vietnam (44 percent), Zambia (50–75 percent) and Cambodia (80 percent). In Cambodia more than a third of the household expenditure goes to private tutoring, while in India about three-quarters goes toward textbooks and other learning materials.[8]

In some countries, including South Africa and China, school fees vary in magnitude across schools and hence contribute to disparities in school quality. Data from one of the wealthiest of South Africa's nine provinces indicate that the fee revenue collected by schools serving middle class students—both white and black—permitted those schools in 2002 to increase their teaching staffs by more than 30 percent on average above their state-paid allotment of teachers and in some schools to double the number of teachers they could employ (Fiske & Ladd, 2004, chapter 7). Though poor schools in South Africa are also permitted to impose fees, their fees tend to be very low and often go uncollected. In China, high quality schools in urban areas, known as key schools, often recruit fee-paying students from other districts. Such fees, which are not allowed under national law, are often described as "education donation and assistance" or "joint construction fees" (World Bank, 2005).

Effects of User Fees on Enrollment

Fees differ from other types of funding for education in that they are triggered only when a child is enrolled in school. Because parents can avoid paying school-related fees by not sending their child to school, there is widespread concern that the use of fees will reduce school enrollment rates, especially among poor families for whom the fees represent a significant financial burden.

By far the most compelling evidence that fees reduce enrollments emerges from the experiences of several African countries that have abolished school fees as part of their effort to promote universal primary education. In Malawi, the 1994 elimination of school fees generated a 50 percent increase in primary school enrollment, from approximately 1.9 million in 1993–94 to nearly three million the following year (Kadzamira & Rose, 2001). Similarly, when Uganda eliminated tuition fees for primary schools in 1996, school enrollment increased by 70 percent in one year and rose an additional 20 percent by 2001 (Hillman & Jenkner, 2002; World Bank, 2002.) Between 1992 (before the initiative) and 1999 (after the initiative) net enrollment rates at the primary level rose from 65.1 percent to 82.1 percent and gross enrollment rates from 84 percent to 123 percent. The latter figure suggests that the elimination of school fees may have attracted a large number of overage children back into the system. In Kenya, the response to the 2003 elimination of fees was an immediate surge of 1.2 million students, many of whom could not be immediately accommodated. Other countries, including Bulgaria, Russia, Azerbijan, Armenia, Tajikstan and the Kyrgyz Republic, Moldova, Romania, and Hungary, provide additional, albeit less compelling, evidence that fees reduce enrollment. Many of those countries have experienced reductions in enrollment rates, especially among the poor and minorities, at the same time that school fees have been rising (Kattan & Burnett, 2004, p. 18).

In many countries, other factors could well be more important than fees in keeping poor children out of schools. Such obstacles to schooling include the opportunity costs to families of having children in school rather than working in the home or fields, expectations of low economic returns from a primary education, social norms that reduce benefits to girls of attending school, the burdens families face in dealing with HIV-AIDS, and the absence of high-quality schools in rural areas. If demand for schooling were low for such reasons, user fees for education could potentially have little or no negative effect on the decisions of low-income families to send their children to school.

Consistent with the possibility that the adverse enrollment effects of user fees might be small, studies during the 1980s showed that the price elasticity of demand for education in developing countries was quite low (Jimenez, 1987, pp. 80–81). More recent studies, however, find far higher price elasticities for girls and poor households. One study, for example, estimated that the price elasticity of demand for schooling in rural Peru was 2-3 times larger for the poorest than for the highest quintile (Kattan & Burnett, 2004, p. 17). Other evidence that the cost of education affects enrollment among low-income households emerges from a careful study of the Progresa program in Mexico, which gave cash grants to families conditional on their sending their children to school (described in Kremer, 2003). By providing compelling evidence that the grants were the cause of increased school enrollment, the study reinforces the conclusion that financial incentives matter to the schooling decisions of low-income households.

Even in countries where school fees may not have inhibited school enrollments, such fees would be undesirable to the extent that they impose financial hardships on poor families. Information gathered by a household survey by income quintile for eight Asian countries document that in many countries not only do school fees place a heavy burden on households in general, but the burdens are highest for families with the lowest income. In China, for example, while all households spend an average of 19 percent on primary education, the proportion for the poorest quintile is 29 percent. In Thailand the disparity is even greater; 16 percent on average versus 47 percent for low income families (Kattan & Burnett, 2004, Table 3, p. 15). Thus, user fees for education force poor families to confront difficult financial tradeoffs.

Both because user fees tend to reduce enrollment and because they put the heaviest burden on low-income households, the growing consensus in the international community is that school fees are undesirable and should be eliminated. If basic education is truly a fundamental human right, the argument goes, it is inappropriate to rely, even if only partially, on a financing mechanism that denies that right to some children. Similarly, if education is intended to play an essential role in reducing poverty, any financing mechanism that disproportionately burdens the poor should be avoided. This consensus against school fees is embodied in Goal 2 of the Dakar Framework, which calls for free and compulsory primary education for all students by 2015.

Why Fees Are so Common

Despite these concerns about school fees and despite the opposition of the international community, many developing countries continue to rely on such fees and even to increase such reliance or to make explicit policy decisions to allow schools to impose fees. They do so primarily because of their inability to generate sufficient public funds—either because of lack of revenue-raising capacity or lack of political will—to provide high quality basic education for all their students.

A second reason for the prevalence of school fees is that until quite recently some international development organizations, including the World Bank, promoted the use of cost-sharing methods in social sectors, including education, as part of their structural adjustment policies. Such policies were typically intended to make developing countries become more fiscally responsible. In addition, the use of cost sharing arrangements—such as having parents pay for textbooks—was rationalized in part on the ground that they would generate greater buy-in from parents and would, by analogy to the private sector, lead to more efficient operation of the schools. We know of no research, however, that documents these alleged beneficial properties of school fees, especially in schools serving low-income families.[9] It is of interest that the World Bank has now made an about-face on the issue of school fees and no longer promotes their use (Kattan & Burnett, 2004).

A third justification for school fees arose most clearly in South Africa at the end of the apartheid era. The new post-apartheid government chose not only to permit, but also to encourage, the governing bodies of each school to levy and collect school fees from the families of its students. Not surprisingly, the schools serving middle class students were able to levy and collect far more fee revenue than those serving poor students. In that context, school fees were rationalized primarily as a way to keep middle-class families—both black and white—in the public school system and thereby to avoid the situation in many Latin American countries where the middle class has fled the public system (Fiske and Ladd, 2004). A secondary goal was to promote a sense of ownership and thereby encourage parental involvement in the schools, especially among poor black families who had become alienated from the public school system during the apartheid period. Though the policy was relatively successful in maintaining the quality of the middle-class schools and thereby keeping middle class families of all races in the public schools, at least through 2002, their main lasting effect has been to perpetuate many of the earlier disparities in quality across schools, with the significant difference being that the new fault line has become family income rather than race.

The Quality Challenge

Though the African countries that abolished school fees were remarkably successful in increasing access, this achievement put huge strains on the existing education systems and thereby reduced the quality of education they could provide. This issue was exemplified in Malawi, where rising enrollments in primary schools led to a drastic deterioration in school quality, as measured by stress on school inputs. That country ended up with extremely high ratios of pupils to permanent classrooms (119:1); of pupils to desks (38:1); pupils to textbooks (24:1); and pupils per teacher (62:1) (Kattan & Burnett, 2004, p. 8). Likewise, in Uganda, the quality of education also plummeted with the change in fee policy despite significant outside donor support. In that country the number of pupils per teacher rose from 40 before the change to 60 in 1999, while the number of pupils to permanent classrooms rose from 85 to 145 (World Bank, 2005, p. 10). Such declines in quality could potentially reduce the demand for schooling, but we know of no study that has explored how enrollment levels respond to declining school quality.

Crucial to the ability of these countries to maintain school quality—and ultimately to maintain the new higher enrollment rates—will be their ability to generate new funding for education. Such new funding must be sufficient to cover not only the loss of fee revenue from the students who would otherwise have been enrolled even with the fees, but also the significant additional costs associated with the larger number of students. In addition, to the extent that the elimination of fees at the primary level succeeds in raising the rate at which children complete primary school, it will also increase the demand for, and, hence the costs of providing, secondary education.

While such additional public funding is clearly a necessary condition for success in meeting the EFA goals of universal free primary education of good quality for all students, it is far from sufficient. As already noted, fees are not the only factor keeping students out of school. Also, many developing countries currently lack the capacity to train an adequate teaching force and the managerial capacity to run a more extensive system of education.

The two main potential sources of new funds are additional public revenues and additional support from the international donor community. Another possibility, mentioned in some documents, is making schools more productive by means such as reducing retention rates and thus allowing children to take fewer years to progress through school. However praiseworthy that latter strategy might be, it is unlikely to be successful. The strategy itself would require additional resources, and in many low-income areas non-school considerations such as HIV-AIDS, cultural norms, and the opportunity costs to families of sending children to school rather than working in the fields make it difficult for many children to progress at the expected rate through school. Reducing corruption and misuse of funds, however, could potentially free up some additional resources for education. Uganda's 1996 Public Expenditure Tracking Survey provides one example of how the provision of information on the flow of funds can reduce the diversion of funds for private or non-education purposes (UNESCO, 2005, p. 83).

Provided the political will is there, some developing countries appear to have the capacity to generate additional public support for primary education because they currently devote relatively low proportions of their GNP to education. Although a 1996 UNESCO report argued that governments should invest at least 6 percent of their GNP in education (Delors et. al. 1996), as of 2002, most developing countries spent far lower percentages. In contrast, some countries, including Togo, South Africa, Algeria and Zimbabwe, spent significantly higher percentages on education. But the Malawi situation is instructive. Even though public spending on education in that country surged to 7.5 percent of GDP in 1994/95 in response to the demands of enrollment growth, educational resources were still inadequate.

The harsh fact remains that developing countries are, by definition, very poor and face a number of competing demands on their public budgets for other essential services, such as health and housing. Thus, it may be the case that the only way for many such countries to achieve the EFA goal of free and universal primary education is through substantially more outside support from the international donor community, not only for education, but also more generally to break the cycle of poverty (Avenstrup, Liang & Nellemann, 2004; Kattan and Burnett, 2004).

CONCLUSION

The Education for All movement has succeeded in assuring that issues of educational equity remain high on the policy agendas of developed and developing countries alike, and that demonstrable progress is being made in enhancing access to education, thereby moving toward specific goals of universal primary education and gender equity. When it comes to the quality of education, however, the picture is much less clear. Measures of progress are imprecise, and developing countries inevitably face tradeoffs between access and quality.

All countries throughout the world struggle with the challenge of providing high quality education, and none has come up with a silver bullet for doing so. This challenge is particularly daunting in developing countries that are simultaneously attempting to meet the goal of universal access to primary education, while increasing the quality of the education they provide. Given their poverty and the size of the challenge, ongoing pressure and enhanced support from the international community—economic, political and technical—seems essential.

The availability of data at the national level, including achievement data, which are increasingly available through international organizations, will provide opportunities for ongoing research on the issues discussed in this chapter. To supplement that national data, the Education Policy and Data Center, which is a joint venture of USAID and the Academy for Educational Development initiated in 2004, is building a database that includes subnational statistics that currently includes data for 80 developing countries (Wils, Yzhao and Harwell, 2006; www.epdc.org). By increasing the amount of information readily accessible to researchers and practitioners in international education, data projects such as this one should make possible additional high-quality research on the topic of international equity in education.

NOTES

1. Consensus on this point is not unanimous. The United States is not a signatory to these treaties, and U.S. official policy rejects the idea of education as a fundamental right. Since education is not mentioned in the U.S Constitution, the legal basis for promoting educational equity in the U.S. context is found in constitutional provisions at the state level that typically require the various states to provide a "uniform" or a "thorough and efficient" system of education rather than in any national consensus that education is a basic human right. Congress has, however, given particular attention to the rights of handicapped and other students who qualify for special education. For them education of a certain quality has become a de facto right.
2. The concept of education as a tool for development can also be found in developed nations, including the U.S. Serious school improvement efforts in the U.S. began in the late 1970s when the governors of various southern states concluded that improving schools was essential to their economic development.
3. TIMSS is the Trends in International Mathematics and Sciences Study and PISA is the Program for International Student Assessment. At least three factors account for the low participation rate. One factor is simply lack of information about the international tests. The second is insufficient technical capacity to carry out the complex surveys. The third is that the students in some countries score so low on assessments such as TIMSS or PISA that policy makers in those countries cannot learn much from the surveys. The development of additional modules with easier items would be required to make these surveys more relevant to such countries. (Based on e-mail correspondence with Andreas Schleicher of OECD, February 2, 2007).
4. For summaries of global assessments of student achievement, see UNESCO (2000b) and Kellaghan and Greaney (2001).
5. As cited in Wilson (2004), CEDAW reports from Egypt and Morocco mention early marriage as a cause of female drop-out in rural areas. They also provide the fullest documentation of the role of early pregnancy in preventing women from receiving a quality basic education. Although countries such as Malawi, Chile, Guinea and Belize permit pregnant women to return to school under law, qualitative studies suggest that pregnancy leads girls to drop out of school in substantial numbers (Kadzamira and Chibwana, 2000; Avalos, 2003; Colclough et. al., 2003; CEDAW, 1996).
6. Whereas the typical challenge for gender equity is to increase access to schooling for girls, the 2006 Global Monitoring Report also noted that in a growing number of countries the enrollment rates for

girls are higher than for boys, especially at the secondary and tertiary levels. This pattern is typically found either in developed countries or in developing ones that are close to achieving universal primary education. For this reason, some developed countries, such as Denmark, Finland, New Zealand and the United Kingdom, are at risk of not achieving gender parity in secondary education by 2015.

7. Survey data were collected from 79 out of a total universe of 145 countries. Survey responses were relatively comprehensive for East Asia and the Pacific, Latin America and the Caribbean, the Middle East and North Africa and South Asia. Only half the countries in Africa are included.
8. Data on household burdens are available for Cambodia, China, Ghana, India, Indonesia, Mauritania, Nepal, Philippines, Tanzania, Thailand, Vietnam, and Zambia, but the data are broken down by category for only five of the countries. Also see Das et al. (2004) for detailed analysis of the burden of private funding in Zambia.
9. Tanzania's experience illustrates the impact of structural adjustment policies on primary schooling. A persistent economic crisis in that country during the 1970s and 1980s forced the country to negotiate with the IMF for a loan, conditioned on the country pursuing a number of structural adjustment policies. Among these was the introduction of user fees in the education sector, which forced it to reintroduce school fees which had earlier been eliminated. The predictable result was that gross rates of enrollment at the primary level declined from about 90 percent in the early 1980s to between 66 and 75 percent a decade later (Vavrus, 2005, p. 182).

REFERENCES

Abu-Ghaida, D. and S. Klasen. (2004). "The Costs of Missing the Millennium Development Goals on Gender Equity." *World Development, 32*(7): 1075–1107.

Avenstrup, Roger, Xiaoyan Liang and Soren Nellemann. (2004). "Kenya, Lesotho, Malawi and Uganda: Universal Primary Education and Rural Poerty Reduction. A Case Study from "Reducing Poverty-Sustaining Growth—What Works, What Doesn't, and Why." Accessed frm http://www.info.worldbank.org/etools/docs/reducingpoverty/case/58/fullcase/East%20Africa%20Edu%20Full%20Case.pdf.

Barro, R. and J. Lee. (1994). "Sources of Economic Growth." *Carnegie-Rochester Series on Public Policy,* 40, 1–46.

Barro, R. and X. Sala-i-Martin. (1995). *Economic Growth.* New York: McGraw-Hill.

Carnoy, M. (2004) Education for All and the Quality of Education: A Reanalysis. Background paper or EFA Global Monitoring Report 2005. Accessed Feb. 10, 2007 from http://unesdoc.unesco.org/images/0014/001466/146633e.pdf

Chinapah, V. (1997). *Monitoring Learning Achievement: Towards Capacity-Building.* Paris: UNESCO.

Das, J. et al. (2004). "Public and Private Funding of Basic Education in Zambia: Implications of Budgetary Allocations for Service Delivery." 2004. Africa Region Human Development Working Paper. World Bank (May). Accessed from http://siteresources.worldbank.org/AFRICAEXT/Resources/AFRHD-62DasZambia022504FINAL.pdf.

Delors, J. et al. (1996). *Learning: The Treasure Within: Report to UNESCO of the International Commission on Education for the Twenty-First Century.* Paris: UNESCO. Accessed from http://www.unesco.org/delors.

Dollar, D. and R. Gatti. (1999). *Gender Inequality, Income, and Growth: Are Good Times Good for Women?* Research Report on Gender and Development, Working Paper No. 1. Washington, DC: World Bank.

Fiske, E.B. and H.F. Ladd. (2004).*Elusive Equity: Education Reform in Post-Apartheid South Africa.* Washington, DC: Brookings Institution Press.

Hewett, P.C. and C.B. Lloyd. (2005). "Progress toward Education for All: Trends and Current Challenges for Sub-Saharan Africa." In *The Changing Transitions to Adulthood in Developing Countries:Selected Studies.* C.B. Lloyd, J.B. Hehrman, N.P. Stromquist and B. Cohen, eds. National Research Council. Washington, DC: The National Academies Press.

Hillman, A.L. and E. Jenkner. (2002). "User Payments for Basic Education in Low-Income Countries." International Monetary Funds Working Paper. Washington, DC.

Jimenez, E. (1987). *Pricing Policy in the Social Sectors.* Washington, DC: World Bank.

Kadsamira E. and P. Rose. (2001). "Educational Policy Choice and Policy Practice in Malawi: Dilemmas and Disjunctures." Working Paper 124. Institute of Development Studies, Brighton, U.K.

Kattan, R.B. and N. Burnett. (2004). "User Fees in Primary Education." The World Bank. Education Sector, Human Development Network. Accessed July from. http://www1.worldbank.org/education/pdf/EFA-case_userfees.pdg.

Kellaghan, T. and V. Greaney. (2001). "The Globalisation of Assessment in the 20th Century."*Assessment in Education, 8*(1), 87–102.

King, E.M. and M.A. Hill. (1993). *Women's Education in Developing Countries: Barriers, Benefits and Policies.* Baltimore: Johns Hopkins University Press.

Klasen, S. (2002). "Low Schooling for Girls, Lower Growth for All? Cross-Country Evidence on the Effect of Gender Inequality in Education on Economic Development." *The World Bank Economic Review, 16*(3), 345–373.

Knowles, S., P.K. Lorgelly, and P.D. Owen. (2002). "Are Educational Gender Gaps a Brake on Economic Development? Some Cross-Country Empirical Evidence." *Oxford Economic Papers*, *54*(1), 118–149.

Kremer, M. (2003). "Randomized Evaluations of Educational Programs in Developing Countries: Some Lessons." *The American Economic Review*, 93(2), 102–106.

Leach, F. (2003). *Gender and Violence in Schools.* Background Paper for EFA Global Monitoring Report 2003/2004. Paris: UNESCO.

Little, A. and E. Miller. (2000). *The International Consultative Forum on Education for All 1990–2000: An Evaluation.* Report to the Forum's Steering Committee. Paris: UNESCO. Accessed from http://www2.unesco.org/wef/en-leadup/evaluation.shtm.

Ohsako, T, ed. (1997). *Violence at School: Global Issues and Interventions.* Paris: UNESCO-International Bureau of Education.

Psacharopoulos, G. and H. Paytrinos. (2002). *Returns to Investment in Education: A Further Update.* Washington, DC: World Bank.

SACMEQ. (1993). *A Southern Africa Proposal for Monitoring Progress Towards Attaining the Goals of the EFA Jomtien Conference Concerning the Quality of Education.* Southern and Eastern Africa Consortium for Monitoring Educational Quality. Accessed from http://www.sacmeq.org/SACMEQ%201/A/1A02.PDF.

Schubert, J. and D. Prouty-Harris. (2003). *Accelerating Paths to Quality: A Multi-Faceted Reality.* Working Paper for Biennial Meeting of the Association for the Development of Education in Africa (ADEA). Paris: Association for the Development of Education in Africa.

Schleicher, A., M. Siniscalco and T.N. Postlethwaite. (1995). *The Conditions of Primary Schools: A Pilot Study in the Le3ast Developed Countries. Report to UNESCO and UNICEF.* Cited in UNESCO 2004.

Schultz, T.P. (1995). *Investment in Women's Human Capital.* Chicago: Union of Chicago Press.

Schultz, T.P. (2001). "The Fertility Transition: Economic Explanations." Discussion Paper No. 833, Economic Growth Center, Yale University. Available online from Social Science Research Network, accessed from http://papers.ssrn.com/sol3/papers.chm?abstract_id=286291.

Schultz, T.P. (2002). "Why Governments Should Invest More to Educate Girls." *World Development, 30*(2), 207–225.

UNESCO. (1990). *Framework for Action: Meeting Basic Learning Needs: Guidelines for Implementing the World Declaration on Education for All.* Paris: UNESCO. Accessed Sept. 3, 1007 from http://www.unesco.org/education/efa/ed_for_all/background/07Bpubl.shtml.

UNESCO. (1996). *Education for All: Achieving the Goal. Final Report of the Mid-Decade Meeting at the International Consultative Forum on Education for All.* 16–19 June 1996. Amman, Jordan. Paris: UNESCO.

UNESCO. (1997). *Adult Education in a Polarizing World: Education for All Status and Trends/1997.* Paris: UNESCO.

UNESCO. (2000a). *The Dakar Framework for Action: Education for All – Meeting our Collective Commitments.* World Education Forum. Dakar, Senegal, 26–28 April. Paris: UNESCO.

UNESCO. (2000b). *Assessing Learning Achievement: Education for All Status and Trends/2000.* Paris: UNESCO.

UNESCO. (2004). Education for All: The Quality Imperative. *Global Monitoring Report, 2005.* Paris: UNESCO.

UNESCO. (2005). Education for All. Literacy for Life. *Global Monitoring Report, 2006.* Paris: UNESCO.

UNESCO. (2003). Gender and Education for All: The Leap to Equality. *Global Monitoring Report, 2003/4.* Paris: UNESCO.

UNESCO. (2002). *Education for All: Is the World on Track? 2002.* Paris: UNESCO.

UNICEF. (2001). "Early Marriage: Child Spouses." *Innocenti Digest 7.* Florence, Italy: Innocenti Research Center. Accessed Sept. 3, 2007 from: http://www.unicef-icdc.org/publications/pdf/digest7e.pdf.

Vavrus, Frances. (2005). "Adjusting Inequality: Education and Structural Adjustment Policies in Tanzania." *Harvard Educational Review,* 75(2), 174–244.

Wils, A., B. Carrol and K. Barrow. (2005). *Educating the World's Children: Patterns of Growth and Inequity.* Washington, DC: Education Policy and Data Center of the Academy for Educational Development and the U.S. Agency for International Development.

Wils, A. Yzhao and A. Harwell. (2006). "Looking Below the Surface: Reaching the Out-of-School Children." Collaborative Working Paper CWP-02-01. Washington, D.C.: Education Policy and Data Center.

Wilson, D. (2004). "Human Rights: Promoting Gender Equality In and Through Education." *Prospects, 34*(1), 11–27.

World Bank. (1988). *Education in Sub-Saharan Africa: Policies for Adjustment, Revitalization and Expansion.* Washington, DC.: The World Bank.

World Bank. (2002). "Achieving EFA (Education for All) in Uganda: The Big Bang Approach." World Bank working paper. Accessed from http://www.world.org/education/pdf/efa.case–uganda.pdf.

World Bank. (2002). "The Elimination of User Fees for Primary Education in Tanzania." Partnership for Poverty Reduction.

World Bank. (2005). "EFA and Beyond: Service Provision and Quality Assurance in China." Accessed from http://sieresources.worldbank.org/EDUCATION/Resources/Education-Notes/EdNotes_China.pdf. Education Notes Series.

IV

CHANGING PATTERNS OF GOVERNANCE AND FINANCE

Section Editor

Andrew Reschovsky

17

The Changing Federal Role in Education Finance and Governance

Nora E. Gordon

INTRODUCTION

This chapter details the transition from a historically nearly absent federal role in education finance and governance, through significant expansions in federal influence in the post-World War II period, to the current peak of federal involvement in educational policy and practice at the classroom level with the implementation of the No Child Left Behind Act (NCLB).

The U.S. Constitution does not explicitly give the federal government jurisdiction over education, and its Tenth Amendment reserves all rights not explicitly granted to the federal government to the states. Thus the relatively (from a comparative international perspective) decentralized educational system in the United States is not surprising. The states, which have final constitutional authority, have allowed school districts to play the dominant role in the governance and finance of elementary and secondary education (see the chapter by McGuire and Papke in this volume). In recent decades, however, the states have become significant contributors to education revenue—on average about equal to local districts, but with great variation across states (see the chapter by Corcoran and Evans in this section). A common and not inaccurate characterization of the federalist evolution of education finance and governance in the United States is that much power has shifted from local districts to states and that the federal role has been relatively small over time. A more complete characterization, however, would acknowledge significant expansions in the federal role in recent decades and the potential for still more to come.

The magnitude of the federal role cannot be measured fully using any one dimension, but its relative magnitude may be quantified most simply by the amount of federal funds directed towards educational activities through the legislative process. The majority of federal funding related to education historically has come from agencies other than the Department of Education. This pattern of funding reflects the fact that federal policies related to education often arise from goals unrelated to education, such as attempting to support key economic sectors through vocational education, strengthening national security post-Sputnik with the increased emphasis on science and math education, or protecting civil rights through desegregation, bilingual education, and other efforts.

Congress may affect educational practice more through the conditions it attaches to the receipt of federal funds than through appropriations alone. Because of constitutional limitations on federal powers, Congress relies primarily on such grant conditions rather than simply enacting laws that dictate behavior by state and local agencies.[1] In principle, state governments and local school districts have the option of passing up federal funding and not complying with whatever conditions have been placed on them. Once Congress has set forth conditions for receiving federal grants, federal agencies such as the Department of Education write policy guidance that interprets the law in greater practical detail and has significant impact on the implementation process. Federal courts also play an important role in influencing the behavior of state and local educational agencies. The evolution of the federal role is marked by important changes by all these players, in all their decision-making capacities.

What Should the Federal Role Be?

While theoretical arguments can be made in favor of both a strong and a weak federal role, the practical political reality in the United States is that local governments, historically, have dominated the control and financing of education. There remains great resistance to reductions in this local control, and voters perceive local control to be closely linked to local finance.

Academic arguments for a relatively small federal role typically draw on the efficiency implications of the Tiebout (1956) model of local public finance, in which many small geographically distinct jurisdictions, such as school districts, provide public goods.[2] The Tiebout model predicts that these jurisdictions and the bureaucrats who run them will compete against one another for residents, thus ensuring that residents receive high quality, low cost services. In this model, households with different tastes can choose the school district that best meets their desired levels of local taxes and school spending. Hoxby (2000) finds that geographic areas with more school districts (and therefore more competition for residents) for reasons of geographic accident, such as more rivers and streams, produce higher test scores for lower educational spending levels, in support of these efficiency arguments and the Tiebout model. (Rothstein, 2005, critiques Hoxby's work; see also her reply in Hoxby, 2005.) Their detailed exchange has been followed closely because there has been so little empirical work, aside from the paper in question, using variation in centralization that is not likely to be correlated with variation in other determinants of efficiency in educational production; there is still less work finding statistically significant positive effects of jurisdictional competition on efficiency.

Arguments for a strong federal role, more akin to the pattern found in other industrialized nations, often emphasize the limited ability of state and local governments to redistribute resources within jurisdictional boundaries in a context of inequality across such boundaries. These arguments also rely on the fact that the quality of education in one school district can affect the well-being of residents of other districts through mechanisms such as worker productivity (Moretti, 2004), crime (Lochner and Moretti, 2004), and civic participation (Dee, 2004; Moretti, Milligan, and Oreopoulos, 2004). Residents, therefore, may wish to subsidize education outside of their own districts, requiring a more centralized level of government to be involved. Finally, to the extent that some education-related activities have large fixed costs, like research and development, centralized provision across local jurisdictional lines allows an efficient pooling of resources.

Growth of the Federal Role

Why has the federal role grown so significantly? In many cases, the federal role in education has grown for reasons not directly related to the previous economic arguments about how to optimally finance and govern an educational system, but rather for reasons more closely related to the political and economic issues of the day. These issues have ranged from concerns about national security to concerns about civil rights and the War on Poverty. As the following summary of key instances of major expansions in federal powers reveals, these non-educational issues were often instrumental in generating the political will necessary to expand the federal role. It is only relatively recently, beginning with the 1983 release of *A Nation at Risk,* a report issued by the National Commission on Excellence in Education at the request of the Reagan administration, that the federal push for greater involvement has focused exclusively on educational quality for its own sake. This coincides with a shift towards focusing on educational quality broadly, rather than attempting to improve conditions for particular categories of typically disadvantaged students, such as the poor or the disabled, through distinct categorical programs.

The remainder of this chapter first provides a brief chronological overview of milestones in the federal role in U.S. education. It then reviews issues of current interest with respect to the federal role, compares the U.S. federal role to that of other countries, and, finally, lays out some of the major issues to be resolved in defining the ongoing federal role.

THE EVOLUTION OF THE FEDERAL ROLE IN THE UNITED STATES

The first federal education agency was established in 1867 with a commissioner and a staff of three (Office of Education Library). This agency changed its name, bureaucratic status, and home several times before gaining the prestige of a cabinet-level agency, the Department of Education, in 1980. (See Goldin, 2006, for more on this bureaucratic evolution.) Throughout most of this period, the federal role in governing and financing schools remained small. Congress did appropriate limited funds to states, but it did not interfere in decisions about curriculum, attendance requirements, graduation and promotion (Goldin, 2006). When the federal government increased its role in educational governance, it tended to do so in conjunction with the award of federal revenue in the form of conditional grants-in-aid.

Changes in federal revenue to local educational agencies reflect many changes in the importance of the federal role over time. The earliest estimate of federal revenue to public elementary and secondary schools is from 1917, when it totaled approximately $1.7 million dollars and comprised just 0.2 percent of total revenue received by local educational agencies, or school districts (Goldin, 2006). By 2002, federal revenue totaled about $37.5 billion dollars and comprised 8.5 percent of total revenue (Digest of Education Statistics). As Table 17.1 shows, this transition was

TABLE 17.1
Federal Revenue for Elementary-Secondary Education, Selected Years, Fall 1919–2003.

Fall of school year	*Federal revenue per student (in current dollars)*	*Federal percentage share of all elementary-secondary revenue*
1919	(rounds to 0)	0.3
1929	(rounds to 0)	0.4
1939	2	1.8
1949	6	2.9
1959	19	4.4
1965	47	7.9
1970	82	8.4
1977	141	8.9
1980	239	9.2
1985	253	6.7
1990	334	6.2
1995	426	6.6
2000	616	7.3
2002	779	8.5

Source: Digest of Education Statistics 2005, Table 152. Retrieved November 6, 2006 from National Center for Education Statistics Web site, http://nces.ed.gov/programs/digest/d05/tables/dt05_152.asp

marked by periods of discontinuous increases in federal spending post-World War II and again in 1965, with the passage of the Elementary and Secondary Education Act (ESEA).

A major theme in this evolution is the extent to which major federal policy changes closely follow social crises outside the education realm.[3] The following chronology emphasizes federal involvement in elementary and secondary education.

Early Federal Education Policy: Support for Manufacturing and Agriculture

The National Vocational Education (Smith-Hughes) Act of 1917, Public Law 347, marked the first major federal foray into elementary and secondary education policy and a substantial increase in federal funding.[4] The Act resulted from concerted advocacy efforts by representatives from manufacturing, agriculture, and labor. The Act allocated $1.5 million current dollars to agricultural and vocational education in 1918. This amount, comprising about 90 percent of total federal spending on education at that time, accounted for well under 1 percent of total revenues for elementary and secondary education. In contrast, as demonstrated in Table 17.2, in fiscal year (FY) 2006 the Department of Education's total spending on elementary and secondary vocational education comprised only 3 percent of the Department's total spending on elementary and secondary education.[5]

Have federal vocational education funds been well spent? It is difficult to assess the success of vocational or "career-technical" education (CTE) because students self-select into vocational coursework. The impact of the coursework itself on later academic and labor market outcomes is thus inextricably linked to the type of student who chooses that curriculum. The literature estimating effects of vocational coursework, therefore, attempts to control for as many student characteristics as possible to limit bias from unobservable student characteristics. Its findings are mixed. In explaining its initial budget proposals to eliminate vocational education funding completely, the Bush Administration cited the National Assessment of Vocational Education's June 2004 Final Report that "found no evidence that high school vocational courses themselves contribute to

TABLE 17.2
Composition of Department of Education Elementary and Secondary Expenditures (FY 2006)

Program	*In thousands of dollars*	*Share of total*
ESEA Title I Grants to Local Educational Agencies	12,713,125	33.6%
Special Education	11,653,013	30.8%
Other	3,847,116	10.2%
Improving Teacher Quality State Grants	2,887,439	7.6%
Vocational Education	1,296,306	3.4%
Impact Aid	1,228,453	3.2%
Reading First	1,132,352	3.0%
21st Century Community Learning Centers	981,166	2.6%
English Language Acquisition	669,007	1.8%
State Assessments	407,563	1.1%
Safe and Drug-Free Schools and Communities	346,500	0.9%
Educational Technology State Grants	272,250	0.7%
Mathematics and Science Partnerships	182,160	0.5%
Indian Education	118,690	0.3%
Teacher Incentive Fund	99,000	0.3%
Striving Readers	29,700	0.1%
Total, Elementary and Secondary	37,863,840	100.0

Source: Education Department Budget History Table. Retrieved November 6, 2006 from Department of Education Web site, http://www.ed.gov/about/overview/budget/history/edhistory.xls.

academic achievement or college enrollment" (Fiscal Year 2006 Budget Summary). Bishop and Mane (2004) review much of this literature and, using National Education Longitudinal Study data for the high school class of 1992, estimate positive effects of high school vocational coursework on later employment and earnings. Perhaps the most convincing evidence comes from a randomized study of career academies by the non-profit policy research organization MDRC.[6] Demand for enrollment at the academies studied outstripped the supply of student slots, so students were randomly accepted to the academies, and researchers followed the treatment group of academy attendees and the control group of those who lost the assignment lottery. They found that academy attendance had a significantly positive impact on labor market outcomes for males, but no labor market impact for females and no impact on educational attainment for either males or females. This provides strong evidence that well-targeted investments in vocational programs can improve job prospects, at least for men, without hurting educational attainment.

World War II: Impact Aid and the GI Bill

The federal government's role in education began to grow in earnest during World War II. The Lanham Act of 1940 provided funds for home construction in communities with tax-exempt military plants and depots, and its 1941 reauthorization expanded the Act to include funds for school construction and operations (Kaestle, 2001). These efforts were extended with the 1950 impact aid laws for school construction and operations, and were later incorporated into the Elementary and Secondary Education Act under Title VIII. While current impact aid legislation still funds school operations and construction in federally-impacted areas, the majority of its funding follows "federally connected children" such as members of Indian tribes to their respective school districts, which need not be impacted districts (About impact aid). Table 17.2 shows that $1.2 billion was appropriated for impact aid in 2006, comprising about 3 percent of the Department of Education's elementary and secondary education budget. Both the Lanham Act aid and the Impact Aid program were uncontroversial at their inceptions; political support for their beneficiaries was strong, and the programs provided funds to districts while explicitly retaining local control over the funds.

The best known federal education response to World War II was the GI Bill (the Servicemen's Readjustment Act of 1944). It included, among other programs, assistance for post-secondary education and training of returning veterans. The education component of the GI Bill provided subsidies for the training of about 7.8 million veterans; approximately 2.2 million attended college (History of the G.I. Bill). The GI Bill was extended in 1952 to cover veterans of the Korean War (Korean War GI Bill of Rights). In 1984 the current version of the law, known as the Montgomery GI Bill, was passed. In 2002, the Department of Veterans Affairs spent $2.1 billion on these education, training, and readjustment provisions (Committee on Ways and Means, 2004). Although the main impetus for the original G.I. Bill likely was to prevent unemployment among returning veterans, the Bill had a substantial impact on educational attainment. Stanley (2003) finds that the World War II and Korean War GI Bill bills increased college attainment of the cohort most likely to be affected, men born between 1921 and 1933, by 15 to 20 percent.

The Cold War and Science Education

The launching of Sputnik in 1957, accompanied by widespread fear about U.S. ability to compete in math and science during the Cold War, generated the political momentum necessary for another categorical federal education bill in 1958, the National Defense Education Act (NDEA). The Department of Health, Education and Welfare actually had produced a bill "nearly identical to NDEA" (Kaestle, 2001) in 1957 prior to Sputnik, reflecting a more general desire for the federal government to improve math and science education. Most of the federal funds allocated under NDEA were for higher education student loans and for math, science and foreign language education at the elementary and secondary levels. A number of different and permanent federal programs since have absorbed the substantive components of NDEA (Clowse, 1981).

The Civil Rights Movement and Racial Desegregation

The federal role continued to expand through key court decisions and legislation, often driven by civil rights concerns. In *Brown v. Board of Education* (1954), the Supreme Court reversed its previous endorsement of the "separate but equal" doctrine of school segregation established by *Plessy v. Ferguson* in 1896. Not until the Civil Rights Act of 1964, however, did Southern schools begin to desegregate in earnest. Recent evidence suggests that this rapid decline in segregation was due not solely to the Civil Rights Act, but to its combined impact with Title I of the Elementary and Secondary Education Act of 1965, which provides compensatory education funding to districts based largely on child poverty. Title VI of the Civil Rights Act of 1964 specified that federal funds could be denied to public agencies not in compliance, and Title I of ESEA of 1965 then provided sufficient federal funds to make Title VI relevant. Many have speculated that without the creation of the Title I program, the Civil Rights Act would have been less effective in inducing school desegregation (Boozer, Krueger, and Wolkon, 1992; Clotfelter, 2001; Rosenberg, 1991). Recent work by Cascio, Gordon, Lewis, and Reber (2006) provides empirical evidence for this hypothesis. They find that school districts with more Title I funding at stake desegregated more intensively than demographically comparable districts eligible for smaller grants.

The ultimate impact of any federal policy depends on state and local responses to it, and one much-discussed local response to desegregation policies is "white flight" to residentially segregated school districts. Reber (2005) uses variation in the timing of implementation of major court-ordered desegregation plans to assess the effects of such plans on segregation and white enrollment. She concludes that court-ordered desegregation plans, largely implemented after 1968, did induce decreases in white enrollment, but on net reduced segregation substantially. Clotfelter (2001) finds that factors historically established as contributing to white flight—the exposure of white students to blacks in local public schools and the availability of alternative public school districts in the metropolitan area with lower black enrollment shares—continued to affect white enrollment in the 1980s and 1990s.

Ashenfelter, Collins, and Yoon (2006) examine the broad impact of federal civil rights policy on outcomes for African Americans. They note that resources began to improve in black schools relative to white schools in the South well before *Brown*. Schools did not effectively desegregate until well after *Brown*, however, following the passage of the Civil Rights Act and ESEA. They find that state efforts to make black schools "equal," at least in easily measurable and litigable dimensions (i.e., expenditures), had significant positive impacts on labor market outcomes for African Americans while schools remained segregated, and that desegregation further improved these outcomes. Their findings on resources are consistent with Card and Krueger's (1992) findings that increased education quality, as measured by teacher-student ratios, teacher salaries, and length of school year, in black schools relative to white schools in the segregated South prior to 1967 explains about 20 percent of the narrowing of the black-white male wage gap from 1960 to 1980. Ashenfelter, Collins and Yoon's findings on desegregation are consistent with research by Guryan (2004), who finds that desegregation plans account for about half of the drop in black high school dropout rates from 1970 to 1980, with no effect on white dropout behavior.

Despite these measured benefits to desegregation, more recent Supreme Court decisions have lessened the federal pressure on school districts to fully desegregate. In *Board of Oklahoma City v. Dowell* (1991), the Court ruled that school districts are freed from court supervision once they have taken all "practicable" steps to eliminate segregation, even if *de facto* school segregation due to residential segregation remains. In *Freeman v. Pitts* (1992), the Court ruled that schools in DeKalb County, Georgia, could be released from some aspects of their district court-ordered desegregation plan even if the schools exhibited other segregated characteristics. Again, the Court emphasized the distinction between segregation caused by "private choices" about residential location as opposed to *de jure* segregation. In *Missouri v. Jenkins* (1995), the Court ruled that while Kansas City schools were unacceptably segregated, lower courts could not order the state of Missouri to pay for continued (and in this case, ineffective) efforts to integrate the district.

Civil Rights and Title IX

The civil rights movement affected federal education legislation related to gender as well as race. Title IX of the Education Amendments of 1972 established that, "No person in the United States shall, on the basis of sex, be excluded from participation in, be denied the benefits of, or be subjected to discrimination under any education program or activity receiving Federal financial assistance." This is analogous to Title VI of the Civil Rights Act, in which a new condition is attached to all existing federal funds but no new funds are established.[7]

A much-studied aspect of Title IX has been its impact on athletic programs at all educational levels, as these were one of the few areas in which schools explicitly devoted different resource levels to males and females. As Kaestner and Xu (2006) report, the rate of girls' participation in organized high school sports rose from 5 percent in 1970–71 to 26 percent in 1977–78, while the participation rate for boys was essentially unchanged. They find that this increase in athletic participation was associated with increased physical activity and decreased weight and body mass increase for girls, presumably with associated health benefits. Stevenson (2006) finds that a 10 percentage point increase in girls' high school sports participation at the state level is associated with a 1 percentage point increase in female college attendance and a one to 2 percentage point increase in female labor force participation.

Civil Rights for Language Minority Students

Congress first legislated how language minority students should be educated, and first allocated federal funds specifically for this group in the Bilingual Education Act of 1968. The Act created Title VII of the Elementary and Secondary Education Act, which awarded grants on a competitive basis to a small number of bilingual education programs, in which students are taught new subject matter content in their primary languages rather than in English. Title VII evolved over time to allow these funds to be targeted to the education of language minority students without restricting their use to bilingual programs. In NCLB, Title VII was eliminated as a separate program, consistent with the current federal emphasis on teaching English to language minority students. The magnitude of federal funding for programs for language minority students consistently has been a small share of federal education spending and has not grown commensurately with the language minority population of U.S. public schools. Table 17.2 shows that current federal funds for English language acquisition programs constitute less than 2 percent of the Department of Education's elementary and secondary budget. Just over 10 percent of all public school students in the United States received some type of services for English language learners in the 2003–04 school year. Less than 1 percent of students in Mississippi and West Virginia received such services, while one-quarter of California public school students did.

Title VII funded some programs directly and may have encouraged states to develop similar categorical programs of their own. Far greater federal impact, however, stemmed from the Supreme Court's interpretation of the Civil Rights Act as applicable to language minority students in the 1974 *Lau v. Nichols* case. It required schools to "establish programs"—and specifically mentioned isolated bilingual classrooms as one acceptable type of such programs—for students who do not speak English so they may have "meaningful" participation in class, and ruled that failure to do so constituted a violation of the Civil Rights Act. As Nelson (2005) discusses, this requirement was particularly burdensome to districts also faced with a requirement that their schools be integrated if possible.

Since *Lau*, there has been considerable controversy over whether bilingual education, in which students are taught subject-specific material in their native languages, or English immersion, in which students are taught academic subjects in English while typically participating in additional English as a second language courses, is a superior method for teaching language minority students. Matsudaira (2005) uses the assignment rule to bilingual education in a large urban school district to compare students with similar initial English language proficiency but different bilingual/immersion assignments. He finds a statistically insignificant difference in reading outcomes across the classroom settings, and a statistically significant but relatively small positive effect of bilingual education on math scores (a 0.08–0.10 standard deviation difference, two years after assignment). The chapter by Rumberger in this volume provides much greater detail on bilingual education, including recent state-level movements towards English immersion.

The War on Poverty: ESEA and Federal Approaches to Redistribution

By far the greatest single increase in federal funding for elementary and secondary education to date came with the passage of ESEA of 1965. The largest component of ESEA 1965 was Title I, designed to assist school districts in providing programs for poor, "educationally disadvantaged" children. As with earlier war-related efforts, the design of Title I reflected the more general social agenda of the times, the Johnson administration's War on Poverty, in its focus on providing "compensatory education" funds to school districts based in large part on the number of poor children in the district. Title I dramatically affected federal school funding almost immediately. During the fall of 1965, Congress doubled federal expenditure on education when it appropriated almost one billion dollars for the new program. For decades, Title I has remained the cornerstone of federal education policy. The 1994 reauthorization, the Improving America's Schools Act, reflected the growing movement for standards-based reform, and the 2001 reauthorization, NCLB, brings the types of accountability provisions previously present in some states, but not at the federal level, to federal policy.

The formula for allocating Title I funds to school districts has changed over the years, but its basic components have not. In the current formula, school districts (rather than states) are allocated funds primarily based on the number of poor children who reside in the district and on the average level of school spending in the state. The program is not fully funded, which means that the amount appropriated for the program does not equal the sum of its grant obligations as determined by the formula. The current funding formula includes a "hold harmless" provision to prevent districts from experiencing declines in funding commensurate with any declines in the number of poor children, and also a "small state minimum" which ensures that the sum of district allocations in each state meets some minimum level. These provisions, in the context of the lack of full funding, disproportionately limit the amount of funds available for districts with growing poor populations as districts with relatively shrinking poor populations are held harmless.

Traditionally, Title I has mandated schools to target funds to students whose academic performance is inadequate rather than to economically disadvantaged students, while the targeting of funds to districts and schools has been driven by child poverty. To the extent that the letter and spirit of the law prevailed, Title I maintained the federal tradition of targeting funds to specific categories of students. As lawsuits from advocacy groups reveal, Title I was in fact treated more like general aid in many cases.[8] Over time, Congress has permitted more general uses of Title I funds, most notably by allowing schoolwide (as opposed to targeted assistance) programs in schools meeting various poverty thresholds over time. These schoolwide programs support general expenditures such as hiring more teachers to reduce class sizes.

The magnitude of the Title I program and its continued existence for over 40 years naturally prompts the question of whether it has improved educational quality and outcomes. Given the targeting of Title I funds to schools serving poor students, and, in particular, to poorly achieving students within these schools, this is a difficult question to answer. Gordon (2004) investigates the possibility that Title I funds are used to substitute for rather than supplement state and local revenue. She finds that the revenue generated by local districts and given to districts by states changes in response to changes in Title I funds, so total revenue and school spending do not increase significantly with Title I grants.[9] Consistent with these findings, van der Klaauw (2006) uses a regression discontinuity approach to compare New York City schools just eligible for Title I funds with their just-ineligible counterparts and finds that the two groups of schools do not have significantly different instructional spending. Given these findings, van der Klaauw's finding that Title I funding does not improve student outcomes is not surprising.

Title I is an important program for redistribution across states, but it also represents the main mechanism through which the federal government is involved in redistribution within states. In 1973, the U.S. Supreme Court ruled in *San Antonio Independent School District v. Rodriguez* that the U.S. Constitution did not require the state of Texas to guarantee students in different school districts equal resources. This decision asserted that education was not among the 'fundamental rights' protected by the U.S. Constitution. Since the *Rodriguez* decision, it has been the states rather than the federal government whose courts have made the key rulings on school finance adequacy and equity.[10]

Civil Rights for Disabled Students

The disabled were the next category of students to have their rights explicitly delineated. In 1975, Congress passed the Education for All Handicapped Children Act (P.L. 94-142) and President Ford signed it into law. It took effect in 1977, and was renamed the Individuals with Disabilities Education Act (IDEA) in its 1990 and subsequent reauthorizations. Unlike Title IX for girls and the *Lau* ruling for language minority students, IDEA does not simply mandate changes in district behavior. It provides funds for the education of students with physical and mental disabilities, and conditions receipt on states providing a "free appropriate public education" in the "least restrictive environment" to all children, regardless of disability status. Just before the law's passage in 1975, the Department of Education spent 3.7 percent of its elementary and secondary budget on special education. By 1980, this share had grown to 12.4 percent, and by 2005, to 27.1 percent. Chambers, Parrish, and Harr (2002) estimate that IDEA funding in 1999 ($605 per student) covered 4.9 percent of total spending on special education. See chapter 7, this volume, for further discussion of special education funding and policy.

Although most special education funding does not come from the federal government, federal laws have been critical in making states and districts increase their spending on special education. Just over 10 percent of students are classified as disabled and receive special education services, and up to 20 percent of all school spending is devoted to special education (Hanushek, Kain, and

Rivkin, 2002). This naturally prompts questions about the efficacy of this spending on outcomes for the disabled, as well as concerns about potential crowding out of resources for other students (see Cullen, 1997). Hanushek, Kain, and Rivkin (2002) compare outcomes for the same students over time as they move in and out of special education services, as well as outcomes for other students in these schools whose non-special education resources are simultaneously fluctuating. They find that the average special education placement has a modest but statistically significant positive impact on math performance for special education students, and that the achievement of students who are not disabled is not affected by placement decisions for the disabled.

A Nation at Risk and the Charlottesville Summit: Moving Towards a Stronger Federal Role

In a departure from the civil rights and anti-poverty motivation driving much federal education policy in the 1960s and 1970s, the National Commission on Excellence in Education's 1983 report *A Nation at Risk* reflected concern with the state of America's schools from the perspective of their impact on national competitiveness. The first two sentences of the report make this clear: "Our Nation is at risk. Our once unchallenged preeminence in commerce, industry, science, and technological innovation is being overtaken by competitors throughout the world" (National Commission on Excellence in Education, 1983, p. 5). Through use of the bully pulpit rather than any new funding or legislation, *A Nation at Risk* prompted what Fiske (1991) describes as "an era of feverish educational reform efforts" in the 1980s. While President Reagan's then Secretary of Education, T. H. Bell, created the Commission and the Administration released the report, the reform efforts following it were largely at the state rather than federal level.

President George H. W. Bush, who had run for office as "the education president," began his term by convening a meeting of the nation's governors to discuss education policy. At this meeting, at the University of Virginia in Charlottesville in September of 1989, attendees set goals for the country's schools to meet by 2000. With a new Secretary of Education, Lamar Alexander, in place, President Bush released his America 2000 plan for school reform in April 1991. While *A Nation at Risk* pointed out deficiencies in American schools, America 2000 made specific proposals to address these problems. These included school-based innovation (through New American Schools, a not-for-profit effort to implement and evaluate promising comprehensive school reform models); national standards and tests; school report cards; and some federally-supported school vouchers. Though New American Schools was established, most of the content of the original proposal never made it into federal legislation. In many ways, some components of NCLB are a direct response to the criticisms of America 2000. For example, the push for national standards and tests, even a voluntary national test, drew so much criticism that it is unsurprising that NCLB mandates state-determined standards and tests.

Federal Education Aid from Outside the Department of Education

Given the tendency for federal education policy to come from other social, political, and economic pressures, it is not surprising that until 2003 more than half of spending by the federal government on elementary and secondary education came from agencies other than the Department of Education. In 2005, an estimated 44 percent of federal spending on elementary and secondary education came from other agencies. The Department of Agriculture spent more than any other agency through its support of school lunches and related programs. Other sizeable federal programs include Head Start (under the jurisdiction of the Department of Health and Human Services), job training programs (under the Department of Labor), schools for children of military personnel (under the Department of Defense), and spending on Indian education (under the Department of the Interior).

The Department of Agriculture spent over $7.1 billion in fiscal year 2003 serving over 28 million children per day through the National School Lunch Program (National School Lunch Program), and also provides breakfast, milk, snack (for after-school programs), and summer feeding programs. These programs provide fully and partially subsidized meals and snacks to economically disadvantaged school children using surplus commodities, purchased from farmers who otherwise would face excess supply or low prices (Gunderson, n.d.).

Research on the impact of school meals on child health has yielded mixed results. Schanzenbach (2005) finds that participation in the National School Lunch Program increases consumption of calories per day, and estimates that these additional calories are responsible for a 2 to 4 percentile point increase in the incidence of overweight children. Bhattacharya, Currie, and Haider (2006) examine the effects of the School Breakfast Program (SBP). Using data from serum measures of nutrients, they find that the SBP has positive impacts on several measures of child nutrition and do not find any evidence of the increased caloric intake Schanzenbach found from the lunch program.

The Head Start program began in 1965 as part of the War on Poverty and provides early childhood education along with health and nutrition services for economically disadvantaged children, mostly ages three and four. The program is politically popular, in part due to the findings of the Perry Preschool Study in which Head Start participants and a control group were followed from enrollment in Head Start through adulthood. Participants fared significantly better than a control group into adulthood, but this may not be generalizable as the educational component of the Perry Preschool was of higher quality than the average Head Start program (Garces, Thomas, and Currie, 2002). Much of the more recent literature looking at a wider sample of Head Start programs has identified positive but short-lived effects on academic achievement (for a review, see Karoly et al., 1998). Garces et al. (2002) compare outcomes across siblings with differential exposure to Head Start. They find that effects vary by the race of the student, with positive educational attainment and labor market outcomes for whites, and significant reductions in criminal activity for blacks. Ludwig and Miller (2007) find quite large and statistically significant positive effects of Head Start on reductions in child mortality due to diseases for which children can be tested and treated, but not due to other causes of death. Despite this history of generally favorable research findings, the Head Start program has never had sufficient funding to serve all eligible children (children in households below the federal poverty line). About half of eligible three- and four-year-old children currently are served by Head Start.

THE FEDERAL ROLE AS REDEFINED BY NO CHILD LEFT BEHIND

With its enactment in 2001 of NCLB, Congress reauthorized and fundamentally changed ESEA. The subsequent years have been filled with the issuance of rules and regulations for its implementation, and the federal response to challenges to NCLB by states, districts, and advocacy groups. While many constituencies have protested the new law, it was in fact crafted and pushed through by a diverse political coalition (Rudalevige, 2003). Although most input from the nation's governors in the 1989 education summit did not translate into immediate changes in federal education legislation, the summit was critical in establishing the role of the states as advisors to the federal stance on education, and NCLB draws heavily on the experiences of individual states' accountability systems. NLCB has resulted in a stronger federal influence at the school and classroom level than ever before.

Content of the Law

NCLB reauthorizes the funding stream for ESEA, but adds significant accountability provisions and other conditions to federal aid from ESEA. Both the full text of the law and the regulations governing its implementation are available at the Department of Education Web site (www.ed.gov). The law and the regulations alone paint an incomplete picture of the policy as enacted, as parts of the law have been waived at the state or district level. Some conditions of NCLB apply only to schools which receive federal Title I funds, while others apply to all schools in any state receiving Title I funds (historically and currently, all states receive these). I describe only some of the most notable characteristics of the law here and refer the reader to the chapter in this volume by Figlio and Ladd on accountability.

The stated goal of NCLB is to close the academic achievement gap that currently exists among students of different races and between those from economically disadvantaged and other families. NCLB as written requires states receiving Title I funds to implement annual standardized testing in grades three through eight in reading and math and to set state standards of proficiency on those tests.[11] The law mandated that by 2005–06, all schools in Title I states must be staffed entirely by "highly qualified" teachers, with bachelors degrees, state certification and some proof of subject-level competency in each subject they teach.

Title I schools are monitored for their annual yearly progress (AYP) in working towards having all students and all sufficiently large "subgroups" of students (defined by racial/ethnic category, free lunch eligibility, English proficiency, and disability) meet state standards by 2014. Various penalties exist for failing to meet AYP with the severity of the penalty depending on the number of consecutive years of failing to meet the standards. Key sanctions include giving students the option to transfer to another public school and giving low-income students the opportunity to use part of the Title I funds previously allocated to the school on their behalf. Students can use these funds with the supplemental educational services (tutoring) provider of their choice, including a private provider. While take-up of these private services has been low so far, this change in the law represents a significant and largely unregulated expansion in the use of federal education funds in the private sector, as some school districts are explicitly prohibited from providing these tutoring services themselves, leaving private providers as the sole option in those districts. All Title I schools, regardless of progress in meeting state standards, must use federal funds only for programs grounded in "scientifically based research." This requirement is both ambiguous and highly controversial.

While states retain authority over what constitutes proficiency on their own tests, the federally-determined sanctions for failure to make AYP provide an incentive for states to set lower proficiency thresholds that schools are more likely to attain (or, alternatively, to choose easier tests that yield higher scores). In lieu of a national test, the National Assessment of Educational Progress (administered to a changing sample of all schools in each year) has provided the opportunity to benchmark perceived gains in state test scores against a measure of achievement that cannot be manipulated by state-level policy.

Costs of NCLB: An Unfunded Mandate?

States, districts, and advocates have raised too many objections to NCLB to list here. Among these, litigation has focused on the cost to the states of complying with the NCLB conditions for receipt of Title I funding and the question of whether NCLB is an unfunded mandate. This was the central issue in *Pontiac v. Spellings*, a lawsuit brought by the National Education Association, its affiliates in ten states, and several school districts in Michigan, Texas, and Vermont.[12]

In reviewing this issue before the lawsuit was filed, the General Accounting Office found that NCLB did not meet the definition of an unfunded mandate, as specified in the Unfunded Mandates Reform Act of 1995, "because the requirements placed on states and local school districts were a condition of federal financial assistance" (General Accounting Office, 2004, p. 27). The GAO's reasoning, notably, does not depend on the actual costs of complying with NCLB. Some states have considered legislation to pass up Title I funds and effectively to opt out of NCLB, but so far, no state has done so. Imazeki and Reschovsky (2006) show that the costs of complying with NCLB in Texas exceeded the accompanying *increase* in Title I funding. States would lose all Title I funding, not just new funding, if they did not comply, so compliance is to be expected so long as the *total* amount of Title I funding exceeds these compliance costs.

Impact of NCLB

However much controversy surrounds NCLB, there is consensus that it has sparked significant changes in educational practice. The Center for Educational Policy has conducted one of the most comprehensive data collection efforts tracking the impact of NCLB since its implementation. Jennings and Rentner (2006) describe major findings from this tracking effort. These include changes in activities undertaken by state education agencies, ranging from adopting standards and creating corresponding standardized tests to establishing state-specific criteria of what constitutes a highly qualified teacher. The bulk of NCLB-induced changes, however, have been at the school level. Jennings and Rentner describe schools increasing time spent teaching reading and math (the only subjects currently mandated for testing), aligning their curricula to better match state standards and tests, and increasing attention to the subgroups of students most likely to cause schools to fail to meet AYP goals.

THE FEDERAL ROLE IN COMPARATIVE PERSPECTIVE

While NCLB is viewed by many as an excessively large role for the federal government, this does not change the fact that the U.S. federal role is small in both absolute and relative terms compared to most other countries, particularly in Europe.[13]

The OECD provides 2002 data (OECD statistics) for 28 countries on total primary and secondary education spending and total central government primary and secondary education spending. Among these countries, the United States, with 8.3 percent, has the third smallest central government share, behind Switzerland (2.3 percent) and Poland (7.0 percent). Essentially, all of total spending is done at the central government level in the Slovak Republic, Ireland, New Zealand and Turkey. In both the mean and the median country in the sample, just over half of all primary and secondary education expenditures are attributed to the central government.

Centralization in finance provides only part of the picture. The regulation of educational decision-making is another important aspect of educational policy, which could vary independently of financing arrangements (for example, the regulatory role of the U.S. federal government has recently expanded without a correspondingly large increase in its funding role). Of 25 OECD countries responding to a 2003 survey about secondary education, 13 countries reported that the central governments had full control over teacher salary scales and 10 reported that the central government had full autonomy over required hours of instruction (Education at a glance: OECD indicators). In a similar pattern, many European countries have long traditions of centralized secondary school exit examinations, which require centralized curricula. In the United States, none of these decisions are made by the federal government.

This comparison is admittedly a broad one, and the countries with full central government control over pay scales and hours requirements are disproportionately countries with large central government roles in education financing. Using either definition of centralized decision making (control over salary scales or minimum instructional hours), the average share of government education spending coming from the central government is about 69 percent for countries where the central government has total control over the decision, well above the full sample mean of 53 percent. Ideally, we would like to know how large the U.S. federal role in governance is compared to other countries with similarly small central government roles in school financing. There are, however, few countries that meet these criteria in the OECD sample. When we limit our focus to other countries with less than 25 percent of total government education spending coming from the central government responding to the survey (Belgium, the Czech Republic, Germany, Japan, and Spain), we see only one country, the Czech Republic, with full central autonomy over hours of instruction and none of the five with full central decision making power over setting teacher salary scales. In summary, the United States has an unusually small central government role in both spending and regulation, and regulatory and spending roles appear to be correlated for most countries.

Claudia Goldin (2003) discusses the virtues and vices of American decentralization in international perspective. She argues that the relative decentralization of the U.S. system hastened the high school movement in the United States, which took place more quickly than its European counterparts. In part, this is likely because smaller jurisdictions could decide when they were ready to open a high school rather than waiting for a democratically elected central government to push for the expansion of high school education nationwide. At the same time, Goldin notes that decentralization allows for greater inequality in school resources. As Corcoran and Evans show in their chapter in this volume, spending differences between states remain quite large.

OPTIONS FOR THE FEDERAL ROLE MOVING FORWARD

Legislation like the 1941 Lanham Act reauthorization and the 1950 Impact Aid Act provided new federal funds for schools but emphasized that increased federal revenue did not imply an increase in federal control over local schools. NCLB, which at least some consider "the greatest extension to date of federal authority over public school governance" (McDermott and Jensen, 2005), takes nearly the opposite approach. It transforms Title I grants from essentially an entitlement into a reward for compliance with federal policies that significantly depart from existing state and local practice. While controversial, this strategy is not new to federal education policy. The Second Morrill Act of 1890, for example, conditioned receipt of higher education funds on the availability of institutions for blacks. Nor is the presence of conditions new to Title I, as the historical experience of Southern school districts opposed to desegregation emphasizes. Furthermore, NCLB was not the first time the federal government conditioned Title I funds on state standards and accountability policies. The 1994 ESEA reauthorization (the Improving America's Schools Act) did so eight years earlier, albeit less stringently and with less enforcement.

The impact of federal education policy in the near future depends critically both on how the current version of NCLB is enforced and on how NCLB is amended and enforced in its next reauthorization. Increased federal expenditures may be necessary in order to induce districts and states to comply with the increasingly demanding conditions of federal aid. As Rudalevige (2003) writes, "Even if it were willing to use its sticks, the Department of Education has small sticks to brandish." Despite the small magnitude of Title I relative to overall district revenues, no large district or state has yet been willing to incur the loss of Title I revenue in order to opt out of some of NCLB's requirements.

As schools face real penalties under NCLB, questions inevitably arise about whether all schools are equipped to meet the standards assigned to them and if a greater federal role in financing is needed to ensure that they are. Evans, Murray, and Schwab (1998) decompose the variation in 1992 levels of local spending per-pupil and estimate that 65 percent of the total variance comes from across the states. This suggests that state-level redistributive policies (i.e. school finance equalization) alone will be insufficient in moving towards greater equalization of resources.

If the federal government is to assume a greater role in redistributing resources to districts, it could do so either through a new general, foundation-type program or by expanding its revenue to districts through categorical programs. Though the federal government historically has not distributed aid through a program as general as a foundation aid system, such as the one Rothstein (2001) proposes, there have long been unsuccessful movements for one (Kaestle, 2001). The existence of many federal funding streams, each with their own devoted constituencies, may limit the ability of the federal government to move to a more streamlined and flexible approach to funding education and necessitate continued reliance on categorical programs. Ladd and Hansen (1999) review these two possible approaches in detail, while Kaestle (2001) cautions against viewing them as distinct when implementation may render categorical spending general in practice, particularly over time.[14]

The Federal Role in Flux

Through NCLB, the federal government is affecting educational practice at every level—state, district, school, and, perhaps most notably, inside the classroom. The full effects of NCLB will not be known until details of implementation are resolved through regulatory guidance and the courts. Key issues to watch for include the definition of AYP and sanctions associated with failure to meet it, the possibility of national curricular standards and tests (as proposed in America 2000 and supported by the American Federation of Teachers but insufficiently popular for inclusion in NCLB), and the level and distribution of federal funds. We can be sure, however, that the federal role in elementary and secondary education at this time is greater than ever before in our history, and that it has the potential to grow greater still.

NOTES

1. McDermott and Jensen (2005) provide several examples of policies outside of the education realm which were struck down by the courts when implemented in a regulatory framework, but then ultimately prevailed when instituted as conditions for the receipt of grants, suggesting that this strategy increases the power of federal agencies over the states more broadly.
2. Education exhibits more private good qualities than public good ones, but the general argument of the Tiebout model holds.
3. Kaestle (2001) provides a useful discussion of how this historical evolution is often framed as "episodic" in its responsiveness to other social issues, but also reveals how in many cases episodic shifts have followed periods in which support for the agenda at hand grew incrementally, as well as examples of crises that did not ultimately change education policy and policies that changed without any precipitating external event. Kaestle refers the reader to Nelson Polsby's (1984) work on "acute" versus "incubated" policies.
4. The first major federal education legislation was the Morrill Land Grant Act of 1862, in which Congress gave federal land to the states (those remaining in the Union during the Civil War) in proportion

to their populations for the establishment of agricultural and technical colleges. The Second Morrill Land Grant Act, in 1890, appropriated land to the Southern states, and also appropriated federal funds from sales of public lands to the states for land grant colleges. New conditions were added with the new funds: the states could not use them to support colleges "where a distinction of race or color is made in the admission of students", but did allow this if the state maintained separate colleges for different races and divided the federal funds equitably among those colleges. This condition prompted the establishment of what are now known as "historically black colleges" (Goldin, 2006), and provides an early example of conditional grants, which emerge as a favored mode of federal education policymaking. The Morrill Land Grant Acts have had a lasting legacy on the geographic landscape of American higher education. Their impact is so significant that Moretti (2004) is able to use the original grants as an instrument for the city-level distribution of educational attainment in 1990. He finds that having a land-grant college in a city is associated with a 20 percent increase in the share of college-educated adults. The Smith-Hughes Act of 1917, however, was the most significant federal legislation applicable to elementary or secondary education at that time.

5. The Bush administration proposed zero funding for one politically popular federal funding stream, through the Perkins Act, in its 2005 and 2006 budgets. Ultimately President Bush did sign a version of the reauthorized act (Cavanagh, 2006), but the prolonged process is reflective of No Child Left Behind's focus on academic achievement and the corresponding decline in support for vocational programs.
6. Career academies are public high schools with academic and vocational content organized around particular professions, and linked to relevant local employers. The findings therefore should be interpreted as relevant to career academies but not necessarily to other types of vocational education.
7. In the case of the Civil Rights Act, however, significant new funds were made available the next year through Title I of the Elementary and Secondary Education Act, and districts would be ineligible if not in compliance with the Civil Rights Act.
8. See, for example, Washington Research Project (1969).
9. These changes in Title I grants, however, are much smaller than the full grant amount received by any district, so it is not possible to extrapolate from these estimates to predict district spending levels in the complete absence of the program.
10. See Nelson (2007) for discussion of the tension between the Supreme Court's resistance to mandating redistribution in *Rodriguez* and willingness to require that states redistribute to particular categories of students in *Lau v. Nichols* and *Milliken v. Bradley* (both in 1974).
11. Beginning in 2007-08, all states must test students in science as well.
12. The suit was filed in April, 2005, and dismissed by a federal court in November, 2005. The plaintiffs have since appealed the decision.
13. Given the large size and important education policy and finance roles of many states, it should be noted that a small federal role in the United States is not equivalent to a highly decentralized system, as states themselves play a centralized role with local districts.
14. For example, Title I funds under ESEA are nominally categorical funds in that they are based on district-level child poverty and are to be spent on a particular program, "compensatory education." Over time, Title I has turned into a program present in over half of public schools; with high poverty schools now allowed to use Title I funds for schoolwide programs, including class size reduction, Title I funds are essentially general revenue for many schools.

REFERENCES

About impact aid. Retrieved August 23, 2006, from Department of Education Web site: http://www.ed.gov/about/offices/list/oese/impactaid/whatisia.html

Ashenfelter, O., W. J. Collins, and A. Yoon. (2006). Evaluating the role of *Brown v. Board of Education* in school equalization, desegregation, and the income of African Americans. *American Law and Economics Review*, forthcoming.

Bhattacharya, J., J. Currie, and S. J. Haider. (2006).Breakfast of champions? The School Breakfast Program and the nutrition of children and families. *Journal of Human Resources, 41*(3), 445–466.

Bishop, J. H. and F. Mane. (2004). The impacts of career-technical education on high school labor market success. *Economics of Education Review, 23*(4), 381–402.

Boozer, M., A. Krueger, and S. Wolkon. (1992). Race and school quality since Brown v. Board of Education. *Brookings Papers on Economic Activity, Microeconomics,* 269–326.

Card, D. and A. B. Krueger. (1992). School quality and black-white relative earnings: a direct assessment. *Quarterly Journal of Economics, 107*(1), 151–200.

Cascio, E. U., N. E. Gordon, E. Lewis and S. Reber. (2006). Financial incentives and the desegregation of Southern schools. Working paper.

Cavanagh, S. (2006, Aug. 30). Bush signs measure renewing Perkins Act. *Education Week,* 39.

Chambers, J. G., T. B. Parrish, and J. J. Harr. (2002). *What are we spending on special education services in the United States, 1999–2000?* Retrieved August 28, 2006 from Center for Special Education Finance Web site: http://www.csef-air.org/publications/seep/national/AdvRpt1.PDF

Clotfelter, C. T. (2001). Are whites still fleeing? Racial patterns and enrollment shifts in urban public schools, 1987–1996. *Journal of Policy Analysis and Management, 20*(2), 199–221.

Clowse, B. B. (1981). Brainpower for the Cold War: the Sputnik crisis and National Defense Education Act of 1958. Westport, CT: Greenwood Press.

Cullen, J. B. (1997). Essays on special education finance and intergovernmental relations. Ph.D. dissertation, Massachusetts Institute of Technology.

Dee, T. (2004). Are there civic returns to education? *Journal of Public Economics, 88*(9), 1697–1720.

Digest of Education Statistics. (2006). Table 153, retrieved August 31, 2006 from National Center for Education Statistics Web site: http://nces.ed.gov/programs/digest/d05/tables/dt05_153.asp.

Education at a glance: OECD indicators. (2005). Paris: Organisation for Economic Co-operation and Development.

Education Department budget history table. (2006). Retrieved August 23, 2006, from Department of Education Web site: http://www.ed.gov/about/overview/budget/history/edhistory.pdf.

Evans, W. N., S. Murray, and R. Schwab. (1998). Education finance reform and the distribution of education resources. *American Economic Review, 88*(4), 789–812.

Fiscal Year 2006 Budget Summary. (2005, Feburary 7). Retrieved August 31, 2006, from Department of Education Web site: http://www.ed.gov/about/overview/budget/budget06/summary/edlite-section2c.html.

Fiske, E. B. (1991). *Smart schools, smart kids.* New York: Simon & Schuster.

Garces, E., D. Thomas, and J. Currie. (2002). Longer term effects of Head Start. *American Economic Review 92*(4), 999–1012.

General Accounting Office. (2004). *Unfunded mandates: analysis of reform act coverage.* GAO-04-637. Washington, D.C.: Government Printing Office.

Goldin, C. (2003). The human capital century. *Education Next, 2003*(1), 73–78.

Goldin, C. (2006). A brief history of education. In Carter, S. B., S. S. Gartner, M. R. Haines, A. L. Olmstead, R. Sutch, and G. Wright (Eds.), *Historical statistics of the United States: millennial edition* (pp. 2-387–2-397). New York: Cambridge University Press.

Gordon, N. (2004). Do federal grants boost school spending? Evidence from Title I. *Journal of Public Economics 88*(9–10), 1771–1792.

Gordon, N. E. (2007). Challenges in redistributing resources across local school districts: evidence from Title I and state school finance equalizations. In Kaestle, C. F. and A. E. Lodewick (Eds.), *To educate a nation: federal and national strategies of school reform* (pp. 95–116). Lawrence, Kansas: University Press of Kansas.

Gunderson, G. W. (n.d.). *The National School Lunch Program background and development.* Retrieived August 24, 2006, from USDA Web site: http://www.fns.usda.gov/cnd/lunch/AboutLunch/ProgramHistory_4.htm.

Guryan, J. (2004). Desegregation and black dropout rates. *American Economic Review, 94*(4), 919–943.

Hanushek, E. A., J. F. Kain, and S. G. Rivkin. (2002). Inferring program effects for special populations:

does special education raise achievement for students with disabilities? *The Review of Economics and Statistics, 84*(4), 584–599.

History of the G.I. Bill. Retrieved August 23, 2006 from Veterans Administration Web site: http://www.75anniversary.va.gov/history/gi_bill.htm.

Hoxby, C. M. (2000). Does competition among public schools benefit students and taxpayers? *American Economic Review, 90,* 1209–1238.

Hoxby, C. M. (2005). Competition among public schools: a reply to Rothstein (2004). NBER working paper no. 11216.

Imazeki, J. and A. Reschovsky. (2006). Does No Child Left Behind place a fiscal burden on states? Evidence from Texas. *Education Finance and Policy, 1*(2), 217–246.

Jennings, J. and D. S. Rentner. (October 2006). Ten big effects of the No Child Left Behind Act on public schools. *Phi Delta Kappan, 88*(2), 110–113.

Kaestle, C. R. (2001). Federal aid to education since World War II: purposes and politics. In *The future of the federal role in elementary and secondary education* (pp. 13–35). Washington, D.C.: Center on Education Policy.

Kaestner, R., and X. Xu. (2006). *Effects of Title IX and sports participation on girls' physical activity and weight.* NBER Working Paper No. 12113. Cambridge, MA: National Bureau of Economic Research.

Karoly, L. A., P. W. Greenwood, S. S. Everingham, J. Hoube, M. R. Kilburn, P. C. Rydell, M. Sanders, and J. Chiesa. (1998). Investing in our children: What we know and don't know about the costs and benefits of early childhood intervention. Santa Monica, CA: RAND MR-898.

Kemple, J. J. (2004). *Career academies: impacts on labor market outcomes and educational attainment.* New York: MDRC.

Ladd, H. F. and J. S. Hansen (Eds.). (1999). *Making money matter: Financing America's schools.* Washington, D.C.: National Academy Press.

Lochner, L. and E. Moretti. (2004). The effect of education on criminal activity: Evidence from prison inmates, arrests and self-reports. *American Economic Review, 94*(1), 155–189.

Ludwig, J. and D. Miller. (2007). Does Head Start improve children's life chances? Evidence from a regression discontinuity design. *Quarterly Journal of Economics, 122*(1).

Matsudaira, J. (2005). Sinking or swimming? The impact of English immersion relative to bilingual education on student achievement. University of Michigan working paper.

McDermott, K. A. and L. S. Jensen. (2005). Dubious sovereignty: Federal conditions of aid and the No Child Left Behind Act. *Peabody Journal of Education, 80*(2), 39–56.

Moretti, E. (2004). Estimating the social return to education: Evidence from longitudinal and cross-sectional data. *Journal of Econometrics, 121,* 175–212.

Moretti, E. (2004). Workers' education, spillovers and productivity: Evidence from plant-level production functions. *American Economic Review, 94*(3), 656–690.

Moretti, E., K. Milligan, and P. Oreopoulos. (2004). Does education improve citizenship? Evidence from the U.S. and the U.K. *Journal of Public Economics, 88*(9–10), 1667–1695.

National Commission on Excellence in Education. (1983). *A nation at risk: The imperative for educational reform.* Washington, D.C.: Government Printing Office.

National School Lunch Program. Retrieved from USDA Web site August 24, 2006, http://www.fns.usda.gov/cnd/lunch/AboutLunch/NSLPFactSheet.pdf.

The National Vocational Education (Smith-Hughes) Act. Public law no. 347, sixty-fourth Congress-S. 703. Retrieved August 23, 2006, from http://www.cals.ncsu.edu/agexed/sae/smithugh.html

Nelson, A. R. (2005). *The elusive ideal: equal educational opportunity and the federal role in Boston's public chools, 1950–1985.* Chicago: University of Chicago.

Nelson, A. R. (2007). *Rodriguez, Keyes, Lau,* and *Milliken* revisited: The Supreme Court and the meaning of "equal educational opportunity," 1973–1974. In Kaestle, C. F. and A. E. Lodewick (Eds.), *To educate a nation: federal and national strategies of school reform* (pp. x–y). Lawrences: University Press of Kansas.

Orfield, G. and Lee, C. (2006). *Racial transformation and the changing nature of segregation.* Cambridge, MA: The Civil Rights Project at Harvard University.

OECD statistics. Retrieved via data query from OECD Web site August 24, 2006, http://www.oecd.org/statistics.

Office of Education library-early years. (n.d.). Retrieved August 23, 2006, from http://www.ed.gov/NLE/histearly.html.

Patterson, J. T. (2001). *Brown v. Board of Education: A Civil Rights milestone and its troubled legacy.* New York: Oxford University Press.

Polsby, N. (1984). *Political innovation in America: The politics of policy initiation.* New Haven, CT: Yale University Press.

Reber, S. J. (2005). Court-ordered desegregation: Successes and failures in integration since *Brown vs. Board of Education. Journal of Human Resources, 40*(3), 559–590.

Rosenberg, G. N. (1991). *The hollow hope: Can courts bring about social change?* Chicago: University of Chicago Press.

Rothstein, J. (2005). Does competition among public schools benefit students and taxpayers? A comment on Hoxby (2000). NBER working paper no. 11215.

Rothstein, R. (2001). New federal roles in education. In *The future of the federal role in elementary and secondary education* (pp. 37–43). Washington, D.C.: Center on Education Policy.

Rudalevige, A. (2003). No Child Left Behind: forging a congressional compromise. In Peterson, P. E. and M. R. West (Eds.), *No child left behind? The politics and practice of school accountability* (pp. 23–54). Washington, D.C.: Brookings Institution Press.

Schanzenbach, D. W. (2005). Do school lunches contribute to childhood obesity? Harris School Working Paper Series 05.13.

Stanley, M. M. (2003). College education and the mid century GI Bills. *Quarterly Journal of Economics, 118*(2), 671–708.

Stevenson, B. (2006). Beyond the classroom: using Title IX to measure the return to high school sports. Wharton School working paper.

Tiebout, C. M. (1956). A pure theory of local public expenditures. *Journal of Political Economy, 64*(5), 416–424.

U.S. House of Representatives Ways and Means Committee. (2004). *2004 Green book.* Washington, D.C.: Government Printing Office.

van der Klaauw, W. (2006). Breaking the link between poverty and low student achievement: an evaluation of Title I. *Journal of Econometrics*, forthcoming.

Washington Research Project. (1969). Title I of ESEA: Is it helping poor children? Washington, DC: The Washington Research Project of the Southern Center for Studies in Public Policy and the NAACP Legal Defense and Education Fund, Inc.

18

The Role of Nongovernmental Organizations in Financing Public Schools

Janet S. Hansen

INTRODUCTION

Financing K–12 public schools in the United States is overwhelmingly a governmental responsibility. The National Center for Educational Statistics reports that in 2003, sources other than federal, state, and local governments accounted for just 2.3 percent of all the revenues received by public schools.[1] Even this figure overstates the financial contribution of nongovernmental organizations that provide funds to support or improve public schools, since it includes income from various fees[2] as well as contributions and donations from private sources.

Despite the small share of public school revenues provided by nongovernmental organizations, this funding source is of increasing interest from a policy perspective. There is a growing perception that, as one newspaper headline recently put it, "private funds [are] padding public school coffers" (Carr, 2004). Tight school budgets are reported to be leading to a situation in which "parents buy in to paying for the basics" (Galley 2003) through voluntary donations and fundraising activities. Foundation activities in education, most recently that of the well-funded Bill & Melinda Gates Foundation, garner widespread public attention. Researchers[3] have suggested that changes in public school finance systems (especially the growing dependence on state rather than local revenues) have encouraged districts and schools to turn to private fund-raising. Nongovernmental funding helps them to overcome state-imposed constraints on local spending and to meet new demands for improved educational performance. While private funds supporting public education are nothing new, anecdotes and some research evidence suggest that districts and schools "are now pursuing private support with increased sophistication and aggressiveness" (Zimmer et al., 2003, p. 485).

Educators appreciate nongovernmental revenues. These funds often come with fewer restrictions than public dollars, and they support activities and programs that would otherwise be unaffordable. At the same time, a growing reliance on private donors raises a number of issues and concerns. Chief among them is whether nonpublic funding negates some of the equity gains that school finance system reformers have achieved in the distribution of public funds. There are questions about whether private funding offered for specific purposes inappropriately affects the decisions of public officials charged with making resource allocation and other strategic decisions for schools. Concerns have been raised about whether private donors, especially the large foundations, are sufficiently attentive to the effectiveness, impact, and sustainability of their spending. As schools and businesses have increasingly become involved in commercial relationships, alarms have been sounded over possible negative consequences for children.

This chapter provides an overview of nongovernmental funding of public schools. It begins by identifying the wide variety of organizations that contribute to public education and the kinds of private giving that will be the focus of this essay. An explanation of the data limitations plaguing this aspect of education will serve to indicate why it is impossible to say with any precision exactly how much nongovernmental revenue is directed at public schools and for what purposes. Whatever the amount, it is clearly a very small fraction of what government spends. Nongovernmental organizations support education in ways that range from enhancing traditional activities to fostering comparatively ambitious reforms and do so for reasons ranging from the purely altruistic to the largely self-interested. Even though the overall contributions of these organizations to education budgets may be small, it is important to understand who they are, the roles that they play, and the influence their spending has on educational policy and practice.

Nongovernmental Organizations That Finance Public Schools

There is no accepted typology of nongovernmental organizations that provide revenues to or on behalf of public schools. Nor are there common reporting arrangements that would allow an accurate and complete picture of this universe. A reasonable list of organizations (many of which will be defined further in subsequent sections) that make financial contributions would include:

- School-based organizations (parent associations, alumni associations, booster clubs)
- School foundations
- Local education funds
- Community foundations
- Local businesses
- Independent foundations
- Corporations (via direct giving, corporate foundations, business/school partnerships, and commercial relationships)

Some of these organizations do not limit themselves to financial contributions. For some the value of volunteer time or other in-kind contributions, for example, may far outweigh their monetary assistance. Some organizations that infrequently make financial contributions to schools are not on this list; for example, colleges sometimes give money as well as other services to local schools (e.g., Nichols, 2006). The list emphasizes one type of "nontraditional revenue source"—donors (Addonizio, 2001)—over enterprise activities such as user and developer fees. The list does, however, discuss one kind of enterprise activity—commercial relationships—because this activity more than others reaches inside the school building and even inside the classroom. The chapter focuses on organizations that provide at least some financial resources to schools. It generally ignores other kinds of contributions from some of these donors, such as foundation support of education-related research at universities and think-tanks or of education advocacy activities that may have as much or more impact on schools than direct contributions.

In short, the first challenge in examining the role of nongovernmental organizations in public school finance is to create a coherent framework for exploring this dizzyingly diverse set of actors and activities. While acknowledging that the boundaries are fuzzy and that the organizations and activities sometimes overlap, the chapter will examine nongovernmental organization financing provided to or on behalf of K–12 education by three distinguishable groups of donors: (1) locally-based voluntary contributors, (2) independent foundations, and (3) corporate supporters. Because charter schools are the subject of other chapters in this handbook, this chapter will not discuss the substantial role nongovernmental donors have played in their development.

What Donors Give: The Limits of Data

As already indicated, there is no good source of data on the number of nongovernmental organizations that provide revenue to public schools or on the amount that they give. The important point to keep in mind is that in overall terms private giving is at best a very small proportion of the $450+ billion[4] in total revenues devoted annually to public elementary and secondary education.

While some evidence will be cited in the sections below about magnitudes of, and changes in, levels of private giving, no attempt will be made to do the impossible and develop a credible estimate of totals. Researchers who have examined various nongovernmental funders have chronicled some of the difficulties in painting a statistical portrait of these organizations and their donations:

- National statistics on district revenues typically draw on data collected by the U.S. Census Bureau in its "Annual Survey of Local Government Finances: School Systems." This survey has traditionally collected information on contributions and donations from private sources in a single reporting line that includes rentals, gains and losses on capital assets, refunds of prior year's expenditures, and miscellaneous local revenues.[5] States and local districts may have more finely-grained reports, but definitions and categories are inconsistent across sites and are difficult to interpret on their face.[6]
- Efforts to quantify giving by studying donor statistics run into similar problems of incompleteness and inconsistency. Many donors channel their contributions to public education through non-profit entities established under section 501(c)(3) of the Internal Revenue Code. Such organizations with gross receipts greater than $25,000 must annually file a form 990 with the Internal Revenue Service, and some researchers[7] have used these reports to try to develop a portrait of education giving. However, many local contributors fall under the $25,000 threshold.[8] For those above it, it can still be difficult to consistently identify those whose purpose is support of public education. Studies based on data that charities must report to individual states[9] can surmount some, but not all, of the problems in pinning down giving that is targeted on public education.
- Despite the effort of foundations to reduce the ambiguity over the purposes and amounts of their giving by voluntarily providing data to the Foundation Center, uncertainty still abounds. In a recent study attempting to quantify philanthropic support of public K–12 education, Greene (2005) (who comes up with an estimate of $1.5 billion annually) describes the imprecision of the Center's education reporting categories and inconsistent reporting across classifications by the foundations themselves.

Researchers attempting to understand philanthropic giving in just three school districts expected to find the task straightforward but discovered that no one in the districts had a comprehensive grasp of nongovernmental funding. "Preparing a coherent account of this topic was therefore less like telling a story and more like assembling a puzzle from widely scattered pieces" (Jenkins and McAdams, 2005, p. 134). This chapter, too, has had to depend on scattered pieces of information to provide insight into nongovernmental funding for public schools.

LOCALLY-BASED VOLUNTARY CONTRIBUTORS

Local individuals and organizations have long provided financial support to public schools. What is new is the growing number of such contributors and the increasingly formal and sophisticated way in which many are approaching their fundraising activities.

A Picture of Local Contributors

While individuals and local businesses sometimes provide money, equipment, and other gifts directly to schools on an ad-hoc basis, private giving is increasingly channeled through a variety of organizations with missions that explicitly include fundraising for schools and/or districts.

School-Based Parent, Alumni, and Booster Clubs. These familiar organizations are sometimes taking on unfamiliar roles in raising money for their schools. While many may bring in just a few hundred dollars, others are raising tens of thousands and using the money for such things as athletic tracks, computers with wireless Internet access, a new phonics curriculum, or salaries of instructors and teacher aides (Luttrell, n.d.).

School Foundations. Some districts and schools have moved to make local fundraising more formal and sophisticated by establishing foundations (tax-exempt 501(c)(3) organizations set up to support individual schools and/or whole districts). School foundations (as distinct from local education funds described below) were generally created to raise extra dollars for schools. They do not attempt to operate independently from the schools they support and may have staff appointed by the school or district and/or have school officials sitting on or chairing their boards (Lampkin and Stern, 2003).

One study (Lampkin and Stern, 2003) identified over 1,200 school foundations nationwide that were required to file Form 990s in 2001. The National School Boards Association, in a guide on establishing school foundations (Coventry, 2004), indicated that there were more than 4,800 of these groups, suggesting that many raise only small amounts of money and/or support private rather than public schools. A handful, however, are quite large as measured either by absolute dollars or as a proportion of district or school spending. For example, the Hillsborough (CA) Schools Foundation reports that its contributions increase the district budget by 22 percent.[10] In New York City, the Fund for Public Schools received over $124 million in donations and pledges from fiscal year 2003 through December 2005 (Fund for Public Schools, 2005).

Statewide and national associations exist to support the formation and programs of these foundations. The California Consortium of Education Foundations assists 500+ foundations.[11] The Oklahoma Foundation for Excellence supports the work of 195 foundations.[12] The National School Foundation Association[13] provides resources to help schools and school districts that want to establish foundations or improve and expand their financial performance.

Local Education Funds. While the boundaries are not always neat (and similar names may be used for different kinds of organizations), activists and researchers distinguish local education funds (LEFs) from school foundations on a number of dimensions. LEFs, most of which belong to the Public Education Network (PEN), are also non-profit organizations that support public schools, but they operate on a district, regional, or statewide level and act independently of the schools and districts themselves. They focus on areas with significant numbers of low-income families. While school foundations use their resources mainly to support school programs, many LEFs see system wide reform efforts as a key part of their missions. LEFs are on average larger than school foundations in terms of both revenues and expenditures and have larger paid staffs (Lampkin and Stern, 2003). They sponsor a variety of activities aimed at creating a supportive civic environment for public education; enhancing school and community capacity to support student achievement; and raising community status as measured by educational attainment, higher education participation, and economic development. In 2005 this work was carried out by 85 U.S. LEFs (there are also three international ones) in 34 states and the District of Columbia, reaching 22 percent of the nation's public schoolchildren. They had $200 million in revenues, with a median of $819,000, and 880 staff members (Public Education Network, 2005).[14]

The earliest LEFs were established in the 1970s, but their expansion was spurred by a 1983 Ford Foundation grant that seeded 53 LEFs across the country via the Public Education Fund. The Public Education Network, a successor to the Fund, is a membership organization that continues to support LEF activities both financially and through the provision of information and networking opportunities.

Community Foundations. A final type of local contributor to public education is the community foundation. Legally distinct from private foundations—like the independent and corporate foundations to be described below—community foundations are a type of public foundation that operates a grant program addressing broad public needs of the geographic community or region in which it is located.[15] There were 700 such foundations in 2004 providing $2.9 billion in grants. A study of 86 of the larger community foundations found that education accounted for 24 percent of their giving (Foundation Center, 2006a).

Concerns Arising From the Growth in Local Voluntary Contributions

Even though local voluntary contributions represent only a small fraction of expenditures on public education, they can be sizeable in specific circumstances, as the Hillsborough example above suggests. They have therefore raised a number of concerns, chief among them the possibility that growing reliance on local contributions would undo some of the effects of school finance reforms meant to reduce spending disparities among districts and schools.

Equity. School finance reform and tax limitation laws in California in the 1970s had the effect of centralizing finance decisions at the state level, limiting what local officials could spend on public education, and reducing spending disparities among districts. These changes spurred growth in organizations to channel private contributions to schools and also stimulated research aimed at assessing the extent and effects of this private giving. Much of what is known about local voluntary contributions to education comes from this California-based research.

Brunner and Sonstelie (1997) demonstrated that in 1992 294 educational foundations, 523 Parent Teacher Associations, and 447 other organizations filed Form 990s and raised nearly $100 million for California public schools. (A total of 2,634 organizations supported public schools, but many were not required to file 990s.) Statewide, these private contributions amounted to just $20 per student. Contributions were not uniformly distributed, however. About a third of the districts whose school spending was most constrained by school finance reform and tax limitations had nonprofit support organizations reporting revenues, and these organizations raised an average of $141 per pupil. Districts with high family incomes ($70,000 or above in 1990) were the most likely to have nonprofits reporting revenues (79 percent) and had the highest average per pupil revenue ($244).

Motivated by new concerns that state budget cuts were further spurring new levels of school fundraising, Brunner and Imazeki (2005) updated this research with figures for 2001. They found that voluntary contributions had just about doubled in inflation-adjusted terms but still amounted to less than $40 per pupil, if distributed equally across the state. Again, though, they found that the distribution was unequal and that the districts that benefited the most from private contributions were high-income districts. They also observed, however, that the use of voluntary contributions was not as widespread as they had expected, even for high-income districts and schools. They concluded that when the source of local discretionary spending changes from local property taxes to voluntary contributions, some people will "free ride" on those willing to contribute. This free-riding diminishes the willingness of would-be contributors to pay more to support the schools. Brunner and Imazeki believe that only in the smallest and wealthiest schools and districts is voluntary giving likely to be of more than limited appeal; and the contributions data support this view.

While acknowledging some disparities in the distribution of voluntary contributions, Brunner and Imazeki conclude that private giving has not led to large inequalities across jurisdictions. Furthermore, because of its nature, they believe that private giving is unlikely ever to be the source of wide-scale disruptions in the distribution of resources. Zimmer et al. (2003) also found in a sample of districts in Los Angeles County that while poorer communities might have fewer monetary contributions from parents, they might be more apt to benefit from donations from organizations that concentrated on support for less-advantaged communities, including the philanthropic and corporate donors to be described below. These analyses are largely echoed by research on education foundations in Michigan (Addonizio, 2000).

Nevertheless, some districts have adopted policies to guard against the potential disequalizing effects of voluntary giving, especially among individual schools in the district. In Montgomery County, Maryland, the school board in 1989 prohibited outside groups from paying for teachers' salaries. More recently, the board specified that some kinds of facilities-related costs, such as stadium lighting and landscaping, can, with board approval, be paid for with private funds. A new gymnasium cannot be privately funded unless it will be available to the community at large. In Portland, Oregon, outside groups that raise more than $5,000 for teachers' salaries must send one-third of the money to the Portland Schools Foundation to use at schools in low-income neighborhoods (Galley, 2003).

Sustainability. Questions arise about whether voluntary contributions can be sustained, especially if they are used to pay for schools' routine operating expenses. There are uncertainties about whether volunteer fundraisers can keep the money flowing in year after year. Moreover, the leadership of local groups like parents' organizations and booster clubs may change frequently, with new leaders having new priorities for their funds. The concern for sustainability is one factor that motivates some local individuals to form education foundations to act as full-time fundraisers and watchdogs over spending. It also has encouraged some of these foundations to focus on setting up endowments to sustain beneficiaries in the future (Galley, 2003). As suggested earlier, some school boards address the sustainability issue by limiting private giving to one-time expenditures and "extras" rather than paying for items that should be covered by routine operations. Some school supporters also argue that private givers need to focus their activity not just on fundraising but on building community support for public education more generally and for public funds to address important school needs (Luttrell, n.d.).

New Developments and Transparency

The paucity of data about local voluntary giving for public schools has severely hampered research efforts to assess its scope and impact. In 2002, the Governmental Accounting Standards

Board (GASB) issued a statement aimed at clarifying and making more consistent the accounting of organizations that are closely related to a primary government. The new rules, which went into effect for financial statements for periods beginning after June 15, 2003, require state and local governments to include the financial activities of "qualifying" foundations in their own financial statements. Generally, Statement No. 39 requires the primary government agency (in this case, a school district) to report "as a component unit, an organization that raises and holds economic resources for the direct benefit of a governmental unit" (GASB, 2002). This rule appears to hold promise for making more transparent at least some of the contributions flowing into school districts from independently-governed but closely affiliated groups.

Beginning with its Fiscal 2006 survey of school system finances, the U.S. Census Bureau is requiring separate reporting of contributions and donations from private sources. Distinguishing these funds from other miscellaneous sources of local revenue should in the future provide better information on the private giving that is included in the financial recordkeeping systems of local districts.

INDEPENDENT FOUNDATIONS

Considering that independent foundations have been providing support for public education since early in the 20th century, it is surprising how little their contributions have been studied by researchers. As foundation donors increasingly turn from ad-hoc project support to "reform-oriented giving," their activities arguably warrant more outside scrutiny and accountability.

Independent Foundations and Public Education

The foundations discussed in this section are the so-called independent foundations, one of three types of private foundations as defined by the Foundation Center.[16] A second, the corporate foundation, is discussed below. The third, the operating foundation, is not relevant to this examination of organizations that provide funds for public schools.

> Independent foundations are the most prevalent type of private foundation, comprising 89 percent of those in the Foundation Center's database. An individual or family usually provides these foundations' assets in the form of gifts or bequests that are held as an endowment. Because of the narrow base of their support, they are subject to the private foundation laws intended to assure that they serve the public good.[17]

There were about 60,000 independent foundations in 2004.[18] The top 100 foundations (ranked by total giving for all purposes) account for about a third of all independent foundation giving.[19] The best available estimate of total foundation giving (from foundations of all types) to public elementary and secondary education is "probably about $1.5 billion per year and almost certainly does not exceed $2 billion" (Greene, 2005, p. 53). The disparity in giving levels among foundations is apparent within the top 30 givers: the biggest K–12 donor (Bill & Melinda Gates Foundation) gave $246 million in 2002; No. 30 (Paul G. Allen Charitable Foundation) gave $415,000 (Greene, 2005, p. 65).[20] Not all this K–12 giving goes into the coffers of public schools or of organizations that directly support public education activities. Research and advocacy funding, for example, is directed in some part to organizations specializing in these kinds of endeavors.

The Track Record of Independent Foundation Philanthropy

Independent foundations have a long history of supporting public education, and their efforts have been so diverse that summarizing them is impossible. As Frumkin (2005) notes:

> One of the oldest and most popular targets for philanthropy is education. Going all the way back to the start of modern, large-scale giving, donors have found the idea of supporting education—in all its many form—attractive because it offers one of the clearest and most compelling ways to increase opportunities. (p. 275)

An early example was the General Education Board (GEB), established by John D. Rockefeller in 1902 with an initial endowment of $33 million. The largest of a number of endeavors created after the Civil War to foster education for black students, the GEB supported teacher training, rural school agents, and the development of state education departments and sponsored studies, demonstrations, and conferences. A few recent foundation-funded initiatives suggest the diversity of foundation grantmaking: the New American Schools Development Corporation, the National Board for Professional Teaching Standards, Teach for America, and the Comer School Development Program (Lenkowsky, 2005).

Undoubtedly, many foundation-sponsored efforts have left their mark on public schools. Colvin (2005) points out that "many of the features of public schools that are taken for granted can be traced to foundation-funded projects" (p. 25). He cites as examples classroom aides, the Advanced Placement Program, the creation of schools and colleges of education, the Educational Testing Service and achievement testing programs, middle schools as a replacement for junior highs, the academic standards movement, and the research and advocacy projects that spawned lawsuits across the country challenging the constitutionality of disparities in spending and tax rates between rich and poor communities.

Nevertheless, there is a belief among both researchers and foundation officials themselves that the result of a century of foundation philanthropy has been disappointing. Loveless (2005) states the argument bluntly: "The record of philanthropic foundations in promoting education reform is known more for its failures than its successes" (p. 105). His view is echoed by many of the other researchers and practitioners who undertook studies for Frederick Hess's pioneering volume on K–12 philanthropy (Hess, 2005) and by Fleishman (2007) in his recent book on American foundations. They do not quarrel with the proposition that many individual projects positively affected their beneficiaries. But they argue that foundations have not had a significant impact on improving the overall quality of American education.

Two major programs, separated in time by more than 30 years, symbolize for many the disconnect between the money and time invested and the results achieved in too many foundation undertakings.

In 1960 the Ford Foundation launched the Comprehensive School Improvement Program (described in Manno and Barry, 2001). It was not a "one-off" effort, but part of a larger systemic reform agenda with "a distinctive, well-articulated reform vision" aiming at social change. The foundation spent $30 million throughout the 1960s on 25 projects in school systems (not individual schools) encouraging a variety of innovations designed "to create a critical mass—a chain reaction of change that would overcome the inertia of school systems and produce significantly different educational institutions" (quoted in Manno and Barry, 2001, p. 2). The foundation undertook ongoing evaluation of the projects, cross-site conferences, and frequent site visits. In its 1972 report *A Foundation Goes to School,* the foundation itself (as reported by Manno and Barry,

2001, pp. 3-4) documented the failure of CSIP to spur significant change because its sponsors failed to grasp the complexity of improving schools.

In the 1990s the largest philanthropic grant ever made to American schools, the Annenberg Challenge, had similarly large ambitions but was ultimately also judged to have been generally ineffective. Walter Annenberg's $500 million gift to nine large city school systems, a consortium of rural schools, two national school-based-reform groups, and several arts education projects were viewed in the end as supporting more of what was already going on in schools, rather than fostering major change (Colvin, 2005; Fleishman, 2007). Colvin reports varied explanations offered for the project's lack of impact, including among others: not enough foundation staff to guide such a big effort; money spread too thin; activities focused too much on the margin instead of on radical reform that started with an empty slate and radically redesigned school operations; and insufficient attention to systemic shortcomings such as adequate, equitable, and reliable funding of schools.

The difficulties of achieving lasting improvement in elementary and secondary education caused some major foundation donors to withdraw from the field. The Ford Foundation, the Edna McConnell Clark Foundation, the Pew Charitable Trusts, the Rockefeller Foundation, and the David and Lucile Packard Foundation have all decided for now to focus their funding elsewhere (Hess, 2005; Manno and Barry, 2001).

Recent Developments in Foundation Philanthropy

Despite the scaling back of some traditional foundation donors, philanthropic contributions to K–12 education continue to flow, but with some new emphases.

New Players. While some old hands have withdrawn from the field, new players have emerged in the K–12 philanthropic arena. The top two donors in 2002 and subsequently, the Bill & Melinda Gates Foundation with total 2002 giving of $246 million and the Walton Family Foundation at $77 million, rose rapidly to the number one and two positions. In 1998 the Walton Family Foundation was number 26 on the Foundation Center's list of the 50 largest givers to K–12 education. The Gates Foundation, which was not founded until 2000, did not appear at all.[21] Gates is now the largest foundation in the world and is about to see its assets (roughly $30 billion) doubled over the next several years when Warren Buffett donates most of his assets to it (Strom, 2006). The foundation has become the focal point for much of the current debate about how and whether philanthropists are influencing education reform.

"Higher-Leverage" Agendas. A key explanation offered by some researchers for the relative failure of foundation philanthropy to spur major education reform is that much of the giving has gone to support what schools already do, rather than to encourage systemic reform and significantly new ways of operating. Greene (2005) argues that too much of philanthropy goes for "lower-leverage" activities (e.g., providing training to educators, offering pedagogical or curricular innovations, giving schools additional resources or equipment). Given the size of philanthropy relative to total school budgets, such gifts are like "buckets into the sea," too small to make a significant impact. He argues that "higher-leverage" activities, aimed at trying to redirect how future public expenditures are used, have more potential to effect real long-term systemic changes. Such activities include supporting research and advocacy efforts that inform education policy debates, creating new types of public schools or administrative structures through which public dollars will flow, and developing alternative professional associations and credentials.

Greene analyzed the K–12 education giving by the 30 largest educational donor foundations in 2002 and found that overall 61 percent of their gifts were going for the kinds of lower-leverage activities described in the previous paragraph. Gates and Walton were better than most, however, in the higher-leverage category, as were a few of the older foundations. The former, however, tended to focus their higher-leverage activities on specific reforms (small public schools for Gates and charter schools and vouchers for Walton). The older foundations with high proportions of higher-leverage activities (Pew Charitable Trusts, Charles Stewart Mott Foundation, William Penn Foundation, and James Irvine Foundation) concentrated on research and advocacy rather than direct funding for schools.

Hands-on Involvement and Venture Philanthropy. Unlike the older foundations whose founders and family members are often long gone, many of the newer and most visible foundations are actively managed by the business leaders who endowed them. The Broad Foundation (founded in 1999 with an exclusive focus on K–12 urban education) reflects "the beliefs and core values" of founder Eli Broad in its efforts to improve education through better governance, management, labor relations, and competition (Hassett and Katzir, 2005). Michael Dell (Dell Foundation), Donald and Doris Fisher (Pisces Foundation), John Walton (Walton Family Foundation, before his untimely 2005 death in an accident), and John Doerr (NewSchools Venture Fund) are other examples of donors with active hands-on involvement in the decisions about the operations and beneficiaries of their charities. Bill Gates has announced that in July 2008 he will step away from day-to-day management of the Microsoft Corporation to devote more time to the Gates Foundation.[22]

These "new givers" are described as bringing "a flashier, more entrepreneurial, more aggressive approach to both giving money and insisting on results." They are "more intrusive, ask much tougher questions, have a much more hands-on relationship. They bring a degree of impatience…." (Colvin, 2005, pp. 29–30)

Some foundations are explicitly following a new approach called "venture philanthropy," which the Foundation Center defines as creating "vehicles that allow the donors to be highly engaged in the management of a relatively small number of grantees" and which "are said to follow a venture capital model of investment."[23] An example is the NewSchools Venture Fund, which raises early-stage capital from a variety of institutional and individual donors and invests it in promising education entrepreneurs.[24]

While newer foundations are more apt to follow this "new giver" model, there are flashes of more aggressiveness in the older foundations as well. Though it is now working in youth development rather than education, the Clark Foundation is following "a more hands-on, results-oriented approach to grantmaking focusing on developing partnerships with and supporting exceptional nonprofit organizations" much as venture philanthropists do (Manno and Barry, 2001, p. 9). In 2002, three foundations (the Grable Foundation, the Heinz Endowments, and the Pittsburgh Foundation) announced they were suspending all their education grantmaking in the Pittsburgh school district because of "a sharp decline of governance, leadership, and fiscal discipline" (Galley, 2002, p. 7).

Use of Intermediaries. Because of the concern that the forces of tradition and the politics of education are so hard to overcome in public schools, some donors (especially the larger ones) have turned to intermediary organizations through which to channel their K–12 giving, rather than funding schools and districts directly. For example "[i]ntermediary organizations were integral to the Annenberg Challenge" (Rothman, Winter 2002/03, p. 2). Private groups (some national or regional in scope, some working with just one district) were the recipients of Challenge funds. The Gates Foundation directed funds for high school reform in North Carolina and Texas to newly-established public-private partnerships.

Collaboration and Coordinated Giving. Finally, there seems to be more of a tendency for foundations to collaborate with districts and with each other to maximize the impact of their giving as opposed to seeing their influence dissipated on numerous, uncoordinated projects. Colvin (2005) cites two superintendents (Alan Bersin in San Diego and Thomas Payzant in Boston) as working to encourage foundations to avoid fragmentation by supporting a district's reform strategy rather than insisting on the foundations' ad hoc projects and preferences. In a recent example of collaboration, ten foundations led by Gates are investing $20 million to fix the nine worst-performing high schools in Baltimore and to create at least six new ones.[25]

Challenges Facing Foundation Philanthropy.

Will new approaches to foundation philanthropy be more successful than old ones in spurring significant K–12 improvement? It is too early to tell, but already some echoes of history can be heard in the experiences of the newest generation of foundation donors to take on education reform. In just its first six years, the Gates Foundation might be said to have evolved to a third generation of education giving. After focusing for several years on principal and teacher training, mostly in the use of technology, the foundation abandoned these efforts in 2002 and turned toward high school reform and the creation of small schools (Colvin, 2005). While not abandoning these interests, the foundation subsequently decided to become more strategic in its reform efforts and to focus more heavily on district-wide reform efforts and on research and advocacy in the policy arena (Robelen, 2006). Frumkin (2001) has asked whether the new venture philanthropy will really turn out to be substantially different than its forebears or whether the apparent changes in operating style are more a matter of semantics than reality (with, for example, "investments" equating to "grants," "investors" to "donors," "social returns" to "impact," "performance measurement" to "evaluation," "due diligence" to "grant review process," and so on).

Frederick Hess (2005), who spearheaded one of the few efforts to assess the role of independent foundation philanthropy in K–12 education, poses five challenges raised by philanthropic involvement in efforts to influence the course of America's schools.

- "Strategic" giving: how donors can advance strategic visions of reform without stifling experimentation.
- The political economy of evaluation: how to obtain good evaluations in the face of such political realities as donor reluctance to incur criticism and researchers whose present or future prospects may be tied to donor support.
- The lure of geniality: how to overcome philanthropists' frequent unwillingness to provoke controversy, which can lead them to shy away from structural reforms that challenge established arrangements.
- Pipelines versus programs: how to increase donor appreciation of the value of pipelines that seek to alter the composition of the education workforce by attracting and keeping new talent, as contrasted to programs that focus on a limited population of children and educators. Pipelines (examples include Teach for America, Troops to Teachers, and the National Board for Professional Teaching Standards) have less immediate and direct impacts on individual schools than programs such as reading programs or computer labs, but they offer longer-term levers for systemic change.

- Balancing performance and patience: how to reconcile the new focus on disciplined management strategies and measurable results in the near term with the reality that worthwhile efforts may not demonstrate near-term effects but can more broadly contribute to reshaping education.

Hess also makes the point that as foundations engage in higher-leverage giving intended to influence public policy they should expect to be held to higher standards of public accountability. His preference (echoed in Fleishman, 2007) is for accountability that is fostered through transparency and openness to public scrutiny rather than through formal governmental regulation.

CORPORATE SUPPORTERS

America's business community has had an off-again, on-again relationship with the nation's public schools. Beginning with the West Indies Company which started schools in New Amsterdam (later New York City) in the 1640s to attract settlers (Lenkowsky, 2005), businesses were important in founding schools for America's children. After publicly-provided education became widespread, business involvement shifted from the creation to the support of schools, both financially and through such activities as service on school boards. While many business leaders pulled back from K–12 education during the politically tumultuous 1960s and 1970s, they began to reengage again in the 1980s in response to global economic changes that focused attention on the quality of the nation's workforce. Reinvigorated business involvement with the schools was accompanied by a shift in corporate contribution programs toward a new emphasis on pre-collegiate education (Timpane and McNeill, 1991).

As with other kinds of private givers, it is difficult to portray succinctly the myriad of educational activities of the diverse business community. There is a continuum of involvement, and individual businesses and business people work with schools for reasons both altruistic and self-interested. Some key points related to corporate support can most effectively be conveyed by a brief discussion of two types of activities: philanthropic support and commercial partnerships.

Corporate Philanthropic Support of K–12 Education

Businesses small and large contribute to schools in a variety of ways, both financial and nonfinancial. Employees donate time to work in classrooms and mentor students or teachers. Their employers give equipment and money to individual schools and districts, sometimes directly and sometimes through LEFs and other community groups. Timpane and McNeill (1991) describe four "patterns" of business involvement:

- Helping-hand relationships: these encourage businesses to supplement or enhance existing school programs through donations of tangible goods and services such as equipment, mini-grants, tutors, speakers, and special materials.
- Programmatic initiatives: more intensive, more complex partnerships between business partners and schools aimed at improving one particular program or school through, for example, career academies and mentoring programs.
- Collaboratives and compacts: joint efforts involving several businesses and one or more school districts, such as the LEFs mentioned earlier.
- Policy change: through their involvement with such organizations as the national Business Roundtable and its state affiliates, the Committee for Economic Development, and various

> state and city business associations, business leaders have engaged with public policy debates over higher standards, accountability for outcomes, and restructured schools.

Corporate financial giving to K–12 education is done both directly and through corporate foundations, which are private foundations that receive their assets from a company rather than an individual or family. These foundations may have an endowment, but the bulk of their giving generally comes from annual gifts from the company. Companies may give both directly and through their foundations. The latter are subject to IRS regulation; the former have no public disclosure requirements, though the Foundation Center tries to include them where it can.[26] According to the Center (Foundation Center, 2006b) there were 2,956 corporate foundations in 2004 (a doubling since 1987) that gave away $3.4 billion, representing 5 percent of all private philanthropic giving. About a quarter of corporate foundation giving was directed to education at all levels, not just K–12.

Corporate foundations face many of the same criticisms and challenges that independent foundations do in terms of the impact their activities have on creating a more effective K–12 education system. Hill (2001) believes that corporate foundations —and independent foundations closely associated in the public eye with the business of the philanthropist who endowed them, such as Gates and Microsoft—may shy away from aggressive philanthropy that challenges the educational status quo for fear of offending potential customers. Rotherham (2005) suggests that corporate foundations are thus even more inclined than their independent brethren to invest in lower-leverage rather than higher-leverage activities. Frumkin (2005) finds corporate philanthropists more likely to make gifts in a relatively detached way, in order to avoid exposure to negative publicity if their charitable programs backfire or fail. Corporate donors are also more apt to be detached because their foundations and giving arms do not often have enough staff to permit deeper involvement.

As in the independent foundation world, there are some signs that corporate foundations are feeling the pressure to become more aggressive and hands-on, more strategic, and more collaborative. Even though its efforts at 22 schools in 17 cities aimed at increasing the percentage of students going to college were showing positive results, the General Electric Foundation in 2004 began pulling back from a school-by-school approach in favor of new activities designed to influence district-wide transformation (*Business Week* Online, 2006). Leaders of corporate foundations participated in a September 2005 conference organized by Jobs for the Future to talk about how they could collaborate to overcome the isolation and disconnectedness of their "commendable but 'siloed'" projects (Borja, 2005a).

Commercial Partnerships

One type of school-oriented business activity that has grown in size and visibility over the last 15 years involves explicitly commercial relationships. The change has been so noticeable and controversial that Congress asked the General Accounting Office (now the Government Accountability Office, GAO) to undertake a study looking at the nature and extent of commercial activities in schools and the laws, regulations, and policies that govern them (GAO, 2000).

GAO found that school-business commercial partnerships had been growing because of limited school budgets, an increased demand for educational services, and the growing purchasing power of American youth. GAO described the benefits perceived by schools and businesses from the increase in commercial arrangements:

> In general, schools want cash, equipment, or other assistance in providing services and technology during a period when revenues from traditional tax sources are, for many school districts,

essentially flat. Businesses want to increase their sales, generate product loyalty, and develop climates favorable to their products, although some businesses are involved with schools primarily to help local communities. (GAO, 2000, p. 5)

GAO classified the commercial activities it found in a sample of schools as product sales, direct advertising, indirect advertising (e.g., via corporate-sponsored educational materials, teacher training, contests or incentives, or grants and gifts), and in-school market research. Product sales were the most common and lucrative type of school-oriented commercial activity, especially the sale of soft drinks. Advertising appeared especially on soft drink machines and high school score boards, though some was delivered to classrooms via media (e.g., Channel One[27]). Indirect advertising was "limited and subtle,"[28] while in-school market research was nonexistent in the sampled schools (though one principal had been approached about doing research). GAO found that high schools had more commercial activities than middle or elementary schools, that state laws and policies were spotty and varied, and that most decisions about whether to engage in commercial activities were left up to local officials. The revenues generated by commercial activities were tiny percentages of district revenues, but their intensity varied from place to place.

Commercial activities such as soft drink contracts (which guarantee schools some amount of per-pupil revenues or a percentage of sales) and electronic advertising in classrooms have been especially controversial. The former have been under attack because of concerns about rising levels of obesity in children. The latter have raised the ire of groups opposed to the over commercialization of society and concerned about the effects of advertising on young children.[29] Some states have enacted restrictions on the sale of sugary beverages and unhealthy snack foods in schools (Greifner, 2006). In 2006 the soft-drink industry (in an agreement among beverage distributors, the American Heart Association, and former President Clinton's William J. Clinton Foundation), voluntarily agreed to curb soda sales, a development that occurred as several organizations were planning to sue soda companies over the obesity issue (Samuels, 2006). What such developments will mean for school revenues depends on the popularity of the substitute products that the companies will provide.

CONCLUDING THOUGHTS

The universe of nongovernmental organizations providing financial resources to public schools is diverse, and our understanding of it is fragmentary. While the total amounts of revenue involved are very small compared to government funding of elementary and secondary education, in "niches" private funders can have an important impact both for good, such as when they spur important improvements in educational offerings or in the operation of the system, or for ill, such as when they encourage unhealthy habits in children. As private donors engage more systematically in efforts to spur major reforms in America's educational enterprise, their actions take on aspects of public as well as private interest. Thus enhanced efforts to accumulate better data and understanding of the role of nongovernmental organizations in financing public schools are of ongoing importance.

NOTES

1. Http://nces.ed.gov/programs/digest/d05/tables/dt05_153.asp. Accessed October 8, 2006.
2. For example, districts may receive tuition payments from various sources and rental fees from patrons who use school facilities.

3. See, for example., Zimmer, Krop, and Brewer, 2003; Addonizio, 2000; Brunner and Sonstelie, 1997; Brunner and Imazeki, 2005.
4. Total revenues from all sources for public elementary and secondary schools in 2002–03 were $440 billion according to the National Center for Education Statistics. Revenue statistics online at http://nces.ed.gov/programs/digest/d05/tables/dt05_153.asp. Accessed October 8, 2006.
5. The F-33 form used by the Census Bureau to collect finance data on school systems is online at http://ftp2.census.gov/govs/forms/2003/03f33.pdf, accessed October 8, 2006. The accounting codes used on the F-33 form are from National Center for Education Statistics (NCES), 2004. NCES also collects information on public school revenues by source on the National Public Education Finance Survey (ED Form 2447), but this survey is based on state-wide rather than district-level data; and the "other revenue from local sources" category in which contributions and donations from private sources are to be reported includes an even larger number of other revenue types than does the F-33.
6. For example, in attempting to quantify philanthropic giving to public education in five southwestern states, Born and Wilson (2000, p. 3) report: "[W]e noticed a huge amount of gift and grant revenue reported for a small Texas district where nothing like it had appeared before. When we called to ask what it represented we were told that it was actually part of an arrangement whereby a large corporation was recruited to the community with the incentive of a substantial property tax abatement (which withheld potential revenues from the district). In return, the corporation now makes a significant charitable contribution to the district each year. The donation, of course, is claimed as an income tax deduction. Texas Education Agency guidelines define gift and grant income as anything other than local tax and other local revenue, state funds, or federal entitlement funds, so this is reported the same as a foundation grant." Imazeki and Reschovsky (2004) found such tax abatement arrangements to be growing in popularity in wealthy school districts in Texas because they reduced local tax revenues and therefore decreased the amount of local tax dollars that could be "recaptured" by the state as part of school finance equalization efforts.
7. See, for example, Brunner and Sonstelie, 1997; Brunner and Imazeki, 2005; Lampkin and Stern, 2003.
8. For example, Lampkin and Stern (2003, p. 17) report that fewer than 40 percent of the members of the California Consortium of Education Foundations are represented in a database of organizations that file Form 990s.
9. See, for example, California, as used by Brunner and Sonstelie (1997) and Brunner and Imazeki (2005); Michigan, as used by Addonizio (2000).
10. Http://www.hsf.org/faq/applications/FaqsManager/faqshsf.asp?ItemID=56. Accessed September 9, 2006.
11. Http://www.cceflink.org. Accessed September 9, 2006.
12. Http://www.ofe.org/lef/index.htm. Accessed October 12, 2006.
13. Http://www.schoolfoundations.org. Accessed October 12, 2006.
14. These statistics describe the organizations that belong to PEN.
15. Http://foundationcenter.org/findfunders/statistics/pdf/01_found_fin_data/2004/02_04. Accessed October 9, 2006.
16. Http://foundationcenter.org/getstarted/onlinebooks/ff/text.html. Accessed October 9, 2006.
17. Http://foundationcenter.org/getstarted/onlinebooks/ff/text.html. Accessed October 9, 2006.
18. Http://foundationcenter.org/findfunders/statistics/pdf/02_found_growth/03_04.pdf. Accessed October 9, 2006.
19. Author's calculation from Foundation Center statistics.
20. Greene notes that his estimates of individual foundation giving to K–12 education differ from giving reported by the Foundation Center, sometimes dramatically. I have chosen to use his figures for the top 30 foundation givers because he calculated their donations based on information they reported on their IRS 990 forms. The Foundation Center relies on foundation announcements of grant amounts rather than on public filings of actual expenditures.
21. Http://foundationcenter.org/findfunders/statistics/pdf/04_fund_sub/1998/50_found_sub/sub_b2_8.pdf. Accessed October 9, 2006.

22. Http://www.microsoft.com/presspass/press/2006/jun06/06-15CorpNewsPR.mspx. Accessed August 13, 2006.
23. Http://foundationcenter.org/getstarted/onlinebooks/ff/text.html. Accessed October 9, 2006.
24. Http://www.newschools.org/strategy/index.htm. Accessed October 9, 2006.
25. Association of Baltimore Area Grantmakers, at http://www.abagmd.org/info-url2446/info-url_show.htm?doc_id=103573. Accessed July 23, 2006.
26. Http://foundationcenter.org/getstarted/faqs/html/cf_v_cg.html. Accessed October 9, 2006.
27. Channel One, in operation since 1990, provides television sets, VCRs, and satellite receiving equipment to schools in return for their agreeing to show a 10-minute daily current-events broadcast to students, accompanied by 2 minutes of advertising. For a recent article on some problems facing Channel One, see Borja (2005b).
28. Were the GAO report to be repeated today, this finding might be modified. Keen (2006) reports that a growing number of cities and schools are selling naming rights to gyms, locker rooms, kitchens and cafeterias, classrooms, and even the principal's office.
29. See, for example, the organizations Commercial Alert (http://www.commercialalert.org/, accessed October 8, 2006) and the Commercialism in Education Research Unit at Arizona State University (http://epsl.asu.edu/ceru/, accessed October 8, 2006).

REFERENCES

Addonizio, Michael F. (2000). "Salvaging Fiscal Control: New Sources of Local Revenue for Public Schools," in Neil D. Theobald and Betty Malen, eds., *Balancing Local Control and State Responsibility for K-12 Education*, 2000 Yearbook of the American Education Finance Association, Larchmont, NY: Eye on Education, Inc.

Addonizio, Michael F. (2001) "New Revenues for Public Schools: Blurring the Line Between Public and Private Finance," in Stephen Chaikind and William J. Fowler, eds., *Education Finance in the New Millennium*, 2001 Yearbook of the American Education Finance Association, Larchmont, NY: Eye on Education, Inc.

Borja, Rhea. (2005a)."Business Leaders Call for More Cooperation in K-12 Giving Efforts," *Education Week*, September 28.

Borja, Rhea. (2005b). "Channel One Struggling in Shifting Market," *Education Week*, July 27.

Born, Laurie, and Dave Wilson (2000). *Philanthropic Support for Public Education in the Southwest Region*, Environmental Scanning Brief 00-06, Austin, TX: Southwestern Educational Research Laboratory.

Brunner, Eric J., and Jennifer Imazeki (July 2005). "Fiscal Stress and Voluntary Contributions to Public Schools," in W. J. Fowler, ed., *Developments in School Finance: 2004*, Washington, DC: National Center for Education Statistics, pp. 39–54.

Brunner, Eric J., and Jon Sonstelie. (1997). "Coping with Serrano: Private Contributions to California's Public Schools," Proceedings of the 89th Annual Conference on Taxation, National Tax Association. pp. 372–381.

Business Week. Online, June 26, 2006, http://www.businessweek.com/magazine/content/06_26/b3990007.htm.

Carr, Sarah. (2004). "Private Funds Padding Public School Coffers," *Milwaukee Journal-Sentinel*, November.

Colvin, Richard Lee. (2005). "A New Generation of Philanthropists and Their Great Ambitions," in Frederick M. Hess, ed., *With the Best of Intentions: How Philanthropy is Reshaping K-12 Education*, Cambridge, MA: Harvard Education Press.

Coventry, Kate. (2004). "Starting a School Foundation," *Leadership Insider: Practical Perspectives on School Law and Policy*, National School Boards Association, January.

Fleishman, Joel L. (2007). *The Foundation: A Great American Secret*, New York, NY: Public Affairs.

Foundation Center, Key Facts on Community Foundations. (2006a). Online at http://foundationcenter.org/gainknowledge/research/pdf/communitykeyfacts.pdf.

Foundation Center, Key Facts on Corporate Foundations. (2006b). Online at http://foundationcenter.org/gainknowledge/research/pdf/corporatekeyfacts.pdf.

Frumkin, Peter. (2001). "Inside Venture Philanthropy," in *Seven Studies in Education Philanthropy*, Washington, DC: The Thomas B. Fordham Foundation. Online at http://www.edexcellence.net/foundation/publication/publication.cfm?id=318

Frumkin, Peter. (2005). "Strategic Giving and Public School Reform: Three Challenges," in Frederick M. Hess, ed., *With the Best of Intentions: How Philanthropy is Reshaping K–12 Education*, Cambridge, MA: Harvard Education Press.

Fund for Public Schools, *Private Investment in Public Education: Supporting Change in NYC*, Annual Report 2005. Online at http://schools.nyc.gov/NR/rdonlyres/C70B432F-CF17-49B8-AFF9-80851F7C9426/10030/FPSannual2005singlepgs2.pdf. Accessed July 23, 2006.

Galley, Michelle. (2002). "Freeze on Grants Roils Pittsburgh District," *Education Week*, August 7.

Galley, Michelle. (2003). "Parents Buy into Paying for the Basics," *Education Week*, February 12.

General Accounting Office. (2000). *Commercial Activities in Schools*, GAO/HEHS-00-156, Washington, DC, September.

General Accounting Standards Board (GASB), "Summary of Statement No. 39: Deterining Whether Certain Organizations Are Component Units—an amendment of GASB Statement No. 14," May 2002, http://www.gasb.org/st/index.html. Accessed October 16, 2006.

Greene, Jay P. (2005). "Buckets into the Sea: Why Philanthropy Isn't Changing Schools, and How It Could," in Frederick M. Hess, ed., *With the Best of Intentions: How Philanthropy is Reshaping K-12 Education*, Cambridge, MA: Harvard Education Press.

Greifner, Laura. (2006). "Connecticut Moving to Curb Soda Sales in Schools," *Education Week*, May 10.

Hassett, Wendy, and Dan Katzir. (2005). "Lessons Learned from the Inside," in Frederick M. Hess, ed., *With the Best of Intentions: How Philanthropy is Reshaping K-12 Education*, Cambridge, MA: Harvard Education Press.

Hess, Frederick M. (2005). *With the Best of Intentions: How Philanthropy is Reshaping K-12 Education*, Cambridge, MA: Harvard Education Press.

Hill, Paul T., "Education Philanthropy for the 21st Century," in *Seven Studies in Education Philanthropy*, Washington, DC: The Thomas B. Fordham Foundation, 2001. Online at http://www.edexcellence.net/foundation/publication/publication.cfm?id=318. Accessed July 23, 2006.

Imazeki, Jennifer, and Andrew Reschovsky. (2004). "School Finance Reform in Texas: A Never-Ending Story?" in John Yinger, ed., *Helping Children Left Behind: State Aid and the pursuit of Educational Equity*, Cambridge, MA: MIT Press.

Jenkins, Lynn, and Donald R. McAdams. (2005). "Philanthropy and Urban School District Reform: Lessons from Charlotte, Houston, and San Diego," in Frederick M. Hess, ed., *With the Best of Intentions: How Philanthropy is Reshaping K-12 Education*, Cambridge, MA: Harvard Education Press.

Keen, Judy. (2006). "Wisconsin Schools Find Corporate Sponsors," *USA Today*, July 26.

Lampkin, Linda M. and David D. Stern. (2003). *Who Helps Public Schools: A Report on Local Education Funds*, Washington, DC: Urban Institute and Public Education Network, November.

Lenkowsky, Leslie. (2005). "The 'Best Uses' of Philanthropy for Reform," in Frederick M. Hess, ed., *With the Best of Intentions: How Philanthropy is Reshaping K-12 Education*, Cambridge, MA: Harvard Education Press.

Loveless, Tom. (2005). "How Program Officers at Education Philanthropies View Education," in Frederick M. Hess, ed., *With the Best of Intentions: How Philanthropy is Reshaping K-12 Education*, Cambridge, MA: Harvard Education Press.

Luttrell, Sharron Kahn. (n.d.). "Can Parents Do Too Much?" *PTO Today*. Online at http://www.ptotoday.com/0302ptogroups.html. Accessed October 9, 2006.

Manno, Bruno, and John Barry. (2001). "When Education Philanthropy Goes Awry," in *Seven Studies in Education Philanthropy*, Washington, DC: The Thomas B. Fordham Foundation. Online at http://www.edexcellence.net/foundation/publication/publication.cfm?id=318. Accessed July 23, 2006.

National Center for Education Statistics. (2004). *Financial Accounting for Local and State School Systems, 2003 Edition*, NCES 2004-318, Washington, DC: U.S. Department of Education.

Nichols, Russell. (2006). "Colleges Pledge $10m Boost to 10 Boston Schools," *Boston Globe*, September 29.

Public Education Network. (2005). *A Portrait of the Network: Local Education Funds' Impact in Schools and Communities*, 2005 annual membership survey, Washington, DC: November 13.

Robelen, Erik. (2006). "Gates Learns to Think Big," *Education Week*, October 11.

Rotherham, Andrew J. (2005). "Teaching Fishing or Giving Away Fish? Grantmaking for Research, Policy, and Advocacy," in Frederick M. Hess, ed., *With the Best of Intentions: How Philanthropy is Reshaping K-12 Education*, Cambridge, MA: Harvard Education Press.

Rothman, Robert. (2002/03)."'Intermediary Organizations' Help Bring Reform to Scale," *Challenge Journal*, The Journal of the Annenberg Challenge, Winter.

Samuels, Christina A. (2006). "Stricter School Soda Limits Offered," *Education Week*, May 10.

Strom, Stephanie. (2006). "Gates's Charity Races to Spend Buffett Billions," *New York Times*, August 13.

Timpane, P. Michael, and Laurie Miller McNeil. (1991). *Business Impact on Education and Child Development Reform*, New York: Committee for Economic Development.

Zimmer, Ron W., Cathy Krop, and Dominic J. Brewer. (2003). "Private Resources in Public Schools: Evidence from a Pilot Study," *Journal of Education Finance*, 28, Spring, 485–522.

19

Equity, Adequacy and the Evolving State Role in Education Finance

Sean P. Corcoran and William N. Evans

INTRODUCTION

All fifty state constitutions mandate a statewide system of public education, charging state governments with providing a "thorough and efficient system of free public schools" (or similar language). State legislatures fulfill this obligation by establishing compulsory schooling laws, curriculum standards, and institutions governing the formation and operation of school districts. Despite constitutional goals, states historically played only a minor role in the *financing* of public schools, leaving the funding and day-to-day management of schools in the hands of local governments.

This long-standing devolution of fiscal responsibility to local school districts all but dissolved over the past century. State aid in the form of flat grants and "minimum foundation" programs became common practice in the first half of the century; later, legal challenges to state school finance systems led to far-reaching reforms that further expanded the fiscal responsibilities of the states. As shown in Section III of this handbook, these challenges originated as "equity" suits that sought to break the link between local property wealth and school resources. A later wave of litigation instead sought "adequacy" in school expenditure, as defined by the level of spending necessary to reach some performance standard. Despite the disparate objectives of these challenges, the result was more often than not an increased state role in school funding. On this matter, states frequently had few alternatives, as most major reforms to state school finance systems were legislative responses to a court order. In several cases, though, legislatures enacted significant reform without the prompting of the courts.[1]

In this chapter, we examine the evolving role of the states in the financing of primary and secondary education in the United States. We begin in the next section by documenting the increased importance of states as a source of revenue for schools, show how reliance on state funding varies across states and within states over time, and briefly explore some of the key explanations for these trends. In the following section we examine the extent to which finance reform has increased the states' role in education funding, and how in turn these reforms have affected the level and distribution of per-pupil expenditure between and within states. Finally, prior to a brief concluding section, we review how an increased state role in education finance has affected various non-fiscal aspects of the public education system, most importantly student outcomes.

EDUCATION FINANCE AND THE ROLE OF THE STATES

U.S. education's early roots in the English tradition of locally provided private or religious schools influenced the division of fiscal responsibility for education for nearly two centuries. Not until the mid-19th century "common school" movement did states formally recognize public education in their constitutions, creating statewide systems of public schools to be funded almost entirely by local taxes (Odden and Picus, 2004). Such a shift from private to public education arguably would have been politically infeasible without an implicit promise that tax dollars and administrative control, via a myriad of community school boards, would remain in local hands.[2]

As late as the 1920s, local taxes accounted for the vast majority of funds for public education (83.2 percent, see Figure 19.1) with the remainder coming from states (16.5 percent), predominately through flat per-student grants. During these early years of the 20th century, federal contributions to public education were negligible at less than 1 percent of all school revenues. The 1930s saw a doubling in the state share of school expenditure, as state governments sought to assist localities whose property tax base had eroded during the Depression with new "minimum foundation" programs (Benson and O'Halloran, 1987; see also Picus, Odden, and Goertz, this volume). The state share of revenues continued to rise in the 1940s as localities coped with the effects of the baby boom on primary school enrollment, but then stalled at just under 40 percent of public school expenditures for the next 25 years. Meanwhile, the 1965 passage of the Elementary and Secondary Education Act caused the federal contribution to school spending to jump from 4.4 percent in 1960 to 8 percent in 1970, later peaking near 10 percent in 1980.

As seen in Figure 19.1, the state share of public K–12 expenditure again surged in the 1970s, rising from 39.9 percent in 1969–70 to 46.8 percent at the end of the decade. Perhaps surprisingly, the state share in the aggregate has risen only slightly since 1978 to its present level of 49

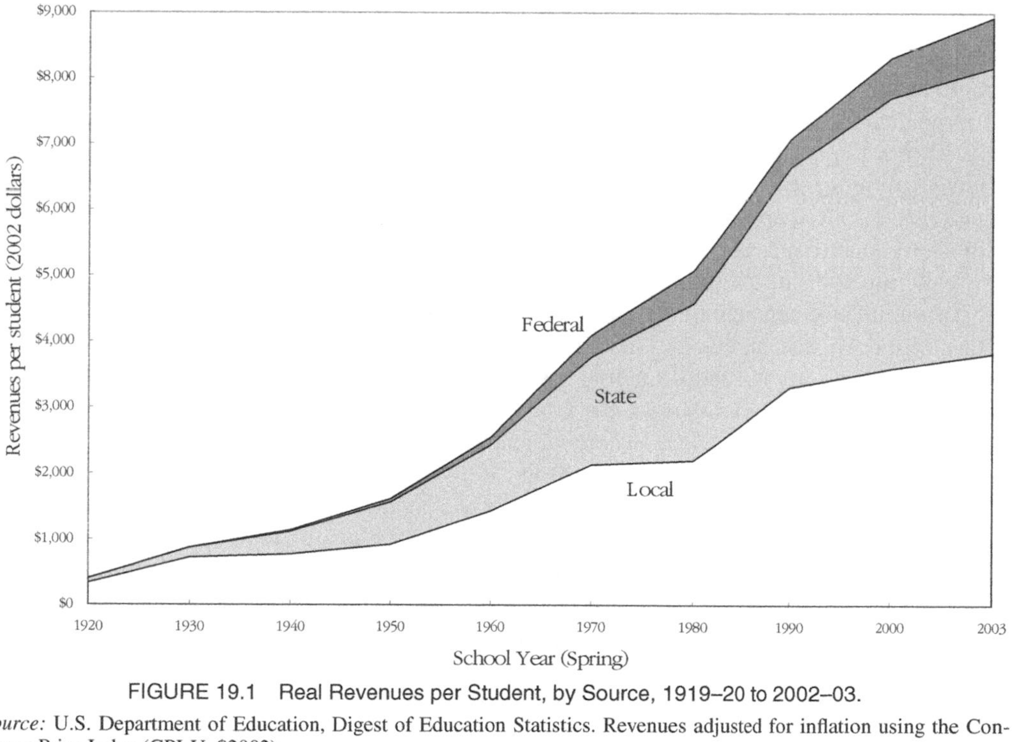

FIGURE 19.1 Real Revenues per Student, by Source, 1919–20 to 2002–03.

Source: U.S. Department of Education, Digest of Education Statistics. Revenues adjusted for inflation using the Consumer Price Index (CPI-U, $2002).

percent—despite reforms of the 1980s and 90s that in some states vastly increased state funding. In any case, not since the mid-1970s have local school districts contributed more to education revenues than state governments. The federal share has never surpassed 10 percent, though its contribution appears to be rising again in response to No Child Left Behind (see Gordon, this volume, for more on the evolving role of the federal government in education finance).

The national trend in state funding masks considerable variation across states in aid to local school districts. In 1970, for example, the fraction of school revenues from state sources varied across states from a low of 10–18 percent in New Hampshire, South Dakota, and Nebraska to a high of 60–70 percent in New Mexico, Alaska, and Delaware.[3] By 2001, the variation across states in the state share was much smaller, ranging from lows of 20–35 percent to a high of nearly 80 percent. Almost every state increased its share of public school revenues over this period, with Florida, Texas, and Pennsylvania being notable exceptions.[4] Generally speaking, increases in the state share appear to reflect increases in state spending on education rather than declines in local revenues.

Explanations for this dramatic shift in fiscal responsibility for public schools from local to state can be found in part in a series of legislative and court-mandated reforms to state finance systems that originated in California's *Serrano I* ruling (1971) and continue to this day. These reforms arose initially in response to inequities generated by reliance on local property taxes for school funding, but in recent years have been driven by concerns over the adequacy of funding for public education, in particular the funding of education for students from disadvantaged backgrounds.[5]

Pressure to reform state school funding originated in state legislatures and—more frequently—in the courts. At last count, litigants had challenged the constitutionality of state school finance systems in all but five states.[6] As Table 19.1 indicates, state supreme courts have ruled on the legality of school funding systems in 39 states since 1970, with 17 declaring their system to be unconstitutional and 27 upholding the existing state program (five states have had both types of ruling; see Appendix Table A19.1 for a more detailed inventory).[7] In most cases, a decision by a high court to overturn a state education financing system has been accompanied by a direct order to make fundamental changes to school funding formulas, an order to which the legislature has responded in full (e.g., Kentucky, Washington), in incremental steps (New Jersey) or barely at all (Ohio). Legislatures have also initiated their own far-reaching reforms to school finance systems, in the wake of unsuccessful litigation (e.g., Georgia and Idaho), under the threat of litigation (e.g., Missouri and Oklahoma; see Minorini and Sugarman, 1999), or in response to political pressure (e.g., Michigan).

While much of the literature has focused on the *effects* of these finance reforms, a smaller body of work has examined the circumstances under which reform arises. Baicker and Gordon (2006), Figlio, Husted, and Kenny (2004), and Card and Payne (2002) all demonstrate that high court rulings overturning school funding systems are notoriously difficult to predict, even after researchers account for variation in the constitutional language upon which such rulings are purportedly based.[8] Consequently, empirical research investigating their effects typically treats court-mandated reform as an exogenous event. Reforms initiated by the legislature cannot, of course, be viewed in this way and perhaps for this reason have been less frequently studied.[9]

Several authors have examined the growth in state aid to local school districts more comprehensively, relating redistributive state aid to state demographics and political measures in addition to exogenous court orders. De Bartolome (1997), for example, attributes much of the growth in state aid between 1970 and 1990 to rising income inequality. His logic is that a rise in income inequality raises mean income relative to that of the median, or decisive, voter in the political process and encourages a greater redistribution from high-income to low-income school districts through state aid. Recognizing that the same level of state aid can be distributed in more or less

TABLE 19.1
State Supreme Court Rulings on School Finance Constitutionality

Rulings Against School Finance System Constitutionality			*Rulings Upholding School Finance System Constitutionality*		
State	*Case*	*Year*	*State*	*Case*	*Year*
Arkansas	*DuPree*	1983	Alaska	*Matanuska*	1997
	Lakeview III	2002	Arizona	*Shofstall*	1973
	Lakeview V	2005	Colorado	*Lujan*	1982
California	*Serrano II*	1976	Florida	*Coalition*	1996
Connecticut	*Horton I*	1977	Georgia	*McDaniel*	1981
	upheld in:	1985	Idaho	*Thompson*	1975
Kansas	*Montoy II*	2005	Illinois	*Committee*	1996
	upheld in:	2006		*Lewis*	1999
Kentucky	*Rose*	1989	Kansas	*USD 229*	1994
Massachusetts	*McDuffy*	1993	Maine	*SAD 1*	1995
Montana	*Helena*	1989	Maryland	*Hornbeck*	1983
	Columbia Falls	2005		*Bradford*	2005
New Hampshire	*Claremont II*	1997	Massachusetts	*Hancock*	2005
	Claremont III	1998	Michigan	*Milliken*	1973
	Claremont V	1999	Minnesota	*Skeen*	1993
	Claremont VI	2000	Missouri	*Committee*	1998
	Claremont VII	2002	Nebraska	*Gould*	1993
New Jersey	*Robinson*	1973	New York	*Levittown*	1982
	upheld in:	1976		*REFIT*	1995
	Abbott II	1990		*Paynter*	2003
	Abbott III	1994	North Carolina	*Britt*	1987
	Abbott IV	1997	North Dakota	*Bismarck*	1994
	Abbott V	1998	Ohio	*BOE*	1979
New York	*CFE*	2003	Oklahoma	*Fair School*	1987
North Carolina	*Leandro II*	2004	Oregon	*Olsen*	1976
	(Hoke)			*Coalition*	1991
Ohio	*DeRolph I*	1997	Pennsylvania	*Danson*	1979
	DeRolph II	2000		*PARSS*	1998
	DeRolph III	2001		*Marrero*	1999
	DeRolph IV	2002	Rhode Island	*Pawtucket*	1995
Tennessee	*Small Schools I*	1993	South Carolina	*Richland Co.*	1988
	Small Schools II	1995	Virginia	*Scott*	1994
	Small Schools III	2002	Washington	*North Shore*	1974
Texas	*Edgewood I*	1989	Wisconsin	*Kukor*	1989
	Edgewood II	1991		*Vincent*	2000
	Edgewood III	1992			
	upheld in:	1995			
	West Orange	2005			
Vermont	*Brigham I*	1997			
Washington	*Seattle I*	1978			
West Virginia	*Pauley*	1984			
Wyoming	*Washakie Co.*	1980			
	Campbell I	1995			
	upheld in:	2001			

Source: see Appendix Table A19.1.

targeted ways, Figlio, Husted, and Kenny (2004) instead relate within-state revenue inequality to various state characteristics. Holding constant court rulings on school finance constitutionality, these authors find fewer spending disparities (i.e., greater redistributive state aid) in states with stronger constitutional language toward equity and states under Democratic control and greater disparities in states with more heterogeneous populations.

EDUCATION FINANCE REFORM AND THE LEVEL AND DISTRIBUTION OF SPENDING

As just discussed, the expanded state role in funding public education occurred in part as a consequence of legislative and court-mandated reforms addressing the equity or adequacy of school spending. A natural question to ask is whether these reforms have generated changes in the level and inter-district distribution of school resources within affected states. There are good reasons why one might not observe the expected change in the level or distribution of spending, even as courts have ordered and states have designed policies specifically targeting these objectives. State aid formulas vary widely in their framework (Loeb, 2001; Hoxby, 2001; Fernandez and Rogerson, 2003; Yinger, 2004) and—in the case of judicially-mandated reforms—may be designed more with an eye toward satisfying court requirements than institutionalizing incentives that yield desired outcomes. Reforms deemed to meet constitutional requirements may in fact embody incentives that yield unintended consequences. It thus remains an empirical question whether these reforms have—in practice—affected the level and distribution of school funding.

In this section, we assess how finance reform has altered the role of states in funding public education, and in turn how these reforms have affected the level and distribution of school resources. We focus primarily on court ordered reform, but briefly address the literature on the effects of reforms originating in the legislature. In conducting our analysis, we have chosen not to adjust reported school expenditure for differences in student populations or other district-specific cost factors, as doing so would introduce a number of complications. For example, there is little consensus in the literature about how to properly adjust for cost differences (see Duncombe and Yinger, this volume), and it is likely that the weights on various cost factors have changed over time. Most importantly, the data required to carry out comprehensive cost adjustments over a four-decade period are not readily available.

Trends in PerPupil Spending Inequality

In Table 19.2, we use two panel datasets of school districts spanning the 1972–2004 period to compute four measures of inequality in perpupil current school expenditures, using school districts as the unit of analysis and weighting by district enrollment. For the earlier years of our analysis, we rely on a panel of unified school districts originally constructed by Harris, Evans and Schwab (2001) that includes revenue and expenditure data from the *Census of Governments*.[10] For years 1990 and following we use a similar panel from the U.S. Department of Education, the *Longitudinal School District Fiscal-Nonfiscal File*, supplemented by data from the annual Census survey of school districts, 2001–2004. Our first measure of inter-district spending inequality presented here—the ratio of the 95th percentile of per-pupil expenditure and the 5th percentile—captures inequality by comparing the extremes of the spending distribution, while the other three (the Gini coefficient, Theil index, and coefficient of variation) provide measures of inequality that take into account the entire distribution of spending.[11] The Theil index is particularly useful in that it can be decomposed into disparities *within* and *between* states. All of these measures increase as the level of inequality in expenditure increases.

Each measure of inequality in Table 19.2 follows a similar pattern over time.[12] Inequality in per-student funding fell sharply between 1972 and 1982 and then rose steadily during the 1980s.

TABLE 19.2
Inequality in Per-pupil Current Expenditures, United States, 1972 to 2004

School Year Ended	Gini (x100)	95-to-5 Ratio	Coefficient of Variation (x100)	Theil Index (x1000)	Theil Decomposition			
					Within States	Between States	% Within	% Between
1972	16.2	2.73	30.57	43.1	14.0	29.2	32.4	67.6
1982	13.7	2.21	25.53	30.7	13.8	16.9	45.0	55.0
1990	15.7	2.53	30.02	41.1	12.9	28.2	31.3	68.7
1992	14.9	2.32	28.81	37.6	12.2	25.4	32.4	67.6
1994	14.5	2.26	28.27	36.1	10.7	25.4	29.6	70.4
1996	13.5	2.13	26.45	31.5	9.5	22.0	30.1	69.9
1998	12.5	2.00	24.59	27.3	8.6	18.8	31.3	68.7
2000	12.3	1.98	24.52	27.1	8.2	18.9	30.3	69.7
2002	12.9	2.12	25.58	29.4	8.6	20.8	29.2	70.8
2004	13.7	2.24	27.51	33.7	9.3	24.4	27.6	72.4

Notes: Unified districts only in all years, excluding Alaska, Hawaii, Montana, Vermont, and the District of Columbia. Districts with per-pupil current expenditure greater than 150 percent of the state's (unweighted) 95th centile of per-pupil expenditure, or less than 50 percent of the state's 5th centile of per-pupil expenditure were omitted.
Sources: Authors' calculations from U.S. Department of Commerce (1972, 1982), U.S. Bureau of the Census (2002, 2004) and the U.S. Department of Education Longitudinal Unified School District Fiscal-Nonfiscal file (1992–2000). All inequality measures are calculated using district enrollment as weights.

The 1990s saw an almost monotonic decline in inequality—as much as 18 to 22 percent, depending on the measure (the Theil index suggests an even greater decline of 34 percent). Recent years, however, have witnessed a steady uptick in inequality—the Gini coefficient, for example, rose from 12.3 in 1999–2000 to 13.7 in 2003–04, an 11 percent increase.

Our decomposition of the Theil index into between and within state inequality illuminates several interesting properties of spending inequality in the United States. First, in nearly every year, 60–70 percent of the variation in spending can be attributed to *between*-state differences in per-pupil expenditure. Second, declines in between-state inequality have been the source of most of the decline in national inequality, accounting for roughly 64 percent of the fall in the Theil index. This decline in between-state spending disparities can almost certainly be attributed in part to income convergence across states. Variation in state per capita income follows a similar time series pattern to that of between-state inequality in school funding—sharp declines in the 1970s, followed by a sizable increase in the 1980s and a moderate decline in the 1990s (Bernat, 2001; see also Hoxby, 1998). Finally, both within- and between-state inequalities have risen in recent years, with between-state inequalities accounting for the lion's share (about 85 percent) of the 2000–04 rise in the Theil index. Reschovsky (2004) and Kalambokidis and Reschovsky (2005) attribute this recent uptick in inequality, and the small but parallel decline in the state share of school funding, to a post-recession fiscal crisis experienced by many state governments that led to sharp cuts to state education aid.

Time series trends in national spending disparities mask considerable differences within states. Figure 19.2 plots each state's Gini coefficient of per-pupil spending inequality in 2001–02 against its Gini in 1971–72, with points weighted by their relative 1972–2002 growth in real per-pupil current expenditures. Measured by the Gini, the vast majority of states experienced a decline in inter-district disparities between 1972 and 2002, with most states in Figure 19.2 falling below the 45-degree line.[13] Some states saw sizable reductions in inequality over this period—California, Delaware, and North Carolina, for example, saw a greater than 50 percent decline in within-state spending inequality. Others—such as Arizona, Missouri, and Idaho—actually

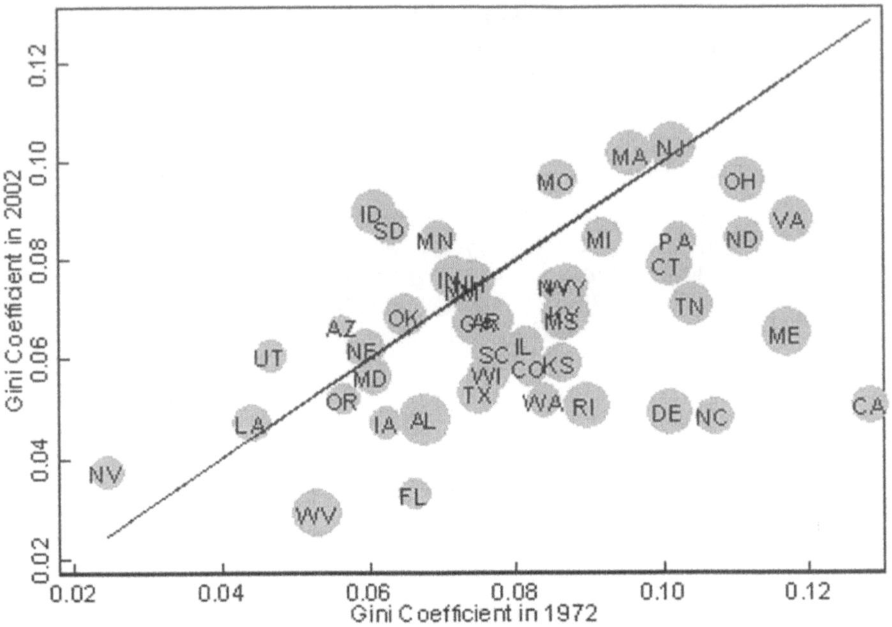

FIGURE 19.2 Gini Coefficient of Inequality of Per-pupil Current Expenditures, 1971–72 and 2001–02.
Source: Authors' calculations using a balanced panel of unified school districts (Harris, Evans, and Schwab, 2001, as modified by Corcoran and Evans, 2004). Alaska, Hawaii, Montana, Vermont and the District of Columbia have been omitted. Points are weighted by relative 1972–2002 % growth in real per-pupil current expenditures.

became more unequal over this period.[14] A comparison of state Gini coefficients in 1990 and 2004—an era notable for courts' emphasis on resource *adequacy* rather than equity—also shows evidence of equalization in spending, though reductions in inequality were less dramatic (states such as Georgia, Oregon, Maryland, and Texas, however, became substantially more equal).

A recurring question in the school finance literature is whether or not finance reforms achieve their goals by "leveling up" or "leveling down" overall spending on education (Manwaring and Sheffrin, 1997; Hoxby, 2001). "Leveling up" may be loosely defined as a reduction in spending disparities accomplished by a rise in spending in historically low-spending school districts, a condition under which average spending will rise. "Leveling down," in contrast, is a reduction in spending disparities accomplished by reducing spending at the top of the distribution, either absolutely or relative to what it would have been in the absence of the reform.

If there were indeed a strong "leveling down" effect of finance reform, one would expect to observe a negative correlation between the extent of equalization over time and relative growth of per-pupil expenditure. In Figure 19.2, a strong leveling down effect would be apparent if expenditure growth were lower (the point size were smaller) the further the state appears below the 45-degree line. In fact, this doesn't appear to be the case. Bivariate correlations between equalization and spending growth do not offer any obvious evidence of leveling down—i.e., it is not generally true that states with the greatest reduction in spending disparities tend to have the smallest growth rates—but there are some clear exceptions (California, North Carolina, Washington, and Florida, for example). Of course, Figure 19.2 and bivariate correlations are only suggestive. We turn next to a more systematic analysis of the effects of court-ordered finance reform on school spending, considering first the literature on individual state reform experiences and then estimates of the average effect of reform across states.

The Fiscal Effects of Education Finance Reform—Evidence from Specific States

As the first and arguably the most stringent state effort to equalize education spending across districts, California's response to *Serrano v. Priest* (1976) has received considerable attention. Silva and Sonstelie (1995) note that the post-*Serrano* reduction in spending disparities in that state was accompanied by a significant reduction in real spending growth, with mean expenditures per student dropping from 11th to 30th in the nation. By 1990, the state was spending nearly 10 percent less per-pupil than the U.S. average. This collapse in expenditure growth was certainly attributable to Proposition 13, the 1978 property tax limitation that followed *Serrano* (see Downes and Figlio, this volume), and Fischel (1989, 1996) convincingly argues that voter support for Proposition 13 was a direct reaction to the *Serrano* reforms.[15] Ultimately, Silva and Sonstelie attribute more than half of California's "leveling down" to the effects of *Serrano*.[16]

While California has become the most visible example of the fiscal effects of finance equalization, most scholars of school finance view it as an exception to the rule, or at least an extreme case. In contrast to California, school finance reform in many other states appears to have been accomplished through a leveling up of overall spending. For example, Roy (2004) and Cullen and Loeb (2004) document both a sharp reduction in spending inequality in Michigan after its 1995 reform and a growth in mean per-pupil expenditure that surpassed the national average.[17] Clark (2003) and Flanagan and Murray (2004) found considerable equalization in current expenditure after Kentucky's 1990 reform responding to *Rose v. Council for Better Education, Inc.*, yet Kentucky ranked third in the nation in per-pupil expenditure growth between 1990 and 2004; hardly evidence for leveling down. Nearly all studies of individual state reforms—Kansas (Duncombe and Johnston, 2004), Vermont (Downes, 2004), and Massachusetts (Guryan, 2001), for example—show reductions in inequality with little evidence of leveling down. Given the recent vintage of these reforms, however, it may be too early to provide a full assessment of their long-run effects.

The effects of finance reform on expenditure can occur through a variety of channels (Manwaring and Sheffrin, 1997; Fernandez and Rogerson, 2001; Downes and Shah, 2006). For example, increased centralization of school finance may alter the public choice mechanism relevant for the determination of school spending. Under local school finance, households sort into communities based on their demand for school quality, which is determined in part by income. A fully centralized system effectively creates a single jurisdiction. According to a simple collective choice model in which spending is determined by the median voter, one would predict lower school expenditure (i.e., a "leveling down") under a centralized system than under a decentralized system if median state income lies below the mean.[18] Hoxby (2001) shows that when local school districts retain some discretion over expenditure, a reformed state aid formula can reduce incentives to spend at the top of the expenditure distribution more than it raises the incentive to spend at the bottom, again resulting in a leveling down. Further, aid formulas may contain additional features that result in a mechanical leveling down of expenditure. For example, Hoxby and Kuziemko (2004) argue that the "recapture" feature of the redistributive "Robin Hood" formula in Texas destroyed property wealth in rich districts, upon which the system depended.[19] Finally, leveling down may arise as a long-run "general equilibrium" response to finance reforms, whereby tax revolts, increased private school enrollment and political fractionalization reduced the support for public education (Nechyba, 2004).

Given the diversity of finance systems, political and constitutional histories, demographics, and preferences for public education across states, it is reasonable to ask how finance reforms *on average* have affected within-state inequities and the overall level of spending on public schools. We turn next to this question.

The Fiscal Effects of Education Finance Reform—Evidence Across States and Over Time

Estimates of the average impact across states of school finance reform typically involve some variation on the following empirical model:

$$y_{it} = X_{it}\beta + D_{i}\alpha + \mu_{i} + \eta_{i} = \varepsilon_{i} \quad (1)$$

(see Murray, Evans, and Schwab, 1998; Evans, Murray, and Schwab, 1997 and 1999; Corcoran et al., 2004; Berry, 2007; and Springer, Liu, and Guthrie, 2006). In this model, y_{it} is some measure of per-pupil spending or spending inequality for state i in year t, X_{it} is a vector of state demographic characteristics, D_{it} is an indicator of the status of finance reform in state i in year t, μ_i and η_t are state and year fixed effects, respectively, and ε_{it} is an idiosyncratic error. State fixed effects allow for the possibility that reform states differ in systematic ways from non-reform states; for example, in the form of differences in existing spending equality or school governance. Year effects control for secular trends in the dependent variable common to all states, and the demographic controls account for correlates with school expenditure (such as age, race, or income) that may also influence reform legislation. Taken together, in the case where y_{it} is—say—spending inequality and D_{it} is an indicator that equals one in all subsequent years after reform, α can be interpreted as the average impact of finance reform on within-state spending inequality.[20]

Murray, Evans, and Schwab (1998) were the first to use a national panel of school districts to estimate the effects of court-ordered finance reform on the level and distribution of school expenditure within states. That paper covered reforms to 1992, while Corcoran et al. (2004) extended their work through 1997. Here, we use state-level data from the *Digest of Education Statistics* (2005) together with a balanced panel of more than 10,300 school districts to further extend this analysis through 2002.[21] Following the existing literature, we estimate model (1) for four separate measures of within-state spending inequality and for per-pupil spending at various points in the state expenditure distribution. State- and year-fixed effects are included along with an indicator variable indicating whether or not the school finance system in that state had been declared unconstitutional in the current or an antecedent year. Only high court rulings on constitutionality are considered (those listed in Table 19.1), a slightly more stringent inclusion criteria than that followed in past literature. Murray, Evans, and Schwab (1998) showed that the estimates of these models are generally not sensitive to the inclusion of demographic covariates or measures of within-state population heterogeneity, so for ease of exposition we exclude them here as well.

Table 19.3 summarizes the estimated effects of court-mandated school finance reform on the level and distribution of spending within states. In this table, each row summarizes the results of a separate regression, where the dependent variables used are listed in the left-hand column. Column (1) presents the estimated coefficient on our reform indicator (D_{it}) from each regression, while column (2) provides results from an alternative specification of D_{it} (described below). In the following discussion, the marginal effects reported in Table 19.3 have been converted to percentages using the baseline (1972) mean values of the relevant dependent variable.

With 1972 as a baseline, we find within-state inequality fell as much as 15–19 percent between 1972 and 2002 in states with court mandated finance reform, relative to those without such orders (Panel A, column (1)).[22] The decrease is considerably higher, at 36.7 percent, for the Theil index. All of these estimates are statistically precise, and are comparable to those in Murray, Evans, and Schwab (1998) and Corcoran et al. (2004) who found a 19–34 percent decline in inequality in reform states, relative to non-reform states. Not surprisingly, the average effect on inequality over the full 1972–2002 period examined here is somewhat smaller than that found in earlier work covering a shorter time horizon; these smaller estimates are likely attributable to the preponderance of adequacy (in contrast to equity) rulings in the additional years of data. Berry (2007) and Springer, Liu, and Guthrie (2006) have also examined the effects of court mandated reform on within-state equity over this period. Although their criteria for defining court rulings and empirical specifications differ somewhat from ours, their findings are not notably different from those in Table 19.3.

TABLE 19.3
Impact of Court Mandated Education Finance Reform on the Level and Distribution of School Funding, 1971–72 to 2001–02

Dependent variable	*Mean in 1972*	*(1)* *Court Overturn*	*(2)* *Court Overturn*	*Adequacy Ruling*
A. Within-state inequality in per-pupil current expenditure:				
Log (95th/5th percentile)	0.462	–0.070	–0.104	0.064
		(0.029)	(0.038)	(0.040)
Gini coefficient	0.080	–0.015	–0.022	0.014
		(0.005)	(0.007)	(0.007)
Theil index	0.012	–0.004	–0.006	0.004
		(0.002)	(0.002)	(0.002)
Coefficient of variation	0.152	–0.029	–0.044	0.028
		(0.010)	(0.014)	(0.014)
B. Per-pupil current expenditure:				
Log (Mean)	3,576	0.092	0.056	0.068
		(0.025)	(0.037)	(0.049)
Log (95th percentile)	4,472	0.055	–0.014	0.130
		(0.037)	(0.052)	(0.062)
Log (Median spending)	3,535	0.100	0.070	0.055
		(0.026)	(0.037)	(0.048)
Log (10th percentile)	2,948	0.119	0.093	0.049
		(0.026)	(0.037)	(0.048)
Log (5th percentile)	2,812	0.125	0.090	0.066
		(0.027)	(0.039)	(0.049)
C. Revenues by source:				
Real total revenues per pupil	4,285	701	478	416
		(256)	(360)	(445)
Real state revenues per pupil	1,658	786	489	556
		(202)	(199)	(271)
Real local revenues per pupil	2,185	-91	-31	–112
		(266)	(404)	(452)
Real federal revenues per pupil	442	6	20	-26
		(23)	(34)	(48)
State share of school revenues	39.5	6.69	3.13	6.68
		(3.14)	(3.71)	(4.35)
State and local revenues as a share of per–capita personal income	21.6	2.25	2.48	0.43
		(0.78)	(1.07)	(1.28)

Robust standard errors in parentheses.
Source: Authors' calculations based on a panel of unified school districts. Districts in Alaska, Hawaii, Montana, Vermont and the District of Columbia are omitted. Expenditures and revenues are expressed in real 2002 dollars, using the CPI-U deflator.

Table 19.3 also summarizes estimates of the average effect of court-ordered finance reform on the *level* of spending, on average and at various points in the spending distribution (Panel B column (1)). During this period, the level of spending per-pupil rose by a statistically significant 9.2 percent more in states under judicial orders than in states without a court order. Further, as found in earlier work, we see that spending in reform states grew more at the bottom of the distribution than at the top. After a high court order, spending per student at the 5th percentile in reform states grew 12.5 percent more than comparably low-spending districts in non-reform states. Spending grew 10 percent more at the median, and 5.5 percent more at the 95th percentile relative to states without reform orders, with the latter result statistically indistinguishable from zero. Taking all of the estimates in column (1) of Panels A and B together, we find little evidence of "leveling down" after court mandated reform—at least in the aggregate—consistent with Murray, Evans, and Schwab (1998), Corcoran et al. (2004) and Berry (2007).

A natural extension of model (1) tests for differences in the impact of court rulings made on the basis of *equity* and those made on *adequacy* grounds. Our comparison of the results in Table 19.3 column (1) to earlier estimates in the literature suggests that court-ordered reforms based on adequacy may have had weaker effects on spending disparities than those related to equal protection. One might also expect adequacy rulings to have more of a "leveling-up" effect on spending than equity orders. Berry (2007) and Springer, Liu, and Guthrie (2006) test for a differential effect of adequacy over equity rulings, and we present the results of a similar analysis in column (2) of Table 19.3. Column (2) re-estimates model (1) with an added indicator variable denoting that a court ruling was based on adequacy. The estimated coefficient on this variable may be interpreted as the differential effect of adequacy versus equity rulings.[23]

Not surprisingly, estimates of the effect of court-ordered reform on inter-district spending disparities are considerably smaller for rulings based on adequacy. For every measure, we find that adequacy-based rulings reduced spending inequality by roughly half that of equity rulings (although for two measures, the Theil index and log 95/5 ratio, the difference is not statistically significant). These point estimates are similar to those in Berry (2007), and Springer, Liu, and Guthrie (2006), although the former is unable to reject the hypothesis of equivalent effects. When considering the *level* of expenditure, adequacy rulings appear to increase spending to a greater extent than equity rulings at all points in the distribution (the effect size is roughly 50 percent larger), though these differences are not always precisely estimated. Interestingly, when equity rulings are distinguished from adequacy rulings, we find that equity rulings may have *decreased* spending at the 95th percentile, though this estimate is statistically insignificant. In contrast, adequacy rulings are estimated to have increased spending at the mean, median, 95th and 5th percentile by 14.0, 12.5, 11.5, and 16.6 percent, respectively. In general, adequacy rulings have increased spending more at all points in the distribution, but as a result have had much less of an impact on within-state inequality.

One can further ask how these changes in the level and distribution of school expenditures within states were achieved in states subject to court-mandated reform by looking directly at changes in revenues by source. Evans, Murray, and Schwab (1997), Corcoran et al. (2004) and Berry (2007) examine the local and state responses to court-ordered finance reform by looking separately at the effects of court-ordered reform on each revenue source, and we do the same in Panel C of Table 19.3. As in earlier work, we find that states under court-ordered reform on average increased revenues per-pupil by $701 (or 16.4 percent) more than non-reform states (column (1)). Further, this increase appears to have been financed entirely by state funding, which rose on average $786 more per-pupil in reform states. If anything, localities reduced their own funding in response to court-mandated reform (on average $91), though we cannot rule out the hypothesis of no reduction in local funds.[24] Though we do not present such estimates here, Evans, Murray, and Schwab (1997) show that per-pupil revenues rose the most in the lowest spending districts in reform states, and that state aid provided the most tax relief to these districts (that is, local tax revenues fell the most in these districts). As would be expected, we find no differences in federal funding growth between reform and non-reform states. Taken together, the net effect of court mandated reform appears to have been a 6.7 percentage point increase in the state share of education funding, relative to non-reform states.[25]

When looking at the differential effect of adequacy-based court orders (column (2)), we find that adequacy rulings in most cases have a larger effect on the level of spending than non-adequacy rulings, but differences in most cases are statistically insignificant. One exception is state funding, where we estimate that adequacy rulings increase revenues from state sources nearly twice as much as other ruling types. Consequently, adequacy reforms appear to have increased reliance on state funds (as measured by the state share of total education revenues) more than other reforms.

Table 19.4 presents estimates of model (1) applied to the 1989–2004 "adequacy" era, using annual financial data from the National Center for Education Statistics from 1989 (see also Berry, 2007, and Springer, Liu, and Guthrie, 2006).[26] Over this recent period, we find the average impact of court-mandated reform on within-state spending disparities to be statistically indistinguishable from zero (Panel A column (1)), although most point estimates are negative in sign. When looking at the effect of court-ordered reform on the *level* of spending during the 1990s (Panel B), we

TABLE 19.4
Impact of Court Mandated Education Finance Reform on the Level and Distribution of Current Expenditures per Pupil, 1989–90 to 2003–04

Dependent variable	*Mean in 1990*	*(1)*	*(2)*	
		Court Overturn	*Court Overturn*	*Adequacy Ruling*
A. Within-state inequality in per-pupil current expenditure:				
Log(95th/5th percentile)	0.436	0.0006	–0.1261	0.1314
		(0.0187)	(0.0161)	(0.0101)
Gini coefficient	0.076	–0.0028	–0.0220	0.0200
		(0.0030)	(0.0025)	(0.0015)
Theil index	0.011	–0.0013	–0.0066	0.0055
		(0.0009)	(0.0008)	(0.0004)
Coefficient of variation	0.146	–0.0069	–0.0438	0.0383
		(0.0049)	(0.0042)	(0.0029)
B. Per-pupil current expenditure:				
Log (Mean)	5,798	0.0330	0.0512	–0.0188
		(0.0234)	(0.0200)	(0.0093)
Log (95th percentile)	7,426	0.0421	–0.0290	0.0737
		(0.0268)	(0.0233)	(0.0117)
Log (Median spending)	5,629	0.0409	0.0774	–0.0378
		(0.0252)	(0.0219)	(0.0094)
Log (10th percentile)	4,919	0.0320	0.0869	–0.0568
		(0.0282)	(0.0243)	(0.0100)
Log (5th percentile)	4,760	0.0415	0.0971	–0.0576
		(0.0275)	(0.0242)	(0.0099)

Standard errors adjusted for clustering by state.

Source: Authors' calculations using the Longitudinal School District Fiscal-Nonfiscal panel database and U.S. Department of Commerce (2001, 2002, 2003, 2004). Districts in Alaska, Hawaii, Montana, Vermont and the District of Columbia are omitted.

again find a pattern that differs from that observed between 1972 and 2002. Surprisingly, court orders during the 1990s based on equity had a larger effect on spending in reform states than did adequacy-based rulings. The level effects of adequacy rulings are all estimated to be positive (if imprecise), and—as our inequality results would suggest—fairly uniform across the spending distribution. Together, columns (1) and (2) indicate that adequacy-based reforms have increased spending in reform states relative to non-reform states on the order of 3–4 percent, at the mean, median, 5th and 95th percentiles.[27]

All of the estimates provided here of the equalizing or level effects of school finance reform have relied exclusively on court rulings as a plausibly exogenous indicator of a structural change to a state system of school funding. A related literature has sought to move beyond "black box" estimates of the effects of finance reform by exploring the *channels* by which fiscal reform impacts spending. Manwaring and Sheffrin (1997) and Downes and Shah (2006) each interact reform indicators with key state-level determinants of school expenditure, in recognition that reform may fundamentally alter these underlying relationships. For example, as discussed above, Silva and Sonstelie (1995) identified one such possibility in that centralization may change the relationship between income and school spending in a state, as expenditure adjusts to reflect the demands of the median versus the mean income household. Downes and Shah (2006) also argue that the relationship between spending and the racial or ethnic composition of a state, its elderly share, and membership in teachers unions may also change in response to finance reform, as the political determination of spending changes post-reform. Both Manwaring and Sheffrin (1997) and Downes and Shah (2006) find some evidence to support the hypothesis that a state's response to fiscal reforms will depend to some degree on its own population characteristics.

Evans, Murray, and Schwab (1997), Manwaring and Sheffrin (1997), and Downes and Shah (2006) further contrast the effects of reforms that were a response to court mandates with those originating in legislatures. Court-mandated reform is reputedly more stringent and more restrictive of local discretion, and thus may be more likely to "level down" education spending. Indeed, each of these papers found evidence of a stronger impact of court-mandated reform on reducing spending disparities than legislative reform. Of course, it is more difficult to treat legislative reforms as exogenous events to which spending changes can be attributed, so such findings should be interpreted with caution.

Finally, an alternative approach taken by Hoxby (2001) avoids the legislative versus court-mandated reform typology and looks to state aid formulas themselves to predict whether a finance program will level up or level down school expenditure. As aid formulas in effect determine each district's "tax price" of per-pupil school expenditure, finance reforms can significantly alter a district's incentives to spend on education.[28] How a reform may be expected to affect the level and distribution of spending in a state will depend how—on net—districts respond to changes in their tax price. Hoxby's empirical estimates show that states with the most dramatic equalization programs (such as California, New Mexico, South Dakota, and Utah) had much lower per student expenditure than would be expected under a finance scheme with less distortionary tax prices, or under a purely local system of finance.

Effects of Education Finance Reform on Other Public Expenditures

Model (1) has also been used to estimate the effects of finance reform on other public expenditures at the state and local level. As shown above, court-ordered reform—particularly when based on equity considerations—has increased the level of spending at the low end of the distribution of school districts while leaving expenditure in high-spending districts relatively unchanged. Further, the increase in per-pupil revenues necessary to support these changes has occurred almost entirely through increased state funding with only a minimal decline in local funds. As state governments have increased their aggregate contribution to public education, one could ask whether this increase has occurred at the expense of other public programs.

Murray, Evans, and Schwab (1998) look at the impact of increased state support of public education on welfare, health, corrections, transportation, and higher education, and find no evidence of a reduction in per-capita expenditure in any of these categories. In contrast, Baicker and Gordon (2006) found over a longer time period that states reduced aid to localities for other public programs in response to court ordered reform, and to a greater extent in counties with lower median income. They estimate that each additional dollar of state aid for education crowded out 22 cents in aid for public programs such as welfare, hospitals, and transportation. They further show that local governments respond to higher state taxes—necessary to support increased state aid to schools—by reducing their own taxes and expenditure (see also Berry, 2007, for additional evidence on this).

NON-FISCAL EFFECTS OF EDUCATION FINANCE REFORM

Student Achievement

The shift in fiscal responsibility for education from local school districts to the states has ultimately been driven by a desire to raise the level of student performance, for all or at least some students. Despite the claim by some researchers (e.g., Hanushek, 2003) that changes in the level of spending are unlikely to have much effect on educational outputs, the push for resource equity and adequacy has long rested on the assumption that shifts in the level or distribution of funding will have real consequences for students' educational opportunities and success. An important question, then, is whether the fiscal transformation described above has in fact improved student outcomes. The evidence on this question is decidedly mixed.

For example, in looking at the relationship between state funding of education and SAT scores, both Peltzman (1993) and Husted and Kenny (1997) found that states with more centralized school funding have lower test scores (or lower test score growth) than decentralized states. Card and Payne (2002), on the other hand, showed that states under court-ordered finance reform saw greater reductions in the test score gap between low- and high-income students on the SAT than states with no court-mandated reform. Of course, these studies are somewhat limited by their use of college admissions tests relevant only to a select population of students in each state.

Downes and Figlio (1998) showed using two longitudinal surveys of high school seniors from 1972 and 1992 that—controlling for state tax and expenditure limitations that in some cases coincided with school finance reform—court-mandated and legislature-originated reforms improved mean school performance, as measured by test scores, particularly in initially low-spending districts. Tax limitations themselves, however, were shown to have a negative effect on student outcomes (see also Figlio, 1997; and Downes and Figlio, this volume). Both Downes (1997) and Hoxby (2001) considered the impact of school finance equalization on high school dropout rates. Downes (1997) found little to no evidence that state intervention into local school finance improved high school dropout rates, while Hoxby (2001) likewise found no evidence that states with stronger equalization schemes saw greater reductions in dropout rates. One plausible explanation for these findings may be that many finance reforms based on equalization of taxable property wealth do not benefit central city districts, which have historically poor student outcomes but relatively high per-pupil property wealth.

Several papers have assessed the impact of individual state reforms on student outcomes.

For example, Downes (1992) found virtually no difference between the distributions of 6th grade scores on a California state achievement test across school districts before and after *Serrano,* despite substantial equalization in per-pupil expenditure. Likewise, Clark (2003) evaluated Kentucky's Education Reform Act of 1990 that drastically reduced per-pupil spending inequities by increasing funding to low-income districts and found no evidence of a reduction in the achievement gap between high- and low-income students. Flanagan and Murray (2004) also found a small but statistically insignificant effect of increased spending on test scores in Kentucky. Guryan (2001) showed that 4th grade test scores improved—particularly at the bottom of the test score distribution—after a 1993 reform in Massachusetts, but 8th grade scores were unchanged. Papke (2005) found a positive and statistically significant effect of spending equalization on math test pass rates in Michigan after its 1994 reform (see also Cullen and Loeb, 2004 and Roy, 2004). Taken together, assessments of the effects of finance reform on achievement have yielded quite varied results, quite likely due to the varied nature of these reforms.[29]

If a lesson can be drawn from the burgeoning research on education finance reform and its effects on student outcomes, it is that reform—no matter how extensive or well-intended—is by no means a guarantee of improved adequacy or equity in student achievement. Our cursory review of the literature offers several possible explanations for this. First, even the most generous estimates of the spending—test score gradient would suggest that extraordinarily large increases in spending are necessary to observe any real increase in student outcomes. It may be that few finance reforms to date have been aggressive enough for much of an effect on test scores to surface. Second, the institutional details of school funding reforms, the unique circumstances of individual states and local and state responses to changes in finance systems vary considerably. A firm understanding of these differences is likely to be critical for understanding how a new finance regime will ultimately affect outcomes of the education process. Finally, the ability of a finance reform to improve outcomes may depend on more than just changes to the level and distribution of spending. Arguably, the most successful reforms pay as much attention to the use of funds as to the level of expenditure.

Some Broader Consequences of Education Finance Reform

The increased role of the states in promoting equity and adequacy in education funding has affected economies, politics, and public education systems in ways that extend beyond short-run changes to state and local revenue sources or student test scores. An expansive body of research has examined the role school finance reform has played in the productive efficiency of schools, economic growth, spending volatility, property values, the political support for tax limitations, the influence of state teacher unions, and numerous other indicators of support for public education. Finance restructuring in some cases has produced incentive structures that result in quite unintended consequences, including the strategic reclassification of students as disabled (Cullen, 2003) and the intensification of local efforts for more off-formula categorical aid (Timar, 1994). To the extent that success in acquiring off-formula aid depends on the political power or wealth of local districts (as opposed to genuine cost differences or student needs), such practices may serve to partially undo the intended effects of finance reform. Further, the recent linkage of funding formulas to school accountability has introduced an entirely new dynamic between school districts and states (Figlio, 2004).

A comprehensive review of this literature is beyond the scope of this chapter, and a more thorough discussion of many of these topics can be found elsewhere in this volume. To close, we briefly address two additional consequences of finance reform observed in practice—increases in private donations to local school districts, and enrollment in private schools.

School finance equalization by definition is designed to remove or at least weaken the link between local resources and educational opportunity. A state's ability to achieve this objective is in part a function of the latitude granted individual school districts to set spending levels and to supplement state funds. Variation in preferences for school spending across districts, coupled with a long history of local decision-making suggests that at least some households are likely to be dissatisfied with the loss of local control associated with certain finance reforms. Brunner and Sonstelie (2003) and Brunner and Imazeki (2005) show that private funding of local schools has increased in importance in California, as public school districts solicit contributions to supplant revenues lost through *Serrano* and Proposition 13. Brunner and Imazeki (2005) found that private contributions in California soared in the 1990s, though these contributions remain small on a per-pupil basis, and only represent a significant share of revenues in a handful of wealthy districts.

Parents may also respond to a loss of local control over public schools by moving to the private education sector. Downes and Schoeman (1998), for example, argued that finance reform in California played a significant role in the growth of private schooling in that state, although Sonstelie, Brunner, and Ardon (2000) reached the opposite conclusion. Looking at metropolitan areas over the 1970–90 period, Husted and Kenny (2002) found that private school enrollment rose with school finance centralization at the state level, while Hoxby (2001) found that districts facing a higher tax price (i.e., were subject to a more stringent equalization scheme) saw greater increases in rates of private schooling than districts which did not.

CONCLUSION

Over the course of the 20th century, states emerged as the predominant source of funding for public K–12 education in the United States, reversing a long-standing tradition of local school finance. This role increased markedly in recent years in the wake of court-ordered and legislative reforms targeting improved equity and adequacy in student resources. As this chapter has demonstrated, the increased state role in funding public education has indeed affected the level and distribution of school resources within states—on average, states affected by court-mandated finance reforms have increased expenditures and reduced inter-district disparities to a much greater extent than those states unprompted by litigation. Although there are a few notable exceptions, states in general do not appear to have "leveled down" expenditure in their ongoing efforts to improve equity and adequacy.

The U.S. experiment in greater centralization of school funding remains, however, in its infancy. To date, we have very little evidence of how increased state control over education finance is likely to affect public spending on schools over the long run. Simple models of collective choice would suggest that the dynamics of school spending at the state level are likely to be quite different than those experienced at the local level. Competing state budget interests, greater voter heterogeneity and a more volatile tax base are but three challenges schools are likely to encounter under a more centralized system. The increased involvement of states in funding local schools has in some cases been further accompanied by greater accountability for school performance, or an increased role for school choice, the effects of which are only beginning to be studied. How greater state control over the funding of local schools will ultimately affect the support for public education remains an open and important question.

APPENDIX 19A.1
State Supreme Court Rulings on School Finance System Constitutionality, and Pending Cases

Case	*Citation*	*Year*	*Ruling*	*Case Type*
Alaska				
Matanuska-Susitna Borough School District v. State	931 P.2d 391	1997	Upheld	Equity
Moore v. State	Civil 3-AN-04-9756	Pending		Both
Arizona				
Shofstall v. Hollins	110 Ariz. 88, 515 P.2d 590	1973	Upheld	Equity
Crane Elementary School District v. State		Pending		Adequacy
Arkansas				
DuPree v. Alma School District No. 30	279 Ark. 340, 651 S.W.2d 90	1983	Overturned	Equity
Lake View School District No. 25 v. Huckabee (Lakeview III)	351 Ark. 31, 91 S.W.3d 472	2002	Overturned	Both
Lake View School District No. 25 v. Huckabee (Lakeview V)	___ S.W.3d ___ , 2005 WL 3436660	2005	Overturned	Both
California				
Serrano v. Priest (Serrano II)	18 Cal.3d 728, 557 P.2d 929, 135 Cal. Rptr. 345	1976	Overturned	Equity
Colorado				
Lujan v. Colorado State Board of Education	649 P.2d 1005	1982	Upheld	Adequacy
Lobato v. Colorado		Pending		Adequacy
Connecticut				
Horton v. Meskill (Horton I)	172 Conn. 615, 376 A.2d 369	1977	Overturned	Equity
Horton v. Meskill (Horton III)	195 Conn. 24, 486 A.2d 1099	1985	Upheld	Equity
Connecticut Coalition for Justice in Education Funding (CCJEF) v. Rell		Pending		Adequacy
Florida				
Coalition for Adequacy and Fairness in School Funding v. Chiles	680 So.2d 400	1996	Upheld	Equity
Georgia				
McDaniel v. Thomas	248 Ga. 632, 285 S.E.2d 156	1981	Upheld	Both
Consortium for Adequate School Funding in Georgia v. State		Pending		Adequacy
Idaho				
Thompson v. Engelking	96 Idaho 793, 537 P.2d 635	1975	Upheld	Equity
Illinois				
Blase v. Illinois	302 N.E. 2d 46	1973	Upheld	
Committee for Educational Rights v. Edgar	174 Ill.2d 1, 672 N.E.2d 1178	1996	Upheld	Both
Lewis v. Spagnolo	186 Ill.2d 198, 710 N.E.2d 798	1999	Upheld	Adequacy
Kansas				
U.S.D. 229 v. State	256 Kan. 232, 885 P.2d 1170	1994	Upheld	Both
Montoy v. State (Montoy II)	278 Kan. 769, 102 P.3d 1160	2005	Overturned	Both
Montoy v. State (Montoy IV)		2006	Upheld	Both
Kentucky				
Rose v. Council for Better Education	790 S.W.2d 186	1989	Overturned	Adequacy
Young v. Williams		Pending		Adequacy

Case	*Citation*	*Year*	*Ruling*	*Case Type*
Maine				
S.A.D. No. 1 v. Commissioner Leo Martin	659 A.2d 854	1995	Upheld	Equity
Maryland				
Hornbeck v. Somerset County Board of Education	295 Md. 597, 458 A.2d 758	1983	Upheld	Adequacy
Maryland State Board of Education v. Bradford	387 Md. 353, 875 A.2d 703	2005	Upheld	Adequacy
Massachusetts				
McDuffy v. Secretary of Executive Office of Education	415 Mass. 545, 615 N.E.2d 516	1993	Overturned	Adequacy
Hancock v. Driscoll	443 Mass. 428, 822 N.E.2d 1134	2005	Upheld	Adequacy
Michigan				
Milliken v. Green	390 Mich. 389, 212 N.W.2d 711	1973	Upheld	Equity
Minnesota				
Skeen v. Minnesota	505 N.W.2d 299	1993	Upheld	Adequacy
Missouri				
Committee for Educational Equality v. Missouri	967 S.W.2d 62	1998	Upheld	Both
Montana				
Helena Elementary School District No. 1 v. Montana	236 Mont. 44, 746 P.2d 684 as modified 784 P.2d 412	1989	Overturned	Adequacy
Columbia Falls Elementary School District No. 6 v. Montana	326 Mont. 304, 109 P.3d 257	2005	Overturned	Adequacy
Nebraska				
Gould v. Orr	244 Neb. 163, 506 N.W.2d 349	1993	Upheld	Adequacy
Nebraska Coalition for Educational Equity and Adequacy v. Heineman		Pending		Adequacy
Douglas County School District et al. v. Heineman		Pending		Both
New Hampshire				
Claremont School District v. Governor (Claremont II)	142 N.H. 462, 703 A.2d 1353	1997	Overturned	Adequacy
Opinion of the Justices—School Financing (Claremont III)	142 N.H. 892, 712 A.2d 1080	1998	Overturned	Adequacy
Claremont School District v. Governor (Claremont V)	144 N.H. 210, 744 A.2d 1107	1999	Overturned	Adequacy
Opinion of the Justices—School Financing (Claremont VI)	145 N.H. 474, 765 A.2d 673	2000	Overturned	Equity
Claremont School District v. Governor (Claremont VII)	147 N.H. 499, 794 A.2d 744	2002	Overturned	Adequacy
Londonderry v. State		Pending		Adequacy
New Jersey				
Robinson v. Cahill (Robinson I)	62 N.J. 473, 303 A.2d 273	1973	Overturned	Equity
Robinson v. Cahill (Robinson II)	69 N.J. 449, 355 A.2d 129	1976	Upheld	Equity
Abbott v. Burke (Abbott II)	100 N.J. 269, 405 A.2d 376	1990	Overturned	Equity
Abbott v. Burke (Abbott III)	136 N.J. 444, 643 A.2d 575	1994	Overturned	Equity
Abbott v. Burke (Abbott IV)	149 N.J. 145, 693 A.2d 417	1997	Overturned	Adequacy
Abbott v. Burke (Abbott V)	153 N.J. 480, 710 A.2d 450	1998	Overturned	Adequacy

(*continued*)

APPENDIX 19A.1
Continued

Case	Citation	Year	Ruling	Case Type
New York				
Levittown v. Nyquist	57 N.Y. 2d 27, 439 N.E.2d 359, 453 N.Y.S.2d 643	1982	Upheld	Equity
Reform Educational Financing Inequities Today (REFIT) v. Cuomo	86 N.Y. 2d 279, 655 N.E.2d 647, 631 N.Y.S. 2d 551	1995	Upheld	Equity
Campaign for Fiscal Equity, Inc. v. New York	100 N.Y.2d 893	2003	Overturned	Adequacy
North Carolina				
Britt v. North Carolina Board of Education	86 N.C. App 282, 357 S.E. 2d 432 affd mem. 320 N.C. 790, 361 S.E. 2d 71	1987	Upheld	Equity
Hoke County Board of Education v. North Carolina (Leandro II)	599 S.E.2d 365	2004	Overturned	Adequacy
North Dakota				
Bismarck Public School District No. 1 v. North Dakota	511 N.W.2d 247	1994	Upheld	Equity
Williston v. State		Pending		Both
Ohio				
Board of Education v. Walter	58 Ohio St.2d 368, 390 N.E.2d 813, cert denied 444 U.S. 1015	1979	Upheld	Equity
DeRolph v. Ohio (DeRolph I)	78 Ohio St.3d 193, 677 N.E.2d 733, as clarified 78 Ohio St.3d 419, 678 N.E.2d 886	1997	Overturned	Adequacy
DeRolph v. Ohio (DeRolph II)	89 Ohio St.3d 1, 728 N.E.2d 993	2000	Overturned	Adequacy
DeRolph v. Ohio (DeRolph III)	93 Ohio St.3d 309, 754 N.E.2d 1184	2001	Overturned	Adequacy
DeRolph v. Ohio (DeRolph IV)	97 Ohio St.3d 434, 780 N.E. 2d 529	2002	Overturned	Adequacy
Oklahoma				
Fair School Finance Council v. Oklahoma	87 Okla 114, 746 P.2d 1135	1987	Upheld	Adequacy
Oklahoma Education Association et al. v. Oklahoma		Pending		Adequacy
Oregon				
Olsen v. Oregon	276 Or. 9, 554 P.2d 139	1976	Upheld	Equity
Coalition for Equitable Funding, Inc. v. Oregon	311 Or. 300, 811 P.2d 116	1991	Upheld	Equity
Pennsylvania				
Danson v. Casey	484 Pa. 415, 399 A.2d 360	1979	Upheld	Equity
Pennsylvania Association of Rural and Small Schools v. Ridge	558 Pa. 374, 737 A.2d 246	1998	Upheld	Both
Marrero v. Commonwealth	559 Pa. 14, 739 A.2d 110	1999	Upheld	Adequacy
Rhode Island				
City of Pawtucket v. Sundlin	662 A.2d 40	1995	Upheld	Both
South Carolina				
Richland County v. Campbell	294 S.C. 346, 364 S.E.2d 470	1988	Upheld	Equity
Abbeville County School District v. South Carolina		Pending		Adequacy

Case	*Citation*	*Year*	*Ruling*	*Case Type*
Tennessee				
Tennessee Small School Systems v. McWherter (I)	851 S.W.2d 139	1993	Overturned	Equity
Tennessee Small School Systems v. McWherter (II)	894 S.W.2d 734	1995	Overturned	Both
Tennessee Small School Systems v. McWherter (III)	91 S.W.3d 232	2002	Overturned	Both
Texas				
Edgewood Independent School District v. Kirby (Edgewood I)	777 S.W.2d 391	1989	Overturned	Equity
Edgewood Independent School District v. Kirby (Edgewood II)	804 S.W.2d 491	1991	Overturned	Equity
Carrolton-Farmers Branch ISD v. Edgewood Independent School District (Edgewood III)	826 S.W.2d 489	1992	Overturned	Equity
Edgewood Independent School District v. Meno (Edgewood IV)	893 S.W.2d 450	1995	Upheld	Equity
West Orange-Cove Consolidated ISD v. Neeley		2005	Overturned	Other
Vermont				
Brigham v. Vermont (Brigham I)	166 Vt. 246, 692 A.2d 384	1997	Overturned	Equity
Brigham v. Vermont (Brigham II)		Pending		Equity
Virginia				
Scott v. Commonwealth of Virginia	247 Va. 379, 443 S.E.2d 138	1994	Upheld	Equity
Washington				
North Shore School District No. 417 v. Kinnear	84 Wash.2d 685, 530 P.2d 178	1974	Upheld	Equity
Seattle School District No. 1 v. Washington	90 Wash.2d 476, 585 P.2d 71	1978	Overturned	Adequacy
West Virginia				
Pauley v. Bailey	174 W.Va. 167, 324 S.E.2d 128	1984	Overturned	Both
Wisconsin				
Kukor v. Grover	148 Wis.2d 469, 436 N.W.2d 568	1989	Upheld	Equity
Vincent v. Voight	236 Wis.2d 588, 614 N.W.2d 388	2000	Upheld	Equity
Wyoming				
Washakie County School District No. 1 v. Herschler	606 P.2d 310, cert denied, 449 U.S. 824	1980	Overturned	Equity
Campbell County School District v. Wyoming (Campbell I)	907 P.2d 1238	1995	Overturned	Adequacy
Campbell County School District v. Wyoming (Campbell II)	19 P.3d 518	2001	Upheld	Adequacy
State v. Campbell County School District		Pending		Adequacy

Notes:

1) does not include rulings related strictly to capital or facilities financing (e.g. Arizona's Roosevelt decisions)

2) does not include high court procedural rulings—e.g. a high court reversal of a lower court's dismissal of the suit, remanding the case to trial

3) does not include intermediate court rulings (e.g. Serrano, 1986 and Charlet, 1998 in Louisiana)

Sources:

ACCESS, Education Finance Litigation (http://www.schoolfunding.info/states/state_by_state.php3); Education Law Center, State Laws Relating to Pre-K (http://www.startingat3.org/state_laws/index.html); Odden and Picus (2004), Yinger (2003) Appendix A, Murray, Evans, and Schwab (1998), Evans, Murray and Schwab (1997), Minorini and Sugarman (1999), Card and Payne (2002), Downes and Shah (2006), Corcoran et al. (2004), Springer, Liu and Guthrie (2006).

NOTES

1. Some authors treat the terms "reform" and "equalization" in school finance as synonymous. Indeed, early state interventions into local school finance were attempts to equalize differences in local fiscal capacity (through foundation and guaranteed tax base formulas, for example). As the more recent wave of court challenges and legislative reforms have focused less on equalization or "fiscal neutrality," we generally prefer to use the term "reform" to refer to any significant program change intended to alter the level and/or distribution of education spending. We refer to "reform states" as any state that has enacted or has been ordered to enact such a program change.
2. Walters (2001), for one, makes this argument.
3. Hawaii and the District of Columbia are ignored here. Hawaii—with its single school district—had 100 percent of its non-federal funding classified as state; the District of Columbia had 100 percent of its non-federal funding classified as local.
4. It may not be immediately obvious how one can reconcile the observation that most states increased their share of K–12 revenues between 1970 and 2000 with our earlier statement that the aggregate state share rose only slightly between 1978 and 2003 (45.6–48.7 percent). Part of the explanation lies in timing (the aggregate state share rose 6 percentage points between 1970 and 1978). More importantly, however, is the observation that—in any given year—the aggregate state share is a weighted sum of individual state enrollment shares, where the weights are the relative size (in terms of revenue) of the 50 states. Thus, changes in the aggregate state share are driven primarily by trends in larger states, states that significantly changed their state share, or both. A number of large states with higher than average state shares in 1978—Pennsylvania, Illinois, and Louisiana, for example—saw their state share decline over this period (they also lost relative size).
5. See Section III of this volume. Note that concerns over appropriate funding for at-risk students are not exclusively tied to the "adequacy" movement—see, for example, Berne and Stiefel's (1984) discussion of vertical equity in school finance.
6. These states are Delaware, Hawaii, Mississippi, Nevada, and Utah (ACCESS, 2006).
7. Our list of court rulings has been substantially revised and updated from earlier work (Murray, Evans, and Schwab (1998), Corcoran et al. (2004)) and reconciled against other frequently cited reform inventories (Odden and Picus (2004), Appendix A of Yinger (2004), Minorini and Sugarman (1999), Card and Payne (2002), Springer, Liu, and Guthrie (2006), and others). Our list is more conservative in that it includes only rulings made by the highest court in the state explicitly addressing the constitutionality of the school finance system; it also omits rulings that pertain only to capital financing, as we would not expect these rulings to necessarily impact current expenditures. High court rulings on the justiciability of a dispute related to school financing are not included. We do not deny that such rulings can send strong signals to state legislatures, and in many cases states have responded to these rulings by enacting serious reform. However, in other cases states have not acted until ordered to do so by the state supreme court. For uniformity we consider only orders issued by high courts.
8. See also Campbell and Fischel (1996). Howard and Roch (2001) and Wood and Theobold (2003) provide an alternative view.
9. Exceptions include Evans, Murray, and Schwab (1997) and Downes and Shah (2006). We discuss this literature in greater detail in the following section.
10. We use a modified version of this panel, constructed by Corcoran and Evans (2004).
11. See Berne and Stiefel (1984), Murray, Evans, and Schwab (1998) and Section III of this volume for more on the measures of spending inequality implemented here.
12. A more detailed analysis of spending inequality for select years of this period can be found in Moser and Rubinstein (2002) for 1991–92 and 1994–95, Wyckoff (1992) for 1979–80 and 1986–87, Schwartz and Moskowitz (1988) for 1977–85, and Hussar and Sonnenberg (2000) for 1979–94.
13. For reasons explained in Harris, Evans, and Schwab (2001), the sample of school districts upon which these measures are based is somewhat smaller in 1971–72 than in 2001–02. The missing districts in 1971–72 are predominately rural, low-enrollment districts, which suggests (if these districts are relatively low spenders) that we may be underestimating inequality in that year. Our calculations are weighted by district enrollment, however, which should alleviate this problem.

14. These comparisons are similar when other measures of inequality (such as the 95–5 ratio) are used in place of the Gini coefficient.
15. As Silva and Sonstelie (1995) point out, it does not necessarily follow that California's relative drop in spending was a direct consequence of the *Serrano* judgment. Most of the loss of school revenue was due to Proposition 13, not *Serrano*, and while *Serrano* was an exogenous event, Proposition 13 was an endogenous decision by voters to cap tax revenues. In fact, California had the capacity to increase school funding post-Proposition 13 through other tax sources, but opted not to do so. Therefore, Silva and Sonstelie argue, *Serrano* fundamentally altered the political determination of education expenditure.
16. See also Downes (1992) for an additional case study of reform in California. Picus (1991) and Sonstelie, Brunner, and Ardon (2000) are excellent resources on the history of finance reform in California.
17. Courant and Loeb (1997) provide details on this reform.
18. Silva and Sonstelie (1995) refer to this as an "income effect." There may also be a "price effect" if the tax price facing the median voter differs from that of the mean (say, due to the deductibility of local taxes and differing marginal tax rates). The simple model described here also assumes the median voter has the state's median income.
19. It is not clear, however, that Texas "leveled down" in the 1990s. While per-pupil spending inequality fell moderately (see Imazeki and Reschovsky, 2004), Texas actually ranked fairly high (15th) in real expenditure growth during the 1990s. "Robin Hood" did, however, result in a system of escalating property tax rates that was ultimately found to be unconstitutional (*Neeley v. West Orange-Cove Consolidated Independent School District*).
20. The specification of D_{it} takes a number of forms in this literature. In its simplest form, D_{it} is an indicator variable that equals one in the year of reform and all subsequent years. Alternative specifications have allowed the effect of reform to vary over time, where D_{it} represents the number of years since reform, or is a vector of two or more categorical variables (e.g.,1–5 years since reform, 6 or more years since reform).
21. Our school district panel is described in Corcoran et al. (2004). For reasons outlined there, we exclude Alaska, Hawaii, Montana, Vermont, and the District of Columbia, and we restrict our analysis to unified (K–12) districts to control for differences in cost structures across district types. According to the *Common Core of Data* (2001–02), over 92 percent of all public school students attend unified districts. Non-unified districts are disproportionately located in a few states (e.g., Arizona, California, and Illinois).
22. Recall that a decrease in each of these inequality measures represents a drop in inter-district disparities in per-pupil expenditure.
23. We relied on Odden and Picus (2004), Springer, Liu, and Guthrie (2006) and ACCESS (2006) for the classification of rulings as equity- or adequacy-based.
24. Bahl, Sjoquist, and Williams (1990) found among early finance reforms that in nearly all cases increased state aid was offset by reductions in local property taxes.
25. This can be compared to Evans, Murray and Schwab (1997) who estimate an average increase of 4 to 6 percentage points in the state share in reform states. Our larger point estimate here suggests that recent adequacy-based reforms had a more significant effect on the state revenue share than earlier reforms, a hypothesis our column (2) findings confirm.
26. Here we use the *Longitudinal Fiscal-Nonfiscal* panel of school districts compiled by the National Center for Education Statistics, supplemented by more recent financial data for 2000–01 through 2003–04 from the U.S. Census Bureau. As noted by Berry (2007), panel estimates using high-frequency (in this case, annual) data call for standard errors to be clustered at the state level, which we do here.
27. In the interest of space, we do not present the equivalent of Table 19.3 Panel C for the 1990s. The pattern of effects on total, state, and local revenues per-pupil is qualitatively similar to that in Table 19.3, although in this case we found that the positive effects of equity-based rulings on state and total revenues are larger than those for adequacy rulings. Adequacy rulings during this period are estimated to have a negative and statistically significant effect on local revenues per-pupil.
28. The "tax price" implicit in a state aid formula represents the additional tax revenue that must be raised locally in order to increase school expenditure by a dollar. A purely local system of school funding would involve a tax price of $1 in every district. Matching grants from the state can significantly lower

the tax price below $1 for some districts, while systems with property tax revenue "recapture" can increase the tax price above $1 in high-property wealth districts. See Picus, Odden, and Goertz, this volume, for more details.

29 For additional examples, see also Duncombe and Johnston, 2004 (on Kansas) and Downes, 2004 (on Vermont).

REFERENCES

ACCESS Education Network (2006). http://www.schoolfunding.info/states/state_by_state.php3. Accessed November 15, 2006.

Bahl, Roy, Sjoquist, David, and Williams, W. Loren. (1990). School Finance Reform and Impact on Property Taxes. *Proceedings of the Eighty-Third Annual Conference on Taxation.* 163–171.

Baicker, Katherine, and Gorden, Nora. (2006). The effect of state education finance reform on total local resources. *Journal of Public Economics*, 90, 1519–1535.

Benson, Charles S., and O'Halloran, Kevin. (1987). The Economic History of School Finance in the United States. *Journal of Education Finance*, 12, 495–515.

Bernat, G. Andrew, Jr. (2001). Convergence in State Per Capita Personal Income, 1950–99. *Survey of Current Business*, 81, 36–48.

Berne, Robert, and Stiefel, Leanna. (1984). *The measurement of equity in school finance: conceptual, methodological, and empirical dimensions.* Baltimore: Johns Hopkins University Press.

Berry, Christopher (2007). The Impact of School Finance Judgments on State Fiscal Policy. In Martin R. West and Paul E. Peterson, (Eds.), *School Money Trials: The Legal Pursuit of Educational Adequacy* (pp. 213–242). Washington, D.C.: Brookings Institution Press.

Brunner, Eric, and Imazeki, Jennifer. (2005). Fiscal Stress and Voluntary Contributions to Public Schools, *Working Paper.* San Diego: San Diego State University.

Brunner, Eric, and Sonstelie, Jon. (2003). School Finance Reform and Voluntary Fiscal Federalism. *Journal of Public Economics*, 87, 2157–2185.

Campbell, Colin D., and Fischel, William A. (1996). Preferences for School Finance Systems: Voters versus Judges. *National Tax Journal*, 49, 1–15.

Card, David, and Payne, A. Abigail. (2002). School Finance Reform, the Distribution of School Spending, and the Distribution of Student Test Scores. *Journal of Public Economics*, 83, 49–82.

Clark, Melissa A. (2003). Education Reform, Redistribution, and Student Achievement: Evidence From the Kentucky Education Reform Act.

Corcoran, Sean P., and Evans, William N. (2004). Income Inequality, the Median Voter, and the Support for Public Education. *Working Paper.* College Park, MD: University of Maryland.

Corcoran, Sean P., Evans, William N., Godwin, Jennifer, Murray, Sheila E., and Schwab, Robert M. (2004). The Changing Distribution of Education Finance, 1972 to 1997. In Kathryn M. Neckerman (Ed.), *Social Inequality* (pp. 433–465). New York: Russell Sage Foundation.

Courant, Paul N., and Loeb, Susanna. (1997). Centralization of School Finance in Michigan. *Journal of Policy Analysis and Management*, 16, 114–136.

Cullen, Julie Berry. (2003). The Impact of Fiscal Incentives on Student Disability Rates. *Journal of Public Economics*, 87, 1557–1589.

Cullen, Julie Berry, and Loeb, Susanna. (2004). School Finance Reform in Michigan: Evaluating Proposal A. In John Yinger, (Ed.), *Helping children left behind: state aid and the pursuit of educational equity* (pp. 215–249). Cambridge, MA: MIT Press.

de Bartolome, Charles A. M. (1997). What Determines State Aid to School Districts? A Positive Model of Foundation Aid as Redistribution. *Journal of Policy Analysis and Management*, 16, 32–47.

Downes, Thomas A. (1992). Evaluating the impact of school finance reform on the provision of public education: The California case. *National Tax Journal*, 45, 405.

Downes, Thomas A. (1997). The Effect of *Serrano v. Priest* on the Quality of American Education: What Do We Know? What Do We Need to Know?, *Proceedings of the Eighty-Ninth Annual Conference on Taxation, 1996*, 336–342.

Downes, Thomas A. (2004). School Finance Reform and School Quality: Lessons from Vermont. In John Yinger, (Ed.), *Helping children left behind : state aid and the pursuit of educational equity* (pp. 283–313). Cambridge, MA: MIT Press.

Downes, Thomas A., and Figlio, David N. (1998). School Finance Reforms, Tax Limits, and Student Performance: Do Reforms Level-Up or Dumb Down? Mimeo. Tufts University.

Downes, Thomas A., and Schoeman, David. (1998). School Finance Reform and Private School Enrollment: Evidence from California. *Journal of Urban Economics*, 43, 418–443.

Downes, Thomas A., and Shah, Mona P. (2006). The Effect of School Finance Reforms on the Level and Growth of Per-Pupil Expenditures. *Peabody Journal of Education*, 81, 1–38.

Duncombe, William, and Johnston, Jocelyn M. (2004). The Impacts of School Finance Reform in Kansas. In John Yinger, (Ed.), *Helping children left behind: state aid and the pursuit of educational equity*. Cambridge, MA: MIT Press.

Evans, William N., Murray, Sheila E., and Schwab, Robert M. (1997). Schoolhouses, Courthouses, and Statehouses after Serrano. *Journal of Policy Analysis and Management*, 16, 10–31.

Evans, William N., Murray, Sheila E., and Schwab, Robert M. (1999). The Impact of Court-Mandated School Finance Reform. In Helen F. Ladd, Rosemary Chalk, and Janet S. Hansen (Eds.), *Equity and adequacy in education finance issues and perspectives*. Washington, D.C.: National Academy Press, 72–98.

Fernandez, Raquel, and Rogerson, Richard. (2003). Equity and Resources: An Analysis of Education Finance Systems. *Journal of Political Economy*, 111, 858–897.

Figlio, David N. (1997). Did the "Tax Revolt" Reduce School Performance? *Journal of Public Economics*, 65, 245–269.

Figlio, David N. (2004). Funding and Accountability: Some Conceptual and Technical Issues in State Aid Reform. In John Yinger, (Ed.), *Helping Children Left Behind: State Aid and the Pursuit of Educational Equity* (pp. 87–110). Cambridge, MA: MIT Press.

Figlio, David N., Husted, Thomas A., and Kenny, Lawrence W. (2004). Political Economy of the Inequality in School Spending. *Journal of Urban Economics*, 55, 338–349.

Fischel, William A. (1989). Did Serrano Cause Proposition 13? *National Tax Journal*, 42, 465–473.

Fischel, William A. (1996). How *Serrano* Caused Proposition 13. *Journal of Law and Politics*, 12, 607–645.

Flanagan, Ann E., and Murray, Sheila E. (2004). A Decade of Reform: The Impact of School Reform in Kentucky. In John Yinger, (Ed.), *Helping children left behind : state aid and the pursuit of educational equity* (pp. 195–213). Cambridge, MA: MIT Press.

Guryan, Jonathan. (2001). Does Money Matter? Regression-Discontinuity Estimates from Education Finance Reform in Massachusetts. NBER Working Paper. National Bureau of Economic Research.

Hanushek, Eric A. (2003). The Failure of Input-Based Schooling Policies. *Economic Journal*, 113, F64–F98.

Harris, Amy Rehder, Evans, William N., and Schwab, Robert M. (2001). Education Spending in an Aging America. *Journal of Public Economics*, 81, 449–472.

Howard, Robert M., and Roch, Christine H. (2001). Policy Change and the State Courts: The Case of Education Finance Reform. *The Justice System Journal*, 22, 137–153.

Hoxby, Caroline M. (1998). How Much Does School Spending Depend on Family Income? The Historical Origins of the Current School Finance Dilemma. *American Economic Review*, 88, 309–314.

Hoxby, Caroline M. (2001). All School Finance Equalizations Are Not Created Equal. *Quarterly Journal of Economics*, 116, 1189–1231.

Hoxby, Caroline M., and Kuziemko, Ilyana. (2004). Robin Hood and His Not-So-Merry Plan: Capitalization and the Self-Destruction of Texas' School Finance Equalization Plan. *NBER Working Papers*. Cambridge: NBER.

Hussar, William J., and Sonnenberg, William. (2000). *Trends in Disparities in School District Level Expenditures per Pupil*. National Center for Education Statistics report 2000–020, U.S. Department of Education. http://nces.ed.gov/pubsearch/pubsinfo.asp?pubid=2000020.

Husted, Thomas A., and Kenny, Lawrence W. (1997). Efficiency in Education: Evidence from the States. *Proceedings of the Eighty-Ninth Annual Conference on Taxation, 1996*, 358–365.

Husted, Thomas A., and Kenny, Lawrence W. (2002). The Legacy of Serrano: The Impact of Mandated Equal Spending on Private School Enrollment. *Southern Economic Journal*, 68, 566–583.

Imazeki, Jennifer, and Reschovsky, Andrew. (2004). School Finance Reform in Texas: A Never-Ending Story?. In John Yinger, (Ed.), *Helping children left behind: state aid and the pursuit of educational equity* (pp. 251–281). Cambridge, MA: MIT Press.

Kalambokidis, Laura, and Reschovsky, Andrew. (2005). States' Responses to the Budget Shortfalls of 2001–2004. *Challenge*, 48, 76–93.

Loeb, Susanna. (2001). Estimating the Effects of School Finance Reform: A Framework for a Federalist System. *Journal of Public Economics*, 80, 225–247.

Manwaring, Robert L., and Sheffrin, Steven M. (1997). Litigation, School Finance Reform, and Aggregate Educational Spending. *International Tax and Public Finance*, 4, 107–127.

Minorini, Paul A., and Sugarman, Stephen D. (1999). School Finance Litigation in the Name of Educational Equality: Its Evolution, Impact, and Future. In Helen F. Ladd, Rosemary Chalk, and Janet S. Hansen, (Eds.), *Equity and Adequacy in Education Finance: Issues and Perspectives*. Washington, D.C.: National Academy Press, 34–71.

Moser, Michele, and Rubenstein, Ross. (2002). The Equality of Public School District Funding in the United States: A National Status Report. *Public Administration Review*, 62, 63–72.

Murray, Sheila E, Evans, William N., and Schwab, Robert M. (1998). Education-Finance Reform and the Distribution of Education Resources. *American Economic Review*, 88, 789–812.

Nechyba, Thomas. (2004). Prospects for Achieving Equity or Adequacy in Education: The Limits of State Aid in General Equilibrium. In John Yinger, (ed.), *Helping Children Left Behind: State Aid and the Pursuit of Educational Equity* (pp. 111–143). Cambridge, MA: MIT Press.

Odden, Allan R., and Picus, Lawrence O. (2004). *School finance: A policy perspective*. Boston: McGraw-Hill.

Papke, Leslie E. (2005). The Effects of Spending on Test Pass Rates: Evidence from Michigan. *Journal of Public Economics*, 89, 821–839.

Peltzman, Sam. (1993). The Political Economy of the Decline of American Public Education. *Journal of Law and Economics*, 36, 331–370.

Picus, Lawrence O. (1991). Cadillacs or Chevrolets? The Effects of State Control on School Finance in California. *Journal of Education Finance,* 17, 33–59.

Reschovsky, A. (2004). The Impact of State Government Fiscal Crises on Local Governments and Schools. *State and Local Government Review*, 36, 86–102.

Roy, Joydeep. (2004). Impact of School Finance Reform on Resource Equalization and Academic Performance: Evidence from Michigan. Working Paper. Princeton, NJ: Education Research Section, Princeton University.

Schwartz, M., and Moskowitz, J. (1988). *Fiscal Equity in the United States, 1984–88*. Washington, D.C.: Decision Resources Corp.

Silva, Fabio, and Sonstelie, Jon. (1995). "Did Serrano Cause a Decline in School Spending?" *National Tax Journal*, 48, 199–215.

Sonstelie, Jon, Brunner, Eric, and Ardon, Kenneth. (2000). *For Better or Worse? School Finance Reform in California*. San Francisco: Public Policy Institute of California.

Springer, Matthew G., Liu, Keke, and Guthrie, James W. (2006). The Impact of Education Finance Litigation Reform on Resource Distribution: Is There Anything Special About Adequacy? Peabody College of Vanderbilt University, unpublished manuscript.

Timar, Thomas B. (1994). Politics, Policy, and Categorical Aid: New Inequities in California Finance. *Educational Evaluation and Policy Analysis*, 16, 143–160.

Walters, Pamela Barnhouse. (2001). Educational Access and the State: Historical Continuities and Discontinuities in Racial Inequality in American Education. *Sociology of Education*, extra issue, 35–49.

Wood, B. Dan, and Theobold, Nick A. (2003). Political Responsiveness and Equity in Public Education Finance. *Journal of Politics*, 65, 718–738.

Wyckoff, James H. (1992). The Intrastate Equality of Public Primary and Secondary Education Resources in the U.S., 1980–1987. *Economics of Education Review*, 11, 19–30.

Yinger, John. (2004). *Helping children left behind: State aid and the pursuit of educational equity*. Cambridge, MA: MIT Press.

20

Local Funding of Schools: The Property Tax and Its Alternatives

Therese J. McGuire and Leslie E. Papke

INTRODUCTION

The property tax has long been the primary local source of funding for schools and, along with state aid, provides the lion's share of total resources for schools. In recent decades, though, the property tax has come under siege as a source of revenue for schools. The principal charge has been that, since property wealth is unequally distributed across school districts, reliance on this source of revenue results in unacceptable differences in property tax rates, property revenues per pupil and, most importantly, spending per pupil across districts. The property tax is also criticized for being inequitable, inefficient, and complex. Dissatisfaction with the tax appears to be growing as evidenced by the number of attempts to constrain spending and limit access to taxes, including the property tax (Downes & Figlio, this volume).[1] Among the possible explanations for the declining support for property taxes are demographic shifts in the form of a rising elderly share and a declining school-age share of the population. Our goals are to examine the various charges against the property tax as a means of funding schools and to compare alternative sources of revenue such as sales and income taxes with the property tax.

The Role of the Property Tax in Funding U. S. Education

The property tax has been and remains the predominant *local* source of revenue for school districts. Not all school districts, however, have independent authority to raise revenue. In 36 states, districts have the power to generate their own revenue by setting property tax rates. In the other states, some school districts are dependent for revenue on a city, town, or county. Most dependent districts are on the East Coast. For example, most school districts in Connecticut, Massachusetts, and Rhode Island are city- or town-dependent, while districts in Maryland and North Carolina are primarily county-dependent (Hoo, Murray, & Rueben, 2006). Other states have a mix of both dependent and independent school districts. Dependent school systems receive most of their local revenue from appropriations by their parent government. Most of this revenue comes from property tax collections, but the exact amount of parent government revenue from property taxes often cannot be determined from accounting records of state education agencies (U.S. Census Bureau, 2004).

For 2003–04, the most recent year for which Census data are available, the federal government provided 8.9 percent of public school system revenue, states provided 47.1 percent, and local governments provided 43.9 percent. Of the local government share, 85.2 percent was comprised of taxes and parent government contributions. There was substantial variation across states, however, in the percent of revenue provided by local governments. Local governments provided over half of total revenue in 12 states and the District of Columbia, while in 23 states, state governments provided over half of the revenue.[2] In most of the remaining 15 states, K–12 funding was relatively evenly shared.

In nearly all states, local revenue is raised primarily from taxes, and almost all tax revenue comes from the property tax. Table 20.1 lists sources of local school district revenue in 2004. Over 65 percent of local revenue comes from the property tax. This figure underestimates the importance of the property tax, however, because much of the 17.3 percent of local revenue from parent government contributions also comes from the property tax. In 2004, the property tax collected by independent school districts provided over 80 percent of local revenues in 17 states and over 50 percent of revenue in 32 states.[3] Only six states received more than 10 percent of local revenues from an alternative source, typically from other local governments.

A shorter time series of district finances is maintained by the National Center for Education Statistics (NCES) of the Department of Education. The NCES data, which come from a survey of state education agencies, include property tax revenue by state for both independent and dependent school districts annually between 1990 and 2004. Using the NCES data, it is possible to calculate the percent of property taxes in dependent school districts as a percent of total property tax revenue (1990: 17.0%, 1995: 15.8%, 2000: 18.0%, 2004: 17.3%). These percentages are quite close to parent government contributions as a share of local school district revenues as indicated in the Census data, suggesting that most parent government contributions do in fact come from the property tax.[4]

School finance reform and the move away from heavy reliance on the property tax began in the 1970s. Table 20.2 reports the percent of K–12 revenue from state sources, local sources, and the property tax from 1957 to 2004. In 1957, the local share comprised 61.8 percent of total revenues, and the state share was 36.0 percent. The fraction of revenues from local sources remained at least 60 percent until 1967, when it fell to 56.4 percent. It remained at least 50 percent until 1982, when it fell to 48.2 percent. Since 2000, the fraction of revenues from local sources has hovered around 40 percent.[5]

The decline of reliance on local revenue sources is a story of the decline in the use of local property taxes for education. In 1957, the local property tax comprised 46.6 percent of total revenues and remained at least 40 percent until 1977 when it fell on average to 36.6 percent. The fraction from the property tax continued to decline, but remained above 30 percent until 2000, when it dropped to 27.8 percent. The reversal of this trend with the slight increase in 2004 to 29.4 percent of K–12 revenues[6] may reflect the fact that many states responded to the budgetary crises between 2000 and 2004 by cutting (absolutely or relatively) state assistance to local school districts (Kalambokidis & Reschovsky, 2005). Districts in states that have not enacted limitations on the local use of the property tax have the flexibility, in principle, to respond to state cuts by raising local revenue. In a recent paper, Dye and Reschovsky (2007) present evidence that on average local school districts increased property taxes between fiscal years 2002 and 2004 on the order of 37 cents for each one dollar cut in state aid.

Hoo, Murray, and Rueben (2006) report that much of the shift to state financing occurred in the 1970s. However, they point out that the shift masks differences across school districts—many dependent districts have always received a substantial share of their revenue from state aid. For the 36 states that contain independent school districts, state aid increased from 46 percent in

1972 to 60 percent in 2002. A similar, though less dramatic, shift occurred in states with both dependent and independent districts. County-dependent districts in Maryland and North Carolina averaged 60 percent of total funding in the form of state aid over the entire period, while city-dependent districts averaged considerably less.

Currently, the local property tax comprises about one-third of the revenue of K–12 school districts. Although property taxes remain a substantial fraction of revenue, this figure understates the importance of the property tax because it includes only local property tax revenue. In several states, statewide property taxes have replaced or supplemented the local property tax. California and Michigan, for example, have both capped the ability of their school districts to use the property tax and have in effect adopted state-wide property taxes to fund K–12 schools. In other cases, including, for example, New Hampshire, states have implemented a foundation formula with a required minimum tax rate contribution by local school districts that is labeled as a statewide property tax. A number of states have enacted property tax limits that restrict the amount of additional property tax revenue that can be raised each year. For example, Proposition 2½ in Massachusetts limits annual increases in property tax levies to 2.5 percent a year.[7] An implication of moving to a state property tax or of putting limits on revenue from local property taxes is that the property tax is no longer the marginal source of funds for local school districts. Generally, there are efficiency gains when the last dollar of school funding comes from a *local* tax—the property tax in most states—so that spending decisions can reflect local preferences for education. Thus, the shift to state-wide property taxes or the imposition of limits on local property tax revenue could lead to a less efficient distribution of spending across districts.

In 1994, Michigan replaced local property taxes as the primary funding source for K–12 funding with a combination of a flat-rate state property tax and a portion of the state sales tax.[8] Prior to the reform, in 1992, local property taxes accounted for 55.9 percent of K–12 funding. By 1997, this percent had fallen to 22.0 percent and has not reached 25 percent since that time. In 2004 the local property tax contributed 24.4 percent. The state-level property tax for education in Michigan is levied at six mills on both homestead and non-homestead property.[9] Proposal A, as the funding reform was called, established a minimum per pupil foundation grant and imposed a cap on property tax revenue.[10] These changes resulted in an overall net drop in property taxation. In 1993, the average statewide millage rate for all property was 56.6 mills. In 2000, the statewide average homestead millage rate was 31.5 mills, and the non-homestead rate was 50.1 mills.

California's Proposition 13, which passed by voter initiative in 1978, limited local government's ability to fund education by establishing a maximum local property tax rate of 1 percent, rolling back assessments to 1975 levels and limiting reassessments to an increase of 2 percent per year, except upon the sale of a property. The property tax revenues do not stay in the local jurisdiction where they are raised. Rather, the revenues from the uniform 1 percent property tax are disbursed by the state through grant programs to local jurisdictions. These changes essentially converted the local property tax into a state property tax. In 1957, the property tax comprised 48.9 percent of total revenues and remained about 50 percent of revenue through 1977, but by 1982 it had fallen to 21.5 percent of total revenues. In 2004, property tax revenues stood at 23.1 percent of revenues, local funding (which includes property tax revenues) was 34.1 percent, and state funding 54.5 percent.[11]

Even though the median percent of school revenue from the local property tax fell from 47.2 in 1957 to 28.7 in 2004, it remains a substantial revenue source. Eight states (Colorado, Illinois, Nebraska, New Jersey, Ohio, Pennsylvania, South Dakota, and Texas) continue to receive over 40 percent of all revenues for K–12 schools from the local property tax. However, in Texas, in response to a Supreme Court ruling mandating a reduction in reliance on the property tax, the legislature enacted legislation to lower property taxes by about one-third. Despite these actions

TABLE 20.1
Percent Composition of Local Source School District Revenue, 2003/4

Property taxes	65.3
Other taxes	2.6
Parent government contribution	17.3
Nonschool local government	2.3
School lunch charges	3.1
Tuition and transportation charges	0.5
Other charges	2.3
Other local revenue	6.6

Source: Public Education Finances, Annual Survey of Government Finances, U.S. Census Bureau, 2004.

limiting use of the property tax, no other local source of revenue has arisen to challenge the property tax as the primary source of own-source revenues for schools.

IMPLICATIONS OF 35 YEARS OF COURT CHALLENGES AND LEGISLATIVE ACTIONS

Many charges have been made against the property tax to justify actions that reduce reliance on the tax for school funding. Critics have argued, for example, that the property tax is regressive, that it distorts economic behavior, that it is difficult to administer, and that its burden is unrelated

TABLE 20.2
Sources of School District Funding: Average across States 1956/7–2003/4

	Percent of total revenue from state sources	*Percent of total revenue from local sources*	*Percent of total revenue from local property tax*
1956/7	36.0	61.8	46.6
1961/2	37.1	60.5	46.4
1966/7	41.3	56.4	41.4
1971/2	43.6	54.4	43.1
1976/7	35.4	53.1	36.6
1981/2	46.1	48.2	33.6
1986/7	49.2	44.9	34.6
1991/2	49.0	44.9	32.3
1996/7	50.5	42.8	32.2
1999/2000	52.7	40.4	27.8
2000/1	52.3	40.9	28.4
2001/2	51.9	40.5	28.9
2002/3	51.5	40.3	28.9
2003/4	51.9	41.1	29.4

Source: Authors' calculations using data from the Census of Governments, Finances of School Districts or Public Education Finances Report. Years 1992 and later are available at www.census.gov/govs/www/school.html.

to the ability of taxpayers to pay. But these charges—some valid, others not so valid, as we argue below—pertain to the property tax in general, whether the tax is used to fund education or parks. Another charge—that disparities in property wealth lead to disparities in spending—is applicable to any type of local government expenditure but is particularly relevant to local schools. It is this aspect of the local property tax that has motivated the school finance court cases. Plaintiffs have used provisions in state constitutions for equal protection and fair and adequate provision of education to argue for reduced reliance on local property taxes for funding schools. None of the legal arguments employed specifically condemns the property tax as a means of financing education. Rather, it was the use of the property tax by *local* jurisdictions, whose per pupil property tax bases varied considerably, that was deemed problematic. From the arguments made it would seem that any locally-imposed tax whose base varied greatly across jurisdictions would have been challenged.

Legal challenges brought under equal protection clauses of state constitutions attempted to reduce the interdistrict variation in per pupil spending and to weaken the link between local property wealth and school spending. California is widely viewed as having gone the farthest down this path with the changes implemented in response to the two California Supreme Court decisions related to school funding (*Serrano I* and *II*) in the early to mid-1970s and the subsequent passage in 1978 of the tax limitation measure, Proposition 13. As discussed above, local school districts (and other local taxing bodies) continue to derive significant revenues from property taxes in California,[12] but the tax has effectively become a state tax—imposed at a uniform rate of 1 percent.

Another set of legal challenges has been brought under education clauses of state constitutions. The argument in most of these cases has shifted away from the concept of spending equity with its focus on the variation in per pupil spending across districts or fiscal neutrality with its attention to the relationship between property tax wealth and district spending toward the newer standard of educational adequacy. Under this standard, the state attempts to insure that every student has access to an adequate level of education. (See Koski and Hahnel, this volume and the chapters in Section III, this volume.) Thus, state policy attention shifts almost exclusively to the low-spending districts. The shift in emphasis from equity to adequacy could have fairly dramatic implications for the property tax. For example, if concerns about adequacy, rather than equity and fiscal neutrality, had driven the *Serrano* decisions, the California state legislature could potentially have satisfied the State Supreme Court by proposing a school financing system that preserved access to the local property tax for those districts wanting to spend more than average as long as the system guaranteed a reasonably high minimum level of spending across the board.[13] In fact, the system the state implemented after the first *Serrano* decision focused on raising the spending of low-spending districts, but the State Supreme Court ruled that this new system continued to violate the equal protection clause of the constitution because it continued to allow districts to override the limit on property taxes. Whether any system proposed under an adequacy standard would have forestalled the subsequent passage of Proposition 13 is a highly debatable matter, but the breaking of the link between local property wealth and school spending that the Court demanded, and that Fischel (1989) argues was central to the support for Proposition 13, might not have occurred.

Evans, Murray, and Schwab (2001) describe the consequences of court-ordered reform for spending per pupil (as well as for the composition of spending, the demand for private schools, and student outcomes). They present descriptive statistics for the 19 states where plaintiffs successfully challenged the existing system and regression findings using data for all states. They find that (1) court-ordered reform resulted in a significant decline in within-state inequality in spending per pupil; (2) after court-ordered reform, spending rose in the lowest spending school districts and remained essentially constant in the highest spending districts; and (3) state spending on education increased, while state spending in other areas remained virtually unchanged.

Missing from Evans, Murray, and Schwab (2001) is any direct evidence on how court-ordered reform has affected the level or structure of property taxes. Using calculations provided to us by Kim Rueben (personal communication), we compare the percent of elementary and secondary expenditures financed by property taxes in states subject to court-ordered reform to the corresponding figures in states without court-ordered reform.[14] For states with early (pre-1985) court orders, the share of expenditures financed by the property tax fell from 28.1 percent in 1982 to 23.7 percent in 2002. During that same period, the share of expenditures financed by the property tax in states with no court order fell from 36.5 percent to 31.7 percent, a similar percentage point drop. For states with late (post-1985) court orders, the share of expenditures financed by the property tax fell from 38.0 percent in 1992 to 30.6 percent in 2002, a drop of nearly 7.5 percentage points in ten years. The corresponding figures for states without court orders show a drop from 36.2 percent in 1992 to 31.7 percent in 2002, a fall of less than five percentage points. Clearly, the property tax is diminished in all states, whether subject to court-ordered reform or not. In the most recent decade for which we have data, it appears that the decline in the role of the property tax may have been greater in states subject to court-ordered reform.

The shift in emphasis in school-reform court challenges from equity and fiscal neutrality to adequacy may hold out hope for the property tax. While the emphasis on equity and fiscal neutrality generally has led to less reliance on *local* property taxes, how the new emphasis on adequacy will affect property taxes is not obvious. On the one hand, because adequacy is likely to require an increase in total spending on education, the shift may lead to an even greater role for the state in funding education. At the same time, though, it need not lead to a reduced reliance on property taxes. Adequate funding could potentially be achieved through the use of a (perhaps, significantly enhanced) state foundation aid program in conjunction with a fully functioning local property tax. Under some interpretations of adequacy there would be no need to limit local property taxes or to restrain spending by high wealth districts.[15] As long as the foundation level was set at a high enough level to achieve adequacy and the level was guaranteed with funding from the state, the goal of providing access to an adequate level of education could be achieved without eliminating or severely crippling the local property tax. In other words, if districts chose to spend more than the state guarantee, they could do so by tapping into their property tax wealth, and this behavior would not compromise the adequacy goal. Of course, policy makers may wish to pursue both adequacy *and* equity, in which case limits on the property tax, additional equalizing state aid programs, or restrictions on the supplements that districts can add to the foundation level may be desirable in order to keep high-wealth districts from spending more than low-wealth districts.[16]

IS THE PROPERTY TAX STRUCTURALLY FLAWED?

Another set of criticisms pertains to the nature or structure of the property tax itself—that it is inefficient, inequitable (in that the incidence falls disproportionately on lower-income taxpayers), and difficult to administer. These criticisms are not specific to the funding of school districts, and, in large part, they would pertain to the property tax whether it is a local or a state tax.

The property tax consists of many taxes. It may be a tax on land, a tax on improvements to land, including residential buildings and commercial and industrial buildings, and a tax on personal property, including tangible personal property such as furniture, machinery and equipment, and intangible personal property such as stocks and bonds. The property tax is a tax on property valuation and placing values on many of the components of the property tax base can be difficult.

For example, one acre of land in the center of a large city can be more or less valuable depending on what the parcel of land is proximate to (a port?, a large condominium building?, a public housing project?), the history of the use of the parcel (is it contaminated with toxic materials?), and the predictions for the future economic health of the neighborhood. It is a tax on capital wealth, and yet property represents consumption of housing and other services. The particular structure of the property tax has implications for the efficiency, equity and simplicity of the tax.

The charge that the tax is inefficient refers to distortions in decisions regarding factors of production, such as capital, that can be moved either across jurisdictions or among sectors of the economy in response to property tax rates. Zodrow (2001) summarizes the basic argument that the use of property taxes to finance local public services results in inefficiently low levels of public services, as jurisdictions try to keep the property tax low in an effort to keep mobile capital, such as manufacturing firms, from moving to other lower-tax jurisdictions. Competition of this form for mobile capital is inefficient because it creates a fiscal externality—when a given jurisdiction increases its tax rate and drives capital out, it creates a fiscal benefit for the jurisdictions to which the capital flows (see Wildasin, 1989). Still, Inman (2001) argues that the property tax is likely to be no more inefficient than other local taxes that might be alternative sources of revenue. He argues that mobile workers, capital and consumers (but not land) can escape any local tax by moving to other cities. If these other cities are similar in the efficiency of their governments and economies, which may be plausible in suburban America, then there will be little loss in social welfare associated with a local property tax.[17]

Fischel (2001) makes an alternative argument for the property tax. He argues that the tax is a benefit tax and therefore is an efficient and nondistortionary source of local revenue. This argument rests on the assumption that there is a tight link between taxes paid and services received, an argument that is quite plausible for services such as police and fire protection. With respect to schools, especially inner-city schools, however, the argument is difficult to make because the value of school services received is likely to have little relation to housing value and therefore to a taxpayer's property tax liability. While competition among school districts in the suburbs can lead to capitalization of school services quality into housing values, thereby providing the requisite link for the property tax to act as a benefit tax, in school districts in large central cities, which serve a large percentage of public school children, competition is usually lacking. Thus, the argument that the property tax acts like a benefit tax is not particularly persuasive.

In his history of the property tax from the early 1900s until 1992, Wallis (2001) offers a perspective on why the property tax is the most important source of local government revenue but plays such a small role at the state and national level.[18] In brief, Wallis argues that only local governments can effectively use the property tax as a benefit tax because they spend money on services that are geographically specific and they are better able than state governments to match taxes paid to services received for their taxpayers. He also argues that over the course of the 20th century the political and administrative costs of raising state-level revenues by new automobile, sales and income taxes fell relative to the costs of raising revenue with a state-wide property tax. Thus, over time the property tax, which had originally been an important source of revenue at the state level, has maintained its role at the local level while being usurped by other revenue sources at the state level.

The question of the incidence of the property tax has long been the subject of debate among scholars. The traditional view (see Netzer, 1966) argues that the tax is similar to an excise tax on housing, and, because expenditures on housing fall as a percentage of income as income rises, the tax burden is distributed regressively. Beginning with Mieszkowski (1972), scholars began to argue for a "new view" of the burden of the property tax.[19] Since the property tax is widely used across the country and applies to land and structures, they argued that the property tax functions nationally like a tax on capital. The fact that capital is in relatively fixed supply in the aggregate means that the property tax serves to reduce the overall average net-of-tax return to capital. Hence, under this view, the tax burden is progressive since high income individuals receive higher proportions of their income from capital than lower income individuals. The observation that there is not one monolithic national property tax and that local tax rates differ, modifies the conclusion only somewhat. The local tax differentials are likely to be borne by the owners of the least mobile input, namely land. To the extent that the returns from land as a share of income rise with income, the burden of the local proportion of the property tax would also be progressive.

These theoretical conclusions rest on some strong assumptions regarding relative supply and demand elasticities and the corresponding ability to shift taxes. The question of the distribution of the burden of the property tax is ultimately an empirical one. Conclusions about the distribution of the tax burden also depend on the definition of income used to calculate tax burdens. Metcalf (1994) uses a measure of lifetime income (total consumption expenditures in a year) to examine the incidence of various taxes, including the property tax. He finds that the burden of the residential property tax is close to proportional. Chernick and Reschovsky (1993) challenge Metcalf's measure of permanent income. They argue that annual consumption expenditures are or can be highly variable as unexpected and non-recurring expenditures arise. Chernick and Reschovsky use longitudinal data to calculate 11-year averages for both income and tax payments and conclude that the tax is mildly regressive. Plummer (2003) examines the incidence of residential property taxes in Dallas County, Texas across thousands of owner-occupied homes. Arguing that individuals rely on expectations of their lifetime earnings when purchasing housing, she uses residential property value as a measure of a household's lifetime income and finds the burden of the property tax to be distributed essentially proportionally.

The question of whether to use annual income or some measure of permanent income in calculating tax burdens is unresolved. Poterba (1989) argues that permanent income is a better measure since in any given year annual income may be unusually low (because, for example, the individual is in college) or high (the individual's firm handed out unexpectedly high bonuses). At the same time, lifetime income can be hard to measure. Metcalf (1994) and Poterba (1989) use annual consumption expenditures, but these are likely to be more variable than lifetime income. In our view, housing expenditures are likely to reflect permanent income better than any other measurable variable. Using this measure of permanent income (as in Plummer, 2003), our reading of the pertinent evidence is that the tax is broadly proportional.

Despite the view of many economists that the property tax burden is not distributed regressively, the layman's view is largely fixed on the tax being regressive. In part, this view reflects aspects of the tax that have little to do with determining incidence, but strike people as unfair attributes of the tax: the fact that the tax is paid in lumpy increments and that tax liabilities do not closely track current incomes. Still, the notion that the tax is regressive influences public policy. Nearly all states have instituted various exemptions and credits to try to relieve the burden of the tax on the elderly (with the argument being that the elderly are on fixed incomes) and on low-income taxpayers. Also, the argument that the tax is regressive has been used in some states to justify the enactment of various property tax limitations.

A third view of the incidence of the tax is that to the extent that the tax can be viewed as a benefit tax—that is, a price paid for services received—issues of redistribution and incidence are irrelevant. Fischel is a strong proponent of this view (see, for example, Fischel, 2001). For the property tax to act as a benefit tax several strong conditions must hold, including free mobility of households among many communities differentiated by their tax and public service packages. These conditions might accurately describe the suburbs of large metropolitan areas, but they are not likely to hold in central cities or rural areas.

The property tax is open to criticism because it is difficult to administer fairly. In some jurisdictions, assessment of property value for taxing purposes may include measurement error, special treatment for certain classes of taxpayers (such as the elderly), and the possibility of political influence.[20] Assessing the volume of property in large cities is a daunting and potentially costly task, and maintaining assessed values in line with current market values may not be possible in areas and periods of rapid housing price inflation. In addition, it is difficult to determine the value of property when sales of similar property are infrequent or, as is often the case for non-residential property, when no similar properties exist. Consider in contrast, the income tax for which individual taxpayers have frequent observations and reports on the income on which to base their calculations of liability. Similarly, with the sales tax, taxes are easily calculated at the time of purchase. In comparison, the property tax may appear more arbitrary and clumsy. Further, multiple overlapping jurisdictions generate the aggregate statutory tax rate on a given parcel. The presence of overlapping jurisdictions makes it difficult for taxpayers to know how much tax they are paying to which governments. And the efforts to relieve the burden on select taxpayers or to redress perceived inequities and inefficiencies lead to complex exemptions, credits, and limitations measures. Although most taxes have problems with administrative complexity (for example, most general sales taxes have exemptions), the property tax seems more complex and less transparent than income or sales taxes.

ARE DEMOGRAPHIC AND ECONOMIC TRENDS UNDERMINING THE PROPERTY TAX?

Even if economists generally agree with Wallace Oates (2001, p.29) that the property tax is "well suited for use at the local level," there is no denying that the tax is unpopular and is being increasingly crippled by the enactment of various limits and restrictions. In the modern era, the passage of Proposition 13 in California in 1978 started a wave of similar limitations and restrictions in states as diverse as Arizona and Massachusetts. These measures limited property tax rates, property tax revenues and property tax assessments. More recently, voters in Colorado in 1992 approved the Taxpayer's Bill of Rights (TABOR), a sweeping constitutional limit on taxes and expenditures for all levels of government.[21] Interest remains high in limiting taxes as witnessed by the number of states that have proposed measures similar to TABOR. The cumulative impact of these limits and restrictions is to render the property tax (and other taxes subject to the limits) ineffective as a means for providing local governments with fiscal autonomy.

Current demographic and policy trends may add to the difficulties with the tax. The aging of the U.S. population, for example, could well reduce support for the property tax. Menchik (2004) documents that the percentage of the population below the age of 19 is expected to decline from 28.6 percent in 2000 to 26.3 percent in 2035. Perhaps more importantly, the percentage of the population aged 65 or over is expected to increase from 12.4 to 20.5 percent over the same period. As they move away from their children and grandchildren to retirement homes and come to rely on relatively fixed sources of income, the elderly may be less willing to support high property taxes for schools. Poterba (1997) finds support for this notion. Using state-level panel data for the period 1960 to 1990, he finds that per child spending is negatively related to the elderly share of the population.[22] Harris, Evans, and Schwab (2001) use a national panel of individual school districts to study the effect of an aging America on education spending. They find that while the elderly have only a modest negative effect on education spending at the district level, a large share of elderly depresses education spending at the state level. They interpret these results to be consistent with the notion that differences in local, but not state, spending are capitalized into housing values, which homeowners, including the elderly, presumably care about. Brunner and Balsdon (2004) examine evidence from a survey of potential voters on two initiatives on public school spending in California. They find that support for school spending declines with age, and that older voters are more willing to support local than state spending on schools.

Another potentially relevant development is that the number of taxpayers subject to the Alternative Minimum Tax (AMT) has exploded in recent years. Initially enacted as a means of ensuring that rich taxpayers were not able to use various exemptions, deductions and credits to avoid paying federal income taxes, it has become commonplace for upper middle-class taxpayers to find themselves subject to the AMT. Approximately 20,000 taxpayers were subject to the AMT in 1970. By 2006, 3.5 million taxpayers paid the AMT, and projections under current law indicate that more than 32 million taxpayers (one-third of total taxpayers) will be subject to the AMT by 2010.[23] Taxpayers subject to the AMT cannot deduct property taxes paid from their federal taxable income. This inability to deduct them raises the marginal price of an extra dollar of local government spending funded with the property tax (including education spending) from $0.66 or $0.75 to one full dollar. Without the federal discount provided to the property tax, political support for the property tax (and other deductible state and local taxes) may be diminished.[24]

ALTERNATIVES TO THE PROPERTY TAX FOR FUNDING SCHOOLS

Suppose policy makers are persuaded that the property tax is structurally flawed or that it is too hampered by restrictions to be useful for school funding. Where would they turn for revenues to support schools? Would they turn to a local income or sales tax? If so, how would they address the problems of these other local sources? Would they move all funding of local schools to the state level? If so, how would they address the problems associated with breaking the link between spending responsibility and revenue-raising authority?

McGuire (2001) begins her analysis of possible alternatives to the local property tax by asking whether local governments need a local source of revenue. She notes that local governments in Europe are largely financed by the central government and that in many U.S. states local governments are heavily reliant on state grants because their access to local revenues is severely restricted. Yet, the arguments for fiscally empowering local governments, including schools—at least fiscally empowering them at the margin—are compelling: the ability to cater to differences in tastes for local public goods is enhanced when local governments have authority to raise their own revenues. In addition, when local governments are grant financed the incentive to spend monies responsibly is weakened, especially when grants fund the marginal dollar of spending.[25]

Assuming that a local source of revenues is desired, McGuire compares the local property tax to its two main alternatives—a local sales tax and a local income tax—and argues that the property tax compares favorably along efficiency and equity criteria.[26] In particular, differences across local jurisdictions in sales and income taxes distort purchases and employment decisions perhaps as much as property tax differences distort investment decisions.[27] The typical sales tax is considerably more regressive than the property tax, and while income taxes can be more progressive than property taxes, sub-national income taxes are usually nearly proportional or only modestly progressive by design.

Oates and Schwab (2004) set up a horse race between the property tax and the income tax as the primary source of revenues for local governments (they do not focus on schools). On the standard economic criteria of equity and efficiency, neither tax gets the nod over the other. Both taxes are likely to distort economic decisions, but either tax is likely to work well as a signal to mobile residents choosing among local jurisdictions. Although income taxes can be designed to be more progressive than property taxes, in practice they rarely are at the state and local level. Also, under the new view that the property tax is largely a tax borne by owners of capital or under the view that lifetime income should be used in assessing the incidence of the property tax, the property tax compares favorably. On the question of visibility or transparency of the tax, they argue that the property tax—largely because there is only one level of government relying on the tax—is superior to the income tax.

Reschovsky (2004) challenges the argument that the property tax is more transparent than the income tax. He points out that while local governments are the primary users of the property tax, the tax is still complicated because of its use by overlapping layers of local governments such as cities, counties, and schools districts. Reschovsky also argues that the income tax has advantages over the property tax as a local revenue source. Depending on the design of the two taxes and assumptions regarding incidence, he contends that a shift toward income taxes would result in a modest decline in the regressivity of the local tax system.

On the crucial criticism of the property tax as a source of funding for education—that there are significant disparities in tax base across districts—both McGuire (2001) and Oates and Schwab (2004) present empirical evidence that the income tax base is distributed more evenly across space than is property wealth. McGuire studies the distribution of adjusted gross income per capita and equalized assessed property value per capita across municipalities in Illinois in 1997, and she finds that the coefficient of variation in adjusted gross income per capita is 0.8 compared to the coefficient of variation in equalized assessed property value per capita at 2.8.[28] Oates and Schwab examine income per pupil and property wealth per pupil across school districts in four states (Massachusetts, New Jersey, New York, and Texas) in 1990 and find property wealth per pupil to be one and a half to two times more unevenly distributed across space than income per pupil. Still, because the income tax base also varies across districts, inequities in spending would nevertheless emerge if school districts relied on local income taxes.

Two practical considerations, however, heavily favor the property tax. First, income and sales taxes are highly pro-cyclical revenues, whereas property taxes are more stable over the economic cycle.[29] It is problematic to fund education expenditures, which vary with characteristics of the population and not the business cycle, using economically volatile revenues. Second, the property tax is a highly productive revenue source. For example, in Illinois in 2004 school districts raised $11 billion in property taxes. In comparison, the state raised $7 billion through the state general sales tax and $8.5 billion through its individual and corporate income taxes combined. If the local property taxes for schools were replaced with a local income or sales tax or with state aid financed through either state sales or income taxes, the required combined sales or income tax rate would be extraordinarily high and could potentially generate large distortions in economic behavior.[30]

IS THERE A FUTURE FOR THE PROPERTY TAX IN SCHOOL FUNDING?

As discussed, there are two fundamental sets of criticisms of the property tax as a source of funds for schools. The first is that because the tax is a local revenue source and the base is unequally distributed across local jurisdictions, it often leads to unacceptably large interdistrict disparities in per pupil spending. The solution to this problem is to reduce or eliminate reliance on the tax at the local level.[31] The recent shift from equity to adequacy as a focus of court challenges, however, may mitigate the force of this argument. In contrast to policies designed to reduce wealth-related spending disparities, a policy aimed at raising the spending of low-spending school districts to an adequate level need not require a concomitant decline in spending by high-spending districts. If the dominant goal of a state government's school finance policy is to assure that all its students are provided with an adequate education, the state may be willing to allow individual districts to supplement the state-guaranteed adequate level of spending by levying local property taxes, even if the property tax base is unevenly distributed across jurisdictions.

The other set of criticisms pertains to the nature or structure of the tax itself—that it is inefficient, inequitable, and difficult to administer. These criticisms are not specific to the funding of school districts and in large part they would pertain to the property tax whether it is a local or a state source. Nonetheless, if the property tax comes up short on the criteria of equity, efficiency, and simplicity, the primary reliance of local school districts on the tax is called into question. We think that, with the exception of simplicity and ease of administration, these criticisms are largely without merit. In comparison with local income and sales taxes, the property tax holds its own in terms of efficiency and equity. Of course, the tax in practice is often not a theoretically pure tax. Like all taxes, its ability to score well on economic criteria depends on the base being broadly defined, the marginal tax rates being relatively low, and the tax administration being transparent. Many property taxes operating today do not meet these requirements. Instead, the base is reduced through preferential treatment of residential property relative to commercial and industrial property; nominal tax rates exceed effective tax rates because assessments are far below market values; and the tax price of local services is not clear. In addition, access to the tax by local governments is complicated where states have imposed (or voters have supported) limitations and restrictions on the tax. Still, assessing its structure and design using normative criteria, we believe the property tax, in practice, holds up well compared to its main alternatives, especially as they would be implemented, and likely compromised, in practice. Although the property tax clearly fails with regard to simplicity and transparency, its productivity as a revenue source and the stability of the tax base over the economic cycle give it two important practical advantages over income and sales taxes.

We conclude that the property tax will continue to have an important role, actually two roles, to play in financing schools.[32] First, the property tax can be used as a source of revenues for state school aid programs either through a statewide property tax or through state capture of locally raised property taxes. Moving from reliance on local property taxes to a state-level property tax has been championed by Sheffrin (2001). He argues that it is hard to justify reliance on the local property tax for funding schools given efforts to "delegitimize differences in educational support across districts" (p. 316). He reasons that a state-level property tax might alleviate concerns of unfairness.[33] Sheffrin notes that a statewide property tax is, in fact, what we have to varying degrees in states as varied as California and New Hampshire. Second, to enhance economic efficiency, the property tax can be a marginal revenue source—to supplement state aid—at the local school district level.

Despite decades of criticism, the property tax remains the major source of local tax revenue for schools. Given that policy makers would find fault with any local tax alternative for funding education, the property tax must play an important, if perhaps diminished, role in funding schools now and into the foreseeable future.

ACKNOWLEDGMENTS

We thank Andrew Reschovsky for helpful comments, and Shannon Wobbe and Jonathan Gemus for excellent research assistance.

NOTES

1. Several states have considered tax and expenditure limits (TEL) in recent years. In 2006 alone, nearly a dozen states considered adoption of a TEL. The National Conference of State Legislatures tracks TEL actions. See http://www.ncsl.org/programs/fiscal/tels2006.htm.
2. See Table 1 of Public Education Finances, Annual Survey of Local Government Finances, 2004.
3. Authors' calculations using data from Table 4 of Public Education Finances, Annual Survey of Local Government Finances, 2004.
4. It should be noted that in a handful of states the amounts reported by the NCES and the Census for property tax revenues and for total local school district revenue differ substantially. These differences are as yet unexplained, but they exist only in a few, relatively small states, and the differences go in both directions. We thank Andrew Reschovsky for pointing out these data discrepancies.
5. All averages are unweighted. That is, the number reported is the average of the share in each state. This provides a measure of the typical share that local revenue, for example, comprises in each state. An alternative calculation would be to divide the sum across all states of locally raised revenue for elementary and secondary education by the sum of total education revenue. Averages calculated this way in effect give more weight to larger states. For example, in 2004, the weighted average for the entire country was 43.9, nearly three percentage points higher than the average for the typical state (as indicated in Table 20.2).
6. These calculations omit the property tax revenues used in states that obtain funds from the parent government.
7. See the chapter by Downes and Figlio in this volume for a discussion of the impacts of tax and expenditure limits on school funding and education quality.
8. Papke (2005, 2007) describes the effects of Proposal A in Michigan on K–12 school funding and student performance.
9. The property tax rate is often expressed in term of mills, or dollars per thousand dollars of assessed valuation.
10. See the Michigan Department of the Treasury (2002) for detailed discussion of this reform.
11. These figures come from the authors' calculations from the state-level Census data.
12. In 2004 aggregate property taxes in California generated $34.5 billion compared to the state individual income tax, which generated $36.4 billion.
13. This interpretation—that local reliance on property taxes is more compatible when the goal is adequacy rather than equity—finds support in Figlio (2004) and Yinger (2004). Figlio notes, "adequacy definitions are entirely child-centered, rather than taxpayer-focused..." (p. 90), thus implying that equity among taxpayers is not necessary, and Yinger concludes that, with adequacy as the goal, a (well-designed) foundation plan would appear to be sufficient.
14. The figures are restricted to the 36 states with independent school districts. Of these 36 states, 24 did not experience court-mandated school reform, five experienced court-mandated school reform before 1985, and seven experienced court-mandated school reform after 1985.
15. Evans, Murray, and Schwab (2001) interpret adequacy along these lines. They contend that adequacy can be achieved through a well-designed foundation aid program coupled with local control over spending above the amount required for an adequate education.
16. Yinger (2004) discusses the various ways in which states supplement foundation programs to achieve greater equity. Loeb (2001) argues that a system of state grants coupled with unlimited ability to raise additional revenues at the local level may not be politically sustainable.
17. While the portion of the property tax that applies to land (which is clearly immobile) is arguably nondistortionary, the portion that applies to buildings and other structures is likely to discourage taxpayers from improving their property. See Netzer (1998) for a discussion of the rationale for and issues surrounding land taxation.
18. At the beginning of the 1900s, property taxes made up 45 percent of state government revenues; by 1992 property taxes were only 1.2 percent of state revenues.

19. See Mieszkowski and Zodrow (1989) and Zodrow (2001) for interpretive surveys of the relevant literature.
20. Dye, McMillen, and Merriman (2006) describe and evaluate a rather byzantine assessment limit on residential properties in Cook County that was championed by the county assessor, an elected official.
21. And even more recently (in November 2005) Colorado voters chose to suspend TABOR's restrictions for five years.
22. In a study that challenges this result, Ladd and Murray (2001) use data on county-level expenditures on education and find that differences in the share of county population that is age 65 or older has no impact on the level of education spending per student.
23. These figures are taken from "The Individual Alternative Minimum Tax: Historical Data and Projections," updated November 2006, prepared by Greg Leiserson and Jeffrey Rohaly, available at the AMT page of the Tax Policy Center's Web site: http://www.taxpolicycenter.org/newsevents/amt.cfm.
24. This effect may be much weaker than anticipated. After the Tax Reform Act of 1986 eliminated deductibility of state sales taxes but retained deductibility of state income taxes, many commentators predicted that states would reduce reliance on sales taxes in favor of the deductible income tax. Instead, the vast majority of state tax increases post TRA86 involved increases in sales taxes.
25. The well-known flypaper effect, whereby recipient governments spend a much greater proportion of a grant dollar than a dollar of local income, is a likely manifestation of this phenomenon. See Hines and Thaler (1995).
26. Oates (1991) argues similarly.
27. See Haughwout et al. (2004) for an analysis of the effect of Philadelphia's wage tax on employment in the city.
28. McGuire (2001) provides evidence that the sales tax, with a coefficient of variation of 2.6 in sales per capita, is distributed as unequally across space as the property tax.
29. See Giertz (2006).
30. In neighboring Wisconsin, where state aid plays a more important role, school districts raised about \$3.4 billion in property taxes, while the state raised \$5.9 billion from the individual and corporate income taxes and \$4.2 billion from the sales tax. While requiring smaller increases in state taxes then in Illinois, the elimination of the school property tax would, nevertheless, require very substantial state tax increases.
31. Note that this criticism is not per se about the property tax; rather it applies to any local tax whose base is unevenly distributed.
32. See, Evans, Murray and Schwab (2001), McGuire (2001), Sheffrin (2001) and Oates and Schwab (2004) for similar conclusions on the continued importance of the property tax.
33. Ladd and Hansen (1999) also argue the case for state-level property taxes on equity grounds.

REFERENCES

Advisory Commission on Intergovernmental Relations (ACIR). (1995). Tax and Expenditure Limits on Local Governments, Information Report, M-194, Washington DC: ACIR.

Brunner, Eric, and Balsdon, Ed. (2004). Intergenerational Conflict and the Political Economy of School Spending. *Journal of Urban Economics*, 56, 369–388.

Chernick, Howard and Reschovsky, Andrew (1993). Evaluating the Long-Run Burden of the Residential Property Tax and Selected State and Local Consumption Taxes. Paper resented at the eighty-sixth Annual conference on Taxation, National Tax Association, November 10. St. Paul: Minnesota.

Dye, Richard F., McMillen, Daniel P., and Merriman, David F. (2006). Illinois' Response to Rising Residential Property Values: An Assessment Growth Cap in Cook County. *National Tax Journal*, Vol LIX (3), 707–16.

Dye, Richard F. and Reschovsky, Andrew (2007). Property Tax Responses to State Aid Cuts in the Recent Fiscal Crisis. Paper presented at a conference *State and Local Finances After the Storm: Is Smooth Sailing Ahead?*, March 30. The Urban Institute, Washington, DC.

Evans, William N., Murray, Sheila E., and Schwab, Robert M. (2001). The Property Tax and Education Finance; Uneasy Compromises. In Wallace E. Oates (Ed.), *Property Taxation and Local Government Finance; Essays in Honor of C. Lowell Harriss*. Cambridge, MA: Lincoln Institute of Land Policy, 209–35.

Figlio, David N. (2004). Funding and Accountability: Some Conceptual and Technical Issues in State Aid Reform. In John Yinger (Ed.), *Helping Children Left Behind; State Aid and the Pursuit of Educational Equity*. Cambridge, MA: The MIT Press, 87–110.

Fischel, William A. (1989). Did *Serrano* Cause Proposition 13?. *National Tax Journal*, Vol XLII (4), 465–73.

Fischel, William A. (2001). Municipal Corporations, Homeowners and the Benefit View of the Property Tax. In Wallace E. Oates (Ed.), *Property Taxation and Local Government Finance; Essays in Honor of C. Lowell Harriss*. Cambridge, MA: Lincoln Institute of Land Policy, 33–77.

Giertz, J. Fred (2006). The Property Tax Bound. *National Tax Journal*, Vol LIX (3), 695–705.

Harris, A. R., Evans, W. N., and Schwab, R. M. (2001). Education Spending in an Aging America. *Journal of Public Economics*, 81, 449–472.

Haughwout, Andrew, Inman, Robert, Craig, Steven, and Luce, Thomas (2004). Local Revenue Hills: Evidence from Four U.S. Cities. *The Review of Economics and Statistics*, MIT Press, Vol 86 (2), 570–585.

Hines, James R., Jr. and Thaler, Richard (1995). The Flypaper Effect. *Journal of Economic Perspectives*, Fall, 9 (4), 217–226.

Hoo, Sonya, Murray, Sheila, and Rueben, Kim. (2006). Education Spending and Changing Revenue Sources. *Tax Notes*, April 10, 223.

Inman, Robert (2001). Commentary. In Wallace E. Oates (Ed.), *Property Taxation and Local Government Finance; Essays in Honor of C. Lowell Harriss*. Cambridge, MA: Lincoln Institute of Land Policy, 148–151.

Kalambokidis, Laura, and Reschovsky, Andrew. (2005). 'States' Responses to the Budget Shortfalls of 2001–2004. *Challenge*. January-February, 76–93.

Ladd, Helen F., and Hansen, Janet S. (1999). *Making Money Matter: Financing America's Schools*. Washington, DC: National Academy Press.

Ladd, Helen F., and Murray, Sheila E. (2001). Intergenerational conflict reconsidered: county demographic structure and the demand for public education. *Economics of Education Review*, 20, 343–357.

Loeb, Susanna. (2001). Estimating the Effects of School Finance Reform: A Framework for a Federalist System. *Journal of Public Economics*, 80 (2), 225–47.

McGuire, Therese J. (2001). Alternatives to Property Taxation for Local Government. In Oates, Wallace E. (Ed.), *Property Taxation and Local Government Finance; Essays in Honor of C. Lowell Harriss*. Cambridge, MA: Lincoln Institute of Land Policy, 301–14.

Menchik, Paul L. (2004). Consumption Patterns, Demographic Change and Sales Tax Revenue: Is Yet Another Fiscal Shock on the Horizon?. In *Proceedings of the Ninety-Sixth Annual Conference on Taxation*, 367–378. Washington, DC: National Tax Association.

Metcalf, Gilbert (1994). The Lifetime Incidence of State and Local Taxes: Measuring Changes During the 1980s. In Joel Slemrod (Ed.), *Tax Progressivity and Income Inequality*. New York: Cambridge University Press, 59–88.

Michigan Department of the Treasury (2002). School Finance Reform in Michigan: Proposal A Retrospective. Office of Revenue and Tax Analysis, December.

Mieszkowski, Peter (1972). The Property Tax. An Excise Tax or a Profits Tax?. *Journal of Public Economics*, 1(1), 73–96.

Mieszkowski, Peter, and Zodrow, George R. (1989). Taxation and the Tiebout Model: The Differential Effects of Head Taxes, Taxes on Land Rents, and Property Taxes. *Journal of Economic Literature*, 27, 1098–1146.

Netzer, Dick (1966). *Economics of the Property Tax*. Washington, DC: Brookings Institution.

Netzer, Dick. (1998). *Land Value Taxation; Can It and Will It Work Today?* Cambridge, MA: Lincoln Institute of Land Policy.

Oates, Wallace E. (1991). The Theory and Rationale of Local Property Taxation. In Therese J. McGuire and Dana Wolfe Naimark (Eds.), *State and Local Finance for the 1990s: A Case Study of Arizona*. Tempe, AZ: Arizona Board of Regents, 407–424.

Oates, Wallace E. (2001). Property Taxation and Local Government Finance: An Overview and Some Reflections. In Wallace E. Oates (Ed.), *Property Taxation and Local Government Finance; Essays in Honor of C. Lowell Harriss*. Cambridge, MA: Lincoln Institute of Land Policy, 21–31.

Oates, Wallace E. and Schwab, Robert M. (2004). What should local governments tax: income or property? In Amy Ellen Schwartz (Ed.), *City Taxes, City Spending; Essays in Honor of Dick Netzer*. Cheltenham, UK: Edward Elgar, 7–29.

Papke, Leslie E. (2005). The Effects of Spending on Test Pass Rates: Evidence from Michigan. *Journal of Public Economics*, 89, 821–39.

Papke, Leslie E. (2007). The Effects of Changes in Michigan's School Finance System. Working paper, Michigan State University, May.

Plummer, Elizabeth. (2003). Evidence on the Incidence of Residential Property Taxes Across Households. *National Tax Journal*, Vol. LVI (4), 739–53.

Poterba, James. (1989). Lifetime Incidence and the Distributional Burden of Excise Taxes. *American Economic Review*, 79 (2), 325–330.

Poterba, J. M. (1997). Demographic Structure and the Political Economy of Public Education. *Journal of Policy Analysis and Management*, 16, 48–66.

Public Education Finances. (2004). Annual Survey of Loca Government Finances.

Reschovsky, Andrew. (2004), Comment. In Amy Ellen Schwartz (Ed.), *City Taxes, City Spending; Essays in Honor of Dick Netzer*. Cheltenham, UK: Edward Elgar, 30–41.

Reschovsky, Andrew. (2004). The Impact of State Government Fiscal Crises on Local Governments and Schools. *State and Local Government Review*, 36 (2), 86–102.

Sheffrin, Steven M. (2001). Commentary. In Wallace E. Oates (Ed.), *Property Taxation and Local Government Finance; Essays in Honor of C. Lowell Harriss*. Cambridge, MA: Lincoln Institute of Land Policy, 315–119.

U.S. Census Bureau, *Annual Survey of Local Government Finances*, selected years.

Wallis, John Joseph (2001). A History of the Property Tax in America. In Wallace E. Oates (Ed.), *Property Taxation and Local Government Finance; Essays in Honor of C. Lowell Harriss*. Cambridge, MA: Lincoln Institute of Land Policy, 123–47.

Wildasin, David E. (1989). Interjurisdictional Capital Mobility: Fiscal Externality and a Corrective Subsidy. *Journal of Urban Economics*, 25, 193–212.

Yinger, John. (2004). State Aid and the Pursuit of Educational Equity: An Overview. In John

Yinger (Ed.), *Helping Children Left Behind; State Aid and the Pursuit of Educational Equity*. Cambridge, MA: The MIT Press, 3–57.

Zodrow, George. (2001). Reflections on the New View and the Benefit View, in Wallace E. Oates (Ed.), *Property Taxation and Local Government Finance; Essays in Honor of C. Lowell Harriss*. Cambridge, MA: Lincoln Institute of Land Policy, 79–111.

21

Tax and Expenditure Limits, School Finance and School Quality

Thomas A. Downes and David N. Figlio

INTRODUCTION

The rapid escalation in real estate prices in the United States over the last several years has led to a resurgent interest in tax and expenditure limitations at the state level. As their name suggests, tax and expenditure limitations place caps on the degree to which states and localities can raise or spend money. While the limitations that have been recently proposed vary substantially in their design and attributes, they share a common purpose—to provide tax relief for populations feeling increasingly burdened by tax collections, and particularly, the property tax.

This recent push for limitations on the ability of states and localities to raise or spend money is by no means the first time in recent years that the United States has experienced a "tax revolt." In the late 1970s and early 1980s, one in three states (most notably California, whose Proposition 13 was not the first but was the most influential of the modern tax and expenditure limitations) acted to limit revenue or expenditure levels or growth, and amidst another economic downturn in the early 1990s, another ten states either enacted or strengthened their fiscal constraints. By early 2007, 30 states had active tax and expenditure limitations (TELs) in place.

These limitations are among the most hotly debated elements of state and local government finance today. In 2005, the Maine legislature enacted a new limitation on expenditure growth, which it capped at the 10-year average personal income growth or 2.75 percent, whichever is lower. In that same year, however, Colorado voters relaxed several key provisions of what most observers considered the nation's most restrictive TEL (McGuire and Rueben, 2006). In other states, voters rejected proposals to strengthen existing TELs (as in California and Oregon) or to enact new, highly restrictive TELs (as in Nebraska) in 2005 and 2006. Still elsewhere, courts removed TEL proposals due to petition fraud (as in Michigan, Montana and Oklahoma) or technicalities (as in Missouri and Nevada). In sum, while few new TELs have been enacted in the 21st century, the fiscal environment throughout the United States appears ripe for new fiscal constraint proposals.

Tax and expenditure limitations are important for education finance and policy because education spending is today the single largest component of state and local budgets. K–12 education spending accounts for over 20 percent of combined state and local expenditures, and higher education spending accounts for over 10 percent of state spending. If TELs restrict the size or growth of state and local budgets, they may lead either to reductions in education spending, or to reallocations in spending from one education category (say, higher education) to another education category (such as K–12). Some state TELs, such as in Oregon, explicitly "protect" state spending on K–12 education at the expense of other state budget categories. This protection of state spending on K–12 education has led to dramatic cutbacks in higher education spending in some states (Archibald and Feldman, 2006). Still, even though K–12 education spending has been protected relative to other categories of spending, the level of K–12 education spending and the distribution across school districts of this spending may have been influenced by TELs. In the case of local education agencies that are their own taxing authorities, TELs that limit their revenue or spending either reduce spending on education or change the mix of revenues used to finance education spending. TELs can also influence the distribution across school districts of education spending as well, as some school districts are more likely to be constrained by TELs than are others. It is therefore of important to understand the degree to which TELs affect overall revenues for, and spending on, K–12 education and the distribution across districts of revenue and spending.

Understanding the impact of TELs on both the average level and distribution of educational outcomes such as student achievement is of equal importance. Even if TELs reduce education spending, they may not reduce achievement. Studies of the 1970s-era limitations (e.g., Citrin, 1979; Courant et al., 1980; Ladd and Wilson, 1982; Stein et al., 1983) indicate that supporters of TELs believed that these limits would lead to increased efficiency in government; that is, that governments would cut waste without reducing service levels.[1] On the other hand, analysts of TELs have argued that these policies could lead to reductions in student outcomes that are far larger than might be expected given the changes in spending. The literature we summarize below indicates that this latter outcome is most consistent with the data.

In this chapter, we first briefly describe the different types of TELs active in the United States today. We then summarize the literature on the relationship between TELs and the fiscal structure of local governments and provide an overview of the literature that has examined the impact of limits on student performance. After offering potential explanations for why TELs could influence student outcomes to a different degree than might spending changes in general, we close with a discussion of gaps in our knowledge.

TAX AND EXPENDITURE LIMITATIONS IN THE UNITED STATES

TELs that affect school districts and other local governments take a variety of forms that differ in their restrictiveness. The most common form of TELs prior to the 1978 passage in California of Proposition 13 was a limit on specific property tax rates. For any local jurisdiction, such as a school district or a water authority, the property tax revenues of that jurisdiction are determined by the following relationship:

Property tax revenue = (Tax rate levied by the jurisdiction)*(Taxable value of property).

Total tax payments made by the residents of any jurisdiction equal the revenues of that jurisdiction and any payments made to overlying jurisdictions. As a result, limits on specific tax rates, that is, setting a maximum tax rate that specific local jurisdictions can levy, may not reduce the property tax payments of residents of those jurisdictions. This follows, in part, because spending responsibilities could be shifted from the jurisdictions constrained by the specific limit to overlying jurisdictions that are not constrained and in part because the limits do not control the growth in the taxable value of property in the jurisdiction, also known as the assessed value of property.

Other TELs limit the overall property tax rate levied by all overlapping taxing authorities within a geographic area, but, as with specific tax rate limits, they can be circumvented with changes in the assessed value of property in the affected jurisdictions. The majority of post-1978 TELs either limit both property tax rates and growth in the assessed value of property or directly limit the growth in property tax revenues. Less common but potentially more restrictive still are limits on overall revenue growth from all sources, or limits on expenditure growth.

These "modern" TELs are more likely to be effective in restricting the total revenues and expenditures of all jurisdictions within a geographic area than are the earlier forms of limits. The extent to which a limit constrains the ability of local governments to raise revenues or make expenditures depends not just on the type of limit, but also on how restrictive it is. For instance, a TEL that limits annual revenue growth to 1 percent is much more likely to constrain local governments than would a TEL that limits growth to 10 percent. Figlio (1997) and others have attempted to quantify variation in the extent to which limits constrain local governments, and (as discussed later in this chapter) have found that variation in the extent to which limits constrain matters less for student outcomes than the presence of any limit that could be "binding"; that is, that could impose an effective constraint on local fiscal behavior.[2]

Today, nine states (Arizona, California, Colorado, Iowa, Kansas, Maine, Minnesota, Nevada, and New Jersey) impose restrictions on aggregate spending by all local governments, and Wisconsin imposes limits on non-federal revenues of school districts. Other states limit property tax revenues but do not restrict total revenues (i.e., revenues from all sources including intergovernmental aid) of all local governments; these states are Idaho, Indiana, Kentucky, Louisiana, Michigan, Mississippi, Missouri, New Mexico, Ohio, Oregon, Texas, Utah, West Virginia, and portions of Illinois. Several of the states with overall spending limits, such as Colorado and Minnesota, also limit total revenue of all local governments. Arkansas, Florida, Maryland, Oklahoma,and Washington do not directly limit either revenues or expenditures but effectively do the same thing with combinations of tax rate limits and limits on property assessments. It is not likely that the TELs imposed in other states have had any real effect on revenue.

THE EFFECT OF TELS ON EDUCATION REVENUES AND SPENDING

The most natural place to begin a discussion of the effects of TELs on schools is to consider whether TELs have influenced school finances at all. McGuire (1999) and Mullins and Wallin (2004) summarize much of the early literature on the fiscal effects of TELs. TELs apparently slowed the growth of property tax revenues, but did not significantly slow the growth of total revenues received by all local governments. Indeed, the most compelling estimates indicate that TELs have little or no effect on total revenues of local governments, where revenues are aggregated across all local governments. The research also points to three changes in the fiscal systems in states with local limitations that have blunted the effects of TELs on the revenues of local governments. First, increased state aid, funded by increased state taxes, compensates for the decline in local revenues (Mullins and Wallin, 2004). Second, overrides, in the states that permit overrides, have permitted voters in some localities to allow post-limitation spending to continue along the path it would have followed in the absence of the limit (McGuire, 1999). Third, in localities constrained by TELs, there has been an increased reliance on other local taxes and user fees (Mullins and Wallin, 2004).

Recent research confirms the results of the earlier work and provides a richer picture of the effects of TELs on the revenue and expenditure of local governments. Shadbegian (1998, 1999, 2003) documents the varied effects of state and local tax and expenditure limitations on revenues and expenditures of local governments. Examining the impact of TELs on all local revenue sources and accounting for differences in limit stringency, he finds that TELs reduce per capita property tax revenue, local own-source revenue (i.e., revenue from all sources other than intergovernmental aid), and local expenditures. TELs reduce local reliance on the property tax and on own-source revenues, though an increase in the use of miscellaneous revenues mitigates the extent to which the decline in property tax revenues translates into a decline in own-source revenues. The estimated impacts of TELs vary, however, with the stringency of the limits.[3] Localities in states with more stringent limits rely more on other taxes and less on miscellaneous revenues to compensate for the decline in property tax revenues.

Shadbegian (2003) narrows the focus to the impact of state and local limits on the provision of public education. Using data aggregated to the state level, Shadbegian establishes that, on net, TELs have almost no effect on total spending on public education because increases in direct and indirect spending by state governments compensate for the decline in spending from local own-source revenue. Not surprisingly, the presence of a limit on the state government revenues of expenditures reduces the extent to which state spending can compensate for reductions in local own-source revenue.

Recent research also indicates that, while TELs had limited impact on the size of the state and local sectors, the limitations did affect the relative importance of different sources of revenues for local governments. For example, Joyce and Mullins (1991), Mullins and Joyce (1996) and Mullins (2004) find that limits increase centralization of revenue raising, state government spending growth, and growth in the local use of non-tax revenues. In addition, TELs reduce the share of revenue raised through local broad-based taxes. The variation across localities in the extent to which the limits constrained local spending (Figlio, 1997) means, however, that state-level data provide an imperfect picture of the full impact of TELs, since spending data from constrained localities are averaged with spending data from localities unaffected by the constraints. Nevertheless, the results from this series of papers establish that, for all local governments, the extent to which TELs affect spending on education or on any other publicly-provided service provided by a local government depends upon the ease with which that government can generate non-tax revenue and the change in the amount of state aid distributed to that government.[4]

Mullins (2004) uses county-level fiscal data on within-county variation in spending by local governments from all counties in the United States to determine whether TELs affect some parts of a state differently from others. He finds that, on average, TELs increase the within-county variation in both general and education expenditures. The more binding the limit is, the more within-county inequality grows after the TEL. Given that TELs are more likely to bind in initially low-spending districts, TELs may lead to greater disparities in spending across districts within a state because state aid has typically not fully compensated for the impact of the constraints.

Mullins also finds that the impact of TELs on affluent suburban fringe counties differs from the average impact of these limits. For these counties, more binding limits reduce variation in education expenditures across school districts and have no impact on the within-county variation in general expenditures. Why these counties look different from all others is not clear, though differential ability to pass overrides and differential access to non-tax revenues are two possible explanations.

Case studies of the evolution of local public spending in California provide some final useful evidence on the impact of TELs. Proposition 13, the voter-approved initiative that was the first in a series of local and state revenue and expenditure limitations imposed on governments in California, limited the overall tax rate on any property to 1 percent of the taxable value of that property. The initiative also limited the growth in the taxable value of property to at most 2 percent, unless that property changed hands, at which time the taxable value would be set equal to the sales price of the property. Although local and state revenue and expenditure limitations co-exist in a number of states other than California, the stringency of these key provisions of Proposition 13 as well as the state and local limitations that have since been approved by California voters resulted in a context in California that was unique—at least until the passage in 1992 in Colorado of the Taxpayer's Bill of Rights. As importantly, the elapsed time since Proposition 13 has made it possible in the California case to examine the long-term effects of stringent fiscal limits. For that reason, a brief summary of the research focusing on California is warranted.

In general, the evidence from California indicates that the evolving fiscal structure of its state and local governments has constrained the ability of cities and counties to increase spending in areas that might substitute for education spending. The evidence from California also sheds light on the extent to which TEL-induced restrictions on education spending are circumvented by increases in noneducation spending by overlying jurisdictions with access to unconstrained revenue sources. In California, a combination of legislation and voter initiatives has resulted both in a reallocation of property tax revenues from cities and counties to school districts and in earmarking portions of state revenues for school districts (Wassmer, 2006). This favored status of school districts, relative to cities and counties, has limited the flexibility of cities and counties and has accentuated the extent to which cities and counties rely on nontraditional revenue sources (Hoene, 2004; Wassmer and Anders, 1999). These trends in the fiscal status of cities and counties have apparently limited the relative growth in expenditures by these governmental units on such services as libraries and parks and recreation, which could substitute for declines in inflation-adjusted education spending. While city and county governments have greater access to nontraditional revenue sources, this access has been used primarily to maintain the share of noneducation spending. Hoene (2004), for example, shows that the shares of total expenditures by California cities on libraries, parks and recreation, and social services have stayed constant or declined slightly since 1977. For California cities, housing and community development was the only spending category that might substitute for education for which the share of total expenditures increased. And for the period from 1990–91 to 1994–95 per capita expenditures by county governments in California were not higher in those counties in which a larger percentage of the population was non-adult (Wassmer and Anders, 1999), even though a larger percentage would have been expected if substitution had occurred. While California's experience with TELs is unique, the weight of the evidence from elsewhere indicates that California mirrors the general national experience with TELs.

TELS AND STUDENT PERFORMANCE

Even if TELs reduce both the revenues that school districts and other local government generate and the amount that these governments can spend, these limits might not adversely affect student outcomes. As mentioned in the introduction, one primary rationale for TELs cited by supporters is that they could lead to more efficient provision of services. In the case of education, this logic might imply that resources may be deployed in times of fiscal constraint to preserve instructional spending rather than administrative spending. Evidence regarding general school reactions to fiscal stress (e.g., Ladd, 1998) suggests that fiscally constrained districts are more likely than other districts to cut back on administrative and capital spending in order to preserve instructional spending. While this result need not imply that the districts are becoming more efficient (i.e., are able to produce improved student outcomes with the same level of spending), the result does mean that it is theoretically an open question as to whether TELs would lead to reduced school service levels or student performance.

Even if inefficiency is not pervasive, if the argument made by Hanushek (1986, 1996, 2003) that increases in spending per se are unlikely to result in large improvements in student performance is correct, then cutbacks in spending could well generate no adverse effects on student outcomes.

An obvious alternative is that the cut resources are productive, so resource cuts would result in reductions in student outcomes. Further, if the resource cuts were concentrated in the most productive areas of education spending, the declines in student performance might be larger than would be expected given the magnitude of the declines in education spending. As a result, assessing the impact of TELs on student performance can only be done by estimating directly this impact.

Early case studies of TELs like those of the Joint Budget Committee (1979) and Schwadron (1984) for California and Greiner and Peterson (1986) for Massachusetts consistently show that residents of the studied states perceived a drop in the quality of publicly-provided services. That this perception reflected reality is sometimes, though not always (Greiner and Peterson 1986), confirmed by objective measures of service quality. According to the case studies, government officials responded to TELs by first making cuts in capital expenditures and in areas of current expenditure that these officials felt were peripheral. For example, in California school administrators sought to protect the core academic subjects, choosing instead to make cuts by pursuing such strategies as reducing the diversity of course offerings and the number of pupil service employees.[5]

Given their timing, these case studies could not be used to draw any conclusions about the long-run effects of TELs. Also, even though these case studies moved beyond examination of the fiscal impacts of TELs, the absence of any clear prediction about the impact of TELs on student performance meant that only by examining student outcomes directly, and by determining how these outcomes had changed relative to the pre-limit baseline, could researchers ascertain the effect of limits.

Downes (1992) offers the first over-time comparison of the effects of TELs on student performance. Comparing performance on the California Assessment Program test for 170 unified (K–12) districts in 1976–77 and 1985–86, Downes finds that student performance actually increased by five points, on average, and that the cross-district distribution of student performance was essentially unchanged over this time period. This research implies that California's Proposition 13 did not reduce student performance at any point on the performance distribution.

Such a conclusion is unwarranted, however. Contemporaneous with the state and local response to Proposition 13 the state implemented school finance reforms made necessary by the *Serrano v. Priest* decision of the California Supreme Court.[6] This reality raises a problem that faces any researcher attempting to isolate the impact of TELs on public schooling. Frequently, states have implemented major school finance reforms close in time to the passage of TELs. Thus, the effects of TELs can only be isolated by looking across the states or by examining the long-run experience in a state in which a limit was passed and no major changes in the school finance system had occurred (Blankenau and Skidmore, 2004).

Three recent papers take this lesson to heart and, thus, provide a model for future empirical research on the impact of TELs. Using a cross-section of student-level data from the National Education Longitudinal Survey (NELS), Figlio (1997) finds that, *ceteris paribus*, revenue and expenditure limits significantly reduced tenth grade performance in mathematics, reading, science, and social studies. Using variation generated by the imposition of property tax limits on some, but not all, school districts in Illinois, Downes, Dye, and McGuire (1998) conclude that, in the short term, these limits led to slower growth in the performance of third graders on a standardized test of mathematics, but did not do so for eighth graders or in either grade in reading.

While these papers provided improved estimates of the effects of TELs, they had potential flaws. For example, Figlio's (1997) work drew upon cross-sectional comparisons, making it impossible for him to rule out the possibility that the school districts subject to TELs were a nonrandom sample of all U. S. school districts.[7] Downes, Dye, and McGuire's (1998) comparison of cross-time changes in performance in districts subject to TELs to similar changes in Illinois districts not subject to TELs could have resulted in flawed estimates of the impact of TELs because of the existence of only three post-limit years[8] of data and the possibility that the limited districts might be a nonrandom selection of Illinois districts. Nevertheless, these two papers clarified that evaluating the effects of TELs requires not only before-and-after data on students in districts subject to limits but also a control group of students from states in which no limits have been enacted.

With this observation in mind, Downes and Figlio (2000) attempted to determine how the TELs of the late 1970s and early 1980s affected the distribution of student performance in states in which limits were imposed and how student performance has changed in these states relative to student performance in states in which no limits were imposed. The core data used in the analysis were drawn from two national data sets, the National Longitudinal Study of the High School Class of 1972 (NLS-72) and the 1992 (senior year) wave of the NELS. The NELS data were collected sufficiently far from the passage of most TELs to permit quantification of the long-run effects of these limits by analyzing changes in the distributions of student performance between the NLS-72 cross-section and the NELS cross-section.

Downes and Figlio confirm Figlio's (1997) earlier finding that TELs reduce mathematics test scores by 1 to 7 percent, depending on model specification, as well as Downes, Dye, and McGuire's (1998) finding of no observable impact of TELs on reading scores.[9] Given the age of the test-takers, it is sensible to believe that high school mathematics differences may be more attributable to differences in schooling than are high school reading differences. Thus the generally stronger effect of TELs on mathematics than on reading should come as no surprise. Moreover, this pattern of stronger effects for math is also fully consistent with Figlio and Ladd's findings with respect to school accountability programs elsewhere in this handbook

Both Downes, Dye, and McGuire (1998) and Downes and Figlio (2000) find that TELs have more negative effects on student performance in economically-disadvantaged localities, though these estimated differences are frequently imprecisely estimated and so should be taken with a grain of salt. That said, the general pattern of these results is consistent with the finding that TELs affect low-income communities more than higher-income communities and the increased likelihood that they would bind poorer communities may exacerbate existing inequalities across school districts.

For the most part, when researchers examine the impact of TELs on student performance, they limit their analysis to students who remain in the public schools. Downes and Figlio (1999a) provide the only attempt to study the *performance* effects of TELs (and school finance reforms) on private school students. Using a methodology similar to Downes and Figlio's (2000) study of public school performance, they find evidence of a modest, though imprecisely estimated, negative effect of TELs on student test scores in the private sector. Determining whether these negative effects are attributable to lower, private sector quality because of diminished public sector competition or to changes in the composition of students served by private schools[10] requires analysis of the enrollment effects of TELs. To date, the only such analysis is provided by Bradbury, Case, and Mayer (1998), who analyze the relationship between grade-level enrollment patterns and various indicators of the extent to which TELs affect the ability of affected towns to increase education spending. Since differences between actual enrollment patterns and the patterns of enrollment implied by the decennial Censuses reflect primarily withdrawal from the public schools, either to private schools or nonenrollment status, the results from this paper shed some light on the effect of TELs on dropout rates. Bradbury, Case, and Mayer find that the share of the potential student population served by the public schools is lower in districts in which more initial cuts were necessary when the limits were first imposed. This result suggests that limits could increase dropout rates or could result in students switching from the public to the private sector. Further research on the impact of limits on school completion and on the share of students attending private schools is clearly needed.

IF MONEY DOES NOT MATTER MUCH, WHY MIGHT TELS SIGNIFICANTLY REDUCE PERFORMANCE?

The weight of the evidence on TELs suggests that these limits lead to small reductions in school spending and significant reductions in student performance. Readers who believe that spending cuts necessarily translate into achievement declines might find these parallel results to be obvious. Those who interpret the literature as supporting the conclusion that increases in education spending do not translate into increases in student achievement might find this seemingly asymmetric result surprising: small declines in spending appear to translate into relatively large declines in performance. As Hanushek (1986, 1996, 2003) points out, the existing research relating spending to student outcomes overwhelmingly suggests that the relationship between spending and outcomes is weak, if present at all. Re-analyses of Hanushek's surveys, conducted by Dewey, Husted, and Kenny (1999) and Hedges, Laine and Greenwald (1996), indicate that Hanushek may have overstated the case for no empirical relationship, but much of their evidence still points to modest relationships. That said, some of the estimated effects found in the Hedges et al. meta-analyses are almost implausibly large. Modern analyses that better deal with the question of causal inference, such as Angrist and Lavy (1999), Krueger (1999), Ferguson and Ladd (1996), Ludwig and Bassi (1999), and Figlio (1999) also suggest that additional dollars may be productive, but these implied productivity gains are still quite modest.

There are numerous commonly-suggested explanations of why additional dollars allocated to schools might not lead to proportional (or any) gains in student outcomes. In addition to Betts and Johnson's (1997) finding that there exist decreasing returns to school spending, most of the remaining arguments boil down to suspicions about either intentional or unintentional resource misallocation, at least from an efficiency perspective. Unintentional resource misallocation could occur if, for instance, a school district spends additional dollars on school services that are intended to be beneficial to students but do not actually have much effect. A good example of such an action might be to hire additional teachers to reduce class size without making any changes in curriculum or instructional techniques. The evidence cited by Murnane and Levy (1996) suggests that such a strategy, while well meaning,[11] may have little effect.

Other explanations are less charitable to the schools. For instance, results suggesting no relationship between additional spending and student outcomes are also consistent with additional dollars being captured as union rents or administrative rents, with no additional productive inputs being provided. By "rents," we mean that individuals currently in control of resources (either administrators, or experienced teachers, through bargaining in the union) may be able to direct new resources to expenditure categories that most benefit them *personally*, rather than necessarily choosing the most effective use of additional resources. Administrative rents could accrue, for example, if the additional dollars are used to hire more administrative staff or to improve central office buildings. Teacher union rents could accrue if the additional school spending tends to boost salaries of more experienced, vested teachers who are unlikely to leave the school. The weight of the existing empirical evidence suggests that there are few if any performance benefits to increased teacher experience after the first several years, or to a teacher's master's degree in education. These findings suggest that the higher salary premiums for experience, or for a master's degree, result in higher spending on salaries with little discernable impact on student outcomes.[12]

Interestingly, most of these types of explanations for little relationship between adding spending and increased achievement do not have obvious symmetric implications for student outcomes when spending is reduced. If rent-seeking is an explanation for the small gains associated with increases in expenditures, relatively large reductions in outcomes could result when equal-sized reductions in resources are imposed, as is likely in the case of TELs. Consider, for instance, the case of administrative rents. Reductions in spending would be more likely to be borne by instruction, rather than administration, just as increases in spending accrued to administration, rather than instruction. If instructional spending matters for student achievement per se, then this logic would imply that reduced spending, leading to reduced instructional spending, would have impacts on student outcomes that are larger in magnitude than would similarly-sized spending increases. Note, also, that reductions in spending that lead to cuts in instruction, rather than administration, are also consistent with a story of an efficiently-run school already operating with the minimal necessary fixed administrative costs. In such a situation, even an efficiently-run school would need to cut its instructional budgets, which would, in the current example, harm student outcomes.

In general, if reductions in spending do not change (or exacerbate) the premium to a less productive input, then outcomes should fall, just as outcomes would not be expected to rise as spending increases. This observation implies that the case of teacher union rents is similar to the administrative rents case. If reductions in spending increase the relative salary of experienced teachers in a district because starting salaries are cut, the school district may end up holding on to its more experienced teachers while running off its less experienced teachers and reducing the ability to attract high quality teachers from the outside.

If teacher union rents are a partial explanation of the findings of a negative relationship between tax limitations and student outcomes, then one should expect that tax limitations are associated with changes in the teacher labor market. Figlio and Rueben (2001) find that tax limitations substantially reduce the average qualifications of new entrants into a state's teaching force. Several researchers, such as Ehrenberg and Brewer (1994) and Goldhaber and Brewer (1997), demonstrate that teacher characteristics such as the selectivity of the teacher's undergraduate institution, as a proxy for native ability, or teacher subject matter expertise have statistically significant influences on student outcomes. Thus the finding that these teacher attributes fall with tax limitations is consistent with a reduction in student achievement. This evidence could also partially explain the differences between Downes, Dye, and McGuire's (1998) results suggesting relatively small achievement effects of TELs and Downes and Figlio's (2000) results suggesting larger achievement effects because the teacher labor market responses to TELs should be relatively long-term.

Moreover, Figlio and Rueben's (2001) results are consistent with an explanation of union rents, because they find that teacher quality responds to TELs by even more than what would have been predicted by changes in teacher salaries alone. Further evaluation of different data, though not part of the Figlio and Rueben paper, suggests that school districts subject to TELs tend to cut the salaries of starting teachers while maintaining teacher salaries for more experienced teachers. This finding helps to explain why TELs apparently led to reduced teacher quality among new teachers that is larger even as the salary reductions per se associated with tax limitations were comparatively modest.

Asymmetry in the impact of TELs could also result because school districts might not respond to budget reductions in a manner consistent with increasing efficiency. Even if schools in the districts affected by the limits are capable of reducing waste and thus maintaining the pre-limitation level of student performance, the limits typically provide no explicit incentive to administrators of these districts to eliminate waste. Figlio and O'Sullivan (2001) provide evidence of strategic behavior of municipalities, townships, and school districts in response to the imposition of a limit. One goal of this behavior seems to be to encourage voters to override the limit. For school districts, if school district administrators are budget maximizers and if technical inefficiency in the schools persists because insiders in school systems have more information than outsiders about how resources can be used productively, then administrators may have an incentive to allow student performance to decline by more than is dictated by changes in financial circumstances and to use this decline to argue for additional resources.

Figlio (1997) finds results consistent with this argument, showing that in school districts bound by TELs, measured school inputs are reduced but administrative expenditures are not. Similarly, Figlio (1998) establishes that school districts affected by Oregon's Measure 5 are more likely to cut instructional expenditures than administrative expenses.[13]

Dye and McGuire (1997), on the other hand, exploring the short-term effects of a tax limitation affecting only portions of Illinois, find very little evidence to suggest that school districts cut instruction to preserve administration expenses; if anything, affected school districts may have cut administration more. This finding is wholly consistent with Downes, Dye, and McGuire's (1998) evidence that this Illinois tax limitation has not appreciably affected student outcomes in the constrained school districts, at least in the short run. It is possible that the administrative-rents explanation can provide some reconciliation between the findings of little achievement implications in Illinois versus larger achievement implications found using other methods from a national study. One factor that might explain why Illinois school districts did not cut instruction, relative to administration, following their tax limitation, while other school districts facing other limitations apparently did, involves Tiebout competition. The attributes of the Illinois tax cut that facilitate nice quasi-experiments—that is, the fact that some Chicago-area school districts were affected while others were not—also makes it possible that the unaffected school districts could put competitive pressure on the affected districts. This finding is confirmed by Millimet and Rangaprasad (2007), who find evidence of competition among Illinois school districts only in those counties in which school districts are subject to TELs.

While Dye and McGuire (1998) indicate that, in instances in which interjurisdictional competition might provide incentives for administrators to use resources efficiently, instructional spending might be protected, Dye, McGuire, and McMillen's (2005) update suggests that the discipline provided by competition may disappear when the limits become more widespread. Over time in Illinois, voters in many more school districts have chosen to adopt limits. Using data on both the early and later adopters, Dye, McGuire, and McMillen find that, in the long run, instructional spending is not protected. Such a result could indicate that the more widespread adoption of limitations in the Illinois context has eliminated some of the competitive discipline that existed when limits applied to a small subset of districts in the state. Thus, in the aftermath of limits, competition may constrain rent-seekers only if the limits do not apply universally.

The magnitude of private responses to constraints provides additional indirect evidence on the limited scope of competitive pressure as a disciplining mechanism. The central lesson from the work on private schooling and private contributions seems to be that the private responses to constraints tend to be small. For example, Brunner and Sonstelie (2003) note that, while private contributions are a substantial portion of district revenues in a small number of school districts, overall these contributions have little impact on the post-*Serrano* distribution of education expenditures. Brunner and Imazeki (2005) confirm this finding based on data from 2001. They show that less than one-fifth of California students attend schools where combined contributions to the school and district exceed $50 per pupil. In Vermont, a court-mandated finance reform in 1997 imposed fiscal constraints on some but not all school districts. Downes and Steinman (2006) took advantage of this variation to show that while contributions may have slightly muted, the impact of constraints and the overall effect of contributions on the distribution of spending in Vermont was limited. In a similar vein, Anderson and Butcher (2006) demonstrate that fiscal constraints imposed by TELs lead school districts to enter into more junk-food contracts in an apparent attempt to boost revenues. They find, however, that the additional revenues have not resulted in improved student performance, while the increased availability of junk food seems to have led to increased obesity.

An additional explanation for why tax limitations may reduce student outcomes is put forward by Aaronson (1999). Aaronson demonstrates that communities constrained by TELs become more heterogeneous over time. If educating a more heterogeneous population is more costly, then one might expect that fiscally constrained school districts would experience reduced outcomes for any given level of spending. In addition, if reduced spending leads some students to leave the public sector for the private sector (Downes and Schoeman, 1998; Husted and Kenny, 1997; Evans, Murray, and Schwab, 1998; Bradbury, Case, and Mayer, 1998), especially the highest ability students (Epple, Figlio, and Romano, 2004), mean performance levels in the public sector would fall and the remaining students in the public sector would be costlier still to educate.

Downes and Figlio (1999a, 1999b) present complementary evidence on the school choice responses to TELs and school finance reforms. Using school-district-level data, they find that school finance reforms, and to a smaller extent TELs, reduce the share of students from high income families attending public schools and increase the share of such students attending private schools. This result, coupled with those of Aaronson on community composition and of Lankford and Wyckoff (2000) and Figlio and Stone (2001), which suggest that factors correlated with TELs, such as student-teacher ratios, are important determinants in private school selection for relatively high-socioeconomic status families,[14] indicates that tax limitations have the potential to dramatically alter the student composition in the public schools. This resulting change in school composition can help to explain why tax limitations might affect student outcomes (for the students remaining in the public schools) to a greater degree than would be predicted from the corresponding reduction in the level of spending.

In the space available, we cannot offer a comprehensive explanation of all of the possible causes of the negative relationship between TELs and student outcomes. Nevertheless, the preceding discussion demonstrates that it is plausible that student outcomes could fall with the reductions in spending induced by TELs in more dramatic fashion than outcomes would be expected to rise if school districts faced equal-sized spending increases. At a minimum, the results imply that a central desire of voters for TELs—that they would receive reductions in taxes but not face appreciable reductions in student outcomes—appears to have not been realized. Since TELs provide no explicit requirements to spend money in a particular way, there is no reason to believe that adding an additional constraint would necessarily eliminate waste and inefficiency even if the system was inefficient or wasteful at the outset. Moreover, if school administrators or teacher unions extract rent from the system, tax limitation measures may exacerbate existing inefficiency if the most flexible components of spending are the ones that, if reduced, would result in the largest relative declines in student performance. These results may or may not imply that governments fail to allocate resources to those inputs most strongly linked to student performance. But, even if waste exists, the evidence does not suggest that tax limitation measures reduce this waste, or at least reduce waste at low cost.

DISCUSSION

The last 20 years have provided researchers with an opportunity to determine if TELs are good public policy. The proponents of the argument that government insiders seek to maximize the size of government contend that constitutional constraints like Proposition 13 could reduce the size of local governments and, at the same time, have little or no effect on the quality of public services provided. This "free lunch" would be realized, the argument goes, because the limits would force governments to eliminate waste.

In this chapter, we summarize the research that has shed light on the validity of the argument that TELs provide a costless mechanism for constraining government spending. The research we summarize produces a relatively consistent conclusion; the imposition of TELs results in long-run reductions in the performance of public school students. We also provide evidence that reconciles these reductions with the most often-reported result of the education production literature: dollars matter little per se, if at all. Still, whether TELs are good public policy remains an open question, we contend, since work remains on the quantification of the costs and benefits of TELs. This quantification requires information on the magnitude of the reductions in tax liabilities that result, on the changes in the mix of revenue sources used, on the impact of limits on student performance and on schooling services more broadly, and on the impact of limits on the distribution of spending across levels of education and non-schooling services. Further, how TELs affect the net well-being of individuals at different locations on the socio-economic spectrum must be assessed.

As this discussion reveals, we know the most about the impact of TELs on tax liabilities, on the mix of revenue sources used, and on the mix of expenditures. Yet, even in these areas, gaps in our knowledge remain. Assessing the distributional implications of limits requires further analysis, adding to that of Shadbegian (1999, 2003) and Mullins (2004), of the extent to which TELs affect some communities and school districts more than others. Additional work on the impact of limits on nontraditional revenue sources, such as private contributions to fund education and other publicly-provided services, is needed. Larger gaps remain in our knowledge of the impact of limits on student performance. Since those gaps have existed, in part, because of the absence of pre- and post-limit data on student performance, the now universal existence of accountability systems that require annual testing of all students should make it possible to assess the impact of newer limits.

Finally, Reschovsky (2004) suggests that the existence of fiscal constraints could serve to exacerbate the impact of downturns on education spending, both by limiting the ability of localities to respond to state aid cuts and by shifting local revenue away from a stable source, the property tax, to less stable sources. Further research into the extent to which TELs make education spending more cyclical is warranted, as is research into the degree to which limits add to the uncertainty of those individuals with the responsibility for crafting budgets.

NOTES

1. Anderson (2006) reviews several other potential explanations for voter support for statewide limitations on the ability of local governments to raise revenue or make expenditures.
2. The convention in the literature has been to classify a limit as binding if the limit constrains overall revenue growth from all sources, constraints overall expenditure growth, or combines a limit on the growth the assessed value of property with a limit on the overall property tax rate.

3. Using the terminology of Figlio (1997) and others, all of the TELs considered in Shadbegian (1999) are potentially binding. Shadbegian classifies limit stringency based on the maximum permitted growth rate in nominal property tax revenues.
4. Growth of non-tax revenue may be an explanation for Dye, McGuire, and McMillan's (2005) findings that, in Illinois school districts subject to a tax cap, growth in operating spending had declined less than had growth in school district tax revenues and that the different changes in growth rates were not attributable to compensating changes in state aid.
5. The results in Downes (1996) suggest that school administrators in California did not respond to the limits by cutting the administrative staff. For a national cross-section, Figlio (1997) also finds no evidence of cuts in administration.
6. Fischel (1989, 1996) makes a strong case that, in fact, the prospective school finance reforms that were compelled by the *Serrano* decision stimulated enough additional support for tax limits to make passage of Proposition 13 inevitable. If this logic is right, any observed changes in the distribution of student performance in California should ultimately be attributed to the finance reforms, not the resultant tax limits.
7. Shadbegian and Jones (2005) also use cross-sectional data in their analysis of the impact on student achievement of the stringency of the constraints imposed by Proposition 2½ in Massachusetts. Again, as is the case with Figlio (1997), the possibility exists that some combination of sorting and unobserved tastes for education resulted both in towns being constrained by the limits and having lower levels of student performance. In this particular case, the absence of data on pre-Proposition 2½ test performance means that the authors are unable to rule out the possibility that there existed unobservable factors that resulted in lower test performance and that are correlated with the extent to which a locality was constrained by Proposition 2½.
8. Dye, McGuire, and McMillan's (2005) finding that the Illinois limits have become more binding over time suggests strongly that the long-term effect of the limits may be different.
9. Downes and Figlio find stronger evidence of a negative effect of TELs on reading scores when they treat TELs as endogenous—that is, that factors influencing reading scores might also influence the likelihood of TELs in a state. See their paper or Figlio (1997) for more of a discussion of the potential endogeneity biases, as well as a detailed treatment of the issue of reverse causality.
10. Epple and Romano (1998) theoretically describe stratification patterns between the public and private sectors that predict that reduced public sector spending leads to the movement of "top" public school students into the private sector, reducing the average performance level of both the private and public sectors. Epple, Figlio, and Romano (2004) offer some empirical justification of the stratification patterns identified in the theoretical model.
11. While the more modern evidence on class size (e.g., Krueger, 1999; Ding and Lehrer, 2005) indicates that large reductions in class size may be beneficial, if not necessarily cost-effective, Murnane and Levy (1996) suggest that estimated class-size effects may confound the impact of class size alone with the combined effect of class size reductions with changes in what happens in the classroom made possible by the class size reductions.
12. We are not advocating flat teacher salary schedules, as teacher salary steps and career ladders may be very important in attracting highly-qualified potential teachers into the teaching force. For instance, Figlio (2002) offers some evidence that this may be the case.
13. Hadbegian's (2003) finding that student-teacher ratios appeared to increase a small amount in states in which local school districts were subject to TELs even though total spending on public education was unaffected provides additional evidence of instructional resources being reduced in states with binding TELs even when these reductions appeared to be unnecessary.
14. This finding, again, is fully consistent with the stratification patterns predicted in a slightly different context by Epple and Romano (1998), in which relatively high-ability students would leave the public sector for the private sector as the public sector looks less attractive to them, thereby reducing the average socio-economic-status in both the public and private sectors.

REFERENCES

Aaronson, Daniel. (1999). The Effect of School Finance Reform on Population Heterogeneity. *National Tax Journal* 52, 5–30.

Anderson, Patricia, and Butcher, Kristin. (2006). Reading, Writing and Refreshments: Are School Finances Contributing to Children's Obesity? *Journal of Human Resources* 41, 467–494.

Angrist, Joshua, and Lavy, Victor. (1999) Using Maimonides' Rule to Estimate the Effect of Class Size on Student Achievement.*Quarterly Journal of Economics* 114, 533–575.

Archibald, R., and Feldman, D. (2006) State Higher Education Spending and the Tax Revolt. *Journal of Higher Education* 77, 618–644.

Betts, Julian. R., and Johnson, E. (1997). A Test for Diminishing Returns to School Spending. Unpublished manuscript, Department of Economics, University of California, San Diego.

Blankenau, William F., and Skidmore, Mark L. (2004). School Finance Litigation, Tax and Expenditure Limitations, and Education Spending. *Contemporary Education Policy* 22, 127–143.

Bradbury, Katherine L., Case, Karl E., and Mayer, Christopher J. (1998). School Quality and Massachusetts Enrollment Shifts in the Context of Tax Limitations. *New England Economic Review* July/August issue, 3–20.

Brennan, Geoffrey, and Buchanan, James. (1979). The Logic of Tax Limits: Alternative Constitutional Constraints on the Power to Tax. *National Tax Journal Supplement* 32, 11–22.

Brunner, Eric, and Imazeki, Jennifer. (2005). Fiscal Stress and Voluntary Contributions to Public Schools. In William C. Fowler, (Ed.), *Developments in School Finance: 2004*. Washington, DC: National Center for Education Statistics, 39–54.

Brunner, Eric, and Sonstelie, Jon. (2003). School Finance Reform and Voluntary Fiscal Federalism. *Journal of Public Economics* 87, 2157–2185.

Citrin, Jack. (1979). Do People Want Something for Nothing: Public Opinion on Taxes and Government Spending. *National Tax Journal Supplement* 32, 113–129.

Courant, Paul, Gramlich, Edward, and Rubinfeld, Daniel. (1983). Why Voters Support Tax Limitations: The Michigan Case. *National Tax Journal*, 38, 1–20.

Cutler, David M., Elmendorf, Douglas W., and Zeckhauser, Richard J. (1999). Restraining the Leviathan: Property Tax Limitations in Massachusetts. *Journal of Public Economics* 71, 313–334.

Dewey, James, Husted, Thomas, and Kenny, Lawrence. (1999). The Ineffectiveness of School Inputs: A Product of Misspecification? *Economics of Education Review* 19, 27–45.

Ding, Weili, and Lehrer, Steven. (2005) Class Size and Student Achievement: Experimental Estimates of Who Benefits and Who Loses from Reductions. Working paper, Queens University.

Downes, Thomas A. (1992). Evaluating the Impact of School Finance Reform on the Provision of Public Education: The California Case. *National Tax Journal* 45, 405–419.

Downes, Thomas A. (1996). An Examination of the Structure of Governance in California School Districts Before and After Proposition 13. *Public Choice* 86, 279–307.

Downes, Thomas A., Dye, Richard F. and McGuire, Therese J. (1998). Do Limits Matter? Evidence on the Effects of Tax Limitations on Student Performance. *Journal of Urban Economics* 43, 401–417.

Downes, Thomas A., and Figlio, David N. (1999a). What are the Effects of School Finance Reforms? Estimates of the Impact of Equalization on Students and on Affected Communities. Mimeograph. Tufts University.

Downes, Thomas A. and Figlio, David N. (1999b). Economic Inequality and the Provision of Schooling. Federal Reserve Bank of New York. *Economic Policy Review* 5, 99–110.

Downes, Thomas A. and Figlio, David N. (2000). School Finance Reforms, Tax Limits, and Student Performance: Do Reforms Level-Up or Dumb Down*? Mimeograph.* Tufts University.

Downes, Thomas A. and Schoeman, David. (1998). School Financing Reform and Private School Enrollment: Evidence from California. *Journal of Urban Economics* 43, 418–443.

Downes, Thomas A., and Steinman, Jason. (2006). Alternative Revenue Generation in Vermont Public Schools: Raising Funds Outside the Tax Base to Support Public Education. Mimeograph. Medford, MA: Tufts University.

Dye, Richard F., and McGuire, Therese J. (1997). The Effect of Property Tax Limitation Measures on Local Government Fiscal Behavior. *Journal of Public Economics* 66, 469–487.

Dye, Richard F., McGuire, Therese J., and McMillen, Daniel P. (2005). Are Property Tax Limitations More Binding over Time? *National Tax Journal* 58, 215–225.

Ehrenberg, Ronald and Brewer, Dominic. (1994). Do School and Teacher Characteristics Matter? Evidence from *High School and Beyond*. *Economics of Education Review* 13, 1–17.

Epple, Dennis, Figlio, David N., and Romano, Richard. (2004). Competition Between Private and Public Schools: Testing Stratification and Pricing Predictions. *Journal of Public Economics* 88, 1215–45.

Epple, Dennis, and Romano, Richard. (1998). Competition Between Private and Public Schools, Vouchers, and Peer-Group Effects. *American Economic Review* 88, 33–62.

Evans, William N., Murray, Sheila E., and Schwab, Robert M. (1999). Public School Spending and Private School Enrollment. Mimeograh. College Park, MD: University of Maryland, College Park.

Ferguson, R. F., and Ladd, H. F. (1996). How and Why Money Matters: An Analysis of Alabama Schools. In Helen F. Ladd (Ed.), *Holding Schools Accountable: Performance-Based Reform in Education.* (pp. 265–298). Washington, DC: The Brookings Institution.

Figlio, David N. (1997). Did the 'Tax Revolt' Reduce School Performance?. *Journal of Public Economics* 65, 245–269.

Figlio, David N. (1998). Short-Term Effects of a 1990s-Era Tax Limit: Panel Evidence on Oregon's Measure 5. *National Tax Journal* 51, 55–70.

Figlio, David N. (1999). Functional Form and the Estimated Effects of School Resources. *Economics of Education Review* 18, 241–52.

Figlio, David N. (2002). Can Public Schools Buy Better-Qualified Teachers? *Industrial and Labor Relations Review* 55, 686–99.

Figlio, David N., and O'Sullivan, Arthur. (2001). The Local Response to Tax Limitation Measures: Do Local Governments Manipulate Voters to Increase Revenues? *Journal of Law and Economics* 44, 233–257.

Figlio, David N., and Rueben, Kim. (2001).Tax Limitations and the Qualifications of New Teachers. *Journal of Public Economics* 80, 49–71.

Figlio, David N. and Stone, Joe A. (2001). Can Public Policy Affect Private School Cream-Skimming? *Journal of Urban Economics* 49, 240–66.

Fischel, William A. (1989). Did *Serrano* Cause Proposition 13? *National Tax Journal* 42, 465–473.

Fischel, William A. (1996). How *Serrano* Caused Proposition 13. *Journal of Law and Politics* 12, 607–645.

Goldhaber, Dan and Brewer, Dominic. (1997). Why Don't Schools and Teachers Seem to Matter? *Journal of Human Resources* 32, 505–523.

Greiner, J. M., and Peterson, G. E. (1986). Do Budget Reductions Stimulate Public Sector Efficiency? Evidence from Proposition 2½ in Massachusetts. In G. E. Peterson and C. W. Lewis (Eds.), *Reagan and the Cities*, 63–93. Washington, DC: Urban Institute Press.

Hanushek, Eric A. (1986). The Economics of Schooling: Production and Efficiency in the Public Schools. *Journal of Economic Literature* 24, 1141–1177.

Hanushek, Eric A.(1996). School Resources and Student Performance." In Gary Burtless, (Ed.), *Does Money Matter? The Effect of School Resources on Student Achievement and Adult Success.* Washington, DC: The Brookings Institution.

Hanushek, Eric A. (2003). The Failure of Input-Based Schooling Policies. *Economic Journal* 113, F64–F98.

Hoene, Christopher. (2004). Fiscal Structure and the Post-Proposition 13 Fiscal Regime in California's Cities. *Public Budgeting and Finance* 24, 51–72.

Husted, Thomas A., and Kenny, Lawrence W. (2002). The Legacy of Serrano: The Impact ofMandated Equal Spending on Private School Enrollment. *Southern Economic Journal* 68(3), 566–583.

Joint Budget Committee. (1979). *An Analysis of the Effects of Proposition 13 on Local Governments.* Sacramento: California Legislature.

Joyce, Philip G., and Mullins, Daniel R. (1991). The Changing Fiscal Structure of the State and Local Public Sector: The Impact of Tax and Expenditure Limitations. *Public Administration Review* 51, 240–253.

Krueger, Alan B. (1999). Experimental Estimates of Education Production Functions." *Quarterly Journal of Economics* 114, 497–532.

Ladd, Helen. (1998). How School Districts Respond to Fiscal Constraint. National Center for Education Statistics, *Selected Papers in School Finance, 1996.* Washington, DC.

Ladd, Helen, and Wilson, Julie Boatright. (1982). Why Voters Support Tax Limitations: Evidence from Massachusetts' Proposition 2 ½. *National Tax Journal* 35, 121–147.

Lankford, Hamilton, and Wyckoff, James. (2000). The Effect of School Choice and Residential Location on the Racial Segregation of Students. Albany: State University of New York-Albany. Mimeograph.

Ludwig, Jens, and Bassi, Laurie. (1999). The Puzzling Case of School Resources and Student Achievement." *Educational Evaluation and Policy Analysis* 21, 385–403.

McGuire, Therese J. (1999). Proposition 13 and Its Offspring: For Good or for Evil? *National Tax Journal* 52, 129–138.

McGuire, Therese, and Rueben, Kim. (2006). The Colorado Revenue Limit: The Economic Effects of TABOR. *State Tax Notes* 40 (6).

Millimet, Daniel L. and Rangaprasad, Vasudha. (2007). Strategic Competition Amongst Public Schools. *Regional Science and Urban Economics* 37, 199–219.

Mullins, Daniel R. (2004). Tax and Expenditure Limitations and the Fiscal Response of Local Government: Asymmetric Intra-Local Fiscal Effects. *Public Budgeting and Finance* 24, 111–147.

Mullins, Daniel R., and Joyce, Philip G. (1996). Tax and Expenditure Limitations and State and Local Fiscal Structure: An Empirical Assessment. *Public Budgeting and Finance* 16, 75–101.

Mullins, Daniel R. and Wallin, Bruce A. (2004).Tax and Expenditure Limitations: Introduction and Overview. *Public Budgeting and Finance* 24, 2–15.

Murnane, Richard J., and Levy, Frank. (1996). Evidence from Fifteen Schools in Austin, Texas. In Gary Burtless, (Ed.), *Does Money Matter? The Effect of School Resources on Student Achievement and Adult Success* (pp. 93–96). Washington, DC: The Brookings Institution.

Reschovsky, Andrew. (2004). The Impact of State Government Fiscal Crises on Local Governments and Schools.*State and Local Government Review* 36, 86–102.

Schwadron, Terry, editor. (1984). *California and the American Tax Revolt: Proposition 13 Five Years Later.* Berkeley: University of California Press.

Shadbegian, Ronald J. (1998). Do Tax and Expenditure Limitations Affect Budgets? Evidence from Panel Data. *Public Finance Review* 26, 218–236.

Shadbegian, Ronald J. (1999). The Effect of Tax and Expenditure Limitations on the Revenue Structure of Local Government. *National Tax Journal* 52, 221–247.

Shadbegian, Ronald J. (2003). Did the Property Tax Revolt Affect Local Public Education? Evidence from Panel Data. *Public Finance Review* 31, 91–121.

Shadbegian, Ronald J., and Jones, Ronald T. (2005). Did Proposition 2 1/2 Affect Local Public Education in Massachusetts? Evidence from Panel Data. *Global Business and Economics Review* 7, 363–380.

Sonstelie, Jon. (1979). Public School Quality and Private School Enrollments. *National Tax Journal Supplement* 32, 343–353.

Stein, Robert, Hamm, Keith, and Freeman, Patricia. (1983). An Analysis of Support for Tax Limitation Referenda. *Public Choice* 40, 187–194.

Stocker, Frederick D. (1991). Introduction. In Frederick D. Stocker, editor, *Proposition 13: A Ten-Year Retrospective*. Cambridge, MA: Lincoln Institute of Land Policy.

Tiebout, Charles M. (1956). A Pure Theory of Local Public Expenditures. *Journal of Political Economy* 64, 416–424.

Wassmer, Robert W. (2006). The 'Roller Coaster' of California State Budgeting after Proposition 13. Atlanta: Fiscal Research Center, Andrew Young School of Policy Studies, Georgia State University. FRC Report Number 131, July.

Wassmer, Robert W., and Anders, Charles. (1999). County Fiscal Stress: Cause and Consequence in California after Proposition 13. Sacramento, CA: Graduate Program in Public Policy and Administration, California State University, Sacramento, January. Mimeograph.

V

EDUCATIONAL MARKETS AND DECENTRALIZATION

Section Editor

Henry M. Levin

22

Issues in Educational Privatization

Henry M. Levin

INTRODUCTION

Throughout most of the world, private schooling preceded public schools. Private schools were largely religious in their founding and operations and emphasized values and character as much as literacy and secular knowledge. It was not until the middle or latter part of the nineteenth century that industrializing countries established broad-based government sponsorship and operation of public schools—eventually dwarfing the importance of the private sector in the education of the overall population. In the United States, private or independent schools account for only about one-ninth of enrollments today and more than 80 percent of their enrollments are in religiously-affiliated institutions.

Towards the end of the twentieth century, however, a movement that is broadly referred to as educational privatization arose in the United States and in other industrialized or industrializing societies (Levin, 2001). This phenomenon has coincided with a broader and more general, even global, shift of political and economic institutions towards greater reliance on markets in the last two decades. Thus, educational privatization represents just one component of a much larger trend away from government provision of services.

In education, the privatization movement has taken a variety of institutional forms that are discussed in subsequent chapters in this volume. For example, a movement has developed in the nation to establish charter schools that are publicly authorized and financed, but governed by their own private boards. A significant portion of charter schools are managed by private educational management organizations (EMOs) comprised mainly of for-profit firms. Public school systems have also joined in contracts with EMOs to operate particular district schools independently of conventional district governance and management.

Another form of privatization is embodied in educational vouchers, whereby public funds are provided to families in the form of a certificate or voucher that can be applied towards the costs of private school. Milwaukee and Cleveland have adopted voucher programs for low-income students. Florida made vouchers available for students in failing schools before the state's Supreme Court rejected the plan because it violated the separation of Church and State established in the state's constitution. The U.S. Congress established and funded a limited voucher plan for lower-income students in Washington, D.C., and in 2007 Utah passed a state-wide voucher plan with a $3,000 voucher for children from low income families and a $500 voucher for families with higher incomes. In some states, taxpayers have been granted tax credits, or deductions from taxable income covering some portion of their tuition payments to private schools (Huerta &

d'Entremont, 2007). The purest form of privatization has been the practice of home schooling where parents reject formal schooling and undertake responsibility for the education of their own children, a trend that has been increasing (Belfield, this volume; Cooper, 2005).

Educational privatization is controversial and politically contentious, largely because it reaches into deep ideological and societal divisions in our society (Belfield & Levin, 2005a). The traditional rationale for government funding and provision of schooling is premised on the need to provide a common and equitable educational experience that will prepare all students for their economic, political, and social roles in a democracy. In contrast, privatization focuses on market provision of education, allowing families to choose the type of school that best meets the needs of their own children. In this respect privatization is mainly devoted to meeting the private goals of families rather than the broad public goals for social and democratic participation in society. As I discuss below, conflicts arise between addressing the private goals of education through choice and the public ones through a common educational experience.

This chapter provides a framework for understanding this conflict between public and private goals and for evaluating different forms of educational privatization. Since this section of the Handbook offers detailed chapters on educational vouchers (Bettinger & Zimmer), charter schools (Bifulco & Buckley), educational management organizations (Miron), home schooling (Belfield), and decentralized approaches to education (Plank & Smith), the reader is referred to these chapters for details on specific approaches to privatization. Instead, I explore here the commonalities among these phenomena and develop a framework that encourages comparison and analysis of their provisions and consequences. The main themes are that privatization can take many forms and that even within a specific form of privatization, differences in design features can induce vastly different consequences. Finally, the general term "educational privatization" carries little meaning without detailed information on the forms it takes.

DEFINING EDUCATIONAL PRIVATIZATION

Defining the term *educational privatization* is less straightforward than it might appear because almost all forms of education have both public and private components. The term *private* refers to the provision of schooling for and by individuals, groups, institutions, or entities that is primarily devoted to meeting the private goals of both the school clientele and the institutional sponsors. In contrast, the term *public* characterizes entities and purposes that are dedicated to a broader societal impact beyond that conferred upon the direct participants and is usually (but not always) associated with a government role. Given these working definitions of public and private, it is clear that there is considerable overlap between them in their application to the educational arena.

Dimensions of Privatization

Public and private aspects of education can be viewed through at least five key lenses: sponsorship, governance, funding, production, and outcomes.

Educational *sponsorship* defines who establishes schools and who is ultimately responsible for the schooling that is provided. This is the most common concept used in distinguishing public from private schools. Clearly private schools are sponsored by private entities, but so is home schooling. Public schools, in contrast, are sponsored by government. Charter schools cannot be so easily categorized because they are initiated by private groups, but subject to official approval and funding by governments.

Governance encompasses the overall authority and responsibility for school operations. In the United States, even private schools and home schooling, although privately sponsored, are jointly governed by both public and private entities. Under the decision of the U.S. Supreme Court in *Pierce v. Society of Sisters* (1925), state governments are responsible for the regulation, inspection, supervision, and examination of all schools, their teachers, and pupils. Home schooling and private schools, though privately sponsored, are regulated (often lightly) by state governments. Charter schools, though sponsored by privately constituted governance boards and given considerable autonomy from many public laws and regulations, are still subject to the overall authority of their states. Public schools are governed by public authorities under state constitutions and legislatures and state authorized agencies. The management of schools can be delineated from governance in the sense that even some public and charter schools, though subject to public governance, employ private, Educational Management Organizations (EMOs) (Miron, this volume) to manage their organizations.

Sources of *funding* for all types of schools can be public or private. Although, in theory, the funding streams for the two forms of schooling types are distinct, in practice they frequently commingle. Home schooling and private schools are funded mainly through the private resources of families. Nonetheless, they may also receive considerable public support. Home schoolers can receive public funding when attending public schools part-time or enrolling in virtual charter schools where instruction is provided through the internet (Huerta, Gonzalez, & d'Entremont, 2006). As non-profit entities, almost all private schools receive public services without paying taxes, and many receive federal funding for the instruction of handicapped, low-income, and bilingual students. States such as Ohio also provide transportation and textbooks to private schools for core academic subjects. When states adopt voucher or tuition tax credit programs, private schools are able to benefit from public funds or tax reductions. Charter schools receive both public funds and extensive private philanthropy. Although the predominant share of public school funding is from government sources, private funds are also sought through both philanthropy and parental charges for specified services

With respect to the *production* of education, schools rely on inputs of students, teachers, administrators, facilities, supplies, and other resources. These resources are provided by both public and private suppliers. The most important input to the educational process, however, is the socioeconomic status of the student's family. Because the family is the most "privatized" entity in society, the co-production of education between schools and families must depend upon a major private component, regardless of the sponsorship, governance, or funding of the school organization. Not only are the educational attainments of individual children conditioned heavily by their private circumstances, but the productivity and character of the school as a whole is also influenced by the socioeconomic composition of its students. Thus, the private character of the student body influences the public character of the educational process (Zimmer & Toma, 2000).

Schools also enlist other resources from the private sector to produce education. Public schools purchase textbooks, equipment, maintenance, food services, staff development, and consulting services from private vendors. Even more encompassing is the private role played by EMOs (Miron, in this volume), organizations that have been contracted to operate both traditional public schools and charter schools. Such organizations, usually for-profit, not only manage entire schools, but they also provide publicly-funded, supplementary services such as tutoring, after-school, and summer-school services.

It is also possible to categorize the *outcomes* of education into both private and public benefits. Private outcomes benefit primarily the individuals being educated and their immediate families, whereas public ones benefit the larger society. Clearly, what students learn in schools confers private benefits in terms of skills, knowledge, values, behaviors, and understanding. These, in turn, enhance their capabilities in the workplace and other settings, increase access to further educational opportunities, and translate into better jobs, earnings, health, and personal satisfaction.

Beyond these private benefits, children's experiences at school can also provide benefits for the larger society—the main justification for public funding. Under ideal conditions, schools provide students with a common set of values and knowledge to contribute to their functioning in a democratic society. Schools can also contribute to equality of social, economic, and political opportunities among persons of different racial and social class origins—thus making for a fairer society. Schooling is expected to contribute to economic growth and high employment as well as cultural and scientific progress and the defense of the nation.

The debate over the various forms of privatization is driven largely by controversy over how much each type of school contributes to public or private outcomes. Presumably, home schools and private schools—with their dedication to the individual quests of families—are weighted more heavily in the direction of the private benefits. Charter schools in many states and traditional public schools are usually required to ensure greater public outcomes by virtue of their conformance with standardized state curriculum and testing requirements.

Advocates of vouchers and tuition tax credits argue that all types of schools—whether they be public or private—deliver both public and private benefits and they point to public schools in wealthy neighborhoods attending to the private goals of their families as much as private schools with similar families. Opponents of vouchers and tax credits, however, suggest that a singular stress on market competition by schools on the basis of their narrow appeals to individual families tends to preclude broader consideration of the public benefits of education. They argue that yielding primacy to the self-serving instincts that drive school choice undermines the democratic functions of schooling that are necessary to build a socially cohesive and more equitable society. But, advocates of privatization reply that the political conflicts over the roles and operations of existing public schools blunt their efficiency in meeting the specific and diverse educational needs of their constituents. They conclude that market choice over privatized alternatives would serve children and families more effectively (Chubb and Moe, 1990). These underlying contentions about the virtues of government versus markets drive much of the controversy over recent initiatives for expansion of public funding for private schools and other forms of privatization (Belfield & Levin, 2005a).

ISSUES IN EDUCATIONAL PRIVATIZATION

Central to an understanding of educational privatization is the recognition that much of the controversy surrounding privatization is rooted in different values and objectives of the protagonists on both sides of the debate. A scrutiny of the literature and the debates suggest that four criteria for evaluating particular forms of educational organization are central to the debate over privatization: freedom of choice, productive efficiency, equity, and social cohesion (Levin, 2002).

Freedom of Choice

In a democratic society dominated by free markets, most families value the freedom to choose the experiences that affect their wellbeing. Indeed, this freedom is viewed as a basic right with respect to childrearing: the liberty to provide children with the education that is consistent with parental values and educational goals. Those who push for greater privatization of sponsorship, governance, and public funding for private schools tend to place great weight on freedom of choice whereby parents select schools for their children and bear the consequences of those decisions.

Productive Efficiency

Education is a costly undertaking, so there is deep concern about how to use resources most efficiently. In general, there is widespread agreement that policy makers should seek forms of educational organization that yield the largest educational result for any given resource investment. Proponents of educational privatization assume that market competition for students among schools will create strong incentives, not only to meet student needs, but also to improve productivity. Opponents are skeptical of this claim because they believe that privatized approaches to education will create competition only for the "best" students. Students with greater needs will have fewer choices and will be isolated in segregated school environments with other students like themselves. Further, they believe that a preponderance of resources will be used to produce private outcomes at the expense of publicly-valued ones.

Equity

A common public goal of education is the quest for fairness in access to educational opportunities, resources, and outcomes by gender, social class, race, language origins, disability, and the geographical location of students. Advocates of greater privatization argue that the ability to choose schools will open up possibilities for students who are locked into inferior neighborhood schools and that the competitive marketplace will provide greater incentives to meet student needs than existing public schools. Opponents argue that a move towards greater privatization, such as vouchers, will generate greater inequities because parents with education and income are better informed and have greater resources for making use of choice, such as access to transportation. They also believe that the choices themselves will further segregate and disenfranchise the poor because those with power and status will select schools with student demographics like their own, and schools will also select students by such criteria.

Social Cohesion

The main argument for public funding and operation of schools has been its fostering of a relatively, common, educational experience that will orient all students to grow to adulthood as full participants in the social, political, and economic institutions of a given society. Government funding and sponsorship of schools enables the implementation of a curriculum and pedagogy devoted to a common knowledge-base, social values, goals, language, and political and economic institutions for promoting social cohesion of both youth and adults. Opponents of greater privatization believe that, educational privatization will undermine social cohesion by giving schools the incentives to differentiate their approaches to enhance their narrow market appeal at the expense of their social mission (Wolfe, 2003).

The One Best System

The basic policy problem in designing an educational approach comprising these four goals is that they may not be fully compatible with each other. Although it may be possible to establish a plan employing both public and private components, any particular plan will not be able to maximize results on some of the criteria without sacrificing performance on others. In this sense the "one best system" is that which conforms most closely to the preferences of individuals or social groupings regarding the four dimensions of choice, efficiency, equity, and social cohesion. Unfortunately, different groups in different settings will make widely varying judgments regarding the relative importance of each dimension and how each would fare under different forms of public/private organization (Belfield & Levin, 2005a). This complexity can be illustrated by considering the specific designs proposed for publicly-funded, educational vouchers. Three prominent design tools are: (1) finance, (2) regulation, and (3) support services.

Finance. Finance refers to the monetary value of the educational voucher, how it is allocated and whether families are able to supplement the voucher to send their children to a more costly school. A larger voucher will allow more options in the marketplace with greater freedom of choice, possibly increasing productive efficiency as well as greater competition for students. But, if families can add-on to vouchers from their private resources as Milton Friedman (1962) proposed, there will be advantages for families with higher incomes and a potential decrease in equity.

Alternatively, the educational voucher can be differentiated by educational need by providing larger vouchers for those with handicaps and from poverty backgrounds to address equity. Schools will have greater incentives to attract educational needy students and provide the resources and programs to address their needs. Clearly, the financial arrangements can have profoundly different consequences for equity.

Regulation. Regulation encompasses the requirements set out by government for eligibility of schools to participate in the voucher system as well as guidelines for participation of families. Only schools that meet certain requirements will be eligible to redeem vouchers, and these requirements are designed to achieve certain policy goals. A particular source of contention is the eligibility for public funding of schools sponsored by religious entities. Although the U.S. Supreme Court approved the participation of religious schools in the case of the Cleveland voucher plan, many of the states have much stronger proscriptions against public funding for religious institutions than the U.S. Constitution (*Zelman vs. Simmons-Harris*, 2002).

Some voucher plans have emphasized a common curriculum and uniform testing as a condition of school participation. The purpose is to ensure that students are exposed to experiences that support social cohesion and that schools can be compared for their productive efficiency along common measures of student achievement. Some voucher analysts advocate that when schools have more applicants than places, applicants should be selected by lottery to provide fair access. Those who are more preoccupied with freedom to choose tend to favor government policies by which schools make all admissions decisions encompassing the premise that freedom of choice must also apply to schools in selecting the types of clientele that they prefer. Eligibility for vouchers may be restricted to certain populations in the name of equity. For example, public and private voucher programs in Milwaukee and Cleveland are limited to children from poorer families in order to give them choices outside of their neighborhoods. The Florida legislation limited vouchers to children in failing public schools. In each of these cases the regulatory aspects of design tend to favor some social goals over others.

Support Services. Support services can be used to enhance the effectiveness of the market in providing freedom of choice, productive efficiency, and equity. Competitive markets operate on the assumption that consumers will have access to a wide variety of choices as well as to useful information for selecting among them. In the United States, the availability of public transportation is very limited, necessitating a system of school transportation from children's neighborhoods to schools of choice. In the absence of school transportation, school choices and competition for students will be limited, reducing both the competitive efficiency of schools and creating inequities for those who cannot afford private transportation.

In order to make informed choices about the schools that they select for their children, families need good information. Accurate information on school programs and effectiveness as well as other important aspects of school philosophy and practice would need to be collected and disseminated to parents in appropriate forms to assist them in making decisions (Schneider et al., 2000). Schools have incentives to provide their own information through promotional materials and informational sessions for parents. However, there is little assurance that such information will be accurate and balanced, and it may be especially difficult for less-educated parents to process. Technical assistance might also be provided by government agencies through information and training to assist new schools and to advance the productivity of the entire sector. But comprehensive systems of information and effective systems of school transportation, though essential for extensive and informed choice, are very costly. In this respect, they will compete for resources that would otherwise be available to schools for instruction.

Tradeoffs in the Design of Different Voucher Plans

The different provisions that are set out in an educational policy such as a voucher plan reflect the diverse values and purposes for pursuing privatization. More specifically, the application of the three policy tools of finance, regulation, and support services in designing a privatization plan will determine its impact on choice, efficiency, equity, and social cohesion. In essence, each plan uses the design tools to construct a plan that either implicitly or explicitly places greater weight on some goals rather than others.

Designs for Freedom of Choice

A voucher plan that seeks to maximize choice would incorporate a wide range of school types; would provide either a large voucher to all students or a smaller basic voucher with provision for supplements from family resources; would minimize the regulation of curriculum, admissions, and other dimensions of school operations; and would provide comparative information on schools and an adequate system of transportation. Such a design would ensure that parents would have a large number of alternatives from which to choose. Much of this plan is attractive to persons who prefer to see the least government interference in the marketplace, especially if the voucher is modest and parents are able to add to it. But, Libertarians may view the support services of information and transportation as unwarranted because of high cost and government intrusion, and they would favor private tuition supplementation by families rather than a large basic voucher from public funding.

Designs for Efficiency

Productive efficiency is maximized when schools produce a given level and type of education for the least cost. This concept is somewhat difficult to assess, in part because under a system of freedom of choice, schools may be producing very different types of education, which makes it hard to compare outcomes across schools. The matching of educational offerings to the preferences of families in a competitive environment is viewed by market advocates as an efficient use of resources, even in the absence of comparative efficiency measures that demonstrate that conclusion. Accordingly, designs that focus on efficiency would ensure that the voucher is large enough (when combined with parental add-ons) to attract many competitors into the marketplace. Regulations would be minimal because they would tend to inhibit competition. Some would argue that academic achievement is so central to the productivity of all schools that testing of students should be required and reported as a check on academic efficiency. Although support services such as information and transportation might increase competitive pressures on schools, the cost of those services would have to be taken into account relative to the effectiveness gains.

Designs for Equity

Equity in education refers to equality in access, resources, and educational outcomes for groups that have traditionally faced differences on these dimensions.[1] From a finance perspective, an equitable design would seek compensatory vouchers where more funding was available for students with greater educational need such as those in educationally at-risk and handicapped categories. To assure that income differences would be neutralized, families would not be permitted to add on to the voucher.

The most fundamental regulation determining equity relates to who is eligible to receive and use a voucher. Thus far, the publicly-funded voucher plans in the United States have been limited to students from lower income families or those enrolled in failing schools. The exception is Utah where all students are eligible for vouchers with larger vouchers for students from poor families than for those from more affluent families. Equity-oriented regulations would also embrace non-discrimination in admissions, with schools being required to choose some portion of their students by lottery in the event that there are more applicants than openings. Provisions encouraging or requiring that schools not limit themselves to a narrow social or ethnic population would also be needed in light of the evidence that peers have an important impact on educational outcomes (Zimmer & Toma, 2000). With respect to support services, transportation would be required to provide access to those who are less advantaged and information would be needed for promoting informed parental choices among schools.

Designs for Social Cohesion

To promote social cohesion, the voucher would have to be large enough to provide a common educational experience for all students. It would have to be structured so that all students could gain access to schools where they would be exposed to peers from a variety of backgrounds. Such diversity in student composition means that parental add-ons to the voucher would probably be proscribed because they would tend to place students from different income strata into different schools. Regulations would focus on establishing common elements in curriculum and certain school activities including the possibility of all students engaging in community service. Support services might focus on the provision of technical assistance in helping schools develop a common educational core as well as the information and transportation to enable families to find and gain access to schools with heterogeneous student bodies.

Incompatibilities and Tradeoffs

As this example should make clear, no single system provides maximal results for all four objectives. Ultimately, the choice of design features will depend upon specific preferences and values as transmitted through democratic institutions. Those who place a high value on freedom of choice will probably be willing to sacrifice some equity and social cohesion provisions by eschewing regulations and support services and allowing parental add-ons to vouchers. Conversely, those who place a high value on social cohesion will be willing to sacrifice some freedom of choice through establishing a common curriculum core and other standardized features of schools. Ultimately, much of the debate over the specifics of educational voucher plans revolves around the political power and preferences of the stakeholders.

This conclusion becomes obvious if one reviews the two most prominent early voucher plans. The seminal plan of Friedman (1962) focuses on freedom of choice and productive efficiency through heightened competition, arguably at the expense of equity and social cohesion. Friedman would provide a modest, flat voucher at public expense. Parents could add to the voucher out of private resources, and schools could set their own tuition. Regulation would be minimal, and there would be no provision for transportation and information. This approach would promote a very large number of alternatives at different levels of tuition, *for those who could afford them*, with few restrictions on schools that enter the marketplace, which would promote a large supply of alternatives. Clearly, social cohesion and equity goals would not be paramount.

Conversely, plans that emphasize social cohesion and equity tend to reduce freedom of choice through extensive regulation and may inhibit productive efficiency by establishing costly support services. For example, the Jencks plan (Center for the Study of Public Policy, 1970) would regulate admissions and curriculum and would require standardized testing and reporting of results (see also the proposal by Godwin and Kemerer, 2002). It would also provide larger (compensatory) vouchers for the poor and a system of transportation and information. Moreover, vouchers could not be augmented from private resources. Relative to the Friedman plan, a fixed-government voucher with no private augmentation would reduce freedom of choice. The high costs of providing information and transportation and monitoring the regulations for eligible schools would add considerably to the costs of the voucher system (Levin and Driver, 1997).

Although certain design provisions would improve outcomes for one or more goals, they typically would also reduce outcomes for other objectives. For example, provision of information and transportation would promote equity by improving choice options for those with the least access to information and transportation. But such provision would also raise considerably the non-instructional costs of the educational system, thereby reducing academic efficiency unless the academic gains from competition due to better information and access offset the high costs of transportation and information. Empirical studies of school competition suggest that this outcome is unlikely (Belfield and Levin, 2005b, Chap. 6). Likewise, the establishment of regulations with continuous monitoring and enforcement could be used to increase equity and social cohesion, but at the sacrifice of freedom of choice and productive efficiency.

Advocates of vouchers may agree on the general case for vouchers or increased educational privatization, but may disagree profoundly on specifics. Strong differences arise even among persons with the same general political persuasion. Thus, many liberals want to see greater freedom of choice for students in the inner-city through educational vouchers, even though liberals are usually viewed as antagonistic to market-based approaches for the delivery of government services. At the same time, cultural conservatives are deeply committed to a common curriculum and knowledge framework that should be required of all students and the schools where they are enrolled; which represents a substantial commitment to regulation (Hirsch, 1987). Political conservatives with libertarian views reject regulatory requirements entirely in favor of complete market accountability; that is letting consumers decide what they want. The classic Friedman (1962) proposal is very close to this stance in its almost complete omission of regulation, despite his willingness to provide public funding for vouchers on the basis of the contribution of schools to a "stable and democratic society."

SUMMARY

The term *educational privatization* can thus mean different things depending on how it is applied and which dimensions of education are privatized. There are many different institutional forms of privatization, and even profoundly different versions of the same form, with potentially different educational consequences. The specific provisions for finance, regulation, and support services can create very different educational outcomes. Moreover, in many cases the improvement of one outcome through the use of these provisions will be accomplished at the expense of other outcomes. For all of these reasons it is best to address issues about educational privatization by grounding them in the details of specific provisions such as those on finance, regulation, and support services. As a corollary, broad generalizations about the impacts of educational privatization should be viewed with skepticism unless buttressed by supportive details and evidence.

Finally, it appears that claims of particular educational results for privatization are colored more heavily by ideological leanings than by supportive evidence. As the chapters in this section and other summaries of research on privatization demonstrate, the evidence on the consequences of the different forms of privatization is often mixed and contradictory (e.g., Gill, Timpane, Ross, & Brewer, 2001; Belfield & Levin, 2005a). In this respect the ideological claims seem to have trumped the validity of the empirical evidence in the debate over educational privatization.

NOTE

1. It is important to note that the present quest in school finance for addressing "adequacy of funding" is an equity concept. Adequacy does not mean that the level of funding must be the same for each child, since it generally assumes that the funding for each child will reflect differences in educational needs.

REFERENCES

Belfield, Clive R. & Levin, Henry M. (2005a) Vouchers and Public Policy: When Ideology Trumps Evidence, with Clive Belfield. *American Journal of Education*, 11, 548–567.

Belfield, Clive R. & Levin, Henry M. (2005b). *Privatizing Educational Choice: Consequences for Parents, Schools, and Public Policy*. Boulder, CO: Paradigm Publishers.

Center for the Study of Public Policy. (1970). *Education Vouchers, a Report on Financing Elementary Education by Grants to Parents*. Cambridge, MA.

Chubb, John & Moe, Terry. (1990). *Politics, Markets, and America's Schools*. Washington, D.C.: The Brookings Institution.

Cooper, Bruce S., ed. (2005) *Homeschooling in Full View: A Reader*. Greenwich, CT: Information Age.

Friedman, Milton. (1962). The role of government in education. In M. Friedman, *Capitalism and Freedom*. Chicago: Chicago University Press.

Gill, Brian, P. Timpane, Michael, Ross, Karen E., & Brewer, Dominic J. (2001). *Rhetoric vs. Reality: What We Know and What We Need to Know About Vouchers and Charter Schools*. Santa Monica, CA: The Rand Corporation.

Godwin, Kenneth & Kemerer, Frank. (2002). *School Choice Trade-offs*. Austin: University of Texas Press.

Hirsch, Ed. Jr. (1987). *Cultural Literacy: What Every American Needs to Know*. New York: Houghton-Mifflin.

Huerta, Luis A. & d'Entremont, Chad. (2007). Education Tax Credits in a Post-*Zelman* Era. *Educational Policy*, 21(1), 73–109.

Huerta, Luis A., Gonzalez, Maria-Fernanda, & d'Entrement, Chad (2006). Cyber and Home School Charter Schools : Adopting Policy to New Forms of Public Schooling. *Peabody Journal of Education*, 81(1), 103–139.

Levin, Henry M. (2002) A Comprehensive Framework for Evaluating Educational Vouchers. *Educational Evaluation and Policy Analysis,* 24, 159–174.

Levin, Henry M. (2001). *Privatizing Education*. Boulder, CO: Westview.

Levin, Henry M. & Driver, Cyrus. (1997) Costs of an Educational Voucher System. *Educational Economics*, 5, 303–311.

Schneider, Mark, Teske, Paul, & Marschall, Melissa. (2000). *Choosing Schools: Consumer Choice and the Quality of American Schools.* Princeton, NJ: Princeton University Press.

Wolfe, A. (2003). *School Choice. The Moral Debate.* Princeton, NJ: Princeton University Press.

Zelman v. Simmons-Harris (00-1751) 536 U.S. 639 (2002) 234 F.3d 945, reversed.

Zimmer, R. & Toma E. (2000). Peer Effects in Private and Public Schools Across Countries. *Journal of Policy Analysis and Management*, 19, 75–92.

23

Autonomous Schools: Theory, Evidence and Policy

David N. Plank and BetsAnn Smith

INTRODUCTION

For much of the 20th century, government efforts to build comprehensive public school systems relied on the instruments of central control and standardized practice. In centralized polities such as France and the Soviet Union, national ministries worked to extend public school systems to all corners of the nation, and to manage those systems under direct central authority (Archer, 1979). In developing countries, international agencies including UNESCO and the World Bank sought to extend State capacity and authority to deliver educational opportunities to all children (Bruns, 2003). Even in less centralized nations, including the United States, schools established and administered by local communities were steadily consolidated into professionally managed bureaucracies, often characterized as "the one best system" (Tyack, 1974; Katz, 1975). Through these developments, education systems around the world enrolled ever-growing numbers of children for an increasing number of years, and provided them with an expanded array of services (Meyer & Hannan, 1979). Schools were expected to serve as the standardized, regulated constituents of a system seeking to ensure equality by delivering prescribed educational services under similar conditions to all.

As public school systems have grown larger and more costly, an array of critics has expressed skepticism about the capacity of the State to build and administer efficient and effective education systems (e.g., Friedman, 1955; Carnoy & Levin, 1985). They have protested government efforts to use schools to advance contested goals such as integration and multiculturalism for fear that these efforts undermine academic rigor and the cultivation of a shared national identity (Brighelli, 2005; Schlesinger, 1998). They have also targeted size, standardization, and bureaucratic control as obstacles to efficiency, accountability, and responsiveness (Chubb & Moe, 1990; Meier, 1995; see also Levin, 2002a). As one consequence, many recent reform proposals have shifted from aspirations to perfect the "one best system" toward policies that seek to encourage administrative decentralization, local engagement, and school autonomy by making schools the unit for management, finance, and accountability in the education system (Hill, Pierce, & Guthrie 1997; Fiske, 1996).

In this chapter we review the main theoretical arguments supporting the move to decentralize responsibility to the school level. We assess the empirical evidence on how decentralization affects key outcomes including student learning, giving particular attention to the problems of low-performing schools. We conclude with a number of questions about the prospects for autonomous schools.

THEORY AND POLICY

The policy turn toward treating individual schools as the key unit for management, finance, and accountability is rooted in two very different theoretical traditions. One draws on public choice economics and principal-agent theories to advance policies that seek to align the interests of local educators with those of their students, and to shift the burden of failure from students onto the shoulders of those responsible for educating them (Hanushek & Raymond, 2002; see also Thernstrom & Thernstrom, 2003). The other tradition calls on communitarian and social capital theories, and on the idea that local affinities and loyalties among and between educators and parents are critically important assets for schools (Coleman & Hoffer, 1987; Bryk, Lee, & Holland 1993; Furman, 2002; Katz, Noddings, & Strike, 1999). Both lines of theory derive empirical support from nearly four decades of research on effective and improving schools (Edmunds, 1979; Cohen, 1985; Elmore, 2004; Hopkins, 2001; OECD, 1999; Jansen, 1995).

Some advocates of shifting authority and accountability to the school argue that the institutions of bureaucratic governance, including teachers unions, represent obstacles to improved performance in the educational system (e.g., Moe, 2001). They argue that educators—like other public officials—are more concerned with their own interests in job security, higher incomes, and enhanced prestige than they are with the achievement of the students under their care. Accordingly, they call for shifts in power and responsibility that locate responsibility for performance in the schools and classrooms where students are educated (Hanushek & Raymond, 2002).

Other advocates of shifting authority and accountability to schools begin from very different premises, arguing for the development of schools as communities (Bryk & Driscoll, 1999; Coleman, 1985; Furman, 2002; Noddings, 1996; Sergiovanni, 1994). Underscoring the records of religious, independent and small rural schools (Ashton-Warner, 1963; Lightfoot, 1983; Neill, 1995; Bryk, Lee, & Holland 1993; Hill, Foster, & Gendler, 1990), they assert that smaller, flatter school organizations will orient parents, teachers, and students towards the achievement of common purposes, thus enhancing school effectiveness. These authors portray community as a critical source of social capital, which can enhance the educational successes of children generally, and of poor and marginalized children in particular.

Proponents of shifting authority and responsibility to individual schools have lately brought public choice and communitarian theories together, arguing that autonomous schools are squarely in the public interest not simply because they call upon the strengths of local communities but also because they are more efficient, requiring less governmental inducement, compensation, supervision, and monitoring (Brandl, 1998; Chubb & Moe, 1990; Hill, Pierce, & Guthrie, 1997; Murray, 1988).

Policy Implications

Policies that make schools the key unit for management, finance, and accountability may serve either of two quite different policy goals (Plank, 2006). On the one hand, they may feature in a larger set of policy initiatives aimed at reinventing the State by decentralizing authority to local and private-sector actors (e.g., Osborne & Gaebler, 1992; World Bank, 1997). On the other, policies that shift responsibility to the school may free schools from the burdens of central regulation in order to encourage specialization, innovation, and diversification (Nathan, 1996; Mintrom,

2000; DFES, 2001). The grounds for differentiation are often religious or cultural but sometimes pedagogical as well. In some instances distinctive school missions can depart from or even oppose educational objectives approved by the State.

EFFICIENCY AND ACCOUNTABILITY

Enhancing Efficiency

A familiar set of strategies for increased efficiency in education systems relies on administrative and instructional changes developed and implemented by central authorities. These include the adoption of administrative practices based on business principles (Callahan, 1962; Peters & Waterman, 1982); the development of teacher-proof curricula (Darling-Hammond, 1996); the intensification of teachers' work through double-shifting, multi-grade instruction, year-round schedules and larger class sizes (World Bank, 1995); and the use of new technologies including film, radio, television, and now computers (Cuban, 2001). In contrast, recent strategies that encourage school-site management (SSM) typically give councils comprising principals, teachers and parents (and sometimes students) the power to make decisions about budgeting, curriculum and improvement according to local needs and circumstances.

Advocates of SSM claim that centralized systems waste scarce resources on administrative sinecures and activities far removed from classrooms. They argue for policies that push money and responsibility down the system on the grounds that local actors know best how to deploy scarce resources to advance student learning (Thomas B. Fordham Institute, 2006) and that central efforts to micro-manage local decisions are bound to fail (Cohen, 1990; Kennedy, 2005; McLaughlin, 1991). They also point out that decentralizing administrative and financial responsibility may enable educators to mobilize resources (both financial and otherwise) unavailable to central authorities. At the limit, as in some African and Latin American countries, the State may not be able to provide schools at all, and communities step forward to build their own schools and hire their own teachers (DeStefano et al., 2006).

Strengthening Accountability

Advocates of decentralization further argue that holding educators accountable requires that power and resources be located as close as possible to the schools and classrooms where instruction takes place. Under traditional arrangements resources are controlled by central administration, while educational services are delivered in schools. Under these circumstances, local educators cannot readily be held accountable for students' performance because they have little control over the conditions of their work (Bryk, Sebring, Kerbow, Rollow, & Easton, 1998; Meuret, 2007; Kogan, 2002; Wise, 1989). By the same token, however, it is difficult to hold bureaucrats responsible because the principal and teacher decisions that govern student learning are made outside their direct supervision and control.

To strengthen accountability, governments have adopted two sets of policy innovations aimed at aligning educators' incentives with the objectives of the State. First, they have asserted greater central control over learning objectives in national education systems (Finn, Petrilli, & Julian, 2006; Schmidt et al., 2001). Mechanisms include explicit goals for student and school performance, regular assessments of student learning and mandatory interventions in schools that fail to meet legislated targets. Second, they have introduced policies that shift accountability for student performance to individual schools and imposed consequences upon local educators for the performance of their students (Macpherson, 1998). Under the No Child Left Behind Act (NCLB) in the United States, for example, schools that fail to meet established performance expectations may face sanctions ranging from public stigmatization to reconstitution and closure. School choice policies similarly raise the stakes for educators, allowing parents to identify unsuccessful schools by voting with their feet (Plank & Sykes, 2003).

Fiske and Ladd (2000) characterize this new pattern of school governance as a "tight-loose-tight" accountability system, in which the State asserts strict control over goals and the specification of acceptable outcomes, while allowing schools to adopt their own preferred strategies for achieving those goals. Increasing the autonomy and responsibility of actors at the school level is valued mainly as a policy instrument deployed in the service of goals that are defined under increasingly tight central control.

Innovation and Specialization

Advocates of SSM also express the hope that schools freed from government regulation will find new and better ways to improve the performance of their students (e.g., Meier, 1995; Nathan, 1996). As early as 1986 in the United States, for example, the National Governors' Association proposed reforms based on "some old-fashioned horse trading" to educators: "We'll regulate less, if schools and school districts will produce better results." The Governors expected the removal of regulations to "change dramatically the way most American schools work" (Vinovskis, 1999). Their view was premised on the assumption that one-size-fits-all federal and state policies were preventing schools from discovering and implementing more innovative and successful educational programs.

Subsequent federal and state legislation has allowed schools and school districts to seek waivers to regulations in return for assurances that student performance will improve.[1] Other countries including the U.K. and France have also adopted waiver policies (Meuret, 2007; DFES, 2001). Similar assumptions inspired enthusiasm for charter schools, which were expected to pioneer new and better ways of organizing schools and teaching students (Nathan, 1996; Fuller, 2002). Charter school laws typically include provisions that waive many of the regulations that govern traditional public schools (Bulkley & Wohlstetter, 2003).

A related motive for shifting authority to schools is to allow them to tailor their programs to the needs and preferences of particular students and parents. In the one best system the exercise of preferences is muted, as all schools are required to conform to a common set of goals and regulations. If some approaches to schooling work better for particular students, however, then allowing schools to specialize and differentiate enables students and parents to choose schools that suit their preferences. Some parents prefer to send their children to schools that require uniforms and strict discipline; others prefer environments that encourage student choice. Some students may wish to focus on technical subjects while others prefer art and music.

Many school choice policies, such as charter schools in the United States and *écoles experimentales* in France, have been designed to stimulate innovation and specialization (Mintrom, 2000; Meuret, 2007). In the U.K. the Labour Government recently tried but failed to win approval for an initiative requiring all secondary schools to adopt a specialized identity and mission (DFES, 2001). As above, the guiding idea is that schools perform better when their practices align with the aptitudes and preferences of their students, which requires that schools differ sufficiently from one another to provide parents with meaningful alternatives from which to choose.

Similar hopes animate a new wave of "autonomy for accountability" initiatives in the U.S., many linked to mayoral and state takeovers. Following Hurricane Katrina in September of 2005, for example, the Louisiana legislature created a Recovery School District jurisdiction that authorized the state to take control of 102 of New Orlean's 117 schools (National Governors Association, 2005). The state intends to reopen most New Orleans schools as charter schools, pioneering what stands to become the nation's first all-chartered public school system. New York City has moved to expand its Empowerment Schools program, offering principals full independence from district oversight and full authority over lump sum budgets. In exchange, schools must purchase all materials and services on their own, and provide quarterly student performance data to authorities (New York City Department of Education, 2006). Chicago has created a Renaissance 2010 venture that will replace up to 100 low performing schools with schools operated by educational management companies, community groups, university foundations and local charter school founders (Chicago Public Schools, 2006). Groups can operate schools as district performance schools freed from certain regulations, as charter schools or as contract schools.

The combination of centralized goal setting and decentralized execution that is reflected in these initiatives has come to represent the modal policy framework for education systems in countries around the world (Macpherson, 1998; Thélot, 2004). Recent policy initiatives have assigned increased authority and responsibility to individual schools in efforts to lift schools out of "the depressing ethos of centralized control" (Kogan, 2002, p. 331), to stimulate new practices, and to improve performance. In the following sections we review the available empirical evidence on the impact of these initiatives, and assess whether newly autonomous schools can be expected to improve educational efficiency and effectiveness.

EMPIRICAL EVIDENCE

The idea that the school is the critical unit of change and improvement in the education system has received strong empirical support from four decades of research on effective schools (Edmunds, 1979; Rutter, Maughan, Mortimore, Ouston, & Smith, 1979; Teddlie & Stringfield, 1993). This research has consistently identified key attributes shared by schools that are successful in improving the achievement of poor and minority children. These include, for example, a culture of high expectations (Cohen, 1985; Purkey & Smith, 1983) strong principal leadership (Davis, Darling-Hammond, LaPointe, & Meyerson 2005; Hallinger & Heck, 1998; Her Majesty's Inspectorate, 1977) high quality and coherent instructional programs (Newmann, Smith, Allensworth, & Bryk, 2001; Schmidt et. al., 2001) an emphasis on teachers' learning and development (Elmore, 2004; Darling-Hammond & Sykes, 1999; Smylie, 1995) and mechanisms to foster parent involvement and support (Comer, 1984; Epstein, 2001). Beyond empirical findings, the effective schools research provides an invaluable existence proof for the proposition that the crucial levers for school improvement are to be found within individual schools, and for the corollary claim that individual schools should be the unit for management, finance, and accountability in the education system. The fact that some schools beat the odds is taken both as a demonstration that schools have the capacity to acquire or develop the knowledge and resources for educational success, and as a warrant for policies that hold them accountable for their outcomes (Apthorp et al., 2005).

The effective schools literature simultaneously highlights the fact that schools that consistently exceed expectations are by definition outliers, exceptional in ways that set them apart from their similarly situated peers. Simply knowing that unusually effective schools exhibit (for example) a culture of high expectations and strong leadership does not establish whether and how these attributes can be cultivated in schools where they are not already present. The hopes invested in policies that shift authority and accountability to the school therefore depend for their fulfillment on whether individual schools can muster the necessary mix of social, professional and fiscal capacities to set a new course and improve their own performance. The evidence on whether this can be accomplished in large numbers of schools is mixed, but not greatly encouraging.

School Site Management and Budgeting

A considerable body of empirical work has developed on school-site management (SSM) and budgeting that examines whether these initiatives produce the effects and outcomes promised by theory. A line of studies conducted across many continents and contexts offers remarkably similar conclusions.[2] Overall, the record suggests that outcomes range from the insignificant to the modestly positive. In developing countries the literature is somewhat more encouraging, in large part because initial expectations were considerably less ambitious (King & Ozler, 1998; Sawada, 1999; Shukla, 1999).

The measured outcomes produced by SSM initiatives are generally small. When skillfully supported with fiscal and other resources, SSM reforms have been found to manifest some hoped-for effects, such as a stronger sense of efficacy (Wohlstetter, Symer, & Morhman, 1994); greater commitment to local priorities (Malen, Ogawa, & Kranz, 1990; Williams, Harold, Robertson, & Southworth, 1997); and enhanced teacher influence and engagement (Murray & Grant, 1995; Smylie, Lazarus & Brownlee-Conyers, 1996; Thrupp, Harold, Mansell & Hawksworth, 2000). Some studies suggest that SSM can stimulate improved relations between schools, parents, and their communities (Logan, Sachs & Dempster, 1996; Ryan et al., 1997; Townsend, 1994.) Across continents and contexts, however, successful implementation and positive outcomes have most often been observed in more advantaged schools with an already established tradition of informal, if not formal, participatory governance (Gammage et al., 1996; Hanson, 2000; Malen, Ogawa, & Kranz, 1990; King & Ozler, 1998; Sawada, 1999; Wildy, 1991). The concluding remarks of many studies emphasize the benefits of collaboration and professional community in schools, which might be fostered with or without changes in governance.

Even in conditions where SSM has been found to operate reasonably well, few studies have identified linkages between increased autonomy and changes to instruction. Studies conducted in Canada, Australia, and the U.K. suggest that improvements in planning and communication linked to SSM can shape conditions that influence classroom practice, but they find little direct impact on teaching behaviors or student outcomes (Leithwood, Jantzi, & Steinbach, 1999; Dempster, 2000; Wildy, 1991). In a careful study of relationships between SSM, instructional improvement and student outcomes Smylie, Lazarus and Brownlee-Conyers (1996) conclude that the relationship is at best indirect, turning on the capacities of schools to reduce teacher isolation, increase opportunities for organizational learning and foster a sense of internal accountability among school members. The structures of SSM have clearly proliferated, but like many reforms in education, SSM initiatives often have lacked crucial supports including clear domains of authority, member training, information systems on which to base decisions, and meaningful motivation and reward structures (David, 1989; Dempster, 2000; Smylie, Lazarus, & Brownlee-Conyers, 1996; Wohlstetter & Odden, 1992.).

A variety of cultural conditions that prevail in school organizations have also reduced SSM's potential to stimulate change. Institutionalized assumptions of equality among teachers, tacit prohibitions against passing judgment on peers, and an overall press for collegiality have often discouraged initiative and risk-taking (Leithwood & Menzies, 1998; Malen, Ogawa, & Krantz, 1990; Weiss, 1993). Naiveté about the politics of decision-making likewise jeopardizes school-level initiatives. SSM advocates typically envision unitary or consensual politics in schools, but real decision-making processes present value conflicts and tensions over whose wants and priorities should take precedence (Conley, 1989; Weiss, 1993; Wylie, 1996). Routine splits between educators and parents and between teachers and principals often result in agendas emphasizing symbolic and conflict-mediating actions rather than substantive and transformative change (Lewis & Nakagawa, 1995; Malen, 1994.) Additionally, many teachers, though philosophically supportive of SSM, report that increased responsibility for decision-making drains their instructional time and energy (Fiske & Ladd, 2000; Leithwood & Menzies, 1998; Weiss & Cambone, 1994). As a result, expanded domains of communication and influence rarely seem to lead to new visions or more effective instructional or administrative practices.

Skeptics of SSM point out that the empowering flexibility promised by policy-makers has generally proven to be far more rhetorical than real (Wylie, 1996; Malen, 1999; Townsend, 1994). Most national, regional and local rules remain in place, as do teacher union contracts. Indeed, the regulatory environment surrounding schools in nearly all of the Anglophone countries that pioneered SSM has become *more* crowded with mandates governing curriculum, testing, and accountability, Offers by U.S. governors and ministry officials elsewhere to forego regulations in exchange for better results have drawn little interest. In the U.S., for example, the use of waivers has proven to be modest and uninventive (Raphael & McKay, 2001).

Altered lines of authority between schools and local education authorities (LEAs) took root in some contexts, but many SSM initiatives were subsumed by the institutionalized environment of central control and policy incoherence that they aspired to contravene. Ironically, administrative structures associated with SSM have themselves become familiar features of this institutionalized environment, as participatory decision structures including school-site councils have emerged as obligatory if largely symbolic components of public, private and charter school organizations.

Many of the obstacles noted in SSM studies are also observed in studies of more bounded site-based budgeting initiatives, but this literature is slimmer and less cohesive. The U.S. literature generally portrays mixed promise and disappointment (Archibald, 2001; Goertz & Stiefel, 1998; Odden, 1990; Picus, 1999; Wohlstetter & Van Kirk, 1995). In Chicago, for example, site-based budgeting was central to the district's extensive decentralization reforms. Principals viewed the distribution of significant discretionary dollars to schools as the most potent element of the reform package, as it allowed them to hire added instructional personnel, provide stronger professional development and enhance student support services such as after-school programming (Hess, 1995). Research elsewhere suggests that the impact of more limited experiments has been minimal, however. Many programs were quickly eroded by unclear understandings of authority over funds and by the low level of funds delegated to schools (Goertz & Stiefel, 1998; Wohlstetter & Van Kirk, 1995).

Frequent changes in state and local finance and budgeting systems may be one reason why a cohesive line of empirical work has not emerged to investigate whether individual schools become more productive when they control their budgets. For example, in the late 1990s New York City piloted a Performance Based Budgeting System modeled on systems used in Canada. Studies of the program found that schools that took control of their instructional budgeting systems developed new and effective ways to allocate resources and made small but statistically significant gains in student academic outcomes (Siegel & Fruchter, 2002). Despite these encouraging findings the program was ended and budgeting recentralized. Two years later, however, New York re-piloted school site budgeting under the Empowerment Schools Initiative noted earlier.

Research and debate on site-based budgeting and decentralized administration of financial resources has been greatly overshadowed by the larger debate as to whether money matters (e.g., Burtless, 1996), whether the design of funding formulas matters (Levacic, Ross, Caldwell, &

Odden, 2000), and whether funding allocations matter (Standard & Poors, 2005). Recent efforts to create support for "student-weighted" funding systems that tie resources to individual students may help to revive interest in the topic (Thomas B. Fordham Institute, 2006).

Schools as Communities

Efforts to form more communitarian schools have not produced the same volume of scholarly inquiry as have SSM initiatives. Much of the empirical work in this area is qualitative, seeking to develop conceptual frameworks of community and its relationships to democratic education, the practice of difference, personalization and student engagement in learning (Maier, 1995; Oxley, 1997; Raywid, 1988; Sergiovanni, 1994; Sinclair & Lillis, 1980). The literature intersects heavily with research on small schools, and is typified by illustrative outlier studies. Both case-based and larger scale assessments tend to confirm that smaller, more communal schools support student success and academic achievement through their emphasis on more personalized relationships (Lee & Smith, 1997; Walsey & Lear, 2001; Wehlage, Rattner, Smith, Lesko, & Fernandez, 1989); more focused and rigorous academic programs (Battistich, et al. 1995, Bryk, Lee, & Holland 1993; Phillips, 1997); and higher levels of parent and community engagement (Coleman & Hoffer, 1987; Cotton, 2001; Howley & Bickel, 2000). In almost all cases, the effects are most pronounced among poor, minority or otherwise marginalized students.

Failure to specify the precise mechanisms that produce these positive effects and the acknowledged dilemma of selection bias encumber the empirical literature on schools as communities. Findings are more consistently positive than in research on SSM, but studies often raise as many questions as they answer, especially where policy is concerned. For instance, there is a notable absence of empirical research, qualitative or otherwise, investigating if and whether more autonomous public schools, including charters, are more able to develop positive, communitarian ethos than existing public and private schools.

It is worth noting that many recent analyses of schools as communities have criticized traditional conceptions of community and policies that support them (Fendler, 2006; Furman, 2002; Shields, 2000; see also Plank, 2006). Because democratic or participatory communities are so often built on socio-cultural values rooted in particular racial, ethnic, and religious backgrounds, policies that increase reliance on communities are seen as antithetical to social integration and thus anathema to core educational values. In place of "other mindedness," these critics see considerable risk for segregation, coerced assimilation, selective exclusion, and the suppression of social, racial, and other differences that invoke discomfort among educators and parents. They argue that genuinely nurturing communities cannot be built on the basis of self-selection and exclusion, but only upon norms of inclusion and diversity.

Community Schools

Some countries make the school the key unit of management and accountability as a strategy to cope with fundamental problems of finance and capacity. In some African and Latin American countries, for example, the failure of national governments to provide sufficient educational opportunities has prompted local communities to build and operate their own schools (often with the assistance of international NGOs). These efforts, referred to as community schools, have received favorable attention and financial support from agencies including the World Bank and USAID; evaluations of their performance have often been positive. In a recent review of community schools in Ghana, Honduras, and Mali, for example, DeStefano et al. (2006) concluded that schools managed and financed by local communities were generally comparable and sometimes superior to government schools in terms of learning outcomes and cost-effectiveness, despite the difficult economic and geographic circumstances they faced.

In very poor countries, community schools may exhibit additional advantages. Children in community schools generally travel shorter distances to attend school, and the school calendar is more readily adaptable to local circumstances including variable demand for children's labor. The close supervision of parents and community members ensures that teachers are present in their classrooms during school hours, which is a widespread problem in government schools in South Asia and elsewhere (Duflo & Hanna, 2005). On the other hand, teachers in community schools are generally recruited from the community itself, and they are often significantly less qualified than their government-school counterparts.

Effective and Improving Schools Research

If SSM initiatives have disappointed, so too have many other reform and improvement efforts that cast individual schools as the originators and architects of change. Informed by effective schools research and motivated by new funding and flexibility, educators and others have launched continual efforts to do things better, if not always differently. Research across the U.S., the U.K., central Europe, and other nations evidence hundreds of efforts to improve the performance of schools. Studies profile programs aimed at developing literacy, mathematics and science teaching (Allington, 2001; OECD, 2002; Schmidt, et. al. 2001); the intellectual quality of instruction (Leat, 1999; Levin, 2002b; Mintrop 1999; Sizer, 2004a); teacher knowledge and skill (Lovett & Gilmore 2003; Newmann, King, & Youngs, 2000; OECD, 2002; Wilson & Berne, 1999); school leadership (Elmore, 2004; Firestone & Riehl, 2005; Henderson, 2002; Mulford, 2003); and parent involvement (Epstein, 2001; OECD, 1997). These initiatives and the expansive body of research documenting them originates in a general model of school improvement that develops a set of core organizational domains in schools; namely instruction, leadership, professional development, school culture, and parent-community involvement. Elementary schools have been much more likely to benefit from such efforts (NCES, 2004; OECD, 2005) than secondary schools, which are seemingly immobilized by unclear goals and adolescent turmoil the world over (Csikszentmihalyi & Schneider, 2003; Idriss, 2002; NASSP, 2004; Osborn et al. 2003).

In all, school improvement research inevitably underscores that the demands of advancing a coherent system of supports for effective teaching and learning almost always outstrips the professional, technical and fiscal resources of individual schools. Genuinely innovative schools emerge in some studies, while many others marshal the capacity to deliver improved practices in one or two domains (e.g., primary grade literacy instruction or the use of common assessments). As a rule, however, most schools—public, chartered or private—make these gains while functioning much as they always have. For example, schools often appear to improve their performance by recruiting better students, teachers and leaders, by expanding time spent studying core academic subjects, or by delivering more focused, articulated curricula (Elmore, 2004; Hopkins, 2001). Yet, even these efforts may yield only modest changes in performance; one recent analysis of U.S. data has argued that many accounts of achievement gains, particularly those attributed to low performing schools under new accountability measures, are overstated (Harris, 2006).

Placing schools at the center of the policy frame, freeing them from bureaucracy and exhorting them to do better has not by itself generated many of the systemic improvements, innovations, or productivity gains that policy makers hoped for. Rather, the research record continues to show that school improvement is a Sisyphusian struggle against shortages of money, time, knowledge and imagination plus, more recently, staff and leader turnover and external policy shifts that deflate and reverse commitment and progress (Fullan 1995; Louis, 1994; Peschar & van der Wal, 2000; Sizer, 2004b; Thrupp, 1999).

For many, this catalogue of stubborn challenges has effectively laid to rest the notion that schools can innovate or improve themselves if left to their own devices. This seems especially true when considering schools serving poor and minority communities, the focus of policy attention worldwide. Consequently, recent research has turned its attention to more comprehensive school improvement efforts guided by external partners using specific designs and employing deliberate but locally tailored systems of teacher learning, program implementation, and progress assessment. Examples of comprehensive school reform in the U.S. include the America's Choice network (Supovitz & Perda, 2004) Comer Schools (Comer, et al., 1996), New American Schools (Berends, Bodilly, & Kirby, 2002) and Success for All (Slavin & Madden, 1999); an analogous development in the U.K. is the national Improving the Quality of Education for All (IQEA) program. These more comprehensive approaches, while not successful in every case, have produced compelling cases and more detailed propositions on how to advance school level capacity for effective teaching and learning. They stress the importance of more tightly executed improvement strategies rooted in instruction, a continuous and embedded press on teacher learning and the use of tools such as data analysis and reflection to assess outcomes and progress towards specified benchmarks. Of particular relevance to this discussion, they stress the critical importance of external support structures—professional expertise, technical assistance, and peer learning that reach beyond the boundaries of individual schools.

CHALLENGES AND PROSPECTS

At the end of the day, the proposition that assigning greater authority and autonomy to schools can bring about significant improvements in student and system performance will depend on whether two fundamental challenges are overcome. The first is the general challenge of capacity building at all levels of the education system, but specifically within schools. The second is the challenge of turning around schools where student performance consistently falls below expectations.

Knowledge and Capacity

Rules and regulations have long served as substitutes for technical knowledge in schools. It does not follow, however, that reducing the regulatory burden on schools will create or increase the knowledge available to educators. Even when faced with new responsibilities and accountability pressures, educators can only do what they know how to do, effective or not (Elmore & Burney, 1997). By the same token, schools' capacity to change remains strictly limited by the absence of slack resources that can be deployed to support knowledge development and changes in practice (Arsen, Bell, & Plank, 2003). Within schools, virtually everyone's time and attention are already fully committed to instruction and management. In schools overwhelmed with social and organizational challenges developing new capacities is doubly difficult.

Where this is the case, significant improvements in the performance of schools will require the support of external partners equipped to provide targeted resources and technical assistance. In the United States, this is a task traditionally left to LEAs, including school districts. Given distrust of the central office and the institutionalized arrangements of the one best system, many are pointing to other agencies—mayors' offices, universities, policy entrepreneurs, educational management companies, and private-sector vendors of all descriptions—as prospective partners for schools seeking to improve their performance. The potential of any of these agencies to succeed where LEAs have failed is subject to doubt.

Available evidence on the development of instructional capacity in schools makes it clear that capacity building is a complex process involving multiple agencies and actors. Though a technical focus on teacher knowledge and skill is essential, lasting improvement cannot be accomplished through discrete or short-term interventions. Studies of some of the most promising improvement efforts, such as the America's Choice project, Success for All, and the U.K.'s IQEA initiative link success to relentless attention to the development of school leaders and teachers (including continuous retraining in response to staff turnover), persistence towards full implementation and unyielding attention to staff focus and commitment (Cross, 2004; Elmore & Burney, 1997; Hopkins, 2001; Rowan, Camburn, & Barnes, 2005). Extensive development of technologies for data use, planning and assessment also appear to play a key role (Boudett, City, & Murnane, 2005; Supovitz & Klein, 2003). The cost and complexity of introducing and making good use of comprehensive improvement strategies places them well beyond the reach of individual schools.

Failing Schools

Issues raised by the shift of administrative authority and responsibility to schools are especially urgent in schools that persistently fall short of public expectations. These are almost invariably schools serving the poorest and least advantaged pupils, including racial and linguistic minorities, who rely most heavily on schools for the knowledge and skills needed to enter the economic mainstream. They include inner-city schools in the United States, schools in the *banlieues* of Paris, township schools in South Africa, and rural schools across Africa and South Asia. Academic league tables and other scorecards routinely identify these schools as those in greatest need of improvement, and subject them to the most intense sanctions including reconstitution and closure. School choice policies likewise have their greatest impact in schools enrolling poor and minority pupils, as parents depart failing schools and seek out more promising educational environments for their children (Fiske & Ladd, 2000; Plank & Sykes, 2003). They are often also the schools with the least internal capacity to change.

Governments have traditionally responded to the problems of chronically low-performing schools by providing additional financial and administrative supports, but student achievement outcomes have proven to be largely impervious to such interventions. Four decades of experience with Title I support for high-poverty schools in the United States and two decades of experience with special programs for schools in the ZEPs (*zones d'education prioritaires*) in France have produced limited results in the targeted schools (Doyle & Cooper, 1988; Benabou, Kramarz, & Prost, 2004). Chile's similarly designed P900 program has produced some positive effects, but poor and minority students continue to lag well behind (Tokmani, 2002). The consequence is widespread disenchantment with programs that provide additional resources to low-performing schools without requiring far-reaching changes in the ways these schools are organized and administered.

In keeping with the broader shift of authority and responsibility to the school level, many western governments have recently moved to institute policies that hold low performing schools responsible for their own outcomes, with no excuses allowed for challenging demographic or educational circumstances (Thernstrom & Thernstrom, 2003). Failure to meet common standards now triggers a variety of sanctions and interventions. Such policies are expected to concentrate the minds of educators on the accomplishment of specific learning objectives. Some studies do indeed suggest that heightened pressures can prod chronically failing schools to confront severe dysfunctions through the introduction of stronger leadership and more coherent instructional programs (Hess, 2005; Newmann, Smith, Allensworth, & Bryk, 2001; Plank & Dunbar, 2006). As we have already suggested, however, there are a variety of good reasons to doubt that failing schools can improve their internal processes and outcomes without extensive external support, even under the most favorable circumstances (Harris, 2006; Rothstein, 2004; Hopkins, 2001).

Shifting Authority Relations

Despite the lack of strong evidence that making schools the unit for management, finance, and accountability produces much in the way of systemic school change or improved student performance, efforts to shift administrative authority to schools have not abated. Beyond the autonomy for accountability policies noted earlier, these efforts have found new energy in policy initiatives that aim to accelerate change by shifting the balance of power within schools and eliminating rules and protections that perpetuate and legitimate low expectations for student and teacher performance. On one front, these initiatives seek to enhance the authority of school principals; on another, they propose to reduce or remove the constraints on administrative action imposed by union contracts.

Enhancing the authority and autonomy of school principals has resurfaced as a leading objective for policy makers across continents (Her Majesty's Government, 2005; Hess, 2003; Levine, 2005; Mulford, 2003). Power, Halpin, and Whitty (1997, p. 343) describe dramatic changes in the responsibilities and expectations that school leaders must meet:

> Progressively freed from, or perhaps unprotected from, the intermediary layers of democratic and bureaucratic controls between central government and local stakeholders, especially consumers, such a position requires that (leaders) engage both with the demands of the central state in terms of meeting centrally determined objectives and with the day to day business of running a school and ensuring its survival within an education market.

Policies in several countries now seek to recast school leaders as chief executives who may encourage participation among stakeholders but who nevertheless provide decisive leadership in their schools and exercise final authority over programming, budgeting, and personnel. As the environments of schools have increased in uncertainty, complexity, and external demands, proponents of a new managerialism assert that a school's success in achieving critical objectives increasingly depends on the ability of a strong leader to cut across competing stakeholder interests to align resources, practices and incentives with stated goals and priorities. In this view, the efficient achievement of goals is more likely under unified authority in the school than under more participatory processes that diffuse goals and priorities across multiple interests (Boyd & Crowson, 2002; Meyer, 2002).

A closely related development is the intensifying effort to blame educational mediocrity and stagnation on union contracts that value stability over innovation and suppress the ability of individual schools to attract and reward the best teachers and fire the worst (Moe, 2001; Hoxby, 1996; Loveless, 2000). Because unions typically bargain with LEAs, spinning schools off from these centralized administrative structures might be expected to release schools from the constraints of union contracts (Carnoy & McEwan, 2005; Fiske & Ladd, 2000). Proponents of more flexible labor markets have recently gained policy leverage by highlighting research underscoring the impact of teacher quality (Sanders & Horn, 1998; Rivkin, Hanushek, & Kain, 2005), the link between systematic inequities in the distribution of teachers and contract provisions (Peske & Haycock, 2006), and also by adopting the rhetoric and propositions of schools as communities.

While some efforts to design more flexible and responsive union contracts have been heralded (see e.g., Kerchner, Koppich, & Weeres, 1997; Rothman, 2001) the boundaries of school personnel systems have remained largely unaffected by policy and teachers have remained individually insulated from the incentives and sanctions introduced by most accountability measures. With a handful of exceptions, the authority to hire, assign and fire teachers remains constrained by the retention of strong seniority rights in union contracts (Burgess, Croxson, Gregg, & Propper, 2001; Ladd, 1996), and by union resistance to performance contracting (Jupp, 2005; Koppich, 2005; Solmon, 2005).

CONCLUSIONS

The "tight-loose-tight" approach to educational governance that Fiske and Ladd (2000) described in New Zealand reflects an emerging cross-national consensus on the organization of public school systems. In systems organized along these lines, the State is responsible for distributing resources, establishing performance expectations, administering regular assessments, and managing incentives and sanctions in ways that align the interests of educators with those of their clients. Responsibility for accomplishing the State's purposes is assigned to individual schools, which are offered increased administrative autonomy in exchange for increased accountability. In principle, the State's rules for distributing resources and deploying rewards and punishments should steer schools toward the use of proven practices to improve student achievement, while strengthened autonomy should permit local leaders to mobilize local actors and resources in the effective pursuit of common objectives.

This approach to educational governance leaves vacant the space between the State and the school, which was traditionally occupied by LEAs including U.S. school districts. One key policy question is whether these intermediary institutions can simply be dispensed with, as vestiges of a failed system that consume scarce resources in unproductive ways, or whether schools require more direct supervision and support than the State can provide.

School Autonomy and School Performance

Effective schools research demonstrates that many sources of variation in school performance are located within schools. Schools with talented principals, committed and effective teachers, deep parental engagement, and a culture of high expectations often beat the odds, ensuring a measure of academic success for even the least advantaged students. Though the number of these schools remains small, their success demonstrates that school improvement is a profoundly local process, contingent on the knowledge and orientations of principals, teachers, parents, and students working in individual schools.

The existence of unusually effective schools poses a quandary for policy makers. The qualities of successful schools are widely-known, but many schools plainly lack these attributes, especially those responsible for educating disadvantaged students. Knowing what effective schools look like offers no guidance on the more urgent question of how the attributes of effectiveness can be incorporated into the tremendous number of schools where they are lacking. *Being* effective is very different from *becoming* effective (Cuban, 1984).

Two decades of experience and research provide compelling evidence that simply setting schools free and holding them accountable for results is not in itself sufficient to conjure the attributes of effectiveness into being. Detaching schools from the bureaucratic structures within which they are embedded may enable the most privileged or resourceful schools to strike out in new and positive directions, but the rewards of enhanced autonomy for less advantaged schools are uncertain at best.

The fundamental problems that face low performing schools are acknowledged in policy initiatives that duck the challenge of transforming existing public schools by calling instead for the creation of new schools (e.g., charter schools, contract schools) or the incorporation of private schools into the public system. The prevailing hope for these new schools is that they will attract inspired leaders, sustain a focus on academic achievement, foster stronger teacher work ethics, and reject institutionalized bad habits, including unionization. For now, however, the evidence that new schools perform better than existing schools when working with similar students remains equivocal. Indeed, a recent study suggests that some of the least successful schools in the U.S. are isolated charter schools (Braun, Jenkins, & Grigg, 2006). For most struggling schools, significantly improved performance will require intensive external support because local knowledge and capacity fall far short of what would be needed for them to turn themselves around.

The Need for Intermediary Institutions

If going it alone is not an option for most schools, there is a clear need for intermediary institutions to occupy the space between the State and the school. There are a variety of candidates for this role: traditional LEAs, mayors' offices, universities, educational management organizations, and a growing array of school improvement networks. Each has revealed strengths and weaknesses, and none has proven that it has what it takes to turn around low-performing schools on a consistent basis (Arsen, Bell, & Plank, 2005).

In the United States, renewed scholarly attention has lately focused on the proposition that school districts might function as assets rather than liabilities in the education system. Recent work has shown how districts can operate to drive improved organizational performance through vision creation, the alignment of resources to goals, stronger instructional support systems and strategic human resource development (Hess, 2005; Massell, 2000; Spillane & Thompson, 1997; Campbell, DeArmond, & Schumwinger 2004). Other work has shown that a strong central office is essential to support research and knowledge utilization among practitioners (Elmore & Burney, 1997; Wilson & Easton, 2003). Many school districts, including the large urban districts that serve a disproportionate share of poor and minority students, operate on a scale that would allow them to support technical assistance and capacity building. Success in these tasks would require school districts to radically reframe their purposes, however, and shift from a focus on compliance to a focus on performance and support. The challenge of turning urban school districts around may equal or exceed the challenge of turning around individual schools.

Another set of intermediary institutions receiving increased scholarly attention is the growing array of independent networks that connect schools pursuing similar organizational designs and improvement strategies. Among these are reform networks serving public schools (e.g., Success for All and Little Red Schoolhouse) networks creating new schools (e.g., KIPP (the knowledge is power program) and Big Picture) and networks created by private-sector educational management organizations (e.g., Edison Schools and National Heritage Academies). All of these intermediaries bring together educators engaged in common, long-term school improvement strategies and engage in research and development activities with them (Cross, 2004; Educational Policy Institute, 2005; Rowan, Camburn, & Barnes, 2005). To date, however, independent evidence on the effectiveness of these networks remains scarce.

The emergence of horizontal networks and partnerships with the scale and capacity to provide comprehensive support for continuous improvement in large numbers of schools remains a work in progress. One open question is whether any or all of these networks can in fact mobilize the technical expertise and administrative capacity to guide steady improvement in the growing number of schools in which they work. A second question is whether schools are prepared to commit themselves to comprehensive, full-service reform strategies from a single provider instead of relying on a diverse menu of partners, consultants and vendors to address discrete problems as most do now (Newmann, Smith, Allensworth, & Bryk, 2001). In addition, the survival and effectiveness of these networks is under constant threat in a turbulent policy environment where the State's expectations for schools are subject to frequent changes, as the checkered history of Edison Schools illustrates.

The Role of the State

Those who favor making the school the key unit for management, finance, and accountability often foresee a minimal role for the State, limited primarily to setting standards and aligning incentives. The preceding account suggests that more will be required of the State in at least two respects if schools are to accomplish increasingly ambitious educational objectives.

First, recognizing that most schools lack the knowledge and capacity to significantly improve their own performance, the State must cultivate and support a variety of intermediary institutions to provide technical and other assistance to schools, particularly those schools where performance consistently falls short of expectations. LEAs may be obvious candidates for this role, but in instances where they have consistently failed to provide effective assistance, the State must be prepared to identify or even create alternatives.

Second, the State must invest in knowledge production and capacity building to provide schools with the resources that they need to improve their performance. One focus of these efforts must be the painfully unyielding question of how to increase the effectiveness of poorly performing schools. Four decades of research on this question provide some clear directions, but solid answers remain elusive. It is quite clear, however, that without a good answer to this question the hopes invested in enhanced autonomy for individual schools are likely to be frustrated.

NOTES

1. See for example Section 311 of the Goals 2000: Educate America Act; Section 14401 of the Elementary and Secondary Education Act of 1965 as amended; Sections 502 and 503 of the School-to-Work Opportunities Act.
2. Typically, the first is that identifying and distinguishing the effects of school-site management from other, simultaneous improvement efforts is highly problematic.

REFERENCES

Allington, R. (2001). *What really matters for struggling readers: Designing research-based programs*. New York: Longman.

Apthorp, et al. (2005). *Schools that beat the odds*. Boulder, CO: Mid-continent Research for Education and Learning.

Archer, M. (1979). *Social origins of educational systems*. London and Beverly Hills: Sage.

Archibald, S. (2001). *A case study of dramatic resource reallocation to improve student achievement:* Harrison Place High School. Madison: University of Wisconsin,Consortium for Policy Research in Education.

Arsen, D., Bell, C., & Plank, D. N. (2003). *Who will turn around "failing" schools? A framework for instutional choice*. Working Paper #12. East Lancing, MI: The Education Policy Center.

Arsen, D., Bell, C., & Plank, D. (2004). *Who will turn around "failing" schools? A framework for institutional choice.* Perspectives,10, 1–20.

Aston-Warner, S. (1963). *Teacher.* New York: Simon & Schuster.

Battistich, V., Solomon, D., Kim, D., Watson, M. & E. Schaps (1995). Schools as communities, poverty levels of student populations, and students' attitudes, motives and performance: A multilevel analysis. *American Educational Research Journal,* 32(3), 627–258.

Benabou, R., Kramarz, F., & Prost, C. (2004). Zones d'education prioritaires: Quels moyens pour quels resultats? *Economie et Statistique* 380.

Berends, M., Bodilly, S.J., & Kirby, S.N. (2002). *Facing the challenges of whole-school reform. New American schools after a decade.* Santa Monica, CA: RAND.

Borman, G. D., Hewes, G. M., Overman, L. T. & Brown, S. (2002). *Comprehensive school reform and student achievement: A meta-analysis. Report No. 59.* Baltimore: Center for Research on the Education of Students Placed At Risk.

Boyd, W. L. & Crowson, R. L. (2002). The quest for a new hierarchy in education: From loose coupling back to tight? *Journal of Educational Administration,* 40(6), 521–533.

Boudett, K. P., City, E. A., & Murnane, R. J. (Eds). (2005). *Data wise: A step-by-step guide to using assessment results to improve teaching and learning.* Cambridge: Harvard Educational Publishing Group.

Brandl, J.E. (1998) *Money and good intentions are not enough.* Washington DC: Brookings Institute Press

Braun, H., Jenkins, F., & Grigg, W. (2006). Comparing private schools and public schools using hierarchical linear modeling (NCES 2006-461). U.S. Department of Education, National Center for Education Statistics, Institute of Education Sciences. Washington, DC: U.S. Government Printing Office.

Briggs, K. L., & Wohlstetter, P. (2003). Key elements of a successful school-based management strategy. *School Effectiveness and School Improvement,* 14(3), 351–372.

Brighelli, J-P. (2005). *La Fabrique du Cretin: La mort programée de l'école.* Paris: Broché.

Bruns, B. (2003). *Achieving Universal Primary Education by 2015: A chance for every child.* Washington, DC: The World Bank.

Bryk, A. S., & Driscoll, M. E. (1999). *The high school as community: Contextual influences and consequences for students and teachers.* Madison, WI: Center for Education Research, National Center on Effective Secondary Schools.

Bryk, A.S., Lee, V.L. and Holland, P. (1993). *Catholic schools and the common good.* Cambridge, MA: Harvard University Press

Bryk, A. S., Sebring, P.B., Kerbow, D., Rollow, S & Easton, J. Q. (1998). *Charting Chicago school reform: Democratic localism as a lever for change.* Boulder, CO: Westview Press.

Bulkley, K. & Wohlstetter, P. (2003). *Taking account of charter schools: What's happened and what's next.* New York: Teachers College.

Burgess, S., Croxson, B., Gregg, P., & Popper, C. (2001). *The intricacies of the relationship between pay and performance for teachers: Do teachers respond to performance related pay schemes?* University of Bristol, CMPO Working Paper Series No. 01/35. Retrieved October 16, 2006 from 99/015 http://www.bris.ac.uk/cmpo/workingpapers/wp35.pdf.

Burtless, G. (Ed.) (1996). *Does money matter? The effect of school resources on student achievement and adult success,* Brookings Institution Press, Washington, D.C.

Callahan, R. (1962). *Education and the cult of efficiency.* Chicago: University of Chicago.

Campbell, C., DeArmond, M., & Schumwinger, A. (2004). *From bystander to ally: Transforming the district human resources department.* Seattle. Center for Reinventing Public Education. Retrieved July 20, 2006 from: http://www.crpe.org/pubs/introBystanderToAlly.shtml.

Carnoy, M. & Levin, H.M. (1985). *Schooling and work in the democratic state.* Palo Alto, CA: Stanford.

Carnoy, M. & McEwan, P.J. (2003). Does privatization improve education? The case of Chile's national voucher plan. In Plank, D.N. & Sykes, G. (eds.), *Choosing choice: School choice in international perspective.* New York: Teachers College.

Chicago Public Schools. (2006). Renaissance 2010. Retrieved July 8, 2006 from http://www.ren2010.cps.k12.il.us/index.shtml

Chubb, J.E. & Loveless, T. (2002). *Bridging the achievement gap.* Washington DC: Brookings.

Chubb, J.E. & Moe, T. (1990). *Politics, markets and America's schools.* Washington DC: Brookings Institute Press.

Cohen, D.K. (1990). Governance and instruction: The promise of decentralization and choice. In W. H. Clune & J.F. Witte (Eds.) *Choice and control in American education: Vol. 1 The theory of choice and control in American education* (pp. 337–386). Philadelphia: Falmer Press.

Cohen, M. (1985). Effective schools: Accumulating research findings. *American Education,* 18, 13–16.

Coleman, J.S. (1985). Schools and the communities they serve. *Phi Delta Kappan,* 66(8), 527–532.

Coleman, J.S. & Hoffer, S. (1987). *Public and private high schools: The impacts of communities.* New York: Basic Books.

Comer, J.P. (1984). Home-school relationships as they affect the academic success of children. *Education and Urban Society,* 16, 323–337.

Comer, J.P., Haynes, N. M., Joyner, E. T., & Ben-Avie, M. (Eds.) (1996). *Rallying the whole village: The Comer process for reforming education.* New York: Teachers College Press.

Conley, S.C. (1989). Who's on first? School reform, teacher participation, and the decision-making process. *Education and Urban Society,* 21(4), 366–379.

Cotton, K. (2001). *New small learning communities: Findings from recent literature.* Portland, OR: Northwest Regional Educational Laboratory.

Cross, C. (Ed.) (2004). *Putting the pieces together: Lessons from comprehensive school reform research* Washington, DC: National Clearinghouse for Comprehensive School Reform.

Csikszentmihalyi; M., & Schneider, B. (2003). *Becoming adult: How teenagers prepare for the world of work.* New York: Basic Books.

Cuban, L. (1984). Turning the frog Into a prince. *Harvard Education Review.*

Cuban, L. (2001). *Oversold and underused: Computers in classrooms.* Cambridge, MA: Harvard University Press.

Darling-Hammond, L. (1996). The right to learn and the advancement of teaching: Research, policy and practice for democratic education. *Educational Researcher,* 25(6), 5–17.

Darling-Hammond, L., & Sykes, G. (Eds.) (1999). *Teaching as the learning profession: Handbook of policy and practice.* San Francisco: Jossey-Bass.

David, J. L. (1989). Synthesis of research on school-based management. *Educational Leadership,* 46(8), 45–53.

Davis, S., Darling-Hammond, L.; LaPointe, M.; & Meyerson, D. (2005). *School leadership study: Developing successful principals.* Stanford, CA: Stanford Educational Leadership Institute.

Dempster, N. (2000). Guilty or not: The impact of site based management on schools. *Journal of Educational Administration,* 38(1), 47–63.

Department for Education and Skills (2001). *Schools achieving success.* London: DFES.

DeStefano, J., Hartwell, A., Schuh-Moore, A., & Benbow, J. (2006). *Meeting EFA: Cost-effectiveness of complementary approaches.* Washington DC: USAID/Educational Quality Improvement Project.

Doyle, D.P. & Cooper, B.S. (1988). *Federal aid to the disadvantaged: What future for Chapter 1?* New York: Falmer.

Duflo, E. & Hanna, R. (2005). *Monitoring works: Getting teachers to come to school.* NBER Working Paper # 11880. Cambridge: NBER.

Edmunds, R. (1979). Effective schools for the urban poor. *Educational Leadership,* 37, 15–24.

Educational Policy Institute (2005). *Focus on results: An academic impact analysis of the knowledge is power program (KIPP).* Virginia Beach: Educational Policy Institute.

Elmore, R. F. (2004). *School reform from the inside out: Policy, practice and performance.* Cambridge, MA: Harvard Education Press.

Elmore, R.F. & Burney, D. (1997). *Investing in teacher learning: Staff development and instructional improvement in Community School District #2, New York City.* New York: Teachers College.

Epstein, J. L. (2001). *School, family and community partnerships: Preparing educators and improving schools.* Boulder, CO: Westview Press.

Fender, L. (2006). Others and the problem of community. *Curriculum Inquiry,*36 (3), 303–326.

Finn, C.E. Jr., Petrilli, M. & Julian, L. (2006). *The state of state standards, 2006.* Washington, DC: The Fordham Foundation.

Firestone, W. & Riehl, C. (2005). *A new agenda for research in educational leadership.* New York: Teachers College Press.

Fiske, E.B. (1996). *Decentralization of eduation: Politics and consensus.* Washington DC: The World Bank.

Fiske, E.B. & Ladd, H.F. (2000). *When schools compete: A cautionary tale.* Washington, DC: Brookings.

Friedman, M. (1955). The role of government in education. In Solo, R.A. (ed.), *Economics and the public interest.* New Brunswick, NJ: Rutgers.

Fullan, M.G. (1995).The school as a learning organization: Distant dreams *Theory into Practice*, 34(4), 230–235.

Fuller, B. (2002). *Inside charter schools: The paradox of radical decentralization.* Cambridge, MA: Harvard.

Furman, G. (2002). *School as community: From promise to practice.* Albany: State University of New York Press.

Gammage, D.T., Sipple, P. & Partridge, P. (1996). Research on school-based management in Victoria. *Journal of Educational Administration*, 34 (1), 24–40.

Gibton, G., Sabar, N., & Goldring, E.B. (2000). How principals of autonomous schools in Israel view implementation of decentralization and restructuring policy: Risks, rights, and wrongs. *Educational Evaluation and Policy Analysis,* 22(2), 193–210.

Glewwe, P., & Hanan, J. (1994). Student achievement and schooling choice in low-income countries: Evidence from Ghana. *Journal of Human Resources*, 29(3), 841–864.

Goertz, M. E. & Stiefel, L. (1998). School-level sesource allocation in urban public school. *Journal of Education Finance*, 23(4), 435–446.

Hallinger, P., & Heck, R. (1998). Exploring the prinsipal's contribution to school effectiveness: 1980–1996. *School Effectiveness and School Improvement*, 9, 157–195.

Hanson, M. (2000). Democratization and educational decentralization in Spain: A twenty year struggle for reform. Washington DC: World Bank. Retrieved August 6, 2006 from: www.worldbank.org/education/globaleducationreform.

Harris, D.N. (2006). High flying schools, student disadvantage and the logic of NCLB. Paper presented at the Harvard Achievement Gap Initiative. Cambridge, MA. June 2006.

Hanushek, E.A. & Raymond, M.E. (2002). Sorting Out Accountability Systems. In Evers, W.M & Walberg, H.J. (eds.), *School Accountability* (pp. 75–104). Stanford, CA: Hoover Institution.

Henderson, R. (2002). Educating Leaders in Developing Nations. *Higher Education in Europe,* 27(3), 249–253.

Her Majesty's Inspectorate (1977). *Ten good schools: A secondary school enquiry.* London: Department of Education and Science; Her Majesty's Inspectorate.

Her Majesty's Government (2005). *Higher standards, better schools for all, more choice for parents and pupils.* London: Department of Education and Skills: Her Majesty's Government.

Hess, A. G., Jr. (1995). *Restructuring urban schools: A Chicago perspective.* New York: Teachers College Press.

Hess, F. M. (2003). *A License to lead? A new leadership agenda for America's schools.* Washington, DC: Progressive Policy Institute.

Hess, F. M. (Ed). (2005). *Urban school reform: Lessons from San Diego.* Cambridge, MA: Harvard Education Press.

Hess, F.M. (2006). *Tough love for schools: Essays on competition, accountability, and excellence.* Washington DC: AEI.

Hill, P.T., Foster, G.E., & Gendler, T. (1990) *High schools with character.* Rand Report R-3944-RC Santa Monica, CA: Rand Corporation.

Hill, P.T., Pierce, L.C., & Guthrie, J.W. (1997). *Reinventing public education: How contracting can transform America's schools.* Chicago: University of Chicago Press.

Hopkins, D. (2001). *Improving the quality of education for all: The theory and practice of school improvement.* London: David Fulton.

Howley, C., & Bickel, R. (2000). *Results of a four-state study: Smaller schools reduce harmful impact of poverty on student achievement.* Washington, DC: Rural School and Community Trust.

Hoxby, C.M. (1996). How teachers' unions affect education production. *The Quarterly Journal of Economics*, 111 (3), 671–718.

Idriss, C.M. (2002). Challenge and change in the German vocational system since 1990. *Oxford Review of Education* 28(4), 473--490.

Jansen, J. (1995). Effective Schools? *Comparative Education*, 31(2), 181–200.

Joyce, B., Calhoun, E., & Hopkins, D. (1999). The new structure of school improvement: Inquiring schools and achieving students. Philadelphia: Open University Press.

Jupp, B. (2005). The uniform salary schedule. *Education Next,* 1, 10–12.

Katz, M.B. (1975). *Class, bureaucracy and schools: The illusion of educational change in America.* New York: Praeger.

Katz, M.S., Noddings, N., & Strike, K.A. (Eds.) (1999). Justice and caring: The search for common ground in education. New York: Teachers College Press, Columbia University.

Kennedy, M. M. (2005). *Inside teaching: How classroom life undermines reform.* Cambridge, MA: Harvard University Press.

Kerchner, C.T., Koppich, J.E., & Weeres, J.G. (1997). *United Mind Workers: Unions and teaching in the knowledge society.* San Francisco: Jossey-Bass.

King E., & Ozler, B. (1998). *What's decentralization got to do with learning? The case of Nicaragua's school autonomy reform.* Working Paper on Impact Evaluation of Education Reforms Washington, DC: World Bank. Accessed July 8, 2006 from: http://www.worldbank.org/html/prddr/prdhome/AdobePDFfiles/EKing&BOzler.pdf

Kogan, M. (2002). The subordination of local government and the compliant society. *Oxford Review of Education*, 28(2/3), 331–342.

Koppich, J. (2005). All teachers are not the same. *Education Next*, 1, 13–1. Retrieved September 19, 2006 from: http;//www.hoover.org/publications/ednext/3251891.html.

Lavacic, R., Ross, K., Caldwell, B., & Odden, A. (2000). Funding schools by formula: Comparing practice in five countries. *Journal of Education Finance,* 25(4), 489–515.

Leat, D. (1999). Rolling the stone uphill: Teacher development and the implementation of thinking skills programmes. *Oxford Review of Education,* 25(3), 387–403.

Leithwood, K, Jantzi, D., & Steinbach, R (1999). Do school councils matter? *Educational Policy,* 13(4), 467–493.

Leithwood, K., & Menzies, T. (1998). Forms and effects of school-based management: A review. *Educational Policy*, 12, 325–246.

Levin, H.H. (2002a). A Comprehensive Framework for the Evaluation of Educational Vouchers, *Educational Evaluation and Policy Analysis*, 24(3), 59–74.

Levin, H. M. (2002b). Pedagogical challenges for educational futures in industrializing countries *Comparative Education Review*, 45(4), 537–560.

Levine, A. (2005). *Educating school leaders*. New York: Teachers College, The Education Schools Project.

Lewis, D.A & Nakagawa, K. (1995). *Race and educational reform in the American metropolis: A study of school decentralization*. Albany: State University of New York Press.

Lightfoot, S. L. (1983). *The good high school: portraits of character and culture*. New York: Basic Books.

Logan, L., Sachs, J. & Dempster, N. (1996). *Planning for better primary schools*, The Australian College of Education, Canberra.

Louis, K. S. (1994). Beyond managed change: Rethinking how schools improve. *School Effectiveness and School Improvement*, 5(10), 2–24.

Loveless, T. (2000). *Conflicting Missions? Teachers Unions and Educational Reform* (pp. 189–211). Washington DC: Brookings.

Lovett, S. & Gilmore, A. (2003). Teachers' learning journeys: The quality learning circle as a model of professional development. *School Effectiveness and School Improvement*, 14(2).

Macpherson, R.J.S. (1998). *The politics of accountability: Educative and international perspectives*. Thousand Oaks, CA: Corwin.

Malen, B. (1994). The micropolitics of education: Mapping the multiple dimensions of power relations in school politics. In J. Scribner & D. Layton (Eds.), *The study of educational politics* (147–167). New York: Taylor & Francis.

Malen, B. (1999). The promises and perils of participation on site-based councils. *Theory into Practice,* 38 (4), 209–216.

Malen, B., Ogawa, R.T., & Kranz, J. (1990) .What do we know about school-based management? A case study of the literature. In W. H. Clune & J.F. Witte (Eds.) *Choice and control in American education: Vol. 2 Choice and control in American education* (pp. 389–342). Philadelphia: Falmer Press.

Massell, D. (2000). *The district role in building capacity. Four strategies* (CPRE Research Report RR-32). Philadelphia: Consortium for Policy Research in Education.

May, H., Supovitz, J. A., & Perda, D. (2004). *A longitudinal study of the impact of America's Choice on student performance in Rochester, New York, 1998–2003.* Philadelphia: Consortium for Policy Research in Education.

McDermott, K. A. (2000). Barriers to large-scale success of models for urban school reform *Educational Evaluation and Policy Analysis*, 22 (1), 83–89.

McLaughlin, M.W. (1991). The Rand change agent study ten years later. In A. R. Odden (Ed.) *Education Policy implementation* (pp. 143–156). Albany: State University of New York Press.

Meier, D. (1995). *The power of their ideas: lessons for America from a small school in Harlem.* Boston: Beacon Press.

Meuret, D. (2007). *Gouverner l'école: une comparaison France/Etats Unis.* Paris: PUF.

Meyer, H. (2002). The new managerialism in education management: Corporatization or organizational learning? *Journal of Educational Administration,* 40(6), 534–551.

Meyer, J. & Hannan, M. (1979). *National development and the worldsSystem: Educational, economic, and political change, 1950-1970.* Chicago: University of Chicago.

Miles, K. W & Roza, M. (2006). Understanding student-weighted allocation as a means to greater school resource equity. *Peabody Journal of Education*, 81(3), 39–44.

Mintrom, M. (2000). *Leveraging local innovation: The case of Michigan charter schools.* East Lansing: The Education Policy Center.

Mintrop, H. (1999). Changing core beliefs and practices through systemic reform: The case of Germany after the fall of socialism. *Educational Evaluation and Policy Analysis*, 21(3), 271–296.

Moe, T.M. (2001). *A Primer on America's Schools.* Stanford: Hoover Institution.

Mulford, B., (2003). *School leaders: Challenging roles and impact on teacher and school effectiveness* OECD At: http://www.oecd.org/dataoecd/2/52/37133393.pdf.

Murray, C. (1988). *In pursuit of happiness and good government.* New York: Simon and Schuster.

Murray, C.E., & Grant, G. (1995). *The normative structure of a successful experiment in shared decision making.* Paper presented at the Annual Convention of the American Educational Research Association, San Francisco.

NASSP (2004). *Breaking ranks II: Strategies for leading high school reform.* National Association of Secondary School Principals. Reston, VA.

Nathan, J. (1996). *Charter schools: Creating hope and opportunity for American education.* San Francisco: Jossey-Bass.

National Center for Education Statistics (2004). *NAEP 2004 trends in academic progress: Three decades of student performance in reading and mathematics.* Washington, DC: U.S. Department of Education.

National Commission on Excellence in Education (1983). *A nation at risk: The imperative for educational reform.* Washington DC: Author.

National Governors Association (2005, November 10). *Louisiana seeks state takeover of New Orleans Schools.* Downloaded 6-12-06. Available at http://www.nga.org/portal/site/nga/menuitem.9123e83a1f6786440ddcbeeb501010a0/?vgnextoid=a0f7cecc2da77010VgnVCM1000001a01010aRCRD&vgnextchannel=4b18f074f0d9ff00VgnVCM1000001a01010aRCRD.

Neill, A. (1995). *Summerhill school.* London: St. Martins Press.

New York City Department of Education (2006, June 15). *Empowerment schools FAQ.* Downloaded 08-14-06. Available at http://schools.nycenet.edu/region6/midwood/empowerment.html.

Newmann, F. M & Associates. (1996). *Authentic achievement: Restructuring schools for intellectual quality.* San Francisco: Jossey-Bass.

Newmann; F. S., King, B., & Youngs, P. (2000). Professional Development That Addresses School Capacity: Lessons from Urban Elementary Schools. *American Journal of Education,* 108 (4), 259–299.

Newmann, F. N, Smith, B.A., Allensworth, E. & Bryk, A. S. (2001). Instructional program coherence: What it is and why it should guide school improvement policy. *Educational Evaluation and Policy Analysis,* 23(4), 297–322.

Noddings, N. (1996). On community. *Educational Theory*, 46(3), 245–267.

Odden, A. (1990). School funding changes in the 1980s. *Educational Policy*, 41(1), 33–47.

OECD (1997). *Parents as partners in schooling*. Paris: Organization for Economic Cooperation and Development.

OECD (1999). *Innovating schools*. Paris: Organization for Economic Cooperation and Development.

OECD (2002). *Reading for change: Performance and engagement across countries*. Paris: Organization for Economic Cooperation and Development.

OECD (2005). *Education at a glance – OECD indicators 2005*. Paris: Organization for Economic Cooperation and Development.

Osborn, M., Broadfoot, P., McNess, E.,Plane, C., Ravn, B., & Triggs, P. (2003). *A world of difference? Comparing learners across Europe.* Berkshire: Open University Press.

Osborne, D., & Gaebler, T. (1992). *Reinventing Government: How the entrepreneurial spirit is transforming the public sector*. Reading, MA: Addison-Wesley.

Oxley, D. (1997). Theory and practice of school communities. *Educational Administration Quarterly*, 33, 624–643.

Peschar, J. L. & van der Wal, M. J. (2000). *Education contested: Changing relations between state, market and civil society.* London: Taylor & Francis.

Peske, H. G., & Haycock, K. (2006). *Teaching inequality: How poor and minority students are short-changed on teacher quality.* Washington, DC: The Education Trust.

Peters, T. J., & Waterman, R. H. Jr. (1982). *In search of excellence: Lessons from America's best run companies.* New York: Harper and Row.

Phillips, M. (1997). What makes schools effective? A comparison of the relationships of communitarian climate and academic climate, mathematics achievement and attendance during middle school. *American Educational Research Journal*, 34, 633–662.

Picus, L. O. (1999). Defining adequacy: Implications for school business officials. *School Business Affairs*, 65(1), 27–31.

Plank, D.N. (2006). Unsettling the State: How 'demand' challenges the education system in the US. *European Journal of Education,* 41 (1), 13–28.

Plank, D.N. & Dunbar, C. Jr. (2006). *Michigan: Over the first hurdle.* Paper prepared for a conference on NCLB, American Enterprise Institute, November.

Plank, D.N. & Sykes, G. (2003). *Choosing choice: School choice in international perspective.* New York: Teachers College.

Power, S., Halpin, D., & Whitty, G. (1997). Managing the state and the market: 'new' education management in five countries. *British Journal of Educational Studies,* 45 (4), 342–362.

Purkey, S., & Smith, M. (1983). Effective schools: A review. *Elementary School Journal*, 83, 427–452.

Raphael, J. & McKay, S. (2001). *Analysis of the education flexibility partnership demonstration program. Final report.* Washington, DC: The Urban Institute.

Raywid, M. A. (1988). Community and schools: A prolegomenon. *Teachers College Record*, 90(2), 197–210.

Rivkin, S.G., Hanushek, E.A., & Kain, J.F. (2005). Teachers, schools, and academic achievement. *Econometrica*, 73(2), 417-58.

Rothman, R. (2001). How teachers unions are working with districts to improve schools. *Challenge Journal*, 5(1), 1–8.

Rothstein, R. (2004). *Class and schools: Using social, economic and educational reform to close the Black-White achievement gap.* Washington, DC: Economic Policy Institute.

Rowan, B., Camburn, E. & Barnes, C. (2005). Benefiting from Comprehensive School Reform: A Review of Research on CSR Implementation . Ann Arbor: The University of Michigan Consortium for Policy Research in Education.

Rowan B., & Miskel, C. G. (1999). Institutional theory and the study of educational organizations In J.

Murphy & K. S. Louis (Eds.), *Handbook of research on educational administration*. San Francisco, CA: Jossey-Bass, 359–383.

Rutter, M., Maughan, B., Mortimore, P., Ouston, J. & Smith, A. (1979). *Fifteen thousand hours*. London: Open Books.

Ryan, S., et. al. (1997). *Charting reform: LSCs- local leadership at work*. Chicago: Consortium on Chicago School Research.

Sanders, W.L., & Horn, S. P. (1998). Research findings from the Tennessee Value-Added Assessment System database: Implications for educational evaluation and research. *Journal of Personnel Evaluation in Education,* 12(3), 247–256.

Schlesinger, A. M. (1998). *The disuniting of America: Reflections on a multicultural society*. New York: W. W. Norton.

Schmidt, W.H. et al. (2001). *Why Schools Matter: A cross-national comparison of curriculum and learning*. San Francisco: Jossey-Bass.

Sergiovanni, T. (1994). *Building community in schools*. San Francisco: Jossey-Bass.

Shields, C. M. (2000). Learning from difference: Considerations for schools as communities. *Curriculum Inquiry*, 30 (3), 275–294.

Siegel, D., & Fruchter, N. (2002). *Final Report: Evaluation of the performance based budgeting system*. Institute for Education and Social Policy, New York University.

Simmons, W. & Grady, M. (Eds) (2003). *Research perspectives on school reform: Lessons from the Annenberg Challenge*. Providence: The Annenberg Institute for School Reform.

Sinclair, M.E., & Lillis, K. (1980). *Schools and community in the third world*. London: The Institute of Development Studies.

Sizer, T. R. (2004). *Horace's compromise: The dilemma of the American high school*. Boston: Mariner.

Sizer, T. R. (2004). *The red pencil: Convictions from experience in education*. New Haven, CT: Yale University Press.

Slavin, R. E., & Madden, N. A. (1999). *Success for all: Research and reform in elementary education*. Mahwah, MJ: Erlbaum.

Smylie, M.A. (1996). From bureaucratic control to building human capital: The importance of teacher learning in education reform. *Educational Researcher*, 25(9), 9–11.

Smylie, M., Lazarus, V., & Brownlee-Conyers, J. (1996). Instructional outcomes of school-based participative decision making. *Educational Evaluation and Policy Analysis*, 18(3), 181–198.

Solmon, L. (2005). Recognizing differences. *Education Next*, 1, 16–18.

Spillane, J. P. & Thompson, C. L (1997). Reconstructing conceptions of local capacity: The local education agency's capacity for ambitious instructional reform. *Educational Evaluation and Policy Analysis,* 19(2), 185–203.

Standard & Poors School Evaluation Services. (2005). *The issues and implications of the "65 percent solution."* School Matters: A service of Standard & Poors. Downloaded 930/06. Available at http://www.schoolmatters.com/pdf/65_paper_schoolmatters.pdf

Supovitz, J. A., & Klein, V. (2003). *Mapping a Course for Improved Student Learning: How Innovative Schools Systematically Use Student Performance Data to Guide Improvement*. University of Pennsylvania: Consortium for Policy Research in Education.

Teddlie, C., & Stringfield, S. (1993). Schools do make a difference: Lessons learned from a ten-year study of school effects. New York: Teachers College Press.

Thélot, C. (2004). *Pour la réussite de tous les élèves*. Rapport de la Commission du débat national sur l'avenir de l'École. Paris: CNDP.

Thernstrom, A., & Thernstrom, S. (2003). *No Excuses: Closing the Racial Gap in Learning*. New York: Simon & Schuster.

Thomas B. Fordham Institute (2006). *Fund the Child: Tackling inequity and antiquity in school finance*. Washington DC: Author.

Thrupp, M., Harold, B., Mansell, & Hawksworth (2000). *Mapping the cumulative impact of educational reform: A study of seven New Zealand schools*. Final Report. New Zealand: University of Waikato.

Thrupp, M. (1999). *Schools making a difference: Lets be realistic*. Buckingham: Open University Press.

Tokmani, A. (2002). *Evaluation of the P900 Program: A targeted education program for underperforming schools*. Santiago: Banco Central de Chile.

Townsend, T. (1994). Community involvement: the hidden factor in devolution. *International. Journal of Educational Management*, 8 (4), 24–29.

Townsend, T. (2001). Satan or savior? An analysis of two decades of school effectiveness research. *School Effectiveness and School Improvement* 12(1), 115–129.

Tyack, D.B., & Cuban, L. (1995). *Tinkering toward Utopia: A century of school reform*. Cambridge: Harvard University Press.

Vinovskies, M.A. (1999). *The road to Charlottesville: The 1989 Education Summit*. Washington, DC: The National Education Goals Panel.

Wasley, P.A., & Lear, R.J. (2001). Small Schools, Real Gains. *Educational Leadership,* 58 (6), 22–27.

Wehlage, G.G., Rutter; R. A., Smith, G. A., Lesko, N., & Fernandez, R. R. (1989). *Reducing the risk: Schools as communities of support*. New York: Falmer Press.

Weiss, C.H. (1993). Shared decision making about what? A comparison of schools with and without teacher participation. *Teachers College Record*, 95, 68-92.

Weiss, C.H., & Cambone, J. (1994). Principals, shared decision making and school reform. *Educational Evaluation and Policy Analysis*, 16(3), 287–301.

Wilson, S.M., & Berne, J. (1999). Teacher learning and the acquisition of professional knowledge: An examination of research on contemporary professional development, *Review of Research in Education,* 24, 173–209.

Wilson, R., & Easton, C. (2003). *Using research in educational improvement: The LEAs role*. Paper presented at the British Educational Research Association Annual Conference, Heriot-Watt University, Edinburgh, 11–13 September 2003.

Wohlstetter, P., & Odden, A.R. (1992). Rethinking school base management and research. *Educational Administration Quarterly*, 28, 529–549.

Wohlstetter, P., Symer, R. & Morhman, S. A. (1994). New boundaries for school based management: The high involvement model. *Educational Evaluation and Policy Analysis*, 16(3), 268–286.

Wohlstetter, P., & Van Kirk, A. (1995). Redefining school-based budgeting for high-involvement. In L. O. Picus & J. L. Wattenbarger (Eds.), *Where does the money go? Resource in elementary and secondary schools* (pp. 212–235). Thousand Oaks, CA: Corwin.

Wildy, H. (1991). School-based management and its linkage with school effectiveness: Issues arising from a preliminary study of three government secondary schools in Western Australia. In I. McKay & B.J. Caldwell (Eds.), *Researching Educational Administration Theory and Practice, ACEA Pathways Series 2*, Australian Council for Educational Administration, Hawthorne: Victoria.

Williams, R.C., Harold, B., Robertson, J., & Southworth, G. (1997). Sweeping decentralization of educational decision-making authority: Lessons for England and New Zealand. *Phi Delta Kappan*, 78(8), 626–631.

Willms, J. D., & Somer, M. (2001). Family, classroom, and school effects on childrens' educational outcomes in Latin America. *School Effectiveness and School Improvement* 12(4), 409–445.

Wise, A. (1989). Professional teaching: A new paradigm for the management of education. In T. Sergiovanni (Ed.), *Schooling for tomorrow: Directing reforms to issues that count*. Needham Heights, MA: Allyn and Bacon.

World Bank. (1995). *Priorities and strategies for education*. Washington DC: The World Bank.

World Bank. (1997). *World development report: The state in a changing world*. Washington DC: The World Bank.

Wylie, C. (1996). Finessing site-based management with balancing acts. *Educational Leadership*, 53 (4), 54–59.

24

Charter Schools

Robert Bifulco and Katrina Bulkley

INTRODUCTION

Charter schools have been one of the most significant developments in U.S. education over the last fifteen years. Since the first charter school program was introduced in Minnesota in 1991, 40 states and the District of Columbia have adopted charter school legislation. According to one charter school advocacy group, 3,977 charter schools serving roughly 1,150,000 students were open as of October, 2006.[1] Although, only about 2 percent of students nationwide are enrolled in charter schools, the percentage enrolled in some urban areas is much higher.

While charter school laws vary considerably, charter schools are generally nonsectarian, free, public schools operating with a contract, or charter, granted by a public agency. This contract usually lasts for a set number of years, and must be renewed in order for the school to continue receiving public funding. In most cases students are not enrolled in charter schools unless their parents apply for admission. As public schools, they are open to all who wish to attend within a geographic area, are supported primarily by tax dollars, and are not allowed to charge tuition. Typically, oversubscribed charter schools are required to select students from those who apply by lottery. Unlike traditional public schools, charter schools receive funding based on the number of students they attract and operate with some independence from local school boards. In theory, charter schools trade additional autonomy from state and local regulation for greater accountability to parents (through markets) and government (through the need to have contracts renewed). The fact that students and parents select charter schools, advocates argue, pushes these schools to be more innovative and higher quality than district-run public schools (see Nathan, 1996; Kolderie, 1990).

In this chapter, we survey research that examines the effects of charter school programs on schools and students with an eye both to what it can tell us about the costs and benefits of existing charter school programs, and to what it can tell us about the effects of parental choice, market competition, and school level autonomy more generally. We begin with a discussion of the genesis of the charter school movement, reviewing the intellectual arguments as well as the political dynamics underlying the movement. The following sections review research that evaluates the effects of charter school programs on educational practices, the segregation of students across schools, student achievement, and school efficiency. A concluding section identifies policy implications and challenges for future research.

THE GENESIS OF THE CHARTER SCHOOL MOVEMENT

The first discussion of the idea of "chartering" schools can be traced to Ray Budde, a former professor at the University of Massachusetts (1988, 1989). Budde suggests that groups of teachers should be able to set up special programs, or schools-within-schools, through a charter received from the local school board.[2] He describes a charter as a written agreement, in this case between a group of teachers and the school board, that "spells out the goals, objectives, and responsibilities of both parties" (Budde, 1989, p. 10). Albert Shanker, the President of the American Federation of Teachers, also began to write favorably about the idea in the late 1980s (see Shanker, 1988a, 1988b). For both Budde and Shanker, the primary purpose of charters is to provide greater autonomy and flexibility to teachers interested in designing innovative programs.

Others have also emphasized charter schools as a means to provide more teacher control and to encourage schools that have a clear educational mission (i.e., Rebarber, 1992). For those who argue for charters on the grounds of innovation through autonomy, it is critical that charter schools be "a truly different alternative to what is already offered" (Amsler, 1992, p. 1–2). Choice, for these advocates, is primarily a way to match parents, students, and educational programs, rather than a means of introducing competition to public education.

During the 1990s, charter school advocates began to place more emphasis on the potential benefits of competition. In 1990, the Progressive Policy Institute published an article by Ted Kolderie which argues that monopoly control is the primary problem with public education. With resources guaranteed, he argued, districts have few external incentives to improve educational quality. Unlike Shanker and Budde, who envision charter schools operating within the traditional district structure, Kolderie argues that choice cannot be a powerful force when the school district provides all of the options, and guarantees students and resources to every school. He advocates for *new* schools that receive a charter from a public entity *other than* school districts. More recently, free-market oriented think tanks have become leading advocates for school choice programs, emphasizing the role of charter schools in meeting the demands of parents and students, however innovative or traditional the education programs might be (see, for instance, Cato Institute, 1998).

While charter school advocates emphasize the potential for innovation, competition and improved student achievement, others worry that charter schools might increase student segregation. Many have argued that because of differences in schooling preferences across groups, information inadequacies, or market pressures on schools, school choice programs can increase segregation by race, ethnicity, class, or ability (Fiske & Ladd, 2000; Henig, 1994; Levin, 1998; Wells, 1993). Others argue that by breaking the link between where students live and where they go to school, choice programs allow poor and minority students trapped in racially and economically isolated neighborhoods to attend more integrated schools (Coons & Sugarman, 1978; Lui & Taylor, 2005; Viteritti, 1999). Thus, some charter school programs have added reducing racial, ethnic, and economic isolation as an explicit goal.

Given the complex roots of the charter school idea, it is not surprising that there are multiple, and at times inconsistent, goals for charter school policies (Bulkley, 2005). Multiple rationales for charter school programs have helped to secure broad support that has eluded voucher programs. In some cases, charter schools have won support from groups hoping they could "hold off" the push towards vouchers. Supporters have included "strange bedfellows," with groups of free-market-oriented conservatives and urban African-American leaders joining ranks in favor of charters (Fuller, 2000; Bulkley, 2005; Wells, Grutzik, Carnochan, Slayton, & Vasudeva, 1999). At the same time, differences across groups in the reasons for supporting charter schools has led to conflict over the design of charter school policies.

State charter school laws differ along many dimensions including how their supply is controlled, how they are governed, and the amount of autonomy granted to them. Several studies describe and compare the specifics of laws in different states (Buechler, 1996; Wohlstetter, Wenning, & Briggs, 1995; Bierlein & Bateman, 1995). The criteria used by many to categorize different laws use value-laden language, distinguishing "weak" laws from "strong" laws. Common elements of stronger laws include: the availability of authorizers other than local school boards; the opportunity for multiple types of operators including for-profit organizations and former private schools; automatic waiver from many state and local regulations; fiscal and legal autonomy; high or no limits on the number of charter schools; potential for non-certified teachers to work in schools; and release from local collective bargaining agreements.[3] These schemes for classifying charter schools assume that weakening monopoly control of public schools and engendering competition are the key rationale for charter school programs. Other researchers have sought to develop less politicized ways to analyze charter school laws. For example, Scott and Barber (2002) offer an alternative framework that considers how the laws address issues of choice, productive efficiency, equity, and social cohesion.

Accountability has emerged as a particularly contentious issue in the design of charter school programs. To some observers replacing traditional democratic/bureaucratic forms of control with an alternative model of accountability is at the heart of the charter school concept (Hill et al., 2001), and many charter school laws identify establishing new forms of accountability as an explicit goal. Though charter schools are accountable to parents through the market-based pressures inherent in the need to compete for students, one of the main factors that distinguishes charter schools from voucher programs is that they are also accountable to the state through the chartering process (Hassel, 1998). In practice, states differ in their approaches to accountability with "some following a 'centralized' state agency approach, others a 'market-driven' approach, and still others a 'district-based' approach that relies on local accountability within a framework of state testing" (RPP International, 2000, p. 3). Programs that attempt to mix market and governmental forms of accountability face difficulties related to the role of the charter contract in holding charter schools accountable, assignment of responsibilities for overseeing charter schools, and appropriate use of state curricula and standardized tests in the accountability process.

In principle, contracts are granted for charter schools based on clear goals and expectations and with the understanding that, if the schools do not meet those expectations, their charters will not be renewed. The authorizing agencies charged with approving, monitoring, and evaluating charters thus, play a key role in this state-based form of accountability. Depending on the state law, these agencies can include local educational agencies, state departments of education, universities, or state charter school boards. Many authorizers, however, lack the capacity to carry out their oversight functions in a meaningful way. As documented by Finnigan et al. (2004), only one-third of authorizers report having a charter school office or staff members whose sole purpose is charter schools, although some of them use formal and informal networks that enhance their internal capacity (see also Vergari, 2001). In addition, the political attitudes of authorizers toward charter schools—positive or negative—can adversely affect the integrity of the accountability process (c.f. Bulkley, 2001). A number of authors also note the difficulty of developing and enforcing clear expectations in charter and other educational contracts (Hassel & Batdorff, 2004; Hannaway, 1999; Bulkley, 2001). Research suggests that charters are terminated mainly because of concerns about management or finances, not inadequate student performance (Hassel & Batdorff, 2004; Bulkley, 2001; Hill et al., 2001). For those who believe the market test is sufficient to ensure charter school accountability, the challenges faced by authorizing agencies are not a major concern. To others, shoring up the capacity of authorizing agencies to evaluate charter schools is a top priority.

Additional questions arise regarding the effectiveness of non-profit boards in overseeing charter school operations, the role that statewide testing programs should play in charter school accountability, and the appropriate forms of government oversight. Many charter school laws require that charter schools be operated by nonprofit boards. Hill and Lake (2006) argue that the rationale for this requirement is unclear and that many boards are the cause of mismanagement and school instability. Ascher, Jacobowitz, and McBride (1999) point out that the requirements that charter schools use state established curricula and meet achievement goals defined in terms of statewide tests can inhibit the development of diverse or innovative instructional approaches. Fiske and Ladd (2001) argue that the only way to maintain an appropriate balance between allowing flexibility for charter schools to innovate, offer alternative programs, and take risks, on the one hand, and providing oversight to ensure public tax dollars are spent appropriately, on the other, is to limit the number of charter schools. More generally, Fiske and Ladd highlight the tensions that arise in any effort to hold charter schools accountable to the public. These include accountability for processes versus for outcomes, between support and oversight roles, and between providing direction and allowing innovation.

EFFECTS ON ADMINISTRATIVE AND EDUCATIONAL PRACTICES

Many charter school proponents emphasize their potential for bringing innovation and program diversity to public education (Nathan, 1996; Hassel, 1998). Charter schools are, fundamentally, an institutional innovation involving the ways in which publicly-funded schools are governed. Beyond this institutional innovation, however, one of the motivations for advocates of charter schools has been to foster innovation in the day-to-day operations of schools (although parents' desire for such innovation is not clear).

Determining the extent to which charter schools foster innovation is complicated by the fact that "innovation" is difficult to define. While some argue innovation implies something altogether new, others interpret it as something new to a particular context (Finn, Manno, & Vanourek, 2000). Miron and Nelson (2002) argue that for something to be innovative it must also be shown to be "effective" at producing desired results. Another motivation for charter school programs, which can be distinguished from the objective of fostering innovation, is to expand the range of programmatic offerings and educational environments from which parents and students can choose. Such diversity provides parents opportunities to match programs with their child's needs and educators opportunities to identify effective practices.

This section examines research on the ways in which day-to-day practices in charter schools differ from those in conventional public schools. Following Lubienski (2004), we discuss two areas for potential diversification and innovation—administration and instruction. In addition, we assess evidence on the claim that because charter schools bring together parents by choice and are freed from bureaucratic constraints, they are better able to focus on a coherent mission and develop a sense of community.

Administrative Practices

The evidence on administrative practices suggests some important differences between charter schools and conventional public schools. Wohlstetter and Chau (2004) find that charter schools frequently use partnerships with local organizations and educational management organizations (EMOs). Recent statistics suggest that almost 20 percent of charter schools are managed by for-profit EMOs, and additional schools are managed by non-profit EMOs (Molnar, Garcia, Bartlett,

& O'Neill, 2006). In some states, such as Michigan, EMOs are particularly prevalent (Miron & Nelson, 2002).

One of the most consistent and interesting findings about charter schools is how they spend on teachers. Several studies find that charter schools tend to hire younger, less experienced teachers and more uncertified teachers than the typical public school, which allows them to pay lower salaries and to free up resources for other purposes (Burian-Fitzgerald, Luekens, & Strizek, 2004; Carnoy, Jacobsen, Mishel, & Rothstein, 2006; Guarino, 2003; Miron & Nelson, 2002; Podgurski & Ballou, 2001). To sustain such policies, charter schools need to maintain relatively high rates of turnover (Burian-Fitzgerald, 2005; Podgurski & Ballou, 2001).

Critics see schools with less experienced teachers as a problem because inexperienced teachers might provide inferior instruction, teacher turnover undermines instructional cohesiveness, and a high concentration of inexperienced teachers in charter schools reduces opportunities for mentoring by more experienced teachers (Carnoy et al., 2006). Analysis by Kane, Rockoff, and Staiger (2006), however, suggests that high turnover rates can be consistent with optimal teacher policies if schools are able to induce high performing teachers to stay and low performers to leave.[4] At least one study finds that charter schools are more likely to dismiss teachers for poor performance and to award merit based bonuses—policies that may help to target retention to more effective teachers (Podgursky & Ballou, 2001). Whether charter schools are effective enough at identifying and retaining high quality teachers to compensate for high turnover rates and heavy reliance on novice teachers is unknown.

Instructional Practices

Far less is known about the pedagogical practices of charter schools than about some of their administrative practices. In one of the few studies to look at this issue, Wohlstetter and Chau (2004) find that more autonomous charter schools use more research based literacy practices than either less autonomous charter schools or district schools. While relying on a small sample (only nine schools), this study offers an example of how to build a better understanding of educational practices in charter and non-charter schools.

A few studies consider the influence of state tests on pedagogical practices. Not surprisingly, charter school administrators and teachers have found it challenging to address state standards and testing requirements while also seeking to engage in alternative teaching practices (Ascher, Jacobowitz & McBride, 1999). A RAND study of charters in California includes analysis of survey data on attention to state testing (Hamilton, 2003). They find that charter schools focus less on state testing than matched conventional public schools, and those charters that have converted from conventional schools focus more on testing than start-up charters. However, their qualitative findings suggest tests are more influential in charter schools than the quantitative findings indicate, with testing and standards influencing areas not included in the survey, such as curriculum selection. Thus, emphasis on results-oriented accountability can conflict with the goals of fostering diversity and innovation.

Commitment and Community

A significant literature argues that teacher community and parent involvement are important elements of effective schools (Louis, Kruse, & Bryk, 1995; McLaughlin & Talbert, 2001; Levine & Lezotte, 1990; Haynes et al., 1996). Scholars have also suggested that when parents are able to choose among small, autonomous schools they are more likely to trust school staff (Schneider, Teske, Marschall, Roch, & Mintrom, 1997), to participate in school activities (Brandl, 1998), and to be committed to a school's vision (Hill, Pierce, & Guthrie, 1997). Building on this literature, a number of researchers examine community in charter schools.

Wohlstetter and Griffin (1998) find that charter schools with more autonomy were more able to "create and sustain a learning community" (p. 22). This finding differs from that of Bulkley and Hicks (2005), who in a study of charter schools managed by EMOs, find that the schools with the least autonomy from their EMO have the highest levels of teacher professional community. The small sample sizes and different definitions of community used in these articles may help to explain these differences.

Two recent studies suggest that charter schools achieve more cooperation among parents and teachers, but do so by attracting more involved parents rather than by eliciting more commitment. Bifulco and Ladd (2005) find that more parents participate in school activities in charter schools than in similar traditional public schools. However, they also find evidence that charter schools located in areas with more involved parents and that parent participation in nearby public schools tended to decline after the establishment of charter schools, suggesting that charter schools attract more involved parents away from traditional public schools. Schneider & Buckley (2006) argue that charter schools have important advantages in building effective school communities including smaller size, the ability to implement parent contracts, and waivers from educational mandates to create "niche" schools. They also report findings that charter schools outscored traditional public schools on a number of indicators of school-based social capital. However, the charter school advantage over traditional public schools in generating school-based social capital is small and erodes over time, suggesting that charter schools are not consistently able to develop initial levels of commitment into vibrant school communities.

Effects on Student Segregation

Several studies compare the student composition of charter schools to that of the state or districts in which they are located. Because minorities and lower income groups are over-represented in the urban areas where charter schools tend to locate, district level comparisons are more informative than state level comparisons. Generally, these studies find that a higher percentage of students in charter schools are minority and a slightly higher percentage are free-lunch eligible, although there is some variation across states. In most areas, charter schools serve lower percentages of disabled and LEP students than traditional public schools.[5] Such comparisons provide useful information about who is being served by charter schools, but do not tell us how segregated charter schools are relative to neighboring schools or what effect charter schools programs have had on the isolation of minority and other student groups.

The challenge in estimating the impact of charter schools on segregation is determining the student composition of the schools charter school students would have attended in the absence of charter school programs. Individual student addresses and enrollment histories, as well as information on school feeder patterns can help researchers determine where charter school students are most likely to have enrolled. However, only a few studies have used such data to develop good estimates of the effect of charter schools on segregation.

Cobb and Glass (1999) use detailed maps of Arizona metropolitan areas to subjectively determine the schools from which each charter school is most likely to draw students. They find that charter schools typically enroll 15 to 20 percent more white students than the nearest traditional public school and that roughly half of the charter schools contribute to ethnic/racial segregation. Bifulco and Ladd (2007) use longitudinal data from North Carolina to identify the school a student attended the year before transferring into a charter school. They find that the average black charter school student has transferred from a public school that is 53 percent black to a charter school that is 72 percent black, while the average white charter school student transfers from a school that is 28 percent black to one that is 18 percent black, suggesting that charter schools exacerbate racial isolation for both groups. They also find that students with college educated parents transfer into charter schools with a much higher percentage of college educated parents than in their previous school. Using the same type of data, Booker, Zimmer, and Buddin (2005) report similar findings for black charter school students in Texas and California, although they find that Hispanic charter school students typically transfer into less ethnically isolated environments.

Questions can be raised about each of these studies. The schools that Cobb and Glass (1999) subjectively choose as comparisons might not be the schools from which charter schools actually draw. The other studies rely on students who transfer from traditional public schools into a charter school sometime after the third grade. Students who begin school in a charter or who transfer from private schools might be drawn from different peer environments. Also, although charter school enrollment in Arizona, North Carolina, California, and Texas constitutes a large proportion of charter school students nationwide, the effects of school choice on segregation are likely to vary depending on the local context (Fuller, Elmore, & Orfield, 1996; Wells, Holme, Lopez, & Cooper, 2000), and thus, it is difficult to generalize from these studies.[6] Nonetheless, the best evidence to date suggests that charter schools have exacerbated the isolation of black students, and may increase other forms of stratification as well.

Some suggest that we should not be concerned that charter schools exacerbate segregation. Viteritti (1999) argues that "[i]t is unreasonable . . . to equate the once horrible situation that existed prior to *Brown* with the recent development of charter schools. One involved the exclusion of children from institutions on the basis of race; the other involves voluntary inclusion of children in institutions to advance their educational goals" (p. 13). To determine how concerned we should be about segregation created by charter schools and whether charter school programs can be modified to reduce segregation, we need to know why charter school programs have increased segregation. Three factors that potentially contribute to the segregation of charter schools and which would suggest that high levels of segregation is an important policy problem are "white flight," "cream skimming," and "asymmetric preferences."

White Flight

The history of school desegregation is marked by efforts of white families to avoid racially integrated schools and the willingness of state and local officials to accommodate the wishes of these families (Clotfelter, 2004). Reflecting the concern that some charter schools might develop into white enclaves, several charter school laws place racial and ethnic balance requirements on charter schools.[7] Nonetheless, the findings of Cobb and Glass (1999) suggest that some charter schools in Arizona are facilitating white flight. Bifulco and Ladd (2007), in addition to observing white students transferring into charter schools with lower percentages of black students, also find that in Wake County, North Carolina, a district where desegregation policies have fostered high levels of integration by race and socio-economic status, there are a number of predominantly white charter schools. Thus, concern about white flight is warranted in some places.[8] However, black students selecting into racially isolated charter schools emerges as a much more prevalent phenomenon in the studies discussed above, suggesting that white flight is not the primary driver of segregation in charter schools.

Cream Skimming

"Cream skimming" refers to the worry that under school choice policies, the best schools will primarily serve the most advantaged students, leaving the disadvantaged to languish in underperforming schools. Cream skimming might emerge in charter school programs for two reasons.

First, the availability of information about charter schools and funding for transportation varies by state and in some cases by district within states (Wells et al., 2000; Nelson, Muir, & Drown, 2000). When information and transportation are costly to obtain, economically and educationally advantaged families are better able to exercise choice. Second, because advantaged students are less costly to educate and because schools with advantaged peers are better able to compete for students and teachers, schools face pressure to select high SES and high achieving students (Henig & MacDonald, 2002; Ladd, 2002).

Many charter school laws, including federal legislation governing the distribution of grants to charter schools, require oversubscribed charter schools to select students by lottery, limiting their ability to cream skim. In addition, some charter school laws (i.e., those in Texas and Connecticut) give preference to charter schools that serve poor or at-risk students. Nonetheless, Wells et al. (2000) document several ways charter schools can use targeted recruitment, application procedures, pre-enrollment interviews, and parent and student contracts to select students. Requirements of various forms of parent support and student behavior, which some disadvantaged families and students might have trouble meeting, and decisions to not offer special education or English as second language programs can also contribute to cream skimming. Finally, there is evidence that for most families, location near one's residence is an important criteria in selecting a school (Hastings, Kane, & Staiger, 2006), suggesting that where a charter school chooses to locate can influence the type of students it attracts.

The evidence suggests that the extent of cream skimming depends to a large extent on local context. The fact that charter schools serve high percentages of low-income and minority students suggests that, in aggregate, charter schools are not cream skimming (RPP International 2000; Finn, Manno, & Vanourek, 2001). However, Carnoy, Jacobsen, Mishel, and Rothstein (2005) provide evidence that among the low-income and minority populations in the areas served by charter schools, charter schools are serving those from better educated families. Henig and MacDonald (2002) also show that market-oriented charters in Washington, D.C.,are more likely to locate in minority neighborhoods with high home ownership rates suggesting a strategy to recruit more socially advantaged minority students. Lacireno-Paquet et al. (2002) find little evidence that market-oriented charter schools in Washington, D.C., are cream skimming by focusing on an elite clientele, but do find evidence that they might be "cropping off" service to students whose language or special education needs make them more costly to educate.

Perhaps the most convincing evidence on cream skimming comes from Booker, Zimmer, and Buddin (2005). They find that charter school students in Texas are drawn from schools with below average achievement and were scoring substantially lower than their peers in those schools, which indicate charter schools in Texas are generally not cream skimming. Considering the strong preference it has given to authorizing charter schools for at-risk students, the Texas charter school program might be exceptional. Booker, Zimmer, and Buddin's findings for California are more mixed. Overall, charter school students have lower test scores than their peers in the schools they previously attended; however, white students who select into charter schools tend to be higher achieving than the peers in the schools they left behind. Overall, the evidence suggests that although cream skimming is not typical of the charter school sector, some charter schools do effectively target advantaged students.

Asymmetric Preferences

Two types of preference asymmetries can lead to segregated charter schools. First, if one group prefers a different student composition than another, a tipping process could lead to segregated schools. This type of asymmetry is particularly worrisome because it suggests that any program that allows parents' control over which school their student attends will generate segregation, and that maintaining integrated options for families who value intergroup contact will be difficult. A second type of preference asymmetry arises if students from one group prefer a different set of curricular and programmatic emphases than another.

The evidence on whether these two types of preference asymmetries exist and are generating segregated charter schools is inconclusive. Studies that rely on responses to surveys provide mixed evidence on whether different groups prefer different school attributes. Schneider, Teske, and Marschall (2000) find that minority and lower income parents are more likely to say that high test scores and discipline are important, while parents with a college education cite diversity and values as the most important concerns. In contrast, Klietz, Weiher, Tedin, and Matland (2000) and Armor and Peiser (1998) find that both black and white parents are concerned foremost with academic quality and safety. The only consistent finding from these surveys is that few parents in any group report that racial composition is an important consideration. However, Schneider and Buckley (2002), who observe internet search behavior of parents in Washington, D.C., provide evidence that lack of emphasis on socioeconomic characteristics and race in surveys of school preferences is due to socially desirable response bias. Studies that attempt to infer parent preferences from observed choices, as opposed to expressed values, have found that racial composition is important to parents (Glazerman, 1997; Henig, 1996; Lankford & Wyckoff, 2005).

Only two studies have explicitly addressed the role that preferences might play in generating charter school segregation. Inferring preferences from observed choices, Bifulco and Ladd (2007) find that the racial composition preferred by the typical black charter school student in North Carolina is 40 to 60 percent black, while the optimal composition for the typical white charter school student is less than 20 percent black, a distribution of preferences that makes it difficult to maintain racially integrated charters. Weiher and Tedin (2002), using a sample of charter school parents in Texas, find that although few say that the racial composition of a school is an important criteria in choosing a school, race is a powerful predictor of the schools they choose. These studies suggest that differences in preferences related to the racial composition of schools are playing a role in generating student segregation in charter schools.

Effects on Academic Achievement

Charter schools can influence student achievement in several ways: by providing either higher or lower quality programs than the nearby traditional public schools; by expanding the options offered to parents, helping to improve the match between educational programs and individual student needs; and by influencing the achievement of students who remain in traditional public schools. In this section we review the evidence on charter school quality and the achievement of charter school students.

Much of the research on student achievement has focused on the average effect of charter schools on charter school students, as opposed to the effects of specific charter schools. Some question whether the average charter school effect is an important policy parameter. By design, charter schools offer a diverse set of educational programs and settings, and some argue that treating such a disparate set of schools as a monolithic intervention hides as much as it reveals. Charter school programs, however, are systemic interventions aimed at changing the institutional environment under which public schools operate. Thus, although the effects of particular educational programs offered by charter schools are of interest, the "treatment" that is of primary policy interest is the charter school program as a whole, making the average effect on the achievement of charter school students a crucial piece of information.

Nonetheless, researchers have highlighted an important caveat about the average charter school effect. New schools face considerable startup challenges that can undermine their educational effectiveness during the first years of operation (Hanushek, Kain, Rivkin, & Brand, 2005; Sass, 2006). Conversely, enthusiasm associated with a start-up school may lead to initial gains that are not maintained as the founders' excitement wanes. In either case, one must keep in mind that the average effect of young charter schools might not be a good indicator of what to expect from a mature charter school program.

In addition to the average effect of charter schools, several other effects are of interest. One purpose of charter school laws is to encourage experimentation with new educational approaches, which can lead to many failures as well as a few outstanding successes. In order to determine whether the successes are worth the cost of the failures, we need to know the distribution of achievement effects across charter schools, including how bad the failures are and how outstanding the successes are, as well as the number of failures relative to the number of successes (Carnoy et al., 2006). Knowledge about the effects of different types of charter schools—conversions, startups, those run by EMOs, distance learning schools, or schools targeting at-risk populations—can inform the design of charter school regulations (Buddin & Zimmer, 2005; Sass, 2006). To assess the impact of charter schools on achievement gaps between advantaged and disadvantaged students we need to know whether the effects of charter schools differ across groups of students defined by race, ethnicity, and socioeconomic status (Bifulco & Ladd, 2007).

Methodological Challenges and Approaches

By far the most common approach to estimating charter school impacts has been to compare the achievement of charter school students to that of students who remain in traditional public schools. The challenge is to identify a group of traditional public school students that provide a valid indication of what charter school students would have achieved had they remained in traditional public schools. Because charter school students self-select, they may differ in important ways, such as motivation, even from those students in nearby traditional public schools with similar background characteristics.

The ideal research design for estimating charter school impacts would randomly assign students interested in attending a charter school to a treatment group allowed to attend any charter school or to a control group who would not have access to charter schools.[9] Random assignment would ensure that the control group is comparable to the treatment group, on average, and comparing the achievement of the two groups would provide a valid estimate of the average charter school effect. To date, no one has attempted an experiment of this type.

A second type of randomized, quasi-experimental design takes advantage of the lotteries used by oversubscribed charter schools to select students. Assuming the lottery is conducted properly, one can assume that the students admitted to a particular charter school are comparable to the students who applied but were not admitted. One can then measure how effective the charter school is for the type of students who apply to it by comparing the average achievement of the students admitted with that of the students on the waiting list. This approach is illustrated by Hoxby and Rockoff (2005) in a study of three charter schools in Chicago. They find positive effects on both math and reading for these schools. These results, however, only provide information on the effects of the programs offered in these schools and only on those students interested in those types of programs. Many charter schools either are not oversubscribed or do not select students randomly, and those that are oversubscribed might not be representative of all charter schools.[10] Thus, although useful for evaluating individual charter schools, this approach is unlikely to provide estimates of average charter school effects.

More common are studies based on administrative data that are designed to determine the effects of a whole system of charter schools. Studies not based on randomized experiments must pay close attention to potential selection biases. The most convincing estimates come from studies that track individual students over time. If three or more observations on individual students are available, researchers can estimate models of achievement growth that control for individual fixed effects. This approach eliminates the threat of selection bias, as it is commonly understood, by basing effect estimates on comparisons between the achievement gains made by students in charter schools and the gains made by the same students in traditional public schools.

Individual level growth models that control for student fixed effects eliminate the threat of selection bias. However, this approach has disadvantages as well. First, valid effect estimates require the assumption that, in the absence of intervention, growth rates vary over time in a similar way for different types of students. If temporary changes in school experiences or specific trends in achievement prompt the transfer from one sector to another this assumption would be violated. For instance, if students who are assigned to a bad teacher in one year are more likely to transfer into a charter school the next year, then estimates of charter school effects may be biased upwards (Hanushek et al., 2005). Second, the effects of attending a charter school can be separated from individual fixed effects only for those students who have achievement gains observed in both sectors. If the effects of charter schools on students who switch sectors are not representative of the effects on students who are never observed in traditional public schools, then growth models with individual fixed effects will provide biased estimates of the average charter school effect (Bifulco & Ladd, 2006).

Because of these shortcomings, it is not clear that growth models with individual fixed effects are superior to growth or value-added models that do not control for fixed effects. Value-added models that do not control for fixed effects rely on a comparison of test score gains made by charter school students with those made by students in traditional public schools, and thus are susceptible to selection bias. However, estimates from these models are based on a more complete and perhaps more representative set of charter school students. Which method is superior depends on the size of the bias due to self-selection relative to the bias due to student sampling. The best studies examine estimates using both methods to ensure robust findings.

Results from the Best Studies

Figure 24.1 summarizes the results of eight studies that have used individual level and longitudinal data to estimate charter school impacts in five different states. Estimates of overall average effects are mixed for two states (Arizona and California) and are negative for three states (Florida, North Carolina, and Texas). In each of the studies that find negative effects on average, these effects are substantially larger for charter schools during their first year of operation than during subsequent years, with some studies showing positive results beginning in the fifth year of operation.

Two of the studies disaggregate the impacts both by the length of time the school has been open and the length of time the student has been in the charter schools. Both studies find that most or all of the negative effect of charter schools occurs during a student's first year in a charter. Other studies have found that transfers into any type of school have negative effects on student achievement during the transition year. However, the estimates from these charter school studies control for the general effect of switching schools, and thus, these findings suggest that transfers into a charter school have a larger negative impact than transfers into a traditional public school. Booker et al. (2004) find that the negative effects of a student's first year in a charter is partially offset by larger gains in subsequent years for students who remain in the charter. Bifulco and

Ladd (2006) find that the negative effect of the first year is neither compounded nor offset in subsequent years for those students who choose to stay.

Only two studies report the distribution of charter school impacts across charter schools. Both find considerable variation including high performers and low performers. In Bifulco and Ladd (2006), North Carolina charter schools with unequivocally negative effects outnumbered those with unequivocally positive effects six to one. Hanushek et al. (2005) explicitly compare the variability in charter school quality to that of traditional public schools and find that charter school quality is considerably more variable.[11]

Of the studies in Figure 24.1, Sass (2006) examines variation in effects across different types of charter schools most extensively. He finds that Florida charter schools that target at-risk and special education students have larger negative effects on math than charter schools generally. However, it is not clear that these findings can be generalized. In an earlier study of Texas using similar methods, Gronberg and Jansen (2001) found that charter schools targeted for at-risk students had positive effects, while other charter schools had negative effects. Also, Bifulco and Ladd (2007) find that in North Carolina the effects of attending a charter school targeted for at-risk students were substantially less negative than the effects of other charter schools. Sass (2006) also examines whether charter schools run by EMOs have different effects than those run by non-profits and finds no significant differences.

Studies that examine differences in charter school effects across different groups of students suggest that charter schools are not helping to increase achievement among minority students. Hanushek et al. (2005) and Solmon and Goldschmidt (2004) test for differences in charter school effects across student groups defined by ethnicity and by family income but do not find any statistically significant differences. Buddin and Zimmer (2006) find only small differences in charter school effects across racial and ethnic groups in Los Angeles and San Diego, and conclude that charter schools are not consistently producing increased test scores for minorities. Booker et al. (2004) find some differences in the timing of effects, but the cumulative effects of charter schools differ little across groups. Bifulco and Ladd (2007) find that charter schools have larger negative impacts on the math scores of black students, and conclude that charter schools have increased black-white test score gaps in North Carolina.

CHARTER SCHOOL EFFICIENCY

The studies in Figure 24.1 generally find that charter schools have had negative effects on student achievement on average, and that older charter schools have small positive impacts in Florida, small negative impacts in North Carolina, and no significant impacts in Texas. However, some studies suggest that charter schools receive less funding than traditional public schools in the same district. If charter schools are able to make similar contributions to student learning as traditional public schools with less funding, that would demonstrate that schools operating under different institutional arrangements can be more efficient than schools operating under traditional governing arrangements.[12]

Several factors complicate the comparison of resources available in charter schools to those available in traditional public schools. First, many school districts are responsible for services such as preschool programming, adult education, and community outreach that charter schools do not provide (Nelson, Muir, & Drown, 2003). Second, charter schools often receive facilities, transportation, administrative, special education or other services from local school districts, the value of which is not reflected in standard revenue or expenditure reports (Nelson, Muir, & Drown, 2000). Third, student needs and program goals in charter schools can differ quite

Study	*State (Years)*	*Research Design*	*Average Impacts*	*Variation by Age of School*	*Variation by School*	*Variation by Student Group*
Solmon & Goldschmidt (2004)	Arizona (1998–2000)	Growth model without student fixed effects	Students in elementary charter for three years make larger reading gains than students in traditional public school for three years. Students in secondary charter for three years make smaller reading gains than students in traditional public school for three years. Largest gains made by students who transfer from a charter into a traditional public school.	Not examined.	Not examined. Authors speculate that charter high schools perform poorly relative to traditional high schools because they are less likely to focus on academics and more likely to focus on "at-risk" populations.	Effect of treatment status does not vary significantly by student background characteristics.
Buddin & Zimmer (2003)	California (1998–2002)	Levels and gains models with student fixed effects.	Elementary charters have no effect on reading, negative effect on math. Secondary charters have positive effect on reading, no or negative effect on math	Not examined.	Start-up elementary charters in Los Angeles and San Diego have larger negative effects than conversion charters.	Not examined
Buddin & Zimmer (2006)	California (1998–2002) Los Angeles & San Diego only	Levels and gains models with student fixed effects.	Elementary charters have no effect in LA, negative effects on reading & math in San Diego Secondary charters have small, mixed effects in both cities	Not examined.	Not examined.	Elementary charters have negative effects on black students, no effects on others in LA, and negative effects on all ethnic groups in SD. Differences in secondary charter school effects across ethnic groups small and mixed.

FIGURE 24.1 Studies of Charter School Impacts on Student Achievement (continued)

Study	*State (Years)*	*Research Design*	*Average Impacts*	*Variation by Age of School*	*Variation by School*	*Variation by Student Group*
Sass (2006)	Florida (2000–2003)	Value-added model with student fixed effects	Charters have small negative effects on reading and math of students in grades 3–10.	Negative effects on math remain statistically significant through fourth year. Negative effects on reading remain statistically significant through third year. Small positive effects on reading during fifth year.	Charters targeted to at-risk & special education students have larger negative effects on math than other charters. No difference in effects between charter schools run by EMOs and those run by non-profits.	Not examined
Bifulco & Ladd (2006, 2007)	North Carolina (1998–2002)	Gains models with and without student fixed effects	Charters have negative effects on reading and math of students in grades 4–8.	Negative effects are largest during first year of operation, and remain statistically significant through fifth year.	Some charter schools show positive impacts but majority show negative impacts. Charters targeted to at-risk students have smaller negative effects on math and reading than other charters.	Charters have larger negative effects on math scores of black students than of white students.
Booker et al. (2004)	Texas (1997–2002)	Gains models with student fixed effects	Charters have negative effects on reading and math of students in grades 4–8.	Negative effects are largest during first year of operation. and remain statistically significant through fifth year Positive effects during the sixth year of operations (based on a small sample of schools and students).	Not examined.	No significant differences in cumulative charter school effects across ethnic groups.
Hanushek et al. (2005)	Texas (1997–2002)	Gains models with student fixed effects	Charters have negative effects on combined reading and math of students in grades 4–8.	Negative effect is largest during the first year of operation, and remains statistically significant through second year.	Variation in charter school quality is greater than variation in traditional public school quality.	No significant differences in charter school effects by race or family income.

1. Level models have test scores on the left hand side, gain models have annual change in test scores on the left hand side, value-added models have test scores on the left-hand side and prior year test scores on the right-hand side, and growth models examine change in test scores over a three year period. All these studies include individual student characteristics on the right-hand side. Fixed effects control for unobserved student characteristics that remain constant over time.
2. Solomon & Goldschmidt (2004) does not estimate average charter school effects, but rather compares the effects of various patterns of attendance in charter schools and traditional public schools over a three-year period.

FIGURE 24.1 Continued

substantially from those in traditional public schools. Many charter schools do not provide transportation or services for moderately to severely handicapped, and provide far fewer extra-curricular activities. Fourth, a disproportionate share of charter schools are elementary schools, which might be less expensive to operate than secondary schools. Finally, traditional public schools can often take advantage of economies of size and low cost capital that are not readily available to charter schools.

Two multistate analyses of charter school funding indicate that, although there is considerable variation both across and within states, charter schools generally receive less revenue per pupil than traditional public schools in the districts where charter schools are located (Nelson, Muir, & Drown, 2003; Speakman & Hassel, 2005).[13] Because they differ in their treatment of in-kind services and lumpy capital revenues, the estimated size of the charter school shortfall differs across the two studies.[14] The chief reasons for the revenue shortfalls for charter schools, where they exist and are not driven by differences in student body composition, are less than full access to local tax revenue and to facility funding.

Financing facilities has been a particularly difficult issue for many charter schools. Although, many state funding formulas seek to provide charter schools operating funds equal to traditional public schools serving similar students, few states provide charter schools extra money to pay for facilities. Lack of access to low-cost financing exacerbates this problem. As a result charter schools often either have to redirect funding for instruction to pay for space or make due with substandard facilities. Facilities funding presents a difficult dilemma for charter school programs. Where charter schools are drawing students from schools that are under utilized, spending on new facilities can be a significant source of system-wide inefficiency.[15] On the other hand, failure to provide facilities funding can create resource disparities between charter school and other students. Some states have tried to address this issue by requiring districts to provide unused space to charter schools free-of-charge, and in some cases, EMOs have funded facilities for the charter schools they manage. Nonetheless, the facilities funding dilemma remains a difficult issue for many charter school programs.

The main issue of contention in determining whether charter schools receive their fair share of resources concerns the comparability of service responsibilities and student needs. Nelson, Muir, and Drown (2003) argue that charter schools provide a more limited range of services and are less costly to operate. In a careful analysis of school funding in Michigan, Miron, Nelson, and Nelson (2002) point out that revenue shortfalls in charter schools relative to traditional public schools are offset by lower levels of spending on special, compensatory, vocational, and adult education, as well as transportation, food, and community services. However, it is difficult to determine how much of the lower levels of expenditures in these categories represent lower levels of service responsibility and student needs, and how much represents efficiencies achieved by charter schools. Thus, it remains uncertain whether or not charter schools receive fewer resources than traditional public schools for the set of services charter schools provide and the set of students they serve.

What is needed are studies which combine careful analysis of the impact of attending a charter school on student outcomes with comparisons of the resources available in charter schools and in the schools that charter school students would have attended in the absence of charters. Care must be taken in making funding comparisons to isolate those funds used to serve the classifications of students and to promote the programmatic goals that are shared by both types of schools. Data limitations make such studies difficult to complete. Until such studies are conducted, conclusions about the efficiency of charter schools relative to traditional public schools will remain uncertain.

CONCLUSION

Research to date provides little evidence that the benefits envisioned in the original conceptions of charter schools—organizational and educational innovation, improved student achievement, and enhanced efficiency—have materialized. Although charter schools do appear more willing than traditional public schools to adopt new management strategies such as contracting with EMOs and relying on younger, less expensive teachers, there is no indication that charter schools have generated significant instructional innovations worth emulating. Convincing evaluation of student achievement effects are now in from five different states. In none of these states have charter schools, on average, had large or unequivocally positive effects on student achievement. It does appear that in most states the typical charter school receives less funding than the typical traditional public school. This fact, combined with the findings from Texas and Florida that mature charter schools perform as well, on average, as traditional public schools, suggests that charter schools might be more efficient than traditional public schools. However, the types of studies required to confirm this suggestion have not been conducted, and it is not clear whether any efficiencies that might have been achieved are the result of autonomy from traditional governance structures, the pressures of market competition, or simply the fact that charter schools have been forced to make due with less.

In contrast, concerns that charter schools increase segregation do appear warranted. The three studies that have most carefully examined the effect of charter schools on racial segregation find either that charter schools facilitate white flight, increase the racial isolation of black students, or both. Although there are undoubtedly some instances of "white flight" and "creaming," the more prevalent cause of segregation in charter schools appears to be differences in the preferences of different groups for schools with different student compositions. This finding suggests that given current attitudes towards race and schooling, programs to expand parental choice will tend to increase segregation.

Despite the fact that charter school programs have not yet been able to consistently demonstrate the benefits advocates have emphasized, continued experiments with charter school and charter school-like alternatives to traditional public schools may still be warranted for several reasons. First, expanding parental choice may be beneficial in- and of-itself. Providing choices to families that otherwise might be relegated to a public school that does not meet their child's needs can be empowering. Second, as charter school programs mature, the benefits originally envisioned might begin to emerge, especially as charter school authorizers gain experience. Finally, although current research provides little guidance, careful design of charter school policies might help to mitigate effects on segregation and increase chances of academic success.

This revised set of hopes for charter schools suggests directions for future charter school research. Research on outcomes in addition to student performance on standardized tests is needed. Even where different educational settings do not show impacts on student test scores, they may show positive impacts on school attainment, student attitudes, and behavioral outcomes. Identifying characteristics of charter schools that are more successful at improving achievement or attracting diverse student bodies can help charter school authorizers and policy makers make more informed decisions. Efforts to understand how differences in charter school finance, accountability, and governance matter for the type of charter schools that emerge are needed. Finally, as an increasing number of charter schools become long-standing, it will be worth seeing how the impacts on educational practice, student segregation, and student achievement evolve.

NOTES

1. Center for Education Reform Web site, http://www.edreform.com/_upload/CER_charter_numbers.pdf, accessed October 20, 2006.
2. Nathan notes that Budde actually used the term, "charter," as early as 1975, but did not write about it until 1988 (Nathan, 1996).
3. See for instance CER Web site, http://www.edreform.com/_upload/ranking_chart.pdf, accessed-December 8, 2006.
4. Differences in the effectiveness among teachers of a given experience level are large relative to the differences in average effectiveness between new and experienced teachers. Thus, gains in instructional effectiveness from retaining only high quality teachers can potentially outweigh losses in instructional effectiveness from relying more heavily on novice teachers.
5. Ascher, Jacobowitz, and McBride (1999) and RPP International (2000) are two national studies that make such comparisons. See also Wells et al. (2000) for a review of state evaluations that make these comparisons.
6. In 2000–01 the charter school enrollment in these four states constituted approximately 47 percent of the charter school enrollment nationwide (calculations based on information provided in Frankenberg & Lee, 2003).
7. Frankenberg and Lee (2003) report that of all the states with charter school legislation as of 2002, 19 have specific racial/ethnic balance guidelines. However, Wells et al. (2000) report that "there is little evidence that either state officials or local school districts are monitoring charter schools' compliance" (p. 171).
8. Whether the movement of white students from integrated schools to predominantly white charter schools in these areas is motivated by preferences for white peers or other factors is more difficult to determine.
9. This design is similar to the experimental designs that have been used for investigating the effects of voucher programs, see chapter 11 in this volume.
10. In an early national study, RPP (1997) surveyed charter schools on their admissions processes. Almost three-quarters indicated they were oversubscribed, but only 39 percent of those reported using a lottery to determine admissions. In order to be eligible for some sources of federal funds, charter schools are required to use a lottery to admit students, so we suspect that the percentage of oversubscribed charter schools that use a lottery is higher today. However, legal requirements are no guarantee. A study of private schools participating in the Milwaukee voucher program, who were also required to select students by lottery, found that many were not using lotteries (People for the American Way Web site, http://www.pfaw.org/pfaw/general/default.aspx?oid=1486#, accessed December 8, 2006). Also, as charter school programs mature and more charters schools are established, we might expect that a lower percentage of schools will be oversubscribed.
11. Part of the measured variation in school quality, however, reflects sampling error, and the greater variation in charter school quality results at least in part from smaller school enrollments.
12. The question here concerns productive efficiency, i.e. the extent to which schools are maximizing the achievement of programmatic goals given their level of resources. Allocative efficiency, i.e., whether the programmatic goals furthered by educational spending maximize individual welfare, is a more complicated question not addressed here.
13. Both studies compare total revenues including revenues for debt service and capital outlays, but excluding bond proceeds.
14. Differences between these two studies are most marked for California and Washington, DC. Because the charter school populations in California and Washington, DC, are so large, differences in how revenues are treated in these states can create substantial differences in aggregate estimates of the average charter school funding shortfall.
15. Inefficiency of this kind is not a concern in fast growing areas that face space shortages.

REFERENCES

Armor, D.L., & Peiser, B.A. (1998). Interdistrict choice in Massachusetts. In P.E. Peterson & B.C. Hassel (Eds.), *Learning from school choice* (pp. 157–186). Washington, DC: Brookings Institution Press.

Amsler, M. (1992). *Charter schools* (Policy Brief No. 19). San Francisco: Far West Laboratory.

Ascher, C., Jacobowitz, R., & McBride, Y. (1999). *Standards-based reform and the charter school movement in 1998–99*. New York: Institute for Education and Social Policy.

Bierlein, L. A., & Bateman, M. (1995). *Opposition forces and education reform: Will charter schools succeed?* Baton Rouge: Louisiana Education Policy Research Center.

Bifulco, R., & Ladd, H.F. (2005). Institutional change and the coproduction of public services: The effect of charter schools on parental involvement. *Journal of Public Administration Research and Theory*, advanced access published November 30, http://jpart.oxfordjournals.org/cgi/ content/muj001v1.

Bifulco, R., & Ladd, H.F. (2006). The impact of charter schools on student achievement: Evidence from North Carolina." *Education Finance and Policy,* 1, 50–90.

Bifulco, R., & Ladd, H.F. (2007). School choice, racial segregation and test score gaps: Evidence from North Carolina's charter school program. *Journal of Policy Analysis and Management*, 26.

Booker, K., Gilpatric, S.M., Gronberg, T.J., & Jansen, D.W. (2004). Charter school performance in Texas. Unpublished paper. Texas A&M University.

Booker, K., Zimmer, R., & Buddin, R. (2005). The effect of charter schools on school peer composition. Rand Working Paper WR-306-EDU.

Brandl, J,E. (1998). Governance and educational quality. In P.E. Peterson & B.C. Hassel (Eds.), *Learning from school choice* (pp. 55–82). Washington, DC: Brookings Institution Press.

Brown, H., Henig, J. R., Lacireno-Paquet, N., & Holyoke, T. T. (2004). Scale of operations and locus of control in market- vs. mission-oriented charter schools. *Social Science Quarterly,* 85, 1035–1051.

Budde, R. (1988). *Education by charter: Restructuring school districts*. Andover, MA: Regional Laboratory for Educational Improvement of the Northeast and Islands.

Budde, R. (1989). Education by charter. *Phi Delta Kappan,* March, 518–520.

Buddin, R., & Zimmer, R. (2003). Academic outcomes. In R. Zimmer et al. (Eds.), *Charter school operations and performance: Evidence from California* (pp. 37–62). Santa Monica, CA: RAND.

Buddin, R., & Zimmer, R. (2006). Charter school performance in two large urban districts. *Journal of Urban Economics*, 60, 307–326.

Buechler, M. (1996 (July)). *Charter schools: Legislation and results after four years* (No. PR-B13). Bloomington, Indiana: Indiana Education Policy Center.

Bulkley, K. E. (2001). Educational performance and charter school authorizers: The accountability bind. *Education Policy Analysis Archives*, 9, http://epaa.asu.edu/epaa/v9n37.html. Accessed June 1, 2006.

Bulkley, K. E. (2005). Understanding the charter school concept in legislation: The cases of Arizona, Michigan and Georgia. *International Journal of Qualitative Studies in Education*, 18, 527–554.

Bulkley, K. E., & Hicks, J. (2005). Managing community: Professional community in charter schools operated by educational management organizations. *Educational Administration Quarterly*, 41, 306–348.

Burian-Fitzgerald, M. (2005). *Average teacher salaries and returns to experience in charter schools* (Occasional Paper #101). New York: National Center for Study of Privatization in Education.

Burian-Fitzgerald, M., Luekens, M.T., & Strizek, G.A. (2004). Less red tape or more green teachers: Charter school autonomy and teacher qualifications. In K. Bulkley & P. Wohlstetter (Eds.), Taking *account of charter schools: What's happened and what's next* (pp. 11–31). New York: Teachers College Press.

Carnoy, M., Jacobsen, R., Mishel, L., & Rothstein, R. (2005). *The charter school dust-up: Examining the evidence on enrollment and achievement.* Washington, DC: Economic Policy Institute and Teacher College Press.

Carnoy, M., Jacobsen, R., Mishel, L., & Rothstein, R. (2006). Worth the price? Weighing the evidence on charter school achievement. *Education Finance and Policy*, 1,151–161.

Cato Institute. (1998). *Cato handbook for congress: 105th Congress*. Washington, DC: Cato Institute.

Clotfelter, C.T. (2004). After *Brown: The rise and retreat of school desegregation*. Princeton, NJ: Princeton University Press.

Cobb, C.D., & Glass, G.V. (1999). Ethnic segregation in Arizona charter schools. *Education Policy Analysis Archives,* 7, http://epaa.asu.edu/epaa/v7n1.html. Accessed April 1, 2006.

Coons, J.E., & Sugarman, S.D. (1978). *Education by choice: The case for family control.* Berkeley: University of California Press.

Finn, C.E., Manno, B.V., & Vanourek, G. (2000). *Charter schools in action: Renewing public education.* Princeton, NJ: Princeton University Press.

Finn, C.E., Manno, B.V., & Vanourek, G. (2001). Charter schools: Taking stock. In P.E. Peterson & D.E. Campbell (Eds.), *Charters, Vouchers, and Public Education* (pp. 19–42). Washington, DC: Brookings Institution Press.

Finnigan, K., Adelman, N., Anderson, L., Cotton, L., Donnelly, M. B., & Price, T. (2004). *Evaluation of the public charter schools program: Final report.* Washington, DC: U.S. Department of Education.

Fiske, E., & Ladd, H.F. (2000). *When schools compete: A cautionary tale.* Washington, D.C.: Brookings Institution.

Fiske, E., & Ladd, H.F. (2001). Lesson from New Zealand. In P.E. Peterson & D.E. Campbell (Eds.), *Charter, Vouchers, and public education* (pp. 59–79). Washington, DC: Brookings Institution Press.

Fuller, B. (2000). Breaking away or pulling together? Making decentralization work. In B. Fuller (Eds.), *Inside charter schools: The paradox of radical decentralization* (pp. 230–256). Cambridge: Harvard University Press.

Fuller, B., Elmore, R.F., & Orfield, G. (1996). Policy making in the dark: Illuminating the school choice debate. In B. Fuller & R. Elmore (Eds.), *Who chooses? Who looses? Culture, institutions, and the unequal effects of school choice* (pp. 1–21). New York: Teachers College Press.

Frankenberg, E., & Lee, C. (2003). *Charter schools and race: A lost opportunity for integrated education.* Harvard University: The Civil Rights Project.

Glazerman, S. (1997). *A conditional logit model of elementary school choice: What do parents value? Chicago*: University of Chicago, Harris School of Public Policy.

Gronberg, T. J., & Jansen, D.W. (2001). *Navigating newly chartered waters: An analysis of Texas charter school performance.* Austin: Texas Public Policy Foundation.

Guarino, C. (2003). Staffing in charter and conventional public schools. In R. Zimmer et al. (Eds.), *Charter school operations and performance: Evidence from California* (pp. 143–160). Santa Monica, CA: RAND.

Hamilton, L. (2003). Academic environments of charter and conventional public schools. In R. Zimmer et al. (Eds.), *Charter school operations and performance: Evidence from California* (pp. 115–142). Santa Monica, CA: RAND.

Hannaway, J. (1999). *Contracting as a mechanism for managing education services* (Policy Brief No. RB-28). Philadelphia: Consortium for Policy Research in Education.

Hanushek, E.A., Kain, J.F., Rivkin, S.G., and Brand, G.F. (2005). Charter school quality and parental decision making with school choice. NBER Working Paper 11252. Cambridge, MA: National Bureau of Economics Research.

Hassel, B.C. (1998). The case for charter schoos. In P.E. Peterson & B.C. Hassel (Eds.), *Learning from school choice* (pp. 33–51). Washington, DC: Brookings Institution Press.

Hassel, B. C., & Batdorff, M. (2004). *High stakes: Findings from a national study of life-or-death decisions by charter school authorizers.* Chapel Hill, NC: Public Impact.

Hastings, J.S., Kane, T.J., & Staiger, D.O. (2006). Preference and heterogeneous treatment effects in a public school choice lottery. NBER Working Paper 12145. Cambridge, MA: National Bureau of Economics Research.

Haynes, N.M., Ben-Avie, M., Squires, D.A., Howley, J.P., Negron, E.N., & Corbin, J.N. (1996). It takes a whole village: The SDP School. In Comer, J.P., Haynes, N.M., Joyner, E.T., & Ben-Avie (Eds.), *Rallying the Whole Village: The Comer Process for Reforming Education.* New York: Teachers College Press.

Henig, J.R. (1994). *Rethinking school choice: Limits of the market metaphor.* Princeton: Princeton University Press.

Henig, J.R. (1996). The local dynamics of choice: Ethnic preferences and institutional responses. In B.

Fuller and R. Elmore (Eds.), *Who chooses? Who looses? Culture, institutions, and the unequal effects of school choice* (pp. 95–117). New York: Teachers College Press.
Henig, J.R., & MacDonald, J.A. (2002). Locational decisions of charter schools: Probing the market metaphor. *Social Science Quarterly*, 83, 962–980.
Hill, P., & Lake, R. (2006). Charter school governance. Paper prepared for National Conference on Charter School Research, Vanderbilt University, September 28.
Hill, P., Lake, R., Celio, M. B., Campell, C., Herdman, P., & Bulkley, K. (2001). *A study of charter school accountability*. Seattle: Center on Reinventing Public Education, University of Washington.
Hill, P., Pierce, L.C., & Guthrie, J.W. (1997). *Reinventing public education: How contracting can transform America's schools.* Chicago: University of Chicago Press.
Hoxby, C.M., & Rockoff, J.E. (2005). The impact of charter schools on student achievement. Unpublished paper. Harvard University.
Kane, T.J., Rockoff, J.E., & Staiger, D.O. (2006). What does certification tell us about teacher effectiveness? Evidence from New York City. NBER Working Paper 12155. Cambridge, MA: National Bureau of Economics Research.
Kirst, M. W. (2006). Politics of charter schools: Competing national advocacy coalitions meet local politics (Occasional Paper #119). New York: National Center for the Study of Privatization in Education.
Klietz, B., Weiher, G.R., Tedin, K., & Matland, R. (2000). Choice, charter schools, and household preferences. *Social Science Quarterly*, 81, 846–854.
Kolderie, T. (1990). *Beyond choice to new public schools: Withdrawing the exclusive franchise in public education* (No. 8). Washington, DC: Progressive Policy Institute.
Lacireno-Paquet, N., Holyoke, T.T., Moser, M., & Henig, J.R. (2002). Creaming versus Cropping: Charter school enrollment practices in response to market incentives. *Educational Evaluation and Policy Analysis*, 24, 145–158.
Ladd, H.F. (2002). *Market-based reforms in urban education.* Washington, DC: Economic Policy Institute.
Lankford, H., & Wyckoff, J. (2005). Why are schools racially segregated? Implications for school choice policies. In J.T. Scott (Ed.), *School choice and diversity: What the evidence says.* New York: Teachers College Press.
Levin, H.M. (1998). Educational vouchers: Effectiveness, choice, and costs. *Journal of Policy Analysis and Management,* 17, 373–392.
Levine, D.U., & Lezotte, L.W. (1990). *Unusually effective schools: A review and analysis of research and practice.* The National Center for Effective Schools Research & Development.
Louis, K. S., Kruse, S. D., & Bryk, A. S. (1995). Professionalism and community: What is it and why is it important to urban schools? In K. S. Louis & S. D. Kruse (Eds.), *Professionalism and community: Perspectives on reforming urban schools* (pp. 3–22). Thousand Oaks, CA: Sage Publications.
Lubienski, C. (2004). Charter school innovation in theory and practice: Autonomy, R & D, and curricular conformity. In K. E. Bulkley & P. Wohlstetter (Eds.), *Taking account of charter schools: What's happened and what's next?* (pp. 72–90). New York: Teachers College Press.
Lui, G., & Taylor, W.L. (2005). School choice to achieve desegregation. *Fordham Law Reveiw*, 74, 791–823.
McLaughlin, M. W., & Talbert, J. E. (2001). *Professional communities and the work of high school teaching.* Chicago: University of Chicago Press.
Miron, G., & Nelson, C. (2002). *What's public about charter schools? Lessons learned about choice and accountability.* Thousand Oaks, CA: Corwin.
Miron, G., Nelson, C., & Nelson, F.H. (2002). Charter School Finance. In Gary Miron and Christopher Nelson, *What's public about charter schools? Lessons learned about choice and accountability* (pp. 43–71). Thousands Oaks, CA: Corwin Press.
Molnar, A., Garcia, D. R., Bartlett, M., & O'Neill, A. (2006). *Profiles of for-profit education management organizations: Eighth annual report.* Tempe, AZ: Education Policy Studies Laboratory, Arizona State University.
Nathan, J. (1996). Charter *schools: Creating hope and opportunity for American education.* San Francisco: Jossey-Bass.

Nelson, F.H., Muir, E., & Drown, R. (2000). *Venturesome capital: State charter school finance systems.* Washington, DC: U.S. Department of Education.

Nelson, F.H., Muir, E., & Drown, R. (2003). *Paying for the vision: Charter school revenue and expenditures.* Washington, DC: U.S. Department of Education.

Podgurski, M., & Ballou, D. (2001). *Personnel policy in charter schools.* Washington, DC: Thomas B. Fordham Foundation & Institute.

Rebarber, T. (1992). *State policies for school restructuring.* Denver, CO: National Conference of State Legislatures.

RPP International. (1997). *A national study of charter schools: Second-year Report.* Washington, DC: U.S. Department of Education, Office of Educational Research and Improvement.

RPP International. (2000). *The state of charter schools 2000: Fourth-year report.* Washington, DC: U.S. Department of Education, Office of Educational Research and Improvement.

Sass, T.R. (2006). Charter schools and student achievement in Florida. *Education Finance and Policy,* 1, 91–122.

Schneider, M. & Buckley, J. (2002). *What do parents want from schools? Evidence from the Internet* (Occasional Paper #21). New York: National Center for the Study of Privatization in Education, Teachers College.

Schneider, M. & Buckley, J. (2006). Charter schools: Hype or hope? *Education Finance and Policy,* 1, 123–138.

Schneider, M., Teske, P., & Marschall, M. (2000). *Choosing schools: Consumer choice and the quality of American schools.* Princeton, NJ: Princeton University Press,

Schneider, M., Teske, R., Marschall, M., Roch, C. & Mintrom, M. (1997). Institutional arrangements and the creation of social capital: The effects of school choice. *American Political Science Review,* 91, 82–93.

Scott, J. T., & Barber, M. E. (2002). *Charter schools in California, Michigan and Arizona: An alternative framework for policy analysis* (Occasional Paper #40). New York: National Center for the Study of Privatization in Education, Teachers College.

Shanker, A. (1988a, July 10). Convention plots new course - A charter for change. *New York Times,* p. E7 (paid advertisement).

Shanker, A. (1988b). Restructuring our schools. *Peabody Journal of Education,* 65, 88–100.

Solman, L.C., & Goldschmidt. P. (2004). *Comparison of traditional public schools and charter schools on retention, school switching, and achievement growth.* Phoenix, AZ: The Goldwater Institute.

Speakman, S., & Hassel. B.C. (2005). *Charter school funding: Inequity's next frontier.* Washington, DC: Thomas B. Fordham Foundation & Institute.

Vergari, S. (2001). Charter school authorizers: Public agents for holding charter schools accountable. *Education and Urban Society,* 33, 129–140.

Viteritti, J.P. (1999). *Choosing equality: School choice, the Constitution, and Civil Society.* Washington, D.C.: Brookings Institution Press.

Weiher, G.R.. & Tedin, K.L. (2002). Does choice lead to racially distinctive schools? Charter schools and household preferences. *Journal of Policy Analysis and Management,* 21, 79–92.

Wells, A.S. (1993). *Time to choose: America at the crossroads of school choice policy.* New York: Hill and Wang.

Wells, A. S., Grutzik, C., Carnochan, C., Slayton, J., & Vasudeva, A. (1999). Underlying policy assumptions of charter school reform: The multiple meanings of a movement. *Teachers College Record,* 100, 513–535.

Wells, A.S., Holme, J.J., Lopez, A., & Cooper, C.W. (2000). Charter schools and racial and social class segregation: Yet another sorting machine? In R.D. Kahlenberg (Eds.), *A notion at risk: Preserving public education as an engine for social mobility* (pp. 169–222). New York: Century Foundation Press.

Wohlstetter, P., & Chau, D. (2004). Does autonomy matter? Implementing research-based practices in charter and other public schools. In K. E. Bulkley & P. Wohlstetter (Eds.), *Taking account of charter schools: What's happened and what's next?* (pp. 53–71). New York: Teachers College Press.

Wohlstetter, P., & Griffin, N. (1998). *Creating and sustaining learning communities: Early lessons from charter schools* (No. OP-03). Philadelphia, PA: Consortium for Policy Research in Education.

Wohlstetter, P., Wenning, R., & Briggs, K. L. (1995). Charter schools in the United States: The question of autonomy. *Educational Policy*, 9, 331–358.

25

Beyond the Rhetoric: Surveying the Evidence on Vouchers and Tax Credits

Ron Zimmer and Eric P. Bettinger

INTRODUCTION

Advocates for greater school choice have long hailed school vouchers as a mechanism for improving educational systems. These advocates argue that market incentives, created through the competition for students, can force all schools to be more effective and efficient while creating greater educational opportunities for low-income families and, possibly, increasing racial and socio-economic integration within schools.

Milton Friedman, who is largely credited with introducing the idea, originally proposed vouchers as a government-financed entitlement that students and their families could use to attend any school, including private schools (Friedman, 1955; 1962). Over time, support for voucher programs has made for strange bedfellows as conservative, pro-market advocates (including Friedman), Roman Catholic bishops hoping to reinvigorate parochial schools in urban cities, and more liberal-minded leaders of minority groups have advocated for the use of vouchers.

Voucher opponents, by contrast, argue that vouchers may exacerbate inequities in student outcomes. These opponents maintain that voucher programs can "cream skim" the best students and may increase inequities, especially if selection into voucher programs falls along racial or economic divides. Moreover, voucher programs reduce public school enrollments, thereby intensifying the fiscal strains already felt by public schools. Finally, these critics argue that vouchers can undermine the "common school" model, which instills common values for democratic citizens.

The debate over vouchers has heated up in recent years with the advent of publicly funded voucher programs in Milwaukee, Cleveland, and Florida. Questions about the efficacy and the constitutionality of voucher programs have dominated the policy discussion.[1] The surge in the number of foundations and philanthropists that provide private money for students to attend private schools has intensified. Moreover, tuition tax credits, as an alternative mechanism of providing public money for private schooling, have also spread across many states. Outside of the United States, voucher-like programs have increased in popularity; and while the motivation for these voucher programs differs from those in the United States, debates over these programs rage worldwide. In this chapter we examine many of the claims and counterclaims of the debate by surveying the research literature on both domestic and international programs.

While public funds in the form of grants and transportation subsidies have been provided to private schools in the U.S. for many years, we focus here on tuition support in the form of voucher payments, privately funded scholarships and tuition tax credits.[2] Thus, this chapter represents a bridge between the research on educational choice and the research on private/public schooling differences. Researchers have long been interested in identifying the effects of private schools on student outcomes (e.g., Coleman, Hoffer, and Kilgore, 1982; Evans and Schwab, 1995), and many researchers in discussing educational vouchers have focused on the private/public difference as a central component of large-scale voucher programs (e.g., Carnoy, 1998; Levin, 1998, 1999). In foreign countries, the distinctions between private and public schooling are often vague. In many cases, state governments provide substantial financial support and resources to private schools or to children who attend them (Toma, 1996).

We focus on differences in outcomes between students with and without vouchers. Some research has extended beyond academic and behavioral outcomes or the distributional effects of voucher programs and examined the effects of voucher programs on residential housing markets (Nechyba, 2000), on subsequent public support for vouchers, or lack thereof, (Brunner and Imazeki, 2006), and on who wins and loses under voucher programs (Epple and Romano, 1998, 2003). We discuss these broader effects to the extent that the studies shed light on the specific voucher programs that we review.

Ours is not the first review of vouchers programs. Gill et al., (2001), Levin (2002), and McEwan (2000, 2004) have all provided comprehensive and insightful literature reviews. Their reviews include the conceptualization of, and rationale for, voucher programs as well as the evidence of the efficacy of vouchers. This chapter builds on these reviews but focuses on the achievement and behavioral effects of vouchers on students and the effect these programs have on access and integration.[3] For a review of the competitive effects of voucher programs, we refer readers to the chapter by Gill and Booker within this volume. For a review of the cost effectiveness of voucher programs, we refer readers to Levin (2002).

CRITERIA FOR INCLUSION OF STUDIES

In recent years, a number of research studies have examined the effects of both publicly- and privately-funded voucher programs. In addition, a handful of studies examine tuition tax credits. In synthesizing this research, we have included virtually all of the tuition tax credit research, primarily because there has been so little research. For the more extensive voucher literature, however, we establish criteria for inclusion. Although these criteria are not exhaustive, they provide a framework for organizing and prioritizing lessons from the existing studies.

The first criterion for inclusion is the range of issues probed. The vast majority of the literature is limited to test scores, which makes it difficult to examine other outcomes. Although we highlight student achievement in this review, we also examine how vouchers change the behavior of voucher users and how they affect the distribution of students across schools by ability, race/ethnicity, and socio-economic status.

Second, we paid particular attention to the assumptions required to elicit the causal effects of the voucher program. When examining an educational intervention, researchers try to identify the effects of the intervention by comparing the outcomes with the intervention to those that would have occurred without the intervention. In this case, once a student uses a voucher, we cannot observe the performance of the student without it. Though there are a number of methods for addressing this problem (see McEwan, this volume), each approach is based on one or more assumptions. We draw more attention to studies where the identifying assumptions seem most plausible and lead to the clearest picture of what would have happened in the absence of the program.

Third, we consider the quality of the data utilized for the analyses. Data on voucher programs are difficult to find. Some researchers expend significant resources attempting to track the applicants to a specific voucher program. Other studies rely on school-level data drawing data from administrative records that may or may not fully represent the students in the voucher program. As the chapter by Bulkley and Bifulco in this volume illustrates with respect to the evaluation of charter schools, the ability of researchers to track individual students over time can greatly improve both the range of outcomes upon which it can focus and the likelihood that a study is informative.

Additionally, we should note that attrition, while not necessarily a criterion for inclusion, can be a problem in these studies and needs to be considered when evaluating the quality of the research. For instance, many voucher studies are able to track only 50 to 60 percent of students who originally applied to the voucher program. This level of attrition itself not only has important policy implications, but also can compromise the validity of the research. If the attrition is related to student outcomes, it can affect the ability of the research to identify the causal effects of the program.

STRUCTURE OF VOUCHER PLANS

Voucher programs differ greatly in their specific design. Much of this variation is related in part to the differences in the motivation for vouchers among the voucher advocates (Levin, this volume). For example, the business community and many conservatives believe that vouchers can increase efficiency through increased competition. Thus, advocates from this persuasion argue that voucher programs should have few regulations and restrictions, offer a flat modest voucher amount and make no provision for transportation and information (e.g., Friedman 1955, 1962). By contrast more liberal-minded voucher proponents argue that vouchers can promote equity by providing better educational opportunities to low-income families in inner-city schools. These proponents believe voucher programs should be means-tested, provide free transportation, require wide dissemination of information, strict regulation of admission policies, and require that state policy makers hold schools accountable for performance through testing of students (Jencks et al., 1970; Levin, 2002). Still, others see vouchers as a way to revitalize inner-city Catholic schools.

Ultimately, the differing motives of voucher advocates lead to large differences in the programmatic details of voucher programs. For instance, some proponents argue that the monetary value of the voucher should be higher for children from poor families than for those from higher income families or that eligibility should be restricted to poor children. Others may want to restrict the use of vouchers to nonsectarian schools or schools that charge tuition under a certain amount. Still others may want to assure that any voucher program does not reduce the financial resources available to public schools that lose students to voucher schools. In contrast, other more market-oriented proponents argue for a universal voucher program that would allow students to attend a wide range of private schools, including sectarian schools. These proponents would have the money specifically follow the student, which would have adverse financial consequences for the public schools and thereby spur them, at least in theory, to improve the quality of the education they provide.[4]

Any of these programmatic details could affect who participates in a voucher program and thereby influence the generalizability of individual programs and studies. For instance, programs that restrict participation to low-income students are likely to have different distributional effects than a universal voucher program. Also, programs that allow students to attend sectarian schools are likely to attract a particular set of students—specifically students seeking religious instruction opportunities. In addition, to the extent religious instruction affects the educational experience, this feature may affect outcomes such as student achievement, educational attainment, and other behaviors.[5] Furthermore, in voucher programs that adversely affect the financial situation of public schools that lose students to private schools, such schools may be induced to improve their performance. Finally, the scale of the programs may affect whether these programs will generate general equilibrium effects that may be even larger than the localized effects of voucher programs (e.g., Nechyba 2000; Epple and Romano, 1998, 2003).

Because the programmatic design can affect outcomes, our review highlights the details of each voucher program and the associated outcomes individually. We synthesize the results in the final section and provide a summary of the programs and outcomes in Table 25.1 and Appendix Table A25.1.[6]

DOMESTIC VOUCHER PROGRAMS

Domestic voucher programs have been funded either by public taxes or private donations, primarily through philanthropists or foundations. While the scale and regulation of public and private programs may differ, they are similar in that they both provide a subsidy for students to attend private schools.

Publicly-Funded Programs

The Milwaukee Voucher Program. The first large voucher program of note began in Milwaukee in 1990. With broad support from both liberals and conservatives, many advocates saw the Milwaukee voucher program as a way to extend greater educational opportunities to low-income students. As a result, vouchers were provided only to low-income students. Students could not attend sectarian schools, and available scholarships were capped at 1 percent of the total district population. From its inception, policy makers were interested in whether Milwaukee's program improved academic achievement and educational opportunities for low-income minorities. While the results have been highly debated, the general consensus is that the vouchers slightly improved student math test scores.

The first studies of Milwaukee's program came from researchers at Wisconsin and Harvard. Comparing the performance of voucher students to that of all other students in the Milwaukee school system, University of Wisconsin political scientist John Witte (2000) found no differences in test scores. In contrast, Harvard researchers, led by Jay Greene, Paul Peterson, and Jiangtao Du, found that the programs increased reading and math test scores. This finding emerged from a comparison of the outcomes for voucher recipients who had stayed in voucher schools for multiple years to outcomes for a comparison group of students who had wanted to use the voucher but could not because of a lack of space (Greene et al., 1997, 1998). The differences in results led to a spirited debate over the best and most accurate comparison group for the analysis. [7] The acrimony of the debate confused journalists, policy makers, and others interested in understanding the role and effects of vouchers (e.g., Mitgang and Connell, 2003).

In a widely lauded paper, Princeton economist Cecilia Rouse (1998) attempted to resolve the controversy. Rouse relied heavily on the fact that students who applied to oversubscribed schools were randomly selected for participation in the voucher program. Randomization is the "gold standard" in evaluative research (McEwan, this volume). Using statistical controls to take advantage of the randomization that occurred in a number of the voucher schools,[8] Rouse found slight positive significant effects of the voucher program in math test scores, but none in reading.

Policy makers also hoped that the Milwaukee experience would shed light on the impact voucher programs can have on access and racial integration. Research from the early years of the Milwaukee voucher program showed that the program generally attracted poor performing students from low-income families with a racial makeup similar to the district as a whole.[9] A 1998–99 school year survey of voucher parents also showed that 62 and 13 percent of voucher students were African American and Hispanic students, respectively, which was similar to the district population as a whole (Wisconsin Legislative Audit Bureau, 2000). However, these surveys also showed that the voucher parents had slightly higher educational levels (Rouse, 1998; Witte, 1996; Witte and Thorn, 1996) than other parents in Milwaukee. Overall, these studies suggest that the Milwaukee voucher program (at least in the early years) was attracting disadvantaged students, as intended.

While the early Milwaukee program offered insights to policy makers, the small scale of the program limited the policy implications. In 1995, the state of Wisconsin greatly expanded the scholarship cap and the range of private schools that students could attend. These changes dramatically redefined the scope of the program. While only 341 students attended seven private schools in 1991, by the 2004–05 school year over 15,000 students attended dozens of sectarian and non-sectarian schools (Gill et al., 2001). This expansion led some researchers to investigate whether Milwaukee's program resulted in changes in nearby public schools (e.g., Hoxby, 2001; see Gill and Booker, this volume).

Unfortunately, because the expanded program did not require testing within the private schools, no new studies of how the program has affected the achievement of the vouchers users have been possible. A recently commissioned study (funded by the Bradley and Joyce Foundations among others) seeks to re-evaluate the Milwaukee voucher program by having private schools voluntarily administer a standardized test. While the voluntary nature of participation may limit the interpretation of the results, it will provide the first insights of the impacts of the larger scaled Milwaukee voucher program on voucher recipients.

The Cleveland Voucher Program. A second major voucher program was initiated in Cleveland in 1995. Similar to Milwaukee's voucher program, support for Cleveland's voucher came from both ends of the political spectrum. Cleveland's program is means tested and focuses on students from the Cleveland Municipal School District, one of the poorest districts in the nation. The program was initially intended to allow vouchers to be used at sectarian schools; however, court decisions immediately blocked this provision. Not until many years later were students allowed to choose among both sectarian and non-sectarian schools.[10] Cleveland's program now serves over 6,000 students.

Cleveland's voucher program has not yielded clear answers about how the program affected student academic achievement. As in the Milwaukee program, the problem that arose with the evaluations was whether the researchers used an adequate comparison group. The primary evaluation (Metcalf et al., 2003) compared the academic achievement of voucher users to two groups of students: (1) students offered vouchers who did not use the vouchers, and (2) students who were not offered vouchers. For the second group, the researchers controlled for observable characteristics. Other researchers, including Gill et al. (2001), argued that the study failed to create an adequate control for students self-selecting into the program.

A later study by Clive Belfield (2006) tried to address this issue by comparing the performance of voucher students to students who applied but were rejected because they did not meet requirements, including the level of family income. Belfield acknowledges the limitations of this comparison group, but he suggests that it is better than the alternatives. Overall, he finds little effect from the voucher program on academic achievement, but again, the inadequacies of the control for selection calls into question the reliability of the results.

Another key motivation for establishing the voucher programs was to improve students' access to better schools. Kim Metcalf (1999) found that the vouchers were used primarily by minorities and students from low-income families. The mean income level of students utilizing the vouchers was $18,750, and these students were more likely to be African American students than a random sample of Cleveland students. As in Milwaukee, parents of voucher applicants had slightly higher levels of education (Metcalf, 1999; Peterson, Howell, and Greene, 1999). Nonetheless, the program is serving disadvantaged students, as intended.

Other Publicly Funded Voucher Programs. Voucher programs are also in place in Vermont, Maine, Florida and Washington, D.C., and recently Utah's state legislature and governor signed into law a new state-wide voucher program. However, researchers have not yet examined how these programs affect student achievement.

Tuition Tax Credit Programs

Another mechanism through which students could receive a public subsidy to attend a private school is an Educational Tax Credit (ETC). In describing ETCs, Columbia University researchers Clive Belfield and Amy Wooten (2003) note that existing credits have taken one of two forms: the state grants tax credits either to parents for education-related expenses or to individuals, groups of individuals or businesses for contributions they make to organizations that distribute scholarships for students to attend private schools. In the late 1990s, Illinois, Iowa, and Minnesota initiated tax credit programs. A few years later, Arizona, Florida, and Pennsylvania began similar tax credit programs.

Choice advocates argue that these programs generally have the same advantages as school vouchers and are less likely to be legally challenged because the funds are not directly transferred from the government. Opponents reply, however, that these programs divert money from state coffers while providing subsidizes to families who would have sent their children to private schools anyway. Such programs, they argue, would be disproportionately utilized by wealthier families, since they are most likely to have itemized tax deductions (if the subsidy is offered as a deduction instead of a credit).

In general, ETCs have not received much attention from researchers, and the research that has been done has not focused on student achievement. Instead, researchers have estimated lost state revenue or examined whether the programs are inducing new students to private schools or are simply subsidizing families that already made the choice of sending their child to a private school. Summarizing this research (including research by Frey (1983, 1991), West (1985), and Olsen et al. (2001)), Belfield and Wooten (2003) suggests that, as critics feared, ETCs have generally created subsidies for families that would have sent their children to private schools anyway. They state:

> ...for every student newly induced into the private sector by such a tax credit, there would be on average another 6 or 7 students who would have chosen the private sector anyway and receive the tax break as a windfall. States lose significant tax revenue when the number of new families taking advantage of this choice option is not substantial. (Belfield and Wooten, 2003, p. 2)

Moreover, studies in Illinois and Arizona suggest an overwhelming majority of the families claiming these tax credits are families with incomes greater than the states' median incomes. Belfield and Wooten also note that the research generally shows these programs lead to a significant decrease in state revenue. For instance, Belfield and Wooten highlight a study by Olsen et al. (2001), which estimates that a $500 tuition tax credit would cost the federal government over $600 million of revenue per year. A second study of the first four years of Arizona's tax credit suggests the program cost the state as much as $109 million in potential revenue (Wilson, 2002).

Overall, researchers have yet to examine the achievement, racial/ethnic integration, or competitive effects of ETCs, but they have generally shown that ETCs will lead to a decline in government tax revenue and that the subsidies would disproportionately be used by families already sending their children to private schools.

Domestic, Privately Funded Programs

Roman Catholic dioceses have provided scholarships to students to attend their schools for years. The use of philanthropists and foundation money for private school scholarships was first popularized by J. Patrick Rooney, Chairman of the Golden Rule Insurance Company of Indianapolis, who formed the Educational Choice Charitable Trust in 1991.[11] This trust allocated private scholarships to low-income students to use at private schools in Indianapolis. Other programs quickly sprouted in Milwaukee, Atlanta, Denver, Detroit, Oklahoma City, and Washington, D.C. The motivations for these programs vary by location. Some of the programs were established and financed by conservatives who wanted to either open up sectarian school options to more students or to create competition between private and public schools. Other programs (e.g., Oklahoma City) were funded by liberal voucher proponents who wanted to provide additional schooling opportunities for inner-city students.

In 1994, the Walton Family Foundation threw its support behind the movement by providing a $2 million grant to form Children's Educational Opportunity Foundation (CEO America) to support and create existing and new scholarship programs. In the next few years, the number of privately funded programs quickly expanded to dozens of urban areas across the country. Of these programs, one of the most ambitious was a CEO America program in San Antonio funded at $5 million a year for at least ten years. The program provided full scholarships to over 14,000 "at-risk" students, making it the largest privately-funded voucher program in existence at the time.

In 1998, after the rapid proliferation of these programs, the Walton Family Foundation, through a $100 million grant, formed the Children's Scholarship Fund (CSF), which went beyond giving scholarships to any one particular location. Rather, the program partnered with local funders to provide scholarships in cities across the nation. Due to high demand for these scholarships, in 1999 Walton provided an additional $30 million in funding, and in April of that year 1.25 million low-income students applied for 40,000 partial scholarships.[12] Over the last decade, more and more of the programs developed, often receiving very little national attention, making it difficult to know exactly how many of the programs currently exist.

Of these programs, CSF has received the most national attention partially because of its relatively large scale[13] and partially because its method of assigning private school scholarships is conducive to rigorous research utilizing randomization methods. To distribute scholarships equitably, CSF uses lotteries. The use of lotteries allowed researchers to use the randomized designs, that "gold standard" of evaluative research, and to compare students who participated in the lotteries to determine the effectiveness of these programs. Such studies have been carried out in Charlotte, Dayton, New York, and Washington, D.C., among other locations.[14] For each program, scholarship recipients and applicants in the city programs completed questionnaires and took the Iowa Test of Basic Skills (ITBS) at baseline and at annual follow-up sessions. While Greene (2000) did find a positive overall effect in Charlotte,[15] these studies have generally shown no effect for the overall student population. They have, however, shown some positive effects for African American students, who made up a small portion of the overall voucher recipients (Howell and Peterson, 2002; Myers et al., 2002).[16] [17] However, these results are not without controversy.

In 2002, Princeton economists Alan Kreuger and Pei Zhu reanalyzed the data from the study of New York's CSF program and found an insignificant effect for African Americans. Arguing that Howell and Peterson (2002) and Myers et al. (2002) excluded too many students from their analysis, Kruger and Zhu expanded the analysis by including students with missing baseline test scores. Krueger and Zhu (2002) also redefined who was African American. While the original analysis identified a students' race by the race of her mother, Krueger and Zhu identify as African American students whose mother or father are identified as African American. This more inclusive definition results in a scholarship effect size that is smaller than reported the one in the original study and is not statistically significant. In the end, whichever definition of African American students is used, the implications of the results, at best, would suggest that vouchers are having an effect on a very limited population.

Recently, economists Bettinger and Slonim (2006) examined the impact of the CSF program in Toledo, Ohio on non-academic outcomes. Before beginning their data collection, the researchers interviewed principals at schools where students could have used the voucher. They compiled a list of outcomes that educators felt that they were trying to influence. Using surveys and new methods from experimental economics, they attempted to measure the effects of the vouchers on traditional outcomes such as test scores and on non-traditional outcomes such as student and parents' levels of altruism, patience, and self-confidence. To test the effects of the voucher program on altruism, Bettinger and Slonim gave each student $10 and invited them to share some of their money with charities. In this context, they show that voucher recipients gave more to charities as a result of the voucher program.

While the achievement effects of voucher programs remain controversial, the types of students these programs serve are quite clear. Given that these programs were designed to target impoverished students, it is not surprising to find that participants have relatively low income. Peterson (1998), for example, found that the average income level of families of students participating in the New York scholarship program was only $10,000. The parents' education level of the participants, however, was slightly higher than the average level of the eligible population. In Washington and Dayton, Howell and Peterson (2000) and Wolf et al. (2000) found that the families of participating students had an average income level of $18,000. In terms of race, 100 percent of students participating in the Washington, D.C. scholarship program were minorities, while 95 percent of the students in New York were minority, mostly Hispanic students. In Dayton, the percentage of minorities was lower but was still 66 percent. This research also suggests that the participating students were well below the national averages in test scores (Wolf et al., 2000).

Finally, research has also found that these programs served a low percentage of special education students. For example, in New York, 9 percent of participating students have disabilities compared to the district-wide average of 14 percent of special education students (Myers et al, 2000). In Charlotte, 4 percent of participating students had disabilities, while the district wide average of special education students was 11 percent (Greene, 2000). The situation differs somewhat in Washington, where 11 percent of students were disabled compared to district-wide averages of 11 percent special education students (Wolf et al., 2000). In addition, the students using the vouchers may have less severe disabilities that are not taken into account in these comparisons.

While the research of the private scholarship programs raises some concerns of whether these voucher programs are fully inclusive of special education students, this research suggests that the programs have in general served generally disadvantage students as intended.

INTERNATIONAL VOUCHER PROGRAMS

There are a number of educational voucher or voucher-like programs across the world, including programs in Chile, Colombia, Sweden, Netherlands, Belize, Japan, Canada, and Poland. These voucher programs often differ significantly from the U.S. programs either in terms of the motivating factors or the policy context. For, example, many of the non-U.S. programs are motivated by the goal of increasing school attendance among girls or low-income students. Also, the relationship between church-sponsored private schools and public schools is less defined in other countries where, in many cases, religious groups operate public schools.

We focus our attention on two programs that have received the lion's share of attention from researchers and policy makers—Colombia's PACES voucher program and Chile's national voucher program. These two programs figure prominently in debates on the efficacy of vouchers.

Colombia PACES Program

One of the largest voucher programs in the world operated in Colombia from 1992 to 1997. The Programa de Ampliación de Cobertura de la Educación Secundaria (PACES) offered educational vouchers to over 144,000 low-income students thoughout Colombia. At the onset, the voucher program was fairly generous in that it awarded full private school tuition to secondary school students who wished to transfer from public to private school at the start of their secondary school experience. Over time, the value of the voucher did not keep up with the cost of inflation.

In contrast to the United States, where policy makers or private foundations espouse vouchers as a means of generating more competition between schools or as a way of providing alternatives to disadvantaged students in urban schools, policy makers in Colombia used vouchers to expand the capacity of the public school system. Most high school buildings host multiple high school sessions per day. For instance, one high school might meet in the early morning, another around mid-day, and yet another into the evening. Because most private schools were not overcrowded, Colombia established the voucher program as a means of taking advantage of excess capacity in the private system.

One of the unique features of Colombia's PACES program was its use of randomization in the assignment of vouchers. When the program was oversubscribed, each municipality held a lottery to determine which applicants received the vouchers. Researchers have made use of these lotteries to identify the effects of the educational vouchers by comparing voucher lottery winners and unsuccessful lottery applicants. The strength of this approach is that it provides convincing causal evidence of the effects of the voucher on the type of students who apply for a voucher. Whether these effects would generalize to other populations of students is not clear.

Using this approach, Angrist, Bettinger, Bloom, Kremer, and King (2002) find that within three years voucher students had completed about 0.1 years of schools more than their peers and had test scores about 0.2 standard deviations higher than those who did not receive vouchers. They also find that the incidence of child labor and teen-age marriage was lower as a result of the educational voucher. Based on follow-up research on students' high school careers, Angrist, Bettinger, and Kremer (2006) find that voucher lottery winners were 20 percent more likely to graduate from high school and had more behavioral problems and fewer resources than the academic schools that the voucher losers attended. Nonetheless, the voucher lottery winners in this group had better academic outcomes.

An alternative explanation for the better outcomes is that they reflect changes in student behavior associated with the incentives provided to the students. Students kept their voucher only if they were successfully promoted to the next grade (Angrist et al., 2002). Repeating a grade is fairly common in Colombia, and based on the behavior of voucher lottery losers, voucher winners who repeated a grade would likely have had to enter the workforce prematurely. The prospect of keeping the voucher and avoiding the labor market may have been enough incentive to encourage voucher winners to work harder than other students.

In Colombia, the evidence on the impacts of stratification is less developed and conclusive than the effects on achievement. Colombia's educational vouchers targeted low-income families living in the poorest neighborhoods, and Ribero and Tenjo (1997) reports that the vouchers were largely effective in reaching this population. However, applicants to Colombia's voucher program did not constitute a random sample of families from these neighborhoods. Voucher applicants came from families with higher educational levels than other families in the same neighborhoods (Angrist et al., 2002).

The Colombian voucher program was instituted to increase students' access to schools. No systematic research has evaluated whether Colombia's voucher program has actually improved access to education; as a result, it is unclear whether the voucher program increased overall enrollments among the most disadvantaged families.

Chile

In 1980, Chile embarked on an ambitious series of educational reforms designed to decentralize and privatize education. At the urging of Milton Friedman, who along with other prominent economists advised the Pinochet government at the time (Rounds, 1996), Chile established perhaps the world's largest ongoing voucher program. The program offered tuition subsidies to private schools. Only a small number of elite private schools did not accept the voucher, and new schools entered the educational marketplace in response to the voucher program.

The true value of the voucher has fluctuated not only with business cycles and inflation, but also by school. Prior to the reform, the federal government had subsidized many private schools by giving them about half of the per pupil amount that was spent on government-controlled schools. After the reform, these schools received the same amount as the public schools (Hsieh and Urquiola, 2003). Moreover, as part of the reform, the government decentralized public schooling. Instead of managing all expenses for public schools, the central government ceded control and began giving public schools a per student subsidy. Prior to the reform, the budgets of public schools were insensitive to enrollment; however, after the reform, local public schools lost money when students transferred to voucher schools.

Unlike Colombia, where vouchers targeted poor students, the Chilean system was available to all students. Additionally, unlike other programs that do not allow selective admission, voucher schools in Chile could admit the students they most preferred. As a result of these policies, Rounds (1996) found that the poorest families were less likely than other families to enroll their children in voucher schools.

Because of the nature of this admission policy, research on the efficacy of Chile's voucher program has been much more difficult to interpret than the Colombian research. Some of the early evidence suggested that voucher schools modestly outperformed public schools. This finding was common in many papers (e.g., Bravo, Contreras and Sanhueza, 1999; McEwan and Carnoy, 2000) but was sensitive to the types of controls included in the empirical model, the specific municipalities included in the sample, and the statistical methods used. McEwan (2001), for example, found that Catholic voucher schools tended to be more effective and productive than other schools, but only for certain specifications of the model. McEwan and Carnoy (2000) show that academic achievement is slightly lower in non-religious voucher schools, particularly when located outside the capital. Given that that these voucher schools have less funding, however, McEwan and Carnoy suggest that they could still be more cost-effective than public schools.

As research on the Chilean system continued, many researchers took note of the fact that the voucher program altered the composition of both public and private schools. For example, Hsieh and Urquiola (2003) show that after the reform began in 1981. The drop in public school enrollments was accompanied by a reduction in the average family income and the average achievement of the students who remained in the public schools. Thus, it was the more affluent families who transferred their children to the private sector following the reform. Hsieh and Urquiola suggest that this shift in student populations could account for the finding that private schools appear to be more effective than public schools. McEwan and Carnoy (2000) and Carnoy (1998) offer similar evidence that parents in voucher schools have higher incomes and greater levels of education than parents in public schools. In the early 1990s, many voucher schools began charging tuition in addition to the voucher, and the difference in parents' incomes and education levels between these tuition-charging voucher schools and the other voucher schools was significant (Anand, Mizala, and Repetto, 2006).

How this increased sorting across voucher and non-voucher schools affects student achievement depends on the nature of peer effects.[18] If improvements in peer quality lead to better educational outcomes for voucher users, then the sorting associated with the voucher program could improve their outcomes. At the same time, given the exit of high quality students from the public schools, the students remaining in those schools may have systematically worse outcomes because of the greater disadvantage of their peers. The aggregate effect of the voucher depends on the strength of these two effects.

Hsieh and Urquiola (2003) argue that the only way to identify the overall effects of the voucher program is to focus on aggregate outcomes because it is difficult, if not impossible, to remove the selection bias inherent in comparisons of different schools. The change in aggregate test scores reflects both the direct achievement effects for voucher recipients and the indirect effects for students who remain in public schools. When the authors look at changes in aggregate test scores throughout Chile, they find no evidence that the voucher program increased overall test scores. (See Gill and Booker, this volume, for additional discussion of this research.)

selection bias

Recent research by Gallego (2005) provides new evidence on the Chilean voucher program. Gallego notes that the number of Catholic priests existing in a community in the early 1950s can predict the number of and overall enrollment in voucher schools. This relationship arises because most voucher schools were affiliated with Catholicism both before and after the reform. Gallego (2005) uses this relationship to identify the effects of the voucher program. Specifically, he uses the number of priests as an instrument for the penetration of the voucher program in a specific market. His findings suggest positive effects of the voucher program on the academic outcomes of students throughout municipalities where the voucher program had more penetration. While the result may be indicative of competitive effects, it is driven in part by the effects of the program on voucher recipients. It echoes earlier research (McEwan, 2001; Carnoy and McEwan, 2000) which suggested that voucher schools affiliated with Catholicism had better outcomes than other voucher schools, public or private. As Carnoy and McEwan (2000) show, Catholic schools produced better students at a lower cost than other public or private, voucher schools.

SUMMARY AND CONCLUSION

Table 25.1 summarizes the achievement findings from both domestic and international voucher programs. The table highlights the location, program, methods used in the analysis, and their key findings.

Research on domestic voucher programs has produced inconsistent results. While advocates have often pointed to positive effects for African American students in the CSF program as proof that vouchers can work, the strength of these findings has been questioned–leaving many skeptical about the purported benefits of vouchers. International studies have also found mixed results. The evidence from Colombia indicates that voucher users have better academic and non-academic outcomes than they would have in the absence of the voucher. In Chile, the estimated effects differ across studies, and a number of confounding factors make it difficult to ascertain the true effects. Overall, behind the rhetoric of the voucher debate is a set of mixed results which is less bullish than voucher advocates hoped for.

The research generally shows that students who take advantage of vouchers are disadvantaged students, especially in voucher programs that are means tested and that specifically target such students.[19] Researchers have done a relatively poor job of examining how voucher programs affect the racial and economic integration of schools. Of interest to policy makers is not only the mix of students in the private schools chosen by voucher recipients, but whether the schools are more or less integrated than the schools that the voucher students previously attended. To shed light on this issue, researchers need to use longitudinal student-level data so that they can track the movement of individual students and explicitly compare the mix of students in the schools they leave and enter. In doing so, researchers could also examine more explicitly whether the availability of vouchers is "cream skimming." In addition, because voucher programs are typically small in scale, it is hard to generalize to large scale programs. For a program with massive movements of students, an important policy consideration is not only who is participating in these programs, but what happens to the racial/ethnic and ability distribution of students in public schools.

In sum, researchers have failed to come to consensus on the efficacy of vouchers as a reform effort. This murkiness may be clarified as new studies emerge, including studies of the current Milwaukee program and the federally-funded Washington, D.C. vouchers. Research needs to go beyond focusing on outcomes in isolation from the policy context. Previously, Levin (2002) and Gill and colleagues (2001) argued that policy context matters. To get at this issue, researchers may need to design grander experiments as suggested by a recent National Research report (Ladd and Hansen, 1999). Such experiments may need to be larger scale or be over multiple sites in which the design would allow variation in the voucher amounts, access to information, transportation provisions, and participation constraints. By varying these policy levers, we can gain a greater understanding of how policies affect outcomes.

Also, future research needs to peer "inside the black box" and to examine the mechanism in which outcomes differ among schools. Voucher researchers should take the opportunity to look at private schools that may be doing things differently and how the variation in the operation affects outcomes. Finally, we suggest researchers broaden their scope and go beyond student achievement or even distributional effects and examine other critical outcomes such as behavioral outcomes, educational attainment as measured by college attendance, wages, and cost effectiveness of these programs. Largely ignored by researchers is the question whether vouchers can be a cost-effective strategy.

It is also interesting to consider the value of vouchers programs relative to other forms of choice. When the idea of vouchers was first introduced, the only choices a family could make

TABLE 25.1
Summary of International Research on Vouchers

Voucher Site	*Authors*	*Measures Effects on*	*Identification Strategy*	*Key Results*
Milwaukee WI	Witte (1990)	Voucher Users	Regressions with Controls	No substantial effect
	Greene, Peterson, Jiangtao (1997, 1998)	Voucher Users	Quasi-experimental design	Significant effects in both reading and math
	Rouse (1998)	Voucher Users	Quasi-experimental design with covariate controls	Significant effects in math only and the effects grew over time
Cleveland OH	Metcalf (2003)	Voucher Users	Observational with covariate controls	No effect
	Belfield (2006)	Voucher Users	Quasi-experimental design with covariate controls	Little effect from the voucher program
Privately-Financed Voucher Programs (Children's Scholarship Fund)	Mayer et al. (2002), Howell and Peterson (2002)	Voucher Users	Randomization of Vouchers with Baseline Controls	Positive effects for black students only[20]
	Kruger and Zhu (2004)	Voucher Users	Randomization of Vouchers	No effect for any set of students, including black students
	Bettinger and Slonim (2006)	Voucher Users	Randomization of Vouchers	Little effects of the voucher program on student test scores. Increased altruism among voucher recipients.
Colombia	Angrist, Bettinger, Bloom, Kremer, and King (2002)	Voucher Users	Randomization of Vouchers	Positive Effects on School Yrs Completed and Tests
	Angrist, Bettinger, and Kremer (2006)	Voucher Users	Randomization of Vouchers	Positive Effects on HS Graduation
	Bettinger, Kremer, and Saavedra (2006)	Voucher Users at Vocational Schools	Randomization of Vouchers	Positive Effects on HS Graduation
Chile	Gallego (2005)	Overall System	Instrumental Variable for Voucher Presence	System-wide increase in test scores.
	Mizala and Romaguera (1998)	Voucher Users	Regressions with Controls	No Effects on Users
	Sappelli and Vial (2002)	Voucher Users	Heckman Selection Model	Positive Effects
	Rounds (1996) Hsieh and Urquiola (2003)	Overall System	Regressions with Controls; Aggregation	No system-wide increase in test scores
	Bravo, Contreras and Sanhueza (2000)	Voucher Users	Regressions with Controls	No Effects on Users. Effects Depend on Controls
	McEwan (2001)	Voucher Users	Regressions with Controls	No effects at most voucher schools
	McEwan and Carnoy (2000)	Voucher Users	Regressions with Controls	Mixed Effects but Private Schools more Cost-Effective
	Tokman (2001)	Voucher Users	Regressions with Controls	Mixed Effects Depending on Student Background

were sending their students to private schools without subsidies or choosing among various public schools based on residential location. However, over the last 50 years, a number of other alternatives have evolved including charter schools, magnet schools, and other inter- and intra-district choice programs. A relevant policy question has to do with the advantages and disadvantages of voucher programs relative to these other choice options, especially when many of these choice options are politically more feasible. In sum, we have much to learn about vouchers as a policy tool.

APPENDIX

Here, in this appendix, we list in table format the domestically-funded voucher programs, including educational tax credit programs. As part of the table, we list the location, type of program, who is eligible, how much the subsidy is worth, and the approximate number of students served.

TABLE 25A.1
Domestic, Publicly Funded Programs

Location: When it was started	*Type of program*	*Who is eligible*	*How much is the subsidy worth*	*Approximate number of students*
Vermont: 1869	Voucher	Students in grades 7-12, sometimes K-12, who live in areas too sparsely populated to support a public high school. Parents in these areas, called "tuitioning towns," receive vouchers to send their children to any approved public or private (non-religious) high school in state or out of state.	For government schools, the established tuition rate is used. Private (non-religious) schools set their own tuition, and the district pays either the average tuition for Vermont public high schools (approximately $5,000) or the private school tuition, whichever is lower.	There are approximately 90 "tuitioning towns." In 2001-02, 7,147 students participated.
Maine: Late 1800s	Voucher	All K–12 students who live in areas too sparsely populated to support a public school (sending towns) are eligible to receive a voucher to attend the public or private (non-religious) school of their parents' choice. "Sending towns" are towns that have the option of paying tuition to another public or private (non-religious) school instead of operating their own public schools. Out of 284 school districts, 145 exercise this option.	Public schools use their established tuition rate. Private schools set their own tuition, and the district either pays the average public high school tuition (approximately $5,000) or the actual private school tuition, whichever is lower.	Currently 14,185 children participate in the program; 5,933 attend private schools and 8,252 attend public schools

Location: When it was started	*Type of program*	*Who is eligible*	*How much is the subsidy worth*	*Approximate number of students*
Milwaukee: 1990 (expanded 1995)	Voucher	K–12 students enrolled in either Milwaukee Public Schools (MPS), the Milwaukee Parental Choice Program, grades K–3 of a private school, or not enrolled in any school the previous year.	The state of Wisconsin pays either the amount allotted per pupil for MPS or the voucher school's actual cost to educate a child, whichever is less, up to $6,351.	The program is open to 15%, about 15,000, of Milwaukee public school students. Currently, 7,996 children are enrolled in the program. In 205-06, students chose from about 125 private schools that are either religious or non-religious, five charter schools and over 150 public schools in Milwaukee.
Cleveland: 1995	Voucher	Any Cleveland student, grades K–6, who meets certain income guidelines. The program follows the child through eighth grade.	Scholarships pay either 90% or 75% of tuition, depending on family income, not to exceed $2,700 in scholarship money.	In 2004–05, 5,675 students enrolled in the Cleveland Scholarship Program. In 1999-2000, 56 private schools, 10 non-sectarian and 46 religious or parochial schools accept choice students. Students may also choose from 66 public schools and 16 magnet schools.
Florida: 1999	"Opportunity Scholarship" Voucher	All K–12 students who attend a public school that receives a failing grade for two years in a four-year period.	Children are provided roughly $3,400 to attend a better performing public or eligible private or religious school. Special needs children receive additional funds	By the 2004-05 school year, approximately 730 students were using the Opportunity Scholarships.
Florida: 2000	McKay Scholarship	Students with disabilities are eligible	McKay vouchers can be worth more than $20,000, depending on the severity of the student's disability.	By the 2004–05 school year, approximately 15,500 students were using McKay vouchers to attend private schools.
Florida: 2002	Tuition Tax Credit	Students poor enough to receive free or reduced-price lunches are eligible. The vouchers are awarded through private Scholarship Funding Organizations that collect the donations and issue the vouchers to students.	Approximately $3,500.	About 13,500 students used the tax credit vouchers in the 2005–06 school year.
Washington, D.C.: 2004	Voucher	Students must be from families with income no greater than 185 percent of the federal poverty level.	Up to $7,500	Approximately 1,700 students participated in the 2005-06 school year.

(continued)

TABLE 25A.1
Continued

Location: When it was started	*Type of program*	*Who is eligible*	*How much is the subsidy worth*	*Approximate number of students*
Minnesota: 1997	Tuition Tax Credit	All parents with students in public or private schools, or home-schooling, can benefit by claiming a tax credit or deduction when they invest in eligible expenses, including books, tutors, academic after-school programs, and, in the case of the tax-deduction, tuition fees at private or religious schools.	The state refunds income-eligible parents, via a tax credit, up to $1,000 per child ($2,000 per family) for approved educational expenses. Families can claim a tax deduction of up to $1,625 for elementary school students or $2,500 for secondary students.	The state estimates that 40,000 low-income families invested over $14 million in their children's education in 1998, the first year of the program. The average investment by a low-income family was $400. It is expected that more than 100,000 families claimed the tax deduction in 1998.
Arizona: 1997	Tuition Tax Credit	K–12 kids can receive school tuition help from money given to "student tuition organizations" (STOs). Taxpayers get a dollar-for-dollar refund for giving to STOs or to a public school.	STOs give varying amounts of student aid, usually 50-80% of tuition costs. Taxpayers receive up to $625 back for donating to an STO or $200 back for donating to a public school foundation	Over 500 students received tuition assistance during the 1998–1999 school year. This number is expected to rise dramatically in future years, as legal challenges have been settled in favor of the program. Eighteen student tuition organizations now receive and disperse donations for children's education.
Illinois: 1999	Tuition Tax Credit	All students in public, private, or parochial schools benefit from a tax credit when their parents invest in covered items including tuition, books and lab fees	The state provides a tax credit of up to 25% for education-related expenses exceeding $250 up to $500 per family.	

Note: We could not find information about overall usage and adoption of the Iowa and Pennsylvania Tax Credit Programs.
Source: Much of the information was derived from the Milton & Rose D, Friedman Foundation Web site at: http://www.friedmanfoundation.org/schoolchoice/theprograms.html

NOTES

1. In June 2002, the Supreme Court overturned a lower court decision that Cleveland voucher plan violated the Establishment Clause of the First Amendment (Levin, 2002). However, some state Supreme Courts have been less sympathetic to voucher programs. For instance, in 2006, Florida's Supreme Court stuck down the use of taxpayer-funded vouchers primarily because the state's constitution requires schools to be "uniform" and the justices viewed private schools to lack uniformity both among themselves and in relation to public schools (Toppo, 2006).

2. While school vouchers were originally envisioned to be certificates of entitlements, the programs that fall under the domain of vouchers have expanded over time. These include privately funded scholarships and educational tax credits. In general, throughout the document, we will use the word voucher when we are referring to these various programs.
3. A number of voucher studies focus on parental satisfaction among voucher schools (Howell and Peterson, 2002; Greene and Hall, 2001; Peterson, Campbell, and West, 2001). This literature is difficult to interpret since parental satisfaction is a significant predictor as to whether a family pursues an educational voucher. Not surprisingly, the general finding is that parents whose children are using the voucher tend to have higher levels of satisfaction than parents in the public sector.
4. Others, including John Coons and Stephen Sugarman (1978) along with John Chubb and Terry Moe (1990), suggested further alternatives.
5. Indeed, a large literature in economics has explored whether religious schools improve student academic achievement generally finding that these schools do create modest improvement in test scores (McEwan, 2000). Religious schools also expose students to different types of training, and many researchers have investigated whether religious schools reduce the incidence of disciplinary infractions, truancy, teen-age pregnancy, and other non-academic behaviors (e.g., Figlio and Ludwig, 2000).
6. Appendix Table A-1 focuses on domestically-funded voucher programs. A comprehensive list of currently operating privately-funded scholarship programs can be found at http://www.edreform.com. West (1996) contains a list of international voucher programs.
7. Even the control group in Greene et al. (1998) was somewhat contaminated by students who failed to win random assignment to the private school of choice seeking out alternative private schools and did not attend a public school (McEwan, 2000).
8. Rouse focused on African American and Hispanic students since the publicly available data permitted researchers to infer whether these students participated (and either won or lost) a voucher lottery at a participating voucher school.
9. The average family income of students participating in the program in the early 1990s was $11,600 and the test scores of these students were below the district average as a whole and for a sample of low-income students within the district (Witte, 2000).
10. In 2002 in *Zelman v. Harris*, the U.S. Supreme Court upheld the constitutionality of the publicly-funded voucher program in Cleveland.
11. To see more details about the development of privately funded scholarships, see Center for Education Reform's discussion at http://www.edreform.com/index.cfm?fuseAction=document&documentID=657.
12. It should be noted that these scholarships only fund a portion of the total cost of attending private schools and the families are expected to make up the differences. This was a conscious decision of CSF as they wanted families to have a financial stake in their decision.
13. CSF has provided over 70,000 scholarships nationwide.
14. One challenge these studies have had to address is attrition of the scholarship "winners" in the lottery assignments. A substantial portion of students that are randomly assigned scholarships never use the scholarships. Presumably, a portion of the scholarship "losers" would have also declined the scholarship offers. Therefore, comparing the performance of scholarship winners and losers through random assignment is complicated by not knowing who would have declined the scholarships in the group that was not assigned a scholarship. Two approaches of dealing with this challenge is to examine the effect of those offered the scholarship, whether they take the scholarship or not, to the control group (i.e., "intent to treat" analysis) or to use sophisticated statistical techniques to estimate the actual effect of attending a private school (McEwan, 2004).
15. It should be noted that the Charlotte study was for one year with no follow-up.
16. This effect was significant in all three years in New York and in the second year in Washington, though no significant effect was found in Dayton. Aggregating over the three cities, the effect of 0.28 and 0.30 standards deviations was significant in the second and third years.
17. Greene (2000) did not break out the effects by race.
18. The relationship between peer effects and educational vouchers has been explored in theoretical models presented in Epple and Romano (1998) and Nechyba (2000).

19. The important exception is in Chile where voucher users tend to have better socio-economic characteristics.
20. In Charlotte, the research suggested an overall positive effect, but the vast majority of students were black students. The authors did not break down the results by race.

REFERENCES

Anand, P., Mizala, A., & Repetto, A. (2006). Using school scholarships to estimate the effect of government subsidized private education on academic achievement in Chile. *NEP–Report on Central and South America*, September 16.

Angrist, J., Bettinger, E., Bloom, E., Kremer, M., & King, E. (2002). The Effects of School Vouchers on Students: Evidence from Colombia. *American Economic Review 92*(5), 1535–1558.

Angrist, J., Bettinger, E., & Michael Kremer (2006). Long-Term Educational Consequences of Secondary School Vouchers: Evidence from Administrative Records in Colombia. *American Economic Review 96*(3), 847–862.

Belfield, C.R. (2006). The Evidence on Education Vouchers: An Application to the Cleveland Scholarship and Tutoring Program. Available at http://www.ncspe.org/publications_files/OP112.pdf.

Belfield, C.R. & Wooten, A.L.. (2003). Educational Tax Credits for America's Schools" NCSPE Policy Briefing 3. Available at: http://www.ncspe.org/publications_files/PB03.pdf.

Bettinger, E. & Slonim, R. (2006). Using Experimental Economics to Measure the Effects of a Natural Educational Experiment on Altruism. *Journal of Public Economics 90*(8–9), 1625–1648.

Bettinger, E., Kremer, M., & Saavedra, J. (2006). How Educational Vouchers Affect Students – The Role of Vocational High Schools in Colombia. Case Western Reserve mimeo.

Bravo, D., Contreras, & D., Sanhueza, C. (1999). Rendimiento escolar, desigualdad y brecha de desempeño privado/público: Chile 1982–1997. *Documento de Trabajo* , Departamento de Economía, U de Chile, 1999.

Brunner, E.J. & Imazeki. (2006). Tiebout Choice and the Voucher. Working Paper. University of Connecticut Economics Department.

Carnoy, M. (1998). National Voucher Plans in Chile and Sweden: Did Privatization Reforms Make for Better Education? *Comparative Education Review 42*(3), 309–337.

Chubb, J.E., & Moe, T.M. (1990). *Politics, Markets, and America's Schools*. Washington DC: Brookings Institution.

Coleman, J., Hoffer, T., & Kilgore, S. (1982). Cognitive Outcomes in Public and Private Schools. *Sociology of Education* 55, 65–76.

Coons, J.E., & Sugarman, S.D. (1978). *Education by Choice: The Case for Family Control*. Berkeley, CA: University of California Press.

Epple, D., & Romano, R. (1998). Competition Between Private and Public Schools, Vouchers and Peer Group Effects. *American Economic Review*, 88, 33–63.

Epple, D., & Romano, R. (2003). Neighborhood Schools, Choice, and the Distribution of Educational Benefits, in: C. M. Hoxby (Ed.), *The Economics of School Choice*. The University of Chicago Press, Chicago, 227–286.

Evans, W.N., & Schwab, R. (1995). Finishing High School and Starting College: Do Catholic Schools Make a Difference? *Quarterly Journal of Economics* , *110*(4), 941–974.

Figlio, D., & Ludwig. J. (2000). Sex, Drugs and Catholic Schools: Private Schooling and Non-Market Adolescent Behaviors. NBER Working Paper No. 7990, November 2000.

Friedman, M. (1955). The Role of Government in Education. In *Economics and the Public Interest*, edited by Robert A. Solo. Piscataway, NJ: Rutgers University Press, pp. 123–144.

Friedman, M. (1962). *Capitalism and Freedom*. Chicago, IL: University of Chicago Press.

Frey, DE. (1983). Tuition Tax Credits for Private Education. An Economic Analysis. Iowa State University Press: Iowa.

Frey, D.E. (1991). Optimal-sized tuition tax credits reconsidered—comment. *Public Finance Quarterly, 19*, 347–354.

Gallego, F.A. (2005). Voucher-School Competition, Incentives, and Outcomes: Evidence from Chile. *MIT mimeo*.

Gill, B.P., M. Timpane, P.M., Ross, K.E., & Brewer, D.J. (2001). Rhetoric versus reality: What we know and what we need to know about vouchers and charter schools. Santa Monica, CA: RAND Education.

Greene, J.P. & Hall, D. (2001). *The CEO Horizon Scholarship Program: A Case Study of School Vouchers in the Edgewood Independent School District, San Antonio*. Washington, DC: Mathematica Policy Research.

Greene, Jay P. (2000). *The Effect of School Choice: An Evaluation of the Charlotte Children's Scholarship Fund*. New York: Center for Civic Innovation at the Manhattan Institute.

Greene, Jay P., Peterson, P.E., & Du, J. (1997). *Effectiveness of School Choice: The Milwaukee Experiment*. Cambridge, MA: Harvard University Program in Education Policy and Governance.

Greene, J.P., Peterson, P.E., & Du. J. (1998). School Choice in Milwaukee: A Randomized Experiment. In *Learning from School Choice*, edited by Paul E. Peterson and Bryan C.Hassel. Washington DC: Brookings Institution.

Howell, W.G., & Peterson, P.E. (2000). *School Choice in Dayton, Ohio: An Evaluation After One Year*. Cambridge, MA: Program on Education Policy and Governance, Harvard University.

Howell, W. G., & Peterson, P. E. (2002). *The education gap: Vouchers and urban schools*. Washington, D.C.: Brookings Institute.

Hoxby, C. M. (2001). The rising tide. *Education Next*, Winter (4), 69–74.

Hsieh, C., & Urquiola, M. (2003). When Schools Compete, How Do They Compete? An Assessment of Chile's Nationwide School Voucher Program, NBER Working Papers 10008.

Jencks, C., et al. (1970). Educational Vouchers: A Report on Financing Elementary Education By Grants to Parents. Report prepared under Grant CG 8542 for the U.S. Office of Economic Opportunity, Washington, D.C.

Krueger, A.B., & Zhu, P. (2002). Another look at the New York City school voucher experiment. Working Paper 9418. Cambridge, MA.: National Bureau of Economic Research.

Ladd, H.F., & Hansen, J.S. (1999). *Making Money Matter: Financing America's Schools*. Washington, D.C.: National Academy Press.

Levin, H. (1998). Educational Vouchers: Effectiveness, Choice, and Costs. *Journal of Policy Analysis and Management 17*(3), 373–392.

Levin, H. (1999). The Public-Private Nexus in Education. *American Behavioral Scientist 43*(1), 124–137.

Levin, H. (2002). A Comprehensive Framework for Evaluating Educational Vouchers. *Educational Evaluation and Policy Analysis, 24* (3), 159–174.

Metcalf, K.K., West, S.D., Legan, N.A., Paul, K.M., & Boone, W.J. (2003). *Evaluation of the Cleveland Scholarship and Tutoring Program*, Summary Report 1998–2002 Bloomington: Indiana University School of Education.

Metcalf, K.K. (1999). Evaluation of the Cleveland Scholarship and Tutoring Grant Program: 1996–1999. Bloomington, IN: The Indiana Center for Evaluation.

Myers, D., Peterson, P., Mayer, D., Chou, J., & Howell, W.G. (2000). *School Choice in New York City After Two Years: An Evaluation of the School Choice Scholarship Program*. Washington, D.C.: Mathematica Policy Research.

Myers, D. P., Peterson, P. E., Myers, D. E., Tuttle, C. C., & Howell, W. G. (2002). *School choice in New York City after three years. An evaluation of the School Choice Scholarships Program* (Rep. No. 8404-045). Princeton, NJ: Mathematica Policy Research.

McEwan, P.J. (2000). The Potential Impact of Large-Scale Voucher Programs. *Review of Educational Research*, 70(2), 103–149.

McEwan, P.J. (2001). The effectiveness of public, Catholic, and non-religious private schools in Chile's voucher system. *Education Economics, 9*(2), 103–128.

McEwan, P.J. (2004). The Potential Impact of Vouchers. *Peabody Journal of Education*, 79(3), 57–80.

McEwan, P.J., & Carnoy, M. (2000). The effectiveness and efficiency of private schools in Chile's voucher system. *Educational Evaluation and Policy Analysis, 22*(3), 213–239.

Mitgang, L.D., & Connell, C.V. (2003). *Educational vouchers and the media.* In Levin, H.M. *Privatizing education: Can the marketplace deliver choice, efficiency, equity, and social cohesion?* Boulder, CO: Westview.

Nechyba, T. (2000). Mobility, Targeting and Private School Vouchers. *American Economic Review*, 90, 130–146.

Olsen, DA, Lips, C., & Lips, D. (2001). Fiscal analysis of a $500 Federal Education Tax Credit to help millions, save billions. Policy Analysis #398, Cato Institute.

Peterson, P.E. (1998). *An Evaluation of the New York City School Choice Scholarships Program: The First Year.* Cambridge, MA: Program on Education Policy and Governance, Harvard University.

Peterson, P.E., Campbell, D.E., & West, M.R. (2001). *An Evaluation of the BASIC Fund Scholarship Program in the San Francisco Bay Area, California.* Cambridge, MA: Program on Education Policy and Governance.

Peterson, P.E., Howell, W.G., & Greene, J.P. (1999). *An Evaluation of the Cleveland Voucher Program After Two Years.* Cambridge, MA: Program on Education Policy and Governance, Harvard University.

Ribero, R., & Tenjo, J. (1997). University de los Andes, Department of Economics Working Paper.

Rounds, P.T. (1996). Will Pursuit of Higher Quality Sacrifice Equal Opportunity in Education? An Analysis of the Educational Voucher System in Santiago. *Social Science Quarterly*, *77*(4), 821–841.

Rouse, C.E. (1998). Private school vouchers and student achievement: An evaluation of the Milwaukee parental choice program. *Quarterly Journal of Economics, 113,* 553–602.

Toma, E.F. (1996). Public Funding and Private Schooling Across Countries. *Journal of Law and Economics, 39*, 121–148.

Toppo, G. (2006). Fla. Supreme Court strikes down school vouchers. *USA Today,* January 1, Available at: http://www.usatoday.com/news/nation/2006-01-05-florida-school-vouchers_x.htm?POE, accessed April 9, 2007.

West, E.G. (1985). The real costs of tuition tax credits. *Public Choice*, *46*, 61–70.

West, E.G. (1996). Educational Vouchers in Practice and Principle: A World Survey. http://www.worldbank.org/html/extdr/hnp/hddflash/workp/wp_00064.html#TofC19.

Wilson, G.Y. (2002). The Equity Impact of Arizona's Education Tax Credit Program: A Review of the First Three Years. Education Policy Research Unit (EPRU), Arizona State University.

Wisconsin Legislative Audit Bureau. (2000). *Milwaukee ParentalChoice Program: An Evaluation.* Madison, WI: Legislative AuditBureau.

Witte, J.F. (1996). Who Benefits from the Milwaukee Choice Program? In B. Fuller, R.F. Elmore, & G. Orfield (Eds.), *Who Chooses, Who Looses? Culture, institutions, and the unequal effects of school choice* (pp. 118–137). New York: Teachers College Press.

Witte, J.F. (2000). *The Market Approach to Education.* Princeton, NJ: Princeton University Press.

Witte, J.F., & Thorn, C.A. (1996). Who Chooses? Voucher and interdistrict choice programs in Milwaukee. *American Journal of Education*, *104*, 187–217.

Wolf, P., Howell, W.G., & Peterson, P.E. (2000). *School Choice in Washington D.C.: An Evaluation After One Year.* Cambridge, MA: Program on Education Policy and Governance, Harvard University.

26
Home Schooling

Clive Belfield

INTRODUCTION

Home-schooling represents perhaps the most radical reform of the U.S. education system (Lines, 2000). The ultimate form of privatization, the education of children who home-school is typically privately funded, privately provided, and largely privately regulated. In essence, home-schooling gives primacy to private interests in education over a broader public interest, with limited oversight and legal action by government authorities (Buss, 2000). With the development of the Internet, the distinction between home-schooling and distance learning has essentially blurred. Most distance learning takes place at home. Most home-schoolers use the Internet to obtain some instructional materials such as syllabi and curricula. Moreover, some home-schoolers receive instruction through the Internet; these students might be as accurately called "cyber-schoolers" rather than home-schoolers. So, as the "distance" aspect of distance learning is covered elsewhere in this volume (see rural schooling), the focus here is on home-schooling in all its forms. The efficacy of cyber or Web-based learning per se is not discussed.

Home-schooling is a diverse practice. It is not a discrete and determinate form of education provision, particularly when contrasted with enrollment at a public school, which has a formal governance structure and offers a definite pedagogy and standard curriculum, taught by a teacher as part of a regular instructional program fitted into the academic calendar. Indeed, home-schooling is sometimes lauded for not being "four walls education," with some families explicitly motivated by a desire to "unschool" their children (Stevens, 2001). Home-school regulations vary across states in terms of inspections, assessments, and legal status (Buss, 2000; Lambert, 2001).

But many families adopt some of the procedures of a school. They develop timetables or lesson plans and follow textbooks and curricula comparable to those in the local public school. Home-schoolers do use resources and facilities outside the home, including those of community and religious groups, but many also maintain some affiliation to a school by participating in school courses or activities on a part-time or temporary basis. Indeed, one-fifth of home-school families send their children to school for part of the day (NCES, 2001). A large proportion of home-schoolers are also cyber-schoolers, enrolled in a virtual school which may not be in their district or state and which may be publicly-funded under charter school legislation. Cyber-charter schools may offer instruction, tutoring, and assessments and at their most extensive operate almost as bricks-and-mortar schools do. In California approximately 1 in 6 home- schoolers is enrolled as a cyber-schooler in a virtual school (Collom, 2006); cyber schooling is also popular in Ohio and Pennsylvania.[1] Finally, many home-schoolers attend a regular school over their childhood, with the median home-schooling duration estimated at a surprisingly short, two years (Lines, 2002; Isenberg, 2002).

Counting the numbers of home-schoolers is not easy. NCES (2004) estimates the number of home-schoolers at 1.1 million by 2004, up from 800,000 in 1999 (NCES, 2001).[2] This figure—albeit imprecise—is considerably higher than the numbers of students in charter schools and voucher programs, reforms which have attracted considerably more academic attention, and it is significant given that private school, elementary, and secondary school enrollments are 5.3 million. But the home-schooling numbers are only approximate. Most authorities do require that home-schoolers declare their status outside the public and private systems, typically by submitting a document of notification. However, this requirement is not strictly enforced, is often voluntary, and there appears to be no incentive for home-schoolers to comply as penalties for non-compliance are unclear. The requirements and degree of enforcement also vary across states. Consequently, it is difficult to verify the accuracy of state administrative data on home-schooling.

Home-schooling has been legal across all 50 states since 1993 (Somerville, 2005, 137). Religious exemption from state school was legally affirmed in *Wisconsin v. Yoder* (1972), and this exemption has been extended beyond religious grounds. The first states adopted explicit statutes in 1982 and since then U.S. law has become considerably more favorable toward home-schooling. Non-public schools may be regulated, as established in *Pierce v. Society of Sisters* (1925), but they need not be. Presently in the U.S., both home-schoolers and private schools remain free of obtrusive regulation. The practice of home-schooling is increasingly being accepted across society: whereas in 1985, only 16t% of families thought home-schooling a good thing, by 2001 this figure had risen to 41% (Rose and Gallup, 2001, p. 46).

Finally, home-schooling is not distinctly American: most countries expressly permit or tolerate home-schooling. Glenn (2005) groups countries into those that: permit home-schooling without monitoring (Finland only); permit with monitoring (U.S., Portugal, United Kingdom, New Zealand, Chile, Russia, Australia, Norway, France, Iceland, Italy, and Belgium); generally forbid home-schooling (Spain, Greece, South Africa, Luxembourg, Switzerland, Israel, and Uruguay); and those requiring attendance at a school (Germany, Sweden, Argentina, and Brazil). As far as is known, international rates of home-schooling are low.

WHAT INFLUENCES THE DECISION TO HOME-SCHOOL?

Home-schooling families are not a homogeneous group. Early adopters of home-schooling have been described as either ideologues or pedagogues (Nemer, 2002): either they did not agree with what was taught in public schools or felt they could do a better job of educating their children themselves (Stevens, 2001). As described by Lines (2002, p. 1), relative to public school families, home-schooling families are "more religious, more conservative, white, somewhat more affluent, and headed by parents with somewhat more years of education." But other groups, dissatisfied with public schools and priced out of private school, are becoming involved.

There are two interlocking factors which strongly determine whether a family home schools. The first of these influences on the decision to home-school is the household's characteristics and, specifically, the opportunity cost of the mother's time. Because the mother is substituting for the school in providing education, the mothers' education and earning potential are important factors. Using micro-economic evidence, Isenberg (2003) finds a higher propensity to home-school where the mother's education is higher; the relationship holds for young children but not for older ones (for a more weakly positive relationship, see Belfield, 2004). However, the relationship between home-schooling and family income is complex. Home-schoolers do on average live in families with incomes above the median. But this probably understates the advantage to home-schoolers because the mother is typically not working and yet if she was the household income advantage would be even larger. However, at some point higher total household income will generate a preference for purchasing educational services rather than producing them. Isenberg (2002) finds that exogenous income, i.e., income earned by the father, is positively associated with private schooling rather than home-schooling (as does Belfield, 2004). Finally, larger families should prefer home-schooling over private as the former includes a large fixed cost—having the mother stay home.

The second factor is family preferences. As with private schooling, family religion has been identified as an important determinant of home-schooling (Stevens, 2001). Using data for Wisconsin, Isenberg (2002) finds Evangelical Protestants are more likely to home-school their children than other religious groups. In the sample of home-schoolers who took the SAT in 2001, Belfield (2004) finds almost 20% reported their religion as Baptist. However, the influence of family religion depends on the religiosity of the local community. Where a household's faith is represented in large numbers within the local community, private school supply may be available; this reduces the demand for home-schooling. It is where the household's faith is represented in small numbers within the local community that home-schooling is likely to be more desirable. The local religious community may offer formal or informal support to home-schoolers, e.g., by arranging community activities or providing lesson plans. But it does not have sufficient resources—at least in the short run—to set up a traditional private school.[3] As well as religion, differentiated tastes may play a role, including 'white flight' from the public school system, alienation from the public system, and family ideology (Fairlie and Resch, 1999). Stevens (2001) explores the various family circumstances associated with home-schooling.

Certainly, the decision to home-school will be affected by the quality of the alternatives, both public and private. Families may either face poor-performing public schools or have to pay a significant premium for property near high-quality public schools. Houston and Toma (2003) find that home-school families are responsive to the quality of public schools; in areas where public schools report poor academic results, home-schooling is more common. Private school options may also be very expensive or unavailable in rural locations, raising the likelihood of home-schooling. But, it is the confluence of household composition and instructional preferences which appear to dominate.

THE EFFECTIVENESS OF HOME-SCHOOLING

Few conclusions can be drawn as to the effectiveness of home-schooling. First, because it is a diverse practice it is not clear a priori what aspects of home-schooling might convey academic or cognitive advantages over public schooling. Advocates contend that small class sizes, flexible instruction without age-tracking, and dedicated teacher-parents should make home-schooling more effective than other forms of education. Home-school parents may exert more pressure or have higher expectations, both of which are typically associated with high achievement. However, educational outcomes may be skewed toward those on which the family has competence, and educational progress may be slow if there is no formative assessment or peer-pressure to learn. There is limited evidence to support or refute these arguments, although Cai et al. (2002) find home-school teacher-parents use more controlling teaching styles. Generally, because home-school families are motivated by idiosyncratic goals, it may not be appropriate to measure effectiveness using standardized metrics such as test scores. Thus, both the inputs and the outcomes are not easily identified.

Second, there are very significant methodological and empirical challenges in evaluating home-schooling. There are practical difficulties in obtaining data because in the majority of states, home-schoolers are either exempt from standardized tests or data is not recorded separately (even state-contracted evaluators have difficulty obtaining data, as reported for Pennsylvania by Huerta and Gonzalez, 2004).[4] Even with data, sample sizes are often too small for statistical inference particularly as to which aspects of home-schooling are most effective.

There are also several endogeneity biases. One is the general selection bias that arises in any form of school choice. Because different types of families choose the type of school they believe will be the most effective for their children, little can be inferred from their experiences about the impact of home-schooling for other children. The second is that of test-taking bias. Because test assessment is voluntary for home-schoolers, only those who anticipate doing well on the test will take it. This bias is significant: students may choose which if any test to take, when to take it, and under what conditions or level of supervision. This gives home-schoolers a sizeable advantage. Finally, as home-schoolers may have family characteristics that differ from other students, it is important to include controls for family background. For example, home-schoolers tend to be families with incomes above the median, and this should inflate their academic achievement. Yet there is a danger of over-controlling for family background. Some of the characteristics of the family are actually inputs into home-schooling: controlling for parental education is in effect the same as controlling for teacher education.

Notwithstanding, there has been some attempt to evaluate home-schooling relative to other options (Ray, 2005). Ray (2000) and Rudner (1999) review mean home-schooling achievement levels in language, reading, and math. They find relatively high scores for home-schoolers. But neither corrects for endogeneity bias or includes controls for family background. Also, Ray's data is based on survey response rates of less than 20% and Rudner's data is sampled from a single conservative college, with tests administered in the home. Belfield (2005) analyzes the SAT scores of home-schoolers. This yields a large sample of home-schoolers, but it also shows the extent of selection effects: based on the absolute numbers of home-schoolers, approximately three times as many home-schoolers should take the SAT compared to those who do take it. Home-schoolers obtain high SAT-Total raw scores, with a mean 0.4 standard deviations above public school students but 0.15 standard deviations below those in private-independent schools. Notably, most of the home-schooling premium comes from higher SAT-Verbal scores and not the SAT-Math scores (as also found by Rudner, 1999). After controlling for family background but not selection, there is no clear advantage for home-schoolers over public school students in the SAT-Verbal and some possible disadvantage on the SAT-Math. There is also some evidence that the gradient of test score differences by socio-economic status is sharper for home-schoolers.

Finally, there is evidence from comparisons of cyber charter school students in California by Buddin and Zimmer (2004). Some charter schools are nonclassroom-based or cyber-charter schools whose enrollees could be classified as home-schoolers. Buddin and Zimmer (2004) report that, of the charter school population, 17% of elementary school students and 41% of secondary school students attend nonclassroom-based charter schools. These schools spend considerably less per student on direct instruction, mainly because of lower spending on teachers. But in many cases they receive public funding that is equivalent, per student, to the amounts spent in regular public schools. The educational outcomes of such cyber charter school students are inferior, according to Buddin and Zimmer (2004): controlling for family background and personal characteristics, nonclassroom-based charter school students perform considerably worse in reading and math tests than other charter school students and public school students in California.

Overall, drawing conclusions from test score comparisons must be cautious. So far at least, the results from studies that are far-from-perfect are mixed: they do not indicate home-schoolers are at a significant disadvantage or advantage compared to public school students. But, there is very little information on the variance in achievement of home-schoolers to allow judgements about its equity.[5] Also unknown is the impact on other outcomes which might be valued by society, such as social cohesion or child welfare.[6] Information on college performance is also very limited: very few colleges have home-schooled enrollees and where colleges do have very high proportions, they tend to have very specific missions.

THE COSTS AND FINANCING OF HOME-SCHOOLING

Home-schooling entails a substantial change in household finances because the family is forgoing "free" public schooling. The largest economic change is that one of the parents (typically, the mother) will not be able to participate in the labor market. Given the average education level of the mother, this opportunity cost may be counted at $40,000 annually, not including health and pension benefits. However, as 4 out of 10 mothers do not work, there are many family circumstances such that staying home is worth this cost. If housework and home-schooling are strongly complementary practices, or if the family believes that the mother's responsibility is to raise the children, then the opportunity cost might be much lower.

A second additional cost is that the family will need learning materials and may need extra facilities. Assuming parents spend the same as a public school would do, this adds $1,000–$2,000 annually to the cost of education (Rothstein, 1995). Where families use local community resources such as church centers they may need to contribute either funds or in-kind. Offsetting these two costs, home-schoolers will save on transportation costs and they may purchase property in areas with relatively low house prices.

Government is heavily involved in education and so government policy will influence the incentive to home-school.[7] From the state perspective, the main issue is the extent to which home-schoolers are eligible for, and utilize, public subventions. For the state, a higher proportion of home-schoolers might yield a fiscal gain similar to that accrued when a student attends private school: the number of students and so expenditures is reduced but the revenue base is not. Of course, this does not apply where home-schoolers enroll in nonclassroom-based charter schools unless these schools are substantially more efficient. This fiscal saving will be reduced by several factors. Home-schoolers are entitled to use public school resources on a part-time or temporary basis; legally, they cannot be barred from access to the public school system. Regulation and monitoring of home-schooling may impose additional costs on the state. Also, home-schoolers may claim tax credits and tax deductions at a higher rate. Little is known about the extent to which these cost items offset each other, but it seems likely that school district or state finances are not dramatically affected by increased numbers of home-schoolers.[8] Thus, there appears to be little incentive to publicly fund home-schooling or any willingness by home-schoolers to accept government funding.

Moreover, it would seem very difficult to include home-schoolers in any accountability statutes that governments might impose. Home-schoolers who are enrolled in cyber-charter schools are already included in accountability statutes because the charter school is a public school. But other home-schoolers, as with private school students, are exempt from 'No Child Left Behind' mandates and as noted above state regulations are light. But tightening accountability for home-schoolers would be very challenging. First, it is unclear what educational standard home-schoolers should be held to. In general, states impose educational requirements on schools in regard to attendance, teacher quality and certification, facilities, and curricula. Schools are then evaluated in terms of outcomes that are in some sense a function of the required inputs. For home-schoolers who learn at home, these input requirements are very much weakened: attendance is expected to match that of a school calendar; teacher-parents may—but often need not—be educated to college level; and home facilities and curricula are not regulated. Second, it may be impractical to test home-schoolers to ensure accountability. Home-schoolers may not be registered within a school district and there is only a small incentive for them to participate in state-imposed tests. Third, the consequences of accountability mandates for home-schooler are not straightforward. Schools are typically held accountable. Yet if a home-schooler fails to meet a state standard, it is not clear what actions by the family or by the state would follow. Given the low level of state funding that home-schoolers receive, they are in a similar position to a private school: accountability is assumed by virtue of parental choice of this form of education. Moreover, given their relatively affluent family backgrounds, home-schoolers who choose to take tests are likely to do sufficiently well in terms of raw scores. Whether home-schooling is relatively effective in meeting accountability mandates will not be identifiable with such unadjusted metrics.

CONCLUSIONS

Home-schooling represents an expansion of educational options in terms of how children are educated. Indeed, all aspects of the educational process—including access, administration, use of teacher and physical resources, and assessment—may be chosen openly by the family, such that the education process may be fully liberated. Such opportunities will be attractive to some parents, even for a short duration; and especially where families are able to negotiate with their public school for tailored home-based education. Also, if the broader purpose of education is to create a diverse society, then an array of choices may be socially desirable. Given that home-schooling families do not receive public funds or receive fewer funds than with full-time enrollment, this independent choice has considerable persuasive power. Politically, the home-schooling community is well-organized and influential as a 'single-issue' constituency, i.e., their support is heavily contingent on policy makers' positions about home-schooling.

The debate over home-schooling will grow more intense if home-schooling grows. Such growth will depend on several factors.

First, home-schooling epitomizes freedom of choice as to how education is provided. It may be devised to satisfy many preferences and because existing regulations are either light or lightly enforced the decision to home-school is relatively easy.[9] Although full home-schooling is limited to families with substantial home resources, short-term or part-time home-schooling is an option for many. (It is also more common for two-parent families.) Families may appreciate such freedom particularly when it is compared to the inflexible public system. Change in public education is extremely slow: both institutionally and in terms of pedagogy, educational systems are remarkably unchanged over the last century. (There is considerable debate over the forces that create such inertia and whether it is deleterious or not, but little disagreement that it exists.)

Second, the growth of home-schooling may depend on social acceptance, which thus far appears to be increasing. But this social acceptance is largely devoid of any evidence base. In some countries (such as Spain), high-profile child abuse cases made home-schooling much less tolerated. Social attitudes may also change if home-schoolers receive more public funds, particularly through low-performing cyber-charter schools. But without a significant change in education funding toward per-student vouchers or greater use of tax credits and deductions, increased public financing of home-schooling seems unlikely. The result is likely to be stability: additional funding for home-schooling will only be available if home-schooling is made more accountable, but home-schoolers will likely refuse any funding that is tied to accountability.

Finally, where home-schooling appears to be effective for the individual child in terms of academic achievement then other families will adopt the practice. On this last issue, however, much more high quality evidence needs to be collected as very little about its effectiveness is known.

NOTES

1. Furthermore, some home-schools may be charter schools even if they are not cyber-based. Two states explicitly allow home-school charter schools (27 explicitly prohibit them). Detailed discussion is given by Huerta and Gonzalez (2004).
2. These estimates use the 1999 and 2003 National Household Education Surveys (NHES99, NHES2003). There were 270–285 home-school respondents, which is aggregated to derive a national estimate reported by Bielick et al. (2001). Based on how the NHES99 classifies siblings' schooling, Isenberg (2002) derives a corrected, higher figure, at 2% of all students. Advocacy agencies report higher numbers, at 1.7–2.0 million home-schoolers by 2002 (McDowell and Ray, 2000; for earlier estimates, see Bauman, 2002). Census data are not adequate because questions about home-schooling are not asked.
3. This non-linearity may explain why Houston and Toma (2003) find no statistically significant effect of religion on the decision to home-school. However, Isenberg (2002) finds Evangelical Protestants are more likely to home school, and the rate declines with growing representation in the district
4. The ideal source would be state or district-level data in states where test information is required. However, review of the data available across nine states with high regulation of home-schooling yields very limited information. In five of these states home-school students are not required to take state assessments or their results are not recorded.
5. Home-schooling clearly weakens the opportunity for a community to guarantee or verify that children obtain a reasonable level of education or personal well-being. From society's perspective these parental preferences cannot be taken as given. Moreover, although family resources are the main determinant of all children's education, for home-schoolers they become almost the only determinant. Home-schooling may therefore entrench intergenerational attributes, such that highly educated or wealthy families transfer resources to their children most effectively.
6. Critics argue that home-schooling reduces the social benefits of education (Reich, 2002). It may separate children from their peers, impairing identity formation and an appreciation of social values and norms (e.g., if it elides into indoctrination; see Buss, 2000). In rebuttal, home-schooling need not be isolating: home-schoolers go to school and may have strong ties to their local (religious) community (Medlin, 2000). It need not be incompatible with public values: some home-schooling parents would like public schools to teach communitarian values more intensely. Also, where education is intended to create a diverse society, then a plurality of educational options should be promoted.
7. In terms of eligibility, government policy and legislation will determine who can home-school. Currently, eligibility is extremely broad (to include parents who may not have graduated from high school, for example). In terms of regulation and support services, government places only limited burdens on home-schoolers.
8. The state may also care about the efficiency of home-schooling, i.e., achievement relative to cost. However, as noted above, there are many difficulties in measuring achievement and attributing its levels to home-schooling practices.
9. Reich (2005) argues for basic regulations, including registration, an explicit curriculum, and testing, but it is likely that home-schoolers will oppose these regulations and successfully campaign against them.

REFERENCES

Belfield, C.R. (2004). Modeling school choice: Comparing public, private, and home-schooling enrollment options. *Educational Policy Analysis Archives*, April.

Belfield, C.R. (2005). Home schoolers: How well do they perform on the SAT for college admissions? In Cooper, B.S. (Ed.) *Home-schooling in Full View* (pp. 167–178). Greenwich, CT: Information Age.

Buddin, R. and Zimmer, R. (2004). Charter schools: A complex picture. *Journal of Policy Analysis and Management*, 24, 351–371.

Buss, E. (2000). The adolescent's stake in the allocation of educational control between parent and state. *University of Chicago Law Review*, 67, 1233–1289.

Cai, Y., Reeve, J., and Robinson, D.T. (2002). Home schooling and teaching style: Comparing the motivating styles of home school and public school teachers. *Journal of Educational Psychology*, 94, 372–380.

Collom, E. (2006). The 'ins' and 'outs' of home schooling. The determinants of parental motivations and student achievement. *Education and Urban Society*, 37, 305–335.

Collom, E. and Mitchell, D.E. (2005). Home schooling as a social movement: Identifying the determinants of homeschoolers' perceptions. *Sociological Spectrum*, 25, 273–305.

Fairlie, R. W. and Resch, A. M. (2002). Is there white flight into private schools? Evidence from NELS. *Review of Economics and Statistics*, 84, 21–33.

Glenn, C.D. (2005). Homeschooling: Worldwide and compulsory state education. In Cooper, B.S. (Ed.) *Home-schooling in Full View* (pp. 45–68). Greenwich, CT: Information Age .

Houston, R.G. and Toma, E.F. (2003). Home-schooling: An alternative school choice. *Southern Economic Journal*, 69, 920–935.

Huerta, L. and Gonzalez, M. (2004). Cyber and home charter schools: How states are defining new forms of public schooling. Working paper, National Center for the Study of Privatization in Education, Teachers College, Columbia University.

Isenberg, E. (2002). Home schooling: School choice and women's time use. Working Paper, Washington University.

Lambert, S.A. (2001). Finding the way back home: Funding for home school children under the Individuals with Disabilities Education Act. *Columbia Law Review*, 101, 1709–1729.

Lines, P. (2002). Support for home-based study. *Eric Clearinghouse on Educational Management*, University of Oregon.

Medlin, R.G. (2000). Home schooling and the question of socialization. *Peabody Journal of Education*, 75, 107–123.

Nemer, K. M. (2002). Understudied education: Toward building a home-schooling research agenda. Working Paper, NCSPE, http://www.ncspe.org/publications_files/114_OP48.pdf

Ray, B.D. (2000). Home schooling: The ameliorator of negative influences on learning? *Peabody Journal of Education*, 75, 71–106.

Ray, B.D. (2005). A homeschool research story. In Cooper, B.S. (Ed.) *Home-schooling in Full View* (pp. 1–20). Greenwich, CT: Information Age .

Reich, R. (2002). The civic perils of homeschooling. *Educational Leadership*, 59, 56–59.

Reich, R. (2005). Why homeschooling should be regulated. In Cooper, B.S. (Ed.) *Home-schooling in Full View* (pp. 109–120). Greenwich, CT: Information Age .

Rose, L.C. and Gallup, A.M. (2001). *33rd Poll of the Public's Attitudes toward the Public School*,. http://www.pdkintl.org/kappan/kimages/kpoll83.pdf

Rothstein, R. (1995). *Where's the Money Gone?* Washington, DC: Economic Policy Institute.

Rudner, L.M. (1999). Scholastic achievement and demographic characteristics of home-school students in 1998. *Education Policy Analysis Archives*, 7, 8.

Somerville, S. (2005). Legal rights for homeschool families. In Cooper, B.S. (Ed.) *Home-schooling in Full View*. Greenwich, CT: Information Age.

Stevens, M.L. (2001). *Kingdom of Children. Culture and Controversy in the Home-Schooling Movement*. Princeton, NJ: Princeton University Press.

Welner, K.M. and K. Welner. (1999). Contextualising home-schooling data. A response to Rudner. *Education Policy Analysis Archives*, 7, 13.

27

Education Management Organizations

Gary Miron

INTRODUCTION

This chapter examines one of the fastest growing and increasingly controversial forms of privatization in education—contracting out the management and operation of public schools to private companies called education management organizations (EMOs). The growth and prevalence of EMOs is occurring against the backdrop of a larger movement toward the privatization of education services. Many of these other forms of privatization have been examined in other chapters within this handbook. Proponents of EMOs claim that they will bring a much needed dose of entrepreneurial spirit and a competitive ethos to public education. Opponents worry that outsourcing to EMOs will result in already limited school resources being redirected for service, fees and/or profits for yet another layer of administration.

Increasingly, over the last 15 years, public schools have contracted with privately owned companies for goods and services such as food for school lunches, buses for transportation, janitorial services, and support services for children with special needs. This form of contracting, guided by strict rules and regulations, has generally been accepted. While unions that represent affected employee groups have raised questions, contracting practices by school boards are not generally seen as relinquishing control or ownership of the school.

Since the early 1990s, contracting to private companies has evolved to contracts for the complete management and operation of public schools, including responsibility for recruiting and admitting students. This latest trend toward full service management companies has been widely debated and contested.

DEFINING AN EDUCATION MANAGEMENT ORGANIZATION

An education management organization is a private organization or company that manages public schools—either district schools or charter schools. A contract is prepared to hand over executive authority to run one or more school in exchange for a commitment to produce measurable outcomes within a given time frame. Ideally, this contract arrangement assumes that an EMO will do a better job with the same or fewer resources.

Groups promoting private management of public schools have sought to use other names or labels for EMOs such as education service providers, perhaps because they wish to avoid the obvious association with HMOs.[1] Because the term "education management organization" and the acronym "EMO" are most commonly used to describe these private organizations that operate public schools under contract, this name will be used throughout the chapter.

An important distinction should be made between EMOs that have executive authority over a school and partial service contractors (also known as à la carte management companies) that are referred to as "vendor." Vendors provide specific services for a fee such as accounting, payroll and benefits, transportation, financial and legal advice, personnel recruitment, and special education.[2]

EMO Management Fees

The contracts between school boards and EMOs specify the actual services and responsibilities of the EMOs as well as the fees to be paid to them. The fees paid to EMOs vary considerably, depending on the scope and nature of the services provided. Typically, management fees are about 10 to 15 percent of revenues. Some companies establish a per-pupil fee, but these typically still result in a fee that is equivalent to 10 to 15 percent of total revenues. Beyond the actual management fee, EMOs often receive additional funds to pay for administrators and/or instructional staff who work at the school or rent/lease from the facility and equipment when these are owned by the EMO.

Some of the larger full-service EMOs simply guarantee the school board that hired them a positive year-end balance. In this group, National Heritage Academies (NHA) is unique in that it requests all revenues as its gross management fee but promises to reserve 2 percent of the state aid for the board to spend at its discretion (National Heritage Academies, 2005). NHA, in turn, is responsible for paying for all services and education programs specified in the contract, including the facility lease. The company retains all money remaining after paying for the specified services.

Revenues available for operating schools and paying management fees are dependent on the overall state funding formula for charter schools. Although charter school funding is largely non-negotiable, some EMOs have been successful in negotiating higher per pupil funding from states or districts for contract schools. Edison Schools Inc., for example, has negotiated extra revenues before or after signing contracts to manage schools in a number of sites, including Philadelphia and Chester, Pennsylvania, and Dallas.

Types of Education Management Organizations

EMOs vary on a number of dimensions, such as whether they have for-profit or nonprofit status, whether they work with charter schools or district schools, or whether they are a large national franchise or single-site operator.

For-Profit vs. Nonprofit Status. Most EMOs are private, for-profit organizations. The largest and most recognizable for-profit EMOs include the following companies, which are rank ordered by the number of schools they operate: Edison Schools Inc., National Heritage Academies, the Leona Group, White Hat, Mosaica, and Imagine Schools.[3] All of these companies manage at least 30 schools and typically have substantial financial resources that allow them to help schools leverage loans or purchase facilities. The Education Policy Studies Laboratory at Arizona State University publishes an annual review of the for-profit EMOs (see Molnar, Garcia, Bartlett & O'Neill, 2006).

Although no comparable inventory of nonprofit EMOs is available, it is reasonable to assume that they are fewer in number and that most of them operate only one or two schools each.

In Michigan, for example, three nonprofit EMOs manage a total of four charter schools (Miron & Nelson, 2002). In other parts of the nation, there are three, quite large nonprofit EMOs that are expanding. Aspire Public Schools in California operates more than 15 charter schools, Constellation Community Schools in Ohio operates nearly a dozen charter schools, and Green Dot Public Schools manages ten schools in the Los Angeles area.[4]

Not included within the definition of an EMO are various community groups, many of which are nonprofits that assist and support many charter schools (Wohlstetter, Malloy, Hentschke, & Smith, 2004). Agreements between charter schools and these community groups differ from the contractual obligations and remuneration associated with the EMO contracts. Further, in a number of states, notably Pennsylvania (Miron, Nelson, & Risley, 2002) and New York (Ascher, Echazarreta, Jacobowitz, McBride, & Troy, 2003), various nonprofit community foundations or organizations have established charter schools as extensions of their community service. In nearly all of these cases, the community organizations do not assume executive or contractual authority to operate the school and thus are not considered EMOs, although they do seek to have extensive representation on governing boards. In many cases community organizations provides back office support for the school.

Charter Schools or Contract Schools. EMOs can work with district schools and/or charter schools. Charter schools are a new form of public school—a hybrid that mixes elements of traditional public schools such as universal access and public funding with elements usually associated with private schools such as parental choice and school autonomy (see chapter by Bulkley and Bifulco, this volume, for more information). The traditional public schools operated by EMOs are commonly referred to as contract schools.

The first EMOs predated charter schools; they focused on district schools that they could operate under contract from a district school board. For example, Education Alternative Inc. was under contract to operate schools in Miami; Baltimore; and Hartford, Connecticut, in the early 1990s. Edison Schools Inc. was founded in 1992 just as the charter school idea was taking form. Edison initially planned to set up a system of private schools but soon changed its focus to public schools. Until about 2000, about half of the schools Edison operated were contract schools and half were charter schools. Since 2000 the proportion of charter schools operated by Edison dropped sharply as it increased contractual relationships with contract schools.

There are advantages and disadvantages to operating both charter schools and contract schools. EMOs have greater autonomy in operating charter schools. This is particularly important when it comes to the power to hire and fire teachers and set compensation levels. Working with contract schools, EMOs often must deal with local bargaining units. An important advantage with contract schools is that EMOs can sometimes negotiate higher levels of revenues, while in charter schools the funding is fixed. With charter schools, EMOs are often burdened with securing a facility, while with contract schools, the EMO takes over an existing school including its facility. Finally, while EMOs must devote resources to marketing and recruitment of students in charter schools, this is not required in contract schools, since the schools already have enrolled students.

About 20 percent of all charter schools across the country are operated by for-profit EMOs. Although they were designed to be autonomous and locally run alternatives to rigid school district bureaucracies, charter schools have provided a new entry point for private management companies, many of which run their schools from faraway corporate headquarters.

Among the major problems administrators faced in start-up charter schools were being overwhelmed with paperwork, securing facilities, financial management, and overall lack of resources. These are some of the key areas in which EMOs provide assistance.

Multiple School vs. Single-Site Operator. Most media attention is given to the large EMOs that operate numerous schools in two or more states. Molnar et al. (2006) identified 14 for-profit EMOs that managed 10 or more schools, nine EMOs that managed between four and nine schools, eight EMOs that managed between two and three schools, and 20 EMOs that were single-site operators. The number of single-site operators is likely to be a rather low estimate since decisions by founders or administrators of charter schools to create their own EMOs are not often reported in the media, and not always reported to oversight or regulatory agencies.

While information on the large EMOs is substantial through their annual reports and marketing materials or through reviews prepared by policy analysts (see, Gill, Hamilton, Lockwood, Marsh, Zimmer, Hill, & Pribesh, 2005; Saltman, 2005) or practitioners (Wilson, 2006; Whittle, 2006), little is written on the single-school operators. Arizona and Michigan appear to be the two states where single-site operators have become rather prevalent.[5] In some cases, single-site EMOs have branched out to start a second or third school, but this is the exception. In Michigan alone single-school EMOs are estimated to be operating close to 30 charter schools (Miron & Nelson, 2002).

It is worth looking closely at the single-site EMOs because they provide a mechanism for private ownership of public charter schools. Many private schools that convert to public charter schools create their own EMO to resume or restore ownership and control of the charter school to the original owners of the private school. Also, some of the so-called mom- and pop-operated charter schools have sought to create their own family run EMO, which essentially takes over ownership of facilities.[6]

Information regarding the operation and internal working of EMOs is proprietary with few requirements for disclosure, thus limiting academic research on this topic. Although some EMOs disseminate a lot of information about operation and performance, that information is largely marketing material and is not covered in this review. Many EMOs are guarded about sharing information about their companies. In some cases, state agencies and authorizing agents[7] that sponsor the schools are not aware of the existence of EMOs. This chapter focuses on the large EMOs for which the greatest amount of research and information is available.

HISTORY AND GROWTH OF EMOS

The number of EMOs and their share of the education market have expanded rapidly, both in the charter school sector and, increasingly, in struggling school districts. Molnar (2001) cited a number of sources from EMO advocates, practitioners and investment industries that suggested that EMOs hope or expect to be operating as much as 10 percent of all K–12 education by 2010 or 2015. Chris Whittle, founder of Edison Schools Inc., calls for 100 percent of public schools to be privately managed by 2030.

Currently, more than 60 EMOs are operating schools in the United States. This accounts for about 20 percent[8] of the total number of charter schools and about a quarter of all charter school enrollments. In terms of numbers of schools, district school boards have contracted out management of more than 75 traditional public schools to EMOs. Close to 500 charter school boards have contracted out their schools to EMOs, making this the preferred entry point for private EMOs.[9] It is estimated that EMO-operated schools serve close to a quarter million students in the United States. Edison Schools Inc. has remained the largest EMO since its creation in the early 1990s. It currently operates about 80 schools with a student enrollment of approximately 50,000. Figure 27.1 illustrates the growth in the number of schools operated by EMOs in the United States.

The expansion of private, for-profit EMOs operating charter schools has progressed more

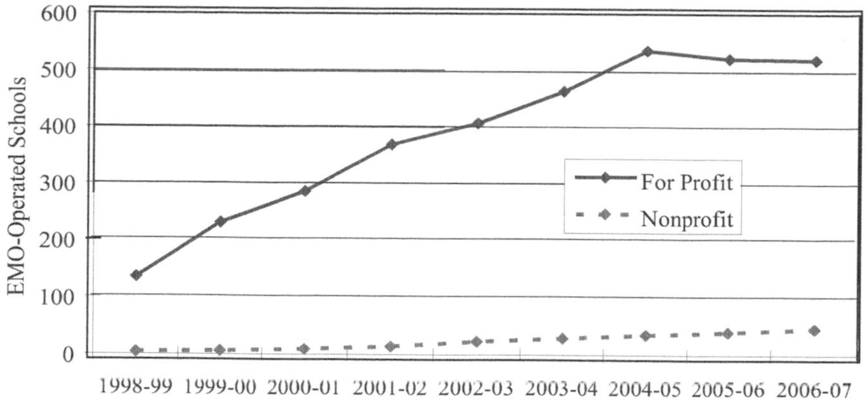

FIGURE 27.1. Number of Schools Operated by For-Profit and Nonprofit EMOs.

Note: This figure represents estimates based on available documentation. The number of for-profit EMO schools from 1998 to 2005 is based on data from Molnar et al. (2006).

quickly in Michigan than anywhere else. There, EMOs operate 75 percent of Michigan's charter schools, representing more than 80 percent of all charter school students in that state. Although the growth and expansion of EMOs is most obvious in the United States, signs of EMO growth also exist in the United Kingdom (Fitz & Beers, 2003), Canada, and elsewhere.

Factors Explaining the Growth of EMOs

One of the most critical factors behind the growth of EMOs is expectation of profit. While private companies and investors have captured most of the health care sector in the United States, they have for a long time been interested in capturing a piece of the public education sector.[10] EMOs have successfully entered this traditionally public sector and during the late 1990s sparked considerable interest among venture capitalists and private investors. Even though only a handful of EMOs have reported profits thus far, the increasing number of EMOs entering the market in the last decade suggests that many more anticipate there are profits to be had.

The growth of EMOs in the charter school sector appears to be related to several factors including demands from schools and authorizers as well as the creation of new regulations[11] Charter school founders often face an uphill battle as they seek to find start-up funding, acquire facilities, and develop programs and curricula. It is during the start-up phase that EMOs are most often contracted to operate charter schools. The EMOs bring with them capital to finance facilities and lease them back to the charter school. The EMOs also have ready-to-use curriculum packages and assessment tools.

Some charter schools either have hired or established their own EMOs in order to privatize their instructional staff; many states do not require charter school staff to be employed by the school board. When staff members are employees of the EMO, it is possible to circumvent the state retirement system and arrange less expensive private benefits and retirement plans.

Several Michigan authorizers have required groups applying for charter schools in Michigan to have an EMO in order to have their applications considered. Some authorizers of charter schools prefer to authorize schools that work with management companies, since these schools will have access to capital and managerial expertise and are likely to have fewer compliance-related problems than charter schools with no outside management help.

The growth of EMOs is also linked to political agendas. For example, in Michigan (Miron & Nelson, 2002), Colorado, Maryland, and Pennsylvania (Rhim, 2005), governors or state officials have gotten involved in the process of contracting out charter schools or district schools to EMOs. Elected district school boards can also influence outsourcing the management and operation of struggling district schools to an EMO.

Some states restrict EMO involvement, while most states impose no restrictions on contracting with for-profit EMOs to operate some or all schools. States like Connecticut with a cap on the enrollment size of charter schools discourage EMOs, which often seek larger schools for economies of scale. Regulations requiring EMOs to use state purchasing systems or regulations prohibiting EMOs from collecting service fees until all other debts are paid by the school also provide structural limitations that discourage EMOs.

State and federal accountability provisions provide a key impetus and rationale for contracting out low performing schools or districts to private EMOs. For example, the federal No Child Left Behind Act identifies five options for schools that continually fail to make adequate yearly progress in student achievement: convert to a charter school, replace all staff, contract with a private EMO, allow for a state takeover, or implement another major governance change. EMO management could well be a more attractive option than conversion to a charter school because the district will retain control of the school through its contract.

Below, seven key trends are described that have affected the growth of EMOs in number of companies, as well as the number of schools and students they serve.

- **Charter schools starting their own EMOs.** Increasingly, charter school founders or administrators are creating their own single-site EMO, which is then contracted by the charter school board to operate the school.
- **Expansion from single-site EMO to multiple school EMO.** A few EMOs that operated single schools have expanded their services to other schools or started additional schools. The new schools created by these single site EMOs often provide a range of grades not provided in their original school.
- **Evolution from partial-service to full-service EMOs.** EMOs that initially provided only partial services in the 1990s or allowed schools to select and pay for specific services have been moving toward full-service management agreements.
- **Growth of nonprofit EMOs**. Nonprofit EMOs or Charter Management Organizations (CMOs) are being used to stimulate the growth of charter schools and bring to scale reportedly successful school models.
- **EMOs starting their own charter schools.** EMOs are increasingly involved in starting their own schools rather than waiting for a school to invite them in. In these cases, the EMO decides where it wants to establish and operate a school and then goes in search of a few community members who can serve as a founding group. In Arizona, EMOs are permitted to hold the charter and do not need to depend on a school board to hire them.
- **Expansion into cyber schooling**. Cyber schools[12] have become a large growth area for charter schools (Huerta, Gonzalez, & d'Entremon, 2006). Nearly all cyber charter schools are operated by EMOs, making this a large growth area for private management.
- **Growth in enrollments in existing EMO charter schools.** The average school size for charter schools is increasing each year and much of this increase is due to the expansion within existing EMO-run schools that add additional grades and/or classes.[13]

Beyond efforts to increase their presence in K–12 schools, several large EMOs are diversifying to cover supplemental education services such as tutoring, after school programs, summer school programs, juvenile services, and technical assistance for accountability. Unlike formal K–12 schools, supplemental services are not as highly regulated and have limited demands for accountability, which makes this sector even more attractive to private EMOs.

One trend that has reduced the number of EMOs has been mergers among the large and medium-sized EMOs. For example, Edison bought LearnNow; Advantage Schools Inc. merged with Mosaica; and JCR & Associates—once a small EMO from Michigan—merged with Beacon Education Management, which later merged with Chancellor to become Chancellor Beacon and, most recently, evolved into Imagine Schools.

Although the number of schools operated by single-site EMOs and nonprofit EMOs are still growing, the number of schools operated by the large for-profit EMOs has been leveling off. Although these for profit EMOs continue to expand to new charter schools and district schools, this growth has been matched or exceeded by the termination or nonrenewal of existing contracts.[14] In some cases contracting districts and charter schools have been disappointed with the performance of their EMO schools. There have also been concerns about costs in excess of district operations for similar schools, as in Dallas and Philadelphia (Gill, Zimmer, Christman, & Blanc 2007). Thus, the overall growth of the large for-profit EMOs has been leveling off and decreasing slightly as noted in Figure 27.1.

PERFORMANCE OF EMO SCHOOLS ON STANDARDIZED TESTS

The role of for-profit entities in public education has been characterized as an attempt to harness private interests in the service of public interests (Friedman, 1953; Schultze, 1977).

The body of research on the performance of EMOs is growing. This research, while still limited, does not show that students in EMO-controlled schools perform better than those in traditional public schools with comparable student enrollments.

Edison Schools Inc. Edison has captured considerable media attention since its inception in 1992. In each of its annual performance reports, the company claims that its schools make substantial gains on standardized tests. In its most recent performance review for 2004–05, Edison claimed its students were making "striking academic progress and posting significant gains" (Edison Schools Inc., 2006). Evaluations conducted by districts that contract with Edison or by other researchers have found, however, that gains made in Edison schools are similar to or slightly lower than gains made by comparable groups of students (Dryden, 2004; Gomez & Shay, 2000; Minneapolis Public Schools, 2000; Miron & Applegate, 2000; Nelson & Van Meter, 2003; Shay, 2000). Two of the most rigorous studies from Miami (Shay, 2000) and Dallas (Dryden, 2004) involved quasi-experimental designs in which the students in the Edison schools were matched with a comparison group of similar students in traditional public schools. Edison students were found to show lower academic improvement relative to demographically matched students at other schools. Two comprehensive reviews, which included more schools but less rigorous designs (Miron & Applegate, 2000; Gill et al., 2005), found mixed or slightly negative results. Edison has been effective at propelling its successful schools into the limelight. Nonetheless, the body of evidence suggests that Edison's schools—on the whole—are doing similarly or worse than comparison groups of schools or students.

National Heritage Academies (NHA). This company commissioned two studies that examined its student achievement data. Wolfram (2002) examined performance on state assessment tests and found that NHA schools were performing quite well, although no demographic controls were used and the comparisons were limited to the average results in their state of Michigan. Hess and Leal (2003) analyzed norm-referenced test data collected and processed by NHA. Their findings suggested that NHA students were making gains on the Metropolitan Achievement Test compared to the national norm.

Given the high socioeconomic background status of the students enrolled in NHA schools, the fact that they perform at or above state averages is not surprising. Horn and Miron (2000) found that Michigan NHA charter schools' results were above state average, but its schools' gains on the state assessment were typically smaller than those of surrounding districts.

Evidence of Performance in Other Large EMOs. Although no independent research or evaluations of Aspire schools exist, the company's Web site claims improvement on the California state assessment, but no comparable data for similar traditional public schools is included (Aspire Public Schools, 2006). Similarly, Leona Group LLC, reports on its Web site that performance is improving, but no technical reports or even data sources are provided (Leona Group, 2006). Miron and Nelson (2002), however, found that Leona Group, along with Charter School Administrative Services, were the two EMOs with the poorest performance records in Michigan in terms of relative change scores. The Web site for Victory Schools (2006) has a section devoted to general achievement claims. However, no technical reports have been made available except for Philadelphia, where Victory Schools and other EMOs did no better than comparable district schools (Gill, Zimmer, Christman, & Blanc 2007). Other EMOs, such as Mosaica, White Hat, and Constellation Schools, had no available research or technical reports, but their web sites did share success stories. Nelson and Van Meter (2003) completed a review of performance in Mosaica schools and found its performance in 9 out of 11 sites to be noticeably lower than demographically similar districts. Like the other EMOs noted above, there are no published evaluations of student achievement for Imagine Schools and Charter Schools USA. These two EMOs did not even_provide evaluation reports that can be assessed for validity.

EMO vs. Non-EMO Charter Schools. Two studies compare the performance of EMO-run charter schools with non-EMO charter schools (Loveless, 2003; Miron & Nelson, 2002). Both studies found that EMO-run charter schools had lower absolute results on standardized tests. The Miron and Nelson analysis, which covered Michigan, found that EMO charter schools showed achievement gains that were less than non-EMO schools. The Loveless study, which covered 10 states, indicated that EMO-run charter schools had exceptionally low starting points, but were making larger gains than charter schools without EMOs. Both of these studies were methodologically weak because the states they covered had only school-level data available. They both also relied on measuring performance only by the percentage of students who met a particular level of performance rather than by an analysis of the overall distribution of achievement gains.

Other Reviews of Research. Other studies have concluded that there was insufficient evidence to evaluate the effectiveness of EMOs. They include evaluations of student achievement in EMO's by The Comprehensive School Reform Quality Center at the American Institutes for Research (CSRQ, 2006) and the U.S. General Accounting Office (GAO, 2002). In 2003, the GAO conducted an analysis of a small number of EMO-operated schools in six cities. Results were "mixed," although a majority of the EMO schools in the study had negative results.

There still is no independent evidence that EMOs are successful in raising student achievement results relative to similar comparison groups. This should not come as a surprise, since earlier research suggested that efforts to outsource school management to private EMOs did not achieve the anticipated results. For example, Ascher, Berne, and Fruchter (1996) and Richards,

Shore, and Sawicky (1996) examined experiments with private management of public schools in the early 1990s. They characterized these experiments as disappointing failures that ended with the termination of management contracts.[15] Similarly, papers presented at a conference sponsored by the National Center for the Study of Privatization in Education (Levin, 2001) expressed caution about the performance claims of EMOs and raised questions about the outcomes of private management in terms of efficiency, equity, and social cohesion.

Although the evidence on student achievement is not promising, evidence from a number of studies and evaluations suggests that EMOs appear to be doing a good job in terms of satisfying customers as measured by satisfaction surveys of parents and teachers and qualitative research (Cookson, Embree, & Fahey, 2000; Gomez & Shay, 2000).[16] However, Miron and Nelson (2002) found that while parents in EMO-run charter schools were more likely to be satisfied with the schools' facilities than parents in non-EMO charter schools, teachers were less satisfied with working conditions in the EMO-run charter schools.

While data limitations preclude hard and fast conclusions, the existing research on student achievement in privately managed public schools casts doubt on privatization advocates' claims that introducing the discipline of the bottom line to education will lead to improved effectiveness.

EMO FINANCE: MEANS AND STRATEGIES FOR PROFIT

The fate of EMOs does not lie directly in their ability to perform well but rather in their ability to make profits. Even though only a few EMOs have reported profits[17] thus far, the large number of EMOs that have entered the market suggests that many perceived this to be a profitable sector. Unfortunately, little is actually published on EMO's business plans or strategies for surviving and succeeding in the marketplace. Because much of this information is proprietary and because these are private entities, it is difficult to gain information about how they work.

EMOs are profit motivated, therefore the overall strategy of EMOs should be to seek all possible sources of revenues and find ways to cut or save on expenditures while maintaining or improving quality. A number of profit-making strategies pursued by EMOs are described below. Some of these strategies are self-apparent, and some have been uncovered from fieldwork and interviews with representatives of EMOs or the schools they operate.

Targeting Less Costly to Educate Students

The most obvious way for an EMO to seek profit is to cater to students who are less costly to educate than the typical student on which the funding is based. On the whole, EMO-operated district schools tend to enroll students similar to those in neighboring public schools. The EMO, typically, is asked to assume responsibility for failing district schools that serve largely disadvantaged populations.

Charter schools differ from district contract schools in that they create specific profiles and market themselves to specific families. The process of marketing and recruiting students makes it possible to target students who are less costly to educate. Although charter schools are not allowed to charge fees, they can make it difficult for low-income or single-parent families to enroll by providing limited or no transportation, requiring parents to volunteer at the school, or establishing a complicated application process that requires interviews and parent information meetings. The implementation of strict disciplinary policies that result in suspensions and expulsions of students can further structure enrollment by removing or "counseling out" students experiencing difficulties.[18]

Depending on state and district funding formulas, and depending on details in the individual education plans, students with special educational needs can be substantially more costly to educate.[19] A number of studies have confirmed that charter schools, particularly those operated by EMOs, enroll substantially fewer students with special education needs (Horn & Miron, 2000; Nelson, Drown, Muir, & Van Meter, 2001) than traditional public schools. Furthermore, the special education students they do enroll tend to have mild and easily remediated disabilities such as speech and language difficulties (Miron & Nelson, 2002). Nelson et al. (2001) and Miron and Nelson (2002) found that most EMO-operated schools served elementary students.[20]

Although patterns indicate that most EMOs tend to focus attention on elementary schools and enroll lower proportions of economically disadvantaged and special education students, there certainly are exceptions to this pattern. While it is hard to prove that EMO-operated charter schools are engaging in intentional cream-skimming, enrollment patterns are compatible with a cost-reducing, profit-making approach to education. For example, when EMOs can target and enroll more homogeneous populations of students, it is easier to increase average class size and cut down on paraprofessional staff that supports students who require extra assistance.

Saving on Costs for Employee Compensation

Salaries for teachers and staff consume a large proportion of the overall budget for schools, which makes cuts in salaries one of the most attractive means of cutting costs. Based on data from state evaluations, EMO-operated charter schools typically have a pay scale that is 10 to 15 percent lower than those of local districts (Miron & Nelson, 2002; Miron, Nelson, & Risley, 2002). Many EMOs report that they use bonus pay to increase base salaries. Teachers' salaries in EMO-operated district schools typically follow the pay scale in the local district.

Teachers recruited to work in EMO-operated schools tend to be younger and have less formal education and training than teachers in surrounding districts (Miron & Nelson, 2002). Employing less qualified teachers helps concentrate teacher salaries at the lower end of the pay scale.[21] Depending on the state, teachers employed by the EMO might also be exempted from state retirement systems,[22] making it possible to achieve savings by providing less comprehensive retirement and fringe benefits.

Two consequences of hiring large proportions of less-experienced teachers at reduced salaries and benefits below prevailing compensation rates are that EMOs cannot compete for the best teachers, and they can be plagued with attrition that will drive up costs for in-service training. This may partially explain the relatively poor gains in student achievement in schools operated by EMOs.

A number of EMOs have designed their models so that more scripted instruction is used, which means the experience and qualifications of teachers becomes less important. NHA uses what it calls "teacher-centered" instruction. Incoming teachers to NHA receive clear and comprehensive lessons, thus reducing time for planning and developing lessons. In many respects, the success that NHA is having with retaining teachers with substantially lower salaries mirrors what has been seen in small private schools where teachers are willing to work for less money in exchange for orderly and eager-to-learn students.[23]

Reduction of Services and Support

EMOs can attempt to increase profits by reducing services and support.[24] Particular areas where services can be cut include transportation, lunch programs, and extracurricular activities. Two of these areas are described here.

Transportation. In some states, charter schools are not required to provide transportation. In Michigan, for example, state funding for transportation is incorporated into per pupil revenues, even though charter schools are not required to provide it. While some EMO-operated charter schools provide extensive transportation services to increase enrollments, others such as NHA do not provide a formal transportation system. An absence of transportation makes the school less attractive to low-income or single-parent families that may find it difficult to drive their children to and from school each day.

Hot Lunch Programs. The absence of a hot lunch program not only saves money but also disqualifies schools from the federally sponsored free and reduced lunch program. Therefore, low-income families that wish to take advantage of this program may need to opt for other schools where they can benefit from the subsidized lunch program.

Negotiating for More

A high official at Edison Schools claims that public schools have been wasteful and ineffective, spending too much on central administration and not properly focusing instructional resources (Chubb, 2001). Based on such claims, Edison seeks to receive the "whole dollar" when it negotiates with districts to operate schools. It requests the typical per pupil expenditures that reach schools as well as a portion of the central administration costs. Negotiating for the "whole dollar" has resulted in substantially higher revenues for the Edison schools than for surrounding district schools, even though the contract requires the district to provide services such as transportation, school health services, and cleaning and maintenance from general district funds. Districts have become more aware of these practices and have given more scrutiny to their contracts with EMOs.[25]

Aside from negotiating with districts for additional revenues, a number of EMOs and CMOs have leveraged donations from foundations or corporate sponsors as a condition for managing schools in states where the per pupil revenues are low.[26]

Building Equity in Facilities and Equipment

If handled effectively, purchasing or construction of facilities can be a profit-maker for EMOs. Many of the large EMOs that operate charter schools and nearly all of the single-site EMOs own the school buildings. In turn, the school leases the building from the EMO. By purchasing the privately owned facilities or equipment with public money, EMOs can create equity.[27]

In many privately operated charter schools, the EMO owns the facilities, equipment, furniture, and even learning materials (Horn & Miron, 2000). The private property holdings of the EMO are completely or partially paid for with federal charter school start-up monies and state and district operational costs. In recent years, charter schools across the country have been making more concerted efforts to secure their "fair share" of capital funds from states. This issue is not easily resolved, however, since state agencies insist that the building be publicly owned by the charter school board so that it can revert to the state in the event of a closure.

Expanding and Diversifying

Creating economies of scale is critical for EMOs if they are to succeed in making a profit. School size and concentration of schools are critical in determining overall efficiency. Many of the large EMOs started in a particular region where schools were closely clustered, and they could benefit from common purchases and share human and material resources. Edison Schools Inc. was unique in that it initially sought a national network of schools that was costly to support. Later, as Edison started losing contracts, the company emphasized the need to concentrate its schools in regional clusters that could be better served by national and regional staff.

EMOs have sought to expand into other service areas, such as cyber schools and the provision of supplemental education services that are less regulated and show growth potential. Some EMOs have packaged and sold or leased their curriculum and accountability systems. Supplemental services such as summer school provide the opportunity for EMOs to use their facilities and human resources during times when many public schools are not productive.

Can EMOs Be Profitable?

The outlook for EMOs is unclear. A number of signs suggest that EMOs are likely to face a more challenging milieu in the years to come. Increasing scrutiny by states agencies, authorizers, and school boards has led to an increasing number of terminated or nonrenewed contracts with EMOs. Given the proprietary nature of the data, it is difficult to obtain precise data on nonrenewals and terminations and the reasons underlying them. However, as one indicator of their magnitude, Edison reported managing more than 130 schools in 2001, but only about 80 in 2006. Even among this smaller number, some newer schools had replaced older ones. In some cases, the EMOs have terminated contracts that are not profitable. District officials and school boards are also becoming more careful in negotiating new contracts, making it less likely that EMOs will receive beneficial treatment in terms of higher financial compensation than for comparable district schools.

Another factor that is likely to undermine the future profitability of EMOs is that if they are successful, they may work themselves out of a job. For example, if an EMO succeeds in turning around a struggling district contact school, the district likely will want to resume control of the school. In the case of charter schools, EMOs can be critical as they navigate the start-up phase which requires the most work and capital. Once the budget is stabilized and operation of the school becomes more routine, the charter school board may wish to resume responsibility for operating the school.[28]

Levin (2002) questioned whether EMOs can be profitable and identified five critical characteristics of education that EMOs have "failed to realize": (1) education is a tough business because it is regulated, monitored, and subject to the demands of multiple audiences and layers of government; (2) EMOs must incur high marketing costs that public schools do not face; (3) relatively short-term contracts (3–5 years) have their own risks in amortizing investments at school sites; (4) the economies of scale that were anticipated do not exist; and (5) a uniform educational model akin to a single business model cannot be owners of nonprofit EMOs and for-profit EMOs that are not profitable[29] can garner generous easily applied (Levin, 2002). These factors as well as changing political climates are critical in determining the further growth and profitability of EMOs.

Even if EMOs prove not to be profitable in the long run, that may not mean they will not survive. Political agendas that promote private management are likely to continue to result in new opportunities for EMOs, including new contracts to operate schools with higher levels of revenues than surrounding schools receive. Furthermore, the fact that investors may perceive the potential of high returns and administrators can command high salaries and benefits (including bonuses) in successful EMOs may motivate others to consider taking risks to establish EMOs. Closer scrutiny by investors and a weak track record of overall profitability, however, is likely to limit or stop many of the new companies from flourishing.

SAFEGUARDS TO ENSURE REASONABLE AND EQUITABLE CONTRACTS WITH EMOS

Reasonable and equitable contracts ensure that there is a balance between the authorizing board's need to fulfill its public obligation to govern the school responsibly and the EMOs need to have sufficient freedom to run the school without micro-management from the board (Lin & Hassel, 2005). Faulty financial incentives, combined with poorly designed contracts can result in EMO-run schools operating in ways that may be at odds with the goals set by the contracting board as well as the overall public interest. Boards that contract with EMOs should consider the following measures to ensure that they engage in "smart buying" (Horn & Miron, 2000; Lin & Hassel, 2005):

- Require at least two competing bids from EMOs.
- Limit the length of a contract to no more than the length of the charter and preferably less. In the case of contract schools, the length of the contract should allow reasonable time for implementation of new models (e.g., at least 3 years), but not more than five years.
- Establish benchmarks for intermediate outcomes and contingency plans to resume control of the schools in the event of poor EMO performance; these will help ensure that the option for terminating a contract early is viable and realistic.
- Require full disclosure of finance and performance data.
- Ensure that the district or a nonpartisan group serves as a broker for information on schools from which parents can choose.[30] This should not be left to the EMOs alone.
- Retain independent legal counsel.
- Budget for internal and external evaluations of contracted schools and EMO performance.
- Ensure that the EMO has no personal connections with the contracting board members (i.e., arm's-length negotiation of contract).
- Ensure that materials developed at the school and equipment and materials purchased with public funds remain under the ownership of the school board.

Although the safeguards noted above are specific to school boards, there are other safeguards that are more specific to state agencies and authorizers that can help ensure a proper balance that protects the public interest while still tapping the entrepreneurial spirit of private management to provide education.[31]

Oversight of EMOs. Policy makers should act to make oversight of EMO-operated schools as transparent to the public as possible.[32] Boards that contract with EMOs are still responsible for the services delivered and should therefore be required to budget for and plan adequate oversight. Authorizers of charter schools should require that they be allowed to review contracts with EMOs before boards enter into agreements.

Technical Assistance for School Boards. District boards or charter school boards that contract with EMOs could benefit from technical assistance and information regarding the contracting process. Many large EMOs have experienced and effective business people promoting their company as well as sophisticated lawyers and accountants negotiating their contracts. Support and guidance from the state may help public school boards negotiate more carefully and effectively.

Create Equitable Funding Formulas. Involving EMOs in the provision of public services creates an opportunity to harness the entrepreneurial interests of private companies. Policymakers should ensure that funding formulas are fair and equitable, and they should be aware of how monetary incentives steer for-profit enterprises. In other words, policymakers should peg funding for schools to variations in the true cost of educating different groups of students (Miron & Nelson, 2002). If it costs more per pupil to educate secondary school students than students in the elementary grades, the funding formula should account for this. If services such as transportation are going to be optional, so too should funding for these services. When funding formulas assume that it costs the same to educate every child, EMOs will have an incentive to target those students who, experience shows, cost less to educate.

Ensure Adequate Start-Up Funds and Timely Payments to Charter Schools. Both the limited amount of start-up money and the fact that many new charter schools need to wait several months after the start of the school year before state or district money arrives create a need and demand for EMOs. While charter schools can benefit from EMOs' access to capital and administrative capacity, they are likely to lose in other areas. They may face higher administrative costs and, in accepting a standardized school model, lose key ideals of charter schools such as autonomy, site-based management, and ability to create diverse school options.

These measures and safeguards presume that EMOs can and should be allowed to manage public schools. Interestingly, some suggest harsh restrictions on EMOs. Conn (2002), for example, suggested that state legislatures enact laws that require for-profit EMOs to post monetary bonds in escrow that will provide remedial education, tutoring, or job training to students whose academic achievement is impaired as a result of attending schools managed by the companies. In addition, she proposed creating a limited private cause of action for education malpractice. Although measures such as these may help protect public interests, they are likely to go too far and serve as a deterrent to EMOs rather than a safeguard to balance school boards' interests and those of private management companies.

CONCLUSION

Private involvement in public schooling is not new. Neither is the notion that private companies can contribute to and profit from public education. Nevertheless, many educators and policy makers are uncomfortable with private management of public education, a relatively new form of privatization (Belfield & Levin, 2005). Most would agree, however, that if a company can deliver a better product for less cost, it should have the right to claim remaining revenues as profit. Education management organizations remain controversial for a number of reasons, including the following:

- Even though democratically elected public officials are responsible for the services that are contracted to EMOs, this responsibility is complicated by the lack of transparency and the fact that important information regarding the operation of these private companies is largely proprietary. There is also concern that public officials may become increasingly dependent on private contractors for information regarding quality and performance of the actual services they are contracted to provide.
- After more than a decade and after hundreds of contracts to outsource management and operation of public schools to private EMOs, there still is a lack of evidence that private

companies can operate public schools more efficiently and with more favorable outcomes than traditional public schools.

The intent of this chapter, with its review of research and available literature on EMOs, is to provide a sound basis for understanding education management organizations and the manner in which they are affecting the control, performance, and public nature of education. As has been illustrated, EMOs represent a relatively new but controversial form of privatization that confounds the basic notions of accountability and further blurs the distinction between public and private.

NOTES

1. HMOs, or health management organizations, have been perceived less positively by the public in recent years due to rapidly increasing costs of health care and the common perception that HMOs have become another layer of health care bureaucracy.
2. Some management companies, such as JCR & Associates (now a part of Imagine Schools), began by providing a menu of services for the schools with which it worked and later evolved to an exclusively full-service EMO. Some EMOs, such as Charter Schools USA, advertise that they can provide either comprehensive management or just back office support.
3. KIPP, which has more than 50 schools in 16 states plus the District of Columbia, is a nonprofit network of schools that many confuse with an EMO. The KIPP model provides assistance and quality control to locally operated schools that follow the packaged model. However, since KIPP does not actually manage the school or have executive authority over the school, it is not actually an EMO.
4. The term charter "management organization" (CMO) is sometimes used to refer to nonprofit groups that manage multiple charter schools and whose goal is to promote expansion of charter schools and address concerns with quality and sustainability (New Schools Venture Fund, 2006).
5. In Arizona, EMOs are allowed to hold a charter. In Michigan, like most states, there must be a school board that holds the charter and then subcontracts to an EMO.
6. In these instances, it is not uncommon to see one spouse running the school as a principal and the other spouse heading the EMO to which the board has subcontracted the operation of the school (Horn & Miron, 2000). The creation of the EMO undermines the authority of the school board, but provides greater assurance to founders that the facilities or school they created will not be taken from them easily. In many cases, founders of charter schools have put considerable personal wealth on the line to start the school.
7. Charter school authorizers—also known as sponsors—are publicly elected or appointed groups that issue and oversee the contracts that govern charter schools. In most states, local and state school boards are authorizers, although in some more permissive states, other groups such as appointed boards and public or nonprofit agencies are permitted to issue charters.
8. This estimate is based on figures from 17 states that account for approximately 80 percent of the nation's charter schools. For these 17 states the figures were based either on existing reports or on estimates made by individuals working with charter schools in the state. For the remaining 20 percent of the charter schools—for which we had no basis for making an estimate—it is assumed that 5 percent of the schools were operated by EMOs, which is a rather conservative estimate. The Center for Education Reform suggests that only 10 percent of the charter schools in the nation are operated by EMOs. Molnar et al. (2006) estimated that approximately 18.8 percent of charter schools are operated by EMOs.
9. Lists of EMOs can be found in Molnar et al. (2006), who have been preparing annual reports on EMOs, and also in Miron and Nelson (2002). The National Association of Charter School Authorizers (2006) identified 22 EMOs and lists them on its Web site (this list includes a few nonprofit EMOs). The list is being updated and will reportedly profile an additional 20 companies. Differences in the total number of EMOs reported by differing sources or groups relate to whether or not the growing number of single school operators is included. Also, some lists do not include nonprofit EMOs.

10. Public education systems consume a large portion of each nation's gross national product. The American public education sector (kindergarten to 12th grade) is estimated to cost around $420 billion per year and consumes nearly 5 percent of the Gross Domestic Product of the United States. Because revenues for education expand moderately from year to year, this sector is both a stable yet potentially lucrative market for exploration and expansion by private entrepreneurs.
11. Hentschke, Oschman, and Snell (2005) highlight five likely factors that can explain the growth of EMOs: (i) districts have a history of outsourcing special education services, (ii) growth in accountability policies, (iii) increasing use of school choice programs, (iv) greater use of school district outsourcing, and (v) increasing numbers of charter schools.
12. Cyber schools, also known as virtual schools or online schools, deliver the majority of their instruction to students through a Web site instead of in a school building. These schools are particularly popular with families that are homeschooling their children. Cyber schools receive recognition and public funding by applying to become a charter school, which is permitted in a large number of states.
13. Several EMOs, have a strategy to start with lower elementary grades and then grow from the bottom. In other words, they add a grade each year until the school reaches its desired range of grades.
14. Edison Schools Inc., for example, has lost contracts for more schools than the total number of schools it currently operates. By 2005, Edison lost contracts for 81 schools (American Federation of Teachers, 2006). Commonly cited reasons for terminating contracts with Edison include poor performance on tests and additional expenses required by the contract. Less commonly cited reasons were low enrollments and teacher attrition.
15. The EMO studied was Education Alternatives Inc. This company ultimately lost its contracts with districts and, after a name change and an attempt to enter the charter school market, went bankrupt.
16. One important limitation in satisfaction surveys is that they include only teachers and parents that remain in the school. Dissatisfied teachers and parents that leave are typically excluded from the samples.
17. Molnar (2001) reported that 5 of 21 EMOs contacted indicated that they were profitable. Four of the five profitable EMOs, however, were rather small in size or had sizeable investments in operating private schools.
18. Lacireno-Paquet (2004) found that enrollment patterns in EMO-operated charters differed substantially. On the whole, she reported that small EMOs were less likely than large EMOs to enroll low-income or minority students.
19. State and federal categorical grants do provide additional revenue for special education and economically disadvantaged students. These additional revenues, however, typically fall short of covering the additional costs of providing educational services to these special needs students.
20. Costs for elementary schools are noticeably lower than secondary schools because of differences in average teacher salaries, extracurricular activities, and demands for specialized subjects with high infrastructure costs such as science laboratories and vocational technical programs.
21. In her study of teacher salaries in charter schools, Burian-Fitzgerald (2005) found that charter school teachers had similar starting salaries as teachers in traditional public schools although charter school teachers gained less salary for additional years of experience.
22. In Michigan, employees of EMOs including teachers, are specifically exempted from the Michigan teacher retirement system. The resulting financial boost is frequently mentioned as an explanation for the growth of private EMOs in Michigan (Prince, 1999).
23. In most NHA schools, teachers are greeted with relatively homogeneous classes of students with supportive parents. Teacher satisfaction surveys from teachers at NHA indicated that they were more satisfied at NHA and less likely to leave than teachers in other Michigan charter schools (Miron & Nelson, 2002).
24. In-depth analyses of Michigan finance data presented in Miron and Nelson (2002) suggest that charter schools realize cost savings by offering a more limited range of services than noncharter public schools. In other words, even while Michigan charter schools received less funding per pupil than traditional public schools, they typically were receiving more funding than traditional public schools once we controlled for the types of services offered and students served. This reduction in services

resulted in an annual $1,033 per-pupil cost advantage for one of the NHA schools that was studied in depth. From this same analysis, it was found that EMO-run schools tend to spend a considerably lower proportion of their total expenditures on instruction and, not coincidentally, have higher administrative costs.

25. In Dallas, an audit revealed that the district was paying around $12 million more for the 7 schools operated by Edison than it did for its remaining schools that were still under district management (Dallas Public Schools, 2001).
26. Many of the large for-profit EMOs have been effective in securing capital resources from investment firms, although much of the interest from the investment sector seems to have fizzled after the collapse of value in Edison shares in 2002. A number of the nonprofit EMOs have secured additional funding from foundations and private individuals who wish to promote the growth of private management of public schools (New Schools Venture Fund, 2006). This capital largely has been used for starting and establishing the EMOs and CMOs.
27. Because NHA leases its facilities from a sister company, it also retains any profits derived from the building lease. In fact, the financial arrangement that NHA has with its boards essentially allows NHA extensive leeway to set the terms of the lease. Annual leases on most of the buildings are above market rates (Miron & Nelson, 2002). Interestingly, NHA doubled the annual lease paid by one of its schools in 1999, which drew questions from the media (Reinstadler, 1999) but not from the school's governing board.
28. In many states, training of charter school boards has become mandatory or at least highly recommended. With boards that are aware of their responsibilities, increasingly autonomous, and empowered, we are likely to see them terminate more contracts with EMOs. In Delaware, the charter school boards terminated all of the contracts for the EMOs that once operated a third of the charter schools in the state (Miron, Cullen, Applegate, & Farrell, 2007). Interestingly, Wilson (2006) claims that EMOs are losing contracts in part because of conflicts with school boards and the unwillingness of authorizers or state regulators to enforce contracts.
29. While shareholders of Edison stock suffered with the collapse of stock value, top administrators in the company were enjoying salaries that were more than twice what large district superintendents would receive. In addition, a number of top Edison administrators cashed in on lucrative stock options and have benefited from low-interest loans from the company.
30. In order to work efficiently, markets must provide cheap and reliable information about products to potential consumers (see, e.g., Stiglitz, 1988). Therefore, at the state or district level, reliable and accurate data should be reported on the schools from which parents can choose, including those under contract.
31. Arsen, Plank, & Sykes (1999) identify and discuss rules that policy makers should consider to encourage positive outcomes and protect students and citizens against the harmful consequences of a poorly-structured market for schooling.
32. Pini (2001) calls for greater oversight and scrutiny of EMOs after she found extensive disparities between what EMOs say and what they actually do.

REFERENCES

American Federation of Teachers. (2006). *Edison school closing and contract/charter cancellations.* Washington DC: Author.

Arsen, D., Plank, D. L., & Sykes, G. (1999). *School choice policies in Michigan: The rules matter.* East Lansing: Michigan State University Educational Policy Center.

Ascher, C., Berne, R., & Fructher, N. (1996). *Hard lessons: Public schools and privatization.* New York: Twentieth Century Fund Press.

Ascher, C., Echazarreta, J., Jacobowitz, R., McBride, Y., & Troy, T. (2003). *Governance and administrative infrastructure in New York City charter schools: Going charter year three findings.* New York: Institute for Education and Social Policy, New York University.

Aspire Public Schools. (2006). *Student academic achievement*. Retrieved September 19, 2006, from http://www.aspirepublicschools.org/results/results.html.

Belfield, C., & Levin, H. M. (2005). *Privatizing educational choice: Consequences for parents, schools, and public policy*. Boulder, CO: Paradigm.

Burian-Fitzgerald, M. (2005). *Average teacher salaries and returns to experience in charter schools*. (Occasional Paper #101). New York: National Center for the Study of Privatization in Education, Teachers College, Columbia University.

Chubb, J. E. (2001). The private can be public. *Education Next, 1*. Hoover Institution: Stanford University. Retrieved October 18, 2006, from http://www.hoover.org/publications/ednext/.

Conn, K. (2002). For-profit school management corporations: Serving the wrong master. *Journal of Law & Education, 31*(2), 129–148.

Cookson, P., Embree, K., & Fahey, S. (2000). *The Edison partnership schools: An assessment of academic climate and classroom culture*. New York: Teachers College, Columbia University.

CSRQ. (2006). *CSRQ center report on education service providers*. Washington, DC: The Comprehensive School Reform Quality Center, American Institutes for Research.

Dallas Public Schools. (2001). *Interim evaluation report on Edison*. Dallas: Author.

Dryden, M. (2004). *The performance of Edison Schools Inc. in the Dallas schools*. Paper presented at the 2004 annual meeting of the American Educational Research Association, San Diego.

Edison Schools Inc. (2006). *Eighth annual report on school performance 2004–2005*. New York: Author.

Fitz, J., & Beers, B. (2003). Education management organizations and the privatization of public education: A cross-national comparison of the USA and Britain. *Comparative Education, 38*(2), 137–154.

Friedman, M. (1953). *Essays in positive economics*. Chicago: University of Chicago Press.

General Accounting Office. (2002). *Public schools: Insufficient research to determine effectiveness of selected private education companies* (GAO-03-11). Washington, DC: Author.

General Accounting Office. (2003). *Public schools: Comparison of achievement results for students attending privately managed and traditional schools in six cities* (GAO-04-62). Washington, DC: Author.

Gill, B., Hamilton, L., Lockwood, J., Marsh, J., Zimmer, R., Hill, D., & Pribesh, S. (2005). *Inspiration, perspiration, and time: Operations and achievement in Edison schools*. Santa Monica, CA.: RAND.

Gill, B., Zimmer, R., Christman, J., & Blanc, S. (2007). *State Takeover, School Restructuring, Private Management, and Student Achievement in Philadelphia*. Santa Monica, CA: RAND.

Gomez, J. J., & Shay, S. A. (2000). *Evaluation of the Edison project schools. Third interim report: 1998–99 school year*. Miami: Miami-Dade County Public Schools.

Hentschke, G., Oschman, S., & Snell, L. (2005). *Trends & best practices for education management organizations*. Policy brief. San Francisco: WestEd.

Hess, F., & Leal, D. (2003). An evaluation of student performance in National Heritage Academies charter schools: 2000–2003. Grand Rapids, MI: National Heritage Academies.

Horn, J., & Miron, G. (2000). *An evaluation of the Michigan charter school initiative: Performance, accountability, and impact*. Kalamazoo: The Evaluation Center, Western Michigan University. Retrieved from http://www.wmich. edu/evalctr/charter/michigan/.

Huerta, L. Gonzalez, M. F., & d'Entremon, C. (2006). Cyber and home school charter schools: Adopting policy to new forms of public schooling. *Peabody Journal of Education, 81*(1), 103–139.

Lacireno-Paquet, N. (2004). Do EMO-operated charter schools serve disadvantaged students? The influence of state policies. *Education Policy Analysis Archives, 12*(26). Retrieved September 14, 2006, from http://epaa.asu.edu/epaa/v12n26/.

Leona Group. (2006). *Leona Group LLC: A new kind of public school*. Retrieved September 19, 2006, http://www.leonagroup.com/index1.html.

Levin, H. M. (Ed.). (2001). *Privatizing education: Can the marketplace deliver choice, efficiency, equity, and social cohesion?* Boulder, CO: Westview Press.

Levin, H. M. (2002). *Potential of for-profit schools for educational reform*. (Occasional Paper #47). New York: National Center for the Study of Privatization in Education, Teachers College, Columbia University.

Lin, M., & Hassel, B. (2005). *Charting a clear course: A resource guide for building successful partner-*

ships between charter schools and school management organizations. Washington DC: National Alliance for Public Charter Schools.

Loveless, T. (2003). *The 2003 Brown Center report on American education. How well are American students learning*? Washington, DC: Brookings Institution.

Minneapolis Public Schools. (2000). *Edison project school information report*. Minneapolis: Author.

Miron, G., & Applegate, B. (2000). *An evaluation of student achievement in Edison schools opened in 1995 and 1996*. Kalamazoo: The Evaluation Center, Western Michigan University.

Miron, G., Cullen, A., Applegate, B., & Farrell, P. (2007). *Evaluation of Delaware's charter school reform: Final report*. Dover, Delaware. Delaware State Board of Education.

Miron, G., & Nelson, C. (2002). *What's public about charter schools? Lessons learned about choice and accountability*. Thousand Oaks, CA: Corwin Press.

Miron, G., Nelson, C., & Risley, J. (2002). *Strengthening Pennsylvania's charter school reform: Findings from the statewide evaluation and discussion of relevant policy issues*. Harrisburg: Pennsylvania Department of Education.

Molnar, A. (2001). Calculating the benefits and costs of for-profit public education. *Education Policy Analysis Archives, 9*(15). Arizona State University. Retrieved October 18, 2006, from http://epass.asu.edu/epaa/v9n15.html.

Molnar, A., Garcia, D., Bartlett, M., & O'Neill, A. (2006). *Profiles of for-profit education management organizations: Eighth annual report, 2005–06*. Tempe: Education Policy Studies Laboratory, Arizona State University.

National Association of Charter School Authorizers. (2006). *Education service providers project*. Retrieved on September 18, 2006, http://www.charterauthorizers.org/site/nacsa/ content.php?type=1&id=8.

National Heritage Academies. (2005). *Management agreement for Worcester Regional Charter School*. Grand Rapids, MI: Author.

Nelson, F. H., Drown, R., Muir, E., & Van Meter, N. (2001). Public money and the privatization of K-12 education. In S. Chaikind & W. Fowler (Eds.), *Education finance in the new millennium: 2001 yearbook of the American Education Finance Association*. Larchmont, NY: Eye on Education.

Nelson, F. H., & Van Meter, N. (2003). *Update on student achievement for Edison Schools, Inc*. Washington, DC: American Federation of Teachers.

NewSchools Venture Fund (2006). *Charter management organizations: Toward scale with quality*. San Francisco: Author.

Pini, M. E. (2001). *The corporatization of education: Education management organizations (EMOs) and public schools*. Unpublished dissertation, University of New Mexico.

Prince, H. (1999). Follow the money: An initial view of elementary charter school spending in Michigan. *Journal of Education Finance, 25*, 175–194.

Reinstaldler, K. (1999). Charter school's rent nearly doubles. *Grand Rapids Press* (September 3).

Rhim, L. M. (2005). *Restructuring schools in Chester Upland, Pennsylvania: An analysis of state restructuring efforts*. Denver, CO: Education Commission of the States.

Richards, C. E., Shore, R., & Sawicky, M.B. (1996). *Risky business: Private management of public schools*. Washington, DC: Economic Policy Institute.

Saltman, K. (2005). *The Edison schools: Corporate schooling and the assault on public education*. New York: Routledge.

Schultze, C. L. (1977). *The public use of private interest*. Washington, DC: Brookings Institution.

Shay, S. A. (2000). *A longitudinal study of achievement outcomes in a privatized public school: A growth curve analysis*. Unpublished doctoral dissertation, University of Miami, Coral Gables.

Stiglitz, J. E. (1988). *Economics of the public sector* (2nd ed.). New York: W.W. Norton.

Victory Schools. (2006). *Victory Schools: Results*. Retrieved on September 19, 2006, from http://www.victoryschools.com/new/schooldesign/index.asp?PageID=results.

Whittle, C. (2006). Crash course: A radical plan for improving public education. New York: Penguin Group.

Wilson, S. (2006). *Learning on the job: When business takes on public schools*. Cambridge, MA: Harvard University Press.

Wohlstetter, P., Malloy, C., Hentschke, G., & Smith, J. (2004). Improving service delivery in education through collaboration: An exploratory study of the role of cross-sectoral alliances in the development and support of charter schools. *Social Science Quarterly*, *85*(5), 1078–96.

Wolfram, G. (2002). *The effect of National Heritage Academies on student MEAP scores: A detailed statistical analysis*. Grand Rapids, MI.: National Heritage Academies.

VI

RACE, SES AND ACHIEVEMENT GAPS

Section Editor

Susanna Loeb

28

Patterns and Trends in Racial/Ethnic and Socioeconomic Academic Achievement Gaps

Sean F. Reardon and Joseph P. Robinson

INTRODUCTION

Racial, ethnic, and socioeconomic disparities in academic achievement remain a stubborn fact of schooling in the United States. National studies consistently show that the average non-Hispanic black student scores well below the average non-Hispanic white student on standardized tests of math and reading skills, as does the average Hispanic student. Likewise, the average student from a low-income family scores much lower on such tests than students from higher-income families. Considerable attention has been focused on achievement gaps, particularly the black-white achievement gap. Scholars and educators have suggested a number of possible explanations for these gaps, and policy makers, principals, and teachers have tried a range of remedies. As this chapter documents, however, the gaps persist despite these efforts. Moreover, our understanding of the causes and patterns of these achievement gaps is far from complete.

HOW SHOULD ACHIEVEMENT GAPS BE MEASURED?

A prerequisite for investigating the patterns, causes, and consequences of achievement gaps is the availability of a meaningful metric for measuring the gaps. The most obvious measure is the difference in mean test scores between the two groups. While this is appealingly simple, it has important flaws. If the tests used at different grades or for different cohorts do not share an identical metric,[1] then the magnitude of the gap will depend on which test is used. There is also a more subtle—and less tractable—problem. An ideal test measures cognitive skill in an interval-scaled metric, so that a difference of one point in mean scores between two groups has the same meaning as a difference of one point in mean scores between two other groups, regardless of where on the test score metric the group means lie. Yet, while a well-constructed test can be assumed to be an ordinal-scaled (higher scores correspond to higher levels of cognitive skill), the assumption of linearity is harder to justify.[2] If a test is not interval-scaled, the meaning of a difference in groups' test score means will depend on where on the scale the difference lies, thus rendering inferences about achievement gaps highly dependent on the choice of a test metric (Reardon, 2007; Seltzer, Frank, & Bryk, 1994).

Given that we often wish to compare the magnitude of achievement gaps measured using different tests, or using a single test that is not clearly interval-scaled, researchers generally eschew using mean test scores and instead measure gaps in standard deviation units. Although standardizing test scores solves the primary problems of the comparability of gaps measured with different tests and in non-interval-scale metrics, there are several potential problems. First, suppose we have some "true" measure of cognitive ability, measured in a meaningful interval-scale. If the variance of cognitive ability, as measured in this metric, were to change over time (either across cohorts, or within a cohort as they progress through schooling), then standardizing the metric at each wave of testing would result in a measure of the gap that confounded changes in the "true" gap with changes in the variance of test scores. Thus, standardized gap measures are measures of *relative* achievement differences: they measure the size of the gap relative to the amount of variation in test scores within each group. If we are interested in *absolute* mean differences, then standardizing destroys part of the information we desire. Second, measurement error in test scores will tend to inflate the variance of the test score distributions, meaning that the achievement gaps measured in standard deviation units will be biased toward zero. If the gaps at different grades, ages, or cohorts are measured with tests that have different amounts of measurement error, then the amount of bias will not be the same in each measure of the gap, leading to potentially erroneous inferences regarding patterns or trends in the magnitudes of the gaps over time. If the reliability of the test is known, then one can correct the estimated gaps for measurement error.

Standardized measures of gaps may be sensitive to the distribution of test scores and the test metric, because a non-linear transformation of the test metric will alter the distributions of each group's test scores differently. So-called "metric-free" measures of achievement gaps, however, rely only on the ordinal aspect of the test metric, requiring no assumption of interval-scaling (Ho & Haertel, 2006).

For example, one can compute the probability that a randomly chosen black student has a score higher than a randomly chosen white student; the less overlap there is of the white and black test score distributions, the lower this probability will be. Moreover, this measure of the gap is invariant under any monotonic transformation of the test metric, obviating the need for assumptions about the metric's interval nature. Metric-free measures, however, do have some drawbacks: they are sensitive to measurement error and they require individual-level test scores to compute, unlike the standardized measures which require only group-specific means and standard deviations.

The empirical literature on achievement gaps has generally relied primarily on standardized gap measures (see, for example, Clotfelter, Ladd, & Vigdor, 2006; Fryer & Levitt, 2004, 2005; Grissmer, Flanagan, & Williamson, 1998; Hedges & Nowell, 1999; Neal, 2005; Phillips, Brooks-Gunn, Duncan, Klebanov, & Crane, 1998; Reardon & Galindo, 2006). Metric-free measures are arguably superior to standardized measures, though they have not yet been widely used (for recent examples of their use, see Ho & Haertel, 2006; Neal, 2005; Reardon, 2007). Finally, some of the literature on achievement gaps has relied on (un-standardized) mean differences in test scores (Hanushek & Rivkin, 2006; LoGerfo, Nichols, & Reardon, 2006; Murnane, Willett, Bub, & McCartney, 2006), and this literature generally points out that the results may be sensitive to the test metric used. However, the implications of using different measures of gaps have not been thoroughly investigated. In one example comparing standardized gaps and metric-free measures, Reardon (2007) shows that metric-free measures yield patterns similar to those using standardized gap measures, while different versions of the test score mean measures yield very different patterns.

HOW HAVE ACHIEVEMENT GAPS CHANGED OVER TIME?

The best source of data on how achievement gaps have changed over time comes from the National Assessment of Educational Progress (NAEP).[3] NAEP includes two different assessments of the math and reading skills of nationally-representative samples of students.[4] The first of these—NAEP long-term trend (NAEP-LTT)—is given about every four years to a nationally-representative sample of children aged 9, 13, and 17 years. Because the tests used for NAEP-LTT have remained essentially unchanged since their first administration in the early 1970s, they provide a consistent instrument to evaluate achievement trends (see, for example, Grissmer, Flanagan, & Williamson, 1998; Hedges & Nowell, 1998; Neal, 2005).

The second of the NAEP assessments has been administered roughly every two years since 1990 and is sometimes referred to as "Main NAEP." The content of the Main NAEP tests is updated periodically to reflect changing curricula, so that it is more appropriate than NAEP-LTT for providing information on how students perform on tests of the material taught in their schools. While this feature has obvious appeal for investigating current achievement patterns, the changing nature of the assessments makes comparisons across years difficult. For this reason, most studies rely on NAEP-LTT to investigate trends in achievement gaps. Using either test, researchers typically report gaps in standard deviation units because the data are collected in a cross-sectional manner and do not follow the achievement trajectories of the same students over time.

One additional difference between the two NAEP datasets deserves particular attention. NAEP-LTT is administered to age-cohorts (9-, 13-, and 17-year-olds), while Main NAEP is administered to grade-cohorts (fourth-, eighth-, and twelfth-graders). Because the populations sampled for the two assessments differ from one another, and because patterns of grade retention differ among racial, ethnic, and socioeconomic groups, the gaps measured by NAEP-LTT and Main NAEP would likely differ from one another even if the same tests were used in each. Moreover, changing patterns of grade retention across cohorts (e.g., if grade retention has increased in recent years) might complicate interpretation of trends in measured gaps, since the average grade level of each age-cohort and the age composition of each grade-cohort will then differ over time.

In Tables 28.1 and 28.2, we report trends in NAEP achievement gaps. Table 28.1 indicates 1971–2004 trends in black-white and Hispanic-white math and reading gaps, and gaps between students whose parents have only a high school diploma and those with a four-year college degree, as measured in standard deviation units on the NAEP-LTT tests. Table 28.2 indicates 1990–2005 trends in black-white, Hispanic-white, Mexican-white, and Asian-white math and reading gaps, measured in standard deviation units on the Main NAEP tests.

Trends in Black-White Achievement Gaps

Trend data on black-white achievement gaps are relatively clear: the black-white achievement gaps in both math and reading narrowed from the early 1970s through the late 1980s (Grissmer, Flanagan, & Williamson, 1998; Hedges & Nowell, 1998, 1999; Neal, 2005).[5] This pattern is evident not only in NAEP, but also in Scholastic Achievement Test (SAT) score trends (Ferguson, 1998), and in comparing nationally-representative samples of students in other large scale studies from the 1960s through 1992 (Hedges & Nowell, 1999). The black-white gap widened in the early 1990s (Ferguson, 1998; Neal, 2005), but the most recent NAEP-LTT results (administered in 2004) show that the black-white gap has narrowed again since the 1990s (see Table 28.1). Likewise, the 2003 and 2005 Main NAEP results also indicate a narrowing of the black-white

TABLE 28.1
Long-Term Trend NAEP Gap Estimates

	Black-White Gap						*Hispanic-White Gap*						*HS-College Degree Gap*			
	Reading			*Math*			*Reading*			*Math*			*Reading*		*Math*	
Test Year	*9-y.o.*	*13-y.o.*	*17-y.o.*	*9-y.o.*	*13-y.o.*	*17-y.o.*	*9-y.o.*	*13-y.o.*	*17-y.o.*	*9-y.o.*	*13-y.o.*	*17-y.o.*	*13-y.o.*	*17-y.o.*	*13-y.o.*	*17-y.o.*
1971	–1.04	–1.08	–1.15													
1975	–0.92	–1.02	–1.19				–0.88	–0.83	–0.92							
1978				–0.88	–1.08	–1.07				–0.59	–0.86	–0.84			–0.53	–0.65
1980	–0.84	–0.91	–1.19				–0.82	–0.78	–0.75				–0.55	–0.57		
1982				–0.84	–1.02	–0.98				–0.58	–0.66	–0.83			–0.58	–0.59
1984	–0.79	–0.74	–0.79				–0.76	–0.65	–0.68				–0.42	–0.53		
1986				–0.74	–0.79	–0.93				–0.63	–0.63	–0.79			–0.56	–0.67
1988	–0.71	–0.53	–0.55				–0.58	–0.61	–0.65				–0.36	–0.48		
1990	–0.79	–0.58	–0.71	–0.81	–0.88	–0.67	–0.62	–0.68	–0.53	–0.65	–0.70	–0.84	–0.43	–0.47	–0.57	–0.72
1992	–0.83	–0.73	–0.86	–0.82	–0.93	–0.87	–0.65	–0.69	–0.61	–0.70	–0.63	–0.65	–0.48	–0.49	–0.64	–0.61
1994	–0.80	–0.77	–0.67	–0.74	–0.90	–0.89	–0.79	–0.75	–0.73	–0.81	–0.76	–0.71	–0.44	–0.55	–0.59	–0.74
1996	–0.74	–0.82	–0.69	–0.75	–0.92	–0.89	–0.64	–0.71	–0.70	–0.66	–0.81	–0.71	–0.46	–0.60	–0.51	–0.64
1999	–0.91	–0.74	–0.73	–0.82	–0.99	–1.02	–0.71	–0.60	–0.57	–0.76	–0.74	–0.72	–0.48	–0.58	–0.67	–0.57
2004	–0.72	–0.59	–0.67	–0.68	–0.80	–0.95	–0.58	–0.64	–0.68	–0.52	–0.70	–0.82	–0.50	–0.54	–0.62	–0.74

Source: Authors' calculations from NAEP-LTT data, available at http://nces.ed.gov/nationsreportcard/ltt/; pooled standard deviations for tests through 1990 come from Phillips et al. (1998), and standard deviations of subsequent years' tests were provided by NCES. Note: Gaps measured in standard deviation units. NAEP-LTT does not report parental education level for 9-year-olds, so we report parental education gaps only for 13- and 17-year-olds.

gap in fourth and eighth grades since the early 1990s (see Table 28.2). In reading and math the black-white gaps for 9- and 13-year-old students are roughly similar in magnitude to those in the late 1980s. The black-white math and reading gap for 17-year-olds in 2004, however, does not appear to have narrowed. Table 28.1 reports the magnitude of the black-white gap in NAEP-LTT from 1971-2004.

A wide variety of explanations have been proposed for the trends in the black-white test score gaps since the 1970s, though none is conclusive. Grissmer, Flanagan, and Williamson (1998) argue that trends in black and white students' family characteristics can only account for a small portion of the narrowing of the black-white gap through the late 1980s; they argue instead that school policies (including desegregation) account for much of the reduction in the gap. Among other things, they demonstrate that achievement gains by region were greatest for blacks in the southeast, which experienced desegregation, and lowest in the northeast, which experienced increased segregation. Ferguson (1998) argues that the accountability movement of the 1980s led to increased advanced course taking among black students, thus narrowing the gap through the 1980s.

Neal (2005) focuses more on explaining the widening of the gap in the late 1980s and early 1990s, and suggests that declines in black incomes relative to white incomes in the 1980s, the changing wage structure of the United States, and the rise in single-parent black families in the 1980s may have contributed to the reversal of the narrowing gap trend. He also suggests that the crack-cocaine epidemic in the late 1980s and early 1990s may have contributed to the widening of the gap because of its disruptive effects on the lives of black children in urban communities affected by the epidemic. In addition, Ferguson (1998) argues that the rise of hip-hop and rap music in the late 1980s may have led to both a decline in the amount of leisure reading among black adolescents, and a decline in black students' identification with schooling and academic achievement.

Trends in Hispanic-White Achievement Gaps

Despite the availability of NAEP-LTT data on a sizable Hispanic student population, there is relatively little research on patterns and trends of Hispanic-white achievement gaps. Tables 28.1 and 28.2 present standardized achievement gaps calculated from NAEP data. In reading, the long-term trend in the Hispanic-white achievement gap has followed a similar pattern as the black-white reading gap—a decline from the mid-1970s through the late 1980s, followed by an increase in the early 1990s, and then another decline from the mid-1990s through 2004. The Hispanic-white reading gap is generally similar in magnitude to the black-white reading gap. In math, however, the Hispanic-white gap has been consistently smaller (by roughly .10–.15 standard deviations) than the black-white gap. Moreover, the Hispanic-white math gap has not changed substantially since the late 1970s, though the gap does appear to have widened in the early 1990s before narrowing again more recently (at least for 9- and 13-year-olds).

Data from Main NAEP also allow the examination of achievement patterns of Mexican-origin students relative to non-Hispanic white students (Table 28.2). In general, the Mexican-white gaps are very similar to the overall Hispanic-white gaps (not surprising, since Mexican-origin students make up roughly two-thirds of Hispanic students). In reading, however, the Mexican-white gap in fourth grade is slightly smaller than the overall Hispanic-white gap, while the eighth- and twelfth-grade Mexican-white reading gaps are similar or slightly larger than the corresponding overall Hispanic-white gaps, suggesting that Mexican-origin students' reading skills have grown less rapidly from fourth to eighth grades than have those of non-Mexican Hispanic students.[6] Again, a more detailed analysis would be required to understand these patterns.

TABLE 28.2
Main NAEP Gap Trend Estimates

	Black-White Gap						*Asian-White Gap*					
	Math			*Reading*			*Math*			*Reading*		
Test year	*4th*	*8th*	*12th*	*4th*	*8th*	*12th*	*4th*	*8th*	*12th*	*4th*	*8th*	*12th*
1990	–1.02	–0.91	–0.89				0.15	0.15	0.30			
1992	–1.09	–1.10	–0.89	–0.91	–0.83	–0.74	0.12	0.37	0.21	–0.23	0.04	–0.21
1994				–0.94	–0.83	–0.78				–0.10	–0.05	–0.41
1996	–1.11	–1.09	–0.96				–0.11		0.05			
1998				–0.82	–0.75	–0.71				–0.26	–0.18	–0.26
2000	–0.99	–1.04	–0.94	–0.82				0.12	0.26	0.01		
2002				–0.83	–0.80	–0.67				–0.12	–0.18	–0.18
2003	–0.96	–0.98		–0.82	–0.78		0.11	0.09		–0.07	–0.06	
2005	–0.92	–0.93		–0.81	–0.80		0.17	0.18		–0.01	0.00	

(continued)

	Hispanic-White Gap						*Mexican-White Gap*					
	Math			*Reading*			*Math*			*Reading*		
Test year	*4th*	*8th*	*12th*	*4th*	*8th*	*12th*	*4th*	*8th*	*12th*	*4th*	*8th*	*12th*
1990	–0.61	–0.66	–0.66				–0.64	–0.76	–0.65			
1992	–0.79	–0.77	–0.56	–0.77	–0.73	–0.58	–0.77	–0.84	–0.59	–0.65	–0.76	–0.61
1994				–0.87	–0.65					–0.76	–0.66	–0.68
1996	–0.80	–0.79	–0.74			–0.63	–0.82	–0.83	–0.72			
1998				–0.83	–0.77	–0.57				–0.79	–0.78	–0.54
2000	–0.85	–0.82	–0.70	–0.84			–0.80	–0.81	–0.73	–0.80		
2002				–0.77	–0.76	–0.53				–0.73	–0.79	–0.59
2003	–0.76	–0.79		–0.76	–0.76							
2005	–0.72	–0.74		–0.73	–0.71							

Source: Authors' calculations from Main NAEP data, available at http://nces.ed.gov/nationsreportcard/naepdata/. Note: Gaps measured in standard deviation units.

Trends in Socioeconomic Achievement Gaps

No existing research has explicitly examined trends in what we might call the socioeconomic status (SES) achievement gap—the gap between children from lower- and higher-income or socioeconomic status families. In part, this reflects the fact that socioeconomic status is a multidimensional construct that is both harder to measure and much less stable than is race/ethnicity. Nonetheless, in Table 28.1 we make an effort to examine socioeconomic achievement gaps using parental education level as a crude indicator of socioeconomic status. Specifically, we use NAEP-LTT data to compare the math and reading achievement of students whose parents have only a high school diploma, to those with a (four-year) college degree.

The high school-college degree gaps in math have been relatively stable over the last 25 years, ranging from roughly one-half to two-thirds of a standard deviation at age 13, and ranging from three-fifths to three-quarters of a standard deviation at age 17. In reading, the parental education gaps have been generally smaller than those in math and show a little more of a trend over time. The reading gaps narrowed through the 1980s before widening again, so that the most recent estimates of the gap (roughly one-half a standard deviation at ages 13 and 17) are now only slightly smaller than they were in 1980.

HOW DO ACHIEVEMENT GAPS CHANGE AS CHILDREN PROGRESS THROUGH SCHOOL?

Research findings on the development of achievement gaps as children progress through school come from two types of studies: those using longitudinal panel data on one or more cohorts of students,[7] and those relying on repeated cross-sectional data of the same cohort to infer developmental patterns (such as the NAEP studies). Under the respective assumptions that attrition (from longitudinal studies) is random, and that changes in cohort composition are unrelated to achievement patterns (in repeated cross-sectional studies), both types of studies will provide unbiased estimates of the development of achievement gaps as students age.[8] Regardless of whether longitudinal or repeated cross-sectional data are used to examine the development of gaps as students progress through school, the value of comparison of the magnitude of the gaps at different ages depends on the comparability of the test metrics used at each age. In fact, different test metrics lead to dramatically different conclusions regarding how achievement gaps change with age (compare, for example, Fryer & Levitt, 2004; Fryer & Levitt, 2005; Hanushek & Rivkin, 2006; see also Reardon, 2007). In the absence of metric-free gap measures, gaps measured in pooled, within-age standard deviation units are likely less sensitive to violations of the interval-scaled metric assumption than other approaches, so we focus here on studies that measure gaps in this type of metric.

The Development of Black-White Achievement Gaps

Almost all research on the topic concludes that the black-white achievement gap in math grows during the school years, particularly in elementary school. Most research shows that the same is true for the black-white reading gap. NAEP-LTT data show that the black-white math gap (though not the reading gap) widens from age nine to 13 (Ferguson, 1998; Neal, 2005; Phillips, Crouse, & Ralph, 1998). The development of the gap from age 13 to 17 is less clear—the gaps generally do not appear to widen much in this period, but these results are less certain because differential dropout patterns may bias the estimates of the gaps at age 17.

The most commonly-cited (and probably the best) contemporary evidence on the development of the black-white gaps in elementary school comes from the Early Childhood Longitudinal Study—Kindergarten Class of 1998–9 (ECLS-K), which includes kindergarten through fifth-grade assessment data on a nationally-representative sample of students who were enrolled in kindergarten in the fall of 1998 (see Table 28.3). ECLS-K data show that the black-white gaps in both math and reading are sizeable at the start of kindergarten—about three-quarters and one-half of a standard deviation, respectively (Fryer & Levitt, 2004; Reardon, 2007; Reardon & Galindo, 2006). Measured in standard deviation units, these gaps widen slightly through kindergarten and first grade, and then widen more rapidly between first and fifth grades, by which time the math gap is about one full standard deviation, and the reading gap is about three-quarters of a standard deviation (Reardon, 2007; Reardon & Galindo, 2006). Measured in metric-free units, both the math and reading gaps increase moderately from kindergarten through fifth grade, with most of the increase occurring in second and third grades (Reardon, 2007).

Analyses of several other large studies, however, have produced somewhat different results than those from ECLS-K. Data from the Prospects study (which includes longitudinal data collected from 1991 to 1993 from three age-cohorts of students) suggest that the black-white math gap grows in first and second grades, and from seventh to ninth grades (though not from third to fifth grades), while the black-white reading gap grows in first to second grades, and third to fifth grades, but not in seventh to ninth grades (Phillips, Crouse, & Ralph, 1998). However, the Prospects data were collected almost a decade before ECLS-K (and on cohorts of children born 9–16 years prior to the ECLS-K cohort), so the data may be less relevant than the ECLS-K sample.

The National Institute of Child Health and Human Development Study of Early Child Care and Youth Development (SECCYD) indicates that the black-white math gap—measured in standard deviation units—narrows slightly from kindergarten through third grade (from 1.1 to 1.0 standard deviations), while the black-white reading gap widens during the same period (from 1.0 to 1.2 standard deviations) (Murnane, Willett, Bub, & McCartney, 2006). Murnane and his colleagues argue that at least part of the difference in the patterns observed in SECCYD and ECLS-K may be due to differences in the tests used in the two studies, since the Woodcock-Johnson tests used in the SECCYD assess a broad range of skills, while the ECLS-K tests are designed to measure skills taught in school.

Finally, analyses of test score data from several U.S. states provide yet another set of conflicting findings regarding the development of the black-white gaps during the schooling years. Data from four cohorts of students in Texas (cohorts in third grade from 1994-1997) indicate that the black-white gap in math grew modestly, in standard deviation units, from third through eighth grades (from .59 to .70 standard deviations) (Hanushek & Rivkin, 2006). Similar data from North Carolina (five cohorts in third grade from 1994-1999), however, indicate that the black-white math gap was relatively stable from third to eighth grades (changing from 0.77 to 0.81 standard deviations); and the black-white reading gap likewise increased only very modestly (from 0.69 to 0.77 standard deviations) (Clotfelter, Ladd, & Vigdor, 2006). It is unclear whether the relatively small differences in the rate of growth of the math gap between Texas and North Carolina are due to differences in the tests used in each state, differences in their black and white student populations, or differences in the features of the two states' educational systems, curricula, and/or instructional practices.

In contrast to their growth during elementary school, black-white achievement gaps appear to change relatively little during high school. Evidence from the National Educational Longitudinal Study of 1988 (NELS), which contains longitudinal data on a nationally representative sample of eighth graders in 1988, shows that the black-white math gap—measured in standard deviation units—is stable from eighth through twelfth grades, while the black-white reading

TABLE 28.3
Race/Ethnic and Parental Education Achievement Gaps, by Subject and ECLS-K Assessment Wave

	Math					*Reading*				
Race / National Origin	*Fall K*	*Spring K*	*Spring 1*	*Spring 3*	*Spring 5*	*Fall K*	*Spring K*	*Spring 1*	*Spring 3*	*Spring 5*
"Black, Not Hispanic, 3rd generation"	–0.73	–0.80	–0.79	–0.93	–1.01	–0.53	–0.56	–0.53	–0.76	–0.80
Asian	0.12	0.14	0.05	0.08	0.29	0.19	0.25	0.26	0.11	0.10
"Hispanic, any Race"	–0.77	–0.68	–0.56	–0.57	–0.50	–0.52	–0.34	–0.29	–0.36	–0.38
Mexican Origin	–0.91	–0.79	–0.60	–0.65	–0.61	–0.56	–0.37	–0.34	–0.37	–0.40
Mexican, 1st generation"	–1.12	–0.98	–0.77	–0.78	–0.71	–0.89	–0.93	–0.68	–0.70	–0.68
Mexican, 2nd generation"	–1.09	–1.00	–0.73	–0.81	–0.74	–0.76	–0.56	–0.47	–0.48	–0.52
Mexican, 3rd generation"	–0.46	–0.35	–0.29	–0.32	–0.33	–0.36	–0.17	–0.21	–0.27	–0.28
Cuban Origin	–0.46	–0.10	–0.15	–0.09	–0.11	–0.25	0.09	–0.15	–0.16	–0.14
Puerto Rican Origin	–0.45	–0.46	–0.46	–0.34	–0.26	–0.36	–0.27	–0.09	–0.18	–0.12
Central American Origin	–1.05	–0.85	–0.87	–0.61	–0.37	–0.58	–0.39	–0.44	–0.18	–0.29
South American Origin	–0.53	–0.38	–0.23	–0.15	–0.09	–0.26	–0.17	–0.03	–0.03	0.00
Parent Educational Attainment										
Less than high school graduate	–1.49	–1.39	–1.30	–1.37	–1.40	–1.33	–1.24	–1.23	–1.44	–1.41
High school graduate	–0.94	–0.89	–0.82	–0.90	–0.98	–0.95	–0.79	–0.74	–0.90	–0.99
Some education after HS	–0.62	–0.57	–0.53	–0.57	–0.61	–0.63	–0.50	–0.45	–0.59	–0.62

Notes: Reference group for Race/National Origin comparisons is "White, Not Hispanic, 3rd Generation." Reference group for parental educational attainment comparisons is "College Graduates and up."
Sources: Race/National Origin comparisons taken from Reardon & Galindo (2006), Tables B1-B6; parental educational attainment gaps from authors tabulations of ECLS-K data.

gap appears to narrow very slightly during this period (LoGerfo, Nichols, & Reardon, 2006). NAEP data on trends in the gap during high school differ slightly, but are ambiguous. Ferguson reports NAEP-LTT data showing that the black-white gap in math narrowed from age 13 to 17 in reading for cohorts born in the 1960s (but was unchanged from 13 to 17 for later cohorts), while the black-white gap in reading widens from 13 to 17 for some NAEP cohorts of students (those born in 1958–1963 and those born 1975–1977), but is stable for other cohorts (those born 1967–1971 and in 1979) (Ferguson, 1998). Ferguson reports test scores in the NAEP scale score metric (which is constant over time), so the patterns he reports are not exactly the same as those inferred from 28.1, which indicates gaps by age, in wave-specific standard deviation units. Phillips, Crouse, & Ralph (1998) conduct a meta-analysis of a number of cross-sectional estimates of the black-white gaps, and find that the black-white gap in math widens, on average, during high school, but is unchanged in reading and vocabulary.

In sum, evidence on how the black-white achievement gap changes during schooling is somewhat unclear. Data from ECLS-K and SECCYD suggest the gap is large at the start of kindergarten, and grows in the early elementary grades (particularly from first to third grades in ECLS-K). Data from NAEP indicates that the gap continues to grow from age 9 to 13 (fourth to eighth grades, roughly), but state-level data from Texas and North Carolina seem to contradict this finding, at least during the late 1990s and early 2000s, by showing that the gap grows relatively little in standard deviation units over the latter half of elementary school. Finally, data from NAEP and NELS suggest that the gaps change relatively little following eighth grade, though there is some uncertainty in these estimates, since most are based on analysis of repeated cross-sectional data.

The Development of Hispanic-White Achievement Gaps

The most detailed evidence on the development of Hispanic-white gaps comes from the ECLS-K, which includes a large sample (roughly 4,000) of Hispanic students that can be disaggregated by national origin, generational status, and English proficiency (Reardon & Galindo, 2006). In addition, because the ECLS-K study administered the math test orally in either English or Spanish, depending on students' language proficiency, ECLS-K estimates of the Hispanic-white math scores are not biased by the changing English proficiency of the students.[9]

ECLS-K data (Table 28.3) indicate that the Hispanic-white math and reading gaps at the start of kindergarten are very similar in magnitude to the black-white gap; yet math and reading gaps decrease for Hispanic students during the first six years of formal schooling, while the black-white gaps widen during the same period (Fryer & Levitt, 2004, 2005; Reardon & Galindo, 2006). In math, the gap shrinks from three-quarters to one-half of a standard deviation; the reading gap narrows from one-half to about one-third of a standard deviation. Most of the narrowing of the gap occurs in kindergarten and first grade; the gaps narrow relatively little following first grade.

Evidence from other studies suggests the Hispanic-white achievement gaps continue to narrow, albeit slowly, through middle and high school. Data from North Carolina indicate that Hispanic students gain ground on white students in both math and reading from third through eighth grades, closing both gaps by over 0.10 standard deviations (Clotfelter, Ladd, & Vigdor, 2006). Data from the NELS study likewise show the Hispanic-white gaps in both math and reading narrow modestly from eighth to twelfth grades, though differential dropout rates for Hispanic and white students during high school may confound these estimates somewhat (LoGerfo, Nichols, & Reardon, 2006).

Hispanic-white gaps do not develop similarly for all subgroups of the Hispanic student population. Using ECLS-K data, Reardon and Galindo (2006) provide a detailed description of the development of achievement gaps from kindergarten through fifth grade, by Hispanic subgroups (as defined by national origin and generational status). They find that students of Mexican and Central American origin perform much worse, on average, in math and reading at the start of kindergarten than do students of Cuban, Puerto Rican, and South American origin (Table 28.3). However, the gaps between Mexican and Central American students' scores and white students' scores narrow quite rapidly, particularly in kindergarten and first grade. Likewise, first- and second-generation students enter kindergarten with math and reading skills far below those of white students (and third-generation Hispanic students), but make up considerable (but not all) ground in the first few years of schooling. Reardon and Galindo speculate that because rapid gains for Hispanics occur generally in the first two years of schooling, and because they are concentrated among recent immigrants and students with the lowest levels of English proficiency at the start of kindergarten, it is likely that much of the narrowing of the gap in kindergarten and first grade is attributable to the development of English language skills among these students. Because most other studies do not have sufficiently large samples of Hispanic subgroups (or do not collect data on national origin and generational status), we know relatively little about the development of achievement gaps by Hispanic subgroups in middle and high school.

The Development of Asian-White Achievement Gaps

There is relatively little detailed evidence regarding the development of Asian-white achievement gaps. Reardon and Galindo (2006) and Fryer and Levitt (2005) report the development of Asian-white gaps using ECLS-K data for the three-quarters of Asian-origin students proficient in oral English at the start of kindergarten.[10] These estimates likely overstate the average achievement of Asian-origin students, since the excluded students are generally from recently-immigrated and lower socioeconomic status families. That said, the ECLS-K data (Table 28.3) show that Asian-origin students who are proficient in oral English at the start of kindergarten appear to have similar levels of math skills as white students through third grade, but better math skills by fifth grade. In reading, the Asian-origin students in the sample have scores roughly two- to three-tenths of a standard deviation higher than white students in kindergarten, an advantage that narrows to non-significance by fifth grade (Fryer & Levitt, 2005; Reardon & Galindo, 2006).

Data from North Carolina show that the Asian-white math gap is statistically indistinguishable from zero in third grade, but widens (in favor of Asian-origin students) to one-third of a standard deviation by eighth grade, while the Asian-white reading gap remains relatively constant at about one-tenth of a standard deviation in third and eighth grades (Clotfelter, Ladd, & Vigdor, 2006). Given the heterogeneity of the Asian population—in terms of national origin, recentness of immigration, socioeconomic status, and context of immigration—generalizations about Asian students as a monolithic group are as problematic as they are for Hispanic students. Certainly more detailed research on Asian-origin students' achievement patterns would be useful.

The Development of Socioeconomic Achievement Gaps

Although considerable research has documented the strong association between family socioeconomic characteristics, and children's cognitive development and school achievement, there is relatively little research that provides a descriptive analysis of the development of the socioeconomic achievement gradient over time. One factor confounding such analyses is the fluid nature of socioeconomic status—unlike race or gender, socioeconomic characteristics of a family change over time, often quite dramatically.

In the absence of extant clear descriptive research on the patterns of cognitive development over time, we present here some new analyses using the ECLS-K and NAEP data. Using an indicator of the highest level of education completed by either parent, we begin by examining trends in NAEP-LTT data. Averaging across all years for which we have NAEP data (see Table 28.1), we compute the gaps between students from families, with each of three levels of parental education (no high school diploma, only a high school degree, and some college) and students with a parent holding a four-year college degree (although only the high school-college degree gap is presented in Table 28.1).

In mathematics, test scores are consistently lower for children of parents at each successively lower parental educational attainment level. That is, at age 13, children of parents with less than a high school degree, a high school degree, and some education beyond high school score an average of –0.93, –0.59, and –0.21 standard deviations below children of college-educated parents, respectively.[11] By age 17, the average gaps have widened to –1.04, –0.66, and –0.31, respectively—an increase in the gaps of roughly one-tenth of a standard deviation from age 13 to 17 for each group. In reading, the story is similar, though the reading gaps are smaller than the corresponding math gaps for each education and age group. Second, the reading gaps widen only slightly from age 13 to 17. At age 13, children of parents with less than a high school degree, a high school degree, and some education beyond high school score an average of –0.82, –0.46, and –0.08 standard deviations below children of college-educated parents, respectively. At age 17 the corresponding gaps are –0.84, –0.54, and –0.13 standard deviations. Of course, if low-achieving students from less educated families leave school before age 17 at higher rates than similarly low-achieving students from families with college-educated parents, then these numbers may underestimate the rate of increase in the socioeconomic gaps as children progress through school.

Data from longitudinal studies such as ECLS-K and NELS also show that socioeconomic gaps widen as students progress through school, except during the first few years of schooling, when they appear to narrow. Our analysis of ECLS-K data suggests that both math and reading achievement gaps narrow by roughly 10 percent during the first two years of schooling, but then widen slowly through fifth grade (Table 28.3). Data from NELS suggest that the socioeconomic gaps continue widening slowly though twelfth grade (LoGerfo, Nichols, & Reardon, 2006).

DO ACHIEVEMENT GAPS GROW DIFFERENTLY ACROSS THE ACHIEVEMENT RANGE?

Most studies examining achievement disparities between groups focus on differences in mean achievement. There are, however, important reasons to examine the disparities across the full distribution of test scores. For example, underlying the debate regarding affirmative action in admissions to highly competitive colleges is the fact that black and Hispanic students are dramatically underrepresented in the upper end of the achievement distribution. Neal (2005, see Figures 2a–2d) shows that roughly 5 percent of black students 13- to 17–years-old in the 1990s had math scores in the top quartile of the white math score distribution. This means that black students are underrepresented by 80 percent in the top quartile of the distribution, a finding that has enormous implications for black students' access to elite colleges and employment in jobs with the highest skill demands (and the highest pay). Such patterns suggest the importance of investigating not only differences in the black and white test score distributions, but also of investigating when and how such differences emerge.

Answering this question turns out to be more complex than it would seem, however, because any comparison of the magnitude of gaps or differences in growth rates relies on the assumption that the test metric used is interval-scaled. Clotfelter, Ladd, and Vigdor (2006) investigate whether the gap in scores between the ninetieth percentiles of the black and white test score distributions grows or narrows faster than the gap between the tenth percentiles of the distributions. They find that in math, racial test score gaps measured in standard deviation units generally narrow from grades three to eight at the tenth percentiles of the score distributions, and widen at the same time at the ninetieth percentiles of the distributions. They find no such pattern for reading. They interpret the math pattern as potentially a result of accountability pressures, arguing that the compression of the gap at the low end of the test score distribution is a result of policies that push schools to reduce the percentage of students scoring below certain thresholds. Likewise, they view the expansion of the gap at the high end as a result of the diversion of resources away from high-achieving minority students (because such students are in schools with many low-achieving students). While this is a plausible explanation, it is also possible that the results are an artifact of the tests used to measure the gaps. If the third- and eighth-grade tests are not both scored in interval-scaled metrics, and if the eighth-grade test metric is more sensitive to variation at the high end of the distribution than is the third-grade test, then the pattern they find would be observed in the absence of any true difference in the rate of the gap growth.

Likewise, determining whether achievement gaps grow faster or slower between initially high- and low-achieving students relies on the assumption that test scores are interval-scaled. In addition, measurement error in test scores will also tend to bias such estimates, because conditioning growth rates on scores measured with error will systematically bias estimates of differences in growth rates (Hanushek & Rivkin, 2006; Reardon, 2007). Relatively little empirical research has attempted to systematically address the question of whether achievement gaps within a cohort grow or narrow differentially across the range of skill distribution.[12] What research there is has focused exclusively on the black-white gap, and generally has not adequately addressed the complexities described here. As a result, there is little we can say with certainty to this point. More research is certainly needed.

HOW MUCH OF RACIAL/ETHNIC ACHIEVEMENT GAPS CAN BE EXPLAINED BY SOCIOECONOMIC STATUS?

A relatively common question addressed in studies of racial/ethnic achievement gaps (particularly the black-white gap) is the extent to which the observed gaps can be explained by socioeconomic differences between the groups. Using ECLS-K data, Fryer & Levitt (2005) show that socioeconomic factors explain almost all (85 percent) of the black-white math gap, and all of the reading gap at the start of kindergarten (in fact, they find that the black students score higher in reading than white students of the same socioeconomic status). By third grade, however, they find that the same socioeconomic factors account for only about 60 percent of both the math and reading black-white gaps. This finding suggests that socioeconomic factors explain, in large part, the black-white differences in cognitive skills at the start of formal schooling, but do not account for the growth of the black-white gap as children progress through elementary school. This observation has significant implications for understanding the role of schooling in producing or exacerbating achievement gaps.

The Fryer and Levitt (2005) analysis is notable for being the only one that shows that the black-white gap at kindergarten entry can be almost completely accounted for by socioeconomic differences between black and white students. Earlier studies, for example, typically found that socioeconomic factors explain roughly half of the black-white gap at kindergarten entry, though these results were based on samples of children that are disproportionately poor (Brooks-Gunn,

Klebanov, & Duncan, 1996; Phillips, Brooks-Gunn, Duncan, Klebanov, & Crane, 1998). Other recent studies, however, show that socioeconomic factors typically account for even less—between 25 and 40 percent—of the black-white math and reading gaps through middle and high schools.[13] Using the same ELCS-K data as Fryer and Levitt, but a different version of the test score metric (the un-standardized scale scores), Murnane and colleagues (2006) report that the socioeconomic differences between white and black students account for only one-third of the math gap, and 15 percent of the reading gap by third grade (though they find that socioeconomic factors fully account for the black-white gap in kindergarten).[14] Similarly, using the SECCYD data, they find that socioeconomic status accounts for one-third of the math and one-quarter of the reading black-white gaps in third grade (Murnane, Willett, Bub, & McCartney, 2006). Phillips, Crouse, and Ralph's (1998) analysis of Prospects and NELS data shows SES explains about 35 to 40 percent of black-white achievement gaps in math, reading, and vocabulary across the span of second through twelfth grades. North Carolina data show similar patterns, with socioeconomic factors (as well as region of the state and urbanism) accounting for about 35 percent of the math and reading gaps from third through eighth grades (Clotfelter, Ladd, & Vigdor, 2006).

The extent to which socioeconomic factors account for Hispanic-white achievement gaps, however, is quite different than for the black-white gap. Using ECLS-K data, Fryer and Levitt (2005) show that socioeconomic factors account for 75 to 85 percent of the Hispanic-white gaps in kindergarten, and 85 to 100 percent of the gaps in third grade. One explanation for this different pattern may be that the Hispanic-white gaps are partly due to Hispanic students' lower levels of English proficiency; as students progress through school, their English skills improve and the gaps narrow (see Table 28.3), so that socioeconomic factors explain an increasing proportion of the gaps. Similarly, Reardon and Galindo (2006; tables B11, B12) show that Hispanic-white gaps, conditional on socioeconomic status, narrow from kindergarten through fifth grade, while the corresponding black-white gaps widen at the same time. North Carolina data show a similar pattern: Hispanic-white socioeconomic-adjusted math and reading gaps are small (one-tenth of a standard deviation) in third grade, non-existent by fifth grade, and reversed by eighth grade, when Hispanic students score higher, on average, in both math and reading than socioeconomically similar white students (Clotfelter, Ladd, & Vigdor, 2006).

DO ACHIEVEMENT GAPS GROW BETWEEN OR WITHIN SCHOOLS?

A central question in understanding test score gaps is the extent to which such gaps can be attributed to differences in average school quality between schools attended by students of different racial, ethnic, or socioeconomic groups. If, for example, black students attend, on average, lower quality schools than white students, we would expect the between-school component of the black-white achievement gap to grow over time. If black and white students receive unequal instructional opportunities when attending the same schools, we would expect the within-school component of the black-white gap to grow over time. Of course, it is difficult to disentangle the effects of school quality from the sorting processes that produce racially and socioeconomically segregated schools, and that may result in lower-ability students, regardless of race or socioeconomic status, attending schools that have lower proportions of white or middle-class students. Likewise, it is not clear that differences in achievement gains can be attributed solely to schooling processes (particularly given the evidence that the gaps predate kindergarten; see Fryer & Levitt, 2004; Lee & Burkham, 2002; Reardon & Galindo, 2006), given unequal family resources, neighborhood context, and opportunity structures (which may lead to unequal motivation even in the presence of equal home and school resources). Nonetheless, an understanding of the relative contribution of between- and within-school factors, as well as of family background and out-of-school social context, is essential for determining the appropriate policy remedies for the gaps.

Despite the importance of disentangling between- and within-school patterns in the growth of achievement gaps, there is relatively little clear evidence on this point. Fryer and Levitt (2005) find that the black-white gap is small or non-existent in kindergarten—net of family socioeconomic characteristics—but grows from kindergarten through third grade (using ECLS-K data), a pattern that suggests that observable family background characteristics are not solely responsible for the post-kindergarten growth in the gap. However, they also find that the black-white gap grows through third grade even between black and white students attending the same school, a finding they interpret to mean that between-school differences in school quality do not account for much of the growth of the black-white gap during elementary school.

Hanushek and Rivkin (2006), however, disagree with the Fryer and Levitt (2005) conclusion that the gap grows primarily within schools. Using the same ECLS-K data (as well as data from Texas), Hanushek and Rivkin (2006) describe a decomposition of the growth of the black-white gap from kindergarten through fifth grade, and conclude that almost all of the growth of the gap in elementary school is attributable to the growth of the gap between schools attended by black and white students. Reardon (2007) shows that the disagreement between these two analyses stems from an ambiguity in the decomposition of the gap into between- and within-school components and argues that no unambiguous decomposition is possible in the absence of a theory of the mechanisms that produce the gap. Hence, it remains unclear to what extent the gaps are attributable to between-school, within-school, and non-school factors. More research is needed here to guide policy.

WHAT ARE THE LABOR MARKET EFFECTS OF ACHIEVEMENT GAPS?

From a labor market perspective, achievement disparities are important primarily because test score disparities in elementary and secondary schools are highly predictive of corresponding disparities in subsequent labor market outcomes. Data from the most recent Annual Demographic Survey (March Supplement) of the Current Population Survey (CPS) show that median black and Hispanic male full-time workers earn 28 percent and 40 percent less than the median white male full-time worker, respectively. For female full-time workers, the corresponding black and Hispanic gaps are 15 percent and 32 percent, respectively.

A sizeable body of research has investigated the extent to which these wage disparities are attributable to differences in cognitive skill obtained prior to entering the labor force (i.e., in childhood, elementary school, and secondary school), typically measured by cognitive achievement test scores. In general, this research finds that roughly one-half of all of the male black-white wage gaps can be accounted for by black-white differences in human capital, as shown proxied by scores on the Armed Forces Qualification Test (AFQT) when individuals were near completing high school (Bollinger, 2003; Carneiro, Heckman, & Masterov, 2003; Neal & Johnson, 1996).[15] Although there is much less evidence regarding the extent to which test score differences account for Hispanic-white wage gaps, evidence from the National Longitudinal Survey of Youth (NLSY) suggests that test score differences account for virtually all of the male Hispanic-white wage gap (Carneiro, Heckman, & Masterov, 2003).[16]

These findings suggest that factors such as racial discrimination in the labor market are not responsible for much, if any, of the black-white wage differential, a conclusion supported by other research that compares the earning differential among different cohorts. For example, O'Neill (1990) reviews possible explanations for the decrease in the black-white wage differential during the twentieth century, and finds that differences in the educational and workplace experiences of black and white men are much more important in explaining the wage gap between the races than is labor market discrimination. Examining hourly wages six years after high school graduation, Murnane, Willett, and Levy (1995) find that cognitive skills predict labor markets outcome more in the mid-1980s than they did in the late-1970s, suggesting the increasing importance of cognitive skills in wage determination.

It is worth noting, however, that not all gains in reducing black-white wage inequality during the twentieth century can be attributed to narrowing skill gaps (O'Neill, 1990). For instance, the relative earnings of blacks increased during the 1960s and 1970s—arguably due to governmental intervention in reducing employment discrimination—for cohorts who had already completed schooling. Likewise, some recent research suggests that labor market discrimination remains an important factor in labor market outcomes (see, for example, Grodsky & Pager, 2001; Pager, 2003), though even this research acknowledges that the majority of the black-white wage differential can be attributed to black-white differences in human capital obtained prior to entering the labor market.

The finding that human capital differences account for a large portion of the black-white wage gap, suggests that efforts to reduce black-white achievement disparities at the end of adolescence may substantially reduce subsequent black-white wage gaps, though such a reduction would take decades to take full effect. Even an immediate elimination of the gaps in human capital among adolescents would not, presumably, reduce wage disparities among cohorts already in the labor force. As a result, wage differentials among older cohorts may persist for decades, until they age out of the labor force.[17]

In addition to concerns regarding the magnitude of the differences in mean test scores among individuals of different racial groups, a number of researchers have called attention to the effects of racial disparities at the upper end of the achievement distribution (see Neal, 2005, discussed above). Recent evidence indicates that the increase in the returns to education in the 1980s was largest for those in the top quartile of the achievement distribution (Heckman & Vytlacil, 2001). Because whites are substantially overrepresented in the highest quartile of the achievement distribution, this pattern suggests that racial disparities at the top of the achievement distribution have become increasingly salient in shaping labor market inequality.

CONCLUSION

In this review, we have attempted to summarize the state of knowledge regarding racial/ethnic achievement gaps and to suggest areas in which more research is needed. Despite the complexity of answering questions about achievement gaps due to the need to rely on imperfect measures of cognitive skills, several key patterns are evident from our summary of the research.

First, racial/ethnic and socioeconomic achievement gaps are narrower now than they were 30 years ago; and this is particularly true for the black-white achievement gaps. Second, the gaps of most interest—the black-white, Hispanic-white, and socioeconomic gaps—remain quite large today, ranging from 0.5 to 1.0 standard deviations. Third, the black-white gap appears to widen during the school years—particularly in early elementary school—in ways that are not explained by socioeconomic family background characteristics, a pattern that suggests that schooling appears to contribute to the growth of the gaps. The same patterns are not found for Hispanic-white and Asian-white disparities, however; for these groups, socioeconomic differences account for a large portion of the gaps, and processes of second language acquisition appear to contribute to a narrowing of the gap as children progress through school. Fourth, achievement disparities have large effects in the labor market, and explain a large portion of racial/ethnic income disparities.

Less clear in extant research are the processes and mechanisms that produce racial and ethnic achievement disparities. Although it is clear that family background and schooling each play some role in the development of achievement gaps, we do not have good evidence on exactly how—or how much—each contributes. Nor do we have any good evidence regarding the extent to which these processes may vary among racial or ethnic groups. Most importantly, without a good understanding of the mechanisms that produce these gaps, we have very little evidence regarding how we might reduce them. In addition to documenting the magnitude, trends, and development of achievement gaps, we need more and better research regarding the effectiveness of social and educational policy to reduce them.

NOTES

1. Formally, two tests share an identical metric if scores on test A can be converted to scores on test B by adding a constant ($Y_B = Y_A + c$).
2. An understanding of the basic principals of cognitive measurement, including Classical Test Theory and Item Response Theory (Hambleton, Swaminathan, & Rogers, 1991; Lord, 1980; Lord & Novick, 1968; National Council on Measurement in Education & Brennan, 2006; Yen & Fitzpatrick, 2006), is essential for careful study of achievement gaps.
3. For more information on NAEP, see http://nces.ed.gov/nationsreportcard/about/.
4. Main NAEP also includes assessments in writing, science, and other subjects. We focus in this chapter on the math and reading NAEP assessments.
5. Although the trend is clear, different studies report the narrowing of the gap in different metrics. Neal (2005) calculates the black-white achievement gap at each assessment wave in standard deviation units, and then compares changes in these gaps across waves (see also Hedges & Nowell, 1999). Grissmer, Flanagan, and Williamson (1998), however, calculate the achievement gains for white students from one assessment to the next (standardizing this gain by dividing by the standard deviation of white students' scores at the first assessment), and do the same for black students (standardizing by the standard deviation of black students' scores at the first assessment). They then calculate the change in the black-white reading achievement gap from one assessment to the next by subtracting the white standardized gain from the black standardized gain. In general, these two methods will give the same answer only if the white and black standard deviations are the same at each wave and the same as one another. In practice, this is not true—the standard deviation of black test scores is generally smaller than that of whites in NAEP-LTT, meaning that the Grissmer et al. approach overstates the gain of black students relative to white students. We think the Neal (2005) approach provides a more meaningful metric for comparing gaps across cohorts.
6. When comparing Hispanic-white achievement gaps across cohorts or grades, some caution is required. Given the dramatic increase of the Hispanic student population over the past few decades, the composition of Hispanic students tested in different grades and different years may vary greatly, and so any comparison across cohorts or grades may be confounded with the changing composition of the Hispanic student population.
7. Examples of such studies include those using panel data from nationally representative samples—such as the Early Childhood Longitudinal Study-Kindergarten Cohort (ECLS-K) (see http://www.nces.ed.gov/ecls), the National Education Longitudinal Study (NELS) (see http://www.nces.ed.gov/surveys/nels88), Prospects: The Congressionally Mandated Study of Educational Growth and Opportunity, and High School and Beyond (HSB) (see www.nces.ed.gov/surveys/hsb)—and those drawn from state administrative data sources in states like North Carolina, Texas, or Florida, each of which has administrative data systems allowing tracking of individual student test scores over multiple years (Clotfelter, Ladd, & Vigdor, 2006; Hanushek & Rivkin, 2006).

8. The assumption of no cohort change may be particularly problematic, however. For example, a sample of 9-year-old students drawn in 1991 and a sample of 17-year-old students drawn in 1999 may not represent exactly the same cohort population, since the 1999 sample would include some students not in the 1991 population (e.g., those born in 1982 who immigrated to the U.S. between 1991 and 1999), and the 1991 sample would include some students not in the 1999 population (e.g., those who dropped out of school between age nine and age 17).
9. Because the ECLS-K reading test was only administered in English, students not proficient in oral English were not assessed in reading; as a result, estimates of the Hispanic-white reading gap are typically generalized only to the subsample of Hispanics proficient in oral English at the start of kindergarten (see, for example, Fryer & Levitt, 2004, 2005; Reardon & Galindo, 2006).
10. The ECLS-K math test was only administered in English or Spanish (and the reading test was only administered in English), so the roughly 22 percent of Asian-origin students in the sample who were not proficient in oral English did not take the tests.
11. These gaps are the average of the corresponding parental education gaps from 1978 to 2004, weighted by the inverse of the estimated sampling variance of the gap in each year. Similar average gaps are produced without weighting.
12. The comparison across cohorts relies much less on the assumption of interval scaling, since it is possible to compare the full test score distributions across cohorts. See, for example, Hedges and Nowell (1999) and Ferguson (1998).
13. One possible reason why Fryer and Levitt's model explains more of the black-white gap in elementary school than other studies may be that they use a somewhat larger list of covariates than other studies, including age, birth-weight, gender, number of children's books (and its quadratic term), mother's age at first birth, WIC receipt, and a composite socioeconomic status variable that includes family income, parental education, and parental occupation measures (Fryer & Levitt, 2005).
14. Murnane et al.'s results differ substantially from those of Fryer and Levitt likely because Murnane, et al report the predicted black-white gap from a random-coefficient growth model while Fryer and Levitt report results from a series of repeated cross-sectional covariate adjustment models (Fryer & Levitt, 2005; Murnane, Willett, Bub, & McCartney, 2006). We prefer the Fryer and Levitt results because they rely less on assumptions regarding interval scaling of the test metric and the stable effects of socioeconomic factors over time.
15. With regard to wage gaps for women, the evidence is less clear because of differential selection into the labor force among women. Among women in the labor force, however, black and Hispanic women earn, on average, the same or more than white women after controlling for AFQT scores (Bollinger, 2003; Carneiro, Heckman, & Masterov, 2003).
16. Note that the NLSY Hispanic sample is made up of Hispanics living in the United States in 1979, so this finding may not be representative of the experiences of the current U.S. Hispanic population.
17. In addition, we might expect that—to the extent that any of the current wage differentials is due to employers' "statistical discrimination" practices (i.e., employers' use of race or education levels as a proxy for unobserved skill levels believed to differ systematically between racial groups)—an immediate reduction in achievement gaps may not yield immediate gap reductions even among the youngest cohorts, because it may take time for employers to adjust their prior beliefs about racial differences in human capital. However, Altonji and Pierret (2001) find little evidence for statistical discrimination on the basis of race, net of educational attainment. Moreover, they find also that although employers may statistically discriminate on the basis of employees' educational attainment in assigning initial wage levels, employees' productivity plays a much larger role in wage determination as the employee accrues more experience; employers appear to adjust their prior beliefs, at least with regard to their own employees, as they gain more information. These findings suggest that the impact of a reduction in the black-white skill gap may have a relatively immediate effect on wage gaps among cohorts for whom the skill gap is reduced.

REFERENCES

Altonji, J. G., & Pierret, C. R. (2001). Employer learning and statistical discrimination. *Quarterly Journal of Economics, 116*(1), 313–350.

Bollinger, C. (2003). Measurement error in human capital and the black-white wage gap. *The Review of Economics and Statistics, 85*(3), 578–585.

Brooks-Gunn, J., Klebanov, P. K., & Duncan, G. J. (1996). Ethnic differences in children's intelligence test scores: Role of economic deprivation, home environment, and maternal characteristics. *Child Development, 67*(2), 396–408.

Carneiro, P., Heckman, J. J., & Masterov, D. V. (2003). *Labor market discrimination and racial differences in premarket factors* (No. w10068). Cambridge, MA: National Bureau of Economic Research.

Clotfelter, C. T., Ladd, H. F., & Vigdor, J. L. (2006). *The academic achievement gap in grades three to eight* (Working Paper No. 12207). Cambridge, MA: National Bureau of Economic Research.

Ferguson, R. F. (1998). Test-Score trends along racial lines, 1971 to 1996: Popular culture and community academic standards. In N. J. Smelser, W. J. Wilson & F. Mitchell (Eds.), *America becoming: Racial trends and their consequences* (Vol. 1, pp. 348–390). Washington, DC: National Academies Press.

Fryer, R. G., & Levitt, S. D. (2004). Understanding the black-white test score gap in the first two years of school. *The Review of Economics and Statistics, 86*(2), 447–464.

Fryer, R. G., & Levitt, S. D. (2005). *The black-white test score gap through third grade* (Working paper No. w11049). Cambridge, MA: National Bureau of Economic Research.

Grissmer, D. W., Flanagan, A., & Williamson, S. (1998). Why did the black-white score gap narrow in the 1970s and 1980s? In C. Jencks & M. Phillips (Eds.), *The black-white test score gap* (pp.182–228). Washington, DC: Brookings Institution Press.

Grodsky, E., & Pager, D. (2001). The structure of disadvantage: Individual and occupational determinants of the black-white wage gap. *American Sociological Review, 66*(August), 542–567.

Hambleton, R. K., Swaminathan, H., & Rogers, H. J. (1991). *Fundamentals of item response theory*. Newbury Park, CA: Sage.

Hanushek, E. A., & Rivkin, S. G. (2006). *School quality and the black-white achievement gap*. Unpublished manuscript.

Heckman, J. J., & Vytlacil, E. (2001). Identifying the role of cognitive ability in explaining the level of and change in the return to schooling. *Review of Economics and Statistics, 83*(1), 1–12.

Hedges, L. V., & Nowell, A. (1998). Black-white test score convergence since 1965. In C. Jencks & M. Phillips (Eds.), *The black-white test score gap* (pp.149–181). Washington, DC: Brookings Institution Press.

Hedges, L. V., & Nowell, A. (1999). Changes in the black-white gap in achievement test scores. *Sociology of Education, 72*(2), 111–135.

Ho, A. D., & Haertel, E. H. (2006). *Metric-free measures of test score trends and gaps with policy-relevant examples* (CSE Report No. 665). Los Angeles, CA: Center for the Study of Evaluation, National Center for Research on Evaluation, Standards, and Student Testing, Graduate School of Education & Information Studies.

Lee, V. E., & Burkham, D. T. (2002). *Inequality at the starting gate: Social background differences in achievement as children begin school*. Washington, DC: Economic Policy Institute.

LoGerfo, L., Nichols, A., & Reardon, S. F. (2006). *Achievement gains in elementary and high school*. Washington, DC: Urban Institute.

Lord, F. M. (1980). *Applications of item response theory to practical testing problems*. Hillsdale, NJ: Erlbaum.

Lord, F. M., & Novick, M. R. (1968). *Statistical theory of mental test scores*. Reading, MA: Addison Wesley.

Murnane, R. J., Willett, J. B., Bub, K. L., & McCartney, K. (2006). Understanding trends in the black-white achievement gaps during the first years of school. *Brookings-Wharton Papers on Urban Affairs*.

Murnane, R. J., Willett, J. B., & Levy, F. (1995). The growing importance of gognitive skills in wage determination. *Review of Economics and Statistics, 78*(2), 251–266.

National Council on Measurement in Education, & Brennan, R. L. (Eds.). (2006). *Educational measurement* (4th ed.). New York: Praeger.

Neal, D. A. (2005). *Why has black-white skill convergence stopped?* Chicago: University of Chicago Press.

Neal, D. A., & Johnson, W. R. (1996). The role of premarket factors in black-white wage differences. *The Journal of Political Economy, 104*(5), 869–895.

O'Neill, J. (1990). The role of human capital in earnings differentials between black and white men. *Journal of Economic Perspectives, 4*(4), 25–45.

Pager, D. (2003). The mark of a criminal record. *American Journal of Sociology, 108*(5), 937–975.

Phillips, M., Brooks-Gunn, J., Duncan, G. J., Klebanov, P., & Crane, J. (1998). Family background, parenting practices, and the Black-White test score gap. In C. Jencks & M. Phillips (Eds.), *The Black-White test score gap* (pp. 103–148). Washington, DC: Brookings Institution Press.

Phillips, M., Crouse, J., & Ralph, J. (1998). Does the black-white test score gap widen after children enter school? In C. Jencks & M. Phillips (Eds.), *The black-white test score gap* (pp. 229–272). Washington, DC: Brookings Institution Press.

Reardon, S. F. (2007). Thirteen ways of looking at the black-white test score gap.

Reardon, S. F., & Galindo, C. (2006). *Patterns of Hispanic students' math and English literacy test scores in the early elementary grades*: National Task Force on Early Childhood Education for Hispanics.

Seltzer, M. H., Frank, K. A., & Bryk, A. S. (1994). The metric matters: the sensitivity of conclusions about growth in student achievement to choice of metric. *Educational Evaluation and Policy Analysis, 16*(1), 41–49.

Yen, W. M., & Fitzpatrick, A. R. (2006). Item response theory. In National Council on Measurement in Education & R. L. Brennan (Eds.), *Educational measurement*, 4th ed. (pp. 111–153). New York: Praeger.

29

Early Childhood and the Achievement Gap

Susanna Loeb and Daphna Bassok

INTRODUCTION

Schools do not create achievement gaps. By the time children enter kindergarten, dramatic socioeconomic and racial school-readiness gaps are deeply entrenched. Data from the Early Childhood Longitudinal Study (ECLS-K), a large, nationally-representative survey, show that at kindergarten entry, the average cognitive scores of children from high socioeconomic backgrounds are approximately three-fifths of a standard deviation higher than those of children from lower socioeconomic backgrounds (Reardon, 2003; Lee & Burkham, 2002; Coley, 2002).[1] Significant differences in cognitive assessment scores are also evident between racial groups, with white students scoring two-thirds of a standard deviation higher than black children on a math assessment, and two-fifths of a standard deviation higher on a test of reading. The Hispanic-white gap is even more pronounced (Fryer & Levitt, 2004; Rumberger & Anguiano, 2004). Study after study confirms this early childhood gap, which seems to surface as early as 18 months and widen throughout early childhood (Shonkoff & Phillips, 2000).

The goal of the No Child Left Behind Act passed in 2001 was to close the achievement gap between low-income and minority students and their peers. Our increasing understanding of the links between early childhood development and life outcomes has provided solid evidence that any effort to meaningfully narrow the achievement gap also must address these early childhood issues (Shonkoff & Phillips, 2000). There are at least two critical and interrelated reasons to also focus attention on the years prior to children's school entry. The first is that children's *ability* when they are young is highly linked with their later life outcomes. That is, children who lag behind early are likely to continue doing so throughout their school experiences. Secondly, what happens to children in the early years of their life has a disproportionately large impact on their life outcomes relative to other experiences. Because children are so influenced by their early childhood environments, and because early abilities are so predictive of later outcomes, devoting resources to early childhood interventions may yield larger returns than investments later in life.

THE IMPORTANCE OF STARTING EARLY

The Role of Early Childhood Experiences

Recent advancements in both the neurobiological and social sciences have vastly expanded our understanding of development in the early years of life (Collins, Maccoby, Steinberg, Hetherington, & Bornstein, 2000; Knudson, Heckman, Cameron & Shonkoff, 2006; Shonkoff & Phillips, 2000; Shore, 1997). While genetic make-up plays a dramatic role, environmental factors including physical surroundings, communication, and nurturing all interact with children's genetic endowment, and play critical roles in their cognitive, social, and emotional development. Further, during early childhood, children's brains develop extremely rapidly, making the early years an optimal time to lay the groundwork for positive lifelong development.

An impressive study conducted by Hart and Risley (1995) highlights the importance of early environmental factors. Forty-two children from professional, working-class, and welfare families were followed through monthly home visits starting when each child was roughly eight months old and continuing through age three. At each visit researchers meticulously recorded every word produced by the child and their parents. As might be expected, the rate of children's language development was highly correlated with the number of words spoken by their parents. Parents in professional families had a much larger vocabulary than those in working class or welfare families, and by age three these gaps were reproduced in their children. For instance, in the welfare group, children's recorded vocabulary size was 525, whereas in the professional group, it was more than double that figure, at 1,116. While it is difficult to truly separate the role of language exposure from the role of social class in driving these results, the study does suggest a strong role for environmental factors.

Focusing specifically on the role of a child's economic well-being, Duncan, Yeung, Brooks-Gunn, and Smith (1998) use the Panel Study of Income Dynamics to assess how family income during three intervals (0–5, 6–10, & 11–15) is linked to high school completion. Their results show that income in the early years is a much stronger predictor of both years of schooling and school completion, than income during the two later periods. The authors offer the importance of early childhood and school readiness as an explanation for their results.

The Link Between Early Abilities and Later Achievement

Studies also demonstrate that children's cognitive and social abilities at school-entry are strongly related to their later school and life outcomes (Chen, Lee, & Stevenson, 1996; Luster & McAdoo, 1996). For instance, Baydar, Brooks-Gunn, and Furstenberg (1993) followed over 200 children born to black, teenage mothers in Baltimore from birth to approximately age 20. The authors attempted to identify observable antecedents to functional illiteracy. They found that early childhood developmental assessments done when these children were between ages four and six were the strongest predictors of illiteracy 15 years later, even controlling for per-person family income, maternal education, and a host of other family characteristics. These early cognitive scores were also strong predictors of high school completion and post-secondary education (Brooks-Gunn, Guo, & Furstenberg, 1993). In their meta-analysis of eight national studies of the black-white achievement gap, Phillips, Crouse, and Ralph (1998) found that the black-white test score gap at the end of high school could be reduced by at least one-half if the gap was eliminated at school entry.

The Benefits of Intervening Early

One of the most celebrated early childhood interventions is the High/Scope Perry Preschool experiment, which randomly assigned 123 at-risk, low-income black children either to a high-quality, two-year preschool intervention or a control group. Researchers have followed these children from age three through age 40 and have reported dramatic and long-lasting effects (Schweinhart, Montie, Xiang, Barnett, Belfield, & Nores, 2005). For instance, while 65 percent of program participants graduated from high school, only 45 percent of the control group did; for females alone the proportions were 84 and 32 percent, respectively. At age 40 the median annual earnings of program participants were $20,800, compared with $15,300 for the control group. Participants were also more likely be employed, raise their own children, and own a home or a car, and they were far less likely to experience arrests or utilize drugs. Researchers estimated that the Perry preschool program had a return of approximately $258,888 per child, or $17.07 per dollar invested. About three-quarters of this return went to the public through savings on crime, education, and welfare, as well as increased taxes. While involvement in a highly-publicized experiment may have influenced the choices and outcomes of program participants, it is unlikely that these large, persistent effects are being driven only by heightened attention. Intensive interventions early in life appear to meaningfully impact the later success of poor children.

A full evaluation of the potential of early investment in child development requires a comparison of the returns of these types of interventions to those achieved through other avenues. Carneiro and Heckman (2003) compare the impact on life outcomes of early childhood interventions to those of school improvement efforts (e.g., class size reduction and teacher salary increases), adolescent interventions (e.g., mentorship and drop-out prevention programs), job training programs, and college tuition breaks. They conclude that the most powerful drivers of adult outcomes are determined by environmental factors during early childhood. Heckman argues that remediation of early childhood deficits is far more expensive then intervention during the first years of life. He concludes that early childhood interventions are "a rare public policy initiative that promotes fairness and social justice and at the same time promotes productivity in the economy and in society at large" (Heckman, 2006).

EXPLAINING THE ACHIEVEMENT GAP

The relationship between socioeconomic status and child outcomes has been well documented (Duncan, Brooks-Gunn, & Klebanov, 1994; McLoyd, 1998; Brooks-Gunn & Duncan, 1997; Bradley & Corwyn, 2002). Lack of income or low levels of parental education could have direct negative effects on children's development through, for instance, inability to access necessary resources. At the same time, it is likely that the socioeconomic gap also is driven by risk factors highly correlated with low levels of income and education, such as depression, stress, hunger, divorce or single parenthood, housing instability, unemployment, unsafe neighborhoods, and inadequate child care options.

While a review of the expansive literature demonstrating associations between environmental factors and children's early development is beyond the scope of this chapter, we note that researchers have found positive relationships between child outcomes and breast-feeding (Anderson, Johnstone & Remley, 1999), exposure to enriched language environments (Huttenlocher, Haight, & Bryk, 1991), access to books and educational resources (Linver, Brooks-Gunn, & Kohen, 2002), and shared book reading (Bus, Ijzendoorn, & Pellegrini 1995; DeBaryshe,

1993). Conversely, divorce (Pagani, Boulerice, Tremblay, & Vitaro, 1997), maternal depression and stress (Cummings & Davies, 1994; Mistry, Vandewater, Huston, & McLoyd, 2002; Petterson & Albers, 2001), and harsh or punitive parenting style (McLoyd, 1998) are among factors that are negatively correlated with child outcomes. Given the interrelatedness of these factors, and the unclear directionality between them, great care must be taken not to confuse strong correlations with causation, and to seriously consider the possibility of omitted variables.

It is also important to note that some environmental factors have more mixed associations with children's well-being depending on the particular outcome or sub-population considered. For instance, while attending center-based care is positively related with children's cognitive outcomes (Currie, 2001; Barnett, 1995), several studies have found negative associations between long hours at centers and children's behavioral outcomes (Belsky, 2002; NICHD ECCRN, 2003). Interestingly, Brooks-Gunn and Markman (2005) note that many of the environmental characteristics that are correlated with children's achievement also vary systematically by ethnicity and race. Black mothers are less likely to read to their toddlers on a daily basis, and both black and Hispanic families tend to have fewer reading materials and educational resources in their homes than do whites. Across all income groups, Hispanic families are far less likely to send their children to center-based care than their black or white counterparts (USDE, 2006).

EXPLAINING INDIVIDUAL DIFFERENCES

Before turning to interventions, it is useful to examine another heavily researched possibility, namely that both socioeconomic and racial gaps are driven by genetic differences. When researchers explore the impacts of various environmental factors using non-experimental samples of children, their results generally capture some combination of the environmental factors in which they are interested, and the genetic parental contributions. For instance, a study examining the impact of regular exposure to sonatas and symphonies on infants will overstate the importance of the music if the genetic characteristics of parents who choose to play such music are vastly different from those who do not. Similarly, an observed relationship between maternal education and child outcomes might be spurious if maternal education is a proxy for genetic differences between mothers.

This is a difficult matter to parse out. Genetic and environmental factors are often correlated because most children are brought up by their biological parents, who both determine their genetic characteristics and play a primary role in determining their environment. Some of the most powerful insights on the importance of environmental and genetic factors have come therefore from adoption and twin studies. In this section we summarize the literature on the role of genetic and environmental factors in influencing child development, and stress recent discoveries that suggest important interactions between "nature" and "nurture."

Scarr and Weinberg (1978), one of the seminal works in this field, measured the extent to which typical estimates of the importance of environmental factors are biased by the omission of genetic factors. They concluded that for their sample of adolescents, ages 16–22, from working to upper middle-class families, environmental factors were negligible in explaining differences in IQ scores. The authors compared a sample of biological families to families of children adopted in the first few months of life. They reasoned that because adoptive children do not share their adoptive parents' genetic characteristics, any correlations between environmental characteristics and child outcomes represent unbiased environmental effects. They found that income, parental education, and parental IQ were all significantly more correlated between biological children and their parents than between adopted children and their adoptive parents. For instance, for biological children the correlation between their IQ and their mother's education level is 0.24, while for adopted children it is only 0.1. Further, the authors also had data on the education levels of the adopted children's biological mothers, and found that that correlation was 0.21—quite similar to what was found for children raised by their biological parents. This provides further support for their argument that genetic factors are far more powerful predictors than the environment.

Next, the authors compare correlations in IQ scores for biological siblings raised together to those of biologically unrelated siblings raised by adoptive parents. The motivation for these comparisons is similar: biological siblings' IQs are likely to be correlated for both environmental and genetic reasons. In contrast, adoptive siblings share only environmental factors and therefore can be used to isolate environmental effects. The correlation in IQ scores are significantly and dramatically higher for biological siblings, 0.35 compared to -0.03. In fact, the authors show that at age 18.5, on average, biologically unrelated siblings hardly resemble each other at all. They conclude that differences in the intellectual abilities of the adolescents in their sample have very little to do with environmental factors, and that studies that do find environmental associates are likely confounding environmental and genetic factors. These results have been replicated repeatedly across various samples and outcome measures, including cognitive and behavioral outcomes, as well as educational attainment (Harris, 1995; Plomin & Petrill, 1997; Plug & Vijverberg, 2003).

How should this body of evidence be interpreted? Does it imply that environmental factors are unimportant for child development? In her presidential address to the Society for Research on Child Development in 1991, Sandra Scarr summarized results from many quantitative genetic studies and concluded that for children living in typical, "good enough" homes, differences in environment or parenting styles are unlikely to make a large difference for outcomes. While she stressed that the difference between having and not having a caring adult in your life is quite meaningful, she argued that within some normal range of parenting, and barring abuse or neglect, environmental factors are unlikely to matter much for child development.

Many researchers have taken serious issue with the notion that child development is so deterministically driven by genetic factors (Baumrind, 1993; Collins, Maccoby, Steinberg, Hetherington, & Bornstein, 2000; McClearn, 2003; Rutter, 2002). One important criticism is that the studies on which these conclusions are based often assume that nature and nurture affect childhood development independently and aim to isolate each ones' contribution ignoring important interaction effects. McClearn (2004) describes the "distorted perception of genetic and environmental factors as antagonistic, competitive factors in a simplistic, either-or causal scheme," and summarizes some compelling non-human examples that highlight how nature and nurture interact. A well-known example involves two lines of rats bred such that one was quite adept at running through a maze while the other continually struggled. By manipulating the environment of the rats in the months prior to their maze run, researchers were able to influence the rats' performance. "Dull" rats placed in an enriched environment showed marked improvement, and the reverse was true for the "brighter" rats that were placed in a deprived environment (Cooper & Zubek, 1958).

Examples involving humans also strengthen the case for an interaction between genetic and environmental factors. Rowe, Jacobsen, and Van den Oord (1999) used the National Longitudinal Study of Adolescent Health to examine whether parental education has a mediating effect on genetic and environmental influence. They consider correlations in IQ scores for over 3,000 sibling pairs, including monozygotic and dizygotic twins, biological siblings, half siblings, and unrelated siblings. As expected, the IQs of identical twins are highly correlated (0.73) while those of unrelated siblings are quite low (0.07). Among the full sibling sample the estimate of IQ heritability is 0.57, while the shared environment effect is estimated at only 0.13. When the authors disaggregate their results by parental education, a more nuanced story emerges. Adolescents in the low education group had a much lower heritability estimate—0.2 compared with 0.7 for the high education group. In contrast, the shared environment estimate was 0.23 compared to 0.00 in the high education sample. The results demonstrate that environmental factors have differential effects by parental characteristics. McLoyd (1998) points out that because many of the twin and adoption studies focus on non-poor samples, they may understate the important role of environmental factors for poor children.

Finally, Duyme, Dumaret, and Tomkiewicz (1999) considered a sample of low-IQ children who were abused and neglected as infants and were adopted between ages four and six. Adoptive parents were defined as low, medium, or high SES based on the father's occupation. When the children were 13.5 on average, their IQs were reassessed. All children showed growth, but the magnitude of IQ change varied with parents' SES, with the low SES group raising their IQ by 7.7 and the high SES group experiencing an increase of 19.5 IQ points. These differing effects imply that intensive interventions providing highly enriched environments are likely to have significant effects on child outcomes. These examples demonstrate that environments can play a critical role in mediating genetic characteristics.

EXPLAINING GROUP DIFFERENCES

Until now, our discussion has concentrated on the role of genetic and environmental factors in explaining differences among individuals. What about achievement differences *between groups*—such as those between blacks and whites? Do environmental factors that help explain the socioeconomic gap explain the racial one? If racial gaps are being driven by socioeconomic differences, then policy makers interested in narrowing the gap might pursue approaches focused on economic factors. If, on the other hand, there is something specific to particular ethnic or racial groups that is leading to disparities, other policy approaches might be warranted.

One approach to parsing out these two issues is to measure statistically how much of the racial achievement gap remains after controlling for a host of socioeconomic factors, such as parental education, poverty levels, and family structure (Duncan & Magnuson, 2005). Phillips, Brooks-Gunn, Duncan, Klebanov, and Crane (1998) use this strategy to examine the black-white test score gap in a large sample of five and six year olds. Without taking background characteristics into consideration, the authors find that five- and six-year-old black children's vocabulary scores are more than a full standard deviation lower than those of white children. However, controlling for a rich set of family background characteristics eliminates two-thirds of this gap. In a more recent study using the ECLS data, Fryer and Levitt (2004) report that controlling for a small set of observable background characteristics the entire black-white test score gap essentially disappears for both reading and math assessments. The same set of controls eliminates the majority of the Hispanic-white gap as well. One reading of these findings is that focusing on improving the economic well-being and environmental conditions of minority children could significantly improve their school outcomes. This interpretation implies that the racial gap is actually just a proxy for the socioeconomic gap. Another possibility is that controlling for a host of family characteristics that are strongly correlated with race masks important racial differences that economic changes alone would not address.

It is important to note that recent efforts to replicate Fryer and Levitt's results using a different data set yielded substantively different results. In Murnane, Willet, Bub, and McCartney's (2006) analysis of the National Institute of Health and Human Development Study of Early Child Care and Youth Development, controlling for a very similar set of socioeconomic controls did not eliminate the black-white test score gap in either math or early literacy skills. The authors attribute the differing results to differences in the types of assessments used in each study.

Critics of the environmental argument posit that perhaps the lower achievement of black and Hispanic children is driven by genetic factors. If this is the case, they argue, excluding a true measure of genetic background in models of the achievement gap would lead to a serious omitted variable bias because genetic characteristics could be related to both low socioeconomic status and children's achievement. Despite these concerns, two comprehensive reviews of the literature have concluded that there is very little evidence to support the notion that significant portions of the achievement gap *between* groups (i.e., the black-white gap) can be explained by genetic factors (Dickens, 2005; Nisbett, 1998). Many of the most compelling arguments against the genetics hypothesis are found in studies that indirectly challenge the "nature" explanation by demonstrating the powerful effects of environmental or "nurture" factors, on child outcomes. For instance, Eyferth (1961) assessed the intelligence scores of children born after World War II to white German women and American soldiers, either black or white. If the genetics hypothesis holds, we would expect those children born to two white parents to outperform their mixed-race counterparts. However, the IQs of the two groups were practically identical (97 and 96.5, respectively), and there were no indications that the results were driven by unusually high or low intelligence scores for the black and white soldiers, respectively (Dickens, 2005).

A recent study uses data from the Early Childhood Longitudinal Study Birth cohort—a nationally representative sample of over 10,000 children between 8 and 12 months—to cast further doubt about genetic explanations for racial differences. Fryer and Levitt (2006) find that only controlling for children's age and gender, the gap between black and white infants on a developmental assessment is only 0.06 of a standard deviation, and is even smaller for Hispanics. This gap is quite small compared to the one observed among older children in other studies, and it is therefore damaging to the genetics argument. The authors conclude that either genetic factors are not the primary drivers of racial achievement gaps or that genetic influences emerge systematically after age one.

Certainly, we have much more to learn about the interplay among genetics, environmental factors, and child development. It is important to emphasize that even if there were genetic differences among racial or ethnic groups, this need not imply that environmental interventions will be ineffectual. Given the strong success of certain early childhood interventions in improving the well-being of poor, minority children, it seems safe to say that altering environmental factors is one critical approach to the narrowing of both socioeconomic and racial gaps.

THE ROLE OF INTERVENTIONS

Though we do not know the specific mechanism by which socioeconomic status relates to child outcomes, two theoretical models are often posited (Linver, Brooks-Gunn, & Kohen, 2002). The "investment model" focuses on the direct role of income as a means for providing children the resources they need. In contrast, the "family stress model" focuses on the negative impacts of poverty on parents' mental health and parenting ability, which in turn negatively influences children. The two models imply distinct types of parental interventions. The first is associated with programs aimed at improving parents' economic well-being through work incentives, income assistance, education supports, or other routes. The second calls for programs that support parents, teaching them effective parenting techniques and reducing stress.

Family Resources

Evaluating the impacts of employment and income on child outcomes is challenging because both are likely to be correlated with other relevant parental characteristics. A series of randomized welfare experiments conducted in the 1990s has provided a unique opportunity to examine the relationship between parental employment and child outcomes (Morris, Huston, Duncan, Crosby, & Bos, 2001; Zaslow, Moore, Brooks, Morris, Tout, Redd, & Emig, 2002; Clark-Kauffman, Duncan, & Morris, 2003). Researchers assessed the impact of several employment-based welfare programs targeted at single-parent families and found that overall the programs did not strongly affect child outcomes. However, programs that also included earning supplements yielded systematic positive effects on the cognitive outcomes of children, two to four years after program entry. These studies suggest that parental employment, when combined with increased resources, can positively impact child outcomes. However, it is important to note that adolescents did not benefit. In fact, there was some evidence that program participation was associated with detrimental outcomes such as more frequent smoking and drug use, and more frequent behavior problems in school.

Magnuson and Duncan (2002) argue that whenever interventions are indirect they are less likely to yield meaningful impacts on child outcomes. As an example, many policy makers have designed interventions aimed at increasing maternal education levels in the hopes that the higher education levels would lead to positive impacts for the children. In order for such interventions to yield the desired results two sequential processes must occur. The intervention would have to successfully raise maternal education, and then that maternal education would have to affect child outcomes either through specific skills learned, increased earnings, or another mechanism. Indeed, experimental studies of these types of interventions demonstrate that even when they do raise maternal education, this increase fails to translate into significant benefits for children (Quint, Bos, & Polit, 1997; McGroder et al., 2000).

Family Processes

A strong association between early literacy practices and child outcomes has led to a variety of parental interventions focused on home reading practices. One strategy involves promoting literacy through children's regularly scheduled doctor's visits. These relatively inexpensive interventions have been associated with improvements in low-income, black and Hispanic parents' literacy behaviors (Golova et al., 1999; High et al., 2000). In addition, program participation appears correlated with children's early language development. The Reach out and Read (ROR) program, for instance, involves reading to children in the waiting room of clinics, giving them developmentally appropriate books to take home, and having pediatricians discuss the benefits of reading during the actual appointment. Mendelsohn et al. (2001) compared the vocabulary development of poor, minority children in two similar inner-city pediatric clinics—one of which had used the ROR for three years, while the other had only recently introduced the intervention. Multivariate regressions showed that those children who had been visiting the clinic that offered ROR had significantly higher scores on measures of both receptive and expressive language. Parental literacy interventions carried out through child care centers and elementary schools also are associated with improved short-term literacy outcomes for children (Whitehurst, Arnold, Epstein, Angell, Smith, & Fischel, 1994; Jordan, Snow, & Porsche, 2000). To our knowledge, there are no experimental studies that demonstrate long-term benefits associated with parent literacy interventions.

Some long-term impacts have been found for more broadly-aimed parenting interventions.

One of the most rigorously studied examples is the Nurse Home Visitation Program, which began in a semi-rural area of New York in 1978 and followed families longitudinally through adolescence (Olds et al., 1997). Five hundred pregnant women were randomly placed in either a treatment or a control group. These women were predominantly white, low-income, and unmarried. Women in the treatment group received regular home visits that focused on maternal health, positive parenting, and personal development. The control group received developmental screenings for their children at 12 and 24 months of age, but no further maternal support services[2]. The 15-year follow-up showed that program participants were less likely to be perpetrators of child abuse and neglect. The subgroup of mothers who were unmarried and low-income at the time of their pregnancy also experienced fewer subsequent births, fewer months on welfare, and fewer arrests.

Further, program participation had meaningful social and health benefits for the children of the unmarried and low-income sub-sample. They displayed lower levels of arrests, lower incidents of running away, fewer sexual partners, and less regular alcohol consumption. No systematic cognitive benefits were reported at age 15. Overall, results from this experiment suggest that parenting interventions *can* have meaningful impacts on certain child outcomes. Further, the experiment indicates that poor children from single-parent homes seem to benefit differentially from this intervention, suggesting that targeted services could be most efficient.

The outcomes of the nurse visitation program aside, findings from most home visitation programs have been decidedly underwhelming. Gomby, Culross, and Behrman (1999) summarized results from six randomized studies of large parental intervention programs. Though interventions differed with respect to target populations and intensity, all aimed to support and promote positive parenting as a strategy for improving child outcomes. While some of the programs resulted in various improvements in parenting practices, they had few measured effects on children's development. The authors considered the few small positive effects identified as unsystematic exceptions. While early attrition and inconsistent participation may partially explain the lack of positive outcomes, the intensity of these home visitation programs is likely the most relevant factor. As Gomby et al. point out, it may be unrealistic to expect programs involving 20–40 hours of direct contact over several years to have such significant impacts on parental behaviors, that children's outcomes are affected in a meaningful and significant fashion. As such, more intensive, directly child-focused interventions might be preferable over parent directed interventions (Magnuson & Duncan, 2002).

Centers

Center-based programs are among the most highly utilized direct child interventions, with 69 percent of four year olds nationwide participating in 2005 (U.S. Department of Education, 2006). And these interventions have shown consistent positive effects on cognitive development.

Experimental Evidence. Some of the most compelling evidence on such interventions comes from a handful of well-designed randomized experiments. The primary advantage of experimental studies is that, when done well, they eliminate doubts about selection bias. Since children are assigned to an intervention or control group by chance, we can be fairly certain that their post-intervention results represent the causal relationship between the intervention and child outcomes. The most famous of these studies is the High Scope/Perry Preschool, which shows significant differences between the treatment and control group at every wave of the study from preschool to age 40. A similar experiment—the Carolina Abecedarian project—randomly assigned 111 infants born to extremely poor, high risk mothers into a treatment and control group

(Ramey & Ramey, 2002). Most of the mothers enrolled in the study were young, black, had less then a high school education, and were single. Both the treatment and the control group received some enriched social services; but starting at age six months, children in the treatment group were enrolled in an intensive, high quality preschool program which ran full-day, full-year through kindergarten entry. While the cognitive performance of the two groups was roughly similar until age nine months, by 18 months a gap rapidly emerged, and a dramatic 14-point difference on an IQ test persisted through the preschool years. In the most recent follow-up, the Abecedarian children are 21, and the treatment group continued to outperform the control group on an IQ test, as well as on a reading and math assessment (Campbell, Ramey, Pungello, Sparling, & Miller-Johnson, 2002). In addition, the treatment group was far more likely to be enrolled in a four-year college (36 percent compared to 14 percent), and far less likely to have been a teen parent (26 percent compared to 45 percent).

Taken together, the Perry and Abecderian preschool experiments convincingly show that intensive, high quality preschool interventions can have powerful and lasting effects, at least for very poor, black children. That said, both interventions targeted extremely at-risk black populations, making it difficult to generalize their results to the population at large. Further, both of these programs offered high-quality care and in turn were far more expensive and intensive then more "typical" preschool programs. Therefore, these studies cannot necessarily help us estimate the effects of programs that, for instance, last only one year, meet only half day, or do not employ highly educated teachers with engaging curriculums.

Non-Experimental Evidence. Results from large-scale, non-experimental studies are the best available source for understanding the relationship between more standard center-based interventions and child outcomes. While determining causality is more difficult in non-experimental analyses, these studies tend to find a positive correlation between center participation and children's cognitive outcomes, though, as might be expected, the magnitude of the effects are smaller than those observed in the more intensive preschool experiments (Barnett, 1995; Currie, 2001).

The Child Parent Centers, which opened in 1967, provide a useful example. These centers offered comprehensive social, health, and educational support services for impoverished children ages three through nine, and their parents. Specifically, the program included a high quality half-day, nine month preschool program, home visitation, outreach services, and comprehensive school-age services (reduced class size, enrichment activities, etc.) for a subsample of participants. Reynolds, Temple, Robertson, and Mann (2002) compared the outcomes of program participants to those of demographically similar children living in the neighborhoods where centers were operating. They found that program participants had higher cognitive and achievement scores through age 15, lower levels of grade retention and special education placements through age 15 and 18, respectively, and higher rates of school completion through age 21.

Several research teams have looked at the effects of center-care participation on child outcomes using the nationally representative ECLS-K (Loeb, Bridges, Bassok, Fuller, & Rumberger, in press; Magnuson, Ruhm, & Waldfogel, 2004; Rumberger & Tran, 2006). All reported a positive relationship between participating in center-based care in the year prior to kindergarten, and children's cognitive outcomes. Controlling for a rich set of environmental variables, Magnuson, Ruhm and Waldfogel (2004) found that center attendees outperformed children who stayed at home on both a reading and math assessment, with effect sizes of 0.13 and 0.09—enough to move the average child from the fiftieth to the fifty-fifth percentile. Consistent with previous studies examining this issue, the ECLS-K data showed that along with the cognitive benefits, participation in center-based care—particularly for extended hours—is associated with somewhat heightened levels of externalizing behavior, which includes fighting, arguing or, disrupting (NICHD, 2003).

One important advantage of the ECLS-K data is that its large sample size allows for meaningful analysis of subgroup differences. Magnuson et al. (2004) found that the relationship between center care and cognitive outcomes is particularly large for very poor children, or for those with low parental education. Loeb et al. (2007) showed important differences in the impact of center participation between racial groups. For example, they found that the gains associated with center attendance (compared to home-based care) are largest for English proficient Hispanics. These results suggest that certain groups are more likely to gain from participation and that targeted interventions might be useful for eliminating gaps.

Researchers are cautious when interpreting these findings because, at least in part, the positive association between center-based care and child outcomes found in non-experimental data is likely driven by a selection mechanism, whereby those children who attend center care have unobserved characteristics that influence both their entrance into this type of care and their eventual outcomes. To get at this, researchers have used a variety of statistical strategies.

Gormley, Gayer, Phillips, and Dawson (2005) used one such strategy to evaluate the effects of Oklahoma's universal preschool program, which established a free, voluntary preschool open to all four year olds in the state. Run through the Oklahoma public schools, the preschool program requires all classrooms to have 20 or fewer children and all teachers to have a bachelor's degree as well as an early childhood credential. Almost three-quarters of the eligible children in Oklahoma participate in publicly funded preschool, which is the highest penetration rate nationwide. To get around selection issues, Gormley et al. used a regression discontinuity design, taking advantage of the program's strict use of birthday cut-off dates for determining program eligibility. The authors compared a treatment group comprised of children who enrolled in one year, and a control group of those children whose birthdays were after the cutoff date but who enrolled in the following year. Adjusting their regressions for age as well as demographic characteristics, the authors found a 0.79 of a standard deviation gap on a letter-word identification measure, and a 0.38 standard deviation gap on an applied problem measure between the treatment and control group. Further, they showed that the positive preschool effects arise in all racial and socioeconomic subgroups, though they were unable to compare the magnitude of the effects across groups. These results are certainly promising, and it will be interesting to see whether the benefits of preschool persist as children progress through school.

A recent analysis of the effects of Head Start, a large-scale, federally funded early childhood intervention, also creatively utilized regression discontinuity. When Head Start was first introduced in 1965, the Office of Economic Opportunity tried to encourage take-up in high poverty counties by providing the 300 poorest districts in the country with intensive technical assistance for funding proposals. This policy created a sharp discontinuity in program funding between those counties on either side of the technical assistance cutoff point. Ludwig and Miller (2007) took advantage of this exogenous discontinuity to assess whether counties that fell just below the cutoff for technical assistance varied systematically on health and educational outcomes from counties that fell just above the cutoff. The authors report significantly lower mortality rates in those counties just below the cutoff line, and they demonstrate these drops in mortality are driven by declines in deaths from "Head Start susceptible causes" such as smallpox, polio, and measles, rather than injuries. They also find slightly weaker evidence of differences in educational attainment. If the authors are correct in their assumption that counties falling on either side of the cutoff were initially quite similar, any differences in child outcomes could be attributed to the Head Start program, without concern over selection issues.

Quality. One limitation of much of the data used to study the effects of preschool is the lack of information on the quality of centers that children attended. While results tell us about the average effects of centers, we do not know whether these effects vary based on characteristics of their curriculum, instruction, or facilities. Magnuson et al. (2004) attempt to get at this issue in the ECLS-K data by separately analyzing program effects for children whose parents indicated they attended a "pre-kindergarten" program and those who attended other types of centers (nursery school, day care, preschool, etc). The authors assume that the pre-kindergarten programs are school-based programs that have higher levels of regulations and a more educational curriculum. Indeed, they find that cognitive outcomes are higher in the pre-kindergarten group, though levels of externalizing also appear higher in these settings.

A large body of literature has more directly examined the effects of observable measures of care quality on child outcomes (Loeb, Fuller, Kagan, & Carrol, 2004; NICHD, 2002; Peisner-Feinberg et al., 2001). These studies all indicate that higher quality centers—in terms of both structural and process measures—have a larger and a more long-lasting effect on children's cognitive and social outcomes. For instance, results from the Cost, Quality & Outcomes Study showed that children who had closer, more nurturing relationships with their care providers displayed stronger cognitive and social skills through second grade. Further, the impact of care variations were largest for high-risk children whose mothers have very low levels of education. This finding strengthens the case for investing most heavily in programs for the neediest children, though, once again, the studies do not unequivocally establish the causal nature of the relationship between center characteristics and children's outcomes.

Sustaining Effects. While the short term effects of preschool programs are encouraging, policy makers and researchers worry about whether or not program effects dissipate as preschool children move through elementary school. Magnuson, Ruhm, and Waldfogel (2004) found that by the spring of first grade, the benefits associated with attending prekindergarten had mostly disappeared. Karoly et al. (1998) synthesized the results from evaluations of nine early childhood interventions, and found similar evidence of diminishing cognitive and academic outcomes in many of the programs considered. Why is it that the effects of programs such as the Perry Preschool, Abecedarian, and the Child Parent Centers last into early adulthood and beyond, while those of more broad-based, naturally occurring interventions seem to fade out after the first few years of school? One explanation is the wide ranging quality of typical preschool interventions. Based on the quality literature presented above, it seems plausible that when aggregating the effects of *all* preschool programs together, the low quality of some programs masks long-lasting effects from other higher quality programs.

Another possible explanation stems from the intensity or dosage of early childhood interventions. Children's exposure to center-based interventions varies dramatically both in terms of age at entry and in terms of hours per weeks. To the extent that more intensive interventions are stronger predictors of long-term benefits for children, aggregating the outcomes of all center attendees irrespective of the amount of time they have spent in center could mask effects. The Infant Health and Development Program (IHDP) provides an illustrative example. The IHDP began in 1985 and randomly assigned low-birth weight infants and their families to a treatment or a control group. Families in the treatment group received regular home visits through the child's third birthday, and children had access to high-quality, year-round, center-based care from age one to age three. At age three, the treatment group significantly outperformed the control on cognitive outcomes, but by age eight there were no significant differences. Hill, Brooks-Gunn, and Waldfogel (2003) hypothesized that, in part, the lack of sustained results at age eight might be related to center exposure. To get at selection issues that could influence which children attend centers most intensively, the authors used a variety of matching strategies, and compared children with high center participation (>350 days or >450 days) to children with very similar characteristics who were in the control groups. As they had predicted, regular center attendees did in fact demonstrate sustained cognitive outcomes at age eight. Further, the group who had the highest intervention dosage (>450 days) showed the greatest benefits, bolstering the notion that intervention intensity matters for sustaining results.

Finally, a third explanation for the "fading" effects of child care interventions has to do with the experiences children have once they enter school. Several studies have considered the possibility that school quality plays an important role in sustaining or negating the effects of center-based programs. Lee and Loeb (1995) test this hypothesis within the context of Head Start, the federally-funded comprehensive preschool program that aims to narrow the school-readiness achievement gap for extremely disadvantaged children. Using data from the National Education Longitudinal Study of 1988, a nationally representative sample of approximately 25,000 eighth graders, the authors compare the school quality of children who reportedly attended Head Start, another type of preschool program, or no preschool intervention. Defining school quality broadly—to include social composition, academic excellence, perceived safety, and teacher student relationships—the authors find that eighth-graders who attended Head Start end up in significantly worse schools compared to children who attended other types of preschools, even when they control for race, parental education, and an income-to-needs ratio. They conclude that the poor quality of schools attended by Head Start participants seriously undermines the likelihood of sustained program effects.

Currie and Thomas (2000) expand on this analysis by first noting that the extent of impact fade out is systematically different for blacks and whites, with the effects on blacks disappearing rapidly, but white children experiencing long-lasting benefits through adolescence. They argue that if, indeed, the school quality explanation is driving fade out effects, the difference in school quality for Head Start participants and non-Head Start participants must be larger for blacks than for whites. Their results support this claim, and they suggest that environmental factors in the years after a child completes a center-based intervention can seriously negate the initial impact of the program. In a separate study, Garces, Duncan, and Thomas (2002) report that white Head Start attendees experience significant long term gains from Head Start participation, including higher levels of high school completion and earnings during early adulthood. This evidence suggests that the benefits of early childhood intervention would be maximized if combined with high-quality experiences for participants as they enter elementary schools.

Evidence from the Chicago Child Parent Centers further supports this notion, because those children who extended their participation into the first years of elementary school displayed higher levels of school achievement from elementary school through high school, and also had significantly fewer special education placements (Reynolds, Temple, Robertson, & Mann, 2002).

CONCLUSIONS

This review has highlighted several crucial points about the early achievement gap. First, systematic differences in development and ability emerge long before children enter school, and those children who start school at a disadvantage are likely to remain behind their peers throughout school and beyond. Second, advances in research have highlighted the importance of the early childhood environment as a contributing factor to this school readiness gap. And third, despite our continuously-expanding understanding of child development, implementing programs that meaningfully narrow the gap is a challenging task. Most interventions directed at parents have lackluster effects on children, and the effects of center programs are both highly dependent on quality and, at times, fleeting.

Nevertheless, there are several compelling examples of interventions that confirm the positive potential of early childhood interventions. We know that the most successful of these programs are intensive and involve substantial investments. We also know that the biggest program benefits are typically seen in the neediest children. Given the vast impediments that very poor children face, neither of these findings is particularly surprising. The bottom line is that there are no easy solutions. Achieving sizeable practical results necessarily means making a highly targeted, long-term commitment to those children most in need.

NOTES

1. The SES gap represents the difference in scores for children who are one standard deviation apart on a continuous SES measure which is a composite of parental income, education and occupation.
2. A subgroup of the control group also received cab fare for prenatal and well-child care.

REFERENCES

Anderson, J., Johnstone, B., & Remley, D. (1999) Breast-feeding and cognitive development: a meta-analysis. *American Journal of Clinical Nutrition*, 70 (4), 525–535.

Barnett, W. (1995) "Long Term Effects of Early Childhood Programs on Cognitive and School Outcomes." In *The Future of Children*, 5(3), 25–50.

Baydar, N., Brooks-Gunn, J., & Furstenberg, F. (1993) Early Warning Signs of Functional Illiteracy: Predictors in Childhood and Adolescence. *Child Development*, 64, 815–829.

Baumrind, D. (1993) The Average Expectable Environment is Not Good Enough: A Response to Scarr. *Child Development,* 64(5), 1299–1317.

Belsky, J. (2002) Quantity Counts: Amount of Child Care and Children's Socio-economic Development. *Journal of Developmental & Behavioral Pediatrics,* 23(3), 167–170.

Bradley, R. & Corwyn, R. (2002) Socio-economic Status and Child Development. *Annual Review of Psychology,* 53, 371–399.

Brooks-Gunn, J. (2003) Do you believe in magic? What we can expect from early childhood intervention programs. *Social Policy Report*, 17(1), 3–14.

Brooks-Gunn, J. & Duncan, G. (1997) "The Effects of Poverty on Children." *The Future of Children,* 7(2), 55–71.

Brooks-Gunn, J., Guo, G., & Furstenberg, F. (1993) Who Drops Out and Who Continues Beyond High School? A 20-Year Follow-Up of black Urban Youth. *Journal of Research on Adolescence*, 3(3), 271–294.

Brooks-Gunn, J., Klebanov, P., & Duncan, G. (1996) Ethnic Differences in Children's Intelligence Test Scores: Role of Economic Deprivation, Home Environment and Maternal Characteristics. *Child Development*, 67(2), 396–408.

Brooks-Gunn, J. & Markman, L. (2005) "The Contributions of Parenting to Ethnic and Racial Gaps in School Readiness." *The Future of Children,* 15(1), 139–168..

Bus, A., Ijzendoorn, M., & Pellegrini, A. (1995) Joint Book Reading Makes for Success in Learning to Read: A Meta-Analysis on Intergenerational Transmission of Literacy. *Review of Educational Research,* 65(1), 1–21.

Campbell, F., Ramey, C., Pungello, E., Sparling, J., & Miller-Johnson, S. (2002). Early childhood education: Young adult outcomes from the Abecedarian Project. *Applied Developmental Science,* 6(1), 42–57.

Carneiro, P. & Heckman, J. (2003) Human Capital Policy. NBER working paper #9495.

Chen, C., Lee, S., & Stevenson, H. (1996) Long-Term Prediction of Academic Achievement of American, Chinese, and Japanese Adolescents. *Journal of Educational Psychology*, 88(4), 750–759.

Clark-Kauffman, E., Duncan, G., & Morris, P. (2003) How Welfare Policies Affect Child and Adolescent Achievement. *American Economic Review*, 93(2), 299–303.

Coley, R. (2002) An Uneven Start: Indicators of Inequality in School Readiness. Princeton, NJ: Educational Testing Service.

Collins, W., Maccoby, E., Steinberg, L., Hetherington, E., & Bornstein, M. (2000) Contemporary research on parenting: The case for nature *and* nurture. *American Psychologist,* 55(2), 218–232.

Cooper, R. & Zubek, J. (1958) Effects of Enriched and Restricted Early Environments on the Learning Ability of Bright and Dull Rats. *Canadian Journal of Psychology,* 12(3), 159–164.

Cummings, E. & Davies, P. (1994) Maternal Depression and Child Development. *Journal of Child Psychology and Psychiatry,* 35(1), 73–122.

Currie, J.(2001) Early Childhood Education Programs. *Journal of Economic Perspectives,* 15(2), 213–238.

Currie, J. & Thomas, D. (2000) School Quality and the Longer Term Effects of Head Start. *The Journal of Human Resources*, 35(4), 775.

DeBaryshe, B. (1993) Joint Picture-book Reading Correlates of Early Oral Language Skill. *Journal of Child Language,* 20(2), 455–461.

Dickens, W. (2005) Genetic Differences and School Readiness. *Future of Children,* 15(1), 55–69.

Downey, G. & Coyne, J. (1990) Children of Depressed Parents: An Integrative Review. *Psychology Bulletin,* 108(1), 50–76.

Duncan, G., Brooks-Gunn, J., & Klebanov, P. (1994) Economic Deprivation and Early Childhood Development. *Child Development*, 65(2), 296–318.

Duncan, G. & Magnuson, K. (2005) Can Family Socio-economic Resources Account for Racial and Ethnic Test Score Gaps? *Future of Children,* 15(1), 35–54.

Duncan, G., Yeung, W., Brooks-Gunn, J., & Smith, J. (1998) How Much Does Childhood Poverty Affect the Life Chances of Children? *American Sociological Review,* 63, 406–423.

Duyme, M., Dumaret, A., & Tomkiewicz, S. (1999) How can we boost IQs of "dull children"?: A late adoption study. *Psychology*, 96, 8790–8794.

Eyferth, K. (1961) Performance of Different Groups of Occupation Children on the Hamburg-Wechsler Intelligence Test for Children. *Archhiv fur die gesamte Psychologie,* 113, 222–241.

Fryer, R. & Levitt, S. (2004). "Understanding the Black-White Test Score Gap in the First Two Years of School," *The Review of Economics and Statistics*, 86(2), 447–464.

Fryer, R. & Levitt, S. (2006) Testing for Racial Differences in the Mental Ability of Young Children. NBER working paper #12066.

Garces, E., Thomas, D., & Currie, J. (2002) Longer-Term Effects of Head Start. *American Economic Review,* 92(4), 999–1012.

Golova, N., Alario, A. Vivier, P. Rodriguez, M., & High, P. (1999) Literacy Promotion for Hispanic Families in a Primary Care Setting: A Randomized, Controlled Study. *Pediatrics,* 103(5), 993–997.

Gomby, D., Culross, P., & Behrman, R. (1999) "Home Visiting: Recent Program Evaluations—Analysis and Recommendations." *Future of Children*, 9(1), 4–26.

Gormley Jr., W., Gayer, T., Phillips, D., & Dawson, B. (2005). The effects of universal pre-k on cognitive development. *Developmental Psychology,* 41, 872–884.

Harris, J. (1995) Where Is the Child's Environment? A Group Socialization Theory of Development. *Psychological Review,* 102(3), 458–489.

Hart, B & Risley, T. (1995) Meaningful Differences in the Everyday Experiences of Young American Children. Baltimore, MD: Paul H. Brookes.

Heckman, J. (2006) Investing in Disadvantaged Young Children is an Economically Efficient Policy. Lecture presented at the forum on "Building the Economic Case or Investments in Preschool". http://www.ced.org/docs/report/report_2006prek_heckman.pdf#search=%22heckman%20invest%20in%20the%20young%22 (accessed September 5, 2007).

Hill, J., Brooks-Gunn, J., & Waldfogal, J. (2003) Sustained Effects of High Participation in an Early Intervention for Low-Birth-Weight Premature Infants. *Developmental Psychology,* 39(4), 730–744.

High, P., LaGasse, L., Becker, S. Ahlgren, I., & Gardner, A. (2000) Literacy Promotion in Primary Care Pediatrics: Can We Make A Difference? *Pediatrics,* 105(4), 927–934.

Huttenlocher, J., Haight, W., Bryk, A., Seltzer, M., & Lyons, T. Early Vocabulary Growth: Relation to Language Input and Gender. *Development Psychology*, 27(2), 236–248.

Jordan , G., Snow, C., & Porche, M. (2000) Project EASE: The Effect of a Family Literacy Project on Kindergarten Students' Early Literacy Skills. *Reading Research Quarterly,* 35(4), 524–546.

Karoly, L., Greenwood, P., Everingham, S., Hoube, J., Kilburn, R., Rydell, P., Sanders, M., & Chiesa, J. (1998) *Investing in Our Children: What We Know and Don't Know about the Costs and Benefits of Early Childhood Interventions.* Santa Monica, CA: RAND.

Knudsen, E., Heckman, J., Cameron, J., & Shonkoff, J. (2006) Economic, neurobiological, and behavioral perspectives on building America's future workforce. *Proceedings of the Natitonal Academy of Sciences*, 103(27), 10155–10162

Lee, V. & Burkam, D. (2002) *Inequality at the Starting Gate: Social Background Differences in Achievement as Children Begin School.* Washington, DC: Economic Policy Institute.

Lee, V. & Loeb, S. (1995) Where do Head Start Attendees End Up: One reason why Preschool Effects Fade Out. *Educational Evaluation & Policy Analysis*, 17(1), 62–82.

Levin, M. (1994) Comment on the Minnesota Transracial Adoption Study. *Intelligence,* 19, 13–20.

Lewit, E. & Baker, L. (1995) "School Readiness" in *The Future of Children,* 5(2), 128–139.

Linver, M., Brooks-Gunn, J., & Kohen, D. (2002) Family Processes as Pathways from Income to Children's Development. *Development Psychology,* 38(5), 719–734.

Loeb, S., Bridges, M., Bassok, D., Fuller, B., & Rumberger, R. (2007). How much is too much? The influence of preschool centers on children's social and cognitive development. *Economics of Education Review,* 26(1), 52–66.

Loeb, S., Fuller, B., Kagan, S., & Carrol, B. (2004). Child care in poor communities: Early learning effects of type, quality, and stability. *Child Development,* 75, 476–65.

Ludwig, J. & Miller, D. (2007) Does Head Start Improve Children's Life Chances? Evidence from a Regression Discontinuity Design. *Quarterly Journal of Economics*, 122(1), 159–208.

Luster, T. & McAdoo, H. (1996) Family and Child Influences on Education Attainment: A Secondary Analysis of the High/Scope Perry Preschool Data. *Developmental Psychology*, 32(1), 26–39.

Magnuson, K. & Duncan, G. (2002) Parent vs. Child-based Intervention Strategies for Promoting Children's Well-Being. Prepared for the JCPR Conference "Family Investments in Children's Potential."

Magnuson, K. A., Ruhm, C. J., & Waldfogel, J. (2004). Does pre-kindergarten improve school preparation and performance? NBER Working Paper 10452.

McClearn, G. (2004) Nature and Nurture: Interaction and Coaction. *American Journal of Medical Genetics,* 124(1), 124–130.

McGroder, S. M., M. J. Zaslow, K. A. Moore, & S. M. LeMenestrel. (2000). *National Evaluation of Welfare-to-Work Strategies Impacts on Young Children and Their Families Two Years After Enrollment: Findings from the Child Outcomes Study*. Washington, DC: United States Department of Health and Human Services Office of the Assistant Secretary for Planning and Evaluation Administration for Children and Families.

McLoyd, V. (1998) Socio-economic Disadvantage and Child Development. *American Psychologist,* 53(2), 185–204.

Mendelsohn, A., Mogilner, L., Dreyer, B., Forman, J., Weinstein, S., Broderick, M., Cheng, K., Magloitre, T., Moore, T., & Napier, C. (2001) The Impact of a Clinic-Based Literacy Intervention on Language Development in Inner-City Preschool Children. *Pediatrics,* 107(1), 130–134.

Mistry, R., Vandewater, E., Huston, A., & McLoyd, V. (2002) Economic Well-Being and Children's Social Adjustment : The Role of Family Process in an Ethnically Diverse Low-Income Sample. *Child Development,* 73(3), 935–951.

Moore, E. (1986) Family Socialization and the IQ Test Performance of Traditionally and Transracially Adopted Black Children. *Development Psychology*, 22(3), 317–326.

Morris, P., Huston, A., Duncan, G. Crosby, D., & Bos, J., (2001) How Welfare and Work Policies Affect Children: A Synthesis of Research. New York: MDRC.

Murnane, R., Willet, J., Bub, K., & McCartney, K. (2006) Understanding Trends in the Black-White Achievement Gap during the First Years of School. *Brookings-Wharton Papers on Urban Affairs, 2006*, 97–127.

NICHD ECCRN. (2003). Does the amount of time spent in child care predict socioemotional adjustment during the transition to kindergarten? *Child Development*, 74, 976-1005.

NICHD ECCRN. (2002) Child-care structure-->process-->outcome: direct and indirect effects of child-care quality on young children's development. *Psychological Science*, 13, 199–206.

Nisbett, R. (1998) "Race, Genetics & IQ" in *The Black-White Test Score Gap*. C. Jencks & M. Phillips, eds, Washington, D.C.: Brookings Institution Press, pp. 86–102.

Olds, D. Eckenrode, J., Henderson, C., Kitzman, H., Powers, J., Cole, R., Sidora, K., Morris, P., Pettitt, L., & Luckey, D. (1997) Long-term Effects of Home Visitation on Maternal Life Course and Child Abuse and Neglect. Fifteen-year Follow-up of a Randomized Trial. *JAMA*, 278(8), 637–643.

Pagani, L., Boulerice, B., Tremblay, R., & Vitaro, F. (1997) Behavioural Development in Children of Divorce and Remarriage. *Journal of Child Psychology & Psychiatry*, 38(7), 769–781.

Peisner-Feinberg, E. et al. (2001). The relation of preschool child-care quality to children's cognitive and social developmental trajectories through second grade. *Child Development*, 72(5), 1534–1553.

Petterson, S. & Albers, A. (2001) Effects of Poverty and Maternal Depression on Early Child Development. *Child Development*, 72(6), 1794–1813.

Phillips, M., Brooks-Gunn, J., Duncan, G., Klebanov, P., & Crane, J. (1998) "Family Background, Parenting Practices and the Black-White Test Score Gap." In *The Black-White Test Score Gap*. C. Jencks and M. Phillips, eds. Washington, DC: Brookings Institution Press, pp. 103–148.

Phillips, M., Crouse, J., & Ralph, J.(1998) "Does the Black-White Test Score Gap Widen After Children Enter School. In *The Black White Test Score Gap*. C. Jencks and M. Phillips, eds. Washington, DC: Brookings Institution Press, pp. 229–272.

Plomin, R., Asbury, K., & Dunn, J. (2001) Why are Children in the Same Family So Different? Nonshared Environment a Decade Later. *Canadian Journal of Psychiatry*. 46(3), 225–233.

Plomin, R. & Daniels, D., (1987) Why are Children in the Same Family So Different From One Another? *Behavioral & Brain Sciences*, 10(1), 1–16.

Plomin, R., Fulker, D., Corley. R., & DeFries, J. (1997) Nature, Nurture and Cognitive Development From 1 to 16 Years: A Parent-Offspring Adoption Study. *Psychological Sciences*. 8(6), 442–447.

Plomin, R. & Petrill, S. (1997) Genetics and Intelligence: What's New? *Intelligence*, 24(1), 53–77.

Plug, E. & Vijverberg, W. (2003) Schooling, Family Background and Adoption: Is it Nature or Nurture? *Journal of Political Economy*, 111(3), 611–641.

Quint, J., Bos, J., &Polit, D. (1997). *New Chance: Final Report on a Comprehensive Program for Young Mothers in Poverty and Their Children*. New York: MDRC.

Ramey, C. & Ramey, S. (2004) Early Learning and School Readiness: Can Early Intervention and Make a Difference? *Merrill-Palmer Quarterly*, 50(4), 471–491.

Reardon, Sean F. (2003) "Sources of Educational Inequality: The Growth of Racial/Ethnic and Socio-economic Test Score Gaps in Kindergarten and First Grade." Population Research Institute, Pennsylvania State University, Working Paper 03-05R.

Reynolds, A., Temple, J., Robertson, D., & Mann, E. (2002). Age 21 cost-benefit analysis of the Title I Chicago Child-Parent Centers. *Educational Evaluation and Policy Analysis*, 24, 267–303.

Rowe, D., Jacobson, K., & Van den Oord, E. (1999) Genetic and Environmental Influences on Vocabulary IQ: Parental Education Level as Moderator. *Child Development*, 70(5), 1151–1162.

Rumberger, R. & Anguiano, B. (2004) Understanding and Addressing the California Latino Achievement Gap in Early Elementary School. Working Paper.

Rumberger, R. & Tran, L. (2006) Preschool Participation and the Cognitive and Social Development of Language Minority Students. Santa Barbara, CA: Linguistic Minority Research Institute.

Rutter, M. (2002) Nature, Nurture, and Development: From Evangelism through Science toward Policy and Practice. *Child Development*, 73(1), 1–21.

Scarr, S. & Weinberg, R. (1978) The Influence of "Family Background" on Intellectual Attainment. *American Sociological Review*, 43(5), 674–692.

Scarr, S. (1992) Development Theories for the 1990s: Development and Individual Differences. *Child Development,* 63(1), 1–19.

Schweinhart, L., Montie, J., Xiang, Z., Barnett, W., Belfield, C., & Nores, M. (2005) *Lifetime Effects: The High/Scope Perry Preschool Study Through Age 40.* Ypsilanti, MI: High/Scope Press.

Shonkoff, J. P. & Phillips, D. A., Eds. (2000). *From Neurons to Neighborhoods: The Science of Early Child Development.* Washington, DC: National Academy Press.

Shore, R. (1997) *Rethinking the Brain: New Insights into Early Development.* New York: Families and Work Institute.

Suomi, S. (2003) Gene-Environment Interactions and the Neurobiology of Social Conflict. *Annals of the New York Academy of Sciences.* 1008, 132–139.

Turkheimer, E. & Waldron, M. (2000) Nonshared Environment: A Theoretical, Methodological and Quantitative Review. *Psychological Bulletin,* 126(1), 78–108.

U.S. Department of Education, National Center for Education Statistics (2006) The Condition of Education 2006. NCES 2006-071. Washington, DC: U.S. Government Printing Office.

Waldman, I., Weinberg, R., & Scarr, S. (1994) Racial-Group Differences in IQ in the Minnesota Transracial Adoption Study: A reply to Levin and Lynn. *Intelligence,* 19, 29–44.

Weinberg, R., Scarr, S. & Waldman, I. (1992) The Minnesota Transracial Adoption Study: A Follow-up of IQ Test Performance in Adolescence. *Intelligence,* 16, 117–135.

Whitehurst, G., Arnold, D., Epstein, J. Angell, A., Smith, M., & Fischel, J. (1994) A Picture Book Reading Intervention in Day Care and Home for Children From Low-Income Families. *Development Psychology,* 30(5), 679–689.

Zaslow, M., Moore, K., Brooks, J., Morris, P., Tout, K., Redd, Z., & Emig, C. (2002) Experimental Studies of Welfare Reform and Children. *The Future of Children,* 12(1), 78–95.

30

Increasing the Effectiveness of Teachers in Low-Performing Schools

Donald Boyd, Hamilton Lankford, and James Wyckoff

INTRODUCTION

Low-income African-American and Latino students often enter elementary school with fewer academic skills and less ready to learn than wealthier, white students. Research shows that achievement gaps often either remain constant or increase as students progress through the education system,[1] and that education policies contribute to this outcome. In particular, the least qualified teachers often work in schools with the lowest performing students. Because teachers can make an important difference in student achievement, improving the quality of teachers in schools with low-performing students may well be the single best opportunity to reduce racial and socioeconomic achievement gaps.

In this chapter we examine how teachers are distributed across schools, analyze research on how that distribution affects student achievement, and consider policies to insure that low-achieving students are taught by more effective teachers. We end with suggestions for additional research.

SYSTEMATIC DIFFERENCES IN WHO TEACHES WHOM

Teachers differ in the qualifications they bring to the classroom, and consistent patterns emerge across the country in how teachers with different qualifications are distributed among schools. Teachers with weak academic credentials, as measured by qualities such as the competitiveness of their undergraduate college, or their scores on general knowledge certification exams, are overrepresented in schools with lower-achieving, non-white, and poor students. The same is true for teachers who are not certified or who have less teaching experience. Thus, the students whose educational success most depends upon their school experiences typically are taught by the least-qualified teachers.

This pattern clearly emerges from detailed analysis of administrative data for California, New York State and New York City, North Carolina, and three midwestern states. In elementary schools in California, for example, the schools in the top quintile—when schools are ranked by the percentage of their students in poverty—have nearly 40 percent more novice teachers than those in the quintile with the least poverty (Betts, Reuben, & Danenberg, 2000). The poorer schools also have four times the percentage of teachers who have, at most, a bachelor's degree, and 10 times the percentage of teachers who are not fully certified. Similarly, at the elementary level in New York State, poor, non-white, and low-achieving students are much more likely than non-poor, white, and higher-achieving peers to have teachers who are inexperienced, lack certification in the subjects they teach, or who have failed the general knowledge certification exam (Lankford, Loeb, & Wyckoff, 2002).

Non-white students in New York, for example, are four times more likely than white students to have teachers who are not certified in the courses they teach. Such patterns also emerge within single districts. Within New York City, for example, non-white students are 40 percent more likely than white students to have a teacher who is not certified in any of the courses she or he teaches, and 40 percent more likely to have a teacher with no prior experience (Lankford, Loeb, & Wyckoff, 2002).

Regardless of whether they focus on elementary, middle, or secondary schools, Clotfelter, Ladd, Vigdor, and Wheeler (2006) find that teachers and principals in North Carolina are sorted in ways that are detrimental to the weakest students. Echoing the pattern in California, for example, is the finding that in 2004, elementary schools in the quartile with the highest concentration of poor students in North Carolina had 40 percent more novice teachers than did schools in the quartile with the lowest concentration. Similar patterns emerge for every other teacher credential included in the study, as well as for credentials of principals—such as their Praxis scores, leadership ratings, school tenure, and measures of undergraduate college competitiveness. In a previous study of fifth graders in North Carolina, three of these same authors (Clotfelter, Ladd, & Vigdor, 2006b) document that, in addition to differences in average teacher credentials across schools, some differences, albeit smaller, emerge across classrooms within schools.

The distribution of teachers, as defined by their credentials, is similarly patterned in Wisconsin, Ohio, and Illinois (Peske & Haycock 2006). The fact that the same patterns emerge from states that differ so much in size and demographic characteristics, and in the power of teacher unions, implies that these patterns are widespread and potentially crucial for understanding differences in student achievement.

Student Sorting

If students were randomly distributed among schools, a student from any group would have the same probability of having a teacher with a given set of credentials as a student from any other group. Thus, one of the conditions for the adverse sorting of the type just described is that students are segregated by characteristics such as their race, socioeconomic status, or prior achievement.

The common policy of neighborhood schoo-attendance zones, combined with residential sorting of families by socioeconomic status, race, and preferences for education, often leads to schools segregated by income, race, and student achievement.[2] In metropolitan areas with school districts that are geographically small, as in many Northeastern states, families often reside in suburban school districts while parents work in central cities. This pattern facilitates the sorting of students across districts by their socioeconomic status. Such across-district sorting is less common in the South where school districts are larger and often have the same boundaries as counties. Nevertheless, residential location choices often result in the socioeconomic sorting of students across schools within districts as well. The result is that some schools end up with large proportions of disadvantaged and low-performing students.

This concentration of students is clearly evident in New York State, where 70 percent of the lowest-performing students on that state's 2004 fourth grade math exam came from 20 percent of the state's elementary schools, which collectively enrolled only 30 percent of the state's students

(Wyckoff, 2006). This pattern has been stable over time. These same schools enrolled more than 60 percent of the lowest-performing students in math and English language arts exams in each year from 2001 through 2004. More than 80 percent of these schools are found in the five largest cities in New York, even though these districts have less than 40 percent of the schools in the state. This concentration of the lowest-performing students in relatively few schools and districts makes it feasible for many teachers to avoid working with low-performing students.

Nature of Teacher Sorting

No single factor accounts for the fact that teachers are sorted among schools in ways that are detrimental to disadvantaged students. Rather, it arises from several aspects of the educational system, including the organization of school districts, personnel policies, and the preferences of teachers for particular working conditions. Research suggests that most of the variance in teacher qualifications occurs either between districts within a labor market, or between schools within a district. Proportionately less variation occurs between labor markets or within schools (Lankford, Loeb, & Wyckoff, 2002; Clotfelter, Ladd, & Vigdor, 2006a).

Lankford, Loeb, and Wyckoff (2002) look at differences in teacher qualifications in New York State across schools within districts, across school districts within regions, and across regions. Of the total variation in student exposure to novice teachers, the researchers find that that 72 percent is attributable to differences across schools within districts, and only 25 percent to differences across districts within regions. Similarly, of the variation in student exposure to uncertified teachers, 36 percent is across schools within districts, and 47 percent is across districts. These differences are important because the nature of sorting between districts differs from the sorting of teachers across schools within districts.

Teacher Sorting Between Districts

Teacher sorting between districts reflects the preferences of both teachers and hiring authorities. These preferences interact with organizational and policy structures to determine the allocation of teachers within and across school districts.

There is ample evidence that teachers prefer positions with higher compensation and better working conditions (Baugh & Stone, 1982; Dolton & van der Klaauw, 1995, 1999; Hanushek, Kain, & Rivkin, 2004; Murnane, Singer, & Willett, 1991; Stinebrickner, 2001; Scafidi, Sjoquist, & Stinebrickner, 2003). Recent research suggests that teachers are more sensitive to working conditions, particularly to the characteristics of the students they teach, than to salary differences. This finding is not surprising given that working conditions differ much more across schools than do salaries (Hanushek, Kain, O'Brien, & Rivkin, 2005). Teachers are drawn to schools with relatively low proportions of students who are poor, of a race different from their own, and low-achieving (Boyd, Lankford, Loeb, & Wyckoff, 2006). Teachers are also more likely to remain in schools with lower concentrations of low-achieving, poor, or non-white students (Betts, Rueben, & Danenberg, 2000; Bohrnstedt & Stecher, 1999; Boyd, Lankford, Loeb, & Wyckoff, 2005, 2006; Hanushek, Kain, & Rivkin, 2004; Ingersoll, 2001; Lankford, Loeb, & Wyckoff, 2002; Scafidi, Sjoquist, & Stinebrickner, 2003). In most of these studies it is difficult to separate the effects of teacher preferences on the achievement of students from the effects of student race or family income. In addition, it is difficult to separate the effects of student characteristics from more difficult-to-measure factors—such as the quality of school leadership—that may affect student achievement. The bottom line, though, is that the schools with low-performing students are relatively unattractive to teachers.

Teachers also appear responsive to working conditions unrelated to student characteristics. Studies have found that higher rates of attrition are associated with greater teacher workload (Johnson et al., 2004), and with poor facilities (Buckley, Schneider, & Shang, 2004; Loeb, Darling-Hammond, & Luczak, 2005). Teacher preferences for better facilities and professional networking lead them away from schools with low-performing students, who disproportionately attend schools with inferior facilities[3] and weaker peer networks. On the other hand, the evidence suggests that attrition can be reduced by providing novice teachers with good mentoring and networking experiences (Smith & Ingersoll, 2004).

Geography also plays an important role in defining the supply of teachers. Estimates from New York State suggest that teacher labor markets are relatively small: 85 percent of teachers take their first job within 40 miles of where they attended high school (Boyd, Lankford, Loeb, & Wyckoff, 2005). Moreover, teachers take their first job in settings similar to where they grew up. Since the supply of teachers who attended urban high schools is insufficient to fill urban teaching vacancies, these districts must hire a substantial number of teachers who attended high school in suburban or rural areas.

Geography also affects teacher retention. An analysis of retention of novice teachers in New York City shows that teachers who lived outside the city prior to taking their job were five times more likely to transfer to suburban schools within the first three years of their teaching careers than teachers who lived in New York City prior to beginning their careers. The preferences of teachers for teaching environments geographically close to, or similar to, those they experienced in their own schooling helps explain inter-district sorting of teachers, and has important policy implications for the recruitment and preparation of teachers.

Research on the preferences of teachers suggests that attracting more qualified teachers to schools with high concentrations of poor, non-white, and low-performing students will require an offsetting benefit in the form of higher compensation or better working conditions. Given the widespread use of the single-salary schedule within a district, pay differentials between low- and high-performing schools *within* a district are either small or nonexistent. Salary differences between districts with concentrations of low-performing students and their higher-achieving neighboring districts, however, could affect the ability of schools to attract teachers.

Lankford, Loeb, and Wyckoff (2002) find that, across the nine largest metropolitan regions of New York State, the average starting salaries for teachers who teach non-white students were about the same as those of teachers teaching white students. The only major exception was in the New York City metropolitan area, where the average salary of those teaching non-white students was 7 percent less than the average for those teaching white students. The same salary patterns hold for teaching poor versus non-poor and low- versus high-achieving students. Nationally, Loeb and Reininger (2004) find that most salary variation is across labor markets, not within labor markets. The variation that does exist within labor markets indicates that districts serving somewhat lower proportions of black students and students in poverty pay slightly higher salaries than the districts that serve black and poorer students. Thus, current salary scales appear to do little to counter teachers' revealed preferences for teaching white, non-poor, and higher-achieving students and, in some areas, tend to make teaching disadvantaged students even less attractive than it would be with uniform salaries.

Preferences of employers also affect how teachers are distributed among districts and schools. Employers generally prefer to hire teachers with superior academic qualifications, such as higher scores on certification exams and graduation from an academically strong college (Boyd, Lankford, Loeb, & Wyckoff, 2006). Ballou (1996) finds that teacher applicants who attended above-average colleges are significantly less likely to take teaching jobs in low-achieving schools than applicants who attended below-average colleges. However, this finding could reflect differences in the jobs to which these candidates apply. For example, highly-qualified candidates may simply not be willing to teach in schools where less-qualified candidates accept jobs.

The timing of hiring decisions also shapes the patterns of teacher hiring because delayed hiring processes can limit options. Based on case studies in four urban districts, Levin and Quinn (2003) find that the pool of applicants, especially highly-qualified applicants, is substantially reduced because these districts wait to make hiring decisions until mid- to late-summer—much later than neighboring districts. Although the four districts received applications from many well-qualified teachers, many of these teachers accepted other positions before the urban districts began hiring. The authors cite three factors that contribute to late hiring: late notification by existing teachers of their intent to leave, experience-based transfer preferences, and budget and enrollment uncertainties. These practices thus work to the disadvantage of urban, low-performing schools.

Teacher Sorting within Districts

Nearly all school districts compensate teachers through a single-salary schedule. That is, teachers with the same experience and education receive the same compensation regardless of the characteristics of the school in which they teach or their performance. With compensation not a factor in their decisions, most teachers choose to teach in schools with better working conditions. This is especially true among teachers in subject areas with teacher shortages, such as math, science, and special education, because these teachers typically have more school and non-school options among which to choose. Thus, under a single-salary schedule, schools with low-performing students typically are disadvantaged, both in recruiting and retaining teachers.

In addition, labor contracts in many districts specify that, in filling teacher vacancies, preference must be given to teachers applying from within the district based on seniority.[4] The result is that experienced teachers are able to transfer out of less appealing schools to schools with higher performing students. Because experience is an important determinant of teacher effectiveness, low-performing students are disadvantaged by this policy. Somewhat to the contrary, a recent study (Koski & Horng, 2007) finds that in California, the language related to seniority transfers is quite flexible so that, in that state at least, the allocation of teachers based on seniority is more the result of the personnel practices of human resource departments and district administrators than that of inflexible contract provisions.

Effective principals also may steer poorly-performing teachers to low-performing schools, where competition for available teaching positions is weak. The prevalence of this practice is difficult to document, but in fall 2006, California enacted legislation that allows principals in low-performing schools to refuse teacher transfers from within the district—suggesting that such transfers are at least a perceived problem. The bill mandates that any seniority-based voluntary transfer process be completed by April 15, more than four months prior to the beginning of the school year. After this date, principals are free to consider all candidates equally, and, in theory, can hire the most qualified applicants.

School district budgeting policies also work against the interests of schools with low-performing students. Typically, within-district personnel allocations to schools are based solely on the number of teaching positions in the school and do not reflect a fixed overall personnel budget. Thus, when filling teaching vacancies, administrators in schools with better working conditions are able to hire more experienced, and thus more highly compensated, teachers without bearing any additional cost in their school-level budget. This separation of personnel decisions from budgetary consequences at the school level, in effect, encourages within-district transfers that, in turn, contribute to the systematic sorting of teachers and results in lower spending per pupil in the less attractive schools.[5]

Each of these district policies contributes to the sorting of teachers and makes it more difficult to attract and retain teachers in schools with disproportionate numbers of low-achieving students. Policy shifts, such as the elimination of preferential transfer rights for experienced teachers, differential pay in difficult-to-staff schools, and the establishment of school-level personnel budgets could potentially enhance the ability of traditionally difficult-to-staff schools to recruit and retain teachers with stronger qualifications.

IMPROVING THE QUALITY OF TEACHERS IN LOW-ACHIEVING SCHOOLS

Although there is substantial evidence that teachers differ in their ability to improve student test performance, there is little consensus regarding what teacher attributes, knowledge, or skills contribute to improved student achievement.

A number of studies find that teachers can significantly influence student achievement (Sanders & Rivers, 1996; Aaronson, Barrow, & Sander, 2003; Rockoff, 2004; Rivkin, Hanushek, and Kain, 2005; Kane, Rockoff, & Staiger, 2006). Sanders and Rivers estimate that differences in teacher quality can provide up to a 50 percent improvement in measures of student achievement, and that these improvements are additive and cumulative over subsequent teachers. Aaronson, Barrow, and Sander find that a two standard deviation increase in teacher quality improves student achievement by 0.25 to 0.45 of a grade equivalent. Kane, Rockoff, and Staiger estimate that the difference in effectiveness between the top and bottom quartile of teachers results in a 0.33 standard deviation difference in student test score gains. In sum, every recent study of student achievement finds that differences in teacher effectiveness contribute meaningfully to differences in student achievement.

Large differences in teacher effectiveness suggest two strategies for closing achievement gaps: reallocating the most effective teachers to the lowest performing students, and increasing the pool of highly-effective teachers. In order to implement these strategies, it is necessary first to identify the teachers who are most effective in helping low-achieving students and, second, to design and implement policies that lead to the desired matching of teachers and students.

Methodological Issues in Identifying High Quality Teachers

The sorting of teachers complicates empirical attempts to determine how their specific qualifications are linked to teacher quality, or even to assess the extent to which effective teachers are teaching in higher- or lower-performing schools. For example, if teachers in schools where students perform best in math are more likely to be certified in math, one might be tempted to conclude that being certified to teach math contributes to higher student achievement. The causal relationship, however, may operate in the other direction; that is, the more qualified teachers may be in schools where students perform well in math because they prefer to teach good students and because employers want to staff their courses with in-field certified teachers. Without good controls for this selection, researchers will overstate the contributions of certified teachers.

Policymakers are keen to understand how improving teachers' knowledge and skills can influence student achievement, but that, too, is subject to selection. If more able and motivated individuals seek out more and better-quality teacher preparation, it is difficult to disentangle the effects of their preparation from their general ability and motivation. Selection issues can be mitigated by research methods that account for both the observed and unobserved attributes of students, teachers, and schools.

Unfortunately, using quasi-experimental data to determine the extent to which teacher attributes influence student achievement faces an additional challenge. If schools are able to attract a given quality teacher because of the wage and non-wage benefits that they offer, then one would expect that the teachers in the school would be of similar quality. Teachers who lack one attribute may have others that compensate within a school. Thus, we rarely observe differences in teacher quality that can be used to identify attributes of teachers that influence student achievement. This realization should encourage caution when researchers using quasi-experimental data conclude that attributes of teachers are unimportant.

A final potential concern is that relatively little variation in many of the relevant teacher variables makes it difficult to identify the underlying effects of these attributes. The range of knowledge and skills observed in teachers is substantially reduced by a variety of institutions, including the state certification. For example, most states require that teachers of core subjects have a subject-matter major in those areas or otherwise demonstrate sufficient content knowledge. If this requirement is effective, then we may not observe an empirical relationship between a teacher's content knowledge and the achievement of his or her students. This methodological problem arises not because content knowledge is unimportant but because teachers without much content knowledge are not observed in the data. There is thus a premium on measuring the differential quality of knowledge and skills that the teacher brings to the classroom, as opposed to some cruder measure of content knowledge such as whether she or he has taken courses in the field.

Teaching Experience

To gauge how additional years of teaching experience affect student achievement gains produced by individual teachers, the analyst must control for compositional changes in the cohort. For example, suppose that 10 percent of a cohort of teachers leave the profession following the first year of teaching and that those who leave are relatively less effective. Even if the effectiveness of the returning teachers did not improve, the observed achievement gains of students taught by second-year teachers would be greater than the gains for students of first-year teachers.

After controlling for such changes in the composition of cohorts, research has estimated that novice teachers produce student achievement gains that are from 0.03 to 0.20 standard deviations less than otherwise similar teachers with 10 to 15 years of experience (Rockoff, 2004; Rivkin, Hanushek, & Kain, 2005; Kane, Rockoff, & Staiger, 2006). These studies also suggest that most of these gains from experience occur within the first four years of teaching. While other research based on data from Florida finds that teacher experience exerts only modest effects on student achievement (Harris & Sass, 2006), the smaller effect may simply reflect the less flexible way in which the experience variable was specified in the analysis.

The research does not identify what it is that teachers learn over their first few years that accounts for their increased effectiveness. However, the meaningful gains in effectiveness associated with experience underscores the importance of trying to retain teachers who have at least a few years of experience. A focus on retention may be particularly important for raising the performance of low-achieving students because, as described above, these students often attend schools with above-average teacher attrition and substantially higher proportions of novice teachers.

Teacher Certification

Historically, most schools have hired graduates of teacher preparation programs in college- and university-based schools of education. Many low-performing schools, however, are unable to recruit sufficient numbers of teachers from such programs—especially in difficult-to-staff subject areas such as science and special education—and have resorted to hiring uncertified teachers. Increasingly, state-level accountability policies and the federal No Child Left Behind Act of 2001 (NCLB) have challenged this practice. NCLB requires states to ensure that teachers of core academic subjects (reading or language arts, math, science, foreign languages, civics and government, economics, arts, history, and geography) are "highly qualified." New teachers typically are judged highly qualified if they receive full state certification and demonstrate content knowledge of the material they teach. Experienced teachers must meet similar criteria. States must also ensure that poor and non-white students are not taught disproportionately by teachers who are not highly qualified. These requirements place a floor under the qualifications of teachers hired in low-performing schools.

Many studies examine the effect of teacher certification on student achievement, and they differ, sometimes substantially, in their findings. Most have weak controls for teacher sorting, and few differentiate their analysis for low-performing students. However, three recent studies with strong research designs and solid data address how teacher certification affects student achievement (Goldhaber, 2006; Clotfelter, Ladd, & Vigdor, 2006; Boyd, Grossman, Lankford, Loeb, & Wyckoff, 2006). In both North Carolina and New York City, these studies find that the students of teachers with certification outperform those whose teachers are uncertified. The achievement effect of certification is approximately two to four percent of a standard deviation in math, which is about half as large as the effect of second-year teachers relative to first-year teachers. The effect in reading is about half this size. These measurements do not represent the full differential effect of requiring teachers to be certified; many uncertified teachers are in the process of meeting certification requirements, and have more knowledge and skills than they would have had if certification were not required.

In response to shortages of qualified teachers, states and school districts have developed alternative certification programs. These alternate-route programs have become an important source of teachers for many schools, especially traditionally difficult-to-staff schools. Alternative-route programs typically allow teachers to enter the classroom by delaying or bypassing many of the requirements for entry into traditional teacher preparation programs. Forty-six states and the District of Columbia report they have at least one type of alternate route to teacher certification.[6] Some states and school districts rely heavily on alternate routes as a source of supply. New Jersey, Texas, and California in some years obtain more than one-third of their new teachers from alternative routes. These programs are a rapidly growing source of supply in many other states and school districts.[7]

The growth of alternative routes reflects a shift away from emergency and temporary certification. In 2001, for example, about half of the 9,000 new teachers hired by New York City were not certified. Thanks to the New York City Teaching Fellows program, an alternate-route program that was started in 2002, the city hired fewer than 300 uncertified teachers in 2005 (Boyd et al., 2006). Some alternative certification programs have been able to recruit teachers with very strong qualifications compared to those entering teaching through traditional teacher preparation programs and, especially, to those having emergency or temporary certification. Teach for America (TFA), an alternative-route teacher program whose mission is to place teachers in high-poverty urban and rural schools, exemplifies this approach.

TFA recruits teachers nationally and targets recent graduates of elite liberal arts colleges; it has been very successful. In 2003, for example, it had 16,000 applicants for 1,800 available slots.[8] As a result, it is able to be highly selective in terms of the academic qualifications of its teachers. In New York City, both TFA and Teaching Fellows teachers have qualifications—certification exam scores, undergraduate college rankings and SAT scores—that, on average, substantially exceed those of unlicensed teachers and teachers prepared in traditional preparation programs (Boyd et al., 2006). These alternative route teachers are also, on average, a more diverse group than traditionally prepared teachers, with more males and 50 percent more Hispanics and blacks. Both TFA and Teaching Fellows teachers are initially placed in more difficult-to-staff schools than are teachers from traditional preparation programs.

Several studies examine the relative effectiveness of TFA teachers.[9] Although these studies generate similar results in some ways, they also differ in other important ways, depending on how the analysis was performed and the school districts examined. The most persuasive evidence suggests that, on average, students of entering TFA teachers perform at least as well in math as students of other entering teachers, including those from traditional preparation programs. They score slightly worse in English language arts. By their second or third year teaching, TFA teachers generate student gains that are somewhat higher than non-TFA teachers in math and about the same in reading. Similar, though somewhat less positive, results hold for New York City Teaching Fellows (Boyd et al., 2006; Kane et al, 2006).

These evaluations do not distinguish between the general ability of teachers and their preparation to teach. Because TFA and the New York City Teaching Fellows programs strongly emphasize recruitment and selection, their teachers have better general qualifications than many other teachers. Thus, the results of these evaluations may mean that the higher general qualifications of TFA and Teaching Fellow teachers compensate for their less substantial preparation. The fact that alternate-route teachers typically teach in more difficult-to-staff schools, however, means that the results might differ if the TFA and Teaching Fellow teachers were compared, not to teachers in the schools in which they teach, but rather to comparably qualified teachers entering the profession by a more traditional route who take positions in easier-to-staff schools. Here again the sorting of teachers may limit our ability to draw policy inferences.

Studies to date that examine how teacher preparation programs affect student outcomes compare one program to another, and do not indicate performance compared to a desired outcome. Thus, all programs may be doing a fine job, or they may all produce relatively weak teachers. Additionally, Kane, Rockoff, and Staiger (2006) show that there is wide variation among teachers within each pathway, suggesting that there remains much to learn about the knowledge and skills of teachers that are most effective in producing student achievement gains.

Variation in the Effectiveness of Teachers by Type of Students

Some teachers are more effective with some students than with others. One factor to consider is the race of the teacher in relation to the race of the student. Ferguson (1998) provides some initial evidence to support the hypothesis that black students taught by black teachers realize higher achievement gains. Using data from the Tennessee Project STAR (Student Teacher Achievement Ratio), an experiment related to class size in which teachers were randomly assigned to students, Dee (2004) finds that black students assigned to black teachers score two to four percentile points higher than those assigned to white teachers. Hanushek, Kain, O'Brien, and Rivkin (2005) also find support for this hypothesis in an urban Texas district where black students perform 0.05 to 0.10 of a standard deviation higher when matched with a black teacher.

Also relevant is the interaction between teacher credentials and the initial performance level of the students. Though the evidence on this interaction is limited, studies based on data from North Carolina and New York City generated consistent evidence. Clotfelter, Ladd, and Vigdor (2006a) find in North Carolina that teachers with stronger qualifications appear to be equally effective with lower- or higher-achieving students. Their evidence suggests that students who are not poor or whose parents are better educated benefit more from teachers with stronger qualifications, although those effects are small. Boyd et al. (2006) find that teachers who score higher on the New York State certification exam generate student achievement gains among low-performing students that are no greater than those for teachers with lower certification exam scores. For students who begin the year with high scores, however, a positive relationship emerges between the teacher's certification exam score and gains in student achievement.

Retaining Teachers in Low-Performing Schools

Much has been made of the high overall attrition rate of teachers, especially in difficult-to-staff schools.[10] Nationally, 23 percent of teachers with one to three years of experience left their current school between the 2000 and 2001 school years.[11] In difficult-to-staff schools attrition often is even higher. For example, Ladd, Clotfelter, Vigdor, & Wheeler (2006) find turnover rates for first-year teachers in high-poverty elementary and middle schools of 23 and 27 percent, respectively. They report five-year attrition rates in high-poverty schools of 73 percent for elementary schools and 78 percent for middle schools. Boyd, Lankford, Loeb, and Wyckoff (2005) find similar attrition rates in New York City schools in the bottom quartile, as grouped by student performance.

A number of studies have shown that the characteristics of students in a school can increase the likelihood that teachers will remain in that school. Teachers are more likely to stay in schools in which student achievement is higher. And teachers, especially white teachers, are more likely to stay in schools with higher proportions of white students. In addition, characteristics of the teachers affect their departure decisions. Teachers whose home town is farther from the school in which they teach are more likely to leave. Furthermore, the attributes of teachers interact in important ways with the characteristics of students they teach. In particular, teachers with stronger qualifications, as measured by scores on a general knowledge certification exam, are more likely to quit or transfer than are less-qualified teachers, and this is especially true for those teaching in schools with low-achieving students (Boyd, Lankford, Loeb, & Wyckoff, 2005).

A strong case has been made that reducing teacher attrition would improve the teacher workforce and the educational outcomes of students. Ingersoll (2001) argues that major school staffing problems result from the "revolving door," whereby large numbers of qualified teachers leave their jobs for reasons other than retirement. How teacher attrition affects the overall quality of the teacher workforce depends upon a number of factors. If teachers leave within the first few years, schools lose the benefits of having more experienced teachers. Low-performing, poor, and black students are disproportionately affected by teacher attrition because their schools have the highest attrition rates, and new hires are invariably novice teachers.

The effect of attrition depends upon the effectiveness of the teachers who leave relative to that of those who stay. One can easily imagine that ineffective teachers become disillusioned most readily and leave to find a more rewarding position or career. There is little research comparing the effectiveness of teachers by retention status. One exception is work by Hanushek, Kain, O'Brien, and Rivkin (2005) who find that the teachers leaving schools in an urban Texas district on average have lower student achievement gains than do the teachers who remain. Boyd et al. (2007) find that New York City teachers who transfer or quit following their first year of teaching also have lower student achievement gains than those teaching in the same school for a second year.

Improving the retention of effective teachers in schools with poor, non-white, and low-performing students remains an important strategy for closing the achievement gap. However, we have much to learn about policies that effectively retain the best teachers. For example, to what extent can mentoring and induction practices, or interventions by principals improve teacher retention of the more effective teachers?

PROMISING POLICIES TO ATTRACT AND RETAIN HIGH QUALITY TEACHERS

Many states and school districts have experimented with various types of salary incentives intended to attract and retain teachers in schools with large portions of low-performing students. Strategies include variations on pay-for-performance, one-time bonuses, loan-forgiveness, and housing subsidies. In 2006, Denver Public Schools and the Denver Classroom Teachers Association initiated ProComp, a teacher compensation system under which teacher pay is linked more closely to teacher performance and student outcomes.[12] Teachers are able to enhance their earnings through four components: knowledge and development, professional evaluation, market incentives, and growth in student achievement. The knowledge and development component allows teachers to earn an additional 2 percent in salary by completing annual professional development courses, an additional 9 percent for acquiring a graduate degree or obtaining national licensure or certification, and $1,000 for tuition reimbursement. Teachers receive salary increases in a variety of other ways, including a 3 percent market incentive to teach in hard-to-staff schools. In the student-growth component, the school principal and teachers collaborate to set student achievement goals, and teacher salaries increase or decrease depending on whether their students meet learning goals, including performance measured by the Colorado Student Assessment Program. Based on a pilot project in 16 Denver schools begun in 1999, ProComp improved student test scores in elementary, middle, and high schools.[13]

Many of the programs intended to attract and retain teachers to low-performing schools are relatively new and have not been evaluated. An exception is an examination of North Carolina's policy to provide math, science, and special education teachers an annual bonus of up to $1,800 to teach in schools serving disproportionate numbers of low-performing or poor students (Clotfelter, Glennie, Ladd, & Vigdor, 2006). This analysis examines the mobility decisions of teachers in schools that are eligible for the bonus, and schools barely missing the eligibility threshold, both before and after implementation of the program. The results suggest that $1,800 was sufficient to reduce teacher turnover in eligible schools by about 12 percent. The authors find that implementation problems, including the failure of the state to communicate clearly who was eligible, reduced the impact of the program. Teachers with 10 or more years of experience were more responsive to the bonus than were teachers with less experience, suggesting that bonus programs may be an effective strategy for retaining teachers who are expected to have a positive impact on student achievement.

In order to attract more qualified teachers, in 1998 Massachusetts instituted a program that included a $20,000 signing bonus to be paid out over fours years, and an expedited certification process. An analysis of the program followed 13 of the 59 teachers hired during the first year of the program and concluded that expedited certification was much more influential in attracting those teachers than was the signing bonus (Liu, Johnson, & Peske, 2004). Although these studies provide some insights, we know little about how to design optimal monetary awards to recruit and retain teachers.

Some research indicates that salary increments will need to be substantial in order to induce teachers, especially those whose qualifications suggest they have a range of alternative job opportunities, to move to schools with high proportions of low-performing students. Hanushek, Kain, and Rivkin (2004) estimate the increase in salary needed to reduce the rate of attrition in a large urban district to that in suburban schools: 9 percent for non-minority male teachers with three to five years of experience; 43 percent for female non-minority teachers with the same level of experience. Research in New York State suggests that salary differentials of $10,000 to $16,000 would be necessary to attract equally qualified new teachers to low-performing urban schools instead of neighboring suburban schools (Boyd, Lankford, Loeb, & Wyckoff, 2006).

Non-monetary incentives might also induce more effective teachers to accept positions in low-performing schools. For example, case-study evidence suggests that teachers value their peers and school leadership. The opportunity to work with a strong instructional team may decrease the wage premium necessary to attract an effective teacher to a school with a disproportionate number of low-performing students. Additional research is needed to determine whether the attractiveness of strong leadership and peers induce effective teachers to work in low-performing schools.

The termination of ineffective teachers is also receiving increased attention. Given the restrictions of due process once teachers have received tenure, most terminations occur during the probationary period. Anecdotal reports suggest that in many schools the threshold for demonstrating effective teaching for tenure is quite low. States differ in their probationary period, though every state has a teacher tenure law. Most states—32—grant tenure after three years of teaching; 10 grant it after only two years, and the remaining states allow a longer probationary period (Loeb & Miller, 2007). Thus, in many schools the short length of the probationary period allows only limited experience on which to judge a teacher's effectiveness.

Kane, Rockoff, and Staiger (2006) suggest that using measures of the effects of teachers on student test score gains during their first few years in teaching may be part of a useful evaluation program to select teachers for tenure. While the creation of effective evaluation procedures is still in the early stages of policy development, it is clear that teachers have the potential to make substantial improvements in their teaching effectiveness during their first four to six years of teaching. Utilizing teachers' demonstrated ability to improve student achievement to shape a school's workforce makes sense. It might well be desirable to make tenure decisions during the fifth or sixth year of a teacher's career, with especially ineffective teachers being terminated sooner.

SUMMARY

Education offers the potential for economic mobility for children from poor families. We know that effective teachers can make a substantial difference in the achievement of students, especially low-performing students. However, the least-qualified teachers typically teach in the schools with the highest concentration of these students. The reasons for teacher sorting are numerous and varied, but they primarily relate to teachers' preferences regarding compensation and working conditions. These preferences combine with substantial differences in working conditions across schools that generally favor more advantaged students. Changing personnel policies may help alter the current situation, but such changes are unlikely to be sufficient. In order to alter this sorting, it will be necessary either to recruit teachers whose preferences are different from those already teaching, or to change teacher compensation or working conditions so as to make teaching in schools with traditionally low-performing students more appealing. States, districts, and schools are experimenting with policies aimed at doing this, yet it is still too early to determine the effectiveness of such policies. While monetary incentives have shown mixed results, however, there is evidence that other policies—particularly those aimed at increasing the pool of teachers by changing entry requirements into teaching—can reduce the differences in teacher qualifications across schools.

The evidence on whether teachers with better qualifications are more effective in increasing student achievement is much less clear. Many of these qualifications do influence achievement positively, but other than in the case of teacher experience, the effects appear to be relatively small. We have a far better understanding of the nature of the problem than we do of the underlying causes. Thus, effective policies for closing the achievement gap remain uncertain.

This uncertainty could be substantially reduced if we had answers to the following sets of questions:

- Is it more effective to target resources toward differential pay or improvement of specific working conditions for hard-to-staff schools? What changes in working conditions such as school leadership, school culture, and facilities are most effective in improving achievement, either directly or indirectly through improving a school's ability to attract and retain more able teachers?
- How effective are various efforts to reward teacher performance in raising student achievement? How should teacher performance be evaluated? Should it rely heavily on student achievement gains or should other forms of evaluation, including portfolios of accomplishments and administrative evaluation, be employed as well?
- To what extent do teacher certification requirements reduce the supply of a more able group of teachers? What types of teacher preparation are most effective in raising the student achievement among low-performing students?

Several ongoing research efforts promise to provide more evidence on these and other strategies to improve low student achievement. For example, understanding whether and to what extent pay for performance could improve student achievement will be important in attempts to motivate teachers to work successfully in schools with low-performing students. Research employing quasi-experimental and random assignment research designs will provide useful guidance. In a different vein, the potential for teacher pre-service education and professional development to improve teaching, especially in low-performing schools, using detailed school district and state databases, as well as random assignment designs, will provide more specific guidance. More generally, we should explore a variety of strategies to attract, nurture, and retain effective teachers to work with low-performing students and, systematically, evaluate these strategies employing a variety of different research designs.

NOTES

1. Fryer and Levitt (2004, 2005) find that the black-white achievement gap grows as students progress from kindergarten through third grade. However, Murnane, Willett, Bub, and McCartney (2006) find that gap narrows between kindergarten and the fifth grade. Clotfelter, Ladd, & Vigdor (2006) find that the black-white gap remains constant between grades three and eight.
2. See, for example, Clotfelter (2004) and Lankford and Wyckoff (2005).
3. National Center for Education Statistics (2005).
4. For a good description of these practices in four districts see Levin and Quinn (2003).
5. Roza and Hill (2004) describe this process in detail.
6. *Quality Counts*, Education Week (2006).
7. From the Web site of the National Center for Alternative Certification, Teach-Now at http://www.teach-now.org .
8. Ashindi Maxton, Teach For America, e-mail, October 8, 2003.
9. Raymond and others (2001); Darling-Hammond and others (2005); Glazerman and others (2006); Boyd and others (2006); Kane and others (2006).
10. For recent work see Ingersoll (2001, 2004); Ingersoll and Kralik (2004); Ingersoll and Smith (2003, 2004); Hanushek, Kain, and Rivkin (2004); Johnson (2004); Boyd, Lankford, Loeb, and Wyckoff, (2005b); Loeb, Darling-Hammond, and Luczak (2005).
11. NCES (2004)
12. For details see a discussion of ProComp at http://denverprocomp.org/.

13. For more details see a report by Community Training and Assistance Center at http://ctacusa.com/denvervol3-front-section.pdf .

REFERENCES

Aaronson, D., Barrow, L., & Sander, W. (2003). "Teachers and Student Achievement in the Chicago Public Schools." Federal Reserve Bank of Chicago. WP-2002-28.

Ballou, D., (1996). "Do Public Schools Hire the Best Applicants?" *Quarterly Journal of Economics, 111*(1), 97–134.

Baugh, W.H., & Stone, J.A., (1982). "Mobility and Wage Equilibration in the Educator Labor Market." *Economics of Education Review, 2*(3), 253–274.

Betts, J., Rueben, K., & Danenberg, K., (2000). *Equal Resources, Equal Outcomes? The Distribution of School Resources and Student Achievement in California*, Public Policy Institute of California.

Bohrnstedt, G.W., Stecher, B.M., & Krist, M. (2000). "Evaluating the Effects of Statewide Class Size Reduction Initiatives: The Need for a Systemic Approach." Paper presented at the National Conference on Taking Small Classes One Step Further.

Bonesrønning, H., T. Falch, B. Strøm (2005). "Teacher Sorting, Teacher Quality, and Student Composition." *European Economic Review*.

Boyd, D., Goldhaber, D., Lankford, H., & Wyckoff, J. (Forthcoming). "The Role of Teacher Preparation and Certification in Improving the Quality of K-12 Teachers." In S. Loeb, C. Rouse, & A. Shorris (eds.), *Excellence in the Classroom: Policies to Improve the Teacher Workforce.*

Boyd, D., Grossman, P., Lankford, H., & Wyckoff, J. (2007). "Who Leaves? Teacher Attrition and Student Achievement." Working paper, University at Albany.

Boyd, D., Grossman, P., Lankford, H., Loeb, S., & Wyckoff, J. (2006). "How changes in entry requirements alter the teacher workforce and affect student achievement." *Education Finance and Policy, 1*(2), 176–216.

Boyd D., Lankford, H., Loeb, S., Rockoff, J., & Wyckoff, J. (2006). "The Narrowing Gap in New York City Teacher Qualifications and its Implications for Student Achievement in High-Poverty Schools." Working paper.

Boyd, D., Lankford, H., Loeb, S., & Wyckoff, J. (2006). "Analyzing the Determinants of the Matching of Public School Teachers to Jobs: Estimating Compensating Differentials in Imperfect Labor Markets." Unpublished manuscript, University at Albany.

Boyd, D., Lankford, H., Loeb, S., & Wyckoff, J. (2005a). The Draw of Home: How Teachers' Preferences for Proximity Disadvantage Urban Schools. *Journal of Policy Analysis and Management, 24*(1), 113–132.

Boyd, D., Lankford, H., Loeb, S., & Wyckoff, J. (2005b). "Explaining the Short Careers of High-Achieving Teachers in Schools with Low-Performing students." *American Economic Association Proceedings, 95*(2), 166–171.

Boyd, D., Lankford, H., Loeb, S., & Wyckoff, J. (2002). "Initial Matches, Transfers, and Quits: Career Decisions and the Disparities in Average Teacher Qualifications Across Schools." Working paper, University at Albany.

Buckley, J., Schneider, M., & Shang, Y. (2004). "The Effects of School Facility on Teacher Retention in Urban Schools." National Clearinghouse on Educational Facilities (www.edfacilities.org/pubs/teacherretention3.html).

Clotfelter, C. (2004). *After Brown: The Rise and Retreat of School Desegregation.* Princeton, NJ: Princeton University Press.

Clotfelter, C., Glennie, E., Ladd, H., & Vigdor, J. (2006). *Would Higher Salaries Keep Teachers in High-Poverty Schools? Evidence from a policy intervention in North Carolina*, NBER Working Paper #12285.

Clotfelter, C., Ladd, H., & Vigdor, J. (2006a). "Teacher-Student Matching and the Assessment of Teacher Effectiveness." *Journal of Human Resources, 41*(4), 778–820.

Clotfelter, C., Ladd, H., & Vigdor, J. (2006b). "The Academic Achievement Gap in Grades 3 to 8." NBER Working Paper 12207.

Clotfelter, C., Ladd, H., & Vigdor, J. (2006c). "How and Why do Teacher Credentials Matter for Student Achievement." Working paper, Duke University.

Clotfelter, C., Ladd, H., Vigdor, J., & Wheeler, J. (2006). *High Poverty Schools and the Distribution of Teachers and Principals.* Working paper, Duke University.

Darling-Hammond, L., & others (2005). "Does Teacher Preparation Matter? Evidence about Teacher Certification, Teach for America, and Teacher Effectiveness." *Education Policy Analysis Archives, 13*(42), 1–47.

Dee, T. (2004). Teachers, Race and Student Achievement in a Randomized Experiment." *Review of Economics and Statistics, 86*(1), 195–210.

Dolton, P., & Newson, D. (2003). "The Relationship Between Teacher Turnover and School Performance." *London Review of Education, 1*(2), 132–140.

Dolton, P. J., & van der Klaaw, W. (1995). "Leaving Teaching in the U.K.: A Duration Analysis." *The Economic Journal*, 105(March), 431–444.

Dolton, P. J., & van der Klaaw, W. (1999). "The Turnover of Teachers: A Competing Risks Explanation." *Review of Economics and Statistics, 81*(3), 543–552.

Education Week. (2006). *Quality Counts.*

Ferguson, R. (1998). "Teachers' Perceptions and Expectations and the Black-White Test Score Gap." In C. Jencks & M. Phillips, *The Black-White Test Score Gap* (pp. 273–317). Washington DC: Brookings Institution Press.

Fryer, R., & Levitt, S. (2004). "Understanding the Black-White Test Score Gap in the First Two Years of School." *Review of Economics and Statistics, 86*, 447–464.

Fryer, R., & Levitt, S. (2005). "The Black-White Test Score Gap Through Third Grade." Working Paper.

Glazerman, S. et al. (2006). "Alternative Routes to Teaching: The Impacts of Teach for America on Student Achievement and Other Outcomes." *Journal of Policy Analysis and Management, 25*(1), 75–96.

Goldhaber, D. (2006). "Everyone's Doing It, but What Does Teacher Testing Tell Us About Teacher Effectiveness?" Unpublished manuscript.

Hanushek, E., Kain, J., O'Brien, D., & Rivkin, S. (2005). "The Market for Teacher Quality." NBER working paper 11154.

Hanushek, E., Kain, J., & Rivkin, S. (2004). "Why Public Schools Lose Teachers." *Journal of Human Resources, 39*(2), 326–354.

Harris, D. and Sass, T. (2006). "Teacher Training and Teacher Productivity." Working paper, Florida State University.

Ingersoll, R. (2001). "Teacher Turnover and Teacher Shortages: An Organizational Analysis." *American Educational Research Journal, 38*(3), 499–534.

Ingersoll, R. (2004) "Why do High Poverty Schools Have Difficulty Staffing Their Classrooms with Qualified Teachers?" *Report for Renewing Our Schools, Securing Our Future.*

Ingersoll, R. and Kralik, J.M. (2004). "The Impact of Mentoring on Teacher Retention: What the Research Says." *Research Review*. Education Commission of the States.

Ingersoll, R. and Smith, T. (2003). "The Wrong Solution to the Teacher Shortage." *Educational Leadership, 60*(8), 30–33.

Ingersoll, R. and Smith, T. (2004). "What are the Effects of Mentoring and Induction on Beginning Teacher Turnover." *American Education Research Journal, 41*(3), 681–714.

Jacob, B. and Lefgren, L. (2005). "Principals as Agents: Subjective Performance Measurement in Education." Kennedy School of Government Working Paper No. RWP05-040.

Johnson, S. M., & the Project on the Next Generation of Teachers. (2004). *Finders and Keepers: Helping New Teachers Survive and Thrive in Our Schools.* San Francisco: Jossey Bass.

Kane, T., Rockoff, J. & Staiger, D. (2006). "What Does Certification Tell Us About Teacher Effectiveness? Evidence from New York City." NBER Working Paper No. 12155.

Kane, T. & Staiger, D. (2002). "Volatility in School Test Scores: Implications for Test-Based Accountability Systems." Brookings Papers on Education Policy, 235–269.

Koski, W. & Horng, E. (2007). *Curbing or Facilitating Inequality? Law, Collective Bargaining, and Teacher Assignment Among Schools in California.* Technical Report, Getting Down to Facts Project, Stanford University.

Lankford, H., Loeb, S. & Wyckoff, J. (2002). "Teacher Sorting and the Plight of Urban Schools: A Descriptive Analysis." *Educational Evaluation and Policy Analysis, 24*(1), 38–62.

Lankford, H. & Wyckoff, J. (2005). "Why are Schools Racially Segregated? Implications for School Choice Policies." In J. Scott (ed.), *School Choice and Diversity: What the Evidence Says.* Teachers College Press, 9–26.

Levin, J. & Quinn, M. (2003) *How We Keep High Quality Teachers Out of Urban Classrooms.* New York: The New Teacher Project.

Liu, E., Johnson, S., & Peske, H. (2004). "New Teachers and the Massachusetts Signing Bonus: The Limits of Inducements." *Educational Evaluation and Policy Analysis.*

Loeb, S., Darling-Hammond, L., & Luczak, J. (2005). "How Teaching Conditions Predict Teacher Turnover in California Schools." *Peabody Journal of Education, 80*(3).

Loeb, S., & Reininger, M. (2004). "*Public Policy and Teacher Labor Markets: What We Know and Why it Matters.*" The Education Policy Center at Michigan State University.

Loeb, S., & Miller, L. (2007). "*A Review of State Teacher Policies: What Are They, What Are Their Effects, and What Are Their Implications for School Finance.*" Technical Report, Getting Down to Facts Project, Stanford University.

Murnane, R., Singer, J., & Willett, J. (1991). "*Who Will Teach?: Policies that Matter.*." Cambridge MA: Harvard University Press.

Murnane, R., Willett, J., Bub, K., & McCartney, K. (2006). "Explaining the Puzzling Patterns in Black-White Achievement Gaps." Harvard Graduate School of Education.

Murnane, R. & Olsen, R. (1989). "Will There be Enough Teachers?" *American Economic Review, 79,* 242–246.

Murnane, R., Singer, J., & Willett, J. (1988). "The Career Paths of Teachers: Implications for Teacher Supply and Methodological Lessons for Research." *Educational Researcher, 17*(5), 22–30.

Murnane, R. (1981). "Teacher Mobility Revisited." *Journal of Human Resources, 16*(1), 3–19.

National Center for Education Statistics (2004). *Teacher Attrition and Mobility: Results from the Teacher Follow-up Survey*, 9.

National Center for Education Statistics (2005). "An Examination of the Condition of School Facilities Attended by 10th Grade Students in 2002."

Peske, H. & Haycock, K. (2006). "Teaching Inequality." The Education Trust.

Raymond, M. & others (2001). *Teach for America: An Evaluation of Teacher Differences and Student Outcomes in Houston, Texas.* Stanford, CA: The Hoover Institution, Center for Research on Education Outcomes.

Rivkin, S., Hanushek, E., & Kain, J. (2005). "Teachers, Schools, and Academic Achievement." *Econometrica, 73*(2), 417– 458.

Rockoff, J. (2004). "The Impact of Individual Teachers on Student Achievement: Evidence from Panel Data." *American Economic Review, 94*(2): 247– 252.

Roza, M. & Hill, P. (2004). "How Within District Spending Inequities Help Some Districts Fail." In Diance Ravitch, ed., *Brookings Papers on Education Policy*. Washington DC: Brookings Institution.

Sanders, W.L. & Rivers, J.C. (1996). "Research Project Report: Cumulative and Residual Effects of Teachers on Future Student Academic Achievement." University of Tennessee Value-Added Research and Assessment Center.

Scafidi, B, Sjoquist, D., & Stinebrickner, T. (2003). "Do Teachers Really Leave for Higher Paying Jobs in Alternative Occupations?" Working paper, Georgia State University.

Smith, T. & Ingersoll, R. (2004). "What are the effects of induction and mentoring on beginning teacher turnover." *American Educational Research Journal.*

U.S. General Accounting Office, (2002). *School Finance: Per-Pupil Spending Differences between Selected Inner City and Suburban Schools Varied by Metropolitan Area.* December.

31

Educational Outcomes of Disadvantaged Students: From Desegregation to Accountability

Douglas N. Harris

INTRODUCTION

Improving educational outcomes for racial minorities and students from economically disadvantaged households has long been a central objective of federal and state educational policies. The federal government's involvement arguably started with the United States Supreme Court's 1954 *Brown v. Board of Education* decision to end racial segregation in schools.[1] Although federal policymakers were initially reluctant to support the decision, they eventually helped to implement and build on it with complementary policies such as the Elementary and Secondary Education Act (ESEA) of 1965.

Federal educational policy has evolved considerably since the initial efforts to desegregate schools and no more so than with the 2001 re-authorization of ESEA, commonly known as No Child Left Behind (NCLB). The law requires that students of various racial, income, and programmatic subgroups make "adequate yearly progress" toward state-determined proficiency standards. Thus, the law is specifically designed to focus attention on students who have historically achieved lower educational outcomes.

Previous policy efforts were designed to improve educational opportunities for disadvantaged students. For example, mandatory desegregation of schools increased the access of black children to schools previously denied to them, and Title 1 of ESEA provided more education funding for poor children. Underlying these policies is the idea that students experience educational deprivation in classrooms and schools with large proportions of disadvantaged peers. That deprivation arises either because of the negative "spillover effects" from their peers or because the schools serving such students typically end up with fewer educational resources than do other schools.[2] For reasons such as these, the court in *Brown v. Board of Education* declared that racially separate schools cannot be equal.

NCLB takes a different approach, re-orienting federal education policy away from attention to access and resources toward accountability for educational outcomes. Here, the belief is that students and schools have sufficient resources, but insufficient incentives to use them. Students can pass through school and receive a diploma with minimal effort. Similarly, educators have low expectations for disadvantaged students and keep their jobs and salaries regardless of whether student performance is high or low. The "theory of action" behind accountability is clearly quite different from the one behind desegregation.

This chapter examines evidence about the effects that desegregation and accountability have had on achievement and long-term outcomes for students. Much of the extant research reviewed here focuses on how policies affect student achievement as measured by scores on standardized tests. This focus on achievement is understandable both because of the primacy given to student achievement in current reform efforts and because it is one predictor of long-term success.[3] The review also focuses on the relatively small number of rigorous studies that measure the long-term effects directly in the form of graduation rates, employment, and wages.

Desegregation Policies and Peer Effects

Central to arguments for racial or economic desegregation is how students' peers affect their educational outcomes. The classic paper on this topic, Jencks and Mayer (1990), provides two main models for why having more advantaged peers may improve a student's educational outcomes. One is the "epidemic" or contagion model in which children's behavior, such as the propensity to do homework, has positive spillovers on other students in the classroom. According to this model, children in classrooms with motivated and high-achieving students are likely to perform at higher levels than those in other classrooms. A second model, called "institutional" theory, highlights the fact that schools serving more advantaged students are likely to have more resources than other schools because of the way political and funding institutions operate. Heavy reliance in the United States on local funding for education, for example, results in less funding per pupil for schools in low-wealth districts. Within districts, similar inequalities often emerge across schools because of the greater political power of the higher-income parents.

While these two mechanisms suggest that having more advantaged peers is beneficial for disadvantaged students, the opposite outcome is also possible. According to Jencks and Mayer's (1990) "relative deprivation" theory, children may simply become more frustrated and put forth less effort in the presence of advantaged peers because of their *relative* social position. A variation on the relative deprivation model, "cultural conflict," posits that students who are low in the perceived social hierarchy choose to disassociate from the dominant group and form alternative peer groups that reject the dominant group's preferences and behaviors. Either of these mechanisms would mean that being in a school or classroom with more advantaged peers could be detrimental. As we show below, the evidence suggests that any harmful effects of having advantaged peers are outweighed by the benefits.

Desegregation Experiments on Black Achievement

During the early period of the school desegregation movement, especially the late 1960s and 1970s, courts required schools to desegregate, usually by busing black students from their homes to predominantly white schools located in predominantly white neighborhoods. In some cases, the children reassigned to more integrated schools were determined by some form of lottery, thus providing the basis for experimental evidence on the effects of desegregation.

One of the most studied programs is the Boston METCO program.[4] This program, the largest and longest-running metropolitan desegregation effort in the nation, has operated continuously since 1966 with the cooperation of Boston Public Schools and various suburban school districts. More black students applied to switch schools than there were slots available, at least in the program's early years, so black students were randomly assigned to be bused to whiter schools in the suburbs (the treatment group) or to remain in a school in Boston (the control group). Both the treatment and control groups were given academic achievement tests before and after busing took place.

Many of the students in the control group were siblings of those who were bused, but who had been denied the right to transfer. Comparing sibling pairs of treatment and control students, Armor (1972) finds no gain in student test scores for the students bused to the suburban schools. While some concerns have been raised about Armor's data and methodology, subsequent analyses of the METCO program, based on different methods and considering students over several different decades, have confirmed Armor's finding that the program did not raise student achievement (Angrist & Lang, 2004).[5]

While the METCO results indicate no effect of desegregation on student achievement, studies of similar programs in other locations do find effects. In 1984, the National Institute of Education (NIE) commissioned seven extensive reviews of the topic, each considering essentially the same group of studies (Armor, 1984; Cook, 1984; Crain, 1984; Miller & Carlson, 1984; Stephan, 1984; Walberg, 1984; Wortman, 1984). An independent review by Crain and Mahard (1983) found that the four studies of desegregation that were based on random assignment of students to the treatment and control groups, were more likely to find a positive and significant effect, and that the (weighted) average effect size was large by traditional research standards.[6] Of the 21 reported effects from these four studies, 17 effects were positive and significant; bused students made large average gains of 0.235 standard deviations, or 8 percentile points, per year compared with the control group.[7] Other longitudinal studies with good control groups also yielded positive, but smaller effects of 0.084 standard deviations. Although researchers differ in their interpretations of these studies, depending in part on which research method they favor, all of the NIE-commissioned reviews concluded that these desegregation programs raised the test scores of the black students who participated (Schofeld, 1995).

Several patterns emerge concerning the design and implementation of desegregation programs. First, desegregation initiated by school districts—often called "voluntary" desegregation—is more likely to generate positive effects than desegregation resulting from court orders (Bradley & Bradley, 1977; Cook, 1984; Schofeld, 1995; Stephan, 1984). Indeed, the review by Bradley and Bradley (1977) suggests that all of the voluntary desegregation programs show positive effects on black achievement.

Students who are moved to a desegregated school during their elementary school years also seem to benefit more than those desegregated later in their school careers (Cook, 1984; Crain, 1984; Crain & Mahard, 1983; St. John, 1975; Stephan, 1984). Crain and Mahard (1983) find that three-fourths of the studies where desegregation occurred in kindergarten showed higher student achievement gains than in desegregation efforts aimed at older students. Harris (2006) suggests two possible reasons for this pattern. First, elementary students may have fewer social adjustments compared with older students who have spent more time in segregated settings. Second, secondary schools are more likely to track students by academic ability (and perhaps race), which could reduce the benefits of desegregation for minorities. The likelihood of younger students benefiting more than high school students from desegregation may partly explain why some high school-focused desegregation programs, such as Boston's METCO program have not yielded positive achievement effects.[8]

It is also important to note that the families who participated in these desegregation experiments did so by their own choice. These groups of volunteers may differ from the average minority family. Therefore, results could differ with more broad-based, non-voluntary desegregation programs.

Housing Opportunity Experiments

Two major programs during the past two decades have attempted to move low-income families out of racially and economically isolated housing projects and neighborhoods to more racially integrated or higher-income neighborhoods. They are Gautreaux in Chicago and the "Moving to Opportunity" (MTO) program in five cities across the country. Compared to previous desegregation programs, these two programs are more recent, include larger samples of students, and involve changes in neighborhoods not just in schools. In addition, the studies of MTO have used more sophisticated research methods to estimate the effects and to address the inevitable problems of attrition and fidelity that arise in experiments. Given the nature of these programs, researchers are not able to distinguish the effects of racial or economic desegregation at the school level from that at the neighborhood level.

In Gautreaux, a non-profit organization relocated more than 7,000 African American families living in public housing to other parts of the metropolitan area, some within the city and others to suburbs. Because the families were not randomly selected for relocation, studies of this program are subject to concerns about selection bias. Nevertheless, the available data indicate that those who moved to the suburbs were much less likely to drop out of school and had higher rates of college attendance compared with students in the inner-city schools from which the students moved (Kaufman & Rosenbaum, 1992).

The apparently positive outcomes of the Gautreaux program inspired the U.S. Department of Education to initiate the more ambitious MTO experiment. Under this program more than 9,227 families in Baltimore, Boston, Chicago, Los Angeles, and New York were randomly assigned to receive one of two "treatments." One treatment group was given Section-8 federal housing vouchers to be used wherever they could find suitable private-sector housing. The second treatment group was given the same vouchers combined with counseling and a restriction that the vouchers only be used to move to neighborhoods where the poverty rate was lower than 10 percent. Participants in the Section-8-only treatment received no counseling and could move to private housing in any neighborhood. The two treatment groups together were 54 percent black and 39 percent Hispanic and had household incomes averaging less than $10,000 per year.

Two studies have examined the effects of the MTO program on student academic achievement.[9] Ludwig, Ladd, and Duncan (2001) examine MTO effects based on data from more then 638 households (198 in the control group) near Baltimore using data from two school district-administered achievement tests. The use of such tests is an important characteristic of the study because the tests are aligned to the curriculum and can therefore be expected to capture intervention effects. A disadvantage in this case, however, is that the State of Maryland has limited testing requirements, which resulted in considerable missing data.[10] Still the results suggest statistically significant differences between the experimental and control groups for students who entered the program when they were less than 12 years old. Compared with the control group, these treatment-group students were 17.8 percent more likely to pass the state standardized test and scored 7 percentile points higher (equivalent to 0.17 standard deviations) on a district test.[11] No effects on state test scores emerged for those students entering the program after age 12. This distinction in effects between younger and older students is consistent with the school desegregation experiments discussed earlier.

A second study of the MTO includes all five cities and used different outcome measures. Instead of district achievement tests, the results reported in Sanbonmatsu et al. (2006) are based on a test that was not part of the cities' standards and accountability system (the Woodcock-Johnson test). In contrast to Ludwig, Ladd, and Duncan (2001), these authors find no achievement effects for students in any age group.

Two possible explanations could account for the different results. First, because the test used by Sanbonmatsu et al. (2006) was not aligned with state standards or accountability, it may not have measured whether students were learning the curriculum taught in schools.[12] Second, the data in Sanbonmatsu et al. (2006) show that the movement of families under the MTO resulted in only small changes in the characteristics of the students' classmates. The differences in the percentages of students who were racial minorities or who were eligible for free or reduced price lunches declined by only 3 to 6 percentage points and the mean percentile test score rank increased by only four points. This relatively small change in school circumstances might be insufficient to generate significant differences in student learning. It is unclear whether these small changes in school and peer characteristics also apply to the Baltimore study because Ludwig, et al. (2001) do not report such school differences, and Sanbonmatsu, et al. (2006) do not report differences by city.

Peer Effects and Achievement

A growing amount of studies use non-experimental methods—sometimes called "value-added" modeling—to measure the relationship between each student's learning and the characteristics of his or her classmates. Utilizing large student-level administrative databases, these studies identify the effects of peers through changes in conditions of individual students over time. Thus, in such studies, each student serves as his or her own control group.

Value-added studies of peers provide more comprehensive information than the previously discussed school and housing integration studies.[13] First, these studies make it possible to disentangle the separate roles of peer race, peer income, and peer achievement in desegregation effects. Second, these studies fill an important gap in the studies of school desegregation by considering, not only the effects on minority students, but also the effects on white students. While the primary purpose of desegregation is to address the needs of minority and disadvantaged students, it is important to know whether benefits for targeted students come at the expense of other students.

A final benefit of value-added peer effect studies is that they avoid the possible confounding influence of disruption that occurred during the early era of desegregation that may have altered the measured effects of the programs (Hanushek, Kain, & Rivkin, 2002). Being one of a handful of black students bused to a suburban school—in some cases accompanied by newspaper headlines, picket lines, and National Guard troops—likely influenced the educational environment in detrimental ways. These disruptions might be avoided with other forms of integration, or might be absent in the present era where such controversy has diminished. The following discussion summarizes findings from five main studies that use value-added-type methods to study peer effects. While there are many consistencies across these studies, some key differences are evident.

The first consistent finding from the peer effect studies is that having more advantaged peers results in better outcomes for minority students. This result is found in each of the three studies that estimate peer effects by race: One study conducted in North Carolina (Cooley, 2006) and two studies in Texas (Hanushek, Rivkin, & Kain, 2002; Hoxby, 2000). These studies also find that the benefits of advantaged peers for whites are smaller than the benefits for minorities. A fourth study, by Burke and Sass (2006), finds that more advantaged peers are beneficial, but this study does not estimate the effects by racial subgroup.

Because minorities benefit from having advantaged peers, and more so than white students, these studies suggest that desegregation could improve outcomes for non-white students and increase average achievement simultaneously. However, some nuances or complexities in these findings are worth noting.[14] In particular, each racial group appears to be influenced most by peers of their own race. Hoxby (2000) finds that peers are influenced more by the percentage of students in their specific racial group (e.g., blacks are more negatively influenced by an increase in percent of black students than by an increase in the percent of Hispanic students) and by the achievement of same-race peers. Hanushek et al. (2002) find negative effects from peer percent black and Hispanic that are larger within-race, as does Cooley (2006), though she combines blacks and Hispanics into a single "minority" category. This general finding of larger within-race effects may be explained by the fact that all students more closely identify with, and are therefore more affected by, students who are similar to themselves.

It is also possible that peer influences depend on the individual student's initial test score. Burke and Sass (2006) find that achievement peer effects occur for students throughout the distribution of test scores, and the effects are largest for students who are among the lowest 20 percent of the test score distribution, and smaller for high-scoring students. Cooley (2006) finds this same result for white students, but that the reverse is true for minorities—high-scoring minorities benefit the most from more advantaged peers. While Burke and Sass (2006) do not break out their results by racial subgroup, it is likely that their results are driven by white students (who represent the majority of their sample), which makes their results consistent with those of Cooley.

Inconsistencies also arise in the specific ways that peers matter. First, Hanushek, et al. (2002) find that peer influences are most closely related to peer percent minority and are unrelated to peer achievement. In contrast, Cooley (2006) and Hoxby (2000) find that both peer percent minority and peer achievement are associated with individual achievement. Second, Vigdor and Nechyba (forthcoming) find that having more minority peers actually has a *positive* impact within racial subgroups (e.g., blacks benefit from having more black peers), after controlling for peer achievement. Harris (2006) finds this same result in a larger sample of students, though he only has access to subgroup-by-race data and for a limited number of years. These inconsistencies in findings are probably due partly to differences in the states being studied, as well as differences in methodology.[15]

For at least two reasons, these estimated peer effects may not be fully causal in nature. First, a second study of North Carolina by Vigdor and Nechyba (forthcoming) finds that the apparently positive effects of advantaged peers are eliminated when unobserved differences in teachers are taken into account. This contrary finding may not be as significant as it seems, however, because part of the benefit of advantaged peers may be that teachers are generally more willing to teach advantaged students. The Vigdor and Nechyba results do not allow for these benefits.[16] None of the other studies account for differences in teachers in this way.

Second, as Harris (2006) points out, some of the estimated peer effects are also implausibly large. For example, Hoxby's (2000) estimates of peer effects imply that moving a black student from a 100 percent black school to a (slightly less than) 100 percent white school would raise individual achievement by an additional 0.7 standard deviations in a single year. To see why this is implausible, consider that the total achievement gap between whites and blacks is about 0.7 to 0.9 standard deviations. Hoxby's results suggest that this could be eliminated in a single year simply by moving students to different schools.[17] There is considerable evidence of substantial achievement gaps even in schools that are mainly white, as highlighted by the well known Shaker Heights example (Ogbu, 2003). If blacks really could catch up in majority-white settings, then these within-school gaps should be considerably smaller than they are. Nevertheless, given the consistency with which researchers find benefits of more advantaged peers, including through experiments, it seems likely that at least part of these effects are causal.

Long-Term Effects of Desegregation on Blacks

The above effects of integration[18] and peer influences on achievement are important because achievement is a predictor of long-term success. But integration might also affect long-term outcomes in ways unrelated to achievement. As described by Wells and Crain (1994), integrated schools or neighborhoods may give black students the confidence and ability to cope with situations involving whites, who make up the majority of people in college and the professional workplace. Integration also establishes networks that provide both information and personal connections that help students as they navigate their educational and career paths. As we will see below, the evidence supports this idea and suggests significant long-term influences of desegregation.

Again, the most convincing studies are those that address the selection bias issue through random assignment and track the randomly assigned students over long periods of time. In the Boston METCO example, Armor (1972) compared the treatment and control groups up to two years after high school graduation. Even though there were no achievement gains, as reported above, Armor finds longer-term educational gains: 84 percent of the bused students went on to college after high school compared with 56 percent in the control group.[19] More modest evidence of long-term effects is found in the MTO housing program. Ludwig, et al. (2001) find some reduction in drop-out rates, but their estimates are significant in only one specification, and only then at the 10 percent level of significance.

Unfortunately, very few of the desegregation experiments involved long-term follow-up of students. It is therefore worth considering other types of analyses, including correlative analysis. Two such analyses include a relatively rich set of control variables and therefore increase the likelihood that the observed correlations reflect causal relationships. Using the High School and Beyond data, Rivkin (2000) finds that having more white classmates is slightly negatively associated with black test scores, but positively associated with black educational attainment and wages. The effects on long-term student outcomes are lower, and in some cases negative, in urban school districts that were under court-ordered desegregation, consistent with the earlier evidence of desegregation on achievement. Using a similar approach, but with different data and somewhat weaker control variables, Grogger (1996) finds a similar positive association between proportion of white classmates and black wages.[20]

Compared with the earlier experiments, it is somewhat more difficult to draw clear conclusions from the studies of longer term effects. There are fewer studies, many of which rely on correlative analysis. Nevertheless, gains for black students, as measured in the most convincing studies of integration, are almost universally positive. Moreover, the evidence, especially from Rivkin (2000), suggests that the long-term benefits are due more to confidence and networking opportunities afforded minority students in majority-white schools than to the achievement gains discussed earlier.

Discussion of Desegregation Effects

While each of the approaches to estimating desegregation effects has its limitations, the studies collectively paint a consistent picture: Having more advantaged peers is beneficial. This is especially true for minority students and at the elementary school level. Peer influences also appear to be complex. Individuals are affected most by peers of the same race, and the effects vary depending on whether the individual student is low- or high-achieving.

Having more minority peers may generate inconsistent effects on student achievement because what sometimes appears to be a race effect may actually reflect the socioeconomic status of the peers, as measured, for example by family income or parental education. While there do not appear to be any studies that provide convincing results regarding this hypothesis, the role of peer family income is important because recent U. S. Supreme Court decisions have limited the ability of school districts to assign students to schools on the basis of race. As a result, at least 40 school districts have already changed strategies and now assign students to schools on the basis of income (Kahlenberg, 2006). At first glance, it might appear that this strategy would have the same effect as assigning students on the basis of race because of the correlation between the two characteristics. However, as Reardon, Yun, and Kerlander (2006) show, income-based desegregation may have relatively little effect on racial integration. Clearly, there are holes in our understanding of how methods of assigning students to schools influence students' outcomes.

ACCOUNTABILITY

Notwithstanding the apparent benefits of desegregation, the national perception in the late 1970s was that the policy had failed or even backfired. As discussed by Harris and Herrington (2006), average college entrance exam scores appeared to be on the decline, and the general public believed that desegregation and other equity-focused reforms of that era had lowered academic standards, making schools more concerned with keeping students from dropping out than with making sure they could read and write.

A Nation at Risk (*NAR*) gave voice to these student achievement concerns (National Commission on Excellence in Education, 1983), and state policymakers made a concerted effort to raise academic standards. These policy efforts seemed to have little effect on test score trends or on the perception that students were inadequately prepared for the "new economy." Combined with broader support for business-oriented approaches to public services, a new shift developed in the early 1990s that focused on measurable results and incentives—what has come to be known as accountability.

Today, accountability takes many forms. The focus of this section is on government-based accountability efforts, especially those that create incentives based on student scores on standardized tests. These high-stakes testing policies that can determine grade promotion or graduation for students are designed to place pressure on students to work harder in their academic pursuits. Other policies, including most of those in No Child Left Behind (NCLB), evaluate schools and school personnel on the basis of student test scores and provide incentives for teachers and administrators to improve these scores. See Figlio and Ladd (this volume) for additional and more general discussion of accountability. Discussion of market-based accountability, including such policies as charter schools and vouchers, is left to the chapters by Bulkley and Bifulco (this volume), and Bettinger and Zimmer (this volume).

High-stakes testing is intended to go beyond the intrinsic or personal motivations of students and educators and has become a source of considerable controversy. One argument against a policy emphasis on high-stakes testing is that education should be driven by the personal motivations, needs, and desires of students; thus external incentives to perform well on standardized tests could be counter-productive. Moreover, since educators who enter the profession have their own internal motivation to serve students, that motivation, too, could be undermined by external pressures. Proponents of accountability argue, however, that external incentives need not undermine internal motivation and, instead, provide a way for students and educators to monitor and improve their performance. Further, they can help induce those students and educators who lack internal motivation to do well and to weed out educators who are not performing. Such pressures are especially important for schools serving disadvantaged students, where student test scores are unquestionably low, and where educators are seen as the primary source of the problem. A counter-argument is that the low test scores among disadvantaged students may be driven by societal factors outside of the control of educators; thus accountability may lead educators to "game the system," reducing education to superficial test preparation and harming the students they are trying to help.

Even if researchers find that test-based accountability leads to higher scores on high-stakes tests, determining whether those gains reflect true improvements in learning is difficult. An alternative research strategy is to study the effects of high-stakes testing on test scores that are not part of the accountability system. As noted earlier in the discussion of MTO, however, such studies are less likely to find positive effects because the content of the low-stakes tests may not be very well aligned with the curricula that students experience. There is no clear solution to this research challenge except to consider evidence from both high and low stakes tests and to be cautious about drawing conclusions where the evidence conflicts. This is the approach taken below.

Evidence on Promotion/Graduation Exams

One of the frustrations voiced in the midst of the desegregation and other equity-focused reforms of the 1970s, was that students were passing from grade to grade, and even from high school to college, without reaching minimum levels of achievement. This frustration has led to calls to end "social promotion" to ensure that students who earn high school diploma have met basic requirements for success as citizens and workers. In at least 22 states, these calls for reform have been answered with promotion and graduation exams (PGEs). These exams require students to achieve a minimum score on a standardized test before being promoted to the next grade, or in the case of high school seniors, before being allowed to receive a diploma.[21] Students who do not pass the graduation exam, initially or in subsequent attempts, cannot graduate from high school. They generally either drop out of school, or settle for a Graduate Equivalent Degree (GED).

PGEs create a variety of complex incentives that vary for different groups of students. The conventional wisdom is that students who are near the score required to pass the test (the test "cut-off") will work harder to ensure passage, while students far above or far below the cut-off are influenced less by the incentive of a high school diploma. They have a fairly clear indication that they will graduate or not, regardless of how much effort they put into improving their test score.

Some studies of PGEs have utilized state and national databases. For example, Jacob (2001) uses the National Educational Longitudinal Survey (NELS) to find no statistically significant effects from PGEs on average achievement. This result might be due to the lack of test alignment because the student test in NELS focused on students' cognitive skills, scores which are more difficult to influence than achievement scores.[22] Two studies of the New York state graduation exam—the Regent's Exam—contradict Jacob's findings. Alexander (2000) finds positive effects on the percentage passing the Regent's Exam, though it is unclear whether the increase is due solely to shifts in the curriculum and test coaching that do not reflect actual learning. This concern is partly alleviated by Bishop's (1998) finding that the exam led to increases in New York's Scholastic Achievement Test (SAT) scores. This latter study can be criticized, however, because it is simply a cross-sectional analysis with insufficient control variables to generate a causal relationship. Importantly, for purposes here, the estimated effects did not vary across racial/ethnic sub-groups in Alexander (2000) and were not reported in Bishop (1998).

A growing number of studies have considered the effects of PGEs in Chicago using an extensive student-level longitudinal database. The district's policy required that students scoring below the required level in grades three, six, and eight take summer school and retake the exam, and earn a passing score before being allowed to go on to the next grade. Roderick et al. (2002) found effects of PGEs on achievement that were almost uniformly positive in grades six and eight, but not grade three. Further, while schools with large portions of high-risk students appear to benefit the most in terms of reading in all three grades and third-grade math, the low-risk students benefit the most in sixth- and eighth-grade math. It is unclear why these differences in results by grade, subject, and risk category would arise. Some possible explanations are discussed below.

The positive effects discussed above may be misleading. In a broader study of the Chicago reforms, Miller et al. (2002) report that gains in achievement made during high school were due to improvements in student preparation and higher academic standards in lower grades, not the PGE.[23] Also, Nagoaka and Roderick (2004) find no effect of PGEs on the achievement of those students who failed and were held back. That is, while students may have increased their test scores to avoid being held back, the Nagoaka and Roderick study suggests that the students who were actually held back did not improve. If the PGEs in the early grades had no long-term effects on students in general, and if the students held back do not benefit, then it is questionable whether the policy resulted in greater learning.

Two studies of the Chicago reforms more directly examine the equally important issue of *why* accountability might raise test scores. An in-depth, small-scale study by Roderick and Engel (2001) based on interviews with students found that, as a result of accountability, two-thirds of elementary students paid greater attention and worked harder on their school work and experienced greater pressure and support from teachers. The other one-third of students, however, was further behind academically and therefore faced greater difficulty in passing the standardized test. Thus, as predicted earlier, students far below the cut-offs did not respond with additional effort.

Jacob (2005) confirms that accountability led to increased test scores in Chicago, especially for middle- and, to a lesser degree, upper-elementary students. Like Roderick and Engel (2001), he also finds that this gain for middle and upper-elementary students was accomplished through increased student effort. Additionally, Jacob identifies some of the factors that contributed to the higher scores: Schools increased the number of students placed in special education, retained more students in grade, and shifted the curriculum away from non-tested subjects such as science and social studies. In short, these findings suggest that accountability produces both substantive improvement and strategic responses of questionable educational value.

The possibility of unproductive strategic responses is also suggested by recent analyses of accountability effects in Texas. Klein et al. (2000) find that, as in most of the studies discussed here, the effects of accountability appears much larger for the high-stakes than for a low-stakes exam, the National Assessment of Educational Progress (NAEP). Again, it is unclear which set of results is the better descriptor of the effects of testing. Those studies using high-stakes exams most likely overstate the effects of accountability policies, while those using low-stakes exams understate the effects.

The studies reviewed above, which examine the effects of accountability using longitudinal data and sophisticated research methods, arguably represent the best available evidence on the effects of PGEs on student achievement.[24] Overall, while the evidence tends to support some achievement effects from PGEs, contrary results found by Jacob (2001) and the hard-to-explain pattern of effects found by Roderick et al. (2002) raise significant concerns. The fact that most of the best studies consider only Chicago adds an additional element of uncertainty regarding whether these effects can be generalized.

Promotion/Graduation Exams and Long-Term Outcomes

Regardless of the short-term effects, it is possible that PGEs improve long-term outcomes by providing students with human capital that makes them better able to obtain work and work productively. Again, this benefit might arise even for students who fail the exam and/or those who drop out, as long as the incentives of the PGEs induce them to work harder in school. The existence of PGEs may also improve the quality of the "signal" that high school diplomas send to employers about student knowledge and skills, thereby improving the efficiency of the labor market for all workers (Bishop, 2001). The empirical evidence on these topics is discussed below

Most studies, especially those using the most rigorous methods, find, as expected, that PGEs increase the probability of dropouts, especially for students who have low academic achievement. Dee and Jacob (2006) used U.S. Census data to find that PGEs increase the probability that average students will drop out.[25] More importantly, they find that the increased probability of dropout is greater for black students than for white students. These represent some of the most convincing findings available because the authors can compare students within states before and after the PGE policies were adopted.

Dee and Jacob (2006) also study district-level data from Minnesota to address several limitations of their initial analysis.[26] The state's basic skills test (BST) was administered in grades eight to twelve. Making use of the fact that the program was phased in, and therefore applied to some groups but not others at different times, they find that the exams reduced the probability that students would drop out in grades 10 and 11, but increased the probability of dropping out in twelfth grade. This suggests many students ultimately failed the test. Interestingly, these effects, both positive and negative, become more extreme in districts with higher percentages of blacks, implying that staying in school longer (in grades 10 and 11) was not enough to reduce dropouts later on.

Consistent with Dee and Jacob (2006), Martorell (2005) finds that while PGEs in Texas reduced the number of students who receive traditional diplomas, failing did not induce students to drop out at an earlier age. Instead, students who fail the promotional exam continue in school at the same rate as students who barely pass the exam, and many eventually receive general education diplomas (GEDs). The Martorell study relies on a regression discontinuity design, and is likely to have high degree of validity.

A similar study was carried out in the Chicago Public Schools, which recently adopted a PGE in eighth grade to allow promotion to high school. Allensworth (2004) finds that the Chicago PGE increased the probability that low-scoring students would drop out, although this was roughly offset by the lower probability of higher-scoring students dropping out.[27] This is the only study reviewed that compares student outcomes based on initial achievement level, and it provides further evidence that blacks gained in achievement but lost in terms of high school graduation. These results are also consistent with those in other studies that rely more on cross-sectional analysis.[28]

So far, the news on PGEs is mixed, suggesting that achievement gains are offset by reduced rates of graduation. The picture becomes somewhat more confused when we consider college enrollment and labor market outcomes. Martorell (2005) finds that PGEs reduce the probability that students just below the cut-off will go on to higher education. This is what we would expect, given that students just below the cut-off are less likely to obtain the high school degrees that are often necessary for admission to college. However, Dee and Jacob (2006) find no effect on college attendance, except a possible positive effect for Hispanic females. Bishop and Mane (2001) find that PGEs appear to increase the probability of Hispanic females attending college, and this effect increases for students who have higher grade point averages. Given the apparent reduction in high school graduation, it is difficult to explain why college attendance would increase, especially for students with high grade point averages who should be least affected by such policies.

The effects of PGEs on employment outcomes are also highly inconsistent and hard to explain. Dee and Jacob (2006) find that while PGEs have no employment effect for the average student, negative effects emerge for black males, and positive effects emerge for white and Hispanic females. In contrast, Bishop and Mane (2001) find that PGEs lead employers to hire more students with low grade point averages compared with students and employers in non-PGE environments.[29] They also find that, for students of nearly all grade point averages, PGEs are positively associated with future earnings. Dee and Jacob find nearly the opposite results: The presence of PGEs had no apparent effect on employment probability for whites and Hispanics, while PGEs reduced earnings for whites and Hispanics, but increased earnings for blacks. The inconsistencies in these employment findings are probably driven by the lack of random assignment experiments, as well as by the general difficulty of studying effects over long periods of time.

Taken together, this evidence suggests that PGEs may have some positive effects in terms of achievement, but the clearer effect is to redistribute long-term success from some groups—mainly, those who fail the exams—to those who pass the exams. Students who fail the test lose because they do not receive diplomas or the educational opportunities that come with them; students who pass the test gain because they earn diplomas and future educational opportunities. Some of the specific effects, especially the mixed findings regarding college attendance and labor market success, are perplexing and probably, despite the best efforts of the above researchers, do not reflect causal relationships. Given that minority and low-income students are more likely than others to be near PGE test score cut-offs, it is likely that these groups are, at best, unaffected and, more likely, negatively affected by PGEs.

Other Forms of Government-Based Accountability

So far, the focus has been on PGEs that place the onus on students: If they fail the exams, they are not promoted or do not graduate. Other forms of accountability, especially those incorporated in NCLB, focus performance burden more on the schools themselves and school personnel. These include school report cards, financial rewards for schools, merit pay for teachers, school takeovers, and reconstitutions. Due to a lack of evidence on the effectiveness of many of these strategies, only studies of school report cards and general levels of accountability are considered here. (See Figlio and Ladd, this volume, for a more complete discussion.)

School report cards publicly report student outcomes, a method sometimes called the "scarlet letter." School report cards are now regularly considered front page news in newspapers throughout the country. As a result, they also influence school board elections and support for superintendents, pressures that undoubtedly filter down to individual schools. Beginning in the 1990s, states began expanding reporting student test scores and instituting sanctions for schools that were considered failing. With NCLB, these government-based pressures have become the national norm.

The NAEP is used as the achievement measures in several analyses of the effects of state-level accountability systems on student achievement. Carnoy and Loeb (2002) find that an index of accountability, measuring the overall level of external pressures on school personnel from a variety of policy mechanisms, is often positively associated with student achievement. Moreover, these gains are largest for blacks and Hispanics.[30] Building on these results, Harris and Herrington (2004) separate the same accountability index into its component parts (PGEs, school report cards, and associated report card incentives) and additional state policy characteristics (e.g., market-based accountability). Consistent with the frequently positive PGE effects discussed earlier, they find that PGEs most likely account for the positive effects found by Carnoy and Loeb. Bishop, Mane, Bishop, and Moriarity (2001) and Raymond and Hanushek (2003) perform similar analyses for school report cards and find some evidence for the scarlet letter argument, though the analysis by Harris and Herrington suggests that these two studies may be capturing effects of PGEs and other policies that are excluded from the Bishop et al. and Raymond and Hanushek analyses.

Even if there is a positive effect of school report cards, it is not clear that this would help low-socioeconomic status (SES) students. For example, Figlio and Lucas (2000) find that housing values in neighborhoods with schools showing very high report card grades are higher than those with more modest grades. Most of these high-grade schools are serving advantaged students, suggesting that school report cards may not place disproportionate pressure on schools serving disadvantaged students. Also, Ladd (1999) finds that the sophisticated school accountability system in Dallas, Texas resulted in relatively large gains for whites, but smaller gains for Hispanics and no gains for blacks. These results suggest no gains in the relative achievement of disadvantaged students, and perhaps losses, reinforcing the idea that accountability may induce schools to improve performance among more advantaged students than disadvantaged ones.

What can we conclude from this evidence on high-stakes testing? First, it seems clear that more stringent accountability increases the *average* level of achievement and that the promotion and graduation exams appear to play a role in this. But with regard to disadvantaged students, the story is much less clear. While the policies do seem to increase achievement for minorities, these benefits are probably offset by losses in graduation, college attendance, and labor market success. In this sense, the benefits depend not only on which group researchers focus on, but also on which outcomes.

CONCLUSION

The strategies used to improve outcomes for disadvantaged students have evolved considerably in recent decades—from desegregation that reduces the isolation of disadvantaged students, to accountability that, instead, focuses attention on educational outcomes. This chapter shows that these strategies have had different levels of success. Evidence from decades-past experiments in school and housing integration, and more recent peer effect studies, suggests that desegregation improves student achievement. Moreover, the evidence from peer effect studies suggests that racial integration has little negative effect on the achievement of whites, but increases outcomes for disadvantaged students and for the average student. Further, some of the evidence from the peer effects literature suggests that it may be the higher achievement or income levels of peers in racially integrated schools rather than the racial mix per se that accounts for the apparent positive effects of racial integration on student achievement. This evidence is important not only for understanding the effects of past policies, but also for future policies that might consider addressing the stagnant or increasing concentration of student disadvantage in some schools (e.g., Orfield, 2001).

The achievement effects that emerge from the desegregation studies are quite consistent in that disadvantaged students seem to benefit on all outcome measures. Moreover, there is growing but still inconclusive evidence that the achievement losses among more advantaged groups are either small or non-existent. The fact that this policy helps disadvantaged students without hurting others means that the policy could improve average achievement as well, making it an attractive policy option.

In contrast, it is difficult to draw clear conclusions about the effects of accountability measures on disadvantaged groups because the research results are inconsistent. For example, although PGEs seem to increase achievement among disadvantaged students, in many cases, they also appear to reduce the probability of graduation and subsequent labor market outcomes such as employment and earnings. Nevertheless, much of the accountability movement is relatively new. We do not yet clearly understand either the net effects or the specific mechanisms and circumstances that determine the effects of accountability we have observed.

NOTES

1. The federal government was involved in education before desegregation through the Vocational Education Act, but this involvement was arguably less significant in its effects on educational practice than was its involvement in desegregation.
2. While there are policies, such as the federal Title I, that target resources to low-income students, there is considerable evidence that financial resources are only loosely related to educational quality. For example, Hanushek, Kain, and Rivkin (2001) find that the supply of teachers is driven not by teacher salaries, but by student demographics such as income. The same is likely true for administrators and other personnel, though there is less evidence on these groups.
3. For example, there is evidence that a one standard deviation increase in student test scores is associated with an 8–20 percent increase in future wages after controlling for a variety of other differences between workers. Currie and Thomas (1999) present estimates that are at the lower end of this range, though they also show that there are independent effects from scores on quantitative and verbal abilities. Adding these together yields an estimate toward the higher end of the range. Neal and Johnson (1996) provide an estimate at the higher end of this range, although this estimate does not control for years of education and is therefore biased upwards.
4. METCO is not an acronym but refers to the "Metropolitan Council" that manages the program.
5. Armor (1972) argues that siblings represent a good control group because siblings have the same home environment. This may be problematic, however, because families may give the bused child more financial resources for college and from higher expectations. This could exacerbate the unmeasured difference between the two groups of students rather than reducing it. In addition, Angrist and Lang (2004) point out that Armor's treatment group and, even more so, the control group was very small—as few as 20 students in some comparisons. They therefore present an alternative analysis based on data recently obtained from a suburban school district in the Boston area that took in large numbers of bused students. Taking a quasi-experimental approach, they make use of the fact that the district only admitted bused students to schools in which the total number of students in a class would be 25 or less. The cap allows for the calculation of the expected number of open slots available in each school and therefore the number of available slots for bused students. This variable helps to control for the possibility that bused students are assigned to schools non-randomly. However, Angrist and Lang, unlike Armor, are still not able to account for non-randomness in the decision to participate in the busing program.
6. Crain (1984) is based substantially on Crain and Maynard (1983). Also, the latter study provides a more detailed breakdown based on research methodology. For this reason, only the latter is discussed.
7. These effects are not reported per time period, which complicates the interpretation. Some of the effects may have occurred after one only year of the treatment (desegregation) while others may have occurred over longer periods.
8. An additional, though arguably less relevant pattern is that desegregation impacts reading scores, but probably not math scores (Cook, 1984). This is somewhat surprising because researchers more typically find that policy and program changes influence math scores. The main reason for this is that reading scores are more likely to be affected by activities in the home (e.g., casual reading), whereas math skills are rarely used outside of school. Effects on math are more likely in high school because there are specific courses in this subject, whereas there are no "reading" courses in high school. The more significant effects on reading also contrast, as we will see, with findings from the research on peer effects.
9. A third study by Katz, Kling, and Liebman (2000) focuses on the effects of MTO other than achievement. This study found considerable benefits in terms of child health and behavior.
10. The authors use scores on the Comprehensive Test of Basic Skills (CTBS) and Maryland Functional Tests (MFT) for elementary and MFT only for middle school. The administration of the tests was not

required by the state, though some districts did so anyway. As a result, only one-third of the full sample has an observed test score. There are also limitations in the ways the data are reported. The authors only had access to percentile rankings for the CTBS and did not convert to normal curve equivalents. Also, the MFT was available only as pass/fail.

11. These are the intent-to-treat effects. The effects of the treatment-on-the-treated were roughly 50 percent larger in both cases. After interpolating the missing data, the intent-to-treat effects declined slightly for the MFT and by about 50 percent for the CTBS. The time dimension of these effects is also somewhat difficult to interpret. The authors collected data for five years beginning in the year preceding the MTO (initial test scores are from 1993–94, and MTO began in 1994). Students varied in the average length of treatment, but the authors indicate that there is insufficient data to analyze the temporal differences.
12. There is evidence to support the argument that achievement tests are more likely than other tests to pick up intervention effects than other types of tests. For example, the Perry pre-school project found long-term term sustained effects on achievement scores, but not on tests of intelligence (Barnett, 1992). The appropriate measure depends partly on which outcome is of greatest interest.
13. In addition to the three mentioned in the test, peer effect studies have the advantage of much larger sample sizes.
14. These studies vary in their modeling specifications. Burke and Sass (2006) include student, teacher, and school fixed effects. This means that their resulting estimates are identified from variations in student assignment to classrooms within schools and that possibly non-random selection of students to teachers is accounted for with the student and teacher effects. Cooley (2006), however, includes only teacher fixed effects and excludes student and school fixed effects.
15. These studies all use quite different methods. Hoxby (2000) estimates the effects of peers from the apparently exogenous "unexpected" changes in cohort racial and achievement composition. Burke and Sass (2006) and Hanushek, Kain, and Rivkin (2002) use value-added models with student (and in some cases other) fixed effects, identifying peer effects from within-student variation in peer characteristics. Cooley (2006) estimates the effects of race and peer achievement, accounting for unobserved classroom characteristics using a two-stage approach to account for selection bias. Vigdor and Nechya (forthcoming) consider the effects of peers from a subsample of schools where between 10 and 50 percent of students are new to the school, changes that would generally arise from changes in school attendance boundaries. Hoxby (2000), as well as Harris (2006), are the only studies discussed in this section that use data aggregated to the school-by-race level. Harris (2006) has only two years of achievement data, while Hoxby has many more years, which allows her to use more sophisticated methods that account for selection bias.
16. Specifically, Vigdor and Nechyba (forthcoming) include teacher fixed effects to account for unobserved teacher characteristics.
17. This statement is based on Hoxby's (2000) estimated effects of he benefits for blacks of moving them to low-minority schools and the low costs to doing so for whites. The difference between the two implies that blacks would gain 0.72–0.16=0.56 standard deviations in a single year.
18. I use the term "integration" throughout much of the chapter because this encompasses both desegregation policies, whose direct aim is to alter the distribution of students, and other ways in which racial diversity occurs. For example, racially diverse schools that arise simply because of housing patterns would not be considered desegregation.
19. Nearly equal percentages of the bused and control groups who went to college went on to a four-year institution; 56 percent of the total bused students went to a four-year college, or 56/84 = 67 percent of the total. Similarly, 38 percent of the control group went to a four year college, or 38/56 = 68 percent. Project Concern in Hartford also involved a form of random assignment and long-term follow-up, although it is difficult to draw any clear conclusions for a variety of reasons. The long-term follow-up sample is extremely small with only 71 follow-respondents, spread among three comparison groups (bused students who graduated, bused students who dropped out and returned to Hartford schools, and students who were never bused).
20. Note that neither the Grogger nor Rivkin studies can identify students who actually switched schools as a result of desegregation. So, the effect here is just the average influence of race (and school quality) on the average black student.

21. No distinction is made here between minimum competency testing and standards-based testing, which are distinguished mainly by the level of achievement required for passage. Some researchers (e.g., Bishop, 2001) use the former term to refer to promotion exams applied before grade twelve.
22. The results from Jacob (2001) are more positive for math, which are generally considered more pliable than reading scores. Jacob does not report results separately, though he does report them according to the initial level of student achievement. Interestingly, the results appear more positive for students whose initial achievement was already near or above average. The results are statistically insignificant for both the overall sample and these subgroups.
23. There was also a compositional change in the students taking the test, caused by several factors including increases in the rate at which high-performing elementary school students remained in the Chicago public school district, apparently due to the creation of college preparatory magnet schools. Also, the percentage of high school students placed in special education increased from 11.5 percent in 1993–94 to 16.4 percent in 1999–2000; special education students are not required to take the high stakes exam (Miller et al. 2002).
24. Several studies have examined the effects of PGEs on NAEP scores and on international tests. Bishop (1998) also compared the performance of countries on the International Assessment of Educational Progress (IAEP) and its follow-up, the Third International Mathematics and Science Study (TIMSS). He finds large effects from PGE for those countries included in the sample. In a separate study, Bishop, et al. (2001) also find positive effects of PGE across U.S. states based on NAEP, especially when the PGEs are tied to specific courses and curricula. While these tend on find positive effects on achievement, they are less convincing than those above, due to the highly aggregated nature of the data and the fact that change in scores were not studied before and after the reforms were implemented.
25. The analysis of Dee and Jacob (2006) is quite similar to Dee (2003).
26. These limitations in their initial include their assumption that students graduated from high school in the state in which they were born (introducing possible measurement error), inability to distinguish between high school completers and GED recipients, inability to identify when students dropped out.
27. One limitation of this analysis is that the test taking rate declined after the eighth grade PGE was put in place. The excluded students almost certainly have a higher probability of dropping out. Allensworth acknowledges this point and addresses it through various selection bias corrections. She indicates that the results are generally insensitive to these corrections. Under some assumptions the benefits for the students who continue in school more than offset the losses for other students; in other cases, the two countervailing effects are roughly equal.
28. Bishop and Mane (2001) analyze these issues using the National Educational Longitudinal Survey (NELS-88) which tracked students a national sample of students who were in the eighth grade in 1988 through 1994, comparing outcomes for those students in states that had PGEs with students in other states. They find that, while PGEs increase the probability of students' dropping out, the main effect is to delay graduation or shift students into GED programs. These effects are largest for students with low grade point averages; that is, the presence of the PGE increases the probability of the average student dropping out or delaying graduation, but the increase is larger for students with low grades. Interestingly, other analyses of the same database have produced more mixed findings (Lillard & DeCicca, 1997). One explanation for the difference in results is that the Bishop and Mane do not separately examine lower achieving students and they therefore average together the negative on low achieving students with the positive or neutral effect for higher achieving students.
29. Bishop and Mane (2001) appropriately include dummy variables for student graduation status (dropout, GED, etc.) in the regressions where employment outcomes represent the dependent variables. Otherwise, a higher rate of employment and higher earnings might be considered negative outcomes, the result of students being less likely to enter college.
30. Extending their analysis of NAEP, Carnoy and Loeb (2002) also find that the index of state accountability is not associated with each state's probability of dropout and graduation. Also, note that their specific measure of student achievement is percent passing the basic level of NAEP proficiency.

REFERENCES

Alexander, Nicola (2000). "The missing link: An econometric analysis of the impact of curriculum standards on student achievement," *Economic of Education Review*, 19, 351–361.

Allensworth, Elaine (2004). *Dropout Rates in Chicago after Implementation of the Eighth-Grade Promotion Gate*. Consortium on Chicago School research.

Armor, David (1972). "The evidence on busing," *Public Interest*, 28, 90–124.

Armor, David (1984). "The evidence on desegregation and Black achievement," In T. Cook, D. Armor, R. Crain, N. Miller, W. Stephan, H. Walberg, and P. Wortman (Eds.), *School Desegregation and Black Achievement* (pp. 43–67). Washington, DC: National Institute of Education.

Barnett, Steven (1992). "Benefits of Compensatory Preschool Education," *Journal of Human Resources*, 27(2), 279–312.

Bishop, John (1998). "*Do Curriculum-Based External Exit Exam Systems Enhance Student Achievement?*" Report RR-40. Consortium for Policy Research in Education, University of Pennsylvania.

Bishop, John and Ferran Mane (2001). "The Impacts of Minimum Competency Exam Graduation Requirements on High School Graduation, College Attendance and Early Labor Market Success." *Labor Economics*, 8, 203–222.

Bishop, John, Ferran Mane, Michael Bishop, and Joan Moriarity (2001). "The Role of End-of-Course Exams and Minimal Competency Exams in Standards-Based Reforms." In Diane Ravitch (ed.) *Brookings Papers in Educational Policy* (pp. 267–345). Washington, DC: Brookings Institution.

Bradley, L.A. and G.W. Bradley (1977). "The academic achievement of Black students in desegregated schools: A critical review," *Review of Educational Research*, 47, 399–449.

Burke, Mary A. and Tim R. Sass (2006) "Classroom peer effects and student achievement." Unpublished manuscript.

Carnoy, Martin and Susanna Loeb (2002). "Does External Accountability Affect Student Outcomes? A Cross-State Analysis." *Educational Evaluation and Policy Analysis,* 24(4), 305–331.

Coleman, James. (1966). *Equality of Educational Opportunity*. Report OE-38000. Washington, DC: U.S. Department of Health Education and Welfare, Office of Education.

Coleman, James (1975). "Recent trends in school integration," *Educational Researcher*, 3–12.

Cook, Thomas (1984), "What have black children gained academically from school integration? Examination of the meta-analytic evidence." In T. Cook, D. Armor, R. Crain, N. Miller, W. Stephan, H. Walberg, & P. Wortman (Eds.), *School Desegregation and Black Achievement* (pp.6–42). Washington, DC: National Institute of Education.

Cooley, Jane (2006). "Desegregation and the achievement gap: Do diverse peers help?" Unpublished manuscript.

Crain, R.L. (1984). *Is nineteen really better than ninety three?* Washington DC: National Institute of Education.

Crain, Robert L. and Rita E. Maynard (1983). "The effect of research methodology on desegregation-achievement studies: A meta-analysis," *American Journal of Sociology*, 88(5), 839–854.

Currie, Janet and Thomas Duncan (1999). "Early test scores, socioeconomic status and future outcomes," *NBER Working Paper No.6943*. Cambridge, MA: National Bureau of Economic Research.

Dee, Thomas (2003). "Standards and student outcomes: Lessons from the 'First Wave' of education reform," In Paul Peterson and Martin West (Eds.) *No Child Left Behind? The Politics and Practice of School Accountability*. Washington, DC: Brookings Institution.

Dee, Thomas and Brian A. Jacob (2006). "Do high school exit exams influence educational attainment or labor market performance?" *NBER Working Paper 12199*, Cambridge, MA: National Bureau of Economic Research.

Figlio, David and Maurice Lucas (2000). "What's in a grade? School report cards and housing prices," *NBER Working Paper #8019*. Cambridge, MA: National Bureau of Economic Research.

Gill, Brian, Michael Timpane, Karen Ross, and Dominic Brewer (2001). *Rhetoric Versus Reality: What we Know and what we Need to Know About Vouchers and Charter Schools.* Santa Monica, CA: The RAND Corporation.

Grissmer, David and Ann Flanagan. (1998). *Exploring Rapid Achievement Gains in North Carolina and Texas*. Washington, DC: National Education Goals Panel.

Grissmer, David, Ann Flanagan, Jennifer Kawata, and Stephanie Williamson (2000). *Improving Student Achievement: What State NAEP Test Scores Tell Us*. Santa Monica:The Rand Corporation.

Grissmer, David, Ann Flanagan, and Stephanie Williamson (1998). "Why did the Black-White Test Score Gap Narrow in the 1970s and 1980s?" In Christopher Jencks and Meredith Phillips (Eds.) *The Black-White Test Score Gap*. Washington, DC: Brookings Institution.

Grissmer, David, Sheila Kirby, Mark Berends, and Stephanie Williamson (1994). "Student achievement and the changing American family." *Report RB-8009*. Santa Monica: The RAND Corporation.

Grogger, Jeffrey T. (1996). "Does school quality explain the recent black/white wage trend?" *Journal of Labor Economics*, 14(2), 231–253.

Hanushek, Eric A., John F. Kain, and Steven G. Rivkin (2001). "Why public schools lose teachers." *Working Paper No. 8599*. Cambridge, MA: National Bureau of Economic Research.

Hanushek, Eric A., John F. Kain, and Steven G. Rivkin (2002). "New evidence about Brown v. Board of Education: The complex effects of racial composition on achievement," *NBER Working Paper no. W8741*. Cambridge, MA: National Bureau of Economic Research.

Harris, Douglas N. (2006). *Lost Learning, Forgotten Promises: A National Analysis of School Racial Segregation, Student Achievement, and "Controlled Choice" Plans*. Washington, DC: Center for American Progress.

Harris, Douglas N. and Carolyn D. Herrington (2004). "Accountability and the Achievement Gap: Evidence from NAEP." Unpublished manuscript.

Harris, Douglas N. and Carolyn D. Herrington (2006). "Accountability, standards, and the growing achievement gap: Lessons from the past half-century," *American Journal of Education*, 112(2), 209–238.

Harris, Douglas N. and Tim R. Sass, (2006). "The purposes, assumptions, and results of educational value-added models," *paper presented at the 2005 conference of the American Education Finance Association*.

Howell, William and Paul Peterson. (2002). *The Education Gap: Vouchers and Urban Schools*. Washington, DC: Brookings Institution.

Hoxby, Caroline M. (2000). "Peer effects in the classroom: Learning from gender and race variation." *Working Paper #7867*. Cambridge, MA: National Bureau of Economic Research.

Hoxby, Caroline M. and Jonah Rockoff (2004). The impact of charter schools on student achievement." Unpublished manuscript.

Hoxby, Caroline M. and Gretchen Weingarth (2005). "Taking race out of the equation: School re-assignment and the structure of peer effects." Unpublished manuscript.

Jacob, Brian (2001). "Getting tough? The impact of high school graduation exams." *Educational Evaluation and Policy Analysis,* 23(2), 99–121.

Jacob, Brian (2005). "Accountability, incentives and behavior: The impact of high-stakes testing in the Chicago Public Schools," *Journal of Public Economics*, 89, 761–796.

Jencks, Christopher and Susan E. Mayer (1990). "The social consequences of growing up in a poor neighborhood," In *Inner City Poverty in the United States*, (eds) Laurence E. Lynn, Jr. and Michael G.H. McGeary (pp. 111–186). Washington, DC: National Academy Press.

Kahlenberg, Richard (2006). *A New Way on School Integration*. Issue Brief. New York: The Century Foundation.

Katz, Lawrence F., Jeffrey R. Kling, and Jeffrey B. Liebman, (2000). "Moving to Opportunity in Boston: Early Results of a Randomized Mobility Experiment," *NBER Working Paper #7973*. Cambridge, MA: National Bureau of Economic Research.

Kaufman, Julie E. and James E. Rosenbaum (1992). "The Education and Employment of Low-Income Black Youth in White Suburbs," *Educational Evaluation and Policy Analysis*, 14(3), 229–240.

Klein, Stephen, Laura Hamilton, Daniel McCaffrey, and Brian Stecher (2000). *What Do Test Scores in Texas Tell Us?* Santa Monica, CA: The RAND Corporation.

Ladd, Helen F. (1999). "The Dallas school accountability and incentive program: An evaluation of its impacts on student outcomes," *Economics of Education Review*, 18, 1–16.

Ladd, Helen and Randall Walsh (2002). "Implementing value-added measures of school effectiveness: Getting the incentives right." *Economics of Education Review,* 21(1), 1–17. ankford, R.H., Lee, E.S. and Wyckoff, J.H. (1995). "An analysis of elementary and secondary school choice," *Journal of Urban Economics*, 38, 236–251.

Lankford, R.H. and J. Wyckoff (1992). "Primary and secondary school choice among public and religious alternatives," *Economics of Education Review*, 11(4), 317–337.

Lillard, Dean and Phillip DeCicca (2001). "Higher standards, more dropouts? Evidence within and across time," *Economics of Education Review,* 20, 459–473.

Ludwig, Jens, Helen F. Ladd, & Greg J. Duncan (2001). "Urban poverty and educational outcomes," *Brookings-Wharton Papers on Urban Affairs*, (Eds) William G. Gale and Janet Rothenberg Pack. Washington, DC: Brookings Institution Press.

Martorell, Paco (2005). "Does failing a high school graduation exam matter?" *unpublished manuscript.*

Miller, Shazia, Elaine Allensworth, and Julie Kochanek (2002). *Student Performance: Course Taking, Test Scores, and Outcomes.* Chicago: Consortium of Chicago School Research.

Miller, N. and M. Carlson (1984). "School desegregation as a social reform: A meta-analysis of its effects on Black academic achievement." In T. Cook, D. Armor, R. Crain, N. Miller, W. Stephan, H. Walberg, and P. Wortman (Eds.), *School Desegregation and Black Achievement* (pp.89–130). Washington, DC: National Institute of Education.

Nagoaka, Jenny and Melissa Roderick (2004). *Ending Social Promotion: The Effects of Retention*, Consortium on Chicago School Research.

Neal, Derek A. and William R. Johnson (1996). "The role of premarket factors in black-white wage differential," *Journal of Political Economy*, 114, 869–95.

Ogbu, John U. (2003). *Black American Students in an Affluent Suburb: A Study of Academic Disengagement.* Mahwah, NJ: Lawrence Erlbaum Associates.

Orfield, Gary (2001). Schools More Separate: Consequences of a Decade of Resegregation. Cambridge, MA: The Harvard Civil Rights Project.

Raymond, Margaret and Eric Hanushek (2003). "Shopping for evidence against school Accountability," *Education Next*, 3, 48–55.

Reardon, S.F., J.T. Yun, & M. Kurlaender (2006). "Implications of income-based school assignment policies for racial school segregation," *Educational Evaluation and Policy Analysis*, 28(1), 49–75.

Rivkin, Steven G. (2000). "School desegregation, academic attainment, and earnings." *Journal of Human Resources*, 35(2), 333–346.

Roderick, Melissa, Brian Jacob, and Anthony Bryk (2002). "The impact of high-stakes testing in Chicago on student achievement in promotional gate grades," *Educational Evaluation and Policy Analysis,* 24(4), 333–357.

Roderick, Melissa and Mimi Engel (2001). "The grasshopper and the ant: Motivational responses of low-achieving students to high-stakes testing," *Educational Evaluation and Policy Analysis*, 23(3), 197–227.

Sanbonmatsu, Lisa, Jeffrey R. Kling, Greg J. Duncan, and Jeanne Brooks-Gunn (2006). "Neighborhoods and academic achievement: Results from the Moving to Opportunity experiment," *NBER Working Paper 11909*, Cambridge, MA: National Bureau of Economics Research.

Schofield, Janet Ward (1995). "Review of research on school desegregation's impact on elementary and secondary school students." In *Handbook of research on multicultural education*, ed. J.A. Banks and C.A.M. Banks. New York: Macmillan.

Stephan, W.G. (1984). "Black and Brown: The effects of school desegregation on Black students. In T. Cook, D. Armor, R. Crain, N. Miller, W. Stephan, H. Walberg, & P. Wortman (Eds.), *School Desegregation and Black Achievement* (pp.131–159). Washington, DC: National Institute of Education.

St. John, N.H. (1975). *School desegregation: Outcomes for children.* New York: Wiley.

Tice, P., D. Princiotta, C. Chapman, and S. Bielick (2006). Trends in the Use of School Choice: 1993 to 2003, (NCES 2007-045) U.S. Department of Education. National Center for Education Statistics, Washington, DC.

U.S. Department of Education (2006a). Institute of Education Sciences, National Center for Education Statistics, National Assessment of Educational Progress (NAEP), downloaded July 20, 2006 from http://nces.ed.gov/nationsreportcard/ltt/results2004/sub-reading-race.asp.

U.S. Department of Education, (2006b). Condition of Education, p. 11.

U.S. Department of Education (2006c). Condition of Education, 2006, Table 2–1.

Vigdor, J.L. & T.J. Nechyba (forthcoming). K–12 education policies and theire effects on educational equity.

Walberg, Herbert J. (1984). "Desegregation and education productivity." In T. Cook, D. Armor, R. Crain, N. Miller, W. Stephan, H. Walberg, & P. Wortman (Eds.), *School Desegregation and Black Achievement* (pp.160–193). Washington, DC: National Institute of Education.

Wells, Amy Stuart and Robert L. Crain (1994). "Perpetuation theory and the long-term effects of school desegregation," *Review of Educational Research,* 64(4), 531–555.

Wortman, P.M. (1984). School desegregation and Black achievement: An integrative review. In T. Cook, D. Armor, R. Crain, N. Miller, W. Stephan, H. Walberg, & P. Wortman (Eds.), *School Desegregation and Black Achievement* (pp. 194–224). Washington, DC: National Institute of Education.

VII
SPECIAL CIRCUMSTANCES

Section Editor

David H. Monk

32

Special Education

Jenifer J. Harr, Tom Parrish, and Jay Chambers

Special education is an important, unique, and growing component of public education in the United States, and it has become a major focus of attention in regard to public policy, appropriate service provision, and levels of spending. This chapter presents data on special education spending in the United States over time, describes the various ways in which special education services are funded, presents some of the primary policy issues associated with special education finance, and discusses some of the implications of this research for possible future policy directions. Although the primary focus is on special education in the United States, many of the trends and issues presented in this chapter also pertain to Canada, Europe, and elsewhere around the globe (Naylor, 2001; McLaughlin & Rouse, 2000; OECD, 1995, 2005).

A BRIEF HISTORICAL PERSPECTIVE

Although institutions for children with particular disabilities such as deafness and blindness were established in the early nineteenth century in several states, they operated almost entirely independently of the public school systems in place at that time. Even after compulsory attendance laws were established later in the century, children with disabilities continued to be excluded from public schools. Although several states began to upgrade the educational programs and services publicly available to children with disabilities, such programs were still relatively few in number at the time of the civil rights movement during the 1960s. By 1966, congressional hearings revealed that only about one-third of the nation's children with disabilities were receiving appropriate special education services (Verstegen, 1994). It was at this time that the parents of students with disabilities began to organize and demand educational services for their children (Mosher, Hastings, & Wagoner, 1979).

At the federal level, special education funding took root with the Elementary and Secondary Education Act of 1965 (ESEA). The ESEA and its subsequent amendments established grants for state-operated schools to serve students with disabilities and later included public schools. The watershed event for special education took place in 1975 when Congress passed the Education for All Handicapped Children Act (Public Law 94-142), subsequently renamed the Individuals with Disabilities Education Act (IDEA). This legislation laid out the blueprint for federal special education law as we now know it.

In addition to establishing funding for special education, the IDEA guarantees eligible students with disabilities the right to a free and appropriate public education (FAPE) and created due process procedures for ensuring FAPE. Each special education student is required to have an individualized education program (IEP) that specifies the special education program and services he or she is to receive as determined by a multi-disciplinary panel of educators and related service providers. The law further states that these students will be educated with non-disabled children to the maximum extent appropriate to their needs, a concept known as the least restrictive environment (LRE).

UNIQUE ASPECTS OF SPECIAL EDUCATION

Students who qualify for special education differ from general education students in important respects, many of which have fiscal implications. First, student receiving special education represent a substantial—and growing—proportion of public school enrollments. The latest federal data available for 2005–06 indicate that more than 6.7 million students, ages 3–21, have been identified for special education.[1] The percentage of students in special education has grown without interruption for nearly 30 years—rising from 8.3 percent of all public school students in 1976–77, the first year such data were collected, to 13.9 percent in 2004–05. Along with expanding enrollments, special education services comprise a significant proportion—an estimated 14 percent in 1999–2000—of spending on elementary and secondary education (Chambers, Pérez, Harr, & Shkolnik, 2005).

Second, as noted above, special education students have a legal right under federal law to a free and appropriate public education (FAPE), an entitlement that distinguishes them from all other students. Unlike general education, the district is legally bound to provide services that are specified on a special education student's IEP, and cost may not be a precluding factor. The IEP is a legal contract between the responsible school district, the special education child, and her or his family that specifies an entitlement to special education services. There is no counterpart for non-special education students.

Third, special education students encompass a population of children with very diverse educational needs. With 13 federal disability categories, students in special education have a range of disabilities that include cognitive, physical, or behavioral impairments. By far the largest category, specific learning disability (SLD) accounted for over 45 percent of all special education students in the 2005–06 school year.[2] As will be shown later, the average cost of educating students in special education varies considerably by category of disability and varies to an even greater extent within each category.

At the same time, the basic educational needs of most special education students are quite comparable to the needs of all students. The vast majority of special education students are held to the same academic standards,[3] and consistent with LRE requirements, over one-half of the special education population spent 80 percent or more of the school day in a general education class in 2005–06.[4] Since special education students are like all other students in fundamental ways, the question arises as to the degree to which special education students should be treated differently than other students from a policy perspective.

SPECIAL EDUCATION SPENDING

While some states have data on annual spending on special education services, the most current information across a broad array of states comes from a survey conducted by the Center of Special Education Finance (CSEF). However, of the 30 states providing estimates of special education spending for 1999–98—the latest school year these data were collected—only seven indicated a "high degree of confidence" in the data they provided. Even the data from these seven states are marred by comparability problems because of the differing accounting conventions used across states to arrive at these estimates.[5]

The most current and comprehensive national estimates of special education spending come from the Special Education Expenditure Project (SEEP), conducted by the American Institutes for Research (AIR), on the basis of data from the 1999–2000 school year. SEEP was the first comprehensive, nationally representative study of special education spending to be undertaken since the late 1980s and the fourth in a series of studies over the past 40 years examining the nation's spending on special education and related services.[6] Employing an "ingredients" approach to cost estimates,[7] AIR used a series of surveys to collect data on the general and special education services received by individual special education students. This standardized approach provides comparable data on how children are served and the cost of those services across all jurisdictions that are not subject to varying accounting practices across states or local school districts.[8]

SEEP used 23 different surveys to collect data for the 1999–2000 school year at the state, district, school, teacher, and student levels.[9] SEEP asked special education teachers and related service providers to select a sample of two students with disabilities from the rosters of students they served. This method yielded a sample of approximately 10,000 students with disabilities from more than 1,000 schools, in well-over 300 local education authorities across 45 states and the District of Columbia. SEEP differs from previous studies in that it is based on comprehensive descriptions of all (general and special) education services received by a large, nationally representative sample of special education students.

In 1999–2000, a total of $360.6 billion was spent on elementary and secondary education for all students in the U.S. In the same year, SEEP estimated that total spending to educate students with disabilities was $78.3 billion. This SEEP estimate includes both special and general education services for special education students, as well as other special needs programs (e.g., Title I, English language learner services, or gifted and talented education). Of the $78.3 billion, about $50 billion was spent on special education services alone; $27.3 billion on general education services; and $1 billion on other special needs programs. Put another way, special education students, who represented about 13.2 percent of all public elementary and secondary students, accounted for about 21.4 percent of the total spending on elementary and secondary education in 1999–2000. Spending on just the special education services these students received ($50 billion) accounted for 13.9 percent of spending.

The SEEP study is the last of four national special education expenditure studies that have been conducted (Rossmiller, Hale, & Frohreich, 1970; Kakalik, Furry, Thomas, & Carney, 1981; Moore, Strang, Schwartz, & Braddock, 1988; Chambers et al., 2002). The Rossmiller, et al. (1970) study was completed prior to the passage of the IDEA. In comparing these results, one must recognize the different methods and data sources employed by the various studies.[10] Of particular interest is the degree to which these estimates reflect differences in research methods or true variations in spending.

The Kakalik, et al. (1981) and the Rossmiller, et al. (1970) studies both relied heavily on existing fiscal data from small samples of school districts. Neither of these first two studies used detailed nationally representative samples of individual special education students.

The Moore et al. (1988) and Chambers et al. (2002) study approaches were quite similar. Both studies estimated costs based on services received by special education students; programs and services were described in terms of the type of provider, their intensity, and their duration. While the Moore, et al. study analyzed special education spending for a nationally representative sample of 60 districts, the SEEP estimates use the full set of services received by over 10,000 special education students. Given the much greater level of detail deriving from student-level analyses, and the much larger sample included in SEEP, the SEEP estimates likely provide the most accurate, and certainly the most detailed, national special education spending and service provision estimates thus far available.

Findings from all four of the national studies are summarized in Figure 32.1 in constant 1999–2000 dollars. Estimated real spending per special education student rose substantially from the time of the first study (1968–69) to the second (1977–78). While the 1985–86 study shows only a slight increase from the prior estimate, spending per student was considerably below the special education spending estimate from SEEP for 1999–2000.

The first of each of the four pairs of bars in Figure 32.1 shows the average total expenditure (general and special education) to educate a special education student. With the exception of the Rossmiller el al. (1970) study, it is possible to disaggregate these total estimates of spending per special education student between the general (GE) and special (SE) education services received._

The second in each set of bars shows the average amount spent on a general education student receiving no supplemental services of any kind. For example, for 1999–2000, the first bar shows an average total expenditure per student in special education of $12,474, consisting of $4,394 for general education services and $8,080 for special education services.[11] The second bar shows that the average expenditure on a general education student receiving no special services was $6,556.

Also of fiscal policy interest, the ratio of average spending on a special education student to spending on a general education student with no special needs increased from 1.92 in 1968–69 to 2.15 in 1977–78, to a high of 2.28 in 1985–86, dropping to 1.90 in 1999–2000.[12] In other words, in 1999–2000, total spending on an average special education student was an estimated 90 per-

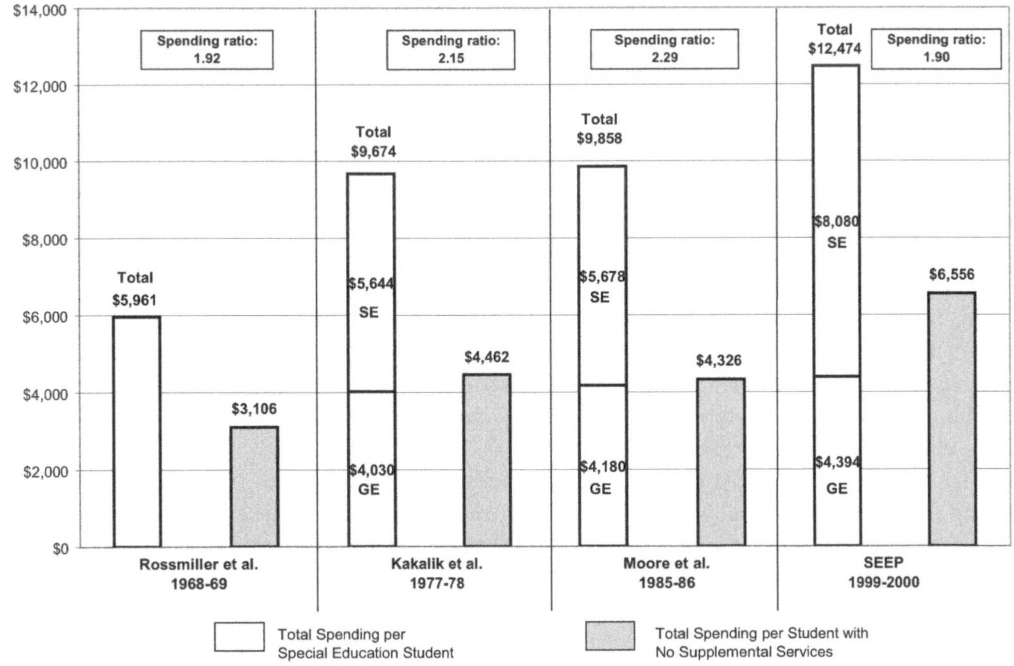

FIGURE 32.1 Total spending per special education student over time, in comparison to the average student receiving no supplemental services (in constant 1999–2000 dollars).

cent more than on the average general education student receiving no supplemental educational services.

The recent decline in the spending ratio breaks the rising trend from the prior three studies. It also seems somewhat counter-intuitive given that total spending on students with disabilities increased from about 16.6 percent of total education spending in 1977–1978[13] to 21.4 percent in 1999–2000.

A primary reason for the decline in the ratio between the last two studies is that increases in spending per general education student outpaced spending per special education student. Average spending per general education student increased by more than 50 percent ($4,326 to $6,556), in comparison to a 27 percent increase ($9,858 to $12,474) for special education students.

In addition, over this same period, the percentage of students aged 3–21 who were receiving special education services increased from about 11 percent to more than 13 percent of total public enrollment. This rise in the percentage of students in special education increased aggregate spending on special education. At the same time, however, it likely lowered the average spending per special education student. While some of the growth in the special education population was in severe disability categories such as autism, the majority of new students were in milder and less costly categories such as specific learning disability, speech or language impairment, and other health impairment. As shown later in this chapter, these three disability categories have the lowest spending estimates per student. The increase in the number of students in these categories had the effect of lowering average special education spending per student.

Variations in Spending Across States

While the national SEEP study does not have samples of sufficient size to be representative of specific states, 11 states opted for individual SEEP studies with samples large enough to generate state-specific results.[14] Among the seven SEEP states whose results are public, total spending on the average special education student ranged from $10,141 to $15,081 (in 1999–2000 dollars),[15] and the spending ratio ranged from a low of 1.57 in Alabama to a high of 2.55 in Maryland. This variation in the spending ratio across states reflects a combination of the overall willingness of a state to spend money on educational services, the relative priority of general versus special education, and the composition of students with respect to needs and expenditures.

While the publicly available SEEP results are limited to these seven states, variations across all states are observed in key special education personnel resources as reported to the federal government. By applying standardized salaries to the total number of special education teachers, related service providers, and aides reported by each state, one can approximate special education personnel spending per student. These estimates suggest special education personnel resources per special education student are over three times greater in the highest versus the lowest allocating states.[16]

Variations in Spending by Category of Disability

As the population of special education students is quite heterogeneous — in the types of disabilities and degree of need — average expenditures mask considerable variation. The highest average total expenditures in 1999–2000 were for students with multiple disabilities ($20,095) as shown in Figure 32.2.[17] In contrast, the two most common disabilities, specific learning disability and speech or language impairment, which make up more than 60 percent of the special education population, show the lowest per pupil expenditures, at $10,558 and $10,958, respectively. Thus, the expenditure for a student with a disability ranges from 1.6 (specific learning disability) to 3.1

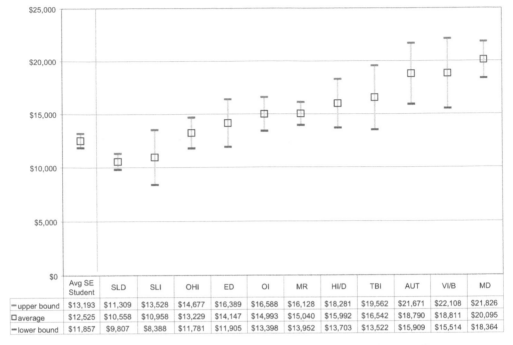

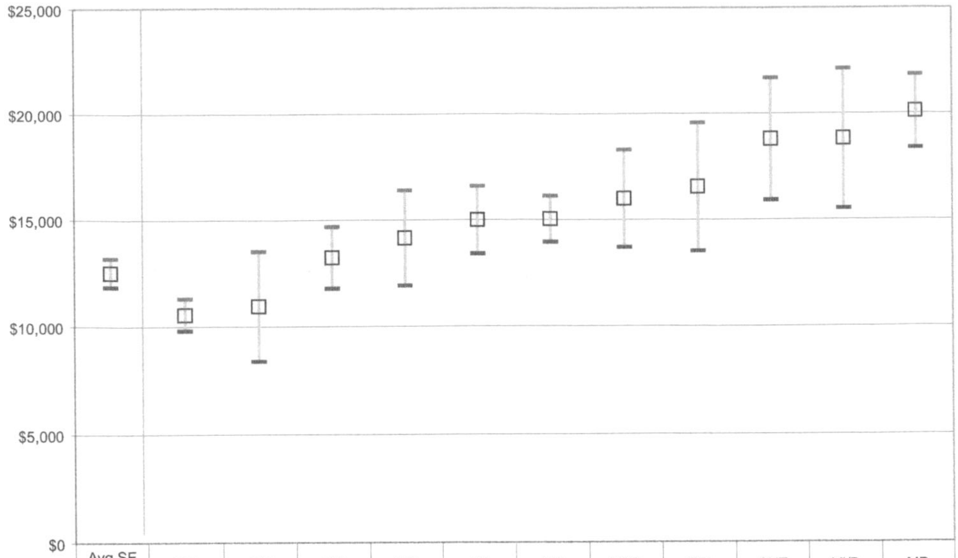

	Avg SE Student	SLD	SLI	OHI	ED	OI	MR	HI/D	TBI	AUT	VI/B	MD
upper bound	$13,193	$11,309	$13,528	$14,677	$16,389	$16,588	$16,128	$18,281	$19,562	$21,671	$22,108	$21,826
average	$12,525	$10,558	$10,958	$13,229	$14,147	$14,993	$15,040	$15,992	$16,542	$18,790	$18,811	$20,095
lower bound	$11,857	$9,807	$8,388	$11,781	$11,905	$13,398	$13,952	$13,703	$13,522	$15,909	$15,514	$18,364

FIGURE 32.2 Total Expenditures on Students With Disabilities, by Disability Category (in 1999–2000 Dollars).

Note: The averages by disability category are for school-aged students served in public schools. The overall average includes students in external placements and preschool students; this figure differs from the earlier figure ($12,474) as it excludes homebound and hospitalized students. The disability labels are as follows: SLD: specific learning disability; SLI: speech/language impairment; OHI: other health impairment; ED: emotional disturbance; OI: orthopedic impairment; MR: mental retardation; HI/D: hearing impairment/deafness; TBI: traumatic brain injury; AUT: autism; VI/B: visual impairment/blindness; MD: multiple disabilities.

(multiple disabilities) times the average expenditure of $6,556 for a general education student.

Disability labels are intended to reflect, to a degree, a particular student's needs, and it is generally accepted that some disability categories are more expensive to serve than others. However, students with the same disability label may have quite different levels of severity, which translate to variations in expenditures within the same disability category. Figure 32.2 also shows the upper and lower bound of the 95 percent confidence interval around each estimate. The estimate for expenditures on students classified as specific learning disability (SLD) has a relatively narrow confidence interval ($9,807 to $11,309), whereas the confidence interval for expenditures on students with visual impairments/blindness (VI/B) is relatively wide ($15,514 to $22,108). In fact, estimates for expenditures on students with visual impairments/blindness are not statistically significantly different from expenditures on students with hearing impairments/deafness (HI/D), traumatic brain injury (TBI), autism (AUT), or multiple disabilities (MD).

The presence of large confidence intervals around some of these expenditure estimates suggests that there is a wide range of needs represented within some of these disability categories. Two students with the same disability may have very different expenditures because they have different needs and therefore receive different types and levels of services. Analysis by Chambers, Pérez, Socias, Shkolnik, Esra, and Brown (2004) show that student disability only explains about 10 percent of the variance in per pupil spending on individual special education students.[18]

FUNDING SPECIAL EDUCATION

Special education services are primarily funded by state and local revenues. According to a state survey conducted by the Center for Special Education Finance (CSEF), federal funds in 1998–99 covered an average of 10 percent of spending on special education services, with state and local funds accounting for an average of 50 percent and 40 percent, respectively.[19] Across the states, however, there are notable differences. The reported local share ranged from zero to 80 percent, and the state share varied from 3 to 90 percent. Given the substantial increases in federal funds in recent years, it is likely that this distribution has changed somewhat since 1998–99.

The formulas used by the federal government and the states respectively to distribute funds for special education differ considerably in their orientation and their detailed provisions. At the most fundamental level, they can be divided across the two broad classifications: Census and non-census systems.

Census-based systems distribute special education funds based on the total enrollment (both special and general education students) in a district (state formulas), or the total school-aged population of the state (federal formula).For example, under the most straightforward implementation of a state-level census-based funding system, districts with identical enrollments would receive the same special education aid regardless of the number of students placed in special education, the disabilities of these students, where they are placed, or how they are served. According to the CSEF 1999–2000 survey, about one-fourth of the states had adopted various forms of census-based special education funding systems (Parrish, Harr, Anthony, Merickel, & Esra, 2003).[20]

Non-census systems, on the other hand, often provide varying funding amounts per student based on some special education attribute, such as the overall number of special education students, the category of disability, the types of services received, and/or the primary placement for these services, e.g., in a general education class, a special education class, or in a separate public or private school.

A frequently-cited advantage of census formulas is that, because funding is not based on the types of services provided, category of disability, or type of placement, they are free of any possible fiscal incentives to identify more students for special education (Parrish & Kaleba, 1998). At the extreme end of this argument, Greene and Forster (2002) concluded that the nation could save over $1.5 billion per year in special education spending if all states were to adopt census-type funding formulas. Although Greene and Forster's analyses and conclusions have been challenged, incentives in special education funding with the potential to affect practice are a major policy concern (Mahitivanichcha & Parrish, 2005).

A counter argument, however, is that such systems simply replace one set of incentives with another. For example, under census-based formulas, the fiscal incentive is to identify fewer students for special education as the revenues for these services are unrelated to the number of identified students (Parrish & Verstegen, 1994).

Federal Funding

The federal government converted to a census approach under the 1997 IDEA amendments. Prior to the formula change, virtually every newly identified special education student generated additional federal funds, whereas under the new formula, federal funds are allocated according to factors that are not directly related to special education: Overall residential population and poverty. Policy deliberations at the time of this change suggest that it was at least partially driven by concerns about the expanding special education population.

Under the new formula, the federal government distributes 85 percent of IDEA grants to the states according to the total age-relevant residential population of each state, with and without disabilities. The remaining funds (15 percent) are allocated according to the relative degree of poverty in the state. To ease the transition to this new formula, the funding levels under the old formula in 1997 were maintained as a constant base for each state, and only the revenues in excess of $4.9 billion are distributed by the new formula. Since 2000, when federal revenues first exceeded this threshold, there have been substantial increases in federal special education funding, and as a result, by 2006, 60 percent of school-age federal IDEA funds were allocated using the new formula.

As an increasing percentage of federal special education funds are allocated under this new formula, the disparity in federal funding per special education student across states will continue to grow (Harr & Parrish, 2005). Due to differing percentages of students served in special education and varying rates of poverty, federal special education funding varied across the states from approximately $1,000 to $1,500 per special education student in 2003. Given projections that this disparity will grow substantially over time, it is possible that the issue of census-based special education funding at the federal level may be revisited in the future.

Overall, however, the biggest special education finance policy issue at the federal level is "full funding." When the IDEA was first passed in 1975, it authorized the federal government to appropriate funding for each special education student up to a level equal to 40 percent of the average per pupil expenditure (APPE) in public elementary and secondary schools in the United States.[21] To clarify, full funding is not 40 percent of the cost of educating special education students, but rather 40 percent of the average per pupil expenditure for all students, including special education students. Although federal funds have increased substantially in recent years, they have never reached even half of this amount. Federal support as a percentage of APPE has steadily increased from its 1996–97 level of 7.3 percent to 17.8 percent by 2006–07 — still considerably below "full federal funding" of 40 percent APPE.[22]

Rising special education costs have increased the pressure for the federal government to provide additional funding up to the 40 percent of APPE, which some have interpreted as a federal commitment or promise. Despite the substantial increases in federal special education funding from 1999–2004, these increases have provided only recent relief on state and local resources, due to a long standing requirement that federal funds could not be used to supplant current state and local efforts. However, the 2004 IDEA amendments now allow up to 50 percent of the increase in the annual federal appropriations for a given district to be used to offset existing local support of special education.

State Funding

State revenues remain the primary source of special education funding, and the debate on how best to allocate these funds among local districts dominates the fiscal policy discussion. The last national survey in 1999–2000 on this topic indicated that approximately one-half of the states were considering changes in the way they allocate special education funds to districts (Parrish, et al., 2003). The survey showed that the vast majority of the states used a non-census approach to special education funding. While only nine states used a census-based approach as the primary component of their special education funding system, these included populous states such as California, Massachusetts, and Pennsylvania.[23] Given the large size of states using this approach and the federal formula, a considerable percentage of special education revenues nationally are allocated on some form of a census approach.

The most common approach for distributing state funds to districts uses pupil funding weights, with 19 states citing such weighting as the primary basis of their special education funding approach. Pupil weights provide a basis for differentiating funding by some characteristic of the student, such as category of disability, location of primary placement, or some combination of the two. Other special education funding approaches include percentage reimbursement (seven states), resource based funding (seven states), and block grants, whereby prior year's funding is adjusted for growth in enrollments, expenditures, or inflation (four states).

Oklahoma's formula illustrates the use of special education funding weights. As an example, the supplemental funding weight attributed to a student with a specific learning disability (SLD) is 0.4 as compared to a student with mental retardation (MR), which has a weight of 1.3. This means that base funding is multiplied by 0.4 for SLD students and by 1.3 for students who are MR to derive the amount of supplemental special education funding for students with these disabilities. Under pupil weighting systems, higher weights are generally assigned to students in higher cost categories of disability or educational placements.

Pupil weights have the advantage of recognizing cost differentials among types of special education students and generating revenue amounts that can follow individual students wherever they are served. These advantages may be particularly relevant as states increasingly move to systems of greater student and family school choice. For example, if a student with a disability chose to go to a charter school, a pupil weight system could clarify the amount of funds that should follow this child to a new school assignment (Parrish & Bitter, 2003).

A common concern in considering alternative approaches to funding special education relates to fiscal incentives. Pupil-weighted formulas that distribute state funds on the basis of some special education attribute (e.g., greater funding for certain categories of disability or placements) may encourage higher identification rates of certain disabilities or more costly placements.

In fact, the 1997 amendments to the IDEA raised concerns about higher state funding for more costly placements which are also found to be more segregated or restrictive. States like New York, which had a special education weighted formula based on placement, were required to show that such a formula had not resulted in failure to educate students in the least restrictive environment (LRE) appropriate to their needs as required by the IDEA. New York responded to this challenge by adding a new weight to its formula that provides more funding for serving special education students in general classes, as opposed to more segregated instructional settings (Parrish, 2000).

There is no single, best approach to funding special education. Criteria for evaluating special education funding formulas were initially developed by Hartman (1992) and expanded by Parrish (1994). These criteria describe such formula attributes as being fair, adequate, cost-based, flexible, and understandable, among others. While each of these criteria likely holds value for some constituency, the relative importance placed on each may differ. No funding formula can fully accommodate all of these criteria. As a focus on one criterion often comes at the expense of one or more of the others, the "best" formula for a given state is one that maximizes criteria that are relevant to the context of that state.

In addition to the base formula, many states have established a "high cost risk pool" to protect districts against extraordinarily high special education costs that may hit some districts harder than others in a given year. Small districts are especially vulnerable to the disproportionate fiscal impact that can result from one or two unusually high cost special education students (Chambers, Pérez, & Esra, 2005). Adjustments for high cost students are especially important in states with census-based special education funding systems, as it is not connected in any way to true variations in special education need or cost.

Irrespective of funding approach, substantial variations in average spending per special education student can occur across districts within a given state. Given that some disability categories are more costly to serve than others, and the distribution of these high-cost disabilities is likely to vary across districts, one would expect some degree of disparity in special education spending. However, in some cases, observed spending disparities do not always appear related to cost factors such as student poverty or the percentage of students with low incidence—and generally higher cost—disabilities.

For example, Wyoming has a special education funding system whereby the state reimburses districts for 100 percent of their eligible special education expenditures. Despite this type of funding system in which disparity in spending would seem clearly linked to differences in student need, variations in special education spending per student ranged from $7,082 in the lowest quartile of districts, to $10,382 in the highest quartile, with no apparent relationship to poverty, the percentage of students in low incidence, or higher cost categories of disability (Parrish, Harr, Pérez, Esra, Brock, & Shkolnik, 2002).[24]

In California, which distributes funds to Special Education Local Plan Areas (SELPAs) based on a fixed amount for each student in average daily attendance (e.g., census-based), the average special education spending per student in the quartile of the highest spending SELPAs was over 1.5 times the amount in the lowest quartile. Similar spending disparities were observed in Oregon, which has a single pupil weight system (e.g., a fixed amount per special education student). Average spending per student in the quartile of the highest spending districts was over twice that of the lowest quartile. Again, differences in poverty levels or the percentage of students identified with low incidence disabilities did not seem to drive these differentials in either state.

OTHER SPECIAL EDUCATION FINANCE POLICY ISSUES

Other important issues are the encroachment of special education on general education revenues, the overall litigious climate surrounding special education, and the interaction between the increased focus on education accountability and how it pertains to special education.

Encroachment

The concept of special education encroachment is a growing policy concern at state and local levels of special education funding (Asimov, 2006; Little Hoover Commission, 1997; Beales, 1993).[25] Encroachment is generally defined as offsetting special education costs with funds that are not specifically designated for this purpose. A recent estimate of special education encroachment in California is that it exceeded $1.6 billion in the 2005–06 school year (Asimov, 2006).

With limited federal and state financial support designated for special education, and with rising special education costs, school districts report that they are increasingly tapping into funding sources that have traditionally supported general education activities to cover the legally-obligated special education services. When growth in required special education spending exceeds the state and federal revenues allocated for this purpose, the additional funds in support of special education services most generally come from the local general fund. As a result, all educational services other than special education may be curbed to accommodate required spending on special education. These program reductions may exacerbate tensions between the special education and all other public school programs and services. It also draws increasing attention to the disparity in treatment between special education and all other students, where the former has a legal entitlement to services that must be provided and the latter does not.

The issue of encroachment is complex and contentious. Synonymous with violation or intrusion, the very term "encroachment" suggests some form of hostile takeover rather than collaborative support. For example, it seems to imply that there is no local responsibility to support special education beyond the funds the federal government and the states provide specifically for special education services. In fact, what was most commonly reported by the states in the 1999–2000 CSEF survey on special education revenues and spending was a three-way support system based on some combination of federal, state, and local funds (Parrish et al., 2004). What one state calls encroachment, another may simply refer to as the expected local share.

Figure 32.1, shown earlier in this chapter, supports one counter-argument to the notion that special education is increasingly taking resources away from non-special education programs. From the time of the first expenditure study shown in this figure, which was conducted in 1968–69 prior to the implementation of federal special education law, to the most recent study using 1999–2000 data, spending per general education student increased at a greater rate than total spending per special education student. Thus, general education has realized a dramatic increase in support over a period of time during which considerable supplemental funds were also allocated to serve students in need of special education services. This trend does not seem to support the claim that overall resources available through the general fund have been disadvantaged by the rise in special education services.[26]

At the same time, rising special education costs can be seen as coming largely from the growing percentages of students being served in special education. Although the most effective way to stem the tide of rising special education spending may be to bolster general education, special education is increasingly seen as a drain against those resources. This reality undoubtedly fuels some of the frustration in regard to what is seen as special education encroachment.

One could argue that special education may be among the least efficient ways to address learning problems that could be addressed better through general education services. This may be one reason why the reauthorization of the IDEA in 2004 included changes in how to identify children with specific learning disabilities (SLD), by far the largest category of children in special education.

Representing a substantial change in special education law, the 2004 IDEA regulations moved away from a discrepancy model for identifying students with specific learning disabilities. This model identifies students in need of special education based on the difference between the student's intelligence and his or her actual achievement. Often described as a "wait and see" approach, in which students can be in third or fourth grade before having a large enough discrepancy, critics of this model have argued that it can be harmful to students by potentially delaying intervention. Furthermore, many students with SLD show minimal gains in achievement after placed in special education, and few actually exit special education (Donovon & Cross, 2002).

As an alternative to the discrepancy model, the "response to intervention" approach uses research-based educational interventions to target at-risk students within general education early, which may preclude subsequent identification for special education. Students who do not respond to increasingly intensive interventions would be subsequently identified for special education. Although too early to determine, this greater increased focus on remediation within general education may provide one source of relief in regard to the growing share of public education spending going to special education.[27]

Another change may lead to targeting students early and more effectively. A new provision in the reauthorized IDEA allows up to 15 percent of the federal funds to be used for early intervention services for students not identified for special education, but who need additional support to succeed in the general education environment. Flexibility of this type has the potential to benefit students who might otherwise be in special education and to bolster general education services.

Litigation

Concerns are frequently raised about the burgeoning costs of special education litigation arising from the legal entitlements associated with special education.[28] The IDEA established procedural safeguards—which include due process hearings, complaint resolution, mediation, and the right to a civil trial—to resolve disputes between parents and school districts regarding the education of students with disabilities.

SEEP estimates show that districts spent $146.5 million on these due process activities (including litigation) in 1999–2000, accounting for only 0.3 percent of total special education spending in that year (Chambers, Harr, & Dhanani, 2003). If we apply this figure to all special education students, the average expenditure per special education student is $24. The rates at which these procedural activities occur are also relatively low, with a reported five due process hearings, seven mediation cases, and less than one litigation case per 10,000 students with disabilities (U.S. General Accounting Office, 2003; Chambers et al., 2003).

While the data seem to suggest that concerns about the cost of special education due process guarantees may be over stated, individual cases can sometimes be quite costly for districts. Furthermore, the SEEP cost estimates do not include the degree to which the threat of litigation may be causing districts to provide more special education services than they believe are required, thus indirectly driving up special education costs (Asimov, 2006; Nussbaum, 2003).

Accountability and Adequacy

A final set of issues pertains to changes in the focus of accountability for special education programs. Historically, most emphasis has been placed on fiscal and procedural accountability. More recently, however, the focus of special education accountability has shifted to educational outcomes. The federal No Child Left Behind (NCLB) legislation and state-specific accountability systems clearly reinforce this conceptual shift. The NCLB specifies participation requirements for the testing of specific subgroups of the student population, including those in special education. It also requires that test scores be reported separately for each racial, economic, and programmatic subgroup within each school, and specifies clear school- and district-level sanctions when these participation or performance goals are not met.

The increased emphasis on education accountability and clearly specified educational outcomes for all students has led to a number of court cases related to the adequacy of education funding (Koski, this volume). The resulting judicial pressure has forced many state policymakers to try to determine the cost of providing an adequate education, given the state's implicit (or sometimes explicit) education outcome standard (Downes & Stiefel, this volume). Virtually all of the adequacy studies that have been conducted in various states incorporate special education to some degree. The attention given to special education adequacy, however, has been mixed and has been far less thorough than that given to general education (Harr, Parrish, Chambers, Levin, & Segarra, 2006).

The term "cost" in such adequacy studies is defined as the minimum expenditure required to achieve a specified standard of educational outcomes. Adequacy debates and litigation proceedings across the nation are complicated by the nature of special education law and the students it is designed to serve. For example, how do outcome standards apply to students with severe disabilities? How can the cost of adequacy be determined across the broad array and mix of services appropriate for individual special education students? In addition, the very nature of the federal law, in which every eligible student must be served in accordance with an IEP, seems counter to the notion of a standardized set of state adequacy resource standards.

The concept of the IEP arguably reflects one basis for considering adequate education for special education students. The IEP is a legal contract in which the unique needs of the student must be fully examined by a multi-disciplinary team of appropriate professionals to establish educational goals and to specify the location, frequency, and duration of services necessary to make progress toward those goals. According to the federal special education law, the cost of the services alone cannot be used as a reason to preclude services considered necessary to provide a student with disabilities with a free and appropriate education. Supplementing these IDEA provisions, the NCLB contains further requirements to ensure that professionals delivering various educational services have the appropriate qualifications.

One concern is that these provisions may lead districts to provide services beyond what is needed to reach a specified education standard, and hence lead to excessive spending. While these concerns are valid, the considerable pressure regarding rising special education spending may serve as a counter balance. In addition, special education law and regulatory provisions require audits and other checks designed to align IEPs with specified education goals and to not authorize services beyond what each child's educational objectives require.

For these reasons, it might be argued that current practice reflects a better and more systematic assessment of what is needed to achieve specified and appropriate educational objectives for special education students than is true for other students. In this sense, studies measuring expenditures (e.g., Chambers et. al., 2002, as described above) and quantities of special education staff, as reported annually by the states to the U.S. Department of Education, provide rational bases for considering special education adequacy given current levels of general education.

Providing an adequate general education (which studies have shown to be higher than current levels) may reduce what is ultimately needed for special education. Considering special education provisions within the context of an adequate general education requires a comprehensive approach to the estimation of adequacy, such as that provided by the professional judgment approach (see chapter by Downes and Steifel, this volume on alternative approaches to estimating adequacy, and also Harr et. al., 2006, which contains further discussion of special education adequacy).

Further consideration of special education accountability and adequacy may also advance the concept of special education service standards. For example, what percentage of special education students might be expected to receive speech therapy in a medium-to-large school district? What is a reasonable caseload for a speech therapist? While these measures will, and should, vary to reflect differing local conditions, a greater understanding of what might be reasonably expected in regard to special education resource allocation may assist districts and states in self-evaluating their service practices, and could be an integral piece of state and federal monitoring (Parrish et al., 2002; Parrish & Harr, 2005; Benzel, 2005).

CONCLUSION

Special education students are like all other students in some fundamental ways. At the same time, the degree of variation in the characteristics and educational needs within the category of students determined eligible for special education is immense. Regardless of where they fit on the broad spectrum of disability needs, students in special education are distinct from all other students by virtue of their educational entitlement. School districts are contractually bound to provide students in special education with a full set of supplemental services appropriate to their individual needs that, according to the judgment of a professional team, will allow the students to meet specified educational outcomes.

This legal entitlement to special education services has sometimes produced tensions. Given escalating special education spending, increased accountability for all students, and the growing adequacy-based school finance litigation across the states, we expect increased discussion of some form of special education service standards to emerge. Such standards could further the consideration of what types and quantities of special education services are adequate for special education students and how this relates to adequacy standards for all students.

Adequate funding for special education cannot be considered in a vacuum. Special education students come from general education student population, and most special education students continue to be highly reliant on a mix of general and special education services. As described by Mittnacht (2005), "Ultimately, it makes sense in our efforts to resolve funding issues that we not start with how to fund special education, but rather with how to fund general education."

NOTES

1. Derived from IDEA data, www.ideadata.org.
2. Derived from IDEA data, www.ideadata.org.
3. In 2004–05, 98 percent of students with IEPs took statewide reading assessments, with about 12 percent being provided alternative assessments (O'Reilly, Fafard, Wagner, & Brown, 2006). This suggests that the vast majority of students with disabilities are held to the same standards as their non-disabled peers.
4. Derived from IDEA data, www.ideadata.org.
5. These state-level data are in *State Special Education Finance Systems, 1999–2000, Part II* available at http:// www.csef-air.org.
6. See Levin & McEwan (2001) for a full description of this approach and why it is considered preferable to more traditional analyses of expenditure reports or budgets for purposes of estimating program costs.
7. However, some states elected to over-sample for the national SEEP data collection. Comparable spending estimates for these seven states are presented in Chambers et al., 2005.
8. The full set of data collection instruments is available at http://csef.air.org/about_seep_instruments.php.
9. Please see Chaikind, Danielson, & Brauen (1993) for a comparative analysis of the first three studies.
10. These figures include preschool special education students.
11. Estimates of per pupil expenditure for a general education student are based on a combination of data from the SEEP school surveys and SEEP surveys for those special education students who spend the vast majority of their time in the general education classroom. Expenditures for these students include both direct instruction as well as administration and support services provided to the typical general education student.
12. The 1977–78 school year was two years after passage of the Education for All Handicapped Children Act, PL 94-142, the predecessor to the IDEA.
13. In addition to the national SEEP, all 50 states were invited to extend their participation in this study to obtain state-representative samples that could be used to address state-level policy concerns related to special education finance. Eleven states opted for a state-specific SEEP study, and 7 of the 11 state provided permission to release the results.
14. For comparability across the states, the figures presented are for school-age students only (excluding preschool).
15. Data used for this analysis included the 2004–05 counts of special education personnel and special education students as reported by the states to the federal government (http://www.ideadata.org), and national teacher salary for 2004–05 from the National Center for Education Statistics (http://nces.

ed.gov/programs/digest/d05/tables/dt05_077.asp). For the aide salary, we applied the ratio of special education teacher's salary to an aide salary to the NCES teacher salary.

16. These expenditures on special education students include personnel and non-personnel expenditures on general education instruction, special education instruction and related services, other special need programs (e.g., Title I, ELL), general school and district administration and support, special education program administration and support, general and special transportation services, and school facilities. Average expenditure estimates for specialized equipment are not unique to the student level and therefore may not reflect the actual expenditures for each disability type. It is expected that the estimates for disability categories with high special equipment needs are understated, and estimates for disability categories that have fewer such needs are overstated. Preschool students are not included in this data. Because of the way in which SEEP staff sampled students served in external placements, expenditures for this subset of students are not included in the expenditures by category of disability, and are reported separately as a group. These students in external placements are generally served in non-public schools or schools operated by other public agencies. This group of students exhibited the highest average total expenditure ($25,580).
17. Chambers et al. (2004) used a multivariate analysis that controlled for other student characteristics such as age and ethnicity and a series of community and state characteristics including district size, a geographic cost of education index, and dichotomous variables controlling for the state in which services were provided (see Exhibit 2 in Chambers et al., 2004).
18. Averages are based on 37 states that reported this information.
19. As described below, the IDEA Part B formula which allocates federal revenues to the states in support of school-age special education programs is census based with an additional adjustment for poverty. State census-based formulas may also have adjustments to the basic concept of special education funding based on total enrollment.
20. These states include Alabama, Alaska, California, Connecticut, Idaho, Massachusetts, Missouri, Montana, North Dakota, Pennsylvania, South Dakota, and Vermont.
21. The 2004 regulations of the IDEA defines APPE, as the aggregate current expenditures of all local education authorities in the 50 States and the District of Columbia, including any direct expenditures by the state for the operation of those agencies; Divided by the aggregate number of children in average daily attendance. Please see §300.717 in the Federal Register (June 21, 2005) for the official regulations: http://a257.g.akamaitech.net/7/257/2422/01jan20051800/edocket.access.gpo.gov/2005/pdf/05-11804.pdf.
22. The 1996–7 figure comes from Harr and Parrish (2005), while the 2006–07 figure is from the Council for Exceptional Children (2006).
23. The census formula was the sole mechanism in only 9 of the 12 states with some form of census-based system. The other three states combined the census system with other distribution methods, such as pupil weights.
24. The lowest and highest spending quartiles of districts in this study had 29 percent and 30 percent poverty, respectively. The lowest and highest spending quartiles were also similar in the percent of the special education population with disabilities other than specific learning disability, speech, and language impairment, and emotional disturbance, with 19 percent and 16 percent respectively.
25. An Internet search of special education encroachment produced several records posted by school districts in California, documenting the amounts of general funds going towards special education expenditures.
26. Also see Greene & Winters (2007), who discredit arguments that private placements for special education students have resulted in general education encroachment.
27. Early work on student study teams, an approach similar to the "response to intervention" model, showed reductions in referrals to special education, including reductions in inappropriate referrals to special education (Sheilds, Jay, Parrish, & Padilla, 1989).
28. See Asimov (2006), Cowan (2005), and Nussbaum (2003) as examples of recent popular media articles on special education litigation.

REFERENCES

Asimov, N. (2006, February 19). Extra-special Education at Public Expense. *San Francisco Chronicle*. Retrieved 2/20/06 from: http://www.sfgate.com/cgi-bin/article.cgi?f=/c/a/2006/02/19/MNG8THBH4V1.DTL&hw=Extra+special&sn=001&sc=1000

Beales, J.R. (1993). Special Education: Expenditures and Obligations. Retrieved 12/22/06 from: http://www.reason.org/ps161.html.

Benzel, B. (2005). Superintendent's Commentary: Reflections on Special Education Funding and Our Commitment to Students. *Journal of Special Education Leadership*, 18(1), 47-49.

Chaikind, S., Danielson, L.C., & Brauen, M.L. (1993). What Do We Know About the Costs of Special Education? A Selected Eeview. *The Journal of Special Education*, 26(4), 344-370.

Chambers, J., Harr, J. J., & Dhanani, A. (2003). What Are We Spending on Procedural Safeguards in Special Education, 1999–2000. Special Education Expenditure Project (SEEP). Palo Alto, CA: American Institutes for Research, Center for Special Education Finance.

Chambers, J., Parrish, T., & Harr, J. J. (2002). What Are We Spending on Special Education Services in the United States, 1999–2000? Special Education Expenditure Project (SEEP). Palo Alto, CA: American Institutes for Research, Center for Special Education Finance.

Chambers, J., Pérez, M., & Esra, P. (2005). Funding to Support the Highest-Need Students with Disabilities. *Journal of Special Education Leadership*, 18(1), 14-21.

Chambers, J.G., Pérez, M., Harr J.J., & Shkolnik, J. (2005). Special Education Spending Estimates From 1999-2000. *Journal of Special Education Leadership*, 18(1), 5-13.

Chambers, J.G., Pérez, M., Socias, M., Shkolnik, J., Esra, P., & Brown, S.C. (2004). Explaining Variations in Expenditures for Students with Disabilities: Comparing the Roles of the IDEA Disability Categories and the Abilities Index. Palo Alto, CA: American Institutes for Research.

Council for Exceptional Children (2006). Full Funding for the IDEA. Retrieved 12/21/06 at: http://www.cec.sped.org/Content/NavigationMenu/PolicyAdvocacy/IDEAResources/FullFunding.pdf

Cowan, A.L. (2005, April 24). Amid Affluence, a Struggle Over Special Education. *New York Times*. Retrieved 12/22/06 from: http://www.nytimes.com/2005/04/24/education/24westport.html?ex=1167109200&en=a88448409e388c78&ei=5070

Donovan, M.S., & Cross, C.T. (2002). *Minority students in special and gifted education*. Washington, DC: National Academy Press.

Greene, J.P. & Forster, G. F. (2002). Effects of funding incentives on special education enrollment. Civic Report No. 32, December 2002, Center for Civic Innovation, Manhattan Institute, New York.

Greene, J.P. & Winters, M.A. (2007). Debunking a Special Education Myth: Don't blame private options for rising costs. *Education Next* (no. 2). Retrieved 3/21/2007 from: http://www.hoover.org/publications/ednext/5895486.html.

Harr, J.J., & Parrish, T. (2005). The Impact of Federal Increases in Special Education Funding. *Journal of Special Education Leadership*, 18(1), 28-37.

Harr, J.J., Parrish, T., Chambers, J., Levin, J., & Segarra, M. (2006). Considering Special Education Adequacy in California. Palo Alto, CA: American Institutes for Research.

Hartman, W.T. (1992). State funding models for special education. *Remedial and Special Education*, 13 (6), 47–58.

Kakalik, J.S., Furry, W.S., Thomas, M.A., & Carney, M.F. (1981). *The Cost of Special Education*. Santa Monica, CA: The Rand Corporation.

Levin, H.M. & McEwan, P.J. (2001). *Cost-Effectiveness Analysis* (2nd Edition). Thousand Oaks, CA: Sage Publications, Inc.

Little Hoover Commission (1997, July). Dollars and Sense: A Simpler Approach to School Finance. Report #143. Milton Marks "Little Hoover" Commission on California State Government Organization and Economy. Retrieved 12/22/06 from: http://www.lhc.ca.gov/lhcdir/143/TC143.html.

Mahitivanichcha, K., & Parrish, T. (2005, April). Do Non-census Funding Systems Encourage Special Education Identification? Reconsidering Greene and Forster. *Journal of Special Education Leadership*, 18(1), 38-46.

McLaughlin, M. & Rouse, M. (Eds). (2000). *Special Education and School Reform in Britain and the United States*. London & New York: Routledge.

Mittnacht, M. (2005). Case in Point: Funding Special Education – Are We Asking the Right Questions? *Journal of Special Education Leadership*, 18(1), 50-52.

Moore, M.T., Strang, E.W., Schwartz, M., & Braddock, M. (1988). *Patterns in Special Education Service Delivery and Cost*. Washington, DC: Decision Resources Corporation.

Mosher, E.K., Hastings, A.H., & Wagoner, J.L. (1979). *Pursuing Equal Opportunity: School Politics and the New Activists*. New York: ERIC Clearinghouse on Urban Education, Teachers College, Columbia University.

Naylor, N. (2001). The Ontario Special Education Funding Model. *Journal of Special Education Leadership*, 14(1), 21-26.

Nussbaum, D. (2003, August 31). Reining in Special Education. *New York Times*. Retrieved 12-22-06 from: http://query.nytimes.com/gst/fullpage.html?res=9401E3DF1438F932A0575BC0A9659C8B63&sec=health&spon=&pagewanted=1

Organization for Economic Co-operation and Development (2005). *Students with Disabilities, Learning Difficulties and Disadvantages: Statistics and Indicators*. Paris: OECD.

Organization for Economic Co-operation and Development (1995). *Integrating Students with Special Needs into Mainstream Schools*. Paris: OECD.

O'Reilly, F., Fafard, M., Wagner, M., & Brown, S.C. (2006). *Improving Results for Students with Disabilities: Key Findings from the 1997 National Assessment Studies*. Bethesda, MD: Abt Associates.

Parrish, T. (2000). Restructuring Special Education Funding in New York to Promote the Objective of Higher Learning Standards for All Students. *Economics of Education Review*, 19(4), 431-445.

Parrish, T. (1994). Fiscal policies in special education: Removing incentives for restrictive placements. Policy Paper No. 4. Palo Alto, CA: Center for Special Education Finance, American Institutes for Research.

Parrish, T., & Bitter, C.S. (2003). Special Education in the City: How Has the Money Been Spent and What Do We Have to Show for It? *Journal of Special Education Leadership*, 16(1), 34-40.

Parrish, T. & Harr, J. (2005). *Special Education Funding Issues in Washington*. Palo Alto, CA: American Institutes for Research.

Parrish, T., Harr, J., Wolman, J., Anthony, J., Merickel, A., & Esra, P. (2004, March). *State Special Education Finance Systems, 1999–2000: Part II: Special Education Revenues and Expenditures*. Palo Alto, CA: American Institutes for Research, Center for Special Education Finance.

Parrish, T., Harr, J., Anthony, A. Merickel, & Esra, P. (2003). *State Special Education Finance Systems, 1999–2000, Part I*. Palo Alto, CA: American Institutes for Research, Center for Special Education Finance.

Parrish, T., Harr, J.J., Pérez, M., Esra, P., Brock, L., & Shkolnik, J. (2002). *Wyoming Special Education Expenditure Project and Cost Based Funding Model: Final Report*. Palo Alto, CA: American Institutes for Research.

Parrish, T., & Kaleba, D. (1998). *Movement Toward Census-Based Funding Continues Amidst Questions. The CSEF Resource*. Palo Alto, CA: American Institutes for Research, Center for Special Education Finance.

Parrish, T., & Verstegen, D.A. (1994). *Fiscal Provisions of the Individuals with Disabilities Education Act: Issues and Alternatives for Reauthorization—Policy Paper No. 3*. Palo Alto, CA: American Institutes for Research, Center for Special Education Finance.

Rossmiller, R.A., Hale, J.A., & Frohreich, L.E. (1970). Resource Configurations and Costs (National Educational Finance Project, Special Study No. 2). Madison, WI: University of Wisconsin, Department of Educational Administration.

Shields, P.M., Jay, D.E., Parrish, T., & Padilla, C. (1989). *Alternative programs and strategies for serving students with learning disabilities and other learning problems—Final report*. Menlo Park, CA: SRI International.

United States General Accounting Office (2003). Special Education: Numbers of Formal Disputes Are Generally Low and States Are Using Mediation and Other Strategies to Resolve Conflicts. Report GAO-

03-897 to the Ranking Minority Member, Committee on Health, Education, Labor and Pensions, U.S. Senate. Washington, DC: U.S. General Accounting Office.

Verstegen, D. (1994). *Fiscal Provisions of the Individuals with Disabilities Education Act: Historical Overview.* Palo Alto, CA: American Institutes for Research, Center for Special Education Finance.

33

Resource Needs for Educating Linguistic Minority Students

Russell W. Rumberger and Patricia Gándara

INTRODUCTION

Although all students are expected to meet the same challenging standards, students differ greatly in their initial social and cognitive skills when they first enter school, and in the family and community resources available to support their learning during school. As a result, some students need more support and resources in school than other students. What amount and types of resources do such students need? This chapter addresses this question regarding one of the fastest growing segments of the student population—students who come from households where a language other than English is spoken—so-called linguistic minority (LM) students.

Most linguistic minority students are not yet proficient in English when they start school. These students, referred to as English learners (ELs), require additional resources and support not only to become proficient in English, but also to learn the same academic content as English-only students. Yet while the literature on school finance has recognized the resource needs of English learners—as we illustrate below—the resource needs for all children from non-English homes have been largely overlooked in this literature. For the most part, when students are classified as fluent in English—whether this occurs when they first enter school or sometime later—their needs for specialized educational support are largely ignored, so the task of determining what their resource needs are is more complex. Throughout the chapter we attempt to clarify the distinction between the larger population of linguistic minority students and the subgroup of those students who are not proficient in English.

THE LINGUISTIC MINORITY POPULATION

Linguistic minorities represent one of the largest and fastest growing segments of the school-age population in the United States. According to data from the U.S. Census, there were 10.5 million children, ages 5–17, who spoke a language other than English at home in 2005, representing 20 percent of the school-age population (Table 33.1). The vast majority—77 percent—spoke Spanish. In some states the proportion of linguistic minorities was much higher: in California, for example, 44 percent of the school age population in 2005 were linguistic minorities (Rumberger, 2006).

TABLE 33.1
Linguistic Minority Population in the United States, 1980–2005

	1980		*2005*		*Change 1980–2005*	
	Number	*Percent of total*	*Number*	*Percent of total*	*Number*	*Percent of total*
All speakers, age 5–17	47,493,975	100.0	52,864,512	100.0	5,370,537	11.3
English only	42,925,646	90.4	42,357,558	80.1	–568,088	–1.3
Language other than English	4,568,329	9.6	10,506,954	19.9	5,938,625	130.0
Speak Spanish	2,952,462	6.2	7,529,646	14.2	4,577,184	155.0
Speak non-Spanish language	1,615,867	3.4	2,977,308	5.6	1,361,441	84.3

Source: U.S. Bureau of the Census, 1980 Census of the Population, Volume 1, Characteristics of the population. Chapters C/D, Detailed social and economic characteristics, Parts 1 and 6 (Washington, D.C.: U.S. Bureau of the Census, 1983); U.S. Bureau of the Census, 2005 American Community Survey. Retrieved October 5, 2006, from http://www.census.gov/acs/www/index.html

Over the last 25 years, the linguistic minority population has exploded relative to the English-only population. Between 1980 and 2005, the linguistic minority population in the Untied States more than doubled, while the English-only population actually declined. This means that virtually all of the more than 5 million additional school-age children in the United States over the last 25 years were linguistic minorities.

The LM population consists of two subgroups based on their level of English proficiency: students who are not yet proficient in English are classified as English learners (ELs), while students who are proficient in English are classified as Fluent English Proficient (FEP). FEP students can be further classified based on whether they were proficient when they initially entered school (I-FEP) or whether they became proficient during school, which means they were reclassified from EL to FEP (R-FEP). In general, the proportion of LM students classified as FEP increases as students progress in school. In California, for example, only 15 percent of linguistic minorities were classified as FEP in kindergarten in 2005, whereas 54 percent were classified as FEP in eighth grade.[1]

The process for reclassifying EL students as proficient is an important policy area, and one that has resource implications as well.[2]A number of criteria—including English proficiency and academic achievement—are used to determine whether linguistic minorities are ELs or FEP, and these criteria differ for students' initial classifications when they first enter school (I-FEP), and subsequent reclassification (R-FEP) once they progress in school (Gándara & Merino, 1993; Linquanti, 2001; Zehler et al., 2003). Moreover, local education agencies are accorded considerable latitude in their redesignation practices, leading to widespread differences in reclassification rates (Parrish et al., 2006, Chapter V).[3] Because of these differences, the relative size and characteristics of both the EL and FEP groups can vary greatly from one location to another, and over time. This makes identifying educational needs for both groups of students difficult. Nonetheless, as we show below, students who are reclassified as FEP continue to have needs, even if they initially meet what appear to be high standards when they are first reclassified.

School Performance

The academic achievement of linguistic minority children, particularly those who are not yet proficient in English, lags far behind children from English-only backgrounds. For example, data from the National Assessment of Educational Progress (NAEP) reveal that test scores of EL students range between 0.86 and 1.14 standard deviations below the scores of English-only stu-

TABLE 33.2
2005 NAEP Reading and Math Scale Scores by English Learner Status

	All		*English only*		*English learner*		*Achievement Gap*[a]
	Scale score	*SD*	*Scale score*	*Row percentage*	*Scale score*	*Row percentage*	
Reading							
Grade 4	219	37	222	92	187	8	0.95
Grade 8	262	35	264	95	224	5	1.14
Math							
Grade 4	238	28	240	91	216	9	0.86
Grade 8	279	36	281	95	244	5	1.03

[a]Achievement Gap = [Scale score (English only)-scale score (English learner)]/Standard deviation (All).
Source: NAEP Data Tool. Retrieved July 13, 2005, from http://nces.ed.gov/nationsreportcard/naepdata/

dents (Table 33.2). These are considered large achievement gaps.[4] Of course as English learners become proficient in English, they are reclassified as FEP, so at the higher grades, the proportion of ELs decreases, while the achievement gap for those remaining EL students increases.

Data also reveal that even English learners who are reclassified as FEP and who initially perform higher than English-only (EO) students in the lower grades, begin to fall behind in the secondary grades (Gándara & Rumberger, 2006, Figure 2). Because the population of English learners declines as more and more students are reclassified as FEP, it is important to gauge the combined performance of current ELs and former ELs (R-FEP). Such an analysis conducted with California data reveals that between grades 2 and 11—the period when students are tested—the achievement gap between English-only students and current/former EL students remains essentially unchanged. Of course, it is important to note that any assessment of English learners with tests administered in English only, and that were not designed for or normed on EL students, will yield less-than-valid results. Thus, test data for EL students should be interpreted with great caution. Nonetheless, important decisions are made about students and schools based on these scores.

School Readiness

One reason for the underachievement of linguistic minority students is that they come from more disadvantaged backgrounds than English-only students and, hence, begin school at a significant disadvantage compared to their English-speaking peers. Some indicators of this disadvantage for kindergarten students in 1998–99, based on data from the Early Childhood Longitudinal Study (ECLS), are shown in Table 33.3.

One indicator is socioeconomic status (SES)—a composite measure based on family income, parental education, and occupational status—that provides a useful indicator of family, human, and financial resources. The data reveal a gap of 0.38 standard deviations in SES between EO and LM students at the beginning of kindergarten. Similar gaps exist in oral and written language skills and in math achievement at the beginning of kindergarten.[5] Linguistic minority students suffer from disparities in other areas as well. For example, linguistic minority students are less likely to participate in center-based preschool: 41 percent of linguistic minority students attended center-based preschool, compared to 59 percent of English-only students (Rumberger & Tran, 2006, Table 4).

TABLE 33.3
Selected Indicators of Family Background and School Readiness by Language Background, 1998–99 Kindergarteners

	English only	*Language minority*	*Gap*
Socioeconomic status (SES)	0.09	–0.29	0.38
Language skills	0.10	–0.33	0.43
Math achievement	0.09	–0.31	0.40

Note: Indicators are standardized with national mean of zero and standard deviation of one for the entire population of kindergartners.
Source: Analysis of data from the Early Children Longitudinal Study of the Kindergarten Class of 1998 (N = 17,424)

EDUCATIONAL GOALS FOR LINGUISTIC MINORITY STUDENTS

Identifying the resource needs for educating linguistic minorities requires determining the educational goals for these students, and then specifying the educational programs designed to meet these goals. Ideally, these two things would be specified sequentially—that is, first the goals would be established and then the programs would be developed and implemented to meet these goals. The two activities might also be carried out by different agencies: state educational agencies, for example, might set educational goals for linguistic minority students, along with goals for other students, while local education agencies might design a variety of programs to meet these goals based on local needs and capacity.

In reality, however, the two have been inextricably linked substantively and politically for more than 30 years. A number of different government agencies have specified both goals and programs for linguistic minority students over this period. One reason is that the education of linguistic minorities, as with all students, is the province of local, state, and federal government agencies. Another reason is the education of linguistic minorities has been and continues to be a politically-charged issue at the local, state, and national levels.

Over the last 40 years, federal legislation, federal courts, and state legislation have together specified five educational goals for linguistic minority students, and a number of programs to meet those goals:

1. Access to the core curriculum
2. English language proficiency
3. Native language proficiency
4. Closing the achievement gap
5. Cultural competence

Below we provide a brief history of these policy activities and the educational goals and programs they have endorsed.

Federal Legislation[6]

The education of linguistic minority students was first addressed at the federal level through provisions of Title VI of the 1964 Civil Rights Act, prohibiting discrimination on the grounds of race, color, or national origin. The Equal Educational Opportunities Act of 1974 (EEOA) spelled out more explicitly what constitutes the denial of equal educational opportunity to include "the failure of an educational agency to take appropriate action to overcome language barriers that impede equal participation by its students in instructional programs" (EEOA, 1974, Sec. 1703 [f], p. 136).

The U.S Congress first passed legislation that specifically focused on the education of linguistic minority students in the Bilingual Education Act (BEA) of 1968 (Title VI of the Elementary and Secondary Education Act of 1965). The Act provided funds for local education agencies to develop programs to provide "meaningful and equitable access for English-language learners to the curriculum" (August & Hakuta, 1997, p. 16) without prescribing a particular program of instruction. Thus, the first legislative goal for linguistic minority students was simply access to the core curriculum, with no mention of either primary or English language development, and no mention of the types of instructional programs that might achieve that goal.

In the 1974 reauthorization of the BEA, however, Congress encouraged "the establishment and operation... of education programs using bilingual education practices, techniques, and methods" (BEA, 1974, Sec. 702 [a]). The legislation went on to define bilingual education as "instruction given in... English, and, to the extent necessary to allow a child to progress effectively through the educational system, the native language (BEA, 1974, Sec. 703[a][4][A][i]). In this legislation, the federal government established a second goal for linguistic minority students—English proficiency—and specified an instructional program to meet both this goal and the goal of access to the core curriculum—bilingual education. In this case, native language instruction was not a goal itself, but simply a means for learning the core curriculum.

Subsequent reauthorizations of the BEA in 1978, 1984, and 1988 shifted the focus of instruction to achieving competence in the English language and acceptance of English-only programs, and not simply bilingual instruction. But in the 1984 reauthorization, the Congress also specified a third goal: "competence in English and a second language" (BEA, 1984, Sec. 703[a][5][A]), although no specific funding was provided (García, 2005, p. 96). The 1994 reauthorization reinforced the goal of bilingual proficiency by giving "priority to applications that provided for the development of bilingual proficiency both in English and another language for all participating students" (BEA, 1994, Sec. 7116 [i][1]). At the same time, the legislation reflected the influence of two other pieces of legislation—Goals 2000 and the Improving America's School Act of 1994—that promoted equality and quality education for all students. For the first time, Title VII programs would help linguistic minority students "meet the same challenging State content standards and challenging State performance standards expected for all children and youth" (BEA, 1994, Sec. 7111 [2][B]).

Federal policy for linguistic minority students changed once again with the reauthorization of the Elementary and Secondary Education Act in 2002, called the No Child Left Behind Act (NCLB). The BEA (Title VII) was replaced with the Language Instruction for Limited English Proficient and Immigrant Students (Title III of NCLB) and the term "bilingual" was completely removed from the legislation and all federal offices and programs (Wiley & Wright, 2004, p. 155). The stated purpose of Title III was "to ensure that children who are limited English proficient, including immigrant children and youth, attain English proficiency" (NCLB, 2002, Title III, Sec. 3102), although the law does allow "instructional use of both English and a child's native language." The legislation requires developing and attaining "annual measurable achievement objectives" (AMOs) for English-language proficiency that some critics claim are "strict, complex, and questionable" (Wiley & Wright, 2004, p. 157). The legislation also requires schools and districts to demonstrate "adequate yearly progress" for all students, including EL students, to meet state proficiency standards, with a requirement that all students reach proficiency by the year 2014. The requirement that schools must demonstrate that EL students are making adequate progress meeting the same standards required of native-born English-speaking students, in spite of significantly greater challenges and without specifying additional resource needs to meet them, has placed many schools in jeopardy of losing their accreditation, sometimes in spite of their best efforts. Some critics have also called attention to the ways in which such policies can stigmatize EL students as a source of problems for their schools (Novak & Fuller, 2003). NCLB also established a fourth goal for linguistic minority students: "...closing the achievement gap between high- and low-performing children, especially the achievement gaps between minority and non-minority students, and between disadvantaged children and their more advantaged peers" (U.S. Dept. of Education, 2003, Title 1, Sec. 1001).

Federal Courts

The federal courts have a long history of involvement with the education of linguistic minority students (García, 2005, pp. 77–85). The courts have primarily focused on establishing the rights of linguistic minority students and, in doing so, also specified educational goals for these students.

The most noteworthy court case was *Lau v. Nichols*. The case was filed on behalf of Chinese-speaking students in San Francisco who received instruction only in English while Spanish-speaking students were provided special assistance. Rejecting a lower court ruling, the U.S. Supreme Court ruled "Basic English skills are at the very core of what these public schools teach. Imposition of a requirement that, before a child can effectively participate in the educational program, he must already have acquired those basic skills is to make a mockery of public education" (414 U.S., 563 (1974). Essentially, the Court established the first goal—access to the core curriculum—at the same time the U.S. Congress was specifying the same goal in the BEA of 1974. Yet, like the Congress, the Court did not specify a remedy, or what kind of instructional program would provide students with access to the core curriculum.

Subsequent court cases have tended to weaken the legal underpinnings of the *Lau* decision, and thus have afforded few legal avenues to broaden or even maintain reasonable educational goals for linguistic minority students (Moran, 2004; García, 2005).

State Legislation

The history of state legislation regarding the education of linguistic minority students is varied, in part, because many states have had relatively few linguistic minorities until quite recently. According to a recent tabulation by García (2005), 12 states mandate special services for linguistic minority students, 12 states permit special services, one state prohibits them, and 26 states have no legislation that directly addresses the education of these students (Garcia, 2005, p. 85). For the most part, states that have had sizeable populations of linguistic minorities for some time, such as Texas and California, have a longer history of state legislative activity. California, for example, passed one of the first state-level comprehensive bilingual education bills, entitled the Chacon-Moscone Bilingual-Bicultural Act, in 1976. Texas passed its first such education bill in 1981.

By and large, most state legislation has focused on the second educational goal to "as effectively and efficiently as possible, ... develop in each child fluency in English" (California Education Code, 1976, Section 52161). But 17 states allow or require instruction in a language other than English, and 15 states mandate a cultural component (García, 2005, p. 85).

In three states—California, Arizona, and Massachusetts—state policy regarding the education of linguistic minorities has been dictated by recent ballot initiatives. These initiatives have restricted the educational goals for linguistic minorities to learning English, and they dictated a single educational program to achieve it: structured English immersion. Access to native language instruction is severely restricted and requires a complex process of parental waivers.

In addition to specifying goals and programs, some states have specified instructional materials, assessments, and teacher credential requirements for educating linguistic minorities (García, 2005, pp. 85–89).

EDUCATIONAL PROGRAMS FOR LINGUISTIC MINORITY STUDENTS

Just as there are a number of different goals for educating linguistic minority students, a number of educational programs have been developed to meet these goals. Most educational programs have been developed only to serve LM students who have been identified as ELs. Most of these programs contain a number of specific elements that depend not only on the goals or standards of the program, but also on the characteristics of the EL population at the school and on the school and district context. Salient characteristics of the population that would affect resource needs include family background (income and SES), the number of years in the United States, age and grade level of the students, native language proficiency, and initial English language proficiency and academic achievement. For example, poor EL students with low initial levels of English proficiency would generally need more intensive programs and resources than non-poor EL students with high initial levels of English proficiency (NCSL, 2005). Schools with EL students from a single language background, such as Spanish, may need fewer program elements and resources than schools with EL students from many language backgrounds (Rumberger, Gándara, & Merino, 2006). Of course, the actual programs and services that English learners actually receive is largely unknown—there are some infrequent national surveys, as we describe below, and, at best, states collect general program information on such features as language of instruction.

Instructional Program

The key element of any educational program for English learners is an instructional program that addresses at least two goals: English language proficiency and access to the core curriculum. The defining feature of the instructional program, and the one that has been the focus of most of the policy debates over the last 40 years, is the language of instruction. Some instructional programs for EL students are conducted only in English, while others are conducted in both English and the children's native language, which are commonly referred to as bilingual programs.

Bilingual programs can be further characterized by the extent and goals of the native language instruction (see Table 33.4); in some programs, known as early-exit or transitional bilingual programs, the extent of native language instruction is limited to a relatively short time (one to three years) and the only goals are to facilitate the learning of English and to provide access to the core curriculum during that transition period (which can, and often does, imply early literacy as well). In other programs, known as late-exit programs, the goal of the program is to develop literacy in the native language as well as in English, so the duration of primary language instruction is much longer, usually until the transition to middle school. Still another type of bilingual program, known as a dual-immersion or two-way bilingual program, enrolls native English speakers along with English learners with the goal of full literacy in both languages, and subject matter proficiency for both groups of students.

As discussed earlier, the choice of instructional programs has often been influenced and sometimes prescribed by federal and state policy. And, increasingly, those prescribed instructional programs use only English. Yet an ever-growing body of research supports the value of native language instruction. The most recent and extensive review of the research by the federal government-appointed National Literacy Panel on Language-Minority Youth and Children (August

TABLE 33.4
Major Program Models for English Learners

Program	*Description*
English immersion ("sheltered English")	Use of English-only strategies; English as a second language; specially designed academic instruction in English; usually lasts 1–3 years
Transitional bilingual education/early exit	Instruction using some primary language for transitional support; may teach early reading in primary language but normally makes transition to English only within 2–3 years; goal is literacy in English
Developmental bilingual/late exit	Emphasis on developing competence in two languages; students may receive instruction in primary and second language for many years; goal is literacy in two languages
Two-way immersion ("dual immersion")	English speakers and English learners taught together with focus on two languages; emphasis on strengthening minority language; goal is biliteracy; usually lasts 6 years or more

& Shanahan, 2006) concluded: "Studies that compare bilingual instruction with English-only instruction demonstrate that language-minority students instructed in their native language, as well as in English, perform better, on average, on measures of English reading proficiency than language-minority students instructed only in English" (p. 5).

Despite the growing research base supporting native language instruction, most linguistic minority students in the U.S. are instructed in English. A recent national survey of school LEP coordinators found that 60 percent of LEP students were taught entirely in English; 20 percent were taught with some (2 to 24 percent) native language instruction; and 20 percent were taught with at least 25 percent native language instruction (Zehler et al., 2003, p. 36).

A second key feature of the instructional program is the extent it provides instructional services that are specifically designed for English learners. The national survey also found that 12 percent of EL (LEP) students received no specific instructional services; 36 percent received supplemental instructional services (e.g., aides, resource teachers, and/or fewer than 10 hours a week of ESL instruction); and 60 percent received extensive instructional services where a significant amount of instruction was designed for LEP students (Zehler et al., 2003, p. 36).

A third key feature of the instructional program concerns instructional time. To acquire English and to master the core curriculum, English learners need additional instructional time. In 1963 psychologist John Carroll developed a model of school learning that posited learning as a function of: (1) aptitude, or the time students need to learn (which is inversely related to the quality of instruction and students' ability to understand instruction); (2) opportunity to learn, or the time allowed for learning; and (3) perseverance, or the amount of time students are willing to spend on learning (Carroll, 1963, 1989). The model suggests that some students need more time for learning than other students and that increased time allocated to learning can increase achievement (all else being equal). A number of case studies have documented how effective schools often devote more time to student learning than typical schools (Gándara, 2000; Farbman & Kaplan, 2005) and some experimental evidence has documented that increased learning time can improve student achievement (Gándara & Fish, 1994). Nonetheless, resources for additional instructional time for English learners are not routinely built into school budgets, and schools that attempt to meet this need often have to seek funding from other sources (Gándara & Rumberger, 2006).

A final key feature of the instructional program concerns class size. Two recent reviews of research literature found that small classes generally improve student achievement, although the impact varies in a nonlinear fashion (Ehrenberg, Brewer, Gamoran, & Willms, 2001; Krueger, 2003). One of the largest and most widely studied experimental studies was in Tennessee, where classes were reduced from 22–27 students to 13–17 students (Mosteller, 1995; Finn & Achilles, 1999). Several studies have documented both short-term and long-term benefits of small classes in Tennessee, especially for minority students (Finn, Gerber, Achilles, & Boyd-Zaharias, 2001). Despite the commonsense notions that increased instructional time and reduced class size should also affect the learning outcomes for English learners—and the fact that effective schools for these students often include such modifications (Gándara & Rumberger, 2006)—no study has ever been conducted to demonstrate these effects.

Supplemental Programs

Meeting the educational goals for ELs may require more than an instructional program, even an extensive program based on the primary language. English learners, especially those who come from socioeconomically disadvantaged backgrounds, may require other programmatic services beyond those found in the regular classroom during the regular school day. Such supplemental programs may include preschool, student support (such as peer or adult tutoring), and family supports. Language minority students who become proficient in English may need continued support to match the progress of their English-background peers, and even more support to reach the goal of closing the achievement gap. Of course, other disadvantaged students who come from English-speaking backgrounds may also need more instructional time, smaller classes, and supplemental programs to meet the same academic standards as more socioeconomically advantaged students.

RESOURCE REQUIREMENTS OF EDUCATIONAL PROGRAMS

To provide effective educational programs for linguistic minority students requires both the right amount and the right type of resources. This section discusses three critical resources needed to educate linguistic minority students: teachers, instructional materials, and assessments. The last section of the paper examines the extent to which the type and amount of resources needed to educate linguistic minority students differs from those required to educate other students.

Teachers

The most important resource for educating students is teachers, both classroom teachers and support teachers. While it is critical to provide a sufficient number of teachers to meet the educational goals for linguistic minority students, it is also critical to provide teachers with the proper skills, abilities, and attitudes for dealing with this population. Unfortunately, there is little rigorous empirical evidence on what attributes of teachers are most effective in improving educational outcomes for students generally, let alone for linguistic minority students (Wayne & Youngs, 2003).

But research on effective instructional approaches to educating linguistic minority students does suggest that teachers of such students need several critical competencies. First, teachers of EL and linguistic minority students need specific pedagogical and discipline-specific knowledge. Wong-Fillmore and Snow (2000) argue that all teachers, but especially those who teach EL students, need to know a great deal about the structure of language, its development in the first and second languages, and how to support and enhance it. Understanding how to use cognates in building new vocabulary, using speech markers, and frequent checks for comprehension, are skills that teachers of EL students must have to be effective (August & Shanahan, 2006). Second, teachers of English learners also need to know how to use assessments to measure language proficiency and to monitor student progress (Genesee, Lindholm-Leary, Saunders, & Christian, 2006, pp. 136–139). Third, teachers of EL students should be bilingual. Clearly, teachers instructing in the primary language must be bilingual. But bilingual skills are also useful in English-only classrooms to provide "support" for bilingual students in their native language by previewing and reviewing instructional activities, monitoring their understanding, and motivating students by building rapport with them.[7] And bilingual skills are invaluable for teachers to communicate and work with the parents of linguistic minority students (Gándara & Maxwell-Jolly, 2005). Finally, while disciplinary knowledge and pedagogical skill are important, the following non-cognitive skills may be the most critical characteristics of effective teachers of EL students: compassion; understanding of the challenges that students face; a strong belief in the students' natural abilities; a deep desire to see students succeed; the ability to motivate students; and a willingness to adapt their instruction to meet the distinctive needs of EL students. A recent review of this literature (Gándara & Maxwell-Jolly, 2005) confirms this view, finding that effective characteristics and "active" teaching behaviors were cited more frequently by researchers as characteristics of effective teachers than other types of knowledge.

Existing data find that relatively few teachers of English learners possess even some of these competencies. A national survey of coordinators and teachers in programs for English learners found that only 40 percent of teachers had "significant EL (LEP) training," which the authors defined as having a bilingual or English as a Second Language (ESL) certification, or having received 20 hours or more of in-service training related to the teaching of English learners (Zehler et al., 2003, p. 72). In fact, the study found that 40 percent of all teachers of English learners had received no in-service training in the previous five years.

Appropriate Instructional Materials

To provide a comprehensive and appropriate instructional program requires appropriate instructional materials. In addition to the core instructional materials, linguistic minority students need both strong English Language Development materials and texts; and bridging material that allows them to access the core curriculum with their more limited vocabularies and knowledge of English language structure (these may include primary language materials, as appropriate). Beyond that, linguistic minority students would benefit from computer-based instructional materials. For example, digitalized curriculum (and the hardware to run it) allows students to devote more time to studying subjects outside regular classroom hours. This can be especially beneficial for secondary students who may have little time to catch up for graduation. Library books need to cover a wide range of levels and be available in the languages of the students, both to stimulate reading among those who are not yet fluent in English, and to provide the opportunity for non-English speaking parents to read with their children.

National data show that relatively few EL students receive appropriate materials. Only 57 percent of EL district coordinators in a recent national survey reported that EL teachers in their districts were provided curriculum materials for their EL students to help them align their instruction to state standards (Zehler et al., 2003, p. 62). A recent study in California found that even when specifically designated materials were developed by textbook publishers, in response to state guidelines, they were often difficult for teachers to use and therefore ineffective (Calfee, 2006).

Valid, Comprehensive Assessments

To provide an adequate education for linguistic minority students requires valid diagnostic, formative, and summative assessments. Diagnostic assessments are needed to evaluate the skills and abilities of linguistic minority students when they first enter school, in both their primary language and English; formative assessments are needed to provide teachers with ongoing information on the progress of linguistic minority students in both language development and subject matter competence; and summative assessments are needed to measure the progress of linguistic minority students in reaching standards and other outcomes, including non-cognitive outcomes. Summative assessments are also useful for holding school systems accountable for providing adequate educational opportunities for students. Moreover, accurate assessment of students' skills can accelerate students' learning, allowing teachers to build on what students already know (Darling-Hammond, Ancess, & Falk, 1995), rather than assuming that students do not know material they cannot demonstrate on a test. This can be especially critical in upper grades where students who have received a formal education in other settings may be placed in courses that are below their skill level, unnecessarily handicapping them in meeting academic requirements.

The development of appropriate assessments is a more technically complex and expensive undertaking than the development of textbooks and other curricula (Abedi, 2002). These issues have been long debated within the testing industry, but without a sufficiently large market and with fluctuating state and national testing policies, there has been little incentive to tackle them. Given the numbers of English learners and linguistic minority students, with the proper signals to the test manufacturers, there would undoubtedly be interest in engaging in this test development. For example, the enforcement of NCLB's guidelines that states must use valid and reliable tests for EL students, would provide important incentives for test makers to begin developing better assessment tools for EL students. If the federal government were to insist that states adhere to NCLB guidelines for EL testing, and support the states in meeting those guidelines, the cost to the states should be relatively minimal.

REVIEW OF COST STUDIES

The previous discussion identified a number of resources needed to educate linguistic minority students, but what is the cost of providing those resources? One way to address this question is to examine results from some recent cost studies. A growing number of states are attempting to define an adequate education and provide the resources for schools to provide it (Augenblick, Myers, & Anderson, 1997; Duncombe & Yinger, 2005; Gutherie & Rothstein, 1999). As a result, scholars have undertaken studies to estimate the costs of providing an adequate education, including the differential costs associated with providing an adequate education to students who are disadvantaged due to poverty, language background, and disability. These studies are based on different methodologies. One method estimates costs from a production function that includes student performance measures, pupil characteristics (such as poverty, EL status, and disability), educational inputs (such as teacher salaries), and geographic cost differences (see Duncombe and Yinger, in this volume). Another common method, known as Professional Judgment Panels or PJPs, estimates costs based on educational programs specified by panels of "expert" educators (superintendents, principals, teachers, and resource specialists). Existing studies have only estimated the extra costs of educating English learners, not the larger population of linguistic minorities.

Fiscal Resources

All the methods used to conduct cost studies can be used to generate overall per pupil cost estimates and estimates of per pupil weights associated with poverty, EL, and special education status. Per pupil weights generally range from 0.1, which denotes a 10 percent differential cost, to 1.0 or more, which denotes that the costs are twice as high or higher to educate disadvantaged students. One important question is how the weights associated with poverty compare to the weights associated with EL status, independent of poverty. That is, how do the additional costs of educating poor children compare with the additional costs of educating English learners?

Some estimated weights are shown in Table 33.5. The first studies produced estimates for New York using two different approaches—the first one using the production function approach and the second one using Professional Judgment Panels. The first study (Duncombe & Yinger, 2005) estimated a range of weights based on different techniques for making comparisons among districts and using different measures of poverty. Using Census data on poverty, for example, produced estimates of poverty weights ranging from 1.22 to 1.59 (when special education students are included). That is, these estimates suggest that to educate poor students to the same standard as non-poor students requires per pupil funding levels from 122 to 159 percent higher. Educating EL students, controlling for poverty and special education, requires funding levels from 101 to 142 percent higher still. Using subsidized school lunch data (which is a broader measure that includes both poor and low-income students) produced higher poverty weights—ranging from 1.36 to 2.15—but no additional EL weights.[8] In other words, the second set of estimates suggests there are no incremental costs of educating EL students beyond the costs of educating low-income students.

The second study (Chambers et al., 2004) estimated per-pupil weights for EL students that ranged from 0.18 for elementary schools to 0.20 for middle schools. It should be pointed out that the base funding level in this is much higher than the national funding level of $7,904 in 2001–02 (U.S. Department of Education, National Center for Education Statistics, 2000b, table 162), which may reduce the need for extra expenditures for educating poor and EL students. Yet it leaves open the question of whether uniformly higher spending has any effect on closing achievement gaps.

The third study (National Conference of State Legislatures, 2005) used the PJP approach to estimate per pupil weights for educating two types of EL students in Arizona: low need EL students, who the panel defined as either poor with high English proficiency or non-poor with middle and high English proficiency; and high need EL students, who the panel defined as either poor with low or medium English proficiency or non-poor with low English proficiency. The per pupil weights for low-need EL students range from 0.24 to 0.30, while the per pupil weights for high-need EL students range from 0.48 to 0.61.

The last study (Chambers, Levin, & DeLancey, 2006) used two separate PJPs to generate two independent estimates of per pupil funding levels for three school configurations in California: (1) a base model that represents the "average" school configuration for an elementary, middle, and high school in the state; (2) high poverty schools with a higher concentration of poor (free and reduced lunch) students, but with the same concentration of EL and special education students; and (3) high poverty, high EL schools with both a higher concentration of poor and EL students, but the same concentration of special education students. From the first and second estimates, it is possible to compute a per pupil weight for poverty, and from the second and third estimates it is possible to compute a per pupil weight for EL status.

The results show that the poverty weights are mostly—and in some cases much—higher than the EL weights. The results also show very disparate estimates from the two panels. At the

TABLE 33.5
Estimates of Per Pupil Spending and Weights for Poverty and EL Status

	Base	*Poverty Weight*	*EL Weight*
New York (Duncombe & Yinger, 2005)			
Estimate using Census poverty		1.22–1.59	1.01–1.42
Estimate using subsidized lunch		1.36–2.15	
New York (Chambers, et al., 2004)			
Elementary school	$10,072		.18
Middle school	$9,899		.20
High school	$10,443		.19
Arizona (NCSL, 2005)			
Elementary school			
Low need ELs	$4,198		.29
High need ELs	$4,195		.38
Middle school			
Low need ELs	$4,060		.30
High need ELs	$4,049		.57
High school			
Low need ELs	$4,214		.24
High need ELs	$4,127		.48
California (Chambers, et al., 2006)			
Elementary school			
Panel 1			
Base model	$10,315		
High poverty	$11,562	.38	
High poverty, high EL	$12,978		.38
Panel 2			
Base model	$8,960		
High poverty	$12,023	1.07	
High poverty, high EL	$12,215		.05
Middle school			
Panel 1			
Base model	$8,905		
High poverty	$9,793	.29	
High poverty, high EL	$10,243		.18
Panel 2			
Base model	$7,899		
High poverty	$10,179	.85	
High poverty, high EL			
High school			
Panel 1			
Base model	$9,285		
High poverty	$9,890	.17	
High poverty, high EL	$10,060		.08
Panel 2			
Base model	$7,035		
High poverty	$9,352	.87	
High poverty, high EL			

elementary level, for example, the first panel estimated virtually identical weights of 0.38 for poverty and EL status, whereas the second panel estimated a per pupil weight for poverty of 1.07 and a per pupil weight for EL status of only 0.05. Also, the estimated costs per student in the base models differed as well. This large discrepancy in estimated costs reflects one of the criticisms of the PJP approach—that it can generate very different estimates of the costs of providing an adequate education, probably owing to very different knowledge and experience of the panel members.

Material Resources

One of the benefits of the PJP approach is that the panel first identifies the elements of an educational program and then determines the material resources to provide it. The panels are not required to identify specific programs, simply alternative features of a basic program in terms of resources. For example, the panel may decide that the best way to provide an adequate education to more disadvantaged students is to reduce class sizes for those students or to extend learning time by either lengthening the school day or the school year.

Differences in the resource allocation decisions are illustrated by comparing the two PJP results for the recent California study (Chambers, Levin, & DeLancey, 2006). The material resources allocated to the three configurations of elementary schools by the two panels are shown in Table 33.6. The first panel specified a class size of 20 to 1 and hence the same number of classroom teachers for all grades in all three configurations. However, they specified a higher number of support teachers and instructional aides in the high poverty and high poverty/high EL configurations. They specified a seven-hour school day for all students and an eight-hour school day for all disadvantaged (poor) students. They also specified a 190-day school year for all students and another 10 days per year for teacher planning and coordination. Finally, they specified a small number of disadvantaged students to receive preschool and early childhood programs. The per pupil weight for ELs was 0.38 in the first panel because the panel made substantial increases in the instructional personnel beyond those specified for a high poverty school, primarily for additional support teachers and teacher aides.[9]

The second panel allocated resources much differently than the first panel, specifying larger classes for fourth and fifth grades than kindergarten through third grade, and fewer instructional and non-instructional personnel. They specified a shorter school day (six and one-half hours) than the first panel, but a longer school year (200 days) for most students, with a smaller number of disadvantaged students having a longer school day than was specified by the first panel. Yet they also specified that more students would participate in preschool and early childhood programs. The EL per pupil weight was only 0.05 because the panel did not specify any additional instructional personnel beyond those specified for a high poverty school.

All of these approaches specified the same level of adequacy for all students, and thus did not consider different standards for EL students as discussed above.

Summary of Findings

The cost studies reviewed above provide little consensus on either the amount or types of additional resources that are needed to educate English learners above and beyond those needed for other disadvantaged students, particularly poor and low-income students. This appears to depend, in part, on how the population of economically disadvantaged students is measured and, consequently, the size of the population. Estimates based on a more narrow definition that only includes students living in poverty (Duncombe & Yinger, 2005, table 6) suggest that additional

TABLE 33.6
Resource Allocations for Elementary Schools, California Professional Judgment Panels

	Panel 1			*Panel 2*		
	Base	*High Poverty*	*High Pov/EL*	*Base*	*High Poverty*	*High Pov/EL*
School characteristics						
Enrollment	516	516	516	516	516	516
Percent poor	57	89	89	57	89	89
Percent EL	28	28	60	28	28	60
Percent Spanish ELs	79	79	90	79	79	90
Percent special Education	9	9	9	9	9	9
Program and resources						
1. Class size						
K–3	20	20	20	20	15	15
4–5	20	20	20	24	19	19
2. Personnel						
Classroom teachers	25.5	25.5	25.5	24.0	32.0	32.0
Support teachers	7.0	7.0	9.0	8.0	9.0	9.0
Instructional aides	6.2	6.6	18.9	4.8	5.9	5.9
Substitute teachers	1.6	1.6	1.7	1.7	2.2	2.2
Total instructional personnel	40.3	40.7	55.1	38.5	49.1	49.1
Instructional and pupil support personnel	10.0	14.0	14.0	1.6	3.5	3.5
School administration	5.0	5.8	5.8	4.9	6.4	6.4
Maintenance and operations	1.0	2.0	2.0	2.5	4.5	4.5
Total non-instructional personnel	16.0	21.8	21.8	9.0	14.4	14.4
Professional Development (days/year)	0.0	0.0	0.0	30.5	41.0	41.0
3. School day (hours)						
Instruction						
All students	7.0	7.0	7.0	6.5	6.5	6.5
Disadvantaged students	8.0	8.0	8.0	8.0	8.0	8.0
Number of students served	(294)	(459)	(459)	(103)	(206)	(206)
Number of days served	(190)	(190)	(190)	(105)	(105)	(105)
Teacher planning and coordination	0.5	0.5	0.5	0.75	0.75	0.75
4. School year (days)						
Instruction						
All students	190	190	190	200	200	200
Disadvantaged students	190	190	190	200	200	200
Teacher planning and coordination	10	10	10	9	9	9
5. Preschool program for 4 year olds (#)	43	77	77	65	86	86
6. Early childhood program for 3 year olds (#)	3	3	9	65	86	86

Source: Chambers, Levin, & DeLancy (2006).

resources may be needed to educate English learners because many such students are not poor (see Table 33.4). However, estimates based on a broader definition that includes both poverty and low-income students (as captured by students enrolled in the federal school lunch program), suggest that no additional resources may be needed.[10] But even when a broader and more inclusive definition of *economically disadvantaged* is used, a lack of consensus remains (Chambers, Levin, & Delancy, 2006).

ADDITIONAL RESOURCE NEEDS FOR LINGUISTIC MINORITY STUDENTS

A critical point of discussion in a study of resources for linguistic minority students is the degree to which their needs differ from, or are in addition to, the needs of both all other students and other socioeconomically disadvantaged students. A variety of evidence suggests that *all students* need qualified teachers, additional support personnel, appropriate instructional materials, and sufficient instructional time to meet high performance standards; *all teachers* should possess an array of human resources to make them effective, including subject matter knowledge, pedagogical skills, multicultural skills, empathy, efficacy, and the willingness to learn and work collaboratively (Banks, 1988; Cohen, Raudenbush, & Ball, 2003; Sleeter, 2001); and *all schools* should possess social resources that foster close and caring relationships among teachers, students, parents, and administrators (Ancess, 2003; Barnes, 2002; Bryk & Schneider, 2002; Goodard, Hoy, & Hoy, 2000; Spillane, 2004).

Virtually all cost studies and studies of effective schools also acknowledge that there are additional resources required to educate *all disadvantaged students* who begin school with lower academic skills relative to their more advantaged peers, and thus have more to learn to reach the same achievement standards. Perhaps the most critical resource for schools educating disadvantaged students, above and beyond qualified teachers, is more instructional time, because those students have more to learn to reach the same standards as students who arrive at school with expected initial achievement levels.

What is more difficult is to determine whether the resource needs to educate linguistic minority students—both those who are not proficient in English (ELs) and those who are FEP—are similar to those required for poor and low-income students. We believe the evidence suggests that some needs of linguistic minorities are indeed different from other students with similar socioeconomic backgrounds and their needs cannot all be met with the same set of resources; however, it is not clear to what extent—if at all—they require more resources than those of poor and low-income children. Data from a cohort of children who entered kindergarten in the fall of 1998 indicate that the initial achievement gaps are larger between poor and non-poor students than they are between linguistic minority and English-only students, which suggests that more resources are needed for poor than linguistic minority children (Table 33.7). The data also show that students who are *both* poor and linguistic minority have the largest gaps in initial achievement, which suggests they may need more resources than students who are *either* poor or linguistic minority. Yet by fifth grade, achievement levels for linguistic minority students show greater improvement than achievement levels for poor students. Moreover, achievement levels for poor, linguistic minority students were either similar (in the case of reading) or higher (in the cases of language and math) than poor students from English backgrounds. These data suggest that achievement gaps due to language are more amenable to intervention and therefore may require fewer additional resources than the gaps created by poverty.[11]

Many resource needs appear to be similar for both poor and linguistic minority students, such as access to teachers who are skilled in strategies for developing their linguistic and academic

TABLE 33.7
Selected Background and Achievement Measures by Poverty and Linguistic Minority Status, Fall 1998 Kindergarteners

	Percent	*Mean SES*	*Mean Language K*	*Mean Language 5th grade*	*Mean Reading 5th grade*	*Mean Math K*	*Mean Math 5th grade*
English only	**80.3**	**.11**	**.15**	**.05**	**.11**	**.14**	**.08**
Non-poor	67.4	.30	.24	.14	.24	.25	.21
Poor	12.9	–.89	–.34	–.45	–.57	–.44	–.59
Linguistic Minority	**19.7**	**–.30**	**–.34**	**–.01**	**–.17**	**–.31**	**–.06**
Non-poor	13.4	.03	–.14	.11	.02	–.11	.12
Poor	6.3	–1.01	–.76	–.27	–.59	–.74	–.44
Total	**100.0**	**.00**	**.00**	**.00**	**.00**	**.00**	**.00**

Note: Means are expressed in standard deviations from normalized national mean of zero. Language skills, which cover listening, speaking, reading, and writing, were assessed by students' classroom teachers, whereas reading and math were assessed by trained assessors.
Source: Analysis of data from the Early Children Longitudinal Study of the Kindergarten Class of 1998 (N = 9,796)

skills, and to counselors and other ancillary personnel who can effectively communicate with their parents. But some resource needs are unique to linguistic minority students. In general, these are resources that use the students' primary language and are created with language difference in mind. Students in primary language programs require instructional materials in the students' native language, and all teachers of linguistic minority students, even those in English-only programs, should have access to materials in the students' home languages, to the extent practicable, so that parents who do not speak English can be enlisted in supporting their children's learning. Other material resources include assessments in the students' primary language, or other assessments that can more accurately test their skills, and English Language Development materials that are designed for non-English speakers. The other unique resource consists of teachers and staff who speak the languages of the students. To recruit and attract bilingual teachers may require financial incentives, especially in communities experiencing rapid increases in linguistic minority populations. Some communities have been able to recruit and train teachers from the ranks of bilingual paraprofessionals (Flores, Keehn, & Perez, 2002). Any additional costs for bilingual teachers may be mitigated by decreased use of bilingual classroom aides. For example, research has shown that providing EL students with a bilingual teacher, as opposed to relying on additional support personnel to augment the instruction of monolingual English-speaking teachers, is the less costly alternative and may result in no additional expenditures (Carpenter-Huffman & Samulon, 1981; Parrish, 1994).

In sum, English learners and other linguistic minority students require additional resources above and beyond those of all other students, but their needs appear to differ more in kind than in quantity from those of poor and low-income students who are also struggling with developing broader vocabularies, a command of academic English, and familiarity with the cultural capital that are such important academic assets for the middle class.

CONCLUSIONS

The growing population of linguistic minority and English learner students in the nation's schools has significant implications for the funding and designing of effective educational programs to educate these students. It also has implications for how all students are educated in contexts in which linguistic minority students sit alongside English-speaking peers in the classroom. Both the educational goals for LM students, and whether the educational programs to educate them make use of primary language instruction, have been subject to considerable policy debate over the last 30 years, even while a growing body of research evidence documents the benefits of primary language instruction for both English learners and English speakers, when it provides the opportunity for the latter to acquire a second language. What is less clear from the research literature is the types and amount of resources needed to educate linguistic minority and English learner students, and the extent to which these resources differ from those needed to educate all other students and other disadvantaged students, particularly poor and low-income students. The research does suggest that additional resources are needed to educate all students to higher standards; but to bring linguistic minority students—and others who enter school substantially behind their English-speaking classmates—to the level of their more advantaged peers requires still more educational resources. These include: suitably qualified teachers; appropriate instructional materials; valid, comprehensive assessments; and, probably, additional instructional time. As states continue to struggle with adequate educational funding to help students meet high standards, it is critical that they take into account the specific needs of English learners and other linguistic minorities. While more research will be needed to determine the exact additional costs for these students, if any, it is clear that their needs are, at least in part, different from their native-English-speaking peers, and if not addressed will continue to contribute to low levels of achievement. English learners now comprise at least 10 percent of all students nationwide; in the future this number will grow. It is in the interest of the nation as a whole to invest wisely in these students' education.

NOTES

1. Based on data retrieved September 9, 2006 from the California Department of Education website, *Dataquest* (http://data1.cde.ca.gov/dataquest/).
2. For example, Gándara & Merino (1993) found schools often didn't have the resources to reclassify students.
3. As Parrish, et al. (2006) note, initial classification is primarily based on students' initial score on the California English Language Proficiency Test (CELDT), while reclassification is based on multiple criteria, leading to more variation in reclassification than initial classification (p. V-5).
4. Although there are no strict standards to interpret differences in these values, values above 0.8 SD are often considered large, values above 0.5 are considered moderate, values above 0.2 SD are considered small, and values below 0.2 are considered inconsequential (Cohen, 1988, pp. 24-27).
5. Language skills of kindergarten students in the ECLS were assessed by kindergarten teachers, regardless of their primary language, while math achievement was conducted in English and Spanish (U.S. Department of Education, 2000a). Thus these data can be considered more valid and reliable than assessments of LM students conducted only in English.
6. This section draws heavily from García (2005), pp. 92-98.
7. For example, in California, while only six percent of English learners received primary language instruction in 2005–06, another 21 percent received primary language support (Data from Dataquest, retrieved February 3, 2007, from: http://data1.cde.ca.gov/dataquest/ElP2_State.asp?RptYear=2005-06&RptType=ELPart2_1a
8. The higher weights using the broader population may capture both the effects of poverty and LEP status in the first set of estimates.
9. This begs the question of using bilingual teachers instead of aides and support teachers.
10. In California, for example, 19 percent of students enrolled in first through fourth grades were poor

(meaning their families were at 100% of the federal poverty level) according to estimates from the 2005 American Community Survey (see: http://www.census.gov/acs/www/index.html), whereas 49 percent of students enrolled in California public schools participated in the free and reduced-lunch program (see: http://data1.cde.ca.gov/dataquest/APIBase2006/2005Base_StApiDC.aspx?allcds=0000000).

11. In California, poor linguistic minority students continue to lag behind poor, English-only students, which suggest the former group of students may need relatively more resources (Gándara & Rumberger, 2006).

REFERENCES

Abedi, J. (2002). Standardized achievement tests and English language learners: Psychometric issues. *Educational Assessment, 8,* 231–257.

Ancess, J. (2003). *Beating the odds: High schools as communities of commitment.* New York: Teachers College Press.

Augenblick, J.G., Myers, J.L., & Anderson, A.B. (1997). Equity and adequacy in school funding. *The Future of Children, 7,* 63–78.

August, D. & Hakuta, K. (Eds.). (1997). *Improving schooling for language-minority children: A research agenda.* Washington, D.C.: National Academy Press.

August, D. & Shanahan, T. (Eds.). (2006). *Developing literacy in second language learners: Report of the National Literacy Panel on Language Minority Children and Youth.* New York: Lawrence Erlbaum Associates.

Banks, J. (1988). *Multiethnic Education: Theory and Practice.* New York: Allyn & Bacon.

Barnes, C. A. (2002). *Standards reform in high-poverty schools.* New York: Teachers College Press.

Bilingual Education Act, Public Law 90-247, 81 Stat. 816 (1968).

Bilingual Education Act, Public Law 93-380, 88 Stat. 503 (1974).

Bilingual Education Act, Public Law 98-511, 98 Stat. 2370 (1984).

Bilingual Education Act, Title VII of the Improving America's Schools Act, Public Law 103-382, 98 Stat. 2370 (1994).

Bryk, A. S. & Schneider, B. (2002). *Trust in schools: A core resource for improvement.* New York: Russell Sage.

Calfee, R. (2006). Are California's reading textbooks adequate for teaching English Learners? *UC LMRI Newsletter, V.16, No. 1.* Retrieved April 7, 2007, from http://lmri.ucsb.edu/publications/newsletters/v16n1.pdf

California Education Code, Chacon-Moscone Bilingual-Bicultural Education Act of 1976 (1976).

Carpenter-Huffman, P. & Samulon, M. (1981). *Case Studies of Delivery and Cost of Bilingual Education.* Santa Monica: Rand Corporation. N -1684-ED.

Carroll, J.B. (1963). A model of school learning. *Teachers College Record, 64,* 723–733.

Carroll, J.B. (1989). The Carroll model: A 25-year retrospective and prospective view. *Educational Researcher, 18,* 26–31.

Chambers, J., Levin, J., & DeLancey, D. (2006). *Efficiency and adequacy in California school finance: A professional judgment approach.* Palo Alto: American Institutes for Research. Retrieved April 6, 2007, from http://irepp.stanford.edu/documents/GDF/STUDIES/19-AIR-ProfessionalJdgmt/19-AIR-PJP-Report(3-07).pdf

Chambers, J. G., Parrish, T. B., Levin, J. D., Smith, J. R., Gutherie, J. W. S. R. C., & Taylor, L. (2004). *The New York adequacy study: Determining the cost of providing all children in New York an adequate Education.* Palo Alto: American Institutes for Research.

Cohen, D.K., Raudenbush, S.W., & Ball, D.L. (2003). Resources, instruction, and research. *Educational Evaluation and Policy Analysis, 25,* 119–142.

Cohen, J. (1988). *Statistical power analysis for the behavioral sciences,* 2nd ed. Hillsdale, NJ: Erlbaum.

Darling-Hammond, L., Ancess, J., & Falk, B. (1995). *Authentic assessment in action: Studies of schools and students at work.* New York: Teachers College Press.

Duncombe, W. & Yinger, J. (2005). How much more dose a disadvantaged student cost? *Economics of Education Review, 24,* 513–532.

Ehrenberg, R.G., Brewer, D.J., Gamoran, A., & Willms, J.D. (2001). Class size and student achievement. *Psychological Science, Supplement,* 1–30.

Equal Education Opportunities Act, Public Law 93-380, 88 Stat. 514 (1974).

Farbman, D. & Kaplan, C. (2005). *Time for change: The promise of extended-time schools for promoting student achievement.* Boston: Massachusetts 2020.

Finn, J.D. & Achilles, C.M. (1999). Tennessee's class size study: Findings, implications, misconceptions. *Educational Evaluation and Policy Analysis, 21,* 97–110.

Finn, J.D., Gerber, S.B., Achilles, C.M., & Boyd-Zaharias, J. (2001). The enduring effects of small classes. *Teachers College Record, 103,* 145–183.

Flores, B.B., Keehn, S., & Perez, B. (2002). Critical need for bilingual teachers: The potentiality of *Normalistas* and Paraprofessionals. *Bilingual Research Journal, 26,* 501–524.

Gándara, P. (2000). *The dimensions of time and the challenge of school reform.* Albany: State University of New York Press.

Gándara, P. & Fish, J. (1994). Year-round schooling as an avenue to major structural reform. *Educational Evaluation and Policy Analysis, 16,* 67–85.

Gándara, P. & Maxwell-Jolly, J. (2005). Critical issues in the development of the teacher corps for English learners. In Waxman, H., Tellez, K., *Preparing quality teachers for English Language Learners.* Mahwah, NJ: Lawrence Erlbaum Press.

Gándara, P., Maxwell-Jolly, J., Driscoll, A. (2005). *Listening to Teachers of English Learners.* Santa Cruz, CA: Center for the Future of Teaching and Learning.

Gándara, P. & Merino, B. (1993). Measuring the outcomes of LEP programs: Test scores, exit rates, and other mythological data. *Educational Evaluation and Policy Analysis, 15,* 320–338.

Gándara, P., & Rumberger, R.W. (2006). *Resource needs for California's English Learners.* Santa Barbara, CA: UC Linguistic Minority Research Institute. Retrieved April 7, 2007, from http://lmri.ucsb.edu/publications/07_gandara-rumberger.pdf

Gándara, P., Rumberger, R.W., Maxwell-Jolly, J., & Callahan, R. (2003). English Learners in California schools: Unequal resources, unequal outcomes. *Educational Policy Analysis Archives, 11.* Retrieved October 21, 2006, from http://epaa.asu.edu/epaa/v11n36/

García, E. E. (2005). *Teaching and learning in two languages: Bilingualism and schooling in the United States.* New York: Teachers College Press.

Genao, I., Bussey-Jones, J., Brady, D., Branch, M.T., & Corbie-Smith, G. (2003). Building the case for cultural competence. *American Journal of the Medical Sciences, 326,* 136–140.

Genesee, F., Lindholm-Leary, K., Saunders, W., & Christian, D. (2006) *Educating English Language Learners. A synthesis of research evidence.* New York: Cambridge University Press.

Goodard, R.D., Hoy, W.K., & Hoy, A.W. (2000). Collective teacher efficacy: Its meaning, measure, and impact on student achievement. *American Educational Research Journal, 37,* 479–507.

Gutherie, J. W. & Rothstein, R. (1999). Enabling "adequacy" to achieve reality: Translating adequacy into state school finance distribution arrangements. In H. F. Ladd, R. Chalk, & J. S. Hansen (Eds), *Equity and adequacy in education finance: Issues and perspectives* (pp.209–259). Washington, D.C.: National Academy Press.

Hakuta, K. (1986). *Mirror of Language.* New York: Basic Books

Krueger, A.B. (2003). Economic considerations and class size. *Economic Journal, 113,* F34-F63.

Linguanti, R. (2001). *The redesignation dilemma: Challenges and choices in fostering meaningful accountability for English Learners.* Santa Barbara: UC Linguistic Minority Research Institute. Retrieved April 7, 2007, from http://lmri.ucsb.edu/publications/01_linquanti-redesignation.pdf

Moran, R.F. (2004). Undone by law: The uncertain legacy of *Lau v. Nichols. UC LMRI Newsletter, V.13, No. 4,* 1–8. Retrieved April 7, 2007, from http://lmri.ucsb.edu/publications/newsletters/v13n4.pdf

Mosteller, F. (1995). The Tennessee study of class size in the early grades. *The Future of Children, 5,* 113–127.

National Conference of State Legislatures (NCSL) (2005). *Arizona English Language Learner cost study.* Washington, D.C.: Author.

No Child Left Behind Act of 2001, Public Law 107-110, 115 Stat. 1425 (2002).

Novak, J. R. & Fuller, B. (2003). *Penalizing diverse schools? Similar test scores, but different students, bring federal sanctions.* Policy Brief 03-4. Berkeley, CA: Policy Analysis for California Education. Retrieved April 7, 2007, from http://pace.berkeley.edu/policy_brief_03-4_Pen.Div.pdf

Parrish, T. (1994). A cost analysis of alternative instructional models for Limited English Proficient Students in California. *Journal of Education Finance, 19,* 256–278.

Parrish, T. B., Merickel, A., Perez. M, Linquanti, R., Socia, M., Spain, A., Speroni, C., Esra, P., Brock, L., & Delancey, D. (2006). *Effects of the implementation of Proposition 227 on the education of English learners, K-12: Findings from a Five-Year Evaluation.* Palo Alto, CA: American Institutes for Research and WestEd.

Rumberger, R.W. (2006). The Growth of the Linguistic Minority Population in the U.S. and California, 1980–2005. *El Facts*, Number 8. Santa Barbara, CA: UC Linguistic Minority Research Institute. Retrieved February 5, 2007, from http://lmri.ucsb.edu/publications/elfacts-8corrected.pdf.

Rumberger, R.W., Gándara, P., & Merino, B. (2006). Where California's English Learners attend school and why it matters. *UC LMRI Newsletter, V.15, No. 2,* 1–2. Retrieved February 3, 2007, from http://lmri.ucsb.edu/publications/newsletters/v15n2.pdf

Rumberger, R. W. & Tran, L. (2006). *Preschool Participation and the Cognitive and Social Development of Language Minority Students.* Los Angeles: Center for the Study of Evaluation, Graduate School of Education & Information Studies, University of California, Los Angeles. Retrieved April 7, 2007, from http://lmri.ucsb.edu/publications/06_rumberger-tran.pdf

Sleeter, C. (2001). Preparing teachers for cultural diversity, *Journal of Teacher Education*, 52, 94–106

Spillane, J. P. (2004). *Standards deviation: How schools misunderstand education policy.* Cambridge, MA: Harvard University Press.

U.S. Department of Education, National Center for Education Statistics (2000a). *ECLS-K Base Year Data Files and Electronic Codebook.* Washington, D.C.: National Center for Education Statistics.

U.S. Department of Education, National Center for Education Statistics (2000b). *Digest of Education Statistics, 2000.* Washington, D.C.: U.S. Government Printing Office.

Wayne, A.J. & Youngs, P. (2003). Teacher characteristics and student achievement gains: A review. *Review of Educational Research, 73*, 89–122.

Wiley, T. G., & Wright, W. E. (2004). Against the undertow: Language-minority education policy and politics in the "Age of Accountability." *Educational Policy, 18,* 142–168.

Wong-Fillmore, L. and C. Snow. (2000). *What teachers need to know about language.* US Department of Education, Office of Educational Research and Improvement, Washington, D.C.

Zehler, A. M., Fleischman, H. L., Hopstock, P. J., Stephenson, T. G., Pendzick, M. L., & Sapru, S. (2003). *Descriptive study of services to LEP students and LEP students with disabilities.* Washington, D.C.: Development Associates.

34

Challenges and Strategies Associated with Rural School Settings

John W. Sipple and Brian O. Brent

INTRODUCTION

Rural America is more ubiquitous and its residents more consequential than the caricatures often provided by the popular media (Brown, Swanson, & Barton, 2003; Johnson & Strange, 2005). Sixty million people live in rural communities throughout United States—communities that encompass 97 percent of the Unites States land mass (The University of Montana Rural Institute, 2005). Rural communities educate 8.8 million students, or nearly 21 percent of the school-aged population (NCES, 2003).

Numerous studies have addressed the varying needs and challenges of urban students and schools, but educational policy makers and researchers have not shown comparable interest in finance and policy issues specific to rural schools. While the attention on urban centers is warranted, more scholarly attention to rural schools is also needed if policy makers are to address the needs of these students (Truscott & Truscott, 2005; Roscigno, Tomaskovic-Deveu, and Crowley, 2006).

Defining "Rural"

Some researchers define the term "rural" with reference to socio-cultural traits including lifestyles, values, and behaviors. Others identify rural communities in terms of occupational or land use patterns, such as agriculture and mining, or draw on the concept of "remoteness" and denote such areas by their population density or access to services and economic centers (Witham, 1993).

A quote from the introduction to the *Journal of Education Finance*'s special issue on rural schools is illustrative of the complexity of rural character (Dunn, 2003): "Rural schools typically share the traits of sparsity of population, low property wealth, small student population, less infrastructure, geographic isolation, and a stronger sense of community." Federal and state agencies vary in how they define "rural" for policy making purposes, sometimes even differing even within a single state (Schwob, 2004). The result of such varied definitions is that it makes setting policy for rural schools complicated, and the comparing of results among studies using different metrics suspect.

In 2006, the National Center for Education Statistics (NCES) introduced a new framework for classifying schools. The NCES typology is based on urban-centric criteria and provides a defensible means to identify rural school districts. The framework relies on geographic information systems (GIS) to classify both land areas and the specific location of schools within that territorial region.

Key Challenges Facing Rural Schools

Much research suggests that the socio-cultural and ecological conditions that define rural communities and their schools are great strengths. For example, researchers argue that rural schools foster strong, nurturing, and supportive relationships among community members, staff, and students. Some see the remoteness of many rural schools as providing a focused learning environment without the trappings, influences, and distractions of more populated areas (Beeson & Strange, 2000; Fan & Chen, 1999; Israel, Beaulieu, & Hartless, 2001; Kannapel & DeYoung, 1999, Lyson, 2002). There is also mounting evidence that supports the value of small schools (Jimerson, 2006; Hylden, 2005; Lee & Smith, 1995; Mosteller, 1995; Raywid, 1999; The Bill and Melinda Gates Foundation, 2001). Describing the benefits of small rural schools as the "Hobbit Effect," Jimerson explores and reviews why small school size has many benefits (once controlling for SES), including greater academic success, higher graduation rates, more advanced courses, and greater participation in extracurricular activities.

Nevertheless, educators encounter significant obstacles when trying to provide their students with improved educational opportunities. We now turn to an examination of four of these challenges and the strategies that rural educators have devised to address them.

THE BOUNDED CURRICULUM

The Challenge

Rural schools do not to provide the breadth and depth of course offerings that are available to students in suburban and urban systems, particularly at the secondary-level. Haller, Monk, Spotted Bear, Griffith, and Moss (1990) were among the first to move beyond anecdotal reports and use a national data set (i.e., high school and beyond) to document this phenomenon (see also, Barker, 1985; Monk, 1987; Monk & Haller, 1986). More recently, NCES (2003) offered data that demonstrates that a smaller percentage of rural schools offer instruction in various arts subjects (breadth), and within these subjects, fewer courses (depth) than suburban and urban schools.

A number of scholars now argue, however, that the challenges of a "bounded," or limited, curriculum is exaggerated (e.g., Howley, 1994). A common argument among these skeptics is the notion that offering more types of courses does not necessarily mean that a program is more "comprehensive." Often, images of the "shopping mall" high school are invoked, where students may choose among numerous, though often "inconsequential," courses (Haller, et al., 1990; Haller, Monk, & Tien, 1993).

Policy makers must look closely at findings from studies that link school size and program comprehensiveness. Haller, et al. (1990) report that secondary schools with enrollments of 100 students or more per grade offer basic courses in ways that are comparable to larger schools. However, 51 percent of rural secondary schools enroll fewer than 300 students, and 80 percent enroll fewer than 599 students—suggesting that most of these schools may indeed offer programs limited in depth and breadth (NCES, 2003).

Beyond core courses, researchers are now paying attention to the provision of adequate supplemental academic services. In a study of Academic Intervention Services in New York State, Killeen & Sipple (2005) found urban districts faced great challenges in their ability to offer supplementary services outside of the core academic classes. The sheer number of students requiring additional instruction in multiple subject areas makes it nearly impossible for such schools to meet the state requirement during the normal school hours. Rural districts, however, showed no significant differences when compared to suburban districts in the provision of such services, and did not face the space and capacity challenges found in the larger urban schools.

Though measuring the effect of individual, family, community, and school-based factors on student achievement is complicated (see Section II and Section VI, this volume), rural students consistently exhibit lower levels of student achievement and attainment, and higher drop-out rates than their suburban counterparts. Roscigno et al. (2006), for example, drew from three waves of the National Education Longitudinal Survey (NELS) and the Common Core Data (CCD) to examine the effect of family resources (e.g., income), and family educational investments (e.g., number of household educational items, cultural capital, and parental involvement) on rural student achievement. Controlling for commonly used individual (e.g., gender) and school (e.g., size) attributes, they found that rural areas tend to place a lower premium on educational investment than suburban and urban families with comparable resources. They posit that such differences might be explained by the rural histories and cultures (e.g., economic and social stratification) (see also, Tomaskovic-Devey & Tomaskovic-Devey, 1988).

Strategies

Distance education refers to a variety of instructional delivery methods that use technology to link students and teachers who are separated geographically. One can place these technologies along a continuum of expanded interactions between teacher and student. At the one end, Internet courses using asynchronous (i.e., not simultaneous) computer-based instruction permits student and teacher to interact at the convenience of either party. At the other end, Internet courses using synchronous (i.e., simultaneous) computer-based instruction and two-way, interactive video (ITV) permits "real-time" communication between the teacher and students.

Fifteen percent of rural schools offer distance education courses compared with 5 percent of urban schools and 7 percent of suburban schools (NCES, 2003). In fact, the total number of rural students taking distance education courses varies only slightly from those in non-rural settings.

Ninety-five percent of rural districts report that distance education enables them to offer courses that would otherwise be unavailable (Brent, 1999; Hall & Barker, 1995; Hawkins, Grimaldi, Baker, Dyer, Moeller, & Thompson, 1996). Three in four rural districts indicate that they need the technology to offer Advanced Placement (AP) or college-level courses (NCES, 2003).

Two-way interactive video (ITV) is an efficacious means to expand curricular offerings in rural schools. Researchers have found that student achievement in ITV classrooms does not differ substantially from traditional classrooms (e.g., Kitchen, 1997; Hawkins, et al. 1996), and ITV does not adversely affect students', teachers', and administrators' attitudes toward instruction (e.g., Barker, 1989; Catchpole, 1988; Crowe, 1990).

Studies consistently demonstrate, however, that implementing and supporting ITV technology is costly, both in terms of direct expenditures (e.g., capital outlay) and total cost (Barker & Hall, 1994; Jones & Simonson, 1995). For example, Brent's (1999) analysis of ITV in nine schools indicates that some districts would have incurred substantially less expenditures if they provided classes in traditional settings, albeit in very small class-sizes, rather than through ITV.

Brent's study also revealed several hidden costs that can accompany the use of ITV: Administrators found scheduling problematic because districts operated on different yearly and daily schedules, including holiday schedules, teacher conference days, and snow days. Including system malfunctions, administrators estimated that five instructional days per year were lost while using ITV.

Despite questions about the cost-effectiveness of this instructional delivery mode, rural schools are becoming increasingly reliant on distance education. Most states have categorical aids that support technology maintenance and acquisition (Sielke, Dayton, Holmes, & Jefferson, 2001). In addition, the Federal Telecommunications Act of 1996, commonly known as the "E-Rate," provides discounts to schools and libraries to connect to the Internet. The discounts range from 20 percent to 90 percent depending on the level of poverty and urban/rural status of the population served. They can be applied to telecom services (such as high-speed broadband), to Internet access (but not content), and to internal connections (inside wiring and the creation of LANs/WANs) (Staihr & Sheaff, 2001; Universal Services Administration Company, 2007). In 2005, 95 percent of rural school instructional rooms were connected to the Internet, up from eight percent in 1995 (NCES, 2005). In addition, 96 percent of these schools report Internet access using broadband connections. Furthermore, 74 percent of rural districts with students enrolled in distance education courses plan to expand their offerings in the future, and only 34 percent of these district express concern about receiving funding (NCES, 2003).

Together these findings invite continued inquiry into whether rural school children continue to be hindered by a bounded curriculum despite the increasing use of technology. It is plausible that the gap in course offerings between rural and other schools has decreased considerably from that reported in earlier studies. It is also possible that new and emerging technologies will make distance education a cost-effective alternative to traditional classroom-based instruction.[1]

STAFFING

The Challenge

Adequate staffing of schools represents a particularly salient challenge for high-need rural and urban schools (Ingersoll, 2001). Schools in remote areas have fewer teachers in the labor market from which to draw and hence may need to offer additional incentives to attract and retain applicants. While discussions of teacher staffing are typically linked to an adequate supply of new teachers (and hence discussions related to the supply line of teacher education), the literature is clear that the challenge is linked to teacher mobility and retention (Elfers, Plecki, & Knapp, 2006). Nearly one-fifth of the teachers in the labor force turn over each year with a disproportion of the turnover in high need urban and rural schools. Provasnik and Dorfman (2005) found that three-quarters of newly hired teachers each year are in fact experienced teachers. Only four percent of new teacher hires were brand new to the profession.

The micro-labor markets in which school districts operate limit the numbers of prospective teachers (new and experienced) in rural and urban areas (Guarino, Santibañez, & Daley, 2006). Attempts to model the labor markets for teachers have found them to be more local than was heretofore believed. Researchers found that more than 80 percent of teachers in New York State end up teaching in districts that are located within 40 miles of where they grew up (Boyd, Lankford, Loeb, & Wyckoff, 2003, 2005). In Tennessee, it was found that the vast majority of teachers teach in a public school near the university at which they trained.

As the labor pool shrinks in remote areas, so too does the pool of *qualified* teacher and administrator candidates. This fact is particularly salient given the highly qualified teacher (HQT) provision in the No Child Left Behind Act (NCLB) of 2001 (Russel, 2005). Hammer and colleagues (Hammer, Hughes, McClure, Reeves, & Salgado, 2005; Schwartzbeck, Redfield, Morris, & Hammer, 2003) identify four challenges to recruiting and retaining teachers in rural schools. These include lower pay, geographic and social isolation, difficult working conditions, and NCLB requirements. Rural teachers are often responsible for teaching multiple subject areas and hence, per NCLB regulation, they must be highly qualified in each subject area. Moreover, the provision of professional development opportunities can be scarce in rural areas (Hammer et al., 2005).

Distance to key services is a problem for rural schools. Access to libraries, universities, health services and hospitals, and even shopping opportunities, all represent obstacles for the staffing of rural schools (Murphy & Angelski, 1996/1997). More than just an inconvenience, lack of access to these services signifies a substantial cost to individuals and districts. Lack of access to a larger community or university library may impede her or his teaching. A teacher who must drive for an hour in order to take her or his child to the hospital will miss a greater proportion of a work day than someone who has a five minute drive to an appointment. The district then faces an additional cost of finding a qualified substitute teacher for the time the regular teacher is out of the building. Finally, the students bear the brunt of the cost of less productive day of school with a substitute teacher.

As with teachers, rural schools also have difficulty recruiting and retaining administrators. A number of studies in recent years have suggested that the "quality" of educational administrators in general is in decline (Educational Research Service, 1998; Iowa Department of Education, 1998; O'Connell, 2000, 2001; Esparo & Radar, 2001; Glass, 2001; Castle, 2002). If so, rural schools will be particularly disadvantaged because their circumstances (e.g., limited resources) make them critically dependent on effective school leaders (Browne-Ferrigno & Allen, 2006; DeYoung, 1995; Stephens & Turner, 1988). This challenge is likely to become more pressing in the coming years as rural schools compete for their share of a limited pool of administrators (ERS, 1998).

Scholars suggest that the following factors make it difficult for rural districts recruit and retain administrators: lower compensation (Cooper, Fusarelli, & Carella, 2000) and hence a smaller salary differential between teachers and administrators in rural schools (Stern, 1994); professional isolation due to the physical distance between districts in rural areas, as well as inadequate recreational, educational, or employment opportunities for family members (Grady & Bryant, 1991; Heim & Wilson, 1987; New York State Council of School Superintendent, 2000); and career advancement—the desire to move to a larger, wealthier, or more prestigious district (Dlugosh, 1994; Glass, Bjork, & Brunner, 2000; Shields, 2000).

Strategies

Approaches to reducing social isolation are straightforward, though the cost-effectiveness of such strategies in rural areas is as yet unclear. These include the use of technology, financial incentives, and regional partnerships. As noted above, technology is now in place in many rural areas to offer experiences, coursework, and enrichment to students and their teachers.

The research on teacher recruitment strategies is showing that signing bonuses and other financial incentives are being used by policy makers to staff hard-to-fill positions. In a review of strategies used by different states in 2000, Clewell et al. (2004) summarized policies that have helped local school districts' efforts to recruit more and better teachers. These include loan forgiveness,[2] salary increases,[3] signing bonuses,[4] and allowing the drawing of pension if retired teachers return to the classroom.[5] Mississippi enacted legislation in 1998 to assist rural schools in recruiting teachers to rural areas where there exists a critical shortage of qualified teachers.

Teacher and administrator salaries in rural areas are lower than in suburban and urban districts, though differential compensation is necessary to attract teachers into remote regions located away from the facilities and services of urban life. In a national study of the costs and benefits of altering teacher salaries, Chambers (1995) concluded that salary incentives for rural schools are necessary to overcome what Jimerson (2003) terms the "competitive disadvantage" of teacher compensation in rural areas. Chambers' study calculated that the "average student" attending a rural school would have access to the "average teacher" at a cost-savings of 8 percent when compared to the non-rural average. Another student attending a "remotely-located" district would have access to that same quality teacher at about the average (same) cost of a non-rural school. Hence, to offset the reduced labor market in remote areas, actual labor costs (salaries) should match that of the less-rural school districts.

Regional educational agencies also offset the challenges of providing adequate staffing through the provision of staff development opportunities. Regional labs and intermediate educational organizations serving multiple component districts (e.g., Intermediate School districts in Michigan, and Boards of Cooperative Educational Services in New York State) provide valuable staff development to rural schools (Sipple, 2004; Sipple & Killeen, 2004; Sipple, Killeen, & Monk, 2004). Policies that require such things as a certain number of hours of professional development, or that provide funding and establish programs such as regional service centers), all contribute in positive ways to the promotion and delivery of higher quality professional development (Dean & Lauer, 2001).

Several states have implemented programs to enhance the opportunities for professional development in rural areas. Virginia sponsors a "Satellite Educational Network" which provides electronic classroom coursework for children in small and rural schools. This technology is also used in providing staff development opportunities to the same populations at no cost to the district. Whereas Virginia offers the coursework and professional development opportunities for small and rural districts, other states offer state funding for professional development, but with no special adjustments for rural schools. Kentucky allocates $15 per pupil to each district and then provides free access to the state-sponsored programs, regardless of location. Kentucky sponsors professional development programs for certified personnel, while Alabama provides a salary allocation for two days of professional development for all 9-, 10-, and 11-month professional and support personnel.

Hammer, et al. (2005) offers a promising set of strategies, including some rural-specific themes, to improve the recruitment and retaining of teachers in rural schools. Overall, the strategies for effective recruitment and retention must be strategic, targeted toward the hard-to-staff grades and subject areas, sustained year after year, and grounded in the local community. Specifically, they recommend specific strategies that have found to be effective in attracting and retaining teachers, including basing recruitment on data, building partnerships, offering targeted incentives, regular evaluation, using building level staff in hiring, formal induction programs, and involving the community in the welcoming of new hires.

The use of emerging technology can also reduce the especially heavy recruiting and hiring costs to small rural districts. Districts can purchase access to a Web-based service to facilitate efficient advertising, recruiting, communication, and reviewing potential candidates for teaching positions. While large districts offer the economies of scale to hire human resource professionals, very small districts rely on administrators and teachers to do the advertising, recruiting, and hiring. The cost of advertising in a regional newspaper is the same for a district of 300 as it is for a district of 10,000. One example of such a service is SchoolSpring (www.schoolspring.com), a private service that posts positions for a fee and then provides an archiving service for application materials. Currently serving the entire state of Vermont, this service has the potential to reduce costs and increase the labor pool for rural school districts.

While the literature describes a wide array of strategies, the number and quality of relevant policy evaluation studies is limited (Guarino et al., 2006). Hence, the long-term effect of using these strategies and incentives to increase the size of an applicant pool, to recruit a teacher once an offer is made, and to retain teachers in remote locations is not well understood.

The use of alternative pathways to teaching in rural areas warrants increased attention. Emergency-credentialed math and science teachers are as effective other teachers in teaching twelfth grade students (Goldhaber & Brewer, 2000), and *Teach For America* teachers are virtually indistinguishable (in terms of student learning gains) from their traditionally certified colleagues in high need rural and urban schools (Glazerman, Mayer, & Decker, 2006). The evaluation work on alternative pathways to teaching is in its infancy, though in New York (Boyd, Lankford, Loeb, and Wyckoff (2005), concluded that the "variation in effectiveness within pathways is far greater than the average differences between pathways."

Some researchers argue that it is possible to decrease professional isolation by establishing formal networks for rural administrators who can not find mentors or supportive colleagues near by (Howley, Chadwick, & Howley, 2002). However, given the economic hardships faced by many rural communities, improving salary and benefits seems unlikely in the absence of additional state or federal fiscal support.

Rural schools can benefit from state programs that aim to recruit and retain principals and superintendents in high-need schools of all kinds by providing salary enhancements (Education Commission of the States, 2007). Arkansas, for example, provides a bonus of $25,000 to principals who receive a master school principal designation from the Arkansas Leadership Academy and are employed in a school in "academic distress" (ARK. CODE ANN. § 6-17-1602). Similarly, Georgia principals are given a salary incentive if they are willing to take the principal position at a school that is considered "in need of improvement" [GA. CODE ANN. § 20-2-214 (SB. 468 passed 4/19/06)]. As part of NCLB, the Federal government has also promised to fund efforts to train and recruit "highly qualified" principals. Thus far, about $50 million has been awarded for this purpose, mostly to fund university-district principal training partnerships.

SPARSITY, TRANSPORTATION, AND PARENTAL INVOLVEMENT

The Challenge

Rural schools face heightened transportation costs. Using national data, Killeen and Sipple (2000) calculated per-pupil transportation expenditures in rural districts to be twice as high as urban districts and 50 percent higher than for suburban districts. Moreover, Howley and Howley (2002) analyzed the length of student bus rides and found that students often spent an hour or more on the bus each way. They argued that student time was an unmeasured cost never calculated in district consolidation expenditure analyses.

In addition to costs of transporting students, the lengthy bus rides also pose challenges to the educational program and the well-being of the students (Howley & Howley, 2001). One study on school consolidation reported lengthy student ride-times and documented other costs such as sleep deprivation, lower grades, poor fitness, and inability to participate in extracurricular activities (Schwartzbeck, 2003). Fox (cited in Howley & Howley, 2001) found that long rides in rural Ontario reduced the number and variety of positive household activities and reduced students' sleep time, recreational time, academic attentiveness, and extracurricular participation. More than just depriving rural students of participation in extracurricular activities, Howley and Howley (2001) argue that long bus rides may well erode the social capital of rural communities (Coleman, 1988; Putnam, 1993).

Finally, as the distance from home to school increases, it is reasonable to expect reduced parent involvement in curricula and extracurricular activities. However, little available data support this conjecture. In fact, an NCES study found no difference in the involvement of rural versus non-rural parents (NCES, 2006). The same study found that parental participation varies more by income and education level than by race, family structure, or community type. For example, 87 percent of parents with graduate or professional degrees attend school events, while fewer than 45 percent of parents without a high school diploma attend school events. While the research is sparse in measuring involvement across rural schools, the literature is robust as to the value of close parent-teacher-student involvement to students, parents, and teachers (Lareau, 1987; NCREL, 1996; Neuman, Hagedorn, Celano, & Daly, 1995).

Strategies

Transportation costs impacted by sparsely populated areas can be offset by state aid adjustments. State policies compensating for the costs associated with sparsity most frequently target transportation costs. Some states (e.g., Alabama, Delaware, and Wyoming) provide 100 percent reimbursement for transportation costs, while others provide most of the expenditures (e.g., Arkansas 90 percent, Massachusetts 80 percent, and Ohio 90 percent). Montana offers 85 percent of all transportation expenditures, but institutes a penalty for the proportion of miles the buses are on the road and are less than 50 percent full. Wisconsin offers a graduated reimbursement schedule ranging from $12 per pupil for those students transported less than 2 miles up to $85 per pupil for those transported more than 18 miles each way.

Several states offer aid adjustments to compensate for the special costs of sparsely populated areas, though this number has not changed in more than a decade (Verstegen, 1990). Specifically, Arkansas, Kansas, Kentucky, Minnesota, and New York offer sparsity adjustments for some school districts, though the specifics of these adjustments employ widely different criteria. The Florida legislature offers sparsity aid for school districts with fewer than 20,000 pupils, while in New York, sparsity aid is provided to districts with fewer than 25 pupils per square mile. In Georgia, multiple criteria define those districts eligible for sparsity aid, including the inability to offer adequate educational programs due to small student counts and the lack of feasibility of merger (Sielke, 2000).

SMALL ENROLLMENT

The Challenge

Debate over the costs and benefits of small schools has raged for a century (Callahan, 1962; Lee & Smith, 1997; Tyack, 1974; Tyack & Hansot, 1982). Improving technology and growing support for the small-school movement (Hylden, 2005) has tempered concerns about the educational opportunities available to rural students. However, little has changed over the past 100 years to quell concerns about the perceived diseconomies of scale (i.e., inefficiency) inherent in these schools (Kannapel & DeYoung, 1999). Because 80 percent of rural districts enroll fewer than 600 students, concerns about scale economies are particularly pressing (NCES, 2003).

Strategies

Many state-level policy makers subscribe to the belief that consolidation (i.e., the merging of two or more districts into a single, larger district) is a means to improve the cost-effectiveness of rural schools, though there is little evidence that such actions improve efficiency. For example, Arkansas' Omnibus Education Act 60 requires that any school district with an enrollment of fewer than 350 students either (1) consolidate with one or more other district(s) to create a new district that would meet the minimum size requirements, or (2) be annexed into an existing district meeting those requirements. Through April 2006, 67 of the state's original 307 districts have been consolidated or annexed (Johnson, 2006). Other states encourage consolidation by providing incentives through operating or building aid programs (Lawrence et al., 2002; Sielke et al., 2001).

Scholars have examined whether the resulting consolidated districts are, or likely to be, more efficient. Cost-effectiveness analysis techniques (demanding that the effects *and* costs of policy actions be considered) suggest that the efficacy of these strategies is, at best, ambiguous. Proxies for "educational effectiveness" have included measures of student achievement, student social development (e.g., extracurricular participation), graduation rates, school climate (e.g., disciplinary actions and student and teacher attitudes), curriculum comprehensiveness, and community responsiveness (Arum, 2000; Fowler & Walberg, 1991; Haller, 1992; Haller & Monk, 1988; Howley, 1989; Howley & Howley, 2004; Monk & Haller, 1988; Nathan & Febey, 2001; Sipple, 2004; Verstegen, 1990). With the exception of curriculum comprehensiveness, researchers offer no convincing evidence that students of small rural schools have less of an educational experience than those in larger schools.

Scholars have also considered how district consolidation affects rural communities more broadly. These efforts generally conclude that the loss of a rural school adversely affects the community's economy, by eliminating a sizable employer and thereby fostering a decline in retail sales, property values, and tax revenues (Lyson, 2002; Sederberg, 1997; Sell & Leistritz, 1996). Rural schools are often the center of community social life, offering a reason and site for recreational, cultural, and civic events (e.g., sports, plays, dances, and political meetings) (Lyson, 2002; Peshkin, 1978).

It is not clear that consolidation yields economies of scale. In principle, larger schools should be able to offer a given instructional program at a lower expense than can smaller schools. However, Bard, Gardener, and Wielan's (2005) recent review of rural consolidation studies indicates that consolidation does not necessarily reduce per pupil expenditures (Reeves, 2003; Sher & Schaller, 1986; Sher & Tompkins, 1977).

Scholars have also nested discussions of the costs of consolidation within broader analyses of size economies in education. For example, Duncombe, Minor, and Ruggiero (1995) found that districts with very low enrollments (less than 500 students) do have higher per pupil costs than larger systems, particularly administrative and transportation costs. However, slight instructional, operating, or transportation cost savings are likely to result from the consolidation of geographically large, sparsely populated districts (i.e., typical rural districts). Further, districts that are best suited for consolidation on cost grounds are often wealthy, suburban districts that adjoin urban areas, which for a variety of reasons have maintained their independence.

Many policy makers also believe that educational service agencies (ESA) offer a means to overcome diseconomies of scale in small rural schools. Known variously as Boards of Cooperative Educational Services (New York), Intermediate School Districts (Michigan), and Educational Service Centers (Texas), ESAs are organizational units positioned between districts and the state. Though these units vary greatly regarding their governance and organizational structure, all are expected to provide services to component districts more cost-effectively than if the districts provided these services on their own (Stephens & Harmon, 1996; Cabray, 1998; Fletcher & Cole, 1992; Galvin, 1995; Helge, 1984; Morgan, 2001; Stephens, 1998; Stephens & Christiansen, 1995).

One or more of the following features typically characterize ESA services (Stanley, 1995; Stephens & Harmon, 1996): costly services that necessitate a concentration of students (e.g., programs for disabled students); services that warrant staff expertise that is in limited supply (e.g., curriculum development); and services that require expensive equipment or facilities (e.g., vocational education). Despite their *raison d'être*, few studies investigate the ESAs ability to improve rural school efficiency.

Nevertheless, three tangible lines of evidence suggest that ESAs might be cost-effective in assisting rural school districts. First, researchers have demonstrated that component districts are satisfied with the "quality" of services provided by their ESA (Adams & Ambrosie, 1987; Hayden & Fielder, 1999; McKinney & Gauntt, 2000; Talbott, 1995; Thew, 1994; Thomas, 1997; Talbott, 1995). Second, several studies have compared the costs of locally provided versus ESA provided services, typically favoring districts' use of ESAs (Brey, 1981; Campbell, 2001; Massachusetts Organization of Educational Collaboratives, 1989; Southwest and West Central Educational Cooperative Service Units, 1988; Stanley, 1992; Wallerstein, 1997). Third, a few studies have documented that administrators believe that ESAs provide services more cost-effectively (i.e., efficiently) than do individual districts (Stanley, 1992; Thomas, 1997; ECM, Inc., 1997).

Most states provide aid to districts when they use ESAs. This policy enables the district to pass along a portion of their local cost to the state. Thus, though it may be less costly for a district to contract for services because it is able to receive aid, it does not follow that the total cost to the broader system is always less than if they provided these services on their own. We are aware of no study that accounts for the role of state aid when studying the cost-effectiveness of ESA's. Given the importance of ESAs to rural schools, more definitive work in this area in warranted.

Many states have U-shaped aid formulae, with increased aid flowing to high need rural and urban districts (Sielke et al., 2001).[6] Districts are not eligible for additional aid just because they are rural, but because they are small, isolated or both. Most often districts or schools are identified as small because their enrollments fall below a legislatively defined threshold, which can vary substantially among states. Vermont, for example, identifies small districts as having an average daily membership below 100, while West Virginia uses 1,400 students (Griffith & Byrnett, 2005). Districts or schools identified as isolated are typically designated as such because of the physical distance between one school and another, again with substantial variation among states. Oregon requires a distance of eight miles between schools, while North Dakota requires 20 miles. Alternatively, Washington defines a school as isolated if a student has to travel more than one hour to reach his or her destination. Some states simply need the approval of the State Superintendent of Schools to identify a school as isolated for aid purposes, as is the case in Wyoming (Griffith & Byrnett, 2005).

CONCLUSION

In reviewing the unique challenges facing rural schools and the effective policies and strategies to assist in overcoming the challenges, we stress the lack of existing research on rural schools. While much research has targeted the challenges and policies related to quality curriculum, teacher recruitment, and school size and scale economies, the explicit study of these issues in rural settings is rare. Without more and better research taking place on specifically rural populations and taking into account remote location, sparsity, and size of rural schools and communities, there is a danger in perpetuating the stereotypes, misunderstandings, and misdirected policy initiatives surrounding rural schools (Arnold, 2005; Arnold, Newman, Gaddy, & Dean, 2005; Howley, 1997).

One example of this contextualized rural research was recently published by Howley & Howley (2004). In this study, the authors tackle this issue and provide a reanalysis of national data with attention for the unique attributes of small schools in rural settings rather than small schools in urban settings. They provide evidence of how very small schools in rural areas provide effective educational environments (especially for poor children) when students are used as the unit of analysis, rather than the school or district.

Each of the four challenges we have discussed, and the strategies aimed to overcome the challenges, motivates a healthy array of future research questions. For instance, what are the long-term costs and benefits of the use of technology to reduce social and academic isolation in remote areas? Such work has implications for distance learning, the reduction of teacher turnover and incentives, and transportation costs. To what degree does distance traveled from home to school impact student achievement, participation in extracurricular activities—which are known to improve achievement (Coladarci & Cobb, 1996)—and parental involvement in schools? In light of the rapid technological advances in personal and group communication, how does the new technological environment impact the scale economies in schools?

The findings of such research may document the disadvantage of rural schools and press for further consolidation. Conversely, as broadband access to rural communities grows, it may reduce the isolation and turnover of teachers and students. These are just a few of the many research and evaluation studies necessary to fully understand the challenges confronting rural schools and their communities and to assist policy makers in their quest for more equitable and adequate school resource policies.

NOTES

1. See chapter 26 in this volume for a discussion of a new form of distance education, "virtual schools," as it relates to home schooling. See also, Southern Regional Education Board (2006) for a report on the future of virtual schooling.
2. Arizona, Arkansas, California, Connecticut, Florida, Kentucky, Maine, Maryland, Massachusetts, Minnesota, Nebraska, Oklahoma, Oregon, Pennsylvania, South Carolina, Texas, Utah, Virginia, and Wisconsin.
3. Alabama, Arkansas, California, Connecticut, Iowa, Louisiana, Michigan, North Carolina, Oklahoma., Texas, and West Virginia.
4. Maryland, Massachusetts, New York, and South Carolina.
5. Maryland, North Carolian, South Carolina, and Texas.
6. Earlier in this volume Duncombe & Yinger provided a thoughtful treatment of the theories that ground the conception and measurement of cost-differentials in education, including size and regional variations. We do not revisit these issues here. Instead, we draw attention to how policy makers currently use aid formula to provide additional funding to rural schools.

REFERENCES

Adams, C. F., & Ambrosie, F. (1987). *Improving educational quality: A role for the regional educational agency*. ERIC Document Reproduction Service No. ED 284 348.

Adams, J. P. (1987). *Superintendents and effective schools*. Unpublished doctoral dissertation, University of California, Santa Barbara.

Arnold, M. L. (2005). Rural education: A new perspective is needed at the U.S. Department of Education.

Journal of Research in Rural Education, 20(3), Retrieved May 15, 2005 from http://www.umaine.edu/jrre/2020-2003.pdf.

Arnold, M. L., Newman, J. H., Gaddy, B. B., & Dean, C. B. (2005). A look at the condition of rural education research: Setting a direction for future research. *Journal of Research in Rural Education*, 20(6), Retrieved May 15, 2005, from http://www.umaine.edu/jrre/2020-2006.pdf.

Arum, R. (2000). School and communities: Ecological and institutional dimensions. *Annual Revue of Sociology,* 26, 395–418.

Baker, B. D. (2005). The Emerging Shape of Educational Adequacy: From Theoretical Assumptions to Empirical Evidence. *Journal of Education Finance*, 30(3), 259–287.

Bard, J., Gardener, C., & Wieland, R. (2005). *Rural School Consolidation Report.* Prepared for the National Rural Education Association: NREA Consolidation Task Force.

Barker, B. (1985). *A study reporting secondary course offerings in small and large high schools.* ERIC Document Reproduction Service No. ED 256 547.

Barker, B. (1989). *Distance learning case studies.* ERIC Document Reproduction Service No. ED 332 661.

Barker, B. & Hall, R. F. (1994). Distance education in rural schools: technologies and practice. *Journal of Research in Rural Education*, 10, 126–28.

Beeson, E. & Strange, M. (2000). Why rural matters: The need for every state to take action on rural education. *Journal of research in Rural Educa*tion, 16(2), 63–140.

Bickel, W. E. (1983). Effective schools: Knowledge, dissemination, inquiry. *Educational Researcher,* 12, 3–5.

Bill and Melinda Gates Foundation (2001). Chicago High School Redesign Initiative. Chicago.

Bourdieu, P., & Passeron, J.C. (1977). *Reproduction in education, society, and culture.* Beverly Hills, CA: Sage.

Boyd, D., Grossman, P., Lankford, H., Loeb, S., & Wyckoff, J. (2005). *How changes in entry requirements alter the teacher workforce and affect student achievement.* Albany: State University of New York.

Boyd, D., Lankford, H., Loeb, S., & Wyckoff, J. (2003). Understanding Teacher Labor Markets: Implications for Equity. Albany, NY: Educational Finance Research Association, www.albany.edu/edfin.

Boyd, D., Lankford, H., Loeb, S., & Wyckoff, J. (2005). The draw of home: How teachers' preferences for proximity disadvantage urban schools. *Journal of Policy Analysis and Management*, 24(1), 113–132.

Brent, B. O. (1999). Distance education: Implications for equity and cost-effectiveness in the allocation and use of Educational Resources. *Journal of Education Finance*, 25(2), 229–254.

Brent, B. O., Sipple, J. W., Killeen, K. M., & Wischnowski, M. W. (2004). Stalking cost-effective practices in rural schools. *Journal of Education Finance*, 29(3), 237–256.

Brookover, W. & Lezotte, L. (1979). *Changes in school characteristics coincident with changes in student achievement.* Lansing, MI: Institute for Research on Teaching (Document Reproduction Service No. ED 181 005).

Brown, D. L., Swanson, L. E., & Barton, A. W. (2003). *Challenges for rural America in the twenty-first century.* University Park: Pennsylvania State University Press.

Browne-Ferrigno, T. & Allen, L. W. (2006). Preparing principals for high need rural schools: A central office perspective about collaborative efforts to transform school leadership. *Journal of Research in Rural Education*, 2, 1–15.

Bullard, P., & Taylor, B.O. (1993). *Making school reform happen.* Boston: Allyn & Bacon.

Cabrey, P. A. (1998). *The Interorganizational Relationship Between Selected School Districts and an Intermediate Unit.* Unpublished Doctoral Dissertation, University of Pittsburgh.

Callahan, R. E. (1962). Education and the cult of efficiency; a study of the social forces that have shaped the administration of the public schools. Chicago: University of Chicago Press.

Campbell, D. C. (2001). Proving the worth of ESAs: A cost-efficiency study for an ESD in Oregon," *Perspectives,* 7, 25–28.

Castle, S.D. (2002). *Job satisfaction of Ohio city, local, and exempted village school superintendents and their perceptions of a career crisis in the school superintendency.* Unpublished doctoral dissertation, Bowling Green State University.

Catchpole, M. J. (1988). *Student response to a distance education course Incorporating live interactive television* (Document Reproduction Service No. ED 311 886).

Chambers, J. G. (1995). Public School Teacher Cost Differences Across the United States: Introduction to a Teacher Cost Index (TCI), NCES 95758. Washington, DC: National Center for Education Statistics.

Clark, D., Lotto, L. S., & Astuto, T. A. (1984). Effective schools and school improvement: A comparative analysis of two lines of inquiry. *Educational Evaluation and Policy Analysis,* 11(2), 181–199.

Clewell, B. C., Darke, K., Davis-Googe, T., Forcier, L., Manes, S., & Washington, D. C. (2000). Literature review on teacher recruitment programs. Prepared for the U. S. Department of Education Planning and Evaluation Service. Washington, DC: The Urban Institute.

Coladarci, T. & Cobb, C. (1996). Extracurricular participation, school size, and achievement and self-esteem among high school students. *Journal of Research in Rural Education*, 92–103.

Coleman, J. (1988). Social capital in the creation of human capital. *The American Journal of Sociology,* 94, S95–S120.

Cooper, B. S., Fusarelli, L. D., & Carella, V. A. (2000). *Career crisis in the superintendency? The results of a national survey.* ERIC Document Reproduction Service No. ED 143 167.

Crowe, D. J. (1990). Distance education utilizing two-way interactive and special features: A 4th year evaluation study — perceptions by students and parent (Interactive Video). Unpublished doctoral dissertation, Wayne State University.

Cuban, L. (1984). *Transforming the frog into a prince: Effective schools research policy and practice at the district level. Harvard Educational Review,* 54, 129–151.

Darling-Hammond, L., & Sykes, G. (1999). Teaching as the learning profession : handbook of policy and practice (1st ed.). San Francisco: Jossey-Bass Publishers.

Dean, C. B., & Lauer, P. A. (2001). State policy support for professional development in the Central Region. Aurora, CO: Mid-continent Research for Education and Learning.

Desimone, L. (1999). Linking parental involvement with student achievement: Do race and income matter? *Journal of Educational Research,* 93, 11–31.

DeYoung, A. J. (1995). Bridging multiple worlds: The school superintendent as change agent in a rural and poor school district. *Journal of Research on Rural Education*, 11, 187–197.

Distance Learning Evaluation: Final Report 1994–95. Dutchess County, New York. New York: EDC Center for Children and Technology.

Dlugosh, L.L. (1994). *Why administrators move: Factors contributing to the turnover of school administrators in Nebraska.* Lincoln, NB: Department of Educational Administration. ERIC Document Reproduction Service No. ED 375 505.

Duncombe, W., Minor, J., & Ruggiero, J. (1995). Potential cost savings from rural school district consolidation: A case study of New York. *Economics of Education Review,* 14, 265–284.

Dunne, R. J. (2003). Introduction to the special issues in rural education finance. *Journal of Education Finance,* 29(2), 101–106.

ECM, Inc. (1997). *Potential Savings in Rural Public School Non-instructional Costs through Shared Services Arrangements: A Regional Study.* ERIC Document Reproduction Service No. ED 426 822.

Edmonds, R. (1979). *A Discussion of the literature and issues related to effective schooling.* ERIC Document Reproduction Service No. ED 170 394.

Education Commission of the States (2007). Leadership in hard to staff schools. Retrieved January 15, 2007 from http://mb2.ecs.org.reports/Report.aspx?id=852.

Education Research Service (ERS) (1998). *Is there a shortage of qualified candidates for openings in the principalship? An exploratory study.* Report prepared for the National Association of Elementary School Principals and the National Association of Secondary School Principals.

Elfers, A., Plecki, M., & Knapp, M. (2006). Teacher Mobility: Looking More Closely at "The Movers" Within a State System. *Peabody Journal of Education,* 81(3), 94–127

Esparo, L.J. & Rader, R. (2001). The leadership crisis: The shortage of qualified superintendents is not going away. *American School Board Journal*, 188, 46–48.

Fan, X., & Chen, M. J. (1999). Academic achievement or rural school students: A multi-year comparison with their peers in suburban and urban schools. *Journal of Research in Rural Education,* 15(1), 31–46.

Firestone, W. A., & Pennell, J. R. (1993). Teacher commitment, working conditions, and differential incentive policies. *Review of Educational Research,* 63(4), 489–525.

Fletcher, R., & Cole, J. T. (1992). Rural educational collaboratives: An economic and programmatic viewpoint, *Journal of Rural and Small Schools,* 5, 32–33.

Fowler, W. J. & Walberg, H. J. (1991). School size, characteristics, and outcomes. *Educational Evaluation and Policy Analysis,* 13, 189–202.

Galvin, P. F. (1995). The physical structure of regional educational service agencies: Implications for service and equity goals. *Journal of Research in Rural Education,* 11, 105–113.

Glass, T.E. (2001). *State education leaders view the superintendent applicant crisis.* Education Commission of the States. Retrieved January 15, 2006 from http://www.ecs.org/clearinghouse/29/09/2909.htm

Glass, T.E., Bjork, L., & Brunner, C. C. (2000). *The study of the American school superintendency 2000. A look at the superintendent of education in the new millenium.* Arlington, VA: American Association of School Administrators. ERIC Document Reproduction Service No. ED 440 475.

Glazerman, S., & Tuttle, C. (2006). *An evaluation of American Board Teacher Certification: Progress and plans.* Washington, DC: Mathematica Policy Research.

Glazerman, S., Mayer, D., & Decker, P. (206). Alternative routes to teaching: The impacts of teach for America on student achievement and other outcomes. *Journal of Policy Analysis and Management,* 25(1).

Goldhaber, D. D., & Brewer, D. J. (2000). Does Teacher Certification Matter? *High School Teacher Certification Status and Student Achievement Educational Evaluation and Policy Analysis,* 22(2), 129–145.

Grady, M.L. & Bryant, M.T. (1991). School board turmoil and superintendent turnover: What pushes them to the brink? *The School Administrator,* 2, 19–26.

Griffin, G. W. (1992). *Principals' and Superintendents' Perceptions of Superintendent Behaviors and Activities which are linked to School Effectiveness.* Unpublished doctoral dissertation, University of Oklahoma.

Griffith, M., & Byrnett, P. (2005). State funding issues for small and isolates school districts. Education Commission of the States. Retrieved January 15, 2007 from http://www.ecs.org/html/Document.asp?chouseid=6362.

Guarino, C. M., Santibañez, L., & Daley, G. A. (2006). Teacher recruitment and retention: A review of the recent empirical literature. *Review of Educational Research,* 76(2), 173–208.

Hall, R. F. & Barker, B. O. (1995). Case studies in the current use of technology in education, *Rural Research Report,* 6, 1–12.

Haller, E. J. (1992). High School Size and Student Indiscipline: Another Aspect of the School Consolidation Issue. *Educational Evaluation and Policy Analysis,* 14, 145–56.

Haller, E. J. (1992). *Small schools and higher order thinking skills.* New Brunswick: NJ, Consortium for Policy Research in Education.

Haller, E. J. & Monk, D. H. (1988). New reforms, old reforms, and the consolidation of small rural schools, *Educational Administration Quarterly,* 24, 470–83.

Haller, E. J., Monk, D. H., & Tien, L. (1993). Small schools and higher order thinking skills. *Journal of Research in Rural Education,* 9, 66–73.

Haller, E. J., Monk, D. H., Spotted Bear, A., Griffith, J., & Moss, P. (1990). School size and program comprehensiveness: Evidence from high school and beyond. *Educational Evaluation and Policy Analysis,* 12, 109–120.

Hammer, P. C., Hughes, G., McClure, C., Reeves, C., & Salgado, D. (2005). *Rural teacher recruitment and retention practices: A review of the research literature.* National Survey of Rural Superintendents and Case Studies of Programs in Virginia: Appalachia Educational Laboratory (AEL) at Edvantia.

Hawkins, J., Grimaldi, C., Baker, T., Dyer, P., Moeller, B., & Thompson, J. (1996). Distance learning. *CCT Reports,* 9.

Hayden, J. G., & Fielder, R. (1999). A comprehensive study of Iowa's AEA System, *Perspectives,* 5, 1–8.

Heim, J.M., & Wilson, A.P. (1987). *Situational factors contributing to administrator turnover in small Kansas school districts.* (ERIC Document Reproduction Service No. ED 279 444).

Helge, D. (1984). *Problems and strategies regarding regionalizing service delivery: Educational cooperatives in rural America.* ERIC Document Reproduction Service Document No. ED 242 449.

Horn, J. G. (1991). Rural/small school effectiveness as perceived by stakeholders. *The Rural Educator*, 12, 21–26.

Howley, A. & Howley, C. (2001). *Rural school busing*. Charleston WV.: ERIC Clearinghouse on Rural Education and Small Schools.

Howley, A., Chadwick, K., & Howley, C. W. (2002). Networking for the nuts and bolts: The ironies of professional development for rural principals. ERIC Document Reproduction Service No. ED 463 908.

Howley, A., Pendarvis, E., & Gibbs, T. (2002). Attracting principals to the superintendency: Conditions that make a difference to principals. *Education Policy Analysis Archives*, 10(43). Retrieved January 15, 2007, from http://epaa.asu.edu/epaa/v10n43.html.

Howley, C. & Howley, A. (2004). School size and the influence of socioeconomic status on student achievement: Confronting the threat of size bias in national data sets. *Education Policy Analysis Archives*, 12(52). Retrieved January 15, 2007, from http://epaa.asu.edu/epaa/v12n52/v12n52.pdf.

Howley, C. (1989). Synthesis of the effects of school and district size: What research says about achievement in small schools and school districts, *Journal of Rural and Small Schools,* 4, 2–12.

Howley, C. (1994). *The academic effectiveness of small-scale schooling (an update).* ERIC Document Reproduction Service No. ED 372 897.

Howley, C. B. (1997). How to make rural education research rural: An essay at practical advice. Research in Rural Education, 13, 131–138.

Howley, C. B., & Howley, A. A. (2004). School size and the influence of socioeconomic status on student achievement: Confronting the threat of size bias in national data sets. *Education Policy Analysis Archives*, 12(52), http://epaa.asu.edu/epaa/v12n52/.

Hylden, J. (2005). What's so big about small schools? The case for small schools: Nationwide and in North Dakota. Retrieved January 15, 2007 from http://www.ksg.harvard.edu/pepg/PDF/Papers/PEPG05-05Hylden.pdf.

Ingersoll, R. M. (2001). Teacher turnover and teacher shortages: An organizational analysis. American Educational Research Journal, 38(3), 499–534.

Ingersoll, R. M. (2003). Is There Really a Teacher Shortage?: University of Washington, Center for the Study of Teaching and Policy.

Iowa Department of Education. (1998). *Policy statement on the school administrator shortage*. Retrieved on August 10, 2004, from http://www.state.ia.us/educate/stateboard/shortage.html.

Israel, G. D., Beaulieu, L. J., & Hartless, G. (2001). The influence of family and community social capital on educational achievement. *Rural Sociology,* 66(1), 43–68.

Jimerson, L. (2003). *The competitive disadvantage: Teacher compensation in rural America*. Washington, DC: Rural School and Community Trust.

Jimerson, L. (2006). *The Hobbit Effect: Why Small Works in Public Schools.* Arlington, VA: Rural School and Community Trust.

Johnson, J. (2006). *An investigation of school closures resulting from forced district reorganization in Arkansas*. Arlington, VA: Rural and Community Trust.

Johnson, J. & Strange, M. (2005). Why rural matters 2005: The facts about rural education in the 50 states. Rural School and Community Trust. Retrieved September 1, 2006, from http://files.ruraledu.org/whyruralmatters/.

Jones, J. I. & Simonson, M. (1995). *Distance Education: A Cost-analysis* (ERIC Document Reproduction Service No. ED362 171).

Kannapel, P. F. & DeYoung, A. J. (1999). The rural school problem in 1999: A review and critique of the literature. *Journal of Research in Rural Education*, 15(2), 67–79.

Killeen, K., & Sipple, J. W. (2000). School consolidation and transportation policy: An empirical and institutional analysis. Rural School and Community Trust. Retrieved August 2006 from http://www.ruralchallenge.org/publications.html.

Killeen, K., & Sipple, J. W. (2005). Mandating Supplemental Intervention Services: Is New York State Doing Enough to Help All Students Succeed? Education Policy Analysis Archives, 13(19), Retrieved Fenruary 10, 2005 from http://epaa.asu.edu/epaa/v13n19/.

Kitchen, W. (1997). *Education in telecommunications: Partners in progress.* ERIC Document Reproduction Service No. ED282 551.

Ladd, H. F., & Hansen, J. S. (1999). *Making money matter: Financing America's schools.* Washington, D.C.: National Academy Press.

Lareau, A. (1987). Social class differences in family-school relationships: The importance of cultural capital. *Sociology of Education*, 60(April), 73–86.

Lawrence, B.K., Bingler, S., Diamond, B.M, Hill, B., Hoffman, L., Howley, C.B., Mitchell, S., Rudolph, D., & Washor, E. (2002). *Dollars & Sense: The cost-effectiveness of small schools.* Cincinnati: KnowledgeWorks Foundation/Rural School and Community Trust.

Lee, V. E. & Smith, J. B. (1995). Effects of high school restructuring and size on early gains in achievement and engagement. *Sociology of Education*, 68, 241–70.

Lee, V. E. & Smith, J. B. (1997). High school size: Which works best and for whom? *Educational Evaluation and Policy Analysis*, 19(3), 205–227.

Local Educational Service Delivery Systems in the State of Wisconsin. Unpublished Doctoral Dissertation, Vanderbilt University.

Lyson, T. A. (2002). What does a school mean to a community? Assessing the social and economic benefits of schools to rural villages in New York. *Journal of research in Rural Education*, 17(3), 131–137.

Massachusetts Organization of Educational Collaboratives (1989). *Analysis of savings.* Framingham, MA: Massachusetts Organization of Educational Collaboratives.

Mathis, W. J. (2003). Equity and Adequacy Challenges in Rural Schools and Communities. Paper presented at the annual meeting of the American Education Finance Association, Orlando, FL.

McKinney, B. & Gauntt, K. (2000). An evaluation of product and service awareness, utilization and quality, *Perspectives,* 6, 20–36.

Monk, D. H. & Haller, E. J. (1986). *Organizational alternatives for small rural schools: Final report to the legislature of the State of New York.* Ithaca, NY: Department of Education, New York State College of Agriculture and Life Sciences at Cornell University. (ERIC Document Reproduction Service No. ED 281 694).

Monk, D. H. (1987). Secondary school size and program comprehensiveness. *Economics of Education*, 6, 137–50.

Morgan, P. E. (2001). *A comparative study of rural school district cooperatives: A qualitative study.* Unpublished doctoral dissertation, Washington State University.

Mosteller, F. (1995). The Tennessee study of class size in the early school grades. *Future of Children*, 5, 113–27.

Mulhall, P. F., Flowers, N., & Mertens, S. B. (2004). Are middle level principals an endangered species? *Middle School Journal*, 58–62.

Murnane, R. J. (1987). Understanding teacher attrition. *Harvard Educational Review*, 57(2), 177–182.

Murphy, P. J., & Angelski, K. (1996/7). Rural teacher mobility: A report from British Columbia. *Rural Educator,* 18(2), 5–11.

Nathan, J. & Febey, K. (2001). Smaller, Safer, Saner, Successful Schools. National Clearinghouse for Educational Facilities, Washington, D.C. Retrieved on January 15, 2007, from http://www.edfacilities.org/pubs/saneschools.pdf.

National Center for Education Statistics (2005). Distance education courses for public elementary and secondary school students: 2002–03 U.S. Department of Education, Washington, DC.

National Center for Education Statistics (2007). Internet access in U.S. public schools and classrooms: 1994–2005. U.S. Department of Education. Washington, DC.

NCES. (2006). Navigating resources for rural schools: Educational changes taking place in rural America. Washington, DC: Institute of Education Sciences.

NCREL. (1996). Supporting ways parents and families can become involved in schools (Pathways Project): North Central Regional Educational Laboratory (NCREL).

Neuman, S. B., Hagedorn, T., Celano, D., & Daly, P. (1995). Toward a collaborative approach to parent involvement in early education: A study of teenage mothers in an African-American community. *American Educational Research Journal*, 32(4), 801–827.

New York State Council of School Superintendents. (2000). Snapshot 2000: A study of school superintendents in New York State. New York State Council of School Superintendents: Albany.

O'Connell, R.W. (2000). A longitudinal study of applicants for the superintendency. Paper presented at the Annual Meeting of the Northeastern Educational Research Association. Ellenville, NY. (ERIC Document Reproduction Service No. ED 452 590).

Odden, A., Archibald, S., et al. (2002). A Cost Framework for Professional Development. *Journal of Education Finance*, 28(1), 51–74.

Onyx, J. (2000). Measuring social capital in five communities, *The Journal of Applied Behavioral Science*, 36, 23–42.

Peshkin, A. (1978). *Growing up American: Schooling and the survival of community*. Chicago: University of Chicago Press.

Provasnik, S., & Dorfman, S. (2005). *Mobility in the teacher workforce.* Washington, DC: Institute for Education Sciences.

Powell, A. G., Farrar, E., & Cohen, D. K. (1985). *The shopping mall high school: Winners and losers in the educational marketplace.* Boston: Houghton Mifflin.

Purkey, S. C. & Smith, M. S. (1983). Effective Schools: A Review. *The Elementary School Journal*, 83, 427–452.

Putnam, R. (1993). What makes democracy work? *National Civic Review,* 82(2), 101–107.

Raywid, M. A. (1999). Current literature on small schools. Document Reproduction Service No. ED 425 049.

Reeves, C. (2003). *Implementing the No Child Left Behind Act: Implications for rural schools.* Educational Policy Publications. North Central Regional Educational Lab. Document Reproduction Service No. ED 475 037.

Reeves, E. B., & Bylund, R. A. (2005). Are Rural Schools Inferior to Urban Schools? A Multilevel Analysis of School Accountability Trends in Kentucky*. *Rural Sociology*, 70(3), 360.

Riehl, C., & Sipple, J. W. (1996). Making the most of time and talent: Secondary school organizational climates, teaching task environments, and teacher commitment. *American Educational Research Journal*, 33(4), 873–901.

Roscigno, V. J., Tomaskovic,-Devey, D., & Crowley, M. (2006). Education and the inequalities of place. *Social Forces*, 84, 2121–45.

Rowan, B., Bossert, S.T., & Dwyer, D.C. (1983). Research on effective schools: A cautionary note. *Educational Researcher*, 12, 24–31.

Russel, A. (2005). The facts and fictions about teacher shortages. *Policy Matters, American Association of State Colleges and Universities*, 2(5).

Schwartzbeck, T. D. (2003). Declining Counties, Declining School Enrollments [Electronic Version]. AASA, 2006. Retrieved September 2006 from http://www.aasa.org/government_relations/rural/Declining_Counties.pdf.

Schwartzbeck, T. D., Redfield, D., Morris, H., & Hammer, P. C. (2003). How are rural school districts meeting the teacher quality requirements of No Child Left Behind? Charlestown, WV: AEL.

Schwob, T. J. (2004). Rural education: Its nature and history. Retrieved December 20, 2004 from http://www.potsdam.edu/educ/cre/Minutes?VtfFuture.pdf.

Sederberg, C. H. (1997). Economic role of school districts in rural communities, *Research in Rural Education*, 4, 125–130.

Sell, R. S. & Leistritz, F. L. (1996). Socioeconomic impacts of school consolidation on host and vacated communities. *Journal of the Community Development Society,* 28, 186–205.

Sher, J., & Shaller, K. (1986). Heavy meddle: a critique of the North Carolina DPI's plan to mandate school district mergers throughout the state. ERIC Document Reproduction Service No. ED 270 245.

Sher, J., & Tompkins, R. (1977). Economy, efficiency, and equality: the myths of rural school and district consolidation. *CEFP Journal*, 15, 13–14, 16.

Shields, B.A. (2000). Administrator turnover: Causes and implications. Unpublished doctoral dissertation, State University of New York at Buffalo, New York.

Sielke, C. C. (2000). Georgia. Retrieved September 10, 2006, from http://nces.ed.gov/edfin/pdf/StFinance/Georgia.pdf.

Sielke, C., Dayton, J., Holmes, & Jefferson, A. (2001). *Public School Finance Programs of the United States and Canada, 1998–99* Washington, DC: U.S. Department of Education.

Sipple, J. W. (2004). Local anchors versus state levers in state-led school reform: identifying the community around public schools. In W. K. Hoy & C. G. Miskel (Eds.), *Educational administration, policy, and reform: Research and measurement* (Vol. 3, pp. 25–57). Greenwich, CT: Information Age.

Sipple, J. W. & Killeen, K. (2004). Context, capacity and concern: A district-level analysis of the implementation of standards-based reform. *Education Policy*, 18(3), 456–490.

Sipple, J. W., Killeen, K., & Monk, D. H. (2004). Adoption and adaptation: New York State school districts' responses to state imposed high school graduation requirements. *Educational Evaluation and Policy Analysis*, 26(2).

Southern Regional Education Board (2006). Report on State Virtual Schools. Retrieved January 15, 2007 from http://www.sreb.org/programs/EdTech/SVS/State_Virtual_School_Report_06.pdf.

Southwest and West Central Educational Cooperative Service Units (1988). *Cost Savings Analysis 1998–1989.* Marshall, MN: Southwest and West Central Educational Cooperative Service Units.

Staihr, B. & Sheaff, K. (2001). The success of the e-rate in rural America. Center for the Study of Rural America. Retrieved January 15, 2007 from http://www.Kansascityfed.org/ruralcenter/mainstreet/MSE_0201.pdf.

Stanley, M. C. (1992). Analyses of potential effectiveness of educational collaborative service expansion. Unpublished Doctoral Dissertation, Boston College.

Stanley, M. C. (1995). Proving ESAs save dollars: A Research Design that Works. *Perspectives,* 1, 13–22.

Stephens, E. R. (1998). *Expanding the vision.* Charleston, WV: Appalachia Educational Laboratory.

Stephens, E. R. & Christiansen, L. (1995). Filling the vacuum: The beginnings of National database on educational service agencies. *Perspectives,* 1, 1–8.

Stephens, E. R. & Harmon, H. L. (1996). Cost-Analysis Studies of Programs and Services of State Network of ESAs. *Perspectives*, 2, 7–21.

Stern, J.D. (1994). *The condition of education in rural schools.* Washington, DC: U.S. Department of Education.

Talbott, B. L. (1995). ESA Cost-effectiveness documented in Washington State Study. *Perspectives*, 1, 9–10.

Tennessee Advisory Commission on Intergovernmental Relations. (2002). Teacher Mobility Among Tennessee School Districts: Author, http://www.state/tn.us/tacir/Migration.pdf.

Thew, M. D. (1994). Perceptions of Key Stakeholders Toward the Intermediate Unit. Unpublished doctoral dissertation, University of Maryland.

Thomas, K. (1997). Client views of Texas service centers: Research findings from the service centers 2000 study. *Perspectives*, 3, 22–29.

Tomaskovic-Devey, B. & Tomaskovic-Devey, D. (1988). The social structural determinants of ethnic group behavior: single ancestry rates among four white American ethnic groups. *American Sociological Review*, 53, 650–659.

Truscott, D. M. & Truscott, S. D. (2005). Differing circumstances, shared challenges: Finding common ground between urban and rural schools. *Phi Delta Kappan*, 87(2), 123–130.

Tyack, D. B. (1974). *The one best system: A history of American urban education.* Cambridge, Mass.: Harvard University Press.

Tyack, D. B., & Hansot, E. (1982). *Managers of virtue: Public school leadership in America, 1820–1980.* New York: Basic Books.

United States Department of Labor (2007). *Occupational Outlook Handbook, 2006–07.* Bureau of Labor Statistics. Retrieved January 15, 2007 from: http://www.bls.gov/oco/print/ocos007.htm.

Universal Service Administration Company (2007). *E-Rate discounts for schools and universities.* Retrieved January 15, 2007 from http://www.universalservice.org/sl/about/overview-program.aspx.

University of Montana Rural Institute (2005). *Update on the demography of rural pisability part one: Rural and urban.* Retrieved January 15, 2007, from http://rtc.ruralinstitute.umt.edu/RuDis/RuDemography.htm.

Verstegen, D. A. (1990). *School finance at a glance.* Denver, CO: Education Commission of the States.

Verstegen, D. A. (1990). Efficiency and economies-of-scale revisited: Implications for financing rural school districts. *Journal of Education Finance*, 16, 159–179.

Wallerstein, S. O. (1997). Connecticut RESC Cost-Effectiveness. *Perspectives*, 3, 30–35.

Winter, P. A., & Morgenthal, J. R. (2002). Principal recruitment in a reform environment: Effects of school achievement and school level on applicant attraction to the job. *Educational Administration Quarterly*, 38, 319–340.

Winter, P. A., Rinehart, J. S., & Munoz, M. A. (2002). Principal recruitment: An empirical evaluation of a school district's internal pool of principal certified personnel. *Journal of Personnel Evaluation in Education*, 16, 129–141.

Witham, M. (1993). Definition of rurality. Retrieved January 15, 2007 from: http://www.nexus.edu.au/Teachstud/dexed/docs/ruraliry.html.

Yerkes, D. M., & Guaglianone, C. L. (1998). Where have all the high school administrators gone? *Thrust for Educational Leadership*, 28, 10–14.

Yinger, J. (2004). *Helping children left behind: state aid and the pursuit of educational equity*. Cambridge, Mass.: MIT Press.

Zars, B. (1998). White paper on the impact of long bus rides on the education of rural children. Randolph, VT: Rural Challenge Policy Program.

35

The Organizational and Fiscal Implications of Transient Student Populations

Kieran M. Killeen and Kai A. Schafft

STUDENT TRANSIENCY: DEFINING THE ISSUES

The United States is a mobile nation, with about 16 percent of its population changing residence each year (Schachter, 2001). Americans frequently think of residential mobility as a voluntary and opportunity-related behavior in which people choose to move in order to take advantage of social and economic opportunities at migration destinations, and this generality is accurate with respect to the movement of households with relatively high and stable socioeconomic status (Cadwallader, 1992). However, demographers have long noted that households at the wealthiest *and* poorest ends of the spectrum are most likely to be residentially mobile (Long, 1973; Nord, Luloff, & Jensen, 1995; Schachter, 2001). Unlike wealthier households, low-income families often move for largely unplanned and unpredictable reasons, including household crises such as family breakup, inability to pay rent, or movement away from unsafe, unaffordable or otherwise unacceptable living conditions (Fitchen, 1992, 1994; Schafft, 2005, 2006).

One of the consequences of family instability is student transiency, which refers to the repeated non-promotional and unscheduled movement of students from one school or school district to another. Highly mobile students tend to come from low-income families, migrant or limited English proficiency backgrounds, and/or single-parent families (Rumberger, Larson, Ream, & Palardy, 1999; US General Accounting Office, 1994; Wood, Halfon, Scarlata, Newacheck, & Nessim, 1993). The lives of children are socially and academically disrupted through these frequent and unpredictable school and residence changes.

Despite significantly negative consequences for both children and schools, student transiency is not well recognized within the research and policy arenas. This is the case for several reasons. First, transient students are an institutionally untargeted population. Federal aid for education flows towards schools serving children of migrant workers and homeless students. Although migrant and homeless students may often experience frequent residential mobility, many students from poor mobile households do not fit the socio-demographic profiles of either migrant or homeless students (Hartman, 2002; Schafft, 2006). In fact, poverty-related student mobility is often highly localized and may have no connection to migrant labor and/or seasonal agricultural economies (Schafft, 2005, 2006). Similarly, while low income transient students may often live in temporary and/or inadequate housing, they may not technically be homeless.

Additionally, although schools may experience significant churning of student populations, the numbers of entering and exiting students are often roughly equal and thus in many instances have only negligible effects on net enrollment (Schafft, 2005). This further contributes to the "invisibility" of student movement. As a superintendent in a rural New York district remarked on the incidence of transiency within his district:

> Most of the community does not recognize (student movement) as an issue. But it creates a huge problem... the aid is frozen by the state. To pay for the needs of these kids we will have to go to the local taxpayer. It's a hard sell to the community at large that we have this unknown group that requires some substantial resources that don't even exist to most people here but nonetheless are very real to us. (Schafft, 2005, p. 10)

Despite the relative invisibility of these students, however, a number of studies have identified the scope and magnitude of student transiency, especially within economically disadvantaged school districts and among economically disadvantaged students. A nationally representative study conducted in the early 1990s found that about 17 percent of third graders overall had attended three or more schools since kindergarten. Of children from families with less than $10,000 annual income, 30 percent changed schools frequently, as did 25 percent of children in inner city schools (U.S. General Accounting Office, 1994). In California one out of five high schools was found to have annual mobility rates greater than 30 percent, and one in 10 had mobility rates greater than 40 percent (Rumberger et al., 1999). A Florida study showed that schools with poverty rates falling into the highest quartile had student mobility rates of 46 percent—double that of schools in the lowest poverty quartile (Office of Program Policy Analysis and Government Accountability (OPPAGA), 1997).

Student transiency has serious implications for students and schools, and deserves further attention within educational, administrative, and public policy arenas. It disrupts the social and academic lives of students, reduces academic achievement, and leads to a higher risk of drop out. Student transiency also creates distinct fiscal, administrative, and record-keeping challenges for schools. In the era of high-stakes testing, schools face additional threats of sanctions resulting from the test scores of low-achieving, high-need students who may well have spent only limited time receiving academic preparation from the school or district being held accountable for their learning. We explore all of these social, academic, and institutional issues in the following sections.

THE ACADEMIC IMPACTS OF TRANSIENCY

Research consistently points to profoundly negative social and academic outcomes associated with student transiency (Buerkle & Christenson, 1999; Grey, 1997; Hartman, 2002; Ingersoll, Scamman, & Eckerling, 1999; Lash & Kirkpatrick, 1990; Mehana & Reynolds, 2004; Nelson, Simoni, & Adelman, 1996; Rumberger et al., 1999; Wood et al., 1993). Using data from a nationally stratified sample of elementary school children in the third grade, the United States General Accounting Office (1994) found that about 41 percent of highly mobile third graders scored below grade level in reading, and about 31 percent scored below grade level in math. In comparison, only 26 percent of stable students (those who attended only one school since kindergarten) tested below grade level in reading, and about 16 percent tested below grade level in math. The study also found that highly mobile third graders were far more likely to repeat a grade than stable students.

The impact of enrolling and un-enrolling from school may be likened to the academic and social effects of absenteeism. In a study of student mobility in the Pittsburgh, Pennsylvania, School District, researchers standardized the impact of mobility by the equivalent academic effect of classroom absence. This study found that a change in schools in year one was equivalent being absent 32 days in year two, and 14 days in year three (Dunn, Kadane, & Garrow, 2003). In classrooms where students frequently enter and exit without warning, instructional pace is slowed both from month to month and from grade to grade. Instruction is more likely to be review-oriented and focused on getting new students academically up to speed (Kerbow, 1996). Furthermore, the negative social and academic consequences of high mobility are not limited to mobile students. As transient students are integrated and reintegrated into classroom instruction, attention and resources are diverted from resident students (Lash & Kirkpatrick, 1990). This is particularly true among mobile students with behavioral problems (Malmgren & Gagnon, 2005).

Transiency and disrupted social relationships may also contribute to adolescent behavioral problems and losses in pro-social friendship networks (Osher, Morrison, & Bailey, 2003; Simpson & Fowler, 1994; Tucker, Marx, & Long, 1998). Children of families that move frequently (defined as six or more times before age 17) are nearly eight times more likely to have significant and reoccurring behavior problems in school than those who move less often (Wood, et al., 1993). Behavior problems include attention problems, delinquent rule-breaking behavior, and social difficulties (Wood, et al., 1993). South and Haynie (2004), in an analysis of National Longitudinal Study of Adolescent Health data, find that the harmful effects of mobility are more pronounced among older adolescents and among girls and appear to persist for several years. More recent research has also linked mobility with early instances of sexual intercourse (Baumer & South, 2001; Haynie, South, & Bose, 2006).

Although some researchers have found mixed results, questioning the academic consequences directly attributable to student movement (Alexander, Entwisle, & Dauber, 1996; Hanushek, Kain, & Rivkin, 2004; Pribesh & Downey, 1999; Swanson and Schneider, 1999), empirical evidence consistently demonstrates how transiency is associated with multiple social and academic risk factors. This research in total suggests how mobility disrupts social and academic stability, and it underscores the need to better understand its causes, consequences, and the most appropriate responses for policy and practice.

STUDENTS MOST LIKELY TO BE MOBILE

Student turnover is highly associated with household-level economic distress and tends to occur with greater intensity in economically disadvantaged communities and neighborhoods. However, other student sub-populations are also highly mobile for a variety of reasons, sometimes related to economic distress, and sometimes not. These subpopulations include migrant students, homeless students, and children from military families. We discuss each in turn, concluding with a discussion of chronically mobile students from poverty backgrounds who are not technically migrant or homeless students.

Students from Migrant and Immigrant Backgrounds

American society is becoming increasingly ethnically diverse in large part due to new waves of immigrant populations (Lichter & Johnson, 2006; Kandel & Cromartie, 2004). Among immigrant populations, families employed within agriculture or related industries are those most likely to be mobile. Data from the Title I Migrant Education Program for the 2000–2001 academic year indicate that the migrant student population was nearly 900,000, a growth of 9 percent from two years earlier, with just over half of that population in California, Texas, and Florida. Ninety percent were Hispanic and one-third had limited English proficiency. Over one-half received some type or combination of social work, advocacy, or outreach services (United States Department of Education, 2004).

Because the average yearly earnings for a migrant adult is under $8,500 (United States Government Accounting Office, 1998), migrant students are disproportionately more likely to live in poverty than the non-migrant student population. Immigrant and migrant students must therefore confront challenges of poverty and academic instability in addition to linguistic and cultural barriers to educational achievement (Green, 2003; Hanna, 2003). These challenges are reflected in significantly reduced levels of academic achievement among migrant students. Only 40 percent of migrant students enter ninth grade in comparison to 96 percent of non-migrant students. Similarly, only 11 percent of migrant students enter twelfth grade as compared with 80 percent among non-migrant students (Olsen & Jaramillo, 1999).

A recent trend is for migrant families to relocate to areas that offer work in physically demanding and low paying meat-packing or food processing plants, particularly in the rural South and Midwest (Dalla & Christenson, 2005; Saenz & Torres, 2003). These industries have increasingly established themselves in declining rural communities that are eager to attract new economic activity. With little to no presence of organized labor, these plants can offer low wages and target foreign and migrant (and often undocumented) workers to fill labor needs (Stull, Broadway, & Griffith, 1995). The increased population diversity can create tension, particularly in communities and neighborhoods that historically have been ethnically homogeneous (Gouveia & Stull, 1997; Ream 2003) and ill-equipped to educate immigrant children (Saenz & Torres, 2003). Rapid population growth of immigrant and migrant families can strain community solidarity, as well as a community's capacity to provide housing, education, and social services. This is especially the case as the fiscal burdens for these sectors in the past several decades have shifted increasingly to state and local revenue sources (Dalla & Christenson, 2005).

Nonetheless, structures are in place to assist migrant students and their families. By law, school administrators must identify migrant children eligible for receiving services, and school funds are available to support recruitment efforts to actively enroll migrant students (Green, 2003). The Migrant Education Program, part of the Title I program, is a federally funded effort that offers supplementary instruction and supportive services, and is structured to address the interrelationships between poverty, mobility, and academic underachievement (Branz-Spall, Rosenthal, & Wright, 2003). While unable to meet all the needs of migrant children, the Migrant Education Program has proven an important resource for schools and districts in developing flexible programming and in facilitating records transfer for highly mobile migrant students. However, migrant students face overwhelming social, academic, and economic odds. Academic achievement gaps continue to starkly illustrate how much more progress still must be made in the effort to provide adequate and appropriate education to migrant students.

Homeless Students

The Institute for Children and Poverty in 2003 estimated that 1.35 million children in the United States are likely to experience homelessness on an annual basis. Popular stereotypes of what constitutes homelessness tend to be urban-oriented, and conjure up images of street people and those staying in inner-city homeless shelters. Nevertheless, the federal definition of homelessness among youth covers a much wider range of housing-insecure situations. These situations include children and youth who lack a regular or adequate nighttime residence; those sharing the housing of others (or "doubling up") because of housing loss or economic hardship; and children in substandard housing or living in motels, trailer parks, or campgrounds because of the lack of other, alternative housing arrangements.[1] While this is a broad and flexible interpretation of homelessness, it also leaves much to interpretation, and identification of homeless children requires a more detailed knowledge of a child's living circumstances than may be available to school personnel.

The federal McKinney-Vento Homeless Assistance Act of 2002 mandates that every school district designate a local "liaison" for homeless children and youth, often a guidance counselor, social worker, or school psychologist. The liaison is responsible for identifying and advocating for students living in homeless circumstances. In the broadest sense, the liaison's responsibility is to ensure that homeless children and youth have the same opportunities for academic success as their non-homeless peers. Local liaisons are mandated to assist homeless children and youth by facilitating school enrollment, helping students access a variety of school services, obtaining student records, and ensuring that homeless students have appropriate access to support services.

Local liaisons play potentially vital roles in ensuring that homeless students have equal educational access. Their responsibilities include ensuring that transportation services are provided to reduce the *academic* transiency of residentially mobile homeless children. By law, the McKinney-Vento Homeless Assistance Act ensures that if a child becomes homeless and relocates outside the school district, the student is entitled to remain in the district of origin for the duration of the homelessness, in accordance with state education department plans and policies determining how districts will apportion the provision of transportation to homeless youth.

Some researchers argue that more information is needed within schools and communities, not only about the services to which homeless children and families are entitled, but also concerning *who* is entitled and under which circumstances (Julienelle & Foscarinis, 2003; Schafft, 2006). Homeless parents are rarely aware of rights guaranteed to their children, and districts are often in non-compliance with these regulations because they are either not fully aware of either the circumstances of the child or the specifics of the law. District administrators are responsible for identifying homeless students who may be eligible for transportation services. Recently, 13 Long Island, New York, school districts lost a 2004 federal class action lawsuit in which the districts in question were found to have obstructed homeless students from enrolling in school, by not providing adequate transportation. This resulted in a lack of access to school for up to months at a time for some of the plaintiffs. School districts must develop protocols to ensure that mobile students who meet the criteria as homeless are accorded the rights guaranteed them and are provided with the opportunity to remain within the school district despite uncertain housing circumstances.

Mobile Students from Military Families

Regardless of the type of school in which they are enrolled—public, private, or Department of Defense schools[2]—hildren from military families are highly mobile. Schools within the Department of Defense Education Activity (DoDEA) system, for example, typically experience 35 percent or greater student turnover annually (Smrekar, Guthrie, Owens, & Sims, 2001; Smrekar & Owens, 2003). In addition, children from military families often have socio-demographic backgrounds frequently associated with lower academic achievement. Eighty percent of all children in Department of Defense schools have a parent who is enlisted, and most enlisted personnel have no greater than a high school diploma, and have incomes at or near the poverty line[3] (Smrekar & Owens, 2003). Additionally, 40 percent of the students are from minority backgrounds (Military

Family Resource Center, 2001), and as many as 50 percent of students in Department of Defense schools qualify for free or reduced-price lunch (Smrekar, Guthrie, Owens, & Sims, 2001).

Despite elevated mobility and other factors that would generally be associated with decreased academic achievement, children from military families, and especially those attending DoDEA schools, typically score at or above national averages when taking into account the level of parental educational attainment (Popp, Stronge, & Hindman, 2003; Smrekar & Owens, 2003). Several factors likely account for this. About 90 percent of children in DoDEA schools come from two-parent families in comparison to about 70 percent of children in public schools nationwide. In addition, these children, while mobile, come from families with a steady source of income, and housing is provided if families live on military bases. Therefore, children from military families do not experience the chronic physical and psychological stress that accompanies prolonged economic and housing insecurity. Additionally, military communities are tight knit, often with family support mechanisms to ease the stress of transitions associated with residential relocations and deployments (Popp et al., 2003; Smrekar & Owens, 2003). Last, there is no social stigma attached to family and student mobility associated with military family relocation as there is with poverty-associated mobility (Popp et al., 2003).

DoDEA schools, in particular, are structured to handle the social and academic needs of mobile students and accommodate the associated administrative and fiscal demands. Measures include full time registration and records clerks as well as institutionalized orientation procedures for new students. Family Readiness groups and Family Care plan, coordinated through school and military units, provide care and support systems for children when parents are deployed. There is also a high level of expected parental involvement in DoDEA schools. Military personnel are granted leave time to take part in parent-teacher conferences, as well as to volunteer in the school each month if they choose to do so (Smrekar & Owens, 2003). In sum, while mobile children from military families experience the psychological and social stress of frequent moves, support systems are in place socially and academically to help children adjust, and movement is neither directly caused by, nor a contributing factor to, family disorganization.

Transiency and Poverty-Related Household Mobility

Unlike students from military or migrant farm-working families, other students are mobile due to poverty-related reasons and the inability to secure adequate, affordable housing. These conditions have been worsened by declining rates of homeownership among low income families, rising rent burdens, limited access to housing assistance, and short-term tenancy in overcrowded and often unsafe housing (Crowley, 2003; Fitchen, 1995; Schafft, 2006). In essence, housing-insecure families do not move in response to economic or other opportunities. Rather, these families move when they find themselves without housing or having to vacate current housing because of safety issues and/or affordability. The number of transient students mobile for poverty-related reasons is difficult to estimate. However, they arguably constitute America's largest group of chronically mobile students.

Because they are an institutionally untargeted group, transient students face particular disadvantages. Unlike homeless and migrant students, or students from military backgrounds, there are neither programs nor mandates to meet the particular academic and social needs of the transient student who, while not technically "homeless," may frequently change residence and schools for reasons of poverty and housing insecurity. Regardless, transient, low income students are at high risk of social and academic problems. As a guidance counselor from an Upstate New York school district explained, "No one owns these kids. They have no political or economic power. The chances of reform happening (for them) are certainly less than they might be for other groups. No

THE RELATIONSHIP BETWEEN POVERTY, TRANSIENCY AND ACADEMIC UNDERACHIEVEMENT: A PARENT'S OWN WORDS

In earlier research in upstate New York, the second of the two authors conducted interviews in a set of high need districts with low income parents whose children had made one or more unscheduled school changes during the academic year. The single mother quoted below was 28 years old at the time of the interview, with two daughters, a nine-year-old and a three-year-old. In the five years preceding the interview, she and her daughters made five residential changes. Her oldest daughter had just transferred into the district, which was her sixth unscheduled school change. The mother's story helps to illustrate the interrelationships between poverty, residential mobility, and student transiency, as well as its frequent inter-generational characteristics.

You told me that when you were growing up, you moved around a lot too. What was that like?

A lot of tearful nights.... because I never really knew anybody. I never got to where I could say "hey this is my long-time good friend," because I never got to stay anywhere for too long. When I was ready to learn and put in all I had and just go gung ho, every time I got to that time, I got snatched up and moved somewhere else. I never looked forward to anything because I was always pulled in halfway through something, or right at the end of something and I never felt like it was complete. It was bits and pieces of everything, is how I felt. You get bits and pieces and bits and pieces and pretty soon you don't care no more.

The one time we stayed where we were for a while, I doubled up my school years because I had failed a grade and I had a chance to double up and take them both at once, and get back to where I was supposed to be. I worked really, really hard at it and then I achieved it and when I got up here, the program I went through down in Florida was not acknowledged. So I was right back at square one again and at that point I had given up. I didn't care no more.

I have learning disabilities. I'm dyslexic and that made it that much harder for me. So when I took off, I didn't care no more. I got picked on because I talked "southern" and like I said, the education level up here is way higher than it is down there. You just give up. I didn't care no more, and by the time I did start caring again I ended up with my daughter and had to go to work so I didn't have time for school by that point anyway.

So you grew up down south?

Yeah, mostly down south. I moved up here when I was 15. I lived in Florida, I lived in Georgia, I lived in New Jersey. I lived in Arizona and then I moved back to Florida, and then moved back up here. We moved all the time.

Why did your family move?

Sometimes it was for job purposes. Other times it was to get away from my biological father that had pulled a bunch of stuff on my mom. And then the last move that we made to up here was because my grandfather passed away and my mom couldn't handle it down south any more and she wanted to be closer to her family and so we moved back up here again.

one speaks on behalf of these kids and they are less likely to advocate on behalf of themselves" (Schafft, 2005).

SCHOOLS AND SETTINGS MOST LIKELY TO EXPERIENCE STUDENT TRANSIENCY

Within urban areas, transiency rates have been found to vary. Bruno and Isken (1996) reported average school-level transiency rates (the number of students entering and leaving a school over an academic year as a percentage of the school's total enrollment) within the Los Angeles Unified School District at 42.6 percent. They further found rates to be variable and especially high at the elementary level, with some schools experiencing transiency rates as high as 95 percent. A 1992 study of Chicago, IL public schools noted an average student transiency rate of 36 percent (Beruckzko & Reynolds, 1992), while Kerbow (1996) reported that only 38 percent of sixth graders had attended the same school throughout their elementary years, and 13 percent had attended four or more schools during that period. Ligon and Paredes (1992) reported transiency rates in Austin, Texas at an average of 23 percent. In Baltimore, MD schools, Alexander et al. (1996) found that over a five-year period, transiency rates averaged between 14 and 21 percent.

Some studies have suggested that student transiency is, in fact, a predominantly urban phenomenon. For instance, one study found that about 25 percent of inner city third graders were highly mobile, as compared with only about 15 percent of suburban and rural third graders (United States General Accounting Office, 1994). This may be explained in part, however, by the relationship between poverty and student transiency, the concentration of poverty within the urban core, and the aggregating of rural and suburban data.

A New York State study examined the collection of five-year residential and educational histories from 22 families of students eligible for free or reduced price lunch who had recently transferred into a rural district in upstate New York. It found that, on average, families had lived in six different residences over the five-year period with some respondents having lived in as many as 13 different places. In total, the children of these 22 households made 166 school changes over the five-year period, 92 percent of which were directly attributable to residential relocation. Most of the movement was between rural districts (Schafft, 2006). This is consistent with work in other locations that has examined rural residential instability and school change (Colton, 2004; Fitchen, 1995; Foulkes & Newbold, 2005; Morgan, 2005; Paik & Phillips, 2002).

In short, research on student transiency has tended to focus on its occurrence within urban locations or use aggregated data gathered across the urban-rural continuum. This pattern is curious given that research has consistently shown how rates of poverty are higher in rural areas than in urban ones (Jensen, McLaughlin, & Slack, 2003). However, despite the limited research on transiency in rural areas, mobility of low income students should not simply be considered an urban phenomenon in either its incidence or its consequences for students and schools. Moreover, as we discuss below, the smaller size of rural schools and districts means that the fiscal and human resource impacts of student transiency may be less easily absorbed than in a larger urban district.

RESOURCE AND ORGANIZATIONAL IMPLICATIONS OF TRANSIENCY FOR SCHOOLS AND DISTRICTS

While there is now substantial empirical research on student transiency and its effects on social and academic outcomes, there is a pronounced lack of research on the organizational or fiscal impact of transience on schools as institutions. At the micro level, the entrance or exit of a child from a school initiates a sequence of administrative record keeping steps (e.g. enrollment forms, eligibility analysis, course scheduling, and curricular alignment). These can result in increased staffing demands, reduced per-pupil resources, slowed school improvement, and a reduced capacity to engage in community-building efforts (Hartman 2006). This section examines how mobility interacts with issues such as school/district size, state aid calculations, and accountability.

Mobility, School/District Size, and Absorption Capacity

Transient students may represent liabilities to districts in terms of both increased fiscal costs and lowered test scores, particularly in economically disadvantaged areas. These are the districts that are least likely to have the resources or economies of scale to absorb large and unexpected costs affiliated with mobility (Paik & Phillips, 2002). The unexpected shifts in student population due to mobility represent a type of fiscal stress in these circumstances. As a superintendent from a rural New York district with an enrollment of about 650 explained:

> There is increased pressure on school budgets. One sixth of our budget is targeted towards special needs kids. This year we had budgeted \$100,000 for expenses associated with kids we anticipated would move into the district. We figured that we could expect four special needs kids to move into the district. We actually had ten move in, and we ended up needing to spend \$250,000 to meet their needs, so we went \$150,000 over our budget. We are a small district and so this was significant. (Schafft, 2005, p. 10)

Fiscal stress occurs in this example due to the enrollment of high cost students and associated instructional planning (e.g., staffing, facilities, and accommodations). Stress is also experienced through delayed reimbursement for those costs. Though state governments will reimburse districts for costs associated with the enrollment of special education students, these reimbursements are not immediate and rarely are they complete.

Although student transiency poses significant fiscal, administrative, and academic challenges across both urban and rural contexts, evidence suggests that larger, urban school districts may more easily absorb the challenges. In addition to district size and the enhanced ability of a larger urban district to absorb costs associated with individual students, some research in urban settings has suggested that much of the student movement is school-to-school from within the same district (Kerbow, 1996). In large urban districts there are more opportunities for mobile students to make school-to-school moves, without crossing district boundaries. Movements within the same school district and across schools pose administrative and record-keeping challenges, yet challenges are eased by circumstances like aligned curricula, consistent academic calendars, instructional pacing, and centralized record-keeping. Such consistencies may not be enjoyed when mobile children cross district boundaries, which is frequently the case in small or rural school districts. Among rural districts, by contrast, there is often just one school for each set of grade levels. Therefore a child's movement out of a school would likely mean entrance into a wholly different curriculum and course sequencing within a new district.

Mobility, Enrollment Counts, and Impact on State Aid Formulas

Student mobility also frustrates state aid formulas. Often aid formulas are simply not sensitive enough to adjust for the impact of mobility. Be it need-based aid or wealth equalization formulas, a common feature in the calculus of state aid involves the development of an enrollment count for any one school district or school. Noting that enrollments vary over time, state aid policies commonly define enrollment as an average daily membership (ADM) and then enter this figure into a variety of allocation schemes (e.g., flat grants, foundation formulas, categorical, or need-based aid).

When enrollment is measured infrequently, state aid formula and resource allocations are less likely to be responsive to the effects of mobile student populations. For example, in Vermont, ADM is calculated as a two-year average of enrollment counts taken on the fortieth day of school. Some states, such as California, utilize two or more counts during the year to calculate their average. In general student transiency, particularly in impoverished communities, reflects a "revolving door" where student exits and entrances are generally balanced. However, when enrollment counts are calculated infrequently, they become more biased to situations in which the churning of student populations are not even.

State aid formulas may be particularly unwieldy in instances of small and/or rural districts with high mobility. For example, small districts often enter into contractual relationships with supervisory districts for vocational or special education services. Yet state aid formulas, to the extent they are based on average ADM figures, may not fully reimburse districts for sending and receiving transient students for some time. Moreover, if the students move prior to the calculation of ADM, it is possible that districts may not receive reimbursement at all for services they provide.

The state of Minnesota has addressed this problem by utilizing an individualized student enrollment system that minimizes the impact of mobility in their state aid formula.[4] Minnesota's foundation formula guarantees a fixed amount of revenue per pupil to ensure a minimally adequate education, some of which comes from the schools, and some from the district. Other categorical aid programs exist, but general state aid for the foundation plan constitutes the State's largest funding stream. Though grade level pupil weighting is used in this system, at the heart of the formula is a weighted average daily attendance calculus (WADM) that is calculated using enrollment data from each day of the school year. State resources are allocated based on initial or expected WADM estimates. Yet, school districts also may submit enrollment updates at any time before the end of the school year and receive revenue adjustments. Minnesota's finance formula is greatly aided by an individualized student information system that is more than a decade old. The system allows state administrators and school district personnel to track students as they enter and exit schools to properly direct resources to schools for the costs incurred in providing services. Minnesota's individual student database is akin to a spigot that allows resources to flow towards a school when students are in attendance at that facility.

Mobility and Performance Accountability

Mobility also confounds efforts to promote performance accountability within education. School-based performance accountability systems typically contain four main elements: clear educational goals; assessments of student achievement; methods to judge the effectiveness of schools in meeting the goals; and consequences, particularly for low-performing schools (Stecher & Kirby, 2004; Figlio & Ladd, this volume). The issue of how to account for mobile schoolchildren is most relevant in test administration and in the overall analysis of school performance.

Regardless of the how a school's performance is measured, schools face pressures to exclude mobile students from being tested and/or to exclude their test scores from school reports. For example, based on his examination of recent accountability models, Weckstein (2003) argues that current accountability policies can create incentives for administrators to exclude such students—many of whom are low-scoring—from school-wide assessments. School officials might defend that action on the ground that the school often has limited time to teach such students. Further, given that mobile students may transfer out of the school before the testing at the end of the academic year, schools may have little incentive to devote much attention to them.

In some cases, accountability pressures are so strong that administrators attempt to manipulate measures of their school's progress. For example, in case study research in five New York State school districts, school administrators admitted to purposefully leading students at risk of dropping out into GED programs. Administrators described the practice as a mechanism to reduce drop out rates by labeling students as transfers (Sipple, Killeen, & Monk, 2004). In short, when schools are held accountable for changes in annual test scores at a particular grade level, administrators become quite sensitive to the sudden enrollment of students likely to upend those scores.

School mobility also complicates the task of measuring school progress, a central feature of current accountability policies. Schools are generally scored and comparatively ranked in one of two ways. In the first, schools are ranked based on either the level of the year-to year change or in the aggregate performance of their students. Interestingly, state and local provisions differ in how they treat mobile school children for this purpose. Offenberg (2004) examined the relationship between school ranking and student mobility in Philadelphia and found that school rankings differ depending on the inclusion or exclusion of mobile schoolchildren. Figlio (2005) highlights this feature of school accountability policies for Florida school districts. He argues that the exclusion of test scores from high mobility children may cause policymakers to overestimate the success of a school and lead to the misinterpretation of the success of a school in reaching the specified learning goals (Figlio & Ladd, this volume).

Accountability systems also rely on growth or value-added modeling to calculate school performance. In these multivariate regression models, changes in student performance at the individual level are tracked over time. The goal of the more sophisticated of these approaches is to parse out known factors that contribute to student performance from those attributable to the school itself. In practice, though, as Figlio (2005) notes, it is not possible to control for the complete set of background characteristics associated with student performance (e.g. wealth, race, and mobility), and thereby to disentangle factors contributing to school performance. Unmeasured student, family, and community characteristics—including student transiency—represent a major shortcoming of the growth models that are attempting to isolate the contribution schools make to student learning.

Beyond the calculation of student and school performance, student transiency invokes more fundamental questions about educational accountability itself. How much time is necessary for an educator or a school to have an impact on children's educational outcomes? Which part of the educational system (e.g. teachers, schools, or districts) ought to be held accountable if a child's enrollment has been too brief, or too close to the date of comprehensive testing in any one school? These are important questions that are not resolved simply by removing mobile students from testing opportunities, or by policies that remove their scores from aggregate measures.

CONCLUSION: SOME DIRECTION FOR POLICY INTERVENTIONS

While schools have relatively little control over the household-level economic circumstances that place children at higher risk of frequent school change, school-based interventions may offer possibilities for ameliorating the impact of such moves. At the conclusion of one of the most robust empirical studies of the deleterious effects of frequent mobility on student achievement, Hanushek et al. (2004) state:

> A policy challenge… is to devise schooling approaches that mitigate the academic losses due to school turnover. Whether, for example, such things as more standardized curricula, specialized transition, and remedial programs for entering students, or more careful classroom placement of new students, could help, remain open questions. (2004, p. 1746)

Though empirical evaluations of interventions for highly mobile students are limited in number (Beck, Kratzer, & Isken, 1997; Jason et al., 1989; Weine et al., 1993), recent qualitative research supports school-based interventions focused on heightening school attachment among students. School attachment is generally defined as a sense of connectedness and commitment that results from a perceived sense of caring from peers and teachers (Libby, 2004; Wilson, 2004). As school attachment increases among students, positive achievement and pro-social outcomes become more likely, including improved academic achievement, reduced delinquency rates, and decreased likelihoods of harmful health practices (Kelley, Denny, & Young, 1997).

Fisher et al. (2002) interviewed 18 administrators from 18 schools in seven urban school districts about interventions at the elementary school level meant to address student mobility. Of the interventions designed to reduce the disruption of a move among students, most of the interventions focused on improving interpersonal skills (e.g., social skill activities, participation in after-school clubs, team building, or cooperative problem solving) and strengthening family supports. Similarly, focus group findings as part of a recent Annenberg Foundation Study of Student Mobility across Maryland, also support school programs that improve student attachment to reduce the effects of mobility (Rogers, 2004).

The inclusion of parents in programs to enhance student attachment in schools is also worth exploring in the context of student mobility (Jason, et al., 1989). Literature on parental participation in school programs stresses the development of strong collaborative value systems among parent-professional partnerships (Lake & Billingsley, 2000; Muscott, 2002). Strong partnerships can ameliorate barriers to optimal parent participation in schools (Furney & Salembier, 2000; Lovitt & Cushing, 1999), improve attention to diverse race and ethnic subgroups in schools (Callicott, 2003; Harry, 1992; Kaylanpur & Harry, 1999), as well as improve individual and systemic educational service provision for children with exceptional needs (Lopez, Scribner, & Mahitivanichcha, 2001; Rao, 2000).

Strengthening parental engagement clearly should be considered part of the portfolio of intervention strategies, but many challenges remain. Parents of low-achieving, highly mobile students are likely themselves to have had mixed academic experiences. Their own negative academic experiences may make them hesitant partners in such efforts. Secondly, the social and economic circumstances of mobile, low income parents, including uncertain employment and child care arrangements, and potentially limited access to transportation and communication, pose additional barriers. Finally, the nature of high mobility in and of itself means that parents may not be residentially stable long enough to develop effective partnering relationships with schools.

Other interventions supercede the institutional level of the school, but nonetheless have significant implications for addressing transiency. For example, scholars have[5] recently started to evaluate federal and state efforts to move low-income households located in socially, economically, and racially segregated neighborhoods into more heterogeneous and middle class communities. Initial evidence suggests that policies like housing vouchers can work to stimulate residential homeownership and desegregation among low income and minority households (Clarke, 2005; Johnson, Ladd, & Ludwig, 2002; Rosenbaum et al., 2002). These policies are hopeful for their apparent embracing of a richer and more complex understanding of population movement, housing and poverty dynamics.

Regardless of the innovative interventions that may be devised, a significant extent of childhood mobility is a consequence of deep seated and structural inequalities in the United States (Rank, 2005). Its causes are multidimensional and cannot be meaningfully disentangled from the varied dimensions of poverty and social inequality that are woven into the fabric of contemporary American society. Given the current educational mandates and institutional realities, it is appropriate that education policy facilitate the social and academic adjustment—and ultimately the *success*—of high need, at-risk youth who are quite literally "moving targets." Therefore, educational researchers make important contributions by generating knowledge about the causes and consequences of student mobility and the potentials of various intervention models. We argue however, that fully grasping the problem of student transiency requires widening the analytic focus beyond the school walls, and indicators of learning achievement. Absent a wider analytic lens, educational researchers may miss the true root of the problem: Many American adults and children lack the basic means to lead socially and economically just lives.

NOTES

1. See Title X, Part C, Section 725(2) of the No Child Left Behind Act of 2001.
2. About 106,000 children are enrolled in Department of Defense schools, located within the United States and overseas. Another 600,000 children of military personnel are enrolled in U.S. K-12 public schools located near military bases (Military Family Resource Center, 2001).
3. However, the income level does not factor in the multiple benefits that accrue from military employment, such as housing allowances, that offset the lower pay scale for enlisted personnel.
4. See http://education.state.mn.us/mde/static/004111.pdf#search=%22Minnesota%20WADM%20define%22.

REFERENCES

Alexander, K.L., Entwistle, D.R., & Dauber, S.L. (1996). Children in motion: School transfers and elementary school performance. *The Journal of Educational Research, 90*, 3–12.

Baumer, E.P. & South, S.J. (2001). Community effects on youth sexual activity. *Journal of Marriage and the Family, 63*, 540–54.

Beck, L., Kratzer, C., & Isken, J. (1997). Caring for transient students in one urban elementary school. *Journal for a Just and Caring Education, 5*, 7–18.

Bezruczko, N. & Reynolds, A. (1992). Schools, families and children: Sixth grade results from the 1992 Longitudinal Study of Children at Risk. Performance Evaluation Summary. Chicago: Chicago Public Schools.

Branz-Spall, A.M., Rosenthal, R., & Wright, A. (2003). Children on the road: Migrant students, our nation's most mobile population. *Journal of Negro Education, 72*, 55–62.

Bruno, J.E. & Isken, J.A. (1996). Inter and intraschool site student transiency: Practical and theoretical implications for instructional continuity at inner city schools. *Journal of Research and Development in Education, 29*(4), 239–252.

Buerkle, K. & Christenson, S.L. (1999). A family view of mobility among low-income children. *CURA Reporter, 29*(2), 7–12.

Cadwallader, M. (1992). *Migration and residential mobility: Macro and micro approaches.* Madison: University of Wisconsin Press.

Callicott, K.J. (2003) Culturally sensitive collaboration within person-centered planning. *Focus on Autism and Other Developmental Disabilities, 18*(1), 60–68.

Clark, W. A. V. (2005). Intervening in the residential mobility process: Neighborhood outcomes for low-income populations. *Proceedings of the National Academy of Sciences, 102*(43), 15307–15312.

Colton, R.D. (2004). *Paid but unaffordable: The consequences of energy poverty in Missouri.* Washington, DC: National Low Energy Housing Consortium.

Crowley, S. (2003). The affordable housing crisis: Residential mobility of poor families and school mobility of poor children. *Journal of Negro Education, 72*, 150–157.

Dalla, R.L. & Christenson, A. (2005). Latino immigrants describe residence in rural Midwestern meat-packing communities: A longitudinal assessment of social and economic change. *Hispanic Journal of Behavioral Sciences, 27*, 23–42.

Dunn, M., Kadane, J.B., & Garrow, J.R. (2003). Comparing harm done by mobility and class absence: Missing students and missing data. *Journal of Educational and Behavioral Statistics, 28*, 269–288.

Figlio, D. (2005). Measuring school performance: Promises and pitfalls. In L. Stiefel, A.E. Schwartz, R. Rubenstein, & J. Zabel (Eds.) *Measuring school performance and efficiency: Implications for practice and research.* (pp. 119–136). Larchmont: Eye on Education.

Fisher, T.A., Matthews, L., Stafford, M.E., Nakagawa, K., & Durante, K. (2002). School personnel's perceptions of effective programs for working with mobile students and families. *The Elementary School Journal 102(4)*, 317–333.

Fitchen, J.M. (1992). On the edge of homelessness: Rural poverty and housing insecurity. *Rural Sociology, 57*, 173–93.

Fitchen, J.M. (1994). Residential mobility among the rural poor. *Rural Sociology, 59*(3), 416–436.

Fitchen, J.M. (1995). Spatial redistribution of poverty through migration of poor people to depressed rural communities. *Rural Sociology, 60*(2), 181–201.

Foulkes, M. & Newbold, K.B. (2005). Geographic mobility and residential instability in impoverished rural Illinois places. *Environment and Planning, 37*, 845–860.

Furney, K.S. & Salembier, G. (2000). *Rhetoric and reality: A review of the literature on parent and student participation in the IEP and transition planning process.* Issues influencing the future of transition programs and services in the United States. Minneapolis, MN: National Transition Network at the Institute on Community Integration.

Gouviea, L, & Stull, D.D. (1997). *Latino immigrants, meatpacking, and rural communities: A case study of Lexington, Nebraska.* JSRI Research Report #26. Lansing, MI: Julian Samora Research Institute, Michigan State University.

Green, P.E. (2003). The undocumented: Educating the children of migrant workers in America. *Bilingual Research Journal, 27*, 51–71.

Grey, M. A. (1997). Secondary labor in the meatpacking industry: Demographic change and student mobility in rural Iowa schools. *Journal of Research in Rural Education, 13*(3), 153–164.

Hanna, W.J. (2003). Mobility and the children of Langley Park's immigrant families. *Journal of Negro Education, 72*, 63–78.

Hanushek, E. A., Kain, J. F., & Rivkin, S. G. (2004). Disruption versus Tiebout improvement: The costs and benefits of switching schools. *Journal of Public Economics, 88*, 1721–1746.

Harry, B. (1992). Restructuring the participation of African-American parents in special education. *Exceptional Children, 59(2)*, 123–131.

Hartman, C. (2002). High classroom turnover: How children get left behind. In D.M. Piché, W.L. Taylor, & R.A. Reed (Eds.), *Rights at risk: Equality in an age of terrorism* (pp. 227–244). Washington DC: Citizens' Commission on Civil Rights.

Hartman, C. (2006). Students on the move. *Educational Leadership, 63*(5), 20–24.

Haynie, D. L., South, S. J., & Bose, S. (2006). The company you keep: Adolescent mobility and peer behavior. *Sociological Inquiry, 76*, 397–426.

Ingersoll, G. M., Scamman, J. P., & Eckerling, W. D. (1999). Geographic mobility and student achievement in an urban setting. *Educational Evaluation and Policy Analysis, 11*(2), 143–149.

Institute for Children and Poverty. (2003). *Miles to go: The flip side of the McKinney Vento Homeless Assistance Act.* New York: Institute for Children and Poverty.

Jason, L.A., Betts, D., Johnson, J., Smith, S., Krueckeberg, S, & Cradock, M. (1989). An evaluation of an orientation plus tutoring school-based prevention program. *Professional School Psychology 4*(4), 273–284.

Jensen, L., McLaughlin, D.K., & Slack, T. (2003). Rural poverty: The persisting challenge. In D.L. Brown & L.E. Swanson (Eds.), *Challenges for Rural America in the Twenty-first Century* (pp. 188–134). University Park: The Pennsylvania State University Press.

Johnson, M. P., Ladd, H. F., & Ludwig, J. (2002). The benefits and costs of residential mobility programmes for the poor. *Housing Studies, 17(1)*, 125–138.

Julianelle, P.F. & Foscarnis, M. (2003). Responding to the school mobility of children and youth experiencing homelessness: The McKinney-Vento Act and beyond. *Journal of Negro Education, 72*, 39–54.

Kalyanpur, M., & Harry, B. (1997). A posture of reciprocity: A practical approach to collaboration between parents and professionals of culturally diverse backgrounds. *Journal of Child and Family Studies, 6*, 487–509.

Kandel, W. & Cromartie, J. (2004). *New patterns of Hispanic settlement in rural America*. Rural Development Research Report No. (RDRR99) Washington, DC: USDA Economic Research Service.

Kelley, R.M., Denny, G., & Young, M. (1997). Abbreviated Hare self-esteem scale: Internal consistency and factor analysis. *American Journal of Health Studies, 13*, 180–186.

Kerbow, D. (1996). Pattern of urban student mobility and local school reform. *Journal of Education for Students Placed at Risk, 1*(2), 147–169.

Lake, J.F. & Billingsley, B.S. (2000). An analysis of factors that contribute to parent-school conflict in special education. *Remedial and Special Education, 21*(4), 240–251.

Lash, A. A., & Kirkpatrick, S. L. (1990). A classroom perspective on student mobility. *The Elementary School Journal, 91*(2), 177–191.

Libby, H.P. (2004). Measuring student relationships to school: Attachment, bonding, connectedness and engagement. *Journal of School Health, 74*(7), 274–291.

Lichter, D.T., & Johnson, K.M. (2006). Emerging rural settlement patterns and the geographic redistribution of America's new immigrants. *Rural Sociology, 71*, 109–131.

Ligon, G, & Paredes, V. (1992). *Student mobility rate: A moving target*. Austin, TX: Austin Independent School District.

Long, L. (1973). Migration differentials by education and occupation: Trends and variations. *Demography, 10*(2), 243–258.

Lopez, G.R., Scribner, J.D., & Mahitivanichcha, K. (200a). Redefining parent involvement: Lessons from high-performing migrant-impacted schools. *American Educational Research Journal, 38*(2), 253–288.

Lovitt, T.C. & Cushing, S. (1999). Parents of youth with disabilities: Their perceptions of school programs. *Remedial and Special Education, 20*(3), 134–142.

Malmgren, K.W. & Gagnon, J.C. (2005) School mobility and students with emotional disturbance. *Journal of Child and Family Studies, 14*, 299–312.

Mehana, M. & Reynolds, A. J. (2004). School mobility and achievement: A meta-analysis. *Children and Youth Services Review, 26*, 93–119.

Military Family Resource Center. (2001). *Profile of the military community: 2000 demographics*. Arlington, VA: Military Family Resource Center.

Morgan, A. (2005). *Student mobility in Vermont schools: A multi-level evaluation of educational equity.* University of Vermont, Burlington. (Unpublished Doctoral Dissertation)

Muscott, H.S. (2002). Exceptional partnerships: Listening to the voices of families. *Preventing School Failure, 46*(2), 66–69.

Nelson, P. S., Simoni, J. M., & Adelman, H. S. (1996). Mobility and school functioning in the early grades. *Journal of Educational Research, 89*(6), 365–369.

Nord, M., Luloff, A. E., & Jensen, L. (1995). Migration and the spatial concentration of poverty. *Rural Sociology, 60*(3), 399–415.

Offenberg, R. M. (2004). Inferring adequate yearly progress of schools from student achievement in highly mobile communities. *Journal of Education for Students Placed at Risk, 9*(4), 337–355.

Office of Program Policy Analysis and Government Accountability (OPPAGA). (1997). Improving student performance in high-poverty schools. Report No. 96-86. Tallahassee: OPPAGA.

Olsen, L. & Jaramillo, A. (1999). *Turning the tides of exclusion: A guide for educators and advocates for immigrant students*. Oakland: California, Tomorrow.

Osher, D., Morrison, G., & Bailey, W. (2003). Exploring the relationship between student mobility and dropout among students with emotional and behavioral disorders. *Journal of Negro Education, 72*, 79–96.

Paik, S. & Phillips, R. (2002). Student mobility in rural communities: What are the implications for student achievement? North Central Regional Educational Laboratory. Accessed February 23, 2007 at: http://www.ncrel.org/policy/pubs/html/rmobile/.

Popp, P.A., Stronge, J.H., & Hindman, J.L. (2003). *Students on the move: Reaching and teaching highly mobile children and youth*. Urban Diversity Series 116. Greensboro, NC: National Center for Homeless Education at SERVE.

Pribesh, S. & Downey, D. B. (1999). Why are residential and school moves associated with poor school performance? *Demography, 36*(4), 521–534.

Rank, M. (2004). *One nation underprivileged: Why American poverty affects us all*. New York: Oxford University Press.

Rao, S.S. (2000). Perspectives of an African-American mother on parent-professional relationships in special education. *Mental Retardation, 38*(6), 475–488.

Ream, R.K. (2003). Counterfeit social capital and Mexican-American underachievement. *Educational Evaluation and Policy Analysis*, 25(3), 237–262.

Rogers, L. (2004). Student Mobility in Maryland. Baltimore: Maryland State Department of Education.

Rosenbaum, J. E., Reynolds, L., & Deluca, S. (2002). How do places matter? The geography of opportunity, self-efficacy and a look inside the black box of residential mobility. *Housing Studies, 17*(1), 71–82.

Rumberger, R., W., Larson, K. A., Ream, R. K., & Palardy, G. J. (1999). *The educational consequences of mobility for California students and schools*. Berkeley, CA: Graduate School of Education, University of California.

Saenz, R. & Torres, C.C. (2003). Latinos in rural America. In D.L. Brown & L.E. Swanson (Eds.), *Challenges for Rural America in the Twenty-first Century* (pp. 57–70). University Park: The Pennsylvania State University.

Schachter, J. (2001). Geographic mobility March 1999 to March 2000. (Current Population Reports). Washington, DC: U.S. Government Printing Office.

Schafft, K.A. (2005). The incidence and impacts of student transiency in Upstate New York's rural school districts. *Journal of Research in Rural Education, 20(15)*,1–13. Retrieved February 23, 2007 (http://www.umaine.edu/jrre/20-15.pdf).

Schafft, K.A. (2006), Poverty, residential mobility, and student transiency within a rural New York school district. *Rural Sociology, 71*, 212–231.

Simpson, G. & Fowler, M. G. (1994). Geographic mobility and children's emotional/behavioral adjustment and school functioning. *Pediatrics 93*, 303–309.

Sipple, J. W., Killeen, K.M., & Monk, D. (2004). Adoption and adaptation: School district responses to state imposed learning and graduation requirements. *The Journal of Education Evaluation and Policy Analysis,* 26(2), 143–168.

Smrekar, C., Guthrie, J.W., Owens, D.E., & Sims, P.G. (2001). *March towards excellence: School success and minority student achievement in Department of Defense schools*. Washington DC: National Institute on Early Childhood Development and Education, and Nashville, TN: Peabody College of Vanderbilt University.

Smrekar, C.E., & Owens, D.E. (2003). 'It's a way of life for us': High mobility and high achievement in Department of Defense schools. *Journal of Negro Education, 72*, 165–177.

South, S. J. & Haynie, D. L. (2004). Friendship networks of mobile adolescents. *Social Forces, 83*(1), 315–350.

Stecher, B. & Kirby, N. (2004). *Organizational improvement and accountability: Lessons for Education from other sectors*. Santa Monica, CA: Rand Corporation

Stull, D.D., Broadway, M.J., & Griffith, D. (1995). *Any way you cut it: Meat processing and small town America*. Lawrence: University of Kansas Press.

Swanson, C. B. & Schneider, B. (1999). Students on the move: Residential and educational mobility in America's schools. *Sociology of Education, 72*, 54–67.

Tucker, C.J., Marx, J., & Long, L. (1998). 'Moving on': Residential mobility and children's school lives. *Sociology of Education, 71*, 111–129.

United States Department of Education. (2004). Title I Migrant Education Program Trends Summary Report: 1998–2001. Washington, DC: U.S. Department of Education. Accessed February 23, 2007 at: http://www.ed.gov/rschstat/eval/disadv/migrant/report01.pdf.

United States General Accounting Office. (1994). *Elementary school children: Many change schools frequently, harming their education* (Report No. GAO/HEHS-94-45). Washington, DC: U.S. Government Printing Office.

United States General Accounting Office. (1998). *Child labor in agriculture: Changes needed to better protect health and educational opportunities.* (Report No. GAO/HEHS-98-193). Washington, DC: U.S. Government Printing Office.

Weckstein, P. (2003). Accountability and student mobility under title I of the No Child Left Behind Act. *Journal of Negro Education*, 72(1).

Weine, A. M., Kurasaki, K. S., Jason, L. A., Danner, K. E., & Johnson, J. (1993). An evaluation of preventive tutoring programs for transfer students. *Child Study Journal, 23*(2), 135–152.

Wilson, D. (2004). The interface of school climate and school connectedness and relationships with aggression and victimization. *Journal of School Health, 74*(7), 293–299).

Wood, D., Halfon, N., Scarlata, D., Newacheck, P., & Nessim, S. (1993). Impact of family relocation on children's growth, development, school function, and behavior. *Journal of the American Medical Association, 270*(11), 1334–1338.

VIII
HIGHER EDUCATION

Section Editors

David W. Breneman and Michael S. McPherson

36

The Financing of Public Colleges and Universities in the United States

Paul E. Lingenfelter[1]

Despite the universal and growing importance of higher education, the policies and techniques for public financing and budgeting vary dramatically among countries, among the 50 United States, and over time. These differences have been shaped by many factors, including changing public needs and goals; the blend of personal and public benefits derived from higher education; public administration practices and fads; competition among institutions of higher education; and the ebb and flow of competing social priorities (Layzell & Lyddon, 1990).

Although a full analysis of these forces would take more than the available space, this chapter illustrates them by briefly reviewing the history of higher education in the United States, describing trends, and acknowledging the milestones that have shaped the evolution and financing of public colleges and universities, especially during its rapid expansion in the 20th century. A more extensive analysis of state funding for higher education since 1970 shows how the states have responded to enrollment growth and inflation; how financing for higher education has fared in comparison to other public priorities; how the states differ; and how costs and prices have increased. The chapter then examines the techniques states have used to determine the amounts and allocations of funds among institutions and purposes. Finally, it concludes by considering the fundamental question of public objectives, who is responsible for paying the costs, and the future challenges facing public higher education.

A BRIEF HISTORICAL REVIEW OF HIGHER EDUCATION IN THE UNITED STATES

Although most institutions of higher education chartered during the colonial and early American periods were private and founded principally for religious purposes, they nonetheless received support from state governments. It was not until 1819, following the U.S. Supreme Court's opinion in the *Dartmouth College v. Woodward* case, that the line separating public interests and private sovereignty was drawn (Whitehead & Herbst, 1986).[2] Despite "private" control, the widely acknowledged public contributions of independent colleges and universities are still legitimately used to justify direct and indirect public subsidies for their missions.

States began establishing public institutions near the onset of the Revolutionary War, and additional public colleges were established around the time of the Dartmouth College opinion. These commitments were later advanced by the Morrill Act of 1862,[3] which provided land grants to Federal (Union) states and territories to develop public colleges and universities offering programs in applied and professional disciplines. While higher education became more visible and important as the nation grew in size and sophistication during the 19th century (more than 500 institutions existed by the end of the Civil War), the rate of participation remained modest. In 1870 the national enrollment totaled 52,000, only 0.14 percent of the U.S. population.[4] Enrollments by sector are unavailable for 1870, but surely most of these students were enrolled in privately governed institutions.

Between 1870 and 1920, total enrollment grew more than ten-fold to almost 600,000, and college students accounted for 0.57 percent of the national population. The era between the World Wars marked the beginning of mass higher education in the United States (Trow, 1974). Junior colleges and urban public universities were established and expanded, and urban private universities established large programs to serve part-time and summer students. By the beginning of World War II, total enrollments had more than doubled to 1.5 million. The public and private sectors each accounted for approximately one-half the student enrollment in higher education, but for the first time the public sector had become larger. Public institutions enrolled 800,000 students and spent $392 million, compared to 700,000 students and spending of $367 million in the private sector.

After World War II, the Servicemen's Readjustment Act of 1944 (commonly known as the GI Bill) and the report of the Truman Commission (1947) fundamentally changed public thinking about higher education and its role in American society. The GI Bill advanced social mobility and prosperity throughout the United States by providing widespread financial access to higher education to students from working class families. The Truman Commission[5] anticipated and recommended policies to achieve even wider participation in higher education, though responses to its recommendations did not emerge until later.

As a response to the launching of Sputnik and America's intensifying "Cold War" with the Soviet Union, the 1958 National Defense in Education Act expanded and broadened federal investments in research and training and introduced governmentally subsidized and forgivable loans as a public policy tool to stimulate enrollment and guide students toward needed professions. It was followed by the Higher Education Act of 1965,[6] which established an even more explicit and direct federal interest in higher education.

In the 1960s and early 1970s states rapidly expanded existing public institutions and built new ones. Many states established new higher education institutions in virtually every region within their borders. Statewide coordinating boards were established in about one-half the states to plan and coordinate these expanded systems, and existing statewide governing boards shouldered similar responsibilities in the others. As a result, the public sector of higher education grew rapidly during this period, eventually accounting for 77 percent of all fall FTE enrollments in 1975; community colleges enrolled 29 percent of all fall FTE enrollments that year.

Enrollments continued to grow between 1975 and 2000, although not as dramatically as during the previous quarter century. All sectors grew (in the aggregate by more than 50 percent), but both for-profit and non-profit private institutions grew faster than public institutions in the last quarter of the 20th century, with a collective gain in market share from 23.1 percent in 1975 to 28.7 percent in fall 2004. The for-profit private sector grew most dramatically, with a rise in market share from 0.6 percent in 1980 to 5 percent in 2004. These enrollment trends were undoubtedly shaped by the growing importance of higher education to individuals; by increasingly sophisticated marketing in the private and for-profit sectors; and especially by the 1978 Middle Income Student Assistance Act, which lifted income caps off federally subsidized student loans (Grubb & Tuma, 1991).

Figure 36.1 summarizes key events and statistics in the evolution of higher education in the

Timeline of Historical Events in Higher Education Finance and Statistics for Selected Years

Year	Event
1636	Founding of Harvard College
1819	Dartmouth College v. Woodward
1862	Morrill Act (Land-grant Act)
1944	Servicemen's Readjustment Act (G. I. Bill)
1947	Truman Commission Report
1958	National Defense Education Act
1964	Economic Opportunity Act
1965	Higher Education Act
1978	Middle Income Student Assistance Act

Year	Relevent Statistics
1869-70	Total Institutions: 563 Total Enrollment: 52,286 Percent of U.S. Population in College: <1%
1939-40	Total Institutions: 1,708 Total Enrollment: 1,494,203 Percent of U.S. Population in College: 1.1% Public sector enrollment and spending exceeds private sector for the first time.
1959-60	Total Institutions: 2,004 Total Enrollment: 3,639,847 Percent of U.S. Population in College: 2.0%
1969-70	Total Institutions: 2,525 Total Enrollment: 8,004,660 Percent of U.S. Population in College: 3.9%
1979-80	Total Institutions: 3,152 Total Enrollment: 11,569,899 Percent of U.S. Population in College: 5.1%
1989-90	Total Institutions: 3,535 Total Enrollment: 13,538,560 Percent of U.S. Population in College: 5.4%
1999-00	Total Institutions: 4,084 Total Enrollment: 14,791,224 Percent of U.S. Population in College: 5.3%

FIGURE 36.1 Timeline of Historical Events in Higher Education FInance and Statistics for Selected Years.
Sources: Digest of Education Statistics, National Center for Education Statistics; Statistical Abstracts of the United States, U.S. Census Bureau.

United States, paralleling the nation's development from an agrarian to an industrial, then to a knowledge-based economy that demands increasingly higher levels of educational attainment.

The American values of democracy, equality of opportunity, individual liberties, and limited government are reflected in that history, but in practice these fundamental values sometimes point in opposite directions. Although the public commitment to higher education and the inexorable trend toward universal participation are unmistakable, the extent of public funding and the mechanisms through which it is provided continue to stimulate vigorous public policy debate.

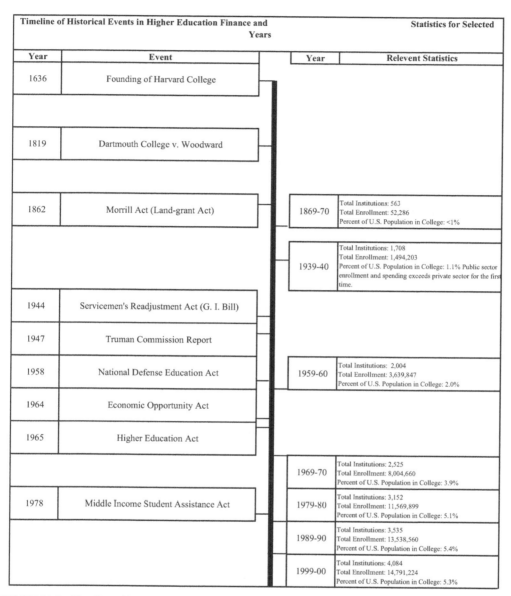

State Support of Public Higher Education

While the federal government promoted the expansion of public higher education in the Morrill Act, and now plays a central role in financing student assistance and research, the states have been and remain the principal source of funding for instruction in public institutions.

Trends in the State Commitment to Higher Education. In 1960, M. M. Chambers at Illinois State University began his "Grapevine" surveys of state appropriations to higher education to monitor state support and advocate its expansion.[7] According to these surveys, which have continued for nearly one-half century, aggregate state support grew from $1.4 billion in Fiscal Year (FY) 1961, to $7.0 billion in FY1971, more than a four-fold increase in 10 years. Headcount enrollments in public institutions grew from 2.3 million in fall 1960, to 6.4 million in fall 1970. During the 1960s, public institutions became established as the predominant provider of higher education in the United States, even though the private sector also enjoyed the benefits of increasing demand. Public enrollments grew further to 9.4 million by fall 1980, and state appropriations grew to $19.1 million by FY1981.

Despite budgetary cycles of alternating stringency and prosperity, state support for higher education generally kept pace with enrollment growth and inflation from 1970 to 2000. During recessions, higher education enrollments generally grow (apparently because a weak labor market reduces the opportunity costs of enrolling) and the economic down-turn causes state revenues to decline or lag behind inflation. The average amount of state support per student (in constant dollars deflated by the Higher Education Cost Adjustment [HECA]) has declined during every economic recession since 1970, but has rebounded to even higher levels during each subsequent recovery. The data on Figure 36.2 from 1980 to 2006 nicely illustrate this pattern.

State support for public institutions peaked in FY2001 when per student support reached $7,370 (in 2006 dollars). In the succeeding four years, however, enrollments grew by 14.4 percent, inflation increased by 14.2 percent, and state support increased only 7.4 percent.[8] The resulting FY2005 level of state support per student ($5,987) was the lowest in constant dollars (HECA adjusted) since 1980. Although it remains to be seen whether the post-FY2005 recovery will match those following earlier recessions, recent data point to a recovery: State and local support appropriations grew 7.9 percent in FY2006, and due to modest enrollment growth, per student support increased to $6,292. Grapevine reports an additional increase of 7.1 percent for FY2007.

Constant dollar net tuition grew from $1,667 to $3,430 in the quarter century from 1980 to 2005. In 2005 students paid 37 percent of total educational costs, up from 2 percent 25 years earlier. In FY2006 net tuition continued to grow in real dollars, but for the first time in several years, state support per student grew slightly faster (State Higher Education Executive Officers [SHEEO], 2007).

The growth of federal student grants, loans, and tuition tax credits from 1970 to 2005 may help explain why these "real dollar" tuition increases apparently did not lead to reduced enrollments. For all sectors in the aggregate, grants and tax credits per FTE (adjusted for inflation by the CPI) grew from $1,654 in 1970, to $2,112 by 2005. Loans per FTE grew steadily from $1,039 in 1970, to $4,816 in 2005, again in constant dollars.[9]

Figure 36.2 also shows trends for "total educational costs" (state support plus tuition revenues net of student aid), over the same time period.

When real dollar increases in tuition are combined with state support, constant dollar total educational costs per student show an upward trend from $7,976 in FY1980, peaking at $10,417 in FY2001, declining to $9,417 in FY2005, and recovering to $9,845 in FY2006 (SHEEO, 2007).

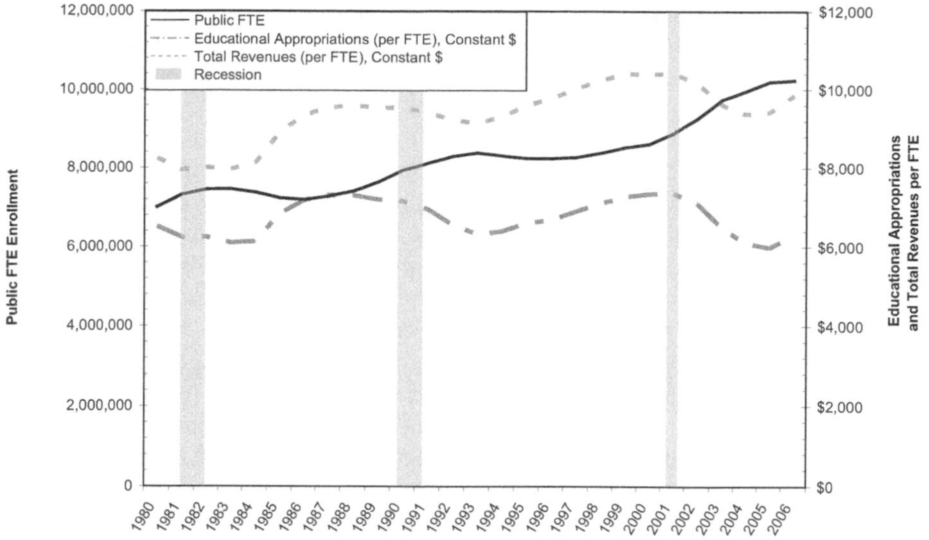

FIGURE 36.2 Enrollment Growth and Public Higher Education Appropriations per FTE U.S., 1980–2006.
Note: Constant 2006 dollars adjusted by SHEEO Higher Education Cost Adjustment.

Variation among the States. While the general pattern of Figure 36.2 can be found in most states, state figures vary substantially around the national mean. For example, in FY 2005, tuition and required fees at state research universities averaged $6,172, but they varied from about $3,000 in Florida to $11,500 in Pennsylvania. Tuition and fees for community colleges averaged about $2,800, but community college fees ranged from about $800 in California to $5,600 in New Hampshire. At the national average, net student tuition and fees account for about 37 percent of total educational costs, but this percentage varies from 13 percent in New Mexico, to 77 percent in Vermont.

The average state provides about $500 per full-time-equivalent student in financial aid grants. Some states, however, provide virtually nothing, and two states, Georgia and South Carolina, provide grants that average $1,500 per student. In these two states, virtually all of the state grant aid is based on academic achievement rather than financial need.

The states also differ greatly in total expenditures per student in higher education. Excluding funds designated for medical education, research, and agricultural extension services, the national average for public institutions is about $9,200, and most states fall between $8,000 and $11,000 per student in spending. The lowest level of spending is below $7,000; the highest exceeds $14,000 per student.[10] Moreover, the trend for state finance differs remarkably among the states. Some states decreased real dollar per student funding as much as 20 percent from FY1991 to FY2005, and others show increases as high as 40 percent.[11]

While the variation among the states is driven by many factors (including general wealth), the relative size and maturity of the private sector of higher education in each state is associated with higher tuition rates and higher levels of spending in public institutions. Where private institutions are numerous and mature (the New England states, as well as Pennsylvania and New York), public institutions tend to have higher rates of tuition and spending. The Western states tend to have lower tuition and spending levels, and the Midwest and Southern states tend to fall in the middle on these variables.

Other factors, including tax policy changes, demographic trends driving (or depressing) enrollment demand, the introduction of new funding sources (typically state lotteries), and unusually rapid or slow economic growth also explain differences among the states in financing levels and trends.

Are the States Abandoning Their Commitment to Public Higher Education? It would be difficult to find a time when higher education leaders did not fret about the adequacy of public support, but between 2001 and 2005, these concerns seemed to reach a new level of urgency. In their 2006 book, *The True Genius of America at Risk: Are We Losing Our Public Universities to De Facto Privatization?,* Katherine C. Lyall and Kathleen R. Sell assembled literature and data to argue that the nation faces a crisis. At the same time, others, including members of Congress and the National Commission on the Future of Higher Education created by Secretary of Education Margaret Spellings, decried the growth of tuition and questioned whether higher education is doing all it should to increase productivity and control costs (The Commission on the Future of Higher Education, 2006). Clearly, different conclusions about the nature of the problem depend not only on one's perspective, but also on *which* facts are observed and analyzed. (Ehrenberg, 2006; Longanecker, 2006; Lyall, 2006), all in the January/February 2006 issue of *Change Magazine.*)

The variety of measures employed in this public discourse illustrate the complexity of this issue. No single measure can fairly assess the adequacy or appropriateness of higher education funding. For example, policymakers and the general public tend to view the growth of higher education costs in relation to the growth of the Consumer Price Index (CPI). Higher education leaders argue that the Higher Education Price Index (HEPI), developed by Kent Halstead in the 1970s, is more appropriate because it reflects the faculty salary market and other higher education costs.[12] Others, including Lyall (2006), Mortenson (2002), and Kane and Orzag (2003), point with alarm to higher education's declining share of state budgets, the decreasing percentage of research university budgets financed by the state, and the dwindling rate of higher education funding per $1,000 of personal income. And given the fluctuation of state economies, state support, and enrollments over time, an analysis can yield very different results when different years are used to make comparisons.

Appendix Table 36A.1 provides a full overview from 1970 to 2005 of the most relevant indicators of: (1) inflation, income, and spending in higher education, in state government, and in the general economy; (2) tuition and student aid; and (3) enrollments. The highlights from Table 36.1 (see boxed text) make clear the direction and extent to which trends for these indicators have diverged over this period; the subsequent discussion draws the various findings together.

In view of the enormous variation among the states discussed earlier, these national figures have limited applicability in particular places. But a few summary observations may add perspective and help explain the divergence of views on higher education spending and public support.

State support per public student since 1970 has *not* kept pace with the HEPI, but it *has* kept pace with the CPI. Because tuition has grown much faster than the CPI, total spending per public student *has* more than kept pace with the HEPI. Higher education spending per student, however, has not kept pace with real growth in income per capita in the U.S. or with state expenditures per capita. Higher education as an industry, both public and private institutions, has doubled in enrollment since 1970 and it accounts for a growing share of Gross Domestic Product (GDP). Real GDP *per capita*, however, has grown considerably faster than *per student spending* in higher education.

In summary, per student spending in public higher education, considering all sources of revenue, has grown faster than inflation (whether measured by the CPI or HEPI), but not as fast as per capita income or per capita state spending in the United States.

INFLATION, INCOME, AND SPENDING 1970–2005—HIGHER EDUCATION, STATE GOVERNMENT, AND THE GENERAL ECONOMY

- The HEPI grew 506 percent; the CPI grew 407 percent.
- Real dollar state and local support per student declined by 11 percent using HEPI, and grew by 7 percent using the CPI.
- Real dollar total educational revenues per student for public institutions grew by 10 percent using HEPI, and by 31 percent based on the CPI.
- Personal income per capita grew 744 percent, in current dollars, and by 66 percent in real terms, deflated by the CPI.
- Real per capita state and local expenditures (CPI) grew by 103 percent.
- Total spending in higher education (all sectors) grew from 2.0 percent to 2.6 percent of GDP.

Tuition and Financial Aid

- Average tuition for four-year public institutions grew by 177 percent in constant dollars (CPI).
- Average tuition for 2-year public institutions grew by 105 percent in constant dollars (CPI)
- Federal grants and tax credits per student (all sectors) grew by 28 percent in constant dollars (CPI), from $1,654 to $2,112.
- Federal loans per student (all sectors) grew by 364 percent in constant dollars (CPI) from $1,039 to $4,816.

Enrollments

- FTE enrollments grew by 183 percent in public 2-year institutions and by 90 percent for the other sectors of higher education.
- The market share for 2-year public institutions increased from 20.8 percent to 28.1 percent of FTE. (Because community colleges spend the lowest amount per student among the sectors of higher education, their increased share of the total market would tend to make the overall average cost of higher education less expensive in 2005 than it was in 1970.)

The share of higher education costs borne by students and their families has increased dramatically when one considers only state and net tuition revenues for public higher education in 2005 compared to those in 1970. But since 1970, federal student grants and tax credits have increased from $2.1 billion to $27.5 billion and subsidized loans have grown from $1.3 billion to $62.6 billion. Some of this financial assistance is inadequately distributed to the students who most need help,[13] but increases in aid of this magnitude certainly help address the issue of affordability.

Public students in 2005 received $37.3 billion in federal grants and loans.[14] Accurate information on the use of federal tax credits by students attending public institutions is unavailable,[15] but estimating that public students receive perhaps 50 percent of the tax credit benefit, or $3.8 billion, means that a total of $41.1 billion in federal grants, tax credits, or loans was available in

2005. In comparison, net tuition for public institutions (net of state and institutional aid) generated $34 billion in 2005. Because student assistance is provided for living costs as well as tuition, it is unlikely that increases in federal aid have totally offset the growth in tuition prices. But they have helped.

Both those who argue U.S. higher education costs are wildly out of control, and others who argue U.S. higher education has been starved of essential resources, must be very selective to find support in the data.

Without question, however, state investments in higher education have not grown as rapidly as state spending for other purposes. As documented by Kane and Orzag (2003), other priorities, especially health care, are consuming more of state revenues. Also, during recessions, the states have tended to reduce higher education appropriations disproportionately by relying on tuition and other revenues to fill the gap (Hovey, 1999; Hauptman, 1997). Few other public services can turn to user fees in a recession; when economic times improve, the states have tended to restrict tuition increases and increase state funding. These trends reflect a struggle to balance state priorities during the ebb and flow of state revenues more than an abandoning of the public commitment to higher education. Over the long haul the public commitment to higher education has been strong and resilient. Whether the level of past commitments will be adequate to meet future challenges is another question.

BUDGETING FOR HIGHER EDUCATION: AN ART, NOT A SCIENCE

Budgeting for higher education, at the state level and even at the institutional level, is complicated and difficult. No other conclusion can explain the variety of approaches employed and the continuous search for a better way. Why is it so difficult?

First, the fundamental mission of higher education—advancing, transmitting, and applying knowledge—knows no bounds. Howard Bowen's (1980) famous "revenue theory of costs," that institutions raise and spend all the money they can, is less a description of insatiable gluttony than of expansive aspirations. Bowen contends that non-profit institutions of higher education endeavor to maximize prestige-enhancing activities rather than profit-maximizing ones. For-profit institutions, where shareholders demand financial returns, act as traditional profit maximizing firms.[16] That is, they also will pursue all the marginally productive dollars the market will provide, and spend them on programs that yield higher returns. While variation in wealth and the ability to attract revenues is substantial, even among institutions with similar missions, every institution, for profit or non-profit, public or private, will raise all the revenue it can.

Second, the many facets of institutional missions are interdependent in fundamental ways and separable in others. Research and instruction can be separated, but not entirely. The budgets for academic departments may be determined by the revenues they generate (commonly known as "every tub on its own bottom" budgeting), but the inflexible application of this principle leads to the starvation of essential disciplines (such as philosophy), which may be less favored in the current marketplace (Froomkin, 1990). Cross-subsidization, based on values, judgments, and politics, has proven unavoidable, even desirable.

Third, the cost structure of the enterprise varies enormously among disciplines, purposes, and functions (Wellman, 2006). Instruction becomes progressively more expensive (by several orders of magnitude) as students advance from lower-division undergraduate courses to doctoral study. Instruction in the lab and in clinical practice settings requires costly equipment and individualized attention, which make it much more expensive than instruction by lecture. Economies of scale are possible at large institutions or in high demand courses, but individual and social goals often require less efficient, small institutions (in rural areas, for example) and small enrollment programs. The many ways such variation can be aggregated at the institutional level (as well as differences in revenue generating capacity) have produced great differences among institutions in per student costs.

Fourth, the principal institutional characteristics used as proxies for quality in higher education—prestigious faculty and highly selective student admissions—are pervasively associated with higher spending. "Quality" institutions (as identified by various ranking schemes) tend to have small classes, higher faculty salaries, heavy commitments to research and graduate education, comfortable facilities, access to advanced technology, and other amenities for students and faculty. The characteristics associated with quality, coupled with the "revenue theory of costs," generate an endless spiral of budgetary demands.

Fifth, the growing importance of a quality higher education to individuals has increased student demand and willingness (among those who can afford it) to pay more. Higher education is now a sellers' market in which institutions compete for relative market position, more so than absolute market share, by enhancing quality and the amenities needed to attract stronger students. Where enrollment demand permits, prices are frequently raised. Institutional costs have also been increasing faster than the CPI, because per capita incomes and competitive compensation in a labor intensive industry have grown faster than the CPI.[17]

These five factors have made it very difficult for public budget makers to know what is "enough" money for higher education and how to allocate those funds among different institutions and purposes. "More" is unfailingly the request, and a "fair" allocation is imperative; but more is never enough, and fair varies in the eyes of different beholders[18] (Wildavsky, 1964; Lingenfelter, 1974).

Two basic techniques—formula budgeting (usually based on some form of cost analysis) and base plus/minus budgeting—have been employed to address these problems in state and system budgeting. Although institutional budget procedures may be less formally structured, formula and base budgeting techniques are also commonly used within institutions. Both approaches have their advantages and limits, and, in some respects, both must be employed to obtain good results. They also have many variations, two of which, performance funding and contracts for service, also are discussed below.

Formula Budgeting with Cost Analysis

For more than 50 years, many states have used formulas which seek to establish "adequacy," that is, based on external standards, what the budget "should" be. These standards have been determined by examining actual costs, funding levels at "peer" institutions, or analytically developed standards for faculty workloads, building operations, libraries, administrative support, etc. Budgeting formulas typically base funding primarily on enrollments and the amount of space occupied, possibly (but not always) with variation depending on the level of enrollment (undergraduate lower division, upper division, and graduate) and the cost of instruction in different disciplines (McKeown-Moak, 2001).

Formula budgeting is predictable, it is generally perceived as fair, and it usually responds to changes in workload quantity and program mix. Many policymakers also consider its "automatic" features (the provision of more or less funding based on changes in workload, space occupied, or programs offered) an advantage, because these features reduce the transaction costs of decision-making from year to year. But formula budgeting's "automatic" features can be a problem. Formulas inevitably limit the number of factors considered in budgeting, which can provide incentives for dysfunctional behavior, such as excessive marketing for student enrollment growth, reduction of academic standards, mission creep, and so on[19] (Shulock & Moore, 2007). Also, when enrollments decline or grow more rapidly than available revenues, the "automatic" elements of formulas become a problem for budget predictability. In the end, virtually every formula budgeting state has made significant "non-formula" budget allocations to address "non-formula" (perhaps political) priorities.

Formula budgeting also fails to encourage gains in quality and productivity, unless such measures are added to the formula in some way. But the more formulas attempt to account for complex goals and conditions, the more they become unwieldy, incomprehensible, and mistrusted. Finally, no formula really resolves the adequacy of funding question, even when based on peer institutions or rationalistic analysis of workload, staffing, and space requirements. Many formulas purporting to establish "adequacy" have been persistently funded at some fraction of the "adequate" amount. Then the formula becomes a straightjacket on the budget process; no discussion of priorities and issues is possible because "there is no money." When formulas are persistently "unfunded," decision-makers eventually will not pay serious attention to the formula "requirements" for the bottom line.[20]

Base Plus/Minus Budgeting

The starting point for base plus/minus budgeting is funding in the current year. This approach is simpler and more transparent than formula budgeting, because all changes (the pluses and minuses)—inflation, salary increases, program improvements, productivity gains or reallocation, changes in workload, etc.—are visible and justified on some basis. Base plus/minus budgeting is entirely flexible in the issues it addresses and the methods it uses. Everything is on the table or can be put there.

At its worse, base plus/minus budgeting perpetuates the status quo. Past decisions have great, perhaps undue weight, and the budget process may be inadequately responsive to quality issues, inequities, or changes in workload and priorities.

The flexibility of base plus/minus budgeting is an asset, but to work well this approach requires continuous analysis and negotiation of need, quality, productivity, and "fairness" issues, the questions formula budgeting seeks to resolve mechanistically. Consequently, base plus/minus budgeting can be more of a decision-making burden—and an occasion for attracting political heat—than some decision-makers can tolerate. This is why formulas were invented. In base-plus budgeting the decision makers are more explicitly people, not a disembodied, pre-negotiated formula.

Finally, base plus/minus budgeting *also* has no direct way to address the question of adequacy. It can use external reference points (just like formula budgeting), but base plus/minus budgeting may be less credible than an explicit formula, even one that is flimsy in substance. These limits of formula and base budgeting and the desire to achieve better outcomes from higher education have led to many experiments, including performance funding and "contracts" between states and institutions which are briefly considered below.

Performance Funding

Performance funding explicitly allocates some portion of an entity's budget based on past performance. It focuses attention on outcomes, provides incentives for improvement, and rewards high or improving performance. It is difficult to argue with popular slogans offered for performance funding: "You get what you measure," and "Money changes behavior, and a lot of money changes a lot of behavior!" Many policymakers have found these approaches very attractive, and performance funding has been advocated as a means of increasing political and financial support for higher education (Burke, 1998; Burke & Minassians, 2002).

Performance funding is related to an earlier budget tradition of Program Planning/Budgeting Systems (PPBS) intended to guide rational resource allocations based on program goals, the evaluation of program effectiveness, and subsequent allocations of resources to the most cost-effective programs. Because performance funding is formula budgeting with an explicit allocation tied to performance outcomes, it shares the advantages and disadvantages of formula budgeting. But the disadvantages are amplified. Performance funding tends to have high transaction and negotiating costs, because the stakes are high and indicators and measurement techniques are debatable. If substantial amounts of money are tied to performance, the systems tend to be politically unsustainable. Why? When the stakes are high, financial stability is put at risk, lower performing institutions are denied resources they may need to improve, and higher performing institutions are likely to become less efficient because they receive budget increases based on already established levels of performance. If a small fraction of the budget is involved, the stakes may be too small to have the desired effect.

After witnessing its popularity grow and then recede, Joseph Burke,[21] who has written extensively and sympathetically about the performance funding movement, concluded that performance funding is more useful and feasible for budgeting purposes at the institutional level than the state level (Burke, 2005).

Contracts for Services

A few states have recently employed yet another budgeting innovation—a contract for services between a higher education institution and the state[22]—purportedly as a means of improving accountability while reducing direct regulation. This approach focuses attention on outcomes and provides incentives for improving performance or meeting explicit state priorities, such as expanding degree production in high demand fields, greater minority participation and success, etc.

The contract for services approach has the great benefit of establishing mutual goals, but some of its drawbacks are obvious. First, a "contract" between an institution and the state for core functions is not the same as an enforceable contract for a specific task or service. Neither the state nor the institution is truly a free agent with viable options. State and public institutional contracts are like agreements between parents and children. Due to dependency and commitment, breaking the relationship or turning to another vendor is not an option. Second, contracts also tend to have high transaction costs with extensive negotiations, lots of fine print, and compliance reviews. Such an approach is hardly likely to reduce bureaucracy. Finally, like all other approaches, contracts do not resolve tension over adequacy (Breneman, 2005).

Intelligent Eclecticism

Each of these approaches to higher education budgeting addresses an important issue, but they all fail to solve the fundamental question of adequacy, and each tends to fall short on one or more essential requirements—continuity, equity, responsiveness to changing conditions, and efficiency. On the question of adequacy, for example, a recent analysis at the National Center for Higher Education Management Systems (Jones & Kelly, 2005), has found wide variation among the states in spending per student and degree production, and a very small correlation between these variables. While the amount of money available is obviously relevant, the mix of institutions in the system, student characteristics and preparation, and how money is used within institutions appear to be even more important.

Although some decision-makers persistently seek a higher education budgeting system that can run on "automatic pilot," effective budgeting requires analysis, engagement, adaptation, and negotiation over ends, means, and values. Cost-analysis, at the core of formula budgeting, is required for fairness and efficiency. The assessment of performance is essential for improving results. Continuity and predictability are necessary for good management. And the effectiveness of the entire system requires institutions and states to agree on common purposes, to develop straightforward, transparent approaches for allocating resources to priorities, and to avoid perverse incentives.

The most important question about budgeting procedures is whether they contribute to progress toward high priority educational goals. A thoughtful, eclectic approach drawing on all of these traditions is most likely to be successful.

HIGHER EDUCATION: WHO PAYS? WHO BENEFITS? WHO SHOULD PAY?

These questions, the title of a 1972 study by the Carnegie Commission on Higher Education, are at the core of the public dialogue on higher education finance. After considerable debate and analysis (engaging numerous economists, several of whom later won the Nobel Prize), the Carnegie Commission concluded: "No precise—or even imprecise—methods exist to assess the individual and societal benefits as against the private and the public costs."[23]

After conceding that the ratio between individual and social benefits cannot be accurately determined, the Commission concluded that the following allocation of costs was appropriate: Students should pay one-third of the direct costs and two- thirds of the sum of direct costs and foregone income. Government and philanthropy, according to the Commission, should cover two-thirds of the direct cost, or one-third of the total of direct costs plus foregone income. The Commission also urged financial assistance to low-income students and state efforts to narrow the price gap between private and public institutions. In practical terms, these recommendations led some states to establish one-third of instructional costs as a standard for tuition, to provide need-based financial aid, and to provide direct grants to private institutions educating state residents.

In 1972, this conclusion challenged the then prevailing philosophy in some states (and traditionally in Europe) of free, or nearly free higher education, for those who qualified for admission. The Carnegie report reflected and in some respects sought to resolve a vigorous public debate in the late 1960s concerning the social justice of low tuition policies led by economists W. Lee Hansen and Burton Weisbrod (1969). The public sector was rapidly expanding during these years, and the competition for students between public and higher tuition private institutions also was (and continues to be) a factor in this debate.

Low tuition in public institutions, to its critics, is a regressive subsidy to the rich, because higher income people enroll disproportionately and benefit unfairly from the taxes of lower income citizens, whose enrollment rate tends to be lower. In response, low-tuition advocates argue that individuals who receive economic benefits from subsidized higher education return the public investment by paying higher taxes; furthermore, all citizens benefit from the larger social contributions of educated people. Its advocates also argue low tuition encourages participation and builds widespread public support for higher education. Low tuition critics respond that taxes are determined by income, not education, and any social benefits, separate from the individual benefits of higher education, are ephemeral.[24]

Higher, or even full-cost tuition in public institutions, combined with generous, need-based financial aid, has been proposed as an alternative to low tuition and a less regressive means of providing access to higher education by Hansen, Weisbrod, Alchian, and others (Hansen & Weisbrod, 1969; Breneman et al. 1993). Despite the logic of this argument, the implementation of the "high tuition/high aid" model has been limited by the political attractiveness of low-tuition to the middle class: concerns that "sticker shock" will discourage low and moderate-income participation (regardless of need-based aid); and concerns about the effectiveness and political durability of need-based aid for providing access. The debate continues. But even though the questions of subsidy and social equity remain relevant, they are becoming less salient as the need for participation in higher education becomes more universal. The extent of unfair subsidies to a privileged few, largely higher income students, who participate in public higher education becomes less relevant to the extent higher education enrollment becomes universal.

Increasingly, virtually all individuals in the United States and other developed economies must obtain some form of postsecondary education in order to join the middle class. In recognition of this new reality, 80 percent of high school sophomores surveyed by the National Center for Education Statistics (NCES) in 2000 intend to obtain at least a bachelors degree, and 40 percent also plan to obtain a graduate or professional degree (NCES, 2005). Most remaining students expect to get technical postsecondary education after high school. Actual participation may fall short of these aspirations, but it is increasingly clear that developed economies must have a highly educated workforce to maintain or improve their standards of living (Friedman, 2005).

Under these circumstances, the central question for the U.S. is no longer how should we subsidize higher education for a privileged fraction of the population, but what financing strategies are most conducive to widespread, successful participation? From this perspective, the need to generate revenues to support instruction is deeply interwoven with questions of cost sharing and the fair distribution of opportunity. As a practical matter, free or nearly free higher education has proven to be sustainable only when the participation rate is low, or instructional expenditures (and perhaps quality) are extremely modest. The growth of public tuition and fees in the past quarter century is unlikely to be reversed, and in the places where tuition is still relatively low, additional real dollar growth in tuition rates and revenues is likely to be required to finance quality programs (Jones et al., 2003).

To the extent that tuition "sticker prices" continue to grow, adequate need-based financial assistance becomes even more critically important for achieving widespread educational attainment in the United States. But the most visible response to growing tuition rates has been more financial aid based on academic merit and tuition discounting in private (and increasingly in public) institutions to attract talented students, regardless of financial need. Middle class subsidies are popular (Baum, this volume).

Another strategy for increasing educational attainment more effectively than pure merit scholarships, has been to provide additional need-based financial aid as an incentive for better academic preparation. Indiana and Oklahoma led this trend with state financial aid programs that provide extra assistance to low-income students taking a rigorous high school curriculum, and the U.S. Congress recently added a bonus for Pell Grant recipients who have done so.

Future Needs and Prospects

As in the past, state support for higher education will continue to be shaped by demographic and economic forces. Enrollment almost certainly will continue to grow—driven by economic necessity, population growth among the young, and the needs of a substantial number of adults already in the workforce who must acquire further education to become or stay competitive in the job market.

Simultaneously, countervailing economic and demographic forces will make it difficult for states and the federal government to finance the demand for higher education. In the United States, the only age group *not* expected to grow over the next 15 years is that of people in the prime working years, 25–55. The number of retirees needing more health care will grow enormously, and the number of young people requiring education will grow steadily, albeit more modestly. Elementary and secondary education enrollments will continue to grow, and without unprecedented new economies in its delivery, health care will consume an increasingly larger share of the GDP and tax revenues.

Based on these demographics and the current tax structure of the states, the National Center for Higher Education Management Systems (NCHEMS) and the Rockefeller Institute have projected that every state will have a revenue shortfall by 2013, with a national average of minus 5.7 percent of the funding required to sustain current state-financed services (Boyd, 2005).

At the federal level, David M. Walker, Comptroller General of the United States, has projected substantial and persistent deficits based on the following assumptions: sustaining current obligations for Social Security and health care; maintaining current domestic, international, and military spending rates as a percent of GDP; and extending all recent tax reductions, which are scheduled to expire. If these policies, the path of least political resistance, are followed, Walker projects that by 2040 interest payments on the federal debt will nearly equal all federal revenues. Moreover, spending will equal 40 percent of GDP, and revenues will be less than 20 percent of GDP. The *annual* deficit projected by Walker, given these assumptions, will equal or exceed federal revenues.[25]

Clearly, these projections of the challenges confronting the federal and state governments are not prophecies. Their dire implications almost surely guarantee they will not come true. Political leaders will be forced to make hard choices; the providers of public services (including higher education) will be called on to reach new levels of efficiency and productivity; and taxpayers will be asked to pay more.

The case for increasing public investment in higher education has never been stronger than it will be in the first half of the 21st century. In significant ways, however, the challenges facing educators and policymakers are different from those facing their predecessors. Forty years ago the task was to expand the capacity of the existing system in order to accommodate a large infusion of traditional students. Now the task is to educate two-thirds or more of the adult population to a standard that previously was necessary for only the top quarter in aptitude and aspiration.[26]

While this challenge clearly has financial implications, simply increasing spending without making other fundamental changes regarding expectations of students and the delivery of instruction is unlikely to yield desired outcomes. Both K–12 and higher education must significantly decrease their tolerance for student failure and increase the ability of instructors to inspire and generate academic effort and achievement.

As schools improve student attainment, enrollment demand in higher education will grow. Public and private higher education institutions will need additional public subsidies (whether direct or in student assistance) to accommodate the demand, but discretionary income for expanding higher education will be scarce. Educators and policymakers will need to become increasingly thoughtful and intentional about balancing appropriations to public institutions, tuition policies, and need-based student financial assistance in order to achieve the desired level of access and student success. And institutions will face unremitting pressure to restrain price increases and increase productivity by focusing relentlessly on priorities and exploiting technology to improve instructional quality and reduce costs (Jones et al., 2003; Twigg, 1999).

TABLE 36A.1

	% growth 1971 to 2005	*1970*	*1980*	*1990*	*2000*	*2005*
The Higher Education Price Index (FY 1983 = 100) 1	506%	40	78	141	197	240
The Consumer Price Index (FY 1983 = 100) 2	407%	39	79	129	173	195
State + Local support per FTE public higher education, adjusted for inflation using HEPI 2005 3	-10%	7,882	8,579	8,744	8,935	7,127
State + Local support per FTE public higher education, adjusted for inflation using CPI 2005	8%	6,594	6,855	7,759	8,317	7,127
Total Educational Cost per FTE public higher education, adjusted for inflation using HEPI 4	11%	8,270	9,002	9,651	10,334	9,196
Total Educational Cost per FTE public higher education, adjusted for inflation using CPI	33%	6,919	7,192	8,563	9,619	9,196
Personal income per capita, calendar year, adjusted for inflation using CPI-U 2005 5	66%	20,722	24,972	29,396	33,790	34,495
State and local expenditures per capita, FY, adjusted for inflation using CPI-U 2005 6	103%	2,795	3,571	4,408	5,090	5,683
Average tuition 4-year public, academic year, adjusted for inflation using CPI-U 2005 7	177%	1,821	1,821	2,686	3,792	5,038
Average tuition 2-year public, academic year, adjusted for inflation using CPI-U 2005 8	105%	903	877	1,141	1,515	1,847
Federal student assistance grants and tax credits per total FTE, adjusted for inflation using CPI-U 2005 9	28%	1,654	2,055	1,113	1,641	2,112
Federal student assistance loan subsidies and administration per Total FTE, adjusted for inflation using CPI-U 2005 10	364%	1,039	1,344	2,070	3,851	4,816
Total Spending in Higher Education (all Sectors) as a % of GDP 11		2.0%	2.0%	2.3%	2.4%	2.6%
Fall FTE Enrollments in 2-year public institutions, fall of academic year 12	181%	1,318,309	2,333,313	2,751,762	3,075,520	3,707,431
Fall FTE Enrollment Share in 2-year public institutions, fall of academic year 12		20.8%	27.5%	28.1%	28.1%	28.5%

Estimate

Indexed to 1970

	% growth 1971 to 2005	*1970*	*1980*	*1990*	*2000*	*2005*
The Higher Education Price Index (FY 1983 = 100)	506%	1.00	1.96	3.56	4.98	6.06
The Consumer Price Index (FY 1983 = 100)	407%	1.00	2.05	3.36	4.48	5.07
State + Local support per FTE public higher education, adjusted for inflation using HEPI 2005	-10%	1.00	1.09	1.11	1.13	0.90
State + Local support per FTE public higher education, adjusted for inflation using CPI 2005	8%	1.00	1.04	1.18	1.26	1.08
Total Educational Cost per FTE public higher education, adjusted for inflation using HEPI 2005	11%	1.00	1.09	1.17	1.25	1.11
Total Educational Cost per FTE public higher education, adjusted for inflation using CPI 2005	33%	1.00	1.04	1.24	1.39	1.33
Personal income per capita, calendar year, adjusted for inflation using CPI-U 2005	66%	1.00	1.21	1.42	1.63	1.66
State and local expenditures per capita, FY, adjusted for inflation using CPI-U 2005	103%	1.00	1.28	1.58	1.82	2.03
Average tuition 4-year public, academic year, adjusted for inflation using CPI-U 2005	177%	1.00	1.00	1.47	2.08	2.77
Average tuition 2-year public, academic year, adjusted for inflation using CPI-U 2005	105%	1.00	0.97	1.26	1.68	2.05
Federal student assistance grants and tax credits per total FTE, adjusted for inflation using CPI-U 2005	28%	1.00	1.24	0.67	0.99	1.28
Federal student assistance loan subsidies and administration per Total FTE, adjusted for inflation using CPI-U 2005	364%	1.00	1.29	1.99	3.71	4.64
Total Spending in Higher Education (all Sectors) as a % of GDP		1.00	1.01	1.15	1.19	1.30
Fall FTE Enrollments in 2-year public institutions, fall of academic year	181%	1.00	1.77	2.09	2.33	2.81
Fall FTE Enrollment Share in 2-year public institutions, fall of academic year		1.00	1.32	1.35	1.35	1.37

Source Notes:
1. Commonfund Institute
2. Commonfund Institute
3. SHEEO SHEF. Includes all functions. State support in 1970 is from Grapevine (FY 1969-1970), and 1970 local support of $396 million (6%) is estimated based on 1980 data."
4. SHEEO SHEF. Data for 1970 estimated based on Digest of Educational Statistics Fall FTE converted to annual FTE (9.5% higher), net tuition based on 1980 data, and state and local support for 1970. "
5. Bureau of Economic Analysis
6. Economic Report to President: 2006 Report Spreadsheet
7. Digest of Education Statistics 2005, Table 312; The data in 1970 is estimated. The average tuition 4-year public in 1980 as a % of the sum of the average tuition at public universities and " other public 4-year institutions is multiplied by the sum of the average tuitions at both types of institutions in 1970 to get the estimate.
8. Digest of Education Statistics 2005, Table 312"
9. College Board. Includes the following programs: Pell, SEOG, LEAP, Veterans, Military, SSEC, and other grants, Work Study, plus education tax benefits.
The data in 1970 is for the academic year 1970-71. Total FTE includes for-profit FTE as well.
10. College Board. Inlcudes the following programs: Perkins, Income Contingent, Subsidized Stafford. Unsubsidized Stafford, PLUS, SLS, and other loans (both FDLP and FFELP). The data in 1970 is for the academic year 1970-71. Total FTE includes for-profit FTE as well.
11. Expenditure data 1970-2000: Digest of Education Statistics 2005, table 26; Expenditure data 2005: IPEDS DCT GDP: Bureau of Economic Analysis (the most recent data as of 10/23/06 - the revised data (by BEA) on September 2006)
12. Digest of Education Statistics 2005, table 199"

TABLE A36.2

	% growth 1971 to 2005	1970	1980	1990	2000	2005
State + Local support for higher education (Fiscal Year, Nominal)[1]	1004%	6,518,961,055	19,441,100,000	40,796,900,000	63,247,976,899	71,939,936,022
State + Local support per FTE public higher education	441%	1,318	2,776	5,141	7,346	7,127
State + Local support per FTE public higher education, adjusted for inflation using HEPI 2005	-11%	7,990	8,579	8,744	8,935	7,127
State + Local support per FTE public higher education, adjusted for inflation using CPI 2005	7%	6,685	6,855	7,759	8,317	7,127
Total Educational Cost at Public Higher Education (FY, Current)[2]	1257%	6,839,759,129	20,397,800,000	45,027,700,000	73,146,232,520	92.821.475,908
Total Educational Cost per FTE public higher education, adjusted for inflation using HEPI	10%	8,383	9,002	9,651	10,334	9,196
Total Educational Cost per FTE public higher education, adjusted for inflation using CPI	31%	7,014	7,192	8,563	9,619	9,196
Annual Enrollments in all public institutions (SHEF)[3]	104%	4,947,012	7,002,698	7,936,066	8,609,741	10,093,410
Fall FTE Enrollments in all public institutions (Fall of AY, Digest)[4]	104%	4,577,985	6,392,617	7,371,590	8,020,074	9,348,081
Fall FTE Enrollments in 4 year public institutions (Fall of AY, Digest)[4]	73%	3,259,676	4,059,304	4,619,828	4,944,554	5,640,650
Fall FTE Enrollments in 2-year public institutions (Fall of AY, Digest)[4]	181%	1,318,309	2,333,313	2,751,762	3,075,520	3,707,431
Fall FTE Enrollments private institutions (Fall of AY, Digest)[4]	108%	1,756,153	2,094,700	2,409,291	2,923,535	3,652,913
The Higher Education Price Index (FY 1983 = 100)[5]	506%	40	78	141	197	240
The Consumer Price Index (FY 1983 = 100)[6]	407%	39	79	129	173	195
Personal income per capita (Current)[7]	744%	4,085	10,114	19,477	29,845	34,495
Personal income per capita (Adjusted by 2005 CPI-U)[7]	66%	20,722	24,972	29,396	33,790	34,495
GDP per capita (Calendar Year, Current)	729%	5,065	12,249	23,200	34,763	41,990
GDP per capita (Calendar Year, Adjusted by 2005 CPI-U)	63%	25,691	30,244	35,015	39,357	41,990
GDP (Calendar Year, Current, in billions)[8]	1099%	1,039	2,790	5,803	9,817	12,456
Population (Calendar Year, in thosands)[9]	45%	205,052	227,726	250,132	282,402	296,639
State and local expenditures per capita (FY)	931%	551	1,446	2,920	4,495	5,683
State and local expenditures (FY, Current, in billions)[10]	1392%	113	329	731	1,270	1,686
Net tuition in public institutions (FY, Current)[11]	2280%	1,429,730,901	4,263,800,000	11,256,700,000	21,494,593,216	34,025,470,271
Average tuition 4-year public (AY, Current)[12]	1303%	359	738	1,780	3,349	5,038
Average tuition 4-year public (AY, Current, Public Universities Only)	1293%	427	840	2,035	3,768	5,948
Average tuition 4-year private (AY, Current)[13]	1123%	1,540	3,225	8,396	14,588	18,838
Average tuition 4-year private (AY, Current, Private Universities Only)	1315%	1,809	3,811	10,348	19,307	25,600
Average tuition 2-year public (AY, Current)[14]	938%	178	355	756	1,338	1,847
Federal student assistance grants and tax credits (Current, in millions)[15]	1229%	2,065	7,063	7,214	15,858	27,454
Federal student assistance grants and tax credits per total FTE[16] (Current, in millions)	548%	326	832	738	1,449	2,112
Federal student assistance loan subsidies and administration (Current, in millions)[17]	4726%	1,297	4,619	13,414	37,228	62,614
Federal student assistance loan subsidies and administration per Total FTE[16] (Current, in millions)	2251%	205	544	1,371	3,402	4,816

Source Notes:

1. SHEF. Includes research, medicine, and agriculture extension. State support in 1970 is from Grapevine (FY 1969-1970). Local support in 1970 is estimated based on the ratio of local support to state support in 1980.
2. SHEF. Data for local revenues and the portion of state support for research, medicine, and agriculture extension in 1970 are unavailable.Therefore, total educational revenue as a % of state + local support in 1980 is applied to the state and local support in 1970 to estimate 1970 cost per FTE.
3. Except for 1970 Annual FTE is from SHEF. Annual FTE in 1970 is estimated at 108% of Fall 1969 FTE from Digest of Education Statistics, based on average ratio between SHEF annual FTE and associated Fall FTE.
4. Digest of Education Statistics 2005, table 199
5. Commonfund Institute
6. Commonfund Institute
7. Bureau of Economic Analysis, All NIPA Tables
8. Economic Report to President: 2006 Report Spreadsheet Tables; Table B-1
9. Economic Report to President: 2006 Report Spreadsheet Table, Table B-34
10. Economic Report to President: 2006 Report Spreadsheet, Table B-85
11. SHEF. The data in 1970 is estimate based on the ratio of net tution revenue to total educational revenue in 1980
12. Digest of Education Statistics 2005, Table 312; The data in 1970 is estimated. The average tuition 4-year public in 1980 as a % of the sum of the average tuition at public universities and other public 4-year institutions is multiplied by the sum of the average tuitions at both types of institutions in 1970 to get the estimate.
13. Digest of Education Statistics 2005, Table 312; The data in 1970 is estimated. The average tuition 4-year private in 1980 as a % of the sum of the average tuition at private universities and other private 4-year institutions is multiplied by the sum of the average tuitions at both types in 1970 to get the estimate.
14. Digest of Education Statistics 2005, Table 312
15. College Board. Includes the following programs: Pell, SEOG, LEAP, Veterans, Military, SSEC, and other grants, Work Study, plus education tax benefits. The data in 1970 is for the academic year 1970-71
16. Fall FTE. Private for-profit is included
17. College Board. Inlcudes the following programs: Perkins, Income Contingent, Subsidized Stafford, Unsubsidized Stafford, PLUS, SLS, and other loans (both FDLP and FFELP). The data in 1970 is for the academic year 1970-71

NOTES

1. With thanks to David Tandberg, who provided assistance in reviewing the literature and analyzing data sources; to Takeshi Yanagiura, who assisted with data retrieval and analysis; and to Matthew Gianneschi, who provided research and editorial assistance.
2. The majority opinion handed down by the Supreme Court in the Trustees of *Dartmouth College v. Woodward* (17 U. S. 518, 1819), delivered by Chief Justice John Marshall, was that private institutions of higher education are to be free from governmental interference pursuant to the contract clause of the Constitution, which asserts that states may not pass laws that impair contracts. Despite its obvious connection to higher education history, the Supreme Court's opinion in this case is a landmark judgment in American contracts law more than a statement about public policy for higher education.
3. The Morrill Act of 1862 (7 U.S.C. 301 et.seq.) was limited to states and territories within the United States. The Act did not apply to states "in a condition of rebellion or insurrection against the government of the United States." That is, it did not apply to the states in the Confederated States of America. The Second Morrill Act (1890; 7 U.S.C. 322 et seq.) extended the provisions of the 1862 Act to include the development of what would later be known as Historically Black Colleges and Universities.
4. The participation rates here and later are calculated from enrollment data from the Digest of Educational Statistics, and U.S. population data are from the U.S. Census.
5. The publication of *Higher Education for Democracy* signaled a change in the role and mission of higher education in the United States. The report called for an extensive network of community colleges and marked a fundamental shift in public perceptions about higher education. By establishing that, "the social role of education in a democratic society is at once to insure equal liberty and equal opportunity to differing individuals and groups, and to enable the citizens to understand, appraise, and redirect forces, men, and events as these tend to strengthen or to weaken their liberties," the Truman Commission Report reinterpreted higher education as a social good.
6. The Higher Education Act of 1965 included a need-based grant program entitled the Educational Opportunity Grant program (EOG). Amendments to the Higher Education Act in 1972 expanded the EOG program and renamed it the Pell Grant program.
7. See http://www.grapevine.ilstu.edu/ for a comprehensive record of these surveys. Kent Halstead launched a complementary survey of state finance in 1978 (Halstead, *State Profiles: Financing Public Higher Education.* Washington, DC: Research Associates of Washington, 1978–1996), which made comparisons among the states in support per FTE student. The Halstead study is the foundation for the current State Higher Education Finance study (SHEF) now annually conducted by the State Higher Education Executive Officers (SHEEO).
8. State Higher Education Finance, 2006 pre-publication data. Data are adjusted for inflation using the Higher Education Cost Adjustment (HECA), developed by SHEEO.
9. College Board. See Table 36A.1 for details, and note a significant decline and then recovery of grant support per student during the period 1980 to 1990.
10. "Per student spending" consists of state and local support per student plus net tuition. It excludes sponsored research and other non-instructional activities as well as medical instruction. The figures for individual states include all sectors of public higher education, and they are adjusted for differences among the states in the cost of living and the proportion of enrollments in different types of institution, two-year, four-year, and different Carnegie classifications. The technical details for these adjustments are explained in State Higher Education Finance, available at www.sheeo.org.
11. SHEF FY2005.
12. In 2002, the association of State Higher Education Executive Officers developed another alternative, the Higher Education Cost Adjustment (HECA), based on the federal employment index for white collar workers (75 percent) and the GNP Implicit Price Deflator (25 percent). Because personnel costs are roughly 75 percent of HEPI, in most years the simply designed HECA index approaches HEPI and exceeds the CPI. See http://www.sheeo.org for details.
13. For a discussion on the distribution and effects of student financial assistance, please see McPherson & Schapiro (1998) and Heller (1997).

14. Total includes $9.0 billion from Pell Grants, $2.6 billion from campus based programs, $13.9 billion from subsidized Stafford loans, and $11.8 billion from unsubsidized Stafford loans.
15. Estimates of fiscal impact of federal tax credits available from the College Board (2005) do not distribute them among sectors of higher education.
16. For discussions of "prestige maximization" please see *The Costs of Higher Education* (1980) by Howard Bowen, and *Academic Capitalism* (1997) by Sheila Slaughter and Larry Leslie.
17. Baumol & Bowen's (1966) analysis of the difficulty of productivity gains in labor-intensive enterprises such as higher education is valid, but it has been extended too far by those who argue productivity gains in education are impossible. The amount of cost variation among institutions and results from recent applications of technology in instruction suggest real productivity gains are feasible, even if these factors limit the extent.
18. Aaron Wildavsky's classic, *The Politics of the Budgetary Process* (1964), and his subsequent research documented the power of inertia in budgeting. The author's 1974 dissertation research examined 10 years of budgetary decisions in Illinois, Michigan, and Wisconsin, and found that in each state previous decisions could predict nearly all (>97 percent) of the variance in annual appropriations to individual institutions.
19. *Rules of the Game: How State Policy Creates Barriers to Student Completion and Impedes Student Success in California's Community Colleges* provides an extensive discussion of dysfunctional incentives in the budget formulas of California's community college system.
20. C. Warren Neel's transmittal memorandum for "Measuring Performance in Higher Education," a joint study of Tennessee's Comptroller of the Treasury, Office of Legislative Budget Analysis, and Division of Budget and Department of Finance and Administration (February 2001), illustrates this tendency in a state noted for its sophisticated budget formulas: [The Tennessee higher education budget] "formula has not been fully funded for thirteen years and this year the gap is $102 million."
21. Former institutional president and system provost in the State University of New York System.
22. As an example, please see the Colorado Commission on Higher Education's website: www.state.co.us/cche/cof/ffs/index.html.
23. See Carnegie, p. 3 (1973), Commision on Higher Education.
24. See Carnegie, p. 75 for Milton Friedman's view claiming social benefits are "bad economics" and Howard Bowens view to the contrary. Also, see Arman A. Alchian, "The Economic and Social Impact of Free Tuition" pp. 5-14, in Breneman, Leslie, & Anderson.
25. See http://www.gao.gov/cghome.htm and refer to Fiscal, Social Security, and Health Care Challenges, Awakening Conference, Sea Island, Georgia, January 7, 2007, GAO-07-345CG PDF Accessible Text
26. While some still question whether such a substantial increase in educational attainment is necessary or possible, a sea change in public attitudes toward educational attainment is strongly implied by the unremitting drive to reform education since 1983 when *A Nation At Risk* was released.

BIBLIOGRAPHY

Alexander, F.K. (2000). The changing face of accountability: Monitoring and assessing institutional performance in higher education. *Journal of Higher Education*, 71(4), 411–431.

Baumol, W. J. & Bowen, W. G. (1966). *Performing arts—The economic dilemma*. New York: The Twentieth Century Fund.

Bowen, H. R. (1980). *The costs of higher education*. San Francisco: Jossey-Bass.

Boyd, D. (2005). *State fiscal outlooks from 2005 to 2013: Implication for higher education*. Boulder, CO: National Center for Higher Education Management Systems.

Breneman, D. (2005). *Are the state and public higher education striking a new bargain?* AGB Public Policy Paper #04-02. Washington, DC.: Association of Governing Boards.

Breneman, D.W., Leslie, L., & Anderson, R.E. (Eds.). (1993). *ASHE Reader on Finance in higher education*. Needham Heights, MA: Ginn Press.

Burke, J. C. (2005). Reinventing accountability: From bureaucratic rules to performance results. In J. C. Burke & Associates (Eds.), *Achieving accountability in higher education: Balancing public academic and market demands*, (pp. 216–245). San Francisco: Jossey-Bass.

Burke, J. & Minassians, H. (2002). Reporting higher education results: Missing links in the performance chain. *New Directions for Institutional Research*, No. 116. San Francisco: Jossey-Bass.

Burke, J. & Serban, A. (1998). Performance funding for higher education: Fad or trend? *New Directions for Institutional Research*, No. 97. San Francisco: Jossey-Bass.

Callan, P.M. (2002). Coping with recession: Public policy, economic downturns and higher education. *National Center Report* #02-2. Washington, DC: National Center for Public Policy and Higher Education.

Callan, P. M., Doyle, W., & Finney, J. E. (2001). Evaluating state higher education performance. *Change Magazine*, March/April, 10–19.

Callan, P.M., & Finney, J.E. (Eds.) (1997). *Public and private financing of higher education: Shaping public policy for the future*. Phoenix, AZ: American Council on Education and The Oryx Press.

Carnegie Commision on Higher Education (1983). *Higher education: Who pays? Who benefits? Who should pay?* New York: McGraw Hill.

The College Board (2005). *Trends in student aid 2005*. New York.

Ehrenberg, R. G. (2006). "The Perfect Storm and the Privatization of Public Higher Education," *Change Magazine*, January/February, 2006.

Friedman, T. L. (2005). *The World is Flat*, Farrar, Strauss, and Giroux.

Geiger, R. L. (1999). The ten generations of American higher education. In Berdahl, R. O., Altbach, P.G., & Gumport, P. J. (Eds.), *American higher education in the twenty-first century: Social, political, and economic challenges* (pp. 38–70). Baltimore: The Johns Hopkins University Press.

Grubb, W.N., & Tuma, J. (1991). Who Gets Student Aid? Variations in Access to Aid. *Review of Higher Education* 14(3): 359–381.

Hansen, W.L. & Weisbrod, B. (1969) *Benefits, Finance, and Costs of Public Higher Education,* Markham Publishing Company.

Hauptman, A. (2001). Financing higher education in the 1990s. In J. L. Yeager, G. M. Nelson, E. A. Potter, J.C. Weidman, T. G. Zullo (Eds.), *ASHE Reader on Finance in Higher Education*, Second Edition. Boston, MA: Pearson Custom Publishing.

Heller, D. E. (2003). State oversight of academia. In R.G. Ehrenberg (Ed.), *Governing academia*. Ithaca, NY: Cornell University Press.

Heller, D. E. (1997). Student price response in higher education: An update to Leslie and Brinkman. *Journal of Higher Education,* 68(6), 624–659.

Hoxby C. M. (1997). *How the changing market structure of U.S. higher education explains college tuition*. National Bureau of Economic Research Working Paper No. 6323.

Hovey, H. (1999). State funds for higher education: Fiscal decisions and policy implications. In J. L. Yeager, G. M. Nelson, E. A. Potter, J. C. Weidman, and T. G. Zullo (Eds.), *ASHE Reader on Finance in Higher Education*, Second Edition. Boston, MA: Pearson Custom Publishing.

Jones, D. (1984). *Higher-Education budgeting at the state level: Concepts and principles*. Boulder, CO: National Center for Higher Education Management Systems.

Jones, D. & Kelly, P. (2005). *A new look at the institutional component of higher education finance: A guide for evaluating performance relative to financial resources*. Boulder, CO: National Center for Higher Education Management Systems.

Jones, D., Mortimer, K., Brinkman, P., Lingenfelter, P., L'Orange, H., Rasmussen, C., & Voorhees, R. (2003). *Policies in sync: Apppropriations, tuition, and financial aid for higher education*. Boulder, CO: Western Interstate Commission for Higher Education.

Kane, T. & Orszag, P. (2003). *Higher education spending: The role of medicaid and the business cycle*. The Brookings Institution Policy Brief #124.

Kaufman, H. (1960). Emerging conflicts in the doctrines of public administration. *American Political Science Review*, 50(4), 1057–1073.

Layzell, D.T. & Lyddon, J.W. (1990). Budgeting for higher education at the state level: Enigma, paradox, and ritual. 1990 *ASHE-ERIC Higher Education Reports* 4. Washington, D.C.: The George Washington University.

Leslie, L. L. & Brinkman, P. T. (1988). *The economic value of higher education*. New York: MacMillan Publishing Company.

Lingenfelter, P. E. (1974). *The Politics of Higher Education Appropriations in Three Midwestern States*. Ph. D. Dissertation, University of Michigan.

Lingenfelter, P. E. (2005). *Higher education and money: Goals, values, strategies, and tactics*. Boulder, CO: State Higher Education Executive Officers.

Longanecker, D. (2006). A tale of two pities. *Change Magazine*, January/February, 14–25.

Lyall, K.C. (2006). The De-Facto privatization of American public higher education. *Change Magazine*, January/February, 2006.

Lyall, K. C. & Sell, K. R. (2006). *The true genius of America at Risk: Are we losing our public universities to de facto privatization?* Westport, CT: Praeger Publishers.

McKeown-Moak, M. (2001). *Funding formula use in higher education*. MGT of America, a paper prepared for the Pennsylvania State System of Higher Education, Harrisburg, PA

McLendon, M.K. (2003). State governance reform of higher education: Patterns, trends, and theories of the public policy process. In J.C. Smart (Ed.), *Higher education handbook of theory and research* (Vol. 18). New York: Agathon Press.

McPherson, M. S. & Schapiro, M. O. (1991). Keeping college affordable: Government and educational opportunity. Washington, DC: Brookings Institution.

McPherson, M. S. & Schapiro, M. O. (1998). Priorities for federal student aid policy: Looking beyond Pell. Proceedings of the American Philosophical Society, 142(2), pp. 171–190.

McPherson, M. S. & Schapiro, M. O. (1998). The student aid game: Meeting need and rewarding talent in American higher education. Princeton, NJ: Princeton University Press.

McPherson, M. S., Schapiro, M. O, & Winston, G. C. (1991). *Paying the piper:*
Productivity, incentives, and financing in U. S. higher education. Ann Arbor, MI: University of Michigan Press.

Meisinger, Jr., R.J. & Dubeck, L.W. (1984). College & university budgeting: An introduction for faculty and academic administrators. Washington, D.C.: National Association of College and University Business Officers.

Mortenson. T. G. (2002). *The rise and fall of state investment effort in higher education, 1962–2002*. Post-secondary Education Opportunity 115, 5.

Mortenson. T. G. (2005). *College affordability trends by parental income levels and institutional type 1990 to 2004*. Postsecondary Education Opportunity 159.

National Center for Education Statistics (2005). Youth indicators, 2005. Accesses from http://nces.ed.gov/programs/youthindicators.

Shulock, N. & Moore, C. (2007) *Rules of the Game: How State Policy Creates Barriers to Student Completion and Impedes Student Success in California's Community Colleges*. Institute for Higher Education Leadership and Policy, California State University, Sacramento, California.

State Higher Education Executive Officers (2007). *State Higher Education Finance FY2003, FY2004, FY2005, FY2006*. Boulder, CO: Author.

Trow, M. (1974). The transition from elite to mass higher education. Paris: OECD, cited by Geiger, R. L. (1999). The ten generations of American higher education. In R. Berdahl, P. Gumport, & P. Altbach (eds.) *American higher education in the 21st century* (p. 58). Baltimore: Johns Hopkins Press.

The Commission on the Future of Higher Education (2006). *A test of leadership. Report of the national commission on the future of higher education*. Washington D.C.: U.S. Department of Education.

Twigg, C. (1999). Improving learning and reducing costs: Redesigning large-enrollment courses. Available: http://www.center.rpi.edu/PewSym/mono1.html

Wellman, J. V. (2006) *Costs, prices and affordability: A background paper for the Secretary's commission on the future of higher education*. Issue Paper #13. Washington, DC: The Secretary of Education's Commission on the Future of Higher Education.

Wellman, J. V. (2001). Assessing state accountability systems. *Change Magazine*, March/April, 47–52.

Whitehead, J.S. & Herbst, J. (1986). How to think about the Dartmouth college case. *History of Education Quarterly*, 26(3), 333–349.

Wildavsky, A.B. (1964) *The politics of the budgetary process*. Little Brown.

37

Cost and Pricing in Higher Education

William F. Massy

> Our higher education system is increasingly dysfunctional. State subsidies are declining, tuition is rising, and cost per student is increasing faster than inflation or family income. Affordability is directly affected by a financing system that provides limited incentives for colleges and universities to take aggressive steps to improve institutional efficiency and productivity. Public concern about rising costs may ultimately contribute to the erosion of public confidence in higher education.
>
> Spellings Commission (2006, p. 9)

Opinions differ about many of the Spellings Commission's conclusions, but few informed observers contest its finding that for decades, the cost of higher education has increased faster than inflation or family incomes (Spellings Commission, 2006). For example, Vedder (2004, p. 6) reports the mean annual increase in tuition exceeded the mean annual rise in the consumer price index by 3.6 percentage points. Similar conclusions apply, on average across institutions and over time, with respect to instructional cost per student. Financial aid has held down net tuition increases for some segments of the population, but, for most, net as well as gross tuition has been rising. The purpose of this chapter is not to detail or decry what most observers agree is a pervasive phenomenon, but to examine its causes (Detailed descriptions can be found in McPherson, et al., 1993; Hoenack & Collins, 1990; Ehrenberg, 2000; Clotfelter, 1996.) It is only by understanding causes that one can craft meaningful policy recommendations.

The conventional wisdom holds that tuition increases are driven by two factors, both of which are outside the control of university managers: cost escalation and, for the public sector, reductions in state appropriations. Shifts in state funding priorities certainly have increased the pressure on public sector tuition rates. Indeed, we sometimes see implicit understandings between governments and universities that appropriations cuts will be offset by tuition hikes. But that understanding depends on the public's continued belief that the cost side of the tuition-cost equation is being managed effectively—a conclusion that is itself subject to challenge.

COST DRIVERS

University leaders like to say that tuition escalation is driven by cost increases; indeed, I made many such arguments during my tenure as Stanford's Vice President for Business and Finance. Huge increases in the price of energy provided an unassailable example of such cost increases in the 1970s—one that may well be regaining currency. Regulatory policy shifts further added to cost. Universities were brought under the National Labor Relations Board (NLRB), the Occupational Safety and Health Administration (OSHA), and many other state and federal regulatory bodies. The fact that businesses had for years been subject to such regulations was scant comfort when compliance costs, which totaled many millions of dollars, were tallied against higher education's sometimes shaky financial base. Other regulations have affected colleges and universities even more directly. Affirmative action goals and timetables forced their way into student admissions and faculty hiring decisions, further adding to cost. Title IX forced institutions to spend additional millions to equalize athletic expenditures for men and women. And while these particular drivers may have receded, each decade brings a new set. The point is not that the requirements are inappropriate—indeed, most are desirable and some were welcomed. It is that the extra costs seem to justify, or indeed mandate, price increases.

The academic market basket also tends to drive cost escalation. Book and journal prices, for example, have risen faster than inflation despite the introduction of cost-saving technology. Universities' direct expenditures on technology also drive up costs, the dramatic increases in price-performance ratios notwithstanding. The new technological solutions are added on top of the existing expenditure base, so of course costs are increasing. The returns from these investments are realized as quality improvements rather than as cost reductions—even reductions at the levels needed to offset the cost of investment. Increased academic specialization is another cost-push factor. Knowledge expands inexorably, and vibrant institutions want to participate in the expansion; but "old knowledge" does not necessarily become irrelevant. Thus, libraries cannot simply throw away the old books as new ones arrive.

The ultimate argument for cost-driven price increases, and one I used to good advantage in the tuition debates at Stanford, is what economist William Baumol calls the "cost disease" (c.f., Baumol & Blackman, 1983). The cost disease afflicts industries with high labor content and limited opportunities for productivity improvement—a description that, as former Princeton President William Bowen pointed out in his path-breaking 1968 book (Bowen, 1968), aptly characterizes the traditional university. Consider the economics of a string quartet playing to live audiences, for example.

> A thirty-minute piece requires two labor hours, the same is it did centuries ago. Trying to boost productivity by playing faster or dropping the "extra" violin would diminish quality. Yet the musicians' real wages escalate year after year because of productivity growth elsewhere in the economy. If they do not share in the fruits of such growth (to which they have contributed by improving the quality of life), the supply of musicians would dry up. Therefore, the large fraction of the quartet's cost that is represented by salaries will grow inexorably in real terms. The quartet will get steadily more expensive relative to the average of other goods and services.

In Baumol's terms, the string quartet represents a "stagnant industry." Labor costs in traditional higher education will continue to rise faster than inflation and, according to the stagnant industry argument, universities will be unable to offset them with productivity increases. Thus higher education would be doomed to become ever more expensive in real terms—ironically, all the more so as it contributes to productivity increases in the general economy and thus to rises in real wages that it will be forced to match.

ADDITIONAL DRIVERS

The conventional wisdom regarding rising costs is only half right. Far from being outside the control of university managers, the rise in costs and tuitions depends in significant ways upon the individual and collective choices made by higher education institutions. It is such dependence, and the continued reluctance of the academy to acknowledge it, that has produced the climate of mistrust that was reflected in the Spellings Commission report.

Factors additional to the "cost disease" fall under three broad rubrics: unbounded aspirations, markets, and "sticky functions." Unbounded aspirations drive universities to do more... and more, and more. The effect of unbounded aspirations is to exert a continuing upward pressure on cost, one that is driven by choice rather than the effect of external factors. Second, higher education's market structure allows the increased cost to be financed with price increases. Indeed, some would say the markets invite such increases through price-quality associations. Third, higher education's production functions are "sticky." As explained later, the academic culture and the internal structure of universities inhibit productivity improvement and lead to the "layering on" of activities as described earlier for technology. No policy pertaining to higher education cost or pricing can succeed unless founded on a detailed understanding of these three factors. Indeed, policies that ignore these root causes are likely to do more harm than good.

UNBOUNDED ASPIRATIONS

Universities constantly strive to better themselves and are hardly unique in this respect. Public corporations generally see growth as an important objective because growth can bring more revenue, more profit, and a higher stock price. Universities do not necessarily try to grow in student numbers; indeed, most of the elite private institutions have held their enrollments near-constant for decades. However, they do seek growth in sponsored research, breadth of scholarship, faculty entrepreneurial activities, and the like. But above all, they strive for growth in quality, which takes the form of more and better academic work and support services per student. The desired results of such betterment are improved student intake, a stronger and happier faculty, easier fund-raising, and—analogous to the corporation's stock price—greater prestige.

The Nonprofit Economic Model

Such behavior has been verified in countless studies (Brewer, Gates, & Goldman, 2001), and it is consistent with direct observation. But it also predictable from theory: specifically, the theory of nonprofit enterprises that Estelle James and I developed in various publications beginning several decades ago (James, 1986; Hopkins & Massy, 1981; Massy, 2003, 2004). Rooted in classical microeconomic theory, the model describes nonprofit behavior as "maximizing a subjectively determined value function by adjusting outputs and output prices, subject to market, production, and financial constraints." The value function reflects the institution's mission. Market constraints reflect the demand functions of those who purchase its outputs and the supply functions of those who provide its factors of production. The production function describes how input factors are transformed into outputs of a given quantity and quality. The financial function requires that total revenue minus total cost equal zero: the all-important not-for-profit condition.

In contrast, for-profit enterprises maximize profits by adjusting outputs and output prices, subject to market and production constraints. If you look at the two models, you can see that the for-profit objective function is simply revenue minus cost—which is the left-hand side of the nonprofit's financial constraint. All other elements of the theory remain the same.

Nonprofit enterprises regulate the quantity and quality of their outputs using the decision rule: "Marginal Value + Marginal Revenue = Marginal Cost," or $MV+MR=MC$ for short. "Marginal value" means "incremental contribution to mission attainment expressed in dollar-equivalent units." Marginal revenue depends on the level of demand and the price set for the outputs. In the simple example of a college that engages only in undergraduate teaching, an institution's total tuition revenue depends on the rate it charges and how willing prospective students are to pay the price that is set. Marginal cost depends on the institution's production function (i.e., how it organizes its work) and the prices it pays for inputs. A program will be expanded when its $MV+MR>M$—that is, when the expansion's contribution to value and revenue ("love" plus "money") is greater than its incremental cost. The nonprofit value-maximizing solution occurs when $MV+MR = MC$ for all outputs and the university is breaking even. In contrast, for-profit entities use the decision rule $MR = MC$, where (hopefully) the entity does better than break even and mission-based value does not enter the picture at all.

Implications for Price and Cost

The nonprofit model has profound implications for prices and costs. Programs with market power enjoy pricing discretion and thus can generate larger margins than those without market power. Universities do not distribute their earnings to shareholders but they still benefit from the higher prices—because boosting price brings in more money for cross subsidies that boost mission attainment. The incentive to raise price is famously enshrined in a behavioral law first formulated by Howard Bowen (Bowen, 1980): "Universities will raise all the money they can and spend all the money they raise." Bowen's Law is the nonprofit analogue to Adam Smith's profit motivation. Absent specific reasons to the contrary (like competition or political concerns), both nonprofit and for-profit enterprises will raise prices as high as the market will allow.

Policy makers need to recognize that any good university's value function is unbounded, *and that this is good thing*. Does the nation want its higher education sector to rest on its laurels, to stop striving to be as good as it can be? Insisting that universities should limit price increases as a matter of principle amounts to just such an assertion. No matter how good an institution is, additional resources can always make it better. Telling a university to stop growing its quality is like telling a corporation to stop growing its profits.

Like its for-profit counterpart, the nonprofit model contains built-in incentives for productivity improvement—and thus cost containment. The incentives arise because a dollar saved is a dollar freed up for cross subsidies, other things being equal. Suppose an institution produces two outputs. One is valued by the market, and the other has low market demand but is important to the institution's mission. Let price and quality be determined by competition. Producing the high-demand output at lower cost will generate extra margin that can be spent on the output less favored by the market. This situation allows the institution to boost mission attainment; that is, to do more of what it would most like to do.

Market forces drive institutions to consider what they do as well as how they do it. Universities trim subsidies to their least-valued programs in times of financial stringency. Sometimes such thinking unearths more low-priority programs than are needed to balance the budget, in which case schools may shift subsidies toward higher priority programs. Robert Zemsky and I call this "growth by substitution," which is another kind of productivity improvement (Zemsky & Massy, 1990). Such substitutions can occur anytime, but adverse market conditions often provide the impetus. In a similar vein, corporations mount cost-cutting drives in response to competition that eats into their profits. Less-than-necessary functions that grew up during good times get excised when times are tough. Shedding unprofitable lines of business is an example of the same phenomenon.

The juxtaposition of market opportunities and unbounded aspirations also drives universities toward commercialization. Such entrepreneurship is beneficial if its financial contributions add to the cross-subsidy pool without compromising academic values (cf. Clark, 2001). There certainly are cases, however, where commercialization has undermined academic values. Bok (2003) provides a balanced account of the benefits and dangers, and how to mitigate the latter. In summary, the nonprofit model tells us that universities have strong incentives to raise price as high as the market will bear and generate additional revenue through entrepreneurial activities, and also to contain costs through productivity improvement and the trimming of lesser-value programs. The first part of the proposition is well born out in practice, but the productivity-improvement part is empirically questionable. Other factors must be intervening to inhibit cost containment. These factors are rooted in the structure of the academic marketplace and the organizational dynamics that make the university's production function "sticky."

MARKETS

The nonprofit model and its corollary, Bowen's Law, say that universities will raise all the money they can and spend all the money they raise. This speaks to the motivation to raise prices and spend more, but why does the market tolerate such behavior? That universities operate in a competitive marketplace is not open to question. Yet the market permits eye-popping tuition increases year after year. We examine the reasons under the rubrics of price elasticity, financial aid, market information, prestige, and winner-take-all markets.

Price Elasticity

One reason that the market accepts ever-increasing prices surely lies in the fact that a college education is widely viewed as essential for getting ahead in the world. Students and their families are willing to sacrifice for the sake of college, and governments at both the state and Federal levels are willing to subsidize these efforts through scholarships, loans, tax benefits, and direct grants-in-aid to institutions. The effect is to make the overall demand for higher education "inelastic —that is, not very sensitive to price.

Estimating the price elasticity of overall demand for higher education is difficult because the needed time series are short and the data incomplete (estimates for institution-specific demand are easier to develop, to such effect that individual schools are beginning to commission them for purposes of decision making). The available studies suggest that overall demand elasticity lies in a range around –0.5: where, for example, a 10 percent price increase produces a 5 percent decrease in demand (cf . Becker, 1990; Chang & Hsing, 1996). Nevertheless, the demand for higher education appears less inelastic than the correlation between rising demand and stunning price increases might suggest. Growth of family income and financial aid might account for the discrepancy, since the price elasticity estimates seek to net out these effects. But the bottom line, which is sufficient for the arguments of this chapter, is that primary demand is strongly inelastic.

How does the inelasticity of primary demand square with the widespread view that college is becoming unaffordable? Zemsky points out the conundrum:

> When something is unaffordable it means it won't be purchased. Health insurance and with it access to health care is now truly unaffordable for a frighteningly large and growing number of American families. We know that to be the case because of the increasing number of American families who do not have health insurance. That seemingly is not the case for American higher education given that in most years enrollments have continued to rise even as have the prices students are expected to pay and the benefits they expect to garner from their college educations. (Robert Zemsky, private communication, 2006)

There is a difference between what market researchers call "ability to pay" and "willingness to pay," but the strong demand for higher education indicates that most members of the target population are both willing and able. Of course that doesn't mean they like the sacrifices required or that they will not press for lower prices in the political arena. But notwithstanding the complaints, the sector's demand—and thus its pricing power—remains strong year in and year out.

But what about competition among institutions? The demand for a particular school is more elastic than overall demand for higher education, but it is not sufficiently elastic to prevent the observed tuition increases. The reasons why competition among institutions fails to discipline price appear to be: (1) price increases are mitigated by financial aid, (2) the market lacks good information about the delivered quality of education, (3) the dominance of prestige as an institutional and consumer motivator, and (4) "winner-take-all" markets faced by the most prestigious universities and liberal arts colleges and the "pricing umbrella" such institutions provide.

Financial Aid

The prevalence of student financial aid provides one explanation for why the overall demand for higher education is inelastic. Much of the grant aid and loans come from the Federal Government, and some comes from state governments, but individual colleges and universities provide large sums as well. The institutions are motivated by a combination of intrinsic value and market forces. Need-based aid, which allows universities to charge those who can pay more than those who cannot, generally is motivated by intrinsic values associated with access and diversity. No-need or merit-based aid, on the other hand, tends to be more of a market response. Much effort has been devoted to discerning the effects of financial aid on student access and diversity, but the subject is complex and beyond the scope of this chapter. Interested readers should consult McPherson and Schapiro (1991, 1997, 2006).

The nonprofit model suggests that despite their propinquity in budget and financial statements, need and no-need aid arise from different motivations and may not directly compete with each other in university decision-making. Merit aid is a fact of life for many colleges and universities. Failure to meet admissions goals means empty seats in the classroom and empty beds in the dormitory. The empty seats and beds represent sunk costs that cannot be scaled back quickly in response to enrollment shortfalls. Achieving a target student profile provides another reason for offering merit aid. The target profile depends partly on the university's value system (diversity goals, for example), but favorable profiles also produce economic gains. Good test scores boost prestige and top-notch athletes win games. Moreover, higher education depends on what some economists call "customer-input technology." Students learn from other students, so an institution's student profile affects the amount and kind of learning it provides. Hence the motivation to shape the profile of incoming students is very strong. But while need-based aid can help because it tends to remove income from the factors that affect demand, targeted merit aid may still be needed to attract the most desirable mix of students. Indeed, using merit aid to fill classrooms may actually increase the funds available for need-based aid if it makes the delivery of education more efficient.

Market Information

Students can tap a tsunami of information as they confront the task of choosing among schools. They can learn about graduation rates, faculty-student ratios, library and IT resources, athletic facilities, extra-curricular activities, and even a school's "party environment." Unfortunately, though, such information sheds little light on delivered educational quality, especially the kind of value-added a particular type of student can expect to receive. Most of it deals with inputs (student-faculty ratios, campus environment, and the like) that represent the *capacity* to provide high-quality education. The output-centered data tends either to be fairly coarse-grained (graduation rates, for example) or focused on non-academic matters (extra-curricular, service, and athletic achievements). Despite some clear roadmaps for what needs to be accomplished (cf., Dill, 1992; van Vught, 1995), recent work on education quality confirms that there are large variations among institutions—and departments within a given institution—in how the capacity to deliver a quality education is translated into quality classroom instruction (cf., Massy, Graham, & Short 2007).

Prospective students would benefit greatly from information about educational value-added, but generally it is not available. Three recent developments provide hope for remedying this shortfall, but institutional indifference or resistance has limited their impact on the marketplace so far. First, the National Survey of Student Engagement (NSSE) provides normed responses, derived from more than two decades of research, on specific undergraduate student experiences and features of the educational environment (Kuh, 2001, 2003). Such data have great potential relevance for the marketplace, but voluntary participation and institutional desires to keep their individual results confidential have limited its impact (Ewell, 2004). Second, the Collegiate Learning Assessment (CLA), a lengthy written test of "critical thinking" and similar skills, was developed originally by the Rand Corporation and is now marketed by the Council for Aid to Education. Finally, the Collegiate Results Instrument (CRI) provides feedback from recent graduates on the attributes and quality of their undergraduate experience. CRI was developed by the National Center for Postsecondary Improvement and the Knight Collaborative and eventually licensed by Peterson's, but it has yet to achieve wide adoption.

In the end, it will be up to colleges and universities themselves to develop and publicize information about their educational value-added. Adopting the NSSE, CLA, and/or CRI in a spirit of transparency would be a good start, but robust value-added assessment measures also need to be developed by individual departments. Northwest Missouri State's "culture of quality" has produced some good examples of both normed and campus-specific measures (Massy, 2003, pp. 195–203). What is needed goes well beyond the typical student assessment program, which generally has not yielded the hoped-for degree of success (Massy, 2003). We will address the question of how to stimulate the development of market information in the last section of this chapter.

Prestige

Prestige is one item of information that is all too readily available in the marketplace. Earlier I likened it to the stock price of a corporation, which distills the views of a wide range of outside stakeholders. Like a corporation's stock price, prestige serves as a powerful motivator of college and university behavior. Presidents cite enhancements in prestige as measuring the success of their administrations, for example, and admissions directors strive to improve applicants' test scores for the same reason, even when the institution's mission is to serve a less well-endowed population. Indeed, many, if not most, institutions have allowed prestige to assume a dominant position in their value functions (Brewer, Gates, & Goldman, 2001).

Prestige correlates with measures such as application ratios; test scores; faculty research and publications; faculty-student ratios and other dimensions of per-student spending; and, for some types of institutions, on prowess in intercollegiate athletics. Prestige is confirmed, some would say conferred, by the plethora of institutional rankings that have been published in recent years. Many prospective students and their parents peruse the prestige rankings diligently and give them great weight in their college choice decisions.

Pursuing prestige drives up cost. Because spending per student enters the rankings favorably, for example, so spending appears good in and of itself. Moreover, spending delivers better applicants, research outputs, faculty, and all the other factors that correlate with prestige. Prestige makes it easier to raise tuition and thus to finance increased spending, and price-quality associations can produce a self-reinforcing relationship between increases in prestige and spending.

All this would be fine if prestige represented a good surrogate for the delivered quality of education. But there is no evidence that such is the case. Prestigious institutions often cite the success of their graduates as an indicator of educational quality, but this ignores the fact that they get the cream of the applicant crop. They get outstanding students, and as long as they observe the opening words of the Hippocratic Oath—"Do no harm"—the students will still be great after graduation. The key issue is what the educational process actually adds by way of value, and here the evidence is lacking. Going to a prestigious institution confers value in terms of credentialing and life-long peer connections, and thus may well be worth what it costs. However, these considerations mask what one suspects are large variations in educational value-added. Whatever the facts, however, the disclosure of data on educational value-added has the potential, in time, to mitigate the vicious-circle connection between cost, price, and prestige. It might even alter, for the better, the very definition of prestige.

Winner-Take-All Markets and the Pricing Umbrella

The most prestigious colleges and universities find themselves in a winner-take-all market. This situation is a direct consequence of the rankings. Top applicant ratios, student scores, spending per student, and faculty research—not to mention amenities like lavish recreational facilities—are key to high scores in the rankings. And because "only ten institutions can be in the top ten," it is a zero-sum game. If one institution breaks into the elite ranks, another must descend. This is different than the situation for corporate stock prices, where better price-earnings ratios tend to boost market performance even if competitors also earn more. Both situations spawn an unbounded pursuit of success, but the pursuit is more intense and single-minded in winner-take-all situations.

Gordon Winston explains how the zero-sum pursuit of student intake quality has produced a "positional arms race" in higher education (Winston, 2000; see also Ehrenberg, 2000). "In an arms race, there's a lot of action, a lot of spending, a lot of worry but, if it's a successful arms race, nothing much changes. It's the purist case of Alice and the Red Queen where 'it takes all the running you can do to keep in the same place'." The arms race drives institutions to maximize all revenue sources, including tuition, in order to match others' spending increases. It's a race that "has no end—no finish line to get to first—instead, it's a process that can go on and on and on..." The arms race isn't the only cause of cost and price escalation among prestigious institutions; Bowen's Law and the pursuit of prestige are sufficient drivers to keep prices moving. However, the arms race surely has intensified the escalation in recent years.

In a disturbing twist on the arms race, there is a growing tendency for tuition-payers to associate price with quality. Price increases, it is said, actually boost prestige in and of themselves, quite aside from the enhancements the extra revenue make affordable. Such price-quality associations, which arise from a dearth of real marketplace information about quality, are familiar features of consumer and even some industrial markets (cf. Rao, 2005). Confronted with two vials of perfume, for example, the uninformed consumer is likely to view the more expensive one as better. It should not be surprising that relatively uninformed consumers would make the same associations in evaluating colleges, or that colleges would, sooner or later, begin to exploit this phenomenon.

One might say the prestigious schools should not be criticized for charging as high a price as they want as long as people are willing to pay and access for lower-income students is maintained through financial aid. However, this tolerant outlook ignores the effect of such pricing on the rest of higher education. Higher tuitions charged at the tops of the public- and private-sector markets make it possible for institutions in the middle segments to raise their prices as well. This occurs because, as noted above, primary demand for higher education is inelastic, because of price-quality associations, and because the middle segment's tuition rates still seem small in comparison to the elite's. Together with the trend toward substituting tuition revenue for direct state appropriations and the effects of Bowen's Law generally, the pricing umbrella has produced substantial tuition escalation through much of the higher education marketplace.

STICKY FUNCTIONS

I noted earlier that higher education's production functions are "sticky"—that universities find it hard to implement productivity improvements and to avoid the layering on of new activities (Zemsky & Massy, 1995). There appear to be three reasons for this phenomenon: (1) beliefs that quality is closely correlated with cost and thus that cost reductions will reduce quality, (2) perceived "property rights" in activities and programs that limit growth by substitution, and (3) resource allocation processes that are not linked to strategic plans, performance measures, and incentive creation. These factors override the objective, called out by the nonprofit model, to capture efficiency gains and reallocate resources in order to build the cross-subsidy pool and thus boost value creation.

Cost and Quality

The unbreakable linkage between cost and quality is deeply embedded in the academic psyche. Smaller student-faculty ratios and class sizes will produce a better educational experience. More academic support services, including access to the latest technology and the best library resources, will do likewise. Efforts to economize in any such area tend to be resisted on principle because they are seen as threatening quality.

The reality is more complex. While there is no doubt that well-directed increments to expenditure can and do improve quality, there is no reason to believe that a department's current pattern of activities is optimally cost-effective. Technological change provides an existence proof for this assertion, if one is needed. Teaching methods that were optimal two decades ago, before ubiquitous computing power and the Internet, cannot possibly be optimal now. Yet most students on traditional campuses are still taught in the old ways with technology being used, where it's used at all, as an add-on to enhance communication and convenience rather than as a core mediator of learning itself.

Space does not permit exploring the alternatives in any depth, but a few observations will illustrate what is possible. First, Carol Twigg's Program in Course Redesign (National Center for Academic Transformation: www.center.rpi.edu) has produced many demonstrations of how restructuring courses can simultaneously improve learning and effect cost savings. Her "whole-course" models have been applied in many disciplines on dozens of campuses, with the results carefully documented for both learning and cost. Twigg's work shows conclusively that significant and sometimes spectacular cost-effectiveness gains can be achieved when faculty look carefully at the educational production function; she shows that the perceived iron linkage between cost and quality is nothing more than an academic myth.

Twigg's methodology marries "Activity-Based Costing" (ABC) with what I call "Academic Quality Work" (AQW). ABC inverts the cost allocation methodology used in most universities: instead of allocating a portion of departmental cost to a particular course, it analyzes and costs out the activities (such as the teacher's preparation time and the provision of classroom space) needed to field the course (Massy, 2003, p. 251). Analyzing activities opens the door for thinking about how they might be reconfigured to improve quality, reduce cost, or both. Cost allocation, on the other hand, is a dead-end street because it focuses on accounting rules rather than on value-adding activities. Because no special databases or software are required and the need for training is modest, course-level ABC can be performed by faculty members themselves—the very people who know most about what produces effective learning and who will have to implement the changes.

Changing the configuration of activities requires that the goals of the course be articulated and that learning be measured (ideally with pre-and post-tests) relative to the goals. Such things fall under the rubric of academic quality work. AQW involves setting goals for learning, mapping the goals into curricula, determining teaching methods, assessing learning performance, and assuring the quality of implementation (Massy, 2003; Massy, et al., 2007). AQW should be done routinely, whether a course is being redesigned or not, but most departments largely ignore it. One of the mainstream approaches to academic quality assurance, and in my opinion the best one, seeks to improve AQW by subjecting it to peer review (the so-called "academic audit"). Systematic course redesign accomplishes the same thing, because redesign is itself a kind of AQW and because it soon becomes obvious that change without goals and performance measurement is dangerous.

Course redesign may produce better quality with the same cost (though the mix of expenditures may change), the same quality with lower cost, or better quality with lower cost—that is, "more with less." Similar techniques can and have been applied to other university activities: for example, in the continuous improvement and business process reengineering programs that dot the administrative and support service landscape (c.f., National Consortium for Continuous Improvement: www.ncci-cu.org).

The demonstrated successes in course redesign, process reengineering, and continuous improvement challenge the argument that higher education is a stagnant industry. Productivity gains *can* be achieved without undermining quality, especially when technology is factored into the equation (even Baumol's string quartet can leverage its labor by selling CDs). While such gains cannot be extrapolated indefinitely into the future, to ever-increasing student-faculty ratios for example, the present is rich with opportunities to mitigate the effects of growing and changing enrollments, regulation, and the cost of the new technology itself.

Property Rights

Nonprofit theory holds that a university should reevaluate its options every year and then recast its budget to maximize value creation subject to the current market, production, and financial situation. The perception of an iron linkage between cost and quality is not inconsistent with this view; it simply reflects an error in evaluating the production function. However, the assertion of participants' property rights to activities and programs *is* inconsistent; the "behavioral theory of the university" differs from the pure "economic theory." Such differences represent nothing new in economics. For example, Cyert and March's "behavioral theory of the firm" introduced the idea that businesses tend to "satisfice" rather than maximize profits (Cyert & March, 1963). "Satisficing" means one accepts a solution that is "good enough" in lieu of searching for the best possible solution. We will see shortly how satisficing also applies to a university's quest for value.

The idea of property rights arises because faculty, and to some extent other professionals in universities, function as semi-autonomous intellectual entrepreneurs. Tenure can be viewed as a property right (Alchian, 1953; Brown, 1997), but it is by no means the only one. A line of research, a course, or even a degree program may well be the brain child of a particular faculty member or a small group of faculty and their associates. The entrepreneurs are heavily invested in the activity or program, which presumably the university has supported financially or at least encouraged them to develop on soft money. They cannot shift their focus to other activities as easily as, say, business executives or professionals when they get a new assignment. Withdrawal of university support can impose significant penalties on the people so targeted in forms such as the need to innovate anew or change institutions. Further, the faculty reward system depends heavily on external reputation, which is largely fueled by publication and which will suffer if one's productivity is slowed or stopped. It's no wonder, then, that academics assert property rights to the fruits of their labors and the momentum they generate and resist efforts by the university to shift its support to others.

Property rights affect costs in at least three important ways: by creating an academic ratchet, inhibiting growth by substitution, and limiting productivity improvement. "Academic ratchet" describes the "steady, irreversible shift of faculty allegiance away from the goals of a given institution toward the academic specialty" (Massy, 2003, p. 97). This most often means toward research, but it can also refer to specialized teaching programs. The ratchet tends to reduce teaching loads and increase faculty discretionary time—time that can be invested in research and scholarship that enhance faculty reputations. A detailed description of the phenomenon can be found in Massy and Wilger (1995), and empirical support in Massy and Zemsky (1994) and Massy and Zemsky (1997).

Property rights also make it hard for universities to "grow by substitution"—that is, to cut back on or close existing programs to make room for new ones of higher priority. For example, most professors would view the following message from a dean to a program head as a betrayal of trust.

> I've got good news and bad news for you. The good news is that you're doing a fine job and your program is well regarded by your students and peers. The bad news is that I'm cutting your budget to make room for a new initiative that the university believes is more important.

Such a message amounts to the confiscation of property rights. Small reductions may be tolerated but large ones or outright program closures will be resisted fiercely. And because most faculty members view the property rights principle as important, they will come to the defense of beleaguered colleagues.

Adverse budget actions are easier when a program is regarded as weak or its faculty members are not well regarded by their colleagues, but these circumstances tend to be rare in top-flight universities. The usual solution is either to share the burden of budget reduction equally with across-the-board cuts or to engage in elaborate "due process" exercises to decide who gets hit. Across-the-board cuts fail to maximize value-creation unless there was a lot of fat in the system to start with, so their efficacy declines markedly with use. The answer, then, lies with due process; administrators must develop viability and importance criteria and apply them even-handedly after wide faculty consultation. Even then, the process is easier when driven by financial problems that all can see. Cutting programs on a routine basis to build a funds pool for unspecified new initiatives is especially difficult.

The existence of tenure, and property rights in general, makes it harder to effect productivity improvements like those often expected from technology. McPherson and Schapiro (1999, p. 96) argue that tenure "contributes to keeping the university a sort of 'cottage industry,' a loosely constructed agglomeration of individuals who do their work in substantial independence from one another… The division of labor is not extensive and where collaboration occurs, it is frequently based on voluntary cooperative relationships, which are unstable." The answer to this problem is not necessarily to eliminate tenure, which confers benefits as well as costs on the institution, but to develop better methods, incentives, and rewards for collegial action—including the division of labor where applicable—as described later under "Corrective Actions."

Resource Allocation

Resource allocation processes can be drivers of change, or they can reinforce the property rights in existing programs. Universities differ in the degree to which their processes tilt one way or the other. The differences arise largely from the treatment of revenue. Forcing schools, departments, or even individual faculty members to live or die by their ability to generate revenue challenges the idea of property rights in a way that may promote cost saving, but it does so at the cost of academic cohesion and, many would say, fundamental academic values.

One framework for compelling university units to generate revenues to cover their costs is Responsibility Center Management (RCM). RCM systems devolve revenue from the central administration to schools (Whalen, 1991; Strauss et al., 1996; Massy, 1996). This puts each school at risk with respect to enrollments and, in many cases, for overhead recovery on grants and contracts. Schools cannot assert property rights to any particular level of revenue, but neither are there incentives to coordinate, say, the undergraduate curriculum across schools. RCM was originally developed at Harvard under the rubric of "Every tub on its own bottom." Later versions were pioneered at the University of Pennsylvania, the University of Southern California, Indiana University, and the University of Houston, and they have been adopted by a significant number of large and complex research universities.

The alternatives to RCM are line-item budgeting and block budgeting (Massy, 1996), both of which are designed to enhance the central administration's ability to steer the university. Good systems include some kind of "performance contract" or memorandum of understanding that describes what the school is supposed to accomplish during the coming year. As generally practiced, however, none of the three systems focuses with sufficient effectiveness on the sticky functions problem. In line-item and block systems, schools assert property rights to their base budgets even as they seek funding for new programs. And while the central administration can in principle use its line-item allocations or performance contracts to force changes in the production function, doing so would require knowledge that tends to be available only at the local level. Furthermore, changes forced from the top rarely are embraced at the grass roots, which make makes their implementation problematic even if the ideas themselves are well conceived.

CORRECTIVE MEASURES

What is to be done? How can the problems of sticky functions and market imperfections be overcome? Two of the six Spellings Commission recommendations address these issues.[1] The relevant portions are:

> Recommendation 2: "To address the escalating cost of a college education… we recommend that… new incentives be put in place to improve the measurement and management of costs and institutional productivity."

Recommendation 3: "To meet the challenges of the 21st century, higher education must change from a system primarily based on reputation to one based on performance. We urge the creation of a more robust culture of accountability and transparency throughout higher education…"

The first of these deals with sticky functions and the second with imperfections in the marketplace. Whatever one thinks of the Commission's conclusions generally, these two statements identify two very important objectives for change.

Freeing Up the Sticky Functions

How can a university influence the behavior of its intellectual entrepreneurs to restrain cost growth without destroying their initiative and undermining academic values? Economists have encountered similar problems in the efforts of principals to influence independent agents upon whom they rely to accomplish important functions. "Economic Agency Theory" identifies three ways by which this can be accomplished (Massy, 2003 p. 285; after Hoenack, 1983):

- *Regulatory.* The principal restricts the agent's freedom of action: e.g., by requiring prior approval for decisions that involve resources. Tight control prevents resource diversion, but at the cost of efficiency. The costs of regulation ("transaction costs" in the language of economists) become greater as tasks get more complex and the organizational distance between principal and agent lengthens.
- *Formulaic.* The principal devises payment formulas that align the agent's objectives with those of the principal: i.e., so that, in pursuing his or her self-interest, the agent automatically furthers the principal's interest. Unfortunately, such formulas become less effective as tasks become more complex and the opportunities for misinterpretation multiply. They also can be "gamed," as when the agent exploits loopholes or omissions in a cynical way. Devising good formulas and fine-tuning them as conditions change can be a daunting task.
- *Persuasive.* The principal uses persuasion and the prospect of discretionary rewards to align incentives and motivate the agent to further the principal's goals. Discretionary rewards reinforce the message and supply tangible incentives. Persuasion even may convince the agent that his long-term goals coincide with those of the principal—that while resource diversion might be attractive in the short run it would eventually prove dysfunctional. Persuasion-based systems work more slowly than well-functioning formulas, but they may be more effective over the long run.

The tenets of economic agency theory have been applied extensively in higher education. Line-item budgeting reflects the regulatory approach, while block budgeting tends toward the persuasive approach. RCM reflects the formulaic approach and the models used to distribute general-funds appropriations in many states also are formulaic. In my own work, I have usually recommended a combination of the persuasive and formulaic approaches, with the balance tilting toward one or the other depending on the needed degree of integration (Massy, 2006). For example, resource allocation on a single campus would generally have a larger persuasive component than allocations among campuses by a system-wide administration or state funding agency.

The persuasive approach generally works better for the freeing up of sticky functions than does the formulaic one. The persuasive focus needs to be on specifics—whether a department, school, or campus has developed effective programs for course redesign, business process engineering, and continuous improvement, for instance, and whether it can demonstrate growth by substitution. Evidence on performance in these areas is readily obtainable, but it is impossible to capture adequately in a set of formulas.

A persuasive element can be added to any of the three types of budging systems simply by capturing revenue to create one or more funding pools for rewards, incentives, and efficiency-improving projects. Making it known that project funds are available boosts activity. Proposals should include evaluation metrics, provide follow-up to see what has been accomplished and what has been learned, and a plan for disseminating exemplary results widely within the institution.

It also is possible to boost incentives by promising after-the-fact rewards for exemplary performance. Teaching awards fall under this rubric, as do the performance funding awards offered by oversight bodies. One needs to clearly identify the criteria for judging effectiveness, provide multiple venues for conversations about the criteria and their importance, and field a systematic evaluation process. Space does not permit further detail here on the use of budgeting to effect change, but readers wishing to pursue the matter further should consult Massy (2007, 2003).

The Spellings Commission's second recommendation and its subtext align well with solving the sticky functions problem. For example, activity-based costing at the level of the course would "provide better measures of [teaching] cost, beyond those designed for accounting purposes," and improve cost management. Rationalizing the regulatory burdens on higher education would facilitate similar efforts on the non-academic side. And, as already being done in Tennessee and a few other venues, state oversight boards can "provide financial incentives to institutions that show they are… increasing productivity and cutting costs while maintaining or enhancing educational quality." For example, state overseers could easily ascertain whether an institution uses the top-slice methodology and whether it's rewarding the right kinds of things. Accreditation agencies could do much more than at present to incorporate similar criteria in their evaluation standards (Wolff, 2007).

Improving Market Information

Assembling and distributing good market information about educational quality, and especially value-added, would be a giant step toward the improvement of higher education. Such information would enrich discussions of institutional attractiveness among students, their parents, the press, pundits and higher-education leaders themselves. It also would enrich the discussion of cost and efficiency, and the myth that quality is proportional to expenditure would be less likely to persist in an environment replete with contrary evidence.

There is a world-wide wave of interest in the development of performance metrics for higher education (c.f., Burke & Minassians, 2002; Burke, 2007). Graduation rates and related statistics have received the most attention in the United States, but many other indicators are in use or have been proposed. Surveys of graduates and employers are catching on here and abroad: for example, Danish and Australian national quality agencies use such surveys routinely. The real challenge, however, is to persuade institutions to develop their own measures and use to them to effect continuous quality improvement. The process of academic audit, to which I referred earlier, offers the best hope for accomplishing this. The prospect of an audit provides the incentives needed for developing an effective set of indicators. Then the site visitors can audit the resulting indicators to make sure they mean what the institution says they mean, that they are made available to the marketplace, and that they are being used internally to effect improvement.

The idea of auditing performance indicators has been largely missing from America's student assessment programs. Australia, Hong Kong, and undoubtedly other venues are developing methodologies to audit performance indicators at the institution level. Their methodologies could easily be adopted here—provided, of course, that organizational inertia and political opposition could be overcome.

The development of robust systems for auditing the whole range of academic quality work would produce even better results. Student learning assessment is one of the five focal areas of Academic Quality Work, and one reaps great advantages by embedding assessment in a comprehensive program of institution- and department-level quality improvement. Robust audit programs would move higher education toward better education quality work and thus better, and better documented, educational outcome assessments. They also would spur transparency and verify the evidence provided to the marketplace. The analogy to financial audits is obvious. Institutions prepare their own financial statements that are then reviewed by external auditors, a process that provides incentives for good work as well as a check on the work. Provision for external audit implies no disrespect for the institution or its people; the mantra is "Trust but check."

Imagine, in conclusion, that a robust program of academic audits has been around long enough for institutions and departments to become proficient in academic quality work. Such institutions will routinely assess student learning and the attainment of graduates in relation to clearly-stated learning objectives. They will do this mainly for their own purposes, to provide the feedback they need to assure and continuously improve quality. But once the assessment data are available, schools that can document good quality will tout the data publicly. Prospective students and parents will value such reports and come to expect them, so publishers of college guides will start to supply such information whenever they can get it. Even institutions of lower quality will report their data, since mediocre data will serve them better than no data at all.

Consider where such a program could lead. The following scenario might seem far-fetched, but it is not beyond the realm of possibility.

> Institutions across the higher education spectrum are spurred to produce meaningful program-level student learning assessments, which are vetted by auditors from time to time. Those with good assessment results use them in recruiting, fund-raising, and political lobbying. College choice publications take note of these data because readers find them interesting if for no other reason. Elite institutions that do not deliver high value-added may try to discredit the assessments, but this only triggers a long-overdue debate about educational value-added v. prestige. Institutions are challenged to justify their reputations with real data, and soon those with good stories begin to tell them. Eventually all institutions are expected to publish audited assessment reports, perhaps as a condition for accreditation, just as all institutions are expected to publish audited financial reports.

Whether one buys into the whole road-map, the first step—using audit to spur institutions to improve their academic quality work—has considerable merit. As noted above, this would be a giant step toward solving the cost-price problem in American higher education.

NOTE

1. Spellings Commission (2006). The quotations here and later can be found on pages 18 to 20. The recommendations also deal with access which, though extremely important, lies outside the scope of this chapter.

REFERENCES

Alchian, Armen A. (1953), "Private Property and the Relative Cost of Tenure," in P. D. Bradley (ed.), *The Public Stake in Union Power*. Charlottesville: University of Virginia Press, 350–371. Reprinted in Alchian, ed. (1977), *Economic Forces at Work*. Indianapolis: The Liberty Press, 177–202.

Baumol, William J., & Blackman, Sue Anne Batey (1983). Electronics, the Cost Disease, and the Operation of Libraries. *Journal of the American Society for Information Sciences,* vol. 34, no. 3, pp. 181–191.

Becker, William E. (1990). The Demand for Higher Education. In Stephen A. Hoenack and Eileen L. Collins, *The Economics of American Universities*. Albany: State University of New York Press, 55–188.

Bok, Derek (2003). *Universities in the Marketplace: The Commercialization of Higher Education*. Princeton, NJ: Princeton University Press.

Bowen, Howard (1980), *The Cost of Higher Education: How Much do Universities and Colleges Spend Per Student and How Much Should They Spend?* San Francisco: Jossey-Bass.

Bowen, William G. (1968). *The Economics of the Major Private Universities*. Berkley, Calif: Carnegie Commission on Higher Education.

Brewer, Dominic J., Gates, Susan M., & Goldman, Charles A. (2001). *In Pursuit of Prestige: Strategy and Competition in U.S. Higher Education*. New Brunswick, NJ: Transaction Press.

Brown, Jr., William O. (1997). University Governance and Academic Tenure: A Property Rights Explanation. *Journal of Institutional and Theoretical Economics*, September, 441–61.

Burke, Joseph C. (2007), "Performance Reporting: Putting Academic Departments in the Performance Loop." Chapter 9 in J. Burke, *Fixing the Fragmented University: Decentralization With Direction*. Bolton, MA: Anker Publishing.

Burke, Joseph C., & Minassians, H. P. (2002), *Reporting Higher Education Results: Missing Links in the Performance Chain, New Directions in Institutional Research*, No. 116. San Francisco: Jossey-Bass.

Chang, Hui S. & Hsing, Yu (1996), "Testing Increasing Sensitivity of Enrollment at Private Institutions to Tuition and Other Costs." *American Economist*, 40, 4–45.

Clark, Burton (2001), "The Entrepreneurial University: New Foundations for Collegiality, Autonomy, and Achievement," *Higher Education Management*, 13(2), 9–24.

Clotfelter, Charles T. (1996), *Buying the Best: Cost Escalation in Higher Education*. Princeton, NJ: Princeton University Press and the National Bureau of Economic Research.

Cyert, Richard M., & March, James G. (1963). *A Behavioral Theory of the Firm*. Englewood Cliffs, NJ: Prentice-Hall.

Dill, David D. (1992). Quality by Design: Toward a Framework for Academic Quality Management. In *Higher Education: Handbook of Theory and Research*. New York: Agatha Press.

Ehrenberg, Ronald G. (2000). *Tuition Rising: Why College Costs So Much*. Cambridge, MA: Harvard University Press.

Ewell, Peter (2004). The National Survey of Student Engagement. Policy analysis paper for the research program in Public Policy for Academic Quality (PPAQ), The University of North Carolina at Chapel Hill (http://www.unc.edu/ppaq).

Hoenack, Stephan A. (1983)., *Economic Behavior Within Organizations*. New York: Cambridge University Press.

Hoenack, Stephen A. & Collins, Eileen L. (1990). *The Economics of American Universities*. Albany: State University of New York Press.

Hopkins, David S. P. & Massy, William F. (1981). *Planning Models for Colleges and Universities*. Stanford, CA: Stanford University Press.

James, Estelle (1986). How Nonprofits Grow: A Model. In Susan Rose-Ackerman, *The Economics of Nonprofit Institutions*. New York: Oxford University Press, 185–195.

Kuh, George D. (2001). Assessing What Really Matters to Student Learning: Inside the National Survey of Student Engagement. *Change*, 33 (3), 10–17.

Kuh, George D. (2003). Assessing We're Learning About Student Engagement from NSSE. *Change*, 35 (2), 24–32.

Massy, William F. (1996). Value Responsibility Budgeting. In William F. Massy with collaborators. *Resource Allocation in Higher Education*. Ann Arbor: The University of Michigan Press.

Massy, William F. (2003). *Honoring the Trust: Quality and Cost Containment in Higher Education.* Bolton, MA: Anker Publishing Company.

Massy, William F. (2004). *Collegium economicum*: Why institutions do what they do. *Change*, July-August.

Massy, William F. (2007). Using the Budget to Fight Fragmentation and Improve Quality. In J. Burke, *Fixing the Fragmented University: Decentralization With Direction* (chapter 3). Bolton, MA: Anker Publishing Company, Inc.

Massy, William F. & Wilger, Andrea K. (1995). Improving Productivity. *Change* (July-August), 10–20.

Massy, William F. & Zemsky, Robert (1994). Faculty Discretionary Time: Departments and the Academic Ratchet." *Journal of Higher Education,* 65(1)(January–February), 1–22.

Massy, William F. & Zemsky, Robert (1997). A Utility Model for Teaching Load Decisions in Academic Departments. *Economics of Education Review,* forthcoming (November/December).

Massy, William F., Graham, Steven W. & Short, Paula Myrick (2007). *Academic Quality Work: A Handbook for Improvement.* Bolton, MA: Anker Publishing Company.

McPherson, Michael S. & Schapiro, Morton Owen (1991). *Keeping College Affordable: Government and Educational Opportunity*. Washington, DC: The Brookings Institution.

McPherson, Michael S. & Schapiro, Morton Owen (1991). *Keeping College Affordable: Governance and Educational Opportunity*. Washington, DC: Brookings Institution.

McPherson, Michael S. & Schapiro, Morton Owen (1999). Tenure Issues in Higher Education. *The Journal of Economic Perspectives*, 13(1), 85–98.

McPherson, Michael S. & Schapiro, Morton Owen, Eds. (2006), *College Access: Opportunity or Privilege.* New York: The College Board.

McPherson, Michael S., Schapiro, Morton Owen, & Winston, Gordon C. (1993). *Paying the Piper: Productivity, Incentives, and Financing in U.S. Higher Education*. Ann Arbor: The University of Michigan Press.

McPherson, Michael, & Schapiro, Morton Owen (1997). *The Student Aid Game*. Princeton, NJ: Princeton University Press.

Measuring Up 2006: The National Report Card on Higher Education. National Center for Public Policy and Higher Education. http://measuringup.highereducation.org/_docs/2006/NationalReport_2006.pdf

Rao, Akshay R. (2005),. "The Quality of Price as a Quality Cue." *Journal of Marketing Research*, 42(5), 401–405.

Spellings Commission (2006). A Test of Leadership: Charting the Future of U.S. Higher Education. Washington, DC: Report of the Commission Appointed by Secretary of Education Margaret Spellings.

Strauss, Jon, Curry, John, & Whalen, Edward (1996). Revenue Responsibility Budgeting. In William F. Massy with collaborators. *Resource Allocation in Higher Education.* Ann Arbor: The University of Michigan Press.

van Vught, Frans (1995). The New Context for Academic Quality. In D. D. Dill and B. Sporn, eds., *Emerging social demands and university reform: Through a glass darkly*. New York: Pergamon Press, 194–211.

Vedder, Richard (2004). *Going Broke by Degree: Why College Costs Too Much.* Washington, DC: The AEI Press, 163–190.

Whalen, Edward L (1991). *Responsibility Center Budgeting.* Bloomington: Indiana University Press.

Winston, Gordon C. (2000). The positional Arms Race in Higher Education. Presented at the Forum for the Future of Higher Education. Aspen, CO (September).

Wolff, Ralph A. (2007). Accrediting the Public University: Part of the Problem or Part of the Solution? In J. Burke, *Fixing the Fragmented University: Decentralization With Direction.* (chapter 8). Bolton, MA: Anker Publishing Company.

Zemsky, Robert & Massy, William F. (1990). "Cost Containment: Committing to a New Economic Reality." *Change,* 22(6), 16–22.

Zemsky, Robert & Massy, William F. (1995). Expanding Perimeters, Melting Cores, and Sticky Functions: Toward an Understanding of Our Current Predicaments. *Change,* 27(6), 40–49.

38

The Effects of Education on Labor Market Outcomes

Jessica Goldberg and Jeffrey Smith

INTRODUCTION

Human capital represents the most valuable asset held by most individuals. Individuals accumulate human capital through investments in schooling and training. Governments subsidize many forms of human capital accumulation including primary, secondary and post-secondary schooling. This chapter surveys the literature on the labor market effects of human capital with a particular focus on higher education.

The seminal book by Becker (1964, p. 9) defines human capital as "activities that influence future real income though the imbedding of resources in people." Thus, skills as varied as basic literacy, helpfulness, familiarity with Ford Motor Company's parts manual, and expertise in cardiac bypass surgery all represent forms of human capital. Individuals acquire these skills in diverse settings, and over different periods of time, at different costs to themselves and society. These different aspects of human capital also imply different financial and non-financial rewards.

Individuals, firms, and governments make decisions about investments in human capital by focusing on the costs and benefits of particular investments "at the margin," that is, relative to the existing stock of human capital. Individuals care about their private costs, which include tuition, foregone earnings, and the effort cost of learning. These costs differ among people because they depend on individual ability, preferences, and access to financial resources. Individuals balance these private costs against the private benefits, which include not only higher wages, but also the non-pecuniary aspects of particular jobs, such as opportunities to help others or to work outdoors, social opportunities, and effects on health. Firms, many of which provide vocational training, weigh the costs of training against the benefits of increased worker productivity. Firms, too, may face unique costs and benefits that depend on their financial situations, level of technology, and business outlook. Governments consider the private benefits to citizens and the public benefits from higher tax revenue, greater civic participation, lower crime, and so on.

Surveying the vast literature on the labor market effects of education presents a daunting task to both reader and writer. Our chapter builds on the surveys of Rosen (1977); Willis (1986); Card (1999); Ashenfelter, Harmon, and Oosterbeek (1999); Harmon, Oosterbeek, and Walker (2003); and Heckman, Lochner, and Todd (2006). This chapter differs from these earlier efforts on several dimensions: we assume a less technical and more policy-oriented audience, focus on evidence from the United States, and devote most of our attention to higher education. Our central theme, variability among persons in the effects of education due both to the variety of available educational experiences and to individual variability in responses to common experiences, draws inspiration from Card (1999) and Heckman et al. (2006). Drawing on the recent literature in economics and statistics, we call this variability the "heterogeneous effects" of education.

Our chapter begins by considering estimates of the labor market effects of years of schooling. This topic dominates the literature though we argue against the usefulness of many such estimates for all but the very broadest policy questions. We then consider how the labor market effects of schooling vary with the characteristics of the student and the school, such as college quality and program of study. We end with a discussion of heterogeneity in the labor market effects of education more generally, and consider its subtle but important implications for the interpretation of the empirical findings in the literature. Table 38.1 summarizes key papers selected to illustrate particular points and highlight the range of estimates in the literature.

YEARS OF SCHOOLING

The Mincer Model

Nearly all modern empirical work on the labor market effects of education builds on the classic model of Jacob Mincer (1958, 1974) and Becker (1964). Using this model, researchers estimate the association between years of schooling and labor market outcomes such as wages and earnings using data on individuals. The model controls for years of experience (or age) in order to account for the fact that individuals who complete more schooling typically enter the labor market full time at a later age. Despite its simplicity, the Mincer model has multiple theoretical justifications; Heckman et al. (2006) lay out the various models.

Formally, the basic model has

Equation '1' $$\ln(Y_i) = \beta_0 + \beta_S S_i + \beta_1 E_i + \beta_2 E_i^2 + \varepsilon_i,$$

where Y_i denotes earnings or wages of individual "i,", S_i denotes years of schooling, E_i denotes years of experience and ε_i denotes the "error term," which embodies the effects of all of the determinants of wages or earnings besides schooling and experience. In words, the equation states that the natural logarithm of annual earnings or of the hourly wage depends linearly on years of schooling, controlling for experience and experience squared.

The coefficient of interest in the Mincer equation is β_S. The use of natural logarithms allows the interpretation of β_S as (roughly) the percentage effect of an additional year of schooling. Under certain strong assumptions detailed in, e.g., Heckman et al. (2006), including no direct costs (i.e., tuition) of education, this coefficient represents a private internal rate of return to schooling. Because of the implausibility of the assumptions underlying this interpretation we avoid the terms "rate of return" and "returns to schooling" in this chapter.

The Mincer model assumes the same effect of schooling for all individuals. For this reason, β_S has no "i" subscript. Under this assumption individuals choose to complete different amounts of schooling for reasons other than differences in expected outcomes. For example, one person might choose to complete college while another stops at high school because of differences in money costs (e.g., they win different scholarships), differences in non-pecuniary costs and benefits (some individuals like reading, others do not), differences in other aspects of the pecuniary benefits such as the variance in earnings (risk averse persons will prefer schooling choices that imply a lower outcome variance) or differences in discount rates (some individuals weigh the

TABLE 38.1

Citation	*Data*	*Summary*	*Control variables*	*Parameter of interest*	*Estimates*
OLS Papers on Years of Schooling					
Heckman et al. (2006) — Table 2	US Census (1930–1990, results from 1990 data for men only reported here, sample includes only men with non-zero earnings)	The authors estimate simple Mincer earnings equations using Census data for various years.	experience and experience squared	effect of a year of schooling on log annual earnings	0.129*** (whites) 0.152*** (blacks)
Kane and Rouse (1995) — Table 2	NLS-72, NLSY-79 (The sample is limited to people who were working and not self-employed in 1986, had non-zero earnings in both 1984 and 1985, and had average annual earnings in 1984 and 1985 of at least $1000.)	The authors test whether or not a year's worth of credits at a two year college have the same effect on earnings as a year's worth of credits at a four year college by running OLS regressions with controls for test scores and family background.	race, parents' income, percentile rank in high school, NLS-72 test score, experience, experience squared, indicators for region and size of high school, and educational attainment after 1979; separate estimates for men and women	effect of a year's worth of credits at a two or four year college on log annual earnings	0.035** (two year colleges, men) 0.056*** (four year colleges, men) 0.066*** (two year colleges, women) 0.086*** (four year colleges, women)
IV Papers on Years of Schooling					
Card (1999) — Table 5	General Social Survey (1974–1996; sample restricted to heads of households ages 24-61)	Card estimates the effect of years of schooling using mother's education as an instrument for own education.	cubic in age, race, survey year, region; separate estimates for men and women	effect of completing an additional year of schooling on log annual earnings	0.106*** (men) 0.110*** (women)
Acemoglu and Angrist (2000) — Table 6	Census IPUMS (1950–1990; sample restricted to white men who were 40–49 in the Census year)	The authors use compulsory schooling laws as instruments for years of schooling	indicators for Census year, year of birth, and state of birth	effect of completing an additional year of schooling on log wages	0.081***
Non-pecuniary benefits					
Lochner and Morreti (2004) — Table 12	Census, NLSY-79, Uniform Crime Reports (results reported here use NLSY-79; sample restricted to men between 18 and 23 in 1980)	The authors use cumpulsory schooling laws as instruments in estimating the impact of years of schooling on subsequent criminal activity.	current enrollment, parents' highest grade completed, indicator for living with natural parents at age 14, indicators for the following variables: being the child of a teen mother, region, age/cohort, ability, SMSA status, local unemployment rate	effect of completing an additional year of schooling on the probability of committing a serious crime over a seven year period (using self reports of criminal activity)	–0.022** (whites) 0.005 (blacks)

Milligan et al. (2004) — Table 7	National Elections Study, November CPS	Using variation generated by changes in compulsory schooling laws in both the United States and the United Kingdom, the authors estimate the effect of education on civic participation. The authors correct for misreporting of voting behavior.	survey year, quartic in age, indicators for year of birth, indicators for state	effect of graduating from high school on the probability of voting in general elections	0.438*** (US)
Lleras-Muney (2005) — Table 4	Census (1960–1970; sample restricted to white respondents who were 14 years old between 1915 and 1939)	The author uses changes in compulsory schooling laws between 1915 and 1939 as instruments for education.	indicator for Census year, gender, state of birth, cohort of birth, and interaction terms between region of birth and cohort	effect of completing an additional year of education on mortality between 1960 and 1970	−0.051**
Spillovers					
Moretti (2004a) — Table 5	Census (1970–1990), NLSY-79	The author uses the presence of land grant colleges as an instrument for the supply of college-educated workers in a given city. He then estimates the impact of an increased supply of college educated workers on wages in the city.	year effects, city effects, unemployment and other city controls, Katz and Murphy index of demand shifts	effect of an increase of 0.1 in the fraction of workers who are college graduates on the log hourly wages of other workers	0.191** (less than HS degree) 0.167** (HS graduate) 0.124** (some college) 0.047 (college graduate)
Ciccone and Peri (2006) — Tables 4 and 5	Census (1970–1990)	The authors separate the effect of externalities from the effect of a downward sloping demand curve for highly educated workers, both of which imply higher wages for workers with low levels of schooling in locations with a higher proportion of workers with high levels of schooling. The authors use the age and racial composition of cities, plus indicators for region, as instruments for the proportion of college educated workers.	log change in average experience, log change in average employment, indicators for region	effect of a one-year increase in average educational attainment within a city between 1970 and 1990 on the change in the log of average wages in that city between 1970 and 1990	-0.010 (all workers) -0.001 (white males only)

(continued)

TABLE 38.1
Continued

Citation	*Data*	*Summary*	*Control variables*	*Parameter of interest*	*Estimates*
Sheepskin Effects					
Hungerford and Solon (1987) — Table 1	May 1978 CPS (sample restricted to white males age 25 to 64)	OLS estimates of Mincer's model with additional indicators for different levels of educational attainment to estimate non-linear effects of completing key grades. The data do not indicate degrees received, so the authors can estimate the effects of completing "diploma years" but do not know who actually receives a diploma.	none	effect of completing 12 or more years of schooling, above and beyond the linear effect of the number of years of schooling, on log hourly wages	0.0375**
Jaeger and Page (1996) — Table 2	1991 and 1992 March CPS (sample restricted to white men age 25-64)	A change in the wording of the CPS question about educational attainment gives the authors information on both the number of years of schooling and the highest degree completed. They use this information to compute "sheepskin effects" for completing a degree, rather than completing a diploma year.	none	effect of receiving a high school diploma, controlling for years of education, on log hourly wages	0.123**
College Quality					
Dale and Krueger (2002) — Table 6	College and Beyond, NLS-72 (results reported here use NLS-72)	The authors compare the future earnings of students admitted to the same set colleges who choose to attend different schools. They measure the quality of schools by a single parameter, the average SAT score of admitted students.	log predicted parental income, own SAT scores, indicators for race, indicator for top 10% in high school class, average SAT score of schools applied to, indicator for recruited athlete, indicators for one to four additional applications	effect of a 1/100th of a point increase in the school average SAT scores, relative to the SAT scores of other schools to which the respondent was admitted, on log annual earnings	0.013

Black and Smith (2005) — Table 5	NLSY-79 men	The authors use a composite measure of five indicators of college quality (faculty-student ratio, the rejection rate among those who applied for admission, the freshman retention rate, the mean SAT score of the entering class, and mean faculty salaries), instead of a single proxy for quality.	years of schooling, ASVAB scores, indicators for race, quartic in age, indicators for region of birth, home characterisistics, parental characteristics,and high school characteristics	effect of a one standard deviation increase in college quality on log hourly wages in 1988	0.043
Program of study					
Black et al. (2003b) — Table 3	1993 National Survey of College Graduates (sample restricted to full time workers age 25 to 55)	The authors run OLS regressions of wages on indicators for particular college majors and other controls. To make comparisions between majors, one must be excluded as a reference category; the authors choose economics.	indicators for race/ethnicity and age; separate estimates for men and women (effects for men only reported here)	effect of majoring in selected fields, relative to studying economics, on log hourly wages	–0.187*** (biology) –0.270*** (elementary education) –0.111*** (business administration)
Arcidiacono (2004) — Table 8	NLS-72	Wage premiums for different majors could reflect sorting by ability into different majors. The author finds large ability differences between majors, and controls for this selection in his estimates of wage premiums.	coefficients reported are for a hypothetical respondent with SAT scores, grade point averages, college quality, and calendar year equal to the sample mean; separate estimates for men and women (effects for men only reported here)	effect of majoring in different fields on log annual earnings, relative to no college	0.197 (natural sciences) 0.159 (business) 0.094 (social sciences/humanities) –0.012 (education)
Firm Provided Job Training					
Barron et al. (1989) — Table 2	Survey of the Equal Opportunity Pilot Project (1982)	The authors run OLS regressions of log starting wages and growth in log wages on log hours of training and controls.	age, age squared, experience, experience squared, education, plus indicators for the following variables: vocational education, gender, firm unionization, temporary position, size of firm, occupation, and industry	effect of an increase in the log of hours of formal on-the-job training in the first three months of employment on the log of starting wages and wage growth over the first two years in the job	–0.003 (starting wage) 0.035** (wage growth)

(continued)

TABLE 38.1
Continued

Citation	*Data*	*Summary*	*Control variables*	*Parameter of interest*	*Estimates*
Frazis and Loewenstein (2005) — Table 4	NLSY-79, Employer Opportunity Pilot Project (NLSY results reported here)	The authors focus on identifying the proper functional form for the effects of employer-provided job training. They determine that the best specification is log wages as a function of log hours of training, and estimate this via OLS.	age, AFQT score, number of missing training spells, indicators for the following variables: calendar year, black, Hispanic, female, union, managerial position in first year at firm, other white collar position in first year at firm, missing AFQT score, missing union variable, any ongoing training	total effect of the log of current hours of formal training and log of hours of formal training in the previous 1, 2, and 3 years, on log hourly wages, at the median hours of training	1.37**
Public Job Training					
Bloom et al. (1997) — Table 2	National JTPA Study (results for adult men and adult women ages 22 and above only presented here)	Experimental evaluation of the Job Training Partnership Act (JTPA) program, at 16 sites, with random assignment from 1989-1991. JTPA provided classroom training in occupational skills, subsidized on-the-job training at private firms, job search assistance and other services to disadvantaged youth and adults.	Impact estimation via OLS regression controls for a variety of covariates, but these act only to increase the precision of the estimates, which are unbiased due to random assignment	Impact on earnings in the 30 months after random assignment. Because of many treatment group members dropped out and many control group members received similar services elsewhere, the estimate represents the incremental effect of JTPA services, above and beyond the services received by control group members.	$1,176*** (adult women) $978* (adult men)
Schochet et al. (2003) — Table III.1	National Job Corps Study	Experimental evaluation of the Job Corps program, which provides an intensive (and expensive) residential training experience to disadvantaged youth. The sample consists of eligible applicants in 1994 and 1995.	Impact estimation via OLS regression controls for a variety of covariates, but these act only to increase the precision of the estimates, which are unbiased due to random assignment	effect of being randomly assigned to Job Corps in 1994 or 1995, on average calendar year earnings (in 1995 dollars)	-$176.8*** (1996 earnings) $171.8** (1997 earnings) $219.8** (1998 earnings) $32.9 (1999 earnings) –$17.4 (2000 earnings) $7.0 (2001 earnings)

future more highly in making decisions). We return to the important implications of this assumption below.

The Mincer model lacks a causal interpretation because of the implicit assumption that individuals make choices about how much schooling to complete in ways unrelated to all of the other factors, such as ability, family background, family income, motivation, and non-cognitive skills not controlled for in the model. The early literature focused on "ability bias" but the same point applies to other factors affecting labor market outcomes both directly and indirectly via effects on schooling. Suppose that ability affects schooling choices, perhaps because more able individuals find school easier. In addition to this indirect effect operating via the schooling choice, suppose that ability also directly affects labor market outcomes because more able individuals produce more than less able individuals, even with the same years of schooling. As a result, the standard method of estimating the Mincer equation, called Ordinary Least Squares (OLS) regression, produces biased estimates of the causal effect of schooling, because the estimated coefficient on schooling reflects both its causal effect and the selection of more able individuals into higher levels of schooling.

The lack of a causal interpretation means that estimates of equation (1), though ubiquitous in the literature, do not provide a sound guide to policy. In particular, they do not provide a reliable guide to the effects of increases in years of schooling induced by policies such as dropout prevention programs or more generous grants to college students. Nor do they reliably estimate the effects of the existing stock of years of schooling. Despite these shortcomings, we discuss the Mincer model here because of its place in the literature, because it provides a useful introduction to the problem of estimating the labor market effects of education, and because it provides a handy summary measure of the association between labor market outcomes and years of schooling that allows comparisons across groups, locations, and time periods.

In that spirit, the first row of Table 38.1 presents estimates of equation (1) from Heckman, Layne-Farrar, and Todd (1996) using log annual earnings from 1990 Census data and dropping individuals with zero earnings. On average, in that year the earnings of white men increased by about 13 percent (0.1292) for each year of schooling, while the earnings of black men increased by over 15 percent (0.1524). These estimates comport with the large difference in mean earnings observed in recent years between high school and college graduates. Both estimates exceed the corresponding values for the 1950–1980 censuses and reflect the large increase in the labor market value of schooling documented in, e.g., Autor and Katz (1999). Harmon et al. (2003) present estimates (for wages) for many countries using a common data source. See also Psacharopoulos and Patrinos (2004).

CAUSAL EFFECTS

In the last couple of decades researchers have sought to obtain more credible estimates of the causal effect of schooling. Put differently, they have tried to go beyond the non-causal association represented by estimates of equation (1) to obtain estimates that correspond to what individuals would actually experience if they chose to undertake additional years of schooling. As noted in the preceding section, the fundamental problem associated with estimating causal effects springs from the fact that individuals do not choose their schooling level at random. If they did so, a simple tabulation of mean earnings levels for each possible number of years of schooling would yield unbiased estimates of the causal effect of schooling on earnings. In reality, individual schooling choices depend on many different factors, only some of which researchers typically observe.

Selection on Observables

Two basic strategies exist for dealing with the non-random selection into different levels of schooling. Heckman and Robb (1985) call these strategies "selection on observables" and "selection on unobservables." These two basic strategies characterize all of the empirical literatures surveyed below.

Under selection on observables, researchers attempt to control for all of the factors affecting outcomes both directly and indirectly through schooling. The idea is to compare two individuals with similar values of background variables but different levels of schooling. Ideally, the researcher would like to measure and condition on any characteristic whose influence on labor market outcomes might get confused with that of schooling due to non-random sorting into different schooling levels. Statistical methods such as multiple regression hold such background factors constant, which allows estimation of plausibly causal effects of schooling.

Ability, typically measured by test scores, constitutes one potentially important background variable. Other commonly used background variables include the parental age, education and occupation, the presence of both parents in the home, family income, number of siblings, and early health outcomes such as weight at birth. For analyses that examine aspects of college attendance, variables measuring educational quality and performance through high school also play a useful role.

Table 38.1 presents estimates from Kane and Rouse (1995). They analyze the wage and earnings effects of years (measured in college credits) spent in two-year and four-year colleges. Their preferred specifications, which control for a rich set of variables including measures of ability and family background, indicate that a year at a two-year college increases average earnings for men by about 3.5 percent (0.035), while a year at a four-year college increases average earnings by about 5.6 percent (0.056). These estimates, and the modestly larger estimates for women, lie well below the simple Mincer estimates from Heckman et al. (2006). In general, controlling for observable characteristics substantially reduces the estimated effect of schooling (see, for example, Table 5 of Card, 1999). His estimates, as well as those in Table 38.1 and others like them in the literature, make it clear that the causal effect of education is substantially smaller than the estimates from simple Mincer equations suggest.

Selection on Unobservables

Controlling for the available observable characteristics often does not suffice to yield a plausibly causal estimate of schooling effects due to the absence of important factors that affect labor market outcomes both directly and indirectly via schooling. In such cases, researchers must rely on alternative strategies that deal with selection on unobservables. The main alternative consists of something that economists have given the unintuitive name of "instrumental variables" or IV for short.

Despite the obtuse name, IV estimation embodies a simple idea. Find a variable that affects labor market outcomes but only indirectly through its effect on years of schooling, not directly. The ultimate IV is random assignment: the random number that determines assignment to the treatment or control groups in an experiment affects outcomes only through its effect on treatment assignment. Instruments typically arise from institutions, such as state-level variation in the age of legal dropout from school, or from costs, such as state-level variation in tuition at public colleges or individual variation in distance to the nearest college. The instruments employed in the schooling literature aim to mimic random assignment via naturally occurring variation.

To see how instruments work, consider a very simple example. Imagine two adjacent school districts and assume that the two districts do not differ in terms of the parents and students who live there, in the quality of their schools, and so on. The only way they differ is that one district has a special program to prepare students for college and the other does not. Students from the program district, on average, complete more years of schooling (mainly in college) than students from the other district. Put somewhat formally, the program induces some exogenous variation in years of schooling.

Suppose that we collect data on earnings and years of schooling for a random sample of students from the two districts at age 30. In such data, much of the variation across individuals in schooling will result from factors such as ability and motivation that we have not measured. Thus, using the data to estimate equation (1) will not yield estimates of schooling effects we can plausibly call causal. However, we can use the variation in schooling resulting from the program to estimate a compelling causal effect. In particular, we can calculate the ratio of the difference in mean earnings in the two districts and the difference in the mean number of years of schooling. In our simple model, the difference in the district means of years of schooling results solely from the program. Moreover, the difference in mean earnings in the two districts also results solely from the program. Thus, dividing the difference in mean earnings by the difference in mean years of schooling yields an estimate of the casual effect of years of schooling that relies only on the variation induced by the program.

Instrumental Variable Estimates

Table 38.1 presents estimates from two representative studies that use IV methods to estimate causal effects of schooling. Card (1999) uses maternal education as an instrument. That is, his estimates assume that maternal education affects labor market outcomes solely through its indirect effect on years of schooling. Card finds that a year of schooling increases the average earnings of men by over 10 percent (0.106) and of women by 11 percent (0.110). Acemoglu and Angrist (2000) find a somewhat smaller effect using compulsory schooling laws as instruments. Card reviews many IV studies and concludes that 'instrumental variable estimates of the return to schooling typically exceed the corresponding OLS estimates—often by 20 percent or more" (Card, 2001, p. 1155). Heckman et al. (2006) also review the IV literature and criticize many of the instruments it relies on.

The general finding that estimates obtained using IV methods exceed those obtained by controlling for observable characteristics via OLS regression creates a puzzle. The usual selection story suggests that the OLS estimates should be too large rather than too small. For example, if motivation is not controlled for, but affects outcomes both directly and indirectly through schooling, we would expect an upward bias in the estimated effect of schooling because it combines the causal effect of schooling with the effect of its correlate, motivation. IV estimates should not suffer from this bias, and so, by this argument, should be smaller than the regression estimates. We have more to say about this puzzle later on.

Wages or Earnings?

Whether to use wages or earnings as the dependent variable depends on the purpose of the analysis. In the simplest case in which everyone works every period for the same number of hours, it does not matter. When employment and hours choices vary among individuals, using earnings rather than wages captures additional effects of schooling on employment and hours worked. Using the logarithm of earnings raises the question of what to do with individuals with zero earnings (for whom the log is not defined). Using wages as the dependent variable allows estimation of the effect of education on worker productivity (what economists call the "marginal product") independent of its effect on hours worked and employment. Of course, examining wages means dealing with the sample selection bias that results from observing wages only for the non-random subset of individuals who work. Dropping observations with zero earnings or no observed wage can lead to misleading inferences about the effects of education. For examples in the context of black/white differentials, see Heckman, Lyons and Todd (2000), Chandra (2003), and Neal (2005).

Synthetic Cohorts

Many analyses use data on individuals of different ages at a point in time (a "cross section") to estimate the causal effect of schooling. Such analyses assume that the labor market outcomes of older individuals with a particular schooling level provide an unbiased estimate of what younger individuals with the same schooling level will experience when they get old. The literature calls this the "synthetic cohort" assumption. While we can relax this assumption for older cohorts—see the evidence in Heckman et al. (2006)—for younger cohorts we do not yet observe their labor market outcomes at older ages.

If we want to use estimates of schooling effects to guide (or study) the schooling choices of young people or the selection of policies that affect those choices, then this assumption matters. Individuals making decisions about the quality, quantity and type of schooling to undertake look not only at older cohorts, they also attempt to forecast future demand and supply for different skills. Students making such decisions can consult many forecasts, ranging from the sobriety of the Bureau of Labor Statistics, as in Hecker (2005), to the near hysteria of Carnevale and Fry (2001). They can also observe the size of their cohort and attempt to forecast how it will affect the value of schooling, as studied in Card and Lemieux (2001) and Welch (1979). Readers looking to project out the lifetime effects of schooling for current cohorts of young people should keep in mind future changes in the demand and supply of skills due to technology and other factors.

Other Issues

A variety of other issues arise when estimating causal effects of schooling; we mention two here. First, including variables such as experience as controls changes the meaning of estimated schooling effects. Whalley (2006) finds that schooling has a causal effect on experience because individuals with more schooling spend more time in the labor force and less time unemployed. As a result, controlling for experience biases the effect of schooling downward. Moreover, the effect of schooling controlling for experience does not have the interpretation of a "net" effect unless the analysis corrects for non-random selection into both schooling and experience levels. Following a literature that starts with Rosenbaum (1984), we suggest that readers not rely on such estimates unless they have strong reasons for controlling for variables affected by the education whose effects they seek to understand.

Second, the literature shows that survey measures of years of schooling and degree receipt typically include measurement error. Measurement error unrelated to the true value of the variable, called "classical" measurement error, leads to bias toward zero ("attenuation") in the estimated effects, but can be dealt with using IV methods. But many measures of education are binary, such as degree receipt, or categorical, such as years of schooling. With such variables, the measurement error necessarily correlates with the true value due to limits on the number of possible values, and the simple intuitions (and statistical solutions) associated with random measurement error do not apply.

Empirically, Kane, Rouse, and Staiger (1999) find strong evidence of non-random measurement error, particularly in regard to years of schooling between high school and college completion. Black, Sanders, and Taylor (2003a) find evidence of substantial over-reporting of college and professional degrees. This evidence suggests a preference for analyses that rely on transcript data to measure schooling or on carefully verified survey measures.

OTHER EFFECTS OF SCHOOLING

Non-Pecuniary Outcomes

A small literature examines the effects of education on outcomes other than earnings and wages. We highlight three examples here. First, education increases fringe benefits. For example, the incidence of employer provided health insurance increases with education in the United States (see http://www.umich.edu/~eriu/fastfacts/cps2005_2.html). Second, education improves health. Lleras-Muney (2005) provides evidence of a causal effect of education on health using the variation induced by state compulsory schooling laws (as well as citations to the literature on other health outcomes). Third, getting more education means, on average, getting a more educated spouse, through what economists call "positive assortative mating;" see Becker (2005) or McCrary and Royer (2006). In short, education improves many outcomes beyond wages and earnings. As such, analyses of the effects of education that focus solely on wages or earnings generally understate the full gains from additional schooling.

Public Benefits

Many authors have argued for the existence of positive external effects of education. Thomas Jefferson wrote to James Madison in 1787, "Above all things I hope the education of the common people will be attended to, convinced that on their good sense we may rely with the most security for the preservation of a due degree of liberty." Such externalities play an important role in social cost-benefit calculations for policies that increase schooling. Indeed, much of the rationale for public funding (and to a lesser extent public provision) relies on such externalities. Bowen and Bok (1998), Rizzo (2004), and Courant, McPherson, and Resch (2006) offer related discussions.

Solid evidence for the existence of externalities remains scarce and their extent at the post-secondary level remains controversial. Table 38.1 summarizes two of the more convincing studies. Lochner and Moretti (2004) find that each additional year of schooling reduces the probability of committing a serious crime, particularly for whites. Milligan et al. (2004) presents evidence that completing high school increases voting. Dee (2004) reaches a similar conclusion. Overall, while the literature remains sparse (and thus provides fertile ground for future research), we think that the full social effect of schooling likely exceeds its effect on individual earnings by a modest amount.

Spillover Effects on Wages

A small recent literature empirically evaluates the claim that workers with high levels of schooling increase the productivity of workers with lower levels of schooling via spillover effects. Moretti (2004a) examines spillovers at the city level from the number of residents with a college degree. He finds that individuals with a high school education or less have higher wages in cities with more college educated workers. Moretti (2004b) finds higher productivity growth in firms located in cities with a more rapidly growing proportion of college graduates. In contrast, Acemoglu and Angrist (2000) examine spillovers at the state level using the variation induced by compulsory schooling laws and find very little.

Ciccone and Peri (2005) discuss econometric problems with the approach used in these papers. Their alternative approach, which avoids these problems, yields "no evidence of significant… externalities" in U.S. Census data. Table 38.1 summarizes the key papers. Besides the differences in methods, two complications that arise in comparing the studies concern the different geographic units (cities versus states), and the different ways in which they measure schooling, with Moretti (2004a) analyzing spillovers from college educated workers and the other papers analyzing spillovers from the stock of schooling. Overall, we think that Ciccone and Peri's (2005) methodological critique and evidence suggest the absence of substantial spillovers.

HETEROGENEOUS EFFECTS

Subgroups

The simplest form of heterogeneity consists of differences in average effects across groups defined by characteristics such as race or sex. Many of the studies summarized in Table 38.1 present separate estimates for men and women and/or blacks and whites. The evidence from those studies (and the broader literature) suggests that education often has surprisingly different effects for such groups. Thus, we encourage the reporting of subgroup estimates, further investigation into the causes of subgroup differences, and reliance on such estimates when considering the effects of policies likely to differentially affect particular subgroups.

Sheepskin Effects

Many analyses assume a constant (in logs) effect of each year of schooling. Different effects of particular years of schooling might result from diminishing returns, in which each additional year of schooling has a smaller effect, or from "sheepskin" effects associated with degree receipt. Sheepskin effects raise the issue of signaling. In this view, first introduced by Spence (1974), part of the value of a high school diploma or college degree results from the signal it provides about the recipient's ability or persistence above and beyond the value of the skills provided by the schooling underlying the degree. We focus here on the empirical evidence on sheepskin effects rather than entering the debate about signaling.

An early review by Layard and Psacharopoulous (1974) found no evidence of sheepskin effects. More recent work by Hungerford and Solon (1987), Kane and Rouse (1995), Jaeger and Page (1996), Heckman, (1996), Card (1999) and Heckman et al. (2006) finds evidence of substantively important sheepskin effects, typically at both high school and college completion. The point estimates (and the importance attached to them by the authors) vary across these studies. Whether or not the analysis controls for ability and family background variables and whether degree completion is measured by number of years of schooling or via a separate survey question account for some of the variation.

Table 38.1 provides estimates from two papers of the additional effect of high school completion relative to the effect of other years of schooling. Hungerford and Solon (1987) treat high school completion as synonymous with 12 years of schooling while Jaeger and Page (1996) directly measure receipt of a diploma. The larger estimated effect in the latter paper may result from the more recent time period examined or from the reduction in measurement error associated with using actual degree receipt. Both papers estimate simple Mincer specifications so neither carries a causal interpretation.

The evidence points to (at least) modest sheepskin effects. As such it makes sense to allow the effects to vary by year when estimating the effects of years of schooling. Policy makers should keep in mind that, for example, policies that increase college degree attainment may have larger benefits than policies that increase the number of individuals with "some college."

College Quality

Educational programs at all levels differ in the quality of the schooling they offer, where we can define quality either in terms of inputs such as expenditures per student, teacher quality (e.g., ability and experience) and peer quality, or directly in terms of labor market effects. We focus here on the literature on college quality, which provides an interesting contrast to that on primary and secondary school quality. While evidence of quality effects often seems elusive at the primary and secondary levels, it leaps out of almost every study at the college level.

Key issues in this literature include how to measure college quality and how to deal with the non-random selection of students into colleges of different quality. In regard to the first issue, most studies use a single variable to proxy for quality, typically the average Scholastic Achievement Test score of the entering class or some measure of selectivity such as that provided by *Barron's* magazine. Black, Daniel, and Smith (2005) argue that estimating the separate effects of quality measures such as selectivity and expenditures per student proves difficult in practice because the high correlation among the quality measures leaves little variation in one conditional on the other.

Using a single variable as a proxy for quality (a latent concept that we cannot directly observe) may mean measuring quality with substantial error. As a result, the estimated effect of the single proxy may provide a biased guide to the effect of quality defined more broadly. Black and Smith (2005) demonstrate that combining multiple quality measures reduces the measurement error implicit in using a single measure; they estimate that using a single measure understates the quality effect by about 20 percent. Their preferred estimate, shown in Table 38.1, indicates that moving one standard deviation up the quality distribution increases wages by more than 4 percent.

In regard to the second issue, the literature features both of the broad strategies discussed above. Black, Daniel, and Smith (2005) provide estimates that control for a rich set of background characteristics including multiple dimensions of ability in a linear regression context while Black and Smith (2004) use the same data but apply matching methods. The latter paper also documents strong sorting by ability and family background into colleges of different qualities; see Reynolds (2007) for a similar analysis that includes two-year colleges. In contrast, Brewer, Eide, and Ehrenberg (1999) use variables related to the price of college as instruments while Behrman, Rosenzweig, and Taubman (1996) use twins to deal with the selection problem. All of these papers find substantial labor market effects of college quality.

The most influential paper in the recent literature, Dale and Krueger (2002), both controls for a rich set of background variables and compares students admitted to roughly the same set of colleges but who make different choices within that set. The fact that college admissions officers observe otherwise unobservable information about the student that gets incorporated into their admissions decisions motivates this strategy. As shown in Table 38.1, Dale and Krueger (2002) find little effect of college selectivity on wages for either of the data sets they examine, with the exception of a positive effect for low income students.

The literature has not yet reconciled the conflicting results but one possibility, suggested by Dale and Krueger (2002), concerns what it means to get admitted to two schools and then choose one or the other. Consider a student admitted to Princeton and Michigan. Princeton ranks higher on most scales; why then might a student choose Michigan? Dale and Krueger's strategy requires that students choose in a way unrelated to the labor market outcomes associated with each school. If the deciding factor is, say, a social or family tie, then this condition should hold. If, in contrast, Michigan has a certain program that fits better in terms of interests and abilities, then the condition likely fails.

Overall, we think college quality matters. At the same time, the Dale and Krueger (2003) finding represents a provocative challenge to the literature, one that awaits resolution. The literature also has little to say about the mechanisms that underlie the influence of college quality on labor market outcomes. Such knowledge would have great value for policymakers.

College Major

Educational programs differ in the type of human capital they seek to provide. Our discussion focuses on one important example of human capital type: college major. Variation in labor market outcomes across majors may arise from many factors, including differences in the amount of human capital provided (as opposed to consumption value while in school), institutional barriers that restrict access to certain majors and thereby raise wages in related occupations, differences in the average ability of students across majors, and differences in other characteristics valued by the labor market such as career focus, soft skills and so on. They may also represent what economists call "compensating" or "equalizing" differences associated with the non-pecuniary aspects of the major itself and the occupations to which it leads. For example, we would expect pleasant jobs to pay less than unpleasant ones, and dangerous ones to pay more than safe ones, all else equal; see Rosen (1986) for a survey.

Black et al. (2003b) examines how the wages of full time workers in the National Survey of College Graduates vary across 85 different majors. Controlling only for demographic variables (because their data lack measures of ability and family background) their results lack a causal interpretation but do provide valuable descriptive information. As shown (in part) in Table 38.1, they find that engineering students have the highest wages, followed by economics students, then generally lower wages for students majoring in education, business, pre-professional studies, social sciences, and the humanities. Moreover, they find support for both ability differences in sorting across majors (MBAs with economics degrees earn more than MBAs with undergraduate business degrees even though they presumably possess roughly the same skills), and for differences in market value added across majors (math and physics majors make less than engineers but likely have at least equal ability).

Arcidiacono (2004) directly examines ability sorting by major using data from the National Longitudinal Study of the Class of 1972. He finds large differences across major even when controlling for ability measured by test scores. As shown in Table 38.1, he finds much larger earnings effects of college attendance for those who major in the natural sciences or business than for those who major in education, with humanities and social science majors in between.

In other papers Koch (1972) and Grogger and Eide (1995) find some evidence that students respond to market signals regarding what to major in. However, the long term persistence of higher wages for certain fields of study such as engineering—see James et al. (1989) for evidence from an earlier cohort—suggests more to these differences than just transitory changes in demand for particular skill sets. Overall, the literature suggests causal effects of college major that do not represent simply differences in unobserved characteristics, institutional constraints, or compensating differences. In thinking about policy reforms to increase college attendance and completion, it matters what the marginal students affected by the policy choose to study. At the same time, this particular aspect of the economic effects of education warrants further study.

Other Types of Human Capital

Much of the literature reads as if formal schooling from primary school through graduate school represents the only means of human capital accumulation. In fact, both other forms of formal education, such as courses provided by firms to their workers and by the government through programs such as the Workforce Investment Act, and on-the-job training of various degrees of formality, add importantly to the total stock of human capital.

On-the-job training has attracted much attention from economists. However, difficulties in measuring both formal and informal on-the-job training due to firms' reluctance to share data, problems with survey measurement as documented in Barron, Berger, and Black (1997a), and the lack of ability and other background measures (or of good instruments) in many data sets that do attempt to measure on-the-job training has hampered efforts to produce credible estimates of causal effects. Unlike years of schooling, courses on the job come in different lengths as well, meaning that analysts must deal with selection problems related to both incidence and duration.

Recent papers focusing primarily on formal training courses include Barron, Berger and Black (1989, 1997b), Blundell, Dearden, and Meghir (1996), and Frazis and Loewenstein (2005). Most studies find that individuals with more formal schooling (and higher ability) tend to receive more on-the-job training; see, for example, Mincer (1989) or Carniero and Heckman (2003). This pattern has two important implications. First, it suggests that part of the effect of years of schooling in the studies reviewed above comes indirectly via increases in on-the-job training. Second, it suggests that studies of the effects of training on wages and earnings that do not control for ability overstate the effects of such training. Even studies like Frazis and Loewenstein (2005) that control for ability (as proxied by test scores) likely attribute differences in other unmeasured characteristics like motivation and social skills to on-the-job training. Table 38.1 presents estimates from two of the better studies on this topic; both show substantial effects of on-the-job training on wages.

Government funded training for the disadvantaged and for displaced workers includes activities such as classroom training in occupational skills (often provided by community colleges), basic skills upgrading (often aimed at GED receipt) as well as subsidized on-the-job training at private firms and lessons in how to look for work and how to hold on to a job. Smith and Whalley (2007) demonstrate that conventional survey measures tend to underestimate the extent of such activities, with the amount missed higher for activities that look less like formal schooling. Heckman, LaLonde and Smith (1999) survey the methodological literature on how to evaluate such programs and the empirical literature on their effects on earnings and employment. Kluve (2006) provides a meta-analysis of European programs.

The literature on publicly provided training dominates that on training at private firms in both size and average quality as a result of the availability of more and better data as well as the occasional use of random assignment. This asymmetry is not appropriate given the much greater importance of training at private firms to the overall stock of human capital. Table 38.1 highlights results from experimental evaluations of two public programs: the Job Training Partnership Act (JTPA) and the Job Corps. The former has moderate and persistent impacts on adults, particularly adult women, but essentially zero impacts on youth (an as yet unexplained pattern it shares with many similar programs). The latter has substantial positive impacts on earnings (and negative impacts on crime) in the short term, but the impacts fade out well before they outweigh the costs of the program. The use of random assignment designs in both cases makes the estimates clear and compelling by removing concerns about non-random program participation.

The study of on-the-job training at firms would benefit greatly from the collection of better data. Both that literature, and the literature on public programs, would benefit from greater integration with the literature on formal schooling, with particular attention to patterns of lifelong learning.

GENERAL HETEROGENEITY

The recent literature goes beyond looking at how the impacts of education vary along observable dimensions of the student and the schooling, and focuses on heterogeneity in the effects of schooling among individuals with the same observed characteristics undertaking the same schooling. Put differently, recent research considers the case where each individual has their own person-specific effect of any particular educational program. The econometric literature calls this the "correlated random coefficient model;" we call it simply "general heterogeneity." Though it might seem a minor innovation at first blush, moving from thinking about the world in terms of everyone having the same effect of particular years or types of schooling (or having different effects that they do not know in advance and so do not act upon in making their schooling choices) has important implications.

First, rather than just one parameter of interest (or perhaps a small number of parameters of interest corresponding to variation in common coefficients based on individual characteristics or school characteristics), we now have many. We can think about the average schooling effect in the population, among particular subgroups defined by observable characteristics, or among groups defined by the amount or type of schooling completed. We can, most importantly for policy, think about the average effect of schooling among those on particular policy margins, such as the average effect of college for those induced to attend college by a new student loan or grant policy.

In a simple economic model in which potential college students have some idea of the effect of attending college on their labor market outcomes, we would expect that those who presently attend have larger effects of doing so than those who presently do not attend, including those at the margin who would change their mind about going to college in response to policies that reduced its cost. This simple model suggests, for example, that potential students on the margin of attending college will not realize the substantial (on average) labor market benefits from attending college received by those already attending. This is a very important point for policy and one that suggests the value of analyses designed specifically to estimate the effects of college attendance on individuals on the margin of attending.

Second, with general heterogeneity, instrumental variables estimates based on instruments related to program costs or institutions do not estimate the average effect of schooling, but rather the average effect of schooling on those individuals whose schooling status depends on the value of the instrument. To see this, consider distance to college in a model of heterogeneous effects of college. Individuals who live near a college will attend even if they benefit relatively little because they face a low cost of attendance. In contrast, individuals who live far away from a college will attend only if they reap benefits high enough to overcome their higher cost. Using distance to college as an instrument then estimates the mean effect of college attendance on those at the margin, which means those who would attend if they lived near a college but would not attend if they lived far away. We expect these individuals to have a lower average benefit from college attendance than individuals who attend regardless of where they live. Of course, if the policy under consideration subsidizes the cost of living away from home while attending college, then the average effect for individuals on the margin of attending due to distance may represent exactly the effect of interest. See , for example,. Imbens and Angrist (1994), Card (1999), Kling (2001), and Heckman et al. (2006) for more technical treatments of this important point.

Third, general heterogeneity suggests two possible solutions to the puzzle of IV estimates of the effect of schooling that exceed OLS estimates. First, Card (1999, 2001) and others have suggested that individuals whose years of schooling depend on the instrumental variables commonly used in the literature, such as the minimum school leaving age, may have larger effects of education at the margin than other individuals, perhaps because they lack access to the assets or credit required to finance such investments. Second, Heckman et al. (2006) suggest instead that in a world of comparative advantage, OLS estimates of schooling effects embody two conflicting biases: failure to control for all the variables that affect outcomes both directly and indirectly via schooling makes them too high, and selection on comparative advantage (wherein each individual does what they do best) makes them too low. To see the latter effect, consider a simple example of selection on comparative advantage with no covariates: suppose that college graduates earn 20 but would have earned 10 as high school graduates. In contrast, high school graduates earn 15 but would have earned only 12 as college graduates. Comparing the earnings of college and high school graduates (the analog of running an OLS regression in the absence of covariates) suggests an effect of college completion of 5 (= 20–15), while completing college actually increases earnings by 10 (= 20–10) for those who do so (and decreases earnings for those who do not). In this case, the IV estimates exceed the OLS estimates because the latter have a net downward bias, rather than the net upward bias traditionally assumed. This view makes the observed pattern consistent with the simple economic notion that individuals who do not attend college would benefit less from doing so than those who do attend.

We sum up this section simply: the notion of general heterogeneity has very important implications for this literature. We find this model more plausible than the common coefficient model that dominated the literature until recently, but note that adopting this model makes life harder, or at least more subtle, for both researchers and policy makers.

CONCLUDING REMARKS

Our survey omits a number of worthy topics including the sequential nature of schooling choices, in which information revealed at each step of the schooling process affects decisions regarding whether and how to continue on to the next step, the difference between ex ante and ex post effects (and the related issue of how much individuals know about how schooling will affect them) and the effect of school type (e.g., public versus private, or two-year versus four-year college).

We have focused instead on three main points. First, standard Mincer equation estimates of the effect of years of schooling that control only for experience (or age) have little relevance to policy because they lack a causal interpretation. They remain useful for comparisons of the association between labor market outcomes and schooling for different groups, different points in time and different locales. Second, we have emphasized heterogeneity in the effects of schooling that results from both differences in average effects across subgroups and differences in average effects for different levels, qualities, and types of education. These forms of heterogeneity have implications for policy because particular policies encourage or discourage particular forms of schooling for particular subgroups. Finally, we have emphasized the importance of what we called general heterogeneity in the effects of education. When individuals make choices based on their person-specific effects of education, evidence-based policymaking requires careful attention to estimating average effects for precisely those individuals whose educational choices change in response to particular policy changes.

REFERENCES

Acemoglu, D. & Angrist, J. (2000). How large are human-capital externalities? Evidence from compulsory schooling laws. *NBER Macroeconomics Annual*, 15, 9–59.

Arcidiacono, P. (2004). Ability sorting and the returns to college major. *Journal of Econometrics*, 121, 343–375.

Ashenfelter, O., Harmon, C., & Oosterbeek. H. (1999). A review of estimates of the schooling/earnings relationship, with tests for publication bias. *Labour Economics*, 6, 453–470.

Autor, D. & Katz, L. (1999). Changes in the wage structure and earnings inequality. In O. Ashenfelter and D. Card (Eds.), *Handbook of Labor Economics,* Vol. 3 (pp. 1463–1555). Amsterdam: North-Holland.

Barron, J., Berger, M., & Black, D. (1989). Job matching and on-the-job training. *Journal of Labor Economics*, 7, 1–19.

Barron, J., Berger, M., & Black, D. (1997a). How well do we measure training? *Journal of Labor Economics*. 15, 507–528.

Barron, J., Berger, M., & Black, D. (1997b). *On-the-job training*. Kalamazoo: W.E. Upjohn Institute for Employment Research.

Becker, G. (1964). *Human capital: A theoretical and empirical analysis, with special reference to education.* New York: National Bureau of Economic Research.

Becker, G. (2005). *A treatise on the family: enlarged edition.* Cambridge, MA: Harvard University Press.

Behrman, J., Rosenzweig, M., & Taubman, P. (1996). College choice and wages: estimates using data on female twins. *Review of Economics and Statistics*, 77, 672–685.

Black, D., Daniel, K., & Smith, J. (2005). College quality and wages in the United States. *German Economic Review*, 6, 415–443.

Black, D., Sanders, S., & Taylor, L. (2003a). Measurement of higher education in the Census and CPS. *Journal of the American Statistical Association*, 98, 545–554.

Black, D., Sanders, S., & Taylor, L. (2003b). The economic reward to studying economics. *Economic Inquiry*, 41, 365–377.

Black, D. & Smith, J. (2004). How robust is the evidence on the effects of college quality? Evidence from matching. *Journal of Econometrics*, 121, 99–124.

Black, D. & Smith, J. (2005). Estimating the returns to college quality with multiple proxies for quality. *Journal of Labor Economics*, 24, 701–728.

Bloom, H., Orr, L., Bell, S., Cave, G., Doolittle, F., Lin, W. & Bos, J. (1997). The benefits and costs of JTPA Title II-A programs: Key findings from the National Job Training Partnership Act study. *Journal of Human Resources*, 32, 549–576.

Blundell, R., Dearden, L., & Meghir, C. (1996). *The determinants and effects of work related training in Britain.* London: Institute for Fiscal Studies.

Bowen, W. & Bok, D. (2005). *The shape of the river*. Princeton, NJ: Princeton University Press.

Brewer, D., Eide, E., & Ehrenberg. R. (1999). Does it pay to attend an elite private college? Cross cohort evidence on the effects of college type on earnings. *Journal of Human Resources*, 34, 104–123.

Card, D. (1999). The causal effect of education on earnings. In O. Ashenfelter and D. Card (Eds.), *Handbook of Labor Economics*, Vol. 3 (pp. 1801–1863). Amsterdam: North-Holland.

Card, D. (2001). Estimating the return to schooling: Progress on some persistent econometric problems. *Econometrica*, 69, 1127–1160.

Card, D. & Lemieux, T. (2001). Can falling supply explain the rising return to college for younger men? A cohort-based analysis. *Quarterly Journal of Economics*, 116, 705–746.

Carnevale, A. & Fry, R. (2001). *The economic and demographic roots of education and training*. Commissioned by the Manufacturing Institute and the National Association of Manufacturers.

Carniero, P. & Heckman, J. (2003). Human capital policy. In B. Friedman (Ed.), *Inequality in America: What role for human capital policies?* (pp. 77–239). Cambridge: MIT Press.

Chandra, A. (2003). Is the convergence of the racial wage gap illusory? NBER Working Papers No. 9476.

Ciccone, A. & Peri, G. (2006). Identifying human capital externalities: Theory with applications. *Review of Economic Studies*, 73, 381–412.

Courant, P., McPherson, M., & Resch, A. (2006). The public role in higher education. *National Tax Journal*, 59, 291–318.

Dale, S. & Krueger, A. (2002). Estimating the payoff to attending a more selective college: An Application of selection on observables and unobservables. *Quarterly Journal of Economics*, 117, 1491–1527.

Dee, T. (2004). Are there civic returns to education? *Journal of Public Economics*, 88, 1697–1720.

Frazis, H. & Lowenstein, M. (2005). Reexamining the returns to training: Functional form, magnitude, and interpretation. *Journal of Human Resources*, 40, 453–476.

Grogger, J. & Eide, E. (1995). Changes in college skills and the rise in the college wage premium. *The Journal of Human Resources*, 30, 280–310.

Harmon, C., Oosterbeek, H., & Walker, I. (2003). The returns to education: microeconomics. *Journal of Economic Surveys*, 17, 115–156.

Hecker, D. (2005). Occupational employment projections to 2014. *Monthy Labor Review*, 128, 70–101.

Heckman, J., LaLonde, R., & Smith, J. (1999). The economics and econometrics of active labor market programs. In O. Ashenfelter and D. Card, (Eds.), *Handbook of Labor Economics*, Vol. 3 (pp. 1865–2097). Amsterdam: North-Holland.

Heckman, J., Lochner, L., & Todd, P. (2006). Earnings functions, rates of return and treatment effects: The Mincer equation and beyond. In E. Hanushek and F. Welch (Eds.) *Handbook of the Economics of Education*, Vol. 1 (pp. 307–458). Amsterdam: Elsevier.

Heckman, J., Layne-Farrar, A., & Todd, P. (1996). Human capital pricing equations with an application to estimating the effect of school quality on earnings. *Review of Economics and Statistics*, 78, 562–610.

Heckman, J., Lyons, T., & Todd, P. (2000). Understanding black-white wage differentials, 1960–1990. *American Economic Review*, 90, 344–349.

Heckman, J. & Robb, R. (1985). Alternative methods for evaluating the impact of interventions. In J. Heckman and B. Singer (eds.), *Longitudinal Analysis of Labor Market Data* (pp.156–245). New York: Cambridge University Press.

Hungerford, T. & Solon, G. (1987). Sheepskin effects in the return to education. *Review of Economics and Statistics*, 69, 175–177.

Imbens, G. & Angrist, J. (1994). Identification and estimation of local average treatment effects. *Econometrica*, 62, 467–475.

Jaeger, D. & Page. M. (1996). Degrees matter: New evidence on sheepskin effects in the returns to education. *Review of Economics and Statistics*, 78, 733–740.

James, E., Alsalam, N., Conaty, J., & To, D. (1989). College quality and future earnings: Where should you send your child to college? *American Economic Review*, 79, 247–252.

Kane, T. & Rouse, C. (1995). Labor-market returns to two- and four-year college. *American Economic Review*, 85, 600–614.

Kane, T., Rouse, C., & Staiger, D. (1999). Estimating returns to schooling when schooling is misreported. NBER Working Paper No. 7235.

Kling, J. (2001). Interpreting instrumental variables estimates of the returns to schooling. *Journal of Business and Economic Statistics*, 19, 358–364.

Kluve, J. (2006). The effectiveness of European active labor market policy. IZA Discussion Paper No. 2018.

Koch, J. (1972). Student choice of undergraduate major field of study and private internal rates of return. *Industrial and Labor Relations Review*, 26, 680–685.

Layard, R. & Psacharopoulos, G. (1974). The screening hypothesis and the returns to education. *Journal of Political Economy*, 82, 985–998.

Lleras-Muney, A. (2005). The relationship between education and adult mortality in the United States. *Review of Economic Studies*, 72, 189–221.

Lochner, L. & Moretti, E. (2004). The effect of education on crime: Evidence from prision inmates, arrests, and self-reports. *American Economic Review*, 94, 155–189.

McCrary, J. & Royer, H. (2006). The effect of female education on fertility and infant health: evidence from school entry policies using exact date of birth. Unpublished manuscript, University of Michigan.

Milligan, K., Moretti, E., & Oreopolous, P. (2004). Does education improve citizenship? Evidence from the United States and the United Kingdom, *Journal of Public Economics*, 88, 1667–1695.

Mincer, J. (1958). Investment in human capital and personal income distribution. *Journal of Political Economy*, 66, 281–302.

Mincer, J. (1974). *Schooling, experience and earnings*. New York: Columbia University Press for National Bureau of Economic Research.

Mincer, J. (1989). Human capital and the labor market: a review of current research. *Educational Researcher*, 18, 27–34.

Moretti, E. (2004a). Estimating the social return to higher education: evidence from longitudinal and repeated cross-sectional data. *Journal of Econometrics*, 121, 175–212.

Moretti, E. (2004b). Workers' education, spillovers and productivity: Evidence from plant-level production functions. *American Economic Review*, 94, 656–690.

Neal, D. (2005). Why has black-white skill convergence stopped? NBER Working Paper No. 11090.

Psacharopoulos, G. & Patrinos, H. (2004). Returns to investment in education: a further update. *Education Economics*, 12, 111–134.

Reynolds, C. (2007). Where to attend? Estimates of the effects of beginnng at a two-year college. Unpublished manuscript, University of Michigan.

Rizzo, M. (2004). The public interest in higher education. Unpublished manuscript, Federal Reserve Bank of Cleveland.

Rosen, S. (1977). Human capital: A survey of empirical research. In R. Ehrenberg (Ed.), *Research in Labor Economics*, Vol. 1 (pp. 3–40). Greenwich, CT: JAI Press.

Rosen, S. (1986). The theory of equalizing differences. In O. Ashenfelter and R. Layard (Eds.), *Handbook of Labor Economics*, Vol. 1 (pp. 641–692). Amsterdam: North-Holland.

Rosenbaum, P. (1984). The consequences of adjustment for a concomitant variable that has been affected by the treatment. *Journal of the Royal Statistical Society Series A*, 147, 656–666.

Schochet, P., McConnell, S. & Burghardt, J. (2003). *National Job Corps Study: Findings using administrative earnings records data.* Princeton, NJ: Mathematica Policy Research.

Smith, J. & Whalley, A. (2007). How well do we measure public job training? Unpublished manuscript, University of Michigan.

Spence, M. (1974). Job market signaling. *Quarterly Journal of Economics*, 87, 355–374.

Welch, F. (1979). Effects of cohort size on earnings: The baby boom babies' financial bust. *Journal of Political Economy*, 87, S65–S97.

Whalley, A. (2006). Racial differences in the insurance value of education. Unpublished manuscript, University of Maryland.

Willis, R. (1986). Wage determinants: A survey and reinterpretation of human capital earnings functions. In O. Ashenfelter and R. Layard (Eds.), *Handbook of Labor Economics*, Vol. 1 (pp. 525–602). Amsterdam: North-Holland.

39

The Student Aid System: An Overview

Sandy Baum

Federal and state governments, colleges and universities, and employers and other private sources distributed $134.8 billion in financial aid to students during the 2005–06 academic year, 95 percent more in inflation-adjusted dollars than a decade earlier. Without these grants, loans, tax benefits, and work subsidies, many of the nation's 17 million undergraduate and graduate students would be unable to continue their educations in the institutions of their choice.

Nonetheless, finances prevent many students from ever getting to college. Evidence can be seen in differences in enrollment rates among those with similar academic preparation and abilities, but different family incomes. In fact, college enrollment rates among high-achieving students from low-income families are similar to those among the lowest-achieving students from the upper quarter of the family income distribution (Ellwood & Kane, 2000). The discrepancy in completion rates is even starker. Almost all students with high math test scores who are from the highest socioeconomic quartile enter college, and three quarters of them have earned at least a bachelor's degree eight years after graduating from high school. Among those from the lowest socioeconomic quartile with similar test scores, three quarters have entered college, but fewer than 40 percent of those who begin have completed a degree in this time frame (College Board, 2005).

Finances certainly do not explain all of the discrepancy in educational attainment across students from different backgrounds, and some researchers argue that lack of funds can explain only a small percentage of gaps in college attendance (Cameron & Heckman, 2001). But there is considerable evidence that money matters (see, for example, ACSFA, 2006; Kane, 2003; Kane, 2004). Moreover, even for many of those who make it to and through college, money is a significant problem. In addition to the fact that the student aid system relies heavily on loans, postsecondary students are looking beyond student aid and increasing their rates of borrowing from banks and other private sources at an alarming rate. In other words, despite its successes, the student aid system falls far short of assuring access to affordable, high quality, higher education for all who could benefit from it. If we do not improve the effectiveness of our student aid policies, the gaps in educational opportunity that persist in our society are likely to deepen as the demographic composition of our society changes in the coming decades.

The system of financial aid that has developed in the United States is a partnership among the federal government, state governments, colleges and universities, and private sources. A strength of this system is that it serves to increase available funding and to allow multiple approaches to meeting a variety of student needs (Baum, 2002). A weakness is that the system also leads to a proliferation of differing programs and policies and a complicated array of regulations and processes facing students. Table 39.1 provides an overview of the amounts and forms of aid provided by different sources over the past 30 years.

THE FEDERAL GOVERNMENT

The federal government has primary responsibility for furthering the goal of equality of opportunity among Americans. While state governments provide the core funding for public colleges and universities and share in the mission of providing educational opportunities, the reality is that the national social welfare is not their first priority. The federal government has recognized this responsibility at least since it established the Pell Grant program (originally known as Basic Educational Opportunity Grants) in 1972. Targeted at low-income students, these grants provide the foundation funding that allows many students to enroll in college despite their financial circumstances. Providing about $3.3 billion (in 2005 dollars) to students in 1975–76, the Pell Grant program grew to $6.5 billion in 1985–86, $7.0 billon in 1995–96, and $12.7 billion in 2005–06, after adjusting for inflation. Even taking enrollment increases into consideration, the current funding level of about $850 per student for *all* undergraduate students compares favorably to $575 a decade ago, and $617 per undergraduate in 2005 dollars in 1985–86.

Eligibility for Pell Grants is based solely on financial circumstances, and the grants are awarded to the lowest-income college students.[1] Students whose expected family contributions, based on the financial information reported on the federal student aid application (FAFSA), are less than the maximum Pell Grant amount receive aid. The poorest students receive the maximum Pell Grant, and those with higher incomes receive smaller grants. About two-thirds of dependent

TABLE 39.1
Student Aid by Type and Source, Billions of Constant 2005 Dollars

	75–76	*80–81*	*85–86*	*90–91*	*95–96*	*00–01*	*05–06*
Federal Aid	$31.4	$33.9	$29.0	$31.7	$48.3	$62.9	$94.4
Grants	$23.9	$15.9	$9.7	$9.9	$10.4	$12.7	$18.6
Pell	$3.3	$5.6	$6.5	$7.4	$7.0	$9.0	$12.7
LEAP	$0.1	$0.2	$0.1	$0.1	$0.1	$0	$0.1
SEOG	$0.9	$0.9	$0.7	$0.7	$0.7	$0.7	$0.8
Other	$20.5	$10.1	$3.1	$2.4	$3.3	$3.6	$5.9
Loans	$6.4	$16.4	$18.0	$20.7	$36.9	$44.4	$68.6
Subsidized Stafford	$4.6	$14.6	$15.1	$14.9	$21.0	$21.0	$28.8
Unsub Stafford	$0	$0	$0	$0	$11.1	$17.3	$28.8
PLUS	$0	$0	$0	$1.4	$3.0	$4.7	$9.7
Other	$1.8	$1.8	$2.4	$4.4	$1.7	$1.4	$1.3
Perkins Loans	$1.7	$1.6	$1.3	$1.3	$1,3	$1.3	$1.1
Tax Benefits	$0	$0	$0	$0	$0	$4.7	$6.0
Work Study	$1.1	$1.6	$1.2	$1.1	$1.0	$1.1	$1.2
State Grants	$1.8	$1.9	$2.4	$2.8	$3.9	$5.4	$6.8
Institutional Grants	$4.2	$3.8	$5.4	$9.1	$13.4	$18.5	$24.4
Private & Employer Grants	NA	NA	NA	$3.0	$3.6	$6.6	$9.3
Total Student Aid	**$37.4**	**$39.6**	**$36.7**	**$46.6**	**$69.2**	**$93.4**	**$134.8**
Private Loans	NA	NA	NA	NA	$1.7	$5.1	$17.3
Total Funds	$37.4	$39.6	$36.7	$46.6	$71.0	$98.6	$152.1

Source: The College Board, *Trends in Student Aid 2006*, Table 2.

students from families in the lowest 20 percent of the income distribution receive Pell Grants, as do 40 percent of those in the second income quintile. Seven percent of those in the middle fifth of the income distribution and almost none with higher family incomes receive Pell (NCES, 2004). Since the late 1980s, almost 60 percent of Pell recipients have been independent (College Board, 2006). It is difficult to know the family backgrounds of these students, but to qualify as independent undergraduates, they must be either over the age of 24, married, with dependents, veterans, orphans, or wards of the court.

Instead of increasing the funding for Pell Grants, in 2006 Congress instituted two new grant programs for a subset of Pell recipients and introduced an academic component to the determination of funding levels. In the program's first year, Academic Competitiveness Grants provide $750 in additional funding to first year Pell recipients who have completed a rigorous high school curriculum. These students are eligible for $1,300 in additional funding in their second year of college if they maintain a B average. The SMART Grant Program provides up to $4,000 a year for third- and fourth-year Pell Grant recipients majoring in science, mathematics, engineering, and selected languages. How many students will be supported by these grants is not yet clear, but the bureaucracy and complexity surrounding them for the government, institutions, and students is already evident (Burd, 2006).

In 2005–06, the maximum Pell Grant of $4,050 covered 33 percent of the tuition, fee, room, and board charges for the average in-state public four-year college student, down from 57 percent in 1985–86, 35 percent in 1995–96, and 39 percent in 2000–01. Before the $260 increase legislated in 2007, the Pell Grant maximum was last increased in 2003–04, when it went up by $50. And total Pell funding actually declined from 2004–05 to 2005–06, largely because of a technical update to the eligibility formula that reduced measured need for many applicants.

There is considerable evidence that grant dollars awarded to students, particularly those from low-income families, can have a significant positive impact on the probability that they will enroll in college (Kane, 2003; Dynarski, 2003). Because grants are more effective in increasing access than other forms of aid, the role of grants in the array of federal aid programs is particularly important (Heller, 1997). Though it did little more than keep pace with inflation between 1985 and 1995, federal grant aid grew almost 80 percent in inflation adjusted dollars between 1995 and 2005, only slightly more slowly than federal loans. As Table 39.2 reveals, federal grant aid did, however, constitute a much larger share of federal aid before 1993–94, when the unsubsidized Stafford student loan program (described below) was added to existing federal aid programs.

More recently, the implementation of federal tuition tax credits in 1998 and tax deductions in 2002 decreased the share of total federal student aid delivered in the form of grants. The tax system also provides subsidies to families that save for college in specified accounts and allows the deduction of some student loan interest payments. Unlike Pell Grants, these tax benefits are not targeted at low-income students. In fact, tax benefits favor middle- and upper-income families over lower-income families. About 46 percent of the benefit of the federal education tax credits goes to taxpayers with incomes below $50,000 and 54 percent goes to higher-income taxpayers. Taxpayers can choose between the education tax credits and the tuition tax deduction, which provides larger benefits to filers in higher marginal tax brackets and goes farther up the income scale than the tax credit. Only 22 percent of the benefit of the tuition tax deduction goes to taxpayers with incomes below $50,000; 41 percent goes to those with incomes between $100,000 and $160,000 (College Board, 2006).

Although politicians frequently promote increased tax credits or deductions as part of an agenda focused on educational opportunities, these policies are actually directed at making college more easily affordable for the middle class. The strengths and weaknesses of the federal tuition tax credits and deductions provide useful insights into the fundamentals of sound student

TABLE 39.2
Composition of Federal Student Aid, 1975-76 to 2005-06

	75–76	*80–81*	*85–86*	*90–91*	*95–96*	*00–01*	*05–06*
Grants	76%	47%	34%	31%	22%	20%	20%
Loans	20%	48%	62%	65%	76%	71%	73%
Tax Benefits	0%	0%	0%	0%	0%	8%	6%
Work	3%	5%	4%	3%	2%	2%	1%

Source: The College Board, *Trends in Student Aid 2006.*

aid policy. The downside is clear. Because only households with positive federal income tax liability are eligible for these subsidies, they are no help to the poor. Moreover, there is no evidence that the credits and deductions have any measurable impact on college enrollment rates (Jackson, 2006; Long, 2004). Instead, they subsidize students whose college-going behavior is unaltered. Timing is another problem. Reduced tax liabilities put money in people's pockets in the spring of the year following the calendar year in which tuition was paid, sometimes more than a full year later. For students lacking the funds to pay the bills, another solution is necessary.

Unlike other student aid programs, the tax benefits cover only tuition and fees, not room, board, or other education-related expenses. The fact that tuition and fees are a relatively small proportion of the expenses incurred by students at low-price institutions such as community colleges exacerbates the skewing of the benefits away from the neediest students. Also problematic in the current system, taxpayers must choose between the credits and the deduction—not an obvious choice for many. Eligibility requirements vary considerably, and families face a major challenge selecting the strategy that will help them most. Government estimates suggest that about a third of eligible tax payers do not claim the credits and deductions (GAO, 2005). It is important to note, however, that the current process of applying for other federal aid, including Pell and other need-based grants, as well as student loans, is itself quite complex. Students must complete a lengthy form, reporting detailed financial and other information. There is no simple way for them to predict how much aid they will receive until just months before they are due to enroll. Many who would be eligible for grant aid fail to apply (ACE, 2006).

In addition to the timing problem associated with subsidies delivered through the tax system, grant aid that is delivered to the student or the institution at the time of enrollment is a much more direct and transparent means of providing funding than is the tax code. That said, there are political advantages to the tax system. Unlike traditional student aid funds, tax expenditures do not need to pass through the appropriations process. Tax benefits will remain in effect unless they are repealed (Jackson, 2006). The exclusion of low-income students from the benefits could be rectified by making the credits refundable, and the inclusion of middle-income students has definite advantages. Certainly, families with incomes around $100,000—the highest eligible for the credits—struggle to pay the full price of a college education. Moreover, as is the case in other public policy areas, public support for federal subsidies to college students is greatly strengthened by the broad nature of these benefits (Skocpol & Leone, 2001). Unlike policies such as Pell that are narrowly targeted at those with the highest levels of financial need, tax benefits have a large constituency among the voting population. In 2005–06, about 8.9 million tax filers had their tax liabilities reduced by tuition tax credits and deductions, while about 5.4 million students received Pell Grants (College Board, 2006).

In sum, current tax credits and deductions are not well-designed. But it does not follow that the tax code cannot be an effective means of delivering student aid. Grant aid awarded directly to students is potentially more transparent, but the current federal system makes it difficult for students to predict in advance, and involves a complicated application process and diverse eligibility criteria.

The federal government also provides a small amount of funding to institutions to distribute to their needy students. The $3 billion of campus-based aid in 2005–06 consisted of $771 million in Supplemental Educational Opportunity Grants (SEOG), with the remainder about equally divided between Federal Work-Study and Perkins Loan funds. In all of these programs, institutional funds must be added to the federal funds, so the total dollars awarded exceed the federal amounts. The federal funding formula for these programs combines a measure of the financial need of students on individual campuses with a guaranteed base of funding that favors older, better-established institutions. Whereas community college students receive about 32 percent of Pell funds, they receive only 9 percent of campus-based funds (College Board, 2006b). Proposals to modify the funding formula are frequent, but have not passed Congress.

STATE GOVERNMENTS

The major contribution from the state coffers to the funding of higher education comes in the form of subsidies to institutions. In addition to improving educational quality, institutional subsidies serve to lower the prices that students are required to pay. There is a clear inverse relationship between state subsidies and tuition and fee charges at public colleges and universities (College Board, 2006a). A critical difference between institutional appropriations and direct aid to students is that the institutional subsidy is shared across all enrolled students. The institutional approach precludes the targeting of subsidies towards students whose college enrollment and persistence behavior is most price-sensitive. In theory, institutions that tend to enroll less affluent student bodies could be more heavily subsidized than others. But in fact, this seldom occurs, as it is the more affluent students who are most concentrated at the flagship universities that provide relatively high-cost education, and it is the lower-income students who are disproportionately represented at community colleges, where faculty are paid less, campus facilities are less elaborate, and the cost of education is lower (Baum & Payea, 2004; Commonfund Institute, 2006; NCES, 2005, table 341).

Public appropriations are related to student aid, because when relatively low state funding leads to high tuition, higher levels of student aid are required to preserve affordability. Economists have long argued that a high tuition-high aid model is most efficient, but others point to the political risks involved in this approach. There is no guarantee that tuition increases will be accompanied by increases in need-based aid and even when they are, the public response is frequently to the sticker, rather than to the net price students actually pay (Turner, 2005). Overall, states distributed $6.8 billion in grant aid to postsecondary students in 2005–06. This aid constitutes about 12 percent of the total grant aid students receive, and a slightly higher percentage of the grant aid undergraduates receive (College Board, 2006).

All but two states have grant programs that award funds directly to students to supplement the institutional subsidies they receive in the form of low tuition at in-state institutions, but states have taken a wide variety of approaches towards student aid. Some states rely heavily on grant aid. South Carolina spends 34 percent of the amount it appropriates for higher education operations on student grants. Georgia, New York, and Vermont all spend between 21 and 24 percent. At the other end of the spectrum, grant aid equals 10 percent of appropriations in Michigan and Minnesota, and less than 1 percent in Alabama, Alaska, Arizona, Hawaii, South Dakota, and Wyoming. It is difficult to find consistency even across states with similar approaches to tuition.

TABLE 39.3
State Grant Aid: Percentage Not Based on Financial Need, 1984–85 to 2004–05

	Percent non-need-based
1984–85	9%
1989–90	11%
1994–95	13%
1999–00	22%
2004–05	27%

Source: The College Board, *Trends in Student Aid 2006.*

Among high tuition states, New Jersey granted $957 per student in 2004–05, compared to a national average of $562, but New Hampshire awarded only $76 per student. Among low-tuition states, New Mexico awarded $724, while Wyoming awarded only $7 per student in 2004–05 (NASSGAP, 2005).

It is not only the level of grant funding, combined with the level of tuition and fees, that determines college affordability, but also how the funds are distributed. As recently as 1993, eligibility for 90 percent of state grant dollars was determined on the basis of financial need. As indicated in Table 39.3, that percentage had declined to 81 percent by 1998, and to 73 percent by 2004 (NASSGAP, 2005). In 1993, Georgia introduced the Hope Scholarship program, which promised free tuition and fees at state universities to students who graduated from a Georgia high school with at least a B average. While a family income cap of $100,000 was initially imposed, that restriction was lifted in 1995. In 2005, 99 percent of freshmen at the University of Georgia and 40 percent at public institutions statewide paid no tuition and fees (Fischer, 2006). Because of the eligibility criteria, middle- and upper-income students are more likely than lower-income students to receive these grants (Cornwell-Mustard, 2006; Heller & Marin, 2002).

Many states have followed Georgia's example, each with their own variation on the themes of basing awards on academic credentials and letting high school students know from an early age that if they meet the criteria, they will have the funds to enroll.

Not surprisingly, these merit-based state grant programs are controversial. Opinions differ about the extent to which college enrollment rates—as opposed to enrollment specifically at in-state institutions—are actually improved by these programs (Binder, Ganderton, & Hutchens, 2002; Binder & Ganderton, 2004; Cornwell & Mustard, 2002, 2004; Dynarski, 2000, 2004). There is also evidence that the programs in some states exacerbate the gaps in enrollment rates across racial/ethnic groups (Dynarski, 2004; Heller & Rasmussen, 2002). On the other hand, there is widespread support for public programs that provide guarantees to low-income students early on that they will be funded—thereby encouraging them to prepare themselves academically for college (Dynarski & Scott-Clayton, 2006; Heller, 2006). The questions about state merit grant programs relate primarily to their targeting and also to their cost (Heller, 2004a; Marin, 2002).

Merit-based grant programs are not the only recent innovation in state approaches to student aid. Some states, most notably Indiana and Oklahoma, have made considerable strides in developing grant programs designed to encourage economically disadvantaged students to prepare academically for college. The Indiana 21st Century Scholars program and the Oklahoma Higher Learning Access Program (OHLAP) program provide academic support and college counseling, combined with assurances that when students graduate from high school the funds they require to make college a realistic possibility will be available to them. While more evidence is required before the success of these efforts in increasing college enrollment and success will be clear, preliminary findings are encouraging (St. John, 2004; St. John et al., 2006).

A unique program is the Tuition Assistance Program in Washington, D.C. Because there is only one public four-year institution in the District of Columbia, the federal government provides subsidies for students to enroll at public institutions or historically black colleges and universities anywhere in the country, or at only private colleges in the Washington area. This program has dramatically increased college enrollment rates among D.C. high school graduates (Kane, 2004).

The priorities reflected in state policies vary widely. Georgia and South Carolina are examples of states that have very high levels of grant aid per student but virtually no need-based aid. Other states have strong commitments to need-based grant aid for students. New York has the highest level of grant aid per student in the country, and 100 percent of it is need-based. California also has a generous need-based grant program—combined with relatively low levels of tuition and fees (College Board, 2006a; NASSGAP, 2006).

The differing economies, populations, and histories of the states make it unlikely that they will develop higher education funding policies that are consistent enough to significantly diminish the disparities in educational opportunities available to residents of different states. However, the federal government already plays a role, and could play a much larger role in the future, in influencing state student aid policies. In 1974–75, the federal government began a program of matching funds for need-based state grants. Always a small program, funding for the Leveraging Educational Assistance Partnership Program (LEAP, originally, State Student Incentive Grants) peaked in constant dollars in 1979–80 and is now back down to its original level of about $70 million in 2005 dollars—about $6 per undergraduate student. The President's budget has repeatedly proposed eliminating LEAP funds. The apparent argument is that since most states have need-based grant programs, the federal government no longer needs to provide an incentive for their development. On the other hand, it is logical that if the price of providing grant aid to students with financial need is lowered, states will be more likely to put more of their dollars into need-based aid. Accordingly, members of Congress and student aid advocates frequently propose expanding and strengthening federal subsidies to states, in order to encourage better targeting of state student aid funds (Baum, 2002; Reed, 2005).

INSTITUTIONAL GRANTS TO STUDENTS

In 2005–06, colleges and universities awarded about $6 billion more in grant aid to their students than did the federal government. As is the case with state funding, grant aid supplements general institutional subsidies that lower tuition for all students. Public institutions receive funds for student aid from state and local appropriations and, increasingly, from private giving (see Table 39.4). Private colleges and universities rely almost entirely on private sources to supplement tuition and fee revenues. Institutional grant programs constitute discounts to published tuition and fee levels and allow institutions to charge different prices to different students, a process known to economists as price discrimination. Some institutions grant discounts to almost all of the students they enroll because they believe that students respond more positively to an individual award than they would to a lower across-the-board tuition price (Avery & Hoxby, 2003).

As is the case with federal and state student aid, the proportion of institutional grant aid that is distributed on the basis of financial need has decreased over the past decade (NCES, 2004). Institutional grants were originally designed to enable students who cannot afford to pay the published price to enroll and to increase racial/ethnic and socioeconomic diversity on campus. The goals have expanded to include strategic enrollment objectives, such as raising the academic

TABLE 39.4
Institutional Grant Aid: Percentage Not Based on Financial Need, 1992–93 and 2003–04

	*Percent Non-Need-Based**	
	1992–93	*2003–04*
Private Nonprofit Four-Year by 2003–04Tuition& Fees		
< $15,200	63%	66%
$15,200-$19,399	42%	68%
$19,400-$25,349	31%	54%
$25,350 +	11%	25%
Public Four-Year	63%	65%
Public Two-Year	64%	55%

*Non-need based aid is defined as aid distributed without regard to financial circumstances. Some recipients of non-need-based aid do have financial need.
Source: The College Board, *Trends in Student Aid 2006.* Data from National Postsecondary Student Aid Study.

or athletic profile of the student body, increasing the size of the entering class, or maximizing net revenue. The new uses of institutional aid are more likely to affect students' choice among institutions than to affect students who otherwise would be unlikely to enroll in college at all. While these non-need-based scholarships provide significant funding to students who could afford to enroll without them, but some of the funds do help to meet need, filling the gap between the amount students and families can afford to pay and the cost of attendance. The definition of non-need aid is therefore more meaningful if it is narrowed to include only those dollars awarded to students without documented financial need—or beyond the amount of need, as measured by need analysis formulas.

The practice of tuition discounting or price discrimination—charging different students different prices for the same educational opportunities—is a longstanding feature of private higher education institutions. Institutional grant aid has also become more common at public colleges and universities in recent years, with the percentage of full-time undergraduates in public four-year colleges and universities receiving institutional grant aid increasing from 16 percent in 1992–93, to 23 percent in 1999–00, and 28 percent in 2003–04. Fourteen percent of full-time public two-year college students received institutional grants in 2003–04, up from 10 percent in 1992–93, but down slightly from 16 percent in 1999–00 (Berkner, 2005; Horn, 2002). This trend is partially due to a combination of rising tuition prices, which exacerbate financial need, and a concern over access to public institutions for low- and moderate-income students. That a significant portion of the institutional grant aid at public colleges and universities goes to students without financial need, however, suggests that it also reflects attempts by these institutions to compete for more students, or for more desirable students. At private four-year and public two-year colleges, on average about two-thirds of the grants go towards meeting need. At public four-year institutions, only 40 percent of institutional grants go towards meeting need, while, on average, about 60 percent of the funds are awarded to students who, according to the need analysis formula, could afford to enroll without this assistance (Baum & Lapovsky, 2006). Of course, higher tuition levels at private colleges make many students who would not have need in the public sector "needy."

Differences across private institutions are important for understanding the relationship between institutional aid and college access. In high-priced private colleges, which tend to enroll relatively few low-income students, grant aid is inversely related to family income, with the lower-income students receiving the largest subsidies. On the other hand, at lower-priced private colleges, which enroll much larger proportions of low- and moderate-income students, there is a greater focus on the strategic use of discounts to meet enrollment goals (College Board, 2006b). These institutions are less well-endowed than the more expensive colleges and almost never have the option of meeting full need for all of their students. Rather, it is vital to their financial stability that they enroll more students who can bring tuition dollars to their campuses. The result is that those low- and moderate-income students who are fortunate, motivated, and talented enough to gain admission to highly selective institutions are likely to be provided with generous funding. The highly publicized programs of elite privates and flagship publics, including Harvard, Princeton, Stanford, University of Pennsylvania, University of North Carolina-Chapel Hill, and University of Virginia, among others, remove the financial barriers for these select few students. But they do not and cannot solve the problems facing the vast majority of students from similar backgrounds (Tebbs & Turner, 2006).

Private Grant Aid

Grant aid from private sources, including employers, foundations, and other organizations, has increased from about 12 percent of total grant aid in 1995–96, to 15 percent a decade later (College Board, 2006). While foundations and other scholarship organizations frequently target their awards to needy students, employer subsidies are much more likely to go either to adults with significant earnings of their own or to the children of employees of financially secure organizations.

LOANS

Total grant aid to postsecondary students grew by 89 percent in constant dollars between 1995–96 and 2005–06, and total grant aid to undergraduates grew by 144 percent. Grant aid per full-time equivalent (FTE) student increased by 43 percent for undergraduates and by 46 percent for all students over the decade (College Board, 2006). Nonetheless, the cost of attending college has grown more rapidly, and has far exceeded growth in incomes, with the possible exception of families at the upper reaches of the income distribution. The additional grant dollars fill only a fraction of the need generated by the rapid growth in college prices. As a result, students are increasingly turning to loan financing.

Much discussion of student debt focuses on the burden of repayment and the danger that some students will be discouraged from participating in higher education, while others will be forced by excessive debt to abandon career dreams in favor of more lucrative occupations (Draut, 2005). However, analysis of borrowers in repayment generally indicates that student loans are an effective form of student aid that has a positive impact on educational opportunities and that for the majority of borrowers the debt burden is manageable. Still, there are significant minorities of students, including in particular those from low-income families, for whom education debt is a real burden (Baum & O'Malley, 2002). Moreover, average debt levels have increased dramatically over the past decade, and if the price of higher education continues to increase rapidly without commensurate growth in grant aid, there is little doubt that problems with student debt will become more widespread (College Board, 2006).

The federal government provides almost $70 billion annually in education loans. There are two different financing systems for these loans. About 80 percent of federal education loans for students and parents are issued through the Federal Family Education Loan (FFEL) Program, under which the federal government guarantees loans made by banks and other private lenders. Other loans carry similar terms and regulated interest rates but are financed directly by the federal government. Each institution participates in either the FFEL or the Direct Loan program, so individual students do not face this choice. Several government reports have indicated that the cost to the government of lending under the Direct Loan program is much lower than the cost of subsidizing banks to lend under the guaranteed loan program (CBO, 2005; GAO, 2005). Because of complexities in the accounting system, however, controversy about the comparative costs of the two programs is ongoing (Burd, 2005).

The composition of student loans has changed dramatically in recent years, as shown in Table 39.5. A decade ago, subsidized Stafford loans, on which the federal government pays the interest while students are in school, constituted 57 percent of education borrowing. By 2005–06, that proportion had declined to 34 percent. Part of the decline resulted from the increase in borrowing under the unsubsidized Stafford program, which is available to all students regardless of their financial circumstances. Instituted in 1993, this program accounted for 27 percent of student loans in 1995–96 and 34 percent 10 years later. Parent borrowing under the Parent Loans for Undergraduate Students (PLUS) program also increased, from 7 percent to 11 percent of the total, but the real story is in private loans. Relatively insignificant a decade ago, non-federal loans from banks and other private lenders now compose about 20 percent of education borrowing. Eighty percent of the $17.3 billion in private loans issued in 2005–06 went to undergraduate students (College Board, 2006).

We have limited information about private student loans, which involve no subsidy at all and are not actually part of the student aid system. We do know that, unlike the Stafford program, under which dependent undergraduates can borrow a maximum of $23,000 over their undergraduate careers, private education loans can be as high as the cost of attendance less financial aid received. Students do not have to complete the potentially daunting Free Application for Federal Student Aid (FAFSA) forms to get these private loans. Unlike federal loans, private loans have differential interest rates based on credit scores and no limits on the interest rates that can be charged. The deferment and forbearance provisions of federal loans do not apply to private loans. In other words, private lending is serving an important function in providing liquidity for students who might otherwise not be able to enroll in the college of their choice, but these loans do not represent public policy. Rather, they reflect a response on the part of for-profit industry to a very real demand (IHEP, 2006).

As they become more prevalent, these loans will have a significant unintended impact on the effectiveness of student aid policies. Proposals aimed at reducing the burden of student debt frequently focus on lower interest rates, income-contingent loan repayment plans, or loan for-

TABLE 39.5
Types of Education Borrowing, 1990–91 to 2005–06

	1990–91	*1995–96*	*2000–01*	*2005–06*
Stafford Subsidized	91%	57%	44%	34%
Stafford Unsubsidized	0%	30%	36%	34%
PLUS	9%	8%	10%	11%
Nonfederal	0%	5%	11%	20%
TOTAL	100%	100%	100%	100%

giveness programs. But these benefits apply only to federal loans and will become less relevant as greater portions of student debt are not covered. If current limits on Stafford Loan borrowing, which increased slightly for 2007–08 for the first time since 1992, are not raised, there will be little chance of reversing this trend.

Like the movement towards federal tax benefits that exclude the truly needy, the increase in the awarding of state grants based on academic credentials without regard to financial circumstances, and the strategic use of institutional grant dollars for enrollment management purposes, the movement towards private student loans has deepened the gulf between the haves and the have-nots.

THE SYSTEM OVERALL

The student aid system of the United States is in important respects a success story. Responsibility for financing higher education is divided among students, families, state and local governments, colleges and universities, and the private sector. Consistent with the structure of the U.S. economy, there is no master plan for the division of the burden, but an invisible hand has created a partnership that has supported an increase in the college enrollment rate of 18 to 24-year-old high school graduates, from 34 percent in 1967 to 46 percent in 2004 (NCES, 2005, table 184), in addition to a sharp increase over the 1970s in the number of older college students (NCES, 2005, table 172). Much of the aid is in the form of grants that students do not need to repay, and a large federal student loan program provides access to funds for students without credit histories. The majority of these students will be able to repay their loans without undue burden out of the increased earnings that will result from their educational pursuits.

Nonetheless, sizeable gaps in college participation and success persist across students from different socioeconomic backgrounds, and there is no doubt that financial aid does have the potential to significantly affect college participation rates (see, for example, Kane, 2003, 2004; Dynarski, 2003). More money for existing student aid programs would help, as would strategies for reducing the rate of growth in both the cost of producing quality postsecondary education and in the prices institutions charge for that education. But the evidence also suggests that student aid programs could be improved in ways that would generate greater effectiveness for the dollars being spent. The current system allows many students to fall through the cracks and creates an unnecessary bureaucratic and logistical burden for those who do manage to take advantage of it (Dynarski & Scott-Clayton, 2007). Moreover, it directs many dollars in pure subsidies to students whose behavior is not measurably affected by those funds (Baum & Lapovsky, 2006; Heller, 1997; Long 2004).

Policy analysts have proposed a variety of modifications to existing student aid programs, but there are some general areas of broad consensus.

1. Simplify the system. There has been considerable focus on the need to simplify the application process for federal student aid (ACSFA, 2005; Dynarski & Scott-Clayton, 2006). Some argue for fewer separate programs (National Commission, 1993; Spellings Commission, 2006); a more important argument may be that the rules for the different programs should be more consistent. Permanent residents qualify for Pell Grants but not for Academic Competitiveness Grants. Less than half-time students are eligible for Pell Grants, but not for Stafford Loans. Federal grants can be applied to room and board expenses but federal tax credits and deductions cannot. It is unreasonable to expect students and families to be able to successfully navigate this system.

2. Better targeting. Some aid policies may be explicitly designed to encourage study in particular disciplines or to be part of the compensation for military service. But the basic framework for efficient public policy suggests that policies must change behavior in order to meet the goal of increasing educational opportunities. Tax deductions concentrated on households with incomes above $100,000 a year are unlikely to have this effect. General grant programs requiring high standardized test scores are unlikely to have this effect. Straightforward income-based eligibility criteria might go a long way towards solving this problem, but many argue that not all subsidies should be distributed on the basis of pre-college financial circumstances. Earnings levels after the completion of the investment in higher education should also be taken into consideration through programs such as income-contingent repayment plans that subsidize former students whose incomes are too low to support their debt burden (Baum & Schwartz, 2006; Kane, 1999, 2007).
3. Focus on persistence as well as access. Assuring young people from low-income backgrounds that the money will be waiting for them if they are qualified for college is likely to increase the number of young people who graduate from high school prepared to continue their studies (Heller, 2006). But progress in college enrollment rates over time has not been matched by progress in persistence rates. The form and design of student aid programs could be more tailored towards supporting degree completion, rather than just getting students in the door.

In 1961, President John F. Kennedy, proposing federal grants to needy students, told Congress, "We must assure ourselves that every talented young person who has the ability to pursue a program of higher education will be able to do so if he chooses, regardless of his financial means" (Kennedy, 1961). The equity considerations underlying this statement provided the basis for much of the legislation creating student aid programs (Gladieux & Wolanin, 1976). More recently, the efficiency considerations of increasing educational opportunities have also received attention (Baum & Payea, 2004).

We have developed a complex and expensive system of subsidies for college students based on these equity and efficiency arguments. There is strong evidence that while these programs have made important contributions to increased participation in higher education, more effective policies could narrow the persistent gaps in educational attainment across socioeconomic groups.

NOTES

1. A tuition-sensitivity provision in the current Pell eligibility criteria affects only a small number of students attending the lowest-price community colleges, diminishing the size of the grants they receive.

REFERENCES

Advisory Committee on Student Financial Assistance [ACSFA] (2005). *The Student Aid Gauntlet: Making Access to College Simple and Certain*. Washington, DC: Author.

Advisory Committee on Student Financial Assistance [ACSFA] (2006). *Mortgaging Our Future: How Financial Barriers to College Undercut America's Global Competitiveness*. Washington, DC: Author.

American Council on Education [ACE] (2006). Missed Opportunities Revisited: New Information on Student Who Do Not Apply for Financial Aid. www.acenet.edu/ AM/Template.cfm?Section=CPA&Template=/CM/ContentDisplay.cfm&ContentFileID=1374. Accessed February 1, 2007.

Avery, Christopher & Hoxby, Caroline Minter (2003). "Do and Should Financial Aid Packages Affect Students' College Choices?" National Bureau of Economic Research Paper #9482.

Baum, Sandy (2002). "The Financial Aid Partnership: Strengthening the Federal Government's Leadership Role." College Board Research Report.

Baum, Sandy & Lapovsky, Lucie (2006). *Tuition Discounting: Not Just a Private College Practice.*

Baum, Sandy & O'Malley, Marie (2002). *College on Credit: How Borrowers Perceive their Education Debt.* Braintree, MA: Nellie Mae.

Baum, Sandy & Payea, Kathleen (2004). *Education Pays: The Benefits of Higher Education for Individuals and Society.* New York: The College Board.

Baum, Sandy & Schwartz, Saul (2006). *How Much Debt is Too Much? Defining Benchmarks for Manageable Student Debt.* New York: The College Board.

Berkner, Lutz, et al. (2005), *Undergraduate Financial Aid Estimates for 2003–04 by Type of Institution,* National Center for Education Statistics, 2005–163.

Binder, M., & Ganderton, P. T. (2004). The New Mexico Lottery Scholarship: Does it Help Minority and Low-Income Students? In D. E. Heller & P. Marin (Eds.), *State Merit Scholarship Programs and Racial Inequality,* 101–122. Cambridge, MA: The Civil Rights Project at Harvard University.

Binder, M., Ganderton, P. T., & Hutchens, K. (2002). Incentive Effects of New Mexico's Merit Based State Scholarship Program: Who Responds and How? In D. E. Heller and P. Marin (Eds.), *Who Should We Help? The Negative Social Consequences of Merit Scholarships,* 41–56. Cambridge, MA: The Civil Rights Project at Harvard University.

Burd, Steven (2005). "Lenders Mislead in Battle over Cost of Direct Lending, Budget Experts Say." *Chronicle of Higher Education.* July 8, A20.

Burd, Steven (2006). "Rules for New Student Grants Put Burden on Colleges." *Chronicle of Higher Education.* November 2, A25.

Cameron, Stephen & Heckman, James (2001). "The Dynamics of Educational Attainment for Black, Hispanic, and White Males, *Journal of Political Economy,* 109(2): 455–449.

The College Board (2005). *Education Pays: Update.* Washington, DC: Author.

The College Board (2006a). *Trends in College Pricing 2006.* Washington, DC: Author.

The College Board (2006b). *Trends in Student Aid 2006.* Washington, DC: Author.

Commonfund Institute (2004). *HEPI: Higher Education Price Index 2006 Update.* http://www.commonfund.org. Accessed February 1, 2007.

Congressional Budget Office [CBO] (2005). *Subsidy Estimates for Guaranteed and Direct Student Loans.* Congress of the United States.

Cornwell, C. & Mustard, D. (2002). Race and the Effects of Georgia's HOPE Scholarship. In D. E. Heller & P. Marin (Eds.), *Who Should We Help? The Negative Social Consequences of Merit Scholarships,* 57–72. Cambridge, MA: The Civil Rights Project at Harvard University.

Cornwell, C. & Mustard, D. B. (2004). Georgia's HOPE Scholarship and Minority and Low-Income Students: Program Effects and Proposed Reforms. In D. E. Heller & P. Marin (Eds.), *State Merit Scholarship Programs and Racial Inequality,* 77–100. Cambridge, MA: The Civil Rights Project at Harvard University.

Cornwell-Mustard Hope Scholarship Page (2006). http://www.terry.uga.edu/hope/. Accessed February 1, 2007.

Draut, Tamara (2006). *Strapped: Why America's Twenty- and Thirty-Somethings Can't Get Ahead.* New York: Doubleday.

Dynarski, Susan (2000). "Hope for Whom? Financial Aid for the Middle Class and Its Impact on College Attendance" *National Bureau of Economic Research Working Paper* 7756.

Dynarski, Susan (2003). "Does Aid Matter? Measuring the Effect of Student Aid on College Attendance and Completion," *American Economic Review,* April.

Dynarski, Susan (2004). "The New Merit Aid." In Hoxby, C. M., ed. *College Choices: The Economics of Which College, When College, and How to Pay For It.* Chicago: University of Chicago Press.

Dynarski, Susan & Scott-Clayton, Judith (2006). "The Cost of Complexity in Federal Student Aid: Lessons from Optimal Tax Theory and Behavioral Economics." Cambridge, MA: Kennedy School of Government.

Ellwood, David & Kane, Thomas (2000). "Who is Getting a College Education? Family Background and the Growing Gaps in Enrollment." In S. Danzier and J. Waldfogel, eds. *Securing the Future.* New York: Russell Sage.

Fischer, Karin (2006). "It's Hard to Compete with Free", *Chronicle of Higher Education*, October 6, A30.

Gladieux, Lawrence E. & Wolanin, Thomas R. (1976). *Congress and the Colleges: The National Politics of Higher Education.* Lexington, MA: D.C. Heath and Co.

Heller, Donald.E. (1997). "Student Price Response in Higher Education: An Update to Leslie and Brinkman." *Journal of Higher Education,* 68(6):624–659.

Heller, Donald. E. (2004a). The devil is in the details: An analysis of eligibility criteria for merit scholarships in Massachusetts. In D. E. Heller & P. Marin (Eds.), *State Merit Scholarship Programs and Racial Inequality*. Cambridge, MA: The Civil Rights Project at Harvard University.

Heller, Donald. E. (2006). "Early Notification of Financial Aid Eligibility." *American Behavioral Scientist.* 49(12):1719–1738.

Heller, Donald.E. & Marin, Patricia (2002). *Who Should We Help? The Negative Social Consequences of Merit Aid and Scholarships.* Harvard University Civil Rights Project.. http://www.civilrightsproject.harvard.edu/research/meritaid/fullreport.php. Accessed February 1, 2007.

Heller, Donald.E. & Rasmussen, C.J. (2002). "Merit Scholarships and College Access: Evidence from Florida and Michigan." In D.E. Heller and P. Marin (Eds.) *Who Should We Help? The Negative Social Consequences of Merit Scholarship.* Cambridge, MA: The Civil Rights Project at Harvard University, pp. 25–40.

Horn, Laura, et al. (2002). *What Students Pay for College: Changes in Net Price of College Attendance* Between *1992–93 and 1999–00,* National Center for Education Statistics, 2002-174.

Institute for Higher Education Policy [IHEP] (2006). *The Future of Private Loans: Who is Borrowing and Why?* Washington: IHEP.

Jackson, Pamela J. (2006). *Higher Education Tax Credits.* Congressional Research Service. http://www.opencrs.com/rpts/RL32507_20060117.pdf. Accessed February 1, 2007.

Kane, Thomas J. (1999). *The Price of Admission.* Washington, DC: Brookings Institution.

Kane, Thomas J. (2003). *A Quasi-Experiment Estimate of the Impact of Financial Aid on College-Going*, National Bureau of Economic Research Working Paper 9703, May.

Kane, Thomas J. (2004). "Evaluating the Impact of the D.C. Tuition Assistance Grant Program." NBER Working Paper No. W10658.

Kane, Thomas J. (2007). "Reshaping the Student Loan Programs to Fit the Careers of Young College Graduates." The Hamilton Project.

Kennedy, John F. (1961). "Special Message to the Congress on Education." February 20. http://www.presidency.ucsb.edu/ws/index.php. Accessed February 1, 2007.

Long, Bridget Terry (2004). "The Impact of Federal Tax Credits for Higher Education." In Hoxby, C. M., ed. *College Choices: The Economics of Which College, When College, and How to Pay For It.* Chicago: University of Chicago Press.

Marin, P. (2002). Merit scholarships and the outlook for equal opportunity in higher education. In D. E. Heller & P. Marin (Eds.), *Who Should We Help? The Negative Social Consequences of Merit Scholarships,* 109–114. Cambridge, MA: The Civil Rights Project at Harvard University.

National Association of State Scholarship and Grants Programs [NASSGAP] (2005). *36th Annual Report on State Sponsored Student Financial Aid.* http://www.nassgap.org. Accessed February 1, 2007.

National Center for Education Statistics [NCES] (2004). National Postsecondary Student Aid Study (NPSAS). DAS Analysis System.

National Commission on Responsibilities for Financing Postsecondary Education (1993). *Making College Affordable Again.* Washington, DC.

Reed, Jack (2005). S1029. A bill to amend the Higher Education Act of 1965 to expand college access and increase college persistence, and for other purposes. http:// thomas.loc.gov/ gi-bin/bdquery/D?d109:44:./temp/~bd4NKB:@@@D&summ2=m&. Accessed February 1, 2007.

Skocpol, Theda & Leone, Richard C. (2001). *The Missing Middle: Working Families and the Future of American Social Policy.* New York: W.W. Norton.

Spellings Commission (2006). *A Test of Leadership: Charting the Future of U.S. Higher Education.* U.S. Department of Education.

St. John, Edward (2004). "The Impact of Financial Aid guarantees on Enrollment and Persistence: Evidence from Research on Indiana's Twenty-first Century Scholars and Washington State Achievers Programs" in D.E. Heller and P. Marin, ed. *State Merit Scholarship Programs and racial Inequality.* Cambridge, MA: Harvard Civil Rights Project at Harvard University, pp. 123–140.

St. John, Edward P. et al. (2006). Postsecondary Encouragement and Academic Success: Degree Attainment by Indiana's Twenty-first Century Scholars. In St. John, E.P. (ed.) *Readings on Equal Education*: vol. 21. *Public Policy and equal Educational Opportunity: School Reforms, Postsecondary Encouragement and State Policies on Postsecondary Education*, 257–291. New York: AMS Press, Inc.

Stoll, Adam (2005). *The Administration of Federal Student Loan Programs: Background and Provisions.* Congressional Research Service. U.S. Library of Congress.

Tebbs, Jeffrey & Turner, Sarah (2006). "The Challenge of Improving the Representation of Low-Income Students at Flagship Universities: Access UVA and the University of Virginia." In McPherson and Schapiro (eds), *College Access: Opportunity or Privilege?* New York: The College Board, pp. 103–116.

Turner, Sarah (2005). "Higher Tuition, Higher Aid , and the Quest to Improve Opportunities for Low-Income Students in Selective Higher Education." Cornell Higher Education Research Institute.

United States Government Accountability Office [GAO] (2005). *Student Aid and Postsecondary Tax Preferences.* GAO-05-684. http://www.gao.gov/new.items/ d05684.pdf.

United States Government Accountability Office [GAO] (2005). *Federal Student Loans: Challenges in Estimating Federal Subsidy Costs.* GAO 05-074.

40

Bridging the High School-College Divide

Thomas R. Bailey

High schools and colleges are financed, managed, and regulated by separate systems and agencies. This arrangement has resulted in inefficiencies and inequities as students move between the two sets of institutions—reducing retention and completion in college and creating inequities in enrollment and college completion patterns. As college enrollments have grown (Kane, 2004) and the economic value of college degrees has risen over the last two decades (Grubb, 2002; Kane & Rouse, 1995; Levy & Murnane, 1992; Marcotte, Bailey, & Kienzl, 2005),[1] policy makers and educators have sought to improve the alignment between high school and college and thus to facilitate the process by which students move between the two sets of institutions. This chapter reviews three strategies designed to promote these goals.

The first, remediation, provides instruction for students entering college with academic skills that are so weak that they are not prepared for college-level work.[2] Remediation is an attempt to compensate for misalignment and failure of the K–12 system to prepare students for college. Colleges can carry out remediation on their own, without collaboration from the high schools.

The second, dual enrollment is a strategy by which high school students can earn college credit while still in high school. It is a more recent approach than remediation and is designed to facilitate the transition to college by giving students a college experience while still in high school. This strategy requires collaboration between high schools and colleges. It is generally carried out through specific relationships between individual institutions, sometimes within a framework established by the state.

The final, and most recent, of the three strategies is the high school/college alignment movement. This is an explicit attempt to get states to bring together high school graduation and college entrance standards. It requires state-level regulatory changes and collaboration among a wide variety of institutions.

The longstanding organizational separation of the high school and college systems has resulted in misalignment between the completion of high school and the beginning of college. Assessments given to determine eligibility for high school graduation do not coincide with assessments that measure college readiness. Thus many high school graduates arrive at college and find, much to their dismay, that they are not considered qualified for college-level work. In a survey conducted in 2006, Achieve Inc. found that only five states had aligned high school English and mathematics standards with "postsecondary and workplace expectations." (p. 9). Another 21 states were working towards such alignment. In the same survey, Achieve found that eight states had "enacted college and work-ready [high school] graduation requirements."[3] Another 12 states had plans to enact such requirements.

One result of this misalignment is that students are misinformed about what they must do to be ready for college or what to expect when they get there (Venezia, Kirst, & Antonio, 2003; Achieve, 2006). Students who arrive misinformed are more likely to have problems in college, to have less successful experiences, and to leave college before reaching their goals or completing degrees. This is one reason why the growth of college enrollments has outpaced college completion (Turner, 2004).

The separation between high school and college also reinforces inequities with respect to socioeconomic status (SES) in access to college and college completion.[4] High SES students have many advantages over low SES peers in navigating the transition from high school to college. They tend to be in schools that are more effective at preparing them substantively for college; they have access to more extensive and effective counseling services; their parents, relatives, and friends are much more likely to have knowledge about the process; and they have more resources with which to purchase material *and* services to help them find and enroll in an appropriate college.[5] A more organized and aligned transition process could help lower-income students overcome some of these disadvantages.

DEVELOPMENTAL EDUCATION AND SERVICES FOR ACADEMICALLY UNDERPREPARED STUDENTS

The weakness of academic skills of entering college students is a profound problem for college faculty and staff. While estimates vary concerning the number of students who enroll in remediation, virtually every community college and the large majority of four-year colleges offer some form of remediation. Using data from the National Education Longitudinal Study (NELS), Attewell, et al. (2006), found that 58 percent of community college students and 31 percent of students at non-selective four-year colleges take at least one remedial course.

The incidence of remediation may not be a good measure of the need for remediation or of the extent of weak academic skills among entering college students. Judging the need for developmental education is extremely difficult—Michael Kirst (2007) calls it "virtually impossible"—because there is no consensus about the level and nature of capabilities needed to be "college ready." There is no consistency among states in the assessments or cutoff scores used to determine eligibility to take college-level courses, and in many states each college can choose its own criteria (Perin, 2006). Community colleges in California, for example, use more than 100 different tests (Kirst, 2007).

Data on the incidence of remediation almost certainly underestimate the number of students arriving at college with weak academic skills. Many students whose test scores suggest that they need some academic help to prepare them for college-level work do not end up enrolling in developmental education classes. For example, in some states, California being the most prominent, students can enroll in college-level courses even if their scores on assessment tests suggest that they are not adequately prepared. Thus in this sense, enrollment in remediation is voluntary. Some occupational courses in community colleges admit students without requiring them to take assessments to judge their academic readiness. Finally, students, professors, and colleges often find ways around eligibility criteria. Students whose assessment test scores fall below cutoff levels enroll in regular courses anyway using various formal or informal exceptions. In a study of 15 community colleges, Perin (2006) found extensive enrollments of this type, and Calcagno (2006) found significant enrollments of "ineligible" students in college courses in Florida, despite a policy in which remediation is supposedly mandatory for students whose test scores fall below the statewide cutoff point.

Therefore, while 58 percent of community college and 31 percent of four-year college students take some remediation, a higher proportion could reasonably be judged to need extra academic support.[6] Whatever the actual numbers, it is clear that close to one half of students entering higher education arrive with academic skills that are so low that they threaten the student's ability to perform in college-level courses.

Colleges and students spend billions of dollars on remediation. Ten years ago, Breneman and Haarlow (1997) calculated that more than $1 billion was spent on programs to strengthen the academic skills of students arriving in college who are judged to be academically unprepared for college-level work. A comprehensive and up-to-date measure of the cost of remediation would undoubtedly be well over $1 billion. Calcagno (2007) reported that remediation in Florida community colleges in 2004–05 was more than $118 million dollars. Bettinger and Long (2006) reported that in Ohio in 2000 the state and the students together spent more than $23 million on high school level courses for freshmen in all types of colleges.

Beyond the costs to the states and institutions, students who enroll in remediation face both financial and psychological costs. In most cases, students in remediation are not earning credit towards a degree. Some colleges charge tuition for remediation, and students can also use up their eligibility for financial aid taking these non-credit courses. Even if no tuition is charged, remedial students bear the opportunity costs of lost earnings. In practical terms, taking developmental courses lengthens the time required to complete a degree, and research shows that factors that lengthen the time to degrees, such as attending part time or interrupting enrollment, also tend to reduce the probability of degree completion (Horn & Nevill, 2006; Horn & Carroll, 1996). Many students assigned to remediation are surprised and discouraged to learn that they must delay their college education and in effect return to high school. The high attrition rates in developmental classes are indications of student resistance to remediation requirements. In recognition of this resistance, faculty and advisors often try to help students avoid remediation by using loopholes and exceptions that can often be found in the regulations and guidelines (Perin, 2006).

Is the positive impact of remediation worth its financial and psychological costs? Would students, or at least some students, with weak academic skills do better or just as well if they were enrolled directly into college-level courses and therefore were able to begin to earn college credit immediately? Evaluations do show that in some cases, students who enroll in developmental education have better educational outcomes, such as retention and graduation, than similar students who enroll directly in college-level courses. But other studies suggest that students who do not take remediation either fare as well or in some cases do even better than those who do. But definitive conclusions are scarce because of methodological weaknesses in the research. Most research fails to use appropriate control groups against which to compare outcomes for developmental students.[7]

Many studies find that students who enroll initially in developmental courses graduate at lower rates than do students who start in regular credit courses (Muraskin & Wilner, 2004). In a study of college transcripts, Adelman (1998) found that the more remedial courses students were required to take, the less likely they were to earn a degree. Among students who attended two-year and/or four-year institutions and earned more than 10 credits, 45 percent of those who took two remedial courses earned either an associate's or bachelor's degree by the time they were 30 years old, compared with 60 percent of those who took no remedial courses. Students who are judged to have low reading skills in particular are more likely to need extensive remediation and less likely to earn a degree.

But such results can only be considered preliminary since, on average, developmental students start with weaker skills. Thus it is not surprising that they have weaker academic outcomes than other students. These apparently negative results are consistent with the hypothesis that remediation is effective, but not effective enough to compensate for the initial deficiency.

More comprehensive studies have tested the effectiveness of remediation after accounting for other characteristics, such as pre-college academic progress and socio-economic status, that might influence both enrollment in remediation and academic outcomes after remediation. When Adelman (1999) compared students with similar pre-college academic skills, he found no difference in subsequent educational outcomes for students who did and did not enroll in remediation. Attewell et al. (2006) found similar results for community colleges after they controlled for previous academic records and many other demographic variables, and they found that students enrolled in remediation did as well as similar (at least based on measurable characteristics) students who do not take remediation.[8] But they also found that, even among students with similar academic skills, remedial students in four-year colleges had less successful academic careers than their non-remedial colleagues.

These results are discouraging. If students enrolled in remediation do no better, or even worse, than similar students who enter directly into college courses, then the delay and extra expense of remediation is wasted.

But it is possible that unmeasured differences between remedial and non-remedial students might account for the outcomes, rather than any influence of the developmental classes themselves. For example, if among those students with low test scores, the more motivated and aggressive find ways to avoid remediation and enroll directly in college courses, then this might reduce the measured effect of remediation.

Very few studies have addressed the problem of unmeasured differences or selection bias. The Attewell et al. (2006) study cited earlier addressed this problem using propensity score matching, a statistical technique for choosing a control group (Rosenbaum & Rubin, 1983). The extent to which this approach addresses the selection bias is still controversial (Smith & Todd, 2005; Agodini & Dynaski, 2004). In any case, in the Attewell et al. (2006) study, the results using the propensity score approach did not differ substantially from the more straightforward logistic regressions that control for a wide range of personal characteristics.[9]

A series of studies by Bettinger and Long (2005, 2006) exploited differences in placement policies among colleges in Ohio and students' proximity to colleges with different placement policies in order to estimate causal effects of remediation on student outcomes. Because of differences in institutional placement policies, a developmental student at one college may be similar to a student placed into college courses who happens to be enrolled at a different college (with lower cutoff scores). One of their studies looked at full-time traditional aged students who took the ACT test and who enrolled in college in 1998 (Bettinger & Long , 2006). They also included both students starting in four-year colleges and those starting in two-year colleges who stated on their community college application that they intended to complete a bachelor's degree. Five years after initial enrollment, students enrolled in math and English remediation were more likely to have earned a degree and less likely to have dropped out than similar students who had enrolled directly into college courses.

Also using the Ohio data set, Bettinger and Long (2005) studied first time degree seeking community college students who were 18, 19, or 20 years old and who had taken the ACT assessment test. They found students placed in math remediation were 15 percent more likely to transfer to a four-year college and took approximately 10 more credit hours than similar students not placed in remediation. English developmental classes had no positive effects. For both of these studies, the conclusions apply primarily to students who are very close to the cutoff point for determining assignment to remediation and, therefore, are less relevant for students who face very serious academic deficiencies. The community college study does not include remediation for older students who may have a different type of developmental need than the traditional aged students included in the sample.

Studies by Calcagno (2007) and Lesik (2006) used regression discontinuity methods, which yield more reliable causal estimates than ordinary least squares or logistic regressions (Shadish, Cook, & Campbell, 2002). Regression discontinuity can be used when there is a fixed cutoff that determines in a reliable and consistent way who gets assigned to a program or initiative. In the case of remediation, the strategy is valid if everyone who scores below a fixed cutoff point is assigned to remediation and everyone who scores above that cutoff enrolls in college-level courses. The contention is that students just above and just below that cutoff point are essentially identical, yet only the students who score below the point are enrolled in remediation.

Calcagno (2007) exploited a statewide remediation cutoff score in Florida to compare outcomes for community college students just above the cutoff score who did not enroll in remediation, to those just below who did enroll. He used a broader sample of students than Bettinger and Long (2006) because he included all beginning community college students, including older students. He generally found that remediation had a positive effect on the likelihood of passing the first college-level English class, but a negative effect on passing college algebra. There were positive, but not statistically significant, effects on the likelihood of persisting in college or the chances of transferring to a state four-year college and completing an associates degree.

The regression discontinuity study by Lesik (2006) included students in one public university who took developmental intermediate algebra. In this case she found a positive effect on completion of the subsequent college-level math course.

These studies have all analyzed the effect of whatever remediation was offered at the colleges under study, but the content and organization of remediation also varies widely. In her analysis of remediation in 15 colleges in six states, Perin (2006) found more approaches than colleges. Indeed, many colleges used several approaches. The most common strategy is to offer remedial courses in which students meet with a professor in a classroom a given number of times over the course or a semester. This is the type of remedial class that gets counted in the surveys. But within that structure, pedagogic strategies vary widely. These range from traditional lecture formats to more interactive approaches based on active student participation (Grubb, 1999; Perin, 2006). Colleges also use other forms of remediation in which students enroll in regular college-level classes but still have access to assistance in learning centers or special tutors. Moreover, college-level classes often must be taught at a relatively low level because many of the students, including some who passed out of remediation, still have very weak skills. Grubb (1999) refers to this as "hidden remediation."

Some research has attempted to determine the best form and content of remediation. There is a consensus among practitioners that developmental students need comprehensive services. Based on their reviews of the literature on academic achievement in college, Pascarella and Terenzini (1991, 2005) contended that institutions can aid the academic adjustment of poorly prepared students by providing extensive instruction in academic skills, advising, counseling, and comprehensive support services. Pascarella and Terenzini contended that these findings have been replicated in several national studies, and that the results hold even after researchers take account of important student and institutional characteristics.

Researchers have been enthusiastic about learning community formats for remediation.[10] In his review of research on developmental education, Grubb (2001) argued that learning communities did appear to have positive benefits on student performance in subsequent college-level courses. Bailey and Alfonso (2005) also found some support for the model in community colleges based primarily on quasi-experimental research. There is extensive research on learning communities in four-year colleges, although these efforts are not primarily designed for developmental students (Taylor et al., 2003). But the research cited in the reviews discussed so far is for the most part correlational, in some cases with controls for pre-program individual characteristics. These studies do not address the effects of unmeasured characteristics that might distort the estimates of program effects.

A random assignment study of a learning communities program at Kingsborough Community College in New York City provides some evidence for the effectiveness of learning communities (Bloom & Sommo, 2005). This study, carried out by the research firm MDRC, found that, among students who had failed both the reading and writing skills tests prior to enrollment, 33 percent of learning community students had re-taken and passed both tests one year later, compared to just 14 percent of control group of students who only had access to the traditional remediation services at Kingsborough. But with the exception of this MDRC study, there is little rigorous research examining different approaches to remediation.

Addressing the problems caused by weak academic skills is perhaps the most difficult problem facing most community colleges and many four-year colleges. Given the size and importance of this problem, colleges need guidance on how to work with students to strengthen their skills and prepare them for college-level work. Nevertheless, we have seen only a meager harvest of research that either measures the benefits of developmental education compared to enrolling students directly in college-level courses, or that provides guidance on program design.

DUAL ENROLLMENT: "REMEDIATION" THROUGH ACCELERATION

Dual enrollment is an increasingly popular strategy for improving the transition from high school to college. High school students participating in dual enrollment programs take college courses while they are in high school. In many cases, these students simultaneously earn high school and college credit (Bailey & Karp, 2003; Western Interstate Commission on Higher Education, 2006). Thus while students in remediation spend their first semesters or even years in college studying high school or perhaps middle school level material, dual enrollment students spend some of their last years in high school studying college-level material.[11]

Dual enrollment is growing quickly. Research by the National Center for Education Statistics for the 2002–2003 school year found that 1.2 million students attending 71 percent of public high schools took courses for dual credit (Waits, Setzer, & Lewis, 2005). The Gates Foundation has funded an extensive program to promote the early college/high school model (Kazis et al., 2004; Palaich et al., 2006), a strategy to orient whole high schools to providing college credit. In some cases, early college students can come close to completing an associate's degree soon after graduating from high school. By 2004, 49 early college high schools had opened, serving 8,000 students, and 175 more schools were scheduled to open by 2008 (American Institute of Research, 2006; SRI International, 2006).

Enthusiasm among educators for dual enrollment is evident from the growing number of reports and conferences on the topic. The Western Interstate Commission in Higher Education (2006) recently completed a comprehensive review of "accelerated learning options." In 2006, the American Youth Policy Forum (Lerner & Brand, 2006) published profiles of 22 programs that allow students to earn college credit in high school. The U.S. Department of Education's Office of Vocational and Adult Education has funded a multi-year program to study dual enrollment—or as it is referred to in these studies, Credit Based Transition Programs (Hughes et. al., 2006).

Dual enrollment has several potential advantages as a strategy to improve the high school to college transition process. One advantage is that it simply accelerates the education process, and, depending on how the program is financed, can save students, parents, or taxpayers money by requiring fewer years, and therefore less tuition or enrollment funding. Dual enrollment involves the high school directly in the transition process and thereby works to break down the separation between colleges and universities. Often, high school students, in order to be eligible to enroll in college-level courses, must take the college assessment tests; thus they get an early sense of how well prepared they are for colleges. High school teachers and administrators, too, get a much more concrete understanding of how well they are doing in getting their students ready for college.

One of the more interesting aspects of dual enrollment is that, in many schools, it attracts young people who are not among the most academically successful students, including many who in the past would not have been considered "college bound." Thus many dual enrollment students have B averages and have not taken the most rigorous "college prep" sequences (Hughes et. al., 2006). Indeed, advocates of dual enrollment see it as a strategy to improve access to college and reduce the need for remediation through exposing a broad range of high school students to college-level material and college-like experiences (Nathan, 2004; Vargas, 2004; National Governors Association, 2005).

The argument in favor of the broadening of the target dual enrollment population rests on two pillars.[12] The first involves notions about expectations. Many educators believe that teacher and parent expectations are crucial determinants of student performance and that students will respond if their teachers expect them to perform at a higher level. In other words, treating a student like an adult will elicit adult behavior.

This point of view calls into question the effectiveness of explicit tracking, especially for students with weaker academic backgrounds. The contention that tracking can be harmful is more common in discussions of K–12 education than for college-level studies. For example, the Accelerated Schools Project (ASP), a widely used approach to improving K–12 education, follows the slogan, "accelerate don't remediate" (Hopfenberg et al., 1993). The underlying principle is that separating lower performing students into remedial classes puts them on a track from which they will never recover. Henry Levin, the founder of the project, attacks the notion of tracking with the following statement:

> Presumably, children who are put into remedial programs are children who arrive at school with "defects" in their development that require repair of their educational faults. But, even this metaphor falls short of its own meaning because the typical child is never repaired, but remains in the repair shop for many years in enclaves labeled as Title I, or special education, or other categorical programs. And, contrary to gaining needed academic prowess, this approach stigmatizes the child with a label of inferiority and constrains academic development to the limitations of the remedial pedagogy. (Levin, forthcoming)

Thus Levin argues that effective classes for students who are not doing well in elementary or middle school would be much the same as classes for "gifted" students.

Evaluation of the accelerated schools model has shown that it is an effective strategy for teaching students with low academic achievement (Bloom et. al., 2001; Ross et. al., 2001). Dual enrollment, when educators have tried to attract a broad group of students to the program, is, implicitly, an attempt to apply the principles that underlie the Accelerated Schools Project to upper-level secondary school students.

The second reason why college studies in high school could benefit a wide range of students, not just the most advanced, is that exposing students to a college-level experience will both show them what college will be like and actually give them experience or practice in college behavior. The hypothesis is that students with these early experiences will not be surprised—and possibly discouraged—when they do enroll in college. Better preparation will, according to this view, reduce early attrition from college and promote longer-term college success (Karp, 2006; Wolk, 2005).

Despite the outpouring of reports and research, as with developmental education, the evidence that students who participate in dual enrollment have stronger academic outcomes than students who remain in regular high school classes, is remarkably thin (Bailey & Karp, 2003). Evidence shows that students enjoy participating in dual enrollment programs, find them useful and motivating, and are generally satisfied with their experiences (Robertson, Chapman, & Gaskin, 2001). A few studies have tracked dual enrollment students through high school and into college, and these studies usually find that dual enrollment students have higher college enrollment rates and experience more success while in college than comparison students. But dual enrollment programs usually have entrance criteria (many, for example, require a B average in high school). It is not surprising that a selected group of students has better outcomes than the average student. Most studies of dual enrollment fail to address this selection problem (Bailey & Karp, 2003).

The methodological problems common in dual enrollment studies are evident in the recent review by the American Youth Policy Forum of research on dual enrollment and other programs that linked high school and college (Lerner & Brand, 2006). The review encompassed 22 studies of what they refer to as Secondary-Post-Secondary Learning Options (SPLOS). These included dual enrollment as well as Advanced Placement (AP) and International Baccalaureate (IB) programs. The authors of this review set out to "identify scientifically rigorous and third-party evaluation," but they found so few of these that in the end they also included any program that they found that "engaged in comprehensive data collection" (Lerner & Brand, 2006).

Three-quarters of the studies reviewed by Lerner & Brand (2006) made some sort of comparison between students who were and were not enrolled in dual enrollment programs. These comparisons were generally positive with respect to college enrollment, grades, and retention. A quarter of the studies compared the program students to a comparison group with some attempt to narrow the group to "peers." Three others had no control group but compared program students before and after enrollment, pointing out improvements in attendance or grades. Another quarter compared program and non-program students by analyzing individual student records, which allowed them to control for individual characteristics such as high school Grade Point Average (GPA). Only two of these studies that analyzed individual data studied dual enrollment, and one of those was for a highly selective program. The others studied AP and IB programs.

A few other studies not reviewed by Lerner and Brand (2006) found positive results after researchers took account of pre-program student characteristics. For example, a study at the University of Arizona that controlled for prior academic achievement found higher GPAs for dual enrollment students (Puyear, Thor, & Mills, 2001). Another study by Palaich et al. (2006) compared high school and college attainment levels for students in two early college high schools, to those levels for students in the National Education Longitudinal Study (NELS) in the lowest two income quintiles and who were rated as "college ready" by NELS. The early college students needed less time to reach specific educational milestones. For example, the researchers report that early college students who earned BAs on average took seven years from the time they first matriculated in college, while those in the NELS comparison group needed 8.5 years.

Prescott (2006) used Florida data to compare dual enrollment students to other Florida high school students who were eligible for dual enrollment in high school (a high school GPA of 3.0 and appropriate scores on the College Placement Test administered by Florida colleges to determine whether students are prepared for college). No other controls were used. He found that, among those who went to any college, dual enrollment students were more likely to earn a degree, more likely to enroll in a four-year college, and more likely to graduate on time than dual enrollment eligible students who did not participate.

One of the most serious barriers to comprehensive analysis of dual enrollment is the dearth of data that track individual students from high school into college. Recent case studies of high school dual enrollment programs found that most high school staff members working in the programs have little idea about what happens to their students after they leave (Hughes et. al., 2006). Only eleven states have linked college student data with high school records (Ewell & Boeke, 2007).

Thus we are only beginning to get a sense of the impact of dual enrollment programs on students. The research available indicates that participants and educators, both in high schools and community colleges, are enthusiastic about the strategy. Dual enrollment students tend to enroll and persist in college at higher rates than high school students who finish high school with no college credit, although this is hardly surprising, since dual enrollment programs are selective. Some of these positive findings remain even after the researchers control for a student's prior academic record or when they compare groups of dual enrollment students to groups with some similar characteristics. No studies of dual enrollment have addressed the problem of selection bias or unmeasured differences between dual enrollment and comparison group students.

To date, no study has used approaches such as random assignment, instrumental variables or other econometric techniques to address these significant methodological shortcomings. Thus we are left with encouraging descriptive data, enthusiasm on the part of students and faculty, and suggestive evidence that relatively strong high school students can accelerate their college and perhaps save money on tuition by enrolling in dual enrollment. Up to this point, we have not been able to show that it will reduce the need for remediation or improve the prospects of students who would otherwise have been unlikely to attend college.

HIGH SCHOOL-COLLEGE ALIGNMENT

So far, we have discussed two strategies that either try to improve or compensate for the separation and misalignment between high schools and college. Over the past decade, reformers have developed a more ambitious strategy that takes aim at the misalignment itself. The fundamental goal is to create a coherent transition from high school to college in which the standards for high school completion will be the same as the standards for college entrance. Thus students who graduate from high school will know that they are prepared for college.[13] One example of this trend is the changing role of the Regents exam in New York State. Previously, these exams were taken by a minority of students who were "college-bound." Since the early years of the current decade, the state has been moving towards a system in which the Regents exams will become the standard for high school graduation.

Achieve, Inc., an education reform organization, has organized the American Diploma Project (ADP) to work towards high school/college alignment. The ADP has developed "a coalition of 26 states dedicated to aligning K–12 curriculum, standards, assessments and accountability policies with the demands of college and work" (Achieve, 2006). In addition, according to an ADP survey, 44 states were taking some action to improve alignment (Achieve, 2006). As part of the ADP activities, 22 states have established P-16 councils to try to coordinate their pre-school, elementary, high school, and college systems.

While promising, these activities are too new to assess. No research has explicitly tried to determine whether students in states that have formal high school/college alignment are more successful at negotiating the transition process than students in other states.

RESEARCH AGENDA

Two related research themes emerge from the analysis of these three strategies. First, although the amount of research on these three strategies varies, very little analysis establishes a causal effect of these approaches on student outcomes. Second, the research program is hampered by the lack of longitudinal data that allows researchers to track students from high school into college.

There now exists a good deal of research on remediation, a small but growing body on dual enrollment, and none on alignment. With the exception of a handful of studies on remediation, the research on remediation and dual enrollment at best controls for observable characteristics, and often does not even do that. Unmeasured factors are not taken into account.

Thus a straightforward research agenda presents itself. Research on remediation needs to focus on establishing causal relationships and on assessing differences in the form and design of remediation. Dual enrollment research is just getting started, so there is room for more descriptive and corelational analysis. But researchers need increasingly to try to determine whether this strategy improves college enrollment and college outcomes, especially for the types of students who in the past would not have been considered "college bound." Research on high school college alignment is so new that a great deal of work needs to be done in conceptualizing how it can be measured and how its effects might be detected.

Research for all three of these strategies is made much more difficult by the absence of appropriate data. The sine qua non of progress on empirical research on the transition from high school to college is the ability to track students across the high school/college divide and into the college experience. The National Center for Education Statistics has developed excellent national level longitudinal data bases such as the High School and Beyond Data Base (HSB) and the National Educational Longitudinal Survey (NELS). But while these have yielded extensive information on how characteristics of individuals influence outcomes, they allow only limited research on dual enrollment and developmental education. For example, they are not useful for studying specific program designs. Furthermore, the most recent of these surveys—NELS—is now a decade old.[14]

Researchers increasingly use state-level longitudinal data; indeed, much of the best research reviewed in this article used state data bases. They are more up-to-date than NELS, and are large enough for institution-level analysis therefore allowing the study of differences in institutional practice. A survey by the National Center for Higher Education Management Systems found that in 2006, 40 states already had some form of longitudinal data bases for their higher education systems (Ewell, 2007). Although in 2006, only eleven states had linked their high school and higher education data systems, and 16 additional states reported that they were either in the process of implementing this link or had plans to do so (Ewell & Boeke, 2007). This news is encouraging, but this type of statewide data transformation is extremely difficult and many states have experienced years-long problems and delays in their data development projects.

Attempts to strengthen the transition from high school to college have the potential to open college to more students, to improve college outcomes, and to make college access and success more equitable. While we already know a great deal about this transition, research that results in reliable measures of the effectiveness and optimal design of these initiatives is in short supply. New methodologies and especially new data have the potential to increase that supply and provide more concrete guidance

NOTES

1. The average weekly earnings for men with no more than a high school degree who were employed full-time fell by 10 percent in constant dollars between 1973 and 2005. But those weekly earnings for men with a bachelor's degree grew by 17 percent. The equivalent earnings for women with only a high school degree grew by 12 percent while those earnings for women with bachelor's degree grew by 30 percent (Miskel, Bernstein, & Allegretto, 2006).
2. Both "remediation" and "developmental education" are used to refer to instruction given to students who arrive in college and are judged unprepared fro college-level studies. "Remediation" is considered a more negative term suggesting that there is some deficiency for which remedial action is necessary while "developmental education" suggests simply that students need to be taught something that they have not learned. I use these two terms interchangeably in this article and do not mean to suggest any positive or negative connotation by the use of one or the other.
3. Achieve allowed states wide latitude in interpreting the concept of alignment.
4. Of the approximately one quarter of students from the high school class of 1992 who had not earned any college credits by 2000, one half were from the lowest quartile of an index of SES developed by the National Center for Education Statistics. Just over 50 percent of the students from that quartile went to any college and about three fourths of those initially went to a community college. In contrast, over 95 percent of students from the highest SES quartile enrolled in college and over two-thirds of those attended a four-year institution. And even for those who enter college, completion is highly related to SES. For example, eight years after initial enrollment in community colleges, just over 30 percent of students from the lowest two SES quartiles have completed a degree, while almost 50 percent of those from the top half of the SES distribution have a degree (US Department of Education, 2002).
5. See Venezia, Kirst, & Antonio (2003) for a discussion of the problems with the high school college transition process. Haveman & Smeeding (2006) argue that the transition process reinforces SES-based inequalities.
6. After reviewing many sources of data, Kirst (2007) estimates that 60 percent of community college and 30 percent of four-year college students need remediation. But he states that given the confusing evidence, he does not have great confidence in this number.
7. For critical analysis of research on remediation see Grubb (2001); Levin and Calcagno (2006); Bailey and Alfonso (2005); Perin (2006); Moss and Yeaton (2006).
8. Because of the wide variation in remediation among colleges and states, a student assigned to remediation in one college may have exactly the same measured characteristics as a student allowed to enroll in college-level courses at another college.
9. They found that developmental education has no statistically significant effect on community college student outcomes and a negative and statistically significant effect on outcomes for four-year college students.
10. In learning communities, students are kept together in cohorts and tend to take two or three classes together as a group. The classes usually consist of a linked developmental and a substantive college-level courses. By linking developmental and substantive courses, educators hope to provide better motivation for the developmental material.
11. Dual enrollment differs from the College Board's Advance Placement (AP) program in that AP students do not earn credit by taking the AP course, but rather by scoring above a cutoff score on the AP exam and by having colleges accept those scores for credit. Dual enrollment students earn credit by completing the course; as do college students in college.
12. See Bailey and Karp (2003) for a more detailed discussion of the arguments in favor of dual enrollment as a policy to improve college access and success for middle and lower achieving students.
13. This will not eliminate the need for some type of developmental education in college because many college students are adults returning to college after several years in the labor market or they are immigrants who attended high school abroad and who at least need help with English.
14. A new longitudinal survey, the Educational Longitudinal Study of 2002 (ELS) conducted by the National Center for Education Statistics, began following a sample of high school sophomores in 2002.

Data to be released in mid-2007 will begin to allow researchers to study the high school to college transition for this cohort of students (http://nces.ed.gov/surveys/els2002/index.asp, downloaded 3/30/07).

REFERENCES

Achieve, Inc. (2006). *Closing the expectations* gap. Washington, DC: Author.

Adelman, C. (1998). "The kiss of death? An alternative view of college remediation." *Crosstalk: A Publications of the National Center for Public Policy in Higher Education,* 6(3). Retrieved September 10, 2007 from: http://highereducation.org/crosstalk/ct0798/voices0798-adelman.shtm.1.

Adelman, C. (1999). *Answers in the toolbox: Academic intensity, attendance patterns, and bachelor's degree attainment.* Washington, DC: Office of Educational Research and Improvement, U.S. Department of Education. Retrieved from http://www.ed.gov/pubs/Toolbox/toolbox.html.

Agodini, R. & Dynarski, M. (2004). Are experiments the only option? A look at dropout prevention programs. *Review of Economics and Statistics, 86*(1), 180–194.

American Institute of Research and SRI International (2006). *Early college high school initiative: 2003–2005 evaluation report.* Washington, DC: American Institute of Research.

Attewell, Paul, Lavin, David, Domina, Thurston, & Levey, Tania (2006). *The Journal of Higher Education, 77*(5), 886–924.

Bailey, Thomas & Alfonso, Mariana (2005). Paths to persistence: An analysis of research on program effectiveness at community colleges. *Lumina Foundation for Education New Agenda Series,* 6(1), 1–44.

Bailey, Thomas & Karp, Melinda Mechur (2003). *Promoting college access and success: A review of credit-based transition programs.* Washington DC: Office of Vocational and Adult Education, U.S. Department of Education, November 2003.

Bettinger, Eric & Long, Bridget (2006) *Addressing the Needs of Under-Prepared Students in Higher Education: Does College Remediation Work?* Cambridge: National Bureau of Economic Research.

Bettinger, Eric, & Long, Bridget (2005). Remediation and the community college: Student participation and outcomes. *New Directions Research in Community Colleges.,* 129, 17–27.

Bloom, Dan & Sommo, Colleen (2005). *Building Learning Communities: Early Results from the Opening Doors Demonstration at Kingsborough Community College,* New York, MDRC. Retrieved Novermber 20, 2006 from: http://www.mdrc.org/publications/410/overview.html.

Bloom, H., Rock, J., Ham, S., Melton, L., & O'Brien, J., Doolittle, F. & Kagahiro, S. (2001). *Evaluating the accelerated schools approach.* New York: Manpower Demonstration Research Corporation.

Breneman, D. W. & Haarlow, W. N. (1997). Remedial education: Costs and consequences. *Remediation in Higher Education: A Symposium.* Washington, DC: Thomas B. Fordham Foundation. Retrieved September 10, 2007 from: http://www.edexcellence.net/institute/publication/publication.cfm?id=34&pubsubid=592#592.

Calcagno, Juan Carlos (2007). Evaluating the impact of remedial education in community colleges: A quasi-experimental regression discontinuity design. Doctoral Dissertation submitted to Teachers College, Columbia University.

Ewell, Peter & Boeke, Marianne (2007). Cricial connections: Linking states' unit record systems to track student progress. *Lumina Foundation New Agenda Series,* January, 1–40.

Grubb, Norton (2002). Learning and earning in the middle, Part I: National studies of pre-baccalaureate education. *Economics of Education Review, 21,* 229–231.

Grubb, Norton (2001). *From black box to Pandora's box: Evaluating remedial/developmental education.* New York: Community College Research Center.

Grubb, Norton (1999). *Honored but invisible: An inside look at teaching in community colleges.* New York: Routledge.

Haveman, R. & Smeeding, T. (2006). The role of higher education in social mobility. *The Future of Children,* 16 (2), 125–150.

Hopfenber, Wendy, Levin, Henry M., Chase, Christopher, Christensen, Georgia, Moore, Melanie, Soler, Pilar, Brunner, Ilse, Keller, Beth, & Rodriguez, Gloria (1993). *The Accelerated Schools Resource Guide.* San Francisco: Jossey-Bass.

Horn, L. & Nevill, S. (2006). Profile of undergraduates in U.S. postsecondary education institutions: 2003–04: With a special analysis of community college students (NCES 2006-184). U.S. Department of Education. Washington, DC: National Center for Education Statistics.

Horn, L. & Carroll, C.D. (1996). *Nontraditional undergraduates: Trends in enrollment from 1986 to 1992 and persistence and attainment among 1989–90 beginning postsecondary students* (NCES 97-578). U.S. Department of Education. Washington DC: National Center for Education Statistics.

Hughes, Katherine L., Mechur-Karp, Melinda, Fermin, Baranda, & Bailey, Thomas R. (2006). Pathways to college access and success. New York: Community College Research Center, Teachers College, Columbia University, Brief #27.

Kane, T. J. (2004). College-going and inequality. In K. M. Neckerman (Ed.), *Social inequality,* 319–353. New York: Russell Sage Foundation.

Kane, T. & Rouse, C. (1995). Labor market returns to two- and four-year colleges. *American Economic Review, 85*(3), 600–614.

Karp, M. (2006). Learning about the role of college student through dual enrollment participation. Working Paper, New York: Community College Research Center.

Kazis, Vargas, & Hoffman (2004). *Double the numbers: Increasing postsecondary credentials for underrepresented youth.* Cambridge: Harvard Education Press.

Kirst, Michael (2007). Who Needs It? Identifying the proportion of students who require postsecondary remedial education is virtually impossible. *National Crosstalk.* A Publication of the National Center for Public Policy in Higher Education, 15(1). Retrieved September 10, 2007 from: http://highereducation.org/crosstalk/ct0107/voices0107-kirst.shtml.

Lerner, Jennifer Brown & Brand, Betsy (2006). *The college ladder: Linking secondary and postsecondary education for success for all students.* Washington, DC: American Youth Policy Forum.

Lesik, Sally Andrea (2006). Applying the regression—Discontinuity design to infer causality with non-Random assignment. *The Review of Higher Education, 30*(1), 1–19.

Levin, Henry (forthcoming). On the relationship between poverty and curriculum. *The University of North Carolina Law Review.*

Levin, Henry & Calcagno, Juan Carlos (2006). Remediation in the community college, an Evaluator's Perspective. New York: Community College Research Center, Teachers College, Columbia Univeristy. Working paper #9.

Levy, F. & Murnane, R.J. (1992). U.S. earnings levels and earnings inequality: A review of recent trends and proposed explanations. *Journal of Economic Literature, 30*(3), 1333–1382.

Marcotte, D., Bailey, T., Borkoski, C., & Kienzl, G. (2005). The returns of a community college education: Evidence from the National Education Longitudinal Study. E*ducational Evaluation and Policy Analysis, (27)* 2, 157–175

Mischel, Lawrence, Bernstein, Jared, & Allegretto, Sylvia (2006).*The state of working America, 2006–2007.* Ithaca, NY: ILR Press. Tables 3.18 and 3.19.

Moss, Brian G. & Yeaton, William H. (2006). Shaping policies related to developmental education: An evaluation using the regression discontinuity design. *Educational Evaluation and Policy Analysis,* 28(3), 215–230.

Muraskin, L. & Wilner, A. (2004). *What we know about institutional influences on retention.* Washington, DC: JBL Associates.

Nathan, Joe. (2004). More high school options, better information: Low-cost approaches to getting more youth prepared for and into college. In Richard Kazis, Joel Vargas, & Nancy Hoffman (eds.), *Double the numbers: Increasing postsecondary credentials for underrepresented youth.* Cambridge, MA: Harvard University Press.

National Governors Association (2005). *Redesigning the American high school. Getting it done: Ten steps to a state action agenda.* Washington, DC.: National Governors Association.

Palaich, Robert, Augenblick, John, Foster, Samara, Anderson, Amy Berk, & Douglas Rose, Amy Berk (2006). *Return on investment in early college high schools.* Denver, CO: Augenblick, Plalaich and Associates.

Pascarella, Ernest T. & Terenzini, Patrick T. (2005). *How college affects students: A third decade of research* (Vol. 2). San Francisco: Jossey-Bass.

Pascarella, Ernest T. & Terenzini, Patrick (1991). *How sollege affects students: Findings and insights from twenty years of research.* San Francisco: Jossey-Bass.

Perin, Dolores & Charron, Kerry (2006)."Lights just click on every day. In *Defending the community college equity agenda.* Eds. Thomas Bailey and Vanessa Smith Morest (pp. 155–194) Baltimore: The Johns Hopkins University Press.

Prescott, Brian (2006). Follow the students. In Western Interstate Commission on Higher Education (WICHE), 2006. *Accelerated Learning Options: Moving the Needle on Access and Success* (pp. 37–46). Boulder, CO: WICHE.

Puyear, D.E., Thor, L.M., & Mills, K.L. (2001). Concurrent in Arizona: Encouraging success in high school. *New Directions in Community Colleges, 133*, 33–42.

Robertson, P.F., Chapman, B.G., & Gaskin, F. (2001). *Systems for offering concurrent enrollment at high schools and community colleges.* San Francisco: Jossey-Bass.

Rosenbaum, P. R. & Rubin, D. B. (1983). The central role of the propensity score in observational studies for causal effects. *Biometrika,* 70, 41–55.

Ross, M., Sanders, W., Wright, S.P., Stringfield, S., Wang, L., & Alberg, M. (2001). Two-and three-year achievement results from the Memphis Restructuring Initiative, *School Effectiveness And School Improvement*, 12, 323–346.

Shadish, W., Cook, T., & Campbell, D. (2002). *Experimental and quasi-experimental designs for generalized causal inference.* Boston, MA: Houghton-Mifflin.

Smith, J. & Todd, T. (2005). Does matching address Lalonde's critique of nonexperimental estimators. *Journal of Econometics, 125*(1–2), 305–353.

Taylor, K., Moore, W.S., MacGregor, J., & Limblad, J. (2003). *Learning Community Research and Assessment: What We Know Now.* National Learning Communities Project Monograph Series. Olympia, Washington: The Evergreen State College, Washington Center for Improving the Quality of Undergraduate Education, in cooperation with the American Association for Higher Education.

Turner, S. (2004). Going to college and finishing college: Explaining different educational outcomes. In C. Hoxby, (Ed.) *College choices: The economics of where to go, when to go, and how to pay for* (pp. 13–56). Chicago: The University of Chicago Press.

U.S. Department of Education, National Center for Education Statistics (2002). *National Education Longitudinal Study, 1988.* Washington DC: US Department of Education.

Vargas, Joel (2004). Dual enrollment: Lessons from Washington and Texas. In Richard Kazis, Joel Vargas, & Nancy Hoffman (eds.), *Double the numbers: Increasing postsecondary credentials for underrepresented youth.* Cambridge, MA: Harvard University Press.

Venezia, Andrea, Kirst, Michael W., & Antonio, Anthony L. (2003). *Betraying the college dream: How disconnected K-12 and postsecondary education systems Undermine Student Aspirations.* Palo Alto, CA: Stanford University Bridge Project.

Waits, T., Setzer, J.C., & Lewis, L. (2005). *Dual credit and exam-based courses in U.S. public high schools: 2003–03 (NCES 2005-009).* U.S. Department of Education. Washington, DC: National Center for Education Statistics.

Western Interstate Commission on Higher Education (WICHE) (2006). Accelerated Learning Options: Moving the Needle on Access and Success. Boulder, CO: WICHE.

Wolk, Ronald (2005). *It's kind of different: Student experiences in two early college high schools.* Boston: Jobs for the Future.

Index

CPSIA information can be obtained at www.ICGtesting.com
Printed in the USA
LVOW021520221212
312658LV00002B/11/P

9 780805 861457